Historical Dictionary of the Spanish Empire, 1402–1975

Historical Dictionary of the Spanish Empire, 1402–1975

James S. Olson, *Editor-in-Chief*

Sam L. Slick, *Senior Editor*
**Samuel Freeman, Virginia Garrard Burnett,
and Fred Koestler,** *Associate Editors*

Greenwood Press
New York • Westport, Connecticut • London

Library of Congress Cataloging-in-Publication Data

Historical dictionary of the Spanish Empire, 1402–1975 / James S.
 Olson, editor-in-chief ; Sam L. Slick, senior editor ; Samuel
 Freeman . . . [et al.], associate editors.
    p. cm.
  Includes bibliographical references and index.
  ISBN 0–313–26413–9 (alk. paper)
   1. Spain—History—Dictionaries. 2. Spain—Colonies—History—
Dictionaries. 3. Spain—Colonies—Administration—Chronology.
I. Olson, James Stuart, 1946- . II. Title: Spanish Empire,
1402–1975.
DP56.H57   1992
909′0971246′003—dc20   91–8250

British Library Cataloguing in Publication Data is available.

Library of Congress Catalog Card Number: 91–8250
ISBN: 0–313–26413–9

First published in 1992

Greenwood Press, 88 Post Road West, Westport, CT 06881
An imprint of Greenwood Publishing Group, Inc.

Printed in the United States of America

The paper used in this book complies with the
Permanent Paper Standard issued by the National
Information Standards Organization (Z39.48–1984).

10 9 8 7 6 5 4 3 2 1

CONTENTS

PREFACE

On October 12, 1992, the Western world will celebrate the 500th anniversary of Christopher Columbus's historic voyage across the Atlantic and his discovery of the New World. His landfall on San Salvador in 1492 launched the era of European imperialism and set in motion a series of far-reaching changes that have brought about the increasing social and economic integration of the world. Before Columbus's voyage, the world had been divided into a series of island communities that had relatively little contact with one another; after his voyage, the world began to share new forms of social, biological, political, cultural, and economic interaction. The Spanish language, first confined to the Iberian peninsula, was destined to become one of the most widely spoken languages in the world, and Roman Catholicism was about to acquire a global foothold. Spain became an international power whose culture and political institutions shaped world affairs for more than two centuries. By the mid-eighteenth century, Spanish fortunes on the world scene began to decline, for a variety of reasons, and the inevitable contraction of the far-flung empire began. From the position as the preeminent power on earth, Spain declined to political insignificance on the world stage.

The *Historical Dictionary of the Spanish Empire, 1402–1975*, is designed to provide a ready reference tool for students and scholars. Its major focus is the people, institutions, and colonies of the Spanish empire, from Castile's expansion to the Canary Islands in 1402 to the surrender of Spanish Sahara in 1975. The dictionary provides brief descriptive essays on a variety of topics—colonies, individuals, political institutions, legislation, treaties, conferences, wars, revolutions, technologies, social and religious groups, and military battles. Essays on individual colonies usually end with the winning of independence, the formal incorporation into the body politic of Spain, or the sale or loss of the colony to another European power. References at the end of each entry provide sources of additional information for those wishing to pursue the subject further. Cross-references within the text, designated by an asterisk, will help the reader to find related items. Two appendixes provide a chronology of Spanish imperialism and a list of the individuals who presided over the viceroyalties of New Granada, New Spain, Peru, and Río de la Plata.

I wish to express my thanks to the scholars who wrote essays for the dictionary, especially to those associate editors who contributed so much material. The contributors' names appear at the end of each entry that they wrote. All unsigned entries were written by me. I am especially grateful to my senior editor, Sam Slick, for his careful critique and good judgment. I would also like to thank the librarians who assisted me in locating hard-to-find material. Bill Bailey, Shirley Parotti, and Ann Holder of the Newton Gresham Library at Sam Houston State University were particularly helpful.

James S. Olson

INTRODUCTION

Although the Kingdom of Castile reached to the Canary Islands[*] in 1402, the real beginnings of the Spanish Empire did not come until 1492, when Ferdinand[*] and Isabella[*] expelled the Moors from Spain and Christopher Columbus[*] reached the New World. Intent on finding a new water route to the Indies, the Spanish monarchs sponsored three more voyages by Columbus and dozens of other expeditions of exploration and conquest during the next half century. In the 1490s and early 1500s, Spaniards conquered the Greater Antilles—Cuba[*], Puerto Rico[*], and Hispaniola[*]—and reduced the native Arawak[*] population to extinction. Ferdinand Magellan[*] began his voyage around the world in 1519; in the process, he established the Spanish presence in the Pacific Ocean that eventually evolved into colonial establishments in the Caroline Islands[*], the Marshall Islands[*], the Mariana Islands[*], and the Philippines[*]. That same year, Hernán Cortés[*] moved into the Valley of Mexico and conquered the Aztecs[*]. The Spanish conquest of Central America took place between the 1520s and the 1530s, and in the 1530s, Francisco Pizarro[*] conquered the Incan[*] empire. From the bases in New Spain[*], the Spanish Empire expanded north into what is today Florida[*] and the American Southwest; from those in Peru[*], it spread south and southeast into Chile[*], Bolivia[*], Paraguay[*], Argentina[*], and Uruguay[*], and north into Ecuador[*], Colombia[*], and Venezuela[*].

From its very inception, the Spanish Empire was largely a political enterprise governed directly from the mother country. The imperial apparatus was heavy-handed, with power resting in the hands of *peninsulares*[*]—political appointees born in Spain who spent several years in the colonies as a means of moving up through the ranks of the civil service, the military, and the Church. Spain discouraged the development of indigenous political institutions and tried to exercise all power, but nationalistic movements developed in the late eighteenth century in Mexico, Central America, South America, the Caribbean, and the Philippines. By that time, the Spanish economy had already entered its long period of decline, which eventually left Spain one of the poorest countries in Europe. Spain took thousands of tons of gold and silver out of Mexico and South America, but the riches bought pleasure for the Spanish nobility, the royal family, and the Church, not an infrastructure or economic development for the country as a whole. The Spanish mercantilist policy, which tried to control every aspect of the colonial economies centrally, eventually resulted in gross economic stagnation and decline. The Spanish population actually declined from 8 million to 6 million people in the late sixteenth and seventeenth centuries. With a declining population and a shrinking economy, Spain could not sustain the empire it had been building since 1492.

During the Napoleonic Wars of the early nineteenth century, Spain was cut off from the New World colonies, and the colonial nationalists gained a new sense of independence. Between 1810 and 1830, revolutions erupted throughout Latin America, and in the process Spain lost control of its colonies. When the political dust had settled, Spain retained only Cuba, Puerto Rico, and the Pacific and African outposts, but these too were doomed. Cuban nationalists fought sporadically against Spanish rule until the 1890s when full-scale revolution broke out. A similar revolution was occurring in the Philippines. Those revolutions merged with the Spanish-American War* in 1898, in which Spain suffered a humiliating defeat at the hands of the United States. In the subsequent treaty, the United States assumed a protectorate over Cuba, seized Guam* and Puerto Rico, and purchased the Philippines. In 1899, Spain sold the remaining Mariana Islands and the Marshall Islands to Germany.

By the twentieth century, the former Spanish Empire had been reduced to a few African possessions. In 1778, Portugal had ceded what became Spanish Equatorial Guinea* to Spain. To counter British naval activity on the coast of Africa, Spain established a trading post on the Río de Oro Bay; that post evolved into the colony of Spanish Sahara*. Spanish Sahara, Spanish Equatorial Guinea, and the two small zones of Morocco known as Spanish Morocco*, along with Ceuta*, Melilla*, Orán, and Ifni*, constituted the Spanish empire in Africa. Spain abandoned Orán in 1792, and during the period of revolutionary nationalism that swept throughout Africa in the 1950s, 1960s, and 1970s, Spain lost her other African colonies as well, except for Ceuta and Melilla. Both parts of Spanish Morocco were ceded to Morocco in 1956 and 1958 respectively, and Ifni went to Morocco in 1969. Spanish Equatorial Guinea became independent as the Republic of Equatorial Guinea in 1968, and in 1975, Spanish Sahara was divided up between Morocco and Mauritania. The Spanish Empire, which had once reached around the world, existed no more. By the 1980s, all that remained of that great imperial enterprise were Spain's intermittent and futile attempts to regain control of Gibraltar* from Great Britain.

Historical Dictionary of the Spanish Empire, 1402–1975

A

ABAD Y QUEIPO, MANUEL. Manuel Abad y Queipo was born in Asturias, Spain, in 1751. He graduated from the University of Salamanca, entered the Roman Catholic priesthood, and in 1779 went as a church attorney to Honduras.* He had served there for five years when he accompanied Bishop Antonio de San Miguel to Michoacán, Mexico. Although Abad y Queipo steadfastly defended the Crown and the Church in colonial affairs, he acquired a reputation as a liberal reformist because of his public convictions that Indians* shoud be relieved of their tax burden and that uncultivated land should be distributed widely among the social classes. When the wars of independence broke out in the New World in general and New Spain* in particular, Abad y Queipo called for the suppression of the rebellion. The Spanish junta nominated him as bishop of Michoacán in 1810, but, because of his reformist sympathies, the pope never confirmed him. King Ferdinand VII* recalled him to Spain in 1814, and Abad y Queipo never returned to Mexico. He was called before the Inquisition* to defend his views, but survived politically and in 1822 became bishop of Tortosa. Manuel Abad y Queipo was imprisoned again by Ferdinand VII in 1825; he died in Toledo later that year.

REFERENCE: L. E. Fisher, *Champion of Reform: Manuel Abad y Queipo*, 1955.

ABAD Y SÁNCHEZ, DIEGO JOSÉ. Diego José Abad y Sánchez was born in Michoacán, Mexico, on June 1, 1727. He was tutored at home and then attended the Jesuit College of San Ildefonso in Mexico City*. Abad was ordained a Jesuit* priest in 1751, and he became a brilliant teacher and intellectual at a variety of universities in Mexico City, Zacatecas*, and Querétaro. He was also a gifted poet and humanist whose most important work was *De deo deoque homine heroica*. Abad's other written works included highly literate philosophical, legal, and geographic treatises. When

the Jesuits were expelled from the New World, Abad went to Ferrara, Italy, and he finished out his life in scholarly pursuits. He died in Bologna, Italy, on September 30, 1779.
REFERENCE: V. J. Leeber, *El Padre José Abad, S. J.*, 1965.

ABARCA DE BOLEA, PEDRO PABLO (CONDE DE ARANDA). See AR-ANDA, CONDE DE.

ABASALO, MARIANO. Mariano Abasalo was born in Dolores Hidalgo, Guanajuato*, New Spain*, in 1783. The owner of a large fortune, Abasalo was an early supporter of the Mexican independence movement. He provided the necessary funds for the early revolutionaries who used the money to secure guns and ammunition. Abasalo was captured by royal officials at Acatita de Baján and imprisoned in Cádiz, Spain. He died there in prison in 1816.
REFERENCE: Marion Florence Lansing, *Liberators and Heroes of Mexico and Central America*, 1941.

ABASCAL Y SOUZA, JOSÉ FERNANDO. José Fernando Abascal y Souza was born in Oviedo, Spain, around 1748. He selected a military career in the Spanish army, and in 1806 he was appointed viceroy* of Peru*. Abascal soon found himself in the middle of the independence movement. In 1809, he crushed rebellions against royal authority in Ecuador* and Chile*, but he also worked hard at placating the anger of Peruvian *criollos**. He launched a number of reforms, including the elimination of the Inquisition*, in order to satisfy liberals. Whatever Abascal did to mollify revolutionary sentiment in the viceroyalty, however, only angered conservatives back in Spain. In 1816, Ferdinand VII* replaced Abascal with Joaquín de la Pezuela*. Abascal returned to Spain and died there in 1821.
REFERENCES: Leon G. Campbell, *The Military and Society in Colonial Peru, 1750–1810*, 1978; Mariano Felipe Paz Soldán, *Historia del Perú independiente, 1822–1827*, 1929.

ABOLITION. See SLAVERY.

ACAPULCO. The city of Acapulco was established by Spaniards on the southwestern coast of New Spain* in 1530. After the discovery and settlement of the Philippines* in the 1570s and 1580s, Acapulco became a major New World port. Beginning in 1601, the Manila galleon* annually transported goods between Manila* and Acapulco, from where they were then shipped to Spain.
REFERENCE: Silvio Zavala, *The Colonial Period in the History of the New World*, 1962.

ACEVEDO Y TORINO, MANUEL ANTONIO. Manuel Antonio Acevedo y Torino was born in Salta*, in what is today Argentina*, in 1770. He received a doctorate from the University of Córdoba* in 1793 and was then ordained a

Roman Catholic priest. He became the founder and rector of the school of philosophy in Salta in 1799, but he then spent several years working with the Calchaquí and Catamarca Indians. Acevedo became a strong supporter of the May Revolution* in Argentina and provided valuable medical assistance to General Manuel Belgrano's* troops. Acevedo was a member of the Congress of Tucumán* and a signer of the Declaration of Independence of Argentina. He died in 1825.

REFERENCE: Enrique Udaondo, *Diccionario biográfico colonial argentino*, 1945.

ACORDADA. Because of widespread banditry in rural areas of the Spanish Empire in the sixteenth century, the *audiencias** were literally swamped with criminal cases. To relieve the case load, the Crown permitted the creation of special judicial tribunals. In 1553, Luis de Velasco*, viceroy* of New Spain*, established the *Santa hermandad*, a system of rural constables to arrest and punish bandits in rural districts. The constables had total power, including the administration of the death penalty. In 1710, the *Santa hermandad* became known as the *acordada*. Presided over by a *juez*, also known as the *capitán de la acordada*, the *acordada* in each viceroyalty employed thousands of special agents. A local *acordada* judge could convene trials and administer punishments. At first there were no appeals of *acordada* decisions, but later in the eighteenth century, as regular judicial institutions became better established, *acordada* decisions became subject to appeal.

REFERENCE: C. H. Haring, *The Spanish Empire in America*, 1947.

ACOSTA, JOSÉ DE, S. J. Born in Medina del Campo, Spain, in 1540, José de Acosta joined the Jesuits* twelve years later. An excellent poet, he studied in Medina, Coimbra, Lisbon, Valladolid, and Segovia, but it was in Alcalá, the center of the Cisnerian and Erasmian reforms, that he acquired his vast culture and humanism. He was ordained a priest in 1566. He then taught at Ocaña and went to Peru* in 1572. There he traveled widely and taught at the University of San Marcos* and the College of San Pablo; he also played the most important role at the third Liman Council. At the age of 35, Acosta became provincial (the local leader of the Jesuit order), which gave him the opportunity to expand Jesuit colleges all over Peru. In 1586, he traveled to Spain, stayed for a year in Mexico, and arrived in Rome in 1588 to gain approval for the decisions of the Liman Council. It was during his stay at the Holy See that his first books appeared: the *De Procuranda Indorum Salute* and the shorter *De Natura Novis Orbis*. In 1590, his *Historia Natural y Moral de las Indias* was published in Seville. The last decade of his life was spent first as *Visitador* of the provinces of Andalucía and Aragón, and then working in Valladolid and Salamanca. Acosta died in 1600.

His great erudition about antiquity and the Middle Ages, coupled with a rich scientific knowledge, made Acosta the most noted scholastic teacher and philosopher in sixteenth-century Peru. Adviser to both Church and Crown, founder of colleges, and spiritual leader of the Society of Jesus in Peru, Acosta was not only a theologian, moralist, and historian, but also a natural scientist in his own right with a special interest in anthropology and physiography. His *Historia Natural y Moral de las Indias* made him justly famous. It comprises seven volumes dealing with the sky, climate, and population of Peru; the plants, animals, and metals of the area; and the government, religion, and customs of the natives. Alexander von Humboldt* commented that the basis of what was then called the physics of the earth, apart from mathematical considerations, was already contained in Acosta's work. Although the observation of Spanish-American nature made him depart from the strict notions of Aristotle, adopting a more critical and empirical approach, he always remained very balanced and within the theological and philosophical framework of traditional Scholasticism. He thus became "the Plinius of the New World."

In his other great work, *De Procuranda Indorum Salute*, Acosta projected even more strongly his great humanism and his ideal world: the concept of the just war, the human nature of the Indians*, his criticisms of both civil servants and ecclesiastics. He touched on the great problems of humanity, both European and native, and he always bore in mind a great spiritual concern for the moral perfection of both Spaniards and Indians. In the last analysis, these problems reflected a profoundly modern concern—the incorporation of a new continent and its native population into Western civilization. "The Plinius of the New World" was thus able to put his imprint on future generations: an ideal and Christian world with its goal of moral perfection.

REFERENCES: Francisco Mateos, S.J., ed. *Obras del P. José de Acosta de la Compañía de Jesús*, 1954; María Luis Rivara de Tuesta, *José de Acosta: Un humanista reformista*, 1970; O. Carlos Stoetzer, "El mundo ideal del Padre José de Acosta, S.J. (1540–1600), 'El Plinio del Nuevo Mundo,' " *Cuadernos Salmantinos de Filosofía*, 13 (1986), 205–18.

O. Carlos Stoetzer

ACOTAMIENTOS. *Acotamientos* were privileges of enclosure, which permitted the landowner to exclude all but his own animals. The *acotamiento* of arable land abrogated the traditional Castilian right of stubble grazing (or the *derrota de mieses**). The right to enclose certain plots appeared in the municipal *fueros** (law codes) granted to newly founded towns during the Castilian Reconquista, but the norm was the open range. In the second half of the sixteenth century, however, the Crown experimented with selling privileges of enclosure. A royal investigation reported that most landowners favored the idea, so in the late 1560s and the 1570s, the Crown sold a number of enclosure permits. The resulting enclosed areas were variously called *cotos redondos*, *términos redondos*, *cerramientos*, or *dehesas*. But the Crown was disappointed in the amount of revenue to be gained from enclosure permits. Furthermore, the enclosures elicited strong resistance from pastoral interests. The Habsburg monarchs also sold permits to establish hunting preserves (*cotos de caza*), which constituted a different type of enclosure that was desired by large landowners who wished to abolish the traditional communal hunting rights on their lands. The Castilian Cortes protested in 1571 that landowners who had established hunting preserves not only kept outsiders from hunting on their lands, but also denied pasture rights to outsiders. In other words, the hunting preserves were *de facto* enclosed pastures.

Many powerful landowners tried to arrogate to themselves the right to declare their lands to be "enclosed" and off-limits to outside animals. This was contrary to local custom, and the courts usually ruled against them. By the end of the sixteenth century, however, many influential individuals had been able to gain control over municipal governments through the purchase of council seats or by other means. These powerful individuals—often nobles—were able to enclose their lands without fear of prosecution from local officials. In many places, these extralegal enclosures were a serious problem.

In addition to the aforementioned theoretical "enclosures," there were also real enclosures in medieval and early modern Castile[*]. These, called *cercas* or *campos cercados*, were formed by erecting a wall (*tapia*), hedge or fence (*vallado* or *valladar*) around plots that were unusually vulnerable to damage by livestock. Some municipal governments, especially in areas with a predominantly pastoral economy, made walls or fences obligatory around garden plots and vineyards. The percentage of arable land that was literally "enclosed" was miniscule. The boundaries of many grain fields were marked by trees, especially willows, poplars, elms, and fruit trees. These were more prominent in earlier centuries than they are today. Not all parcels were enclosed separately; sometimes many parcels were included within the arboreal borders. The result was a landscape of semi-enclosed fields. Nevertheless, it appears that the *derrota* applied even to fields surrounded by *valladares*.

In the Americas, the Spanish attempted to implant their traditional Iberian customs regarding enclosures, but unfenced crops belonging to Indians[*] soon began to suffer serious damage from wandering livestock. Initially, colonial authorities in New Spain[*] tried to protect Indian fields by holding animal owners responsible for damages. This proved unworkable, and, by the end of the 1500s, the colonial government required all persons planting crops to fence them and to maintain the fences; otherwise they could not collect for damages done by livestock.

REFERENCES: David E. Vassberg, *Land and Society in Golden Age Castile,* 1984; Hilario Casado, *Señores, mercaderes y campesinos: La comarca de Burgos a fines de la Edad Media,* 1987.

David E. Vassberg

ACUERDO. The *acuerdo* was the name given to the administrative sessions of the *audiencia* in the Spanish colonies. Decisions coming out of the *acuerdos* were known as *autos acordados*.

REFERENCE: C. H. Haring, *The Spanish Empire in America,* 1947.

ACULCO, BATTLE OF. Father Miguel Hidalgo[*], after defeating the Viceroy Francisco Venegas's forces at the Battle of Las Cruces (1810), decided not to march his army of 40,000 to 60,000 men toward Mexico City[*] and instead ordered a retreat. Although Hidalgo's army greatly outnumbered the royalist forces facing him, his army was comprised largely of untrained and poorly armed Indians* who fought more like a mob than an army. Hidalgo, therefore, apparently decided that his forces were not sufficient to attack successfully the viceroy's artillery.

At Aculco, on November 6, 1810, Hidalgo encountered advanced elements of the viceroy's army commanded by Brigadier General Félix María del Rey Calleja*, whose 7,000 seasoned troops were primarily *criollo**. There is evidence that, because Calleja's troops were torn between their service to the viceroy and their identification with their native country, they might have gone over to Hidalgo's side had he waited longer to attack. Without hesitation, however, he attacked on November 7. Calleja then advanced against Hidalgo's lines in five separate columns, breaking the lines, putting Hidalgo's forces to rout, and capturing his artillery, munitions, and provisions. Having had their choice made for them by Hidalgo's speed of attack, the *criollos* proceeded to slaughter Hidalgo's forces. Although the figure may have been inflated, Calleja reported having killed over 10,000 Indians during the battle. The defeat was sufficiently severe that Hidalgo could not execute an orderly retreat. His forces became split, with him leading one group to Valladolid* while Ignacio Allende led another to Guanajuato*.

REFERENCES: Christon I. Archer, *The Army in Bourbon Mexico*, 1985; William Robertson, *Rise of the Spanish-American Republics*, 1918.

Samuel Freeman

ACUÑA, CRISTÓBAL DE. Cristóbal de Acuña was born in Burgos, Spain, in 1597. He joined the Jesuit* order as a young man. Acuña became the first rector of the College of Cuenca in Ecuador* in 1630, and from there he helped build the Jesuit mission in Maynas on the upper Amazon River. In February 1639, Acuña launched a scientific expedition down the Amazon River and went as far as Pará before returning to Spain. Back in Madrid, Acuña described the expedition to King Philip IV* and to the Council of the Indies*. In 1641, he published his book *Nuevo descubrimiento del Gran Río de las Amazonas*. Acuña returned to Quito* in 1644 and then moved to Lima*, Peru*, in 1659. He died there on January 14, 1670.

REFERENCE: José Jouanen, *Historia de la Compañía de Jesús en la antigua provincia de Quito, 1570–1774*, 1941–1943.

ADAMS-OÑÍS TREATY OF 1819. In 1819, John Quincy Adams, the secretary of state for the United States, and Spanish diplomat Luis de Oñís met to discuss the Florida* problem. The rapidly growing American population in the South was putting pressure on Spanish sovereignty in East Florida* and West Florida*. Spain realized that with the Spanish American colonies erupting in revolution, it would not be able to defend the Floridas if the United States decided to seize them. After extended negotiations, the Adams-Oñiis Treaty was signed in Washington, D. C., on February 22, 1819. Under the terms of the treaty, the United States received sovereignty over East Florida, and Spain formally recognized the earlier U.S. seizure of West Florida. The treaty also carefully defined the western boundary of the Louisiana* Territory, which the United States had purchased from France in 1803. The new boundary began at the mouth of the Sabine River, moved northwest to the 42nd parallel (what is today the northern boundary of California*), and then headed due west to the Pacific Ocean. Spain also surrendered whatever claim it had to the Oregon region. In return, the United States recognized Spain's claim to Texas* and agreed to assume up to $5 million in claims by American citizens against the Spanish government.

REFERENCE: Samuel F. Bemis, *The American Secretaries of State and Their Diplomacy*, 1928.

ADELANTADO. During the sixteenth century, the Spanish Crown awarded the office of *adelantado* to selected individuals who, at private expense, undertook the discovery and conquest of new overseas territories. Some of Spain's most famous conquistadors*, including Juan Ponce de León*, Vasco Núñez de Balboa*, Ferdinand Magellan*, Francisco Pizarro*, and Hernando de Soto* bore the title. Through the efforts of these *adelantados*, Spain* acquired vast colonial domains. In newly acquired territories of the Spanish empire, the *adelantado* was the first chief executive officer assigned to govern the region. The *adelantado* used the title of governor until the arrival of the viceroy* or viceregal authority. Other levels of authority also carried the title of *adelantado*. The term *adelantado mayor* was reserved for those individuals acting as governors with judicial, administrative, and military authority. To act as the head of military forces at distant frontier outposts, the crown appointed an *adelantado menor*, sometimes called *adelantado fronterizo*. An individual with the authority to represent the crown on official matters was called an *adelantado de la corte* or *adelantado del rey*. Those individuals commanding a military expedition into new territories had the title *adelantado del mar*, which often implied the title of governor for any newly conquered territories.

Historians have traced the office as far back as the tenth century. In Reconquest Spain, *adelantados* served as the king's deputies in frontier regions exposed to Moorish attacks. Under such conditions, they exercised significant authority. When Queen Isabella I* decided to bring the Canary Islands* under Castilian rule, she commissioned *adelantados* to pacify them using their own resources. Successful conquerors received the privilege of distributing the spoils of victory to their followers. Some *adelantados* later became governors of the lands they had vanquished. Christopher Columbus* first transferred the ancient title to the New World when, in 1494, he granted it to his brother Bartholomew on the island of Hispaniola*. Subsequently, the Crown grudgingly approved Columbus's unauthorized action. In 1512, the Catholic monarchs promised the office to Ponce de León, who was one of 29 sixteenth-century conquistadors to gain the honor.

Generally, an *adelantado* signed a royal patent or *capitulación** by which he pledged to finance and effect the subjugation of a particular region. He was required to transport a given number of settlers and clergy within a specified time limit to this remote district. Furthermore, towns and forts had to be founded, and native peoples were to be Christianized. In return, the *adelantado* enjoyed extensive civil, judicial, and military powers, as well as potentially lucrative economic prerogatives. In addition, he answered only to the Council of the Indies* in Spain, not to the local viceroy or *audiencia**. Once the *adelantado* had completed his mission, the Spanish rulers typically appropriated his seignorial rights by dispatching various officials to govern the recently colonized province. Consequently, the office fell out of use after 1600, when the era of Spanish imperial expansion drew to a close.

Most of the conquistadors of the 1500s were not accorded the rank of *adelantado*, yet their *capitulaciónes* specified conditions virtually identical to those contained in the patents of the *adelantados*. Moreover, the latter always held the offices of governor and captain-general simultaneously, thus making it difficult to ascertain exactly which duties specifically applied to the conquistador in his role as *adelantado*. Nevertheless, the title seemed to imply that its bearer directly represented the king to a greater degree than did others who had not received it.

REFERENCES: C. H. Haring, *The Spanish Empire in America*, 1947; Roscoe R. Hill, "The Office of Adelantado," *Political Science Quarterly*, 28 (1913), 646–68.

Frank Marotti

AFRICANUS, LEO. See LEO AFRICANUS.

AGRAMONTE, IGNACIO. Ignacio Agramonte was born in Camagüey Province, Cuba*, in 1841, to a well-to-do *criollo** family. He received a law degree at the University of Havana* and then practiced law and managed the family cattle business. He became a follower of Carlos Manuel de Céspedes* in promoting Cuban independence, and he was a leader in the Ten Years War* against Spain between 1868 and 1878. Agramonte rose to the rank of general in the rebel army. He was killed in combat with royal forces in 1873.

REFERENCES: Gerardo Brown Castillo, *Cuba Colonial*, 1952; Pedro José Gutiérrez, *Historia de la Isla de Cuba*, 1856.

AGRARIAN COMMUNITARIANISM. Communitarian property ownership existed in Spain even in pre-Roman times, but it was during the medieval *Reconquista* that the modern Iberian traditions of public property ownership developed their distinctive forms. The *Reconquista* monarchs encouraged the colonization of newly conquered frontier zones by offering generous land grants to Christian settlers. All lands not specifically apportioned through royal grants were called crown lands (*tierras realengas*). The monarchs allowed settlers to have free access to these lands for hunting, fishing, pasture, forest products, and even for cultivation. This led to the emergence of a strong popular perception that the crown lands, also called *tierras baldías** or *baldíos*, were commons in the public domain, although vaguely subject to royal control.

The *Reconquista* monarchs also made extensive land grants to municipalities. Some municipal property was acquired through royal grant; others came through purchase, bequests, or the appropriation of nearby *tierras baldías*. Municipal property fell into two categories: commons, for the free use of the local citizens, and *propios**, which were usually rented out to supplement the municipal treasury. There were also intermunicipal commons, sometimes extending to federations of dozens of villages. In some Castilian villages, virtually all lands were common, with the local government making periodic allotments to each family head. Furthermore, even private property was available for communal use through the *derrota de mieses**, an old European custom that allowed the public to pasture their animals on the stubble of privately owned grain fields after harvest. The communitarian system was regarded as an essential element in the socioeconomic structure of medieval and early modern Castile.* It was protected not only by custom, but also by local and royal law. The municipalities appointed guards to protect the local commons and *propios*, and to arrest violators.

The Spanish conquistadors* transplanted to the New World the institutions of agrarian communitarianism with which they were familiar, creating Spanish towns with landholding systems modeled on their Old World counterparts. The pre-Hispanic Indians* had developed their own communitarian traditions, in some respects remarkably similar to the Iberian ones. The Aztec* population was divided into *calpulli* (clans), which were both kinship and landowning units. The arable lands of Aztec villages were divided among family heads in hereditary allotments. There were no common pastures in pre-Hispanic Mexico, because there were no domesticated grazing animals to use them. In Incan* Peru*, the *ayllu** (a kinship unit similar to the Mexican *calpulli*) controlled the lands used by the common people, annually alloting each family enough arable land for its survival. The *ayllu* also held grazing land in common, for flocks of llamas and alpacas. In the pre-Hispanic Indian* communal system, the holder of a parcel of land had only the usufruct of the property. The ownership rested in the community, and the individual could maintain possession only so long as he used it.

After conquest, a hybrid communitarian system evolved, containing both Iberian and native American elements. Spanish law initially protected Indian communal landholdings. As the native communities were weakened by the great epidemics of the 1500s and 1600s, however, the colonial government in both Mexico and Peru relocated entire Indian towns and their occupants in the policy of *congregación** and *reducción* (reduction*). The new Indian towns received lands in a communitarian system similar to that of pre-conquest times, but with the addition of common pastures for the livestock introduced from Spain. With the passage of time, powerful colonial landowners were able to encroach progressively upon the lands of Indian, Spanish, and mestizo* towns and villages. This was done through a combination of intimidation, legal maneuvering, and purchase. The communitarian system was similarly eroded in Spain, partly through usurpations by powerful landowners, partly through crown-supported privatization schemes. Nevertheless, in both Spain and America, many vestiges of the traditional agrarian communitarian survived to the twentieth century.

REFERENCES: David E. Vassberg, *Land and Society in Golden Age Castile*, 1984; *The Cambridge History of Latin America: Colonial Latin America*, vols. I and II, ed. Leslie Bethell, 1984.

David E. Vassberg

AGUADO, PEDRO DE. Pedro de Aguado was born in Valdemoro, Spain, in 1538 and became a Franciscan* friar as a young man. In 1560, he left Spain with a contingent of Franciscan friars and landed in Cartagena de Indias*, Colombia.* Aguado did missionary work among various Indian* tribes before going to Bogotá* as guardian of the Franciscan convent there. Aguado is best remembered for his manuscript *Recopilación historial*, a four-volume account of the conquest of Venezuela* and Colombia, which he probably wrote in the early 1570s. The work was not published until 1906 and 1913–1915. He died in Bogotá around 1609.

REFERENCE: O. Fals Borda, "Odyssey of a Sixteenth-Century Document: Fray Pedro Aguado's *Recopilación historial*," *Hispanic American Historical Review*, 35 (1955), 203–20.

AGUALONGO, AGUSTÍN. Born in Laguna, Colombia* in the 1790s, Agustín Agualongo was a South American Indian* loyalist who supported Ferdinand VII* and the Spanish monarchy during the Colombian movement for independence. He rose to the rank of colonel in the Spanish army. Clever, cunning, and an excellent military strategist, he was able to enlist the support of the entire province of Pasto against the patriots. Eventually, he was defeated by Simón Bolívar* and captured by General Tomás Cipriano de Mosquera at Barbacoa, when the loyalist army attempted to occupy Quito*, Ecuador*. Agualongo was tried, convicted, and put to death by a firing squad in Popayán*, Colombia.

REFERENCE: José Manuél Restrepo, *Historia de la Revolución de la República de Colombia*, 1827).

Fred Koestler

AGÜERO, JOAQUÍN. Joaquín Agüero was born in Camagüey Province, Cuba*, in 1816. He was reared and educated in Havana*. As a student, he became an outspoken advocate of freedom for the slaves*. Spanish authorities identified him as a dangerous radical, a posture he only magnified when he began to call for Cuban independence as well. In the late 1840s, Agüero became president of the Liberation Society in Camagüey. He also constructed secret printing* presses that he used to reproduce revolutionary literature coming from New York. Spain found his tracts treasonous, and he was arrested in 1851. After a trial, he was executed.

REFERENCES: Gerardo Brown Castillo, *Cuba colonial*, 1952; Jaime Suchlicki, *Historical Dictionary of Cuba*, 1978.

AGÜEYBANA. Agüeybana was the chief of the Taíno* Indians* in Puerto Rico* when the Spaniards first arrived. Juan Ponce de León* led the conquest of Puerto Rico. Agüeybana became friendly with Ponce de León, but when the chief died, leadership of the Taíno Indians shifted to his younger brother, Agüeybana II. The presence of the Spaniards and their diseases was decimating the Indians, and in 1511, Agüeybana led a widespread rebellion against the intruders. The Spaniards crushed the rebellion, killed Agüeybana II, and set the Indians on a course that led to their extinction.

REFERENCE: Sven Loven, *Origins of the Taíno Culture*, 1935.

ÁGUILA NEGRA CONSPIRACY. The Águila Negra Conspiracy occurred in Cuba* early in the 1820s. Inspired by Mexico's successful revolution, several Cuban exiles in Mexico City*, led by Simón de Chávez, established a Junta Patriótica and tried to secure support from such prominent Mexicans as Guadalupe Victoria* and Antonio López de Santa Anna. The conspirators linked up with José Julián Solís and Manuel Rojo in Cuba, and their calls for independence began to attract a following. Simón de Chávez, a former Roman Catholic priest, was known as Águila Negra, or Black Eagle. Spanish authorities arrested and imprisoned the Cuban leaders in 1825, and the movement fell apart.

REFERENCE: Franklin W. Knight, *Slave Society in Cuba during the Nineteenth Century*, 1970.

AGUILAR, JERÓNIMO DE. Born in Ecija, Spain, around 1490, Jerónimo de Aguilar became a soldier and adventurer. He was shipwrecked while traveling from Darién*, Panama* to Hispaniola* and was captured by Mayan* Indians* on the Yucatán* peninsula of Mexico in 1511. They sacrificed his entire crew. Though a traveling companion's life and his own were spared, Aguilar remained a prisoner under unbearable conditions for the next eight years. He was eventually freed by Hernán Cortés* and proved to be a significant contributing strategist in the conquest and domination of Indian territory because of his knowledge of the Mayan language. He died in 1526.

REFERENCE: Bernal Diaz del Castillo, *True History of the Conquest of New Spain*, 1958.

Fred Koestler

AGUILAR, MANUEL. Manuel Aguilar was born in Tonacatepeque, El Salvador*, in 1750, and was educated at San Francisco of Borja College in Guatemala*. A priest, he eventually became the rector of the college. Along with his brothers Nicolás and Vicente, who were also Roman Catholic priests, he is best remembered for his role in the early independence movement in the city of San Salvador.* He refused to read to his congregation a pastoral letter condemning Miguel de Hidalgo*'s revolt in Mexico. Royal officials accused the Aguilar brothers of having carried on a correspendence with Hidalgo and of being an indirect part of the conspiracy. In September 1811, royal officials arrested and imprisoned him in Guatemala City*; his brothers were subsequently arrested as well. News of his arrest provoked the revolt of November 5, 1811, in San Salvador. He was released from prison in 1813, participated in the revolt of January 4, 1814, and was arrested again, along with his brothers. All three died in prison.

    REFERENCE: Philip F. Flemion, *Historical Dictionary of El Salvador*, 1972.

AGUILAR, NICOLÁS. Nicolás Aguilar was born in Tonacatepeque, El Salvador*, on December 15, 1741. He was ordained a Jesuit* priest in 1767. Despite the expulsion of the Jesuits from the New World, Aguilar remained in San Salvador* as a pastor. By the early 1800s, Aguilar was increasingly in favor of independence from Spain, and in 1811 he joined with José Matías Delgado* in leading a rebellion against Don Antonio Gutiérrez Ulloa*, the unpopular *intendente*. The rebellion failed, as did another one he led in 1814. He died in prison on September 12, 1818, in San Salvador.

    REFERENCE: Philip F. Flemion, *Historical Dictionary of El Salvador*, 1972.

AGUILAR Y SEIYAS, FRANCISCO. Francisco Aguilar y Seiyas was born in Betanzos, Spain; he came to New Spain* in 1679 as the bishop-elect of Michoacán. In 1682, Aguilar was appointed archbishop of Mexico City*, and his tenure in office was marked by an ambitious construction campaign—chapels, schools, and hospitals. He died in Mexico City on October 14, 1698.

    REFERENCE: I. A. Leonard, *Baroque Times in Old Mexico: Seventeenth-Century Persons, Places, Practices*, 1959.

AGUINALDO, EMILIO. Emilio Aguinaldo was born into a prominent landowning Tagalog*-Chinese mestizo* family in Cavite, the Philippine* Islands, on March 22, 1869. He was the sixth of eight children. His father died when he was nine, and the boy dropped out of school at age thirteen to pursue various adventures, including sailing to Mindoro and Mindanao*. To avoid serving in the Spanish military, he became a local tax collector and in 1895 was appointed mayor of the town of Kawit, a post his father had held before him. Aguinaldo may have killed a rival in love that year; at any rate, he was married in early 1896 and had a son by the end of the year.

    Aguinaldo joined Andrés Bonifacio's* secret revolutionary society, the Katipunan*, in March 1895 and adopted the revolutionary *nom de guerre* Magdalo after Mary Magdalene. When the revolution began in 1896, Bonifacio's men were soon pushed out of the Manila* area. By contrast, Aguinaldo, leading the insurrection in Cavite, met rapid success. He drove the Spaniards from three towns and on September 3, 1896, routed a large Spanish force. His victories contrasted sharply with Bonifacio's defeats, and Aguinaldo began to think of himself as the leader of the revolution. The two had a showdown at Tejeros, Cavite, in March 1897. Aguinaldo had his rival apprehended, tried, sentenced, and shot. He was thereafter the undisputed leader of the revolution. More than personal jealousy motivated Aguinaldo. For all his undeniable patriotism, he never fully overcame his provincial outlook and fully trusted only his fellow Caviteños.

Spanish forces launched a counter-offensive. Aguinaldo soon found himself bottled up in the mountains. It seemed that he could hope for little more than a continued stalemate, and he found it hard to take care of his soldiers' dependents. After negotiations, Aguinaldo accepted exile in return for 400,000 pesos. He stayed in Hong Kong from January to May 1898, living on the interest while saving the principal to buy arms with which to resume the struggle. While he was in Hong Kong, the United States declared war on Spain. The Americans hoped to use Aguinaldo to undermine the Spanish position in the islands, while Aguinaldo hoped to use the United States to win Philippine independence. He seems to have believed, and may have been promised, that the Americans would really turn the Philippines over to him once Spain had been defeated. On May 19, 1898, not three weeks after Admiral George Dewey's celebrated victory in Manila Bay, Aguinaldo disembarked from the American ship *McCulloch* to resume his fight.

The Filipinos* quickly grew suspicious of American intentions. Aguinaldo declared Philippine independence on June 12. A congress was convened in Bulacán in August. The first Philippine Republic was inaugurated in January 1899 with Aguinaldo as president, but in practice his power was strictly military for the republic was soon at war with the United States. Hostilities began on February 4, 1899. Aguinaldo's government had to abandon Malolos for a series of temporary provincial capitals as American forces pushed inexorably northward across the central Luzon* plain. Military reverses ate away at the Filipinos' morale. Once again, Aguinaldo eliminated a rival, this time General Antonio Luna, who was shot and hacked to death by Cavite troops loyal to Aguinaldo on June 5, 1899.

After a halt during the rainy season, U.S. troops resumed the offensive in October. They nearly trapped Aguinaldo in Pangasinan*, but the wily general escaped through the Tirad Pass, crossed the central cordillera, and on September 6, 1900, reached Palanan, Isabela, one of the most remote towns on Luzon. He remained there for six months, vainly hoping to direct the guerillas who fought on after all regular Philippine armies had been defeated. He was captured through the inspired trickery of an American officer, Frederick Funston, on March 23, 1901. He was brought to Manila where, after much pleading from his family, he took an oath of allegiance to the United States. He wore a black bow tie from that day forward, in mourning for the first Philippine Republic, until the United States granted Philippine independence on July 4, 1946. Aguinaldo faded into obscurity and lived to be 94 years old. He died on February 6, 1964.

REFERENCE: David Bain, *Sitting in Darkness: America in the Philippines*, 1984.

Ross Marlay

AGUIRRE, FRANCISCO DE. Francisco de Aguirre was born around 1500 in Talavera, Spain. He came to the New World in the early 1530s, accompanying Francisco Pizarro* to Peru* and later Pedro de Valdivia* to Chile* in 1540. During the 1540s, Aguirre served as the *alcalde mayor** in Santiago*, Chile; in 1551, Valdivia named him lieutenant governor over northern Chile. But in the 1560s, Aguirre's good fortune changed. On an expedition to Tucumán*, several people under his command became disgruntled with his leadership and reported him to the Inquisition*. As a result of the politics of the subsequent investigation, Aguirre lost his political office and received a five-year prison term. He died in La Serena, Chile, in 1580.

REFERENCE: José Toribio Medina, *Diccionario biográfico colonial de Chile*, 1906.

AGUIRRE, GUILLERMO DE. Guillermo de Aguirre was the Spanish *oidor** of the *audiencia* of Mexico City* who was catapulted into fame at a fateful meeting of the *junta grande* called by the viceroy* in 1808. As a result of the historic events of Bayonne, both the *cabildo** and *audiencia** of Mexico were propelled to action, although in opposite directions. The *cabildo* of Mexico took the initiative on July 16, 1808; three days later, it decided to arrogate to itself the right to speak on behalf of the entire viceroyalty—what the *cabildos* of New Granada*, Chile*, and Río de la Plata* would do in 1810. The *cabildo* then resolved to consider the abdication of the kings in Bayonne null and void, to assume provisionally the government of the area until the viceroyalty would make a final decision, and to allow the viceroy to remain in his post until further notice.

The decisions of the *cabildo* of July 19, 1808, were officially communicated to the viceroy, who accepted them, and to the *audiencia*, which considered them scandalous and dangerous to the interests of the Spanish Empire. In a *Real Acuerdo* on July 21, 1808, the *audiencia* opposed the action of the *cabildo*, with the net result that the disagreement among the most important branches of government in New Spain* was complete: the viceroy siding with the city and the *audiencia* proving hostile to the move of the *criollos**. The *cabildo* replied to the opinions of the *Acuerdo** on August 3, and expressed its surprise concerning the legal stance adopted by the *audiencia*. In regard to its assumption of the full sovereignty of the viceroyalty of New Spain*, it cited several documents of the sixteenth century in its defense and requested the convocation of a general junta, or *cortes* (as was done later in the Peninsula) in order to have its decisions implemented. Again the *audiencia* of Mexico City disagreed, but Viceroy José de Iturrigaray* decided to go along with the wishes of the *cabildo* of Mexico. Thus he called for the famous meeting of Tuesday, August 9, 1808.

The meeting of this *junta grande* was a heterogeneous assembly of 82 members of the *audiencia*, the *ayuntamiento*, and the *consulado**, including the ecclesiastical authorities and the native governors of the district of Mexico City. The meeting did several things: it officially acknowledged the sovereignty of Ferdinand VII*; it recognized the Bourbon dynasty and the order of succession as established in the *Recopilación de Autos* of Castile* in Book V, Title 7, Law 5; and it stated that as long as the king did not return to his monarchy the junta would obey no order from the French emperor or from any authority that would not emanate from his legitimate rule, nor would they acknowledge any supreme junta of those kingdoms unless ratified by this Catholic majesty. A clash of opinions then resulted, and the mouthpiece of the Spanish or royalist party, the *oidor* Guillermo de Aguirre, expressed what may be termed the colonialist approach. It was a viewpoint that was echoed in Spain by Pablo Vicente, deputy to the Cortes of Cádiz*, and in the Río de la Plata by Bishop Benito de la Lué y Riega; in short, the right of Spain and the Spaniards to rule over Spanish-American territories: "As long as there exists a piece of land in Spain, Spain must rule over the Americas; and as long as there exists a single Spaniard in the Americas, that Spaniard must rule over the Spanish Americans, authority coming to the sons of the country only when there is no longer any Spaniard there."

Opposing the views of the Mexican minority, represented by Francisco Primo de Verdad*, the *peninsulares**, who formed the majority, thus ended the first peaceful attempt at gaining autonomy for the area. In the process, the peninsulares later deposed Viceroy Iturrigaray and had him shipped back to Spain.

REFERENCES: Enrique Lafuente Ferrari, *El Virrey Iturrigaray y los orígenes de la independencia de Méjico*, 1941; O. Carlos Stoetzer, *The Scholastic Roots of the Spanish American Revolution*, 1979.

O. Carlos Stoetzer

AGUIRRE, JUAN BAUTISTA. Juan Bautista Aguirre was born on April 11, 1725, in Daule in what is today Guayas Province, Ecuador*. As a young man, Aguirre took vows in the Jesuit* order and eventually became a professor at San Gregorio University in Quito*, where he taught literature and physics. When the Jesuits were expelled from the New World in 1767, Aguirre relocated to Italy where he taught at Tivoli and Ferrara. An accomplished poet, Aguirre is remembered as the premier literary figure of colonial Ecuador. He died in Tivoli on June 15, 1786.

REFERENCE: Augusto Arias, *Panorama de la literatura ecuatoriana*, 1956.

Sam L. Slick

AGUIRRE, LOPE DE. Lope de Aguirre was born around 1511 in Villa de Oñate, in Guipuzcoa Province, Spain. On April 6, 1536, still in Spain, he received the title of *regidor** for Lima* but on December 1, 1536, his *regimiento* was transferred to Chile*. Aguirre arrived in the Indies in 1539. In 1540, he joined the Diego de Rojas expedition to the Chunchos. He participated in the battles against Diego de Almagro*, *el Mozo*. In the battle of Chupas, he hid at Huamanga* refusing to fight. Melchor Verdugo, *encomendero* of Cajamarca, became his benefactor. On Verdugo's recommendation, Aguirre became sergeant of the guard for Peru's* first viceroy, Blasco Núñez de Vela*. On Núñez's arrest, Aguirre left for Trujillo* with Verdugo. Verdugo rebelled against Gonzalo Pizarro* in 1546 with Aguirre.

They went to Nicaragua* and planned to take Nombre de Dios. Verdugo named Aguirre his *sargento mayor*. They attacked the port and the merchants surrendered, but Pizarro's troops arrived from Panama* and Verdugo departed. Aguirre railed at his fate in the following words: "God, if you are to grant me some good, I want it now, and your glory save it for your saints." Verdugo abandoned Aguirre and went to Spain. Aguirre attempted to join Pedro de la Gasca's* expedition against Pizarro, but Gasca heard about the *verduguistas* and refused to take him. Aguirre remained in Panama until Pizarro's defeat, after which he went to Peru hoping for an *encomienda** because of his services with Verdugo and for the king. Aguirre's request was denied, and he felt that his services had been poorly repaid. He participated in numerous revolts, such as the La Plata rebellion against the *corregidor** Pedro de Hinojosa. He helped to make Sebastián de Castilla a caudillo* of the movement. Later the La Plata rebels killed Castilla and then disbanded. Aguirre wandered the countryside, surviving by stealing from the Indians*.

In 1554, Francisco Hernández Girón rebelled in Cuzco*. Aguirre took advantage of an amnesty offered to those who had participated in Castilla's murder, provided that they joined the king's forces against Hernández Girón. In the battle of Chuquinga, a bullet hit Aguirre's right leg, and the wound left him permanently disabled. Bitter against the king, he became a vagabond known as "Aguirre *el loco*." He went to Lima hoping to gain some recompense for his services. To get rid of the old conquistadors, adventurers, and vagabonds, who were a major problem in Lima, Viceroy Andrés Hurtado de Mendoza organized an expedition to El Dorado*. In February 1559, he named Pedro de Ursúa* as governor of Omagua Province and expedition leader. Ursúa rounded up men and resources in various towns. Aguirre returned from Lima with the widow Doña Inés. Aguirre appeared with his *mestiza* daughter, Elvirica, to sign up for the expedition.

In September 1560, the expedition left Topesana. Ursúa's troops resented Aguirre bringing a woman and his conduct towards them. Aguirre, named *Tenedor de los Bienes de Difuntos*, organized a revolt that others seconded. One group wanted to arrest the governor and simply return to Peru, but Aguirre said it was best to kill him and conquer Peru. Others joined him and chose Fernando de Guzmán, a nobleman and *alférez general del campo*, as leader. On New Year's Day, 1561, in the town of Machifaro, they killed Ursua. They named Aguirre *maestre de campo* and wrote a document to the king justifying Ursúa's assassination. It stated that the governor had no intention of conquering and populating the land, that he was living to make love with Doña Inés, that the troops were on the verge of being lost, and that the crime was a service to the king. Guzmán signed first, and Aguirre, who wrote "Lope de Aguirre, *Traidor,*" was second. Some questioned his act, and he responded that all were traitors for killing the king's governor. Guzmán then renounced Philip II*, King of Spain. In Los Bergantines, the Spaniards stayed for three months building two brigantines. They planned to conquer Peru, where they intended to kill the *vecinos* and avenge themselves on the viceroy who had sent them from the kingdom with false promises.

At this point, Guzmán wanted to renounce being prince, so he organized a meeting without inviting Aguirre. Guzmán decided to explore and populate the land (in the hopes of being pardoned by the king) and to kill Aguirre. Aguirre gave his followers the best arms to protect himself. He had a disagreement with Lorenzo de Zalduendo, captain of the guard, over bringing pillows aboard for Doña Inés. Aguirre killed him without Guzmán's permission and then killed her.

The conquistadors continued their journey down the Amazon. Aguirre, still suspicious, disarmed some and killed others. He left some Indians* who had come with him in the jungle. On July 4, 1561, the brigantines went out to sea and on July 21 they spotted La Margarita* island. More men were killed on suspicion before landing. The island's governor, Juan de Villandrando, met them, but he was captured along with other important personages. The island's capital was taken and plundered. Aguirre continued the killings. He sent his captain, Pedro de Munguía, with orders to take the ship of Fray Francisco Montesinos, a Dominican* provincial (local leader), but Munguía, with twenty men, deserted, pledged loyalty to the Spanish king, and joined Montesinos.

When Aguirre discovered Munguía had returned with Montesinos and a large contingent of troops to La Margarita island, he killed the governor and four others. Aguirre wrote to Montesinos in an attempt to come to terms. Montesinos answered that he did not deal with traitors but would go to Santo Domingo* for help. Aguirre promised that he would make Montesinos "Pope" if he would help him take Peru. Montesinos left, and Aguirre continued the slaughter by killing two Dominicans who had nothing to do with Montesinos.

Although he wanted to continue to Peru, he decided to go to Venezuela* and New Granada*. He left on August 31, when a Caracas* *vecino* arrived with Indians to defend the Spaniards of La Margarita. Aguirre left 14 soldiers, seven *vecinos*, two friars, and two women dead. He arrived at La Burburata and burned his ships and a merchant vessel. The people deserted the town. He threatened New Valencia* if they would not bring provisions, and he killed a merchant. After capturing La Burburata's *alcalde** and his family, he destroyed the town. The town's citizens fled to the mountains. The governor of the province of Venezuela, Pedro Pablo Collado, decided to resist.

After killing some soldiers who appeared weak, Aguirre entered New Valencia, but he was sick and muttered to himself, "Kill me. Kill me." After a few days, he recuperated. In New Valencia, he sent his famous letter to Philip

II, treating the king informally and discourteously, while he explained his actions. He left New Valencia* on October 15, 1561, and arrived at New Segovia* a week later. The deserted town contained *cedulas*, directed to Aguirre's men, pardoning them if they abandoned Aguirre. Two of his men decided to do just that, and they assassinated Aguirre on October 27, 1561.

REFERENCE: José Antonio del Busto Duthurburu, *Biblioteca Hombres del Perú, XXI: Lope de Aguirre*, 1965.

Carlos Pérez

AHMED OULD CAID. See CAID AHMED OULD.

AIX-LA-CHAPELLE, TREATY OF. The weakness of the Austrian Empire in 1740, exacerbated by the lack of a male heir to Emperor Charles VI, led to renewed territorial conflict among the European powers. Although the Pragmatic Sanction had been signed by the major European states (thus guaranteeing Empress Maria Theresa's succession to all the Habsburg domains), in 1740, King Frederick II of Prussia seized the Austrian province of Silesia. This exercise ignited a general conflict, the War of the Austrian Succession*, with Bavaria, Spain, and France also interested in annexing Austrian territory. France joined Spain and Prussia against Great Britain and Austria. Maria Theresa was forced to cede Silesia to Frederick II. Until 1748, the struggle continued in Bohemia and in the Austrian Netherlands where Maria Theresa suffered further setbacks. Austria was ultimately forced to negotiate by the threat of diminished subsidies from Britain. The Treaty of Aix-la-Chapelle, signed on October 18, 1748, resulted in little territory changing hands in Europe. In the European colonies, however, the treaty was marked by the mutual restitution of conquests, including the fortress of Louisbourg on Cape Breton Island, Nova Scotia, to France, and the British reacquisition of Madras in India. The treaty settled little of the economic rivalry between Britain and France in the New World, Africa, and India, thus setting the stage for further colonial conflict. The war itself signaled the emergence of Brandenburg-Prussia as one of the two German powers, with the Habsburgs seriously weakened by the Prussian gain of Silesia.

REFERENCES: Edward Crankshaw, *Maria Theresa*, 1970; Robert A. Kann, *A History of the Habsburg Empire, 1526–1918*, 1974.

William G. Ratliff

ALARCÓN Y MENDOZA, JUAN RUIZ DE. See RUIZ DE ALARCÓN, JUAN.

ALBERONI, JULIO. Born in 1664 to humble parents at Piacenza in the Duchy of Parma, Julio Alberoni gained his education through the Church, receiving Holy Orders in 1690. Alberoni quickly displayed an impressive ability to attach himself to influential personages, a process aided by his mastery of the French language and of Italian cuisine. During the War of the Spanish Succession*, he entered the service of the Duke of Vendôme, the victorious commander of French forces operating in Italy. He later accompanied the duke to France and in 1710 to Spain where Vendôme commanded an army deployed in support of Louis XIV's grandson, Philip V*. Although Vendôme died in 1712, Alberoni retained his access to court through his friendship with the powerful French Princess Ursins; he also came to represent the interests of the Duke of Parma. His decisive role in arranging the marriage in September 1714 of the widowed Philip V to the Parmesan Isabel Farnese, niece of the duke, secured him a position of eminence. When the strong-willed bride ridded the court of French influence and embraced her Italian heritage, Abbé Alberoni soon became the *de facto* prime minister of Spain, dominating the newly organized system of ministries without portfolio. In 1717, he was elevated to cardinal.

Alberoni directed his energies primarily toward peninsular regeneration, above all financial and administrative reform, including an attempt to install the intendant system that did not long survive him. Nevertheless, he left his imprint on colonial policy. Appreciative of Isabel's maternal desire to secure thrones for her sons, Alberoni forcefully addressed the problem of restoring Spanish sea power conquering Italy. To unify the supervision of naval supply and finance, he created the Intendancy-General of Marine in Cádiz; to unite the presidency of the Casa de Contratación* to that same office, by decree of May 12, 1717, he transferred to Cádiz both the *Casa* and the Consulado* of Seville*, which held a legal monopoly on the American trade. That same year, Alberoni, desperate to increase royal revenues, also established the Royal Tobacco Monopoly in Cuba to supply the factory in Seville, which proved the first step in what would become a lucrative government enterprise in the years to come. Finally, it may be inferred that he had a hand in the establishment of the viceroyalty of New Granada* in 1717.

Alberoni's star fell as quickly as it had risen. Succeeding almost miraculously in assembling a respectable navy, he occupied Sardinia in 1717. The following year, however, the English, in a surprise attack off Cape Passero, sank or captured most of the Spanish fleet on its voyage to Sicily. With the Quadruple Alliance of Great Britain, France, the Netherlands, and Austria united against Spain and with foreign armies invading his domains, Philip exiled Alberoni by decree on December 4, 1719. The cardinal found his way back to Italy where, among other things, he entered the service of the papacy. He passed his declining years in Piacenza where he died.

REFERENCE: Simon Harcourt-Smith, *Cardinal of Spain: The Life and Strange Career of Alberoni*, 1944.

Allan J. Kuethe

ALBUQUERQUE. In the spring of 1706, Governor Francisco Cuervo y Valdés of New Mexico* founded the Villa of San Felipe de Alburquerque, about 60 miles south of Santa Fe*. It was originally spelled "Alburquerque" and named after the Duke of Alburquerque, Francisco Fernández de la Cueva, who served as viceroy of New Spain* from 1702 to 1711, and in honor of King Philip (Felipe) V* of Spain and the apostle, San Felipe. The area of Albuquerque had attracted Spanish settlers engaged in farming and ranching. Two leaders of the colonization party were Fray Juan Mingues, chaplain of Santa Fe presidio, and Captain Martín Hurtado, who became Albuquerque's first *alcalde**. Figures concerning the population at the founding of Albuquerque reveal that there were 35 families, numbering 252 adults and children. By 1751, the town had grown to 500 Spaniards and 200 Indians. As the years passed, Albuquerque continued to grow and became one of the important settled urban areas in the Spanish Borderlands*.

REFERENCES: Eleanor B. Adams and Fray Angélico Chávez, *The Missions of New Mexico, 1776*, 1975; Richard E. Greenleaf, "The Founding of Albuquerque, 1706: An Historical-Legal Problem," *New Mexico Historical Review*, 39 (1964).

Raymond Wilson

ALCABALA. The *alcabala* was a sales tax imposed by the Spanish Crown on colonial commerce as a revenue-producing measure. The *alcabala* had deep roots in Spanish history, going back to the *gabella* that the Romans imposed on Spain. Next to royal income from tobacco*, and excepting income from gold and silver, the *alcabala* was the most valuable source of revenue for the Crown in the New World. The tax was imposed at each point of commercial exchange, at both the wholesale and retail level. At the custom house, it was collected whether or not the good was sold. The *alcabala* was first levied in New Spain* at 2 percent in 1575; it was extended to Guatemala* in 1576 and to Peru* in 1591. In 1627, the Crown doubled it to 4 percent to offset the military expenses of protecting the colonies. It immediately became apparent that 4 percent was inadequate, and in 1639 Spain raised the *alcabala* to 6 percent. In 1644, it went up again, this time to 8 percent, where it remained until 1754. For a time it jumped briefly to 10 percent. The *alcabala* dropped back to 6 percent between 1754 and 1780, after which it went up to 8 percent.

REFERENCE: C. H. Haring, *Spanish Empire in America*, 1947.

ALCACOVAS, TREATY OF (1479). This treaty ended the War of the Succession (1474–1479) between Castile* and Portugal. Alfonso V, the king of Portugal, had supported the claim of Juana, a niece of Isabella* of Castile, to the throne of Castile in opposition to Isabella and her husband Ferdinand.* This war merged with a longstanding Portuguese-Castilian rivalry over the Canary Islands.* Castile claimed the Canaries on the basis of a papal grant made in 1344. Early in the fifteenth century, Norman pioneers had established settlements on the islands of Lanzarote, Ferro, and Fuerteventura, in spite of determined opposition from the indigenous inhabitants of the Canaries, the warlike Guanches*. Meanwhile, starting in 1419, the Portuguese had begun exploring the west coast of Africa and established a profitable trade there. They had also settled the Madeira Islands in the 1420s and the Azores and Cape Verde Islands beginning in the early 1460s. As a result, they came to fear Castilian attacks on their trade routes from the settlements on the Canaries and wanted the islands for themselves as a base. They established their own settlements on the Canaries and encouraged the Guanches to attack the Castilians.

Savage piratical warfare broke out between the Castilian and Portuguese settlers in the Canary Islands during the 1460s, becoming part of the War of the Succession in 1474. Although the Portuguese and their allies were defeated on land, they had achieved considerable success at sea by 1479. The Treaty of Alcacovas, which ended the conflict, was the first treaty between European nations to deal with conflicts concerning overseas possessions. While the treaty established the legitimacy of Isabella's claim to the throne of Castile, it also favored the further expansion of the Portuguese Empire. Portugal abandoned all claims to the Canary Islands in favor of Castile. In return, Castile (soon to be united with Aragon in 1481 as Spain) recognized Portugal's monopoly of the African trade and its possesion of the Azores, Madeira, the Cape Verde Islands, and all lands south of the Canaries. The treaty was confirmed by Pope Sixtus IV in 1481 by the bull *Aeterni Regis*. Later John II of Portugal (1481–1495) would use this treaty to lay claim to Christopher Columbus's[*] discoveries of 1492. The resulting confrontation between Spain and Portugal would lead to the Treaty of Tordesillas[*] of 1494 and its division of the Atlantic world between the two countries.

REFERENCE: Bailey W. Diffie and George D. Winius, *Foundations of the Portuguese Empire 1415–1580*, 1977.

Ronald Fritze

ALCAIDE. The *alcaide* was a functionary of the Spanish Crown who was charged with supervising local jails and prisoners.

REFERENCE: Ione S. Wright and Lisa M. Nekhom, *Historical Dictionary of Argentina*, 1978.

ALCALDE. The term *alcalde* was used in the colonial period to describe the office of mayor and judge.

REFERENCE: Richard E. Moore, *Historical Dictionary of Guatemala*, 1973.

ALCALDES DE BARRIO. The office of *alcalde de barrio*, also known as *alcalde de vara*, involved supervisory responsibilities for ward or parish administration in Spanish towns in the New World. That position emerged only after the colonial settlements had urbanized and increased in population.

REFERENCE: Richard E. Moore, *Historical Dictionary of Guatemala*, 1973.

ALCALDES DE LA HERMANDAD. In the Spanish colonies, the *alcaldes de la hermandad* were minor officials serving as police magistrates in rural areas of the colonies, serving under the direction of *cabildo*[*] officials. Sometimes they were referred to as *alcaldes de la mesta* or occasionally as *alcaldes cuadrilleros*. The *alcalde provincial* was in charge of all of the *alcaldes de la hermandad*.

REFERENCE: C. H. Haring, *The Spanish Empire in America*, 1947.

ALCALDES DE LA MESTA. See *ALCALDES DE LA HERMANDAD*.

ALCALDES MAYORES. The office of *alcalde mayor* involved duties as judge and mayor in the Spanish Empire. They were royal appointees whom the viceroy* recommended to the king. They served for a period of three years.
    REFERENCE: Richard E. Moore, *Historical Dictionary of Guatemala*, 1973.

ALCALDES ORDINARIOS. The office of *alcalde ordinario* in Spanish imperial cities and towns was an elected position that involved the administration of routine duties.
    REFERENCE: Richard E. Moore, *Historical Dictionary of Guatemala*, 1973.

ALCEDO, ANTONIO DE. Antonio de Alcedo was born in Quito*, Ecuador*, around 1734. His father was Dionisio de Alcedo y Herrera*, a prominent government official in the New World. Alcedo studied mathematics at the Imperial Institute of Madrid and then studied medicine in Paris. He spent his career in the Spanish army, rising to the rank of field marshal, but his real love was history, literature, and geography. Using his father's diaries and letters, Alcedo wrote *El diccionario geográfico histórico de las Indias Occidentales o América*, a five-volume work. In 1921, historians also discovered another Alcedo work—*Biblioteca Americana o catálogo histórico de todos los autores que han escrito sobre materiales de América en varios idomas con una noticia de sus vidas*. Alcedo died in Coruña, Spain, in 1812.
    REFERENCE: J. R. Páez, "Don Antonio de Alcedo y su Biblioteca Americana," *Boletín de la Academia Nacional de la Historia* (Quito), 37 (1957), 90–91.

ALCEDO Y HERRERA, DIONISIO DE. Dionisio de Alcedo y Herrera was born in Madrid, Spain, in 1690. He came to Lima*, Peru*, in 1706 with the party of Marques de Castel-Dos-Ruis, the new viceroy* of Peru. Bright and well-read, he became a politically influential figure even as a young man and was appointed governor of Canta in 1721, a post he held until 1724. He became president of the *audiencia* of Quito* in 1728 and served there until 1736. Alcedo y Herrera is best remembered, however, for his historical writings. In 1740, he wrote *Aviso histórico, político, geográfico con las noticias más particulares de la América*, and the next year the *Compendio de la provincia, partidos, ciudades, astilleros, ríos y puertos de Guayaquil*. Dionisio de Alcedo y Herrera served as governor and captain general of Tierra Firme between 1743 and 1749, before returning to Madrid where he died in 1777.
    REFERENCE: J. R. Páez, "Don Antonio de Alcedo y su Biblioteca Americana," *Boletín de la Academia Nacional de la Historia* (Quito), 37 (1957), 90–91.

ALCINA, FRANCISCO IGNACIO DE. A native of Spain born in 1610, Francisco Ignacio de Alcina joined the Jesuit* order as a young man and spent most of his career in the Philippines*. Most of his time was spent in the Jesuit parishes on the islands of Samar*, Leyte*, and the Visayas*. Alcina was also a brilliant observer of ethnography and natural history; his journals and writings have become an invaluable reference for historians looking at seventeenth-century Filipino history. He died in 1674.

REFERENCE: John Leddy Phelan, *The Hispanization of the Philippines: Spanish Aims and Filipino Responses 1565–1700*, 1959.

ALDAMA, IGNACIO DE. Ignacio de Aldama was born in San Miguel el Grande (known today as San Miguel de Allende), New Spain*, in 1780. A lawyer by profession, Aldama earned a fortune through a variety of commercial investments. He actively participated in the movement for Mexican independence following the "Grito de Dolores"* with Father Miguel Hidalgo*. Named by Hidalgo as president of the municipality of San Miguel after the capture of the town, he was later sent to the United States as an envoy for independence. Aldama was captured in Bejar and executed by a royalist firing squad in Monclova, Mexico, in 1811.

REFERENCES: Lucas Alamán, *Historia de Méjico desde los primeros movimientos que preparan su independencia en el año 1808 hasta la época presente*, 5 vols., 1849–1852; L. E. Fisher, *The Background of the Revolution for Mexican Independence*, 1934.

Fred Koestler

ALDAMA, JUAN. A native of San Miguel el Grande, Mexico, Juan Aldama was a Mexican military leader and central figure in the movement for Mexican independence in 1810. He was a principal in the "Grito de Dolores"* rebellion with Father Miguel Hidalgo* when, as captain in the Spanish army, he pledged his regiment of Spanish dragoons toward Mexican independence. Aldama was also part of the Querétaro, San Miguel el Grande, and Dolores conspiracies. Once the "Plan" was finally exposed by the Spanish forces, he traveled to Dolores with Ignacio José de Allende* to warn Hidalgo of the impending danger (September 15, 1810) and to urge an all-out attack against the Spanish forces. He fought valiantly against the Spanish forces at the battles of Guanajuato*, Alhóndiga de Granaditas*, and others. He was promoted to lieutenant general of the revolutionary forces. Captured at Norias de Baján, he was executed by a royalist firing squad in Chihuahua, Mexico, on July 26, 1811.

REFERENCE: Juan E. Hernández y Dávalos, *Colección de documentos para la historia de la guerra de independencia*, 6 vols., 1877–1882.

Fred Koestler

ALDAMA, MIGUEL. Miguel Aldama was born in Havana*, Cuba*, in 1821, to wealthy, Spanish-born parents. The family emigrated from Spain in the early 1800s and became prominent sugar* planters. In 1841, they purchased majority ownership in the Havana Railway Company, which they hoped to use to ship their products to market as well as to foster other investments in Cuba. By the 1860s, the family business was one of the leading economic entities in Cuba. As a young man, Miguel Aldama became unhappy with the political status of Cuba. During the 1840s he was a leader of the Havana Club, a group committed to the U.S. annexation of Cuba. When the Civil War in the United States eliminated any serious hope of annexation, Aldama became a reformist, working to secure political autonomy for Cuba within the Spanish Empire. Eventually, his political thought evolved all the way to revolutionary independence. During the Ten Years War* between 1868 and 1878, Aldama spent a great deal of time in New York trying to raise money for the revolution. In the process, he lost his own fortune through confiscation as well as contributions to the cause of independence. He died a pauper in Havana in 1888.

REFERENCE: Gerardo Brown Castillo, *Cuba colonial*, 1952.

Fred Koestler

ALDANA, LORENZO DE. Lorenzo de Aldana was born in Lorenzo, Spain, and became an important *conquistador** in the early history of Guatemala*. Aldana fought against the Maya* Indians of Guatemala in the early 1530s; in 1534, he went to Quito* with Pedro de Alvarado's* expedition. Under instructions from Francisco Pizarro*, he later assumed the governorship of Popayán* and founded the city of Pasto in 1539. During the 1540s, Aldana supervised the exploration and early settlement of the Cauca Valley of what is today Colombia*. He returned to Lima*, Peru*, and died there in 1557.

REFERENCE: Robert H. Davis, *Historical Dictionary of Colombia*, 1977.

ALEGRE, FRANCISCO JAVIER. Francisco Javier Alegre was born in Veracruz, New Spain*, on November 12, 1729. Alegre attended school in Puebla* and in Mexico City*, and in 1747 he joined the Jesuit* order. For the next 20 years, Alegre taught philosophy, grammar, Latin, mathematics, and rhetoric in Mexico, Havana*, and Mérida*, and during those years he also wrote history. Throughout the late 1750s and early 1760s, at the request of the Jesuit order, Alegre continued the *Historia de la provincia* that Father Francisco de Florencia had started. At the time, he was teaching at the Royal College and Seminary of San Ildefonso. After the expulsion of the Jesuits from the New World in 1767, Alegre continued his history of the order in Europe. His research and writing were badly biased, however, in defense of Jesuit activities. He died in Bologna, Italy, on August 16, 1788.

REFERENCE: E. J. Burrus, "Francisco Javier Alegre: Historian of the Jesuits in New Spain," *Archives of the History of the Society of Jesus*, 22 (1953), 439–509.

ALEXANDER VI, POPE. Pope Alexander VI played a critical role in the early development of the Spanish and Portuguese empires in the New World. He was born in 1431 as Rodrigo Borgia in Jativa, Valencia, Spain, to a prominent family. He studied canon law at the University of Bologna, and in 1458 he was appointed as bishop of Valencia. Borgia possessed great political skills, which he used carefully in managing his own clerical career. On the evening of August 10–11, 1492, he became Pope Alexander VI, head of the Roman Catholic church*. In terms of the history of the Spanish Empire in the New World, Alexander VI vigorously promoted the evangelization of the Indians*; he also negotiated the

agreement between Spain and Portugal that resulted in the Treaty of Tordesillas*
of 1494, dividing the New World discoveries between the two imperial powers.
In addition, he established the Patronato Real* which gave sovereign political
powers to the Church in the colonies. Pope Alexander VI died in 1503.

REFERENCE: Giovanni Soranzo, *Studi intorno a papa Alessandro VI (Borgia)*, 1950.

ALFINGER, AMBROSIUS. Hoping to profit immediately from the New World
possessions, King Charles V* of Spain extended a special monopoly in 1528 to
the House of Welser*, a German banking firm, to explore and settle the coast
of Venezuela*. Ambrosius Alfinger was one of the individuals whom the Welsers
hired to carry out the exploration and conquest. Between 1528 and 1533, Alfinger
directed three expeditions into the interior of Venezuela. The expeditions went
as far east as the present-day site of Maracaibo and as far west as the Magdalena
River in present-day Colombia*. Alfinger quickly earned a reputation as the
"cruelest of the cruel" in his treatment of the Indians.* He was killed in a
skirmish with Indians in Colombia in 1533.

REFERENCE: Germán Arcienagas, *Germans in the Conquest of America*, 1943.

ALGECIRAS, ACT OF. The Act of Algeciras was signed on April 7, 1906,
at the conclusion of the Algeciras Conference. It confirmed Moroccan independence and assured freedom of trade for all nations. The act created a state
bank with equal shares for the Great Powers but controlled by a French bank.
It granted France and Spain joint control of the police forces in Moroccan ports.
It marked the defeat of Germany's efforts to weaken the Anglo-French *entente*
and to move into Morocco. France became the dominant power in Morocco but
did not succeed in making that country its protectorate.

REFERENCES: Eugene N. Anderson, *The First Moroccan Crisis, 1904–1906*, 1930;
Edmund Burke III, *Prelude to Protectorate in Morocco* 1976; *The Cambridge History
of Africa*, vol. 6, 1985.

ALHÓNDIGA DE GRANADITAS, BATTLE OF. After commencing the
revolt on September 13, 1810, in Dolores, Mexico, Father Miguel Hidalgo*
moved quickly to occupy San Felipe and then San Miguel el Grande on September
17 and 18, capturing each in turn and promptly distributing the property confiscated from Spaniards to peasants. In each town, his ranks swelled until he had
an army of 50,000 as he marched on the capital of the intendancy of Guanajuato*,
the second largest city in Mexico with 66,000 inhabitants and renown for the
richness of its silver mines. Upon the collapse of negotiations for the surrender
of the city, royalist forces moved 500 troops, government records, and all the
gold, silver, and quicksilver into the city's granary, the Alhóndiga de Granaditas,
and prepared its defense. This building was a natural fortress; it had been recently
constructed, was solidly built, had only two entrances, had a well within the
premises, and had been provisioned for a siege of three to four months.

Hidalgo's forces attacked the granary on September 28. Poorly armed with
slings, machetes, lances, and bows and arrows, they suffered about 2,000 cas-

ualties from the defending musketeers, who could hardly miss given the density of the attacking throng. But when Guanajuato's population declared in favor of Hidalgo, the fate of those in the granary was sealed. The doors were blown open with dynamite and the defenders were overwhelmed. Some 300 of those inside were then slain, the massacre being a manifestation of the years of pent-up frustration and anger at the exploitation and injustice of Spanish rule. The slaughter would have been complete, but for the arrival of Ignacio José de Allende*, who ordered that those who surrendered not be killed. Over the next two days, Hidalgo's forces thoroughly sacked and pillaged the city. Hidalgo finally issued orders to stop the rampage, but the damage to the revolution had been done. The *criollos**, undecided as to whether to support the revolutionaries or the royalists, rallied in horror to the royalist side.

REFERENCES: Hugh Hamill, *The Hidalgo Revolt*, 1966; Hubert Miller, *Padre Miguel Hidalgo: Father of Mexican Independence*, 1986.

Samuel Freeman

ALLENDE, IGNACIO JOSÉ DE. Ignacio José de Allende was born in 1779 in San Miguel el Grande (renamed in 1862 in his honor as San Miguel de Allende), New Spain.* Committed to the fight for Mexican independence, as captain of the royal dragoons, he conspired against Spain at San Luis Potosí*, Jalapa, and San Miguel. Allende joined forces with Lieutenant José M. Michelena of Valladolid* by organizing a group of patriots at Morelia and Querétaro. Warned of the discovery of his plot, he fled with Juan de Aldama* to Dolores on September 15, 1810, to pressure Father Miguel Hidalgo* for an immediate attack on Spanish forces. He fought against the Spanish forces at Monte de Las Cruces, Aculco y Puente del Calderón, and other areas. On March 21, 1821, he was arrested by Spanish authorities at Norias de Baján, while on his way to the United States to solicit American help. Tried and convicted, he was executed by a firing squad (facing the wall) in Chihuahua, on August 2, 1821. He was later decapitated and his head shown in Alhóndiga de Granaditas*.

REFERENCE: John A. Caruso, *The Liberators of Mexico*, 1967.

Fred Koestler

ALMAGRO, DIEGO DE. Diego de Almagro was born in Almagro, Spain, in 1475. Like so many other early Spanish explorers and conquistadors, he was from the province of Extremadura. His personality matched perfectly the ascetic ambitions of his other compatriots. Almagro was illegitimate; as a young man, he made his way to the seaports to escape the discrimination he faced at home. In 1514, he traveled to Panama* with an expedition led by Pedro Arias de Ávila*. Once he was in Panama, Almagro met Francisco Pizarro* and joined his expedition to South America. Almagro accompanied Pizarro on three expeditions to Peru* between 1524 and 1533. Pizarro appointed Almagro governor of Cuzco* in 1534. Diego de Almagro soon learned, however, that King Charles V of Spain had also named him governor of the province of New Toledo*, which became modern-day Chile*. In 1535, Almagro led an expedition through Bolivia* and northern Argentina* to conquer Chile. As he gradually learned that Chile had no riches to rival those of the Incas* in Peru, he returned to Cuzco in 1537. Diego de Almagro was killed there in 1538 during a violent civil uprising.

REFERENCES: Rolando Mellafe and Sergio Villalobos, *Diego de Almagro*, 1954; H. R. S. Pocock, *The Conquest of Chile*, 1967.

ALMIRANTAZGO. The *almirantazgo* consisted of shipping duties imposed for loading, unloading, and providing anchorage for commercial ships plying the New World trade. The *almirantazgo* provided revenues to the Spanish Crown and to the colonial government.

REFERENCE: Rafael Altamira y Crevea, *Historia de España y de la civilización española*, 6 vols., 1900–1930.

ALMOJARIFAZGO. The *almojarifazgo* was part of Spanish royal revenue, a duty paid on the value of goods from Europe; it was later extended to include goods from the colonies. Other royal revenues included the *quinto** or royal fifth, the king's share of precious metals; the *avería*, a variable tax on imports and exports levied to pay the cost of providing convoys for the merchant fleet; the *alcabala,** a tax on all sales and exchanges; the *mesada* and the *media anata*, a method of raising royal revenues from the sale of public offices (the former corresponds to the exaction of one month's and the latter to a half-year's salary from royal appointees to offices of both Church and state); and the *cruzada*, originally used by the king to finance various crusades against the infidels by selling indulgences, but later a progressive tax the proceeds of which went into the royal exchequer. Until 1543, the *almojarifazgo* was 7.5 percent in the colonies. It was cut to 5 percent in 1543, but 2.5 percent was collected on Spanish goods being exported at Seville*. European goods arriving in American ports after 1566 paid between 5 and 10 percent. In 1720, Spain abolished the *almojarifazgo* in American ports on trade with Spain. By the end of the colonial period, most of the *almojarifazgo* had been abolished. Foreign goods paid 7 percent.

REFERENCE: Rafael Altamira y Crevea, *Historia de España y de la civilización española*, 6 vols., 1900–1930.

Fred Koestler

ALTO PERU. See BOLIVIA.

ALVA IXTLILXOCHITL, FERNANDO DE. Fernando de Alva Ixtlilxochitl was born in 1577 in Teotihuacán, New Spain*. The grandson of the emperor of the Chichimeca* Indians, Alva Ixtlilxochitl was a mestizo* who graduated from Santa Cruz College of Tlaltelolco. Because of that background, as well as the Spanish roots on his paternal side, Alva Ixtlilxochitl received a land grant from King Philip III* of Spain and had the time to write about Mexican history. He also served as governor of Texcoco from 1612 to 1617 and then as governor of

Tlalmanalco. Because of his Indian* heritage, he was able to pave new ground in Mexican historiography by describing the Indian view of the Spanish conquest. He is best remembered for his work *Historia general de la Nueva España*. He died in Mexico City in 1648.

REFERENCE: A. Curtis Wilgus, *The Historiography of Latin America: A Guide to Historical Writing, 1500-1800*, 1975.

ALVARADO, RUDECINDO. Rudecindo Alvarado was born in Salta*, Argentina*, in 1792. He joined the May Revolution* as a teenager and fought throughout most of the major engagements of the Argentinian independence period, including Chacabuco*, Cancha Rayada*, and Maipú*. He also fought and was imprisoned by royal officials in Peru* and Bolivia* in the early 1820s. In 1824, Simón Bolívar* named Alvarado Grand Marshall of Peru*. Alvarado returned to Salta a few years later and spent the rest of his life in a variety of political posts and intrigues in Salta province. He died in 1872.

REFERENCES: Enrique Udaondo, *Diccionario biográfico colonial argentino*, 1945, and *Diccionario biográfico argentino*, 1938.

ALVARADO DE LA CUEVA, BEATRIZ. The wife of Pedro de Alvarado y Mesía*, Doña Beatriz served briefly as the only female governor of Guatemala*. Assuming the office on the news of the death of her husband (June 29, 1541) she served as governor for only two days. She was killed in the earthquake and massive mudslide that destroyed the city of Santiago de Guatemala (now Ciudad Vieja) on September 10, 1541. After the disaster, the city was rebuilt at a new site (now Antigua), under direction of her brother, Francisco de la Cueva, who was named governor after her death.

REFERENCE: R. L. Woodward, Jr., *Central America: A Nation Divided*, 1983.

Virginia Garrard Burnett

ALVARADO HIDALGO, MANUEL. Manuel Alvarado Hidalgo was born in 1775 and entered the Roman Catholic priesthood as a young man. He is best remembered today as a leading republican figure in the independence era in Costa Rica*. Between 1818 and 1824, Alvarado Hidalgo served successively as the head of the *Casa de Enseñanza de Santo Tomás*, president of the *Junta Delgados*, and member of the first and president of the third *Junta Superior Gobernativa*. Before his death in 1836, he also served several times as president of the congress of Costa Rica.

REFERENCE: Francisco Montero Barrantes, *Elementos de historia de Costa Rica*, 2 vols., 1894.

ALVARADO Y MESÍA, PEDRO DE. A professional soldier, Pedro de Alvarado y Mesía was born in Badajoz, Spain, around 1485. He arrived on the North American mainland with Hernán Cortés* in 1519. As Cortés's second-in-command, Alvarado gave the order that led to the disastrous Aztec* uprising during Cortés's absence from Tenochtitlán* in 1520. In December 1523, Alvarado led a Spanish land expedition south from Mexico City*. He arrived in Guatemala* in early 1524, where he found the Quiché and Cakchiquel Maya* locked in civil war. Allying with the Cakchiquel, Alvarado successfully defeated the Quiché at Xelajú* in April 1524. There, according to legend, Alvarado personally killed the Quiché leader, Tucúm Omán*, in hand-to-hand combat.

In July 1524, Alvarado established the first Spanish settlement, Santiago los Caballeros de Guatemala, at the site of the Cakchiquel revolt that began in 1524 and lasted until 1530. In 1527, Alvarado and his brother Jorge relocated the capital to the Almolonga Valley, at the base of Agua volcano, in a location now known as Ciudad Vieja. Always an adventurer, Alvarado continued to press southward. In 1525, he conquered the Pipil* Indians and established a Spanish base called San Salvador* at the Pipil capital of Cuscatlán*. When the rebellion of his former allies, the Cakchiquel, forced Alvarado to return to Guatemala, Salvadoran territory fell into the hands of Pedro Arias de Ávila* (Pedrarias), the governor of Panama, who was attempting to conquer the region from the south. In 1527, Alvarado was granted the title of governor of Guatemala, and Guatemala was established as a formal captaincy-general. In 1528, his brother reclaimed El Salvador* from the forces of Pedrarias and moved the site of the city of San Salvador to the Valley of La Bermuda.

In 1536, Pedro de Alvarado abandoned Central America to join Francisco Pizarro's* expedition in Peru*. Disappointed with what he found, Alvarado returned to Spain in 1539, where he married a noblewoman, Doña Beatriz de la Cueva. The two returned to Guatemala, but in 1540, he traveled to northern Mexico to join Francisco Vásquez de Coronado's* expedition in search of the fabled city of Cíbola*. He died in North America on June 29, 1541, when his horse fell on him.

REFERENCES: John E. Kelly, *Pedro de Alvarado*, 1941; R. L. Woodward, Jr., *Central America: A Nation Divided*, 1983.

Virginia Garrard Burnett

ÁLVAREZ, JOSÉ MARÍA. Born in 1777, José María Álvarez developed into one of colonial Guatemala's* leading legal scholars. He was widely known as an expert on the Justinian Code; his most famous text was the *Instituciones de derecho real de Castilla y de Indias*, published in 1818. It was the first text in Guatemala about the legal code. José María Álvarez died in 1820.

REFERENCE: Richard E. Moore, *Historical Dictionary of Guatemala*, 1973.

ÁLVAREZ, JULIÁN BALTAZAR. Julian Baltazar Álvarez was born in Buenos Aires*, Río de la Plata*, in 1788. He received a doctorate in theology from the University of Córdoba* and a doctorate in law from the University of Charcas. Alvarez abandoned his ecclesiastical responsibilities as a Roman Catholic priest in favor of politics and became an early follower of Mariano Moreno* and a radical advocate of independence from Spain. In 1820, Alvarez moved to Mon-

tevideo*, Uruguay*, and eventually became president of the Uruguayan supreme court. He died in 1843.
REFERENCE: Ione S. Wright and Lisa M. Nekhom, *Historical Dictonary of Argentina*, 1978.

ÁLVAREZ DE ARENALES, JOSÉ ILDEFONSO. José Ildefonso Álvarez de Arenales was born in San Antonio de Arque in Río de la Plata* in 1793. He studied engineering and joined the army at an early age to become part of the army of José de San Martín*. While fighting against the royal army in Upper Peru*, he found time to be elected to the congress of the province of Salta* in Argentina*. He later published *Reseñas históricas y descriptivas sobre el gran país del Chaco y del Río Bermejo, seguidas de observaciones concernientes a un plan de navegación y de colonización* and also wrote an unfinished *Diccionario Geográfico* on Chile*, Peru, and Río de la Plata. He died in 1862.
REFERENCE: Romay Piccirilli, ed., *Diccionario histórico argentino*, 6 vols., 1953– 1955.

Fred Koestler

ÁLVAREZ DE ARENALES, JUAN ANTONIO. Juan Antonio Álvarez de Arenales was born in Spain in 1770. He joined the Spanish army and came to Buenos Aires* as a member of the military garrison in 1784. Álvarez spent time in Bolivia*, where he earned a reputation for championing Indian* rights and came to resent the Spanish government's oppressive attitudes. In May 1809, he joined the patriots in the Chuquisaca rebellion and eventually emerged as the leader of rebel forces. He was captured by royal troops shortly thereafter, but after a short period of time in prison he was released. Álvarez returned to the rebel forces and led a series of guerrilla attacks on the Spanish army. A disciple of General Manuel Belgrano* (1770–1820), he fought in many battles and was appropriately rewarded to become one of the principal figures of Argentina's* independence. He was also a key figure in the Peruvian independence movement, fighting under José de San Martín* and eventually becoming governor of northern Peru.* He achieved the rank of grand marshal before retiring in 1822. In 1823, he was appointed governor of Tucumán.* After being deposed by José Gorriti in 1827, he was exiled to Bolivia where he died in 1831.
REFERENCE: Romay Piccirilli, ed., *Diccionario histórico argentino*, 6 vols. 1953– 1955.

Fred Koestler

ÁLVAREZ DE TOLEDO, JUAN BAUTISTA. Juan Bautista Álvarez de Toledo was born in Antigua*, Guatemala*, in 1655. Orphaned as a child, he entered the Franciscan* order. He was educated in Franciscan schools and eventually received a doctorate from the University of San Carlos*. He is best remembered as the fourteenth bishop of Guatemala but also as the first *criollo* * bishop of the country. He died in 1725.
REFERENCE: Richard E. Moore, *Historical Dictionary of Guatemala*, 1973.

ÁLVAREZ DE TOLEDO Y FIGUEROA, FRANCISCO DE. See TOLEDO Y FIGUEROA, FRANCISCO DE ÁLVAREZ.

ÁLVAREZ PONTE, ANTONIO. Antonio Álvarez Ponte was born in Madrid, Spain, in 1784. He moved to Buenos Aires* as a child and eventually earned a doctorate in law at the University of San Felipe* in Santiago*, Chile*, in 1809. He returned to Buenos Aires during the May Revolution* of 1810 and joined patriot forces. He spent time in Santiago, Chile, securing support for the revolution, and in 1815 went to London to raise money for the creation of a Chilean navy. He became a close friend of José de San Martín*. He returned to South America in 1818 and died in Pisco, Peru*, in 1820 with the Army of the Andes.*

REFERENCE: Enrique Udaondo, *Diccionario biográfico colonial argentino*, 1945.

ALVEAR, CARLOS ANTONIO JOSÉ DE. Born in the village of San Angel de la Guardia on the Argentine-Brazilian border in 1789, Carlos Antonio José de Alvear spent his first eleven years in this remote place where his father Diego was a member of the Spanish-Portuguese border commission. In 1800, his parents returned to Buenos Aires*, and in 1804, the family embarked for Spain. In a tragic naval encounter with the British, one of the ships on which the Alvears were traveling sank; only father and son survived and landed in Portsmouth. Young Alvear went to a school near London, with the result that he kept a lifelong admiration for English institutions and for liberal ideas.

The events in Bayonne and the rise of the Spanish people against the Napoleonic usurpation brought the father with his son and new English wife to Spain. Here both men enlisted in the *Carabineros reales* with the father being awarded a captaincy and later becoming the military commander of Cádiz while the son was promoted to *alférez*. Young Alvear participated in some of the major battles of the Pensinular War (Talavera, Yébenes, Ciudad Real, and Vitoria) but soon his father obtained a transfer for the son to Cádiz where he watched closely the growing crisis unfolding between the Peninsular authorities and the Spanish-American territories. It was in Cádiz that young Alvear met other Spanish-Americans who had formed a revolutionary group called the *Sociedad de Lautaro**. It profoundly inspired him, as well as José de San Martín* and José Miguel Carrera*. In 1812, he left Spain for London and soon arrived in Buenos Aires.

Once in Buenos Aires, Alvear immediately plunged into politics. He joined the *Sociedad Patriótica*, which he soon dominated, using it for his own ends. This revolutionary group soon adopted the name of the Lautaro Society of Cádiz, in memory of that association, and succeeded in overthrowing the first triumvirate of 1811–1812. The new (second) triumvirate then convoked the Constituent Assembly of 1813 for the purpose of reorganizing the defunct viceroyalty of the Río de la Plata*. Alvear was the domi-

nant figure and imposed Bourbon centralism as a result of his experience in
the Peninsula. While San Martín and Manuel Belgrano* took charge of military matters in the northwest, Alvear aimed at ridding Montevideo* of the
Spaniards. With the creation of a navy, Alvear succeeded in capturing Montevideo but then had to deal with the legendary José Gervasio Artigas*, the
gaucho* patriot who had refused to accept *porteño* centralism in 1813. Artigas defeated him. Alvear's uncle, General Gervasio Antonio de Posadas,
then gave him a new command. This was thwarted by rising opposition
from José Rondeau*. The new alliance between Rondeau and Artigas forced
the resignation of Posadas. Alvear then became Supreme Director of the
United Provinces* on January 9, 1815, at the age of only 27. It was his
greatest political triumph, but a year later he had to resign in view of increasing resistance to his arrogance. He fled to Río de Janeiro where he was
hated by both Spaniards and *orientales*. In deep depression, he wrote a memorial to Ferdinand VII* in which he repudiated the May Revolution*, but
this did not help matters. When this about-face became known later, his
prestige suffered further.

With the Portuguese occupation of the Banda Oriental*, Alvear moved to
Montevideo where he intrigued with the discredited Carrera for a return to power;
Carrera wished to displace Bernardo O'Higgins* in Chile* and Alvear desired to
capture Buenos Aires. The arrangement became known as the secret treaty of
Pilar. Sensing the increased hostility in the interior to the policies of Buenos
Aires, Alvear allied himself with Estanislao López*, the caudillo* of Santa Fé,
but the alliance did not produce results. Again Alvear had to flee and moved
back to Montevideo. A semblance of order in Buenos Aires under the government
of Martín Rodríguez enabled him to return. The Act of Oblivion of 1822 gave
him this opportunity despite his five years of counterrevolutionary activity. Bernardino Rivadavia*, the new minister of foreign affairs, demonstrated his faith
in Alvear by appointing him as minister in Washington in 1824. Alvear thus
opened official relations with Washington and found an opportunity to clear
himself from the tarnish of the past.

Alvear went to the United States by way of England; he met with George
Canning in London and James Monroe in Washington, discussing such problems
as the threat of the Holy Alliance and Brazil's occupation of the Banda Oriental.
In 1825, he was back in Buenos Aires, not having accepted an appointment to
Colombia*. Instead he led a mission to Upper Peru* to meet Simón Bolívar*.
The mission failed, since Alvear found himself at odds with the Liberator on
almost everything. Upon his return home, Alvear found his country on the verge
of war with Brazil over the Banda Oriental. At long last, he obtained a military
command, invaded Brazil, and achieved victory at Ituzaingó. Buenos Aires,
however, threw away this opportunity. With the country disintegrating and Rivadavia falling from power, Alvear's career was again interrupted, since his
fortunes were closely linked to the cause of the *unitarios*.

When the Federalists who opposed centralizing power in Buenos Aires won with Juan Manuel de Rosas[*] in 1829, Alvear seemed vulnerable because of his being identified with the *unitarios*, but since he was not really implicated in any conspiracies, he was left undisturbed. Rosas's increasing troubles on both domestic and foreign fronts led to Alvear's appointment as minister to the United States in December 1832, but his departure was postponed for four years in view of domestic uncertainties, the Falkland (Malvinas[*]) crisis, and illness. The last phase of his turbulent life thus included his years in the United States (1838–1852) where he faced difficult subjects: the Falklands, French and British intervention in the old Banda Oriental, and U.S. expansionism. He never returned to Buenos Aires but died in New York on November 2, 1852.

REFERENCE: Thomas B. Davis, Jr., *Carlos de Alvear, Man of Revolution: The Diplomatic Career of Argentina's First Minister of the United States*, 1955.

O. Carlos Stoetzer

ALVEAR Y PONCE DE LEÓN, DIEGO DE. Diego de Alvear y Ponce de León was born on November 13, 1749, in Mantilla, Spain. He spent his career in the Spanish navy and engaged in conflict in the Philippines[*] in 1700 and against the Portuguese in Montevideo[*] in 1775. Alvear was part of the joint Spanish-Portuguese commission that drew up the border between Spanish and Portuguese colonies in 1783; in 1794, he was promoted to the rank of captain. In 1807, Alvear was named commandant of Cádiz. The Treaty of San Ildefonso[*] in 1777 had established boundaries between the Spanish and Portuguese colonies. In 1783, as part of the commission to define those boundaries in more detail, Alvear traveled to the New World and visited throughout what are today Paraguay[*], Uruguay[*], and southern Brazil. He wrote extensively about the Guaraní[*] Indians, the Jesuit[*] missions[*], and the natural history of the region; his writings have become an important historical source for colonial Latin America. The book was titled *Relación geográfica e histórica de la provincia de Misiones* and published in 1836. Alvear decided to return to Spain in 1804, but a British fleet attacked his squadron, killing his wife and seven of his children. He was briefly imprisoned in London before being released to return to Spain. Alvear was promoted to brigadier general. Diego de Alvear y Ponce de León died in Madrid on January 15, 1830.

REFERENCE: Efraín Cardozo, *Historiografía paraguaya*, 1959.

ALZAGA, MARTÍN DE. Born in 1756 in the Basque region of Spain, Martín de Alzaga came to Río de la Plata[*] where he succeeded in becoming one of the most important and wealthy Spanish merchants in Buenos Aires[*]. He held important positions in the viceregal capital, including that of chief *alcalde*[*] of the city; as such, he played a significant role in the defense of Buenos Aires during the British invasions. Hero of the defense of the capital and leader of the royalist group, Martín de Alzaga was a major protagonist in the fateful events of the early nineteenth century in the Río de la Plata[*].

He was instrumental in the removal from office of Viceroy Rafael de Sobre-monte at the time of the first British invasion. When the invading forces entered Buenos Aires in the second invasion (June 28, 1807), Santiago Liniers* mistakenly believed that his forces could repulse the enemy; his defeat caused dismay. At this critical juncture, Alzaga fortified the city and thus saved it. The British then surrendered.

Alzaga was involved in the intrigues of Princess Carlota Joaquina, the sister of Ferdinand VII* and wife of the Portuguese Prince Regent Dom João. With the arrival of the Portuguese royal family in Río de Janeiro (January 23, 1808), Saturnino Rodríguez Peña negotiated a transfer for her to Buenos Aires where a throne would be waiting for her. The princess herself denounced the plans to the authorities in Buenos Aires, however. Alzaga also headed the coup of 1809 in Buenos Aires. On May 13, 1808, Liniers had been appointed acting viceroy, thus replacing the Marqués de Sobremonte who had fled to the interior at the time of the first English invasion (1806). The confusion that arose in Buenos Aires upon receipt of news of the events of Aranjuez (abdication of Charles IV*) and those of Bayonne (the forced abdication of Ferdinand VII), compounded by the brief arrival on August 13, 1808 of the Marquis de Sassenay, emissary of Napoleon, led to a plot headed by Alzaga. Relations between Alzaga and Liniers had been fairly good until the middle of 1808 but then turned sour. The tragic events in the Peninsula propelled Alzaga into fame with his coup of January 1, 1809. He intended to set up a junta in Buenos Aires based on those in the Peninsula as the result of the spontaneous rising of the Spanish people against the Napoleonic usurpation.

On May 25, 1808, the Junta of Asturias had officially declared war on France, which meant that Spain and its empire were in a state of war with Napoleon. This event not only determined the future actions of the various juntas but pitted *afrancesados* (pro-French) and traditionalists against each other—in this case, Liniers and Alzaga in Rio de la Plata. Alzaga's idea had been put into practice in Montevideo* on September 21, 1808; through his friend Governor Francisco Javier de Elío*, Alzaga had actually prepared the establishment of this junta. Alzaga and his friends Esteban Villanueva, Olaguer Reynals, and Juan Antonio de Santa Coloma, among others, endeavored to set up a junta in Buenos Aires on January 1, 1809, as had been done in Montevideo. On the list of the revolutionaries also appeared the name of Mariano Moreno*. Interpreting Napoleon's march through the Peninsula as the final loss of Spain to the French emperor, the Alzaga group—which represented much of Buenos Aires—planned to form a junta to establish a kind of New Spain on the Río de la Plata in which the Spanish element would be dominant; they also planned to demand the resignation of Liniers and to call on the interior to send delegates to Buenos Aires for each provincial *cabildo*. Their plot failed when Cornelio de Saavedra, leading his *criollo* grenadiers, came to the aid of Liniers. Later, during the May Revolution, Alzaga was responsible for the dismissal of Viceroy Baltasar Hidalgo de Cisneros*.

Finally, the name of Alzaga reappears in connection with the conspiracy of 1812 at a time when independence was threatened from both Peru[*] and from across the Río de la Plata. Again Alzaga headed a secret plot which at the time was by no means an isolated case. The conspiracy of 1812 was linked again to Princess Carlota Joaquina who pledged aid to the group. After all, Portuguese troops were quite close in the Banda Oriental. The plot was foiled and Alzaga was shot. The energetic response to the plot by the triumvirate (ruling government in Buenos Aires) was due mainly to Bernardino Rivadavia[*]. Alzaga thus followed his rival Liniers, who had plotted earlier and been executed in 1810 (in the conspiracy of Córdoba[*]). In sum, Alzaga was a faithful Spaniard whose activities were always on behalf of a royalist and loyalist solution.

REFERENCE: Ricardo Levene, *A History of Argentina*, 1963.

O. Carlos Stoetzer

ALZATE Y RAMÍREZ, JOSÉ ANTONIO. José Antonio Alzate Ramírez was born in Mexico City[*], in November 1737. He graduated from the University of Mexico[*] with a degree in the arts in 1753 and a degree in theology in 1756. He went on to become one of New Spain's[*] greatest minds—a scientist, philosopher, and journalist. Alzate was blessed with a tremendous intellect and a philosophy shaped by the Enlightenment. His major published work was the *Gacetas de literatura de Mexico*, a multivolume description of Mexican culture written in a popular style. Some historians have described Alzate as the "Benjamin Franklin of Mexico." He died in Mexico City on February 2, 1799.

REFERENCE: A. Aragón Leiva, *Elogio a Alzate*, 1942.

Fred Koestler

AMADEO I. Prince of the House of Savoy, Duke of Aosta, and King of Spain, Amadeo I was born in Turin in 1845. He was the second son of Vittorio Emmanuele II, king of Italy. Amadeo spent most of his early life at the castle of Moncalieri. He trained in the Italian army and achieved the rank of lieutenant colonel, distinguishing himself at the Battle of Custozza (1866) against the Austrians. Amadeo joined the Italian navy where he obtained the rank of vice admiral in 1869. He married Princess Maria Vittoria del Pozzo della Cisterna. Amadeo I was elected King of Spain by the Cortes under General Juan Prim y Prats in November 1870, but he abdicated his crown after an attempted assassination by Carlista insurrectionists in 1873. He returned to Italy and resumed his title as Duke of Aosta, removing himself totally from political life. He died in 1890.

REFERENCE: Guillermo Stefano, *Il Conte Verde: Ricordi storici*, 1853.

Fred Koestler

AMAR Y BORBÓN, ANTONIO. A native of Spain, Antonio Amar y Borbón became the last viceroy of New Granada[*] in 1803. His government was blamed for the general discontent and economic depression throughout New Granada.

Eventually, on July 20, 1810, an uprising led to his imprisonment and expatriation to Spain. Amar y Borbón died there in 1819.

REFERENCE: Artemio de Valle-Arizpe, *Virreyes y virreynas de la Nueva España*, 1933.

Fred Koestler

AMAT Y JUNIENT, MANUEL DE. Born to a very prominent family in Spain, Manuel de Amat y Junient distinguished himself in military service in Spain, Italy, and Africa and had been knighted in the Order of St. John before being posted to Chile* as captain-general* and governor in 1754. Amat did not arrive in Chile to assume duty as its first Catalonian governor, however, until December, 1755. In 1761, he was promoted to the viceroyalty of Peru*. Amat was a coarse, aggressive, inconsiderate, ruthless, and, in many ways, objectionable person who appeared to take little interest in Chile. Nevertheless, his administration was capable, efficient, and generally honest. Amat's most notable accomplishment as governor was the creation of Chile's first police force in Santiago* in 1758 as a consequence of his ultimately unsuccessful determination to end the banditry rampant in the city and throughout much of the countryside. Amat's other contributions as governor were to take an interest in and significantly improve the academic quality of the University of San Felipe* and of maps of the Chilean countryside.

Because of his record as governor of Chile, Amat was appointed viceroy* of Peru where he once again performed capably from 1761 to 1776. Amat's accomplishments as viceroy included the founding of the *Real Convictorio de San Carlos* and becoming the first viceroy in the Americas to establish his own militia*. Amat also authored *Memoria de gobierno*, a famous document that examined corruption in Peru, in which he argued that corruption was the consequence of the greed of provincial *audiencia** officials.

REFERENCES: Agustín Edwards, *Peoples of Old*, 1929; Luis Galdames, *A History of Chile*, 1964; Anthony Hull, *Charles III and the Revival of Spain*, 1980.

Samuel Freeman

AMERICA. The term "America" or "Americas" has been used for the past 480 years to describe the New World discoveries of North America, South America, Central America, and the islands of the Caribbean. The use of the name "America" was practically an accident. Amerigo Vespucci*, a Florentine sailor, claimed to have visited the New World in 1497. Although scholars now consider his claim of the 1497 voyage to be a fabrication, he did sail to the New World in 1499 with the expedition of Alonso de Ojeda*. He then claimed to have sailed under the Portuguese flag in 1501–1502 and 1503–1504. Vespucci wrote many highly descriptive letters describing the New World, and those letters received wide attention in Europe in the early 1500s. In 1507 the geographer Martin Waldseemuller published a new version of the ancient Ptolemy book on world geography and, aware of Vespucci's letters, he named the New World

"Amerigo." Waldseemuller's geography was widely circulated in Europe north of the Pyrenees, and the name "Amerigo" or "America" became the accepted reference. In Spain, however, the term "The Indies" was the most common for the next two centuries.

REFERENCES: Germán Arciniegas, *Amerigo and the New World: The Life and Times of Amerigo Vespucci*, 1955; Clements R. Markham, trans. and ed., *The Letters of Amerigo Vespucci and Other Documents Illustrative of His Career*, 1894.

AMERICAN REVOLUTION. The American Revolution, in which the thirteen North American colonies rebelled against British authority, posed a real diplomatic dilemma for Spanish authorities. On the one hand, the Spanish despised Great Britain. Spain held the British responsible for the decline of her national glory, and the loss of Gibraltar* to Great Britain in 1704 remained a source of great bitterness. The idea of assisting the American colonies in humbling the British appealed to Spain, but at the same time, Spanish authorities feared a strong, independent America on the northern flank of her Caribbean and Latin American empire. Charles III* worried that an American republic might expand and take control of some of the Spanish colonies; even if that did not happen, the rhetoric of rebellion might spread throughout Latin America, depriving Spain of its empire. Charles III also worried that if he assisted the Americans, Great Britain might seek revenge by stirring up rebellion in the Spanish colonies. Eventually, in the secret Treaty of Aranjuez of 1779, Spain agreed to assist the French in helping the Americans, in return for a French agreement to take Gibraltar from Great Britain and return it to Spain.

In the end, Spain's worst fears were realized. The treaty ending the American Revolution in 1783 created the United States of America and did not snatch Gibraltar from Great Britain. The rhetoric of the revolution did indeed spread throughout the Western Hemisphere, destabilizing the Spanish colonies, and Great Britain did assist the revolutionary movement in Latin America.

REFERENCES: Samuel F. Bemis, *The Diplomacy of the American Revolution*, 1935; Samuel F. Bemis, *Pinkcney's Treaty*, 1960.)

AMERICAN TREATY OF 1670. Actually called the Treaty of Madrid of 1670, the American Treaty between Spain and Great Britain gave Britain its legal foothold in the Caribbean. Although Spain agreed to relax trade restrictions in the Caribbean and to suppress piracy*, the key to the agreement was Spain's formal acknowledgment of the doctrine of effective occupation. Spain abandoned the claim that only Spain and Portugal had settlement rights in the New World. In effect, Spain extended recognition of British sovereignty to whatever territories Britain had already occupied.

REFERENCE: Roger B. Merriam, *The Rise of the Spanish Empire in the Old World and the New*, 4 vols., 1918–1934.

ANDA Y SALAZAR, SIMÓN DE. Simón de Anda y Salazar was born in 1719 in Subijana, Spain. After years of study at the University of Alcalá, he was sent to the Philippines* to discharge the duties of *oidor**. Although the *alcalde** of Manila* chose to surrender immediately, Anda demonstrated talent and responsibility during an attack by British naval forces against Manila in 1762. Taking charge, he abandoned the capital and fled to Pampanga* where he reorganized the Spanish army and surrounded Manila, thus preventing the British from exiting to their ships. The British admiralty offered 5,000 pesos for Anda, dead or alive. Following a temporary period of peace, he returned triumphantly with his army to Manila. Anda was named governor-general of the Philippines in 1770, and he remained in the post until 1776. During his tenure, he was quite critical of Spanish and clerical policy in the Philippines, a position that won him the respect of Filipinos but the ire of the Church and Crown. He died in office in 1776.

REFERENCE: C. H. Cunningham, *The Audiencia in the Spanish Colonies as Illustrated by the Audiencia of Manila, 1583–1800*, 1919.

Fred Koestler

ANDAGOYA, PASCUAL DE. Pascual de Andagoya was born in Spain in 1495. He came to the New World in 1514 with Pedro Arias de Ávila* and served as a *regidor** in Panama*. His book, *Narrative of the Proceedings of Pedrarias Dávila in the Provinces of Tierra Firme or Castilla de Oro*, has become an important primary source for historians. Andagoya led an expedition down the western coast of Colombia* in 1522, going as far south as the San Juan River and collecting information on the Chocó peoples in the area. That was the first European exploration of the west coast of Colombia. Andagoya returned to Panama and passed his information on to Francisco Pizarro*, who used it in his conquest of Peru*. Andagoya returned to the region as *adelantado** of the San Juan River area in 1539. In the early 1540s, Sebastián de Benalcázar* brought charges of corruption against Andagoya, forcing him to return to Spain, where he died in 1548.

REFERENCE: Robert H. Davis, *Historical Dictionary of Colombia*, 1977.

ANDONAEGUI, JOSÉ DE. José de Andonaegui was born in Spain in 1685 and spent his career in the Spanish army. In 1745, he was appointed governor and military commander of Buenos Aires*. During his 13 years in office, he surveyed the entire coast of Patagonia, pacified Indian* groups in what are today Uruguay* and southern Argentina*, subdued the Guaraní* Indians who refused to accept Portuguese rule under the provisions of the Treaty of Madrid* of 1750, and provided stable royal government in Montevideo*. Andonaegui returned to Spain in 1759 and was promoted to the rank of lieutenant general. He died in Madrid in 1760.

REFERENCE: Enrique Udaondo, *Diccionario biográfico colonial argentino*, 1945.

ANGOSTURA, CONGRESS OF (1819). The military and political career of Simón Bolívar* reached a high point in the Congress of Angostura on February 15, 1819, but his political thought also found its highest expression in this little town on the Orinoco River, formerly known as Santo Tomás de la Guayana and now as Ciudad Bolívar. It was a milestone in Bolívar's third and final attempt to free Venezuela* from royalist rule, this time from the east. It was here that he was confirmed as commander-in-chief of the patriot army and proclaimed president of the republic of Venezuela.

After the *Manifiesto* of Cartagena* and the *Carta* of Jamaica*, the *Discurso* that he delivered on this occasion in Angostura ranks as a first-class monument to his statesmanship. It showed his fundamental political wisdom with an even mixture of noble idealism and remarkable realism. In his *Discurso* to the delegates, he dealt first with such issues as political tempestuousness, bloody campaigns, popular will, and liberty; he also warned of excesses. It was in Angostura that he tried to find an answer to an old problem: the reconciliation of individual liberty with civil authority. Exotic formulae, such as the North American example, would not do, since there existed a fundamental cultural difference between North and South America. It was to Bolívar's merit that he rejected both pure democracy and a reactionary autocracy, even though he firmly believed that a strong hand was necessary in his country. His ideal was "a government eminently popular, eminently just, eminently moral, which could enchain oppression, anarchy, and guilt," where innocence, humanity, and peace would reign. In his view, only Rome in antiquity and Britain in contemporary times could serve as guides. He then reconciled the British model within a republican framework: a strong executive; a two-chamber parliament—a hereditary upper house, the senate, and a democratic and popular lower house, the chamber of representatives, in order to achieve the necessary balance of political and social forces; and a judicial power. Time and again, Bolívar appealed for moderation, prudence, and a middle-of-the-road approach since absolute liberty always degenerated into absolute power.

It was also here that the *Libertador* proposed his famous "Moral Power," which would be closely linked to the other three branches of government. This moral power reflected his great concern for popular education. It was a kind of modern Areopagus but also, in the view of Víctor Andrés Belaúnde, a fascinating secular version of the old Inquisition*. It also had two houses: a moral chamber to direct the moral opinion of the country, with jurisidiction over individuals, families, courts, authorities, and even the government itself, and the chamber of education to watch over the physical and moral well-being of youth—in the view of Charles Minguet, a kind of ministry of national education. Some of the concepts of Bolívar's moral power found a rebirth in the *Casas del Pueblo* of José Vasconcelos when he was Mexico's minister of education in Alvaro Obregón's government. As the fourth power in Bolívar's Angostura project, it also represented an echo of the European currents of political thought of those times— the Bolivarian version of the *pouvoir neutre* of Benjamin Constant and of the Doctrinaire Liberals like Pierre-Paul Royer Collard.

REFERENCES: Gerhard Masur, *Simón Bolívar*, 1948; O. Carlos Stoetzer, "Bolívar y el Poder Moral", *Revista de Historia de América* (Mexico), 95 (1983), 139–58.

O. Carlos Stoetzer

AÑIL. SEE INDIGO.

ANTE, ANTONIO. Born in 1771 in Quito*, Ecuador*, Antonio Ante received a law degree at the University of Quito and then set up a legal practice there. He was one of the leading liberal figures in the early Ecuadorean independence movement. Royalists thought that they could hinder the movement in Quito if they could eliminate Ante, but an assassination attempt failed in 1816. They then exiled him to Africa. Ante returned to Quito after the independence movement had succeeded, served as a member of the constituent convention that met at Riobamba* and declared Ecuador a republic in 1830, and died in Quito in 1836.

REFERENCE: Federico González Suárez, *Historia general de la República del Ecuador*, 7 vols., 1890–1903.

ANTEQUERA Y CASTRO, JOSÉ DE. José de Antequera y Castro was born in Panama* in 1690. He was sent to Asunción*, Paraguay*, in 1717 by the *audiencia* of Charcas* to investigate charges of corruption brought against Governor Reyes Balmaceda. Antequera, however, soon far exceeded his instructions. He deposed Balmaceda and took charge of the government himself. His movement became known as the Revolt of the *Comuneros*** and lasted until 1735. In 1725, government troops from Buenos Aires* captured Asunción and forced Antequera into exile. He was later arrested in Chuquisaca and transferred to Lima* for trial. Antequera went to Lima in 1731. He was there executed for sedition and rebellion.

REFERENCE: Alberto Montezuma Hurtado, *Comuneros del Paraguay*, 1983.

ANTIOQUIA. Antioquia is a region in northwestern Colombia near the Isthmus of Panama.* Spaniards first arrived in the region in 1537 as conquistadors* sought new tribes to conquer and new treasures to be found. Settlers began arriving a few years later. Antioquia was part of the province of Popayán* until 1579 when it received its own governor. In that year, Antioquia became a separate province under the authority of the *audiencia* of New Granada.* The last Spanish governor left Antioquia in 1811. After the end of the wars of independence in Colombia, Antioquia became part of Gran Colombia*.

REFERENCE: Juan Friede, *Descubrimiento y conquista del Nuevo Reino de Granada*, 1965.

ANWAL, BATTLE OF. Anwal was the site of the great Spanish military disaster in Morocco in 1921. In January 1919, General Damaso Berenguer* became high commissioner of Spanish Morocco*; along with General Fernando Silvestre, he soon began sending troops deeper into the central Rif Mountains.

The expansion of Spanish power, combined with poor harvests, triggered an extremely hostile reaction from Berber tribesmen. The opposition coalesced around the leadership of Abd al-Krim*, who led a successful guerrilla war against Spanish forces. On July 22, 1921, Krim launched an all-out attack on the Spanish installation at Anwal. The Spanish troops began a hasty retreat toward Melilla*. When the battle was over, the Spanish had suffered 8,688 killed and another 4,500 wounded. Krim took 570 Spanish prisoners of war. Although Spanish forces eventually retook most of the lost territory, the defeat at Anwal was a political disaster in Madrid, undermining Conservative Party rule and leading to the imposition of a military dictatorship under General Miguel Primo de Rivera. For Krim, the victory at Anwal allowed him to expand his power base among the Berber tribes and extend the rebellion into the Ghmara and the Jbala. He proclaimed the Rif Republic in February 1923. It survived until a combined Franco-Spanish military force defeated him in May 1926.

REFERENCE: C. R. Pennell, *A Country with a Government and a Flag: The Rif War in Morocco, 1921–1926*, 1986.

APACHE. Though some controversy exists over the Apache migrations into the American Southwest and Mexico, there is general agreement that they traveled south from Lake Athapasca and other areas of western Canada, possibly down both sides of the Rockies into the region they now inhabit. This migration began around A.D. 1100, with smaller units arriving earlier and others much later. When this primary group divided into separate entities (Navajo and Apache) is not certain. Anthropologists usually divide the Apachean peoples into western and eastern groupings, with the Eastern (Lipan, Kiowa-Apache, Cuartelejo, Carlana, etc.) having more of a Plains culture with a linguistic relationship to the original Athapascans. The western Apache include the Chiricahua, Warm Springs, White Mountain, San Carlos, and to some extent the Mescalero. Though there is not always agreement about where these bands fit, there is when it comes to describing the characteristics of both the people and the geography of this varied and rugged jumble of mountains, deserts, and canyons.

Apacheria, a harsh yet beautiful land, produced a strong, harsh warlike people numbering about 6,000 individuals by the time of the Spanish arrival. (Their population is about double that today.) Though they have been described as cruel and vindictive, it must be remembered that they were fighting for a home territory. They have also been described as having great love of family and a fondness for children. With primitive weapons and a tremendous understanding of guerrilla tactics, the Apache, once mounted, became a true warrior. They preferred the bow and war club. All members carried select knives and food pouches for survival.

The Spanish used their Indian allies as buffers between themselves and other European groups during their early years in the New World. This did not always work, as they were to discover when they tried to develop an Indian policy and a series of *presidios* along the frontier to prevent French and, to some extent,

Comanche encroachment. The Spanish feared both groups, and they believed that the Apache, having already felt the sting of defeat at Comanche hands, would possibly provide a good buffer. The Plains Apache had already fallen prey to the Comanche many times but finally stood their ground. Then the Comanche spread further into what is now known as Apacheria, an area of about 3,000 square miles ranging both north and south of the border lands. It was a region of conflict and administrative failures for several centuries. Spanish reports for the period from about 1748 to 1770 indicate that the Apache had murdered over 4,000 people and destroyed or stolen an undetermined amount of property and stock. Because of these major conflicts with the Spanish until 1821, they were constantly regrouping and forming alliances of their own. They had come into contact with the Pueblos of the Southwest and preyed on these sendentary tribes as sources for food, women, and other supplies. Spanish settlers, miners, and soldiers were terrorized.

In terms of material culture, the Apache as raiders did not produce many durable goods, nor did they farm or keep large herds as their cousins, the Navajo, had learned to do a century before. Their baskets were light, portable, and easy to carry on the trail. The traditional Apache home was a domed brush arbor in summer and covered with skins for warmth in winter. Tipis were also used, especially by those with Plains affiliations. Both structures were easy to erect and were quickly deserted when danger threatened. They also used a functional sweat lodge and to some extent do so now, though all of these shelters are, at present, used primarily for ceremonial purposes. Their ceremonies, especially the maiden's puberty rites and the dance of the mountain spirits, are well known. Traditional foods included roots, fruits, berries, flint and flour corn, mesquite beans, small game, deer, and, when available, horse and mule.

REFERENCE: Jack D. Forbes, *Apache, Navajo, and Spaniard*, 1960.

George A. Agogino and Lynda A. Sánchez

APARICIO, SEBASTIÁN DE. Born in Aparicio, Spain, in 1502, Sebastián de Aparicio came to New Spain[*] as a young man and earned a reputation as a skilled wheelwright and engineer. He played a key role in constructing the highway from Zacatecas[*] to Mexico City[*], by which huge volumes of silver were transported; he also managed to do it through the land of the Chichimeca[*] Indians, whom he pacified peacefully. As an elderly man, Aparicio joined the Franciscan[*] order. He died in 1600 and was beatified by Pope Pius VII in 1789.

REFERENCES: Donald C. Briggs and Marvin Alisky, *Historical Dictionary of Mexico*, 1981.

APATZINGAN, CONSTITUTION OF. The Constitution of Apatzingan was formulated by Mexican revolutionaries meeting as the Congress of Chilpancingo in October 1814. At the time, they were convened in Apatzingan, a city in Michoacán. Although the constitution was never implemented because of the capture of José María Morelos[*] y Pavón and the dissolution of the congress, its provision for a federal government of three branches, with the legislative branch electing a three-person executive board and a five-person judicial court, became a model for later constitutional discussions.

REFERENCES: John A. Caruso, *The Liberators of Mexico*, 1954; Hugh M. Hamill, Jr., *The Hidalgo Revolt*, 1966.

ARANDA, CONDE DE (PEDRO PABLO ABARCA DE BOLEA). Born in Aragón, Spain, in 1718, Pedro Pablo Abarca de Bolea was the tenth count of Aranda, a descendant of the Jiménez de Urrúa family that since the end of the fifteenth century had carried the titles of viscount of Rueda and count of Aranda. He followed a military career and distinguished himself brilliantly, reaching the rank of field marshal during the reign of Philip V*. He then transferred to the diplomatic service and served as ambassador to King Augustus III of Poland. Again he changed his profession and was appointed captain general of Valencia, then of Aragón, and finally, president of the Council of Ministers. It was he who succeeded in pacifying the country after the famous Esquilache mutiny of 1766.

Aranda was basically a man of action who showed determination and strength of character in all his official positions; at the same time, he was known for his obstinacy and partiality. A firm believer in the Enlightenment*, he applied the tenets of the Age of Reason as the solution for Spain's problems. He was a strong supporter of the societies of the *Amigos del País* and a great admirer of the *philosophes* in France; Voltaire, Guillaume Raynal, and Jean d'Alembert were among his friends. As a foe of ultramontanism, though within the bounds of Catholic orthodoxy, he viewed the papacy with hostility and saw the Church as an obstacle to the ideals of the eighteenth century. Thus, once propelled into the highest office in government in 1765, he used his position to combat the Church in the pursuit of progress and science. In the same year, he was also elected grand master of Spanish freemasonry, which added to his power and gave him another opportunity to further his anticlerical goals. Aranda was very much responsible for the campaign against the religious orders, especially the Jesuits*, who were being blamed for many real and imagined plots (the Esquilache riots, obstructing the Treaty of Madrid* of 1750 between Portugal and Spain regarding the borderlands of Paraguay*, and especially the Jesuit political philosophy based on popular sovereignty and aimed against divine-right theories). As a result of an orchestrated policy joined by Sebastião de Carvalho Pombal in Portugal, Bernardo Tanucci in Naples, Etienne François, the duke of Choiseul,* and Madame de Pompadour in France (1762), the Jesuit order was exiled from the Spanish Empire in 1767, a measure quite detrimental to the interests of the country. In Spanish America, it meant the closing of 120 colleges and the exile of some 2,000 Jesuits, hurting Spanish-American education, and leaving the Indians* in Paraguay to their own devices.

At the same time, Aranda guided Spain on the path of economic reforms within the guidelines of the Age of Reason. Many of the economic reforms of the age in agriculture, mining*, and shipping bear his stamp. He was also responsible for many of the beautiful buildings in major Spanish cities. Perhaps he will be best remembered for the famous Memorandum of 1783, in which, with prophetic insight in regard to both the possible independence of Spanish America and the encroachments of an expanding United States, he proposed to King Charles III* the establishment of three independent Spanish-American kingdoms (New Spain*, Peru*, and *Costa Firme*), headed respectively by the three *infantes* and linked to Spain only dynastically—a proposal later aired in a different manner by Manuel Godoy* in 1804.

Aranda consistently opposed British policies. He was responsible for recognizing the new United States, and he stood for vigorous action against Britain in regard to the various Falkland (Malvinas*) crises (1766, 1770). At the end of the 1770s, he switched back to diplomacy, serving as ambassador to Versailles, though he later returned to Madrid where he again headed the Council of Ministers in 1792. At the beginning of the French Revolution, he showed much sympathy for it, but the imprisonment of the French royal family on August 10, 1792, forced him to change his mind. His sympathy for the French Revolution also cost him the friendship of Godoy, who then replaced and exiled him. Aranda died in 1799 in Aragón. Whatever the opinion about this important personality in Spanish history, the Count of Aranda remains an impressive historical figure of the Spanish eighteenth century.

REFERENCE: Richard Herr, *The Eighteenth Century Revolution in Spain*, 1958.

O. Carlos Stoetzer

ARANGO Y PARREÑO, FRANCISCO. Born in Havana*, Cuba*, in 1756 to a distinguished family, Francisco Arango y Parreño began his study of law in the colonial capital and completed it in Madrid. He soon stood as the most articulate apostle of enlightened thought in Cuba and ranked among the leading intellects of Spanish America. Influenced by the laissez-faire doctrines of his time, particularly the thought of Adam Smith, he authored a host of learned essays championing primarily the cause of commercial deregulation to the benefit of his birthplace. His travels included a 1794 tour of Portugal, England, Jamaica*, and Barbados* to study technological, agricultural, and commercial practices that might enhance Cuban prosperity.

A shrewd advocate of modernization and progress, Arango served as spokesman for the Cuban sugar * aristocracy as it maneuvered to secure greater liberties within the Spanish mercantile* system and to gain direct access to world markets for its products. When acting as Havana's lobbyist at court, he successfully championed the Free Slave Trade Regulation promulgated in 1789 and worked to gain royal approval for the establishment of a *consulado* in Havana, which was granted in 1794. As *consulado syndic*, he did much to procure broad Cuban privileges in neutral trade during the wars of the French Revolution and of Napoleon. At war's end, his influence at court helped secure for Cuba the abolition of the royal tobacco* monopoly (1817) and the right to free trade in the world marketplace (1818).

Arango endorsed theoretically the ideal of egalitarianism for whites and expressed his opposition to legal privilege concretely by rejecting a title of nobility offered him in later life. Yet his liberalism did not extend to free blacks* and mulattoes, whom he mistrusted as threats to social stability. The owner of a sugar plantation, Arango viewed slavery* as a necessary evil for tropical agriculture. He urged the just treatment of slaves to safeguard against a servile uprising, but his humanitarian exhortations had little practical effect. Although in his declining years he came to favor the gradual abolition of slavery, his voice may have been decisive in thwarting the abolitionist movement in the Cortes of 1813.

On July 26, 1808, Arango led a band of conspirators who presented a petition to Governor Marqués de Someruelos urging the establishment of a Junta Suprema de Gobierno to govern Havana during the royal captivity. An implacable critic of the commandancy of marine, the intendancy, and the royal tobacco factory as impediments to free market practices, he aimed to suppress the autonomy of these agencies through a centralized authority. When his revolutionary movement failed to gain the support of the military, which feared for its privileges, he prudently withdrew the petition. Arango later feverishly denied that he wanted Cuban independence. He was soon co-opted by the royal administration of Ferdinand VII*, which first elevated him to the Council of the Indies* and later assigned him innumerable official commissions and showered him with honors. An idealist and a visionary, Arango was above all a realist. He died in 1837.

REFERENCES: Allan J. Kuethe, *Cuba, 1753–1815: Crown, Military, and Society*, 1986; Levi Marrero, *Cuba: Economía y sociedad*, 13 vols., 1972–1986, IX-XIII; William Whatley Pierson, "Francisco Arango y Parreño," *Hispanic American Historical Review*, 16 (1936), 451–478.

Allan J. Kuethe

ARANJUEZ, TREATY OF. The Treaty of Aranjuez of 1777 between France and Spain settled the boundary between the French and Spanish portions of Hispaniola*, between what became Haiti* and the Dominican Republic.

REFERENCE: Roland I. Perusse, *Historical Dictionary of Haiti*, 1977.

ARAUCANIAN. The Araucanians (Araucano) are one of the largest South American tribes of Amerindians. Alonso de Ercilla* y Zuñiga, the sixteenth-century Spanish poet, first coined the term "Araucanian" to describe the fierce Amerindians of what is today Chile*. During the period of Incan* expansion and Spanish conquest in the fifteenth and sixteenth centuries, the Araucanians lived between the Choapa River, in the north, to northern Chiloé Island, in the south of Chile. They included three major groups who designated themselves by their geographical location. The northern Araucanians were known as the Picunche, the central and dominant Araucanians as the Mapuche, and the southern Araucanians as the Huilliche. In the seventeenth and eighteenth centuries, while they were resisting Spanish conquest, the Araucanians themselves expanded eastward and conquered the Pehuenche, Puelche, and Chiquillanes, all of whom were absorbed into Araucanian culture. Other Araucanians, primarily Mapuche and Huilliche, expanded into Argentina*, particularly southern Mendoza, Neuquén, and Buenos Aires* provinces, where they became known as Aucas.

Before the Spanish conquest, the Araucanians totaled more than one million people and practiced a slash-and-burn agriculture to raise maize, potatoes, beans, squash, chili peppers, and quinoa. They also domesticated the llama and the wild chicken. When Spaniards arrived, the Araucanians quickly adopted the cultivation of wheat, the use of the plow, and the domestication of cattle, horses, sheep, goats, mules, and pigs*. Political cohesion was very loose among the Araucanians, with little emphasis on centralized values, but they fiercely resisted Spanish expansion. In 1541, Pedro de Valdivia*, the Spanish explorer of the southern reaches of the continent, established the city of Santiago*, but six months later the Araucanians destroyed the settlement. Valdivia then attacked the Araucanians with a vengeance, placing them on *encomiendas** and exacting tribute from them. He founded the city of Concepción in 1550, but the Araucanians destroyed it in 1553; Valdivia died in the battle. By the end of the 1500s, the Araucanians had adopted the horse and had become expert guerrilla fighters. Still, the toll of war and disease on the Araucanians was great. By the early 1600s, the Araucanian population had been reduced to approximately 100,000 people and the Picunche were rapidly disappearing as an identifiable group. Araucanian culture by that time was confined primarily below the Bio-Bio River.

In the seventeenth century, Roman Catholic* missionaries and neo-Chileno settlers began moving into Araucanian land, by now primarily Mapuche and Huilliche territory. During those years, the Araucanians adopted many items from Spanish material culture, as well as a number of Roman Catholic values, first from the Jesuits* until 1767, then from the Franciscans* until the mid-1850s, and finally from the Capuchins. Throughout the 1700s and 1800s, there was violence between the Spanish and the Araucanians, and then between the Araucanians and the neo-Chilenos and the Chilean government. The Indians resented the increasing pressure of settlers on their lands and periodically rebelled. But in 1866, the government established the first reservations for the Araucanians, now primarily the Mapuche, and in 1884, after the final subjugation of them, the reservations were implemented on a wide scale.

By the mid-1980s, the Mapuche numbered nearly 600,000 people living on several thousand reservations between the Laja River and the Gulf of Reloncavi in the region of La Araucanía. Another 50,000 Mapuche live in the cities of Santiago, Concepción, and Temuco, while more than 20,000 are Aucas living in Argentina. The Huilliche have for all intents and purposes ceased to exist as a separate social unit, having merged over the years with the expanding Mapuche people.

REFERENCES: Bernardo Berdichewsky, *The Araucanian Indian in Chile*, 1975; Maria P. Dillon, *The Fighting Araucanians*, 1964; Herbert Lee Ellis, *The Indian Policy of the Republic of Chile*, 1956; Louis Faron, *The Mapuche Indians of Chile*, 1986.

Frank Marotti

ARAUJO, JUAN DE. Juan de Araujo was born in Villafranca, Spain, in 1646. He moved to Lima*, Peru*. There he studied music as a young man and became a royal scholar at the University of San Marcos*. Juan de Araujo earned a reputation as one of the great musicians and composers of the colonial era. He became *maestro de capilla* of the Lima cathedral; in 1680, he assumed the same post in La Plata (now known as Sucre*), Bolivia*. Araujo remained there the rest of his life, writing more than 200 compositions. He died in Sucre, Bolivia, in 1714.

REFERENCE: R. M. Stevenson, *The Music of Peru: Aboriginal and Viceroyal Epochs*, 1960.

ARAWAK. The term "Arawak" is used to describe a wide variety of Amerindian groups native to the Greater Antilles and South America, as well as to a broad group of related languages. More particularly, Arawak (Aroaqui, Aruac, Aruaki, Aravaco, Arouage) refers to the Locono (Lokono) groups, since the word "Locono" is a self-designation meaning "Arawak proper." Those groups today are confined to the coastal and geographically related areas of Guyana, Surinam, and French Guiana. Most of the Locono Indians are bilingual in English, Dutch, or French, depending upon their residence. Many of them are in an advanced state of acculturation. The Locono population numbers approximately 13,000 people in about 40 villages, with the largest concentration in Guyana. Traditionally, the Locono were a horticultural people who lived off the production of manioc and other products, with hunting and fishing used as dietary supplements. Western-style education as well as Western technologies have undermined that subsistence lifestyle, forcing increasing numbers of Locono to work as laborers in the regional cash economy. That economic integration has also politicized the Locono as they have worked to preserve their tribal land titles and fishing and hunting rights.

Before the arrival of Christopher Columbus* and the Spaniards, the Arawakan Indians found themselves losing a struggle for survival with the more aggressive Karib* Indians, who were expanding out of South America into the Lesser Antilles. The Karibs had already conquered the Lesser Antilles and were poised to assault the Arawakan peoples of the Greater Antilles when Columbus arrived. In their conquest of the Arawak Indians, the Karibs often killed the men, married the women, and then witnessed the survival of the Arawakan language in their children. The arrival of the Spaniards stopped the Karib expansion.

The first people whom Columbus encountered in the New World were the Arawakan-speaking Taíno* people who occupied Cuba*, the Bahamas, and Hispaniola*. From the very beginning, the Spaniards classified the Arawaks as peaceful Indians and the Karibs as violent ones, even cannibals. But despite their peaceful presence, the Arawakan peoples in the Greater Antilles did not survive Spanish contact. Scholars estimate that there were as many as two million Arawak Indians occupying the Greater Antilles at the time of the conquest. By 1519, there were only a few thousand left, the others victims of disease, violence, slavery, and the environmental changes that occurred when the Europeans introduced new species of plants and animals to the islands. By 1600, Arawakan Indian society in the Greater Antilles had ceased to exist as a differentiated social unit.

Arawakan groups on the mainland of South America survived because they were more isolated and because European penetration occurred more slowly there. Also, the Arawak groups on the continent were organized into small, secluded, and seminomadic societies that allowed them to avoid European contact for a long time. The English in Guyana and the Dutch in Surinam approached the Arawak Indians from the perspective of commerce rather than conquest, setting up trading posts along major rivers and encouraging the Indians to exchange forest products for metal goods and textiles. In addition, the Arawaks were drawn to the trading posts because they felt safer there, not so much from other Europeans as from their Karib enemies. Not surprisingly, they acculturated more quickly than Karibs to European ways. In the seventeenth and eighteenth centuries, when the plantation economy emerged in the Guianas and large numbers of African slaves[*] were imported as workers, the planters paid money to the Indians to keep control of the slaves and to track down escaped slaves. The Indians lost that revenue when slavery was abolished in the 1830s and entered a long period of economic and population decline, which did not stabilize until the twentieth century.

REFERENCES: *Encyclopedia of Indians of the Americas*, II:220–226, 1974; Fred Olsen, *On the Trail of the Arawaks*, 1967.

ARCE, MANUEL JOSÉ. Born in 1787, Manuel José Arce was one of the founding fathers of political independence in Central America. He was a leading figure in the antiroyalist rebellions in San Salvador[*] in 1811 and 1814; he spent five years in prison for the latter. During the early 1820s, Arce led the Salvadoran forces opposed to annexation by Mexico, and when the Mexicans prevailed, Arce fled to the United States. Arce returned when the Central American regions seceded from Mexico in July 1823, and he became one of the three-man executive triumvirate that ruled the area. In March 1825, Arce was elected president of the Federal Republic of Central America[*]. He eventually gravitated to the conservative forces in the political struggles of the 1820s, but retired in 1828 after failing to achieve a settlement in the struggle between El Salvador[*] and the federation. When Francisco Morazán[*] and the liberals came to power in 1829, Arce went into exile in Mexico. He did not return to El Salvador until 1844. He died in 1847.

REFERENCE: Philip F. Flemion, "Manuel José Arce and the Formation of the Federal Republic of Central America," Ph.D. dissertation, University of Florida, 1969.

Virginia Garrard Burnett

ARDILES, MIGUEL DE. Miguel de Ardiles was born in Spain in 1515 but decided as a young man to seek his fortune in the New World. He was part of Diego de Rojas's expedition that discovered Tucumán*, and in 1545 he reached the Paraná River with the expedition of Francisco de Mendoza. Ardiles returned to Peru* in the late 1540s and fought against the forces of Gonzalo Pizarro* during the civil wars there. He came back to Tucumán with the expedition of Juan Núñez de Prado and left behind excellent written accounts of the tribulations of the first settlers there. Ardiles played key roles in the founding of Santiago de Estero in 1553, San Miguel de Tucumán in 1565, and Salta* in 1582. He died in 1586.

REFERENCE: Enrique Udaondo, *Diccionario biográfico colonial argentino*, 1945.

AREILZA, JOSÉ MARÍA DE, COUNT OF MOTRICO. José María de Areilza, the Count of Motrico, was born in Bilbao, Spain, in 1909. He was a strong advocate of the continuation of the Spanish colonial empire. During World War II, he hoped that a German victory over France would allow Spain to expand her African empire. In 1941, he coauthored the book *Revindicaciones de España*, in which he called for the enlargement of the Spanish empire into French-held territory in Morocco and Algeria. The German defeat in World War II ended those dreams, as did the guerrilla nationalist movements that emerged in the 1950s in Western Sahara*, Morocco, and Algeria. In 1975, Areilza was appointed foreign minister in the first post-Franco government in Spain, where he ironically presided over the beginning of the demise of Spain's African empire.

REFERENCES: Antonio Rumeu de Armas, *España en el Africa Atlántico*, 1956; Tony Hodges, *Historical Dictionary of Western Sahara*, 1982.

ARENALES, JUAN ANTONIO ÁLVAREZ DE. See ÁLVAREZ DE ARENALES, JUAN ANTONIO.

AREQUIPA. Arequipa is a southern province of Peru*. In 1784, as part of King Charles III's* reforms, Arequipa was established as an intendancy*. The first intendant was José Menendez y Escalada. Spain maintained its control of the area until the latest time in the colonial period, not departing until 1825. At that point, Arequipa became a Peruvian province.

REFERENCE: Carlos Deustua Pimental, *Las intendencias en el Peru (1790–1796)*, 1965.

AREQUIPA, DIOCESE OF. The Roman Catholic diocese of Arequipa*, Peru*, was first established in 1577 but it really did not become functional until 1609 when the first bishop, Pedro de Perea, arrived. Perea and his immediate suc-

cessors set out to convert the Indian tribes in the region, and by 1680, there were 56 parishes in the diocese. Arequipa became an archdiocese in 1943.
REFERENCE: *New Catholic Encyclopedia*, I:776–777, 1967.

ARGENTINA. At the time of the initial Spanish conquest of Mexico* and Peru* in the early 1500s, the region of present-day Argentina was inhabited by a variety of native American tribes. Argentina's conquest by Spain came from two directions: expansion out of the original settlements in Peru and Bolivia* and exploration of the Atlantic coast and up the Río de la Plata. The rich silver mines* in Bolivia needed supplies and pack animals, and the first settlements in northwestern Argentina were designed to fill those needs. Spaniards came to Argentina from Peru, Upper Peru*, and Chile.* Francisco de Aguirre* founded Santiago del Estero in 1553. Juan Pérez de Zorita established Catamarca in 1559, and two years later Pedro del Castillo founded Mendoza. Other settlements soon followed: Tucumán* (1565), Córdoba* (1573), Salta* (1582), La Rioja (1592), Jujuy (1593), and San Luis (1594).

Spanish exploration of the Atlantic coast was proceeding at the same time. Juan Díaz de Solís* discovered the Río de la Plata in 1516, and Ferdinand Magellan* reached Patagonia and the southern straits in 1521. In 1527–1528, Sebastián Cabot* explored the Uruguay and the Paraná rivers and discovered the Paraguay and Pilcomayo rivers. He established Sancti Spiritus near present-day Rosario, but Indians* destroyed the settlement in 1529. Pedro de Mendoza* founded Buenos Aires* on the Río de la Plata in 1536, but the expedition then headed up the Paraná and the Paraguay rivers to establish Asunción* in 1537, abandoning the Buenos Aires settlement. Asunción prospered, and from there, explorers established Santa Fe in 1573, Buenos Aires in 1585, and Corrientes in 1588. By 1600, the cattle industry, feeding the American and European empire, was flourishing.

Portugal founded the Colônia do Sacramento across the Río de la Plata from Buenos Aires in 1680, and the settlement soon became a source of imperial rivalry. Spain thought Portugal had designs on Argentina. For nearly a century, the two countries struggled, militarily and diplomatically, over the settlement, until the issue was resolved with the Treaty of San Ildefonso* in 1777: the Colônia do Sacramento and the missions east of the Uruguay River went to Spain, while Portugal kept Santa Catarina, Guaira, Mato Grosso, and both banks of the Jacuy River and the Río Grande in Brazil.

During the seventeenth century, a frontier society emerged in northwestern Argentina. The Indian tribes underwent a rapid population decline. The *encomienda** exploited Indian labor, but the Argentine economy originally revolved around cattle ranching, pack animals, and grains to supply Asunción and the Bolivian mines. By the time those mines declined in the mid-eighteenth century, northwestern Argentina was thriving economically. To institutionalize control over the region, Spain created the viceroyalty of the Río de la Plata* in 1777. Juan José Vertiz* y Salcedo* was the first viceroy. Within a year, Spain defined the viceroyalty boundaries to include Argentina, Uruguay,* Paraguay,* and southern and eastern Bolivia. Spain also established a royal treasury there in 1778, an *audiencia** in 1785, and a *consulado** in 1794. With the demise of the old fleet system, which had given Panamanian and Peruvian merchants monopolies on New World trade, the economy of Buenos Aires boomed, with northwestern Argentina becoming a breadbasket for much of Spain's New World empire.

Argentina remained loyal to Spain until the Napoleonic Wars allowed Generals Manuel Belgrano*, J. M. de Pueyrredón*, and José de San Martín* to deliver Argentina to self-rule. The independence movement in Argentina had several sources. By the turn of the century, Buenos Aires merchants were increasingly critical of Spanish imperial regulations, which they viewed as stifling and expensive. At the same time, the American Revolution* had deprived Great Britain of her North American colonies, and Britain turned to South America as a new trade source. Argentine merchants welcomed the attention. Spain allied itself with France in the Napoleonic Wars, and in 1805, at the Battle of Trafalgar, Great Britain destroyed much of the Spanish fleet, leaving the Spanish colonies unprotected. Great Britain invaded Buenos Aires in 1806 and 1807. Local forces managed to expel the British, but the combination of nationalism and a new self-confidence, born of their successful military campaigns, inspired the independence movement. When Napoleon invaded Spain in 1808 and deposed King Ferdinand VII*, *criollo** leaders in Buenos Aires refused to recognize the puppet government of Joseph Bonaparte. In 1810, they deposed Viceroy Baltasar Hidalgo de Cisneros*, installing their own government. This event is known as the May Revolution*. They established a provisional revolutionary junta to govern the area, but their hopes that a spontaneous independence movement would sweep through the area did not materialize. On the contrary, spontaneous uprisings against the junta developed in Montevideo* and Asunción, guaranteeing that Argentina would eventually not include what is today Uruguay and Paraguay. During 1812 and 1813, the revolutionaries successfully resisted several invading royalist armies. In the liberated area of northern Argentina, demands for formal independence escalated. The region was divided into 14 separate provinces, and in 1816, representatives from each province convened in the Congress of Tucumán*. On July 9, 1816, they declared their independence from Spain and established the United Provinces of South America*. The delegates were, however, unable to agree on a government. Intense ideological differences emerged between those favoring a strong central government and federalists demanding local autonomy. Civil war erupted between the factions in 1819–1820, and in 1825, the United Provinces went to war with Brazil over the possession of Uruguay. Brazil was defeated in the conflict and Uruguay emerged as an independent nation.

Argentine politics stabilized somewhat in 1829 when General Juan Manuel de Rosas* was elected governor of Buenos Aires. A strong believer in federalism, Rosas reached out to surrounding provinces, building political relationships while assuring that the province of Buenos Aires was not interested in dominating them. Slowly, during the 1830s and 1840s, Rosas extended his authority over the United Provinces. In 1852, with the assistance of Brazil and Uruguay, however, General Justo Urquiza deposed Rosas, and the next year, the United Provinces adopted a federal constitution, creating the Argentine Republic. The province of Buenos Aires refused to cooperate, however, and rebellions broke out there in 1859 and again in 1861. That problem was resolved in 1861 when General Bartolomé Mitre, leader of the Buenos Aires army, was elected president of Argentina and Buenos Aires was designated the country's new capital.

REFERENCES: Jonathan C. Brown, *A Socio-Economic History of Argentina, 1776–1860*, 1979; Tulio Halperin-Donghi and Richard Southern, *Politics, Economics, and Society in Argentina in the Revolutionary Period*, 1975.

Mark R. Shulman

ARIAS DE ÁVILA, PEDRO. See ÁVILA, PEDRO ARIAS DE.

ARIAS DE SAAVEDRA, HERNANDO. Also known as "Hernandarias," Hernando Arias de Saavedra was born in Asunción*, Paraguay*, in 1560, and he became the first *criollo** to serve as governor of colonial Paraguay. He served as governor for more than twenty years, and during his administration, the Jesuits* established their missions* in Paraguay. Arias was especially interested in incorporating the Guaraní* Indians, as well as other tribes, into colonial society. He is largely responsible for establishing the process by which Paraguay became a bilingual—Spanish and Guaraní—society. He died in 1634.

REFERENCES: Philip Caraman, *Lost Paradise: The Jesuit Republics in South America*, 1976; Charles J. Kolinski, *Historical Dictionary of Paraguay*, 1973.

ARIAS DE UGARTE Y FORERO, HERNANDO. Hernando Arias de Ugarte y Forero was born in Spain in 1561 and entered the Roman Catholic priesthood as a young man. He rose relatively quickly through the clerical ranks and in 1613 was consecrated as bishop of the diocese of Quito* in Ecuador*. He was there several years before assuming the archbishopric of Bogotá* in 1618. Arias spent seven years in Bogotá before being named archbishop of Lima*. He assumed that post in 1630. Arias's tenure as bishop in all of those areas was marked by consistent attempts to limit the exploitation of the Indians* by Spanish officials and settlers. He died in 1638.

REFERENCE: J. M. Henao and C. T. Arrubla, *History of Colombia*, 1938.

ARIAS NAVARRO, CARLOS. Carlos Arias Navarro was born to a working-class family in Madrid, Spain, on December 11, 1908. He received a law degree from the Central University and then entered the Spanish civil service. Arias worked as an attorney in the ministry of justice between 1929 and 1933 and then as public prosecutor in Málaga until the outbreak of the Spanish civil war. He spent some time in prison before joining the insurgent forces and serving as a prosecutor for the military judicial corps. In 1944, Arias became civil governor of León; he subsequently filled the same post in Santa Cruz de Tenerife and in Navarre. He became director general for security in the government of Francisco Franco[*] in 1957. Between 1965 and 1973, he served as mayor of Madrid. He became minister of justice in the Franco cabinet in June 1973, and in January 1974, Franco made him premier. From that position, Arias presided over the great challenges of 1975: Basque terrorism, the illness and death of Franco, the transition to constitutional government, and the Spanish withdrawal from the Spanish Sahara[*]. King Juan Carlos forced Arias to resign as premier in July 1976, after which he went into retirement.

REFERENCE: R. C. Carr and J. P. Fusi, *Spain: From Dictatorship to Democracy*, 1979.

ARMADA DE BARLOVENTO. In 1643, Spain formed a special naval force known as the Armada de Barlovento (today, the Windward Islands) for the defense of the Americas. The maintenance of such fleet was supported entirely by colonial taxation. The fleet was soon withdrawn but the tax remained. There were other fleets assembled by the Spanish Royal Navy, such as the Armada del Mar del Sur, the Armada de la Carrera, and the Catalonian deputation fleet. They all gradually disappeared by the end of the seventeenth century. Also not uncommon were private *armadas* engaged principally in the protection against Moslem naval vessels. Although privateering was prohibited by law, the kings looked favorably on such activities.

REFERENCE: James Anthony Froude, *The Spanish Story of the Armada and Other Essays*, 1892.

Fred Koestler

ARMADA DE LA CARRERA DE INDIAS. See FLOTA.

ARMY OF LIBERATION. The Army of Liberation was a Moroccan-led movement of Berber peasants who fought against Spanish control in Western Sahara and against French control in northern Mauritania in the mid–1950s. The army was formed out of a variety of peasant guerrilla bands in 1955. By June 1956, the army was attacking French positions in the frontier zone with Algeria; one year later, they were conducting terrorist campaigns against the Spanish in Ifni[*] and Western Sahara, forcing Spanish troops to withdraw from their posts in the interior. Not until early 1958, when a combined French-Spanish military force launched Operation Ouragan, was the Army of Liberation crushed. By that time, it was already riddled by internal dissension.

REFERENCES: Rafael Ortega Canadell, *Provincias Africanas Españolas*, 1962; John P. Halstead, *Rebirth of a Nation: The Origins and Rise of Moroccan Nationalism, 1912–1944*, 1967.

ARMY OF THE ANDES. The Army of the Andes was composed of Argentine patriots and Chilean refugees, totaling approximately 6,000 men, formed by General José de San Martín[*] to liberate the United Provinces of South America[*] (Argentina[*], Chile[*], Bolivia[*], and Paraguay[*]) from Spanish domination. In the middle of the Argentine summer on January 18, 1817, the army started an impossible march across the Andes, towing cannons, ammunition, baggage, and equipment over icy passes and precipices toward Chile. The march was one of the most heroic and surprising accomplishments in the annals of Latin American movements for independence. Climbing to elevations over 13,000 feet—an altitude that produces nausea, headaches, accelerated heartbeat, and a general weakening of the body ("soroche" or mountain sickness)—the army marched over 300 miles, facing the hot sun during the day and bitter cold at night. After 21 days, the Army of the Andes surprised the Spaniards on February 12, and defeated them decisively at the Battle of Chacabuco*. The defeat of the Spaniards in central Chile secured Chilean independence and provided San Martín with a secure base of operations for the assault on Peru*.

REFERENCE: J. C. J. Metford, *San Martín the Liberator*, 1950.

Fred Koestler

ARRIAGA, PABLO JOSÉ DE. Pablo José de Arriaga was born in Vergara, Spain, in 1564. He studied in Madrid before becoming a Jesuit* novitiate in 1579. He taught rhetoric in Madrid before moving to Peru* in 1585. During his stay in Peru, Arriaga served as the rector of the College of San Martín in Lima and the College of Arequipa. He worried about the welfare of the Indians* and focused his energies on studying them and providing them with Church assistance. He also wrote much and is best remembered for his book *Extirpación de la idolatría del Peru* (1621). He died in a shipwreck near Cuba on September 6, 1622.

ARRIAGA Y RIVERA, JULIÁN DE. Julián de Arriaga y Rivera was born in Spain in 1696 and joined the navy as an ensign in 1728. Blessed with courage and a clear, analytical mind, he was noticed by those in power, especially Zeñón de Somodevilla, the minister of finance, war, marine, and the Indies. When the *criollos** of León, Venezuela*, revolted against the Caracas Company* in 1749, Arriaga was named military governor of Venezuela and was sent with an expedition to crush the rebellion. He did the job efficiently and with a minimum of violence. His success led quickly to his appointment in 1752 as president of the Casa de Contratación*. In 1754, Arriaga succeeded Somodevilla as minister of the Indies and marine. In that position, he served with efficiency and good judgment, although his innate conservatism led him to oppose the creation of the *intendencias** and the rise of free trade policies. Arriaga died on January 28, 1776.

REFERENCE: V. Rodriguez Casado, *La política y los políticos en el reinado de Carlos III*, 1962.

ARTIGAS, JOSÉ GERVASIO. Born in Montevideo* in 1764, the future founding father of Uruguay* distinguished himself early in the Cuerpo de Blandengües, a border patrol created in 1796 to repel increasing Portuguese encroachments into the *Banda Oriental*. On September 21, 1808, Montevideo set up a royalist junta that expressed the traditional antagonism between Buenos Aires* and Montevideo in a different way. This antagonism became even more acute with the May Revolution* in Buenos Aires in 1810. The *orientales* had sided first with the royalist cause against Buenos Aires. By 1811, this unity had cracked, and a new revolution developed against Montevideo. Its leader was Artigas and his gauchos.

The *Grito de Asencio* against Montevideo in February 1811 favored Bueno Aires. It was then that Artigas rallied to the cause of Buenos Aires, soon becoming the leader of the *orientales*. His gauchos won at San José de las Piedras and laid siege to Montevideo. An Argentine army entered the Banda Oriental that same year, in alliance with Artigas's gauchos against the new viceregal center of Montevideo. The Portuguese invaded the area, but since neither Buenos Aires nor Portugal wanted a war, an armistice was signed; both *porteños* and Portuguese evacuated their forces.

Artigas was clearly left in the lurch by the action of the Argentines. It forced him to lift the siege and to cross the Uruguay River with his gauchos and their families—the *éxodo*. Buenos Aires reopened hostilities and made its peace with Artigas. Thus, the Banda Oriental again became a theater of operations. Artigas was now appointed commander-in-chief of the patriot army of the Banda Oriental by Buenos Aires, although the supreme command was given to Manuel de Sarratea. The revolutionary armies once again laid siege to royalist Montevideo, winning at the Cerrito, but soon the harmony between Artigas and the Argentines collapsed. Buenos Aires insisted on a centralist policy, while Artigas, like those in other Argentine provinces, wanted autonomy within a new Argentine federal state. In 1813, a General Constituent Congress was convened in Buenos Aires to solve the constitutional problems of the Río de la Plata*. Artigas then sent delegates to Buenos Aires with his famous *Instrucciones del Año XIII*, which had been worked out in Peñarol and which summarized his political views: autonomy of the provinces, including his own, within a federal republic. Buenos Aires refused and proceeded to occupy Montevideo, which fell to Carlos María de Alvear* on June 22, 1814. It was a short-lived victory.

Artigas's victory over the Argentines at Guayabo (January 10, 1815) opened the gates of Montevideo. The *cabildo**, interpreting the people's will, gave him the title "Protector and Patron of the Freedom of Peoples" and appointed him captain general* of the Banda Oriental. The new Portuguese invasion of 1816 brought new troubles and Artigas's own demise. His defeat at Tacuarembo in 1820 and the annexation of the area (now called Provincia Cisplatina) to Portugal forced him into exile in Paraguay*, where his friend, Dr. José Gaspar Rodríguez de Francia*, the *Supremo*, welcomed him. He died there in 1850.

Once his goal of autonomy for the Banda Oriental was doomed, Artigas aimed to establish a strong buffer state joining together his own Banda Oriental to Entre Ríos and Corrientes, a plan the British would later pursue unsuccessfully. Juan E. Pival Devoto called Artigas "the last Spaniard" for his austere simplicity and his devotion to the *fueros** and to local rights.

REFERENCES: Juan E. Pival Devoto, *Raíces coloniales de la Revolución oriental de 1811*, 1957; Lorenzo Belinzón, *La revolución emancipadora uruguaya y sus dogmas democráticos*, 1932.

O. Carlos Stoetzer

ASIENTO. The *asiento* was a franchise, established by the Spanish Crown, granting individuals or companies the right to ship slaves* for sale in the Spanish colonies. It is not known precisely when the first African set foot in the New World, but the really massive, concentrated effort at slave trade began in 1510 when King Ferdinand I succumbed to the demand for laborers from the Casa de Contratación* to send 250 slaves to the New World. The earliest slaves were bought from the Portuguese, as the Spanish were excluded from the African coast by the Treaty of Tordesillas* of 1494. Spain granted its first *asiento* to a company in Genoa in what is today Italy with instructions to deliver 1,000 slaves to the New World by 1525. The Welser* banking house received an *asiento* in 1528 to deliver 4,000 slaves to Venezuela*. The Spanish Crown later granted *asientos* in 1552, 1595, 1609, 1696, 1701, and 1713. The 1713 *asiento*, guaranteed by the Treaty of Utrecht* of 1713, gave the British the right to deliver 4,800 slaves annually to Spanish colonies for the next 30 years.

REFERENCES: Rafael Altamira y Crevea, *Historia de España y de la civilización española*, 6 vols., 1900–1930; J. H. Elliott, *The Count-Duke of Olivares: The Statesman in an Age of Decline*, 1986; James F. King, "Evolution of the Free Slave Trade Principle in Spanish Colonial Administration," *Hispanic American Historical Review*, 22 (1947), 36–46.

Fred Koestler

ASIENTO, TREATY OF (1713). After defeat in the War of the Spanish Succession* (1702–1713), Spain ceded to Great Britain the monopoly of supplying African slaves* to the West Indies. Although the treaty limited the number of slaves to 4,800 per year for 30 years, British slavers far exceeded those restrictions. Spain grew increasingly upset over British violations of the treaty limits, which precipitated in part the War of Jenkins' Ear* between Great Britain and Spain in 1739. The Treaty of Asiento was not renewed in 1743.

REFERENCE: Peter Kemp, *The Oxford Companion to Ships and the Sea*, 1976.

ASUNCIÓN. The capital city of Paraguay*, Asunción was founded by Juan de Salazar y Espinosa* in 1537 on a high bluff of the Paraguay River, just north of where the river meets the Pilcomayo River. It is about 1,000 miles up the Paraná-Paraguay river system from Buenos Aires. During the sixteenth century, Asunción was the point from which many exploration parties headed into the South American lowlands, but by 1600 Buenos Aires* had assumed that role. Because Paraguay was a landlocked, isolated province of the Spanish Empire, Asunción was a small, backward city throughout the colonial period. Its population had reached only 10,000 people by the independence period.

REFERENCE: Dwight B. Heath, *Historical Dictionary of Bolivia*, 1972.

ASUNCIÓN, DIOCESE OF. The Roman Catholic diocese of Asunción was established in 1547 and covered most of present-day Paraguay*. It became an archdiocese in 1929.

REFERENCE: *New Catholic Encyclopedia*, I:993, 1967.

ATAHUALLPA. The son of Huayna Cápac*, the ruler over the Inca* empire in the early 1500s, Atahuallpa inherited the northern part of the empire at the time of Huayna Cápac's death. A dynastic struggle then ensued between Atahuallpa and his brother Huáscar*, who had inherited the southern portion of the empire. In the midst of that Inca civil war, Francisco Pizarro's* expedition of conquest reached Peru*. Atahuallpa assassinated Huáscar to prevent his brother from cooperating with the Spaniards, but Pizarro then executed Atahuallpa in 1533, even after promising the Incan emperor to release him if he supplied Spain with enough gold.

REFERENCE: George Kubler, "The Behavior of Atahuallpa," *Hispanic American Historical Review*, 25 (1945), 413–27.

AUDIENCIA. The *audiencia*, based on a judicial institution that existed on the Spanish peninsula, had administrative and judicial functions in the Spanish imperial system. The *audiencias* existed in the principal cities of important provinces in the New World and the Philippines*. The first *audiencia* was established in 1511 in Santo Domingo* and then in Mexico City* after the conquest of the Aztec* empire. *Audiencias* soon appeared in the newly conquered territories of the Americas where they shared power with the viceroy* or captain general* and served to check his arbitrary use of it.

The number of bureaucrats who staffed the *audiencia* depended on the importance of the location. The two principal *audiencias* in Mexico City, New Spain*, and Lima*, Peru*, each initially had a president and four judges (*oidores**) but, as the empire gained in complexity, the number of judges grew. In the seventeenth century Mexico City *audiencia*, there were twelve judges divided into two chambers: civil, composed of eight judges, and criminal, composed of four. There were also both civil and criminal attorneys (*fiscales*) for the Crown. The viceroy or captain general was the ex officio president who had no vote in judicial matters and was forbidden to meddle in judicial affairs. There were also many lesser officials, including reporters, notaries, and a lawyer and solicitor for the poor. At the end of the eighteenth century, there were ten civil judges, five criminal judges (*alcaldes de crimen*), and three attorneys. The Lima *audiencia* operated in much the same way. In the less important *audiencias*, there were three to five judges, who tried both civil and criminal cases, and one or two attorneys. Many times these lesser *audiencias* did not have the requisite members because of death, illness, and failure to fill the vacancies. In order to ensure governmental continuity at the highest level, the appointment of a judge was for life.

The *audiencia* had manifold judicial duties. They heard appeals from the lower courts and their decision in criminal cases was final. Any appeal of decisions in important civil cases, on the other hand, went to the Council of the Indies*. One of the most important functions of the *audiencia* was the protection of the Indians*. Two days a week were set aside to hear suits between Indians or between Indians and Spaniards. Moreover, the Indians did not have to pay lawyer fees. This duty was later taken up by the *juzgado de indios* a special court for Indians. The *audiencia* also had original jurisdiction over criminal cases that occurred in the city or within a radius of five leagues from where it resided. It also sat in judgment of ecclesiastical cases of a secular nature.

In addition to its judicial functions, the *audiencia* also had administrative ones. As a council of state, it conferred with the president on political administration. Through these sessions, known as *acuerdos**, and the decisions arrived at, known as *autos acordados*, the *audiencia* was able to exercise administrative and legislative power. It also made sure that all royal decrees and orders were carried out. If the viceroy or captain-general died, the *audiencia* would rule until his replacement arrived. Whether the viceroy or *audiencia* would dominate depended on the personality of the viceroy.

Following the establishment of the first *audiencia* in 1511 in Santo Domingo, the Spanish Crown tried to prevent *audiencia* members from becoming *radicados* (rooted in the New World community where they resided), because *audiencia* members were much more permanent than the viceroy. During the period from 1687 to 1750, the age of impotence, the Spanish Crown was forced to bow to its fiscal needs by selling *audiencia* posts to those who had the money. This situation allowed many *criollos**, or New World Spaniards, to acquire an *audiencia* office and increase their influence in government. During this period, there were also many *radicado* peninsulars, or Old World Spaniards, on the *audiencias*. This trend shifted during the age of authority, from 1751 to 1808, under the later Bourbons who fought against this increase in local influence by appointing *peninsulares* who had few local ties. By the end of the Spanish colonial period, there were far fewer *criollos* who sat on the *audiencia*. The Spanish-American independence movement put an end to this institution. Still, the newly independent Spanish-American nations often had as their borders the colonial *audiencia* jurisdictional limits.

REFERENCES: C. H. Haring, *The Spanish Empire in America*, 1947; Mark A. Burkholder and D. S. Chandler, *From Impotence to Authority: The Spanish Crown and the American Audiencias, 1687-1808*, 1977.

Carlos Pérez

AUDIENCIA OF CARACAS. See CARACAS, *AUDIENCIA* OF.

AUDIENCIA OF CHARCAS. See CHARCAS, *AUDIENCIA* OF.

AUDIENCIA OF CHILE. See CHILE, CAPTAINCY-GENERAL OF.

AUDIENCIA **OF CUZCO.** See CUZCO, *AUDIENCIA* OF.

AUDIENCIA **OF GUADALAJARA.** See NEW GALICIA, *AUDIENCIA* OF.

AUDIENCIA **OF GUATEMALA.** See GUATEMALA, *AUDIENCIA* OF.

AUDIENCIA **OF LOS CONFINES.** See GUATEMALA, *AUDIENCIA* OF.

AUDIENCIA **OF MANILA.** See MANILA, *AUDIENCIA* OF.

AUDIENCIA **OF MEXICO CITY.** See MEXICO CITY, *AUDIENCIA* OF.

AUDIENCIA **OF NEW GALICIA.** See NEW GALICIA, *AUDIENCIA* OF.

AUDIENCIA **OF NEW GRANADA.** See NEW GRANADA, *AUDIENCIA* OF.

AUDIENCIA **OF NEW SPAIN.** See MEXICO CITY, *AUDIENCIA* OF.

AUDIENCIA **OF PANAMÁ.** See PANAMÁ, *AUDIENCIA* OF.

AUDIENCIA **OF PUERTO PRINCIPE.** See SANTO DOMINGO *AUDIENCIA* OF.

AUDIENCIA **OF PUERTO RICO.** See PUERTO RICO, *AUDIENCIA* OF.

AUDIENCIA **OF QUITO.** See QUITO, *AUDIENCIA* OF.

AUDIENCIA **OF SANTA FE DE BOGOTÁ.** See NEW GRANADA, *AUDIENCIA* OF.

AUDIENCIA **OF SANTO DOMINGO.** See SANTO DOMINGO, *AUDIENCIA* OF.

AUGUSTINIANS. The Augustinian Order (OSA-Order of Augustinian Society) was founded by Augustine of Hippo (354–430), a theologian, philosopher, and spiritual leader. Along with Tertullian and Ciprian, Augustine is considered to be one of the fathers of medieval Roman Catholicism. Born in Tagaste, Numidia, now known as Suk Ahras, Algeria, Augustine provided the impetus for religious fervor and fanatic nationalism. The Augustinian order in the New World was deeply involved in the administration of various hospitals. From Lima[*] to Mexico City[*], Augustinians not only provided treatment for the sick but also extended help to the aged, the blind, and the indigent. In fact, the expansion of the Spanish Empire in the sixteenth and seventeenth centuries stimulated the growth and influence of the Augustinians. They established missions in New Spain* in 1533, Peru* in 1551, the Philippines* in 1565, India in 1572, Colombia* in 1575, China in 1575, Angola and the Congo in 1578, Malacca in 1587, Chile* in 1595, Arabia in 1596, Kenya in 1598, Japan and Persia in 1602, Ceylon in 1606, and Iraq in 1623. By 1595, there were 72 Augustinian institutions in New Spain with more than 600 friars working in them. By the end of the eighteenth century, Augustinians in particular and the Church in general had become a prosperous enterprise. After the expulsion of the Jesuits* from the New World in 1767, the Augustinians took over some of their mission settlements, although the Franciscans* and Dominicans* were more active there.

REFERENCE: *New Catholic Encyclopedia*, I:1075–76, XII: 304, 1967.

Fred Koestler

AUSTIN, MOSES. A North American pioneer, Moses Austin received the first *empresario* grant from the Spanish government to settle in the "Internal Provinces"* of northern New Spain* in 1821. Because these provinces (now Texas*, New Mexico*, Arizona, California*, and the Mexican states that they border) were underpopulated, isolated from Mexico City*, and vulnerable to foreign penetration, the Spanish government implemented the *empresario* system to attract permanent, sedentary settlers to the area. The first province to be parceled out was Texas, which had only 7,000 permanent settlers in 1800 and was considered particularly susceptible to foreign encroachments due to its proximity to the territory acquired by the United States in the Louisiana* Purchase in 1803. Austin was the first *empresario* to win land under the plan, receiving his grant from General Joaquín de Arredondo, the Spanish commandant of Monterrey*, in January 1821. Moses Austin died and Mexico gained its independence before the project began, but his son, Stephen F. Austin, ratified the agreement with the new Mexican government. Under the terms of the concession, Austin was authorized to bring in 300 families in the first year, if each individual proved to be of good moral character, would profess Roman Catholicism, and agreed to abide by Mexican law. Austin established his settlement between the Colorado and Brazos Rivers in Texas in 1821.

REFERENCES: Michael C. Meyer and William L. Sherman, *The Course of Mexican History*, 1983; T. R. Fehrenbach, *Lone Star: A History of Texas and Texans*, 1985.

Virginia Garrard Burnett

AUSTRIAN SUCCESSION, WAR OF THE. The War of the Austrian Succession was the direct result of the death, on October 20, 1740, of Charles VI, Holy Roman Emperor, without leaving a male heir. Charles VI had negotiated the Pragmatic Sanction, signed by the European powers including Prussia, which guaranteed that all the possessions of the Austrian Habsburgs would be inherited intact by the heiress, Maria Theresa. The new king of Prussia, Frederick II, saw a chance, however, to annex Silesia, which adjoined Prussia, before the other powers could take advantage of Austria's predicament. On December 16, 1740,

30,000 Prussian troops crossed the border into Silesia, meeting little resistance and capturing the capital, Breslau, on January 3, 1741. In response, Maria Theresa ordered troops into Silesia. On April 10, they engaged Frederick's main army at Mollwitz. Initially, Frederick and his cavalry were driven from the field, but the well-trained Prussian infantry was able to turn the Austrian cavalry's assault, forcing Neipperg to retreat. The Austrian defeat demonstrated its vulnerability to a watching Europe, which was waiting to plunder the empire's holdings. Eventually, Bavaria, Spain, and France joined in the attack.

Maria Theresa requested aid from those countries that had signed the Pragmatic Sanction, but only George II of England was willing to come to Austria's aid, and then only because he wanted a strong Austria to check French expansion on the continent. His aid was tempered, however, by the fear that Prussia would attack Hanover. Parliament voted £300,000 and urged Maria Theresa to cede Lower Silesia to Prussia, which she refused to do. Frederick, therefore, concluded a treaty with France that guaranteed him Breslau and Lower Silesia in return for his vote to elect Charles Albert of Bavaria to the imperial throne. If successful, Charles Albert would rule Bavaria, Upper Austria, the Tyrol, Bohemia, and part of Swabia. Maria Theresa would be left with Hungary, Lower Austria, and the Austrian Netherlands. With monetary support but without support of arms, Maria Theresa turned to Hungary for help. Hungary had little reason to aid her, having suffered under Austrian rule. Nonetheless, when she met with the Diet at Pressburg on September 11, 1741, they were moved by her impassioned plea and raised 100,000 troops, pledging Hungary's loyalty. She also reluctantly concluded the Convention of Klein-Schnellendorg on October 9, 1741. This secret agreement ceded Lower Silesia to Frederick, thus taking him out of the conflict temporarily. Neipperg's army was now able to secure the threatened Austrian capital. The pressure on Vienna was further eased when Saxony entered the war against Austria. Charles Albert now feared that Saxony would seize Bohemia and therefore turned back only a few days' march from Vienna. Three armies now converged on Prague. The Bohemian capital fell on November 25. Disaster awaited Charles Albert, however. An Austrian army under the command of Count Ludwig von Khevenkuller invaded Bavaria, capturing Munich on February 12, 1742. Ironically, Charles Albert was crowned Emperor of the Holy Roman Empire, as Charles VII, on the same day that Munich fell.

In December 1741, events took another turn when Frederick rejoined his former allies, claiming that Maria Theresa had violated their secret convention by revealing it to the French. Frederick now undertook an invasion through Moravia into Lower Austria where he planned to combine with Saxon and Franco-Bavarian forces and then march on Vienna. The failure of his allies and harassment by Hungarian cavalry, which severed his lines of communications with Silesia, forced him to turn back to Bohemia. On May 12, 1742, an Austrian vanguard under Charles of Lorraine attacked the Prussian rear guard but were defeated. This latest defeat convinced Maria Theresa to come to terms with Frederick. The Treaty of Berlin of 1742 ceded to Prussia almost all of Silesia.

In the fall of 1742, the Austrian armies moved into Bohemia, surrounding the French army, which had not taken advantage of the chance to escape, in Prague. France sent a relief army into Bohemia, liberating the English army, which had been held in check to protect Hanover, to enter the war. The English promptly dispatched 16,000 troops to Austrian Flanders. Meanwhile, using money she had obtained from England and the United Provinces, Maria Theresa raised an army to check Maillebois's advance. Finding his position in Prague threatened, Belle-Isle, who had taken command from de Broglie, retreated through the Beraun valley to Eger, reaching it after heavy losses on December 27. This left the rest of Bohemia in the hands of Maria Theresa.

The year 1742 also saw the war extended into Italy when Maria Theresa found her Italian possessions threatened. She was able to secure an alliance with Charles Emmanuel, king of Sardinia, on February 1, 1742, thus checking the invading Spanish-Neapolitan army and forcing it to retreat. Her fortunes appeared to be changing and, with the defeat of the French at Dettingen on June 27, 1743, she even held hopes of regaining Silesia and taking Bavaria and Alsace-Lorraine. France attempted to bring Frederick back into the war and, on August 5, 1744, Frederick opened the second Silesian war with an invasion of Bohemia. Prague fell on September 16, whereupon Frederick moved his main force against Vienna. Again threatened, Maria Theresa turned to the Hungarians for troops. She also ordered Prince Charles of Lorraine to break off the attack on Alsace and to lead the main Austrian army against Frederick. Frederick had expected the French to deal with the Austrians. When they did not, he once again found himself in hostile territory with his lines of communications threatened. He was, therefore, forced to abandon Prague and return to Berlin.

On January 20, 1745, Charles VII died. Following his father's advice, Maximillian Joseph renounced all claims to the imperial throne and supported the election of Duke Francis Stephen (husband of Maria Theresa). Austrian troops could now be withdrawn from Bavaria. Events were going badly for the English, however. On May 11, 1745, the French successfully repulsed the English army at Fontenoy. Furthermore, England was forced to withdraw from Flanders to counter a Jacobite insurrection in Scotland. With Flanders weakened, Marshal de Saxe was able to capture a number of towns for France, including the main English base at Ostend. Again fearful for Hanover, George II attempted to coerce Maria Theresa to come to terms with Frederick. When she refused, England signed a separate peace, the Convention of Hanover, on August 26, 1745. The agreement reaffirmed the provisions in the Treaty of Berlin, and France agreed to support the election of Duke Francis Stephen as emperor. On October 4, 1745, Francis was crowned emperor and Maria Theresa empress. The French were also victorious in Italy, capturing most of southern Piedmont. With her Italian possessions threatened, Maria Theresa reluctantly signed the Peace of Dresden. With Silesia definitely ceded to Prussia, Frederick withdrew from the war.

Fighting in Europe continued, however. France fought Austria and England in Flanders, and France and Spain fought Austria and Sardinia for dominance in Italy. French reversals in the Americas finally brought that nation to the peace table in 1748. France had lost Fort Louisbourg on Cape Breton Island, while the British had driven the French from the seas, blockading the rich French West Indies. This had a devastating effect on French finances. The Treaty of Aix-la-Chapelle*, ending the War of the Austrian Succession, guaranteed Maria Theresa's rule of the Habsburg Empire. It also allowed Prussia to keep Silesia, thereby doubling its population. After eight years of fighting, only Prussia could show any territorial gains.

REFERENCE: Walter L. Dorn, *Competition for Empire: 1740-1763*, 1940.

Michael Dennis

AUTOS ACORDADOS. See *ACUERDO*.

AVELLANEDA, GERTRUDIS GÓMEZ DE. See GÓMEZ DE AVELLANEDA, GERTRUDIS.

AVERÍA. The *avería* was a colonial tax paid by merchants to finance the costs of trade convoys. When the Consulado de Comercio was established in 1793, 1.5 percent of import-export profits was given to the *consulado* for use on internal improvements. Spain had raised the *avería* to 2.5 percent by the end of the colonial period.

REFERENCE: Richard E. Moore, *Historical Dictionary of Guatemala*, 1973.

ÁVILA, FRANCISCO DE. Francisco de Ávila was born in Cuzco*, Peru*, in 1573. He was ordained a Roman Catholic priest in 1591 and then pursued higher education at the University of San Marcos* in Lima*, Peru. He received a doctorate in law there in 1606. During those years, Ávila also served as a pastor in Huarochiri, where he passionately tried to eliminate what he considered Indian* idolatry. A linguist with special skills in Quechua*, Ávila wrote a number of important works dealing with Indian* culture, the most important of which was his *Tratado de los evangelios*, published in 1646. On several occasions, Ávila was accused of being overzealous in his approach to the Indians, but he was exonerated in the formal investigations of his conduct. He died in Lima on September 17, 1647.

REFERENCE: H. R. Trimborn, "Francisco de Ávila," *Ciencias*, 3 (1936), 163–74.

ÁVILA, PEDRO ARIAS DE. Pedro Arias de Ávila, also known as "Pedrarias" and "Pedrarias Dávila," was born in Arias, Segovia, Spain, in 1442, to Jewish parents. He spent his career in the military and civil service of Spain. Early in the 1500s, he distinguished himself in North Africa* where Spanish troops were still battling the Moors. In 1513, Ávila received an appointment as governor of Darién* in the New World, a post he assumed in 1514. But the traits that had distinguished him as a soldier—ferocity and aggressiveness—were not nearly so useful in colonial administration. Ávila quickly earned a reputation for cruelty and the nickname "Wrath of God." Ávila came to Panama* in 1514 to relieve Vasco Núñez de Balboa*. Balboa had been the first Spaniard to reach the Pacific Ocean on September 29, 1513, at which time he had claimed all the lands that bordered the "Southern Sea" for Spain. He had also nurtured the small Spanish colony of Darién in Panama into a viable settlement. Pedrarias, though Balboa's superior officer, was suspicious of his subordinate and covetous of the latter's titles of *adelantado** of the South Sea and captain general of Panama and Cloba (on the west coast of Panama). In 1517, Pedrarias had Balboa tried and beheaded on dubious charges of treason, a particularly heinous deed in light of the fact that Pedrarias was Balboa's father-in-law. The death of Balboa, however, left Pedrarias in control of the two Panamanian provinces. The colony prospered financially under Pedrarias, and in 1519, he established a new capital at Panama City, a location more healthful and pleasant than the malarial wastelands of Darién. Darién was abandoned completely by 1524.

Using Panama as his base, Pedrarias expanded his authority through southern Central America by lethal power plays with competing conquistadors and the merciless exploitation of the Indian population. One of his most bitter competitors was Gil Gonzales* Dávila, a Spaniard who arrived in Panama in 1519 and explored the coast of Costa Rica* and as far north as Lake Nicaragua in 1522. The rivalry between Pedrarias and Gonzales eventually forced the latter to flee Panama, but without relinquishing his claim to Nicaragua*. In 1524, Pedrarias ordered a large military force under the command of Francisco Hernández de Córdoba to travel to Nicaragua to claim the territory for Pedrarias. While in Nicaragua, Hernández founded the towns of Grenada (on Lake Nicaragua) and León (on Lake Managua), but on his return, Hernández turned in rebellion on Pedrarias. In 1526, Pedrarias had Hernández* de Córdoba executed and established himself as governor of Nicaragua. His authority eventually extending from El Salvador and Honduras to Panama, Pedrarias ruled southern Central America until his death in 1531 in León*, Nicaragua.

REFERENCE: Pascual de Andagoya, *Narrative of the Proceedings of Pedrarias Dávila*, 1865.

Virginia Garrard Burnett

AYACUCHO, BATTLE OF. Ayacucho is located on a plateau in southwestern Peru*. At this site on December 8 and 9, 1824, the forces of Antonio de Sucre* defeated the royalist army, under the command of José de la Serna*, in the last great battle of the wars of independence. Sucre brought 5,780 troops to the battle, compared to la Serna's 9,310 soldiers. The royalist troops were already reeling from their earlier defeat at the Battle of Junín*. Sucre caught up with them at Ayacucho, about 200 miles southeast of Lima. The Battle of Ayacucho, also known as the Battle of Candorcanqui, resulted in 2,100 dead and wounded royalist troops, with another 3,500, including la Serna himself, captured. The patriots suffered only 979 casualties. On December 9, 1824, the royalist army surrendered. At the time, the only remaining portion of South America still in Spanish hands was the Banda Oriental*, and the Battle of Ayacucho inspired a new series of rebellions there.

REFERENCE: Peter Young, *A Dictionary of Battles (1816–1976)*, 1977.

AYCINENA, JOSÉ DE. José de Aycinena, son of Juan Fermín Aycinena*, was a member of a prominent *criollo** aristocratic family in Guatemela* during the independence period. The family made its fortune in commerce, and Aycinena was a vocal advocate of liberalism and the Bourbon reforms. In 1811, Aycinena was appointed intendant of San Salvador*, replacing a *peninsular** who had been unable to quell a rebellion that had begun there earlier that year. Although Aycinena successfully put down the rebellion, the family's prominence and liberal political views made them suspect in the eyes of José de Bustamante*, who became captain general of the kingdom of Guatemala* in 1811. Eager to suppress the Aycinenas and other members of the *criollo* aristocracy, Bustamante refused the Aycinenas positions of high office, pressed a legal suit against them for back taxes, and denied them the government protection and advantage they had earlier enjoyed. Aycinena was a strong supporter of the liberal Cortes that met in Cádiz, Spain, from 1810 to 1814, during the Napoleonic occupation of the Iberian peninsula. In 1813, he was named councilor of state for the Cádiz government.

REFERENCE: R. L. Woodward, Jr., *Central America: A Nation Divided*, 1983.

Virginia Garrard Burnett

AYCINENA, JUAN FERMÍN. A native of Navarre, Juan Fermín Aycinena came to Guatemala* by way of New Spain* in the mid-eighteenth century. Of modest origins, Aycinena was an astute businessman; although his initial wealth had come from the ownership of pack mules, he invested his profits in indigo* and livestock in Guatemala and El Salvador* and in silver mining* in Honduras*. Of all his enterprises, indigo was the most profitable. In the more open economic climate of the Bourbon period, Aycinena established an indigo export business in Guatemala City* in the mid-1700s. In 1780, he purchased the title of Marquis from Charles III*, making him the only resident holder of a noble title in the kingdom of Guatemala* at the time. Juan Fermín Aycinena was the patriarch of a large family that would be active in liberal politics in Guatemala during the independence period, including José de Aycinena*. Through blood and marriage, the Aycinena family became principal members of the local *criollo** elite.

REFERENCE: R. L. Woodward, Jr., *Central America: A Nation Divided*, 1983.

Virginia Garrard Burnett

AYLLU. In the pre-Conquest Inca* empire, the *ayllu* was a basic kin unit of community government and administration. It included the people of the community and all of the land they worked. The highly organized state of Inca government, from the emperor down to the basic *ayllu*, made it relatively easy for the Spaniards to conquer the Incas. Today the term *ayllu* is still used to refer to a community of Indians[*], although the internal legal arrangements vary from place to place.

REFERENCE: Karen Spaulding, *Huarochiri: An Andean Society Under Inca and Spanish Rule*, 1984.

AYMARA. The Aymara people constitute a vast Amerindian group that is second in size only to the Quechua[*]-speaking people among the aboriginal people of South America. The Aymara language, part of the Jaqí (Aru) language family, is spoken by more than 600,000 people in Argentina[*], Bolivia[*], Chile[*], and Peru[*]. Perhaps 50,000 Aymara live in northern Chile. Before the Inca[*] conquests of the fifteenth century and the Spanish conquest of the sixteenth century, there were a number of independent Aymara states, each of which had its individual Aymara dialect. The differences among the dialects, however, were quite minimal, and they were mutually intelligible. The major Aymara groups were the following: the Canchi (in the Vilcanota Valley between Combapata and Tinta in what is today the department of Cuzco[*], Peru); the Cana (between Tinta and Ayaviri in the department of Puno[*], Peru); the Colla, Kolla, or Qolla (on the plains of the Pucara and Ramis rivers north to the city of Puno, Peru); the Lupaca (on the southwestern shore of Lake Titicaca between the city of Puno and the Desaguadero River); the Collagua (north of the city of Arequipa[*], Peru, along the upper Colca River); the Ubina (east of the city of Arequipa, Peru, in the Tambo River drainage area of the department of Moquegua); the Pacasa or Pacaje (south of Lake Titicaca on both sides of the Desaguadero River in Bolivia; the Caranga or Caranca (south of the Desaguadero River to Lake Coipasa in Bolivia); the Charca (northeast of Lake Poopo near Chuquisaca, Bolivia); the Quillaca, Quilaco, or Quillagua (southeast of Lake Poopo in Bolivia); the Omasuyo (east of Lake Titicaca in Bolivia); and the Kollahuaya, Collahuaya, Kollasuyo, or Qollahuaya (in the provinces of Muñecas and Caupolicán in Bolivia). Other subtribes were the Sicasica and Paria. Although the forces of acculturation and assimilation are powerful in Peru and Bolivia, most of those subgroups still survive linguistically. Aymara has also spread to Mariscal Nieto province of Moquegua and to Tarata province of Tacna, Peru. Approximately 100,000 Aymara people, also known as Colla, live in Argentina, where they have migrated in recent years to find work. In many areas of Peru and Bolivia, Aymara has become the *lingua franca* of the general population, even among those people who no longer function socially as Indians. They live in the lowlands, central plateaus, and highlands of the Andes Mountains. A small number of Aymara dwell in the Yungas, a subtropical rain forest on the eastern slopes of the Andes. Most of the Aymara live in an area known as the Altiplano, a plateau at 12,000 to 14,000 feet elevation between the eastern and western ranges of Bolivia and Peru. They pursue an agricultural lifestyle in small villages of between 50 and 150 people. In the highlands, they raise potatoes, coca, quinoa, and barley; at lower altitudes they produce wheat and maize. Along Lake Titicaca, they fish and raise beans and onions. At higher altitudes of 14,000 to 17,000 feet, Aymara herders graze alpacas, llamas, and sheep, and those animals provide the Aymara with cheese, fertilizer, milk, leather, wool, rope, and meat.

The Incan* Empire conquered the Aymara in the fifteenth century, scattering many of them to distant places; in the sixteenth century, the Spanish Empire reduced the Aymara to near slave status on the *encomiendas**. When the great mines opened up in Bolivia, the Aymara were forced to work and die in them. By 1600, there were only 35,000 Aymara still alive; more than 75 percent of the pre-Conquest population was gone. In the 1600s, the Spanish tried to bring the Aymara onto *reducciones** where they could be converted to Roman Catholicism by Jesuit* and Franciscan* missionaries. On the *reducciones*, the Aymara were prohibited from speaking their own language, dressing like Indians*, using body paint, or sleeping on the floor. Mass uprisings by the Aymara against Spanish rule occurred in 1781 and in 1814. Since the period of Bolivian independence, the neo-Bolivian government has been trying to incorporate the Aymara into the larger political and social order through individual rather than communal land ownership and through formal connections between Aymara political organizations and the local and national government. Increasingly large numbers of the Aymara people today are acculturating to neo-Peruvian and neo-Bolivian values, speaking Spanish or Quechua as their primary language, accepting Roman Catholicism as their religion, attending state-run public schools, and becoming more and more integrated into the local regional economy. They are adapting to increasing land shortages by turning to cattle fattening, circular migration for temporary jobs, or permanent migration into the major cities looking for work. Approximately 600,000 of the nearly 1,800,000 Aymara people retain strong linguistic and religious ties to their aboriginal heritage, still speaking Aymara, avoiding contact with non-Indians, and practicing an ancient religion that involves worship of the earth and natural environment as the source of all life.

REFERENCES: Lucy Therina Briggs, "Dialectical Variation in the Aymara Language of Bolivia and Peru," Ph.D. Dissertation, University of Florida, 1976; Hans C. Buechler, *The Bolivian Aymara*, 1971; Hans C. Buechler, *The Masked Media: Aymara Fiestas and Social Integration in the Bolivian Highlands*, 1980; T. C. Lewellen, *Peasants in Transition: The Changing Economy of the Peruvian Aymara, A General Systems Approach*, 1978; Harold Osborne, *Indians of the Andes: Aymaras and Quechuas*, 1952.

AYOHUMA, BATTLE OF. In 1813, an attempt was made to secure the independence of Upper Peru* (modern Bolivia*) from Spain and to secure the area for Buenos Aires*. Manuel Belgrano* was ordered to march his rebel army to confront Spanish forces operating in the region. Belgrano was not a professional soldier and had no formal training in the art of war, but he had been successful as a military leader in previous campaigns and Buenos Aires had high expectations of him. Unfortunately, his army met defeat at Vilcapugio and disaster at Ayohuma where his now rabble army was dispersed and swept ignominiously out of Upper Peru by the forces of Viceroy Joaquín de la Pezuela*. Belgrano's defeat at Ayohuma forestalled the independence of Upper Peru for 12 years, until José de San Martín*, who was sent to relieve Belgrano and take command of whatever remained of his army, and Antonio José de Sucre* liberated it in 1825.

REFERENCES: Hubert Herring, *A History of Latin America*, 1961; John Lynch, *The Spanish American Revolutions, 1808-1826*, 1973; Ricardo Rojas, *San Martín: Knight of the Andes*, 1945.

Samuel Freeman

AYUNTAMIENTO. See CABILDO.

AZARA, FÉLIX DE. Félix de Azara was born in Barbunales, Spain, on May 18, 1752. He graduated from the University of Huesca in Spain and spent his career as an engineer and soldier. In 1783, he was appointed to the Spanish-Portuguese commission determining the boundary between the Spanish and Portuguese colonies in the New World. He arrived in Paraguay* in 1784 and spent the next 17 years writing about the history and geography of the Río de la Plata* region. He returned to Spain in 1801 and died in Huesca on October 17, 1821.

REFERENCES: Efraím Cardozo, *Historiografia paraguaya*, 1959; Charles J. Kolinski, *Historical Dictionary of Paraguay*, 1973.

AZPILCUETA, MARTÍN DE. Born in Barátoain in Navarre, Spain, in 1491, Martín de Azpilcueta belonged to the famous family of St. Francis Xavier and was one of the early members of the Jesuit* order. He took up legal studies at the universities of Alcalá and Toulouse; after graduation, he held the chair of law, first at the latter university and thereafter at that of Cahors. His reputation for excellent teaching and his erudition grew, to such an extent that despite being a foreigner he was offered a seat in the Parlement of Paris. He declined this honor, however, and instead returned home where he obtained the chair of canon law at the University of Salamanca, a position he held for some 14 years.

The Age of Discoveries, the Renaissance, and the Reformation, with the decline of both emperor and papacy and the rise of the modern nation state, had brought about changes in political theory. Azpilcueta joined the new trend toward internationalism and the incipient modern law of nations as expressed by Francis Vitoria and Domingo de Soto. He thus belonged to the group of *magni Hispani* of Late Scholasticism, mostly Jesuits and Dominicans*, who, like Francisco Suárez, Luis de Molina, and Diego de Covarrubias, among others, were deeply concerned about the Protestant Reformation and the rise of Gallicanism (French pride). He thus defended the spiritual power of the pope and especially the concept of popular sovereignty, at a time when the spirit of the Renaissance enhanced both the concept of the reason of state (Níccolo Machiavelli) and the absolute monarchies (Jean Bodin). In this respect, Azpilcueta argued that when the ruler, through the translation theory, received the *potestas*, there actually exist two authorities, one in the king and another in the state—what he called "constituent" and "constituted" sovereignty. The latter is *impedita in actu*, that is, it does not function while the king asserts the rights given by the people. But should royal power be abolished or left vacant, the nation can make free use of its rights and can resist the ruler if he governs contrary to the medieval concept of the *bonum commune*. In other words, under certain conditions (the *tyrannus ab origine* and the *tyrannus a regimine*), revolution was justified and legitimate.

Due to Azpilcueta's great prestige, Emperor Charles V* asked him to take charge of the University of Coimbra, which he did for some 14 years and where one of his famous pupils was the mentioned Covarrubias. He was also offered a miter by the king of Portugal and the archbishopric of Santiago de Compostela, but he declined both. Instead, he accompanied Bartolomé Carranza to Rome, where he defended him against attacks by the Inquisition. In Rome he lived his last 19 years, holding the position of apostolic penitentiary.

His extraordinary reputation earned him the title *Doctor Navarro*, and prominent personalities, including kings, consulted him for his sound knowledge and judgment. Religious fervor, profound erudition, and a noble feeling for charity marked his entire life. He also founded a hospital in his native Barátoain. Among his works, the *Manual de confesores y penitentes* and the *De Redditibus ecclecisasticus* should be mentioned. He died in 1586.

REFERENCES: O. Carlos Stoetzer, *The Scholastic Roots of the Spanish American Revolution*, 1979; Juan Beneyto Pérez, *Historia de las Doctrinas Políticas*, 1958.

O. Carlos Stoetzer

AZTEC. The term "Aztec" (or Aztlaneca), literally meaning the people of Aztlán ("the place of the heron"), came into common usage with the historian Francisco Clavijero* and was popularized among English speakers by William Prescott as the name for the group of Nahuatl* speakers who referred to themselves as México or Culhua México. Aztlán, the mythico-historical homeland of the México, was an island located somewhere to the northwest of present-day Mexico City*. In the aftermath of the collapse of the Toltec* Empire, which was centered at Tula, the México and other nomadic Chichimeca* groups filtered south into the Valley of Mexico. After a long period of migration, the México established Tenochtitlán* on an island in the western arm of Lake Texcoco.

During their migration and early years in Tenochtitlán, the México were led by a priest-ruler. Seeking to increase their prestige and to strengthen their alliance with the dynasty descended from the legendary Toltec, the México selected Acamapichtli ("handful of reeds or arrows") as their first *tlatoani* ("he who speaks"). Acamapichtli was the son of a México woman and the grandson of a *tlatoani* of Culhuacán. Because of this connection, the México were called Culhua in a number of early sources. Robert Barlow has suggested that they be called the Culhua México.

During their early years in the Valley of Mexico, the México were subject to the city-states of Culhuacán and Axcapotzalco. In alliance with two other Nahuatl-speaking groups, the Acolhua of Texcoco and the Tepanec of Tlacopan, the México defeated the Tepanec of Azcapotzalco and went on to forge an empire commonly referred to as the Aztec Empire. Between the founding of this triple alliance in 1428 and the Spanish conquest in 1519–1521, the México gradually became the dominant partner. Cortés's defeat of the México led to the incorporation of the Aztec Empire into that of Spain. Mexico City, the capital of this New Spain*, rose from the ruins of Tenochtitlán.

During the reigns of the first three *tlatoani*—Acamapichtli, Huitzilihuitl ("hummingbird feather"), and Chimalpopoca ("smoking shield"), the México were subject to Azcapotzalco and participated in campaigns against rival states within the Valley of Mexico, in Morelos, and in Puebla* (ca. 1372–1427). Following the death of Tezozómoc ("he who is frequently angered") and the accession of Maxtla as *tlatoani* of Azcapotzalco, relations between the two states deteriorated, culminating in Maxtla's having Chimalpopoca put to death. Nezahualcoyotl ("hungry coyote"), *tlatoani* of Acolhua Texcoco, was forced to flee Maxtla's wrath. The new Mexica *tlatoani*, Itzcóatl ("obsidian serpent," who reigned from 1427 to 1440), joined with Nezahualcóyotl in a campaign that resulted in the defeat of Maxtla and the fall of Azcapotzalco. These new allies, joined by the Tepanec of Tlacopan, launched campaigns against states controlling very productive lands around the freshwater lakes in the southern Valley of Mexico. Campaigns were also waged against Tula to the north and against states in Morelos and northern Guerrero to the south.

Upon the death of Itzcoatl, Motecuhzoma I* ("angry one," "archer of the skies," who reigned from 1440 to 1468) became *tlatoani*. Motecuhzoma I and his brother Tlacaélel had been able military leaders during the reign of their uncle Itzcoatl. Occupying the post of Cihuacoatl ("serpent woman") during the reigns of Itzcoatl, Motecuhzoma I, and Axayacatl, Tlacaélel was second in power only to the *tlatoani* and played a crucial role in shaping México imperial policy and ideology. During the reign of Motecuhzoma I, there were campaigns against Chalco in the southern Valley of Mexico, the Tuxpan area in northern Vera Cruz*, and states in central Puebla, central Vera Cruz, and northern Oaxaca. Motecuhzoma I is generally agreed to have been the greatest of the Mexica *tlatoani*.

During the reign of Axayacatl ("water mask," who reigned from 1468 to 1481), there were campaigns in the Tuxpan region of northern Vera Cruz and against states in central Vera Cruz and central Puebla. The fact that the same states appear as conquests more than once suggests that the México had to reassert their domination repeatedly. Most of these conquered states were not physically occupied, but they paid tribute to the México. This tribute was collected locally by native elites or by México-appointed *calpixqui* (imperial tribute collectors). During Axayacatl's reign, the México extended their control in the west to the area that is now the border between the states of Mexico and Michoacán. Expansion in this direction was halted by the complete routing of México forces by those of the Tarascan Empire in a battle near Lake Cuitzeo in 1478. Tlacaelel and Nezahualcoyotl (1472) died during Axayacatl's reign. Also during Axayacatl's reign, Tenochtitlán's sister city, Tlatelolco, was defeated and annexed.

Tlatelolco had been founded shortly after Tenochtitlán on an adjacent small island. As the two cities developed, the area between them was filled, and the islands became one. Tlatelolco became an important market center and continued to be one after its fall in 1473.

The reign of Axayacatl's brother Tizoc ("he who made people bleed;" who reigned from 1481 to 1486) was brief and relatively uneventful. To the west, Toluca was recaptured; in northern Oaxaca, Yanhuitlán was subjugated. There was significant expansion during the reign of Ahuitzotl ("otter;" who reigned from 1486 to 1502). The Pacific Coast, from southern Guerrero and Oaxaca, the Isthmus of Tehuantepec and Chiapas* to the modern border with Guatemala*, was incorporated into the empire. Although there were campaigns in central and southern Oaxaca*, northern Puebla*, and adjacent Vera Cruz, the reign of Ahuitzotl's successor Motecuhzoma* II ("the angry one," "the younger;" who reigned from 1502 to 1520), was primarily a period of consolidation after the period of rapid expansion under Ahuitzotl. Many of the conquests recorded during Motecuhzoma II's reign were expeditions to quell rebellions among previously conquered groups.

Hernán Cortés* and his small band of Spaniards arrived in Tenochtitlán in early November 1519 after Motecuhzoma II's efforts to appease and delay him had failed. Relations between the Mexica and the Spanish quickly deteriorated. Motecuhzoma II was taken captive by the Spanish and was later killed (June 27, 1520) by his own people for trying to prevent open hostilities between them and the Spanish. On July 1, 1520, the Spanish were forced to flee Tenochtitlán with a great loss of life. Cuitláhuac ("excrement-owner"), brother of Motecuhzoma II, was *tlatoani* briefly (September to November 1520). He was succeeded by Cuauhtémoc* ("descending eagle," who reigned from 1520 to 1525). Rested and reinforced, Cortés and his men laid seige to Tenochtitlán in May 1521. Cuauhtémoc, the last independent Mexica *tlatoani*, was captured on August 13, and the Culhua Mexica Empire was then incorporated into that of Spain. Cuauhtémoc was held hostage and accompanied Cortés on the first part of his march to Honduras*. During this march, in February 1525, Cuauhtémoc was hanged on Cortés's orders.

Upon its arrival in the Valley of Mexico, México society was relatively egalitarian. With the growth of the empire, it became more complex and stratified. At the top of the social pyramid were the *tlatoani* and his family. As the ruler of a city or province, the *tlatoani* was the center of civil, military, and religious power. The ruling families, along with other "lords" or *tecuhtli*, composed an internally subdivided noble class, the *pipiltin*. Social mobility was possible through success in activities such as warfare, administration, and trade, especially long-distance trade. It was thus possible for common people, *macehualtin*, to become *quauhpipiltin*. When the empire was expanding rapidly and before the *pipiltin* class had grown large and become institutionalized, such mobility would have been more common.

The majority of the people were *macehualtin*, common people who were neither *pipiltin* nor slaves. Many were farmers. The *macehualtin* provided the bulk of the México military forces. *Macehualtin* youth were trained for this role in the numerous *calpulli* schools known as *telpochcalli* ("young men's house"). Some might receive training in the priestly houses, the *calmecac*, but this was primarily a prerogative of the *pipiltin*. The *calmecac* trained youths for leadership roles as priests and administrators. *Mayeque* were tenant farmers residing on lands controlled by the nobility. People became slaves, *tlatlacotin*, as a result of being captured in war, as tribute payment, as a form of punishment, and as a way of paying their debts. Slaves could be bought and sold as personal property. They could buy or be given their freedom. Children of slaves were not automatically slaves.

The economic bases of this stratified society and empire included the abundant agricultural production of the rich *chinampa* systems located around the freshwater lakes (Chalco, Xochimilco, and the western arm of Texcoco) of the Valley of Mexico; trade; and war, which exacted tribute from subject city states. The *Matrícula de Tributos* and its colonial copy, the *Codex Mendocino*, reveal the extent of the annual tribute exacted.

México warfare was justified ideologically by the need for sacrificial victims. These sacrifices to the tribal god Huitzilopochtli ("hummingbird of the left"; "the sun of the south") and to other gods assured the continuity of the current creation of the world. As a consequence of this warfare, new tribute-paying states were incorporated into the empire. It has been suggested that Tlacaélel was the mastermind who intentionally manipulated Mexica history and religious ideology to promote warfare that benefited the empire economically. Although the México occasionally established military garrisons and colonies, they usually relied on alliances with native nobility to maintain control in conquered territories. These alliances were fragile and quickly dissolved when confronted by the Spaniards.

REFERENCES: Frances F. Berdan, *The Aztec*, 1989; Francisco Clavijero, *The History of Mexico*, 1979; Nigel Davies, *The Aztecs: A History*, 1980; Charles Gibson, *The Aztecs Under Spanish Rule: A History of the Indians of the Valley of Mexico, 1519-1810*, 1964; William Prescott, *The Conquest of Mexico*, 1931; Jacques Soustelle, *The Daily Life of the Aztecs*, 1964.

Edward B. Sisson

AZURDUY DE PADILLA, JUANA. Juana Azurduy de Padilla was born in Chuquisaca (today Sucre*, Bolivia*) in 1781. She received a convent education but decided not to become a nun. She married Manuel Asencio Padilla in 1805. He was a soldier, and together they joined the patriot forces and fought for Argentine independence. He was killed in 1816 at the Battle of Viloma, and she then withdrew to Salta* where she continued to fight. That year she achieved the rank of lieutenant colonel in the rebel army. After the end of the independence struggle, Azurduy retired to Chuquisaca and quietly lived out her life. She died in 1862.

REFERENCE: Enrique Udaondo, *Diccionario biográfico colonial argentino*, 1945.

B

BABA OULD HASSENA. See HASSENA, BABA OULD.

BACARDI MOREAU, EMILIO. Emilio Bacardi Moreau was born in 1844 in Santiago, Cuba*. A prominent writer and journalist, Bacardi was also a successful businessman who founded the famous Bacardi distilleries. He became an outspoken advocate of Cuban independence. Spanish authorities jailed him in 1876 for revolutionary activities; in 1879, they exiled him from the country. The early 1890s found him in Ceuta* on the North African coast where he was arranging for the shipment of weapons to the Cuban insurgents. Spanish authorities arrested him again in 1895. After the revolution, Bacardi returned to Cuba and was elected mayor of Santiago de Cuba in 1901. He later served as a member of the senate. His major published works include *La condesa de Merlín* and *Crónicas de Santiago de Cuba (1516 to 1902)*. He died in 1922.
  REFERENCE: Juan J. Remos, *Proceso histórico de las letras cubanas*, 1958.

BACHIR, AHMED OULD BRAHIM OULD EL. Ahmed Ould Brahim Ould El-Bachir was born on May 1, 1918, in El-Ayoun, Western Sahara. A commercial businessman, he was a close associate and collaborator with Spanish imperial officials. He served as a member of the *Djemma** and the Spanish Cortes, and he vehemently opposed all Moroccan claims to Western Sahara. In 1975, his daughter was killed in a car bomb explosion, which he blamed on the Polisario Front*. After the Madrid Agreement* of 1975, in which Spain began its withdrawal from Western Sahara, he switched his allegiance to Morocco. In 1976, El-Bachir became the president of the municipal council of El-Ayoun and in 1977 was elected to the Moroccan Chamber of Deputies.
  REFERENCES: Rafael Ortega Canadell, *Provincias Africanas Españolas*, 1962; Tony Hodges, *Historical Dictionary of Western Sahara*, 1982.

BACHIR MUSTAPHA SAYED. ·Bachir Mustapha Sayed was born around 1950 to a poor Reguibi tribal family, and he grew up in Tan-Tan, Morocco. An intelligent young man, he earned a government scholarship and attended the lycée in Agadir, where he joined nationalist student groups calling for independence. He was arrested by French police in Tan-Tan in 1972 for leading several anti-Spanish demonstrations. In 1973, he joined the Polisario Front*. Bachir Mustapha Sayed played a key role in directing the front's war against Spain in 1974–1975. After the Madrid Agreement* of 1975, he turned his attention to the Moroccans. He became a leading figure in the Polisario Front during the 1970s and 1980s.

REFERENCES: Tony Hodges, *Historical Dictionary of Western Sahara*, 1982; John Mercer, *Spanish Sahara*, 1975.

BAHAMAS. Some 700 coral islands, stretching approximately 600 miles from southeastern Florida* to northwestern Haiti*, form the Bahamas, known to the early Spaniards as the Lucayas. Hazardous shoals, poor agricultural conditions, and a lack of precious metals discouraged European settlement, but the islands' strategic location adjacent to the Florida Straits and the Windward Passage, afforded them periodic prosperity based upon wrecking, privateering, piracy*, and smuggling*, much to Spain's consternation.

Christopher Columbus's* initial encounter with the New World took place in the Bahamas when, on October 12, 1492, he made his landfall at modern Samona Cay, which he christened San Salvador*. Here he met the Lucayans, a gentle, handsome Arawak* people whom he dubbed Indians.* After bartering with them, Columbus ominously commented that they would make ideal "servants." Anxious to reach the gilded dominions of the great khan, the admiral departed from San Salvador, spending the next two weeks threading his way through the island chain en route to Cuba*.

The deaths of large numbers of Indian laborers on Hispaniola* prompted Governor Nicolás de Ovando* to commence a steady series of slave raids in 1509, with the approbation of King Ferdinand I*. The Bahamas were regarded as the easiest place from which to obtain human chattel. Their relatively small islands and flat terrain offered the docile Lucayans scant refuge from slavers. By 1513, the archipelago had become the first New World territory to undergo depopulation. More than 40,000 Lucayans were shipped to Hispaniola* or Puerto Rican* gold fields and to the pearl fisheries of Margarita* Island, off northern South America. In the midst of these depredations, the Crown granted a patent to Juan Ponce de León*, the conquistador* and former governor of Puerto Rico, for the purpose of colonizing the isles beyond Cuba's northern shores, the purported locale of Bimini, the Fountain of Youth. The aging adventurer embarked from Puerto Rico in March 1513 and explored the Bahamas for three months. More importantly, he discovered Florida, as well as the Gulf Stream, whose warm currents would soon carry Spain's treasure fleets from America to Iberia.

For more than a century after Ponce de León's explorations, no nation permanently settled the deserted Lucayas, though Spaniards occasionally called to gather ambergris, dyewood, and medicinal bark. Meanwhile, the Florida Straits developed into the key corridor through which Spain funneled its American riches. In 1536, by the Treaty of Lyon, France prohibited its nationals from preying on the commerce between Portugal and northwestern Africa. The same year a renewal of Franco-Spanish animosity broke out. French freebooters, attracted by the abandoned archipelago that stood so near to Spain's treasure routes, now frequented the Bahamas.

During the opening decades of the 1600s, the English feared that France might interpose itself between their North American colonies and Cuba by securing Bahamian footholds. Attempts by both countries to populate the chain failed until 1648, when religious dissenters from Bermuda* arrived on the island of Eleuthera. The British occupied neighboring New Providence in 1666. Great Britain established a colonial government in the Bahamas in 1670. Spanish and Bahamian wreckers frequently clashed in their competition to salvage sunken bullion. Friction over a disputed wreck, coupled with the desire to punish an attack upon St. Augustine, Florida, led the Spaniards to sack New Providence twice in 1684. The island was not recolonized until 1686. Following France's effort to eliminate buccaneering from its new colony of St. Domingue, which Spain recognized by the Treaty of Ryswick (1697), more corsairs fled to the archipelago from the island of Tortuga*, their former headquarters close to northwestern Hispaniola.

Cuba's governor regarded Nassau, New Providence's main settlement, as a den of thieves. When the War of the Spanish Succession* erupted in Europe, a Franco-Spanish force from Havana* plundered the town in 1704, causing a complete breakdown in the colony's government. Pirates ran the Bahamas until 1718, when a new royal governor, Woodes Rogers, restored British control. Rogers later repelled a powerful Spanish invasion force in 1720.

Between 1739 and 1782, the Bahamas flourished as a privateering base against Spain. Ironically, the islands also functioned as an *entrepot* for illegal trade between British North America and the French and Spanish West Indies. In 1782, while the American Revolution* raged, the governor of Cuba seized Nassau, occupying it for a year. Although the preliminary peace ending the conflict returned the Bahamas to Britain, Colonel Andrew Deveaux, a South Carolina loyalist, hastened Spain's departure by recapturing the city in April 1783. During Cuba's Ten Years War* (1868–1878) against Madrid, rebels obtained weapons and supplies from the Bahamas.

REFERENCES: Michael Craton, *A History of the Bahamas* (1968); Paul Albany, *The Story of the Bahamas*, 1976.

Frank Marotti

BALBOA, VASCO NÚÑEZ DE. Vasco Núñez de Balboa was born in 1475 in Jerez de los Caballeros, a small village in the province of Badajoz, Spain. In 1501, Balboa set sail for the New World with Rodrigo de Bastidas*, hoping to find pearls along the northern coast of South America. After the voyage, which found few pearls but explored hundreds of miles of coastline, Balboa settled in Hispaniola* to become a planter. Economic miscalculation soon destroyed his plantation and left him with an enormous debt; he fled to Darién* to escape his creditors. In 1513, Balboa led an expedition across the isthmus and discovered the Pacific Ocean. After several months collecting pearls and gold from conquered Indian* tribes, Balboa returned to Darién as a hero. But his exploits and financial success had raised the jealous ire of Pedro Arias de Ávila* (Pedrarias), the governor of Darién. For several years, Pedrarias plotted against Balboa and in 1517 brought him to trial on trumped-up charges of treason. Balboa was convicted of treason and executed in 1517.

REFERENCES: Charles L. G. Anderson, *The Life and Letters of Vasco Núñez de Balboa*, 1941; Kathleen Romoli, *Balboa of Darién: Discoverer of the Pacific*, 1953.

BALBUENA, BERNARDO DE. Often described as a transitional poet bridging the Renaissance and Baroque movements in literature, Bernardo de Balbuena was undoubtedly one of early Mexico's most important poets. Born in Spain, he was the illegitimate son of a Spaniard who settled in New Spain with him in the early 1560s. Balbuena was ordained as a priest in 1592 and later, in 1606, traveled to Spain where he studied theology. He returned to the New World, first to Jamaica*, and eventually to Puerto Rico* where he became bishop in 1620.

Balbuena left several major literary works. Perhaps the best known is *La Grandeza Mexicana* (1604), a long, 40,000-line poem written in tercets and divided into nine parts. The purpose of the work was to describe in detail the splendor of Mexico: its people, geography, customs, flora, and fauna. Balbuena's descriptive powers were immense and he used them readily in *La Grandeza Mexicana*. Another major work by Balbuena was *El Siglo de Oro en las Selvas de Erífile* (1608), a sort of novel in verse, written in eclogues, displaying the influence of Vergil and Sannazzaro. This work was so well received in Spain that the Royal Academy of the Spanish Language produced a special edition of it in 1821.

Most critics consider Balbuena's masterpiece to be *Bernardo o Victoria de Roncevalles* (1624), a sort of long epic poem reflecting the influence of Ariosto. Divided into 24 cantos, the work describes the adventures of Bernardo de Carpio. The work is generally associated with opulence of style and color, flashes of baroque adornment, and an exciting dash of fantasy, all girded by an old-fashioned tendency toward chivalric literature. The hallmark apparent in all of Balbuena's literary work and endeavors was his love for Mexico and its people. He must be considered one of the first genuinely New World poets. He died in 1637.

REFERENCES: Aurora M. Ocampo de Gómez and Ernesto Prado Velásquez, *Diccionario de escritores mexicanos*, 1967; Carlos Gonzales Peña, *History of Mexican Literature*, 1968.

Sam L. Slick

BALCARCE. See GONZALES BALCARCE.

BALDORIOTY DE CASTRO, RAMÓN. Ramón Baldorioty de Castro was born in San Juan*, Puerto Rico*, in 1822. He studied in San Juan and for many years in Paris before returning to Puerto Rico in 1853. Baldorioty de Castro taught school in San Juan for most of his career. He won election as the delegate from Mayagüez in the Spanish Cortes in 1869. After returning from Spain in 1872, Baldorioty de Castro founded the newspaper* *El Derecho* in San Juan and turned it into a pulpit for his demands for Puerto Rican independence. He founded a second newspaper in 1880, *La Crónica*, which proclaimed the same message. In 1887, Ramón Baldorioty de Castro became the first president of the Autonomist Party. Spanish authorities arrested and imprisoned him for sedition a few months later. They released him from prison in 1888, and he died in Ponce, Puerto Rico, in 1889.

REFERENCE: Lidio Cruz Monclova, *Baldorioty de Castro: Su Vida, Sus Ideas*, 1973.

BANANA. The banana was one of the key products that show the biological expansion of western civilization. It was not native to the New World but was brought by Spaniards from the Canary Islands* in the sixteenth century. The banana thrived in the tropical forests of Central and South America and of the Caribbean. It became a primary food source not only for Spanish colonists but for indigenous peoples as well, who began to cultivate the banana. Because of its perishability, the banana was used for domestic consumption and local trade, not for commercial export abroad. It was not until the nineteenth and twentieth centuries that new transportation and refrigeration technologies created a truly international market for bananas.

REFERENCE: Charles D. Kepner, *Social Aspects of the Banana Industry*, 1936.

BANDA ORIENTAL. See URUGUAY.

BANDEIRANTES. The term *bandeirantes*, or *bandeiras*, refers to Portuguese settlers, often mestizo* people, who in the sixteenth and seventeenth centuries expanded out of the Sao Paulo region in Brazil into Mato Grosso and Paraguay* in search of gold, diamonds, and slaves. The first real *bandeirante* was Antonio Raposo Tavares, who led an expedition in 1628. Other prominent *bandeirantes* included Fernão Días País Leme, Bartolomeu Bueno de Siqueira, and Pedro Teixeira. Although they were usually not official representatives of Portugal, the *bandeirantes* played an important role in extending the western and southern reaches of the Portuguese Empire in Brazil.

REFERENCE: John Hemming, *Red Gold: The Conquest of the Brazilian Indians*, 1978.

BANDERAS, QUINTÍN. Quintín Banderas was born in Cuba* in 1834. The descendant of African slaves*, Banderas became a prominent military leader in the Cuban struggle for independence. He fought in the Ten Years War* (1868–1878), and in 1879, with José Maceo, he led the Guerra Chiquita* rebellion. During the 1895 rebellion, Banderas was a rebel leader in Matanzas Province. He concentrated his efforts in the eastern reaches of Cuba, and, although Spanish General Valeriano Weyler* surrounded him there, Banderas kept up a protracted guerrilla war that proved extremely costly to the Spanish army. Quintín Banderas died in 1906.

REFERENCES: Franklin W. Knight, *Slave Society in Cuba During the Nineteenth Century*, 1970; Jaime Suchlicki, *Historical Dictionary of Cuba*, 1988.

BÁÑEZ, DOMINGO. The Spanish Golden Age excelled in the field of theology, and the new spirit radiated in particular from Salamanca. The fusion of Scholasticism with the new currents crossing the Pyrenees—Renaissance ideas and humanism—produced the Spanish (Christian) Renaissance. As it developed in the sixteenth century, this movement was essentially the work of Dominicans* and Jesuits*; it was first linked to such Dominicans as Francisco de Vitoria* (1480–1546), Domingo de Soto* (1494–1560), Melchor Cano (1509–1560), and Domingo Báñez (1528–1604), and then to the Jesuits, especially Francisco Suárez* (1548–1617), Luis de Molina (1535–1600), and Juan de Mariana (1535–1624). In the sixteenth century, the Dominicans represented the great champions throughout Europe and overseas of both missionary enterprise and of Scholastic thought. In spite of differences among them, they steadily held to the principles of individual liberty and free conversion. The great Spanish theologians of the Golden Age "understood the great task of bringing Scholastic philosophy up to date," a task they performed brilliantly. It was in this intellectual context that Báñez and his work have to be placed.

Born in Valladolid, Spain, in 1528, young Domingo Báñez went to Salamanca where he studied humanities at the very time when the university was at its peak. Among his teachers was Cano; he also befriended such erudite Dominican theologians and jurists as Vitoria and Soto. His life evolved basically within the Castilian-Leonese triangle of Valladolid, Salamanca, and Avila. In 1546, Báñez joined the Dominican order in Salamanca. On the recommendation of Soto, he began his teaching career in theology and philosophy in 1552 at that city's Convent of St. Stephen. He held this position for some nine years until 1561. After that year, he taught at a number of prestigious learning centers, including the University of Ávila, specializing in theology, until 1567. It was also here that he developed a deep friendship with Saint Theresa precisely during the time when her great works became the subject of much debate (1561–1562). In the years from 1561 to 1567, he became her spiritual director and confessor, even though she also had a Jesuit confessor. Báñez took up the defense of her reforms—her first monastery in Avila—and was instrumental in launching her to fame through her *Camino de Perfección*, which he encouraged her to write. She herself spoke highly of his spiritual influence on her and mentioned him several times in her works.

Thereafter, Báñez lectured on theology for two years at the Dominican convent in Alcalá but returned to Avila in 1569 when he was appointed president of the College of St. Thomas. In the year 1570, he was back in Salamanca; three years later, he was appointed president of the College of St. Gregory in Valladolid where he also taught a variety of subjects to young Dominicans for the next four years (1573–1577). In the year 1577, he was back in Salamanca where he succeeded in obtaining a desired teaching position at the University of Salamanca, which he held until 1581. In that same year, he submitted his candidacy for the main chair in theology at the same university and again succeeded in obtaining it. For the next twenty-four years, Báñez lectured at Salamanca University on theology, philosophy, and law, until 1601. He then asked to be relieved of his duties in view of his failing health, which no longer permitted him to pursue his intellectual goals. He withdrew to Medina del Campo where three years later, in 1604, he died peacefully in the Convent of St. Andrew.

Báñez was a prolific writer and one of the greatest commentators of the *Summa Theologica* of Saint Thomas Aquinas. He holds a prominent place in Spanish philosophy. But he was not only a brilliant scholar whose erudition was widely acclaimed; he was also known for his remarkable memory and his clear logic. Upon request of the University of Salamanca, he worked on the reform of the Gregorian calender and frequently intervened in the periodic revisions of prohibited books for the Index. Finally, he also contributed to the molding of the political ideas that predominated in theory and practice during three centuries of Spanish rule in the Indies, a political thought that was based on Scholasticism and Late Scholasticism. These ideas included the teaching that any political authority was of human law, not divine law, and hence could legitimately be chosen by the people. By natural law, sovereign authority originating in God belonged to the people, who could not totally reject such authority; if the governors could not provide an order for the common good, then the people were entitled to take the necessary steps to remedy the situation. Civil authority was legally acquired only with the consent of the people, since the people were the only subject of sovereignty. The authority thus conferred on the king could not be despotic, so resistance to oppression became legal. Finally, kingship without a legal successor meant that sovereignty automatically reverted to the political community, the people.

His works could be found in libraries all over the Spanish Empire, and his teachings were quite popular. Thus, Alonso Guerra, the fifth bishop in the Río de la Plata* and first teacher of philosophy in Buenos Aires after its second founding in 1580 (he had come from Asuncion in 1586) established a small academic center in which the preferred theories taught were those of Báñez and Soto.

Finally, Báñez was very much involved in the sixteenth-century dispute over the concept of grace, in which the traditional point of view, based on free will, collided with the Protestant interpretation, which denied it. The Spanish theologians of the sixteenth century answered the Reformist assertions with a position that linked free will to the act of faith and to justification. The dispute in which Báñez got involved began in 1582 and ended only after his death in 1607. Báñez had come to the defense of Fr. Francisco Zumel, a Mercedarian*; this brought about a collision between the Dominicans and the Jesuits. It became a cause célèbre, with Fr. Luis de León and the Jesuits, especially Luis de Molina, denouncing Báñez's position on grace as Lutheran to the Inquisition.*

REFERENCES: Otis H. Green, *Spain and the Western Tradition*, 1968; Vicente Beltrán de Heredia, OP, *Domingo Báñez y las controversias sobre la gracia: textos y documentos*, 1966; O. Carlos Stoetzer, *The Scholastic Roots of the Spanish American Revolution*, 1979.

O. Carlos Stoetzer

BARANGAY. The *barangay* is a Philippine[*] village or hamlet; it was the smallest unit of government there. When the Spaniards reached the Philippines in the late sixteenth century, they found no kingdoms or empires. Natives lived in largely autonomous coastal villages called *barangays*. The word can also mean "ship," leading many scholars to conclude that the villages were settled by kin groups arriving from adjacent islands. The *barangays* were ruled by chiefs or headmen, so the easiest way for Spain to institute local government was simply to designate the local leaders *cabezas de barangay*; in most respects, life then went on as before. Eventually the term *barangay* was dropped and replaced by *barrio*, but the original term has now been reinstated.

REFERENCE: Emma H. Blair and James Alexander Robertson, eds., *The Philippine Islands, 1492–1898*, 55 vols., 1903–1909.

Ross Marlay

BARAYA, ANTONIO. Antonio Baraya was born in Colombia[*] in 1770 to a *criollo*[*] family, and he eventually became a hero of the independence movement. He rose to the rank of general and led the victorious patriot forces at the Battle of the Palacé on March 28, 1811. Baraya later occupied the city of Popayán[*] and promoted the organization of a junta presided over by Joaquín Caicedo. He was taken prisoner near the city of Neiva by the royalist forces under General Pablo Morillo[*] and executed in Bogotá[*] on July 20, 1816.

REFERENCE: José Manuel Groot, *Historia eclesiástica y civil de Nueva Granada*, 5 vols., 1953.

Fred Koestler

BARBADOS. Barbados is the most easterly of the Lesser Antilles, located about 100 miles outside the arc of the Caribbean archipelago. This single 166-square-mile limestone and coral based island is relatively flat, has rolling hills of fertile soil rising to just over 1,000 feet at a couple of points. While Barbados lies midway between the Leeward and Windward Islands, which were sighted by Christopher Columbus[*] on his second to fourth voyages, Barbados was not discovered by Columbus during his famous voyages to the Americas. On account of its relatively small size and the absence of a distinctive mountain range, Barbados was difficult to detect by seafarers, except those within a few miles of its shores. It was therefore initially passed over by the Spanish conquistadors[*] because of both its location and their inability to identify its land mass.

Prior to the Columbian era, however, populations of Barrancoid and Saladoid-Amerindian peoples, and later Arawaks[*] and Karibs[*], occupied significant areas of Barbados during consecutive periods from the beginning of the Christian era.

These pre-Columbian peoples arrived in Barbados from the South American mainland in specific waves. Forty years of modest and periodic archaeological studies on prehistoric Barbadian life have documented a number of permanent Arawak villages throughout the island. The Arawak community remained for about 450 years before they were replaced by the Karibs during the early thirteenth century. The fierce war-oriented and cannabalistic Karibs exercised complete control of Barbados until after the arrival of the Spaniards in the Caribbean in the early sixteenth century. The Karibs used Barbados as a stopover on their canoe voyages to neighboring larger northern islands of the archipelago. Small Karib communities also lived in many Barbadian caves, as well as near its ponds, fresh-water springs, and small rivers. Some have also suggested that African seafarers may have stumbled on the island during the early fourteenth century and cohabited with the Karibs.

Barbados was known to the Spanish seafarers during the early 1500s but held little significance in terms of their interest in the eastern Caribbean basin. Barbados has a geological origin different from most of its neighboring islands. A distinctively large number of huge ''evergreen'' fig trees called attention to the island's mostly uninhabited state. The Spanish navigators identified the island as ''the bearded one'' because of the trees. Its identity and location were included in the early maps of the sixteenth-century Caribbean, including the Egerton Chart (1512–1513) and the Maggila chart (1519), as well as the Turin Map (1525) naming the island Barbudoso or Barbudos. The Spanish colonists of the sixteenth century were not interested in settling the island but the Spanish decree of 1511 allowed the early Spanish settlers of the larger islands to capture Karibs living in Barbados and transport them to Hispaniola[*] to work there as slaves. Portuguese seamen also visited the island on their increasingly frequent voyages to and from their new colonies in northeastern South America but never considered settling there. During one of his visits to Barbados in 1536, however, Pedro Campos, a Portuguese captain, left a herd of hogs on the island in order to increase the supply of food available to himself and other seafaring travelers who stopped off there. For over a century, neither the Spanish nor the Portuguese made any serious attempts to settle Barbados. When the first English ship, the *Olive*, stumbled on the island on May 14, 1625, on its way from the city of Pernambuco in the Portugese-American colony to England, the English sailors determined that the island was uninhabited, and they quickly sought to make it a British settlement. Within two years, British merchants financed and outfitted an expedition that arrived on February 17, 1627, making Barbados a British colony for over the next 340 years.

REFERENCES: J. H. Parry, Philip Sherlock, and Anthony Maingot, *A Short History of the West Indies*, 1987; Jerome Handler and Frederick W. Lange, *Plantation Slavery in Barbados*, 1971.

Glenn O. Phillips

BARBOSA, JOSÉ. José Barbosa, a descendant of African slaves[*], was born in Bayamón, Puerto Rico[*], in 1857. He received a medical degree from the University of Michigan in 1880 and then established a medical practice in San

Juan*. Late in the 1880s, he became active in Puerto Rican politics as a member of the Liberal Reform Party, which demanded political autonomy for Puerto Rico. He became head of the party in 1894. When the Treaty of Paris of 1898* made Puerto Rico an American possession, Barbosa joined the political movement demanding full statehood. He became a member of the executive council, which had been established as the governing body of Puerto Rico by the Foraker Act of 1900, and he served there until 1917. When the Jones Act of 1917 created a senate as the governing body of Puerto Rico, Barbosa served as a member until his death in 1921.

REFERENCE: Antonio Salvador Pedreira, *Un Hombre del Pueblo: José Celso Barbosa*, 1937.

BARINAS. Spain created the province of Barinas in Venezuela* in 1782. It was the last province established in Venezuela before the wars of independence. Fernando Miyares y González arrived in 1786 and served as the first governor. Spanish control of the province deteriorated rapidly after 1810 because of the military situation. In 1819, Barinas became part of Gran Colombia.* It was later incorporated into the Republic of Venezuela.* See VENEZUELA.

BAROQUE LITERATURE. Originating in Europe, the Baroque spread to all of the arts: literature, painting, music, the theater, and even architecture. Although the Baroque existed in various forms throughout most of Europe, to a greater or lesser degree, as an artistic movement it was embraced to its highest degree in Spain. This meant that it was inevitably exported to Spanish colonial America. The Baroque period extended from 1600 to 1750 and went through distinct phases. Although literary periods in Latin America usually began and ended somewhat later than their European counterparts, the Baroque in Spanish colonial America was essentially contemporaneous with that of Europe, although it remained in vogue a bit longer in the colonies. Many critics view the Baroque and its art as a reaction against the Renaissance. The latter was recognized by its classical form and tendency toward order, clarity, and equilibrium, while the Baroque was characterized by affectation, adornment, obscurity, exaggeration, and ostentation. It was expressive, filled with warmth and color. Religion was a center of concern, and in Spain, this preoccupation often found expression in mysticism.

Spanish Baroque literature was one of contrasts and counterpoints. It was dynamic, hyperbolic, and often bitingly satiric. Through the use of obscure and difficult metaphors, it was elevated to a literature of the well-educated elite and hence became the literature of the minority. There was, to be sure, a moderate Baroque and an extreme Baroque. In Spanish literature, the period of the Baroque corresponds to the Siglo de Oro, or the Golden Age. It included such luminaries as Lope de Vega, Tirso de Molina, and Calderón de la Barca in theater, Mateo Alemán and Quevedo in narrative, and Luis de Góngora in poetry. These writers were avidly read, idealized, and imitated in the Spanish colonies.

In Spanish colonial America, the Baroque also thrived. Its tendency toward flourish and the exotic went hand in hand with the bizarre world that the Spaniards inherited in their colonies. As figures of transition from the Renaissance to the Baroque, Bernardo de Balbuena* (Mexico*) and Diego de Hojeda* (Peru*) were notable. The greatest single figure in Baroque literature in colonial America was Sor Juana Inés de la Cruz* (Mexico). Other worthy representatives included Juan del Valle y Caviedes* (Peru), Juan de Espinosa* Medrano (Peru), Carlos de Sigüenza* y Góngora (Mexico), Pedro de Peralta* y Barnuevo* (Peru), Hernando Domínguez* Camargo (Colombia*), and Juan Rodríguez* Freile (Colombia).

REFERENCES: John Englekirk, *An Anthology of Spanish American Literature*, 1965; Orlando Gómez-Gil, *Historia crítica de la literatura hispanoamericana*, 1968.

Sam L. Slick

BARRIENTOS, PEDRO NOLASCO. Pedro Nolasco Barrientos was born in Paraguay* in 1734, the son of Juan Barrientos and Francisca Díaz Barbosa. He became a member of the Franciscan* order in 1749. After a career of teaching philosophy, he became the rector of the University of Córdoba*, in what is today Argentina*, in 1768. While rector, he also occupied the chair of sacred theology. Barrientos died in Buenos Aires* on October 15, 1810.

REFERENCE: *New Catholic Encyclopedia*, II:124, 1967.

BARROS DE SAN MILÁN, MANUEL. Manuel Barros de San Milán was born in Segovia, Spain, and spent his career as a public official in the Spanish imperial bureaucracy. In 1587, he was appointed president of the *audiencia* of Quito* in present-day Ecuador*. His term in office is best remembered for his quelling of the popular uprising in 1592 against the imposition of the *alcabala** sales tax. Barros de San Milán retired from the presidency of the *audiencia* in 1593 and died in Quito in 1599.

REFERENCES: Albert William Bork and Georg Maier, *Historical Dictionary of Ecuador*, 1973; Federico González Suárez, *Historia general de la República del Ecuador*, 7 vols., 1890–1903.

BARRUNDIA, JOSÉ FRANCISCO. José Francisco Barrundia was born in 1784 and became a leading Guatemalan* patriot. In 1813, he was a leading figure in the Belén conspiracy*, an abortive attempt to declare independence from Spain. Although Spanish authorities sentenced him to death in absentia, Barrundia eluded capture for six years. By that time, Spain had granted amnesty to the conspirators. In 1829, Francisco Morazán* appointed him president of the Federal Republic of Central America* to fill the unexpired term of President Manuel Arce*, who had been ousted. Barrundia spent the 1830s as a member of the national senate. When Guatemala left the United Provinces of Central America* in 1848, Barrundia moved to Honduras*, where he was appointed minister to the United States in 1852. He died in 1854.

REFERENCES: Richard E. Moore, *Historical Dictionary of Guatemala*, 1973; Ramon Salazar, *Los hombres de la independencia*, 1899.

BASCO Y VARGAS, JOSÉ DE. José de Basco y Vargas was a Spanish native and career military officer who in 1778 was appointed governor-general of the Philippines*. He is remembered as one of the most able Spanish administrators. Basco founded the Economic Society of Friends and the Philippines Company, both of which helped to make the Philippines more economically independent of New Spain*. Basco also conducted large-scale military campaigns against the Moros* and Kalingas, and he is credited with the conquest of the Batanes Islands north of Luzon.

REFERENCE: Ester G. Maring and Joel M. Maring, *Historical and Cultural Dictionary of the Philippines*, 1973.

BASSIRI, MOHAMMED SIDI IBRAHIM. Mohammed Sidi Ibrahim Bassiri was born around 1942 near Tan-Tan in what is today Morocco. He attended school on government scholarships in Casablanca and then graduated from the Universities of Cairo and Damascus. By that time, he had become an inveterate opponent of European imperialism. Bassiri returned from Syria to Morocco in 1966 and in 1967 moved again to Western Sahara, where he taught lessons on the Koran in Smara. In December 1967, he began to form the nucleus of what became the Movement for the Liberation of Saguia el-Hamra and Oued ed-Dahab. His goal was the independence of Western Sahara from Spanish colonial rule. At a demonstration that he staged at Zemla on June 17, 1970, Spanish troops slaughtered a number of protesters. Mohammed Sidi Ibrahim Bassiri was arrested. Although Spanish authorities claimed to have sent him to Morocco, he was never seen again.

REFERENCE: Tony Hodges, *Historical Dictionary of Western Sahara*, 1982; John Mercer, *Spanish Sahara*, 1975.

BASTIDAS, RODRIGO DE. Rodrigo de Bastidas was the first Spanish conquistador after Christopher Columbus* to explore "Tierra Firme," the South American mainland. He was born in Seville, Spain, in 1460. In March 1501, Bastidas arrived at the mouth of the Magdalena River in Colombia*. From there, he sailed westward to the Gulf of Darién* and discovered the narrow isthmus now called the Isthmus of Panama. In the course of this exploration, Bastidas became the first European to set foot on the land mass of Central America. He failed to establish any settlements, but he returned to Hispaniola* with tales and trinkets, prompting further Spanish interest in the area. He was shipwrecked in 1502 and was later imprisoned by Francisco de Bobadilla*, who sent him back to Spain in chains. In Spain, Bastidas was freed and given a pension by the Spanish Crown. He eventually returned to the New World and established a colony at Santa Marta*, Colombia*, in 1525. He prohibited Indian slavery* in the colony, but the decision made him enemies, one of whom stabbed him in anger. Bastidas went to Cuba* but died there of his wounds in 1526.

REFERENCE: Mario Góngora, *Los grupos de conquistadores en Tierra Firme*, 1962.

Virginia Garrard Burnett

BASTIDAS, RODRIGO DE. Rodrigo de Bastidas, the son of the great Rodrigo de Bastidas who accompanied Vasco Núñez de Balboa* to the Isthmus of Panama*, was born in Spain in 1498. Unlike his father, however, the younger Bastidas decided on a career in the priesthood. He went to the New World as a young priest and traveled widely, describing his journeys in a variety of published works. Eventually, he became bishop of Puerto Rico* and then archbishop of Santo Domingo*. His clerical administration was notably marked by his opposition to the Inquisition* and his attempt to protect the Indians* from the worst of Spanish exploitation. Rodrigo de Bastidas died in 1570.

REFERENCE: Kenneth R. Farr, *Historical Dictionary of Puerto Rico and the U.S. Virgin Islands*, 1973.

BECERRA TANCO, LUIS. Luis Becerra Tanco was born in Taxco, New Spain*, in 1602. He graduated from the University of Mexico and then taught mathematics there. Throughout New Spain, Becerra was acknowledged as the colony's greatest intellect—a linguist, chemist, physicist, biologist, mathematician, poet, philosopher, and historian. Becerra was ordained a Roman Catholic priest in 1631 and filled several clerical and pastoral assignments during his career. He is best remembered, however, for his work *Origen milagroso del Santuario de Nuestra Señora de Guadalupe* (1666), a description of the apparitions of the patron saint of Mexico, the Virgin of Guadalupe*. Becerra died in Mexico City in 1672.

REFERENCE: *New Catholic Encyclopedia*, II:211, 1967.

BEDÓN, PEDRO. Pedro Bedón was born in Quito*, Ecuador*, in 1555. Bedón was tutored in Quito by teachers from the University of San Gregorio in Valladolid; he then studied theology at the University of Lima. While in Lima*, Bedón also studied painting under Bernardo Bitti, a Jesuit* priest. Bedón joined the Dominican* order and returned to Quito in 1587 to teach theology and philosophy. He went on to become one of the great painters of the colonial period. He also served as the Dominican provincial. He traveled widely throughout the *audiencia*, investigating the condition of the Indians* and becoming one of their chief protectors. Bedón died in Quito on February 27, 1621.

REFERENCE: J. M. Vargas, "El venerable padre maestro fray Pedro Bedón, O.P.: Su vida, sus escritos," *El Oriente Dominicano*, 8 (1935), 115–17.

BELALCÁZAR, SEBASTIÁN DE. See BENALCÁZAR, SEBASTIÁN DE.

BELÉN CONSPIRACY. In 1813, several leading Guatemalan radicals—including José Francisco Barrundia*, Joaquín Yudice, Tomás Ruiz, and Fray Victor Castillo—conspired to seize Governor José Bustamente* y Guerra and Archbishop Ramón Casas y Torres and to declare Guatemalan independence from Spain. They met in the cells of the convent of Belén. They were discovered and sentenced to death, except for Barrundia, who hid in Guatemala* for the next six years. For political reasons, Spain decided not to execute them. In 1818, the Crown granted amnesty to Yudice, Ruiz, and Castillo. Ten other participants, also sentenced to execution, were later pardoned.
REFERENCE: Ramon A. Salazar, *Los hombres de la independencia*, 1899.

BELGRANO, MANUEL. Born in Buenos Aires* in 1770, Manuel Belgrano studied at the College of San Carlos where many of the future Argentine leaders also received their education. He then completed his training in Spain: Oviedo (1782–1787), Salamanca (1787–1788) and Valladolid (1789). He graduated as a lawyer. In Spain he fell very much under the spell of the leaders of the Spanish Enlightenment*, especially Pedro Rodríguez Campomanes, and like Gaspar Melchor de Jovellanos, was much influenced by Adam Smith; he also welcomed many of the ideas of the French Revolution. He returned home in 1794, at a moment when the Crown had founded the Commercial Tribunal in Buenos Aires. With his expertise in economic matters, he became the secretary of the new *consulado*. Belgrano annually delivered reports on economic subjects, in which he championed public education, free trade, and the promotion of science, agriculture, and industry. "A theoretical preacher of the new principles of political economy," he fought against ignorance and urged professional, technical, and practical education. He stood for free public schools, and his concepts on elementary schools were adopted by the royal authorities. As a result of his initiatives, two institutions were created in 1799: the School of Navigation, necessary for the protection of commerce, and the School of Design, "indispensable for every artist, carpenter, embroiderer, tailor, smith." He also planned the establishment of schools of agriculture (to teach the farmer to increase and improve production), commerce, and experimental chemistry, the latter related to the tanning industry (for which he urged the participation of women). He also favored the cultivation of hemp and flax.

Belgrano fought in the *patricios* regiment during the English invasions (1806–1807) and played a most conspicuous role in the May Revolution*, together with patriots like Mariano Moreno*, Juan Castelli*, and Bernardino Rivadavia*. On May 25, 1810, he voted that the authority of the viceroy* should pass *ad interim* to the *cabildo* "until such time as the junta which should exercise it is established." Belgrano became one of the nine members of the Provisional Junta of 1810 and subsequently led a *porteño* army against Asunción*, which was defying the authorities in Buenos Aires. He was twice defeated (at Paraguarí, on January

11, 1811 and at Tacuarí, on March 5, 1811), however, thus sealing the *de facto* independence of Paraguay[*]. The next year, near Rosario, where he was in command of the battery defending the area against Spanish warships, Belgrano unfurled the new Argentine flag, the blue and white banner of the *patricios*, on February 27, 1812; he did so again on May 25, 1818, in the town of Jujuy, after having been appointed commander of the Army of the North in its second attempt to reconquer Upper Peru[*]. At first he was victorious (at Tucumán[*] and Salta[*], 1812), for which the government rewarded him with the sum of 40,000 pesos; this he declined and instead asked that the money be assigned for the creation of four elementary public schools. Belgrano was later defeated in 1813 (at Vilcapugio and Ayohuma[*]). In 1814, he was replaced by José de San Martín[*], who had just returned home from Spain.

With the military situation seemingly stabilized but the country in further anarchy, Belgrano and Rivadavia, were entrusted with a diplomatic mission to Europe to seek the support of the British government and to negotiate in Spain for a Platean monarchy. At the end of 1814, they left for Brazil, with Belgrano arriving in England during 1815. Belgrano decided to return to Buenos Aires in 1816 and was at first supposed to lead an army against José Artigas[*] in the Banda Oriental[*]. In that year, under Director Juan Martín de Pueyrredón[*], the United Provinces of South America[*] seemed at last to be showing some stability. The time thus seemed ripe for a declaration of independence and a constitution. Belgrano arrived in Tucumán in early July. There he wielded great influence among the delegates to the congress in favor of such a declaration and of a constitutional monarchy; for the latter he was much helped by San Martín. Belgrano favored a United Kingdom of the United Provinces, Chile[*], and Peru[*], and even went so far as to propose the restoration of an Incan[*] monarchy in Buenos Aires. Later, when the Constitution of 1819 was proclaimed, the interior revolted, in view of the constitution's centralist nature. Belgrano, now commander of the army group in Tucumán, was ordered to return for the defense of Buenos Aires. He was too ill to do so, but eventually reached the capital. By 1820, the United Provinces had collapsed and the interior caudillos[*] were in command. On the very day when the Province of Buenos Aires was ruled by three governors, June 20, 1820, the worst day of Argentine anarchy, Belgrano died in Buenos Aires. Though neither a philosopher nor a military commander by profession, Belgrano was the great revolutionary hero, whose ideas and actions put his imprint on the May Revolution and guided it toward its goals.

REFERENCES: Ricardo Levene, *A History of Argentina*, 1963; O. Carlos Stoetzer, *The Scholastic Roots of the Spanish American Revolution*, 1979.

O. Carlos Stoetzer

BELICE. See BRITISH HONDURAS.

BELIZE. See BRITISH HONDURAS.

BELLO LÓPEZ, ANDRÉS. Andrés Bello López was born in Caracas*, Venezuela*, on November 30, 1781. A gifted intellectual, Bello studied law and medicine at the Central University of Venezuela. He spent much of his life in Caracas, Venezuela, and Santiago*, Chile*, as well as in Quito*, Ecuador*, where he earned a reputation as a poet, philosopher, and jurist. During the revolutionary movement, he was a close associate of Simón Bolívar* and an articulate spokesman for independence from Spain. He was especially adept at raising money and recruiting troops. Between 1810 and 1829, Bello lived in London representing the revolutionary government, but he then relocated to Santiago, Chile, where he spent the rest of his life. In 1843, he was appointed rector of the University of Chile, a post he held until his death. Bello is also credited with being the founder of the university. He is best remembered for his grammars of the Spanish language and his legal textbook *Principles of International Law*. Andrés Bello López died in Santiago on October 15, 1865.
    REFERENCE: R. Caldera Rodríguez, *Andrés Bello*, 1953.

BENALCÁZAR, SEBASTIÁN DE. Sebastián de Benalcázar was born in 1490 in the small village of Benalcázar in the province of Córdoba, Spain. Illiterate and with a lower-class background, Benalcázar decided to seek his fortune in the New World. He settled in Panama* in 1516, participated in the Spanish conquest of what is today Nicaragua*, and then joined Francisco Pizarro's* third expedition to Peru* in 1531. With Peru as his base, Benalcázar then led his own expedition north into Colombia*, where he founded the cities of Popayán* in 1536 and Cali in 1537. Benalcázar then returned to Quito for a year and set out again for Colombia in 1538. His hopes of becoming the conquerer of northern Colombia were dashed, however, when he learned that Jiménez* de Quesada had already conquered the Chibcha* Indians there. In 1540, Benalcázar was named governor of the province of Popayán. The next year, Benalcázar had Jorge Robledo* executed for trespassing on his territory, but in the shifting politics of the sixteenth-century Spanish empire, Benalcázar's actions backlashed on him. Several years later, Benalcázar was arrested for the killing of Robledo, convicted, and sentenced to death. He died in 1551 while awaiting execution.
    REFERENCE: J. Jijón y Camano, *Sebastián de Benalcázar*, 2 vols., 1936–1938.

BENAVENTE, FRAY TORIBIO DE. Fray Toribio de Benavente was born in Spain between 1482 and 1491 in Paredes, a small town northeast of Benavente, which is located south of León in the modern province of Zamora. Sometime prior to 1521, he became a Franciscan*, serving in the provinces of Santiago and Gabriel until 1523. He was then chosen by Fray Martín de Valencia as one of the twelve original Franciscans who arrived in Mexico* in May 1524.
    That same month or early in the next, he arrived in Tlaxcala and assumed his alias of Motolinía. Derived from the Nahuatl* *mo*, an honorific form of address, plus *tolinía*, "to be impoverished," this name is usually translated as "the poor little one." Hearing the Indians* repeat the word several times, Motolinía inquired

as to its meaning. Claiming that it was the first Nahuatl word that he had learned and appreciating its appropriateness, he took it as his own. Motolinía served in various capacities in New Spain* and Guatemala*. He first served in Mexico City as guardian of the monastery of San Francisco. In 1529, while serving as guardian in Huejotzingo, Motolinía came into conflict with representatives of the first *audiencia*. His struggle with the secular authorities on behalf of the Indians* was to continue throughout his career. In 1531, he participated in the founding of Puebla de los Angeles. In 1532–1533, Martín de Valencia*, Motolinía, and others spent half a year in Tehuantepec after a proposed mission to Asia failed to materialize.

From 1536 to 1539, Motolinía was guardian in Tlaxcala. In 1539, he became guardian in Texcoco. From there he made numerous trips. While staying in Tehuacán on one of these trips, he finished the introduction for his *Historia de los indios de la Nueva España*. In 1543, he led a Franciscan mission to Guatemala. In 1545 or 1546, he returned to Mexico after trouble with the Dominicans*. From 1548 to 1551, he served as the provincial of the Franciscan order in New Spain. As provincial, he was in charge of collecting Bartolomé de Las Casas'*s *Confesionario*, which had been banned. Viceroy Antonio de Mendoza* subsequently had the banned work burned. From 1553 until 1556, he was once again guardian of the convent in Tlaxcala*. It was here that he wrote his letter to Charles V*, criticizing Las Casas's confessional rules governing the granting of absolution to penitents. There is no biographical information on Motolinía after this until his death on August 9, 1569. The last of the original twelve Franciscans to die, Motolinía was laid to rest in the convent of San Francisco de México.

Motolinía's writings are regarded as the principal published source for early Franciscan history. His material is included in works by Las Casas, Jerónimo de Mendieta*, and Juan de Torquemada*. His major works include *De moribus indorum*, a lost manuscript; *Historia de los indios de la Nueva España*; and *Memoriales*. *De moribus indorum* was written in central Mexico in the period between 1536 and 1552. It was based on information from Indian informants, personal observation, and probably the works of Fray Andrés de Olmos. Alonso de Zorita refers to the manuscript in his *Breve y sumaria relación de los señores*, thus testifying to its existence. It was also used by Francisco Cervantes* de Salazar, Francisco López de Gomara, Las Casas, Mendieta, and Torquemada. The contents deal with the missionary work of the Franciscans and the conversion and customs of the Indians. Joaquín García Icazbalceta regarded *Memoriales* as a draft of the *Historia*. In 1925, Atanasio López suggested that there was a lost earlier work from which both were derived. In 1933, Robert Ricard argued that Zorita and others had relied on this earlier work. Since Mendieta and Torquemada referred to a work by Motolinía entitled *De moribus indorum*, it was suggested that this was the lost earlier work. *Historia de los indios de la Nueva España* was written in Spanish, probably in central Mexico in the period from 1536 to 1543. Las Casas may have seen this and other manuscripts in 1538 or 1539.

There are two sixteenth-century manuscripts of this work. One is in Spain in the Escorial and the other in a private collection in Mexico. The work consists of three *tratados*, or "treatises," preceded by an *epistola proemial* or introductory letter. The contents deal with the history of the Franciscan missionary effort; the conversion of the Indians; and Indian life, religion, superstitions, human sacrifices, gods, feasts, temples, and so forth. With the exception of some 14 chapters, the material is repeated in *Memoriales*. A copy of Motolinía's letter to Carlos V is printed in O'Gorman's edition of *Historia de los Indios de la Nueva España* (Editorial Porrua, 1969). *Memoriales* was written in Spanish, probably in Central Mexico in the period from 1536 to 1543. It contains approximately 30 chapters not contained in the *Historia*. This material includes information on the native calendar and Michoacán. The material is organized in two parts. The first deals with customs prior to the Conquest. The second is poorly arranged and deals with a miscellany of topics.

REFERENCES: Toribio de Benavente Motolinía, *History of the Indians of New Spain*, tr. and ed. by F. B. Steck, 1951; *New Catholic Encyclopedia*, X:42–43, 1967.

Edward B. Sisson

BENAVIDES, ALONSO DE. Alonso de Benavides was born in San Miguel in the Azores Islands in 1580. He came to New Spain* as a young man and joined the Franciscan* order in 1603. Benavides carried out a number of assignments before assuming the post of regional superior of the Franciscan missions in New Mexico* in 1625. He remained in New Mexico until 1629 when he returned to Spain to report on Franciscan activities in New Mexico. Benavides remained in Spain until 1636, when he was appointed auxiliary bishop of Goa in India. He died later in 1636 on his way to India.

REFERENCE: *New Catholic Encyclopedia*, II:269, 1967.

BENAVIDES, MIGUEL DE. Miguel de Benavides was born in Varrión de los Condes, Palencia, Spain, in 1552. He became a Dominican* priest and studied and taught at Valladolid before going to Manila* in the Philippines*. There he helped establish a Dominican province. Benavides learned Chinese so that he could minister to the Chinese people in Manila. In 1595, Benavides was named bishop of New Segovia* in the Philippines, two years later, he became the archbishop of Manila. Miguel de Benavides died in Manila in 1607.

REFERENCE: *New Catholic Encyclopedia*, II:269, 1967.

BENAVIDES, VICENTE. Vicente Benavides was born in 1777 and eventually became a leading royalist figure in the Chilean war for independence. In 1811, Benavides joined the army of Juan José Carrera* Verdugo and fought against Spain for a few years. In 1813, he switched sides and returned to the royalist fold. Benavides fought at the Battle of Rancagua* in 1814, but he was captured by independence forces in 1818. Just before his execution, however, several former friends got him released and he went into exile in Argentina*. In 1819, he returned to Chile* at the head of a royalist troop contingent and fought for several years. Benavides was captured at the Chilean-Peruvian border trying to escape Chile in 1822. After a trial, he was executed on February 23, 1822.

REFERENCE: José Toribio Medina, *Diccionario biográfico colonial de Chile*, 1906.

BENS ARGANDONA, FRANCISCO. Francisco Bens Argandona was born in Havana*, Cuba*, in 1867. He graduated from the Cuban Military Academy in 1885 and joined an infantry regiment in Madrid. Between 1887 and 1893, Bens fought against the rebel forces in Cuba before being posted to Melilla* in Africa, where indigenous guerrillas were opposing all attempts to extend Melilla's boundaries into the interior. Bens returned to Cuba during the rest of the revolution there, from 1894 to 1898, but after Cuba won its independence, he was sent to the Canary Islands*. In 1903, he was appointed military governor of the Río de Oro* colony in Africa. He carefully cultivated relations with the Saharawi tribesmen and tried to expand Spanish influence up and down the African coast as well as into the interior. Bens left the governorship in 1925 and died in Spain in 1949.

REFERENCE: Tony Hodges, *Historical Dictionary of Western Sahara*, 1982.

BENZONI, GIROLAMO. Although ethnically Italian, Girolamo Benzoni was born in Spain in 1519 and came to the New World as a young man. In 1544, he sailed with Diego Gutiérrez on the adventure and conquest expedition to parts of Central America, and he kept elaborate notes of his experiences and observations. His book *Dell'Histore del Mondo Novo* (1565) is one of the first published accounts of the explorations and history of Central America. Girolamo Benzoni died in 1572.

REFERENCE: Theodore S. Creedman. *Historical Dictionary of Costa Rica*, 1977.

BERENGÜER Y FUESTE, DÁMASO. Dámaso Berengüer y Fueste was born in Remedios, Cuba*, on August 4, 1873, to an aristocratic family whose ancestry was Catalonian. He graduated from the General Military Academy in Spain in 1892. He was stationed in Cuba in 1894 and saw action against Cuban guerrillas in the rebellion of the mid-1890s. Berengüer earned battlefield promotions for bravery and left the war in Cuba with the rank of major. He returned to Spain in 1898 and served as an aide to the captain-general of Andalucía. In 1902, he began a series of assignments with the Spanish army's tactical commission and in 1909 became a lieutenant colonel and aide to the minister of war. At the end of the year, Berengüer went to Melilla* as head of a cavalry regiment. In 1911, he took command of a contingent of Moroccan troops serving in the Spanish army. He moved to Tetuán in Spanish Morocco* in 1912 to pacify the region. In 1916, Berengüer became a brigadier general and captain-general of Málaga. After a short stint in 1918–1919 as under-minister of war in Madrid, Berengüer was appointed high commissioner of Spanish Morocco. He was ultimately held responsible for the military debacle that occurred at the hands of Abd al-Krim* in 1921 at Anwal*. Berengüer managed to survive the event politically, however, and in 1930 became prime minister of Spain. But in 1931, when the government changed hands, Berengüer was arrested and charged with monarchical sympathies. He spent more than a year in prison at the Alcázar in Segovia before being released and deactivated from the military. Dámaso Berengüer y Fueste died in Madrid on May 19, 1953.

REFERENCE: Damaso Berengüer y Fueste, *Campañas en el Rif y Yebvala*, 1923.

BERGANO Y VILLEGAS, SIMÓN. Simón Bergano y Villegas was born in 1781 and immigrated to Guatemala[*]. At the time of his arrival, he was known as Simón Carreno. A liberal journalist and writer, Bergano edited the *Gazeta de Guatemala* between 1803 and 1808. He was often resentful of the attitudes of superiority assumed by *peninsulares* vis-à-vis *criollos*, so his editorials frequently created controversy. In 1808, royal officials arrested Bergano and exiled him to Spain, where he died in 1828. Bergano is also known for his written works, including *Cuatro piezas poéticas* (1803) and *La vacuna* (1808).

REFERENCE: Richard E. Moore, *Historical Dictionary of Guatemala*, 1973.

BERMUDA. Bermuda is located outside the Caribbean Sea off the southeastern coast of North America but along the path of the Spanish mariners. It lies about 580 miles to the east of Cape Hatteras. This close cluster of small coral islands rising from the submerged plateau under the Atlantic totals a mere 20.5 square miles of land mass and is surrounded by reefs that were especially dangerous to early marine navigators. Bermuda's highest elevation is just over 250 feet and could not be easily seen from the deck of the early Spanish ships except from a few miles off shore. Bermuda therefore remained mostly unknown and unexplored by the early Spanish seafarers well into the sixteenth century.

Juan de Bermúdez was the first Spanish captain to acknowledge this small cluster of islands in 1503, and he reported about the location in 1506. Bermúdez did not land on the islands until 1515, however, when he arrived on board the *La Garza* (hawk) while in the company of courtier and historian Oviedo y Valdes. Oviedo recorded a detailed description of Bermúdez's stopover at the islands. These early reports of the islands resulted in their being named after Bermúdez. A dozen years later in 1529, Hernando Camelo, a Portuguese from the Azores, applied to the Spanish Crown to colonize the islands. After delayed attempts by Camelo to mount an effective program (he lived there briefly in the mid-1540s), the colony was abandoned and the islands remained uninhabited for decades. A second attempt at colonial settlement was made in 1587 by Pedro de Aspide, who sought Spanish royal consent to develop a pearl fishing industry; these plans were not enthusiastically endorsed by financiers, and the project failed.

Bermuda became well known to many Spanish seafarers by the late sixteenth century, however, as rich galleons and Spanish convoys moved from the Spanish colonies to Spain. The islands were located near the path of the westerly winds that the Spanish sailing ships needed to help them return from their adventures in the Indies to Spain and the rest of Europe. Many of these Spanish mariners were also aware of the danger of being shipwrecked on the reefs that surrounded the Bermuda islands. For this reason, they frequently referred to them as "the Isles of Devils."

During late 1593, Henry May, an English interpreter for the East India Company, was shipwrecked on the Bermuda reefs while traveling on a French ship bound for Europe. May and his fellow survivors spent five months on these islands building another ship in which to complete their voyage to Europe. During 1603, a Spanish captain, Diego Ramírez, was shipwrecked off the Bermudian coast and spent a number of weeks repairing his vessel as well as carefully mapping these beautiful small islands. Ramírez's account and drawings were registered on his return to Spain but the islands were still regarded as having little significance to the Spanish authorities, who saw the great wealth and lands of the Spanish Main as far more important than these uninhabited and mineral-less little islands off the North American mainland.

Bermuda remained unsettled by the Spanish for almost a century after its discovery. The establishment of the British colonial settlement at Jamestown, Virginia, in 1609, however, quickly placed Bermuda within the view and interest of British colonists who moved quickly to settle there. On July 28, 1609, British Admiral George Somers of Dorsetshire, on his way to the new colony of Jamestown, was shipwrecked off Bermuda's east end in his flagship, the *Sea Venture*. Somers and his men spent ten months in Bermuda building two ships, *The Patience* and *The Deliverance*, to take them to Virginia. William Strachey, one of the survivors, wrote a detailed account of the shipwreck, as well as of the natural vegetation of the islands. This report contrasted with the famine-stricken conditions the British colonists found at Jamestown on their arrival in 1610. Somers and company quickly returned to Bermuda, which he described in a report to the Earl of Salisbury as "the most plentiful place that I ever came to for fish, hogs, and fowl". Somers died in Bermuda and his body was taken back to Britain, as were his beautiful accounts of these unclaimed islands which were named the British Somers Islands after him. In July 1612, 60 British settlers were sent on board the *The Plough* by the Virginia Company, whose third charter was extended to include the right to colonize the "Somers Islands." These islands quickly became a thriving British colony.

REFERENCES: Mary Gray, *A Brief History of Bermuda, 1503-1973*, 1976; Jean de Chantal Kennedy, *Isle of Devils*, 1971; Terry Tucker, *Bermuda Today and Yesterday, 1503–1973*, 1975.

Glenn O. Phillips

BERMÚDEZ, JOSÉ FRANCISCO. José Francisco Bermúdez was born in 1782 and became a prominent Venezuelan patriot and hero of the wars of independence. Between 1810 and 1817, he fought with the patriot forces. In 1817, Simón Bolívar* named him general-in-chief of the Army of the East. After the war, Bermúdez supported the Constitution of 1826 but he also opposed the separatist movement that emerged in Venezuela* in the late 1820s. Bermúdez was assassinated by political enemies on December 15, 1831.

REFERENCE: Vicente Dávila, *Diccionario biográfico de ilustres próceres de la independencia suramericana*, 2 vols., 1924–1926.

BETANCES, RAMÓN EMÉRITO. Ramón Emérito Betances was born in Puerto Rico* in 1827 and pursued a medical education. His real passion, however, was Puerto Rican independence and the creation of what he called an Antillian Confederation out of the West Indies. Spanish authorities viewed Betances as a threat to their authority, and he was harassed and jailed for years. He also spent much of his life in exile, where he wrote and campaigned for an independent Puerto Rico. He also campaigned for an end to slavery*, a position that threatened to undermine the Spanish planter class in Cuba*, Hispaniola*, and Puerto Rico. Betances spent the last 20 years of his life in Europe. He died in 1898, the year in which Puerto Rico became an American colony.

REFERENCE: Kenneth R. Farr, *Historical Dictionary of Puerto Rico and the U.S. Virgin Islands*, 1973.

BETANCOURT, PEDRO DE. Pedro de Betancourt was born in Chasna, Tenerife* Island, in the Canary Islands*, in March 1626. He emigrated to Guatemala* in 1650 and began to study for the priesthood, eventually being admitted to the Third Order of St. Francis; he took the tertiary habit as his clothing. Betancourt spent the rest of his life doing good deeds and assisting the poor and the sick. Before his death in 1667, Betancourt was widely known for his charitable works, and in 1735, Pope Clement XIV beatified him.

REFERENCE: Fernando Vásquez, *Vida y virtudes del venerable Hermano Pedro de San José Betancur*, 1962.

BETANCOURT Y DÁVALOS, PEDRO. Pedro Betancourt y Dávalos was born in Matanzas, Cuba*, in 1858. He studied medicine in the United States and in Spain before returning to Matanzas to set up his practice. He remained there until the insurrection of 1895. Betancourt then went to New York and visited with José Martí* about the revolution. He returned to Matanzas to participate in the rebellion, but he was arrested by Spanish authorities and imprisoned in Spain. Betancourt escaped and made it to New York by way of Paris. In New York, he joined up with Calixto García's* forces, returned to Cuba, and led rebel forces in Matanzas Province. He rose to the rank of major general. After the revolution, Betancourt served in the national legislature and a term as minister of agriculture during the republican era. Pedro Betancourt y Dávalos died in 1933.

REFERENCES: Gerardo Brown Castillo, *Cuba colonial*, 1952; Jaime Suchlicki, *Historical Dictionary of Cuba*, 1988.

BETHLEHEMITES. The Bethlehemites were a religious order of Roman Catholic men founded in Guatemala City*, Guatemala*, in 1668, by Rodrigo de la Cruz. The order revolved around vows of chastity, poverty, obedience, and hospitality, which meant an obligation to care for the sick. In 1672, Pope Clement X confirmed the new order but did not exempt it from diocesan control; three years later, the pope gave it partial exemption. During the next decade, the Bethlehemites took over the operation of a number of hospitals in Mexico City* and Puebla*, New Spain*. By 1700, the Bethlehemites were operating 18 hospitals in the New World. During the eighteenth century, the Bethlehemites also took on educational responsibilities, particularly in establishing and operating elementary schools.

REFERENCE: *New Catholic Encyclopedia*, XII:304–5, 1967.

BIAKNABATO REPUBLIC. On November 1, 1897, Emilio Aguinaldo* proclaimed the Biaknabato Republic on Bulacan, Philippines*. At the time, the Philippines Revolution was gaining momentum, and the nationalists were demanding secularization, representation in the Spanish Cortes, and equality for Filipinos*. Spain reacted quickly to the declaration, and in December 1897, the rebels signed the Pact of Biaknabato, which offered amnesty to the rebels and a Spanish indemnity in return for the end of the rebellion and the exile of Aguinaldo. Because the pact did not address the major grievances, it did little to stem the tide of the nationalist rebellion.

REFERENCE: W. Cameron Forbes, *The Philippine Islands*, 2 vols., 1945.

BLACK LEGEND. Apparently coined by Julían Juderias y Loyot (1877–1918), who took exception to the anti-Spanish view of history, the term "black legend" refers to a body of literature as well as to an attitude critical of Spain's alleged cruelty in the conquest of the New World and its presumed decadence, political corruption, hypocrisy, laziness, bigotry, and pride as a nation. Ironically, a Spaniard, Father Bartolomé de las Casas,* created the image. In 1552, Las Casas documented the harshness of Spain's treatment of the native populations in a polemic entitled "Very Brief Recital of the Destruction of the Indies." His motive was humanitarian; he hoped to reform Spanish policies toward the Indians*. Driven by less noble impulses, however, Spain's enemies quickly saw in Las Casas's pamphlet "proof" of Spanish rapacity. Replete with lurid illustrations, the bishop's work was soon translated into French, English, Dutch, and other languages. Since the early twentieth century, many scholars have challenged the veracity of the black legend, suggesting that it was at least an exaggeration if not an outright distortion of Spanish history. The result has been a more balanced treatment of Spain in the New World, frequently at the expense of Las Casas's reputation as an unbiased observer.

REFERENCE: Charles Gibson, ed., *The Black Legend*, 1971.

John W. Storey

BLACKS. When the Indian* population began to decline rapidly in the early 1500s, undermining the labor supply that Spaniards felt they needed, Spain turned to Africa for slaves*. They were primarily used in the great plantations of the West Indies. By 1600, there were more than 40,000 slaves in the Spanish possessions of the New World, the vast majority of them confined to the West

Indies. They became the source of the black population of Spanish America, which reached approximately 700,000 in 1800. The largest black populations were in the West Indies and in contiguous areas of mainland Colombia* and Venezuela*. See SLAVERY.

BOBADILLA, FRANCISCO DE. Francisco de Bobadilla was born in Spain, trained in the law, and was a member of the Spanish Order of Calatrava. By the late 1490s, Queen Isabella* was growing increasingly concerned about the political administration of the Spanish colony at Hispaniola*. In 1499, she appointed Bobadilla as a royal commissioner and governor of Hispaniola and charged him with investigating abuses and the torture of Indians. Following his arrival in Hispaniola in 1500, he arrested Bartholomew, Diego, and Christopher Columbus.* He soon shipped the three brothers back to Spain in chains, a decision that was not approved by the king of Spain. Bobadilla further exceeded his authority by announcing that Spanish citizens would no longer have to pay the 10 percent tax to Colombus or the 50 percent tax to the Crown for mineral discoveries. He replaced those levies with a simple one-eleventh tax to be paid to the Crown. The Crown removed him from his post, and he died when the ship transporting him to Spain was lost at sea in 1502.

REFERENCE: Joaquín Mariano Inchauéstegui Cabral, ed., *Francisco de Bobadilla*, 1964.

Fred Koestler

BOGOTÁ. From the early colonial period to the present, Santa Fe de Bogotá, later simply Bogotá, has been the administrative and political center of what is now the nation of Colombia*. It is situated 4° 30′ north of the equator at an altitude of 8,660 feet in the Sabana of Bogotá, a fertile plateau in the eastern *cordillera* (range) of the Andes. It is approximately 500 miles from Barranquilla on the Caribbean coast and about half that distance from Buenaventura on the Pacific. The average temperature is 65° Fahrenheit. It has a beautiful and dramatic setting but until recent times was relatively isolated. It was hard to reach from the coast, and communication with other regions of the nation was slow. Hence, Bogotá's authority over other centers was often weak, and regionalism was strong.

Bogotá was founded as the capital of the Nuevo Reino de Granada or New Kingdom of Granada (later often called Nueva Granada or New Granada*) by the Spanish conquistador* Gonzalo Jiménez* de Quesada on a site originally occupied by the Chibchas*, from whom the name Bogotá derives. The commonly accepted date for the founding is August 6, 1538; there are, however, several versions given by commentators as to the precise sequence and derivation of the name of the city. From 1539 on, Santa Fe was governed by a *cabildo** (town council). The city served as the center of colonial administration for much of present-day Colombia and at times Venezuela*, Ecuador*, and Panama*. The end of the period of conquest and the beginning of the colonial period can be taken as the establishment of the royal *audiencia** (supreme court) in Santa Fe, which was decreed by Emperor Charles V* on July 17, 1549, and installed April 17, 1550. In 1564, because of too frequent disturbances, the king established the position of president with civil and military functions and with some dependency on the viceroyalty of Peru*. A viceroyalty was established at Santa Fe between 1717 and 1723 and again on a permanent basis by a 1739 decree.

In the Spanish colonies, towns like Santa Fe played a central role. They were the anchor of European culture, commerce, politics, administration, and military power. The larger landowners from the surrounding area commonly had a home there. Santa Fe became a cultural and intellectual center. The Dominicans* began founding schools in 1563. Several universities were established, including Santo Tomás (1580), Javeriana* (1622), and El Rosario (1653). The first use of a printing* press in the city was in 1738. During the 1790s, the first theater and newspapers appeared. The intellectual ferment at the end of the eighteenth century and beginning of the nineteenth contributed to the independence movement. The Catholic church* played a central role in Santa Fe, as in all the Spanish colonies. The archbishopric of Santa Fe* was established in 1563. By 1773, there were about 20,000 residents in the city, most of European descent.

Because of its central geographical location and its role as the colonial capital of New Granada, Santa Fe played a major role in the independence movement. On July 20, 1810, the *criollos** of Santa Fe rose against the peninsular authorities and created a regional junta. The following year, the state of Cundinamarca (named for the surrounding province) was created. Initially, the *criollos* did not declare independence; they still recognized Ferdinand VII* as their lawful ruler. Nevertheless, July 20 is now celebrated as independence day. Most of the other regional centers (such as Cartagena*, Antioquia*, and Tunja) quickly followed suit. There ensued a period referred to as the *patria boba* (foolish fatherland), in which there was armed and verbal conflict between the major towns over regional ascendancy, centralism vs. federalism, and the question of independence. This situation facilitated the reconquest by the Spanish, who reentered Santa Fe de Bogotá in 1816 and began a reign of terror that produced the execution of many of the leading patriots. The victory of the Liberator, Simón Bolívar*, at the Battle of Boyacá* on August 7, 1819, finally freed New Granada from the Spanish.

On December 17, 1819, the Congress of Angostura* created the Republic of Colombia (later called Gran Colombia by historians), consisting of New Granada (with Bogotá as its capital), Venezuela, and Ecuador. The name New Granada was suppressed in favor of Cundinamarca, and Santa Fe was dropped, leaving simply Bogotá. In 1821, the Congress of Cúcuta* named Bogotá the provisional capital. By the mid–1820s, a renaissance of education and ideas could be clearly seen in Bogotá. The Republic of Colombia, however, was racked by regionalism; by 1829–1830, Venezuela and Ecuador had separated. The remaining portion then reorganized, and in 1832 became the Republic of New Granada with Bogotá remaining as the capital. Throughout the remainder of the nineteenth century,

the conflict between centralism (generally represented by Bogotá) and regionalism was a central fact in the life of the capital. The conflict stunted the city's
growth, according to some, and the central government never had the power to
suppress regionalism completely, yet Bogotá has remained the nation's political
and cultural center.

REFERENCES: Thomas Blossom, *Nariño: Hero of Colombian Independence*, 1967;
R. B. Cumminghame Graham, *The Conquest of New Granada: Being the Life of Gonzalo
Jiménez de Quesada*, 1922; Jesús María Henao and Gerardo Arrubla, *History of Colombia*,
1938; Gerhard Masur, *Simón Bolívar*, 1969.

Robert E. Biles

BOGOTÁ, DIOCESE OF. The first Roman Catholic diocese established in
Colombia* was placed in Santa Marta*, where the first economic and population
center of the colony was. In 1549, the bishop of Santa Marta recommended that
the see be relocated to Santa Fe de Bogotá*, a move that was completed in 1562.
Two years later, the diocese was raised to an archdiocese, covering all of present-
day Colombia and much of western Venezuela*.

REFERENCE: *New Catholic Encyclopedia*, II:634–35, 1967.

BOHOL. Bohol is an oval-shaped island of about 1,500 square miles located
in the central Philippines*, about 400 miles southeast of Manila*. Its people speak
Cebuano. Bohol has no high mountains, but rather two ridges on the east and
west, joined by an upland plateau of 1,000 to 2,500 feet elevation. The whole
island is cultivable, but the people tend to cluster along the coast. The soil is
not favorable to wet-rice agriculture, so Bohol's economy is based rather on
corn, copra, cattle, hemp, and fishing. During Spanish times, coffee*, abaca,
sugar* cane, and tobacco* were also grown. The island is not rich in minerals
except for a manganese deposit on the Anda Peninsula.

Bohol is famous for its bloody religious resistance to the Spanish friars. Things
started out well enough in 1565 when a native chief, Sikatuna, concluded a
blood pact with the explorer Miguel Legazpi*. Thirty years later, the Jesuits*
began missionary work, but their excesses caused the Bohol Revolt of 1621–
1622, in which a messiah named Tamblot called his followers to a golden age
free of Spanish Catholics. Two thousand people from four towns rose in revolt.
Churches and Christian images became special targets for the peasants' wrath.
The insurrection eventually spread to the neighboring island of Leyte*. In January
1622, a small contingent of Spaniards with a larger army of Cebuanos crushed
the revolt and hanged its leaders.

A far longer-lived rebellion, led by Francisco Dagohoy*, denied Spain control
of the interior of Bohol for 85 years (1744–1829). The immediate cause was an
incident in the town of Inabanga, on the northwest coast of Bohol. Dagohoy's
brother died in a duel with a constable and was denied a Christian burial by a
Jesuit priest. The priest himself was killed in retaliation and his body left by the
roadside. Three thousand Boholanos followed Dagohoy to the interior, where
they became self-sufficient and repelled all Spanish attacks. Efforts to lure them

out with offers of pardon were futile. Finally, an expedition of 3,200 men defeated the rebels and resettled them in coastal Christian towns, which by then were under the authority of the Recollects (a Roman Catholic order). The Jesuits had been expelled from the Philippines. Bohol was less intensively developed than other Visayan* islands. Boholanos did not play a major role in the Philippine revolution against Spain (1896–1898), but did fiercely resist American troops until 1901.

REFERENCES: Renato Constantino, *A History of the Philippines*, 1975; Frederick Wernstedt and J. E. Spencer, *The Philippine Island World*, 1967.

Ross Marlay

BOHÓRQUEZ, PEDRO. Pedro Bohórquez was born near Cádiz, Spain, around 1602. He ran away from home as a child and was raised by Jesuits*. In 1620, he went to Peru with his uncle, Martín García, and he lived there for the next 30 years. In 1650, Bohórquez moved to the high Andes region to search for fabled Inca* treasures and in 1656 made his way to Catamarca and Salta* in the Río de la Plata* area. There he masqueraded as a royal Inca* prince named Hualpa Inca. New Spaniards believed him, and even some Indians did. He promised them that he would lead them to victory over the Spaniards. Some Calchaqui Indians followed him. Governor Alonso de Mercado* y Villacorta named him captain general over northern Tucumán* when Bohórquez promised to give him a percentage of all the Inca gold and silver he discovered. Bohórquez then promptly led several Indian* uprisings against the governor. He was not captured and executed until 1667.

REFERENCES: Enrique Udaondo, *Diccionario biográfico colonial argentino*, 1945; Ione S. Wright and Lisa M. Nekhom, *Historical Dictionary of Argentina*, 1978.

BOLAÑOS, LUIS DE. Luis de Bolaños was born in Marchena, Spain, in 1550. He joined the Franciscan* order while still a young man and in 1572 accompanied the Juan Ortiz de Zárate expedition to Asunción*, Paraguay*. He immediately began founding *reducciones** among the Guaraní* Indians. These centers were later handed over to the Jesuits* and became the beginning of the great Jesuit republics. In 1585, Bolaños founded the famous *reducciones* of San Blas de Ita and San Buenaventura de Yaguarón. By the early 1600s, Bolaños was busy founding missions south of Asunción in territory that remained under Spanish control. Bolaños was also a linguist and a scholar. He wrote a Guaraní catechism in 1603, as well as a variety of poems and hymns in Guaraní. He died in Buenos Aires* on October 11, 1629.

REFERENCE: B. R. Oro, *Fray Luis de Bolaños*, 1934.

BOLÍVAR, SIMÓN. Simón José Antonio de la Santisima Trinidad Bolívar was born July 24, 1783, in Caracas*, Venezuela*, to a wealthy and aristocratic *criollo** family that had lived for two centuries in the New World. Orphaned at an early age, he was most influenced by his tutor, Simón Carreño (also known as Rodríguez and Robinson), a man of revolutionary thought. Sent to Europe to complete his education, Bolívar met and married María Teresa del Toro in 1802. She, however, died the following year in Venezuela. Bolívar kept his vow never to remarry, but he had numerous affairs, most notably with his cousin Fanny Dervieu de Villars, Josefina Machado, and Manuela Sáenz. Following a second trip to Europe and the United States, he played a minor role in the revolutionary ferment of Caracas following Napoleon's invasion of Spain in 1808. Already a part of the *criollo* elite, his influence increased rapidly. In 1810, he was sent to London to seek aid for the Caracas junta. The mission failed, but he did persuade Francisco de Miranda* to return and command the independence movement. Following the declaration of independence the following year, Bolívar established himself as a military leader. He clashed with Miranda and collaborated with the victorious Spanish in his arrest. Bolívar then fled to independent Cartagena*, where on December 15, 1812, he published the first of his influential political statements, the "Cartagena Manifesto." He assisted in Cartagena's war against the Spanish and was named commander of an expeditionary force to Venezuela. After a hard-fought campaign, he entered Caracas on August 6, 1813, and was given the title "Liberator." Bolívar ruled Venezuela's second republic as military dictator; without the support of the lower classes, however, he was defeated by the royalist *llaneros* (plainsmen) under José Tomás Boves* in 1814. Later that year, Bolívar led forces in the civil war in New Granada*. The following year, he went to Jamaica*, where he issued the "Jamaica Letter," widely considered his greatest statement.

Bolívar returned to Venezuela in late 1816, soon basing his operations in the lower Orinoco region. He received assistance from foreign volunteers, whose military skills proved very helpful. He established himself as the major patriot leader and was joined by several others, most notably José Antonio Páez* and Francisco Santander*. By 1818–1819, patriot forces controlled the *llanos*, while the Spanish, under General Pablo Morillo*, dominated the Venezuelan Andes and neighboring New Granada*. In 1819, following his "Angostura* Address" to the patriot congress, Bolívar made a daring march across the plains and over the Andes to defeat the Spanish at the Battle of Boyacá* on August 7, 1819. The victory liberated Andean New Granada and proved a turning point in the war. He then proposed, and the Congress of Angostura* approved, the union of New Granada, Venezuela, and Ecuador as the republic of Colombia (later called Gran Colombia*). Bolívar was named president, a position he held until 1830. Because of his almost continuous absences on military missions, however, he had little to do with the actual running of the government until 1827. In November 1820, Bolívar signed an armistice with the Spanish commander Morillo, who had been weakened by the revolution in Spain. When fighting resumed, the patriots' superior forces quickly defeated the royalists in Venezuela, the Battle of Carabobo* on June 24, 1821, being decisive. The same year, Gran Colombia's Congress of Cúcuta* approved a highly centralist and moderately reformist constitution influenced by Bolívar on the former point. On May 24, 1822, one of Bolívar's chief lieutenants, General Antonio José de Sucre*, won the Battle of

Pichincha*, the decisive engagement in the liberation of Ecuador* and southern New Granada. On July 13, Bolívar decreed the incorporation of Guayaquil* into Colombia, thus completing the liberation and unification of Gran Colombia. Conflict continued into the mid-1820s.

On July 26, 1822, Bolívar met in Guayaquil with José de San Martín*, the liberator of southern South America. The content of their discussion is not known; because of Bolívar's stronger position, however, San Martín received neither the assistance he apparently wanted in ousting the Spanish from the highlands of Peru* nor agreement on borders and governmental arrangements. In any event, on returning to Lima*, San Martín resigned and went into exile. In 1822, Bolívar sent two forces to Peru and went himself the following year. In February 1824, the Peruvian congress named him dictator; on August 6, he won the battle of Junín*; and on December 9, Sucre won the Battle of Ayacucho*, the last major battle in South America. Peru was liberated. By April 1825, royalist resistance in Upper Peru had broken in the face of internal dissension and the invasion by Sucre. Upper Peru took the name Bolivia in honor of its liberator, who also drafted its first constitution. This document proved unpopular because of its lifetime presidency and other authoritarian or monarchical features. When Bolívar left Peru in September 1826, the Peruvians appear to have been relieved.

Bolívar's time in Peru and Bolivia represents the high point of his career. He was president of two nations and held sway from Venezuela to Bolivia. He then began a decline. He was always one to think in broad sweeps—about continents instead of nations. The 1826 Panama* congress that he called had limited attendance and meager accomplishments. In Gran Colombia, the removal of the royalist threat brought nationalist sentiment to the fore, and the nation began to break apart. Acting president Francisco Santander*, from New Granada, increasingly came into conflict with other regional leaders, particularly the Venezuelans. Previously, the differences between Bolívar and Santander had generally complemented each other. when Bolívar returned in 1826, however, relations between the two deteriorated. To maintain order and unity, Bolívar wanted to slow the pace of reform and was willing to make concessions to Venezuelan nationalism. Santander not only objected to both of these but worried increasingly about Bolívar's predilection for authoritarian rule.

In September 1827, Bolívar took active control of the government and attempted to rebuild unity. In 1828, he called the Convention of Ocaña to revise the constitution, but it deadlocked between Santander's federalist party and Bolívar's attempt to strengthen the executive. With conditions deteriorating, Bolívar assumed dictatorial powers in June 1828 and began a conservative reaction against the reforms of the Congress of Cúcuta. On September 25, there was an attempt on Bolívar's life, which produced a wave of repression and the exile of Santander. In 1826, General Páez led a revolt in Venezuela against Santander and Bogotá's dominance of the federation. Bolívar was able to regain José Antonio Páez's* allegiance, but in 1829–1830, Paéz* led Venezuela against Bolívar and out of the confederation. In January 1830, another convention, the

Congreso Admirable, was called in a last attempt to save the nation. It produced a new constitution but came too late to stop the break-up. Nationalism in the other regions of the confederation and the forces represented by Santander in Colombia had defeated Bolívar. On March 1, sick and politically beaten, Bolívar stepped down from the presidency. Further rebuffed, even by his friends, he departed from Bogotá, sad, ill, and poor on May 8, intending to go into exile in Europe. On December 17, 1830, he died, ironically on the estate of a Spanish admirer near Santa Marta*.

The interpretations of Bolívar, like the man himself, are contradictory: good and bad, Masonic and Catholic, anti-American and pro-American, republican and authoritarian. Bolívar has been described as ambitious, craving adulation, and enjoying the exercise of power but also as generous, uninterested in personal enrichment, and the consummate *caballero* (gentleman). He was a talented organizer but focused on the grand scale and cared little for detail. There does appear agreement that Bolívar was shaped by the eighteenth-century Enlightenment* but perhaps more by the Enlightened Despotism current than by more democratic and radical ones. He was a republican but thought representation should operate only within narrow limits in order to maintain stability. He was often frustrated by legal formalities. He sought to reconcile a degree of civil liberties and popular participation with a largely self-perpetuating and centralized political authority. He was a moderate conservative out of a sense of realism, not ideology; he was skeptical about the possibility of changing Spanish-American society rapidly. His dreams focused on the continent. He wanted an independent but united continent—hence, such projects as Gran Colombia and a league of South American nations. Ultimately, he failed because his goals did not correspond with the objectives of those he liberated. Their loyalty was to their own region—not the whole that Bolívar sought to unite. He was also out of step with the two leadership patterns of the period—the caudillo* (strong man), such as Páez, or the man of law, such as Santander.

Few can match the range of Bolívar's accomplishments. He participated in the independence movement from beginning to end, leading during most of it. Though he made mistakes and lost battles, he showed considerable military skill coupled with the energy, perseverance, and personality to dominate over the long run. His skills fit the times. He was also a prolific writer who appears to have understood well the problems of Latin America but not their solutions.

REFERENCES: Simón Bolívar, *Selected Writings*, comp. by Vicente Lecuna, ed. by Harold A. Bierck, Jr., trans. Lewis Bertrand, 2 vols, 1951; David Bushnell, ed., *The Liberator, Simón Bolívar: Man and Image*, 1970; Salvador de Madariaga, *Bolívar*, 1952; Gerhard Masur, *Simón Bolívar*, 1969.

Robert E. Biles

BOLIVIA. Bolivia's long and turbulent history has roots in the colonial period with its clash of cultures, peoples, and social classes. What became known as Bolivia after independence was known as Upper Peru (Alto Peru) during this earlier period. The territorial jurisdiction of this area was under the *audiencia* of Charcas* with its seat in Chuquisaca (now Sucre*). The *audiencia* was a part of the viceroyalty of Peru* until the late eighteenth century when it became attached to the new viceroyalty of the Río de la Plata*.

Bolivia's discovery and conquest was made from two directions: from north to south and from the east. The north to south conquest was begun after the final defeat of the Incas* in July 1535 by Diego de Almagro*, Francisco Pizarro's* associate. When this expedition returned from the *altiplano* to Lower Peru, Almagro rebelled, but he was defeated and beheaded in 1538. That same year, Pizarro sent an expedition to Charcas, or Upper Peru, which founded the towns of Chuquisaca and Porco near Potosí*. The eastern expeditions came from Río de la Plata and had outposts in the Chiquitos and Mojos regions by the 1540s. They were forced to settle in the Santa Cruz region by the Lima* and Cuzco* groups. In 1544, Francisco Pizarro revolted against the first Peruvian viceroy* who tried to implement the New Laws*. In 1545, the Potosí silver veins were discovered, and, with Pizarro's defeat in 1548, its wealth attracted Spaniards who started the city as a mining camp. After the civil wars, La Paz*, which became a commercial and agricultural center, was founded in the middle of Aymara* Indian country. Other rebellions in the region occurred. On September 18, 1559, the *audiencia* of Charcas*, was installed in Chuquisaca.

From 1569 to 1581, under Viceroy Francisco de Toledo's* rule, major changes occurred in the region. The declining Indian* communities and the prevention of the development of a *criollo* nobility made Toledo pass legislation to have existing *encomiendas* revert to the Crown. The *mita* (a form of labor tribute) was reorganized to provide labor for the mines. The scattered Indian communities were put in *reducciones* and forced to pay tribute in specie, not in goods, forcing their participation in the Spanish market system. To increase silver production, he introduced the mercury amalgam system, created a royal mint, and established a mining* code. He founded new towns along the eastern frontier to control the Indians and provide agricultural products for the mines. Upper Peru became one of the richest jewels of the Spanish Empire.

In the seventeenth century, there were struggles between the *Vascongados*, who came from Spain's Basque provinces and had political, social, and economic power in Potosí because of their control of mining and the *cabildo**, and the *Vicuñas*, composed of Castilians, Extremadurans, and *criollos* who did not have any opportunities. The most virulent struggles lasted from 1622 to 1625 and ended with the defeat of the Vicuñas, but animosity continued and was exacerbated by the decline in silver production in the middle of the century. This century was Chuquisaca's golden age, reflected by the establishment of a university in 1624, but the decline of silver had profound effects. An exodus from urban to rural areas or out of the region altogether because of lack of opportunities affected the relationship between the cities and supply networks as demand for agricultural products decreased as well. Cochabamba*, a typical example, drifted into self-subsistence as its products became too costly to transport. Indian *mita* participation decreased and a call for the system's abolition was sounded. In 1647, silver coins were falsified, and revolts began near the end of the century. The Jesuits* explored and set up missions* in the frontier regions. Potosí's position within the imperial system changed.

The eighteenth century began with regional decline. In 1730, a Cochabamba* revolt broke out, centered around the grievances of mestizos* and *criollos*, who resented their inclusion on tribute lists because it was an affront to their exemptions; it failed, but others followed. The Jesuit expulsion from the Spanish Empire in 1767 affected the frontier missions. On August 8, 1776, the viceroyalty of Río de la Plata* was created and included the *audiencia*. The change had an impact on Upper Peru's trade patterns. They tended to shift from Lima to Buenos Aires*. The *audiencia*'s powers were curtailed, and administrators arrived to stimulate silver production and economic growth.

The Túpac Amaru* rebellion of 1780–1782 had a profound impact on all social and ethnic classes. The attempts to increase royal revenues had made Indian tribute the second largest source of royal income. The Indian population had increased since its sixteenth- and seventeenth-century declines, leading to the growth of Indian communities. The rebellion was fueled by the Indians' dissatisfaction with the situation because of the *corregidor*'s* and *hacendado*'s exactions. They were led by their *kurakas* (Indian nobility) who felt the decline of their privileges and the attack on their religious beliefs. Beginning in Lower Peru, the revolt spread to Upper Peru, where it continued as all social and ethnic classes became involved against the Spanish. La Paz was put under siege by the rebels, and other regions were engulfed in violence. After its defeat, the *corregimientos* were abolished and the *kuraka* class destroyed; Spaniards were put in their place to rule directly over the Indians. Although the destruction of lives and property was great, population and economic production reached prerebellion levels by the late 1780s. In 1784, intendancies*, which took over most of the *audiencia*'s duties, were established in La Paz, Cochabamba, Potosí, and Chuquisaca. In the 1790s, silver production was again disrupted as mercury shipments from Spain failed to arrive. Besides a general crisis in mining, agricultural production suffered and epidemics occurred at the beginning of the nineteenth century. The economy went into severe depression.

On May 25, 1809, a rebellion in Chuquisaca proved the harbinger of independence. This initial revolt led to one in La Paz on July 16, 1809, under Pedro Domingo Murillo's* leadership. On July 27, independence was declared but was answered by the raising of royalist forces in Peru and Buenos Aires to invade Upper Peru. The rebellion was put down with the execution of its leaders on January 10, 1810. Events moved quickly after Buenos Aires declared independence on May 25. The *audiencia*, in royalist hands, returned to the viceroyalty of Peru. New rebellions occurred in the principal cities. Between 1810 and 1817, four Argentine expeditionary forces invaded Upper Peru to liberate it but were defeated. On their retreat, they caused many depredations and took Chuquisaca's coffers. Internally, the struggle for independence was carried on by the *repub-*

liquitas, irregular guerrilla units representing the popular forces, which harassed the royalists. The Peruvian and Argentine depredations fixed the idea of an autonomous state in the minds of the elites who would declare independence.

In 1823, absolutism was once more installed in Spain and, in early 1824, General Pedro Antonio Olaneta[*], a royalist and conservative in control of Upper Peru, got the news. He had been against Spain's previous liberal regime and had broken with Viceroy José de la Serna[*], a liberal. He declared himself head of Upper Peru. La Serna sent a force against him, but signed the Treaty of Tarapaca on March 9 when he realized Olaneta's strength. In Peru, Simón Bolívar's[*] forces won the Battle of Ayacucho[*] on December 9, but Olanata, not recognizing the royalist surrender, remained in control of Upper Peru. On April 1, 1825, his troops rebelled in Tumusula and he was shot by his own men. On August 6, 1825, Bolivia declared its independence.

REFERENCES: Herbert S. Klein, *Bolivia: The Evolution of a Multi-Ethnic Society*, 1982; Humberto Vásquez Machicado, José de Mesa, and Teresa Gilbert, *Manual de Historia de Bolivia*, 1983; Enrique Finot, *Nueva Historia de Bolivia*, 1976.

Carlos Pérez

BOMBONA, BATTLE OF. The Battle of Bombona was a crucial but indecisive battle in the war of Colombian[*] and Ecuadorian[*] independence. On April 7, 1822, Simón Bolívar[*] attacked Pasto, an inland town absolutely controlled by the clergy and completely loyal to the Spanish Crown. The town was defended by about 4,000 troops under the command of Don Basilio García. Bolívar had a force of about 2,000, which he had marched overland from Cali, in the Cauca Valley. Arriving at Pasto, Bolívar surrounded the city and attacked. The monarchist forces held their positions, inflicting heavy casualties on Bolívar's forces and killing several republican officers. Fighting from established defensive positions and substantially outnumbering the attackers, royalist losses were a fraction of Bolívar's.

Bolívar realized that he could not capture Pasto and withdrew, causing some to see Bombona as a senseless battle and accusing Bolívar of exercising poor judgment. Perhaps it was, within the immediate context of taking Pasto, but not necessarily within the larger context of the revolution. Although the battle was technically a draw, in that neither side suffered a decisive defeat and each maintained the integrity of its forces, the immediate advantage went to the Spanish because they had not been dislodged from Pasto. The battle, however, represented a significant republican gain, in that Bolívar's efforts at Pasto made it easier for Antonio José de Sucre[*] to move against Quito[*]. When García learned that Sucre had seized Quito, he realized that he could not hold Pasto against the combined forces of Bolívar and Sucre, so he negotiated a surrender to Bolívar.

REFERENCE: Gerhard Masur, *Simón Bolívar*, 1948.

Samuel Freeman

BONAPARTE, NAPOLEON. Napoleon Bonaparte was born in Ajaccio, Corsica, on August 15, 1769, to a family which was part of the minor nobility. He graduated from the military school in 1785 with a specialty in artillery. Napoleon entered the French army and became a devoted advocate of the Revolution in 1789. He distinguished himself at the Battle of Toulon in 1793 and was promoted to general of a brigade. In 1796 Napoleon took command of the French Army of Italy, and during the next two years he fought a number of successful battles against Austrian troops. In an attempt to strike at British trade routes, Napoleon seized Egypt in 1798, but he was subsequently defeated by Admiral Horatio Nelson. Napoleon left Egypt and returned to France in 1799, and there he overthrew the Directory and took over the national government. French voters overwhelmingly named him consul for life in 1802 and emperor in 1804.

Napoleon envisioned a French empire with hegemony over the entire continent, but his dreams brought him into conflict with the British, Austrians, and Russians, who feared and resented his aggressiveness. France was embroiled in major wars throughout his reign. Napoleon invaded Portugal in 1807, and in 1808 he took control of Spain and deposed the Spanish Bourbon ruling family. He named Joseph Bonaparte king of Spain. Spanish guerrillas resisted the French invasion, and for the next five years Iberia was embroiled in what became known as the Peninsular War. Great Britain provided military and financial support to the Spanish guerrillas fighting Napoleon. As for Latin America, the Napoleonic invasion of Spain and overthrow of the Bourbons proved to be a liberating event. Spain had neither the energy nor the resources to maintain tight control of the empire, and Latin American nationalists launched the independence movements that would eventually destroy the Spanish empire. The Peninsular War proved to be terribly expensive for France, but it was the invasion of Russia which led to Napoleon's military and political defeat. In 1814 he abdicated the throne and was sent to the island of Elba.

In a tremendous reversal of fortune Napoleon escaped from Elba in March 1815 and headed for Paris. Along the way he picked up the support of thousands of French troops. Cheering crowds greeted him in Paris and he took control of the government. Napoleon immediately set out to rebuild the army. Hoping to catch the Allied powers off guard, Napoleon invaded Belgium, but he was defeated at the Battle of Waterloo on June 18, 1815. Napoleon abdicated again and went into exile on the island of St. Helena. He died of stomach cancer on May 5, 1821.

REFERENCE: Jean Mistler, ed., *Napoléon*, 1969.

BONELLI HERNANDO, EMILIO. Emilio Bonelli Hernando was born in Zaragoza, Spain, in 1854. He lived in Morocco as a young man, learning fluent Arabic, and in 1884, he arrived at Dakhla in Western Sahara[*]. Bonelli explored the coast with financing from the Society of Africanists and Colonists[*]. He signed a variety of treaties with local chiefs, giving Spain a foothold in the area. Spain used those treaties to proclaim a protectorate over the region at the end of 1884. Bonelli served there for a few months as the royal commissioner in 1885, but then he departed for other assignments. He spent many more years on African exploration trips for Spanish economic and political interests. He died in 1910.

REFERENCES: Antonio Rumeu de Armas, *España en el Africa Atlántico*, 1956; Tony Hodges, *Historical Dictionary of Western Sahara*, 1982.

BONIFACIO, ANDRÉS. Andrés Bonifacio was born in Tondo, Manila*, in 1863. His class background is a matter of dispute. On the one hand, his mother was a Spanish mestiza* and his father was the *teniente mayor* of Tondo. On the other hand, there were six children, the family seems never to have had much money, the parents died young, and Andrés Bonifacio had to drop out of school to support his brothers and sisters. He could read Spanish, however, and we know his tastes from a report of the Spanish police who raided his home: the novels of José Rizal*, books on the French Revolution, the lives of U.S. presidents, and even Victor Hugo's *Les Misérables* in Spanish translation.

Bonifacio was with Rizal when Rizal founded the reformist Liga Filipina on July 2, 1892. When Rizal was arrested only four days later, Bonifacio concluded that asking Spain for freedom was hopeless. Instead he organized the Katipunan*, a secret society whose aim was to prepare Filipinos* for a war of independence. Bonifacio was a great organizer, with an intuitive sense of how to attract middle- and lower-class Filipinos accustomed to a posture of defensive civility toward Spaniards. Where Rizal had written in Spanish, Bonifacio used Tagalog. He was less successful in attracting support from wealthy Filipinos, most of whom preferred to cast their lot with Spain. Bonifacio took care of them by forging incriminating documents that made it appear that they were secret Katipuñeros and then leaking those papers to the Spanish police who executed some prominent men who had never been disloyal.

Bonifacio was at first the undisputed leader of the Philippine Revolution, which began in August 1896. He encountered immediate military reverses, however, and he soon found his forces confined to the mountains east of Manila while Spanish troops controlled the densely populated lowlands. Revolutionary forces in Cavite* fared better under a prominent officer, Emilio Aguinaldo*. Bonifacio came down from the hills to mediate a dispute between two rival factions of the Cavite Katipunan and soon found himself at odds with Aguinaldo. Bonifacio was outvoted, and Aguinaldo made himself president. Bonifacio left, vowing to continue as the leader of his own men. Aguinaldo's men chased, wounded, and captured Bonifacio, then tried him for sedition and treason, and shot him on May 10, 1897. Bonifacio was only 34 years old. He is honored as nationalist hero in the Philippines today.

REFERENCE: Renato Constantino, *A History of the Philippines*, 1975.

Ross Marlay

BORDERLANDS. The term ''Borderlands'' has traditionally been used to describe the Spanish colonial settlements of northern Mexico and the southern United States. The borderlands settlements generally included the Mexican settlements north of San Luis Potosí* (Durango, Zacatecas*, Sinaloa*, Sonora, Chihuahua, Coahuila*, and Nuevo León); the Gulf of Mexico settlements of

West Florida* and East Florida*; the mission settlements along the coasts of Upper California*; the colonies at Albuquerque* and Santa Fe in New Mexico*; and the mission settlements in Texas*. Spain lost the Florida* settlements to the United States in 1819 and the rest of mainland North America during the Mexican Revolution. Scholars continue to disagree on a geographical definition of the Borderlands, or Spanish Borderlands. At present, it seems that the trend is to focus on the area north of the border between Mexico and the United States, from Texas to the Pacific Coast. Others, however, include the southeastern part of the United States, from Florida to Louisiana*, and the northern tier states of Mexico.

The Borderlands was a field of American history long neglected by historians until the early twentieth century, when Herbert Eugene Bolton established the field as a legitimate and important area of study. Bolton and the hundreds of Ph.D. and M.A. students whom he trained demonstrated the significance of Borderland history to understanding the complete story of U. S. history. Indeed, before the founding of Jamestown by the English, Spain had erected a thriving empire in the New World and had sent many expeditions to what would become the United States.

REFERENCES: John Francis Bannon, *The Spanish Borderlands Frontier, 1513-1821*, 1970; Oakah L. Jones, Jr., ed., *The Spanish Borderlands: A First Reader*, 1974; David J. Weber, *Myth and History of the Hispanic Southwest*, 1988.

Raymond Wilson

BORJA, JUAN DE. Juan de Borja was born in Spain in 1564 to a prominent family. He was named president of New Granada* in 1605. During his first decade in office, Borja conducted a successful military campaign against the Pijao Indians*, finally subduing them in 1618. During his tenure of office, the Inquisition* was established in the colony and the Casa de Moneda was established. Borja died in 1628.

REFERENCES: Robert H. Davis, *Historical Dictionary of Colombia*, 1977; José Manuel Groot, *Historia eclesiástica y civil de Nueva Granada*, 5 vols., 1953.

BOURBON REFORMS. In 1700 Philip V*, the grandson of King Louis XIV, became king of Spain and launched the era of the Bourbon dynasty. Although the early years of the dynasty were consumed by the War of the Spanish Succession*, the Bourbons eventually introduced sweeping reforms into the administration of the empire. Those reforms were steadily introduced over the course of the eighteenth century, although it was during the reign of Charles III* that the most ambitious reforms were implemented. In terms of administrative structure, the Bourbons introduced new levels of efficiency into the system. They abandoned the old council system of government, replaced the Council of the Indies* with the Ministry of Marine and the Indies, established new viceroyalties at Santa Fé de Bogotá* and Río de la Plata* to provide more direct government, phased out the Casa de Contratación,* and replaced the *corregidores** with the new *intendencia**.

The Bourbons also introduced a measure of freedom into the empire's cumbersome, inefficient economic system. The Casa de Contratación, which had regulated and monopolized imperial trade, was moved from Seville* to Cádiz* in 1717 and then abolished outright in 1790. Instead, the crown allowed private companies, like the Caracas Company* or the Havana Company*, to conduct the imperial trade. The crown also abolished the fleet system gradually in the eighteenth century. That mass movement of goods in crown-controlled fleets, which was often victimized by pirates and war, was eliminated from South America in 1740 and from New Spain in 1789. Charles III also liberalized trade restrictions, opening up South American markets to other countries in hopes of creating new world markets for Spanish products. In 1778 he issued the "Free Trade"* decree. As a result, dramatic increases in exports and imports occurred throughout the empire.

In spite of the new levels of efficiency and profits in trade, the reforms did not address the fundamental problems of the Spanish empire—the resentments between *peninsulares** and *criollos**, the hierarchical racial structure of society, the stifling oppressiveness of the imperial bureaucracy, and the economic weaknesses of the Spanish economy. The Bourbon reforms were not able to eliminate the resentments which eventually led to the revolutions of the early 1800s.

REFERENCE: T. S. Floyd, ed., *The Bourbon Reforms and Spanish Civilization*, 1966.

BOVES, JOSÉ TOMÁS. José Tomás Boves was born to a poor family in Asturias, Spain, around 1770. As a young man, he made his way to the New World and labored as a smuggler* in Venezuela*. When the revolution broke out, Boves sided with royalist forces and rallied some anti-*criollo** peasants to his cause, creating animosity against Simón Bolívar*. Boves formed guerilla bands that fought valiantly against the revolutionary forces of Simón Bolívar, whom Boves ridiculed as a "*criollo* aristocrat." Boves's soldiers were motivated less by political ideology than by personal greed. They plundered the property of their enemies at every opportunity. At the Battle of La Puerta* in 1814, Boves defeated Bolívar's army and seized control of Caracas*. José Tomás Boves died six months later fighting against revolutionary forces in eastern Venezuela.

REFERENCES: Pedro Manuel Arcaya, *Estudios sobres personajes y hechos de la historia venezolana*, 1911; Donna Keyse Rudolph and G. A. Rudolph, *Historical Dictionary of Venezuela*, 1971.

BOYACÁ, BATTLE OF. The victory of the patriots, led by the Liberator, Simón Bolívar*, over the royalist army at the Battle of Boyacá on August 7, 1819, was the culmination of a campaign that effectively ended Spanish control of what is now Colombia*. By early 1819, the independence forces under Bolívar controlled eastern and southern Venezuela*, while the Spaniards held the northern Andean region. Early in the decade, much of New Granada* had declared independence of Spain, but the Spanish had reasserted their control over the area except for the *llanos* (plains) of Casanare. Bolívar had long considered New

Granada key to the independence of the entire region. Moreover, Colombia and Venezuela were, in his mind, one nation. Therefore, he decided on a surprise strike over the Andes from Venezuela to liberate the Colombian highlands. The Venezuelan *llanero* General José Antonio Páez* would stay behind to keep the Spanish forces occupied. (Authors vary as to how cooperative Páez actually was.) Those accompanying Bolívar included General Carlos Soublette*, chief of staff; General José Antonio Anzoátegui, commander of the infantry; and Colonel James Rooke, commander of the British legionnaires. The Colombian *llanero* general, Francisco Santander*, joined the march en route. Reports as to the exact strength of the force vary but were probably around 3,000. In late May 1819, following Bolívar's famous discourse at the Congress of Angostura*, the army left the banks of the Apure, in the western Venezuelan *llanos*. The rainy season had just begun, which served to protect the patriot positions in Venezuela and to conceal their movement. The weather made the plains exceedingly difficult and costly to traverse. The army then crossed the high Andes (passes over 12,000 feet) following a little-used route. The altitude and bad weather took a heavy toll on the ill-clad plainsmen, animals, and equipment. All the horses and many men perished. Nevertheless, this unexpected and dangerous march gave the patriots the advantages of surprise and dispersal of the enemy forces.

The royalist third division under Colonel José María Barreiro was stationed in New Granada. Although considered an able commander, Barreiro has been criticized for dispersing the perhaps 5,000 troops he had in the highlands and not providing for adequate intelligence to warn of the advancing army. He had the original advantage of superior numbers, equipment, and location. The patriots won the first encounter—at Paya—while still ascending. After crossing the last major pass, the patriot army rested briefly, regrouped, and replaced some of its lost men, horses, and supplies from the local population. Reports vary as to the friendliness of the civilians toward Bolívar's army. The opposing forces engaged on the Gameza river. Then Bolívar outflanked the enemy and moved to the Sogamoso valley. On July 25, the two armies met on the banks of the Sogamoso. The resulting battle of El Pántano de Vargas (Vargas swamp) was militarily inconclusive but is generally considered the turning point in the campaign. Barreiro appears to have lost his belief in the inevitability of victory over the ragtag patriot band. On August 3, Bolívar forced Barreiro out of Paipa and two days later, after a stealthy march, captured Tunja, the capital of the province of Boyacá. Barreiro was then in danger of being cut off from Bogotá. The route he chose to take toward the capital required the crossing of the bridge of Boyacá, near Tunja.

The two armies met for the decisive battle at two in the afternoon of August 7, 1819. In many respects, the situation of the two sides was reversed. The patriots were rested and confident, while Barreiro's forces were tired and had lost their reserves. The details of the two-hour battle are still disputed. The key was control of the bridge that led to Bogotá. There were perhaps two separate major skirmishes—one at the bridge and another at a distance. The *llaneros* are commonly credited with making a major contribution. Casualties on both sides were light. Still, 1,600 of the 3,000 royalist troops were captured, including Barreiro and his staff. The road was cleared to Bogotá, from which the royal officials fled upon hearing the news. Bolívar entered the capital on August 10 to the acclaim of the residents. There he established a provisional government with Santander as vice-president and acting president. Bolívar then returned to Angostura, where the Republic of Colombia was proclaimed, uniting Venezuela, New Granada, and Ecuador[*] (although the latter was as yet unliberated).

The significance of the Battle of Boyacá, indeed of the campaign, was more political than military. For a variety of reasons, New Granada was in a situation of divided loyalty. Bolívar's bold stroke in defeating the royalist army and capturing the capital swung loyalty toward the independence cause. Fighting with royalist elements would go on until 1824, but the Spanish would never again control what is now Colombia. More broadly, the victory was the first part of a chain of events leading to the liberation of northernmost South America—a sequence including the Riego revolt in Spain, the truce in Venezuela, Bolívar's victory at the second Battle of Carabobo[*], and Antonio José de Sucre's[*] victory at Pichincha[*].

REFERENCES: Jesus María Henao and Gerardo Arrubla, *History of Colombia*, 1938; Salvador de Madariaga, *Bolívar*, 1952; Gerhard Masur, *Simón Bolívar*, 1969; Daniel Florencio O'Leary, *Bolívar and the War of Independence*, 1970.

Robert E. Biles

BRAVO, LEONARDO. Leonardo Bravo was born in 1764 to a prominent *criollo*[*] family in New Spain. He became a follower of José María Morelos[*] in the early 1800s and fought energetically for the revolution. He was an important military leader under Morelos and spent some time as the governor of the province of Tecpán. Royalist forces captured and executed him in 1812.

REFERENCE: John A. Caruso, *The Liberators of Mexico*, 1967.

BRAZIL. Colonial Brazil must be viewed in the wider context of European and Portuguese overseas expansion in the fifteenth and sixteenth centuries. European powers reached out to Africa, India, and Asia, eager to tap the rich commerce available there. Portugal first ventured seaward under the leadership of Prince Henry (1394–1460), christened "the Navigator" by an appreciative English writer. By 1488 Bartolomeu Dias had rounded the Cape of Good Hope and the Portuguese were soon deeply involved in a commercial empire stretching the length of the Indian Ocean and beyond. Under the leadership of Afonso d'Albuquerque, Governor of India[*] (1509–1515), the Portuguese extended their commercial control over the Indian Ocean sea routes. In these early decades of the sixteenth century, the Portuguese were mainly interested in establishing commercial footholds, with an emphasis on merchants, not settlers. As a result of such enterprises, a small nation exerted an enormous influence over the developing world system of the sixteenth century through its factories, trading forts and commercial agents.

The discoveries of Columbus* in the 1490s created friction between the Portuguese and Spanish that was settled by the Treaty of Tordesillas* (1494), granting to Portugal a large part of the eastern coast of South America. Neither country could legitimately claim the Americas exclusively, and they were soon challenged by French, Dutch, and English explorers. In fact, the vastness of the new discoveries played a role in the Portuguese decision to settle Brazil. In early 1500, Pedro Alvares Cabral left with a large fleet bound for India to follow the earlier discoveries of Vasco Da Gama. During the voyage he changed course, sailed further west than intended, and made landfall on the Brazilian coast in April. However, the discovery was greeted with no great enthusiasm at home, as the commercial empire in the East commanded far keener attention. In the years after 1500, sporadic voyages to Brazil uncovered no great Amerindian empires and no vast treasures to be plundered. In fact, the only item of commercial value uncovered was the bark of a native tree—brazilwood—which was processed into a valuable commercial dye.

It was this dyewood which forced the Portuguese to guard their possession more closely. French ships regularly visited the coast of Brazil in the years 1502–1530, bartering trade goods with Tupí-Guaraní people for the red bark found in abundance along the coast. After years of complaining in vain to the French monarch, Portugal sent Martim Afonso da Souza with five ships and 400 men to found permanent settlements in Brazil in 1532. They built the town of Sao Vicente, near the modern port city of Santos, along the southern coast.

Although a success, it soon became clear that other settlements had to be established to effectively control the vast Brazilian coast. The Portuguese king offered large grants to those with the means to undertake colonization of the new land, and by 1536 fifteen huge grants, called captaincies, existed, extending from the northern Amazon coast to the border of present-day Uruguay*. However, most of these captaincies failed due to lack of population, adverse conditions for agriculture, and constant intrusions by foreigners.

Two of the hereditary grants succeeded. In Pernambuco, on the northeastern coast, Duarte Coelho achieved great success through the cultivation of sugar cane, tobacco, and cotton. He avoided conflict with local Indians and soon had over fifty sugar mills processing cane. By the 1580s his heirs were sending hundreds of sugar ships annually to Europe and were among the wealthiest of all Portuguese. The captaincy at Sao Vicente also flourished with sugar and reported six mills by mid-century. The others languished, however, and the king soon instituted changes. In 1549 he sent Tome da Souza as the first governor-general of Brazil. Salvador da Bahia, a major disappointment as a captaincy, became the seat of a new central administration and the king committed one thousand soldiers and artisans to ensure the success of da Souza.

In the years that followed, sugar quickly became the dominant agricultural enterprise and Brazilian producers supplied the insatiable European markets. A pattern of monoculture, heavily dependent upon fickle world markets, was set in place in Brazil. Sugar was followed by gold and diamonds in the early eighteenth century, coffee and cotton in the nineteenth century, and rubber in the early twentieth century. The prosperity of the colony and its development was tied to the waning fortunes of its export products. This is a trend that has plagued Brazil throughout its history.

One serious problem Tome da Souza and his successors faced was the need for a steady, reliable source of labor. Local Amerindians at first supplied these needs, but as plantations grew in size and complexity, they could no longer fill the demand. Harsh working conditions, susceptibility to European diseases, and a lack of Crown officials to supervise Indian-Portuguese relations led to a disastrous decline in Amerindian numbers. Despite attempts by Portuguese Jesuits[*], such as Manoel da Nobrega, and official policy that forbade exploitation, mortality rates as high as 80 percent were recorded in many areas in the sixteenth century. Survivors fled to the interior, although they were hunted by slave-catching expeditions for another century.

The continuing labor problem led to the importation of Africans in large numbers after 1550. More than 3.5 million Africans came to Brazil in the next three centuries. A racial heritage of African, Amerindian, and European mixtures grew out of the institution of plantation agriculture. Labor conditions remained harsh, and slaves imported to the sugar areas of northeastern Brazil or to the developing center-south region, with its mineral resources and cattle ranches, often survived less than a decade. The colony had its share of slave revolts, with runaway slaves at times forming refuge communities in the interior. The famous slave republic, or *quilombo*, known as Palmares appeared in 1603 and eventually encompassed a dozen villages spread over a 100-square mile area. Palmares survived nearly a century.

As the eighteenth century began, local and international events altered the path of Brazilian development. Northeastern Brazil began a long and serious decline as its grip on the world sugar market loosened and then faded completely. In 1630 the Dutch West India Company invaded the northeast and held it for nearly a quarter century. Although ultimately expelled, they took the valuable knowledge of sugar production with them to the Caribbean. Within fifty years, Caribbean colonies were out-producing Brazil and had captured three-fourths of its sugar business.

This unfortunate turn was partially saved by the discovery of gold in the center-south region known as Minas Gerais in 1695. Thirty-four years later, a major diamond strike occurred there, drawing population and commerce from the northeast and leading, along with increased Portuguese interest in the Plata River region (present-day Uruguay), to the establishment of Rio de Janeiro as the colonial capital in 1763. Although the mineral cycle played out within a half-century, it did spark economic development in Brazil's southern regions. The cattle industry began producing large herds after the mineral discoveries and soon extended from the northeast interior to the extreme south.

The ironic situation of a small Atlantic kingdom governing a huge Latin American colony became more apparent as the nineteenth century began. By

1800 Brazil possessed a handful of small port cities and a few mining centers, with its remaining population dispersed over a 2,000-mile frontier. The masters of large plantations and cattle ranches governed themselves and Portuguese royal authority was confined to the small urban centers. In the interests of tightening control, Portuguese ministers, such as the capable Marquis de Pombal, instituted new regulations in the 1760s and 1770s that strengthened the mother country's hold, but Brazil was too large and geographically diverse for the small number of Portuguese officials to govern it. However, Brazilians were affected by the new fiscal policies and chafed under restrictions that favored Portuguese interests over their own. There were several abortive revolts in the 1780s and 1790s.

The last revolution began in 1807 when Napoleon invaded the Iberian peninsula. The result for Portugal was the improbable escape of the monarch, Dom João (John VI), and thousands of his royal retinue, courtesy of an English fleet, to Brazil. João remained in Brazil until 1821, long after Napoleon's defeat and the restoration of Portuguese independence. He and his family enjoyed life in the colony and their presence brought prosperity and a closer connection with Europe. The eager purveyors of European goods to the now suddenly elevated colony (João decreed Brazil a kingdom co-equal with Portugal in 1815) were the English. They flooded Brazil with all manner of formerly scarce merchandise and eagerly bought raw materials. When a political crisis in Portugal forced João's hand in 1821, he returned to claim his throne, but left his son Pedro behind as regent. When the Portuguese formally attempted to abrogate Brazil's new status and demanded the return of the popular young prince, Pedro refused, and with the backing of the Brazilian elite, he declared the country independent on September 7, 1822. After several months of slight resistence, Pedro became Brazil's constitutional emperor. Brazil retained an emperor until 1889, when a mild revolution created a republic.

REFERENCES: C. R. Boxer, *The Golden Age of Brazil*, 1967; E. Bradford Burns, *A History of Brazil*, 1984.

Craig Hendricks

BRITISH HONDURAS. Now the modern nation of Belize, British Honduras was the territory lying directly east of the Guatemalan Petén, bordering the Caribbean. Originally part of the province of Guatemala* (and still considered so by Guatemalan nationalists), British Honduras was an underpopulated and isolated region of the kingdom of Guatemala*. During the 1660s, British logwood cutters, in violation of Spanish commercial and trade restrictions, began to settle illegally at the mouth of the Belize River and to exploit the area for valuable dyewoods and hardwoods, particularly mahogany. The name "Belize" comes from a corruption of the name of Peter Wallace (or Willis), a British buccaneer who, according to legend, sought refuge from Spanish authorities on the Belize River sometime around 1650. The Belize originally referred to the English settlement on the Belize River, while the territory was referred to as Honduras, later British Honduras.

British Honduras became a pawn in the rivalry between England and Spain during the sixteenth and seventeenth centuries. During this period of the wars of the Protestant Reformation and Britain's desire to trade with Spain's valuable colonies, the circum-Caribbean area—the "Spanish Main," as it was called by the British—became a lawless zone ruled by British, French, and Dutch privateers. By the late seventeenth century, British Honduras had beome an important contraband entrepôt and a base for British pirates* and buccaneers who harassed Spanish settlements along the Central American coast. In 1670, the Godolphin Treaty between England and Spain acknowledged that England had a right to certain islands and countries in the West Indies*. The treaty did not specify, however, that British Honduras fell under British jurisdiction, and the area remained a source of dispute. In 1713, in the Treaty of Utrecht*, Spain denied British log cutters the right to work there, but because there was no effective Spanish occupation of the area, the British residents of British Honduras remained unchallenged. By the Treaty of Paris in 1763*, the British officially recognized Spanish sovereignty over British Honduras, while the Spanish conceded the right of the English to cut dyewoods and retain their settlements in the territory. Despite these negotiations, British Honduras remained a British colony for all practical purposes from 1660 to 1981, when it gained its independence from Great Britain and took the name of Belize.

In 1713, Spain granted Britain an *asiento** (a monopoly to supply African slaves* to Spanish colonies). The first black slaves were brought to the colony around 1720 from Jamaica*. By the end of the eighteenth century, the population of British Honduras was predominantly black; 2,132 of the total population of 2,915 were slaves, although some of these were Amerinds from the Mosquito Coast* of Honduras* and Nicaragua*. Slaves worked in British Honduras's primary industry, timber, especially in the harvesting of mahogony. They also labored on sugar* plantations, which developed in the colony after slavery was introduced. In 1807, British law forbade its subjects from trading in African slaves. The passage of this law simply allowed yet another contraband trade to flourish in Belize—the smuggling of slaves. In 1833, slavery was outlawed in all British colonies, and the contraband trade in slaves ended, as did British Honduras's slave-based labor system. The legacy of slavery in British Honduras is that the vast majority of the population are black, Protestant, and English-speaking. This fact reinforced Belize's autonomy from Guatemala, which continues to claim sovereignty over the territory to the present day.

REFERENCE: Narda Dobson, *A History of Belize*, 1973.

Virginia Garrard Burnett

BUCARELI Y URSÚA, ANTONIO MARÍA DE. Antonio María de Bucareli y Ursúa was born in Spain in 1717 and spent the first half of his career as an officer in the Spanish army. In 1760, Bucareli was appointed governor of Cuba*,

116

BUENOS AIRES

a post he kept until 1771 when he was appointed viceroy* of New Spain*. Bucareli was known as an efficient administrator interested in economic development and political stability. He worked deliberately at pushing the frontiers of New Spain further into the Borderlands*, especially up the California* coast, and he actively saw to the construction of hospitals, schools, and improved facilities for the mentally ill. Bucareli died in 1779 while serving as viceroy.

REFERENCE: Bernard E. Bobb, *The Viceregency of Antonio María Bucareli in New Spain, 1771–1779,* 1962.

BUENOS AIRES. Sebastián Cabot* explored the Río de la Plata* in the 1520s. In 1530, thinking that the river was a conduit to Peru*, Pedro de Mendoza* established a settlement at the site of present-day Buenos Aires. When it became clear that the river would not reach all the way to Peru, the settlement was abandoned. Buenos Aires was permanently established in 1580 by Juan de Garay*, who brought settlers from Asunción* to build a livestock industry. At the time, the entire region was under the political jurisdiction of the viceroyalty of Peru*. Spain established the province of Buenos Aires in 1618 by splitting the province of Río de la Plata into Buenos Aires and Paraguay*. The *audiencia* of Buenos Aires* was created in 1661 to handle the population growth and economic development in the area, but the *audiencia* was discontinued in 1671 and the area continued to fall under the direction of the *audiencia* of Charcas*. By the end of the seventeenth century, Buenos Aires was a major exporter of hides*, tallow, and beef jerky, the premier products of its burgeoning cattle industry. Wheat farming began in the late eighteenth century. In 1776, the Spanish Crown created the viceroyalty of the Río de la Plata*, separating what is today Argentina*, Uruguay*, Paraguay, and Bolivia* from the viceroyalty of Peru. The population of Buenos Aires then totaled 24,000 people. The Spanish Crown designated the province an intendancy in 1783. By 1800, Buenos Aires totaled nearly 50,000 people and had become a center of the independence movement, which achieved success in the area by 1816.

REFERENCES: Woodbine Parish, *Buenos Aires and the Provinces of the Río de la Plata,* 1958; Stanley R. Ross and Thomas F. McGann, *Buenos Aires: 400 Years,* 1982.

BUENOS AIRES, *AUDIENCIA* OF. The city of Buenos Aires* was founded permanently in 1580, but its population grew relatively slowly until the mid-eighteenth century. The crown established the *audiencia* of Buenos Aires in 1661 to deal with the legal and judicial problems in the region; the *audiencia* was subordinate to the viceroyalty of Peru*. But the *audiencia* was suppressed in 1671. By the mid-1700s, Spain had begun to relax its restrictive mercantilist* policies, and Buenos Aires became a major exporter of tallow, hides*, and meat to the rest of the empire. The population of Buenos Aires increased from only 2,500 people in 1720 to nearly 24,000 people in 1776. That year the Crown created the viceroyalty of Río de la Plata*, with jurisdiction over Upper Peru*, Paraguay*, Argentina*, and Uruguay*. The *audiencia* of Buenos Aires began to function again in 1783. At that point, the viceroy* became the head of the *audiencia* of Buenos Aires.

REFERENCES: Mark A. Burkholder and D. S. Chandler, *From Impotence to Authority: The Spanish Crown and the American Audiencias, 1687-1808*, 1977; James R. Scobie, *Argentina: A City and a Nation*, 1971.

BUENOS AIRES, DIOCESE OF. The Roman Catholic diocese of Buenos Aires was established in 1620, but it was not raised to an archbishopric until 1865.

REFERENCE: *New Catholic Encyclopedia*, II:857–58, 1967.

BURGOS, JOSÉ. José Burgos was the most prominent of the three Filipino* priests martyred in February 1872 for their alleged role in instigating the Cavite Mutiny*. Burgos was three-fourths Spanish, from an elite *mestizo** family from Vigan, Ilocos* Sur. He had received a very distinguished education at the College of San Juan of Letran and the University of Santo Tomás. He was awarded a doctorate in theology the year before his public execution at the age of 30. Burgos's real sin, in the eyes of fearful colonial officials, was that he championed native priests in their campaign to take over parishes from Spanish friars. The Spanish governor-general believed that Spanish rule would be undermined if native Filipinos ran the churches. Father Burgos was falsely accused and condemned. In death, he symbolized Spanish persecution of Filipinos.

REFERENCE: Teodoro Agoncillo, *Filipino Nationalism 1872–1970*, 1974.

Ross Marlay

BURGOS, LAWS OF (1512). The first phase of the Spanish discovery and conquest of America took place on the larger islands of the Caribbean—Hispaniola*, Puerto Rico*, Cuba*, Jamaica*—between 1492 and 1515. It was a bitter encounter between two different civilizations, Spanish and Indian, Christian and pagan, and resulted in the gradual destruction and absorption of the Arawak* population. But there were also protests, and "the first cry on behalf of human liberty in the New World," in the words of Lewis Hanke, occurred in Hispaniola on the Sunday before Christmas 1511 when the Dominican* friar Antonio de Montesinos delivered a sermon, followed by many others, in which he protested the treatment that the conquistadors* were inflicting on the natives. He was aiming at the *encomienda**, officially introduced by Governor Nicolás de Ovando* in Hispaniola in 1502, which was a royal grant to a meritorious Spaniard for the purpose of exacting labor or tribute from the vanquished Indians*, in line with the Aristotelian concept of slavery*. The conduct of the settlers ran counter to the official policy of both Church and Crown, and thus the dispute spread quickly to the Peninsula. Since the issue was important, it could not be entrusted to normal channels. The two parties therefore sent their respective delegates: the Franciscan* Alonso del Espinal was to represent the point of view of the settlers; Montesinos himself was to speak on behalf of the Dominicans for the natives.

This was the beginning of an extraordinary debate on both sides of the Atlantic, the great controversy of the sixteenth century that lasted for more than fifty years and concerned three interrelated subjects: the treatment of the Indians, the concept of just war, and the titles for the conquest. It was also in this context that Erasmus and St. Thomas More became influential in the Indies. When King Ferdinand* was confronted with the grievances, he immediately ordered a council of theologians and civil servants to meet and debate the issues and to come up with the necessary legislation. The council met in Burgos, and the result of the deliberations was the Laws of Burgos, of December 27, 1512, which brought about two main changes.

In the first place, the papal donation as the legal title for the *Conquista* was no longer considered a sufficient case as argued by Juan López de Palacios Rubios, Matías de Paz. This argument led to the *requerimiento** (valid until 1543), which was a document that potential conquistadors had to carry with them and read to the Indians, who were then asked to pay homage to the pope as their spiritual leader and to the king as their temporal head. The second change involved the *encomienda*; it was confirmed but the Laws of Burgos specified in detail the Christian duties and responsibilities of the settlers in regard to their Indian vassals. When the Laws of Burgos became known in Hispaniola, they did not satisfy the Dominican friars who then insisted on changes. The amendments that were subsequently introduced—the further protection of Indian women and children, the compulsion for Indians to wear clothes, and the possibility for children to learn a trade—resulted in the clarification of 1513.

The Laws of Burgos represented the first step to set things straight and were part of the need to make royal and civil actions conform to the natural law. They also explain the great official concern with the ethical foundation of Spain's policy in the Indies. After all, no empire in modern times has been built upon such solid and extensive theological and philosophical foundations as the one that the Spanish conquistadors carved out in the sixteenth century and that among others, resulted in the modern law of nations.

REFERENCES: Lewis Hanke, *The Spanish Struggle for Justice in the Conquest of America*, 1949; O. Carlos Stoetzer, *The Scholastic Roots of the Spanish American Revolution*, 1979.

O. Carlos Stoetzer

BUSTAMANTE CARLOS INCA, CALIXTO. See CONCOLORCORVO.

BUSTAMANTE, CARLOS MARÍA DE. Carlos María de Bustamante was born on November 4, 1774, in Oaxaca*, New Spain*. He studied law in France and began a legal practice in Guadalajara*, New Spain, in 1801. Bustamante became involved in the early independence movement, and he published a revolutionary newspaper, *El juguetillo*. During the Mexican war for independence, Bustamante was an army officer. After the war, he served as Emperor Agustín de Iturbide's* secretary. Bustamante was a member of the national legislature for 22 years. A prolific writer and historian, Bustamante's most famous work was the *Caudro histórico de la Revolución de la América Mexicana*, a liberal history of the independence movement. Carlos María de Bustamante died in Mexico City on September 21, 1848.

REFERENCE: Victoriano Salado Alvarez, *La vida azorosa y romantica de don Carlos María de Bustamante*, 1933.

BUSTAMANTE Y GUERRA, JOSÉ DE. The president of the *audiencia* of Guatemala* from 1811 until 1817, José de Bustamante was the archetypal Bourbon bureaucrat. A military man who held the title of captain general, Bustamante firmly upheld the traditional political values of centralism and royal absolutism. This position pitted him directly against the emerging wealthy, *criollo**, liberal merchants of Guatemala*. Bustamante's efforts to limit the power of José de Aycinena*, the wealthy *criollo* merchant, symbolized the emerging struggle between conservative centralism and liberalism that would typify Central America's political struggles during most of the nineteenth century.

In 1811, Bustamante arrived to serve as intendant of the kingdom of Guatemala*, a managerial post created by the Bourbon rulers. He had previously served as governor-general of Montevideo*, where he had earned a distinguished reputation in combating the vast contraband trade on the Río de la Plata*. In 1806, he had failed to repel a British attack on a Spanish settlement, and had been recalled to Spain. Bustamante's experience in Montevideo had hardened him against the contraband trade, so upon arriving in Central America, he immediately curtailed all illegal foreign trade. This made him an enemy in the eyes of the merchants of Guatemala, led by Aycinena, who sought greatly expanded markets for their indigo*, cotton, and wool*. The merchants openly defied Bustamante's strict orders not to engage in illegal trade with the British. Eager to quash the merchants' insubordination, Bustamante struck at the powerful Aycinena family. He prevented family members from holding high public office, pressed a legal suit for back taxes against them, and denied them the government protection and advantage that they had enjoyed as members of the *criollo* aristocracy. His strong-arm rule and suspicion of the *criollos* led to two uprisings, one in Belén* and the other in El Salvador*, which the captain general successfully put down. In 1818, pressure from powerful *criollo* merchants and liberal *oidores** on the Guatemalan *audiencia** forced Bustamante to step down from office. A few years later, when the restored government of Ferdinand VII* sought to strengthen ties with Guatemalan merchants, Bustamante was indicted for malfeasance in office.

REFERENCE: Miles L. Wortman, *Government and Society in Central America, 1680-1840*, 1982.

Virginia Garrard Burnett

C

CABALLERO, PEDRO JUAN. Pedro Juan Caballero was born in 1786 and became a hero of the independence movement in Paraguay*. When General Manuel Belgrano* of Argentina* invaded Paraguay in May 1811 in order to keep Paraguay in the Argentine sphere of influence, Caballero played a central role in Belgrano's defeats at Paraguarí and Tacuarí. On May 14, 1811, Caballero became a member of the first governing junta of Paraguay. Nine years later, after being accused and arrested on charges of plotting to overthrow the government, Caballero committed suicide in a prison cell.

REFERENCE: Charles J. Kolinski, *Historical Dictionary of Paraguay*, 1973.

CABALLERO DE LA TORRE, JOSÉ AGUSTÍN. José Agustín Caballero de la Torre was born in Havana*, Cuba*, in 1771. He was extremely active in educational reform and eventually became the director of science for the Economic Society of Cuba, editor of *Papel Periódico*, founder of the Society of Friends (an elitist think tank that counted among its members José de Luz y Caballero, Félix Varela y Morales, José Antonio Saco*, and others), and author of the document "A Constitutional Project" (1811), an early call for Cuban autonomy. He also wrote *Memorias para reformar los estudios universitarios* (1797) and *Lecciones de filosofía ecléctica* (1797). In terms of his politics, Caballero de la Torre was an early advocate of Cuban autonomy within the Spanish Empire. He died in 1835.

REFERENCE: Antonio Bachiller y Morales, *Apuntes para la historia de las letras y las instrucciones en la isla de Cuba*, 3 vols., 1953.

Fred Koestler

CABALLERO Y GÓNGORA, ANTONIO. Antonio Caballero y Góngora was born of noble lineage in 1723 in Priego, province of Córdoba, in Spain. The second surviving son of his family, he studied for the priesthood in Granada where he received holy orders in 1750. Thereafter, he served as chaplain of the royal chapel in Granada and, from 1753 to 1775, as canon in the chapter house of the cathedral of Córdoba. His impressive merits gained notice at court, and Charles III* presented Caballero y Góngora's name to the papacy as bishop of Yucatán* in 1775. He took possession the following year. Soon after, he was promoted to archbishop of Santa Fe de Bogotá*, a position he occupied in early 1779.

Unusual circumstances soon propelled Caballero y Góngora into the secular sphere. In May 1781, the viceroy* on the coast was directing its wartime defenses and the remaining authorities were cowering in the face of the massive popular resistance to the radical revenue reforms of Regent Visitor Juan Francisco Gutiérrez de Piñeres. The archbishop accepted responsibility for confronting the *comuneros** and negotiated a settlement that kept them out of the viceregal capital. Second in line for emergency succession to the viceregency, he became interim viceroy when Manuel de Flores, stricken by illness, resigned and when the first in line, Governor Juan Pimienta of Cartagena*, died soon after reaching Santa Fe. Caballero y Góngora received a full appointment the following year.

An aggressive, imaginative administrator, the archbishop-viceroy is best remembered for the enlightened tone of his rule. He championed educational reform and he secured royal approval for the botanical expedition of José Celestino Mutis, for a mining reform mission under the direction of Juan José D'Elhuyar, and for an economic society to promote applied learning. He advanced the cause of administrative centralism and forcefully raised treasury receipts to levels unequaled during the colonial period. Caballero y Góngora also closely associated himself with the military. To sustain royal authority in the interior, he secured both the establishment of a regiment of regular troops for Santa Fe and the creation of a disciplined militia* under the command of Spanish officers; he began work on fortifying the capital. Assisted by Colonel Anastasio Zejudo, he imposed order on the colonial army, from Quito* to Panama* to Cartagena. Finally, he committed some 1,000 combat troops to pacify the aboriginals of Darién* and to facilitate permanent colonization. Supervising that operation, he resided on the coast at Turbaco during much of his administration. Despite improved treasury receipts, the archbishop-viceroy left a huge debt, resulting in large measure from military expenditures and the growing bureaucracy. To improve colonial finance, his successors undid much of his work, including the Darién expedition, the militarization of the interior, and the mining reform mission. Caballero y Góngora transferred power to Francisco Gil y Lemos in January 1789, becoming archbishop of Córdoba, where he remained until his death in 1796.

REFERENCES: Allan J. Kuethe, *Military Reform and Society in New Granada, 1773–1808*, 1978; José Manuel Pérez Ayala, *Antonio Caballero y Góngora, virrey y arzobispo de Santa Fe, 1723–1796*, 1951; John Leddy Phelan, *The People and the King: The Comunero Revolution in Colombia, 1781*, 1978.

Allan J. Kuethe

CABELLO Y MESA, FRANCISCO ANTONIO. Francisco Antonio Cabello y Mesa was born in Extremadura, Spain, in 1764. He received a legal education but pursued a career in the Spanish army; in 1790, he was posted to Peru*. An intellectual intrigued with the ideas of the Enlightenment, Cabello's interests were more political than military. In 1790, he founded the first periodical published in South America—*El Diario Curioso, Erudito, y Comercial*. He moved to Buenos Aires* late in the 1790s and in 1801 published the first issue of another periodical—*El Telégrafo Mercantil, Rural, Político e Histórico*. Cabello gradually developed ideas about democracy, natural rights, and independence, and he was eventually charged with collaborating with the British during their occupation of the Río de la Plata* area in 1806–1807. He was exiled to Spain by the viceroy* and lived in Seville*, where he remained active in liberal politics. Cabello was executed by firing squad in 1814 after the restoration of Ferdinand VII* to the Spanish throne.

REFERENCES: Enrique Udaondo, *Diccionario biográfico colonial argentino*, 1945; Ione S. Wright and Lisa M. Nekhom, *Historical Dictionary of Argentina*, 1978.

CABEZA DE VACA, ALVAR NÚÑEZ. Alvar Núñez Cabeza de Vaca was born in Jérez de la Frontera, Spain, around 1490, to a locally prominent family. Cabeza de Vaca entered the military and fought in several Mediterranean campaigns before going to the New World in 1527 as treasurer and financial officer for an expedition led by Pánfilo de Narváez* to explore the Gulf coast of North America. Narváez led an exploring group inland from the Florida* coast, but they eventually lost contact with their ships, which sailed for New Spain*. The land expedition headed north toward the Florida panhandle, unsuccessfully looking for gold among the Indians*. Late in 1528, they constructed several barges and sailed west along the Gulf coast toward Texas*. They reached Galveston Island after several months.

In the spring of 1529, the Spaniards departed from Galveston, leaving Cabeza de Vaca behind because of illness. He lived with several Texas Indian tribes, and in 1533 he met up again with three survivors of the original expedition. Between 1533 and 1536, they marched from the Gulf coast to San Antonio, out to present-day New Mexico*, south through Sonora, and down to Mexico City*. Their description of the American Southwest led to the expedition of Francisco Vásquez de Coronado* in 1542.

Cabeza de Vaca returned to Spain in 1537, but he was appointed governor of the province of Río de la Plata* in 1542. He arrived at Asunción* in 1542. After just two years, he was deposed as governor and sent back to Spain. The subsequent litigation and trial took years before Cabeza de Vaca was convicted of abuse of power while in office. He died in poverty in 1556.

REFERENCES: Morris Bishop, *The Odyssey of Cabeza de Vaca*, 1933; Cleve Hallenbeck, *Alvar Núñez Cabeza de Vaca: The Journey and Route of the First European to Cross the Continent of North America*, 1940.

CABILDO. The *cabildo* or municipal council, patterned after a similar institution that had existed on the Iberian peninsula since Roman times and that later evolved into the Castilian municipality of the Middle Ages, was brought to the New World and the Philippines* by the Spanish conquistadors* who founded new towns as they entered recently conquered territories. The *cabildo* not only ruled over these towns but also over the surrounding rural areas that comprised the district. It would play an important role in the Spanish imperial system because it represented local interests in contradistinction to other institutions that represented the interests of the Spanish Crown and Spain.

*Alcaldes ordinarios** (magistrates) and *regidores** (councilors), whose number would depend on the importance of the city and surrounding district that they administered, composed the *cabildo*. In the smaller towns, there would be between four and six *regidores* and one *alcalde*, while in the larger cities, such as Mexico City* and Lima*, there would be eight or more *regidores* and two *alcaldes*. There were other municipal offices attached to the *cabildo*, such as *alférez real* (herald or municipal standard bearer), *alguacil mayor* (chief constable), *receptor de penas* (collector of judicial fines), and so forth. The *regidores* or *alcaldes** would often exercise these extra functions.

During the initial period of conquest and colonization, the *adelantado** (first governor of a conquered territory) chose the *cabildo*'s first *alcaldes* and *regidores*. After this period, all the *vecinos* (citizens) or property owners elected the *cabildo* members. Under Philip II*, the fiscal necessities of the empire led to the sale of these offices to the highest bidder. By the beginning of the seventeenth century, most of these offices had become not only proprietary but also hereditary. In other towns, these offices were part proprietary and part elective. In the less important towns, the *cabildo* seats often remained vacant because of a lack of buyers.

The *cabildo*'s functions were many and could be quite lucrative to the *cabildo* officeholders. They distributed land to the citizens, imposed local taxes, levied a militia* for self-defense, gave building permits, maintained jails and roads, supervised market prices, and so forth. They also had the added privilege of communicating directly with the king. The *cabildo* ceased to be a functional institution near the end of the colonial period because of the increasing centralization of the Crown.

Besides the Spanish *cabildo*, there was a parallel Indian* *cabildo* that administered the local government in the Indian towns and maintained order through its policing functions. The Indian *cabildo* contained the offices of *alcalde*, *regidores*, *escribano* (scribe), and *alguacil* (sheriff). The Indian *cabildo* had functions similar to the Spanish one. The main difference was that the Indian *alcalde* could only investigate, capture, and bring criminals to the jail located in the

Spanish city of the district, which was where major offenses were punished. He could, at times, punish minor offenses, such as public drunkenness or failure to attend Mass. The Indian *cabildo* shared jurisdiction with the cacique[*] or dynastic ruler, the *corregidor*[*] (Spanish lieutenant governor), Spanish priests, and the *encomendero* (holder of an inalienable grant of Indian labor). The caciques were responsible for the distribution of Indian labor, while the Indian *alcaldes* and *regidores* were responsible for the rest of the duties regarding Indian government. The *cajas de comunidad* (community treasuries) paid for municipal expenses.

The *cabildo abierto* (open municipal council) revitalized the Spanish *cabildo* during the Spanish-American independence period. The *cabildo abierto* was a larger assembly that traditionally dealt with grave matters affecting the city or town. The most notable citizens, as well as the bishop and principal clergy, would attend the assembly. The Spanish-American *cabildo* represented the local interests of the *criollos*[*] against the *peninsulares*.[*] During the independence period, it was often the *cabildo* that declared independence from Spain.

REFERENCES: C. H. Haring, *The Spanish Empire in America*, 1947; Constantino Bayle, *Los Cabildos Seculares en la América Española*, 1952.

Carlos Pérez

CABOT, SEBASTIÁN. Sebastián Cabot, the son of explorer John Cabot, was born in Venice, Italy, in 1484. He claimed to have accompanied his father on the 1497 voyage to North America, as well as leading a second voyage there himself in 1508, but evidence for both trips is sketchy at best. In 1512, the younger Cabot joined the Spanish naval service, and fourteen years later, he led an expedition to the New World. Originally the expedition was headed for the Far East, but Cabot changed directions at the Cape Verde Islands and ended up in the port of Recife, Brazil. After hearing rumors of a wealthy white king living in the Río de la Plata[*] region, Cabot set sail south down the coast of Brazil. Between 1527 and 1530, he explored extensively up the Paraná and Paraguay Rivers, opening up this region for Spanish exploitation. In 1530, Cabot returned to Spain. He went to England in 1548 and spent the rest of his life in the employ of the Muscovy Company, trying in vain to find the Northwest Passage[*] to the Indies. Sebastián Cabot died in 1557.

REFERENCE: Henry Harrisse, *John Cabot: The Discoverer of North America and Sebastián His Son*, 1896.

CABRERA, JERÓNIMO LUIS DE. Jerónimo Luis de Cabrera was born in Seville,[*] Spain, in 1528. He came to the New World with his older brother in 1538 and lived in Cuzco[*], Peru[*]. Cabrera opted for the life of a conquistador[*] and explorer; in 1572, he became governor of Tucumán[*]. Cabrera explored widely throughout the region and in 1573 founded the city of Córdoba[*]. He then pushed up the Paraná River and met up with the expedition of Juan de Garay[*]. When Cabrera returned to Tucumán, he learned that he had lost his governorship to Gonzalo de Abreu. Abreu had Cabrera executed in 1574.

REFERENCE: Machain Lafuente, *Los conquistadores de la Plata*, 1943.

CABRERA, JOSÉ ANTONIO. José Antonio Cabrera was born in 1768 in Córdoba*, Argentina*. He received a law degree from the University of San Felipe* and practiced law there until the May Revolution* of 1810. He then joined patriot forces in working to overthrow Spanish domination. In 1811, Cabrera served as first *alcalde** of the *cabildo** in Córdoba, and in 1816, he was a Cordoban delegate to the Congress of Tucumán*. Cabrera signed the Declaration of Independence of Argentina in 1816. He retired to private life in 1817 and died in Córdoba in 1820.

REFERENCE: Ione S. Wright and Lisa M. Nekhom, *Historical Dictionary of Argentina*, 1978.

CABRERA, RAIMUNDO. Raimundo Cabrera was born in Havana*, Cuba*, in 1852. He was imprisoned as an adolescent for anti-Spanish activities and was exiled to Spain where he studied law. He returned to Cuba in the 1870s, and although he did not participate in the Ten Years War*, his commitment to Cuban independence was unwavering. He became the founding father of the Liberal Party in 1879 and campaigned for the abolition of slavery* and political equality for all Cubans. Disgusted with Spanish intransigence, Cabrera went to New York in 1895 and published the magazine *Cuba and America*. It became the leading independence journal, and Cabrera thereby became one of the most prominent people in the Cuban independence movement. When independence was secured, Cabrera returned to Havana where he wrote books and published the newspaper* *La Unión*, which became his forum for advocating the preservation of democracy in Cuba. He died in 1923.

REFERENCES: Ramiro Guerra y Sánchez, *Historia de la nación cubana*, 10 vols., 1952; Jaime Suchlicki, *Historical Dictionary of Cuba*, 1988.

CABRILLO, JUAN RODRÍGUEZ. Little is known about Juan Rodríguez Cabrillo's origins except that he was born in Portugal in the 1490s. In 1520, he served as a soldier in Pánfilo de Narváez's* expedition to Mexico* and Central America. He then served in Pedro de Alvarado's* campaign in Guatemala*. He was a gifted shipbuilder and constructed Hernán Cortés's* ships on the lakes of Mexico City*. He also constructed a number of ships for Alvarado. Cabrillo led an expedition from New Spain* up the coast of California* in 1542, making his way as far north as present-day Santa Barbara. While wintering at the Santa Barbara Channel Islands, Juan Rodríguez Cabrillo died on January 3, 1543, in an accidental fall.

REFERENCES: Henry R. Wagner, *Spanish Voyages to the Northwest Coast of America in the Sixteenth Century*, 1929; Henry R. Wagner, *Juan Rodríguez Cabrillo, Discoverer of the Coast of California*, 1941.

CACAO. Cacao is both a tropical evergreen tree of the family Sterculiaceae and its fruit. The name of the tree is derived from its Nahuatl* name, "cacahuatl." The most common and widely cultivated species is *Theobroma cacao*. Native to tropical America (Southern Mexico and Guatemala), *T. cacao* is now grown around the world on well-drained soils, below 1,000 feet, and within 20 degrees of the equator. This is a lower canopy tree 20 to 40 feet tall with spreading branches. When grown commercially, the trees, especially immature ones, are shaded by taller species. The tree flowers twice a year. The flowers appear on the branches and trunks and are followed by elliptical fruit about 30 centimeters long and 10 centimeters in diameter. These are harvested from October to February and from May to August. A mature tree will produce 60 to 70 fruit per year. The fruit is fleshy and ridged longitudinally. The color varies from red to yellow to purplish to brown. In cells within the fruit and surrounded by an acid pulp are 20 to 40 large brown or purple seeds rich in carbohydrates and cacao butter, a vegetable fat. The seeds also contain small amounts of the alkaloids theobromine and caffeine. Today, the seeds are dried, cleaned, roasted, and ground to produce chocolate liquor. In 1828, it was discovered that cacao butter could be removed from chocolate liquor by hydraulic pressing. The resulting powder is cocoa. The cacao butter is used in the manufacture of pharmaceuticals. In 1847, eating chocolate was developed in England by adding extra cacao butter to chocolate liquor. This made it easier to mold and prevented it from melting so easily.

The Aztecs[*] and other Indians[*] of Mexico prepared a bitter chocolate drink flavored with chile, maize, honey, ceiba seeds, or other substances. The drink was whipped into a froth that dissolved on the tongue. Since the cacao beans were expensive, the drink was consumed in large quantities only by the nobility. In 1502, the first cacao beans were brought back to Spain by Christopher Colombus[*] after his fourth voyage. The Indian drink was praised by the conquistadors and widely drunk by the early Spanish settlers. The drink was mentioned by Hernán Cortés[*] in one of his letters to Charles V[*]. This chocolate drink was taken to Europe where it rapidly gained favor, but it remained a Spanish secret for almost a century. Cacao was also used by the Mexican Indians as a special type of money. During the early colonial period, it continued to be used in Mexico and Guatemala[*] in lieu of small coins.

After the Conquest, the Spaniards took control of the most important areas of cacao production in the Soconusco, the Pacific piedmont slope of Chiapas[*] and western Guatemala. Cultivation was quickly extended along the Pacific coast of Guatemala into what is now western El Salvador[*]. The piedmont zone from the Isthmus of Tehuantepec to the Gulf of Fonseca became the most important cacao-producing area of New Spain[*]. Tabasco and Colima in Mexico and the Sula Plain in Honduras[*], which had been major producing areas before the Conquest, declined in importance. Ironically, the alluvial plain of Tabasco and the adjacent wet northern foothills of Chiapas are the only major producing areas in Mexico today.

Production in areas like the Soconusco, which had been important prior to the Conquest, was left in the hands of Indians. The new areas opened up on the Guatemalan and Salvadoran piedmont were operated as Spanish plantations with skilled Indian labor. Beginning in the second quarter of the seventeenth century,

Venezuela* became a major producer of cacao, and production in Guatemala and El Salvador declined rapidly.

Early in the colonial period, the central Mexican highlands formed the major market for cacao. Although cacao was known in Italy in the early seventeenth century, Spain and the rest of Europe became important markets only in the second half of the seventeenth century. Cacao production was spread to the West Indies* by Spaniards. High winds and fluctuating prices made production there a risky business. Early in the colonial period, cacao also spread to the Canary Islands* and the Philippines*. In the early seventeenth century, there was an Ecuadorian boom in cacao production centered in the Guayas lowlands. Around 1620, the export of cacao to New Spain and Central America was prohibited, so the boom collapsed. It was in Venezuela, however, that cacao became the most important colonial export. It was grown in the mountains and valleys of the central coastal range. Venezuelan production and trade to Europe were a Basque monopoly controlled by the Caracas Company*. The company was most active from the 1720s into the mid-1750s. At that time, it began to lose control, and in 1789, it lost its monopoly. After independence, areas devoted to cacao production were planted in coffee*. Although small amounts of cacao were exported from Brazil in the second half of the seventeenth century, production was limited until after independence. Colonial production centered on wild stands in Amazonas and Para. After independence, production shifted to southern Bahia, especially Ilheus. In the late nineteenth and early twentieth centuries, there was a cacao boom in this area. By the 1930s, the boom was over, as major production shifted to Africa. Today, the major producers of cacao are the Ivory Coast and Ghana.

REFERENCES: Murdo J. MacLeod, *Spanish Central America: A Socioeconomic History, 1520–1720*, 1973; Miles L. Wortman, *Government and Society in Central America, 1680–1840*, 1982.

Edward B. Sisson

CACIQUE. The term cacique is used in Latin American culture to refer to an individual of great influence and political power. Spaniards first heard the term in the early 1500s when they explored and conquered the Caribbean basin, where a cacique was an Indian* chief. Eventually, the Spaniards used those caciques as political intermediaries between European bureaucratic institutions and the Indian tribes. In return, the Spanish extended special privileges to the caciques. As the Spanish Empire evolved, the term cacique came to mean anyone— Spaniard, mestizo*, or Indian—who enjoyed great political power. It also came to be synonymous with nepotism and corruption, with individuals who used their political positions to benefit themselves and their families. By the eighteenth century, every Spanish colony had caciques who had acquired huge amounts of land and cattle.

REFERENCE: Guillermo S. Fernández de Recas, *Cacicazgos y nobilario indígena de la Nueva España*, 1961.

CÁDIZ, CORTES OF. The Cortes of Cádiz was a Spanish court that sat in the city of Cádiz during the Napoleonic occupation of Spain. The Cortes, which met from 1810 to 1814, continued the liberal, "enlightened" policies of the Bourbon rulers. The Bourbon king, Charles IV*, abdicated the throne to Napoleon, who placed his brother, Joseph Bonaparte, on the throne of Spain in 1808. Professing loyalty to the deposed king's legitimate successor, Ferdinand VII*, the Cortes enacted modern, liberal legislation that reached far beyond the reforms that the Bourbons themselves might have enacted.

The Cortes, made up of representatives from both Spain and the provinces, provided for the election of local *ayuntamientos** (on which, in violation of earlier Bourbon restrictions, *criollos** could and did serve); it created a provincial deputation that transferred much authority from the regional *audiencias** to local governments. The Cortes produced the Constitution of 1812* which limited the Church, called for a constitutional monarchy, provided for free trade, and required strong local political participation. This extremely liberal document proved to be divisive. It split the *criollos* and upper-middle sectors in Spanish America into two opposing political factions that would become the primary political rivals in Latin America during the nineteenth century. The Cortes of Cádiz ended in 1814, when Ferdinand VII was restored to the Spanish throne. He promptly repudiated its work.

REFERENCE: Ramón Solís, *El Cádiz de las Cortes*, 1969.

Virginia Garrard Burnett

CAGAYAN. Cagayan is both a river valley and a province in northeast Luzon*, Philippines*. The alluvial flatland around the Cagayan, largest of Philippine rivers, supports a productive agricultural economy. Cagayan is so remote from other developed parts of the Philippines, however, that the region has a raw, frontier quality. The river flows directly north for 150 miles, emptying into the Babuyan Channel at Aparri. All along the eastern rim of the valley stands the forbidding, roadless Sierra Madre, inhabited by extremely primitive non-Christian tribes. Lowland Filipinos* were no more willing than Spaniards to venture into that area and tended likewise to avoid the massive Cordillera Central, the block of mountains that forms the western rim of the Cagayan Valley. A land route from the upper (southern) end of the valley across the Caraballo Range to the central Luzon plain was possible, but the Spaniards did not construct a trail until 1768, and no road was built until the Philippines became an American colony. Thus, the isolation of the Cagayan Valley was nearly complete. Prior to the mid-eighteenth century, its history was practically autonomous from that of the rest of the Philippines.

Spaniards first came to Cagayan in the 1570s for strategic reasons: the region faced north toward China and Japan. In fact, the Spaniards had to expel a band of Japanese pirates before they could build a settlement at New Segovia* (Lallo). The area seemed unpromising for Dominican* proselytizing as the natives spoke different languages (Ibanag, Gaddand, and various tribal dialects) and lived in dispersed kin settlements. Ilocano settlers, dominant today, came later. Cagayan has a rich revolutionary tradition. The Spaniards were compelled to suppress revolts in 1589, 1598, 1621, 1625, 1627, and 1639. The causes varied, but grievances were local. Spanish control was quickly restored, but the scope of violence seemed to grow with each succeeding outbreak. Priests and churches were targets of insurrection, as were the few government officials present. Native resistance assumed a more radical character with the Cagayan uprising of 1763, the first revolt in the valley associated with disturbances elsewhere, namely the revolts that year in central Luzon and Ilocos*.

Being sheltered by mountains on three sides, the Cagayan Valley is drier than most other parts of the Philippines. Conditions are ideal for growing tobacco*. The Spanish administration of the infamous tobacco monopoly was completely irrational: after first introducing the plant, the Spanish then declared Cagayan a "marketing" area, which meant that the people were supposed to stop growing tobacco and instead buy inferior tobacco grown elsewhere at inflated prices. This unsatisfactory arrangement lasted 12 years (1785–1797), after which Manila* again permitted tobacco to be grown in Cagayan. The government remained the sole buyer, however, a situation that led to great corruption.

In the nineteenth century, the Spanish tried to rationalize administration of the distant valley by dividing what had been one province into two, then three. Ilocanos and some Chinese moved in as economic opportunities developed in the final decades of Spanish power in the islands. Cagayan was too far from the fields of battle to play a significant role in the Philippine Revolution.

REFERENCE: Ed. C. de Jesús, "Control and Compromise in the Cagayan Valley," in Alfred McCoy and Ed. C. de Jesús, eds., *Philippine Social History*, 1982.

Ross Marlay

CAID, AHMED OULD. Ahmed Ould Caid was born in Western Sahara* in the late 1930s. In 1957, he joined the guerrilla war against the Spanish Empire. In the late 1960s, he joined the Movement for the Liberation of Saguia el-Hamra and Oued ed-Dahab. He was imprisoned in the Canary Islands* and at Dakhla after the massacre of Zemla in 1970. Upon his release in 1971, Caid became one of the militant organizers of the Polisario Front*. During its war against Spain in 1973–1975, the Polisario Front gave increasing military responsibility to Caid, who emerged as a brilliant guerrilla strategist. After the Madrid Agreement* of 1975, Caid continued both his war against Morocco and his service in the Saharawi Popular Liberation Army*.

REFERENCES: Antonio Rumeu de Armas, *España en el Africa Atlántico*, 1956; Tony Hodges, *Historical Dictionary of Western Sahara*, 1982.

CALAMBA AFFAIR. The Calamba Affair is one of the seminal events in the development of the Philippines* Revolution. In 1887, a group of peasant tenants on the huge Dominican* estate in Calamba, which happened to be the home of José Rizal*, formally complained to the Spanish government about abusive treatment at the hands of the Dominican fathers. After an investigation that lasted five years, the government sided with the clerics and then used troops to expel the rebellious tenants. Rizal's family had its home burned, and several people were deported. The Calamba Affair became a rallying cry for Filipino nationalists who opposed Spanish rule.

REFERENCE: J. E. Spencer, *Land and People in the Philippines,* 1954.

CALANCHA, ANTONIO DE LA. Antonio de la Calancha was born in Chuquisaca, Bolivia*, in 1584. He joined the Augustinian* order in 1598 and eventually earned a doctorate in theology at the University of San Marcos* in Lima*, Peru*. During his career, Calancha served as rector of the College of San Ildefonso in Lima as well as prior of several Augustinian monasteries in Trujillo*, Arequipa*, and Lima. Calancha was also a scholar and historian. His most important work was the *Crónica moralizada del orden de San Agustín en el Perú* (1638–1653). The work has become an invaluable source for subsequent historians, ethnologists, and linguists studying the indigenous people of South America. Antonio de la Calancha died in Lima, Peru, on March 1, 1654.

REFERENCE: *New Catholic Encyclopedia,* II:1055, 1967.

CALARCA. Calarca was the military leader of the Pijao and Quindio Indians* in the early 1600s. The Spaniards, particularly during the tenure of Juan de Borja* as president of New Granada*, conducted punishing conquest expeditions against the Indians. Calarca led the resistance until his death in battle in 1607.

REFERENCE: Robert H. Davis, *Historical Dictionary of Colombia,* 1977.

CALDAS, FRANCISCO JOSÉ DE. Francisco José de Caldas was a leading scientific figure in the late colonial period of New Granada* and one of the leaders and martyrs of the independence movement. He was born in 1770 in Popayán*, New Granada, where he was educated in the local seminary. He completed his education at El Rosario in Bogotá* in 1788, taking a law degree to please his family. Mathematics and astronomy, however, were his favorite subjects, and it is possible that he studied under José Celestino Mutis. He was married to Manuela Barona.

The end of the colonial period in New Granada saw a flowering of ideas and intellectual ferment, in which Francisco Caldas took a major part. Even when the ideas did not question the political regime, they contributed to the development of patterns of thought that eventually challenged the established order. This was clearest in the case of the *tertulias* (discussion groups) associated with such men as Antonio Nariño* the Precursor. Caldas reportedly frequented Nariño's house.

Caldas was associated with one of the major scientific events of the colonial period in New Granada—the botanical expedition led by Mutis, which in 1791 moved to Santa Fe de Bogotá. Caldas distinguished himself in a number of areas. He carried on Mutis's work and, at the time of his death in 1816, had over 5,000 plants in his herbarium. His most important discovery was the determination of altitude through the temperature at which water boils at different elevations. His astronomical observations have also been recognized. In 1808–1809, he directed the weekly publication of the *Semanario del Nuevo Reino de Granada* (*Weekly of the New Kingdom of Granada*), which included scientific notes from the United States. His *State of Geography of the Viceroyalty with Respect to the Economy and Commerce and the Influence of Climate on Human Beings* had both social and scientific value.

During the independence period, he was, according to some authors, one of the five most important leaders. In 1812–1813, during the conflict between the regional centers of Colombia, he was associated with the Tunja federalists and the attack on Bogotá of General Antonio Baraya. In 1813, as a colonel of an engineering battalion he took refuge in the province of Antioquia[*] and assisted in the erection of fortifications. After the royalist reoccupation of New Granada, the Spanish General Pablo Morillo[*] carried out a reign of terror in which many of the leading patriots were killed. One of these was Caldas, who was executed on October 29, 1816, in the Plaza of San Francisco, now Santander Park, in Bogotá. Caldas reportedly asked Pascual Enrile to spare him in order to complete his scientific works in progress—but to no avail. In 1904, his remains were moved to the church of San José in his native Popayán.

REFERENCE: Jesús María Henao and Gerardo Arrubla, *History of Colombia*, 1938.

Robert E. Biles

CALICUCHIMA. Calicuchima was a prominent Inca[*] general who was closely associated with Atahuallpa[*], the Incan emperor. In the dynastic struggles within the Incan Empire in the 1530s, Calicuchima played a major role in the subjugation of much of Peru[*]. In 1553, the Spaniards condemned Calicuchima as a traitor and had him burned at the stake.

REFERENCE: Albert William Bork and Georg Maier, *Historical Dictionary of Ecuador*, 1973.

CALIFORNIA. Spanish explorers discovered the coast of Baja California in 1533. Within the next decade, they explored the entire coast of both Baja and Alta California. There was no settlement there, however, until late in the seventeenth century when a number of missions were set up in Baja California. The impetus behind the development of the Alta California missions[*] was political rather than religious. Spain feared that either the Russians or the English would eventually claim the area and believed that a string of Spanish missions might enhance the Spanish position. Father Eusebio Kino[*] had already established 50 missions and churches in Arizona, Sonora, and Baja California; the belief prevailed that California might be a logical expansion to the northwest. Each Spanish mission would provide an excuse for a military contingent, since Spanish missions usually had military forces attached as a defense against hostile Indians[*]. The first mission in Alta California was San Diego de Alcalá, near the town of

San Diego, completed in 1769. This mission was built by Father José Actimán in 1823. Unlike previous missions, it was built without church authorization but was later accepted by Catholic leadership. Politically, Alta California and Baja California were separate provinces administered jointly by the same governor until 1804 when each received its own governor. In 1821, they both became part of the Republic of Mexico. It had been the dedicated Spanish priests who had the knowledge to develop and repair irrigation systems, who taught the Indians crafts and trades, and who successfully operated the missions and adjacent farmlands. Without their skills, the missions swiftly declined. What had taken a half a century to develop was completely destroyed in less than a decade. Today, all the missions (San Diego de Alcalá, 1769; San Gabriel Archangel, 1771; Santa Clara de Asis, 1771; San Juan Capistrano, 1776; San Francisco of Asis, 1776; San Buenaventura (Ventura), 1782; Santa Barbara Vírgin y Mártir, 1786; San Luis Obispo de Tolosa, 1787; Nuestra Señora de la Soledad, 1791; Mission Santa Cruz, 1791; San Fernando Rey de España, 1797; San Miguel Archangel, 1797; San José de Guadalupe, 1797; San Juan Bautista, 1797; San Luis Rey de Francea, 1798; Santa Yñez Vírgin y Mártir, 1804; San Rafael Archángel, 1817; San Francisco Solano, 1823) have undergone some degree of restoration which still preserves the historic past of Hispanic California.

REFERENCES: H. H. Bancroft, *History of California*, 7 vols., 1888–1890; M. J. Geiger, *The Life and Times of Fray Junipero Serra*, 2 vols., 1959.

George A. Agogino and Mercedes Agogino

CALLAO, BATTLE OF. On November 5, 1820, in the harbor of Callao in Peru[*], Chilean naval forces under the command of British Admiral Lord Cochrane attacked the 44-gun Spanish frigate *Esmeralda* and killed or captured the entire Spanish crew. Cochrane had been blockading Callao for some time. Lord Cochrane went on to receive full command of the Chilean navy and seriously compromised Spanish naval efforts along the Pacific coast of Ecuador[*], Peru, and Chile[*] in the early 1820s.

REFERENCE: Salvatore Bizarro, *Historical Dictionary of Chile*, 1987.

CALLAO, SIEGE OF. Between February 5, 1824, and January 22, 1826, patriot forces under Simón Bolívar[*] and Bartolomé Salom placed the royal fortress of King Philip, located at Callao, Peru[*], under siege. Fort Philip was the last Spanish stronghold on the Pacific coast of South America. When the siege ended on January 22, 1826, and royalist forces surrendered, the wars of independence were over.

REFERENCE: Robert H. Davis, *Historical Dictionary of Colombia*, 1977.

CALLEJA DEL REY, FÉLIX MARÍA. Born in Medina del Campo, Spain, in 1759, Félix María Calleja del Rey arrived in New Spain[*] in 1789. He commanded a brigade of royalists during the first rumblings of political independence and distinguished himself against the insurgents by summarily defeating them on a number of occasions. In 1813, he was appointed viceroy[*] of New Spain, and he concentrated his energy on eradicating all forms of rebellion. Calleja fought against José María Morelos* y Pavón, whom he ordered executed in 1815. In 1816, he was recalled to Spain to become governor of Cádiz. Calleja died in 1828.

REFERENCE: Lucas Alaman, *Historia de Méjico desde los primeros movimientos que preparan su independencia en el año 1808 hasta la época presente*, 5 vols., 1849–1852.

Fred Koestler

CALVARIO. El Calvario is an important Roman Catholic shrine in Guatemala*. When the Spanish conquistadors* entered the Valley of Esquipulas, they encountered no Indian* resistance. In return for Indian cooperation, they established the valley as a trading and religious center. In 1595, the colonial sculptor Quirio Cataño sculpted a balsam figure of Jesus Christ. The Spaniards and Indians* burned incense and candles there, and over the years, the smoke turned the statue black. Pardo de Figueroa, the Bishop of Guatemala, claimed to have received a miraculous cure there. He saw to the construction of a large edifice around the figure. The building was completed in 1758. Since then, it has been a religious shrine known as the "Black Christ" where thousands of Central Americans seek miraculous cures each year.

REFERENCE: Richard E. Moore, *Historical Dictionary of Guatemala*, 1973.

CAMARGO, HERNANDO DOMÍNGUEZ. See DOMÍNGUEZ CAMARGO, HERNANDO.

CAMARINES. Camarines is the northern part of the Bikol region of Luzon* in the Philippines.* Although it was theoretically possible to travel from Manila* to Camarines by land, the route was so tortuous that Camarines might as well have been on a separate island. Even sea travel was difficult, for the ports of Camarines face east to the open Pacific rather than west toward the calmer Sibuyan Sea passage to Manila Bay. Camarines has a drought-free climate and fertile volcanic soil, so rice cultivation can support a relatively dense population.

The Spanish conquistador* Juan de Salcedo explored Camarines searching for the gold mines at Paracale. Nevertheless, in 1573, the Spanish governor sent troops to establish a seat of ecclesiastical power at New Cáceres (modern Naga City). New Cáceres became a bishopric in 1595. Thereafter, it was a center of education and culture for southeast Luzon, at first under the Augustinian* fathers and later under the Franciscans*. Camarines was a backwater of the Spanish Philippines, only modestly affected by commerce and development until the nineteenth century, when the opening of Manila to foreign commerce coincided with a rising demand for rope. Abaca, called Manila hemp but produced from a banana-like tree, had exactly the right qualities for rope-making. The economy of the Bikol region became focused around abaca production. Class divisions sharpened. Economic fluctuations subjected peasants to a roller-coaster economy. Chinese and other merchants penetrated even remote towns and villages. Despite the turmoil, Camarines played little role in the revolution that toppled Spanish rule in the Philippines.

REFERENCE: Norman G. Owen, "Abaca in Kabikolan: Prosperity Without Progress," in Alfred McCoy and Ed. C. de Jesús, eds., *Philippine Social History*, 1982.

Ross Marlay

CAMILLIANS. The Camillians, more formally known as the Fathers of the Good Death, were a Roman Catholic religious order whose primary mission was in caring for the sick. Father Andre Sicli, the first Camillian priest in the New World, arrived in Puerto Rico* in 1666. By the end of the colonial period, the Camillians were running a number of hospitals in New Spain*, Bolivia*, Ecuador*, and Chile*.

REFERENCE: *New Catholic Encyclopedia*, XII: 308–09, 1967.

CAMPESINO. The term "campesino" has been used for several centuries to describe lower-class farmers and agricultural workers in rural areas. Its meaning is synonymous with peasant.

CAMPOMANES, PEDRO RODRÍGUEZ. See RODRÍGUEZ CAMPO-MANES, PEDRO.

CAÑADAS. *Cañadas* were specially designated migratory routes for flocks of sheep. The sharp contrasts of climate and the seasonal variations in rainfall in Spain made it desirable for sheepherders to move their flocks from place to place during the year in search of green pastures. Northern pastures (in the Cantabrians, the Pyrenees, and the central sierras) were often snowbound or frozen in winter; southern pastures (in the plains, especially of Extremadura, La Mancha, and Andalucía) tended to become parched under the summer Iberian sun. Consequently, it made sense to move sheep north in summer and south in winter. The passage of migratory flocks, however, annoyed local residents, because the transhumant shepherds claimed the right to graze their sheep on the *tierras baldías** and other common pastures used by local livestock. To defend the interests of transhumant herding and to regulate (and tax) the pastoral industry, the Castilian monarchs organized the sheepmen of the kingdom into the royal *mesta** in the mid- or late-1200s. A major task of the *mesta* was to defend the right of migrating flocks to move in transit between their northern and southern pastures and for them to graze on common pastures along the way. The cañadas were therefore created. There were three principal *cañadas*: one extending from León to Badajoz; one from Logroño to Extremadura and Andalucía; and one from Cuenca through La Mancha to Andalusia and Murcia. These major *cañadas* were between 150 and 350 miles long and were fixed at 90 *varas* wide (a *vara* was slightly less than a yard). Numerous smaller tributary sheepwalks connected the major *cañadas*. Each spring, flocks of thousands of sheep would head north along the *cañadas*; each fall, they would return to their southern pastures. The *cañadas* were used by *mesta* flocks only for brief periods during their migratory passages. The rest of the time, the sheepwalks served as common pastures for local livestock. The *cañadas* were protected by law as perpetual pasture and transit areas. Nevertheless, farmers with adjacent fields often could not resist the temptation to enlarge their cultivated area by plowing into the *cañadas*. This type of usurpation produced countless lawsuits. In sixteenth century New Spain[*], a transhumant pastoral industry with many similarities to that of the mother country developed. *Cañadas* were established along regular routes of migration and were protected by ordinances patterned after the Iberian model. Municipal *mestas* were also created in New Spain to defend pastoral interests. The Spanish and Mexican *mestas* were dissolved in the early 1800s, but transhumant herding continued in both areas. In the mid-twentieth century, many of the old sheepwalks were still in use, in both Mexico and Spain.

REFERENCE: Julius Klein, *The Mesta: A Study in Spanish Economic History, 1273-1836*, 1920.

David E. Vassberg

CANARY ISLANDS. The Canary Islands are an archipelago in the North Atlantic Ocean, about 70 miles west of the Moroccan coast of Africa. There are seven major islands. In 1927, the Canary Islands became two formal provinces of Spain. Las Palmas Province consists of Gran Canaria, Fuerteventura, and Lanzarote, while Santa Cruz de Tenerife Province is composed of Tenerife[*], Gomera, La Palma, and Hierro. Although the islands were known to the Phoenicians, Romans, Carthaginians, Greeks, Arabs, and medieval Europeans, their modern history began in 1336 when Lanzarote Malocello first led a sailing expedition there. In 1402, French explorer Jean de Bethencourt claimed the Canaries for his sponsor, King Henry III of Castile[*]. Between 1415 and 1466, Portugal tried but failed to conquer the Canary Islands several times. Spain emerged as the dominant power, crushing the native Guanches[*], who numbered approximately 80,000 people. By 1475, the Guanches controlled only three islands—La Palma, Tenerife, and Gran Canaria. Spain then conquered Gran Canaria between 1478 and 1483, La Palma between 1492 and 1493, and Tenerife between 1494 and 1496. The conquest brought diseases, cows, pigs, horses, sheep, and Mediterranean plants to the Canaries and annihilated the Gaunches by 1600. The conquest of the Gaunches was a model for the European conquests of other colonial people around the world in the next three centuries.

REFERENCE: Alfred W. Crosby, *Ecological Imperialism: The Biological Expansion of Europe, 900-1900*, 1986.

CAÑAS, ANTONIO JOSÉ. Antonio José Cañas was born in 1785. He joined the independence movement in El Salvador[*] after the 1814 uprising and in the early 1820s fought against the annexation of El Salvador by Mexico. Cañas served as a deputy in the Constituent Assembly of El Salvador in 1824 and soon was appointed minister to the United States for the Federal Republic of Central

America[*]. He served as acting president of El Salvador for several months in 1839 and again in 1840, but after his election as president in 1842 he was unable to assume office because of ill health. He died in 1845.

REFERENCE: Miguel Angel Garcia, ed., *Diccionario histórico-enciclopédico de la República de El Salvador*, 13 vols., 1927–1951.

CANCHA RAYADA, BATTLE OF. Cancha Rayada is located on the plains of Chile[*] near the city of Talca. On March 16, 1818, an important battle in the war for Chilean independence occurred there. The Spanish army, commanded by General Mariano Osorio[*], routed Chilean forces, under the command of José de San Martín[*], who panicked when they mistakenly heard that royalist troops had surrounded them. Three weeks later, on April 5, 1818, José de San Martín's soldiers defeated Osorio's forces in the Battle of Maipu[*], which proved to be decisive in the independence struggle.

REFERENCE: Stephen Clissold, *Bernardo O'Higgins and the Independence of Chile*, 1969.

Samuel Freeman

CANDELARIA, VIRGIN OF. The Virgin of Candelaria is a prominent Mexican shrine located in the state of Jalisco. In 1524, parishioners at the church of San Juan de Los Lagos claimed to have received an apparition of the Virgin Mary. Since then, the church has been a shrine where miraculous healings of the sick have occurred.

REFERENCE: Donald C. Briggs and Marvin Alisky, *Historical Dictionary of Mexico*, 1981.

CÁNOVAS DEL CASTILLO, ANTONIO. Antonio Cánovas del Castillo was born in Málaga, Spain, on February 8, 1828. Eventually he became one of Spain's most conservative, pro-monarchist politicians. When the Spanish monarchy was restored in 1874, Cánovas came to head the government, a position he enjoyed until 1881 and again from 1883 to 1885. Cánovas had deep reservations about the imperial adventure in Western Sahara[*], but he faced powerful lobbying pressures from the Society of Africanists and Colonists[*] and from the Spanish-African Commercial Company.[*] In response, Cánovas's government declared the protectorate there in 1884. He was assassinated in Basque country in August 8, 1897.

REFERENCE: J. L. Comellas, *Cánovas*, 1965.

CANTERAC, JOSÉ. José Canterac was born in Guiene, France, in 1775. He entered the Spanish army in 1801 and spent his career as a military officer. He saw a great deal of military action in the Mediterranean before being sent to Peru[*] in 1820 as chief of staff of royalist forces. Canterac was part of the Spanish defeat at the hands of Simón Bolívar[*] at the Battle of Junín[*], and he signed the surrender document at the Battle of Ayacucho[*]. He returned to Spain in early 1824 and was killed in 1835 trying to suppress an army rebellion in Madrid.

REFERENCE: Academia Colombiana de Historia, *Historia extensa de Colombia*, 23 vols., 1965.

Fred Koestler

CAONABO. Caonabo was the Indian chief of the kingdom of Maguana, which led the resistance to the Spanish conquest of Hispaniola[*] in the 1490s. His forces led the attack on and destruction of the Spanish settlement at La Navidad. Caonabo was captured and transported to Spain in 1496. He did not survive the voyage, either drowning at sea or starving himself to death in protest of his capture.
REFERENCE: Roland I. Perusse, *Historical Dictionary of Haiti*, 1977.

CAPITULACIÓN. The *capitulación* was a legal license and contract arranged between the Spanish Crown and a prospective conquistador[*].The Crown gave the conquistador permission to take profits from all conquered territories, exploit local labor through a variety of institutional arrangements (including the *encomienda*[*]), appoint municipal officials during the first year after the conquest, recruit soldiers, and attract settlers. In return for that permission and sanction, the Crown received 20 percent of all profits.
REFERENCE: Richard E. Moore, *Historical Dictionary of Guatemala*, 1973.

CAPTAIN GENERAL. The office of captain general in the Spanish Empire was essentially that of a provincial viceroy[*]. In areas where population settlement was somewhat sparse, a captaincy general was established instead of a viceregal authority. The captain general enjoyed considerable autonomy and usually reported directly to the Council of the Indies[*]. The exceptions to that practice involved major policy decisions, in which cases the captain general had to consult with the viceroy. In colonial Guatemala[*], for example, the captain general's jurisdiction included what is today Chiapas[*], Mexico[*], and Belize[*]. The New Laws[*] of 1542 designated the captain general of Guatemala as a governor with semi-autonomy from the viceroyalty of New Spain.
REFERENCE: C. H. Haring, *The Spanish Empire in America*, 1947.

CAPTAINCY GENERAL OF CHILE. See CHILE, CAPTAINCY GENERAL OF.

CAPTAINCY GENERAL OF GUATEMALA. See GUATEMALA, CAPTAINCY GENERAL OF.

CAPTAINCY GENERAL OF VENEZUELA. See VENEZUELA, CAPTAINCY GENERAL OF.

CAPUCHINS. The Capuchin Order of the Roman Catholic church[*] was directly involved in missionary work in the New World, although it was almost exclusively confined to the viceroyalty of New Granada[*]—what is today Colombia[*]

and Venezuela*. Francisco de Pamplona arrived in New Granada in 1646, and prefectures were established in Uraba (1647), Darién* (1648), Cumaná (1650), Los Llanos (1676), Guayana (1678–1680), and Santa Marta* (1693). Capuchins established towns, missions*, and schools; they also wrote Indian* dictionaries and grammars.

REFERENCE: *New Catholic Encyclopedia*, XII:305–6, 1967.

CARABOBO, BATTLE OF. The region of Carabobo sits on open plains southwest of Valencia in Venezuela*. Intent on liberating northern South America from the control of Spanish royalists, Simón Bolívar* had his associate, José Francisco Bermúdez*, attack Caracas in April 1821. Bermúdez succeeded for a time in occupying the city before Spanish forces expelled his troops. The occupation, however, gave Bolívar time to regroup his own forces west of the city. Nearly 5,000 Spanish troops under the command of Miguel de la Torre confronted Bolívar's army on the plains of Carabobo on June 24, 1821. Bolívar had more than 6,000 soldiers divided into two armies, one of which, commanded by José Antonio Páez*, attacked the Spanish troops from the rear. The Spanish army suffered a major defeat and retreated to Puerto Cabello. On June 28, 1821, Bolívar and his troops triumphantly marched into Caracas* and took control of the city. The Battle of Carabobo assured Venezuelan independence.

REFERENCE: Donna Keyes Rudolph and G. A. Rudolph, *Historical Dictionary of Venezuela*, 1971.

CARACAS. Caracas, the capital city of Venezuela*, was established in 1567 as Santiago de León de Caracas. Its founder was Diego de Losada, and it became the colonial capital in 1576. The city was an economic backwater in the sixteenth and seventeenth centuries, but it began to assume commercial importance in the early 1700s when the Caracas Company* began exporting gold, silver, cacao*, tobacco*, hides*, and indigo* to Spain from the region. By the early 1800s, the city had a population exceeding 40,000 people and was a center of revolutionary sentiment. Independence was declared there in 1811, and a terrible earthquake devastated the city in 1812. In 1830, Caracas became the capital city of Venezuela.

REFERENCE: Donna Keyes Rudolph and G. A. Rudolph, *Historical Dictionary of Venezuela*, 1971.

CARACAS, *AUDIENCIA* OF. From the beginning of the colonial period until 1717, the region of contemporary Venezuela* was under the administrative authority of the *audiencia* of Santo Domingo*. From 1717 to 1723, Venezuela came under the authority of the *audiencia* of Santa Fe (de Bogotá*). When the viceroyalty of New Granada* was suppressed, Venezuela returned to the jurisdiction of the *audiencia* of Santo Domingo, where it remained until 1739. For the next three years, Venezuela went back under the authority of the *audiencia* of Santa Fe (de Bogotá), but from 1742 until 1786, Venezuela returned once again to Santo Domingo's jurisdiction. In 1786, however, with the population growing and the economy expanding, Venezuela deserved its own *audiencia*. That year, Charles III* established the *audiencia* of Caracas, which was installed on July 19, 1787. The *audiencia* of Caracas then functioned until the end of the colonial period.

REFERENCE: Mark A. Burkholder and D. S. Chandler, *From Impotence to Authority: The Spanish Crown and the American Audiencias, 1687-1808*, 1977.

CARACAS COMPANY. By the early 1700s, the Dutch had established a near monopoly on the cacao* trade coming out of northern South America, and the Spanish Crown resented the losses of revenue. King Philip V* authorized the creation of the Caracas Company in 1728 to stimulate commerce and trade between Spain and what is today Venezuela*. Also known as the Guipuzcoa Company because Basque investors in Guipuzcoa Province had financed the venture, the Caracas Company first sent a fleet to the New World in 1730. The company was an immediate success, crushing Dutch trade and the pirates* in the lower Caribbean and exporting Venezuelan gold, silver, hides*, tobacco*, indigo*, and cacao to Spain. The Crown granted the Caracas Company a monopoly over the Venezuelan trade in 1742, a move that alienated *criollo* traders in Caracas. They revolted violently against the company in 1749, under the leadership of Juan Francisco de León, prompting the crown to relocate the company's board of directors to Spain in 1751. After two years of rebellion, which even drove the Spanish governor from the capital, royal troops restored order. The revolt, however, did influence company policy. In 1752, the Caracas Company invited and received substantial *criollo* investment and in 1759 allowed small cacao merchants to use company warehousing and shipping space to export their product. Under the economic operations of the Caracas Company, Venezuela came into its own economically and became an important political and economic center in the Spanish Empire. The Caracas Company began to decline in the 1770s when free trade sentiments came to dominate Spanish policymakers. In 1781, the company lost its monopoly, and the company then dissolved into several smaller firms.

REFERENCE: Roland D. Hussey, *The Caracas Company, 1728-1784: A Study in the History of Spanish Monopolistic Trade*, 1934.

CARACAS, DIOCESE OF. The first Roman Catholic diocese in Venezuela* was established in 1531, and its headquarters was at Coro. Because of population shifts, the see was transferred to Caracas* in 1638. The diocese included most of what is present-day Venezuela. The eastern provinces of Cumaná, Margarita*, and Trinidad* were under the archdiocese of Puerto Rico*, while the western provinces depended on the archdiocese of Santa Fe de Bogotá*. The diocese of Caracas became an archdiocese in 1804.

REFERENCE: *New Catholic Encyclopedia*, III:94–95, 1967.

CARACAS, UNIVERSITY OF. The University of Caracas was founded as the Universidad Central de Venezuela by royal decree in 1721 and began classes in 1725 as the Real y Pontífica Universidad de Santiago de León de Caracas, with a curriculum specializing in canon law, philosophy, civil law, and theology.

REFERENCE: Donna Keyes Rudolph and G. A. Rudolph, *Historical Dictionary of Venezuela*, 1971.

CARAVEL. The caravel was a small trading vessel common to the Mediterranean Sea from the fourteenth to the seventeenth centuries. The Spanish and Portuguese both used caravels in their great voyages of exploration in the sixteenth century; Christopher Columbus*, Ferdinand Magellan*, Vasco Da Gama, and Bartolomeu Dias all sailed in caravels. They were originally lateen-rigged on two masts, but the need to lower the long sail and bring the yard to the other side of the ship in order to tack into the wind made the caravel impractical for long ocean voyages. That problem was overcome with the development of three-masted caravels with square rig on the two forward masts and a lateen-rigged mizzen.

REFERENCE: Peter Kemp, *The Oxford Companion to Ships and the Sea*, 1976.

CÁRDENAS, BERNARDINO DE. Bernardino de Cárdenas was born in La Paz* in what is today Bolivia* in 1579. He attended the College of San Martín, a Jesuit* institution in Lima*, Peru*, beginning in 1594 and later joined the Franciscan* order. Cárdenas was fluent in Spanish, Quechua* and Aymara*. He worked diligently among the Indian* tribes east of La Paz and earned a reputation, among Indians as well as Spaniards, for his effectiveness. Cárdenas campaigned against the sale of alcohol and coca to the Indians*. He became the visitor to the mining center of Cailloma in the mid–1630s, and in 1641, he became the bishop of Paraguay*. He was soon embroiled in an intense struggle for control of the Jesuit *reducciones** in Paraguay, a battle he eventually lost. Indian militia from the *reducciones* militarily expelled Cárdenas from his see in 1651. Although the Council of the Indies*, after an investigation that consumed nine years, found in his favor and ordered his return to the bishopric, Cárdenas was by then too old to do the work. He died in Santa Cruz, Bolivia, on October 20, 1668.

REFERENCE: Antonio Guzmán, *El kolla mitrado: Biografía de un obispo colonial, fray Bernardino de Cárdenas*, 1954.

CARIBS. See KARIBS.

CARMELITES. Although the Carmelites did conduct some missionary work in the New World, it was not on the level of the Augustinians*, Dominicans*, Franciscans*, or Jesuits*. Carmelite missionaries reached New Spain* in 1522, Panama* in 1535, and New Granada* in 1560, but their efforts in the New World were poorly organized. In 1588, the Spanish Crown revoked the 1522 charter authorizing Carmelite missionary work in the New World.

REFERENCE: *New Catholic Encyclopedia*, XII:306, 1967.

CAROLINE ISLANDS. The Caroline Islands constitute a huge chain of nearly 1,000 islands in Micronesia, stretching 3,000 miles from Tobi Island in the west to Kosrae Island in the east. The major islands in the group are Palau, Yap, Truk, Ponape, and Kosrae. The population of the islands is primarily Micronesian in composition. Spanish explorers began reaching the Caroline Islands early in the 1500s: Gómez de Siquieros reached Yap in 1526; Alvaro Saavedra reached Ulithi in 1528 and Truk and Kosrae in 1530; and Pedro Fernández de Quiróz explored Ponape in 1595. Despite the frequency of their contacts, the Spanish did not press their claims to the Caroline Islands until late in the nineteenth century, when maps of the Pacific showed the Caroline Islands as Spanish territory.

In the 1870s, the German presence in the Pacific became more visible. In 1878, German traders signed special trade agreements giving them preferred commercial rights in the neighboring Marshall Islands*, and in August 1885, a German naval flotilla captured Yap. Spain bitterly protested the invasion, and both countries submitted the dispute to Pope Leo XIII for arbitration. The settlement at the end of the year gave the Carolines to Spain, the Marshalls to Germany, and allowed Germany free trading privileges in the entire area. In 1898, when Spain lost the Spanish-American War* to the United States, it also lost the Philippine* Islands and Guam* in the Marianas*. For $4.5 million, Germany purchased the Caroline Islands and the rest of the Marianas from Spain.

REFERENCE: F. W. Christian, *The Caroline Islands*, 1967.

CARONDELET, LUIS FRANCISCO HÉCTOR. Luis Francisco Héctor Carondelet was born in Noyelles, France, in 1748. He spent most of his life as a soldier and administrator in the Spanish imperial bureaucracy. Carondelet was only 15 when he fought at the Battle of Pensacola, Florida*, against the French. After an effective career in the military, he was appointed governor of San Salvador* in 1788, a post he held until 1792. Carondelet served as governor of Louisiana* between 1792 and 1797, and in 1798, he received his most prestigious post—the presidency of the *audiencia* of Quito. He remained in that position until his death in Quito on August 10, 1807.

REFERENCE: Mark A. Burkholder and D. S. Chandler, *Biographical Dictionary of Audiencia Ministers in the Americas, 1687–1821*, 1982.

CARRATÁLA, JOSÉ MANUEL DE. José Manuel de Carratála was born in Spain in 1781 and received a degree from the University of Alcalá. He spent his career in the Spanish army and fought against the Napoleonic invasion of Spain in 1808. Carratála went to America with General Pedro Murillo* in 1817 and eventually rose to serve as chief of staff to General José Canterac*. He became a field marshal and governor of Potosí*, but he was present at the final defeat at Ayacucho*. Carratála returned to Madrid. Before his death in 1854, he also served in the national senate and as minister of war.

REFERENCES: Enrique Udaondo, *Diccionario biográfico colonial argentino*, 1945; Ione S. Wright and Lisa M. Nekhom, *Historical Dictionary of Argentina*, 1978.

CARRERA VERDUGO, JOSÉ MIGUEL. José Miguel Carrera Verdugo was born in 1786 to a prominent *criollo** family in Santiago*, Chile*. He received a military education in Spain and spent time in the Spanish army fighting against Napoleon's forces, where he also acquired an intense Chilean nationalism. While in the Spanish army, he met José de San Martín*. Carrera returned to Santiago in 1811 and immediately joined the independence movement. He rose quickly to prominence because of his military abilities, his prominent background, and his charismatic personality. A few months after returning to Chile, Carrera organized a successful military coup against the ruling military junta. Later in the year, for a brief period, he shared power in the government with Bernardo O'Higgins* and Gaspar Marín. When they both resigned at the end of 1811, Carrera was head of state. Defeated by Spanish forces at the Battle of Chillan in August 1813, Carrera lost his political position to O'Higgins, his chief rival for leadership of the independence movement in Chile. While fighting against royalist forces, they engaged in a civil war with one another, with both of them fleeing to Argentina* in 1814 when royalist forces defeated O'Higgins at the famous Battle of Rancagua*. Carrera traveled widely during the next three years, but in the meantime O'Higgins came to power in Chile and refused to let his rival reenter the country in 1817. Carrera never returned to Chile. Instead he became deeply involved in the labyrinth of Argentine politics, actively opposing groups that supported San Martín, O'Higgins, and Juan Martín de Pueyrredón*. In 1818, his two brothers, Juan José and Luis, were executed for plotting against O'Higgins, and Carrera swore revenge. He unsuccessfully led an invasion army from Montevideo* and was arrested by Argentine authorities. They executed him for treason on September 3, 1821.

REFERENCES: Luis Galdames, *Historia de Chile*, 1945; José Toribio Medina, *Diccionario biográfico colonial de Chile*, 1906.

CARRIÓ DE LA VANDERA, ALONSO. See CONCOLORCORVO.

CARTA AUTONÓMICA **OF 1897.** The *Carta Autonómica*, or Autonomous Charter, was given to Puerto Rico* by Spain just before the Spanish-American War*, which led to the transfer of the island from Spanish to American sovereignty. It was immediately preceded by the Sagasta Pact between Luis Muños Rivera of the Autonomist (Liberal) Party of Puerto Rico and Praxedes Mateo Sagasta, head of the Spanish Liberal Party. Sagasta promised to support complete autonomy of Puerto Rico once he became prime minister*, if the Puerto Ricans would support his Caribbean foreign policies. Sagasta then formed a government in Spain in October 1897, and the charter was issued. The charter formally recognized Puerto Rican representation in the Spanish Cortes, and gave the Puerto Rican legislature complete authority over its internal affairs, including tariff and customs regulations and duties. But the charter still made it clear that sovereignty over the island rested with Spain and that Spain retained the right to appoint the governor-general as chief executive officer. At the time the charter was granted,

Spain was embroiled in the Cuban[*] rebellion, and Spanish authorities hoped that the liberalism inherent in the *Carta Autonómica* would blunt the revolutionary movement in Puerto Rico.

REFERENCE: Clifford A. Hauberg, *Puerto Rico and the Puerto Ricans*, 1974.

CARTAGENA DE INDIAS. The city of Cartagena, Colombia[*], was established in 1533 by Pedro de Heredia[*] and became an important port on the Caribbean Sea, especially for the shipment of mineral wealth out of the viceroyalty of Peru[*]. Because of its strategic location and economic significance, Cartagena was frequently the object of British and Dutch attack during the colonial period. In 1618, Cartagena was separated out as a province with its own governor. It was subject to the viceroyalty of Peru until the establishment of the viceroyalty of New Granada[*] in 1740. Cartagena proclaimed its independence from Spain in 1811 but fell under Spanish control again from 1816 to 1821. In 1821, Cartagena became part of Gran Colombia[*]. See COLOMBIA.

CARTAGENA, DIOCESE OF. The Roman Catholic diocese of Cartagena was established in 1534 in what is today Colombia[*]. The first bishop was Tomás Toro, a Dominican[*] priest. The diocese of Cartagena became an archdiocese in 1900.

REFERENCE: *New Catholic Encyclopedia*, III:155–56, 1967.

CARTAGO. Cartago, the first capital of Costa Rica[*], was founded in 1564 by Juan Vásquez de Coronado[*]. Costa Rica was first explored by Gil Gonzáles[*] Dávila in 1522, but Gonzáles's rivalry with Pedro Arias de Avila[*] (Pedrarias), the governor of Panama[*], and strong Indian[*] resistance prevented the effective settlement of the region for several decades. Not until 1561 did a successful colonization party, led by Juan de Cavallón[*], settle in Costa Rica, although they established only a modest settlement on Nicoya Bay. In 1563, Juan Vásquez de Coronado became governor of Nicaragua[*] and Costa Rica, establishing Cartago as his capital the following year in the highland central valley (Meseta Central).

Costa Rica, despite its name and stunning terrain, had few precious metals and relatively few Indians. It attracted few ambitious Spanish settlers and remained a backwater of the Spanish Empire. At its peak, Cartago, the largest town, had a population of less than 4,000. Those few settlers who came to Costa Rica usually settled in and around Cartago to farm the fertile volcanic soil of the central valley. Because the entire province never had a total population of more than 60,000 in colonial times, Cartago never enjoyed full prestige as a regional capital. Few of the administrative affairs of the province were even dealt with in Cartago; judicial and political matters were handled by the *audiencia* in distant Guatemala, and even ecclesiastical concerns fell under the jurisdiction of the bishop of Nicaragua[*], based in León[*]. Spaniards in Costa Rica during the sixteenth and seventeenth centuries repeatedly petitioned to have colonial authority transferred to the *audiencia* of Panama[*]—a location that was remote and inaccessible from Costa Rica, but not so much so as Guatemala. They were unsuccessful in their attempts.

The location of Cartago, a cool and healthful 1,000 feet above sea level, and its rich, volcanic soil seemed promising for Spanish settlement. Its isolation within the central valley, however, remained a problem throughout the colonial period. In 1601, an important road, optimistically christened the Camino Real, connected Cartago for the first time with Nicoya in the north and Panama in the south. The Camino Real was in fact no more than an elaborate footpath and did little to relieve Cartago's, and indeed all of Costa Rica's, isolation. In 1823, Costa Rica's capital was moved to San José*.

REFERENCE: Carolyn Hall, *Costa Rica: A Geographical Interpretation in Historical Perspective*, 1985.

Virginia Garrard Burnett

CARTAS DE RELACIÓN. Written by Hernán Cortés*, *Cartas* is one of the most famous of the Spanish chronicles. It relates Cortés's personal account of the conquistador's arrival and entrance into the interior of Mexico, his contact with the Aztec* Empire, the eventual conquest of Motecuhzoma*, and the beginning of the Mexican colonial era. The work is comprised of five *cartas* (letters), that were sent to King Charles V* between 1519 and 1526. As a whole, their complete title is *Cartas de Relación sobre el descubrimiento y la conquista de la Nueva España*. The five letters were first published as a unified work in 1852, in Madrid.

Cartas is undoubtedly one of the high points of colonial literature. Composed with a polished, terse style, the narrative takes life and presents one of the world's great historical events—the conquest of Mexico. In Cortés's work, the reader views European man's astonishment upon confronting the advanced Aztec Empire and the amazing development of Tenochtitlán*. Since Cortés's primary motivation in writing the letters was to impress his king and thereby win favor and fortune from the Crown, the author's accuracy in his portrayal of the conquest has been brought into question. Stated simply, many historians and literary critics have suggested that Cortés's account of the conquest and, in particular, of his own role, was self-serving and given to exaggeration. Nevertheless, *Cartas* represents an outstanding epic of bravery and audacity in the face of overwhelming odds. Aside from its literary merit, it is one of the great historical documents of the colonial era.

REFERENCE: Carlos González Peña, *History of Mexican Literature*, 1968.

Sam L. Slick

CARVAJAL, FRANCISCO. Francisco Carvajal, an explorer and conquistador* born in Spain in 1468, came to the New World as a member of the Spanish army and rose to the rank of general. After the assassination of Francisco Pizarro* in 1541, Peru* fell into widespread civil and political disorder. Viceroy Cristóbal Vaca de Castro assigned Carvajal to restore order. In 1542, Carvajal defeated the forces of Diego Almagro* in northern Chile*. In 1544, Gonzalo Pizarro* murdered incoming Viceroy Vasco Núñez de Bela*, who had been charged with enforcing the New Laws*. Carvajal joined forces with Gonzalo Pizarro. Four years later, however, the Spanish Crown sent Pedro de la Gasca* as the new viceroy. Gasca raised an army, defeated the Pizarro-Carvajal forces, and executed both men.

REFERENCE: Manuel de Mendiburu, *Diccionario histórico-biográfico del Perú*, 8 vols., 1874–1890.

CARVAJAL, GASPAR DE. Gaspar de Carvajal was born in Trujillo, Extremadura, Spain, in 1504. A Dominican* priest, he accompanied Bishop Vicente Valverde* to Peru* in 1538 to establish the Order of St. Dominic there. In 1541, Carvajal became vicar-general of Quito*, and there he joined Gonzalo Pizarro's* exploration party into eastern Ecuador*. Carvajal then joined Francisco de Orellana's* expedition down the Amazon River. Carvajal earned a reputation as a mediator between various political factions in Ecuador and Peru during the 1540s and 1550s. He became prior of Lima* and Cuzco*, and in 1557, he became the provincial of the Dominicans in Peru. He died in Lima in 1584.

REFERENCE: Gaspar de Carvajal, *Descubrimiento del río de las Amazonas*, ed. J. T. Medina, 1894.

CARVALLO Y GOYENECHE, VICENTE. Vicente Carvallo y Goyeneche was born in Valdivia, Chile*, in 1742. He spent his career in the Spanish and Argentine military, but Carvallo is best remembered as a historian. In 1790, he began to collect documents, a process that eventually took him to Santiago* and then to Madrid, in order to write a history of Chile. He returned to the New World in 1800 and lived in Montevideo*, Buenos Aires*, and Córdoba*, where he continued to write. His best remembered work is *Descripción histórico-geográfica del reino de Chile*. Carvallo died in 1816.

REFERENCE: G. R. Guarda, "Carvallo Goyeneche," *Revista de Estudios Históricos*, 11 (1963), 5–26.

CASA DE CONTRATACIÓN DE LAS INDIAS. The Casa de Contratación was created in 1503 by Juan Rodríguez de Fonseca*, Queen Isabella's* chaplain, specifically for the management of colonial activities and commerce. The Casa de Contratación, or House of Trade, was a part of the Council of the Indies*. It not only served as a clearinghouse for trade but also had dictatorial powers over all shipping sailing to or from the colonies. Each ship carried a public notary whose duties were to keep a complete record of all on-board activities. The House of Trade had the additional responsibility of keeping a record of the economic geography of all sections of the colonies. Conquistadors* or explorers were obliged to send reports on the people, climate, terrain, and resources available in new lands. In 1524, an edict of Charles I established the Real y Supremo Consejo de las Indias allowing the House of Trade to assume additional responsibilities: to direct the political, judicial, and military affairs of the colonies and to serve as an advisory department regarding all civil and ecclesiastical appointments. At the conclusion of the War of Spanish Succession*, Philip V* created a Ministry of the Marine and the Indies, relieving the House of Trade of all responsibilities pertaining to war, finance, navigation, commerce, and the nomination of many officials, including those of the Council of the Indies and the House of Trade themselves. In 1790, all ministries of the Indies were abolished, and their functions were distributed among the ministries of foreign affairs, justice, war, and finance.

REFERENCES: Rafael Altamira y Crevea, *Historia de España y de la civilización española*, 6 vols., 1900–1930; J. H. Elliott, *Imperial Spain, 1469–1716*, 1964; J. H. Mariejol, *The Spain of Ferdinand and Isabella*, 1961.

Fred Koestler

CASAL, JULIÁN DEL. Julián del Casal was born in Cuba* in 1863 and became a poet of the modernist school. He was a follower of the Nicaraguan* poet Rubén Darío. Casal's work was preoccupied with the enchantment of distant places, exotic people and themes, and death. His most memorable works are *Hojas al viento* (1890), *Nieve* (1892), and *Bustos y Rimas* (1893). Casal died tragically in 1893.

REFERENCE: Juan J. Remos, *Proceso Histórico de las Letras Cubanes*, 1958.

CASAS, BARTOLOMÉ DE LAS. See LAS CASAS, BARTOLOMÉ DE.

CASTAS. During the colonial period in the New World, Spanish authorities used the term *castas* to refer to any individual born of mixed parentage— European, Indian*, or African. It had a variety of social, legal, and political implications, but in general Spanish officials used the classification in determining the size of tribute payments and the length of military service. On the social scale, *castas* were usually higher than Indians because of their ability to speak Spanish.

REFERENCE: James F. King, "The Colored Castes and American Representation in the Cortes of Cádiz," *Hispanic American Historical Review*, 60 (1980), 33–64.

CASTELLANOS, JUAN DE. Juan de Castellanos was born in Alañis, Spain, in 1522. He studied in Alañis and then in Seville* before coming to America as a soldier in 1539. Castellanos served throughout the Caribbean in the early 1540s; in 1544, he was ordained a Roman Catholic priest. Castellanos served as a parish priest in Cartagena* for several years and then as curate of Río de la Hacha. In 1568, he was granted the benefice of Tunja, where he spent the rest of his life. During those years, Castellanos wrote a great deal of history and poetry. He is best remembered for his poetry, particularly his epic descriptions of Puerto Rican history and geography. He traveled in Puerto Rico* and then composed his famous "Elegías de varones illustres de Indias," the longest poem in Spanish literature. He also wrote hundreds of other descriptive poems about the Greater Antilles. Juan de Castellanos died in Tunja on November 27, 1607.

REFERENCES: U. R. Rojas, *Juan de Castellanos: Biografía*, 1958; M. G. Romero, *Juan de Castellanos: Un examen de su vida y su obra*, 1964.

CASTELLI, JUAN JOSÉ. Juan José Castelli was born in Buenos Aires* in 1764. He studied law and theology at the University of Córdoba* and earned a doctorate in law at the University of Charcas. Castelli joined the movement for independence in Argentina*. In association with Martín Rodrigo, he convinced Viceroy Hidalgo de Cisneros* (May 10, 1810) to call for a *cabildo abierto*, an open town meeting that eventually led to independence. Castelli became a member of the provisional independent government under Cornelio de Saavedra. Castelli ordered the execution of Viceroy Cisneros along with other counter-revolutionaries from Córdoba*. On June 20, 1811, his forces were defeated by a detachment of the royalist forces under General José Manual Goyeneche. He died in 1812.

REFERENCES: José Ingenieros, *La evolución de las ideas Argentinas*, 1946; Ricardo Levene, *A History of Argentina*, 1937; Ernesto Palacio, *Historia de la Argentine, 1515-1957*, 1960.

Fred Koestler

CASTILE. Castile is the largest region of Spain. Ferdinand I became the first king of Castile in 1035. When Spaniards defeated the Moors at Toledo in 1085, Castile annexed the kingdom of Toledo. Ferdinand III of Castile annexed the kingdom of León in 1230, and in subsequent years, he took much of Andalucía from the Moors. When Isabella* of Castile married Ferdinand* of Aragón in 1469, modern Spain was born. By that time, Castile, driven by an aggressive political nationalism and crusading Roman Catholicism after centuries of the Reconquest, was the dominant political force in Iberia. It was that Castilian spirit that led to the colonization of the New World. Isabella insisted that the New World was a Castilian domain. She made sure in her will that her daughter Juana, not her husband Ferdinand, received title to the New World dominions, and she insisted that all settlers of the New World be Castilian. Castilian laws and institutions were the ones transferred to the New World.

REFERENCES: J. H. Elliott, *Imperial Spain, 1469-1716*, 1963; Juan Manzano, *La incorporación de las Indias a la corona de Castilla*, 1948.

CASTILLA DE ORO. In 1508, Diego de Nicuesa* received from the Spanish Crown a land grant that included territory from Panama* northward. At the time, the region was called Veragua, but it was soon known as the Castilla de Oro, a term born more of wishful thinking than of geographic reality. By 1514, the region was more carefully defined as what is today the province of Darién* and came under the administrative supervision of Governor Pedro Arias de Ávila*. He settled 1,500 Spanish colonists there. Most of them stayed only a few years before moving to the Pacific side of the colony.

CASTILLO, FLORENCIO DE. Florencio de Castillo was born in what is today Nicaragua* in 1778. He went to school in León*, Nicaragua, and then entered the Roman Catholic priesthood. Early in his life, Castillo developed sympathies for the plight of the lower classes, especially blacks* and Indians*, and he became a vocal advocate of the natural rights philosophy. At the Cortes of Cádiz*, Castillo represented Costa Rica* and served as secretary of the assembly. He received appointment as bishop of Oaxaca*, Mexico*, served as *consejero* to Agustín Iturbide*, and filled a term as president of Mexico's Constituent Assembly. Florencio de Castillo died in 1834.

REFERENCES: Francisco Montero Barrantes, *Elementos de historia de Costa Rica*, 2 vols., 1894; Theodore S. Creedman, *Historical Dictionary of Costa Rica*, 1977.

CASTILLO ANDRACA Y TAMAYO, FRANCISCO DEL. Francisco del Castillo Andraca y Tamayo was born in Lima*, Peru*, on April 2, 1716. Plagued by very poor vision, he was nonetheless a brilliant young man who entered the Order of Our Lady of Mercy as a lay brother in 1734. He became a playwright and satirist, as well as a sincere writer of pious works. Among his best known works are *El redentor no nacido* and *Guerra es la vida del hombre*. Castillo died in Lima in 1770.

REFERENCE: *New Catholic Encyclopedia*, III:193, 1967.

CASTILLO Y GUEVARA, FRANCISCA JOSEFA DE, "LA MADRE CASTILLO." Born in Colombia* to a wealthy family in 1671, Francisca Josefa de la Castillo y Guevara, it is believed, was a quiet, introspective girl who was given to melancholy. She entered a convent at an early age, where she was apparently harassed by her fellow sisters who did not understand her contemplative nature. She studied the Spanish mystics and is herself considered to have been one of the great mystics of the Spanish colonial period. Although she also wrote some poetry, her position in Spanish colonial literature is due to her narrative. Her two primary works were *Mi Vida*, a personal diary, and *Afectos*, which was published under the title *Sentimientos Espirituales*. In *Afectos*, the reader encounters an elegant baroque style that reveals a Catholic mystic and her devotion for encounters with a personal God. Madre Castillo began *Afectos* at the age of 23 and she continued adding entries for years thereafter. Unquestionably, she must be considered the most important woman narrator of the colonial period. She died in 1742.

REFERENCE: R. M. Carrasquilla, "Francisca Josefa de Castillo," *Obras completas*, ed. J. E. Ricuarte, 5 vols., 1956–1961.

Sam L. Slick

CASTOREÑA Y URSÚA, JUAN IGNACIO DE. Juan Ignacio de Castoreña y Ursúa was born in Zacatecas*, New Spain*, on July 31, 1668, to a wealthy, prominent family. He studied under the Jesuits* in Mexico City* and received a doctorate in law there. Castoreña then went to Spain where he earned a doctorate in theology at the University of Ávila. He returned to New Spain as the canon of the cathedral of Mexico City, and he served as the censor for the Inquisition*. He was also the founder of the *Gaceta de México*, a news periodical, in 1720. Castoreña was appointed bishop of Yucatán* in 1729. He died in Mérida, New Spain, on July 13, 1733.

REFERENCE: M. Ochoa Campos, *Juan Ignacio María de Castoreña Ursúa y Goyeneche: Primer periodista mexicano*, 1944.

CATARIS REBELLION. The Cataris Rebellion erupted in 1780 among various Andean tribal people in Upper Peru*. The Indians* had steadily grown more and more irritated with labor abuses and their exploitation at the hands of Spaniards and *criollos** in the region governed by the *audiencia* of Charcas*. The leader of the rebellion was Tomás Catari, an Indian. When a white mineowner murdered Catari in 1781, the rebellion assumed the dimensions of a racial revolt. More than 40,000 Indians laid siege to the city of La Paz*. Before Spanish troops relieved the siege nearly four months later, approximately 10,000 whites were dead. The rebellion was not crushed until large contingents of imperial troops arrived from Lima* and Buenos Aires.

REFERENCE: Lillian Estelle Fisher, *The Last Inca Revolt, 1780–1783*, 1966.

CATEAU-CAMBRESIS, TREATY OF. The Treaty of Cateau-Cambresis, concluded on April 3, 1559, brought an end to approximately six decades of strife between the Habsburg and Valois dynasties. After the signing of the pact, Philip II*, Spain's Habsburg king, never again traveled outside of the Iberian Peninsula. Thenceforth, imperial decisions were made from a Spanish perspective, in the interests of the Iberian kingdom, as opposed to those of the other Habsburg holdings in Europe. During the negotiations, Philip's diplomats sought to prohibit French vessels from navigating the waters of the Indies. They based their contentions on papal pronouncements and on the notion that Castile* had expended valuable resources in the discovery of the New World, whose riches therefore, should accrue to it alone. The Valois representatives refused to concede this point, arguing that effective occupation entitled states to territorial sovereignty. Both sides avoided a deadlock by verbally agreeing that the actions of French corsairs west of the Azores and south of the Tropic of Cancer would not officially violate peace in Europe. That is, international rivalries in the Americas would not necessarily cause warfare to erupt in the Old World. The phrase "no peace beyond the line" came to characterize this diplomatic arrangement. Later, beginning with the Treaty of Madrid* of 1670 and other understandings during the course of the next fifteen years, peace in Europe came to be tied to peace "beyond the line."

REFERENCES: F. G. Davenport, *European Treaties Bearing on the History of the United States and Its Dependencies*, vol. I, 1917; A. P. Newton, *The European Nations in the West Indies, 1493–1688*, 1933.

Frank Marotti

CATHAY. In the late fifteenth century, when the European voyages of discovery to the New World began, Cathay was the geographical term used to refer to China. Marco Polo had traveled widely throughout Asia at the end of the thirteenth century, and in his published writings he had used Cathay in describing the land dominated by Genghis Khan. During the next two centuries, Cathay was the reference word for China. In 1492, when Christopher Colombus[*] set out across the Atlantic, he was heading for Cathay where he hoped to find the riches and spices that Polo had described.

REFERENCE: David Quinn, ed., *New American World*. Volume I: *America from Concept to Discovery: Early Exploration of North America*, 1979.

CATHOLIC CHURCH. During the colonial period in Spanish America, the Roman Catholic Church was one of the key institutions of the empire. King Ferdinand[*] and Queen Isabella[*] negotiated the Patronato Real[*] with the papacy. In 1493, Pope Alexander VI[*] recognized Spanish claims in the New World in return for Spanish acceptance of the responsibility for maintaining the Church there and propagating the faith among the Indians[*]. In effect, the Spanish Crown controlled ecclesiastical patronage and church finances in the New World, complete with the power to nominate clerical appointments from archbishops to parish priests, collect tithes, and disburse church funds. Eventually, the Spanish king was recognized by the papacy as the virtual vicar of the Roman Catholic Church in the New World.

From the very beginning of the Spanish presence in the New World, the idea of Christianizing the Indians was a major impetus for the empire. Roman Catholic friars—especially the Dominicans[*], Franciscans[*], Mercedarians[*], and Jesuits[*]—accompanied Spanish settlers and soldiers to the New World and went to work converting the Indians. In particular, they instituted the system of missions[*] or *congregaciones*[*], whereby the Indians were gathered from dispersed settlements into concentrated towns and villages where clerics taught them Spanish, Christianity, and agriculture. Although the friars had noble motives, the mission Indians suffered from disease, forced labor, and culture shock. Rapid depopulation ensued.

The rapid settlement of the New World required the establishment of dioceses and parishes there. In 1511, an archdiocese was established at Santo Domingo[*] with bishoprics at Concepción de la Vega on Hispaniola[*] and at San Juan[*] in Puerto Rico[*]. The Cuban diocese was established at Baracoa in 1518 and was later moved to Santiago in 1522. The first mainland diocese was established at Darién[*] in 1513 and moved to Panama City in 1524. The dioceses in New Spain[*] were Tlaxcala[*] in 1524, Mexico City in 1530, Oaxaca[*] in 1535, Michoacán in 1536, Chiapas[*] in 1538, Guadalajara[*] in 1548, and Yucatán[*] in 1561. Central American dioceses were founded at Comayagua[*], Honduras[*], in 1531; León[*], Nicaragua[*], in 1531; Coro, Venezuela[*], in 1531; Cartagena[*], Colombia[*], in 1534; and Santa Marta[*], Colombia[*], in 1535. Peruvian dioceses were established at Tumbez in 1529, Cuzco[*] in 1536, and Lima[*] in 1539. Until 1545, all the New World dioceses were subordinate to the archbishop of Seville[*]. By the end of the colonial period, there were 10 archdioceses and 38 dioceses in the New World.

The missionary friars were known as "regular" priests; that is, they were members of religious orders who answered to their own governing authorities, not to the "secular" priests in the parishes, bishoprics, and archbishoprics. An intense rivalry developed between the regulars and the seculars. The Spanish Crown favored the seculars, who were directly under Crown control because of the Patronato Real. In answering to their own clerical order instead of to the Crown, the regulars had more independence, which the Crown resented. As the Indian population declined, however, the regulars lost much of their power because they had lost their primary constituency. In the process, royal officials circumscribed the activities of the religious orders more and more, finally expelling the Jesuits from the New World altogether in 1767. That was the ultimate victory for the secular priests.

The Roman Catholic Church eventually became a conservative force in the New World. The Church came to own huge amounts of property, great *latifundia*[*] estates where hundreds of thousands of peasants labored, and it enjoyed enormous revenues from those estates. When the independence movements began early in the nineteenth century, the Church proved to be a close ally of the Spanish Empire by supporting royalist forces over those of the revolutionaries. When the revolutions succeeded, the reputation of the Church had been severely compromised.

REFERENCES: Mariano Cuevas, *Historia de la iglesia en México*, 1946–1947; Richard E. Greenleaf, *The Roman Catholic Church in Latin America*, 1971; Robert Ricard, *The Spiritual Conquest of Mexico*, 1966.

CATTLE. Because of their familiarity with dry pasture lands in Spain, the Spanish settlers of the New World brought cattle with them to the New World. Near the mines of New Spain[*], Bolivia[*], and Peru[*], Spaniards maintained large cattle herds to feed the Indian laborers, and when the mines declined the Spaniards made ranching a major New World industry. But meat was only of minor economic significance to the Spanish settlements. The real profits in cattle ranching came from hides and tallow. Cheap and plentiful candles provided light in the homes and in the mines, while leather was a ubiquitous product used for a variety of products. The Spanish cattle were ideally suited for the rough New World environment. They were lean, fast, and armed with long horns to fend off predators. Cattle spread across Hispaniola[*] and New Spain. In the sixteenth century, as Spanish settlement penetrated the northern reaches of New Spain, cattle ranching developed there too. By the end of the sixteenth century, the world's largest ranches, some with as many as 200,000 head of cattle, were in New Spain. Wild strains of cattle even spread beyond the pale of settlement into Texas[*], California[*], and New Mexico.[*] Ranches also appeared in the savannas and mountains of Central America, the llanos of Colombia and Venezuela[*], the highlands of Peru and Bolivia, and from there to the pampas of Argentina. By the end of the eighteenth century the pampas were exporting a million hides annually.

REFERENCE: Alfred W. Crosby, Jr., *The Columbian Exchange. Biological and Cultural Consequences of 1492*, 1972.

CAUDILLO. The caudillo, or "military strongman," is identified with the turbulent post-independence period in Spanish America. A typical example of this phenomenon is the period between 1826 and 1903 in Bolivia* when 185 "revolutions" were reported, each led by or in favor of a particular caudillo. Some have traced the caudillo's beginnings to the Iberian past during the *Reconquista* (711–1492), identifying El Cid as an example of an early Iberian caudillo. Others believe that the phenomenon has purely American roots that began with the conquest, identifying Hernán Cortés*, Francisco Pizarro*, Lope de Aguirre*, and others as caudillos. In actuality, *caudillismo* as a political system has its roots in the independence period (1808–1824) and developed as a response to fundamental factors in the post-independence period. During the early nineteenth century, these factors included a weak internal market that contributed to regionalism, a depressed export sector, the severing of links with the metropolis leading to a lack of legitimacy in the new governments and their leaders, the civilian sector's search for employment in a public sector unable to support the many aspirants for office, and the continuing militarization of the society, during and after independence, due to internal threats from the popular classes and inter-elite rivalries, as well as foreign threats from neighbors and the European powers.

The caudillo appeared at a time of economic, social, and political disintegration when a power vacuum existed in the new nations. The breaking down of social barriers frequently allowed mestizos* to rise in the military ranks. It gave the caudillo the opportunity to achieve political power because the *criollo*＊ elites needed to utilize mestizos in the struggles against the Spanish colonial state during the independence period and against other *criollo* elites after independence. The caudillo's primary characteristic was his personal virtue or charisma that his followers, mostly from the popular classes, sought and found in him. Not all caudillos came from the military class (for example, Paraguay's* José Gaspar Rodríguez* de Francia), but the majority were military men, such as Mexico's Antonio López de Santa Anna. He had the support of certain elite sectors because he in turn supported their interests. His military prowess earned him the right to achieve political power, which also gave him access to economic resources. This access was important in order to support his followers and ensure their loyalty. The lack of a strong internal market and export sector led to the use of force to acquire wealth for without wealth, his followers might desert him for another.

During this period, both regional and national caudillos vied for power. The national caudillo had to dominate the regional ones if he was to maintain his power, since they were a threat. If this were not possible, he had to eliminate them either through repression or assassination. An example of this national/regional struggle was that between Juan Manuel de Rosas*, a national caudillo, and Facundo Quiroga, a regional caudillo, in Argentina*. The regional caudillo championed the cause of the regional elites against a centralized state that threatened their economic and political interests. In Salta[*], Argentina, Martín Güemes[*], a regional caudillo, was defeated when he lost the support of the regional elites.

At other times, the caudillo either emerged from the popular classes or championed their cause. The social and political chaos of the period allowed individuals from the social classes that had been excluded from power during the colonial period to emerge as leaders because the elites needed to use them in their struggle. They then escaped the control of these elites to identify themselves with the popular classes and to champion the integrity of the nation. This type of caudillo was unique to nineteenth-century Spanish America because of his identification with the popular classes against the interests of the economic, political, and social elites. They represented an incipient nationalism by defending the internal market against foreign penetration and by attempting to develop it. They had many enemies in the elite classes, especially those associated with foreign interests. Guatemala's[*] Rafael Carrera in power (1839–1865), Paraguay's Rodríguez de Francia (1814–1840), Bolivia's[*] Manuel Isidoro Belzu (1848–1855), and Argentina's Rosas (1829–1852) are all examples of the ''folk caudillo.''

Once in power, the caudillo tried to institutionalize that power and give order to the political chaos. *Caudillismo* was a political system that used violence to achieve political power because of the lack of an institutionalized mechanism for the orderly transfer of power. He depended on five major factors to maintain his power: the military, to supply the needed force; the Church, to maintain the social order; the intellectuals, to provide an ideological basis for the regime; the landowners, to supply the needs of the military; and the merchants, to supply the funds for wars or civil strife. He played an important role in developing nationalism through attempting to provide stability and unify the nation.

Once his power was institutionalized and order brought from the political chaos, the age of the caudillo was over. This occurred during the later nineteenth century when civilian regimes replaced military ones. The expansion of the world market and the need for raw materials from the industrialized nations contributed to this process by ensuring a level of economic stability that had not existed in the post-independence period and by providing increased revenues to the state. The professionalization of the military likewise insured a degree of political stability as that institution became subsumed under civilian rule. The military became an instrument for internal control of the masses in order to insure the functioning of the export sector. Technology integrated the various regions through communication and transportation. These developments and the structural changes that occurred spelled the end of *caudillismo*. Society became more complex and new social forces, populist in nature, emerged on the political scene, challenging the economic and political structures that had emerged. Some have tried to identify a Juan Perón or Antonio Somoza as caudillos but *caudillismo* in its pure form, the personalist rule by one man, had disappeared by the beginning of the twentieth century in most Latin-American countries.

REFERENCES: William H. Beezley, "Caudillismo: An Interpretive Note," *Journal of Inter-American Studies*, 11 (1969) 345–52; E. Bradford Burns, *The Poverty of Progress*, 1980; Charles E. Chapman, "The Age of the Caudillos: A Chapter in Hispanic American History," *Hispanic American Historical Review*, 12 (1932), 281–300; James Dunkerley, "Reassessing Caudillismo in Bolivia, 1825–79," *Bulletin of Latin American Research*, 1 (1981), 13–25; Robert L. Gilmore, *Caudillismo and Militarism in Venezuela, 1810–1910*, 1964.

Carlos Pérez

CAUPOLICÁN. Caupolicán was an Araucanian* Indian leader born near Palmaiquen, Chile*. He fought with Chief Lautaro* in resisting Spanish conquest in the mid-1500s, and when Lautaro died in 1557, Caupolicán assumed leadership of the movement. In 1558, García Hurtado* de Mendoza captured Caupolicán and executed him.

REFERENCE: José Toribio Medina, *Diccionario biográfico colonial de Chile*, 1906.

CAVALLÓN, JUAN DE. Juan de Cavallón was a Spanish *adelantado** who led the first successful colonization party into Costa Rica*. Although Gil Gonzales* Dávila had first explored Costa Rica as early as 1522 and the ambitious governor of Panama*, Pedro Arias de Ávila* (Pedrarias), had sent an expedition into the region, the obduracy of the local Indians* and the lack of precious metals had discouraged Spanish settlement in Costa Rica. In 1566, Cavallón, traveling south from Nicaragua*, established a small settlement on the Nicoya Bay, thus beginning the first permanent and effective Spanish occupation of the region.

REFERENCE: Francisco Montero Barrantes, *Elementos de historia de Costa Rica*, 2 vols., 1894.

Virginia Garrard Burnett

CAVIEDES, JUAN DEL VALLE Y. Probably the greatest satirical poet of the colonial period, Caviedes cultivated "popular" poetry. His works, although baroque, reflect not the influence of Góngora, which informs most of colonial baroque literature, but rather of Spain's other baroque genius, Francisco de Quevedo. Caviedes was a popular poet who was inspired by his immediate surroundings. Most of his poetry, although widely circulated during his lifetime, was actually published for the first time only in the nineteenth and twentieth centuries. Caviedes was born in Andalucía around 1652, but he spent most of his life in Lima*. Little documented information exists about his life. His father left him a small fortune, which Caviedes apparently squandered on women and high living. He supposedly then turned to small commercial ventures and has been variously described by historians as a shopkeeper and peddler. But poetry was his passion. From a purely literary point of view, Caviedes can be considered the greatest Peruvian poet of the seventeenth century.

When Caviedes's poetry was first published, it appeared under the title of *Diente del Parnaso*, which includes works written from 1683 through 1691. It is this collection for which he is best known. The organizing principle of vitriolic and biting satire informs virtually all of the works. The author attacks members of Lima society, including doctors (his favorite target), courtesans, clerics, barbers, *criollos*[*], to name but a few. Quite aside from the humor and simple pleasure of reading Caviedes, his works have yet another importance. The works represent a catalog of and commentary on large segments of colonial Lima society. He left behind a rich firsthand view of life in Peru[*] in the seventeenth century. In addition to his masterpiece, *Diente del Parnaso*, consisting of 47 poems, Caviedes wrote three plays: *El entremés del amor Alcalde*, *El baile del amor médico*, and *El baile del amor tahur*. He also wrote numerous sentimental, philosophical, and religious poems. He died in 1697.

REFERENCE: G. L. Kolb, *Juan del Valle y Caviedes*, 1959.

Sam L. Slick

CAVITE MUTINY. The Cavite Mutiny of January 20, 1872, was a Filipino[*] uprising against Spain that was quickly suppressed, but in retrospect, it was the beginning of the Philippine[*] Revolution. Workers at the Spanish arsenal in Cavite, just south of Manila[*] on the bay, rebelled against the imposition of tribute and forced labor from which they had long been exempted. Two hundred soldiers and workers seized weapons and killed their officers. There is little evidence that the mutiny was part of any wider seditious plot, but the Spanish governor thought it was—a classic example of a self-fulfilling prophecy.

The mutiny occurred in the context of a long-standing struggle for scarce parishes between Spanish friars and Filipino secular priests (usually mestizo[*] or darker-skinned *indios*). Spanish policy wavered between reform and repression, In 1872, after a few heady years of liberalism (1868–1871), it was in a particularly repressive phase under Governor-General Rafael de Izquierdo. The mutiny panicked Spanish officials, who used it as an excuse to launch a witch-hunt against liberals in Manila. Izquierdo also forcefully supported the friars in their resistance to turning over churches to Filipino priests.

On January 27, many of the rioters were executed. Fabricated charges were brought against three priests: Father José Burgos[*], a 35-year-old mestizo intellectual; Father Jacinto Zamora, age 37; and Father Mariano Gómez, 84 years old. They were condemned to be garroted, a particularly repulsive method of execution in which the victim is strangled with an iron collar tightened by screws. The three priests were publicly executed on February 17, 1872, along with a fourth man named Zaldua, whom some scholars believe to have been the only man with certain knowledge of the priests' innocence. Izquierdo wanted the archbishop of Manila to defrock the priests before their execution, but the archbishop refused unless their guilt could be proven. He ordered church bells tolled instead. The government never released the evidence.

In life, the three priests hardly threatened Spanish rule. As martyrs, they inspired a generation of reformers, nationalists, and finally revolutionaries. Filipinos had become deeply Catholic during 300 years of Hispanization, but the Church as an institution was perceived as corrupt, hypocritical, debauched, and, underlying everything else, racist. The theme of redemptive suffering, sacrifice, and martyrdom permeated Filipino thought. Fathers Burgos, Gómez, and Zamora perfectly symbolized the unjust persecution of the Philippines by Spain. Violent revolution was held off for 24 years, but in that time the strangled priests became a unifying symbol. The brilliant novelist and patriot José Rizal* dedicated his satirical book, *El Filibusterismo*, to them: "Let these pages serve as a belated wreath of withered leaves on your forgotten graves." In this, Rizal was wrong. Those graves were not forgotten.

REFERENCE: Nicholas J. Cushner, *Spain in the Philippines*, 1971.

Ross Marlay

CAYMAN ISLANDS. The Cayman Islands are a British crown colony in the Caribbean Sea. All three of the islands—Grand Cayman, Cayman Brac, and Little Cayman—are coral formations located south of Cuba and northwest of Jamaica*. The islands were first discovered by Christopher Columbus* in 1503, and he named them Las Tortugas. When Spain's fortunes declined in the seventeenth century, Great Britain filled the political vacuum in the Caribbean. In 1670, Spain ceded the Cayman Islands to England.

REFERENCE: H. H. Wrong, *The Government of the West Indies*, 1923.

CEBALLOS, PEDRO DE. Pedro de Ceballos was born in Cádiz, Spain, in 1715 and joined the Spanish army in 1739. He was brilliant and courageous, and his rapid rise through the ranks reflected those abilities. In 1755, Ceballos was promoted to lieutenant general, and he was apppointed governor of Buenos Aires* in 1757. Much of his tenure there was spent fighting the Indians* and the Portuguese. Ceballos returned to Spain in 1766, where he was appointed captain general of Madrid. Ten years later, he returned as the first viceroy of Río de la Plata*. Ceballos was there for only two years, but he played an instrumental role in seeing to it that the gold and silver taken from Upper Peru* were shipped to Spain via Buenos Aires, not Peru*, and he promoted free trade and agriculture. Ceballos died in Córdoba*, Argentina*, on December 26, 1778.

REFERENCE: Enrique Barba, *Don Pedro de Cevallos: Gobernador de Buenos Aires y virrey de Río de la Plata*, 1937.

CEBU, DIOCESE OF. Ferdinand Magellan* placed a cross in Cebu in the Visayas* of the Philippines* in 1521, and in 1565, Miguel López de Legazpi* and the Augustinian* Andrés de Urdaneta* founded a settlement there. It was the Spanish capital of the Philippines until 1571, when administration was moved to Manila*. The diocese of Cebu was established in 1595, with Pedro de Agurto as the first bishop.

REFERENCE: *New Catholic Encyclopedia*, III:360, 1967.

CEDEÑO, MANUEL. Manuel Cedeño was born in 1781 and became a great Venezuelan* patriot and revolutionary hero. Cedeño fought with Simón Bolívar at both battles of Carabobo*, and he served as a member of Bolívar's Council of Government triumvirate in 1818. After a stint as governor of Guayana, Cedeño returned to the military campaigns and was killed in action in 1821.

REFERENCE: Donna Keyes Rudolph and G. A. Rudolph, *Historical Dictionary of Venezuela*, 1971.

CENSORSHIP. The question of censorship played an extremely important role in the development of the Spanish colonies. For both moral and political reasons, the Spanish throne rigidly controlled not only the kind of publications that could be produced in the colonies, but also the works that could be imported. From almost the time of discovery and continuing until the final independence of the colonies, the Spanish government enacted an impressive array of edicts and decrees concerning the censorship of written materials. Some of the more important ones were:

1502: The Catholic monarchs give the royal council the authority to examine all texts sold or printed in the Spanish kingdom.

1521: Charles V* issues the first edict against the written works of heretics and radicals.

1531: The Spanish government forbids sending works of fiction to the New World, with special reference to novels* of chivalry.

1543: Prince Philip forbids the shipment of fiction to the New World so as not to misguide the Indians*.

1556: King Phillip II* forbids the printing or selling of any book in the Spanish kingdom without the king's permission; also prohibits the reading of books already indexed by the Inquisition* in the Indies.

1557: Publishers of books in the New World are required to send 20 examination copies to the Council of the Indies*.

1798: All books considered to be against the Spanish government must be seized.

The extent to which the many censorship laws were enforced rigorously or at all is a major point of study by historians. The prevailing view is that, for whatever reason, inability to police or simple laxity, large numbers of prohibited books circulated freely throughout the colonial period. This was apparently particularly true of the highly proscribed novels of chivalry that were so very popular among all strata of society. Additionally, much later in the colonial period, central texts associated with the Enlightenment*, especially French social and political treatises, readily made their way to the Spanish colonies.

The motives for strict censorship, in both Spain and particularly the colonies, were uncomplicated. In the first part of the colonial era, the Spanish throne sought to protect Spain's religious mission to the Indians*. To do this, the Crown attempted to eradicate the novel of chivalry, which was viewed as heretical and capable of interrupting the timely conversion and religious instruction of the Indians. This was totally in keeping with Spain's general attitude and position during the Counter Reformation*. It also mirrored the views of the Inquisition. In the latter stage of the empire, the throne's focus changed to politics. As Spain lost its political control in the New World, it desperately tried to thwart the awakening to independence, prompted in part by anti-monarchical writings from France, England, and the United States. Such works were censored.

REFERENCE: Arthur P. Whitaker, ed., *Latin America and the Enlightenment*, 1958.

Sam L. Slick

CERVANTES DE SALAZAR, FRANCISCO. Francisco Cervantes de Salazar was born in Toledo, Spain, in 1514. He earned a law degree at the University of Salamanca. Cervantes's early career involved work with the Council of the Indies*, but he moved to Mexico City* to study and teach there in the early 1550s. Cervantes earned master's and doctoral degrees at the University of Mexico*. He entered the Roman Catholic priesthood in 1554 and then became an administrator at the University of Mexico. He became rector there in 1572. Cervantes taught Latin, rhetoric, and theology at the university, but he was also an historian, collecting documents and writing the early history of New Spain*. His most important scholarly work was the *Crónica de Nueva España*, which remains today a major primary source for colonial Mexican history. Francisco Cervantes de Salazar died on November 14, 1575, in Puebla*, Mexico.

REFERENCE: Aurora M. Ocampo de Gómez and Ernesto Prado Velásquez, *Diccionario de escritores mexicanos*, 1967.

CÉSAR, FRANCISCO. Francisco César was born in Spain but as a young man he came to the New World to find his fortune. He came to Cartagena*, Colombia*, with the expedition of Pedro de Heredia* in 1531. In 1537, he took command of an expedition that traveled from the Gulf of Uraba into the Cauca River Valley. He returned to Cartagena in 1538 and joined the expedition of Juan Vadillo. César died on that expedition in 1538.

REFERENCE: Robert H. Davis, *Historical Dictionary of Colombia*, 1977.

CÉSPEDES, CARLOS MANUEL DE. Carlos Manuel de Céspedes was born near Havana*, Cuba*, in 1819. As a young man, he traveled widely throughout Europe and the United States and acquired a powerful sense of Cuban nationalism. During the 1840s and 1850s Céspedes became a successful sugar* planter, but he continued his agitation for Cuban independence from Spain. He was a leader of local *criollo** nationalists, especially those active in the Masonic movement. Carlos Céspedes became famous throughout Cuba on October 10, 1868, when he proclaimed independence and the establishment of the Republic of Cuba in the town of Yara in Oriente Province. The proclamation launched Cuba on the Ten Years War*. By the end of October, Céspedes had nearly 15,000 followers. By the end of the year, he was in virtual control of Oriente Province.

In 1869, Céspedes convened a constitutional convention that drafted a constitution declaring Cuban independence, abolishing slavery*, and annexing the country to the United States. The delegates to the convention also elected Céspedes as the first president of Cuba. Céspedes, however, was unable to keep control of the movement. His decision to abolish slavery alienated many conservatives, as had his October 1869 decision to destroy many sugar plantations to rob the Spaniards of their economic base in Cuba. When he grew jealous of the popularity of Manuel Gómez and removed him from military command, Céspedes lost his radical support. In 1873, other revolutionary leaders removed him from the presidency. Carlos Manuel de Céspedes was ambushed and killed by Spanish soldiers in 1874.

REFERENCE: Herminio Portell Vila, *Céspedes, el Padre de la Patria Cubana*, 1931.

CEUTA. Ceuta is a Spanish outpost of 7.5 square miles located on the coast of Morocco, at the Mediterranean entrance to the Straits of Gibraltar*. In ancient times, Ceuta had been controlled by a succession of Phoenicians and Romans. The Vandals overran Ceuta in 618, and Arabs seized it in 711, where they used it as a springboard for their invasion of Iberia. Ceuta had great commercial significance as the Mediterranean outlet of the great trans-Sahara ivory, gold, and slave trade routes. But as the Reconquest took place over seven centuries and as the Moors were gradually expelled from the Iberian Peninsula, the Portuguese and the Spanish looked across the Mediterranean for conquests of their own.

Early in the fifteenth century, the Portuguese began looking for commercial opportunities in North Africa; an army led by King John I captured Ceuta from the Arabs on August 24, 1415. Although the Portuguese did not penetrate more deeply into North Africa*, Ceuta was the beginning of Portuguese expansion, first to Madeira and the Azores, then down the east coast of Africa, and finally to the New World. Ceuta remained under Portuguese control until 1580, when Phillip II* of Spain annexed Portugal. The Portuguese struggle against Spain lasted until 1668, when Spain finally recognized Portuguese independence in the Treaty of Lisbon; that treaty also ceded Ceuta to Spain. Except for the British occupation between 1810 and 1814, Ceuta has been Spanish territory ever since. One siege lasted continually from 1694 to 1720. When Morocco gained its independence in 1956, however, Ceuta remained under Spanish control. Today, Ceuta is administered by the province of Cádiz.

REFERENCES: Damiao Peres, *D. Joã I*, 1917; "Rabat: Loose Ends," *National Review*, 37 (September 6, 1985), 45.

CHACABUCO, BATTLE OF. On January 9, 1817, José de San Martín* mobilized the Army of the Andes* for the reconquest of Chile*. San Martín's plan called for an all-land invasion. An army crossing over the heights of the Andes would not only catch the royalist forces by surprise, but it would also allow San Martín to cut through the Spanish defenders' flanks on a direct route toward Santiago*. On January 13, Lieutenant Colonel Ramón Freire* was dispatched with a small force to create a diversion to cover the march of the main army. In order to confuse the enemy, each division of the army would proceed along a different route through the mountains. Colonel Juan Gregorio de las Heras* commanded one division, while the Chilean patriot, Bernardo O'Higgins* and the Argentine General, Miguel Soler, commanded the other. After descending the mountain, the various divisions would link up at pre-established points of concentration.

San Martín's superb leadership in marching the army across the Andes cannot be overestimated. He had to overcome almost insurmountable logistical difficulties. His chief problem was finding enough food for the men and the thousands of animals. The areas through which the army marched were sparsely populated and bereft of decent pasture. Therefore, the food for the 20-day march had to be transported. Furthermore, along a great part of the march, the two six-inch howitzers and ten four-inch field pieces had to be carried by hand with the aid of block and tackle. Many of the men suffered and some died from oxygen deprivation and the extreme cold.

On February 4, 1817, San Martín's advanced guard made contact with the enemy. By February 8, his forces controlled the valley of Anacagua. Originally, San Martín had planned to give battle on February 14, but thought it better to do so sooner, even though he did not yet have his heavy guns, before the royalists could concentrate more troops. On February 12, the army descended onto the plains of Chacabuco by two roads. O'Higgins led his men down one road, while Soler, with the larger force, led his down another. The patriot army, about 2,000 strong, had to march through a field covered with small hills, streams, and forests of soapbark trees, making advance difficult. The royalist army, which numbered about 1,800, awaited San Martín. Its small size was a good indication that the royalists had not expected a large army to cross the Andes. San Martín's battle plan called for O'Higgins to fake an attack on the enemy's flank while Soler, with the main division, made the attack. Instead of feigning an attack, O'Higgins actually attacked the royalists. Although he was initially repulsed, he quickly reformed his men and mauled the royalist forces. When Soler's division finally entered the battle, the royalist force was heavily outnumbered and retreated, suffering heavy losses. When the smoke cleared, 500 royalists lay dead and 600 were prisoners. The patriots, by contrast, sustained 12 dead and 120 wounded. Two days later, San Martín entered Santiago*. Fighting in Chile was not over, however, until April 15, 1818, when San Martín decisively defeated the royalists at Maipu*.

REFERENCE: Jay Kinsbruner, *Bernardo O'Higgins*, 1968.

Michael Dennis

CHAPETÓN. The term *chapetón* was used in colonial Spanish America to describe recent immigrants from Spain. It was a derogatory description ridiculing a newcomer's naïveté, ignorance, and lack of experience. It also referred to the haughtiness of many *peninsulares**. After independence, the term became synonymous with a conservative, authoritarian political philosophy.

CHARCAS. See SUCRE.

CHARCAS, *AUDIENCIA* OF. The *audiencia* of Charcas, headquartered in what is today Sucre*, Bolivia*, was established in 1559 when the growing population of Bolivia made it increasingly difficult for the *audiencia* of Lima* to deal with problems there. The region supervised by the *audiencia* of Charcas had been officially under the authority of the *audiencia* of Lima since 1542. The *audiencia* was under the jurisdiction of the viceroyalty of Peru*. At first, the *audiencia* of Charcas had jurisdiction over most of what is today Bolivia, Paraguay*, southern Peru*, and the Río de la Plata* region. As those areas gained in population and development, however, the geographical reach of the *audiencia*'s authority grew successively limited. In 1568, southern Peru was returned to the authority of Lima. Paraguay and Tucumán* were transferred to the *audiencia* of Buenos Aires* when it was founded in 1661, although they were again transferred when the *audiencia* was suppressed a decade later. With the establishment of the viceroyalty of Río de la Plata* in 1776, the new viceroy* also became the president of the *audiencia* of Charcas, although cases continued to be heard in Charcas. That too stopped in 1783, when an *audiencia* was established in Buenos Aires. The region controlled by the *audiencia* was taken over by the troops of the United Provinces of Río de la Plata* in 1810, reoccupied by Spanish forces from 1816 to 1824, but then liberated once again to become the nucleus of what is today Bolivia.

REFERENCE: Mark A. Burkholder and D. S. Chandler, *From Impotence to Authority: The Spanish Crown and the American Audiencias, 1687–1808*, 1977.

CHARLES I. See CHARLES V.

CHARLES II. Charles II, son of King Philip IV*, was born in 1661 and became the last of the House of Habsburg to rule Spain. Assuming the throne as a small child in 1665, Charles II was officially known as the King of Spain, Naples, and Sicily, but he was intellectually and physically weak and a notoriously ineffective ruler who proved unable to deal with the problems of a worldwide empire. He did not father any children and ended up naming Philip V*, the grandson of King Louis XIV of France, as his successor to the throne. Charles II died in 1700. His death precipitated the War of the Spanish Succession*.

REFERENCE: John Lynch, *Spain Under the Hapsburgs*. Vol. 2: *Spain and America, 1598 1700*, 1969.

CHARLES III. Charles III, the son of King Philip V* of Spain, was born on January 20, 1716. He assumed the throne in 1759, at the time when he was also the Duke of Parma and King of Sicily. Charles III played a critical role in administering the Spanish Empire. Intelligent and concerned about the status of Spain, Charles III embarked on a reform program at home and in the empire. He was an enlightened ruler who proved to be the best of Spain's Bourbon kings. At home, he tried to stimulate the economy, reduce the stifling power of the craft and merchant guilds, curtail the privileges of the *mesta**, and improve the country's infrastructure through an ambitious program of public works. In 1767, concerned about the growing power and influence of the Jesuit* order, he expelled the Jesuits from the New World, leaving a power vaccum that was quickly filled by Augustinians*, Dominicans*, and Franciscans*. Charles III also instituted the so-called Bourbon reforms at the end of his reign. These opened up commercial enterprise in the colonies and made governmental administration far more efficient. The reforms included the creation of the new viceroyalty of Río de la Plata*, the division of the various captaincies into *intendencias**, the termination of Seville's* monopoly on American trade, and the establishment of a public postal service. Charles III died in 1788.

REFERENCE: Anthony H. Hull, *Charles III and the Revival of Spain*, 1981.

CHARLES IV. Charles IV, the son of King Charles III*, was born on November 11, 1748. Unlike his father, who ruled the empire with the efficiency of a benevolent despot, Charles IV had no vision or strength. He assumed the throne in 1788 upon his father's death, but the Napoleonic Wars in Europe and the growing insurgency in Latin America undermined his authority and eroded his power. He also lost prestige because of the transfer of Louisiana* back to France and its prompt sale to the United States in 1803. In 1808, amid growing unrest and dissatisfaction over economic stagnation, Charles IV abdicated the throne in favor of his son, Ferdinand VII*. Charles IV died in 1819.

REFERENCE: David Hilt, *The Troubled Trinity: Godoy and the Spanish Monarchy*, 1987.

CHARLES V (CHARLES I OF SPAIN). Charles V was born in Ghent on February 24, 1500, and died September 21, 1558 at the St. Yuste monastery in Spain. Of the Habsburg dynasty, he was king of Spain (as Charles I) from 1516 to 1556 and Holy Roman Emperor from 1519 to 1556. In 1516, Charles inherited the Spanish throne from his grandfather, Ferdinand II (Ferdinand* of Aragon). In 1519, he was elected emperor and began a policy of expanding Habsburg influence in Europe and in the New World. Charles V waged numerous wars against France, the Habsburgs' main rival in Europe, and also against the Ottoman Empire, which had expanded into southeastern Europe. In fighting the Reformation in Germany, in 1521 he issued the Edict of Worms against Martin Luther and defeated the German Protestant princes in the Schmalkaldic war of 1546–1548. As the result of military setbacks Spain encountered against Protestantism in Central Europe, Charles was forced to sign the religious Peace of Augsburg in 1555.

During Charles V's reign, Spanish possessions and influence in America expanded considerably. In 1515, Juan Díaz de Solís* explored and claimed for Spain the Río de la Plata*. In 1519, Ferdinand Magellan*, a Portuguese who was employed by Charles, won the emperor's support for a voyage of discovery that resulted in the first passage around South America and the first circumnavigation of the earth. Between 1519 and 1521, Hernán Cortés*, seeking the gold of the Aztec* Empire, captured Mexico* for Spain. Charles V also commissioned Francisco Pizarro* with extensive powers in Peru* and, in 1535, Pizarro successfully completed the conquest of the Inca* empire. As Holy Roman Emperor, Charles authorized the exploration of the Caribbean coast, which was carried out by the German adventurers Ambrosius Alfinger[*] and Nikolaus Federmann[*] in 1535–1538. By the end of his reign, Charles V witnessed the boundaries of his empire in the Americas expanded as far north as California[*] and Texas[*].

REFERENCES: Manuel Fernández Álvarez, *Charles V*, 1975; H. G. Koenigsberger, *The Habsburgs and Europe, 1516–1660*, 1971.

William G. Ratliff

CHAVES, CRISTÓBAL DE. Cristóbal de Chaves was born in Badajoz, Spain, in 1533. Like so many other young men from that region of Spain, Chaves decided to seek his fortune in the New World. He was part of Pedro de Alvarado's[*] conquest of Guatemala[*], and in 1561, he reached Costa Rica[*] with Juan de Cavallón's[*] expedition. Chaves acquired a good deal of property in Costa Rica; by 1600, he was serving as an *alcalde*[*] in Cartago[*]. Eventually, Chaves ended up on the short end of a political struggle with local crown authorities and lost most of his land. Cristóbal de Chaves died in 1629.

REFERENCES: Francisco Montero Barrantes, *Elementos de historia de Costa Rica*, 2 vols., 1894; Theodore S. Creedman, *Historical Dictionary of Costa Rica*, 1977.

CHAVES, NÚFRIO DE. Núfrio de Chaves was born in Trujillo, Spain, in 1518, and he has become known in history as the individual who led the conquest of the Gran Chaco in South America. He joined the expedition of Alvar Núñez Cabeza[*] de Vaca to Asunción[*] in 1542; during the 1540s, he led expeditions up the Pilcomayo River, into Mato Grosso in present-day Brazil, and into southern Peru[*]. During the mid-1550s, Chaves led a series of expeditions to pacify various Tupi[*]-speaking tribes that were attacking Spanish settlements in Paraguay[*], and in the late 1550s, he explored much of eastern Bolivia[*] and established the city of Santa Cruz in 1561. Chaves was a leading advocate for the detachment of the province of Paraguay from Río de la Plata[*] control. Núfrio de Chaves died in 1568.

REFERENCE: Charles J. Kolinski, *Historical Dictionary of Paraguay*, 1973.

CHECA, FELICIANO. Feliciano Checa was born on June 8, 1779, in the city of Quito[*], Ecuador[*]. He is best remembered in Ecuadorian national history as an early advocate of independence who fought with Antonio José de Sucre[*] at the Battle of Pichincha[*] in 1822. He died in Quito in 1846 after a career as a military officer and administrator.

REFERENCES: Albert William Bork and Georg Maier, *Historical Dictionary of Ecuador*, 1973; Federico González Suárez, *Historia general de la República del Ecuador*, 7 vols., 1890–1903.

CHIAPAS. Chiapas, the mountainous southernmost state of modern Mexico, originally formed the outer boundary of the Aztec[*] Empire under Motecuhzoma II[*]. It was conquered in 1522 by one of Hernán Cortés's men, Luis Marín, who stayed in the area until 1524 to establish a town known as la Chiapa de los Indios, or simply Chiapas. The name of the town was eventually changed to

Ciudad Real, now known as San Cristóbal de las Casas. In 1527, the Indians[*] of Chiapas, the Chiapenecos, rebelled, and the territory had to be reconquered by Diego de Mazariegos. Chiapas's remote location, far from the major population centers of the Valley of Mexico and the western highlands of Guatemala[*], made Chiapas isolated during pre-Hispanic times, and it remained so during the colonial period. Pedro de Alvarado[*], the conqueror of Guatemala, ventured into Chiapas periodically in search of gold and silver, but more promising ventures ultimately lured him away. During his sporadic periods of interest in the area, Alvarado brought groups of between 20 and 100 Indians to pan the mountain streams for precious metals. Although Chiapas did yield a fair amount of gold, by the 1530s it was clear that Honduras[*] and northern Nicaragua[*] had more promising lodes, so Chiapas was largely abandoned by the Spaniards. Epidemics in the 1550s greatly reduced the population, making the area even less attractive for effective Spanish settlement.

By the mid-sixteenth century, Chiapas had been reduced to a semi-autonomous Indian economy based on the cultivation of subsistence crops, salt, wild cochineal[*], and some cotton grown on the Pacific coast. Life in Chiapas was based in small, self-sufficient agrarian communities around Ciudad Real and on the upper waters of the Grijalva River. The Spanish population of Chiapas remained quite small; the population of Ciudad Real and its environs was never more than 250 at any time during the seventeenth century. Despite a minimal Spanish presence in Chiapas itself, the Indians of the area suffered in many of the same ways as did natives of more colonized regions. Because Chiapas produced little silver or cacao[*] and only little cochineal, local Indians had to migrate as far as Soconusco to get cacao for tribute payments. They were sometimes taken in labor gangs to work in the silver mines of Honduras and Nicaragua.

The early eighteenth century witnessed an economic depression in southern Mexico, the onus of which fell upon the Indians of Chiapas, whom the Spaniards began to exploit more severely. In 1712, the Tzeltal Mayans[*] of Chiapas broke into rebellion. The proximate cause of this revolt was to protest the *salutación*, a widely abused practice whereby clergy took small payments from each village when they made pastoral rounds. The Tzeltal rebellion was large, nativist, and stridently anti-Spanish. It was very difficult to put down, particularly since there were so few Spaniards living in the area. The rebellion of 1712 represented one of the most powerful indigenous revolts against Spanish authority in Mexico during the late colonial period.

Politically, Chiapas fell under the jurisdiction of the kingdom of Guatemala[*]. Its provincial capital was Chiapas until 1744, when Guatemala[*] was made an archdiocese and gained ecclesiastical authority over the region. In 1786, Chiapas was designated as an intendancy[*], and in 1821, like the rest of the captaincy general of Guatemala[*], it became part of the Mexican Empire. On July 1, 1823, Chiapas voted to remain with Mexico rather than become part of the United Provinces of Central America[*]. It was the only province of the kingdom of Guatemala to do so.

REFERENCES: Murdo J. MacLeod, *Spanish Central America: A Socioeconomic History, 1520-1720*, 1973; Michael C. Meyer and William L. Sherman, *The Course of Mexican History*, 1983; Miles L. Wortman, *Government and Society in Central America, 1680–1840*, 1982.

Virginia Garrard Burnett

CHIBCHAS. The Chibchas (also known as Muiscas) were one of three principal sub-Andean indigenous cultures present at the time of the Spanish conquest of what is now Colombia*. The Chibchas occupied the moderately high central plateau (4,000 to 10,000 feet) in the eastern cordillera (east of the upper Río Magdalena) in what are now the departments of Cundinamarca and Boyacá. Little is known of their history prior to the late fifteenth century, although they appear to have had more in common with the culture of Mexico than that of the central Andes. At the time of the conquest, the Chibcha population, estimated variously at 300,000 to over 1,000,000, was the largest and densest between Peru* and Mexico. Chibcha dialects were spoken throughout Colombia, as well as in Ecuador* and Central America, but the dialects were mutually unintelligible.

Although their lack of stone construction has left few present-day archaeological remains, it is generally accepted that the Chibchas obtained a level of development much higher that of the neighboring tropical forest cultures but probably lower than that of the Maya*, Aztec*, or Inca* civilizations. They were highly praised by Spanish chroniclers of the time. The Chibchas were stronger and more united than their neighbors, and without the Spanish, they probably would have come to dominate a much larger area. At the time of the conquest, they were divided into a series of five political units consisting of federations of villages of the same ethnicity united under a chieftain with near absolute powers. The chieftain exercised political, military, and some religious functions. Taxes and tribute were exacted. The largest state, located in the south around Bogotá*, was headed by a chieftain with the title of *zipa*; the Spanish named their capital after the *zipa* they encountered, chief Bogotá. The next largest state, centered around Tunja, was headed by the *zaque*. The states were in turn divided into subdivisions headed by lesser chiefs who were confirmed by the primary chieftain.

The Chibchas were conquered by a Spanish expedition under Gonzalo Jiménez de Quesada* at the end of 1537 and early in 1538. The Chibchas had a large army with professional soldiers and draftees, which had been quite successful in raiding the tropical forest villages and in expanding their territory. There was considerable disunity within and between states, however, with chieftains fighting to expand or retain their realms. Hence, Jiménez de Quesada, with only 166 men left after his 500-mile trek from the Caribbean coast, won easily, suffering only minor casualties in a few skirmishes. Using native allies and pitting group against group, Jiménez de Quesada defeated the Chibcha piecemeal. Although much of their leadership was killed by the Spanish, most of the population survived and became docile tributaries.

The Chibcha had well marked social classes: chieftains, nobles, commoners, and slaves. Class was hereditary, but mobility was possible for outstanding service in war. Inheritance of the positions of chief and priest passed to the son of one's sister, although land passed patrilineally. Polygyny was practiced, especially among the higher classes. Religion centered on a cult of the sun, although other deities were also recognized. Priests were trained in seminary, and temples were of considerable size. Some human sacrifice was practiced. The legend of *El Dorado** apparently came from the consecration of chieftains. The new leader was coated with resin and covered with gold dust. Standing on a raft in the sacred lake Guatavita at sunrise, he was a golden statue who dove into the water, washed off the gold, and emerged as the new overlord.

The Chibcha economy, based on agriculture, was highly developed. With a temperate climate and fertile valleys, the Muiscas practiced intensive cultivation of carefully laid out fields of maize, root crops such as white and sweet potatoes, beans, squash, tomatoes, aji, coca, and tobacco*. They practiced extensive trade within and outside the region, had professional merchants, and held markets every four days in major cities. They appear to have had a form of currency (gold disks) and a crude credit system. Metallurgy was highly developed, particularly gold and copper. There was little stone construction. Houses, temples, and palaces had wattle-and-daub walls and thatched roofs. The Spanish were impressed with the number—reportedly 42—and size of the palisaded Chibcha settlements, although their actual size is unclear.

REFERENCES: Robert L. Carneiro, "The Aboriginal Cultures of Colombia," in A. Curtis Wilgus, ed., *The Caribbean: Contemporary Colombia*, 1962, 22–33; R. B. Cunninghame Graham, *The Conquest of New Granada: Being the Life of Gonzalo Jiménez de Quesada*, 1922; A. L. Kroeber, "The Chibchas," in Julian H. Steward, ed., *Handbook of South American Indians*. Vol. 2. *The Andean Civilizations*, 1963, 887–909; Gerardo Reichel-Dolmatoff, *Colombia: Ancient Peoples and Places*, 1965; Julian H. Steward and Louis C. Faron, *Native Peoples of South America*, 1959.

Robert E. Biles

CHICHIMECS. The term Chichimec refers to a number of nomadic and semi-nomadic tribes that inhabited the northern and northwestern reaches of Mexico in the pre-Spanish and early Spanish periods. Between the twelfth and fifteenth centuries, various groups of Chichimecs moved south into regions of agricultural communities, establishing permanent settlements and merging with already settled groups in central Mexico. The name Chichimeca may be translated as "People of the Dogs" (chichi meaning dog), but more likely the name derives from the placename Chichiman, meaning "Place of the Young." They were indeed the last peoples to move into Mesoamerica, the region of high civilization in Middle America.

The Franciscan* friar Bernardino de Sahagún* describes three types of Chichimecs: the Otomí*, the Tamime, and the Teochichimeca, or true Chichimecs. All these Chichimecs had a number of traits in common: they came from the north; were largely nomadic; lived by hunting, gathering, and a small amount of farming; lived in caves or grass huts; wore clothing of animal skins; practiced monogamy; and were led by chiefs who demanded tribute from successful hunts. The Teochichimeca were considered more "barbarous" than the other Chichimecs, although they have been described as skilled stone and feather workers. Overall, Chichimecs appear to have been partly nomadic hunters and partly settled villagers.

Many of the most noted Mesoamerican groups had their origins as Chichimecs, including the Tlaxcallans*, the Tepaneca of the western Valley of Mexico, the Acolhua of the eastern valley, the Chalca of Chalco, and the ultimately powerful México, or Aztecs*. These groups continued to respect their Chichimec heritage long after settling into cities and building empires, for some of their most exalted titles contained the element "Chichimec."

REFERENCES: Nigel Davies, *The Toltec Heritage*, 1980; Nigel Davies, *The Toltecs*, 1977; Bernardino de Sahagún, *Florentine Codex*, Book 10:170–175, 1950–1982.

Frances F. Berdan

CHILE. Chile is distinctive among Latin American nations in its geography and its isolation, but it shares similar experiences in relationship to imperialism and neo-imperialism. Located on the western coast of South America, Chile is a very long (over 2,600 miles) and narrow (nowhere over 250 miles) country. The harsh Atacama Desert in the north and the wet and stormy forests of the south are inhospitable to settlement and are sparsely populated, while the fertile Central Valley, with its mild climate, is home to two-thirds of the population. Chile's Southern Hemisphere location, the rugged Andes Mountains to the east, the vast expanse of the Pacific to the west, the desert on the north, and the Antarctic region to the south combine to isolate the country. Chile's population of over 12 million is predominantly mestizo*, Catholic and urban. By Latin American standards, the country is relatively industrialized and modern, with a 95 percent literacy rate and a per capita gross national product of over $1,700. Until the Pinochet coup in 1973, it was one of the more democratic countries of the region. The major contradiction to modernity is the poor distribution of wealth, a result of Spanish imperialism and the neo-imperialism of the post-colonial period.

The first permanent Spanish settlements were established in Chile by Pedro de Valdivia* in 1541. An earlier effort in 1536 had been defeated by the Araucanian* Indians, who contested European dominance for more than two centuries. The Spanish authorities issued *encomiendas** to soldiers, allowing them to exploit the land and exact tribute from the Indians*. The Araucanians, who had a history of resisting Incan* demands for tribute and submission, fought the Spanish with great skill and tenacity and restricted the Europeans to the Central Valley area. The resistance of the natives persuaded the Spanish Crown to accept the enslavement of the Indians by the *encomenderos* and to provide a royal subsidy for the maintenance of a standing army. Relations with the natives, in the form of settlement defense, pacification wars, and slave raids, were central to the economic life of the Chilean colony.

Chile was not a profitable colony for the Spanish Empire. The gold, grain, hides*, and wine exported from Chile could not justify the tens of thousands of Spanish soldiers (and the hundreds of thousands of Araucanians) killed or the drain on the royal treasury. The legacy of the incomplete conquest of Chile was a very unequal distribution of land and other wealth. Colonial Chile was a highly stratified society where physical labor was to be avoided, laborers were to be exploited, and arbitrary use of political authority was accepted.

The occupation of Spain by Napoleon Bonaparte's army brought an end to Spanish control of Chile, but independence did not eliminate the imperial patterns of the society. A *cabildo* *abierto* (open council) abolished the royal government in 1810 but failed to agree on a successor government. In 1814, a royal army from Peru re-established control in the name of the Spanish Crown but Argentine independence forces, led by José de San Martín* and joined by the Chilean *criollo* army of Bernardo O'Higgins*, liberated Santiago* in 1817 and formally declared the independence of Chile in 1818.

REFERENCES: Brian Loveman, *Chile: The Legacy of Hispanic Capitalism*, 1979; Robert J. Bauer, *Chilean Rural Society from the Spanish Conquest to 1930*, 1975.

Bruce R. Drury

CHILE, *AUDIENCIA* OF. See CHILE, CAPTAINCY GENERAL OF.

CHILE, CAPTAINCY GENERAL OF. The captaincy general of Chile was originally part of the great southern viceroyalty of Peru* that was established in 1542, one year after Pedro de Valdivia* (1500?–1553) founded Santiago* in the Central Valley of Chile*. During the sixteenth and seventeenth centuries, experiments were made on the southern peripheries of the viceroyalty with the creation of regional *audiencias* in Chile and Buenos Aires*. Ever since the conquest by Valdivia, Chile had been under a government more military than civilian. South of the River Bio Bio, the Spaniards came into contact with the warlike Araucanians* who resisted them almost continuously for 200 years. In 1565, Phillip II* decided to create an *audiencia* in the town of Concepción on the Indian frontier to the south of Santiago, with a president and three judges (*oidores*) who were entrusted with the direction of military as well as civilian affairs. It was not installed for two years, however, and survived less than a decade. Continued military disasters at the hands of the Araucanians, who adopted the white man's tactics and developed a cavalry of their own, as well as factional disputes among the Spaniards themselves persuaded the Crown to invest the president, Bravo de Saravía, with sole powers. When the situation did not improve, decrees of 1573 suppressed the *audiencia* and directed that judicial appeals in the future would be taken to the *audiencia* of Charcas*.

Chile was put under the rule of a military governor until the beginning of the seventeenth century when the experiment of an *audiencia* was tried anew. In 1609, an *audiencia* was created at Santiago, where it remained thereafter until the end of Spanish rule. Its jurisdiction extended over the territories of the modern republic, from Copiapo southward to the Strait of Magellan, and included a region east of the Andes around the settlements of Mendoza and San Juan called the province of Cuyo, later to be famous as the place where General José de San Martín* (1778–1850) was to organize the famous military expedition that crossed the Andes in January-February 1817. The new *audiencia* had a president, who was also governor with the military rank of captain general but who remained subordinate until near the end of the eighteenth century to the viceroy of Peru. Because of its military responsibilities and its remoteness from Lima*, the presidency of Chile, like that of Panama*, seems to have been permitted greater independence of action than were the governments of Charcas* and Quito*.

REFERENCES: Mark A. Burkholder and D. S. Chandler, *From Impotence to Authority: The Spanish Crown and the American Audiencias, 1687-1808*, 1977; C. H. Haring, *The Spanish Empire in America*, 1947.

Neale J. Pearson

CHILOÉ, BATTLE OF. Chiloé is a small island off the coast of southern Chile* and was the last bastion of Spanish power in the colony. On January 19, 1826, more than 4,000 Chileno troops, under the command of General Ramón Freire*, along with a small naval squadron, attacked the islands and its 2,000 Spanish defenders. The battle proved to be a decisive victory for the patriot army. When the Spanish garrison surrendered, Spain lost the last foothold in Chile.

REFERENCE: Anson U. Hancock, *History of Chile*, 1893.

CHILPANCINGO, CONGRESS OF. The Congress of Chilpancingo was convened on September 14, 1813, in Chilpancingo, Mexico, by José María Morelos* y Pavón, a leading Mexican nationalist who had inherited leadership of the independence movement from Miguel Hidalgo* y Castilla. Although the congress was divided by ideological disputes between radicals and conservatives and among *criollos**, mestizos*, and Indians*, it did declare Mexican independence on November 6, 1813, and wrote the Constitution of Apatzingan*. Morelos eventually lost control of the congress, and because it was forced to move from location to location in order to stay ahead of royalist forces, it did not provide much continuity to the independence movement. It dissolved in December 1815 after Morelos was captured by the royalists.

REFERENCE: Michael C. Meyer and William L. Sherman, *The Course of Mexican History*, 1987.

CHINQUINQUIRA, VIRGIN MARY OF THE ROSARY OF. The Virgin Mary of the Rosary of Chinquinquira is an important religious relic and shrine in Colombia*. The image of the Virgin was painted on cloth around 1555, but it was subsequently damaged, according to local belief, and then miraculously restored at Chinquinquira on December 26, 1586. Since then, it has acquired a reputation for bringing about miraculous events in the lives of devotees.

REFERENCE: Robert H. Davis, *Historical Dictionary of Colombia*, 1977.

CHIRIGUANO. At the time of the Spanish conquest, the Chiriguanos (Guarayo, Izocenio, Ava-Chiriguano, Ava-Guaraní, Chaguanaco, Giriguanos) were a slash-and-burn agricultural group of Amerindians who lived in southeastern Bolivia[*]. Originally a Tupi[*]-Guaraní[*] people who were descended from the Paraguayan Guaraní, the Chiriguanos migrated from the area of the Gran Chaco to settle along the Andes foothills between the upper Pilcomayo River to the upper Río Grande in southeastern Bolivia. The migration occurred in successive waves during the sixteenth century. Before the migration, they were primarily a hunting and foraging people, but after arriving in what is today Bolivia they adopted agriculture, raising maize, pumpkins, beans, sweet potatoes, sweet manioc, peanuts, cotton, and tobacco[*].

The Chiriguano resisted Spanish conquest, fighting a guerrilla war against Spanish expeditions throughout the sixteenth century. Franciscans[*], Dominicans[*], and Jesuits[*] all established missions[*] among the Chiriguanos, but the Indians rose up and destroyed them in 1727. Later in the eighteenth century, new Franciscan and Dominican missions began to succeed in converting the Chiriguano. By the nineteenth century, those missions were acculturating the Indians to the neo-Bolivian economy and material culture. There was still violence, however. In 1866, 1874, and 1892, the Chiriguanos revolted because of heavy in-migration by neo-Bolivian settlers. The Roman Catholic mission system exposed the Chiriguano to a regimented labor system. Late in the nineteenth century, the Chiriguano migration to the cattle ranches and sugar[*] plantations of Argentina[*] began, where they became increasingly integrated into the regional cash economy. In 1891–1892, a massacre of the Chiriguanos took place in Bolivia, after which large numbers of them were enslaved on agricultural and cattle-raising haciendas[*]. The Chiriguano population today exceeds 70,000 people, of whom 40,000 live in Bolivia. In Bolivia, there are two centers of Chiriguano Indians: the eastern Andean foothills from Abapo through Monteagudo and from Cuevo to Camantinoi, bordered on the east by a line extending from Santa Cruz to Bacuiba; and the Río Parapeti region. The Chiriguanos in the Andean foothills are known as Ava-Chiriguano, while those in the Río Parapeti area are the Izocenio-Chiriguano. Most of them resent the term Chiriguano and prefer to be called Ava or Izocenio. There are approximately 1,600 Chiriguanos who have migrated to the Paraguayan Gran Chaco in the past several decades. Several thousand are still on the secularized missions in Bolivia, where they work as craftsmen, truck drivers, teachers, and blue-collar workers. There are more than 28,000 Chiriguano in Argentina[*]. They live primarily in the departments of El Carmen, Ledesma, San Pedro, and Santa Bárbara in Jujuy and in the departments of Oran and San Martín in Salta[*]. Most of them work in sugar mills, live with Franciscan missionaries, or function in the local economy as laborers. The Chiriguano have a powerful sense of ethnic identity, and most still speak the native language, although increasing numbers are bilingual. A closely related subtribe, also known as the Ava-Guaraní, are the Simba, who total approximately 500 people and live in the province of Luis Calvo in the department of Chuquisaca in Bolivia.

REFERENCES: Isabel Hernández, "Los pueblos y las lenguas aborígenes en la actualidad," *América Indígena*, 47 (1987), 409–423; Erick D. Langer, "Franciscan Missions and Chiriguano Workers: Colonization, Acculturation and Indian Labor in Southeastern Bolivia," *Americas*, 43 (1987), 305–327; John Renshaw, "Property, Resources and Equality among the Indians of the Paraguayan Gran Chaco," *Man*, 23 (1988), 334–352; Pedro Plaza Martínez and Juan Carvajal Carvajal, *Étnias y lenguas de Bolivia*, 1985; Graciela Zolezzi and J. Riester, "Lenguas indígenas del oriente Boliviano clasificación preliminar," *América Indígena*, 47 (1987), 425–33.

CHIRINO REVOLT. Near the end of the colonial period in Venezuela*, there was much resentment among *criollos**, mestizos*, Indians*, and African slaves* over the authority of the Spanish Crown. José Leonardo Chirino, a freed *zambo**, led a slave insurrection against the Crown near Coro, Venezuela, in 1795. He openly called for the end of white supremacy. Alarmed about the implications of his demands, local *criollos* joined with Crown officials in suppressing the rebellion. Chirino was captured, hanged, and quartered in Caracas*.

REFERENCE: Donna Keyes Rudolph and G. A. Rudolph, *Historical Dictionary of Venezuela*, 1971.

CHIVALRY, NOVEL OF. See NOVEL OF CHIVALRY.

CHOISEUL, ÉTIENNE-FRANÇOIS DE. Étienne-François de Choiseul, Count of Stainville, then Duke of Choiseul, lived from June 28, 1719, to May 8, 1785. In Spanish Empire history, he has importance as the French co-instigator and staunch proponent of the mid-eighteenth-century Family Compact of France and Spain against Great Britain. Choiseul achieved prominence through a combination of his own skills, paternal influence, and a lavish life, including valuable courtly contacts that marriage to an heiress made feasible. After initial experience as an officer in the War of the Austrian Succession*, he used his assets as a courtier to polish his diplomatic talents as ambassador to Rome and Austria. Doing very well, he advanced to foreign minister in 1758. Thereafter he sometimes also handled the war and navy portfolios—and when he did not, his cousin, the Duke of Choiseul-Preslin, usually did. In this manner, he shaped and dominated French foreign policy for a dozen years. At times, he was all but de facto prime minister for Louis XV.

Choiseul, Charles III*, and the latter's minister to France, Abbé Grimaldi (soon foreign minister) negotiated the Family Compact in 1761–1762. In terms of immediate results, both powers quickly lost. Spain's late entry into the Seven Years War* in no way prevented France from being the chief loser. As is well known, Spain, by participating, also lost. Nevertheless, the alliance continued as the keystone of Spanish-French foreign policy. Choiseul entertained long-range expectations of positive results. First, he viewed the compact a means of producing another showdown with Britain. Second, with the help of Francophile personages in or with access to the Spanish court, he expected to exercise a considerable influence on his ally's policies. Third, he envisioned a major expansion of French trade, by means of Spain's granting free trade privileges in the Spanish colonial world to France.

During the 1760s, Choiseul strove to realize these objectives. The harder he pursued them, the more elusive they became. If anything, France's position vis-à-vis her partner diminished. Finally, in the Malvinas Islands* crisis of 1770, Louis XV dismissed his hard-pressed minister. His immediate reason was fear that Choiseul's alliance was about to plunge his country into a war with Britain over what, from France's standpoint, was only a remote archipelago. This brought Choiseul's career to an abrupt and permanent end.

Despite considerable energy and perception, Choiseul in his policies seems to have produced mostly negative returns for both nations. On the plus side, perhaps, he helped Spain in some degree by constantly pressing for rearmament and by joining with Charles III in his anti-Jesuit* campaign. Negatively, however, he played an important part in a disastrous diplomatic setback that Spain suffered in her contest with Britain. Because Choiseul stressed the alliance so much, Charles III and his ministers overrated his ability to deliver France in a situation of impending war. When Louis XV jettisoned his foreign minister and informed Charles III that France simply could not fight, Spain had to concede the Malvinas to Britain. Thus, from Spain's standpoint, the alliance failed of its central purpose at the first great challenge.

For France, too, the partnership did not prosper. Despite Choiseul's expectations, only minor trade advantages ever materialized. As for Spain's pro-French activists, they had much less effect on policies useful to French interests than scholars have thought. Fundamentally, Choiseul's alliance lacked a sufficiently solid base at court or in the public, due to lingering resentments left over from old Franco-Spanish conflicts. Moreover, France's internal strains, caused by the parliaments' recalcitrance and financial instability, precluded shoring up some support. Having lost all valuable colonies except the Caribbean sugar* islands in the Seven Years War and not having obtained the compensating commercial advantages from her partner, France by 1770 lacked a large enough stake in Spain's troubles with Britain overseas to make war worth its risks. Possibly Choiseul would have done better had Spanish officialdom done more to meet France's needs. With circumstances what they were, Choiseul will probably be remembered as a statesman whose reach exceeded his grasp.

REFERENCES: Louis Blart, *Les Rapports de la France et l'Espagne après le pacte de Famille jusqu'a la fin du ministre du duc de Choiseul*, 1915; "Choiseul," *Dictionaire de biographie française*, 8: 1219–1220; H. M. Scott, "The Making of a Diplomat," *International History Review*, 4 (1982), 414–20.

Lowell L. Blaisdell

CHOLO. Throughout much of Latin America, the term *cholo* is synonymous with *mestizo**, but in Peru* and Bolivia* it has a somewhat more specialized meaning, referring to an individual of Indian* or primarily Indian ancestry who nevertheless aspires to assimilation with the mestizo population and integration within the larger commercial economy.

CHRONICLE. The chronicle (*crónica*) occupies a special place in Spanish colonial literature. The majority of such works were written in the form of historical narrative, although a few major works of epic or narrative poetry certainly must be judged as chronicles from at least an historical point of view. The chronicle was and is a record of conquests, explorations, and travels undertaken by the Spaniards in the New World from 1492 to roughly 1675. The works usually include considerable doses of fiction. In any event, the rich descriptions of flora, fauna, and the indigenous civilizations encountered by the Spaniards, as well as historical events such as conquests and battles, stand till this day as important sources for historical documentation.

The chroniclers (*cronistas*) came from many walks of life, although most were either conquistadors*, soldiers, priests, or adventurers. Thanks to their vivid and imaginative works, readers are afforded eyewitness accounts of the New World that the Spaniards discovered. Some of the most important narrative chronicles are: *Diario de viaje* (Christopher Columbus*); *Cartas de relación* (Hernán Cortés*); *Verdadera historia de la conquista de la Nueva España* (Bernal Díaz del Castillo*); *Naufragios* * (Alvar Núñez Cabeza de Vaca*); *Historia general de las Indias* (Francisco López* de Gómara); *Historia General de las cosas de la Nueva España* (Bernardino de Sahagún*); *Historia del Perú* (Pedro Cieza* de León); *Historia general y natural de las Indias y Tierra Firme del mar océano* (Gonzalo Fernández de Oviedo*); *Historia natural y moral de las Indias* (José de Acosta*); *Brevísima relación de la destrucción de las Indias* (Fray Bartolomé de Las Casas*); *Descubrimiento de las Indias y su conquista* (Juan Suárez* de Peralta); *Relación del Nuevo Descubrimiento del famoso río Grande de las Amazonas* (Fray Gaspar de Carvajal*); *Comentarios reales* (El Inca Garcilaso* de la Vega); *Histórica Relación del Reino de Chile* (Fray Alonso de Ovalle*); *Historia general del Reino de Chile* (Fray Diego de Rosales); *Décadas* (Antonio de Herrera* y Tordesillas); *Historia de la conquista de México* (Antonio de Solís y Rivadeneyra); *Historia del descubrimiento y conquista del Perú* (Agustín de Zárate*); *La Argentina manuscrita* (Ruiz Díaz de Guzmán); and *Historia general de las conquistas del Nuevo Reino de Granada* (Lucas Fernández* de Piedrahita). The three great epic poems that qualify for many literary critics as major chronicles are: *La araucana* (Alonso de Ercilla* y Zúñiga); *Arauco domado* (Pedro de Oña*); and *Elegías de Varones Ilustres de Indias* (Juan de Castellanos*).

REFERENCES: Ángel Flores, *The Literature of Spanish America: The Colonial Period*, 1966; Arturo Torres-Rioseca, *The Epic of Latin American Literature*, 1942.

Sam L. Slick

CÍBOLA, SEVEN CITIES OF. The Seven Cities of Cíbola were the chimerical cities, believed to be made of gold, that promoted Spanish exploration of what is now the south and southwestern United States. The origin of the ''seven cities'' myth is obscure, but probably comes from medieval European folk tales. Belief in the existence of the Seven Cities of Cíbola (sometimes believed to be a single city) took root after Álvar Núñez Cabeza* de Vaca, a Spanish soldier who had been shipwrecked off the coast of Texas* in 1528 and had wandered through the southwest for seven years, returned to New Spain* in 1536 with tales of his adventures, including a vague description of such cities. The viceroy of New Spain, Antonio de Mendoza*, sent an exploratory party, consisting of Esteban, a slave who had traveled with Cabeza de Vaca, and a Franciscan friar, Marcos de Niza*, to investigate the tales. Esteban died en route, but Friar Marcos returned to New Spain giving full verification to the claim. It is possible that Friar Marcos, having traveled as far north as present-day New Mexico, confused the site of Zuñi Indian pueblos, decorated with glittering bits of quartz, with the rich cities.

The "discovery" of the elusive cities prompted great excitement in Mexico. In 1540, the viceroy authorized Francisco Vázquez de Coronado* to travel north, where the Indians assured them of a mythical "land of Quiriva," a fabulously wealthy land in the far distance, even more bountiful than Cíbola. Vásquez de Coronado's expedition transversed the region as far north as present-day Kansas and as far west as Arizona, but returned to New Spain in 1542 with nothing more than tales of great "shaggy cows." It would be many years before Spain would try any further exploration or settlement of the vast northern territories.

REFERENCE: Michael C. Meyer and William L. Sherman, *The Course of Mexican History*, 1983.

Virginia Garrard Burnett

CIBONEY. The Ciboney were an Arawak*-speaking people living in Cuba* at the time of the Spanish conquest. They lived in western Cuba and southwestern Hispaniola*. They were essentially a Stone Age culture enjoying only the most rudimentary forms of agriculture. The Spaniards who conquered Cuba and Hispaniola found the Ciboney to be a peaceful, gentle people. The Indians, however, did not survive the Spanish diseases and the labor exploitation of the *encomienda**. By 1520, the Ciboney were extinct.

REFERENCE: Jaime Suchlicki, *Historical Dictionary of Cuba*, 1988.

CIEZA DE LEÓN, PEDRO. Born in Spain in 1518, Pedro Cieza de León arrived in the New World at the tender age of 13. He traveled widely throughout the continent. A man of keen intellect and great literary talent, Cieza de León was also a born historian. He eventually made his way to Peru* where he was named by the government as the official chronicler. This position afforded him an optimal opportunity to collect data for his historical chronicles. Around 1541, he began to write the first of four parts of his ambitious and famous study on Peru, the Incas*, and Francisco Pizarro's* conquest. He finished this work in 1550.

Cieza de León's intention was to provide an all-encompassing view of the Incan Empire. The first part, titled *Primera Parte o Crónica del Perú*, was published in Seville* in 1533 and treated the geography of the Incan Empire. The second part, titled *Del Señorío de los Incas*, a social and historical account of the Indians[*], was not published until 1880; a third part, incredibly, was not published until 1946. The fourth part, dealing with Pizarro's conquest of the Peru, has been lost.

Cieza de León's greatest claim was his ability to create objective and attractive historical tracts that, up until today, remain among the very best sources of information concerning the Incas and early colonial Peru. He died in 1560.

REFERENCES: Albert William Bork and Georg Maier, *Historical Dictionary of Ecuador*, 1973; A. Curtis Wilgus, *The Historiography of Latin America: A Guide to Historical Writing, 1500–1800*, 1975.

Sam L. Slick

CIMARRÓN. In colonial Hispanic America, the term *cimarrón* was used to describe escaped African slaves[*] who had made their way to freedom in isolated, rural areas.

CINTRA, AGREEMENT OF. The Agreement of Cintra was an agreement between Spain and Morocco that went into effect on April 1, 1958. In the agreement, Spain ceded to Morocco the northernmost part of its Saharan territory—the Tekna Zone[*]. The Franco-Spanish Convention of 1912[*] had defined the 25,600-square-kilometer region as the southern sector of the Spanish protectorate zone in Morocco. Morocco had been demanding the region ever since the Spanish-Moroccan Declaration of Madrid of 1956[*], in which Spain ended its protectorate over northern Morocco and recognized Moroccan independence. Spain delayed handing over the Tekna Zone until the Army of Liberation[*] had been crushed.

REFERENCE: John Mercer, *Spanish Sahara*, 1975.

CIPANGU. In the late fifteenth century, when the European voyages of discovery to the New World began, Cipangu was the geographical term used to refer to Japan. Marco Polo had traveled widely throughout Asia at the end of the thirteenth century, and in his published writings, he described a land of riches lying 1,500 miles off the coast of Cathay, which he called Cipangu. During the next two centuries, the term Cipangu became synonymous with Japan. Because Polo had placed Cipangu much too far east of China, Christopher Columbus[*] mistakenly thought that he had reached Cipangu when he landed at Cuba[*].

REFERENCE: David Quinn, ed., *New American World.* Volume I: *America from Concept to Discovery: Early Exploration of North America*, 1979.

CISNEROS, BALTASAR HIDALGO DE. Baltasar Hidalgo de Cisneros was born in Cartagena, Spain, in 1775. Following his father's lead, he joined the royal navy and participated against the British at Trafalgar in 1805 and against the Napoleonic invasion of Spain in 1808. Cisneros spent a year as captain general of Cartagena before his appointment as viceroy[*] of Río de la Plata[*] in 1809. He was destined to be the last viceroy there. He arrived shortly before the May Revolution of 1810[*], and he was replaced by the Primera Junta Patriótica

(First Patriotic Junta) headed by President Cornelio Saavedra. Cisneros returned to Spain. He died in Cartagena in 1829.

REFERENCES: Romula D. Carbia, *Historia crítica de la historiografía argentina, desde sus orígenes en el siglo XVI*, 1925–1940; Ricardo Piccirilli, Francisco L. Romay, and Leoncio Gianello, eds., *Diccionario Histórico Argentino*, 6 vols., 1953–1955.

Fred Koestler

CISNEROS BETANCOURT, SALVADOR. Salvador Cisneros Betancourt was born to wealthy parents in Camagüey, Cuba*, in 1828. He was known as the Marquís de Santa Lucia. By 1851, he was closely associated with the independence movement of Joaquín de Agüero*, and a few years later, Spanish authorities arrested him and imprisoned him in Spain. He was back in Cuba during the 1860s and emerged as a leader of the Camagüey conspiracy of 1868, which set off the Ten Years War* (1868–1878). During the war, Cisneros served as president of the rebel legislature; he succeeded Carlos Manuel de Céspedes* as president of the rebel republic from 1873 to 1875. During the uprising against Spain in the 1890s, Cisneros was once again selected as president of the republic, just after the death of José Martí* in 1895. After the revolution, Cisneros played a leading role in drafting the first constitution of the new republic. Salvador Cisneros Betancourt died in 1914.

REFERENCE: Ramiro Guerra y Sanchez, *Historia de la nación cubana*, 10 vols., 1952.

CISPLATINE PROVINCE. The Provincia Cisplatina was the name given by the Portuguese to the Banda Oriental, today's Uruguay*. The Portuguese had invaded the Banda Oriental in 1811. This move reflected a traditional Portuguese policy of expansion, since the seventeenth century, for the control of the river system of La Plata: the Paraná, Uruguay, and Paraguay rivers. The Portuguese withdrew from the Banda Oriental in 1812, as the result of an armistice concluded between the Argentine forces and Elío in October 1811. They returned in 1816 when Buenos Aires* was in deep trouble, facing military threats from Peru* where General José de San Martín* was organizing his Army of the Andes* for the liberation of Chile*.

John VII, since 1815 "King of Portugal, Brazil, and Algarves," continued the traditional policy of annexation in the Río de la Plata* area. The new Portuguese policy was twofold: to destroy José Gervasio Artigas*, Uruguay's founding father, who since 1815 was in command of the Banda Oriental, and to annex the territory once and for all. Artigas also had to face the continued hostility of Buenos Aires, since it opposed a federal solution; that is, an autonomous Banda Oriental. Artigas, also powerful in Entre Ríos and Corrientes, attempted to fight both Buenos Aires and the Portuguese. He aimed at freeing the seven Uruguayan missions that the Portuguese had occupied in 1801. Already in 1816, Artigas was aware of the Portuguese plans that ironically had been instigated by the Argentines (Manuel José García) to get rid of the *jefe de los orientales*. He then decided to attack first, but his plans failed. The Portuguese invasion provoked the indignation of the Argentines who forced the Buenos Aires government to change its attitude. Under General Carlos Federico Lecor, the Portuguese entered the country and were able to take Montevideo on January 17, 1817. After the battle of Tacuarembó (1820), Artigas was forced to flee to Paraguay*. With false promises, the Portuguese then attempted to gain the hearts of the Uruguayans, and Lecor convoked a congress to decide the future of the country. This Cisplatine Congress in Montevideo reluctantly accepted the incorporation of the Cisplatina oriental as an autonomous province within the Portuguese United Kingdom. The name Provincia Cisplatina was a Napoleonic projection of revolutionary France.

When Brazil became independent in 1822, the Provincia Cisplatina was automatically incorporated into the Brazilian empire, although Uruguayan resistance continued. In 1823, the *cabildo** of Montevideo put its city under Argentine protection, but Brazilian domination continued. The landing of the "Immortal Thirty-Three"* and the subsequent war between Argentina and Brazil, 1825–1828, put an end to the Brazilian occupation. The intervention of British diplomacy led to the establishment in 1828 of today's República Oriental del Uruguay, a buffer state between its two powerful neighbors.

REFERENCE: Lorenzo Belinzón, *La revolución emancipadora uruguaya y sus dogmas democráticos*, 2 vols., 1932.

O. Carlos Stoetzer

CIUDAD BOLÍVAR, DIOCESE OF. The Roman Catholic diocese of Ciudad Bolívar in Venezuela* was established in 1790. It was at first called the diocese of Guayana. The first bishop was Francisco de Ibarra*.

REFERENCE: *New Catholic Encyclopedia*, III:893–94, 1967.

CLAVER, PEDRO. Pedro Claver was born in Spain in 1580; in 1602, he took vows as a Jesuit* priest. He arrived in Cartagena*, Colombia*, in 1610 to complete his novitiate. After he was ordained a priest in 1616, he began a lifelong career working among the black slaves* of the Cartagena region. Eventually, Claver became known as the "Apostle of the Negroes." He died in 1654 and was canonized by Pope Leo XIII in 1888.

REFERENCE: Robert H. Davis, *Historical Dictionary of Colombia*, 1977.

CLAVIJERO, FRANCISCO JAVIER. Francisco Javier Clavijero was born in Veracruz, New Spain*, to *criollo** parents on September 6, 1731. He entered the Jesuit* order in 1748 and was educated at a Jesuit college in Puebla*. A brilliant scientist and philosopher, Clavijero taught at a number of prominent universities in New Spain. When the Jesuits were expelled from the New World in 1767, Clavijero went to Italy. Fluent in several Indian languages, he wrote his famous *Historia antigua de México*, a description of pre-Conquest Mexico based on primary sources. The book was published in 1780 and 1781. He died in Bologna, Italy, on April 2, 1787.

REFERENCE: E. J. Burrus, "Jesuit Exiles: Precursors of Mexican Independence," *Mid-America*, 36 (1954), 161–75; A. Curtis Wilgus, *Historiography of Latin America: A Guide to Historical Writing, 1500-1800*, 1975.

CLOTHING. See Textile Tradition of Middle America

COAHUILA. Spanish settlers first reached Coahuila in what is today northern Mexico* in 1575, but until 1674, the region was governed as part of New Vizcaya*. Coahuila became a separate Spanish province, with its own governor, in 1674. The province included what is present-day Texas* until 1716. Spain placed Coahuila under the jurisdiction of the Internal Provinces* in 1777, and it stayed there until the end of the colonial period. In 1821, Coahuila became part of the newly independent Mexico. See NEW SPAIN.

COARTACIÓN. Unlike much of the rest of North and South America, Cuba* developed a large class of free blacks. Sugar production was not nearly as intense in Cuba in the 1600s as it was on Hispaniola,* Jamaica,* and Puerto Rico,* so the demand for cheap, involuntary labor was not nearly as great. African slaves on Cuba also enjoyed a legal distinction unknown in most other parts of the empire. Early in the 1500s African slaves received the status of *coartación*— the right to negotiate with their owners for emancipation. Slaves could save up to purchase their freedom or the freedom of their children, or they could arrange to pay out their owner in installments. The practice of *coartación* was more widely exercised in urban areas, where slaves knew of the law and where their opportunities for extra wage labor were greater, than in isolated rural areas where most of them were field hands. Slaves could not exercise the *coartación* until they had already served for seven years, but in most cases the emancipated slaves had been born in Cuba, not in Africa. By 1774 the total Cuban population had increased to 171,620 people. Of that number, more than 75,000 were of African descent and nearly 31,000 of them were free.
REFERENCES: H. H. S. Aimes, "Coartación: A Spanish Institution for the Advancement of Slaves into Freedmen," *Yale Review*, 17 (1909), 412–31.

COCHABAMBA. In 1783, Spain established Cochabamba in what is today Bolivia* as an intendancy* within the viceroyalty of Río de la Plata*. Spanish authority in the region disintegrated after 1810, and in 1825 Cochabamba became part of the new nation of Bolivia*. See BOLIVIA.

COCHINEAL. The production of cochineal, a bright red dye made from the bodies of small insects (Dactylopius coccus) found on the nopal cactus, dates to pre-Hispanic times. The Indians* of southern Mexico and Guatemala* traded cochineal widely and used it as a dye for textiles. The process of extracting cochineal was a delicate one; the female layed her eggs on the plant, passed into the chrysalis stage, and was gently brushed into a receptacle and dried out in the sun. It took approximately 25,000 live insects to make one pound of dye, and 70,000 dried ones to make the same amount. The work was tedious and required great skill. During colonial times, cochineal was produced almost exclusively by Indian labor. Although the Indians gathered the cochineal insect in the wild, the Spaniards formed large plantations, called *nopalerías*, where the cochineal was raised and produced. In pre-Hispanic times, cochineal was produced in great quantities in Mexico in the Mixteca, in Oaxaca*, and around Puebla*; these areas continued to be important centers of the trade after the conquest. By 1600, Spaniards in Mexico shipped between 250,000 and 300,000 pounds of cochineal from Vera Cruz* to Spain annually, where it was usually sold to textile makers in the Netherlands.

The successes of Mexican cochineal production encouraged Spaniards in Central America to produce the dye, particularly after the cacao* industry collapsed in the early seventeenth century. The cochineal industry boomed in 1611. With government encouragement *nopalerías* appeared in the western highlands of Guatemala, in Totonicapán, Suchitepequez, Guazacapán, and south of Lake Atitlán, as well as throughout northern Nicaragua*. The boom lasted until 1621 and then ended abruptly, possibly because of plagues of locusts that ravaged the crop in 1616 and 1618. After 1621, the production of cochineal centered almost completely in Mexico, which had remained the primary producer of the crop. Although the lack of skilled Indian labor hampered the industry's expansion during the seventeenth century, the rich red dye was a vital commodity for Mexico throughout the entire colonial period. The growing textile industry in Europe and the expanded economic policies of the Bourbon period in the early eighteenth century greatly encouraged the cochineal industry. By the mid-eighteenth century, cochineal had become, after silver, Mexico's second most valuable export. It was produced mainly in Oaxaca, where as many as 30,000 Indians were employed in the industry. Cochineal remained a vital export well into the independence period.

REFERENCES: Murdo J. MacLeod, *Spanish Central America: A Socioeconomic History, 1520-1720*, 1973; Michael C. Meyer and William L. Sherman, *The Course of Mexican History*, 1983.

Virginia Garrard Burnett

COCOLIZTLI. See MATLAZAHUATL.

CODEX (pl., codices). Codices are the "books" made by the Indians* of Mesoamerica before the Spanish conquest. The earliest known codices were written by the Mixtecs of southern Mexico, who painted scenes in brilliant color on deerskin. They provide valuable historical information about Mixtec society and military victories. The earliest known Mixtec codex dates back to A.D. 692. The Maya* of Yucatán* also produced a great many codices, written on vegetable fiber paper. These codices included not only the kinds of pictorial depictions found in earlier Mixtec codices, but also the hieroglyphic written language used by the great lowland Maya of the classic period. Unfortunately, the 27 Maya codices were burned in July 1562 by the Bishop of Yucatán, Diego de Landa*, who deemed them to be the "works of the devil." The most important codices still in existence are the work of the Aztecs*, who wrote their chronicles using a combination of pictographic, ideographic, and partially phonetic characters (glyphs) representing numbers, calendar symbols, and proper nouns. The Aztecs had an extensive tradition of oral literature that early Spanish friars, such as Bernardino de Sahagún* and Diego de Durán, had the foresight to have native scribes record in written form. The results were post-conquest codices in the traditional form, supplemented by glosses, or annotations, in Spanish or Latin. Sahagún and others also attempted to transliterate native languages into the Latin alphabet, which allowed Indians to record texts in their own words.

REFERENCES: Patricia Reiff Anawalt, *Indian Clothing Before Cortes: Meso-American Costumes from the Codices*, 1981.

Virginia Garrard Burnett

COFFEE. Although coffee was widely known in the Caribbean in the seventeenth and early eighteenth centuries, it did not become a cash crop in Hispanic America until the very end of the colonial period. It was introduced into Colombia* in the 1720s but developed very slowly. French immigrants, fleeing Haiti after the revolt of 1791, brought new techniques for raising coffee to Cuba*, and the industry took root there. French traders brought coffee plants from the Antilles to Costa Rica* and Colombia in the 1790s. By the early 1800s, the first coffee plantations were producing a crop for export. Eventually, coffee became the primary export in Central America and Colombia.

REFERENCE: Robert C. Beyer, "The Quality of Coffee: Its Colombian History," *Inter-American Economic Affairs*, 2 (1948), 72–80.

COFRADÍA. The *cofradía* was a religious club or organization of the Roman Catholic church. Usually, these clubs were organized along parish and diocesan lines, and they were dedicated to the worship of a saint, the care of a shrine, or a charitable concern. In the New World, as the decades passed, some of the *cofradías* acquired substantial resources, including land and income-producing properties. Considerable resentment began to accumulate in some areas, among the poorer classes, about the wealth and power of the *cofradías* and the Church in general. That resentment became part of the revolutionary equation when the independence movements began in the early 1800s.

REFERENCE: *New Catholic Encyclopedia*, IV: 154–56, 1967.

COLLAZO, ENRIQUE. Enrique Collazo was born in Santiago de Cuba in 1848. He studied military science in Spain as a young man and then returned to Cuba* in 1868 to participate in the Ten Years War* (1868–1878). He served as an aide to General Máximo Gómez*; after the Pact of Zanjón, Collazo fled to Jamaica*, where he remained until 1895 when the revolution erupted again. At that time, he joined forces with General Calixto García*. After the winning of independence, Collazo served as a member of the national legislature and founded and edited a daily newspaper* in Havana*, *La Nación*. He died in 1921.

REFERENCES: Ramiro Guerra y Sánchez, *Historia de la nación cubana*, 10 vols., 1952; Jaime Suchlicki, *Historical Dictionary of Cuba*, 1988.

COLOCOLO. Colocolo was an Araucanian* Indian born in Chile* around 1515. He was one of the leading figures in the Araucanian resistance to Pedro de Valdivia*. Along with Caupolicán*, he is credited with defeating the Spaniards at the Battle of Tucapel. In 1554, Colocolo's warriors burned the city of Concepción. Colocolo continued the fight against the Spaniards until he was killed in the Battle of Lumanco in 1561.

REFERENCE: Salvatore Bizarro, *Historical Dictionary of Chile*, 1987.

COLOMBIA. From its founding as a colony to its independence, Colombia was known variously as the New Kingdom, New Granada*, Cundinamarca, and Colombia. Both as a colony and as a nation, Colombia has been shaped by its geography. Its rugged terrain has made communication difficult and regionalism strong. Loyalty has commonly gone to the *patria chica* before the nation, central authority has more often been weak, and the centralist-federalist conflict has marked the nation since colonial times. Located in northwestern South America, between 4° south and 12° north latitude, Colombia has coasts on both the Caribbean and the Pacific, although the latter is not hospitable. Temperature varies with elevation. The nation is divided into three major regions—the Andean (with three mountain ranges and several subregions), the Caribbean, and the East—with authorities disagreeing about subregions. The most advanced indigenous peoples lived in the highlands of the Andes, as has most of the colonial and present-day population. The hot Caribbean coast (known to Colombians as the Atlantic coast) was important in colonial times for its ports and plantation agriculture but was small in population until recent years. The East, with 60 percent of the area and very little population, is divided into the Amazon rain forest in the south and the grassy *llanos* (plains) of the Orinoco River basin. The nation's 440,000 square miles place it between Alaska and Texas* in size. Colombia is ethnically diverse with whites, mestizos*, blacks*, and indigenous groups. Social class and ethnicity have long been strongly correlated, particularly during the colonial period. Class lines were very strong before and after independence, and much of the following is the history of the small group of *peninsulares** and *criollos**.

Estimates of the indigenous population at the time of the conquest vary considerably. Perhaps 700,000 to over 1,000,000 people, divided into eight language groups, lived in Colombia. The most advanced and numerous were the sub-Andean groups, most notably the Chibchas*. By 1650, however, they had largely lost their cultural identity, while some of the tropical forest societies survived into this century. Because of disease and exploitation, the indigenous population declined from the conquest until the end of the seventeenth century. These peoples suffered great loss of land, poverty, and exploitation.

The first European to reach the Colombian coast was Alonso de Ojeda* in 1500, followed by Rodrigo de Bastidas*, who explored much more of the coast. The first permanent settlements were Santa Marta*, founded in 1525 by Bastidas, and Cartagena* (which became the most important colonial port), founded in 1533 by Pedro de Heredia*. By 1539, all but one of the major inland colonial towns had been founded, including Santa Fe de Bogotá* in 1538, which became the major political and administrative center of the colony. Gonzalo Jiménez* de Quesada named the area around Santa Fé the New Kingdom of Granada, and Colombia was also later referred to as the New Kingdom or New Granada (*Nueva Granada*).

In the Spanish Empire, New Granada was neither as important as New Spain* and Peru* nor a backwater. The first two centuries of Spanish rule were marked by slow development, ineffectual government, and the evolution of distinct regions. Isolation predominated over central authority. The Roman Catholic Church* played a crucial role in the colony, particularly in education and welfare. The expulsion of the Jesuits* in 1767 is counted as one of the more important events of the colonial period. Agriculture was the major occupation, although mining played an important role and a small textile industry developed. The *encomienda** system (grants of authority to Christianize and exploit indigenous groups) was more limited than in other colonies. African slaves were particularly used along the Caribbean coast but spread into other areas. As in the rest of the Spanish Empire, Colombian women were treated as chattel and identified primarily with the roles of wife and mother. Peasant women, however, played an important, if seldom recognized, economic role, and upper-class women affected events indirectly through influence on the men in their families. Women did play some role in the independence movement but saw no change in their status as a consequence of independence.

The end of the period of conquest and the beginning of the colonial period are more or less marked by the establishment of the royal *audiencia** in Santa Fé, decreed on July 17, 1549, and installed on April 17, 1550. (Students will note frequent discrepancies in the dates used by authors because of their choice of the date of either the decree or the actual establishment.) In 1564, the king appointed a president with powers of governor and captain general* with some dependence on the viceroyalty of Peru*. The president's authority covered much of present-day Colombia, Panama*, and Venezuela*. Although three areas of southern Colombia were under the presidency of Quito*, the beginning of Colombian nationality is often dated from this period. A viceroyalty was established at Santa Fe in 1717–1723 and again in 1739–1810. The viceroyalty of New Granada* included the captaincy general of Venezuela* and the presidency of Quito (Ecuador). In practice, however, the viceroy's actual administration covered only New Granada (most of present-day Colombia and Panama). The viceroys* left a strong impression on the last century of colonial rule.

After 1750, changes in Spain produced reforms and an acceleration of change in New Granada. Education and trade increased, introducing ideas that eventually led to revolution. By 1800, New Granada had a reputation for intellectual and scientific activity. The reformist *comunero** revolt of 1780–1781, led by *mestizos*, was followed by stirrings among the *criollos*, typified by the precursor of Colombian independence, Antonio Nariño*. The French invasion of Spain in 1808, the 1809 rebellion in Quito, the 1809 meeting of the first consultative body in Colombia, and the constitutional convention in Cádiz, Spain, all moved New Granada toward independence. On July 20, 1810, the *criollos* of Bogotá created a junta and claimed authority over New Granada. (Although July 20 is now celebrated as independence day, the junta actually recognized Ferdinand VII* as their legitimate ruler.) Most but not all other towns also replaced the Spanish authorities. There followed a period known as the *patria boba* (foolish fatherland) in which the regional centers fought over regional dominance, central vs. federal control, and independence. Cartagena, for example, was tied by trade more to the Caribbean than to the interior of Colombia; it thus preferred a federal arrangement to the central authority of Bogotá. Key figures in this period included Nariño, Camilo Torres*, Francisco Santander*, Francisco de Caldas*, and the Venezuelan Simón Bolívar*. The disunity of the patriots facilitated the reconquest by the Spanish in 1815–1816, which was followed by a reign of terror in which many of the patriot leaders were executed. Although conflict would continue until 1824, Bolívar effectively liberated New Granada in 1819 with the campaign culminating in the Battle of Boyacá*.

On December 17, 1819, the Congress of Angostura* created the Republic of Colombia (later called Gran Colombia by historians), consisting of Cundinamarca (previously called New Granada), Venezuela, and Ecuador* (though the latter was not yet liberated). Bolívar was named president, but vice-president Santander acted as president for most of the period from 1821 to 1827. In 1821, the Congress of Cúcuta* produced a relatively liberal, secular, but centralist constitution. The same year, Panama declared its independence from Spain and joined Colombia. By the mid-1820s, there was an intellectual resurgence in Cundinamarca. The republic of Colombia, however, was racked by regionalism. Bolívar, returning to power in 1827, was unable to regain national unity, and by 1829–1830, Venezuela and Ecuador had seceded. The remaining portion then reorganized and in 1832 became the Republic of New Granada with Santander as president.

The wars of independence had not destroyed the civilian elites of Colombia as they had in many other nations. Moreover, the military leaders who liberated the nation were heavily Venezuelan and men of color. Thus, the civilian *criollos* of Bogotá and the other towns continued to dominate the governments. Colombia saw only one military dictatorship in the nineteenth century and one in the twentieth. Still, divisions, ideology, and personalism ran deep. The nineteenth century saw eight civil wars. Two issues from the independence period dominated Colombian politics well into the twentieth century—centralism vs. federalism and the role of the church. These issues led to the formation of the Liberal and

Conservative parties, which still dominate the nation. The Colombia that gained independence was poor and thinly populated. According to the census of 1843, there were 1.9 million inhabitants (compared to 27.8 million in 1989). The *República de Nueva Granada* became the *Confederación Granadina* in 1858, the *Estados Unidos de Colombia* in 1863, and the *República de Colombia* on August 5, 1886. The final major adjustment in Colombia's territory came with the independence of Panama in 1903.

REFERENCES: Harry Bernstein, *Venezuela and Colombia*, 1964; Jesús Henao and Gerardo Arrubla, *History of Colombia*, 1938; Harvey F. Kline, *Colombia: Portrait of Unity and Diversity*, 1983; A. Curtis Wilgus, ed. *The Caribbean: Contemporary Colombia*, 1962.

Robert E. Biles

COLONIAL ADMINISTRATION. In the Spanish Empire, political power rested clearly in the Spanish monarchy, and all authority was then distributed down through the imperial system to lesser appointees. The most important political institution in the governing of the New World was the Council of Indies.* The council was directly subordinate to the monarchy. It advised the monarchy on all imperial matters, drafted legislation for the colonies, and served as an appellate judicial body to hear civil appeals from the colonies. The Council of the Indies was directly responsible for all clerical and political appointments throughout the empire, and it had responsibility for monitoring, investigating, and analyzing the activities of all crown officials in the Americas and in the Philippines. Over the years, the Council of the Indies became extraordinarily bureaucratic in its administration.

The primary imperial officer in the Americas was the viceroy* who was appointed by the king and given responsibility for implementing imperial legislation, collecting revenues, monitoring the welfare of the Indians*, regulating labor requirements, maintaining order, overseeing church affairs, and a host of other duties. In less developed areas of the empire, the Council of the Indies sometimes created a captaincy-general instead of a viceroyalty. The captain-general was a high-ranking military officer who administered colonial affairs until viceroyalty authority developed.

Because there were only four viceroyalties during the colonial period—New Spain,* Peru,* New Granada,* and La Plata*—the viceroys found themselves exercising authority over vast geographical regions. To assist them, the Council of the Indies divided each viceroyalty into a number of *audiencias*.* The *audiencias* were advisory bodies to the viceroy and also served as appellate courts for their jurisdictions, subordinate judicially only to the Council of the Indies. The *audiencias* were governed by ministers who were appointed by the Council of the Indies. In areas far distant from the viceregal center, the *audiencias* also exercised executive authority in implementing imperial edicts and laws.

The *audiencias* were also subdivided into a variety of local jurisdictions. The basic subdivisions were the *alcaldes mayores*,* *corregidores*,* and *gobernadores*.

Although they had different names, there were no major differences in their functions. All were appointed by the crown, and all of them exercised executive, legislative, and judicial authority in their regions of jurisdiction. The *corregidor* was the superior administrator and judge of a district within an *audiencia*. The *corregidor* presided over a municipal council known as a *cabildo** or over a rural area. Sometimes the Council of the Indies would appoint a *gobernador*, *alcalde mayor*, or even a *presidente* over a region, and that individual would exercise powers very similar to those of a *corregidor*. There were a host of lesser functionaries employed to carry out the directions of viceroys, *audiencias*, *corregidores*, *gobernadores*, *alcaldes mayores*, and *presidentes*.

REFERENCES: J. H. Elliott, *Imperial Spain, 1469–1716*, 1963; Clarence H. Haring, *The Spanish Empire in America*, 1947.

COLONIAL ARCHITECTURE. The architecture of the early Spanish empire was unique in that it amounted to building from the ground up, without the influence of indigenous styles or the need to adapt design and construction to local tastes. Since imperial construction, whether for secular or religious buildings, was an affair of state, town planning and architecture went hand-in-hand from the very beginning. The government expected new towns to be laid out in a rectangular grid with an open plaza at the center. Surrounding the plaza would be the church and shops. The town was then divided up into quarters, and homebuilders employed a Hellenistic style. Homes had inner courtyards with simple walls facing out on the street.

Churches were built in the New World from the very beginning of colonization. The cathedral in Santo Domingo* was rib-vaulted, late Gothic in style. Most of the early churches were constructed by the monastic orders, and they usually consisted of single aisle chapels connected to a cloister and monastery. The supreme example of sixteenth century monastic constructions was the San Francisco cathedral in Quito*, Ecuador.* It was built in 1564. It was basically Flemish and Italian in its styles, and it influenced many other cathedral constructions in South America during the sixteenth and seventeenth centuries. In New Spain* and the Caribbean, on the other hand, Spanish influences were primary. Some of the more prominent architects in the sixteenth and seventeenth centuries were Andrés Blanqui, Claudio Arciniega, and Francisco Becerra.

During the eighteenth century, the baroque styles became more prominent. The most important baroque constructions were in New Spain,* and included Diego Durán Berruecos's Santa Prisca in Taxco (1748), Lorenzo Rodríguez's Sagrario in Mexico City* (1768), and Francisco Antonio Guerrero y Torres's Pocito Chapel (1779) in Guadalupe. The baroque style gave way to neoclassical models in the late eighteenth century. Manuel Tolsá's School of Mines (1813) in Mexico City is one of the best examples, as is Francisco Eduardo Tresguerras's Church of El Carmen in Celaya (1807). Another example is Joaquín Toesca's Cathedral of Bogotá, completed in 1805. The neoclassical styles remained popular in Spanish America throughout the nineteenth century.

REFERENCE: Terence Grieder, "Architecture (Spanish American)," in Helen Delpar, ed., *Encyclopedia of Latin America*, 1974, pp. 33–34.

COLONIAL MUSIC. Although ethnoarcheologists know that music was a very important part of indigenous culture in Latin America, they know little about the exact nature of that music, except that it was probably monodic in structure and relied on a variety of percussion and wind instruments. European music in the first 150 years of the empire was composed primarily of church music. The Franciscan* priest Pedro de Gante established a music school at Texcoco, New Spain*, in 1523, and in 1530 he founded the native choir at the Cathedral of Mexico City. Similar choirs and music schools appeared later in the other major capital cities of the empire. Composers like Juan de Lienas and Hernando Franco wrote the polyphonic, chant music performed by the choirs. By the middle of the seventeenth century music in Hispanic America reflected the cultural fusion which was beginning to take place in the population. As the numbers of *mestizos** increased, so did the fusion of European and indigenous musical forms. Some church hymns were translated into Indian dialects, especially Quechua* and Mayan*, and some composers in the colonies even used native melodies for some of their own compositions.

By the middle of the eighteenth century, the works of the greatest European composers were being studied and performed in the major Latin American cities, and European operas had also made their way across the Atlantic, becoming very popular in places like Mexico City*, Lima*, Buenos Aires*, and Santiago de Cuba*. New forms of secular music, like the *cantatas* and *villancicos*, began to appear from the hands of composers like Tomás de Torrejón and Juan de Araujo of Peru. Folk dances also became popular throughout the empire as secular music gained in popularity. By the early nineteenth century, when the revolutionary mood was sweeping across Latin America, the Romantic themes of European music also became popular, and composers and performers throughout the empire were infatuated with Italian, Austrian, and Parisian music forms, such as the waltz and the minuet.

REFERENCE: George List and Juan Orrego-Salas, eds., *Music in the Americas*, 1967.

COLONIAL NARRATIVE. The first incidence of narrative appeared in the form of the chronicles, which included letters, reports, and diaries as well. Indeed, the first example of New World narrative was Christopher Columbus's* *Diario* or travel log, in which he recorded the events of the discovery of the New World. Other, more extensive chronicles formed the first kernel of narrative development in colonial Spain. They recounted epic deeds—conquests, battles, and exotic exploration. These works were often curious mixes of fact and fiction, generated in part by the Spaniards' familiarity with the novel of chivalry, the most important literary genre of its time in Spain. Some of the most important chroniclers and their works were: Hernán Cortés* (*Cartas de Relación**), Bernal Díaz* del Castillo (*Verdadera historia de la conquista de la Nueva España*),

Alvar Núñez Cabeza* de Vaca (*Naufragios**), Fray Bartolomé de Las Casas* (*Descubrimiento de las Indias y su conquista*), El Inca Garcilaso* de la Vega (*Comentarios Reales*).

Pure narrative fiction was slow to develop in the New World. It lagged far behind poetry and even theater as a literary genre, at the very time when fiction had ascended to a place of prominence in Spain, not only in the novel* of chivalry, but even more importantly in the picaresque novel. It was also the period of Miguel de Cervantes and *Don Quijote*. Spain's incredible legacy of fictional narrative did not have a great impact upon the colonies due almost entirely to government regulations. The Spanish throne forbade the importation of fiction to the colonies. More important was the proscription against publishing such works in the New World.

The seventeenth century witnessed some initial movement toward what might be classified as fictional narrative. In New Spain*, Francisco Bramón* wrote a sort of pastoral novel titled *Los sirgueros de la Virgen sin original pecado* (1620). Also in New Spain, the Bishop of Puebla*, Juan de Palafox y Mendoza (1600–1659), wrote several fictional works, including *El Pastor de Noche Buena* (1644). More important was Carlos de Sigüenza* y Góngora, who wrote *Infortunios que Alonso Ramírez padeció en poder de ingleses piratas* (1680), a baroque narrative work with a picaresque structure. In New Granada*, Juan Rodríguez* Freile wrote a picaresque fictionalized history of colonial Colombia*, *Conquista y descubrimiento del Nuevo Reino de Granada—El Carnero* (1636?). Francisco Núñez de Pineda* y Bascuñan composed *El cautiverio feliz*, a record of his seven-month imprisonment among the Araucanian* Indians.

The eighteenth century marks the rise of the "history" (*historia*) as an objective and scientific account of events. An outstanding example is Father Javier Clavijero's* *Historia antigua de México* (1780). Fictional narrative, however, still did not flourish. The most important work of the period was *El Lazarillo de Ciegos Caminantes* (1773), a kind of picaresque travel guidebook written by Alonso Carrió de la Vandera whose pen name was "Concolorcorvo." Reference should also be made of the political writings of the Mexican friar, Servando Teresa de Mier*.

The beginning of the nineteenth century at last saw the arrival of the Spanish-American novel. In fact, the Mexican writer, José Joaquín Fernández de Lizardi (1776–1827) wrote four novels. The most famous, and the one most cited by literary critics as the *first* Latin American novel, was *El Periquillo Sarniento* (1816). With the close of the colonial period and the end of Spanish rule and its totalitarian censorship, the Latin American novel was finally free to develop.

REFERENCES: Fernando Alegría, *Historia de la Novela Hispanoamérica*, 1965; R. Anthony Castagnaro, *The Early Spanish American Novel*, 1971; Ángel Flores, *The Literature of Spanish America: The Colonial Period*, 1966.

Sam L. Slick

COLONIAL POETRY. Of the various literary genres, it was poetry that flourished and reached its highest level of development in colonial literature. When the Spanish soldiers came to the New World, many were quite capable of reciting poetic meter at length. The Spanish romances were extremely popular among all strata of colonial society. It was not only a pastime, but poetry, for both the poet and the reader, was also a mark of intellect and distinction. In the earliest years of the empire, poets made their way to the New World. One early colonist remarked in a joking way that poets were as "common as manure." Not all the poets came from Spain, however, since poetry was also popular among the leisure class of criollos*, and the New World soon had its own homegrown variety of poet. In general terms, colonial poetry followed the same lines of development and literary currents as the mother country. Although always somewhat behind the current vogue in Spain, colonial poetry began in Renaissance form, passed to baroque and rococo, and finally to neoclassical style prior to the period of independence. Quite aside from these four major literary movements, colonial poetry soon took on its own unique disposition and orientation relative to the geography, history, and criollo culture of the New World. Thus, although in form colonial poetry was very similar to that of Spain, it can be quickly differentiated from Spanish poetry in content and attitude toward nature and life. See RENAISSANCE COLONIAL POETRY.

REFERENCES: Guiseppe Bellini, *Historia de la literatura hispanoamericana*, 1986; Ángel Flores, *The Literature of Spanish America: The Colonial Period*, 1966.

Sam L. Slick

COLONIAL THEATER. When the Spaniards arrived in the New World, they discovered that the more advanced indigenous civilizations had a developed, ritualistic sort of drama-pageant. One of the most famous examples is the Mayan* *Rabinal Achi*. These indigenous song, dance, and play formats were rather quickly incorporated by the Spanish clerics in order to forge the "mission* theater," a presentational play format that would be used to convert and instruct the Indians* in religious matters. The mission theater was generally performed outside of the churches and often utilized Indians as actors. This mission theater, performed in Indian languages, flourished in both New Spain* and Peru*. By and large, the works were either original plays produced by the priests or adaptations of peninsular works. In many instances, the plays, almost always *autos sacramentales*, were performed in conjunction with religious pageants and festivals.

Theater as a literary endeavor did not enjoy the same level of development as did poetry and narrative. Nonetheless, it did have a decided place in colonial life. From a literary point of view, the early mission plays were primitive and unpolished. Their sole purpose was to evangelize. Another kind of drama, today known as didactic theater, emerged in college and university centers, primarily those of the Jesuits*. These plays instructed both students and the public on moral issues. One of the earliest known examples was *Historia alegórica del Anticristo y el Juicio Final*, produced in Lima* in 1559. It appears that this sort of scholastic-oriented theater had only limited success, since it did not target popular taste. It was inevitable that a popular criollo* theater would develop, and so it did in the sixteenth and seventeenth centuries. The first leading proponent was Cristóbal de Llerena of Santo Domingo. Yet another leading figure, perhaps the greatest of his era, was Fernán González de Eslava* (1534?–1601?).

With the flourishing of baroque* literature, the theater's leading playwright appeared in the form of a Catholic nun in Mexico. Sor Juana Inés de la Cruz*, the monumental literary figure of the Spanish colonies, was a major force in theater. In addition to Sor Juana, yet another Mexican playwright appeared, Juan Ruíz de Alarcón*. He, however, spent most of his life in Spain and, indeed, wrote his theatrical works in and about Spain. It is during the baroque period that municipal theaters were built in the major colonial cities.

As Spanish America approached the period of independence, neoclassical literature, along with its French models, began to appear in the colonies. In theater, not only did neoclassical plays appear, but also the beginnings of a national theater that was interested in the history and problems of the new continent. A transitional figure from the baroque to neoclassical theater was the Peruvian Pedro Peralta* y Barnuevo (1663–1743), author of *Triunfos de amor y poder* and *La Rodoguna*. One of the leading dramatists of this period was the Argentine Manuel José de Lavardén*. Another precursor of national theater was José Agustín de Castro, a Mexican playwright. In colonial Cuba* the most important figure in theater was Francisco Javier Foxá y Lecanda (1816–1865?).

REFERENCE: José Juan Arrom, *El teatro de Hispanoamérica en la época colonial*, 1956.

Sam L. Slick

COLUMBUS, BARTHOLOMEW. Bartholomew Columbus was born in Genoa, Italy, around 1451. The eminent Columbus scholar, Samuel Eliot Morison, concluded that Bartholomew was Christopher's slightly younger sibling. Both brothers closely collaborated throughout the great New World venture. Bartholomew's cartographic acumen enabled him to operate a flourishing chart-making business in Lisbon, where Portugal's navigators, fresh from knowledge-expanding sea voyages, congregated. Beginning in 1476–1477, he and Christopher worked as partners, and it is not difficult to imagine their frequent geographical discussions. The elder Columbus gained firsthand experience in waters from Africa to Iceland during his Portuguese years. Moreover, some evidence suggests that when Bartolomeu Dias rounded the Cape of Good Hope in 1486, Bartholomew Columbus accompanied him. Afterward, the cartographer traveled to England and France on behalf of his older brother in order to enlist possible support for an expedition aiming to reach the Spice Islands* by sailing westward.

While in France, Bartholomew received word of Christopher's triumphal homecoming from his first trans-Atlantic voyage. Although he failed to reach Spain in time to depart on Christopher's second mission, Bartholomew was able to reach Hispaniola* by the middle of the summer of 1494. Unfortunately, Christopher had already gone off to explore Cuba*. When he returned seriously ill in September, he found himself in a rapidly deteriorating colony. Acting in his capacity as viceroy*, he granted the powerful office of *adelantado** to Bartholomew, who was the first to hold this title in the Western Hemisphere. Christopher's conferral of considerable authority upon his abrasive brother angered many colonists. One mutinous group found their way back to the peninsula, where they spread slanderous rumors about the Columbus clan. Meanwhile, on Hispaniola, problems with Indian tribes worsened, leading Christopher and Bartholomew to launch a punitive expedition to the island's interior. An arduous, ten-month campaign quelled the disturbances, thanks mostly to the *adelantado*'s forceful personality. Approximately 500 Arawak* captives were shipped to Spain to be sold as slaves.

When the Catholic sovereigns sent Juan Aguado to look into Hispaniola's affairs, the indignant admiral journeyed to Iberia to defend his honor, leaving Bartholomew in charge of the colony from 1496–1498. The *adelantado* was instructed to secure recently identified gold deposits on the southern coast and to relocate the capital from the northern settlement of Isabela to the same area. Both tasks were accomplished admirably. In addition to erecting a fort, San Cristóbal, in the bullion-rich territory, a chain of military posts was established between the island's northern and southern shores. Bartholomew's excellent siting of Santo Domingo*, named after the brothers' father, enabled the new seat of government to endure as the first truly permanent New World. settlement.

The *adelantado* made the initial Spanish *entry* into Xaragua, the western chiefdom containing the island's highest native culture. Local caciques* peacefully agreed to provide the Spaniards with tribute in cotton and cassava. This success, however, did not continue. An uprising spearheaded by Francisco Roldán in Isabela ended in a stalemate. Roldán and his followers moved to Xaragua, adopted Arawak ways, and removed the west from Spanish jurisdiction. Don Bartholomew vented his frustrations by harshly punishing Roldán's native supporters in central Hispaniola.

Discord prevailed by the time of the admiral's return to the Indies. Bartholomew's stern demeanor earned him the dubious distinction of being the most hated member of the Columbus ruling family. In 1500, another royal investigator, Francisco de Bobadilla*, promptly shipped the brothers back to Spain. Nevertheless, two years later, Christopher embarked upon his final journey to the Americas, with Bartholomew as his second in command. Together they reconnoitered the littoral of Central America from Honduras* to Panama*, and both were marooned on Jamaica*. Bartholomew led several shore parties in addition to presiding over a brief, abortive settlement on the Panamanian coast.

Subsequent to Christopher's death in 1506, Bartholomew traveled to Rome to enlist papal support for another trip to Veragua (Panama). His efforts in the Eternal City proved fruitless. When Christopher's son, Diego Columbus*, was appointed governor of Hispaniola in 1509, Bartholomew accompanied him there. Not satisfied, he journeyed back to Spain after a brief stay, still hoping to colonize Veragua. Instead, the king tactfully awarded him the isle of Mona, a *reparti-*

*miento** of 200 Indians, and a lucrative position as Cuba's* mining superintendent. In 1512, he sailed to Hispaniola for the final time. Bartholomew Columbus died on the island shortly after Diego was summoned to Castile*.

REFERENCES: Samuel Eliot Morison, *Admiral of the Ocean Sea: A Life of Christopher Columbus*, 2 vols., 1942.; Troy S. Floyd, *The Columbus Dynasty in the Caribbean, 1492-1526*, 1973.

Frank Marotti

COLUMBUS, CHRISTOPHER. Christopher Columbus was born in Genoa, Italy, in 1451, and as a teenager he went to work as a seaman. By 1476, he had traveled widely throughout the Mediterranean and northern Europe, and he decided to live for a while in Portugal. He continued to sail, making a long trip down the African coast in 1478 and learning more and more about geography, cartography, and navigation. By the 1480s, Columbus was obsessed with one idea: reaching the Far East by sailing around the world rather than going overland or south around Africa. After studying the geographic speculations of Ptolemy, the Greek geographer, and reading the accounts of Marco Polo, Columbus was convinced that Cipangu*, or Japan, was only 2,400 miles west of the Canary Islands*. In 1484, Columbus presented his proposal to King John II of Portugal, only to have it rejected. Irritated by what he considered Portuguese ignorance, Columbus presented his case to King Ferdinand* and Queen Isabella* of Spain in 1486. They too rejected the proposal in 1490 but then approved it on appeal in 1491.

In 1492, Columbus sailed west from Spain, stopping over at the Canaries for repairs, and then headed out into the Atlantic. Two months later, his crew sighted land and stopped over at Watling Island in the Bahamas*. Two weeks later, they landed at Cuba*, which Columbus believed was Cipangu. They plied the northern coast of Cuba* for seven weeks and then landed on Hispaniola*. Columbus left a party of 39 men on Hispaniola, at a settlement that he called La Navidad. On January 3, 1493, he sailed back to Spain.

Columbus's second voyage to the New World was far more ambitious than the first. He left Cádiz, Spain, on September 25, 1493, with 17 ships and 1,500 men who were intended to colonize their discoveries. The expedition landed on the island of Dominica* on November 3, 1493, and reached Hispaniola at the end of the month, only to find La Navidad completely destroyed, probably by Indian attack. In April 1494, Columbus left his son in charge of Hispaniola, and then he set sail for the southern coast of Cuba, still intent on finding the riches of Cipangu. After reaching Jamaica*, Columbus decided to return to Spain in 1496, bringing back with him a supply of Indian slaves.

The third voyage to the New World began with eight ships in January 1498. The fleet split at the Canary Islands, with one group heading for Hispaniola and with Columbus taking the other group south to Cape Verde and from there to the Venezuela* coast, where Columbus was certain that he had reached a large continent—Asia. After several weeks of exploration he reached Hispaniola, only to find a rebellion against his other brother Bartholomew Columbus*. An emissary from Ferdinand and Isabella, Francisco de Bobadilla*, arrived in Hispaniola in 1500 and arrested both the Columbus brothers. They returned to Spain, where Ferdinand and Isabella quickly released them both.

Still convinced that he had reached Asia, Columbus requested and received approval for a fourth voyage to the New World. He sailed from Cádiz on May 11, 1502, and reached Martinique* on June 15. He sailed west and explored the eastern coast of Central America, which he decided had to be the Malay Peninsula. After finding some gold and being shipwrecked, Columbus returned to Spain in November 1504, still convinced that he had reached Asia, not a new land mass. Christopher Columbus died on May 20, 1506.

REFERENCE: Samuel Eliot Morison, *Admiral of the Ocean Sea: A Life of Christopher Columbus*, 2 vols, 1942.

COLUMBUS, DIEGO. Diego Columbus, the son of Christopher Columbus*, was born in 1480. At the beginning of the conquest era, the Spanish Crown extended almost unlimited power to the conquistadors and to their families to govern and profit from their discoveries. As the magnitude of the New World discoveries became clear, however, royal officials decided to limit that power in order to aggrandize their own position and profits. The Columbus family, of course, wanted to retain its monopoly on the New World discoveries, but the Crown would have none of it. Diego Columbus was named governor of the Indies in 1508, two years after the death of his father, but he spent the rest of his life trying to protect the family's New World claims against the encroachments of people like Juan Ponce* de León and the royal family itself. Eventually, of course, his efforts were in vain, and he lost the jurisdictional effort to maintain the family monopoly. Diego Columbus died in 1526.

REFERENCES: Samuel Eliot Morison, *Admiral of the Ocean Sea: A Life of Christopher Columbus*, 2 vols., 1942; Troy S. Floyd, *The Columbus Dynasty in the Caribbean, 1492–1526*, 1973.

COMAYAGUA. Established by Alonso de Cáceras in 1540, Comayagua was one of the first areas of Honduras* to be exploited by the Spaniards. Comayagua seemed to hold great potential because the area had been known for its silver and gold production during pre-Hispanic times. The first Spanish exports of silver from Comayagua were large and encouraging, and Comayagua, along with Gracias a Dios* and Trujillo*, enjoyed a boom of prosperity based on silver production from 1540 to 1542. In 1543, the Spanish Crown selected Comayagua to serve as the base for the *audiencia* of Los Confines*, but the decline in silver production caused the Crown to reconsider. By 1548, the *audiencia* was firmly established in Santiago* de Guatemala. Nonetheless, during the sixteenth century, Comayagua served as a virtually autonomous administrative center for Honduras, although the region technically fell under the jurisdiction of Santiago de Guatemala.

Despite its early flowering Comayagua's importance was short-lived, due to the decline in gold and silver production that had reached serious proportions by 1550. The decline in the Indian population, royal restrictions in the 1540s that limited the work of Indians in mines, and limitations in sixteenth-century technology all hindered the mining industry. The introduction of black slaves to supplement the work force, which began in the mid-1540s, failed to revive the industry, for although the lodes of precious metals were by no means exhausted, they were largely unobtainable with the Spaniards' primitive methods of extraction. By the end of the sixteenth century, Comayagua was reduced to a minor colonial administrative center, although some mining* activity continued throughout the entire colonial period.

REFERENCE: Murdo J. MacLeod, *Spanish Central America: A Socioeconomic History, 1520-1720*, 1973.

Virginia Garrard Burnett

COMMON LANDS. Medieval and early modern Castile* had a hybrid landowning system, with communal property coexisting alongside private property. The roots of Iberian communitarianism may be traced to pre-Roman times, but the system developed its characteristic forms during the eight centuries of the *Reconquista*. Virtually all Castilian municipalities had common lands, and they were of fundamental importance for the rural economy. Common lands may be defined as those that members of the community could use freely for certain purposes. The Castilian system of communal ownership was highly complex. It included lands for pasture and cultivation; the woodlands (*montes**) were considered to be commons for pasture, lumber, firewood, wild fruits and nuts, and various other naturally occurring benefits. Among the commons that were used for pasture were the *ejido* or *exido* (a multipurpose tract near the town's exit), and the *dehesa boyal* (for draft animals). Municipalities often also had various *prados* (meadows) or other *dehesas** used for pasture. Moreover, the Crown lands (*tierras realengas*, also called *tierras baldías**), were treated as commons for most purposes. Even private property was converted into temporary commons through the custom of the *derrota de mieses**, or stubble grazing, which required every possessor of a field to allow the animals of the general public to graze on his stubble and fallow after the harvest until the next sowing time, when the owner could reestablish his exclusive right to the field.

Castilian municipalities often shared pasture privileges with other towns in a form of intercommunal use. In some places, there were dozens of towns united in common-pasture federations. The lands that were common to the residents of one town were clearly distinguished from those common to the federation. Common lands were used not only for pasture, but also for cultivation, which usually required stricter rules. In some places where land was abundant, a person could cultivate whatever amount of common land he wanted, use it as long as he wished, and abandon it at his pleasure, with no restrictions. Custom usually dictated that arable commons be cultivated annually, in order to maintain possession. If the occupier of a common plot allowed a year and a day to pass without plowing it, he forfeited his claim, and the land could be used by someone else.

But many Castilian municipalities—perhaps most of them in the fifteenth and sixteenth centuries—supervised the apportionment of their arable commons by holding a periodic lottery (*sorteo periódico de tierras comunes*) designed to give each family an equal share. The arable commons were divided into roughly equivalent lots (comprising one or more parcels), and a random drawing was held, often by drawing names out of a hat or a jar, to determine which family head would get each lot. Tenure of possession varied, depending upon local custom. If the holder of a lot died before his tenure expired, his spouse might be permitted to complete the term. Otherwise, the lot would lie fallow until the next lottery or until an additional lot was needed by a newly married resident. Only rarely was possession passed to one's descendants, because the principle of common lands was that possession depended upon use and was non-transferable.

The pre-Columbian Indians* had developed their own common landholding customs. The Aztec* *calpulli* (clans) were both kinship and landowning units that supervised the division of their arable lands among family heads, in hereditary allotments. The Aztecs, having no domesticated grazing animals, had no need for common pastures. In Incan* Peru*, the *ayllu** (a kinship unit similar to the Aztec *calpulli*) controlled the people's arable lands, annually alloting each family the land needed for survival. The *ayllu* held grazing lands in common, for flocks of llamas and alpacas. In Aztec Mexico and Incan Peru, land ownership for the common people rested in the community, and the individual had only the usufruct of what was alloted to him.

REFERENCES: David Vassberg, "The Tierras Baldías: Community Property and Public Lands in 16th Century Castile," *Agricultural History*, 48 (1974), 383–401; Alejandro Nieto, *Bienes comunales, Serie J, Monografias Practicas de Derecho Español*, vol. 40, 1964.

David E. Vassberg

COMUNEROS, WAR OF THE (COLOMBIA). Like the earlier War of the *Comuneros** in Paraguay*, the War of the *Comuneros* in New Granada* was also based on the premise that unjust laws should not be obeyed. This serious uprising began in Socorro in 1781 as the result of the imposition of taxes (tobacco*, navy) and soon blossomed into a league of towns—the *Común*. The *Común's* political ideology was "the defense, or advantage, care, and good government of the republic" and opposition to what it termed the despotism of the royal authorities. The rebellion of the *Común* was rooted in republicanism and in medieval philosophy, as the earlier Paraguayan "War of the *Comuneros*" had been. It took its inspiration from the rebellions of Tunja in 1592 and 1641. Based on the concept of popular sovereignty, it also foreshadowed the political independence of New Granada in the early nineteenth century. At first, the *Común* was successful, but the tide turned and the movement was crushed. Its leaders, like Juan

Francisco Berbeo and José Antonio Galán, were executed in 1782 and 1783, respectively.

As seen in the revolutionary slogans, the thought of their revolutionary leaders like Berbeo, Salvador Plata, Antonio Monsalve, Diego de Ardila, and Francisco Rosillo, the Cedula, and the preamble of the *Capitulaciones*, the revolution of New Granada of 1781 was based on the philosophy of the Spanish Golden Age, with its concept of the popular source of the state and its limitations, the social contract, resistance to tyranny, the invalidity of unjust laws, popular consent for the imposition of taxes, the primacy of the common good, and the Christian natural law.

REFERENCES: Pablo E. Cárdenas Acosta, *El movimiento comunal de 1781 en el Nuevo Reino de Granada*, 2 vols., 1980; Rafael Gómez Hoyos, *La revolución granadina de 1810: Ideario de una generación y de una época, 1781–1821*, 2 vols., 1962; O. Carlos Stoetzer, *The Scholastic Roots of the Spanish American Revolution*, 1979.

O. Carlos Stoetzer

COMUNEROS, WAR OF THE (PARAGUAY). The eighteenth century witnessed two serious revolts in Spanish America that go under the name War of the *Comuneros*. In both cases, the events represent a Spanish-American, eighteenth-century version of the *Comuneros* and *Germanias* of Iberian history: the last attempt in Spain to maintain local freedoms against royal encroachments—an echo of the Renaissance politics of Emperor Charles V[*]. The first of these events occurred in Paraguay between 1723 and 1725. The viceroy of Peru[*] had appointed Diego de los Reyes as governor of Paraguay. After many complaints had been received in Lima[*], José de Antequera[*] y Castro, the *fiscal* of the *audiencia* of Charcas[*] and protector of Indians[*], was sent to Asunción[*] to investigate. Antequera's inquiries led to the imprisonment of Reyes; the latter, however, escaped and reassumed his position as governor. Antequera then returned to Asunción, and with the support of both the *cabildo*[*] and the *audiencia*, he opposed the reinstatement of Reyes, who continued to enjoy the backing of the viceroy[*] in Lima. The latter now sent García Ros to take over the government on a temporary basis and to calm things down. But Antequera succeeded in recapturing Reyes and again had him arrested. When García Ros arrived with troops, Antequera confronted him with a *cabildo abierto* whose wholehearted support he had obtained.

In reality, the entire controversy between Antequera and Reyes concealed a deeper problem: the opposition of the Jesuits[*], the protectors of the Indians, to the desires of the *vecinos* and *encomenderos* for increased Indian labor. Antequera was able to defeat García Ros with the promise of Indian labor and booty. When he later turned against the Jesuits[*], his victory was overturned and he was forced to return to Asunción. A new viceroy, the Marqués de Castelfuerte, together with an able bishop, José de Palos, now took steps. They forced Antequera to flee, and a new governor, Martín de Barúa took over and released Reyes. Antequera was finally captured in Lima in 1726, where he spent five years in jail.

Still, he enjoyed so much freedom that he sent another rebel, Fernando de Mompóx, to Asunción at a time when the viceroy[*] had sent a new governor and a new *pesquisidor*. Mompóx now organized a second uprising, which became known as "the revolt of the *comuneros*." The resentful Barúa now joined the *vecinos* and directed his anger at the Jesuits. For months, the *comuneros* would rule Asunción and the countryside, and when Barúa stepped down they adopted republican forms; they set up a *junta de justicia*, the chairman of which, José Luis Barreyro, was called the *presidente de la provincia*. The revolt continued with further strange developments: Barreyro turned out to be a loyal royalist who took hold of Mompóx and was later replaced; Antequera was executed in Lima in 1731. Another development was the fact that the uprising had started as an aristocratic affair in 1723, linked to the wealthy elements in Paraguay. It then turned into a democratic and popular rebellion, the republican tendencies of which attracted members of other religious orders that were hostile to the Jesuits. The revolt was finally suppressed by the governor of Buenos Aires but not without difficulty. It already foreshadowed the forces of regionalism that exploded there in 1809 and 1810. Finally, it should be noted that both the rebels and the clergy who sympathized with their aims based their stand intellectually on the Etymologiae of St. Isidore, the Councils of Toledo, and the tenets of Late Scholasticism; that is, that in case of an unjust law, the king ought not to be obeyed.

REFERENCES: Salvador de Madariaga, *El ocaso del imperio español en América*, 1955; O. Carlos Stoetzer, *The Scholastic Roots of the Spanish American Revolution*, 1979; Alberto Montezuma Hurtado, *Comuneros del Paraguay*, 1983.

O. Carlos Stoetzer

CONCEPCIÓN, DIOCESE OF. The Roman Catholic diocese of Concepción was created in 1564 and named the Diocese of Imperial. It was designed to meet the needs of the vast region between Santiago[*] and southern Chile[*]. The first bishop was a Franciscan[*], Antonio de San Miguel Avendano. The massive uprising of Araucanian Indians in 1598 forced the relocation of the diocese from Imperial to Concepción. The diocese was raised to an archdiocese in 1939.

REFERENCE: *New Catholic Encyclopedia*, IV:106–07, 1967.

CONCEPCIÓN VALDÉS, DIEGO GABRIEL DE. See VALDÉS, DIEGO GABRIEL DE CONCEPCIÓN.

CONCOLORCORVO. Concolorcorvo was the pseudonym of the author of *El Lazarillo de ciegos caminantes*, one of the most important colonial literary works. The original published text identified Concolorcorvo as the alias of one Don Calixto Bustamante Carlos Inca, and for many years the latter was presumed to be the author. In the mid-twentieth century, however, a student of the famous French hispanist, Marcel Bataillon, discovered in the *Archive of the Indies* (Spain) that the true author was Alonso Carrió de la Vandera (1715?–1780?). Carrió, apparently for reasons of censorship or to avoid possible recrimination, chose to hide his true identity. The first printing of *El Lazarillo*, made clandestinely in Lima (1775–76), carried Gijón (Spain) as the place of printing. Moreover, Carrió predated the work to 1773, obviously to confuse authorities and protect himself.

Carrió was a Spaniard who established himself in Lima in 1746. He was a minor government functionary who had the title of Inspector of Postal Routes between Buenos Aires and Lima. *El Lazarillo de ciegos caminantes* was conceived as a sort of traveller's guide for stagecoach passengers making the trip from the Río de la Plata (Buenos Aires and Montevideo) to Lima. The work is divided into two parts and a prologue. It is both picturesque and picaresque in flavor. It is a lively description of life as it was in colonial times in southern South America. *El Lazarillo* contains elements of humor, satire, irony and criticism; the work, although entertaining, is clearly didactic in nature. Carrió employed colloquial language and numerous digressions, so typical of picaresque literature still popular at that time in the New World. Quite aside from its literary merit, *El Lazarillo* is important as a valuable source of historical information for the analysis of eighteenth-century colonial life in Argentina and Peru.

REFERENCES: Fernando Alegría, *Historia de la novela hispanoamericana*, 1965; Jean Franco, *An Introduction to Spanish American Literature*, 1969.

Sam L. Slick

CONDORCANQUI, JOSÉ GABRIEL. See TUPAC AMARU II.

CONGREGACIONES. During the colonial period, Spanish authorities used the *congregaciones* to concentrate and settle the Amerindians as a means of pacifying them. Beginning in the mid-sixteenth century, Spain forced widely scattered Indians* into *congregaciones* or *reducciones**. Although the Indians usually resisted resettlement, the Spaniards implemented the policy, violently if necessary, because they were convinced that only in the *congregaciones* could Indians be effectively "civilized" (converted to Roman Catholicism and acculturated to a lifestyle of small farming and wage labor). It was also easier for *encomenderos* and labor recruiters to get the workers they needed from *congregaciones* than from scattered Indian populations. The policy thus had the effect of making more land available to Spaniards. See also MISSIONS.

CONGRESS OF TUCUMÁN. See TUCUMÁN, CONGRESS OF.

CONQUISTADORS. Conquistador is the Spanish word for conqueror. In English literature, conquistador has been used to describe the Spanish explorers who conquered the various tribes in Central America, South America, the Caribbean, the Pacific, and Africa.

CONSTITUTION OF 1812. The Constitution of 1812 was produced by the Cortes of Cádiz* during the Napoleonic occupation of Spain. Written by representatives of Spain and the provinces that professed their loyalty to the exiled

Bourbon king, Ferdinand VII*, the constitution was a great deal more liberal than anything ever produced by the Bourbons. It reflected the ideas of the Enlightenment* and called for a constitutional monarchy, limitations on the Church, open trade, and greater local political representation, particularly by the *criollo** aristocracy in the New World. Many of the representatives to the Cortes were themselves *criollos*, most of them members of the merchant sector that had thrived under the expanded economic policies of the Bourbon leadership. The constitution, though widely supported by many in the aristocracy and middle sectors, was considered too liberal by many Spaniards and *criollos*. The constitution generated a political controversy that eventually crystallized into the two opposing political camps, liberal and conservative, that would dominate the Latin American political landscape for most of the nineteenth century. The Constitution of 1812 was abrogated in 1814, when Ferdinand VII returned to power. It was restored in 1820, however, when the Riego revolt in Spain forced Ferdinand VII to accept its terms.

REFERENCE: Fernando Suárez, *Las Cortes de Cádiz*, 1982.

Virginia Garrard Burnett

CONSULADO. The *consulado* was a private institution of Spanish capitalism that acquired considerable political authority because of its economic power during the colonial period of the Spanish Empire. In the late Middle Ages, several commercial centers in Spain established *consulados*, which were essentially merchant guilds with monopolistic power over exports and imports in the respective cities. Each *consulado* functioned with a royal charter. Once the huge shipments of gold began returning from the New World in the 1530s, Spain established a *consulado* at Seville* to handle the bullion traffic. For most of the rest of the century, the *consulado* of Seville financed the fleets to New Spain* and Peru*. By the end of the sixteenth century, the volume of trade was too heavy for the Seville *consulado* to handle, so the Crown authorized new *consulados* at Mexico City* in 1594 and Lima* in 1613. Between 1793 and 1795, new *consulados* were also established in Buenos Aires*, Caracas*, Cartagena*, Guadalajara*, Guatemala City*, Havana*, Santiago*, and Vera Cruz*. By that time, the *consulados* had become a conservative, royalist elite, intent on keeping the Spanish Empire intact so that their own monopoly on commerce and trade profits could be maintained. The independence movements throughout Latin America dealt death blows to the *consulados*.

REFERENCE: Robert S. Smith, "The Institution of the Consulado in New Spain," *Hispanic American Historical Review*, 24 (1944), 61–83.

CORCHADO Y JUARBE, MANUEL M. Manuel M. Corchado y Juarbe was born in Puerto Rico* in 1840. He spent his career as a writer and painter, but his main aim was always to generate a revival of Spanish cultural greatness. He lived for years in Barcelona, where he published the magazine *Las Antillas* and tried to advertise life in the Caribbean colonies. Corchado returned to Puerto

Rico in 1879 and spent the remaining years of his life opposing the independence movement and working to achieve complete political and cultural assimilation with Spain. He died in 1884.

REFERENCE: Kenneth R. Farr, *Historical Dictionary of Puerto Rico and the U.S. Virgin Islands*, 1973.

CÓRDOBA. Córdoba, a major city in Argentina*, was established in 1573 by Spaniards traveling from Chile*. Because of its location (390 miles northwest of Buenos Aires*) on the trade route between Buenos Aires* and Peru* and because of the development of a successful livestock industry in the countryside, Córdoba prospered and grew in population. Jesuit* missionaries established the University of Córdoba* in 1623, and it evolved into one of the finest in Latin America. In 1783, Spain established an intendancy* there by dividing the province of Tucumán* into Córdoba and Salta*. Revolutionary forces deposed the intendant, José Gutiérrez de la Concha, in 1810; the region was eventually incorporated into Argentina. At the time of the independence movement, the population of the city of Córdoba exceeded 10,000 people.

REFERENCE: Jonathan C. Brown, *A Socio-Economic History of Argentina*, 1979.

CÓRDOBA, DIOCESE OF. The Roman Catholic diocese of Córdoba, covering northern and central Argentina*, was established in 1570. The diocese of Buenos Aires* included only the northeastern part of Argentina. It was first called the diocese of Tucumán, and the see was located in the city of Tucumán*. The see was transferred to Santiago del Estero in 1580 and to Córdoba in 1699. The first bishop was Francisco de Victoria. It became an archdiocese in 1934.

REFERENCE: *New Catholic Encyclopedia*, IV:321–22, 1967.

CÓRDOBA, JOSÉ MARÍA. José María Córdoba was born in Río Negro, Colombia*, on September 8, 1799. As a teenage engineering student, Córdoba became passionately committed to the independence movement. When he was fifteen, he joined the rebel forces and quickly acquired a reputation for courage and intelligence. By 1822, he commanded the Bogotá battalion, which played a key role in the victory at the Battle of Pichincha*. After his successes at the Battle of Ayacucho*, Córdoba was decorated by Generals Antonio José de Sucre* and Símon Bolívar*. Córdoba served as minister of war in the Bolívar government, but when he rebelled against the Liberator, by putting together a small army of 300 people, he was defeated and killed on October 17, 1829.

REFERENCES: Albert William Bork and Georg Maier, *Historical Dictionary of Ecuador*, 1973; Federico González Suárez, *Historia general de la República del Ecuador*, 7 vols., 1890–1903.

CÓRDOBA, MATIAS DE. Matias de Córdoba was born in Chiapas*, New Spain*, in 1750. He joined the Dominican* order as a priest and spent his career as a teacher and academic at the University of San Carlos* in Guatemala*. In 1795, he founded the Economic Society, a group committed to economic growth and the liberalization of trade regulations. Writing under the pseudonym "Bondesir," Córdoba edited such periodicals as *Para-rayos* and *El Expeciero*. He was also the author of *La tentativa del León*. He died in 1828.

REFERENCE: Richard E. Moore, *Historical Dictionary of Guatemala*, 1973.

CÓRDOBA, PEDRO DE. Pedro de Córdoba was born in Córdoba, Spain, in 1482. He became a Dominican* priest in Salamanca in 1510 and served as a missionary priest in the Caribbean. Bartolomé de las Casas* credited Córdoba with convincing him to give up his *encomiendas**, join the Dominican order, and become the great protector of the Indians*. Most of Córdoba's work was conducted on Hispaniola* and Cuba*. What he most desired was the Christian conversion of the Indians without the sufferings of colonization. Córdoba wrote a number of epistles to the Spanish Crown and to various church leaders campaigning for protection of the Indians. He died in Santo Domingo* in 1521.

REFERENCE: *New Catholic Encyclopedia*, 1967.

CÓRDOBA, TREATY OF. As the newly appointed superior political chief of New Spain, General Juan O'Donoju realized shortly after his arrival at Vera Cruz* that there was little he could do to end the Mexican Revolution. He had been posted to New Spain without military forces beyond those already stationed there, and it was clear that forces sufficient to quell the rebellion would not be forthcoming. With all of the provinces having declared independence, O'Donoju consequently decided that the best he could do for Spain was to secure the most favorable terms possible within the context of Mexican independence. Having reached this decision, he wrote to revolutionary General Agustín de Iturbide*, requesting safe passage through insurgent lines for the purpose of a meeting to negotiate an end to the conflict. Iturbide accepted the offer and suggested Córdoba as the conference site.

The Treaty of Córdoba, which established Mexican independence, was agreed upon by O'Donoju and Iturbide on August 24, 1821. The treaty provided for a member of the Spanish ruling dynasty, King Ferdinand VII* himself if he so chose or one of three princes, to rule over what now would be known as the Mexican Empire. If no member of the royal family chose to assume the Mexican throne in the imperial capital of Mexico City*, the Crown would be offered to whomever the Cortes of the Mexican Empire selected. There was no requirement that future monarchs would have to be from a European dynasty. Drawing heavily on the Plan of Iguala, the treaty proposed that a council would be formed to choose a president and a regency of three members who would exercise the executive authority of the nation until the new monarch could be enthroned. While the viceroy* was excluded from membership in the council, O'Donoju was to have a position. The interim government would rule in accordance with existing law and the principles of the Plan of Iguala. All dissident Spaniards were guaranteed free exit from the country with their families and property. The potentially contentious issue of abolishing the caste system and preserving clerical privileges that were specified in the Plan of Iguala were dealt with only by implication.

Since O'Donoju had negotiated the treaty without the express authorization of the Spanish government, both Governor José Dávila and Marshal Francisco Novella rejected it, and Archbishop of Mexico Pedro José de Fonte also opposed it. After substantial pressure, Marshal Novella agreed to meet with O'Donoju at La Patera Hacienda on September 13, 1821. Novella, persuaded that O'Donoju was in fact the captain general* and superior political chief of Mexico, reluctantly agreed to abide by O'Donoju's instructions with respect to the Treaty of Córdoba. Although Spain subsequently rejected the treaty and declared it void, the independence of Mexico was established.

REFERENCES: William Robertson, *Iturbide of Mexico*, 1952; William Robertson, *Rise of the Spanish-American Republics*, 1918.

Samuel Freeman

CÓRDOBA, UNIVERSITY OF. The University of Córdoba was founded in 1613 in the city of Córdoba* in what is today Argentina*. Bishop Fernando de Trejo y Sanabria was the leading force behind its establishment; the institution opened for classes in 1614. The first degrees were granted in 1622, and both the Church and the Crown formally approved it in 1664. The University of Córdoba was an exclusively Jesuit* institution until 1767, when the Jesuits were expelled from the New World. Franciscans* then took control of the university. They added the school of law in 1791. During the colonial period, the University of Córdoba was widely known for its scholasticism and conservatism.

REFERENCE: Ione S. Wright and Lisa M. Nekhom, *Historical Dictionary of Argentina*, 1978.

CORN. Mexican Indians* grow corn (maize) for its high food value and ease of production to maturity. Before commercial fertilizers were available, new areas had to be developed every few years. Thus, when corn could be grown close to ceremonial centers with a minimum of attention, the Maya* had a surplus of food, and men could work almost full-time on the development of large religious complexes. The average pre-Columbian religious center lasted five to seven centuries. At the close of this period, freshly developed cornfields, by necessity now miles from the ritual complex, forced the abandonment of those centers, and new centers were developed in the area of the fresh fields. This recurred in an endless cycle. Corn played the dual role of developer and destroyer of many impressive ritual "cities."

Corn was probably domesticated fairly early in the central valley of Mexico, as shown by its rather sudden appearance in the early Tehuacán levels. Based on the morphology of the specimens, corn appears to be the result of the development of a wild *Zea* rather than a mixture of *Zea* and teosinte. The addition of teosinte genetic material appeared much later. Certainly maize was domesticated prior to 5,000 B.C. By 4,000 B.C., maize had spread southward into southeast Guatemala* where hybridization with Guatemal teosinte occurred fairly quickly; this phenomenon may have stabilized the gene pool of the species. R. Mck. Bird has suggested that this early form probably reached highland Peru* by 1,000 B.C. An improved race was already in Mexico, at Tehuacán, by 3500 B.C. This improved variety spread quickly into Central America and Mexico.

The tripartite theory for the origin of corn was first proposed in 1939. Objections to the theory were vocal, and the discovery of a perennial diploid teosinte required a revision of the theory. The tripartite theory now reads: (1) a form of wild maize was the direct ancestor of domesticated maize; (2) annual teosinte is no longer considered the forerunner of domesticated maize; and (3) teosinte introgression into maize in North America and Tripsacum introgression in South America were major lines in the evolution of the domesticated variety. The first two points are just as controversial now as they were in 1939.

The teosinte-maize hypothesis now occurs in two forms, neither of which is entirely supported by the archaeological record. Some researchers have proposed, based on modern genetic studies, that the jump was step-wise. The teosinte of 80,000–15,000 B.C. was probably the direct ancestor of modern maize. The genetic similarity of maize and teosinte indicates that theirs is probably a parent-progeny type of relationship.

The question remains regarding the pollen size of the various strains of maize and teosinte. Some authors argue that the large size of very ancient pollen recovered from the lake bed beneath Mexico City indicates that the progenitor of modern maize was a primitive maize. This deposit was originally dated at 80,000 years B.C. Two explanations have been proposed to reevaluate this date. First, G. W. Beadle has suggested that the grains are derived from an autopoly-ploid native grass. The polyploidy was induced by heat generated by volcanic eruption. There is some indirect evidence for this, as the level containing the large pollen grains is sandwiched between two deposits of volcanic ash. More recently some have suggested that the level in question dates to only 2,000 B.C. In any event, the 80,000-year-old age for these grains is now pretty well discredited.

It is clear that maize was domesticated by the early natives of the New World. The result, over thousands of years, has been the creation of a cereal crop that is undoubtedly superior to other forms. Maize had assumed most of its modern characteristics by 7,000 B.C. in the central valley in Mexico. The first domesticates from the maize-teosinte hybrid were adapted to shorter day length, and thus the early spread was in a southerly direction. The spread of maize into northern areas, such as the United States, was not possible until specific adaptations to the plant occurred. These included a shift to long-day growing, as evidenced by the eight-row variety of Maize de Ocho. This adaptation permitted the spread into the southern United States and eventually the Northeast and Canada. Maize de Ocho did not appear in the American Southwest until A.D. 200–700; this maize spread to the northeast. The southeastern varieties of maize range from the coastal regions of eastern and western Mexico and include at least three races. Dent corns may have spread with Spanish trade into the United States during the historic period.

REFERENCES: R. Mck. Bird, "South American Maize in Central America?" In N. S. Stone, ed., *Pre-Columbian Plant Migration: Papers of the Peabody Museum of Archaeology and Ethnology*, 76 (1984), 39–67; G. W. Beadle, "The Ancestry of Corn," *Scientific American*, 242 (1979), 112–19.

George A. Agogino

CORONADO, FRANCISCO VÁSQUEZ DE. Francisco de Coronado was born in Salamanca, Spain, around 1510, and he came to New Spain* in 1535. After marrying the daughter of a prominent royal official, Coronado was appointed governor of New Galicia* on the western coast of New Spain in 1538. In 1540, he accompanied an expedition under the command of Antonio de Mendoza* into the northern territories to search for the fabled cities of Cíbola*. In April 1540, Coronado led an expedition of 100 Spaniards, including his brother Juan Vásquez de Coronado*, from Culiacán north into present-day Arizona, northern New Mexico*, the Texas* and Oklahoma panhandles, and central Kansas. They located Cíbola, which turned out to be the Zuñi pueblo of Kawikuh. Some of Coronado's men explored further west into Arizona and discovered the Grand Canyon. After being thrown from a horse and injuring his head, Coronado returned to Mexico in 1542. He served as governor of New Galicia until 1544 and then moved to Mexico City* to serve on the municipal council. The expedition had not discovered the legendary wealthy cities of Cíbola but had considerably expanded Spain's land claims in the New World. He died in 1554.

REFERENCES: Herbert E. Bolton, *Coronado on the Turquoise Trail: Knight of Pueblos and Plains*, 1949; George P. Hammond, *Coronado's Seven Cities*, 1940.

CORONADO, JUAN VÁSQUEZ DE. Juan Vásquez de Coronado was born in 1523. As a teenager, he accompanied his brother, Francisco Vásquez de Coronado* on the exploratory journeys in what is today the southwestern part of the United States. They were searching for the legendary Seven Cities of Cíbola*. During the late 1540s and 1550s, Coronado was an *alcalde mayor* of Honduras* and El Salvador*, and in 1562, he was appointed an *alcalde mayor* in Nicaragua*. That same year, he headed for Costa Rica*, where he spent months trying to subdue various Indian tribes. He was appointed governor of Costa Rica, a post he held until 1565. He founded the city of Cartago* in 1564, but on a return trip to Spain in 1565 he was shipwrecked and died.

REFERENCES: Francisco Montero Barrantes, *Elementos de historia de Costa Rica*, 2 vols., 1894; Theodore S. Creedman, *Historical Dictionary of Costa Rica*, 1977.

CORREGIDOR. The *corregidor* was a very important official in Spanish colonial administration. His origins can be traced back to the *praesis provinciae* of Roman times. The Emperor Constantine first used the term *corrector* from which *corregidor* is derived. The term first came into general use in Spain under Alfonso XI. Initially, the *corregidor* was only a judicial officer but under Ferdinand* and

Isabella* he also became a political officer. In 1597, in Madrid, Jerónimo Castillo de Bobadilla first published his *Politica para Corregidores y Señores de Vassallos en Tiempo de Paz, y de Guerra: y para Perlados en lo Espiritual, y Temporal entre Legos, Juezes de Comisión, Regidores, Abogados, y otros Oficiales Públicos, y de las Jurisdiciones, Preeminencias, Residencias y Salarios dellos: y de lo tocante a las Ordenes y Cavalleros dellas*. This was a practical as well as theoretical work on politics and government. It outlined the duties and functions of *corregidores* within the administrative apparatus.

In Spain, the term of office could be one, two, or three years, depending on the Crown's decision. In the New World, the term of office was for five years if chosen from Spain; if chosen from the New World, the term was for three years. In Peru*, the *corregidor* was chosen for one year, and the term could be extended for a second year. He remained in office until a successor arrived. If he died, a temporary one could be selected by the *cabildo**.

At first, one had to be a *hidalgo** (noble) to be appointed but with the expansion of the empire this condition changed. In Spain, the *corregidor* was usually a civil lawyer but not necessarily in the New World. The *corregidor* appointed *tenientes* to administer those cities and towns under his jurisdiction. He could have numerous *tenientes* depending on how many cities he had. If he was not versed in legal matters, he had to appoint a *teniente* who was, which led to confrontations between the *corregidor* and his *teniente* at times.

Corregidores governed local jurisdictions, known as *corregimientos*, much like the *gobernadores* and *alcaldes mayores**. The *gobernador* governed a larger area than did the *corregidor* or *alcalde mayor*. No *corregidor* could hold office in the district in which he lived. *Encomenderos* or mineowners could not hold the office where they had their property. He could not engage in any business transactions while in office. He also could not marry within his jurisdiction. A viceroy* could not appoint a close relative to the office. The *corregidor* was associated with the local *cabildo*, although he was not a member of it. The *ayuntamiento* could not meet without an order from him, and when they did meet, he or his *teniente* had to be present. He regulated the price of all foodstuffs in his district and could prohibit grain exports during times of famine. He also had to maintain the streets, plazas, and public buildings, and he regulated sanitary conditions.

When he first arrived in the New World, he made a *visita** in which he toured the district under his jurisdiction to find out about local conditions. Some of the most important *corregimientos* in the New World were Cuzco*, Cajamarca, and Arequipa* in Peru* and in New Spain* those of Ciudad de México and Nuestra Señora de los Zacatecas*. At the end of his term of office, a *residencia** was held by his successor. It lasted 30 days, and the *corregidor* had to explain all of his acts during his term. Any complaints had to be presented before the end of the fifteenth day. This was the juridical and idealistic framework of his office.

In reality, the *corregidor* was paid very little, so he tried to make his term of office as lucrative as possible. One of the most lucrative positions was that of *corregidor de pueblos de Indios*. The *corregidor* became associated with the merchants because a merchant usually paid off the corregidor's debts or revenues owed to the Crown. The merchant would then advance him goods, which he then sold to the Indians*. The merchant would often appoint the *teniente* who was responsible for these business transactions.

These practices led to many abuses against which the Indians revolted. Tupac Amaru's* revolt in 1780 was directed against the *Corregidor* Antonio de Arriaga. Under Carlos III*, the Bourbon Reforms were designed to eliminate the abuses and increase royal revenues, but the *subdelegados* appointed by the intendants often reverted to the practices of the *corregidores de indios*

REFERENCES: C. H. Haring, *The Spanish Empire in America*, 1947; C. E. Castaneda, "The Corregidor in Spanish Colonial Administration," *Hispanic American Historical Review*, 9 (1929), 446–70; Robert S. Chamberlain, "The *Corregidor* in Castile in the Sixteenth Century and the *Residencia* as applied to the *Corregidor*," *Hispanic American Historical Review*, 23 (1943) 222–57.

                                                                                Carlos Pérez

CORTÉS, HERNÁN. Hernán Cortés was born in Medellin, Extremadura, Spain, in 1485. His family was part of the petty nobility, so Cortés had the opportunity to enter the University of Salamanca in 1499. He was not committed as a student, however, and in 1501 he returned home. In 1504, Cortés headed for Santo Domingo* in the New World, becoming a minor bureaucrat in Azua before joining Diego Velásquez's* conquest of Cuba* in 1511. After seven years in Cuba, Cortés received an appointment from Velásquez to lead an expedition to Yucatán* to investigate rumors of fabulous Indian wealth there.

In February 1518, Cortés's expedition landed in Yucatán, where he met a woman named Malinche, his Doña Marina*, who became his mistress and interpreter. He fought his way toward Tenochtitlán, overwhelming some tribes and forming alliances with others, and eventually defeated Monteczuma (Motecuhzoma*) and the Aztec* empire. In October 1522, King Charles I* of Spain rewarded Cortés by naming him governor of New Spain*. Cortés tried to be an effective colonial administrator, but his heart was in exploring and conquest. Gradually, as Spanish administration became better developed in New Spain, Cortés found his prerogatives growing narrower. In 1524, Cortés participated in a conquering expedition to Honduras*, and after spending some time in Spain in the late 1520s, he received authorization to explore the Pacific Coast of Mexico. Those expeditions, which Cortés either supervised or personally led, took place in the 1530s. He returned to Spain in 1540 and in 1541 led a military expedition to Algeria. He died on December 2, 1547.

REFERENCE: Salvador de Madariaga, *Hernán Cortés, Conqueror of Mexico*, 1941.

CORTÉS, MARTÍN. One of two sons of Hernán Cortés,* both of whom were named Martín, Martín was the illegitimate son of Doña Marina* (also known as Malinche, the adviser and lover of Hernán Cortés during his conquest of Tenochtitlán*). The elder of the two sons, Martín was technically a mestizo*, but he received almost all of the honors and titles normally accorded a Spaniard, due to his father's position. At the age of five, he traveled to Spain with his father and, while still a child, was made a knight in the prestigious Order of Santiago. Later, he served as a page to Prince Philip, later Philip II*. Like his father, Don Martín became a celebrated soldier, although he never returned to fight in the New World. He served in the Spanish army in Algeria and Germany. He died in battle, fighting the Moriscos in Granada.

REFERENCE: Michael C. Meyer and William L. Sherman, *The Course of Mexican History*, 1983.

Virginia Garrard Burnett

CORTÉS, MARTÍN (Marqués del Valle de Oaxaca). One of the two sons of Hernán Cortés, both of whom were named Martín, Martín, the Marqués del Valle de Oaxaca, was the only legitimate son of the conqueror of Mexico. Born of a Spanish noblewoman, the daughter of a count, in Cuernavaca around 1532, Martín was the younger brother of the son of Doña Marina*, Hernán Cortés's Indian adviser and mistress. As a Spaniard and the legitimate child of Cortés, Martín traveled to Spain as a child and enjoyed great favor in court, where he later became part of the entourage of Prince Philip, later Philip II*. As a young adult, Martín returned to New Spain* to claim his father's title and properties as the Marqués of the Valley of Oaxaca, which was one of only three *encomiendas** granted in perpetuity after the passage of the New Laws* in 1542–1543. Although his estate was large and his prestige great, Martín, an arrogant and ambitious young man, was not content with his lot. In 1562, when a group of young *criollos** in Mexico City* who had not been permitted to inherit their fathers' *encomiendas* began to plot to assassinate royal officials, to relinquish their allegiance to the crown, and to name Martín as king of Mexico, the young Cortés was willing to oblige. Although the conspiracy was not well planned and included at most only 120 people, it was put down by the royal government with great severity. The key conspirator, Alonso de Ávila, and his brother were both beheaded, and despite their high status in the colony, their heads were publicly displayed on spikes. Martín Cortés was not punished, but was greatly chastened by the affair and was content to live out the remainder of his life quietly. The conspiracy represented the last battle in the struggle for power between the early conquistadors and the Crown in Mexico.

REFERENCE: Michael C. Meyer and William L. Sherman, *The Course of Mexican History*, 1983.

Virginia Garrard Burnett

CORTES OF CÁDIZ. When Napoleon invaded the Iberian peninsula and forced Charles IV* and his son, Ferdinand VII*, to abdicate the Spanish throne, a shortlived republican movement got underway in Spain. In 1810, a number of prominent, liberal Spanish citizens called for a constitutional convention to consider drastic political reform. They convened the Cortes of Cádiz to consider those constitutional changes, and the Spanish colonies sent 63 of the 303 delegates to the convention. It met between September 1810 and September of 1813. Although the Cortes of Cádiz dealt with a wide range of issues, its decisions dealing with the empire involved the abolition of the *encomienda**, the elimination of Indian tribute and forced labor, and the liberalization of Crown-imposed trade restrictions. The Constitution of 1812* that emerged from the Cortes of Cádiz promoted popular sovereignty, separation of powers, equal representation of all male citizens, a strong legislature, and the replacement of legal estates by social classes. It also extended citizenship to adult males in the Spanish colonies and gave permanent representation in the national Cortes to the Spanish colonies. When Ferdinand VII recovered the throne in 1814, all of the decisions of the Cortes were immediately abolished. They were restored between 1820 and 1823 and then again permanently in 1836.

REFERENCE: Fernando Suarez, *Las Cortes de Cádiz*, 1982.

CORTINA Y MAURI, PEDRO. Pedro Cortina y Mauri was born in Spain in 1908 and spent his career in the Spanish diplomatic corps. During the early 1970s, he became Spain's foreign minister, and from that vantage point, he observed the rebellions against Portugal in Angola and Mozambique after the coup d'état in Lisbon in April 1974. Cortina became convinced that Spain should end its colonial involvement in Africa. He thought too that such a posture would make it easier for Spain to recover Gibraltar* through United Nations mediation. In 1974, he announced a plan for self-government in Western Sahara*, but by 1975 he decided that the Polisario Front* had the upper hand and that Spain should withdraw altogether, giving the region independence. He pledged such an arrangement to the Polisario Front leaders, but in the Madrid Agreement* of 1975, Spain caved in and agreed to allow Morocco and Mauritania to seize the region. Cortina felt betrayed by the Polisario Front. Cortina left the foreign ministry and resigned in 1975.

REFERENCE: Tony Hodges, *Historical Dictionary of Western Sahara*, 1982.

COSA, JUAN DE LA. Juan de la Cosa was born in Spain and became a prominent Spanish navigator and cartographer. He is best remembered for a series of expeditions he joined to Colombia* in the 1490s and early 1500s. He was with Christopher Columbus* on the voyages of 1492 and 1493, and he made two expeditions with Alonso de Ojeda* in 1499–1500 and 1509–1510. He completed one expedition with Rodrigo de Bastidas* in 1501 and led one expedition by himself between 1504 and 1507. The maps that Cosa drew during his expeditions became invaluable for subsequent explorers and settlers. Juan de la Cosa died in 1510 during the expedition with Ojeda.

REFERENCE: Robert H. Davis, *Historical Dictionary of Colombia*, 1977.

COSTA RICA. During the colonial period, Costa Rica, a province of the Captaincy General of Guatemala*, was one of four *gobiernos* established to control the region and one of the last Central American provinces to come under

Spanish control. It was a peripheral area in a backwater region of the Spanish Empire and had a small Indian* population. The Spanish population soon outnumbered the Indians, although migration to the region was never large. Isolated and lacking mineral wealth, its inhabitants were condemned to poverty and a harsh existence because of its frontier character. It was on Christopher Columbus's* fourth voyage that he reconnoitered its coasts, which he named Veragua. This territory was under litigation by his heirs against the Spanish Crown because they felt entitled to it because of the Crown's contracts with Columbus*. On June 9, 1508, as these proceedings were taking place, the king named Diego de Nicuesa* governor of Veragua (also named Castilla del Oro*) and included Nicaragua* in his territory. In 1510, Nicuesa went across some of the territory on the Atlantic side.

In 1513, Pedro Arias de Ávila* (Pedrarias) was named governor and captain general of Castilla de Oro but Veragua province was not included. In 1522 and 1523, Gil González Dávila* explored all of Costa Rica on the Pacific side. When Pedrarias heard of the discoveries, he sent Francisco Hernández de Córdoba* to conquer and settle the region. In 1524, he founded the first Spanish town, Bruselas, in Costa Rica, which was depopulated in 1525 by Hernández de Córdoba who rebelled against Pedrarias. Pedrarias ordered the town repopulated in 1526 but it was destroyed by Honduras's* governor in 1527. Columbus's heirs continued their legal fight and in 1536, his nephew, Luis, won both the title of Duke of Veragua and part of the territory. In 1556, the territory reverted to the Crown but the title was kept. The conquistadors* of Panama* and Nicaragua called the territory Costa Rica to distinguish it from the territory that comprised the Veragua dukedom.

In 1539, the *audiencia* of Panama* named Hernán Sánchez de Badajoz *adelantado*and *mariscal* of Costa Rica with authorization to conquer and colonize the territory. A dispute between him and Nicaragua's governor led to his arrest and return to Spain. The king disavowed Sanchez's conquest because the *audiencia* of Panama had no authority over the territory. In 1540, the king contracted Diego Gutiérrez to conquer and settle it, but the latter's cruelty to the Indians led to his death.

Not much of the territory (except Nicoya, which came under Spanish control in 1524) was under Spanish rule after this, but the conquistadors continued their attempts because they thought the area contained great wealth. In 1560, the *audiencia* of Guatemala* gave Juan de Cavallón* license to settle and conquer the territory. He brought the first livestock and founded towns, and by 1562, when he returned to Guatemala, the territory was definitely under Spanish control. Juan Vásquez de Coronado* continued the area's colonization but various Indian revolts plagued these attempts. In 1565, Coronado went to Spain to petition for the title of *adelantado* and governor of the province but he drowned on his return voyage. In 1568, the Indians rebelled but they were put down by governor Perafán de Ribera* who put them in *encomiendas**. After Ribera, the conquest phase was definitely over. It was through the efforts of Cavallón, Coronado, and Ribera that Costa Rica became part of the Spanish Empire.

The first settlers in the region came from Nicaragua. In 1573, there were about 50 families living in the towns of Cartago* and Aranjuez. In 1601, a road was opened from Cartago to Chiriquí, which was very useful because it allowed trade with Panama and mule-breeding for export. The Talamanca Indians were one group that fought against the occupation of their territory. In 1608, Gonzalo Vásquez de Coronado gained permission to conquer the Talamanca territory. Various attempts were made to conquer the region, and a frontier fort was finally established in Chirripo. Costa Rica's lack of minerals and population made it an extremely poor region besieged by many external and internal problems. In 1619, in an attempt to restore an Indian labor force, governor Alonso de Castillo y Guzmán re-entered Talamanca and brought 400 Indian prisoners back to Cartago; they were then divided among his soldiers. In 1622, the province requested incorporation into Panama but was rejected. Various attempts were made to open ports. In 1662, Talamanca's reconquest was attempted again by Governor Rodrigo Arias Maldonado.

Besides the Indians, the Spaniards had the added burden of protecting their borders from outside incursions by pirates who attacked the region frequently during the seventeenth century. The Matina Valley was a prime target because of its cacao* plantations and the town of Cartago. The Miskito* Indians, who were used by the English, raided cacao plantations and took African slaves working there. Cartago's citizens engaged in illegal trade with the English and the Dutch to acquire the goods they needed. As Cartago's population grew, individuals moved to the valley to grow agricultural goods. The region's poverty was such that in 1709 the governor defined cacao as money.

By the eighteenth century, Costa Rica's situation had not improved greatly. In 1709, the Talamancan Indians rebelled against the missionaries because of their excessive zeal. The *audiencia* of Guatemala sent an expedition to put down the rebellion in 1711. Various peace gestures by the Miskito Indians came to naught as the attacks against towns, haciendas, and populations continued. On February 16, 1723, the Irazú volcano erupted. Various new towns, such as San José* and Heredia, were founded as the population increased. After the Talamanca rebellion of 1709–1711, no new attempts at colonization were attempted until 1742. Taxes on cacao and mule exports were raised by the Crown for the defense of the valley. In 1766, the tobacco* *monopoly* was created, and the San José and Heredia tobacco growers, who previously had grown it freely, were required to bring it to a factory. Militias were created to protect the province from Indian and pirate attacks. Because of the province's poverty, it was given an exclusive monopoly in 1787 to grow tobacco; this was abolished in 1792 because of the tobacco's poor quality. The tobacco growers thus found themselves in a precarious situation. In 1804, new indigo, cotton, cacao, coffee*, and sugar* plantation were exempted from paying taxes but this did not help the province's situation. In 1808, an insurrection occurred in San José with the goals of freedom for growing tobacco.

When Napoleon invaded Spain in 1808, Cartago declared itself in favor of

Charles IV* and the next year in favor of his son, Ferdinand VII*. The Costa Rican militia put down a revolt in Nicaragua in 1811. As a reward, in 1813, Cartago was given the title of *muy noble y muy leal*, San José the title of *ciudad*, and Heredia that of *villa*. In 1811, the *audiencia* of Guatemala prohibited Costa Rican trade with Panama which obligated Costa Rica to buy costlier goods from Guatemala. The Cartago, Heredia and San José *ayuntamientos** protested this policy, before the Spanish Cortes in 1813, as did the governor. In 1815, the *Casa de Enseñanza de Santo Tomás*, a school, was founded in San José. Because the province did not have the 60,000 inhabitants necessary to elect a deputy to the 1820 *Cortes*, the district of Nicoya and towns of Santa Cruz and Guanacaste were attached to it. In October 1821, news of the independence declared in Guatemala City* arrived in Cartago and on October 29, Costa Rica declared independence from Spain. A *junta superior gubernativa* was formed that November.

REFERENCES: Ricardo Fernández Guardia, *Cartilla Histórica de Costa Rica*, 1909; Leon Fernández Guardia, *Historia de Costa Rica*, 2 vols., 1937; León Fernández Guardia *Historia de Costa Rica durante la Dominación Española 1502-1821*, 1975.

Carlos Pérez

COUNCIL OF THE INDIES. The Council of the Indies, or *El Real y Supremo Consejo de las Indias*, was established in August 1524 as the supreme legislative and juridical body governing the Spanish colonies in the New World. The Council of the Indies answered only to the king. In 1493, after Columbus's original discoveries, Queen Isabella* appointed Juan Rodríguez de Fonseca* to provide administrative direction to the new discoveries. Fonseca kept that power until his death in 1524. At that point, the Crown decided to institutionalize the governing process, and the Council of the Indies became that governing body. The Council of the Indies heard all cases coming up from the *audiencias** in the New World and also rendered decisions on cases coming to it from the Casa de Contratación*. The council's greatest weakness was its inability to enforce its regulations with any degree of efficiency or strength. In the eighteenth century, the Council of the Indies gradually lost power, primarily because the empire had grown so large and complex that centralized direction was all but impossible. In 1714, its military role was given to the new Ministry of Navy and the Indies, and in 1790, the council lost its legislative and judicial authority as well, becoming purely an advisory body. It was abolished in 1812, re-established in 1814, and permanently dissolved in 1834.

REFERENCE: Ernesto Schafer, *El Consejo real y supremo de las Indias*, 2 vols., 1935–1947.

COUNCIL OF TRENT. On December 13, 1545, the first session of a general church council met in Trent, a city in northern Italy. Called by Pope Paul III, it would meet intermittently until December 4, 1563. The rapid spread of Protestantism in the sixteenth century had elicited calls for a general council of bishops to reform Catholicism, the Protestant threat notwithstanding. Prior to

Pope Paul III, the Church had been reluctant to call a general council for fear of reviving conciliarism, a movement that had sought to replace the pope as head of the church with a general council of bishops. For that reason, from the outset and throughout the Council of Trent, the papacy maintained and strengthened the doctrine that the pope was supreme in all matters temporal and spiritual. Although no pope actually attended the council, the views of the papacy were defended by a preponderance of Italian delegates, especially by the Jesuits[*].

The Council of Trent was not the first attempt to reform the abuses of the Church. The Fifth Lateran Council, meeting from 1512–1515, had decreed reforms, but they were never implemented. After 1517, the Holy Roman Emperor, Charles V[*], began calling for a general church council. Although Charles V was a voice not to be ignored, Paul III was reticent about calling a general council for fear that papal prerogatives would not be exempt from the zeal to reform. If a council had to be called, Paul III looked to it more to enunciate and strengthen church doctrine than to correct abuses, which he viewed as the legitimate task of the pope alone. It was impossible, however, to resist the emperor altogether. That, coupled with the rising demand within the Church itself for reform, forced Paul to act. Therefore, on May 22, 1542, a bull was published, summoning a general council to meet at Trent on November 1, 1542. The continuing conflict between Charles V and Francis I of France caused the council to be delayed until December 13, 1545.

The two main goals of the council were to reform the abuses of the Church and to define Catholic dogma more clearly. Paul III considered the former goal of secondary importance to the latter, which had been his reason for summoning the council. There was considerable debate, however, over the order in which the two issues would be considered. It was finally decided that both issues would be dealt with simultaneously. In reality, the consideration of doctrinal issues took precedence. At the first session in 1545, the council emphatically reaffirmed the right of the Church to interpret scripture. The participants accepted the Latin Vulgate as the official Bible of the Church, including the books of *Judith*, the *Maccabees*, and the *Epistles of James*. The council also reaffirmed that the traditions of the Church held equal authority with the Bible. The most important issues that the council had to consider were the doctrines of free will and justification. Paul III was determined to define these issues in such a way as to make the breach between Catholicism and Protestantism undeniable. With regard to the Protestant doctrine of justification by faith alone, the council ruled that both faith and good works were necessary for salvation. It further stated that all seven sacraments were established by Christ and that therefore all were needed for salvation. The sole attempt to end the practice of bishops' holding multiple sees was voted down. By 1547, attendance began to dwindle and, under the pretext of a typhoid epidemic, Paul III gave permission to move the council to Bologna. Only a few of the delegates made the journey, and the council was suspended.

The council reassembled in Trent on September 1, 1551 under Pope Julius

II. On January 24, 1552, the Protestant delegation, which had been given safe conduct to attend the council, addressed the assembly. The representatives argued that the council's authority should be above that of the Pope. This message was not received very well by the Italian delegation and the papal legates. The most important doctrinal issue it considered at this time was the nature of the Eucharist. Protestants maintained that the Eucharist was merely symbolic, but the council ruled that Christ was actually present in the Eucharist. On April 28, 1552, the council was suspended as an army led by Maurice of Saxony approached Trent.

The Council of Trent had a number of positive effects on Catholicism. It defined the basic beliefs and doctrines of the Catholic Church[*] and distinguished them from Protestant doctrines, which were now considered heresies. With the weapon of a clearly defined doctrine, the faithful could close ranks and stem the Protestant challenge in Europe. Finally, the Council of Trent instilled a new religious vigor into the faithful to sustain them in their attempt to win Europe back to the Catholic Church.

REFERENCE: Edward McNall Burns, *The Counter Reformation*, 1964.

Michael Dennis

COUNTER-REFORMATION. The early beginnings of the Catholic Reformation can be traced to the religious fervor exhibited by the Spanish in the second half of the fifteenth century. A result of successfully driving the Moors from Spain, that nation's religious zeal found expression in attempts to reform the church. One result of this reform zeal was the creation of the Spanish Inquisition[*] in 1480. Its purpose was to eliminate heresy and to convert or drive out Spanish Jews and Moors. Early reformers included men like Cardinal Francisco Ximenes de Cisneros who attempted to reform the Spanish clergy, implementing stricter discipline and raising the educational requirements for all the clergy. This early Spanish movement for reform was driven as much by an attempt to unify the nation as it was by religious fervor. It had begun before Martin Luther posted his Ninety-five Theses, and it was carried out by the authority of the Crown. Once Protestantism became established, however, and began to threaten the Church throughout Europe, the attempt at reform had to be strengthened, with the impetus and authority coming from the papacy.

This more vigorous papal reform in Italy was spurred on by the zeal exhibited in Spain. One phase of reform was manifested in the creation of new religious orders and the reform of old ones. In 1517, the year of Luther's Ninety-five Theses, the Oratory of Divine Love was founded in Rome. This order sought to revive the spirituality of the Church through prayer and preaching and by returning to the simplicity of the early Church. Many of those involved in the oratory soon realized that personal devotion would not be enough to arrest the moral deterioration that they witnessed within the Church. Many of the members, subsequently, left the oratories and sought other means for furthering the reform of the Church.

Among the first of the new activist orders were the Theatines, founded in

1524 by Gaetano de Thiene, a member of the Oratory of Divine Love. The Theatines sought to reform the Church by identifying young men who had potential for future leadership in the Church and educating them to the new reform ideas. Eventually, it was hoped, these young men would become reform-minded cardinals and bishops. Many of the older orders were also reformed to counter the ever-encroaching Protestantism. The Dominicans*, for example, were purged of members who held strong Protestant views by Pope Paul III in the 1540s. Of all the new reforming orders, none was more successful at countering Protestantism than the Jesuits*. Founded in 1534 by Ignatius Loyola, the Jesuits not only devoted themselves to serve God in poverty, chastity, and missionary work, but they also vowed strict obedience to the pope and were at his disposal. The Jesuits considered themselves soldiers sworn to defend the faith. Through teaching and diplomacy, the Jesuits were able to halt the spread of Protestantism and even regained territory formerly lost to the Church, most notably in Poland, Germany, and France.

The reform movement did not take complete hold of the papacy until the election of Pope Paul III in 1534. Concerned with the status of the Church, Paul III called a general church council to convene in Trent. The Council of Trent* began in 1545 and completed its work in 1563. The council reaffirmed Catholic doctrine, rejecting all Protestant interpretations. It further reformed some of the more glaring abuses within the Church. Succeeding popes continued the reforms begun at Trent. Pope Pius IV published a list of condemned books in 1564 and began a revision of the breviary and the missal. Pope Pius V increased the power of the Inquisition in order to root out heresies. He also sent troops to fight the Huguenots in France. Pope Gregory's XIII's most notable achievement was the revision of the Julian calendar. The Gregorian Calendar brought uniformity to Church festival days. The result of the actions of the reform Popes was to reestablish the authority of the papacy and to enable that office to play a leading role in European affairs. More importantly, Catholicism, reinvigorated with a new religious spirit and purged of its worst abuses, could withstand the assault of the new Protestant doctrines.

REFERENCE: A. G. Dickens, *The Counter Reformation*, 1969.

Michael Dennis

CREOLE. See *CRIOLLO*.

CRIOLLO. The term *criollo* was used in Spanish America to describe an individual of European ancestry who was born in the New World. The term *peninsular** referred to individuals of European ancestry born in Spain. In most of the New World colonies, the *criollos* were an elite group who dominated business, commerce, plantation agriculture, and ranching, while real power in the Spanish military, bureaucracy, and Church was exercised largely by *peninsulares*. For the most part, the *peninsulares* looked down upon *criollos* as provincial, undereducated people, while *criollos* resented the arrogance of the *peninsulares*. When the independence movements developed in the late eighteenth and early nineteenth centuries, *criollos* were frequently leaders of the patriot forces who wanted to expel the *peninsulares* from their countries.

REFERENCES: John K. Chance, *Race and Class in Colonial Oaxaca*, 1978; J. I. Israel, *Race, Class and Politics in Colonial Mexico, 1610-1670*, 1975.

CROMBET, FLOR. Flor Crombet was born in Oriente Province, Cuba*, in 1851, and early in his life, he became an advocate of Cuban independence. Exiled for political reasons, Crombet spent the late 1870s and 1880s in Central America, primarily Honduras*, where he served as a militia commander. Crombet returned to Cuba in 1889, but in 1890, Spanish authorities deported him again. When the revolution erupted in 1895, he returned to the island and joined up with the forces of General Antonio Maceo*. Crombet was killed in combat in 1895.

REFERENCE: Ramiro Guerra y Sánchez, *Historia de la nación cubana*, 10 vols., 1952

CRUZ, SOR JUANA INÉS DE LA. Born in Nepantla, New Spain* in 1651, Sor Juana Inés de la Cruz was without a doubt the most important literary figure of colonial Spanish America. Moreover, her literary works rate among the best ever written in the Spanish language. She was a person of awesome intelligence. She was a brilliant student and devoted much of her life to study. By the age of three, she could read; by eight, she had won a literary prize. Because of her immense intellectual and academic powers, her fame spread throughout New Spain, and in her early teens, she was taken to the viceroy's* court in Mexico City*, as a lady-in-waiting. Her forceful personality and broad culture earned her a position of influence, respect, and curiosity there. She astounded court members with her insight and information, but suddenly, at the age of sixteen, she entered the convent. Her motivation for doing so has long been debated. According to her, she left the court in order to pursue her studies. Others, however, suggest that she sought the solitude of the convent in order to escape amorous involvement in the court (she was an uncommonly beautiful woman.)

Whatever her reason for entering the convent, Sor Juana sought the protection of a religious life, even though she herself openly admitted that such a life included aspects repugnant to her. Still, for her, a religious life was superior to that of the secular world and marriage. She therefore entered the convent to study, amassing a personal library of over 4,000 volumes. Nonetheless, not all passed well in convent life, for Sor Juana's intelligence, studies, and writings were not always well received by her superiors. In the later years, she abandoned her humanistic studies entirely in favor of religious contemplation. She died at the age of 44, in 1695, while attending to her fellow sisters during an epidemic. Sor Juana's literary works were numerous and varied. She wrote different types of poetry, plays, and prose. In general terms, she is viewed as a major figure in baroque* literature, but her baroque tendencies were nearly always controlled.

Although at times given to exaggerated adornment and affectation, by and large her works reflect a direct, clear, and simple approach to communication.

In poetry, Sor Juana excelled in both religious and profane love verse. She utilized a wide variety of poetic forms, including sonnets, redondillas, decimes, and romances. Her religious love poetry is marked with mysticism, and her profane love poetry is so knowing and telling that it suggests to some a real-life experience with physical passion. The bulk of her poetry was published in *Inundación Castálida* (1689) and in *Segundo Volumen de las Obras de Sor Juana Inés de la Cruz*. Her greatest single poetic composition, according to most critics, was *Primero sueño*, a philosophical poem. In summary, Sor Juana was the greatest of all colonial lyric poets, producing abundant examples of exquisite baroque and semi-baroque poetry.

Sor Juana also excelled in drama. Her religious *autos* include *El Divino Narciso* (1690), generally viewed as her greatest dramatic piece, and the two historical allegories, *El cetro de José* and *El Mártir del Sacramento: San Hermenegildo*. She wrote at least two comedias: *Los empeños de una casa* (1683), and *Amor es más laberinto* (1689). Although most of Sor Juana's prose has been destroyed or lost, she was a very capable prose writer, particularly in the field of the essay. Her best-known essay is *Respuesta de Sor Filotea de la Cruz*, in which she responded to the Bishop of Puebla by defending her life as a student of broad-based studies. Also of note is her splendid *Neptuno alegórico*. She died in 1695.

REFERENCES: A. Mendez Plancarte and A. G. Salceda, eds. *Obras completas*, 1951–1957; F. T. Royer, *The Tenth Muse*, 1952.

Sam L. Slick

CRUZADA NACIONAL DE LIBERACIÓN DE GUINEA ECUATORIAL (National Crusade for the Liberation of Equatorial Guinea). The Cruzada Nacional de Liberación de Guinea Ecuatorial (CNLGE) was established in 1947 by a number of prominent Fang people and residents of Fernando Po to oppose the Spanish Empire. During the 1950s, the Spanish Civil Guard imprisoned and assassinated a number of CNLGE leaders. Bubo Maho Sikacha took over the CNLGE in 1961, but he was forced to flee to Cameroon and the organization fell apart in a series of ideological disputes among its members.

REFERENCE: Max Liniger-Goumaz, *Historical Dictionary of Equatorial Guinea*, 1988.

CUAUHTÉMOC. Cuauhtémoc was the eleventh and final pre-conquest ruler of the México, the military leaders of the Aztec* Triple Alliance. He was the son of the eighth ruler, Ahuítzotl (who ruled 1486–1502), and cousin of Motecuhzoma Xocoyotzin (who ruled 1502–1520) and Cuitláhuac (who ruled a few months in 1520). Cuauhtémoc (''Eagle That Descends'') succeeded Cuitláhuac just prior to the Spanish siege of Tenochtitlán* while many, including Cuitláhuac, were already dying of smallpox.* Cuauhtémoc was only 18 or 19 years old.

Cuauhtémoc inherited a desperate situation, for he was besieged not only by

Spaniards but also by numerous of his former Indian allies and subjects. He sent messengers to neighboring provinces to secure arms, supplies, and reinforcements, but was unsuccessful. He commanded the México defense in fierce rooftop, street, and lake battles. But between the fighting and the depletion of necessary supplies, the México finally capitulated on August 13, 1521 (the formal attack having begun on April 28). Cuauhtémoc himself was captured in a canoe, fleeing the city. He was easily spotted, boldly flying the banners of his exalted office rather than departing surreptitiously. Cuauhtémoc and other indigenous leaders were later taken with Hernán Cortés[*] on his expedition to Honduras[*] territory. During that journey, Cortés claimed to have suspected Cuauhtémoc and others of treachery; he hanged Cuauhtémoc from a silk-cotton tree. The year was 1525, and Cuauhtémoc was still a young man.

Cuauhtémoc symbolized all the ideals of the Aztec warrior: he was strong, courageous, and skilled in martial technique and strategy. He and these ideals are immortalized in a prominent statue in downtown Mexico City.

REFERENCES: Arthur J. O. Anderson and Charles E. Dibble, *The War of Conquest*, 1978; Tzvetan Todorov, *The Conquest of America*, 1984.

Frances F. Berdan

CUBA. Cuba, whose area approximates that of all other West Indian islands combined, is situated 90 miles south of the Florida Keys. When sighted by Christopher Columbus[*] on October 27, 1492, it was inhabited by 16,000 to 60,000 Amerindians representing three cultures: the Guanajatabey, Ciboney[*], and Taíno[*]. Raids by cannibalistic Karibs[*] were threatening the dominant Taino, a peaceful, agricultural, Arawak[*] people. In 1511, three years after Sebastián de Ocampo's circumnavigation of the 746-mile-long island, Diego Velásquez[*] arrived from nearby Hispaniola[*]. By 1514, he had pacified the natives, though he encountered heroic resistance, notably by Chief Hatuey. To consolidate his power, Velásquez utilized the *encomienda*[*] system, which gave settlers the right to exploit Indian labor as payment for Christianizing and "protecting" them. Bartolomé de las Casas[*], a Dominican[*] friar, embarked upon a lifetime mission of defending America's aborigines as a result of witnessing the ill effects of the Cuban conquest. Velásquez founded Havana[*] and Santiago, modern Cuba's two largest cities, and governed until his death in 1524.

Black slaves were introduced in 1523 to replace the dwindling Amerindian workforce. Slavery[*] would not be completely abolished until 1886. After Hernán Cortés[*] left the island to conquer Mexico in 1518, other Spaniards used Cuba as a springboard for lucrative mainland enterprises. Havana, with its fine harbor and strategic location along the Gulf Stream, served as the key port of call for treasure fleets returning to Europe. It became Cuba's governmental seat in 1538. Cattle-raising developed into an important industry, providing salted meat and hides[*] for export. Still, the island was primarily a "service colony" rather than a producer of goods.

Bullion-laden galleons attracted pirates.[*] The French Huguenot, Jacques de

Sores, sacked and burned Havana in 1555. Pedro Menéndez de Aviles, who governed Cuba in the 1560s, improved the convoy system that guarded Spanish shipping and transformed the capital into a military bastion. Santiago was torched by the infamous Henry Morgan in 1662. Nevertheless, despite a series of foreign attacks, Spain held the island until 1762. Ironically, the English capture of Havana in that year, during the Seven Years War[*], breathed new life into the colony. The port was opened to free trade for 11 months. Capital and slaves poured into the island. When Spain regained Cuba, it was forced to reconsider its monopolistic policies. In 1796, a Haitian revolution led to a flood of refugees and the elimination of the world's top sugar[*] producer. Commercial reforms, combined with growing trade with the United States, further stimulated cane planting. Coffee[*] cultivation increased and peaked from 1820 to 1840. Consequently, by the late 1820s, Cuba had blossomed into the wealthiest colony on earth. Tobacco[*] had boomed in the early 1700s, but now, sugar was "king".

Cuba and Puerto Rico[*] were Spain's last remaining American colonies after 1825. As the century progressed, however, Spanish rule was questioned. Cries for fiscal and political reform went unanswered. In October 1868, Carlos Manuel de Céspedes[*] launched an unsuccessful rebellion ending in February 1878, with the Pact of Zanjón. After the Ten Years War[*], Madrid still refused to implement major colonial changes. Economic depression ignited another uprising in 1895 led by José Martí[*], Máximo Gómez[*], and Antonio Maceo[*]. Rebel victories induced Spain to offer Cuba status as a self-governing province. This proposal was rejected.

In February 1898, the U.S.S. *Maine*[*] mysteriously exploded in Havana's harbor. Since the Ten Year's War, United States businesses had increased their Cuban investments significantly. President William McKinley, pressured by a public outcry fueled by yellow journalism, declared war on Spain on April 25, 1898. Although it had attempted to purchase the island earlier in the century, in the Teller Amendment the United States promised not to annex Cuba. In less than four months, Spain surrendered. The rebels, unfortunately, were not represented at the peace talks. From January, 1899, until May, 1902, the United States militarily occupied the former colony. Some improvements were made, especially in sanitation. Washington approved the Cuban Constitution of 1901 only when the Platt Amendment was attached, which granted the United States the option to intervene for the purpose of protecting Cuba's "independence" or American "lives and property." On May 20, 1902, Tomás Estrada Palma assumed office as the first elected president of the Republic of Cuba. Before Franklin D. Roosevelt abrogated the Platt Amendment in 1934, the United States reoccupied Cuba from 1906 to 1909 and landed Marines there in 1912. Moreover, it acquired a perpetual lease to a 45-square-mile naval base at Guantánamo Bay, which it continues to hold.

REFERENCES: Hugh Thomas, *Cuba: The Pursuit of Freedom*, 1971; Jaime Suchlicki, *Cuba: From Columbus to Castro*, 1985.

Frank Marotti

CÚCUTA, CONGRESS OF. See GRAN COLOMBIA.

CUENCA, DIOCESE OF. The Roman Catholic diocese of Cuenca, which today includes the provinces of Azuay and Canar in Ecuador*, was established on July 1, 1786, with José Carrón y Marfil as the first bishop. It became an archdiocese in 1957.
REFERENCE: *New Catholic Encyclopedia*, IV:519, 1967.

CUITLÁHUAC. Cuitláhuac was born in Tenochitlán* in what is today Mexico City* in 1476. After the death of Motecuhzoma*, Cuitláhuac emerged as the new Aztec* leader. He was a successful military tactician who managed to drive the Spaniards out of Tenochtitlán on June 30, 1520. He died of smallpox in December 1520.
REFERENCE: Donald C. Briggs and Marvin Alisky, *Historical Dictionary of Mexico*, 1981.

CUSCATLÁN. Cuscatlán was the capital of the Pipiles*, a Nahuatl* people who migrated from the Valley of Mexico to El Salvador* sometime during the first millenium A.D. Although the Pipiles successfully defended Cuscatlán from Spanish attack in 1524, they were conquered by Pedro de Alvarado* in 1525. Alvarado renamed Cuscatlán San Salvador* and established it as a Spanish base. In 1528, Alvarado relinquished control of El Salvador to his brother Jorge. Jorge de Alvarado relocated the capital to the Valley of La Bermuda, and Cuscatlán was abandoned.
REFERENCE: R. L. Woodward, Jr., *Central America: A Nation Divided*, New York, 1983.

Virginia Garrard Burnett

CUZCO. "In the year 1000 A.D.," wrote Pedro Cieza* de Leon, "in the name of Tici Viracocha and of the sun and the rest of his gods, Manco Cápac founded the new City." These are the origins of the city of Cuzco in the upper Andean sector of Peru*. The inhabitants, called the Incas*, created a civilization ahead of its time within the Cuzco valley. They domesticated the llama, developed irrigation techniques, possessed an innate sense of organization and unsurpassed architectural and construction methods, and had as the basis of their society the social territorial commune or *ayllu*. The city of Cuzco was conquered by Francisco Pizarro*. It became the seat of a Spanish intendencia* in 1784. Spain crushed a rebellion in Cuzco in 1813, but in 1824, the city was liberated by patriot forces. See PERU.
REFERENCE: Clements R. Markham, *A History of Peru*, 1982.

Fred Koestler

CUZCO, *AUDIENCIA* OF. Throughout the colonial period, the area of Cuzco* was subject to the *audiencia* of Lima*, which was the viceregal *audiencia* for most of South America. By the late eighteenth century, however, economic development and population growth had become so great that it was increasingly difficult for the *audiencia* in Lima to handle all of the matters coming out of southern Peru*. In 1784, the Spanish crown created the *audiencia* of Cuzco with jurisdiction over southern Peru. Benito de la Mata Linares served as the first intendant. The *audiencia* of Cuzco functioned until 1824 when Peruvian rebel forces took control of the region.

REFERENCE: Mark A. Burkholder and D. S. Chandler, *From Impotence to Authority: The Spanish Crown and the American Audiencias, 1687-1808*, 1977.

CUZCO, DIOCESE OF. The Roman Catholic diocese of Cuzco was established in 1537, and its first bishop was Vicente de Valverde*. It was a very prominent diocese in the early colonial period because of its location in the heart of the Incan* civilization and because of the numbers of *encomiendas** and *repartimientos** granted there. Its area was reduced in size in the early 1600s with the creation of the dioceses of Arequipa*, Huamanga*, and La Paz*. In 1600, the diocese of Cuzco had 138 parishes, and that number had increased to 164 parishes by 1800. It became an archdiocese in 1943.

REFERENCE: *New Catholic Encylcopedia*, 1967.

D

DAGOHOY REBELLION. See BOHOL.

DARIÉN. See PANAMA.

DAVILA, PEDRO ARIAS. See ÁVILA, PEDRO ARIAS DE.

DEHESAS. Derived from the Latin *defensa* (enclosed), the *dehesa* was a plot of land that was at least theoretically enclosed. Actually, most *dehesas* were neither walled nor fenced, but were merely restricted, or reserved, for some specific purpose. Some *dehesas* were private property, reserved for the exclusive use of the owner; others were commons or *propios*. Although usually for pasture, the *dehesas* frequently had some trees growing on them and often were partially cultivated. Virtually every medieval and early modern Spanish municipality had at least one common *dehesa*. If a town had only one *dehesa*, it was almost certainly a *dehesa boyal*, a pasture reserved exclusively for oxen and other draft animals. The size, location, and character of these special pastures varied widely, but the typical *dehesa boyal* was located near the town, at a site where there was ample grass, shade, and water. Larger and more prosperous municipalities were likely to have several *dehesas boyales*, for the convenience of their residents.

Normally, the *dehesa boyal* was reserved exclusively for draft animals of local residents. Municipal ordinances prohibited the introduction of non-draft animals and of livestock owned by nonresidents. Some towns reserved their *dehesa boyal* for draft animals only during certain times of the year, at other times allowing other types of animals to pasture there. Still other towns rented out parts of their *dehesa boyal* to provide extra funds during financial emergencies. Some places also had *dehesas de yeguas*, reserved exclusively for broodmares, to encourage horse-breeding. The *dehesa carnicera* was a special municipally owned pasture reserved for the town butcher to fatten his animals prior to slaughter, with the goal of providing better and cheaper meat. The *dehesa*, both as private property and as commons, was transported to America by the conquistadors[*].

REFERENCES: David E. Vassberg, *Land and Society in Golden Age Castile*, 1984; Francois Chevalier, *Land and Society in Colonial Mexico: The Great Hacienda*, 1970.

David E. Vassberg

DELGADO, JOSÉ MATÍAS. José Matías Delgado was born in San Salvador[*] in what is today El Salvador[*] on February 24, 1767. He trained for the Roman Catholic priesthood in Guatemala[*] and in 1797 was appointed the vicar of San Salvador. Because of his intense opposition to royal power, Delgado is widely considered as the father of the independence movement in El Salvador. Delgado played a key role in the uprising of November 5, 1811, and in 1821, he signed the Act of Independence composed in Guatemala City. He was appointed governor of San Salvador in 1821 and spent several years fighting the Mexican attempt to annex El Salvador. When the Mexican Empire collapsed in 1823, Delgado became a leading figure in the constituent assembly in Guatemala City[*] that drew up a constitution for Central America. During his later years, he became a political enemy of Manuel José Arce[*]. José Delgado died in 1832.

REFERENCE: R. Barón Castro, *José Matías Delgado y el Movimiento insurgente de 1811*, 1962.

DE LÔME LETTER. Enrique Dupuy de Lôme (1851–1904) was the Spanish minister to the United States during the critical period before the Spanish-American War[*] of 1898. He was an experienced diplomat who had previously served as first secretary of the Spanish legation in Washington in 1882 and as minister in 1892 and 1895. He was a competent representative of Spain's affairs in the United States; during the hectic months of 1897 and early 1898, he appeared to be having some success with the administration of President William McKinley in countering hostile attitudes toward Spain over its policy in Cuba[*], an attitude inflamed by influential newspapers and supported by factions in Congress and the public. Two events in February 1898 as reported in the "yellow press," outraged public opinion and pushed the McKinley administration toward war with Spain. The first of these events was the publication of the "de Lôme Letter" on February 9, 1898, by William Randolph Hearst's New York *Journal*. The second event was the explosion aboard the U.S. battleship *Maine*[*].

The offending letter was apparently provoked by de Lôme's reaction to McKinley's "State of the Union" address in December 1897. In what de Lôme presumed to be the sanctity of a private letter, he expressed his frustration with the McKinley administration's meddling in Cuban affairs, and he included what can be adjudged a fairly accurate but insulting appraisal of the president himself. In unburdening himself to a friend, de Lôme said of the president and his address:

"Besides the ingrained and inevitable coarseness with which it repeated all that the Press and public opinion in Spain have said about Weyler,* it once more shows what McKinley is, weak and a bidder for the admiration of the crowd, besides being a common politician who tries to leave a door open behind himself while keeping on good terms with the jingoes of his party."

Canalejas had recently left the United States after a brief visit, and de Lôme's letter followed him to Havana*, Cuba. It was stolen from his desk by someone sympathetic to the insurgency and forwarded to the Cuban junta in New York. To make the most of the opportunity to embarrass the Spanish government, the junta turned the letter over to William Randolph Hearst. On February 8, de Lôme was made aware that the letter had fallen into hostile hands and would be published the next day. He immediately realized that his own usefulness would end with the publication of the offending letter. He quickly cabled his government and tendered his resignation.

As de Lôme had anticipated, on February 9, 1898, the headlines of Hearst's *Journal* indignantly screamed the contents of the stolen letter. The cry was taken up by numerous newspapers across the United States, and editorial writers demanded the recall of the Spanish minister. But by the time the United States Department of State had instructed its minister to Spain, General Stewart L. Woodford, to demand de Lôme's recall, the Spanish government was able to inform Woodford that de Lôme had already been relieved of his duties. This maneuver helped to some extent to mitigate the damage to Spanish-United States relations, and the crisis seemed to be ebbing after a few days, only to be followed by a far greater crisis over the destruction of the U. S. S. *Maine* in Havana harbor on February 15, 1898.

REFERENCES: Walter Millis, *The Martial Spirit*, 1931; David F. Trask, *The War With Spain in 1898*, 1981; Robert Ferrell, *American Diplomacy*, 1969; Salvador de Madariaga, *Spain: A Modern History*, 1958.

Joseph M. Rowe, Jr.

DERROTA DE MIESES. The *derrota de mieses* was the custom of common stubble-grazing, as practiced in medieval and early modern Iberia and contemporaneously in most of the rest of Europe. The *derrota de mieses* transformed the post-harvest stubble of all fields into common pasture for the animals of the general public. The person who cultivated the field—whether a tenant farmer or the landowner—could not legally exclude the animals of his neighbors. The entire territory of a town, including pasture and arable land, thus became a continuous common pasture until the next planting season, when individual rights were restored.

In a legal sense, the *derrota de mieses* created a system in which a "privately owned" piece of land had not one ownership, but two: an individual ownership of the field and crop during the period when the plot was planted; and a collective ownership of the stubble and weeds on the plot between harvest and the next sowing. Even fenced or walled fields were subject to the *derrota de mieses*, and gates had to be provided to admit flocks and herds after harvest.

The *derrota de mieses* provided a mixed system of individual and communal rights admirably suited to a rural economy based upon a complementary relationship between pastoral and arable agriculture. The typical agriculturalist of the day could not work his fields without oxen or mules, and these animals needed pasturage, particularly in winter when many mountainside pastures were snowbound. In semi-arid Castile*, the sparse weeds and post-harvest stubble provided a welcome pasture resource for work animals. Furthermore, the typical peasant owned a few sheep, goats, or other animals that needed grazing space. The *derrota de mieses* was of benefit to everyone owning animals, and the grazing flocks and herds compensated the landowner by enriching the soil with their droppings. The *derrota* was regarded as one of the irrevocable rights of the Castilian peasantry, and it was defended even by jurists who tended to be hostile toward communalism. It is not surprising that the custom was transplanted to America, along with the animals that benefited from it. The *derrota de mieses* was remarkably long-lived; it survived in Spain down to the latter half of the twentieth century.

REFERENCES: Jesús García Fernández, "Champs ouverts et champs clôturés en Vieille Castille," tr. P. X. Despilho, *Annales, Economies, Sociétés, Civilisations*, 20 (1965), 692–718; David E. Vassberg, *Land and Society in Golden Age Castile*, 1984.

David E. Vassberg

DIARIO DE VIAJE (Columbus's logbook). Properly speaking, this work is the very first example of New World (colonial) literature. *Diario* recounts, on a daily basis, Christopher Columbus'* first voyage to the New World, including landfall and a rich description of the white man's initial encounter with indigenous peoples. It is a highly personal presentation, written in the first person. *Diario* would have been lost to posterity, were it not for the good Friar Bartolomé de las Casas* who rescued the work, reconstructed it in part, and preserved it.

REFERENCE: Christopher Columbus, *Diario de Viaje*, tr. Cecil Jane, 1960.

Sam L. Slick

DÍAZ DE ARMENDÁRIZ, LOPE. Lope Díaz de Armendáriz, the Marqués of Cadereyta, was born around 1575 in Quito*, Ecuador*. His father, Lope Díaz de Armendáriz, was the president of the *audiencia* of Quito*. Díaz de Armendáriz was educated at the Royal College of Madrid and then spent his career as a diplomat and military official in the royal service. He was *mayordomo* to Queen Isabel, ambassador to the German Court, and head of the West Indian Fleet before becoming viceroy* of Mexico in 1635. He served as viceroy until 1640 and is best remembered for constructing the Great Drainage Canal from Lake Texcoco. He died in 1640.

REFERENCE: Albert William Bork and Georg Maier, *Historical Dictionary of Ecuador*, 1973.

DÍAZ DE ARMENDÁRIZ, MIGUEL. Miguel Díaz de Armendáriz was born in Spain to a prominent family. He received a number of important assignments in the Spanish colonial service, the most important of which was being named to conduct the first *visita** and *residencia** in New Granada (see Colombia*). Between 1544 and 1550, Díaz conducted investigations in Cartagena*, Santa Marta*, Bogotá*, and Cali. He also authorized a number of new exploration and colonization expeditions and tried to enforce the New Laws*. Díaz also lobbied for creation of the *audiencia* of Bogotá*, which was established in 1550. He died that year in Bogota.
REFERENCE: Robert H. Davis, *Historical Dictionary of Colombia*, 1977.

DÍAZ DE ESPADA Y LANDA, JUAN JOSÉ. Juan José Díaz de Espada y Landa was born in Arroyave, Alava, Spain, in 1756. After filling a number of successively more important clerical posts in Spain, Díaz de Espada came to Cuba* in 1802 as the bishop of Havana*. He presided over the diocese for the next 30 years, earning a well-deserved reputation for hard work, fairness, and a sense of reform. Juan de Espada died on August 13, 1832.
REFERENCE: C. García Pons, *El obispo Espada y su influencia en la cultura Cubana*, 1951.

DÍAZ DEL CASTILLO, BERNAL. Bernal Díaz del Castillo was born in Medina del Campo in 1492, the year Christopher Colombus* discovered the New World. A soldier and fortune-seeker, Díaz came to the New World as a young man in 1514, where he served Pedrarias (Pedro Arias de Ávila*) at Nombre de Dios, Panama*. After three years, Díaz went to Cuba*, from where he participated in the first two expeditions to the Mexican coast, led by Francisco Hernández* de Córdoba and Juan de Grijalva*. In 1519, Díaz joined the expedition of Hernán Cortés* and participated as a common soldier in the conquest of Mexico (New Spain*). Díaz eventually returned to Spain. At the age of 76, he wrote the work for which he is remembered, *Historia verdadera de la conquista de la Nueva España*, usually translated into English as *The Conquest of New Spain*. This was a firsthand account of the Spanish conquest of Mexico and the intrigues in Hispaniola*, Cuba, and Spain in the post-conquest period. Díaz recorded his memoirs in response to the published stories of Francisco López de Gómara*, Cortés's confessor, who Díaz believed had misrepresented both Cortés and the details of the conquest of the Aztecs*. Díaz died in Spain around 1580, the last surviving conqueror of Mexico.
REFERENCE: Luis González Obregón, *Cronistas e historiadores*, 1936.

Virginia Garrard Burnett

DÍAZ DE PIÑEDA, GONZALO. Gonzalo Díaz de Piñeda was a close associate of Sebastián de Benalcázar* in the conquest of Ecuador*. An explorer, soldier, and administrator, Díaz de Piñeda served briefly as captain general of Quito*, and he founded the city of Sevilla de Oro (Macas) on the eastern slopes of the Andes in 1539. Along with Gonzalo Pizarro*, he rebelled against the New Laws*

in the early 1540s. The idea of restoring land and rights to Indians* was ludicrous as far as he was concerned. Because of his opposition to the New Laws, Gonzalo Díaz de Piñeda had to flee Quito for the Ecuadorean Sierra, where he died in 1544.

REFERENCES: Albert William Bork and Georg Maier, *Historical Dictionary of Ecuador*, 1973; Federico González Suárez, *Historia general de la República del Ecuador*, 7 vols., 1890–1903.

DÍAZ DE SOLÍS, JUAN. See SOLÍS, JUAN DÍAZ DE.

DIRECCIÓN GENERAL DE MARRUECOS Y COLONIAS (General Administration for Morocco and the Colonies). Established in 1925, the Dirección General de Marruecos y Colonias was the Spanish governmental agency responsible for colonial affairs. It was renamed the Dirección General de Plazas y Provincias Africanas (General Administration of African Towns and Provinces) in 1960. Its status was substantially reduced after the independence of Equatorial Guinea in 1968 and the withdrawal from Spanish Sahara* in 1975.

REFERENCE: Max Liniger-Goumaz, *Historical Dictionary of Equatorial Guinea*, 1988.

DISEASE. Although most historians have focused on the violent confrontation which occurred between the first Spaniards in the New World and the indigenous peoples, it was disease, not war, which explains the dramatic decline in the native populations. For thousands of years, the Indians of the New World had been isolated, geographically and biologically, from the peoples of Europe, Africa, the Middle East, and Asia, and in the process they had not developed any natural immunities to Old World illnesses. Within a few weeks of their first contact with Spaniards, the Indians of the New World fell victim to massive epidemics—pandemics—of smallpox, diptheria, whooping cough, chicken pox, mumps, influenza, malaria, dysentery, and a host of other biological calamities. Of all the diseases the Europeans brought with them to the New World, smallpox was the most devastating. Since it could spread from one victim to another by breath, smallpox was one of the world's most communicable diseases. The 14-day incubation period made it possible for a person to flee a smallpox-ridden area for safety and carry the disease to another region. Smallpox, along with the other European diseases, killed tens of millions of native Americans. The largest number of people died in the dense populations of New Spain* and Peru*, but the highest mortality rates were in the warm, wet lowlands of the Caribbean.

Although the flow of diseases in the other direction—from the New World to Europe—was much less dramatic, many scholars believe that the Indians gave syphilis to the Spanish conquistadors. The question of the origins of syphilis is extremely controversial among epidemiologists. Some people argue the Unitarian theory—that the varieties of syphilis around the world are all part of the same strain and that human beings have shared it for tens of thousands of years. But others argue, quite convincingly, that syphilis was a New World disease. Archaeologists have discovered syphilitic lesions in the bones of ancient Americans, and historians note that Europeans first began writing about the disease in 1493— within months of the return of Christopher Columbus's[*] crew to Spain.

REFERENCES: Alfred W. Crosby, Jr., *Ecological Imperialism: The Biological Expansion of Europe, 900-1900*, 1986; Alfred W. Crosby, Jr., *The Columbian Exchange: Biological and Cultural Consequences of 1492*, 1972.

DJEMAA. The Djemaa was a territorial assembly established by Spain in the colony of Western Sahara[*] in 1967 to give tribal leaders some input into colonial policymaking. Its 82 members were proportionately represented according to the size of their tribes, and they were chosen in tribal elections. By 1973, when Spain began thinking about independence for the region, consideration was given to converting the Djemaa into a formal legislature. After the Madrid Agreement[*] of 1975, which provided for a Moroccan and Mauritanian takeover of Western Sahara, the members of the Djemaa voted to dissolve the body and pledged their support for the Polisario Front[*].

REFERENCE: Tony Hodges, *Historical Dictionary of Western Sahara*, 1982.

DOMÍNGUEZ CAMARGO, HERNANDO. Hernando Domínguez Camargo was born in Colombia[*] in 1601 and spent all of his life in New Granada. He joined the Jesuit[*] order, but later he abandoned it to become a secular priest. Domínguez was well-educated for his time. He held a doctorate degree and was apparently known in New Granada as Doctor Domínguez. His surviving literary work is most likely only a portion of his actual production. He wrote baroque[*] poetry. Perhaps his best-known work is *San Ignacio de Loyola, fundador de la Compañía de Jesús* (1666), which deals with and is dedicated to Ignatius Loyola; the poem is divided into 24 cantos. Domínguez's best poetry comes in the form of separate and diverse poems, particularly sonnets and romances; his poetry has been unevenly received by critics over the years. At the very least, Hernando Domínguez Camargo stands out as one of New Granada's better baroque poets. He died in 1659.

REFERENCES: Ángel Flores, *The Literature of Spanish America: The Colonial Period*, 1966; José Manuel Groot, *Historia eclesiástica y civil de Nueva Granada*, 5 vols., 1953.

Sam L. Slick

DOMINICA. Dominica was the first island in the Caribbean that Christopher Columbus[*] sighted on November 3, 1493 during his second voyage from one of his 17 ships to the Americas. Columbus named the island Sunday, after the day of the week, to commemorate when his crew had spotted it. It had been exactly three weeks since he left the Canary Islands[*] heading west. Nicolo Syllacio of Milan, who accompanied Columbus on this voyage, was very impressed with what he saw from the deck of his ship and wrote: "Dominica is remarkable for the beauty of its mountains . . . and must be seen to believe. In many places, huge trees come down to the shore as in Thessalain Tempe." One of Columbus's ships sought to land but on sighting a Karib[*] settlement at Ovyvhao, it rejoined the main caravan. Columbus also encountered Dominica during his fourth voyage in 1502, but few Europeans sought to settle the island.

Dominica, the largest of the Leeward Islands in the Lesser Antilles, is of volcanic formation, mountainous, having a higher peak than all the other Antilles at over 5,000 feet. Dominica was well-watered and possessed over 365 rivers, most teeming with fish. This fertile land supported crops for a large Karib population who quickly earned a reputation among the Spanish and later other Europeans as being among the fiercest Amerindians in the region. These Karibs called the island Wittagabussee (also spelled Waitukubuili), meaning "tall is her body," and they sought to protect it from any European intrusion. The Spanish first referred to the island's inhabitants as "Caribales," from which the word "cannibal" is believed to be derived. The natives, however, referred to each other as "karina" for men and "karifuna" for women. The Karibs had arrived from South America centuries before, replacing the Arawaks[*] who had lived there since the first Christian century. They desired to be left alone and to live free in their settlements along the coast of the island. Among them were the settlements of Calibishi, Koliho, Makusari, Mero, Kulibistri, Layou, Taro, Batali, Bataki, Itassi, Uyuhao, Sairi, and Kuliru.

As late as the mid-sixteenth century, Dominica remained extremely dangerous to non-Karibs who were found wandering near its coasts. Lennox Honychurch, in the *Dominica Story*, has pointed out that a dozen years after Columbus's final contact with Dominica, Pedro Arias de Ávila[*], a Spanish captain, led an expedition to Dominica that arrived on June 3, 1514. Avila was accompanied by 19 vessels with about 1,500 men on board. Immediately, the Karibs sought to defend their settlements by launching poisonous arrow attacks, but Avila's convoy remained anchored offshore for about half a week. Avila had observed enough about Dominica to appeal later to the Council of the Indies[*], urging the officials to consider settling Dominica. He felt that the island could be a valuable center for Spanish trade in the Lesser Antilles. In 1519, Dominica and other neighboring islands were formally added to the Diocese of Puerto Rico[*], and it seemed that interest had grown in the Spanish settlement of the island. The following year, Antonio Serrano, a government official on Hispaniola[*] was selected to colonize Dominica and neighboring Guadeloupe, but his attempts in 1525 to settle were repulsed by the Karibs and Serrano had to withdraw. This did not prevent a few adventurous Spaniards from seeking to trade with the island.

During 1564, a Spanish crew shipwrecked off the Dominican coast was killed by the Karibs; their bodies were reportedly all devoured by the Karibs, supporting the belief of many that the islands were inhabited by cannibals. Some Spanish entrepreneurs, however, were brave enough to attempt to make slave raids on the Dominican coasts, as they did on other islands of the Lesser Antilles. In Dominica, they were less successful. Still, the Dominica Karibs were themselves known to lead raids on some European settlements as far south as Trinidad[*]. In

1569, fewer than 100 captive Spaniards and Africans lived among the Karibs on Dominica. From the early seventeenth century, both the English and the French were eager to establish settlements in Dominica, as the Spanish continued to ignore events on the island while maintaining their "right" to total possession of all the islands of the eastern Caribbean. It was not until 1763 that Spain formally ceded the island to the English.

REFERENCES: Lennox Honychurch, *The Dominica Story*, 1984; Samuel Eliot Morison, *Admiral of the Ocean Sea*: *A Life of the Admiral Christopher Columbus*, 2 vols., 1942.

Glenn O. Phillips

DOMINICANS. The Order of Friars Preachers (OP), also known as the Dominicans, was founded early in the 1200s and was formalized by papal confirmation in 1216. The order was a synthesis of the contemplative approach and the apostolic ministry, in which vows of monasticism, chastity, poverty, and obedience were combined with a commitment to worldwide preaching and the defense of the faith. By 1277, there were 404 organized Dominican priories in the world, and they increased in number to 590 in 1303 and 635 in 1358. Although the order suffered losses during the Reformation, it more than made up for them by overseas expansion. While many Dominicans played important roles as missionary priests in the New World, most of the important mission work was carried out by Franciscans* and Jesuits* in Mexico, Central America, and South America; there were also Dominican missionary priests in the Philippines*. The Dominicans came to America in 1510 and founded the province of the West Indies; by 1724, there were 11 Dominican provinces in the Spanish colonies. The Philippine province was created in 1595, and from that base, Dominican missionaries fanned out into China, India, Japan, and southeast Asia.

REFERENCE: J. B. Reeves, *The Dominicans*, 1959.

DRAFT ANIMALS. In Roman times and during the entire medieval period, the traditional draft animal in the Iberian peninsula was the ox, and the rural norm was for fields to be plowed with yokes of oxen. During the sixteenth century, Spain witnessed a revolution in draft technology, and the mule gradually displaced the ox as the typical source of plow power. By 1600, oxen predominated only in isolated or backward areas, particularly in the mountains. The sixteenth century was a period of rapid expansion of the area under cultivation, both to feed the burgeoning population and to supply the lucrative overseas markets in the Spanish empire. Mules were preferred over oxen because a mule could plow nearly twice as much land as an ox. Moreover, the mule was a better choice in vineyards and orchards, where it was difficult to maneuver a yoke of oxen. In addition, the nucleated pattern of Spanish rural settlement favored the swifter mule over the proverbially slow-footed oxen, for moving from village to field and from one field to the next. Finally, mules could serve as pack and saddle animals when not needed for field work. The disadvantage of mules was that they required grain (normally barley) in order to work effectively. This meant that a significant proportion (as much as a quarter) of the harvest produced by mule power was consumed by the mules themselves, whereas oxen could get along quite well on pasture alone. Furthermore, the mule was a sterile hybrid that could not reproduce. Strictly speaking, the ox (a castrated male) was also sterile, but many "oxen" were actually cows, which might not be as strong as males but had the advantage of being able to provide milk and even calves for their owners.

In the late 1500s the Spanish economy entered a period of decline that extended throughout the next century. Many intellectuals blamed the mule for the ills of Spain, asserting that mules performed superficial work and encouraged idleness in the rural population. Despite various governmental efforts to encourage a return to oxen, the mule remained the prevalent draft animal in Spain until displaced by the tractor in the twentieth century. In America, there were no draft animals until the Spaniards introduced European bovines and equines. Some Indian communities under Spanish rule long remained loyal to their pre-conquest digging sticks, whereas others readily adopted Spanish plows and oxen. By the eighteenth century, oxen and plows had become fairly common in the Indian communities of New Spain[*]. Colonial plowing was performed largely by yokes of oxen.

REFERENCE: David E. Vassberg, *Land and Society in Golden Age Castile*, 1984.

David E. Vassberg

DRAKE, FRANCIS. Francis Drake was born in Devon, England, in 1543, to a small farming family. He went to sea as an apprentice in 1556, and by the time he was a young man, he had already traveled widely throughout the world. In 1572, with his own ship, Drake attacked Spanish transports at the isthmus of Panama[*] and brought home considerable gold to England. In 1577, Drake set out on his most famous voyage. He sailed along the southern coast of South America and through the Straits of Magellan. On his sweep north of the western coast of South America, Drake attacked Spanish shipping all the way, capturing huge amounts of gold from the treasure galleons. Drake went on to the Moluccas (Spice Islands[*]) and picked up a load of cloves, and then returned to England via the Cape of Good Hope, arriving in Plymouth in 1580. Queen Elizabeth I knighted him. Drake attacked Santo Domingo[*], Cartagena[*], and St. Augustine[*], Florida, in 1585, destroyed the port at Cádiz in 1587, and attacked Puerto Rico[*] and Panama in 1595–1596. He died of dysentery near Puerto Bello on January 28, 1596.

REFERENCE: Derek Wilson, *The World Encompassed: Drake's Great Voyage, 1577-1580*, 1977.

DURÁN, DIEGO. A Spanish critic, historian, and Dominican priest, Diego Durán was born in Seville[*], Spain, in 1537. From early childhood, he was a resident of Texcoco, New Spain[*], where he learned to speak Nahuatl[*]. He taught in the Convent of Santo Domingo in Mexico City*, but he is best remembered as a historian and chronicler, the author of *Historia de las Indias de la Nueva España*, completed between 1574 and 1581. The manuscript was discovered in the National Library of Madrid and published between 1867 and 1880. The work is an invaluable primary source for the study of early colonial Mexico. Diego Durán died in Mexico in 1588.

REFERENCE: Diego Duran, *Historia de las Indias de Nueva-España y islas de tierra firma*, ed. J. Fernández Ramírez, 1867–1880.

Fred Koestler

DUTCH WAR. In April 1672, Louis XIV of France declared war on the Dutch Republic after signing a military treaty with Sweden. Although the Dutch held their own at sea, the land war generally favored the French who were allied with the British. That Spain should become engulfed in the war is not surprising, given that Louis XIV was eager to fight the Spanish because of his desire, based on rather tenuous claims, for control of the Spanish Netherlands. Indeed, one reason for Louis's attack in the Dutch Republic was to neutralize it so that he could move against the Spanish Netherlands, dealing with Spain as necessary in the process. Although Louis's ultimate objective in the war was probably Spain, he hesitated to instigate war against Spain directly because of opposition by his British allies, whose merchants' prosperity was heavily dependent on Spanish trade. He hoped that Spain would decide to attack France, thereby giving Louis the war he wanted without endangering his alliance with Great Britain.

In late August 1673, Louis got his wish when Spain and the Duke of Lorraine joined a military alliance with the Dutch. France declared war on Spain in October after Spanish troops retaliated for a series of small French raids against Spanish territory. Although there were some setbacks, France enjoyed general success on the battlefield. Strategically, France overextended itself by trying to fight on too many fronts at once. Politically, France alienated its allies by pursuing a chaotic military strategy and crassly pursuing France's interests regardless of the welfare of its allies. The war ended in late 1678. In this treaty, of Nijmegen of 1679, the Netherlands lost no territory to France and actually won a reduction in French tariffs. Although France originally went to war with the Dutch, Spain was the big loser, losing Franche-Comté to France as well as several fortified places in Artois, Hainaut, and Flanders.

REFERENCE: Carl Ekberg, *The Failure of Louis XIV's Dutch War*, 1979.

Samuel Freeman

E

EAST FLORIDA. Florida was the first part of the North American mainland to be colonized by Europeans. In 1513, Juan Ponce* de Leon discovered what he assumed to be an island, and since he landed at the time of the spring flowers (on Easter Sunday), he named the land Florida*. Disaster overwhelmed every early Spanish attempt to explore and colonize the new land, however. The first permanant settlement was St. Augustine, founded in 1565 by Pedro Menéndez de Avilez. Although the Spanish had ambitious plans for the development of Florida, the dream was never realized, and the colonial period was troubled by frequent conflicts with the French and British along the Atlantic and Gulf coasts. In the Treaty of Paris of 1763*, ending the Seven Years War, Florida was transferred to British control. The next 20 years marked a period of prosperity, increased population, and development. During the American Revolution*, the people of Florida remained loyal to Great Britain. But in 1779, Spanish forces from New Orleans took the English post in West Florida* and captured Pensacola in 1781.

In the Treaty of Paris of 1783*, Florida was returned to Spain. Disputes ensued between the United States and Spain over the boundary. Treaty provisions between the United States and Britain had set the boundary at the 31st parallel, but Spain claimed considerable land north of that line. The matter was settled in the Treaty of San Lorenzo between the United States and Spain in 1785, and both nations accepted the 31st parallel.

Although the United States annexed West Florida to the Pearl River in 1810 and to the Perdido River in 1813, East Florida remained under Spanish control. During the War of 1812, General Andrew Jackson invaded Florida and seized Pensacola (November 1814), but he quickly withdrew to go to the defense of New Orleans. In 1818, during the First Seminole War, Jackson again invaded

in pursuit of Seminole Indians and to punish the Spanish for assisting them.
When Secretary of State John Quincy Adams supported Jackson and demanded
that Spain either police the territory or give it up, Spain agreed to negotiate.
The outcome was the Adams-Oñís Treaty* of 1819, part of which ceded East
Florida to the United States in exchange for the U.S. government's assumption
of $5 million in claims of American citizens against Spain. Spain also surrendered
West Florida. The treaty was ratified by the U.S. Senate on February 24, 1819.
Florida was formally organized as an American territory in March 1822.

REFERENCES: Michael J. Curley, *Church and State in the Spanish Floridas (1783–
1822)*, 1940; Gloria Jahoda, *Florida: A History*, 1984.

Joseph M. Rowe, Jr.

ECHAVE IBIA, BALTASAR. Baltasar Echave Ibia was born in Mexico City*
around 1580 to a prominent artistic family. His father, Baltasar Echave Orio*,
was a noted Mexican painter. Although most of Echave Ibia's paintings do not
survive, he is considered an important transitional figure between Renaissance
and baroque art in Mexico. He died in 1660.

REFERENCE: Donald C. Briggs and Marvin Alisky, *Historical Dictionary of Mexico*,
1981.

ECHAVE ORIO, BALTASAR. Baltasar Echave Orio was born in Guipuzcoa,
Spain, in 1548. He came to live in Mexico City* in 1580 and became one of
colonial New Spain's* best known painters and artists. His works "La Visita-
ción" and "La Anunciación," which today hang in the Escuela de Artes Plásticas
in Mexico City, are the most important. Echave Orio, nicknamed the "Old
one," died in 1630.

REFERENCE: Donald C. Briggs and Marvin Alisky, *Historical Dictionary of Mexico*,
1981.

ECUADOR. On Francisco Pizarro's* second expedition in 1526, Bartolomé
Ruíz, a ship's pilot, first landed in Ecuador's Esmeraldas province. This province
received its name from the emeralds that the Indians* of the region wore. On
his return from Spain, Pizarro undertook a third expedition in 1531 in which he
landed at Esmeraldas to begin a trek to Peru*. A dynastic feud between Atahualpa*
of Quito* and Huáscar* of Cuzco* was under way, and on November 16, 1532,
Pizarro captured Atahuallpa at Cajamarca. After Pizarro's conquest of Peru, the
conquest of Quito took place.

The conquistador* Sebastián de Benalcázar* organized the conquest of the
kingdom of Quito. After Atahuallpa's capture, an Indian noble, Ruminahuí,
retreated to Quito and began to organize its defense. In October 1533, Benalcázar
left San Miguel for Quito, meeting stiff Indian resistance along the way. Many
Indian enemies of Ruminahuí joined the Spaniards. Before the Spaniards' arrival
in December 1533, Ruminahuí had devastated and depopulated Quito. Meanwhile, Diego de Almagro* arrived to ask why Benalcázar had abandoned San

Miguel. On August 15, 1534, Almagro founded Santiago de Quito. Pedro de Alvarado*, the conquistador of Guatemala* who had heard about the wealth of Peru, landed on the coast and marched to Quito. Almagro met him and convinced him to abandon the enterprise for 100,000 pesos. Alvarado left but many of his men stayed. Before leaving for Peru, on August 28, 1534, Almagro founded the Villa de San Francisco de Quito where the principal city of the Inca* had been. Almagro chose Benalcázar as *teniente gobernador* (lieutenant governor) of Quito and gave him the responsibility of finishing the conquest. Indian resistance continued in the surrounding region. Benalcázar did not enter Quito again until December 1534. Ruminahuí was captured and executed in January 1535, which ended the major Indian resistance. In 1535, Santiago de Guayaquil* was founded but was twice destroyed by the Indians. Francisco de Orellana* founded it for the third time.

After pacification, the eastern territory, the *Oriente*, was penetrated by various expeditions. In September 1538, Gonzalo Díaz de Piñeda* organized an expedition that found none of the riches sought. In March 1541, the Governor of Quito, Gonzalo Pizarro* organized a second expedition. One of his captains, Orellana, discovered the Amazon River. Pizarro's expedition also produced no wealth. Other explorations of this territory followed during the colonial period as missionaries also went into the region. In 1637, an expedition, organized in Brazil, went up the Amazon and then to Quito, but the *audiencia* of Quito had already laid claim to this territory. The New Laws* of 1542 provoked a rebellion from the conquistadors of the territory. The Quito *cabildo* * sided with Pizarro and organized a large group of rebels. He entered Quito in July 1545. In June 1547, Pedro de Puelles, the *Teniente de Gobernador* chosen by Gonzalo and a conquistador of Quito, was assassinated in the name of the Crown. The rebellion ended with Pizarro's execution in 1548.

The viceroyalty of Peru* had jurisdiction over Quito during the colonial period until the eighteenth century. The *audiencia* of Quito*, which had authority over most of present-day Ecuador, was established by *Cédula Real* on August 29, 1563. There were *corregidores* * in Guayaquil*, Cuenca, Loja, Guaranda, Ríobamba, Otavalo, and Ibarra. The administrative divisions did not change for two centuries.

Between July 1592 and April 1593, the *Revolución de las Alcabalas* took place in Quito. It began as a revolt against the new *alcabala* * tax, which the population said it could not pay because it had already given a large donation to the king and had paid ransom to the pirates who had taken Guayaquil. The *audiencia*'s president rejected the petition of the *vecinos*, and this action escalated the rebellion. Help came to the president from Lima*; the revolt was put down and the rebels were jailed or executed.

Ecuador's economy was based on agricultural exports, mining, and textile production. The port of Guayaquil was used for shipbuilding and transporting the *audiencia*'s exports to other parts of the empire along the Pacific coast. Mining, located around Zaruma and Zamora, was not a primary economic activity. A primary agricultural export was cacao* until the ban on its exportation to Mexico in the 1620s caused its collapse. Pastoral farming also developed to supply the textile producers not only for the internal market but also as a major export to other areas of the empire.

Indian attacks, piracy* along the coast, and numerous volcanic eruptions (the worst one in February 1797) plagued the region. The first time that pirates took Guayaquil was in 1587 but the attacks continued into the eighteenth century; the city was razed in 1705 and 1764. In 1739, the *audiencia* became a part of the new viceroyalty of New Granada*. Many scientific missions came to the area in the eighteenth and early nineteenth centuries to study its natural wonders. On May 22, 1765, a revolt broke out not only in Quito but also in other towns because of the establishment of the Spanish economic controls. For two months, the revolt was successful. The rebels exiled the Spaniards from the city, but they returned later when the viceroy retook possession. During the late eighteenth century, Francisco Eugenio de Santa Cruz y Espejo*, of mixed blood, became an influential political thinker with Enlightenment ideas. He was jailed in 1789 and 1795 for his political ideas and died in custody.

The early nineteenth century saw the standard of revolt and independence raised. Beginning in December 1808, a group of Espejo's friends decided to form a *junta de gobierno* because of the situation in Spain, but they were arrested. Another attempt was on August 9, 1809, when a *junta soberana de gobierno* was established; the next day a message from this body was taken to the *audiencia* telling the president that he had been relieved of his duties. This junta lasted for eighty days and acted as an autonomous and representative institution. This was, however, an elite revolt with no support from the masses. The question of which form of government should be installed, as well as personal interests, contributed to the demise of the revolt. The surrounding provinces also condemned the movement, and the two viceroyalties blockaded the rebels and sent troops. On October 28, 1809, the rebels surrendered to the former *audiencia* president and were given assurances that they would not be harmed.

The second phase of the movement began once the troops entered Quito and the rebels were imprisoned. The elite members of the revolt were arrested, as well as the others who had taken part in the battalions organized by the junta. In the surrounding provinces, the troops sacked towns and countryside, enraging the masses. On August 2, 1810, Quito's masses reacted violently and stormed the prisons where the rebels were held. The royalist troops began to kill the prisoners in their possession. After 48 hours of violence from both sides, an assembly was held and the junta resurrected.

Carlos Montufar*, the son of one of the rebel leaders, was sent to Spain to gain support from Spain's *junta central* and Ferdinand VII*, but he sided with Quito's junta. Some of the surrounding town *cabildos* and the Peruvian viceroy* rejected this resurrected junta. The viceroy put Guayaquil and Cuenca under the jurisdiction of the viceroyalty of Peru. Numerous battles were fought between the various forces in the territory. Royalist troops had moved into Quito by

November 1812, and the final battle was fought on December 1. The patriots were persecuted, jailed, and executed. Royal authority was established in the *audiencia* for ten more years. Ecuador's final independence struggle began when a revolt occurred in Guayaquil on October 9, 1820. The royal authorities were overthrown and a revolutionary junta set up putting the royalists' principal port in rebel hands. The final battle for independence was fought on May 24, 1822, at Pichincha*.

REFERENCES: Oscar Efren Reyes, *Breve Historia del Ecuador*, vol. 1, 1955; Pedro Fermin Cevallos, *Historia del Ecuador*, vols. 1–3, 1985–1986; John Leddy Phelan, *The Kingdom of Quito in the Seventeenth Century*, 1967.

Carlos Pérez

EDUCATION. Throughout the colonial period, educational opportunities in the Spanish American colonies were extremely limited. Although the church assumed responsibility in the missions* for educating Indian* children, it was a rudimentary process at best, geared to indoctrinating children with Roman Catholic dogma rather than making them literate. Even that minimal education was unavailable to African slaves. There were no public schools and no sense of the need to create widespread literacy. On the contrary, literacy was generally viewed as the domain of the upper classes. Consequently, there were few opportunities for mestizo children to get an education. Formal education, therefore, was confined to the children of the *peninsular** and *criollo** elites, who hired home tutors or sent their children to private academies or, more likely, to *colegios* established by Dominican* or Jesuit* priests. The Dominicans and Jesuits also established universities in New Spain,* the Caribbean, Central America, and South America. The first of them was the University of Santo Domingo*, founded in 1538, and eventually the two most important of the colonial institutions were the University of Mexico* in Mexico City and the University of San Marcos* in Lima, Peru. Until the late eighteenth century, the university curricula remained static and very traditional, with an emphasis on rote memorization and mastery of older texts. Because of strong sexual and racial biases, university enrollments were confined to the sons of the *peninsular* and *criollo* elites.

REFERENCE: J. T. Lanning, *Academic Culture in the Spanish Colonies*, 1940.

EGUIARA EGUREN, JUAN JOSÉ DE. Juan José de Eguiara Eguren was born in Mexico City* in February 1696. He received bachelor's and doctorate degrees from the Real Pontifica Universidad in Mexico City in 1712 and 1715. During his career, he taught at the university, held several civil service positions in local government, and served for a time as treasurer of the *cabildo** in Mexico City. He is best remembered, however, for his oratorical and scholarly skills. He was an active defender of the Church and worked diligently at collecting and cataloging major documents on the early history of New Spain*. During the 1730s and 1740s, he published a number of important bibliographical works on the pre-conquest era and early history of Mexico. Eguiara died on January 29, 1763.

REFERENCE: Aurora M. Ocampo de Gómez and Ernesto Prado Velásquez, *Diccionario de escritores mexicanos*, 1967.

EL DORADO. In recent years, the term "El Dorado" has become synonymous with a fantasy region of incredible wealth, but the term originated in Hispanic America in the sixteenth century, when rumors of a fabulously wealthy Indian king named El Dorado circulated throughout the European community and inspired dozens of expeditions by Spaniards. The legend originated in the Chibcha* practice of annually covering their chief with gold dust and having him then swim in the waters of Lake Guatavita, Colombia*. The legend of El Dorado led to the expeditions of conquest of Hernán Cortés*, Francisco Pizarro*, Gonzalo Jiménez de Quesada*, Gonzalo Pizarro*, Pedro de Ursúa*, and Sir Walter Raleigh.

REFERENCE: Walker Chapman, *The Golden Dream: Seekers of El Dorado*, 1967.

ELÍO, FRANCISCO XAVIER DE. Born in Navarre, Spain, in 1767 Francisco Xavier de Elío entered the military profession at the Military Academy of Puerto de Santa María and joined first the regiment of cadets and later that of Seville*. He fought in North Africa* in the defense of both Orán* and Ceuta*, and later joined the forces of the Duke of Medinaceli in southern France. It was in 1805, with the rank of colonel, that he arrived in the Río de la Plata* where he took part in the struggle against the English invasions of 1805–1807. As a result of his exploits against the British, he was appointed acting governor of Montevideo* and commander of the Voluntarios de Río de la Plata. At the same time, the liberation of Buenos Aires* led to the appointment of Santiago de Liniers* as acting viceroy*; Elío later resigned in view of his differences with Liniers. The people demanded the reinstatement of Elío, however, foreshadowing later events. In 1808, Elío was confirmed in his position, and the king also appointed him commanding general of the entire Banda Oriental. His government in Montevideo represented another stage in the evolution of the future Uruguay*.

The constitutional crisis of Bayonne, the threat of a Napoleonic expansion, and the fears of further Portuguese encroachments added to the already existing antagonism between Buenos Aires and Montevideo and between Liniers and Elío. The events of Bayonne resulted in Elío's recognition of the Peninsular Regency while maintaining good relations with Río de Janeiro. Liniers, however, believed Elío was furthering Portuguese aims, while Elío feared that Liniers would eventually side with Napoleon. Liniers then tried to depose his subordinate, but Elío, with the spontaneous support of the *cabildo* of Montevideo resisted. On September 21, 1808, a loyalist junta was set up, with the goal of maintaining unswerving loyalty to Spain and freedom from Buenos Aires. Elío had correctly interpreted the popular will of his city. The principle of popular sovereignty, which was invoked in the constitution of the junta, was the same that was to serve the abortive Junta of Buenos Aires of January 1, 1809, and the May Revolution of 1810*: in other words, the *pactum translationis*, whereby civil authority reverted to the source from whence it had come in view of the kingdom now having no head or leader.

Believing that the crisis between the two cities could be solved, the peninsular authorities dismissed Liniers in Buenos Aires and appointed Baltasar Hidalgo de Cisneros* as viceroy of Río de la Plata. He in turn dismissed Elío who then was appointed inspector and second-in-command of all troops in Buenos Aires. As a result, the Montevideo junta was dissolved on June 30, 1809. The crisis, however, was not solved, and the May Revolution aggravated the situation still further. The new Buenos Aires junta now demanded loyalty from Montevideo, which the newly appointed governor, Joaquín de Soria, resisted. Gaspar de Vigodet, the successor to Soria, increased the tension after his arrival (October 7, 1810) when he set up a Junta of finance and administration. Open warfare broke out when Elío returned to Montevideo on January 12, 1811, this time as viceroy of Río de la Plata. Montevideo had now become the effective seat of the viceroyalty of Río de la Plata*, though its power was actually limited to the Banda Oriental. On February 13, 1811, Elío declared war on Buenos Aires.

The events that followed—Argentine and Portuguese invasions, as well as the revolt of the interior of the Banda Oriental against Elío's royalist Montevideo—would gradually lead to the collapse of the Spanish position. Buenos Aires concluded an armistice with Elío on October 20, 1811, and abandoned the Banda Oriental; the Portuguese did likewise by the agreement of May 26, 1812. Before the Spanish bastion of Montevideo collapsed, however, Elío left for Spain in the year 1812 when he was recalled by the regency. He was first appointed Commander of the Island of León (Cádiz) and later fought as Commanding General of the Armies of Catalonia and Valencia against the Napoleonic forces. When King Ferdinand VII* returned to Spain from his forced exile in France in 1814, he rewarded Elío for his distinguished service: Elío became captain general and governor of Valencia.

A bizarre episode followed: On alleged orders of the king, Elío was to be shot; luckily for him, the Count of Cervelló, the oldest general in the Valencia region, postponed the execution. The matter was clarified and proved to be false. Elío interpreted the episode as one more hostile act by the liberals and he reacted accordingly by increasing the repression of liberalism. When the liberals returned to power after the Riego revolt of 1820, he was forced to resign from his position. The leader of the liberals in the area, the Count of Almodovar, whom Elío had jailed earlier, became the new captain general. With the tables turned in 1822, Elío was imprisoned, courtmartialed, and executed by garrote—an ordeal he faced with his customary gallantry.

REFERENCES: Lorenzo Belinzón, *La revolución emancipadora uruguaya y sus dogmas democraticos*, 2 vols., 1932; O. Carlos Stoetzer, *The Scholastic Roots of the Spanish American Revolution*, 1979.

O. Carlos Stoetzer

EL-OUALI MUSTAPHA SAYED. El-Ouali Mustapha Sayed was born in Spanish Sahara* around 1948 to nomadic Reguibi tribesmen. During the Army of

Liberation's[*] war with French and Spanish troops in 1957, his family was forced to move north and settle in Tan-Tan in the Tekna Zone[*]. They were destitute there, but he won a scholarship to good government schools and there met other Saharawi students interested in liberating their homeland from European colonialism. In 1970, when he heard that the Spanish Foreign Legion[*] had carried out a massacre of Saharawi demonstrators in Zemla, El-Ouali Mustapha Sayed became a passionate convert to independence. In 1972, he helped form the Embryonic Movement for the Liberation of Sahara and abandoned his law studies; the next year he was a full-fledged member of the Polisario Front[*] and a leader in its campaign against Spain. He felt betrayed when Spain turned over Western Sahara to Morocco and Mauritania in the Madrid Agreement of 1975[*] rather than giving the country outright independence. El-Ouali Mustapha Sayed continued the struggle against Mauritania and was killed in battle in June 1976.

REFERENCES: Tony Hodges, *Historical Dictionary of Western Sahara*, 1982; John Mercer, *Spanish Sahara*, 1975.

EL SALVADOR. During the colonial period, El Salvador was a province of the captaincy general of Guatemala[*]. San Salvador[*] was an *alcalde mayor*[*] until 1786 when it became an intendancy (*intendencia*[*]). Sonsonate was independent of San Salvador and Guatemala and did not become a part of El Salvador until after independence. Before the arrival of the Spaniards, there were two major linguistic groups who inhabited the territory: the Pipil west of the Lempa River and the Lenca east of it.

In 1522, Andrés Niño and Gil González[*] Dávila left Panama[*] on an expedition to explore Central American territory. Niño was the first European to discover Salvadorean territory. His damaged ships went as far as the Bay of Fonseca, named after Bishop Fonseca, the Council of the Indies[*] president. The next group to enter the region came from New Spain[*] and Guatemala. The competition in Central America between the conquistadors[*] sent by Hernán Cortés[*] and those coming from Panama sent by Pedrarias (Pedro Arias de Ávila[*]) led to two struggles: one among the Spaniards, which lasted six years, and another between the Spaniards and the Indians[*], which lasted 15 to 25 years. Those coming from the north were under the command of Pedro de Alvarado[*]. In June 1524, Alvarado defeated the Indians near Acajutla and reached Cuscatlán[*], the Pipil capital, but this expedition did not succeed in putting the territory under Spanish control. In 1525, another expedition under Gonzalo de Alvarado, Pedro's brother, founded the Spanish settlement of San Salvador but it was destroyed the following year. In 1526, Pedro de Alvarado returned to the region but left when an Indian rebellion occurred in Guatemala. He returned two years later and put the region under Spanish control through the brutal repression of the Indian population. In 1528, Diego de Alvarado, another brother, reestablished San Salvador, and *encomiendas*[*] were given to the settlers. The last major Indian revolt was between 1537–1539 when the town of San Miguel de la Frontera, founded in 1530, was attacked.

Pedrarias sent Martín de Estete to San Salvador at the end of 1529 to claim the territory as part of Nicaragua*, but his attempt failed. Pedro de Alvarado founded San Miguel to protect the region from further incursions from Nicaragua and as a base against the Lenca Indians. When Pedro de Alvarado left for Peru*, he took most of San Miguel's inhabitants with him. Some gold was found around San Miguel, which made a few dozen *encomenderos* rich, but El Salvador's real wealth was in agricultural exports.

Cacao*, the most exportable product, was grown around the Los Izalcos region, which was settled after San Salvador and San Miguel. The Spanish settlement of Sonsonate, founded in 1552, became a collection center for cacao and the second important export, balsam. The Indians kept control of cacao production in the region. In 1558, when the Sonsonate merchants petitioned the Council of the Indies* that the *alcalde mayor* should be chosen directly by the king and the council instead of being under the jurisdiction of San Salvador or Guatemala City, Los Izalcos was granted local autonomy. This was a victory for the local merchants over the Guatemala *encomenderos* who controlled the Indian population. The third important export crop was indigo*. The Indian population precipitously declined between 1550–1560, due to death and to Indians fleeing their villages to get away from paying tribute. This led to the gradual *ladino*ization of the population as peasants moved out of the villages and into the countryside where the *haciendas** were also located.

In 1549, El Salvador was placed under the jurisdiction of the *audiencia* of Guatemala. In 1551, monastic orders arrived in the region. The Dominicans* and Franciscans* established monasteries in Los Izalcos by the early 1570s. In the first half of the seventeenth century, the *repartimientos**, which remained through the eighteenth century, were introduced into the region. This labor institution gradually replaced the *encomienda*, although the latter also remained through the eighteenth century as a means of labor procurement. The lack of an adequate labor supply led to the importation of African slaves in the first quarter of the seventeenth century. In 1625, 2,000 blacks gathered in San Salvador to celebrate Holy Week festivities and to rebel, but the ringleaders were discovered and executed. Constant pirate attacks were another problem that plagued the province. In 1579, Sir Francis Drake* appeared in El Salvador. As attacks continued throughout the seventeenth century and the fear continued into the eighteenth century, the inhabitants moved inland. A militia was established to protect the region.

Until the 1750s, agricultural exports went from the port of Acajutla to Acapulco*, then across Mexico to Veracruz. In 1751, work began on the port and fortress of Omoa, which changed the direction of exports toward Guatemala City* on to Omoa, then to Havana*, and finally to Cádiz*. In 1782, there was an attempt to stimulate the cultivation of indigo by small producers but this did not work out because the large *hacendados* and merchants got hold of the credits. Peninsular authorities were the only check on this economically and politically powerful group.

Cacao had declined by the eighteenth century because of economic competition from Guayaquil* and Venezuela*. In 1722, the Izalco volcano eruption also ruined the region's cacao plantations. Moreover, the Indians destroyed the cacao groves when a one *real* tax was levied on each tree. In the second half of the eighteenth century, indigo production and some cattle ranching became the main economic activities. The few mines had worked themselves out. Few idle or unemployed people lived there as compared with other regions in El Salvador. Cloth and clothes from Spain and China reached even the lower classes in the rural areas. San Salvador became an intendancy in 1786, which removed some of the local elite's power. There was hostility between the *hacendados*, who controlled agricultural production, and the Guatemala City merchants, who controlled purchase and distribution. By the end of the colonial period, one-half to two-thirds of the land was in the hands of subsistence cultivators, and the rest was controlled by the *hacendados*.

These contradictions in the socioeconomic system began to be felt by the beginning of the nineteenth century. Local autonomy, participation in government, and Crown concessions to *criollo** economic interests were demands that spurred the revolts of this period. In 1799, a dispute between Guatemala and the San Salvador *criollos* about who should exercise the office of intendant when the previous one had died was won by San Salvador's *criollos*, who exercised power until 1802. On November 4, 1811, the San Salvador intendant was overthrown, and the local *criollos* exercised power for one month. The other towns of the province pledged their loyalty to Guatemala. Two Guatemalan envoys were sent, and the disturbance was put down. In January 1814, Pedro Pablo Castillo, a leader of the 1811 revolt, led a second uprising against the intendant who created a volunteer militia, annulled municipal elections three times, and arrested two prominent *criollos*. The uprising was defeated when two rebels were shot. This time the repression was harsher than in 1811. The Salvadorean elites, who were interested in trading directly with foreign buyers and against Spain's trading monopoly, were much more open to liberal ideas than their counterparts in Guatemala. On September 22, 1821, San Salvador pledged allegiance to the independence declared in Guatemala City on September 21.

REFERENCES: David Browning, *El Salvador: Landscape and Society*, 1971; Alastair White, *El Salvador*, 1973.

Carlos Pérez

EMANCIPATION. The practice of exploiting indigenous labor in the Spanish Empire began with the *encomienda** in the sixteenth century. By the twentieth century, Spaniards were still forcing native people in Africa to fulfill certain labor requirements. In the twentieth century, the Spanish government granted "emancipation" to African natives who had received a higher education and had earned an annual income of at least 500 pesetas for more than two years. The individual also had to demonstrate a Christian religious faith and a "progressive" attitude. Roman Catholic missions and the Patronato de Indígenas* issued the emancipation certificates. An emancipated native was not required to work on European plantations and could appeal to Spanish rather than to native jurisdiction in court cases.

REFERENCE: Max Liniger-Goumaz, *Historical Dictionary of Equatorial Guinea*, 1988.

ENCOMIENDA. Derived from the Spanish verb *encomendar*, to entrust, the *encomienda* was a manorial concept based upon reciprocal rights and obligations. More specifically, it was a relic of medieval feudalism that was used by the Spaniards to rationalize the virtual enslavement of New World Indians*. Just as European peasants theoretically entrusted themselves to a manorial lord, for whom they performed special services in return for protection, Indians in Spanish America were to labor for *encomenderos* (favored conquistadors*), who in turn were expected to protect and Christianize the natives. Contrary to common belief, the *encomienda* was not a landed estate, but rather a legal arrangement by which Spaniards justified the extraction of labor from the aborigines.

On paper, the *encomienda* was ideally suited to balance the dual and often conflicting religious and material aspirations of the Spanish Crown and the conquistadors. With regard to the Indians, the Crown was in a difficult position. On the one hand, it sought to civilize the aborigines and to defend them against exploitation, thereby placating the papacy and the religious orders; on the other, it was dependent upon Indian labor to operate the mines and harvest the fields. The *encomienda* offered a solution that, theoretically, was mutually beneficial to all. For their labor, the Indians would receive protection and religious instruction, while the Crown and the conquistadors would reap the material rewards of colonization.

In 1503, Queen Isabella*, mindful of both the spiritual welfare of the aborigines and the material needs of the crown and the conquistadors, gave royal approval to the *encomienda*. From the outset, theory and practice diverged. Freed by distance from close royal scrutiny, the *encomenderos* either ignored their obligations to the Indians or performed them perfunctorily. In essence, the practice became little more than a ruthless system of forced labor, and in the sixteenth and seventeenth centuries, it frequently prompted heated exchanges between the religious orders, the Crown, and the conquistadors. Attempts to abolish the *encomienda*, such as the New Laws* of 1542, not only aroused the anger of the conquistadors but also jeopardized the prosperity of the Crown. Despite its sympathy for the Indians and its sensitivity to the protests of friars, such as Bartolomé de las Casas*, the Crown was unprepared to sacrifice its material interests to the spiritual and humanitarian claims of the Indians. In 1573, King Philip II* of Spain released a detailed directive on future conquest and settlement policies. One of his decisions was to prohibit the extension of the *encomienda* system into any new areas. It survived where it already existed, but no future *encomiendas* were to be granted. Spain still needed an institutional vehicle to direct its goals of conquest and settlement, and the mission* became that institution. So the *encomienda*, with all its abuses, survived throughout Spanish

America until the early 1700s and lingered in the Yucatán* and Chile* until the late 1780s.

REFERENCES: Lesley B. Simpson, *The Encomienda in New Spain*, 1950; C. H. Haring, *The Spanish Empire in America*, 1947; John H. Parry, *The Spanish Theory of Empire in the Sixteenth Century*, 1940.

John W. Storey

ENLIGHTENMENT. The Enlightenment was a broad intellectual movement which swept through Europe and the Americas in the late eighteenth century. It drew its major philosophical assumptions from political philosophy, economics, and science. From the American and French Revolutions came the ideologies of equality, natural rights, and liberty, while the economic theories of Adam Smith gave birth to laissez-faire liberalism. The scientific revolution provided European thought with a new faith in rationalism, secularism, and natural law. The Enlightenment gave science a supremacy over religion and rational observation a supremacy over faith and dogma. The writings of Benito Feyjóo y Montenegro first introduced Enlightenment ideas to Spain, and those ideas spread quickly to Spain's New World possessions. Scientific expeditions became much more common and included those of Charles-Marie de La Condamine to Ecuador (1735), Nikolaus von Jacquin to Venezuela (1755–1759), Hipólito Ruiz to Chile (1777), and Alexander von Humboldt to much of South America (1799–1804).

The Enlightenment in the Spanish Empire also included important intellectual developments. Patriotic and economic societies appeared in the major Latin American cities in order to discuss contemporary issues and disseminate useful knowledge. Emphasis on education—from elementary schools to universities— became much more important in the late eighteenth century. Curriculum changed from the study of classics and theological writings to an analysis of more contemporary political and economic arguments, as well as a much greater emphasis on the study of science. Major newspapers appeared, such as the *Diario de México* (1805) in Mexico City, as did literary and scientific publications, such as the *Mercurio Peruano* (1791) in Lima and the *Papel Periódico* in Havana.

The Enlightenment also had important consequences for politics and economics in the empire. The economic ideas of Adam Smith and the rise of classical liberalism led to the Bourbon Reforms of Charles III, which opened the Spanish Empire to global commerce, while the political ideas emanating from the United States and France in the 1790s eventually led to the rebellions and independence movements of the early 1800s.

REFERENCES: Arthur P. Whitaker, ed., *Latin America and the Enlightenment*, 1958; R. J. Shafer, *The Economic Societies in the Spanish World, 1763-1821*, 1958; Richard Herr, *The Eighteenth Century Revolution in Spain*, 1958.

ENRÍQUEZ DE RIBERA, PAYO. Payo Enríquez de Ribera was born in Seville*, Spain, in 1612. He entered the Roman Catholic priesthood and in 1657 was appointed bishop of Guatemala*, a position he held until 1668. During his decade in Guatemala, Enríquez was known for his intellectual open-mindedness.

He is credited with bringing the first printing* press to Guatemala. In 1668, Enríquez became archbishop of Mexico, a clerical post he held until his death in 1685.

REFERENCE: Richard E. Moore, *Historical Dictionary of Guatemala*, 1973.

EQUATORIAL GUINEA. See SPANISH EQUATORIAL GUINEA.

ERCILLA Y ZÚÑIGA, ALONSO. Unquestionably the greatest epic poet of the New World, Alonso Ercilla y Zúñiga is the author of *La Araucana*, one of the most important literary works of Latin America. It was published in Spain in three separate parts in 1569, 1578, and 1589. Born in 1533, Ercilla was a Spanish nobleman who spent his childhood in the Royal Palace in Madrid. He was a close personal friend of Phillip II*, and he eventually served the latter as ambassador to various countries. Prior to that, however, in search of adventure, he went to Chile* at the young age of 22. He subsequently took part in the Spanish campaign, under the command of García Hurtado de Mendoza*, against the Araucanian* Indians in southern Chile. Previous attempts to subdue the fierce Araucanians had failed miserably. So impressed was Ercilla by the Indians'* capacity to fight and suffer that he composed his famous poem in large part in their honor.

Ercilla's primary purpose was to portray the battles that informed the bloody campaign against the indomitable Indians. In doing so, there is a constant tone of chivalry and honor, two highly prized commodities in Spanish society of the sixteenth century. The style and tone of the poem are unaffected, classical, direct, and full of verve. While on the one hand the poet describes the valor of the Spaniards, he describes the courage of the Araucanians even more. *La Araucana* is divided into 37 cantos and consists of some 2,700 octaves. Critics agree that the poem owes a certain debt to the Italian epic and specifically to Ariosto. It appears that Ercilla's primary objective, however, was not to write extraordinary poetry, which he did, but rather to record the extraordinary events associated with the war against the Araucanians. Interestingly, the author often composed his cantos during the actual battles. For lack of paper in the field, he would scribble on hides or other surfaces. The immediacy of battle felt by the reader upon reading *La Araucana* is well deserved. Ercilla became famous in his lifetime as a major literary figure, thanks to *La Araucana*, one of the greatest poems ever written in the Spanish language. He died in 1594.

REFERENCE: Walter Owen, *La Araucana: The Epic of Chile by Don Alonso de Ercilla y Zúñiga*, 1945.

Sam L. Slick

ESCALADA, ANTONIO JOSÉ DE. Antonio José de Escalada was born in Buenos Aires* in 1753 to a wealthy, Spanish-born family. He assumed control of the family's businesses and served for a time as a *regidor** on the Buenos

Aires *cabildo** and as first *alcalde**. In 1810, Escalada was chancellor of the royal *audiencia**, and he became an enthusiastic supporter of the May Revolution*. He formed a close friendship with José de San Martín*, and his daughter Remedios married the future liberator. Escalada spent his time raising money for the patriot forces in Argentina*. His sons Francisco, Mariano, and Manuel distinguished themselves in battle. Escalada died in Buenos Aires in 1821. At the time, he was serving in the provincial legislature.

REFERENCES: Enrique Udaondo, *Diccionario biográfico colonial argentino*, 1945; Ione S. Wright and Lisa M. Nekhom, *Historical Dictionary of Argentina*, 1978.

ESCALERA CONSPIRACY. The so-called Escalera Conspiracy was a series of slave uprisings that spread through Cuba* in the early 1840s. In 1821, Spain and England had signed an agreement prohibiting the importation of any more African slaves into Cuba, but Spanish authorities and planters regularly ignored the agreement. The labor demands of the sugar*, coffee*, and tobacco* plantations were too great, at least from their perspective. The English government regularly protested the continuation of the slave trade, and abolitionists in Cuba, both British and Cuban, constantly articulated their opposition to slavery* and the rights of black slaves to be free. David Turnbull, the English consul in Havana*, actually worked to encourage slaves to seek their freedom.

Since more than half of the Cuban population was black by the 1840s, Spanish authorities and Cuban planters began to fear a slave uprising. To counter the abolitionists, Spain sent Lt. General Leopoldo O'Donnell to Cuba in 1843, giving him specific orders to crush any slave insurrection. O'Donnell conducted a witch hunt, arresting hundreds of suspected radicals and executing several dozen slaves whom he believed to be engaged in conspiracies to rebel. The so-called "Escalera Conspiracy" created enormous resentment among black Cubans against Spanish authority.

REFERENCE: Robert L. Paquette, *Sugar Is Made With Blood: The Conspiracy of La Escalera and the Conflict between Empires over Slavery in Cuba*, 1988.

ESCORIAZA Y CARDONA, JOSÉ EURIPIDES DE. José Euripides de Escoriaza y Cardona was born in Puerto Rico* in 1828 and became a *criollo** activist in Spanish politics. In 1866, Escoriaza was charged with political conspiracy and had to flee to France. He returned to Spain in 1868. After serving as governor of Almeria, Valladolid, and Barcelona, Escoriaza was elected as Puerto Rico's delegate to the Spanish parliament. From that post, he campaigned hard for his assimilationist beliefs—that Puerto Rico should be completely integrated with Spain, politically and culturally. He was profoundly disappointed when Spain lost Puerto Rico, Cuba*, Guam*, and the Philippines* in the Spanish-American War*. Escoriaza died in 1921.

REFERENCES: Pedro de Angelis, *Misceláneas puertorriqueñas: Colección de artículos históricos biográficos*, 1894; Kenneth R. Farr, *Historical Dictionary of Puerto Rico and the U.S. Virgin Islands*, 1973.

ESPADA Y LANDA, JUAN JOSÉ DÍAZ DE. See DÍAZ DE ESPADA, Y LANDA, JUAN JOSÉ.

ESPAÑA, JOSÉ MARÍA. José María España was born in 1761 and became a prominent Venezuelan* revolutionary. During his term as justice of Mucuta, he joined with Manuel Gual in leading the first Venezuelan rebellion against Spanish rule in 1799. They had the support of a number of planters and army officers, but the attempt was foiled by Spanish authorities. España was tried and convicted of treason. On May 8, 1799, he was beheaded and quartered.
    REFERENCE: Donna Keyse Rudolph and G. A. Rudolph, *Historical Dictionary of Venezuela*, 1971.

ESPEJO, FRANCISCO JAVIER EUGENIO DE SANTA CRUZ. See SANTA CRUZ Y ESPEJO, FRANCISCO EUGENIO.

ESPINAR, ALONSO DE. Alonso de Espinar, whose date and place of birth are unknown, was a Franciscan* missionary priest in the Greater Antilles early in the 1500s. Some historians place him in Galicia, Spain, in 1499, but he probably arrived in Santo Domingo* in 1502 with a contingent of 17 Franciscans. He became provincial of the Franciscans in Santo Domingo and directed the expansion of Franciscan missionary work into Puerto Rico*, Cuba*, Jamaica*, and northern South America. Espinar walked a middle ground between those Spaniards who wanted to exploit Indian labor and the Franciscan friars, like Bartolomé de las Casas*, who wanted to protect the Indians. In 1512–1513, he helped draft the Laws of Burgos* regulating Indian labor. Las Casas roundly criticized Espinar for siding with the *encomenderos*. In 1513, Espinar died at sea while returning from Spain to Santo Domingo.
    REFERENCE: A. S. Tibesar, "The Franciscan Province of the Holy Cross of Española, 1505–1559," *Americas*, 13 (1956–57), 377–97.

ESPINOSA, GASPAR. Gaspar Espinosa was born in Spain in 1484. Trained as a lawyer, he came to the New World and accompanied the expedition of Pedrarias (Pedro Arias de Ávila*) to Darién* in 1514. Five years later, Espinosa was one of the principal founders of Panama City. He spent several years exploring the region of the Gulf of Nicoya; he was then appointed an *oidor* with the *audiencia* of Santo Domingo*. During the 1530s, Espinosa tried unsuccessfully, several times, to negotiate the differences in Peru* between Francisco Pizarro* and Diego de Almagro*. He died in 1537.
    REFERENCE: Theodore S. Creedman, *Historical Dictionary of Costa Rica*, 1977.

ESPINOSA, ISIDRO FÉLIX DE. Isidro Félix de Espinosa was born in Querétaro, New Spain*, in 1679. He joined the Franciscan* order in 1696 and was ordained in 1703. Espinosa spent his missionary career in northeastern New Spain and Texas* establishing missions* all the way to the border of French

Louisiana*. In 1726, Espinosa went to the college of Querétaro where he spent the rest of his career as a scholar and historian. His most important historical work was *Crónica de todos los colegios de Propaganda Fide de esta Nueva España de misioneros franciscanos* (1746). Espinosa died in Querétaro in 1755.

REFERENCE: *New Catholic Encyclopedia*, V:544, 1967.

ESPINOSA MEDRANO, JUAN. "EL LUNAREJO." Juan Espinosa Medrano was born in a small village in the Andes in 1640 to Indian* parents. As a small child, he displayed a precocious nature and awesome intelligence. He was nicknamed "El Lunarejo" for a mole that he had on his face. He eventually graduated from the University of Cuzco. There is ample evidence to show that he was well known not only throughout much of the colonial world but also in Spain, particularly as a famous orator. He is considered by literary historians to have been the first literary critic of Latin America. Beyond that, he is remembered as a man of erudition who brought much to early colonial letters as an essayist, thinker, and professor. Espinosa Medrano began writing serious literature, including *autos* and *comedias*, while still in his teens. He wrote his most famous work, *El apologético en favor de don Luis de Góngora, principe de los poetas líricos de España* in 1662, while still in his twenties. This work, dedicated to a fervent defense of baroque literature as interpreted by the Spanish writer Luis de Góngora, occupies a major position in colonial literature as the first example of literary criticism in the New World. It was written as a response to a treatise produced by the Portuguese critic Manuel de Faria y Souza who, in writing an homage to Luis de Camoens, attacked the poetry of Góngora. In *Apologético*, Espinosa presented a careful study of Góngora's use of language—its syntax, poetic form and devices, lexical range, and so forth. To that extent, his criticism has a modern dimension, as opposed to the simple, reactive opinion that often passed as criticism in the New World. Other important works by Espinosa include *Curso de Philosophia Thomistica* (1688), *La novena maravilla*, and two plays, *Amar su propia muerte* and *Auto Sacramental del Hijo Pródigo* (written in Quechua*). He died in 1688.

REFERENCE: Raul Garbin D., *Diccionario biográfico del Perú*, 1943.

Sam L. Slick

ESTETE, MIGUEL DE. Miguel de Estete was born in Santo Domingo de la Calzada, Rioja, Spain. He went to Peru* in 1537 and fought with Francisco Pizarro's* forces at Cajamarca. Estete was rewarded handsomely for his participation in the defeat of Atahuallpa*, and in 1553, he became one of the founders of Huamanga*. Estete wrote a book, *Notice on Peru*, describing the conquest of Peru in the late 1530s and early 1540s. It is today considered an important primary source on the conquest.

REFERENCE: Albert William Bork and Georg Maier, *Historical Dictionary of Ecuador*, 1973.

ESTRADA PALMA, TOMÁS. Born in Cuba* in 1835, Tomás Estrada Palma played a leading role in Cuban nationalism in the middle and late nineteenth century. When the Ten Years War* erupted in Cuba in 1868, Estrada was a leading figure in the revolt, and in 1876 he was declared president of the "republic in arms." Royalist forces captured him in 1876 and imprisoned him for a short time. Estrada spent the 1880s and 1890s in the United States, promoting the cause of Cuban independence while operating a private school in upstate New York. During 1895, Estrada replaced José Martí* as leader of the Cuban junta in New York. After the Cuban revolution and the years of U. S. tutelage, Estrada became the first president of Cuba in 1902. Once in office, Estrada soon lost the support of Cuban nationalists, primarily because of his conviction that Cuba should become part of the United States. In 1906, amid political infighting on the island, Estrada asked President Theodore Roosevelt of the United States to invoke the Platt Amendment and intervene in Cuba. When Roosevelt refused, Estrada resigned from office. By that time, it was clear that he would not be re-elected. Tomás Estrada Palma died one year later.

REFERENCES: Jorge I. Domínguez, *Cuba: Order and Revolution*, 1978; Russell H. Fitzgibbon, *Cuba and the United States, 1900-1935*, 1935.

F

FALKLANDS ISLANDS. See MALVINAS ISLANDS.

FEDERAL LEAGUE. The Federal League emerged out of José Artigas's* federalist political philosophy in the Río de la Plata* area between 1812 and 1815. Artigas was committed to the notions of popular sovereignty and provincial autonomy, and he feared the potential of highly centralized governments. The Federal League included Entre Ríos, the Provincia Oriental, Córdoba*, Santa Fe*, and the Corrientes, and he worked to overcome the centralist forces dominant in Buenos Aires*. Artigas hoped that the Federal League would eventually expand to include all of the United Provinces, but his political influence peaked in 1815. Between 1816 and 1820, when Artigas suffered a series of defeats at the hands of the Portuguese, the Federal League lost influence. The Federal League came to an end in 1820 when Artigas went into exile in Paraguay.

REFERENCES: Juan E. Pival Devoto, *Raíces coloniales de la Revolución oriental de 1811*, 1957; Lorenzo Belinzón, *La revolución emancipadora uruguaya y sus dogmas democráticos*, 1932.

FEDERAL REPUBLIC OF CENTRAL AMERICA. When the Mexican Empire of Agustín de Iturbide* collapsed in March 1823, the Central American provinces of Guatemala*, El Salvador*, Honduras*, Nicaragua*, and Costa Rica* convened in a constituent assembly at Guatemala City*. On July 1, 1823, the representatives declared the independence of the United Provinces of Central America. An executive triumvirate governed the region for eighteen months until the representatives approved the constitution of the Federal Republic of Central America in January 1825. The Salvadoran Manuel José Arce* became the first president of the Federal Republic of Central America that March. The Federation was plagued by centrifugal forces of political philosophy, economics, and ethnicity. Guatemalan conservatives became increasingly dominant in the governing councils of the Federal Republic, much to the resentment of the other states. Civil war erupted in March 1827 when El Salvador rebelled against the federal government. When the liberal Francisco Morazán* was elected president of the Federal Republic in 1830, the rebellion in El Salvador subsided. Morazán's liberal reforms alienated conservatives, however, especially those in Guatemala, as did the decision in 1835 to relocate the capital to San Salvador* from Guatemala City. Between 1835 and 1839, Costa Rica, Guatemala, Honduras, and Nicaragua seceded from the Federal Republic. When Morazán tried to re-establish the authority of the federal government over Guatemala in 1840, the subsequent struggle led to his defeat at the Battle of Guatemala City on March 19, 1840. The Federal Republic of Central America then ceased to exist.

REFERENCE: Philip F. Flemion, "States' Rights and Partisan Politics: José Manuel Arce and the Struggle for Central American Union," *Hispanic American Historical Review*, 53 (1973), 600–618.

Virginia Garrard Burnett

FEDERMANN, NIKOLAUS. Nikolaus Federmann was born in Austria in 1501. In 1528, the famous Austrian banker Bartolomaus Welser named Federmann to go to Venezuela*, where the banking house had a small colony on the Gulf of Venezuela. Federmann arrived in Venezuela in 1530 and spent 1531 exploring the interior and searching for El Dorado*, the mythical Indian kingdom. Between 1536 and 1539, Federmann explored the Colombian highlands, eventually crossing the Andes and arriving in the vicinity of Bogotá*. There he discovered that Gonzalo Jiménez de Quesada* had already conquered the Chibcha* Indians and claimed the area. Federmann returned to Austria in 1540 and died there in 1546. His book *Historia indiana* was published in Spain in 1557.

REFERENCES: German Arciniegas, *Germans in the Conquest of America*, 1943; Juan Friede, *Vida y viajes de Nicolás Federmann*, 1960.

FERDINAND OF ARAGÓN. King of Spain during the initial phase of the age of exploration and colonization, Ferdinand II of Aragón was born March 10, 1452, in Sos, and died January 23, 1516, in Madrigalejo. Ferdinand ruled as king of Aragon from 1479 to 1516, king of Sicily from 1468 to 1516, and King of Castile* (as Ferdinand V, called the Catholic) from 1479 to 1504. With his marriage to Isabella* of Castile in 1469, Ferdinand II joined the kingdoms of Aragón and Castile into what became the nascent state of modern Spain. Following Isabella's death in 1504, he was appointed regent for his daughter Juana. As king, Ferdinand II set upon a course to complete the *Reconquista*, the expulsion of the Muslim Moors from Europe, which he accomplished with the capture of Granada from Moors in 1492. In 1493, he added Roussillon and Cerdagne to Spain under the Treaty of Barcelona with France. In 1512, he seized Upper Navarre from the French. In 1504, during the Italian Wars of 1494–1559, he conquered the Kingdom of Naples, where he was proclaimed King Ferdinand

III. Intending to strengthen Catholicism in Spain, Ferdinand and Isabella in 1480 promulgated the Inquisition* in Castile, and in 1492, they issued a decree banishing all Jews from Spain. They also increased the persecution of the Moors, forcing many of them to convert to Christianity.

Ferdinand's reign coincided with the discovery of the New World and the European colonization of the Americas. A sponsor, along with Isabella, of Christopher Columbus*, Ferdinand helped influence Spanish colonization to the extent that, by the middle of the sixteenth century, Spain controlled the Caribbean and the Gulf of Mexico, most of South and Central America, and a large portion of the southwestern North American continent.

REFERENCES: Denys Hay, *Europe in the Fourteenth and Fifteenth Centuries*, 1966; Felipe Fernández-Armesto, *Ferdinand and Isabella*, 1975.

William G. Ratliff

FERDINAND VI. King Ferdinand VI of Spain, the son of King Philip V*, was born in 1712. He succeeded to the throne of Spain upon the death of his father in 1746. Ferdinand VI's rule was undistinguished. The Spanish Empire continued its long decline. Severe economic problems undermined Spanish military power just as sentiment for more independence was growing in the colonies. Ferdinand VI died in 1759 and was succeeded by his son, Charles III*.

REFERENCES: R. S. Herr, *The Eighteenth-Century Revolution in Spain*, 1958; A. A. Hull, *Charles III and the Revival of Spain*, 1981.

FERDINAND VII. King Ferdinand VII of Spain, the son of King Charles IV*, was born in San Ildefonso, Spain, on October 13, 1783. Ferdinand grew up aware of the ongoing affair between his mother, María Luisa de Parma, and Manuel Godoy*, the Duke of Alcudia. In 1807, Ferdinand wrote to Napoleon Bonaparte, asking him to intervene against Godoy at the Spanish court. Napoleon quickly agreed. In 1808, Napoleon intervened, dismissed Godoy, and saw to the abdication of Charles IV.* Ferdinand came to the throne of Spain after deposing his father, but he was destined to preside over the near destruction of the Spanish Empire. He acquiesced in Napoleon's demand that Charles IV be restored to the throne, but Napoleon then removed him from power and imprisoned Ferdinand VII in France. Not until French fortunes were on the wane in 1814 did Ferdinand return to the Spanish throne, but by then, colonial rebellion was spreading throughout Latin America. There was little he could do about that. He immediately rejected all of the reforms enacted by the Cortes of Cádiz* and the constitutional assembly of 1812*, but it was too late. At the time of his death in 1833, all of the Spanish mainland colonies in the New World were lost.

REFERENCES: D. T. Hilt, *The Troubled Trinity: Godoy and the Spanish Monarch*, 1987; G. H. Lovett, *Napoleon and the Birth of Modern Spain*, 1965.

FERNÁNDEZ, MIGUEL. See VICTORIA, GUADALUPE.

FERNÁNDEZ DE ENCISO, MARTÍN. Martín Fernández de Enciso was born in Enciso, Spain, in 1470. He was a well-known cartographer who sailed throughout the Caribbean and along the northern coast of South America in the 1490s and early 1500s. In 1510, he established Santa Marta* la Antigua del Darién, but he got into a political struggle with Vasco Núñez de Balboa* and was deposed. Fernández drew a wealth of maps describing his observations, and his book *Suma de geographia* was published in Seville*, Spain, in 1519. Martín Fernández de Enciso died in 1528.

REFERENCES: Robert H. Davis, *Historical Dictionary of Colombia*, 1977; José Manuel Groot, *Historia eclesiástica y civil de Nueva Granada*, 5 vols., 1953.

FERNÁNDEZ DE HEREDIA Y VALDEZ, JUAN ANTONIO. Juan Antonio Fernández de Heredia y Valdez was born in Madrid in 1478. An historian, he is best remembered for his book *Historia natural y general de las indias*, which is a broad description of the Spanish conquest of the New World, although its best and most detailed section deals with the discovery of the Amazon River and the establishment of the city of Quito*. Fernández died in Valladolid, Spain, on June 26, 1557.

REFERENCES: Albert William Bork and George Maier, *Historical Dictionary of Ecuador*, 1973; Federico González Suárez, *Historia general de la República del Ecuador*, 7 vols., 1890–1903.

FERNÁNDEZ DE LIZARDI, JOSÉ JOAQUÍN. Most critics agree that Fernández was Latin America's first true novelist. Born in Mexico City* in 1776, Fernández was without a doubt the best-known and most popular literary figure in Mexico during the first part of the nineteenth century. Although his limited resources prevented him from completing a degree, he studied various subjects in several schools. Nonetheless, he was a born writer and thinker. Indeed, his nickname in Mexico City was "El Pensador Mexicano" (The Mexican Thinker). Fernández composed in many genres. Although he was not a particularly refined or artistic writer, his works were widely read and appreciated during their time. He did not seek recognition as a literary craftsman, but rather aimed to promote an anti-Spanish, pro-independence agenda. As a product of the Enlightenment and the French encyclopedists, he wrote pamphlets of a political bent and began a well-circulated but short-lived journal, titled *El Pensador Mexicano*, which served to advance the independence movement. He published other periodicals, as well as plays and poetry. But Fernández's subsequent literary fame rests squarely on his four novels: *El Periquillo Sarniento* (1816), *La Quijotita y su prima* (1818–1819), *Noches tristes y día alegre* (1818), and *Don Catrín de la Fachenda* (1819).

Of Fernández de Lizardi's four novels, unquestionably the most important was *El Periquillo Sarniento*, the first Latin American novel. *Periquillo* is largely patterned after the Spanish picaresque novel, with a benign pícaro-observer, narrating a large number of adventures and tales in the first person. The work treats virtually all strata of Mexican colonial society at the end of the Spanish control. The roguish anti-hero, Pedro, interacts with and comments upon Mexico and its people at a pivotal moment in Mexican history. The author of *El Periquillo* employed a didactic approach to his narrative, while at the same time entertaining the reader. Fernández clearly wanted to moralize and criticize in his works. To achieve this, the author filled his narrative with philosophical digressions, a common element in the Spanish picaresque novel. But unlike their Spanish counterparts, Fernández's novels utilize a clear, direct, and unadorned language with which to communicate. Although *El Periquillo* initially suffered from truncated editions due to censorship, it eventually appeared in a complete version in 1830. Fernández died in 1827.

REFERENCE: Carlos González Peña, *History of Mexican Literature*, 1968.

Sam L. Slick

FERNÁNDEZ DE OVIEDO Y VALDÉS, GONZALO. See OVIEDO Y VALDÉS, GONZALO FERNÁNDEZ.

FERNÁNDEZ DE PIEDRAHITA, LUCAS. Fernández is considered by most to be the best Colombian chronicler of the seventeenth century. He was a baroque writer who claimed as his personal vision the task of writing a history of New Granada. Born in New Granada in 1624, Fernández was a mestizo* whose father was a Spaniard and whose mother was a Peruvian Inca. He studied for many years in Bogotá* and received his doctorate in religion from the Thomistic University there. After holding various governmental positions, an open feud with the authorities convinced him to go to Spain where he spent six years. During that time, he did rigorous research in the archives of the mother country, accumulating information that was to serve him in writing his history of Colombia.* When he returned to Colombia, he began occupying a series of important church positions, ending as bishop of Panama*. His master work, *Historia de las Conquistas del Nuevo Reino de Granada*, is highly regarded by scholars. It includes excellent studies and observations of pre-Columbian Colombia, with attention to Indian culture, particularly that of the Chibchas*. The history continues until the government of Venero de Leiva in the year 1563. Although Fernández intended to write a continuation of the work, bringing the work to the year 1630, he died in 1688.

REFERENCES: Antonio Gómez Restrepo, *Historia de la literatura colombiana*, 1940; A. Curtis Wilgus, *The Historiography of Latin America: A Guide to Historical Writing, 1500–1800*, 1975.

Sam L. Slick

FERNÁNDEZ DE RECALDE, JUAN. Juan Fernández de Recalde was born in Bilbao, Spain, and received his education at the University of Salamanca. He spent years as a professor until his appointment as the *alcalde del crimen* in Lima*, Peru*, in 1586. In 1595, he became magistrate of Lima, and the next year he was appointed rector of the University of San Marcos* in Lima. Fernández became governor of the *audiencia* of Quito* in 1609, a position he occupied until 1612. Juan Fernández de Recalde died in Quito in 1615.

REFERENCES: Mark A. Burkholder and D. S. Chandler, *Biographical Dictionary of Audiencia Ministers in the Americas, 1687-1821*, 1982; Carlos Manuel Larrea, *La real audiencia de Quito y su territorio*, 1963.

FILIPINOS. The evolution of the term "Filipino" illustrates the process by which modern European nationalism took root in an Asian colony. Today the term is used in a legal sense (a citizen of the Philippines*) or in a broad racial sense to mean brown-skinned natives of the Philippines, but initially, a Filipino was a white man, a Spaniard who happened to have been born in the islands. Filipinos were distinguished from the highest caste of Manila* society, the *peninsulares**, who were Spaniards born in Spain. Beneath these two Caucasian groups were, in order of descending status, *mestizos* de español* (offspring of a union between a Spanish man and a native woman, no matter how diluted the Malay strain might be); then came *mestizos de Sangley* (part native, part Chinese); and then, at the bottom, the remaining 95 percent of the population who had no Spanish or Chinese blood. Of course, there were economic and social distinctions among the natives (inaccurately and pejoratively called *indios* by the Spaniards). To complicate matters, the natives were divided into a great number of separate regional groups speaking mutually incomprehensible languages.

Economic and social tensions divided the thin stratum of Spaniards. The *peninsulares* saw their stay in the islands as strictly temporary, a way for a man to advance himself before returning to Europe. They mistrusted their fellow Spaniards born in the islands (Filipinos), suspecting them of the kind of separatism and disloyalty to Spain manifested in Mexico* and elsewhere in Latin America. The *peninsulares* tried to monopolize government jobs for themselves, but they could never fully succeed because they were so few in number. As Philippine society reacted to nineteenth-century intellectual and social trends, those of mixed blood (Spanish-Malay and Chinese-Malay) found educational opportunities in Europe and economic opportunities in Manila. By the 1890s, they began to call themselves Filipinos. In Manila, *mestizos* and prominent *indios* from all over the islands met and mixed. In Madrid, students from the islands were forced to recognize their common identity as a people—a nation—with customs and culture distinctly different from those of Spain. In the agony of the Philippine Revolution (1896–1898) and the Philippine-American War (1899–1901), the modern meaning of Filipino was forged: anyone who subjectively identifies himself with the Philippines, regardless of race. Even today, however, many people do not regard Philippine Muslims, non-Christian tribesmen, Chinese, and Negritoes as true Filipinos.

REFERENCE: Domíngo Abella, *From Indio to Filipino*, 1973.

Ross Marlay

FILÍSOLA, VICENTE. Vicente Filísola was the first captain general* of the Mexican Empire after it gained its independence from Spain in 1821. An able military commander and supporter of Emperor Agustín Iturbide*, Filísola was in charge of maintaining the territorial integrity of the empire. Although most of Central America annexed itself to Mexico* in 1822, El Salvador* opposed annexation, and Filísola was sent to force its compliance. Although he succeeded in negotiating a solution whereby El Salvador would be granted independence from Guatemala* while remaining within the Mexican Empire, Iturbide rejected the agreement. With the failure of negotiations, Filísola invaded El Salvador in January 1823, easily conquered the province, and forced its annexation to Mexico.

On November 4, 1822, Iturbide decreed that Central America should be divided into three provinces of Mexico: Chiapas*, with Ciudad Real (San Cristóbal de las Casas) as its capital; Costa Rica*, with León* as its capital; and "Sacatepequez", with Guatemala* as its capital. This division was almost uniformly opposed throughout Central America and caused a contagion of armed revolts to break out. Filísola attempted unsuccessfully to quell these rebellions until early summer 1823 when Iturbide was overthrown in Mexico. On July 1, 1823, Central America declared its independence from Mexico, thus rendering the issue moot.

REFERENCE: Miles L. Wortman, *Government and Society in Central America, 1680–1840*, 1982.

Virginia Garrard Burnett

FLORES, JUAN JOSÉ. Juan José Flores was born in 1801 in Puerto Cabello, Venezuela*. His father was a *peninsular** who had a mercantile business, but his mother was a local Venezuelan. When he was just 14, Flores fought on the side of Spanish forces, but in 1817 he switched sides, joining rebel forces after having been incarcerated by them. Flores served under Simón Bolívar* at the Battle of Carabobo* in 1821, a battle that immediately resulted in Venezuelan independence. Flores became politically prominent in the Republic of Gran Colombia*, serving as governor of Pasto Province in southern Colombia*; in 1826, he became governor of Quito*. When the Republic of Gran Colombia dissolved in 1830, Flores convened an assembly of repesentatives from the Ecuadorean provinces and declared independence. Later in the year, he became the first president of Ecuador*. He served there until 1835 and then again between 1839 and 1845. Flores was exiled from Ecuador in 1845 and did not return until 1859, when he led military forces on behalf of García Moreno. Juan José Flores died in 1864.

REFERENCE: Carlos A. Rolando, *Biografía del General Juan José Flores*, 1930.

FLORIDA. Spanish expansion into Florida began when Spain became concerned about the French presence there. In 1562, Jean Ribaut landed a group of French Huguenots in Florida; eventually they settled on an island off the coast of what is today South Carolina. René Laudonnière established Fort Caroline at the mouth of the St. Johns River shortly thereafter. The Spanish responded by sending Pedro Mendéndez de Aviles from Cuba* to St. Augustine Bay in 1562. From there, the Spanish destroyed the French settlement at Fort Caroline. In 1565, Mendéndez de Aviles founded St. Augustine*, Florida. From there, the Spanish established a series of posts on the Florida and Georgia coast until they were blocked by English settlements in Virginia and South Carolina. The captaincy general of Cuba had administrative responsibility for Florida. In 1764, after the conclusion of the Seven Years War*, Spain ceded Florida to Great Britain. See EAST FLORIDA and WEST FLORIDA.

FLOTA. The term ''Armada de la Carrera de Indias'' literally translates as Fleet of the Trade of the Indies, and refers to the development of the convoy system for moving goods back and forth between Spain and the New World. First established in 1522, the *flota* was an armed fleet that escorted commercial traffic across the seas in order to protect trade goods from pirates and from English and Dutch privateers. Usually the fleet consisted of as many as 80 or 90 ships departing twice a year from Spain. Once the fleet reached the Caribbean, it would split in two, one group heading for Cartagena*, New Granada*, and the other for Veracruz, New Spain*. On the return trip, they would reunite in Havana* and then head for Spain. The *flota* convoy system survived into the late eighteenth century.

REFERENCES: Woodrow Borah, *Early Trade and Navigation between Mexico and Peru*, 1954; Peter Gerhard, *Pirates on the West Coast of New Spain, 1575-1742*, 1960; William R. Schurz, *The Manila Galleon*, 1939.

''FLOWER WARS.'' Standard, traditional sources have regarded the Flower Wars, or *xochiyaoyotl* (from *xochitl* meaning ''flower'' or ''precious'' and *yaoyotl* meaning ''war'' or ''battle'') as a form of ritual combat between the Aztecs* and their neighbors for the purposes of obtaining sacrificial victims and training warriors. Recent writers have suggested that the primary function of the Flower Wars was to provide the Aztecs with scarce protein in the form of human flesh or that the ritual war of flowers was an Aztec fabrication to mask their inability to conquer powerful neighboring states. Such standard sources as Jacques Soustelle's *Daily Life of the Aztecs* and George Vaillant's *Aztecs of Mexico* have been influential in spreading the traditional, ritual interpretation of the Flower Wars among English- and French-speaking audiences. They have argued that the Aztecs could have conquered the enemy states of Huejotzingo, Cholula, and Tlaxcala in the Puebla-Tlaxcala Valley to the east but did not do so in order to maintain nearby enemies with whom they could do battle and obtain the sacrificial victims required by their gods. These ritual wars also provided the Aztec warriors with the training necessary for success in campaigns of conquest.

According to this view, the war of flowers began in response to the famine of 1 Rabbit (1454). The storms and frosts that led to crop failures and the famine were a sign that the gods were angry and required more human sacrifices. Motecuhzoma* I and his adviser Tlacaelel made a treaty with the states of the Puebla-Tlaxcala Valley to engage in battle at specified times and neutral places to obtain sacrificial victims and to train inexperienced warriors. Michael Harner has suggested an ecological explanation for the War of Flowers. He has argued that protein became scarce as a result of the sharp increase in the Late Postclassic population of the Valley of Mexico. These ritual battles began after the famine of 1 Rabbit to supply the population with a quality source of protein. Harner's argument that there was a severe protein shortage in the Valley of Mexico has been challenged by many researchers familiar with the nutritional data.

Nigel Davies has noted in *Los Señoríos Independientes del Imperio Azteca* that even today wars have their conventions and ritual aspects. Perhaps the difference between the Flower Wars and Aztec wars of conquest was a matter of degree rather than of character. This position has been most forcefully argued by Barry Isaac. Isaac has noted the large loss of life recorded in some of the wars of flowers, the decisive Aztec defeat by the Tarascans in 1478, the Aztec defeat by Metztitlán in 1481, and the difficulty that Aztec armies had in subjugating Coixtlahuaca. From these data, Isaac has concluded that the Aztecs were simply unable to conquer Huejotzingo, Cholula, and Tlaxcala despite heroic attempts and great incentive to do so. This interpretation of the Flower Wars makes the institution seem less exotic and easier to understand in terms of state politics. The ritual need for sacrificial victims provided a convenient religious legitimation for state warfare, warfare in which commoners tried to capture sacrificial victims alive as a means of social advancement.

REFERENCES: Jacques Soustelle, *The Aztecs of Mexico*, 1961; Rudolf van Zantwijk, *The Aztec Arrangement: The Social History of Pre-Spanish Mexico*, 1985.

Edward B. Sisson

FOLK CATHOLICISM. Folk Catholicism is a term that refers to the development of a syncretic religious faith among indigenous people who mixed the Roman Catholicism brought by missionary priests with their own pre-conquest spiritual traditions. Most indigenous cultures of Spanish America and the Philippines[*] believed in densely populated spirit worlds that were propitiated only through the most elaborate rituals. With the advent of Christianity in the sixteenth and seventeenth centuries, these indigenous religious faiths survived, although they were inevitably changed by Roman Catholicism. Gradually, however, as the centuries passed, many of the indigenous traditions were incorporated into formal Catholicism or were eliminated. Sometimes this change resulted in national cult figures, as in the case of the Virgin of Guadalupe[*] in Mexico, where the patron saint had actually been preceded in Aztec[*] tradition by the appearance of a feminine goddess. For centuries before the appearance of the Virgin in 1531, a female goddess had appeared at the same site to Aztec worshippers. Faith in divine intervention was the core of indigenous folk religion, especially in the form of miracles, reflecting the willingness of God to intervene in individual affairs. In Cuba[*], folk Catholicism had an African-Hispanic blend in the Santería cult, which mixed African tribal mythology with Roman Catholic rituals. In the Philippines, where linguistic diversity and extreme geographical isolation were the norm, Roman Catholicism was superimposed on an elaborate system of indigenous deities, rituals, and celebrations.

REFERENCE: James S. Olson, *Catholic Immigrants in America*, 1987.

FONSECA, JUAN DE RODRÍGUEZ. Juan de Rodríguez Fonseca was born in 1451 to a prominent Spanish family. He selected a career in the priesthood, which brought him great success. He became archdeacon of Seville* and chaplain to the Spanish monarchs, Isabella* and Ferdinand*. They appointed him bishop of Badajoz and eventually the archbishop of Burgos. From that position at the royal court, Fonseca developed a particular interest in the New World colonies. He was deeply suspicious of Christopher Columbus*, always worried that the admiral was more interested in his own glory than in that of the Church or the monarchy. Fonseca saw to it that Francisco de Bobadilla* was dispatched to investigate Columbus's administration of the New World colonies. In 1503, Fonseca played a key role in the establishment of the Casa de Contratación*, which assisted him in his supervision of imperial policies. When he died in 1524, the Council of the Indies* was established to fill the vacuum.

REFERENCE: Ernesto Schafer, *El Consejo real y supremo de las Indias: Su historia y organización y labor administrativa hasta la terminación de la casa de Austria*, 2 vols., 1935–1947.

FOUNTAINEBLEAU, TREATY OF (1807). The Treaty of Fountainebleau was a secret treaty entered into between Napoleon Bonaparte and Don Manuel de Godoy* ("The Prince of Peace"). Indeed, not even the Spanish ambassador to Paris knew of the treaty until it was announced. The treaty gave France rights to march its troops across Spain to attack Portugal while also providing for the partial fulfillment of Godoy's dream—the Spanish conquest of Portugal. In the agreement, Spain was to occupy northern and southern Portugal while a French army occupied Lisbon and central Portugal. Then the northern portion would be turned over to France while the southern portion remained under Spanish control and in fact would become Godoy's own kingdom. The disposition of the central portion would be determined at a later time.

Napoleon, not waiting for formalities, ordered French troops across the Spanish border nine days before the Treaty of Fountainebleau actually was signed. Five days prior to the signing, Spain declared war on Portugal. With Spain as an ally and Portugal under attack, the Treaty of Fountainebleau represented the high-water mark of the Napoleonic empire. France was on the verge of removing all potential challengers to its hegemony on the European continent, including Russia which, having been defeated by Napoleon on the battlefield, had now been coerced into the anti-English alliance.

For Spain, the picture was less favorable. The campaign against Portugal did not prove successful and Godoy brought it to a premature conclusion in 1809. The French army trooped across Spanish soil, seizing strongpoints along its route to Portugal and conducting itself more like an army of occupation than an allied army. Finally, Napoleon became disillusioned with both Godoy and the alliance and maneuvered successfully to claim the Spanish crown for himself, prompting the Peninsular War which is also known as the War of Independence.

REFERENCES: Jacques Chastenet, *Godoy: Master of Spain, 1792-1808*, 1953; H. Butler Clarke, *Modern Spain, 1815-1898*, 1906; Gabriel Lovett, *Napoleon and the Birth of Modern Spain*, 1965.

Samuel Freeman

FRANCIA, JOSÉ GASPAR RODRÍGUEZ DE. Paraguayan independence, like that of the *Banda Oriental*, is divided into two phases: the first, 1810–1811, is linked to the loyalist cause; the second, beginning with the revolt of May 14, 1811, is revolutionary and connected with José Gaspar Rodríguez de Francia, who was born in 1766. After the May Revolution*, Buenos Aires* sent delegates to Asunción* to make sure that the former obtained recognition of its authority over the entire territory of the old viceroyalty of the Río de la Plata*. Bernardo de Velasco, governor of Paraguay since 1803, however, resisted and received support from the *cabildo* of Asunción. A *cabildo abierto* on July 24, 1810, decided to swear allegiance to the peninsular authorities of Cádiz. Thereupon Buenos Aires deposed Velasco and proceeded with an army to enforce recognition. Manuel Belgrano's* army was twice defeated (Paraguarí, January 9, 1811, and Tacuarí, March 5, 1811); this meant the *de facto* autonomy of Paraguay.

On May 11, 1811, Paraguay set up a junta that at first included Velasco, but a few days later (May 14, 1811) he was deposed. On May 17, 1811, independence was proclaimed. A congress then convened to decide the future relationship with Buenos Aires. This first Paraguayan congress asserted that, pending an overall solution, "this Province would govern itself." It set up a new Junta Suprema Gubernativa or Triunvirato (July 20, 1811), which included Fulgencio Yegros, Pedro Juan Cavallero, and Francia, who was the only person who had the educational ability, the legal training, and the moral strength to carry out a political program. He had studied theology and law at the University of Córdoba* and had been an elected member of the *cabildo* of Asunción. Ambitious and farsighted, Francia made the best use of the political circumstances and believed that isolation was the only way to ensure independence. He established his power by pursuing a tough policy toward Buenos Aires and succeeded in outwitting the other members of the junta. By the time the second congress assembled in 1813, Francia, as consul, was well on his way to ultimate authority in Paraguay.

In quick succession, Francia became Temporary Dictator in 1814 and Perpetual Dictator in 1816. Increasingly, he fell under the spell of Napoleonic influences, although in reality he was the Paraguayan version of eighteenth-century enlightened despotism, much like Bernardino Rivadavia* in Argentina*, Bernardo O'Higgins* in Chile*, and Francisco de Paula Santander* in Colombia*. In his long rule until his death in 1840 (actually also the end of the Enlightenment in Latin American intellectual history), he governed alone and was not subordinated to any control since he never called a parliamentary assembly. He suppressed the *cabildo* because in his view its authority had not emanated from the people. He respected the lower courts, but always reserved the last resort to himself. His government was personal. As Justo Pastor Benítez stated, his rule was not elegant but is was solid. His work was basic and his goals clear; everything was geared toward the achievement of independence. He knew what the vital elements of Paraguayan nationality were, and he nourished its roots. He took his task as an historic mission and dedicated his entire life to it. He lived a solitary life without friendships, was cold and had no compassion, but was honest. He personally assumed all responsibility, even for the smallest details. He relied on the support of the lower classes and the Indian* peasants, and was ruthless in their protection against the privileged few, especially the clergy. When he died, he had achieved his objective of independence and left his successor with a stronger country in terms of self-sufficiency and respect. Francia died in 1840.

REFERENCE: Justo Pastor Benítez, *La vida solitaria del Doctor José Gaspar de Francia: Dictador del Paraguay*, 1937.

O. Carlos Stoetzer

FRANCISCANS. The Franciscan order was founded by Giovanni Bernardone (1181–1226), who later became known as Saint Francis of Assisi. Established as a mendicant brotherhood (Friar Minor), emphasizing a simple, Christ-like life, Franciscans were, in many respects, similar to the Dominican order. Under various capable leaders, such as Brother Leo, Elias of Cortona, and many others the Order of Saint Francis of Assisi grew to be a major religious organization. Beyond their customary religious role, the Franciscans, along with other religious orders, played an important role in the conquest of the New World. In fact, their expansion into the New World was extraordinarily rapid. By 1400, they had established missions from northern Scandinavia to the Congo in Africa, and from the Azores to China. Franciscan missionaries arrived in Santo Domingo* in 1493 and began their work of conversion among the Indians*. The Franciscans organized a province in Santo Domingo in 1505 and then used it as the base for their expansion into Cuba* and Puerto Rico*. By 1513, the Franciscans were on the northern coast of South America and in 1514, they reached Panama*. Franciscan priests entered New Spain* in 1522 and over the next two centuries expanded throughout the colony. Franciscans accompanied Francisco Pizarro* into Ecuador* and Peru*, and they went into Colombia* and Venezuela* in the 1540s. The Franciscans reached Chile* in 1553 and the Río de la Plata* in the 1580s. By 1700, there were 18 Franciscan provinces with more than 5,200 priests in the New World. At the end of the colonial period, the Franciscans had established five provinces in Mexico, two in Central America, one in Cuba

(which included Florida*), one for Venezuela and the Antilles, and one each in Colombia, Ecuador, Peru, Chile, Bolivia*, Paraguay*, and Argentina*.
    REFERENCE: H. H. Holzapfael, *History of the Franciscan Order*, 1944.

Fred Koestler

FRANCO BAHAMONDE, FRANCISCO. Francisco Franco Bahamonde was born on December 4, 1893, in El Ferrol, Andalucía, Spain, to a distinguished Spanish naval family. He graduated from the infantry academy at Toledo in 1910 and volunteered for service in Morocco, where he quickly earned a reputation for good judgment and courage. He had earned the rank of major by 1916, and in 1920 became one of the founding figures in the organization of the Spanish Foreign Legion*. He became its second commander a few months later. Between 1924 and 1926, he played a key role in crushing the nationalist rebellion in Morocco, for which he earned the rank of brigadier general. In 1928, Franco became the first commandant of the new General Military Academy at Zaragoza.
    Franco's political philosophy was monarchist, nationalist, and conservative. By the outbreak of the Spanish Civil War in 1936, he was commandant of Spanish Morocco*. From there, he led his troops back to the peninsula and toward Madrid. By September, he had emerged as the commander-in-chief of monarchist forces, and he proclaimed himself chief-of-state at the end of the month. Franco minced no words about "totalitarianism," which he believed had been part of Spanish history and culture since the fifteenth century. For him, it was synonymous with authority and discipline, both of which he considered to be virtues. He ruled Spain as a dictator from the three years of the Spanish Civil War between 1936 and 1939 to his death on November 20, 1975.
    In 1950, Manuel Alia Medina informed Franco of huge phosphate deposits in Western Sahara*. That economic interest combined quickly with Franco's own deep-seated belief that Spain had an imperial destiny in Africa. He was also convinced that the nomadic tribesmen of the Sahara would be no match for his Spanish Foreign Legion troops. Franco had to surrender Spanish Morocco in April 1956 and the Tekna Zone* in April 1958, but he was determined to maintain the empire in Spanish Sahara*. As international pressure mounted in the 1960s, however, Franco reluctantly agreed to allow an "evolutionary" process toward self-determination. Spain wanted to get Gibraltar* back from Great Britain and believed that, in order to secure support for such a development, Franco had to appear flexible about his own African colony. He had no intention, of course, of surrendering his control of the phosphate deposits, but the guerrilla activities of the Polisario Front* undermined that conviction early in the 1970s. Franco decided to extend internal autonomy to Spanish Sahara, but his own health failed in 1974 and the political pressure was too great. Spain signed the Madrid Agreement* surrendering Spanish Sahara in 1975, and Franco died a week later.
    REFERENCES: S. G. Payne, *The Franco Regime, 1936-1975*, 1981; J. W. D. Trythall, *El Caudillo*, 1970.

FRANCO-SPANISH CONVENTION OF 1900. The Franco-Spanish Convention of 1900 defined the southern and southeastern boundaries of Spain's Sahara territory with French Mauritania, giving France the Idjil salt flats and the Bay of Levrier, although Spain retained the right to fish and land on the Bay of Levrier and to transport salt tax-free from Idjil.
REFERENCE: Tony Hodges, *Historical Dictionary of Western Sahara*, 1982.

FRANCO-SPANISH CONVENTION OF 1904. The Franco-Spanish Convention of 1904 followed up on the convention of 1900 by further outlining the French and Spanish spheres in West Africa. In the convention of 1904, a clear line was drawn between what became Spanish Morocco* and French Morocco.
REFERENCE: Tony Hodges, *Historical Dictionary of Western Sahara*, 1982.

FRANCO-SPANISH CONVENTION OF 1912. The Franco-Spanish Convention of 1912 took place after Great Britain and then Germany had recognized French supremacy in Morocco. It redefined the boundaries of what became Spanish Morocco*, reducing them in size to what became known as Saguia el-Hamra and the Tekna Zone*.
REFERENCE: Tony Hodges, *Historical Dictionary of Western Sahara*, 1982.

FREE TRADE DECREE OF 1778. Designed to modernize Spanish mercantilism*, the Regulation of Free Trade of October 12, 1778, was the capstone of the process of imperial commercial deregulation begun early in the reign of Charles III*. By decree of October 16, 1765, the monarch granted his Caribbean islands access to the Spanish ports of Alicante, Barcelona, Cartagena, Gijón, la Coruña, Málaga, Santander, and Seville* in addition to Cádiz, whose *consulado* until this time had held a legal monopoly over the American trade. The islands were also permitted intercolonial trade in American products, and, after 1774, in European goods. In 1768, Louisiana* was opened to the same Spanish ports but not to the Caribbean trade until 1770, when it gained access to Havana*. Yucatán* was joined fully to the free trade system in 1770, Santa Marta* and Ríohacha in 1776, and a royal decree of February 2, 1778, incorporated Buenos Aires*, Chile*, and Peru*. The number of enfranchised Spanish ports was expanded to include Tenerife* (1772), Palma (1777), Tortosa (1778), and Almeria (1778).

The 1778 regulation confirmed the enfranchisement of the 13 Spanish ports and extended free trade to the rest of the American empire except Venezuela* and New Spain*, which were not brought into the system until 1788 and 1789 respectively. Wealthy New Spain, it was feared, might overwhelm the weaker colonies, while in Venezuela the Caracas Company* still retained rights. As an interim measure, tonnage limits, distributed among the ports of Spain, were applied to New Spain in 1784.

Drafted in the Indies Ministry of José de Gálvez*, the 1778 regulation simplified licensing and inspection procedures; it also converted the tariffs on Spanish exports from levies assessed by weight and volume to an ad valorem basis. The rates on goods destined for ''major'' American ports, of which there were nine, were fixed at 3 percent for national products and 7 for foreign, payable both on departure and arrival. Those for ''minor'' ports, of which there were 15, were 1.5 percent and 4 percent respectively. Exempt from the *almojarifazgo*[*] upon departure, levies on American goods arriving in Spain varied. Most paid 3 percent to customs with another 1 percent designated for the Cádiz *consulado*; other goods, including sugar[*], were exempt. Gold paid a total of 2 percent and silver 5.5 percent.

The Regulation of Free Trade aimed to eliminate contraband, stimulate the imperial economy, and, through a larger volume of trade, increase tax revenues. During the 18 years following 1778, the volume of trade increased impressively, as did customs receipts. Because of its superior facilities, Cádiz retained its dominant role in both exports and imports. Among national goods, which grew to represent slightly over one-half of total exports, agricultural products remained primary, although textiles showed improvement. Re-exports consisted mainly of foreign manufactures. Precious metals continued to dominate American exports, but agricultural products expanded significantly, particularly Venezuelan cacao[*] and Cuban sugar. Spain's involvement in the Wars of the French Revolution and of Napoleon introduced complications unforeseen by the reformers of 1778. The system never had a long-term opportunity to be tested fully.

REFERENCES: John Fisher, *Commercial Relations Between Spain and Spanish America in the Era of Free Trade, 1778–1796*, 1985; Joseph Fontana, Bernal Fontana, and Antonio Miguel, eds., *El ''commercio libre'' entre España y América 1765–1824*, 1987; *Reglamento y aranceles reales para el Comercio Libre de España a Indias de 12 de octubre de 1778*, 1978.

Allan J. Kuethe

FREILE, JUAN RODRÍGUEZ. See RODRÍGUEZ, JUAN FREILE.

FREIRE SERRANO, RAMÓN. Ramón Freire Serrano was born in Santiago[*], Chile[*], in 1787 and became a cadet in the Spanish military in 1811. He joined the independence movement and participated in the Battle of Rancagua[*], where the Chilean army was defeated. Freire escaped into Argentina[*], returning in 1816 with José de San Martín's[*] Army of the Andes[*]. During the early independence period, Freire opposed the leadership of Bernardo O'Higgins[*], and in 1823, he was named Supreme Director of the Nation, a post he held until 1826. Freire spent most of those three years wiping out the last enclaves of Spanish resistance in Chile. Freire served as president for three months in 1827 as a member of the Liberal Party, but he resigned amid a political squabble with the Chilean Congress. During the civil war in 1829–1830, Freire led the army of the liberal forces, which was defeated at the Battle of Lircay[*] in April 1830. The new conservative government sentenced him to death but he escaped into exile in Tahiti. Ramón Freire Serrano died in 1851.

REFERENCES: Lia Cortés and Jordi Fuentes, *Diccionario Político de Chile*, 1967; Luis Galdames, *Historia de Chile*, 1945.

FRITZ, SAMUEL. Fray Samuel Fritz was born in Bohemia in 1650. A missionary Roman Catholic priest, Fritz led a mission to the Omagua Indians on the Marañón River in 1687. After becoming ill, he traveled down the Amazon River seeking medical assistance. He made observations and took notes along the way until he arrived at Belém, where Portuguese authorities arrested him. Eventually he was released and returned to the Omagua mission. Later in his life, Fritz alerted Spanish authorities to the fact that the Portuguese were occupying Spanish territory in the Upper Amazon region. Fritz is also remembered as a skilled engraver, especially of the city of Quito* and the Amazon River.

REFERENCE: Albert William Bork and Georg Maier, *Historical Dictionary of Ecuador*, 1973.

FUENTES Y GUZMÁN, FRANCISCO ANTONIO DE. Francisco Antonio de Fuentes y Guzmán was born in Santiago* de los Caballeros de Guatemala* in 1643 to an important local family. He was self-educated and pursued a career as a military officer. Fuentes also served as mayor of Santiago and then as mayor of Sonsonate in Guatemala. In those positions, he concentrated on road-building to provide an infrastructure that would make the region more economically efficient and governable. Fuentes is best remembered, however, for his poetry and writings. He wrote historical chronicles in poetic form, as well as collecting important documents from colonial Guatemalan history. Although much of his historical writing has been revised by scholars, Fuentes is still an important figure in Latin American historiography. He died in Sonsonate, Guatemala, in 1700.

REFERENCE: Unión Panamericana, *Diccionario de la literatura latinoamericana: America Central; Costa Rica, El Salvador, y Guatemala*, 1963.

FUERO DE GUERRA MILITAR. The *fuero de guerra militar*, or simply the *fuero militar* as it was commonly known, was a judicial privilege that conveyed the right to present cases before military tribunals. It dated as a distinct legal code from the sixteenth century and subsequently developed into a complex body of law. By the eighteenth century, it consisted of two subdivisions, the *fuero militar privilegiado* for special corps, including the artillery, engineers, and provincial militia, and the *fuero militar ordinario* for the regular army. In its most basic dimension, the *fuero militar* granted the military primary control over its soldiery so that in time of mobilization the army need not look beyond its own prisons to assemble its men. The military *fuero* also conveyed highly coveted prestige in that it placed its holders beyond the reach of ordinary justice.

The *fuero militar* varied considerably in its application. It might be limited to criminal cases or include civil actions. It might be defined as passive, applying only when the holder was a defendant, or it might be active, including cases where he was the plaintiff. In the regular army of Spain and America, as confirmed as the 1768 *Ordenanzas de S. M. para el régimen, disciplina, subordi-*

nación, y servicio de sus ejércitos, officers and enlisted men and their families enjoyed the *fuero* in both civil and criminal actions. This privilege was understood to be passive. The 1734 *ordenanzas* for the provincial militia of Spain extended the complete *fuero militar* to officers and their dependents, but the privilege of enlisted men was limited to criminal actions except when the men were mobilized. Like the *fuero* of the regular army, the militia privilege was interpreted as passive. This construction was confirmed by the *Real declaración sobre puntos esenciales* of 1767.

Until the introduction of the provincial, or disciplined, militia system into America during the 1760s, normally only the officers of the volunteer forces possessed the *fuero militar* and, depending upon custom and circumstance, this might or might not include civil actions. Mobilization brought all grades and ranks the same privileges as those for the regular army. Under the 1769 *Reglamento para las milicias . . . de Cuba*, the disciplined militia, including enlisted men, enjoyed the full *fuero militar*, and the *Real declaración* of April 15, 1771, defined the privilege of officers and sergeants as active. Until this time, only special corps, such as the palace guard, had come under the active privilege, but the hope was that this concession might compensate volunteers, who received no pay, for their sacrifices. In that the Cuban regulation was used as the model in most other colonies, this broad definition of the military privilege for disciplined units was widespread in America; the 1778 *reglamento* for Yucatán[*] reaffirmed it. Still, in New Spain[*], only officers were conceded the civil *fuero*, and their privilege was interpreted as passive. When additional regulations were codified for other colonies later in the century, the passive definition prevailed. For nondisciplined units, traditional limitations remained. After 1786, officers were also denied the *fuero* when not on active duty.

Cases coming under the *fuero militar ordinario* were heard by the regional captains general[*] or, if this were not possible, by the local governors, with appeal to the pertinent captain general. These officials ordinarily operated through trained legal assistants, *auditores de guerra*. Appeals entailing matters of sufficient magnitude could be made before the *Consejo Supremo de Guerra* in Madrid, including all cases where the punishment involved death or mutilation. For the *fuero militar privilegiado* of the disciplined militia in Spain, battalion or regimental colonels, assisted by *asesores de guerra*, constituted the courts of first instance with appeals to the *Consejo Supremo*. Colonels functioned similarly in New Spain, where militia practices closely followed the Spanish model, with appeals on up through the military hierarchy. Under the widely applied Cuban regulation, however, volunteer unit commanders were bypassed in favor of the highest ranking officer of the regular army in the particular locality.

Instances of *desafuero*—where the common good or special considerations intervened—limited the military authority. In such cases, jurisdiction was retained by ordinary justice or was granted to other privileged orders. The civil category included matters such as the disposition of civilian wills, the succession to entailed estates, actions in mercantile law, and debts incurred or contracts negotiated prior to enlistment. Among the criminal offenses where the *fuero* did not apply were treason, sedition, defrauding the royal treasury, counterfeiting, smuggling, heresy, and the abuse of ordinary justice. Frequently, the lines of authority were unclear, owing to the confused properties of individual cases, the inability or unwillingness of the authorities to comprehend the limits of their jurisdictions, and the ambiguities in the legal ordinances themselves. Jurisdictional disputes (*competencias de jurisdicción*) could become commonplace, especially in places where civil-military relationships were already strained.

Military commanders viewed the *fuero militar* as essential for promoting *esprit de corps* among both men and officers, and preferential treatment before military tribunals was not uncommon. The *fuero de guerra ordinario* had little impact on society, because the regular army generally remained isolated from the mainstream of community activity. The *fuero de guerra privilegiado* differed in that it brought military privilege into the daily life of many of the most important communities through militiamen who were engaged in civilian pursuits, except during Sunday drills or in times of mobilization. The *fuero militar* converted the army, the militia included, into an autonomous, self-governing institution, largely free from the constraints of civilian justice, and the military viewed this status with a profound sense of corporate pride. Military privileges were not always accompanied by a commensurate sense of responsibility, either during the eighteenth century or in subsequent history.

REFERENCES: A. J. Kuethe, *Cuba 1753-1815: Crown, Military, and Society*, 1986; L. N. McAlister, *The "Fuero Militar" in New Spain, 1764 1800*, 1957.

Allan J. Kuethe

FUEROS. Since the Middle Ages in Europe, political sovereigns had regularly granted certain exemptions and protections to influential constituencies in return for political support. In Spain, the institution was known as a *fuero*, a grant of special rights, tax exemptions, and judicial privileges to a particular group, including criminal and civil jurisdiction over its members. The most common recipients of *fueros* were the clergy, the military, merchant guilds, and some groups of large landowners. The Spanish Crown continued the practice in the New World colonies, with the military, clergy, and merchant guilds the primary recipients. When the crown attempted to limit the privileges of the *fueros*, it often encountered intense opposition from the members, such as the *comunero*[*] movements. Not surprisingly, those groups with *fueros* became conservative elites, one of the targets of the independence movement in the early nineteenth century. The overlapping jurisdictional authorities frequently led to bitter conflict in the colonies. Politics in nineteenth-century Latin America frequently revolved around the struggle by liberals to abolish the *fueros* and by conservatives to protect them. The special courts were not abolished until late in the eighteenth century in the New World, and some of them survived until the end of the colonial period.

REFERENCES: Charles Gibson, *Spain in America*, 1966; C. H. Haring, *The Spanish Empire in America*, 1947.

FUÑES, GREGORIO. Gregorio Fuñes was born on May 26, 1749, in Córdoba* in the Río de la Plata*. He received an undergraduate degree from the Jesuit College of Montserrat, a law degree from the University of Alcalá in Spain, and a doctorate in theology from the University of Buenos Aires*. He pursued a religious career in the Jesuit* order, which eventually brought him to the position of Vicar General in the Diocese of Córdoba in 1793 and Rector of the University of Córdoba* in 1808. Fuñes emphasized geography, history, law, mathematics, and languages in the curriculum, instead of an exclusive emphasis on the classics. Early in the 1800s, Fuñes became involved in revolutionary activity, writing articles for *La gaceta* and proposing independence from Spain and the establishment of a federal political system. Fuñes opposed domination of Argentina* by Buenos Aires. He was a deputy in the Congress of Tucumán*, which eventually declared independence from Spain. Fuñes served in the Argentine legislature and in several other political posts during the 1820s. He was the author of *Ensayo de la historia civil del Paraguay, Buenos-Ayres y Tucumán* (1816–1817). Fuñes died on January 10, 1829.

REFERENCE: Ione S. Wright and Lisa M. Nekhom, *Historical Dictionary of Argentina*, 1978.

FUÑES VILLALPANDO, AMBROSIO DE. See RICLA, CONDE DE.

G

GACHUPIN. The term *gachupin* originated in the sixteenth century to refer pejoratively to an individual who had been born in Spain and had emigrated to New Spain*. The equivalent term in Peru was *chapeton**. *Criollos** usually resented the *gachupines* because of their naïveté, haughtiness, and monopoly on important clerical, military, and political offices. Resentment of the *gachupines* played an important role in the Mexican independence movement.

GAGE, THOMAS. An English priest who traveled to Central America in the early 1600s, Thomas Gage published the chronicle of his trip, *New Survey of the West-Indies*, in London in 1648. The book has been reissued through the years under a variety of different titles. Although Gage was a Jesuit* at the time of his journey, he had converted to Protestantism and become a hispanophobe by the time he wrote his book, which was first published during the protectorate of Oliver Cromwell. As an anti-Catholic, anti-Spanish polemic, the *New Survey* did much to feed the fires of the Black Legend*. Nonetheless, Gage's powers of observation were acute, and his special status as a priest had allowed him a window on Spanish-American society to which few foreigners had access. Despite its obvious biases, Gage's work remains the most in-depth commentary on Spanish Central America available in English.
REFERENCE: R. L. Woodward, Jr., *Central America: A Nation Divided*, 1983.
Virginia Garrard Burnett

GALEANO, HERMENEGILDO. Hermenegildo Galeano was born in Guerrero, New Spain*, in 1762. His whole family became enchanted with the ideas of José María Morelos*, and Hermenegildo joined the revolution in its early stages. He was a leading figure in the siege of Acapulco* of 1813 which drove the royalists from the port. In 1814, Galeano was killed in an ambush set by royalist troops.

REFERENCE: John A. Caruso, *The Liberators of Mexico*, 1967.

GÁLVEZ, JOSÉ DE. José de Gálvez was born in Málaga in 1720. He earned a law degree at the University of Salamanca and then practiced law in Madrid. Gálvez came to the attention of Leopoldo de Gregorio, the minister of finance, in 1761 when he wrote a proposal calling for the large-scale deregulation of the colonial economies. Gálvez subsequently spent his career as a royal official, and King Charles III* appointed him *visitador* to New Spain* in 1765. His charge was to eliminate corruption and inefficiency in colonial administration and to increase royal revenues. His *visita**, lasting from 1765 to 1771, had an enormous impact on colonial administration. After traveling widely throughout New Spain, Gálvez made a number of important recommendations to the king. First, he called for the election of *regidores** to reduce corruption at the municipal level. Second, he advocated free trade and tariff reductions as a means of stimulating commerce and economic growth. Third, he called for establishment of the intendancy* system to reform colonial administration thoroughly. Fourth, to prevent British and Russian expansion along the northern Pacific coast, Gálvez recommended Spanish military expansion into California*. Gálvez was in New Spain when the order to expel the Jesuits* was imposed, and he played a key political role in bringing about their expulsion in New Spain. José de Gálvez returned to Spain in 1771 to accept appointment as Minister of the Indies. He died in 1787.

REFERENCE: H. I. Priestly, *José de Gálvez: Visitor-General of New Spain (1765– 1771)*, 1916.

GAMARRA, AGUSTÍN. Agustín Gamarra was born in Cuzco*, Peru*, in 1785. Between 1810 and 1820, he fought in the Spanish army against revolutionary forces, but he switched sides in 1820 and joined up with José de San Martín*. At the battles of Junín* and Ayacucho* in 1824, Gamarra was with Simón Bolívar's* army. During the rest of the decade, Gamarra fought against royalist forces in Ecuador* and Bolivia*, and for a while he served as governor of Cuzco. A political chameleon, Gamarra deposed the government of José de la Mar in 1829 for getting the country into a war with Chile*, and he became the virtual dictator of Peru for four years, although his official designation was "president." After engaging in several attempts to force Bolivia into a Peruvian-Bolivian confederation, Gamarra was killed on November 8, 1841. At the time, he was serving again as president of Peru, having been elected in 1839.

REFERENCES: Frederick A. Pike, *The Modern History of Peru*, 1967; Alberto Tauro, *Diccionario enciclopédico del Perú*, 1966.

GAMBA, PEDRO SARMIENTO DE. See SARMIENTO DE GAMBA, PEDRO.

GARABITO, JUAN DE SANTIAGO Y LEÓN. See SANTIAGO Y LEON GARABITO, JUAN DE.

GARAY, JUAN DE. Juan de Garay was born in the Basque region of Spain in 1528 to a noble family that had come on hard times. He came to Peru[*] with the retinue of Viceroy Blasco Núñez de Vela[*] in 1544, and in 1549 he was part of Juan Núñez de Prado's expedition into northwestern Argentina[*]. Garay eventually became an *encomendero* and settled in Santa Cruz de la Sierra in Upper Peru (Bolivia[*]). He moved to Asunción[*] in 1568 and served as the *alguacil mayor* there. He established the city of Santa Fe in 1573 and was appointed governor of Paraguay[*] in 1576. A few years later, he was appointed lieutenant governor and captain general of Río de la Plata[*] and in 1580 founded the permanent city of Buenos Aires[*]. He became governor of the settlement, from which he explored widely throughout the region. In 1584, Garay was killed in an Indian attack by Querandí Indians.
    REFERENCE: Paul Grossac, *Mendoza y Garay*, 1949.

GARCÉS, FRANCISCO TOMÁS. Francisco Tomás Garcés was born in Morata del Conde, Spain, on April 12, 1738. He entered the Franciscan[*] order in 1753 and was ordained in 1763. Garcés soon volunteered for missionary work in the New World and was assigned to New Spain[*]. Between 1768 and 1781, Garcés worked among the Papagos, Pimas, Yumas, and Apache[*] Indians[*] of what is today northwestern Mexico and Arizona, traveling widely across the region trying to convert and pacify the various tribes. On July 19, 1781, while trying to quell a rebellion of Yuma Indians along the Colorado River in Arizona, Garcés was murdered by angry Indians.
    REFERENCE: E. R. Coues, ed., *On the Trail of a Spanish Pioneer: The Diary and Itinerary of Francisco Garcés*, 1900.

GARCÉS, JULIÁN. Julián Garcés was born in Munebrega, Aragón, Spain, in 1447, to a noble family. He was educated at the Sorbonne in Paris and then entered the Dominican[*] order. Because of his family connections, intellectual brilliance, and gifted preaching style, Garcés was appointed royal chaplain to King Charles V[*] and confessor to Bishop Rodríguez[*] de Fonseca. In 1526, Charles V named him bishop of Tlaxcala in New Spain[*]. Garcés was a vigorous missionary among the Indians[*], and he earned a reputation as a man who cared for them. His letters to the papacy about the Indians led to the Papal Bull *Sublimis Deus*[*], in which Pope Paul III proclaimed the basic humanity of the Indians. Garcés died in Puebla[*], New Spain, in 1542.
    REFERENCE: *New Catholic Encyclopedia*, VI:283, 1967.

GARCÍA, DIEGO. Diego García was born in Lisbon, Portugal, in 1471 and became a gifted mariner and navigator in the Spanish service. He was part of Juan de Solís's[*] voyage to the Río de la Plata[*] area in 1512, and between 1519 and 1522 he served with Ferdinand Magellan's* expedition circumnavigating the globe. In 1527, he headed up an expedition to the Río de la Plata area. During that expedition, he explored the Paraná and Paraguay rivers. García returned to Spain in 1530. He set out on another expedition to the New World in 1535, but he became ill and died on Gomera in the Canary Islands*.

REFERENCE: Machain Lafuente, *Los conquistadores de la Plata*, 1943.

GARCÍA DE POLAVIEJA, CAMILO. Born in Spain in 1838, Camilo García de Polavieja rose through the ranks of the Spanish officer corps and was assigned to Cuba* in the early 1870s, where he became an aide to General Arsenio Martínez* Campos. García de Polavieja drafted the Pact of Zanjón ending the Ten Years War* and then played an instrumental role in suppressing the Guerra Chiquita* in 1879. In 1890, he was appointed governor of Cuba; by that time, he had earned the rank of general. But García de Polavieja was a troublesome governor, at least from the Spanish perspective, because during the 1880s he had come to believe in Cuban independence. He resigned in 1892 and then was appointed as governor of the Philippines*, where he led the anti-independence forces. Indeed, García de Polavieja signed the death sentence document for José Rizal*. At the time of the Spanish-American War*, García de Polavieja returned to Spain where he died in 1914.

REFERENCES: E. Arsenio Manuel, *Dictionary of Philippine Biography*, 1955; Jaime Suchlicki, *Historical Dictionary of Cuba*, 1988.

GARCÍA GOYENA, RAFAEL. Rafael García Goyena was born in Guayaquil*, Ecuador*, in 1766. He went to Guatemala* to study at the University of San Carlos* and decided to live there after he completed his studies. García became one of the leading poets and writers in colonial Guatemala. He is best remembered for his poem *El pavo, el guarda, y el loro*. García died in 1823.

REFERENCE: Richard E. Moore, *Historical Dictionary of Guatemala*, 1973.

GARCÍA ÍÑIGUEZ, CALIXTO. Born near Havana*, Cuba*, in 1839, Calixto García Íñiguez became committed to Cuban independence as a young student. During the Ten Years War*, he joined the revolutionary forces fighting the Spanish army. By 1872, he was second in command to General Máximo Gómez*. Spanish forces captured him in 1874, and he spent the rest of the war in prison. After his release in 1878, García relocated to New York City. There he organized the Cuban Revolutionary Committee to raise money and promote the independence movement. In August 1879, just a year after the end of the Ten Years War, García met with Antonio Maceo* y Grajales in Jamaica* to plan an insurrection. They issued the Kingston Proclamation, called for insurrection, and went back to Cuba. Convinced that Maceo's African ancestry would be a political liability, García removed him from military command and personally led an invasion of Cuba in May 1880. It failed miserably, and García was captured in August 1880. After spending several years in prison in Spain, García returned

to Cuba in 1895 and once again rose to become second in command to Máximo Gómez. He died in 1898.
REFERENCE: Luis Rodolfo Miranda, *Calixto García Iniguez: Estrategia*, 1951.

GARCÍA JOFRE DE LOAYSA, JUAN. See LOAYSA, JUAN GARCÍA JOFRE DE LOAYSA.

GARCÍA LANZA, JOSÉ MANUEL. José Manuel García Lanza, born in Bolivia* in the late eighteenth century, became a prominent anti-royalist guerrilla leader during the war for independence. Commander of the so-called Republic of Apopaya in the area of La Paz*, Cochabamba*, and Oruro, he regularly harassed Spanish forces. In 1825, he participated in and served as the acting president of the constituent assembly that proclaimed Bolivian independence. Before his death in 1828, he was an aide to President Antonio de Sucre*.
REFERENCE: Dwight B. Heath, *Historical Dictionary of Bolivia*, 1972.

GARCÍA PUMACAHUA, MATEO. Mateo García Pumacahua was a Quechua*-speaking Indian* born near Cuzco*, Peru*, around 1755. During the rebellion of Túpac Amaru II* in Peru in the early 1780s, García sided with royalist forces and even fought against the rebels. But as time passed, he too became increasingly resentful of the power and attitude of superiority of the *peninsulares** who ran the Spanish colonial bureaucracy, the church, and the military. In 1814, García led a rebellion of his own against the Crown and declared himself president of the *audiencia* of Cuzco*. He then led a force of 20,000 Indians* into northern Argentina*, but they were defeated there. He was executed on March 17, 1815.
REFERENCE: Paul L. Doughty, *Peru: A Cultural History*, 1976.

GARCILASO DE LA VEGA. "EL INCA". Garcilaso de la Vega was born in Cuzco*, Peru*, on November 12, 1539. There are many fascinating details about El Inca's life, not the least of which is his lineage. His father was a Spanish captain who was related to various famous literary personalities of Spain, including the famous poet Garcilaso de la Vega. El Inca's mother was an Incan princess and relative of Atahualpa*, the last emperor of the Incan Empire. In Peru, he grew up learning both the Indian* culture and that of the Spaniards, first in Cuzco and later in Lima*. As a child, he was witness to and victim of the Peruvian civil wars. His Spanish father finally disowned El Inca's mother and legally married a Spanish woman. When his father died and the family fortune passed to only the legitimate heirs, El Inca looked for other roads in life. At age 21, he left for Spain, never to return to South America again. He spent these early years attempting to regain the inheritance and property for both himself and his mother, all without success. He then joined the Spanish military, saw duty in various countries, and rose to the rank of captain. After an adventurous and favored lifestyle, El Inca returned to Spain and joined the priesthood to live a monastic life.

Many critics have cited El Inca Garcilaso de la Vega as the greatest prose writer of colonial Spain. He was, at least, the most important of the colonial chroniclers. He wrote two works of importance. The first, *La Florida del Inca o Historia del Adelantado Hernando de Soto*, was published in 1605. As the title indicates, the book recounts the misfortunes of the Spanish explorer Hernando de Soto[*] in Florida[*]. But El Inca's greatest and most important work within the context of Spanish colonial literature was his *Comentarios Reales*, the first part of which was published in 1609 and the second in 1617. *Comentarios* is a historical account of the history of the Inca[*] people and its conquest by the Spaniards. For many years, it was fashionable to criticize *Comentarios* for its lack of objectivity and historical rigor, particularly with regard to the Incan civilization; today that view has been rejected. But when El Inca did embellish and idealize at the expense of historical accuracy *Comentarios* is perhaps at its best, because he was a creative writer. The fact is that El Inca fused significant historical knowledge, often acquired firsthand, with an imaginative, fictional bent. The result is excellent literature. At the same time, posterity is thankful to El Inca for having recorded his intimate knowledge of the facts, customs, legends, and beliefs of the Incan people. He knew about what he wrote, as he had his mother and her family as his personal tutors. Finally, with regard to El Inca's rendition of the conquest and of the civil wars of Peru that he witnessed firsthand, it is now believed that *Comentarios* is an essentially true and accurate account. He died on April 22, 1616, in Córdoba, Spain.

REFERENCES: Hady Ward Keniston, trans., *Works: A Critical Text*, 1925; Arturo Torres-Rioseco, *The Epic of Latin American Literature*, 1942.

Sam L. Slick

GARÍFUNA. The Garífuna, also known historically as "Black Karibs[*]," live along the Atlantic seaboard of Central America from Belize[*] to Nicaragua[*]. Today their numbers exceed 110,000 people, with the majority in Honduras[*] and smaller numbers in Nicaragua, Belize, and Guatemala[*]. More than 63,000 of the Garífuna live in Honduras. They originated as an ethnic group in the seventeenth century on St. Vincent island in the Caribbean when escaped African slaves mixed with the Karib Indians. By the early eighteenth century, they had become a new ethnic group, neither African nor Indian. In 1783, England took control of St. Vincent and, in the 1790s, fought an extended guerrilla war against the Garífuna. The Garífuna were finally defeated in 1796, and the English promptly relocated 5,000 of them to the Bay Islands of the Gulf of Honduras. From there, they have migrated north and south along the coast, becoming a large working-class population of farmers, laborers, and artisans.

REFERENCES: Nancie L. González, *Sojourners of the Caribbean: Ethnogenesis and Ethnohistory of the Garifuna*, 1988; C. J. Gullick, *Exiled from St. Vincent: The Development of Black Carib Culture in Central America to 1945*, 1976; L. Fernando Cruz Sandoval, "Los Indios de Honduras y la situación de sus recursos naturales," *América Indígena*, 44 (1984), 423–46.

GASCA, PEDRO DE LA. Pedro de la Gasca was born in Ávila, Spain, in 1485. Although he was trained as a priest and a lawyer, he spent the first part of his career as an effective administrator in the Spanish colonial bureaucracy. In 1548, Gasca was named president of the *audiencia* of Lima*. He was charged with enforcing the New Laws* and suppressing the rebellions of Gonzalo Pizarro* and Francisco Carvajal*. Gasca crushed the rebellions, executed Pizarro and Carvajal, and then relieved the Peruvian and Bolivian Indians* of many of the worst abuses imposed on them by Spanish *encomenderos*. But Gasca went too far in limiting the rights of the colonists to exploit the Indians, and continuing protests to the crown eventually undermined his authority. In 1551, he was replaced by Antonio de Mendoza*. Gasca returned to Spain to become the bishop of Palencia, a post he held until 1561, when he was appointed bishop of Sigüenza. Pedro de la Gasca died in 1567.

REFERENCE: Manuel de Mendilburu, ed., *Diccionario histórico-biográfico del Perú*, 8 vols., 1874–1890.

GAUCHO. The term "gaucho" first appeared in the eighteenth century in the region of the Río de la Plata* to describe rural male workers laboring in the livestock industry. Usually the gauchos were of mixed European, Indian*, mestizo*, and African ancestry, and because they were so poor and frequently unemployed, they were looked down upon by the rest of the society. In the late colonial period, the Spanish Empire relied heavily on gauchos to serve in military posts at isolated frontier settlements.

GAZISTAS. The Gazistas were a leading political faction in Guatemala* in the late colonial period. Their leader was José del Valle*, editor of *El Amigo de la Patria*. The Gazistas were strongly committed to Guatemalan independence from Spain, and during the federation period they opposed political fusion with Mexico.* They eventually came to advocate a highly centralized government for Guatemala.

REFERENCE: Richard E. Moore, *Historical Dictionary of Guatemala*, 1973.

GENERATION OF 1898. The term "Generation of 1898" refers to a literary and intellectual movement in Spain during the late nineteenth and early twentieth centuries. The backdrop of the movement was the Spanish-American War* and the loss of the last major remnants of the Spanish Empire. That defeat and loss symbolized the decline of Spain from its sixteenth-century greatness to its twentieth-century impotency. A host of writers and intellectuals—including Gabriel Maura y Gamazo, Andres González Blanco, José Martínez Ruiz, Joaquín Costa, Damián Isern, Ángel Ganivet García, Miguel de Unamuno, Pío Baroja, Antonio Machado, and Ramiro de Maeztu—bemoaned the Spanish fate. They called for a regeneration of the national will. The movement had largely run its intellectual course by the 1920s.

REFERENCE: J. L. Abellán, *Sociología del '98*, 1973.

GIBRALTAR. A British colony, Gibraltar is a tiny peninsula on the eastern coast of the Bay of Algeciras. For centuries, Gibraltar has enjoyed great strategic importance in European and African affairs because it guards the entrance and exit from the Mediterranean Sea. Although Gibraltar has been inhabited since ancient times, its modern history began in A.D. 711 when Berber tribesmen crossed the strait and occupied the area, maintaining it as a defensive outpost. The Moorish occupation of the Iberian peninsula led to the establishment in 1160 of an Arab city there, which Spain captured in 1309 as part of the *Reconquista*. The Moors regained the colony in 1333 and held it until 1462, when Spain retook Gibraltar. By that time, the Moorish presence in Iberia was confined to the outpost at Granada. Gibraltar never again fell into their hands.

Spanish control of Gibraltar continued until 1704 when a British fleet commanded by Admiral George Rooke seized the city during the War of the Spanish Succession*. As part of the Treaty of Utrecht*, which ended the war in 1713, Spain ceded permanent control over Gibraltar to England. Over the years, Spain has periodically tried to regain control over Gibraltar. During the American Revolution*, Spain placed Gibraltar under siege between 1779 and 1783, but the Treaty of Paris* in 1783 reconfirmed British sovereignty. Gibraltar became a crown colony in 1830. During the 1960s, in an attempt to squeeze the Gibraltar economy and bring about a repatriation of the region, Spain sealed off its border with Gibraltar and refused to permit any commerce and trade. In 1966, the people of Gibraltar voted overwhelmingly to maintain their association with the British Empire and to remain independent of Spain. The island remains a part of the British Empire today, but continues to be a point of contention between Spain and Great Britain.

REFERENCES: Maxwell Stamp, *Gibraltar: British or Spanish?*, 1976; Howard S. Levie, *The Status of Gibraltar*, 1983.

GILIJ, FELIPE SALVADOR. Felipe Salvador Gilij was born in Bogotá*, New Granada*, in 1721. He joined the Jesuit* order as a young man and then attended the Javeriana University* in Bogotá. Gilij was ordained in 1748 and then spent the next 18 years as a missionary among the Indians* of the Orinoco River basin. When the Jesuits were expelled from the New World in 1767, Gilij relocated to Rome where he spent the next decade writing his *Ensayo de historia americana, o sea historia natural, civil y sacra de los reinos, y de las provincias de tierra firme en la América meridional*, which was published in Rome between 1780 and 1784. Gilij died in 1789.

REFERENCES: Robert H. Davis, *Historical Dictionary of Colombia*, 1977; José Manuel Groot, *Historia eclesiástica y civil de Nueva Granada*, 5 vols., 1953.

GOD, GLORY, AND GOLD. The phrase ''God, Glory, and Gold'' was a catchword used by Spanish conquistadors* in the sixteenth century to justify their drive for wealth and power in the New World. Those three words summarized the motivation behind early Spanish imperialism. The Spanish sincerely wanted to please God by exporting the Roman Catholic faith to the native inhabitants of Mexico*, Central America, South America, and the Philippines*; they wanted to bring adventure into their own lives, since so many of the conquistadors had been born to the grinding poverty of Extremadura, Spain; and they wanted to bring back bullion—gold and silver—to enrich themselves and the mother country.

REFERENCE: Charles Gibson, *Spain in America*, 1958.

GODOY, MANUEL DE. Manuel de Godoy was born in Castuera, Badajoz, Spain, in 1767. He was a sergeant in the royal guard and became the favorite of Queen María Luisa. In 1793, Godoy managed to displace the Count of Aranda*, assuming the office of prime minister for Charles IV*. He became a friend of the king and the lover of the queen, and he received many honors and titles among which was that of "Príncipe de la Paz" (Prince of Peace). Godoy's political role as prime minister was plagued with continuing disasters, including the French invasion of 1808 and the abdication of Charles IV in favor of Ferdinand VII*. Godoy was exiled to France during the reign of Ferdinand VII, and he lived in Paris, until he died there of old age in 1851.

REFERENCE: Jacques Chastenet, *Godoy: Master of Spain, 1792-1808*, 1953.

Fred Koestler

GOICO, PEDRO GERÓNIMO. Pedro Gerónimo Goico was born in Puerto Rico* in 1808. Of *criollo* descent, he came to resent the point of view of *peninsulares* and, inspired by the other successful colonial revolts in Latin America, Goico became an advocate of Puerto Rican independence from Spain. Spanish authorities arrested him for treason in 1866 and again in 1868. Goico was also an outspoken opponent of slavery*. He spent much of his career practicing and teaching medicine in San Juan*, and in 1870 he became president of the Partido Liberal Reformista. Pedro Goico died in 1890.

REFERENCE: Pedro de Angelis, *Misceláneas puertorriqueñas: Colección de artículos históricos-biográficos*, 1894.

GOICOECHEA, JOSÉ ANTONIO. José Antonio Goicoechea was born in Costa Rica* in 1735. He joined the Franciscan* order as a student and graduated from the University of San Carlos* in Guatemala* in 1767. Goicoechea spent his career teaching at the University of San Carlos and laboring as a missionary among the Indians* of Central America. At the university, he taught physics, astronomy, mathematics, and geography. His best known publications included *Acto público de teología dogmática* (1792), *Memoria sobre los medios de destruir la mendicidad* (1797), and *Relaciones sobre los indios gentiles de Pacura* (1799). Goicoechea died in 1814.

REFERENCE: Richard E. Moore, *Historical Dictionary of Guatemala*, 1973.

GOICURIA CABRERA, DOMINGO. Domingo Goicuria Cabrera was born in Havana* in 1804 and became a rich merchant in the city. He was an outspoken opponent of Spanish authority as well as a strong advocate of the continuation of slavery* in Cuba*. During the 1850s, he campaigned for an American annexation of Cuba, and in 1856, he assisted William Walker in the invasion of Nicaragua*, hoping that Cuba would be next. Goicuria continued his anti-Spanish activities throughout the 1860s, at the same time profiting by running supplies from Mexico* to Confederate forces during the Civil War in the United States. In 1870, Goicuria led an ill-fated invasion of Cuba, during which Spanish troops captured and executed him.
    REFERENCE: Jaime Suchlicki, *Historical Dictionary of Cuba*, 1988.

GOLD. See MINING.

GÓMARA, FRANCISCO LÓPEZ DE. See LÓPEZ DE GÓMARA, FRANCISCO.

GÓMEZ, JOSÉ MIGUEL. José Miguel Gómez was born in Sancti Spiritus, Las Villas Province, Cuba*, in 1858. He was just 12 years old when the Ten Years War* erupted in 1868, but he joined with rebel forces nonetheless. When that war came to an end in 1878, Gómez was part of the short-lived Guerra Chiquita* in 1879. During the independence wars between 1895 and 1898, Gómez rose to the rank of major general and was extraordinarily successful in his military leadership. As a member of the Liberal Party, Gómez served in the national legislature and as governor of Las Villas Province after the revolution; in 1908, he was elected president of Cuba. He had political problems with General Mario García Menocal* in 1913 and fled to the United States, where he died in 1921.
    REFERENCES: Gerardo Brown Castillo, *Cuba colonial*, 1952; Ramiro Guerra y Sánchez, *Historia de la nación cubana*, 10 vols., 1952; Jaime Suchlicki, *Historical Dictionary of Cuba*, 1988.

GÓMEZ, JUAN. Juan Gualberto Gómez was born in Matanzas, Cuba*, on July 12, 1854. He studied engineering in Paris but supported himself as a journalist; it was as a journalist that he found his real career interest. After traveling widely through the Caribbean and Latin America, Gómez became editor of *La Discusión* in Havana*. During the 1880s, Gómez lived in Madrid, where he worked for several newspapers, including *El Pueblo*, *El Progreso*, and *La Tribuna*. In Madrid, Gómez became a fervent abolitionist and a leader in the local abolitionist society. Gómez returned to Cuba when the revolution broke out in 1895, but Spanish authorities captured and deported him in 1897. After independence, Gómez came back to Havana, edited the newspaper *La Lucha*, and served several terms in the national legislature. Juan Gómez died in 1933.
    REFERENCES: Gerardo Brown Castillo, *Cuba colonial*, 1952; Ramiro Guerra y Sánchez, *Historia de la nación cubana*, 10 vols., 1952; Jaime Suchlicki, *Historical Dictionary of Cuba*, 1988.

GÓMEZ DE AVELLANEDA, GERTRUDIS. Gertrudis Gómez de Avellaneda was born in Camagüey, Cuba*, in 1814 to a Spanish father. Although she spent her youth in her homeland (her father was a *peninsular*), she spent virtually all of her adult life in Spain where she wrote and published her important works. Gómez was both a poet and a novelist, but it is the latter career for which she is most noted. Critics consider her to be Cuba's greatest romantic writer. Of her novels, two in particular merit attention. *Sab* (1841) is the first published abolitionist novel of Cuba. It deals with the love of a mulatto slave, Sab, for his slavemaster's daughter, Carlota, with whom Sab grew up in childhood. Carlota falls in love with someone else, and Sab steps aside. He then deals with his loss by committing suicide.

Many critics believe, however, that Gómez's greatest contribution to the Latin American novel is *Guatimozín* (1846). It deals with the Spaniards' conquest of Mexico*. The storyline begins with the arrival of Hernán Cortés* in the Aztec* capital and proceeds until the death of Cuauhtémoc, some three years later. Gómez includes historical events associated with Cortés's conquest that are rigorously accurate in detail. As a historical novel, *Guatimozín* is an exceptionally well written and finely structured work. The characters are drawn well; many critics point to the compassionate and compelling portrayal of Motecuhzoma*. Gómez de Avellaneda died in 1873.

REFERENCE: Juan J. Remos, *Proceso histórico de las Letras Cubanas*, 1958.

Sam L. Slick

GÓMEZ Y BAEZ, MÁXIMO. Máximo Gómez was born in Bani, Santo Domingo*, in 1836. He spent his early years fighting against Spanish authority, but in the civil war that devastated Santo Domingo in the 1860s, Gómez lost all of his possessions and fled to Cuba*, where he took up farming. He was no more comfortable with Spanish authority there than he had been in Santo Domingo. When the Ten Years War* began in 1868, Gómez joined up with Carlos Manuel de Céspedes* and quickly rose through the army ranks because of his leadership skills and his unmatched zeal for independence. Eventually he became secretary of war under Céspedes. Disappointed by the Pact of Zanjón* ending the Ten Years War in 1878, Gómez moved to Honduras*. He went to the United States in 1885 and became part of José Martí's* effort to organize a new war for independence in Cuba. Gómez returned to Cuba in 1895 when the war started. After the deaths of José Martí and Antonio Maceo*, he became the military and political leader of the revolutionary effort. When the war succeeded in 1898, Gómez decided not to become Cuba's first president, a position that was his for the asking. Instead, he went into retirement and died in 1905.

REFERENCES: Grover Flint, *Marching with Gómez*, 1898; Ramiro Guerra y Sanchez, *Historia de la Nación Cubana*, 1952.

GONZÁLEZ BALCARCE, ANTONIO. Antonio González Balcarce was born in Buenos Aires*, Río de la Plata*, in 1774. He accepted a military career under the leadership of his father and began his service with the Blandengües. During the British attack on the Río de la Plata* area in 1807, González was captured and imprisoned in London. He was released after a relatively short confinement and went to Spain to fight in the Spanish army against Napoleon's forces. González returned to Argentina* just after the May Revolution* of 1810 and assumed command of patriot forces in Córdoba* and Upper Peru*. He was the pivotal figure in the Argentine victory at Suipacha on November 7, 1810.

González eventually became chief of staff to José de San Martín* and participated in the battles of Cancha Rayada* and Maipú*. He died in 1819 after a short illness.

REFERENCE: Ricardo Levene, *Historia de la nación argentina (desde los orígenes hasta la organización definitiva en 1862)*, 10 vols., 1936–1942.

GONZÁLEZ BALCARCE, DIEGO. Diego González Balcarce was born in Buenos Aires*, Río de la Plata*, in 1784. He accepted a military career under the leadership of his father and began his service with the Blandengües. During the British attack on the Río de la Plata area in 1807, González was captured and imprisoned in London. He was released after a relatively short confinement and went to Spain to fight in the Spanish army against Napoleon's forces. He arrived in Buenos Aires shortly after the May Revolution* of 1810 and joined patriot forces. González accompanied Manuel Belgrano's* army into Paraguay* and Upper Peru (Bolivia*). Eventually he fought in the battles of Tucumán*, Salta*, Vilcapugio, Ayohuma*, and Sipe Sipe. He died in 1816 after a short illness.

REFERENCE: Ricardo Levene, *Historia de la nación argentina (desde los orígenes hasta la organización definitiva en 1862)*, 10 vols., 1936–1942.

GONZÁLEZ BALCARCE, JUAN RAMÓN. Juan Ramón González Balcarce was born in Buenos Aires*, Río de la Plata*, in 1773 and accepted a military career under the leadership of his father. He fought against the British invasion of the Río de la Plata area in 1806–1807, and after the May Revolution* of 1810, he joined patriot forces trying to overthrow the Spanish Empire. Eventually he teamed up with General Manuel Belgrano* and fought at the battle of Tucumán*. After the winning of independence, González held a variety of posts in the government, including governor of Buenos Aires in 1832. He died in Uruguay* in 1836 after being exiled there because of political disputes with Juan Manuel de Rosas*.

REFERENCE: Ricardo Levene, *Historia de la nación argentina (desde los orígenes hasta la organización definitiva en 1862)*, 10 vols., 1936–1942.

GONZÁLEZ BALCARCE, MARCOS. Marcos González Balcarce was born in Buenos Aires*, Río de la Plata*, in 1777. He accepted a military career under the leadership of his father and began his service with the Blandengües. During the British attack on the Río de la Plata area in 1807, González was captured and imprisoned in London. He was released after a relatively short confinement and he went to Spain to fight in the Spanish army against Napoleon's forces. He arrived in Buenos Aires shortly after the May Revolution[*] of 1810 and joined patriot forces. González served as governor of Cuyo and fought in Chile[*] in 1811 and 1812; he was secretary of war under Álvarez Tomás for a brief time. During the 1820s, González served in a variety of ministerial posts in the Argentine government. He died in 1832.

REFERENCE: Ricardo Levene, *Historia de la nación argentina (desde los orígenes hasta la organización definitiva en 1862)*, 10 vols., 1936–1942.

Virginia Garrard Burnett

GONZÁLEZ DÁVILA, GIL. A professional soldier, Gil González Dávila arrived in Panama[*] in 1519 following the execution of Vasco Núñez de Balboa[*] by Pedro Arias de Ávila[*] (Pedrarias) in 1517. Armed with a royal commission to continue the explorations of Balboa, González immediately found himself at odds with the rapacious Pedrarias, who sought control of the wealth and population of the southern part of the Central American isthmus for himself. After some delay, González set forth from Panama in 1522 to explore Costa Rica[*], hoping to find some of the legendary wealth that Christopher Colombus[*] had heard of from Indian[*] reports and that had caused him to christen Costa Rica with its somewhat inappropriate name. Finding only a modestly developed Indian population and no exploitable mineral resources in Costa Rica, González moved northwestward to Nicaragua[*]. Traveling as far north as Lake Nicaragua, González reportedly had priests baptize 32,000 of the Indians living around the lake before returning to Panama. He established no settlements.

González's successes in Nicaragua only heightened his rivalry with Pedrarias, and González was soon forced out to Santo Domingo[*]. He refused, however, to relinquish his claim on Nicaragua, prompting Pedrarias to order Francisco Hernández[*] de Córdoba to travel to Nicaragua in 1524 to conquer the country in Pedrarias's name. Hernández established the first Spanish settlements in Nicaragua, including Uturina (which failed after three years), Granada on Lake Nicaragua, and León[*] on Lake Meagua.

Hernández's incursions into Nicaragua spurred González to return to Central America. In 1524, he sailed from Santo Domingo to Honduras[*], bringing both the first European women and the first Africans to Central America. He marched south to Nicaragua that year and successfully defeated a contingent of Hernández's men. Hernández himself, however, retained an interest in the territory and forced González to retreat to Honduras. In 1525, Hernández rebelled against Pedrarias and attempted to establish an independent kingdom in Nicaragua, which would be ruled by neither González nor Pedrarias. Failing in this, Hernández was executed as a traitor by Pedrarias in 1526, who remained in León as governor of Nicaragua until his death in 1531. González never regained his claim to Nicaragua, but remained in Honduras.

REFERENCES: Hammond Innes, *The Conquistadors*, 1969; William H. Prescott, *The Conquest of Mexico*, 1936.

                                                    Virginia Garrard Burnett

GONZÁLEZ DE SANTA CRUZ, ROQUE. Roque González de Santa Cruz was born in Asunción*, Paraguay*, in 1576 and became a missionary priest in Paraguay. In 1609, González became vicar general of the diocese of Asunción*. In 1615, he founded Encarnación de Itapua on the Upper Paraná River, and he participated in exploration and missionary activities in Paraguay, Uruguay*, and Argentina*. González was a leading figure in the establishment of *reducciones* in the area of what is today Río Grande do Sul, Brazil. González was captured in 1628 and brutally killed by Indians* in Paraguay. Local mythology has it that his heart was cut out of him and, while it was still beating, was thrown into a fire. Some claim that it was recovered from the fire and is today a venerated religious relic in Paraguay.
    REFERENCE: H. T. Thurston, "The First Beatified Martyr of Spanish America," *Catholic Historical Review*, 20 (1934–1935), 371–83.

GORIBAR, NICOLÁS JAVIER DE. Nicolás Javier de Goribar was born in Quito*, Ecuador*. A gifted artist, Goribar studied painting under Miguel de Santiago* and is today remembered as one of the great seventeenth-century Latin American painters. Goribar is especially remembered for his portraits of the Old Testament prophets that are now displayed in the Compañía de Jesús church in Quito. Nicolás Javier de Goribar died in 1736.
    REFERENCE: Albert William Bork and Georg Maier, *Historical Dictionary of Ecuador*, 1973.

GOYENCHE, JOSÉ MANUEL. José Manuel Goyenche was born in 1775 to a politically influential family in Arequipa*, Peru*. He pursued a military career in Spain in the 1790s and early 1800s, but in 1808, he returned to Peru and the Río de la Plata* area, bringing news of the Napoleonic invasion of Spain. Goyenche remained in the New World for six years in command of royal forces. Brutally repressive, he concentrated on preventing Upper Peru (Bolivia*) from falling under the control of the revolutionary *junta* of Buenos Aires*. He was in command of the forces that lost a series of key battles to General Manuel Belgrano* at Tucumán* and Salta* in 1812 and 1813. Goyenche returned to Spain in 1814 and was promoted to lieutenant general. He died in 1846.
    REFERENCE: Ione S. Wright and Lisa M. Nekhom, *Historical Dictionary of Argentina*, 1978.

GOYENCHE Y BARREDA, PEDRO MARIANO. Pedro Mariano Goyenche y Barreda was born on February 22, 1772, in Arequipa*, Peru* to a politically influential family. He graduated from the University of San Marcos* in Lima* in 1792. The university awarded him a degree in canon law in 1793 and a doctorate in 1795. Goyenche began practicing law in 1798, and he was retained as an adviser to the Lima merchants' guild and the Royal Tribunal of Mining. Goyenche became an *oidor** to the *audiencia* of Cuzco* in 1806 and then an *oidor* to the *audiencia* of Lima* in 1813. Goyenche's brother, José Manuel Goyenche*, was a leading royalist military general in Peru, and his other brother, José Sebastián, was bishop of Arequipa between 1818 and 1858. After the revolution, Pedro Mariano Goyenche went to live in Spain. He died on November 30, 1844.

REFERENCE: Mark A. Burkholder and D. S. Chandler, *Biographical Dictionary of Audiencia Ministers in the Americas, 1687–1821*, 1982.

GRACIAS A DIOS. Gracias a Dios, Honduras*, was a settlement established by Pedro de Alvarado* in the 1530s as a gold-washing center. By 1540, Gracias shipped 5,000 pesos worth of gold to Spain, less than the neighboring settlements of San Pedro and Trujillo*, but enough to establish Gracias as an important Spanish outpost. In 1544, the Crown ordered that the new *audiencia* of Los Confines (Guatemala*), which had jurisdiction from Tabasco and Yucatán* to Panama*, be based in Gracias. Even as an administrative center, the town flourished only briefly, for rapid depletion of the region's alluvial gold and its isolated location quickly plunged the city into decline. In 1548, powerful interests in Guatemala and Panama pressured the crown to move the *audiencia* to Santiago (Guatemala), and Gracias a Dios faded from importance.

REFERENCE: Murdo J. MacLeod, *Spanish Central America: A Socioeconomic History, 1520–1720*, 1973.

Virginia Garrard Burnett

GRANADA. Granada, Nicaragua*, was founded by Francisco Hernández de Córdoba* in 1524 on the shore of Lake Nicaragua; it was one of the first Spanish settlements in Nicaragua. Its main inhabitants during its early years were the Indians* native to the lake area, who suffered grievously from disease and at the hands of Pedro Arias de Ávila* (Pedrarias), who became governor of Nicaragua in 1526. Granada was the site of the first Dominican* convent established by Bartolomé de las Casas* on behalf of the Indians' welfare around 1535. Although las Casas endeavored to persuade Spaniards by his preaching and teaching to treat their Indian charges with more humanity, his efforts were largely unsuccessful, and in 1536, las Casas abandoned Granada for Guatemala*.

Granada continued to survive, however, and by the mid-sixteenth century had become a semi-autonomous administrative center for the region. It had a thriving *encomendero* population and a powerful merchant class, who traded in cacao*, indigo*, cattle, and cochineal*. Granada became an entrepot for trade from all over Central America. Its location allowed goods to be shipped via the Desaguadero to Cartagena* and Portobelo, where the fleets were loaded for Spain. By the early seventeenth century, the cacao market had collapsed, precipitating a period of depression, although some merchants who had concentrated their efforts on the profitable indigo trade continued to flourish. By 1620, however, even the indigo trade had begun to decline, forcing the Spanish elite to leave Granada for the countryside; this trend was not as serious as that in Granada's rival, León*. The seventeenth-century depression forced Granada into new economic enterprises. There is some indication that during the middle years of the century, goods from China may have been illegally smuggled though Granada on their way to Cartagena or Portobelo. In 1670, Granada was attacked by English buccaneers, and its importance as a trading center diminished. Although the English did not remain in Granada long, the town never fully recovered the status it had enjoyed in the earlier years of the colonial period.

REFERENCES: R. L. Woodward, Jr., *Central America: A Nation Divided*, 1983; Murdo J. MacLeod, *Spanish Central America: A Socioeconomic History, 1520–1720*, 1973.

Virginia Garrard Burnett

GRAN COLOMBIA. The Republic of Colombia (later called Gran Colombia by historians to distinguish it from its smaller namesake) was the combination of Colombia*, Venezuela*, and Ecuador* that emerged from the independence struggle in 1819 and broke apart on the shoals of regionalism in 1829–1830. In 1819, the great liberator from Venezuela, Simón Bolívar*, led a campaign that freed the Andean highlands of New Granada* from the Spanish. He then proposed to the Congress of Angostura* the permanent union of Venezuela and New Granada. The Republic of Colombia was unanimously approved on December 17, 1818. It was divided into three departments; Venezuela, Quito* (Ecuador, which had not yet been liberated), and Cundinamarca (replacing the name New Granada), with Caracas*, Quito, and Bogotá* as capitals. The national capital was to be a new city called Bolívar. On the same day, Bolívar was unanimously elected president and Francisco Antonio Zea vice president. Francisco Santander* was selected vice-president for Cundinamarca and Juan Germán Roscio for Venezuela.

The congress of the republic met at Rosario de Cúcuta* from May 6 to October 14, 1821, and drew up a liberal, secular, and highly centralist constitution. Bolívar and Antonio Nariño* were major influences on the document. Bogotá was named the provisional capital. An ultimately unpopular provision broke the three component regions into smaller units responsible directly to the central government. Bolívar was elected president, but because of his military duties, he seldom filled the office. Rather, Santander, who was elected vice-president, ran the government, except for a brief period, until 1827 (the two leaders were re-elected in 1826). Santander proved an able administrator and advanced the liberal reforms begun at Cúcuta. The rule of law returned, and government took on a more republican character than the earlier de facto militarized rule. International recognition was obtained (from the United States in 1822). By 1825, however, with the expulsion of the Spanish, nationalist sentiments caused increasing disunity. Santander came increasingly into conflict with the nationalist leaders of Venezuela, notably José Páez*, and eventually clashed with Bolívar.

During the time of Gran Colombia, the patriots of Venezuela finally drove the Spanish forces from their soil, the last major battle being Bolívar's victory at Carabobo* on June 21, 1821. Thinly populated Venezuela, however, had suffered great economic loss and social disorganization as a consequence of the wars. As the best organized element of the society, the military came to predominate, and their spokesman, General Páez, emerged as the most powerful Venezuelan leader. In 1826, he revolted against the administration of Santander and the dominance of Cundinamarca under the centralized government. Bolívar returned to Venezuela and reclaimed Páez's allegiance, but in November and December 1829, Páez led a successful secessionist movement against Colombia and Bolívar. In 1830, Venezuela left the Republic of Colombia and formed its own government.

The critical victory in the liberation of Ecuador from the Spanish was the Battle of Pichincha*, won by the Venezuelan general Antonio José de Sucre* on May 24, 1822. Bolívar then entered Quito, and on July 13, Guayaquil* was formally incorporated into Gran Colombia. A combination of civilian and military elites maintained control of the largely indigenous population of Ecuador. The smallest and weakest part of the union, Ecuador had the most real grievances. In addition to its economic disadvantages, its top officials came from elsewhere and it contributed no national cabinet members or generals. Nationalist tendencies eventually led to secession on May 13, 1830, under the leadership of General Juan José Flores* (himself a Venezuelan).

Cundinamarca suffered much less destruction than Venezuela had; it continued to enjoy greater wealth and prosperity. Its larger population was much less militarized and its social organization less disrupted. As a consequence, it provided most of the high civilian leaders of the central government, while Venezuela provided most of the military leaders throughout the union. Cundinamarca had largely expelled the royalist forces and established order by 1824. It experienced a renaissance during the middle of the 1820s. The Isthmus of Panama* declared its independence from Spain and incorporated itself into Colombia on November 28, 1821.

In addition to the growing regional discontent with the centralized government in Bogotá, there emerged dissatisfaction with Bolívar and a rift between him and Santander. In September 1827, Bolívar took control of the national administration but was unable to prevent the gradual dissolution of the nation. In 1828, the convention of Ocaña deadlocked between Bolívar's plans for a stronger executive and Santander's efforts to create a federal regime. Bolívar then established a dictatorship and carried out a conservative reaction against many of the liberal reforms of the Cúcuta congress. The year 1828 also saw a war between Colombia and Peru* and the exile of Santander under a cloud of suspicion following an attempt on Bolívar's life. In January 1830, the *Congreso Admirable* crafted a new constitution in an attempt to save the union, but it came too late. It was accepted only in New Granada. On March 1, a sickly Bolívar stepped down from the exercise of power. There followed a period of disorder within

New Granada, involving military revolts and the succession and reintegration of several regions. On February 29, 1832, the constitution of the Republic of New Granada, encompassing present-day Colombia and Panama, was adopted. The dissolution of Gran Colombia was accomplished without the clash of national armies, although there was military conflict in southern areas of New Granada that attempted to secede.

REFERENCES: David Bushnell, *The Santander Regime in Gran Colombia*, 1954; Jesús María Henao and Gerardo Arrubla, *History of Colombia*, 1938; Salvador de Madariaga, *Bolívar*, 1952; Gerhard Masur, *Simón Bolívar*, 1969; Guillermo Moron, *A History of Venezuela*, 1963.

Robert E. Biles

GRAND CANARY. Grand Canary in the Canary Islands* was first settled by Spaniards in 1480, when the first governor was appointed, although the governor at Tenerife* supervised him. Each of the Canary Islands was governed separately throughout the 1500s. Because of attacks by British and French forces, a captaincy general for the Canary Islands was established in 1589; it was suppressed in 1594 and then revived in 1625, with the seat of the captaincy general on Grand Canary.

GREEN MARCH. The "Green March" refers to the migration of 350,000 Moroccan civilians into Western Sahara in November 1975. On October 16, 1975, the International Court of Justice upheld the principle of self-determination in the region, to which Spain had already agreed to extend independence. But Morocco and Mauritania both laid claim to the territory, in spite of the demands of Saharawi nationalists for independence. King Hassan II of Morocco ordered the civilians to march into Western Sahara as a way of establishing his claim to the region. The Polisario Front* denounced the migration, but it demonstrated to Spain the power of Morocco in the region and led to the Madrid Agreement* of November 1975, in which Spain agreed to the division of Western Sahara between Morocco and Mauritania.

REFERENCE: Tony Hodges, *Historical Dictionary of Western Sahara*, 1982.

GRIJALVA, JUAN DE. The nephew of the governor of Cuba*, Diego Velázquez*, Juan de Grijalva was born in Cuellar, Segovia, Spain in 1489. He was named by his uncle to be commander-in-chief of the second Spanish expedition to explore Mexico*. On April 8, 1518, Grijalva sailed with four ships and 200 men to investigate the findings that Francisco Hernández* de Córdoba had made on his ill-fated voyage to Yucatán* in 1517. Grijalva sailed up the Gulf side of the Yucatán peninsula, landing at Champotón (Tabasco), where the Spanish engaged the native Maya* in battle. Continuing on, Grijalva sailed along the coast to present-day Veracruz, Mexico, trading European goods with the natives for small gold pieces and finely woven cotton cloth along the way. After five months, having traveled as far up the Mexican coast as Panuco, Grijalva returned to Santiago de Cuba. Although

Grijalva was derided in Cuba by Velázquez for not having returned with more worthwhile goods, his voyage nonetheless produced enormously valuable intelligence for the Spaniards. First, the expedition demonstrated that Mexico was not an island, as had been previously thought. Second, Grijalva and his men brought back Indian* reports of a wealthy kingdom in the interior ruled by the "Lord of Culhua," one of the honorific titles of the Aztec* emperor Motecuhzoma*. Grijalva's voyage paved the way for the expedition of Hernán Cortés* in 1519. He died in 1527.

REFERENCES: John A. Caruso, *The Liberators of Mexico*, 1967; Henry R. Wagner, *The Discovery of New Spain in 1518 by Juan de Grijalva*, 1969.

Virginia Garrard Burnett

GRITO DE DOLORES. The "Grito de Dolores" refers to Miguel Hidalgo y Castillo's* proclamation of Mexican independence on September 16, 1810, at the village of Dolores, near Querétaro, Mexico.

REFERENCES: Jan Bazant, *A Concise History of Mexico from Hidalgo to Cárdenas*, 1977; Hugh M. Hamill, *The Hidalgo Revolt: Prelude to Mexican Independence*, 1966.

GRITO DE LARES. The "Grito de Lares" was a proclamation of independence issued by a number of Puerto Rican leaders in the town of Lares on September 23, 1868. Manuel Rojas, Joaquín Parilla, and Francisco Ramírez led a group of approximately 400 advocates of independence. They hoped to inspire an uprising throughout the island against Spanish rule, but the revolt never took place. Ramón Betances*, a key leader, was not in Puerto Rico* at the time; there was little publicity in other parts of Puerto Rico, and Spanish authorities got wind of the rebellion from spies. They crushed the rebellion, but it became a key date in the history of the Puerto Rican independence movement.

REFERENCE: Kenneth R. Farr, *Historical Dictionary of Puerto Rico and the U.S. Virgin Islands*, 1973.

GUADALAJARA. Guadalajara was founded in 1530 by order of Nuño de Guzmán*. In the beginning, it was called Espíritu Santo and served throughout the colonial period as the capital city of the province of New Galicia* in New Spain*. Guadalajara was also the headquarters for all the expeditions heading north into the Borderlands* during the colonial period. SEE NEW GALICIA AND NEW SPAIN.

GUADALAJARA, DIOCESE OF. The Roman Catholic diocese of Guadalajara*, New Spain*, was established in 1548, more than a decade after the conquest expeditions of Nuño de Guzmán*. At first, it was located at Compostela and called the Diocese of Compostela in the Indies. Pedro Gómez Maraver served as the first bishop. In 1560, the location of the see and of the *audiencia* of New Galicia* was transferred to Guadalajara. The diocese of Guadalajara covered an immense territory, stretching to the Pacific Ocean and from Colima north into the Borderlands* of what is today the United States. The diocese was raised to an archdiocese in 1863.

REFERENCE: *New Catholic Encyclopedia*, VI:820, 1967.

GUADALUPE, VIRGIN OF. In 1531, only a dozen years after Hernán Cortés's* defeat of the mighty Aztec* nation, Juan Diego, one of the earliest Indians* to convert to Christianity, was walking to the village of Tlatelolco (now part of Mexico City*) when he heard a female voice speaking in his native Nahuatl* (Aztec) tongue. Startled, he looked to the top of the hill of Tepéyac, which had once been the Shrine of Tonantzín, the Corn Goddess of the Aztecs. There he saw a bright light, but on close examination, it was a dark-skinned girl in her early teens. The girl seemed to stand in a golden mist and wore a blue robe. "Juanito," she said, "the most humble of my sons, where are you going?" Juan explained that he was on his way to mass. The mysterious lady then said, "Know then, I am the ever Virgin, Holy Mother of the True God. I wish that a temple be erected here without delay. Go to the Bishop's Palace in Mexico City and tell him what I desire."

After two failures to convince Bishop Juan de Zumárraga*, Juan Diego informed the "dark virgin" that he was a poor messenger, since his lowly status made it difficult for the bishop to believe his story. The Holy Mother promised she would provide the necessary proof. She instructed him to climb to the top of the hill and he would find blooming roses, in mid-winter, which he should pick and take to the bishop in a cape as a sign that he was telling the truth. He did so and was admitted to the bishop as soon as it was discovered that he had roses in mid-winter. The bishop was impressed but still not sure that this sign was enough, for roses could be grown in hot houses even at that time of year. Zumárraga opened Juan's cape, then fell to the floor of the palace in prayer, for painted on the cape was a brightly colored portrait of the Virgin Mary. That very morning, the bishop went with Juan to the hillside to be shown where the Holy Mother desired her church to be built. The image is painted on a coarse-woven cloth of cactus fiber. The original image is of the Virgin Mary, but a cherub, moon, stars, and other items have been added at a later date. At the present time, the added features have become dull and lifeless, cracked and flaking, but the original image remains as bright and vibrant as the date it was first shown to Bishop Zumárraga. The miracle of the Virgin of Guadalupe has had enormous religious and cultural significance. Her shrine is built at the site where the goddess Tonantzín, the mother of gods, had been worshipped by the Aztecs. The Virgin's image, as a dark-skinned, dark-eyed maiden, and the symbolism appearing on her cloak and at her feet all had deep significance for the conquered people. The Virgin of Guadalupe would remain a potent symbol of Mexican culture well beyond the colonial period.

REFERENCES: George Agogino, "The Guadalupe Madonna," *Pursuit*, 20 (1987) 127–28; Donald Demarest and Coley B. Taylor, *The Dark Virgin: The Book of Our Lady of Guadalupe*, 1956.

George A. Agogino

GUADELOUPE. Guadeloupe is an overseas department of France, complete with representation in the French national legislature. One of the Lesser Antilles in the West Indies, Guadeloupe is composed of Basse-Terre, a 35-mile-long island also known as Guadeloupe, and Grand Terre, an island just across a narrow channel from Basse-Terre. Together they total 583 square miles. Christopher Columbus* discovered Guadeloupe and most of its constituent islands during his second voyage to the New World in 1493, but because of the hostility of the native Karib* Indians, the Spaniards did little to develop the island. Instead they invested their military and economic resources in conquering Cuba*, Hispaniola*, Mexico*, and Peru*. It was not until 1635 that Europe showed real interest in Guadeloupe, when France established a colony there. Twelve years later, in 1647, the French constructed their first sugar* mill in Guadeloupe and began importing African slaves to work the plantations. By the middle of the eighteenth century, Guadeloupe had become the crown jewel in the French overseas empire, the world's leading producer of sugar.

REFERENCE: Herbert Ingram Priestley, *France Overseas: A Study of Modern Imperialism*, 1966.

GUAM. Guam is an island in the South Pacific, the southernmost of the Mariana* group. It is 30 miles long and averages about 7 miles in width. Guam has little intrinsic economic significance, but its location, 1,400 miles east of the San Bernardino Strait, the entrance to Philippine* waters, made it an excellent stopping point for the westward run of the Manila galleon*. At Guam, ships took on fresh water and fruit.

The natives of Guam were Chamorros, Malay by language and blood but with customs that had evolved in some unique ways due to their isolation. For example, although their navigational skills were impressive and their woodcarving sophisticated, they went naked. As in the pre-Spanish Philippines, no wider political unit than the autonomous village existed. Rank and class were fundamental in their society. Population estimates are unreliable, but it is certain that many Chamorros were killed in battle by Spaniards, and many more died from diseases, especially smallpox, to which they had no immunity. Today there are no pureblooded Chamorros; Guamanians are a mixture of Chamorro, Spanish, and Filipino.

Relations between Spaniards and Chamorros got off to a terrible start. Ferdinand Magellan* (1521) killed seven men and burnt native houses in reprisal for the theft of one of his boats. He left in a pique, bestowing the name Ladrones (Isles of Thieves) on the group of islands now called the Marianas. Later visitors also clashed with the Chamorros. Juan Garcia Jofre de Loaysa (1525) kidnapped eleven. Miguel de Legazpi[*] (1565) retaliated for the murder of a cabin-boy by hanging three natives, wounding others, and burning houses, but he formally claimed the islands for Spain.

The next century and a half are considered a time of obscurity in Guamanian history. Spanish contact was only intermittent. Guam was occasionally visited by Dutch and English ships, including Sir Francis Drake's[*] *Golden Hind*. This hiatus came to a horrible end after 1668 when, by royal order, all westbound galleons had to stop at Guam. Spaniards forced Chamorros to convert to Catholicism. An uprising in 1670 was followed by a generation of warfare and cruel reprisals from Spanish governors, the worst of whom was Don José de Quiroga. By the end of the seventeenth century, native society had been nearly destroyed.

Spanish administration was initially in the hands of priests (first Jesuits[*] and later Augustinians[*]), and then through the governor general of the Philippines and the viceroy of New Spain[*]. The same administrative structure that applied to the Philippines was imposed, on a smaller scale, on Guam. Socially, a property-owning mestizo[*] elite maintained its distance from commoners. When Spanish power waned in the nineteenth century, Guam was all but forgotten, visited only by occasional American whaling vessels. In 1898, when the Spanish-American War[*] commenced, President William McKinley sent the cruiser *Charleston*, under Captain Henry Glass, to seize Guam. Glass arrived in June and found to his delight that not only was Guam undefended but that the Spaniards there did not even know there was a war and thought the Americans were only paying a courtesy call. Spain ceded Guam to the United States in the Treaty of Paris[*] of 1898.

REFERENCE: Paul Carano and Pedro Sánchez, *A Complete History of Guam*, 1964.

Ross Marlay

GUANAJUATO. The region of Guanajuato in central Mexico[*] was organized into an intendancy within the viceroyalty of New Spain[*] in 1787. It remained an intendancy until 1821, when it became a state in the new republic of Mexico.

GUANCHE. The Guanche were the native inhabitants of the Canary Islands[*].

GUARANÍ. Guaraní is an Indian[*] language spoken today by more than 2,500,000 people in Bolivia[*], Paraguay[*], northern Argentina[*], and southern Brazil. Because of its physical isolation from primary trade routes in South America and its lack of attractive resources, Paraguay did not attract massive settlement, and instead of replacing Guaraní, the Spanish language co-existed with it. The entire population of Paraguay is bilingual, in Spanish and Guaraní, although Spanish tends to be the language of business and government, while Guaraní is the private language of friends and family. Another 1,000 people of Indian descent who speak Guaraní live in Argentina. Still another 14,000 Brazilian Indians—Kaiwa, Mbua (Mbia), and Nhandeva (Nandeva)—speak Guaraní. They are widely dispersed throughout a variety of government Indian parks in southern Brazil.

When the Spaniards first encountered the Guaraní in eastern Argentina in the early 1500s, the Indians lived in town systems of communal houses and practiced slash-and-burn agriculture. Many Guaraní had migrated into Bolivia before the arrival of the Spanish; there they reached the outskirts of the Inca* Empire. Attracted by Incan wealth, the Guaraní welcomed the Spaniards as potential allies in securing some of the riches of Incan civilization. After the establishment of Asunción* in 1537, the Guaraní worked as warriors and porters for Spanish expeditions. In Paraguay and northern Argentina, Guaraní and Spanish civilization produced a mestizo* culture. The society was bilingual in Spanish and Guaraní. Those Guaraní who did not adapt to mestizo culture in the towns were gathered by Jesuits* into the mission system, where they converted to Roman Catholicism and European agricultural patterns.

REFERENCES: Moisés Santiago Bertoni, *La civilización Guaraní*, 1956; Philip Caraman, *The Lost Paradise: The Jesuit Republics in South America*, 1976; Isabel Hernández, "Los pueblos y las lenguas aborígenes en la actualidad," *América Indígena*, 47 (1987), 409–23; Arthur P. Sorenson, Jr., "South American Indian Linguistics at the Turn of the Seventies," in Daniel R. Gross, ed., *Peoples and Cultures of Native South America*, 1973; Robert Lee Spires, "As Linguas Faladas do Brasil," *América Indígena*, 47 (1987), 455–79.

GUARANÍ WAR. The Guaraní War, also known as the War of the Seven Reductions, took place between 1753 and 1766. The Jesuits* had converted large numbers of Guaraní* Indians and then assembled them on the *reducciones** (reductions) along the Paraguay River. The Jesuit communities developed a high degree of commercial success and political stability, and the Portuguese began to see these as extensions of the Spanish Empire. The Guaraní, who were frequently attacked by Portuguese slavers and other Indian tribes, were given permission by Spain to raise their own militias, which only threatened the Portuguese in southern Brazil even more. When Portugal established its Nova Colonia do Sacramento settlement in 1680, Spain attacked it frequently, often with the help of the Guaraní militia. With the Treaty of Madrid* of 1750, Portugal agreed to cede the Sacramento colony to Spain; in return, Spain agreed to give Portugal the land that included the Guaraní *reducciones* of the Jesuits. The Guaraní refused to accept the agreement and would not evacuate their homelands, as the Portuguese requested. In 1754, a combined force of 2,000 Spanish and 1,000 Portuguese troops attacked the Guaraní reductions. At the Battle of Caibate on February 10, 1756, the Europeans slaughtered more than 1,500 Guaraní troops, losing only five soldiers of their own. After that, serious Guaraní resistance was over.

REFERENCE: Philip Caraman, *Lost Paradise: The Jesuit Republics in South America*, 1976.

GUATEMALA. Originally, Guatemala, once the seat of the captaincy general of Guatemala* under the jurisdiction of the viceroyalty of New Spain*, included not only the present Guatemala but also the Central American nations of Costa Rica*, Nicaragua*, Honduras*, El Salvador*, the present-day Mexican state of Chiapas*, and British Honduras*. On December 6, 1523, Pedro de Alvarado* left New Spain on an overland expedition to Central America to meet up with a sea expedition sent by Hernán Cortés* to Honduras. This expedition consolidated Spanish control over Guatemala and made it a part of the Spanish Empire. The Guatemalan Maya* population that Alvarado encountered on his journey was decimated by smallpox and was undergoing a factional struggle between two kingdoms, the Cakchiquel and Quiché. Alvarado allied himself with the Cakchiquel against the Quiché and their allies, the Tzutzuhil. On July 25, 1524, after the Quichés' defeat, he established the first Guatemala City at Iximche, the Cakchiquel capital. The region's conquest continued as various Indian revolts sprang up. Spanish demands caused even their former allies to revolt. The region's pacification continued throughout the colonial period.

Guatemala City* was moved various times throughout the colonial period. On November 22, 1527, Jorge de Alvarado, Pedro's brother, moved the city to Almolonga (now Ciudad Vieja, Guatemala). Pedro went to Spain in 1527 to petition the Crown for the title of *adelantado**. As Governor Pedro de Alvarado, he used Guatemala as a base for further expeditions because of the area's paucity of precious metals. When Pedro lost his life, his widow Doña Beatriz de la Cueva Alvarado*, became governor but lost her life two days after taking command, on September 10, 1541, when an earthquake destroyed Santiago de Guatemala.* The city was moved to Panchoy (now Antigua, Guatemala) in November 1541.

During this early phase, many struggles erupted between the various conquistadors, sent by different authorities, who converged on the region. The establishment of the *audiencia* de los Confines* in Honduras on May 16, 1544, attempted to remedy this administrative confusion and give the isthmus political unity. The *audiencia*'s* removal to Santiago de Guatemala in 1549 showed the city's growing importance. The *audiencia* de los Confines was dissolved between 1564–1570 and moved to Panama*; it had jurisdiction over Panama, Costa Rica, and Nicaragua. Isthmian unity shattered as the rest of Central America came under the jurisdiction of the *audiencia* of New Spain. In March 1570, the *audiencia* of Guatemala was re-established in Santiago de Guatemala. The *audiencia*, presided over by the president who also served as governor and captain general, had political and administrative jurisdiction over Central America from Chiapas through Costa Rica. The viceroyalty of New Spain* had jurisdiction over the kingdom, but its authorities were chosen directly from Spain. The kingdom of Guatemala remained unified until the end of the colonial period.

The region's lack of precious metals made Indian* labor an important commodity, and *encomiendas** (grants of Indian labor and tribute to an individual), were given to the region's *conquistadors* by the Crown. The exploitation of

Indian labor for the burgeoning economy of agricultural exports, initially cacao*
and indigo*, led to many abuses. Indigo, a blue dye, survived throughout the
colonial period as an important export commodity, but declined at the beginning
of the nineteenth century. To gain control over the *encomienda* and stop abuses,
the Crown promulgated the New Laws* of 1542. These gave the *encomienda*
grant for two generations only, not in perpetuity. The New Laws legislated a
system of forced labor, the *repartimiento**, whereby individuals could petition
crown officials to procure an allotment of Indian laborers to work in mines, on
agricultural lands, or on public projects. The *encomienda* declined as a labor
institution with the Indian population decline and Spanish population increase,
but the *repartimiento* continued up to and through the eighteenth century.

The sixteenth and seventeenth centuries saw the expansion and contraction of
Guatemala's economy. There were almost 100 years of economic depression
from about 1570 to the 1660s. The Indian population decline, responsible for
much of this depression, contributed to the Spaniards' move from towns to rural
areas as land became available. They acquired title to empty village lands and
drifted into self-subsistence. The kingdom's unity fragmented as internal trade
diminished. English piracy* ravaged the kingdom's coasts. Cultural and biological miscegenation produced the *ladino*; that is, a mixture of Spanish and Indian
blood or an hispanicized Indian. Throughout the colonial period, the antagonism
between *criollos** (New World-born Spaniards) and *peninsulares** (European
Spaniards) increased. The *criollo*, condemned to minor governmental positions
like *corregidor** to ensure his livelihood, could not expect a major colonial post.
The *corregidor* represented the Crown in the Indian villages and often subjected
them to many abuses, leading to resentment and open defiance of this official.
Many Indian revolts occurred throughout the eighteenth and early nineteenth
centuries over village lands as the Indian population again increased.

In the eighteenth century, the replacement of the Habsburg rulers in Spain by
the Bourbons heightened these antagonisms. This change had a profound effect
on the Spanish Empire in general and on the kingdom of Guatemala in particular,
as reforms for modernization encroached on the Indian's and *criollo*'s traditional
life. The Church, which played a profound role in the region's colonization and
administration, was also affected by this trend. The establishment of the University of San Carlos in 1681 portended profound changes as the kingdom's
importance grew within the imperial system. In 1729, the first Guatemalan
newspaper*, the *Gazeta de Goathemala*, appeared, and a mint was established
in 1733. In 1742, Guatemala was elevated to archdiocese status with jurisdiction
over Chiapas, Honduras, and Nicaragua. The British effectively colonized parts
of the kingdom along the Caribbean coast with the help of Miskito* Indians. In
1767, the Jesuits* were expelled from Guatemala. A major burden for the colony
was relocating the city after an earthquake devastated Santiago de Guatemala
on July 29, 1773; the new city was founded on January 1, 1776. The intendant
system's introduction in 1786 infringed on the *audiencia*'s central authority as
intendants were set up in Honduras, El Salvador, Nicaragua, and Chiapas to

maintain closer supervision. The new system also contributed to later fragmentation after independence. A merchants' guild was established in 1794 to encourage the economic development of the kingdom. An Economic Society was formed in 1795 to spread Enlightenment* thought throughout the elite members of the society.

In the early nineteenth century, indigo's decline and Spain's European wars led to Guatemala's economic decline and contributed to the desire for economic and political independence of many *criollos*. Napoleon's invasion of Spain in 1808 increased this desire. The appointment of a new captain general, José Bustamante y Guerra*, who perceived the *criollos* as responsible for the general agitation in the kingdom, led to harsh rule in the kingdom between 1811 and 1818. Guatemalan *criollos* participated in the efforts of the Cortes de Cadiz* to create a constitutional monarchy in 1812. The Spanish-American independence movements influenced the *criollos*, and numerous revolts, such as the 1813 Belén conspiracy in Guatemala, occurred. The Constitution of 1812* was annulled with Ferdinand VII's* return to the Spanish throne in 1814. The constitutional regime's return in 1820 did not prevent Guatemala's declaration of independence on September 15, 1821.

REFERENCES: Ralph Lee Woodward, Jr., *Central America: A Nation Divided*, 1976; J.A. Villacorta Calderón, *Historia de la Capitanía General de Guatemala*, 1942; Jim Handy, *A Gift of the Devil*, 1984.

Carlos Pérez

GUATEMALA, *AUDIENCIA* OF. The *audiencia* of Guatemala grew out of the *audiencia* of Los Confines* that was established by the celebrated New Laws* of November 20, 1542. First located in early 1544 in the town of Gracias a Dios* on the northeastern coast of what is now Honduras*, its jurisdiction covered the territory of all the present Central American republics, as well as the Isthmus of Panama* or Castilla de Oro*, and the provinces of Chiapas* and Yucatán* that now belong to Mexico. For several decades, both the residence and the geographic jurisdiction of this new tribunal—called the *audiencia* de los Confines because it was first set up on what was called the border of Guatemala* and Nicaragua* without a definite location—remained uncertain. In 1550, Panama was separated from Central America and joined to the *audiencia* of Lima* in Peru*; it was made part of the viceroyalty of Peru* but with an *audiencia* of its own. The residence of the Central American *audiencia* itself was moved to Santiago de los Caballeros de Guatemala (now Antigua) and then to Panama in 1564, with a jurisdiction that included El Salvador*, Honduras, Nicaragua, Costa Rica*, and the Pacific Coast of New Granada*, now part of Colombia*. Guatemala and Chiapas were temporarily annexed to New Spain* at the same time. Within five years, in 1570, the *audiencia* was moved back to Guatemala City*, where it remained until the end of Spanish rule in 1821.

Apparently in the beginning, the president of the *audiencia* of Guatemala was not given the powers of a governor. In other words, the executive authority was placed in a commission, in the hands of the whole board of judges, as in the first *audiencia* of New Spain*. But in September 1560, President Juan Núñez de Landecho was named sole governor with all the powers of the viceroy* in Mexico City*. This event evidently marks the beginning of the captaincy general of Guatemala*.

Difficulties of transportation through the mountains and jungles between Mexico City and the Central American provinces made effective communication and consultation slow and unsatisfactory. In addition, some parts of the isthmus were never truly occupied and controlled by the Spaniards, such as the Caribbean coastal regions now occupied by the nation of Belize*, the Bay Islands of Honduras, and the Mosquitia* region of northeast Honduras and eastern Nicaragua. It is therefore not surprising that Phillip II* of Spain felt impelled to set up a local executive in Guatemala with authority virtually independent of Mexico City and directly responsible to the Crown. The *audiencia* de Guatemala was often called a *reino* or kingdom, suggesting the real autonomy that it enjoyed even though the region was technically part of the viceroyalty of New Spain and governed from Mexico City. The president of the *audiencia*, who throughout most of the period also held the title of governor and captain general, was in reality the personal representative of the king of Spain.

The first six presidents of the *audiencia* de Guatemala, from 1570 to 1611, were appointed by King Phillip II. They were true civil servants, well educated in the law in Spain, with considerable judicial experience in the New World before coming to Central America. The appointees of Philip III* and Philip IV*, holding the office from 1611 to 1668, were often men who came directly from Spain and whose education mattered less than did their influence at the royal court. The sacking of Granada*, Nicaragua, by English freebooters in 1665 and 1670, followed by other depredations and the crossing of the isthmus by the English pirate Henry Morgan in the 1680s, led to the appointment of military men to this position, although both of the earlier types reappeared from time to time. The replacement of the Habsburg family of Philip II by Spanish Bourbons made little difference at first. Once British influence along the Caribbean coast increased in the mid-eighteenth century, however, all appointees after 1752 were men of high rank in the Spanish army or navy. Real warfare took place with the British during the term of Matías de Gálvez (1779–1783). Eventually, older semi-retired military officers, such as José Tomás y Valle (1794–1801), who took office at age 93, were considered adequate to fill the post.

REFERENCES: Franklin Parker, *The Central American Republics*, 1964; C. H. Haring, *The Spanish Empire in America*, 1947.

Neale J. Pearson

GUATEMALA, CAPTAINCY GENERAL OF. While Pedro de Alvarado* had been appointed captain general and governor of the kingdom of Guatemala by Charles V* in 1527, no formal government, be it an *audiencia* or captaincy general, was created until 1542. In that year, an *audiencia* was created for Central

America but its president was not given the powers of governor. Executive power was placed in the hands of the board of four judges (*oidores**) and the president, as in the first *audiencia* of New Spain*. In September 1560, however, after its jurisdiction and residence had been moved several times, President Juan Nunez de Landecho was named sole governor with all the powers of the viceroy* in Mexico City*. This evidently marks the beginning of the captaincy general of Guatemala. Its jurisdiction included El Salvador*, Honduras*, Nicaragua*, Costa Rica*, Panama*, and the Pacific Coast of New Granada*, which is now part of Colombia*. In 1564, Guatemala* and Chiapas* were temporarily annexed to New Spain with the other nations put under the jurisdiction of the *audiencia* of Panama*. In 1570, however, the *audiencia* was moved back to Guatemala City* where it remained until the end of Spanish rule in 1821.

Some parts of the isthmus that were theoretically under the jurisdiction of the *Audiencia* of Guatemala were never truly occupied or controlled by the Spaniards, such as the northeastern lowlands of the Petén, much of the territory now occupied by Belize*, the Bay Islands of Honduras, and the Mosquitia* regions of northeastern Honduras and eastern Nicaragua. A group of British buccaneers, seeking refuge from Caribbean storms and profit from cutting tropical hardwoods such as mahogany, established a trading post at the mouth of the Belize River in about 1540; in 1678, the British assumed a quasi-protectorate over the Miskito* Indians on the Caribbean Coasts of Honduras and Nicaragua.

REFERENCES: Vera Kelsey and Lilly de Jong Osborne, *Four Keys to Guatemala*, 1919; Franklin Parker, *The Central American Republics*, 1964; C. H. Haring, *The Spanish Empire in America*, 1947.

Neale J. Pearson

GUATEMALA CITY. The third and present capital of Guatemala*, Guatemala City is located in the Valley of La Hermita. The first capital was what is now known as Ciudad Vieja and was founded by the conqueror of Guatemala, Pedro de Alvarado*. Ciudad Vieja was destroyed by a massive earthquake and flood on September 10, 1541. The capital was then relocated to a site in the Pachoy Valley at the foot of the Agua Volcano, now known as Antigua, Guatemala. In 1773, Antigua was also destroyed by an earthquake, and the capital was moved to its present location. The relocation of the capital provoked a bitter controversy in colonial society. The poor majority of the population, the old landed interests, and the clergy all opposed the move, while the new merchant elite, who had made their money in commerce and trade due to expanded trade regulations, and the Bourbon officials favored the new location. In July 1775, after the Crown issued a royal *cédula* commanding relocation, opposition to the move degenerated into open rebellion. Only government officials, Indian laborers bound by *repartimiento,** and the elite merchant class, soon to be the new aristocracy of the capital, moved to the new location. The archbishop of Guatemala, leading the opposition, excommunicated the *audiencia** when they tried to force the move. In 1799, the archbishop was ordered back to Spain. Ultimately, the conflict was resolved when the outbreak of the American Revolution[*] persuaded Spain to compromise, allowing those who wished to remain in Antigua to do so. The controversy over the relocation of the capital illustrated the growing fissure between the traditional landed and clerical elite of traditional Habsburg Guatemala and the new merchant aristocracy that had emerged from the Bourbon economic reforms. The removal of the capital was a victory for the new elite, and Nueva Guatemala became a thriving commercial center, enjoying a direct trade with Spain through the Bay of Honduras for the rest of the colonial period.

REFERENCE: Miles L. Wortman, *Government and Society in Central America, 1680-1840*, New York, 1982.

Virginia Garrard Burnett

GUATEMALA, KINGDOM OF. See GUATEMALA, or GUATEMALA, *AUDIENCIA* OF, or GUATEMALA, CAPTAINCY GENERAL OF.

GUAYANA. Spain established the province of Guayana in eastern Venezuela[*] in 1591. It included the neighboring island of Trinidad.[*] The colony was subordinate to New Granada[*] administratively. In 1735, Spain separated Trinidad as a colony in its own right and dissolved Guayana administratively, placing it under the authority of New Andalucia[*], its contiguous neighbor. In 1766, the Spanish Crown transferred Guayana to the captaincy general of Venezuela[*]. Spanish authority survived there until 1817 when rebel forces occupied the region. After the wars of independence, Guayana became part of Gran Colombia[*] and then Venezuela.

GUAYAQUIL. Today Guayaquil is the largest city in Ecuador[*]. It was founded by Sebastián de Benalcázar[*] in 1531, destroyed by Indians[*] shortly thereafter, and then rebuilt by Francisco de Orellana[*] in 1537 to serve as a port city for Quito[*]. Because of its location at the Gulf of Guayaquil, the city prospered and grew as a center for the export of cacao[*] and as the major site of the shipbuilding industry in Latin America. It was also known, however, for its abundance of yellow fever, malaria, and smallpox. Guayaquil and the surrounding region had a *corregidor*[*] under the administration of the *Audiencia* of Quito[*] until 1763 when it became a separate province with its own governor. It fell to rebel forces in 1820 and was part of Gran Colombia[*] until 1830 when it became part of Ecuador.

GÜEMES, MARTÍN. Martín Güemes was born in Salta[*], Río de la Plata[*], in 1785. He was an early convert to the independence movement in Argentina[*], and during the wars for independence, he emerged as a skillful military leader. Güemes was appointed governor of Salta in 1815; he then fought for several years against the royal Spanish forces in Upper Peru (Bolivia[*]). He rose to the rank of general and, employing guerrilla warfare tactics leading platoons of 20

men or fewer, he caused havoc against a better equipped and trained Spanish army. Martin Güemes died in battle in 1821.
    REFERENCE: Roger M. Haig, *Martín Güemes: Tyrant or Tool?*, 1968.

                                                                    Fred Koestler

GÜEMES PACHECO DE PADILLA, JUAN VICENTE. See REVILLA-GIGEDO, CONDE DE.

GUERRA CHIQUITA. The Guerra Chiquita, or "Little War," was a brief, abortive rebellion against Spain after the end of the Ten Years War[*] in Cuba[*]. Although the Pact of Zanjón[*] had ended the long rebellion, Generals Antonio Maceo[*] and Calixto García[*] tried to start the war up again. They proved unable to get much support from the exhausted rebel forces, and the war petered out after only a few months.
    REFERENCE: Jaime Suchlicki, *Cuba: From Columbus to Castro*, 1986.

GUERRERO, VICENTE. Vicente Guerrero was born in Guerrero, New Spain,[*] in 1783 to a poor farming family. An early advocate of independence, Guerrero distinguished himself in battle against royalist forces early in the Mexican Revolution. Guerrero fought with José María Morelos[*] y Pavón in the Sierra Madre del Sur campaigns, and after Morelos y Pavón's execution, he joined forces with Agustín de Iturbide[*]. On April 1, 1829, Guerrero became president of Mexico after his followers refused to permit the inauguration of Manuel Gómez Pedraza, who had defeated Guerrero in a close and controversial election. A liberal and a federalist, Guerrero was ousted in a coup d'état late in 1830. After a year as a fugitive, he was captured, tried, and executed for treason on February 14, 1831.
    REFERENCE: John A. Caruso, *The Liberators of Mexico*, 1967.

GUIPUZCOA COMPANY. See CARACAS COMPANY.

GURRUCHAGA, FRANCISCO DE. Francisco de Gurruchaga was born in Salta[*], Río de la Plata[*], in 1766, to a wealthy merchant family. He was educated in Spain and graduated from the University of Granada with a degree in jurisprudence. When Spain went to war against England, Gurruchaga joined the Spanish navy. He fought against both the British and the French before returning to the Río de la Plata area in 1809 with José de Moldes and Juan Martín de Pueyrredón[*]. Gurruchaga was an enthusiastic supporter of the May Revolution[*] of 1810 and was subsequently charged with building the Argentine navy. He used up most of his family's fortune in supporting the revolution over the next decade. Gurruchaga died in relative poverty in 1846.
    REFERENCES: Enrique Udaondo, *Diccionario biográfico colonial argentino*, 1945; Ione S. Wright and Lisa M. Nekhom, *Historical Dictionary of Argentina*, 1978.

GUZMÁN, GONZALO NUÑO DE. Gonzalo Nuño de Guzmán was born to a prominent family in Guadalajara, Spain, in the late 1480s and became a leading diplomat and court official to King Charles I*. In 1525, Guzmán received appointment as governor of northeastern New Spain*, where he earned a reputation for the ruthless suppression and exploitation of the Indians*. He headed the *audiencia* of New Spain* in Mexico City* from 1528 to 1529. Hopelessly corrupt, Guzmán stole *encomiendas** and gave them to his political cronies, sold Indians into slavery*, and earned a reputation for kidnapping and raping women. In 1529, Bishop Juan de Zumárraga* excommunicated him from the Roman Catholic Church* because of his misdeeds. That same year, he set out on a rapacious expedition of conquest into Michoacán and established the city of Guadalajara*. In 1530, Guzmán declared himself governor of ''Greater Spain,'' which was later dubbed New Galicia*. In 1536, shifting political intrigues cost Guzmán his appointment as governor of New Galicia. He was imprisoned for two years by the new governor Pérez de la Torre, and then returned to Spain, where he died in 1558.

REFERENCES: Paul Horgan, *Conquistadors in North American History*, 1963.

H

HACIENDA. Although land ownership had been the key factor in the development of the elite groups in fourteenth- and fifteenth-century Spain, it did not play an important role in the early Spanish colonies. The conquistadors* were initially more interested in Indian* labor, so the *encomienda** became the single most important institution in the early economy. Early Spanish law and early Spanish settlers essentially respected Indian landholding. As long as Indians made their tribute payments and provided their labor quotas, the Spaniards were satisfied. But as disease depopulated Indian society in the sixteenth and early seventeenth centuries, the *encomienda* declined in importance, because Indians could no longer satisfy Spanish labor demands. As the countryside became depopulated, Spaniards gradually turned to the grazing of livestock on the abandoned lands. Between 1550 and 1600, the number of livestock—cattle, sheep, and goats—in central Mexico* increased from 600,000 head to more than 8 million. At that point, Spanish demands for land began to increase dramatically, and competition for land—between Spaniards and Indians and between Spaniards and Spaniards—became more intense. To move the surviving Indians off their remaining land, Spaniards employed illegal usurpation, the legal formation of *congregaciones** (new concentrated Indian communities), purchase, condemnation and legal seizure, and economic competition.

As the Spaniards acquired the land, haciendas emerged as the dominant institutions in the rural economy. Typically, the haciendas practiced a commercial monoculture of what the owners planned on selling for profit, raising a single commodity—cattle, sheep, indigo*, cacao*, coffee*, sugar*, or other crops. Although Spanish law required that haciendas be established at some distance from Indian towns, the reality was that haciendas often absorbed whole Indian communities; they evolved as feudal institutions in which the Indians became serfs and peons who owed labor to the *hacienda* owner—the *patrón*—who in return offered them care and protection, at least in theory. In the Spanish colonies, the wealthy and powerful people—viceroys*, prominent church officials, prosperous merchants, and ranking military officers—acquired ownership of the haciendas. They became the elite who dominated colonial political, social, and economic life, and established the social structure that still directs political life in much of Latin America.

REFERENCES: Ward Barrett, *The Sugar Hacienda of the Marquéses del Valle*, 1970; François Chevalier, *Land and Society in Colonial Mexico: The Great Hacienda*, 1963; Charles Gibson, *Spain in America*, 1966.

HAITI. The Republic of Haiti, Latin America's first independent nation, occupies the western third of Hispaniola*, an island located 50 miles east of Cuba*. Christopher Columbus* reached northwestern Haiti on December 5, 1492. When the *Santa María* was wrecked on a reef, he was forced to construct an outpost, Navidad, at an important Arawak* village near contemporary Cape Hatien. Upon his return from Europe in November 1493, Columbus learned that Navidad's men had perished, most at the hands of the Indians*. The territory comprising modern Haiti contained the island's densest pre-Columbian population, as well as its most advanced culture. During the early sixteenth century, the Spaniards founded five towns in the west that supplied central Hispaniola's gold fields with provisions and labor. The island's remote, sparsely populated western periphery, vulnerable to foreign attack and prone to smuggling, was evacuated by defense-minded colonial authorities in 1605.

Buccaneers, mostly bands of outcasts who harvested the abandoned western region's vast feral herds for hides and dried meat, caused endless headaches for Spain. Campaigns launched to eject them served only to drive the interlopers to Tortuga*, an island off Haiti's northwestern shore, where they preyed upon the Crown's shipping. Santo Domingo* itself was in constant peril, thus making it extremely difficult to ward off intruders in the west permanently. By 1675, a French colony had taken root on Tortuga and in the adjacent Hispaniola valleys and bays. Spanish mercenaries turned on the invaders in 1784, driving them back across the border. European events obliged the Spaniards to surrender eastern Hispaniola to France under the terms of the Treaty of Basle of 1795.

Revolutionary turmoil in the west, however, permitted Spain to rule its ceded colony until Pierre Dominique Toussaint L'Ouverture's occupation of 1801–1802, nominally in the name of the Paris government. Napoleon's frustrated effort to reinstitute slavery in St. Dominique* brought white soldiers to the east who remained after Haiti's 1804 declaration of independence freed the west. A local anti-French uprising, the War of Reconquest (1808–1809), restored the east to Madrid. Cuba's dread of a Haitian-style insurrection among its own rapidly expanding slave* population was a major reason for its loyalty to the mother country during the Spanish-American wars of independence.

REFERENCES: Troy S. Floyd, *The Columbus Dynasty in the Caribbean, 1492-1526*, 1973; Thomas O. Ott, *The Haitian Revolution, 1789–1804*, 1973.

Frank Marotti

HASSENA, BABA OULD. Baba Ould Hassena was born in 1926 at Togba, Western Sahara*, and he was a strong local supporter of the Spanish Empire there. In 1967, he became vice-president of the *Djemma**, and in 1971, he earned a seat in the Spanish Cortes. But in 1975, when Spain signed the Madrid Agreement*, Hassena joined the Polisario Front* to oppose Moroccan control of his homeland. Since that time, he has continued to work against that control.

REFERENCES: Rafael Ortega Canadell, *Provincias Africanas Españolas*, 1962; Tony Hodges, *Historical Dictionary of Western Sahara*, 1982.

HAVANA. Havana, Cuba*, was founded in 1519 by Spanish settlers attracted to its fine harbor and excellent location. After the conquest of Mexico, Havana became the most important port city in the New World. It was critical in Spain's communication link between Iberia and the mainland colonies. In the eighteenth century, Havana grew by leaps and bounds because of the boom in Cuba's sugar* industry and the importation of slaves* through the port.

HAVANA COMPANY. Prior to 1740, Spain relied primarily on the *asiento**, or contract system, for the importation of slaves* to Spanish colonies in the Americas. Theoretically, the private contractor would agree to ship a specified number of slaves to the colonies each year for a fixed royalty to be paid to the Spanish Crown. Such *asientos* were extremely lucrative because of the ease of smuggling additional slaves and other goods into the colonies without paying import royalties. Trade in the Americas was so lucrative that Portugal and other nations chartered royal trade companies and gave them exclusive trading rights, squeezing private contractors out of business. In 1713, the English Royal African Company won slave trading rights in Spain's American colonies. The British introduced smuggling* on a grand scale, flooding the colonies with slaves and cheap manufactured goods. This was highly injurious to the Spanish treasury because of the lost revenues from the smuggled slaves and the loss of trade and profits to the smugglers. Spain's attempts to end British smuggling led to the War of Jenkin's Ear* and the termination of the British *asiento*. At the time, Cuba* was growing rapidly and had a virtually unquenchable demand for slaves. To stimulate Cuban agriculture and protect the treasury, Spain established the Royal Havana Company in 1740. The company was to have exclusive trading rights for slaves and for regulating all other imports and exports. The company hobbled along until it failed in 1760. During this time, it imported almost 5,000 slaves, but could never generate the same high degree of trade and profitability as the royal trading companies established by England, France, and Portugal. To illustrate, in its entire 21-year existence, the Havana Company imported fewer slaves than did the British in a 10-month occupation of Havana in 1762. There were several reasons. First, smuggling continued unabated. Second, operation costs were higher for Spain than for other countries because it had no slave-trading establishments along the African coast. Efforts to acquire such establishments proved unsuccessful. Relatedly, Spain had no African ports of call and therefore could not keep frigates on station there. That meant that Spanish slave ships had to arm themselves and carry larger crews to defend themselves. Third, the duties that Spain set on slaves was so high as to make their cost prohibitive for many farmers. This of course reduced farmers' ability to produce sugar* and tobacco* so that there was a general economic loss for Spain. After the Royal Havana Company failed, Spain returned to awarding *asientos* to private contractors.

REFERENCES: Hubert Aimes, *A History of Slavery in Cuba, 1511–1868*, 1967; Arthur Corwin, *Spain and the Abolition of Slavery in Cuba*, 1967.

Samuel Freeman

HENRÍQUEZ GONZÁLEZ, CAMILO. Camilo Henríquez González was born in Valdivia, Chile*, in 1769. Educated in Lima*, Peru*, to become a priest, Henríquez earned a reputation as an intellectual rebel early in his career. The Inquisition* investigated him for heresy when he was still in his twenties, after which he went to Quito* to found a convent. Henríquez began writing incendiary articles, under the pseudonym of Quirino Lemáchez, in which he demanded independence for Latin America in general and Chile in particular. At the first national congress of Chile in 1811, Henríquez spoke at length about the ideals of democracy and freedom, and he played a leading role in making Chile the first Latin American country to abolish slavery*, which was accomplished that same year. In 1812, Henríquez established Chile's first newspaper*—*La aurora de Chile*—along with several other newspapers in Santiago* and Buenos Aires*. After the Battle of Rancagua*, Henríquez fled into exile in Buenos Aires, but he returned to Chile in 1822. Until his death in 1825, he was the leading liberal in the Chilean national congress.

REFERENCES: Salvatore Bizarro, *Historical Dictionary of Chile*, 1987; Jose Toribio Medina, *Diccionario biográfico colonial de Chile*, 1906.

HEREDIA, JOSÉ MARÍA DE. José María de Heredia was born in Santiago, Cuba*, on December 31, 1803, and received a law degree from the University of Havana in 1821. As a student, he became a strong opponent of Spanish imperialism, and he joined the *Solés y Rayos de Bolívar*, a group that wanted Cuba annexed to Simón Bolívar's* Republic of South America. Heredia was convicted of conspiracy against the Spanish government and exiled in 1823. He spent two years in Boston and New York before settling in Mexico, where he worked against Spanish control of Cuba and wrote the poems that made him one of Cuba's greatest romantic literary figures. Among his most important works are *Al Niágara, En el Teocalli de Cholula, El himno del desterrado*, and *A Emilia*. Heredia died in Mexico City* on May 7, 1839.

REFERENCE: M. P. González, *José María Heredia: Primogenito del romanticismo hispano*, 1955.

HEREDIA, PEDRO DE. Pedro de Heredia was born in Spain, probably in the late 1490s. He came to the New World to seek his fortune and in 1533 founded the settlement of Cartagena* in what is today Colombia*. Using Cartagena as a base, Heredia launched a series of forays into the interior. A domineering individual who made political enemies easily, Heredia was the subject of a number of *visitas** by Crown officials. He died at sea in 1554 when he was returning to Spain to defend himself against charges of corruption.
    REFERENCE: Robert H. Davis, *Historical Dictionary of Colombia*, 1977.

HERMANO PEDRO. See SAN JOSÉ DE BETANCUR, PEDRO DE.

HERNÁNDEZ DE CÓRDOBA, FRANCISCO. Francisco Hernández de Córdoba was born in Córdoba, Spain, in 1475. Like so many other men from southern and southeastern Spain, Hernández sought his fortune in the New World, arriving in Cuba* in 1511. Diego Velásquez* commissioned him to explore the Caribbean islands, the mainland coast of Central America, and the Gulf of Mexico, and between 1512 and 1518, Hernández conducted those explorations. He was wounded on the coast of Mexico* in 1518 and died of his wounds later that year in Cuba.
    REFERENCES: Robert S. Chamberlain, *The Conquest and Colonization of the Yucatan, 1517–1550*, 1966; Henry R. Wagner, *The Discovery of Yucatán by Francisco Hernández de Córdoba*, 1942.

HERRERA Y TORDESILLAS, ANTONIO. Antonio Herrera y Tordesillas was born in Spain in 1559 and educated at the University of Salamanca. King Philip II* of Spain commissioned him to write a history of the Spanish overseas empire. Herrera had the full cooperation of the Crown, and his book was published in Madrid between 1601 and 1605. Entitled *Historia general de los hechos de los Castellanos en las islas y tierra firme del mar océano*, it provides a valuable historical source for the Crown's imperial policies in the late sixteenth century. Herrera died in 1625.
    REFERENCE: Robert H. Davis, *Historical Dictionary of Colombia*, 1977.

HIDALGO. The term *hidalgo* in Spain and Spanish America referred to an individual with a noble background. The actual origin of the word comes from the Spanish phrase, *"hijo de algo,"* meaning "son of something." Very few members of the Spanish nobility settled in the New World, but the New World economy, with its *encomiendas**, *repartimientos**, mines, haciendas*, and government bureaucracies, created a new *criollo** nobility. The new rich quickly claimed the term *hidalgo* and applied it to themselves.
    REFERENCES: Woodrow Borah, "Race and Class in Mexico," *Pacific Historical Review*, 23 (1953), 331–42; John K. Chance, *Race and Class in Colonial Oaxaca*, 1978.

HIDALGO DE CISNEROS, BALTASAR. See CISNEROS, BALTASAR HIDALGO DE.

HIDALGO Y CASTILLA, MIGUEL. Miguel Hidalgo y Castilla was born on May 8, 1753, on a hacienda* in New Spain* to *criollo** parents. He went to a Jesuit* school until the Jesuits were expelled from the New World in 1767, when he transferred to the College of San Nicolás. Hidalgo entered the priesthood and spent much of his life in Valladolid* working as a teacher and school administrator. By the 1790s, he had become enamored of Enlightenment* rationalism and liberalism, intellectual pursuits that brought him considerable difficulty. In 1800, the office of the Inquisition* investigated him for heresy; although the charges were dropped, Hidalgo was never again the same. In 1803, he moved to Dolores as a parish priest and immediately began developing economic projects for poor peasants. His interest in politics also grew at the same pace as the budding Mexican nationalist movement.

In 1808, Hidalgo joined the political crusade to expel the *peninsular** government from Mexico City*. He is best remembered for the "Grito de Dolores*," his September 16, 1810, message to parishioners, calling for the destruction of illegal, repressive regimes. With a flag of the Virgin of Guadelupe* as a symbol, Hidalgo soon had an army of 25,000 peasants demonstrating against the royal government. At the end of September, the peasant army attacked and slaughtered a Spanish garrison at Alhóndiga de Granaditas*. By the end of October 1810, Hidalgo found himself at the head of 80,000 marauding peasants.

Royalist forces resisted Hidalgo on two fronts—military and political. They warned well-to-do *criollos* that Hidalgo was leading a social revolution that would eventually cost all members of the upper class—*peninsulares* and *criollos*—their property. They also defended Mexico City militarily, sending Hidalgo back to Guadalajara* where he tried to organize a provisional government. He outlawed slavery*, eliminated tribute payments, and guaranteed Indian land ownership. On January 11, 1811, Hidalgo led 100,000 peasants into the Battle of Calderón, in which they were badly defeated. Hidalgo and the other leaders of the revolution were captured, tried, and executed in Chihuahua on July 30, 1811. The Mexican revolution would have to wait until it had gained some *criollo* support.

REFERENCES: Luis Castillo Ledón, *Hidalgo: La vida del héroe*, 2 vols., 1948–1949; Mark Lieberman, *Hidalgo: Mexican Revolutionary*, 1970.

HIDES. From the very beginning of the colonial era, the production of hides was an important part of the colonial economies. By the early 1500s, settlers in Cuba*, Hispaniola*, and Puerto Rico* who had imported sheep, cattle, and goats from Spain were exporting hides back to Spain. From there, the production of hides spread to eastern Venezuela*, northern New Spain*, and Chile*. By the late eighteenth century, however, the center of the industry had shifted to the Río de la Plata* area, where more than 1,500,000 hides were exported annually in the 1780s.

REFERENCE: Peter H. Smith, *Politics and Beef in Argentina: Patterns of Conflict and Change*, 1969.

HIERONYMITES. When the New World was discovered at the end of the fifteenth century, the Hieronymites were the most powerful and influential Roman Catholic religious order in Spain. Because they were a contemplative rather than an activist order, however, they did not have a missionary role in the New World. Their real influence came because of their political power in Spain. During the sixteenth and seventeenth centuries, 17 Hieronymites served as bishops of New World dioceses.

REFERENCE: *New Catholic Encyclopedia*, XII:309–10, 1967.

HISPANIOLA. The word Hispaniola is derived from the phrase La Isla Española (the Spanish island), the name that Christopher Columbus* gave to the island. Hispaniola is the Caribbean island that is today made up of the Dominican Republic and Haiti. See SANTO DOMINGO and HAITI.

HOJEDA, DIEGO DE. Hojeda was born in Seville*, Spain, in 1571. He came to Lima*, Peru*, at the age of 15. He was ordained a priest by the Dominicans* in 1591. Presumed to be a true mystic later in his life, Hojeda was obsessed with the culture of the New World. He belonged to and participated in various literary circles, whereby he apparently learned of, read, and discussed both classical and contemporary literature. Hojeda is often classified, along with the Mexican poet Bernardo de Balbuena*, as a poet of transition, bridging the renaissance and baroque movements. He was fundamentally a religious poet whose ultimate literary objective was to exalt God's work. *La Cristiada*, Hojeda's masterpiece, is considered by some to be the greatest religious epic poem ever written in the Spanish language. Although *La Cristiada* was not published until 1833, it was well known during Hojeda's lifetime, as it circulated in manuscript form. Its polished poetic style has consistently been lauded by critics. Sources and influences noted in *La Cristiada* range from Saint Augustine and Saint Thomas to Tasso and Dante. The storyline of *La Cristiada* recounts the last days of Jesus Christ, from the Last Supper to the crucifixion and burial of Christ. Various digressions and adornments mark the poem as decidedly baroque. Also of baroque flavor are the obscure and lengthy theological discussions and concerns. Hojeda died in 1615.

REFERENCE: Enrique Anderson-Imbert, *Historia de la literatura hispanoamericana*, 1970.

Sam L. Slick

HONDURAS. During the Spanish colonial period, Honduras, a province of the captaincy-general of Guatemala*, was divided into two administrative units: a *gobierno* in Comayagua* and an *alcaldía mayor* in Tegucigalpa, which was reorganized in the eighteenth century when Comayagua became an intendancy*. On July 30, 1502, Christopher Columbus discovered Honduras on his fourth voyage. This initial expedition led to others, and the territory was disputed among various conquistadors*. In 1524, Gil Gonzáles* Dávila arrived in Honduras, followed by Francisco Hernández de Córdoba*, sent by Pedro Arias de Ávila* (Pedrarias), governor and captain general of Castilla de Oro* (Panama*), to challenge Gonzáles Dávila's pretensions. On January 11, 1524, Hernán Cortés* sent an overseas expedition from New Spain* under the command of Cristóbal de Olid*. Olid betrayed Cortés, who sent a second expedition under Francisco de las Casas. Olid captured Gonzáles Dávila and las Casas but, on January 15, 1525, they killed Olid in his headquarters. Unaware of this turn of events, Cortés organized a third expedition, this time overland, under his direction. It left Mexico on October 12, 1524. With Cortés's arrival, las Casas and Gonzales Dávila left for Mexico City*. Cortés introduced livestock and founded the town of Navidad de Nuestra Señora, near the port of Caballos. On April 25, 1526, before he left, Cortés named Hernando de Saavedra as governor and captain general of Honduras, and he left instructions to treat the Indians* kindly. On October 26, 1526, Diego López de Salcedo, named by the Emperor Charles V as Honduras's governor, replaced Saavedra.

In the next decade, the personal ambitions of the governors and conquistadors interfered with administrative and governmental organization. The Spanish settlers rebelled against their leaders, and the Indians rebelled against the harsh treatment imposed on them. Salcedo, out to enrich himself, clashed with Pedrarias, now governor of Nicaragua*, who wanted Honduras as part of his domain. In 1528, Pedrarias arrested Salcedo and forced him to cede territory, but the emperor rejected this agreement. With Salcedo's death in 1530, the settlers became the arbiters of power as they put in and took out governors. The settlers petitioned Pedro de Alvarado*, who had been in Honduras in 1526, to come and bring order to this anarchy. In 1536, with Alvarado's arrival, the chaos subsided and the region was brought under his authority.

In 1537, Francisco de Montejo* arrived as governor under royal appointment. Alvarado's followers opposed Montejo, as the latter annulled the *encomiendas*_ granted by Alvarado. Montejo's captain, Alonso de Cáceres, was responsible for putting down the Indian revolt of 1537–1538 led by the *cacique*_ Lempira. In disagreements over the region, the Council of the Indies* sent Montejo to Chiapas* and Alvarado became governor of Honduras. With Alvarado's death in 1541, a new phase began. The New Laws* of the Indies, signed on November 20, 1542, created the *audiencia* de los Confines*, headquartered in Gracias*, whose jurisdiction included Central America. On May 16, 1544, the *audiencia*_ was inaugurated, with Alonso de Maldonado, the governor of Honduras, as its president. Maldonado's noncompliance with the laws brought him into conflict with Bartolomé de las Casas*, bishop of Chiapas. Alonso López de Cerrato replaced Maldonado who was found guilty of not executing the New Laws. Cerrato's arrival in 1548 signaled a consolidation of central power and the application of the laws, which benefited the Indians. The first religious orders arrived, convents were built, and the organized conversion of the Indians was begun. On Cerrato's departure in 1552, the *audiencia* lost direct control over the province. Thus ended the formative conquest phase as Honduras became a political entity.

Although some agricultural products were exported, mining was the province's most important economic activity. Silver production never competed with that of New Spain and Peru* because of limited supply and a lack of workers. Although a few *encomiendas* existed, the most important labor system for work in the mines was the *repartimiento**. The first important silver mines were discovered in Tegucigalpa in 1578. San Andrés de Nueva Zaragoza, also in a rich mining zone, was abolished as an *alcaldía mayor* in 1703 when the veins ran out. In 1649, African slaves* arrived to work the mines. A mining boom occurred between 1730 and 1780, after which a decline commenced. Ranching, another important economic activity, replaced mining near the end of the colonial period. The Bourbons encouraged tobacco* production but transportation costs proved prohibitive. The end of the eighteenth century and the beginning of the nineteenth saw the economy in decline.

The province was under continual assault by the unconquered Indians of the northeast and by the English. Internally, the province suffered from the nonintegration of the northeast, known as Taguzgalpa, which was only sparsely populated by the Spanish. Colonization was left to the religious orders, which underwent many hardships in their attempts to incorporate the region's Indians. The English occupied the region around Belize* in 1667 and along the Río Tinto in 1699. They used these Indians in their struggles against the Spanish. The English also kept the area in constant agitation through piracy*. In 1556 and 1579, pirates attacked Trujillo*. The Dutch also attacked and burned Trujillo in 1643. When piracy was abolished, the English and Spanish struggle continued. New Spanish settlements were established in the Mosquito region during the eighteenth century. In 1778, the new captain general, Matías de Gálvez, used Honduras as a base against the English. On October 16, 1779, the English occupied Omoa, but Gálvez reoccupied it on November 29, 1779. When the English seized Roatan Island, he launched a second campaign against the English, who were then forced to evacuate the region. Gálvez reorganized trade by shifting military and commercial activity from the Guatemalan coast to the Honduran coast. Further struggles between the English and Spanish at the end of the eighteenth century engulfed the area. Contraband penetrated the captaincy general through these English settlements.

During the eighteenth century, the Bourbon reforms restructured the province administratively. Comayagua was made an intendancy on July 24, 1791, and the *alcaldía mayor* of Tegucigalpa was formally put under its direct rule. Tegucigalpa's residents protested this move until the regency reestablished the *alcaldía mayor* in 1812.

The province's political independence came relatively peacefully because the provincial offices were in the hands of the *criollos**. The last *alcalde mayor* of Tegucigalpa, Narciso Mallol, attempted to better the region through public works projects. In 1812, a disturbance in Tegucigalpa against the re-election of the *alcalde* and *regidores** was brought to an end when the captain general sent a battalion to the city. In 1819 and 1820, there were attacks along the Pacific coast by privateers from the Río de la Plata* region. In 1821, independence brought conflict between Comayagua and Tegucigalpa, since Comayagua sided with the independence proclaimed in Mexico and Tegucigalpa put itself under the authority of the independence proclaimed in Guatemala*. War was avoided when Guatemala declared itself in favor of the Mexican Empire in 1822.

REFERENCES: Ralph Lee Woodward, Jr., *Central America: A Nation Divided*, 1976; Miles L. Wortman, *Government and Society in Central America, 1680–1840*, 1982; Luis Marinas Otero, *Honduras*, 1983.

Carlos Pérez

HORSE. The horse became extinct in the New World approximately 10,000 years ago, but in 1493 Columbus* brought several of them to Hispaniola.* The horse provided Europeans with mobility, a necessity in conquering native inhabitants. Spaniards brought horses with them to New Spain* in 1519, and from there they spread up and throughout the Great Plains of North America. Indians adapted to the horse and it transformed their lifestyle, giving them a mobility they had never enjoyed before. Other Spaniards brought the horse to South America, and it similarly transformed the lives and cultures of many Indian tribes. On the great cattle* and sheep* ranches of New Spain and Argentina*, the horse played a key role in managing the livestock and moving large herds of animals from place to place. Throughout the New World, the horse thrived and shaped the European way of life, providing the mobility that allowed for subjugation of the native populations and, in the absence of any formal infrastructure, the transportation mechanism for successful commerce in the interior.

REFERENCE: Alfred W. Crosby, Jr., *Ecological Imperialism: The Biological Expansion of Europe, 900–1900*, 1986.

HOSPITALLERS OF ST. JOHN. The Hospitallers of St. John was a Roman Catholic religious order founded in the early sixteenth century in Granada, Spain, by John the Good. They were committed to caring for the sick and needy. They had launched their work in the New World by the early 1570s. By 1670, the Hospitallers supervised 70 hospitals in the Spanish colonies of the New World.

REFERENCE: *New Catholic Encyclopedia*, XII:311, 1967.

HOSTOS, EUGENIO MARÍA DE. Although Eugenio María de Hostos was born in Puerto Rico* in 1839 and spent most of his life in Latin America, he was educated in Spain. It was there that he met contemporary Spanish intellectuals who were allied with Krausismo. This was the beginning of Hostos's education of reform. He learned from the *krausistas* the social and political philosophy that would serve as organizing principles for his work and writings in Latin America, particularly with regard to Puerto Rico and its independence movement. Hostos traveled and worked in many parts of Latin America; he was truly a Pan-American. He worked for many years in Chile* where he was active in the field of education; he also worked extensively in the Dominican Republic. Wherever he went, Hostos was a tireless fighter for freedom and human dignity. Of particular interest is his major contribution of promoting the rights of women in Latin America.

Clearly a man of vision and great intelligence, Hostos enjoyed a reputation as an intellectual. Although this important Puerto Rican writer produced literature in many forms (novel, theater, and poetry), he is most remembered for his forceful essays. In narrative, Hostos wrote *La peregrinación de Bayoán*, an 1863 novel, and *Cuentos a mi hijo* (1878). He began as a romantic writer but slowly converted to positivism and the philosophies of Herbert Spencer and Auguste Comte. As Hostos did so, his work increasingly reflected the approach and thoughts of a sociologist. Through his works, he advanced his agenda of morals and ethics, the independence of Puerto Rico, and his pet project of education reform. The work for which Hostos is best remembered is his *Moral social* (1888), in which he articulated his views on many matters, including Spain's oppressive control of Puerto Rico. In short, Hostos was Puerto Rico's major writer and intellectual of the nineteenth century. His contributions to the island were many, and his legacy continues to demand respect and homage in Puerto Rico.

REFERENCE: Lidio Cruz Monclova, *Historia de Puerto Rico (siglo XIX)*, 1970.

Sam L. Slick

HUAMANGA. Huamanga is a region of southern Peru* that was organized as an *intendencia** in 1784 as part of King Charles III's* Bourbon reforms in Latin America. It remained a functioning *intendencia* until 1824 when rebel forces drove out the last of the royalist troops. Huamanga then became part of Peru.

REFERENCE: David P. Henige, *Colonial Governors from the Fifteenth Century to the Present*, 1970.

HUANCAVELICA. The region of Huancavelica in central Peru* was well-known in the Spanish Empire because of its extensive deposits of precious metals. The area had long been governed by a superintendent of mines appointed by the viceroy* of Peru or by the Council of the Indies*, but in 1784, Charles III* created an *intendencia** there. Rebel troops seized control of Huancavelica in 1822, eliminating the power of the *intendencia*. In 1824, the region became part of Peru.

REFERENCE: David P. Henige, *Colonial Governors from the Fifteenth Century to the Present*, 1970.

HUÁSCAR. Huáscar, an Inca* prince, was born in 1495, the son of Emperor Huayna Cápac*. When his father died in 1525, Huáscar began a long dynastic struggle with his half-brother Atahuallpa* for control of the empire. Huáscar's base of support and control came from northern Peru and Ecuador*, but when he tried to extend his power base into southern Peru and Bolivia*, Atahuallpa resisted. Francisco Pizarro* and the Spaniards arrived in Peru in the midst of the ensuing civil war, and Pizarro exploited it to the Europeans' advantage. Huáscar died in 1533.

REFERENCE: Burr Cartwright Brundage, *Lords of Cuzco: A History and Description of the Inca People in Their Final Days*, 1967.

HUAXTECS. The Huaxtec Indians inhabited lowland and mountain regions in eastern Mexico at the time of the Spanish conquest. Linguistically related to the Maya*, they have probably been firmly settled in the Tampico-Tuxpan area for at least 3,000 years, and many Huaxtec Indians still reside in that region. In prehistoric times, the Huaxtecs were called Cuexteca by the Aztecs*; their land was Cuextlán. The Aztecs considered the Huaxtecs rather extraordinary but had no qualms about borrowing certain elements of Huaxtec culture (e.g., distinctive styles of warrior costumes and shields). According to an English visitor (John Chilton) to the region in 1572, the Huaxtecs were a tall people who dyed their bodies blue. An Aztec description states that they dyed their hair red, yellow, or other colors and let it hang over their ears, leaving a tuft in the back; the women braided their hair, adding feathers to the braids. They perforated their noses and inserted a feather or gold ornament in the hole, and they filed their teeth to the shape of gourd seeds, coloring them black. The Huaxtecs were particularly noted for expertly weaving cloth into fantastic designs and were quite extravagant in their use of precious stone, shell, and feather ornaments.

Their land was described by the Aztecs (through the Franciscan* friar Bernardino de Sahagún*) as "the land of food, the land of flowers." Farming, fishing, warfare, and weaving appear to have been their primary occupations. These "hot lands" produced reliable crops of cotton, maize, and other important foodstuffs. Much of the region was conquered by the Aztec Triple Alliance in the latter half of the fifteenth century. Following conquest, the Aztecs demanded that the Huaxtecs send them tributes of fine clothing, chilis, balls of down and feathers, warrior costumes, strings of jadeite beads, turquoise, cotton, and live eagles.

Huaxtec society was divided into social classes similar to those found among groups throughout central Mexico. The region was divided into numerous city states, each with its own ruler, cadre of nobles, and large numbers of commoners (farmers, fishermen, artisans, and merchants). Within each city state, commoners paid tribute and nobles received it; nobles also enjoyed certain privileges, such as the practice of polygyny and rights to special clothing, ornamentation, and body tattooing. Warfare was common in the region, and weaponry (especially bows and arrows), fortresses, military organization, and battle strategies were well developed. Also well developed was commerce, and important markets thrived in the region.

REFERENCES: I. Bernal and E. Dávalos, *Huastecos y Totonacos*, 1953; *Codex Mendoza* [tributary provinces of Tochpan, Tzicoac, and Oxitipan]; Bernardino de Sahagún,

Florentine Codex, 1950–1982; Guy Stresser-Pean, "Ancient Sources on the Huastecs," *Handbook of Middle American Indians*, 1971.

Frances F. Berdan

HUAYNA CÁPAC. Huayna Cápac was born around 1450 and became the great king who presided over the Inca* Empire at the point of its greatest expansion in the late fifteenth and early sixteenth centuries. Although Cápac did not have to deal with the arrival of the Spanish, the Inca Empire was already being affected by the European expansion, primarily because European diseases had spread to some Indian* groups in Colombia* and Ecuador* from the Spanish presence in Panama* and the Caribbean. Huayna Cápac died in 1525, and his kingdom was immediately embroiled in a dynastic struggle between two of his sons—Atahualpa* and Huáscar*.

REFERENCE: Burr Cartwright Brundage, *Lords of Cuzco: A History and Description of the Inca People in Their Final Days*, 1967.

HUICHOLS. The Huichol Indians live largely in the state of Nayarit and in parts of Jalisco, Durango, and Zacatecas states in Mexico, extending over 1,000 square miles of rough territory that ranges from deep barrancas to high mountain plateaus. It is this rugged terrain that has protected the Huichol from non-Indian encroachment, but this respite is nearing an end as roads and airfields are built in their territory. The Huichols speak a variety of the Nahuatl* language, the ancient Aztec* tongue. Their present population numbers approximately 10,000 Indians. The rough, remote territory also protected the Huichol from invasion following the conquest. Shortly after the Spanish conquest, a Spanish priest, Father Ortega, wrote of the area: "It is so wild and frightful to behold that its ruggedness, even more than the arrows of its warlike inhabitants took away the courage of the conquerors; because not only did the ridges and valleys appear inaccessible, but the extended range of towering mountain peaks confused even the eye." It was not until the Spanish were about to be driven out of Mexico that their soldiers penetrated the region.

As late as the end of the nineteenth century, anthropologist Carl Lumholtz was told by a local governor that the Huichol still refused to pay taxes, feeling that they received no benefits from the Mexican government. They live as they have lived in the past, free, and proud, of being born Huichol. They live in an arid area, with open valleys and wooded slopes. Their outside contact is through the sale of their crafts (yarn paintings usually representing native lore or ritual, embroidered bags, woven belts, and beaded jewelry) to tourist towns outside their territory. While nominal Christians, they continue to worship their traditional pantheon and readily incorporate saints including Jesus into their number. The two religions are mingled in such a way that they are hard to separate. The Franciscan* missionaries have made few inroads into the traditional lifestyle or religion, although the mission schools are well attended.

They have an independence of thought and spirit that makes them a difficult subject for anthropologists to study. Many Huichols, both men and women, are shamans. Each individual has his own version of his society, his religion, and his role in the universe. This individuality also characterizes their clothes. Both men and women wear colorful and never-standardized garments, even on ceremonial occasions. The hallucinogenic cactus *peyote* (*Lophora williamsii*) is the unifying drug of the Huichol. Every year, they travel over 500 miles to a desert region in northern San Luis Potosí* to collect it. This region they call Wirkuta. Some believed that this must have been the original homeland of the Huichol, for peyote of good quantity and quality can be obtained much closer, yet is ignored. Others believe that the long trek done under strict conditions of abstinence functions like a pre-Christian pilgrimage to hone spiritual power and teach cultural identity. The unique mixture of native religion, including complex shamanistic rituals, and Christianity has produced a folk Catholicism* best exemplified by an icon of the Lady of Guadalupe at the Huichol settlement of San Andrés. Here the icon, dressed in a colorful skirt, is covered with peyote buttons to such an extent that the cloth is hardly visible.

Today, the future of the Huichol is a subject of controversy. One group of government officials believes that the Indians should be left as they are, remote, mysterious, and, at least for the present, safe from outside encroachment. A second group seeks reservation status and stronger governmental control, which is complicated since peyote is an illegal drug in Mexico. Regardless of this argument, the Huichol continue to exist as they have for centuries, blending Christianity with native ritual, removed and remote from the mainstream of Mexican culture. The Huichol, the Tepehuan, and the Lacadones are three Indian groups that are probably fortunate to live in such difficult and remote regions that they can dictate their own lifestyles, at least for the present, apart from the complexity and frustration of what we call the modern world.

REFERENCE: G. A. Agogino, "The San Andrés Huichol," *Discover Mexico*, 21 (1981), 12–18.

George A. Agogino

HUMBOLDT, ALEXANDER VON. Alexander von Humboldt was born on September 14, 1769, in Berlin. Between 1787 and 1790, he received degrees from the University of Frankfurt, the University of Oden in Göttingen, and the School of Mines in Freiburg, Saxony. A gifted scientist, Humboldt's reputation rests on his work as a naturalist, explorer, and scholar. In 1799, Humboldt journeyed to the New World, a trip that took him Venezuela*, New Granada*, Quito*, Peru*, New Spain*, and the United States. For five years, he made scientific and political observations of New World life. He returned to Berlin in 1804 and began to publish his notes. They were eventually published as 30 volumes between 1807 and 1834. Entitled *Personal Narrative of Travels to the Equinoctial Regions of the New World*, they constitute an invaluable source for understanding New World geography at the turn of the eighteenth century. Alexander von Humboldt died in 1859.

REFERENCE: Karl Bruhns, *Alexander von Humboldt*, 1872.

HURTADO DE MENDOZA, GARCÍA. García Hurtado de Mendoza, the son of a Peruvian viceroy (Andrés Hurtado de Mendoza, served 1556–1561) was born in Cuenca, Spain, in 1535. Well-connected politically because of the influence of his father, he was appointed governor of Chile* in 1554 following the death of Pedro de Valdivia*, and he assumed the post in 1557. Hurtado distinguished himself in military campaigns against the Araucanian* Indians. He voluntarily retired as governor of Chile in 1562 to pursue family political and economic interests. In 1588, he followed in his father's footsteps by being appointed viceroy of Peru, a position he held until 1596 when he returned to Spain. García Hurtado de Mendoza died there in 1609.

REFERENCE: Dwight B. Heath, *Historical Dictionary of Bolivia*, 1973.

HUTTEN, PHILIPP. In 1528, hoping to augment crown income from the New World possessions immediately, King Charles V* of Spain gave a monopoly to the House of Welser*, a German banking concern, to colonize Venezuela*. The Welsers financed a number of expeditions to Venezuela, and one of them was led by Philipp Hutten. Between 1541 and 1546, Hutten explored the Colombian and Venezuelan *llanos* (plains), as well as the Caqueta and Amazon river valleys of Colombia*. Upon his return to Coro, Venezuela, in 1546, Hutten was murdered by a political rival.

REFERENCE: Robert H. Davis, *Historical Dictionary of Colombia*, 1977.

I

IBARRA, FRANCISCO DE. Francisco de Ibarra was born in Spain in 1539. Like so many other adventurous Spaniards in the sixteenth century, Ibarra sought his fortune in the New World. As a young man, he came to New Spain* in the mid-1500s and headed north from Mexico City* toward Zacatecas* searching for gold and silver. By the 1560s, Ibarra had launched mining* operations in several areas north of Zacatecas, and he was named governor and captain general of the new province of New Vizcaya*. In 1564, Ibarra founded the cities of Nombre de Dios and Durango; the next year, he established San Sebastian. Ibarra retired as governor of New Vizcaya in 1568 and returned to Mexico City where he spent the rest of his life until he died in 1575.

REFERENCE: J. Lloyd Mecham, *Francisco de Ibarra and Nueva Vizcaya*, 1927.

IFNI. Ifni is a 579-square-mile province of Morocco, located on the Atlantic coast approximately 200 miles southeast of Marrakech. The native people of Ifni were nomadic Berber tribesmen. In 1860, according to the Treaty of Tetuán, Morocco ceded the region to Spain. The population was sparse and natural resources very limited. Spanish control over the area was minimal at best. Spanish ownership was confirmed by the Franco-Spanish Convention of 1912*. In 1934, Spain formalized its colonial supervision of Ifni, and in 1952, Ifni became part of Spanish West Africa.* When Spanish West Africa was divided into Spanish Sahara* and Ifni in 1958, Ifni came under the administrative control of the Canary Islands*. That relationship persisted until 1969 when Spain returned Ifni to Morocco.

REFERENCES: Richard M. Brace, *Morocco, Algeria, Tunisia*, 1964; John Mercer, *Spanish Sahara*, 1975.

IGLESIAS PANTÍN, SANTIAGO. Santiago Iglesias Pantín was born in Coruña, Spain, in 1872, to a working-class family. Iglesias emigrated to Havana[*], Cuba[*], in 1887 and was soon in labor union politics with the Workers' Circle. Spanish authorities were suspicious of labor agitators. Fearing arrest when the Cuban revolution erupted in 1895, Iglesias fled to Puerto Rico[*]. In San Juan[*], he immediately began organizing another labor movement, establishing a newspaper[*], *Ensayo Obrero*, to promote labor-organizing drives. Spanish officials arrested him, and he remained in prison until the United States took control of Puerto Rico in 1898. After that, Iglesias developed a close relationship with Samuel Gompers and the American Federation of Labor (AFL), of which his Free Federation of Puerto Rican Workers was a constituent union. In 1915, Iglesias organized the Socialist Party of Puerto Rico, and in 1925, he became president of the AFL's Pan American Federation of Labor. Throughout the remainder of his life, Iglesias fought for Puerto Rican statehood, which in his opinion was the only way that poor workers could secure any protection from capitalist exploitation. Santiago Iglesias Pantín died in 1939.
    REFERENCE: Alberto López and James Petras, eds., *Puerto Rico and the Puerto Ricans*, 1974.

ILLINGWORTH, JUAN. Juan Illingworth was born May 10, 1786, in Stockport, England. He spent his career as a naval officer and assistant to Lord Thomas Cochrane, who had been hired to head up the Chilean navy. Cochrane gave Illingworth the assignment of harassing Spanish coastal shipping and installations. Eventually Illingworth settled in Guayaquil[*] and founded the Guayaquil Naval Academy. Active in the Ecuadorean independence movement, Illingworth became chief of naval operations for Ecuador[*]. He died on August 4, 1853, in Guayaquil.
    REFERENCE: Federico González Suárez, *Historia general de la República del Ecuador*, 7 vols., 1890–1903.

ILOCOS. The Ilocos region (also spelled Ilokos or Ylocos) of the Philippines[*] includes the present provinces of Ilocos Norte, Ilocos Sur, and La Unión; it includes the entire northwest coast of Luzon[*] from the Lingayen Gulf to Cape Bojeador. The coastal plain is 150 miles long but very narrow. There are only a few spots with enough flat land for rice fields; these are located where rivers drain the cordillera and empty into the South China Sea at the sites of the only three large towns in Ilocos: San Fernando, Vigan, and Laoag. The economy is varied, based on corn[*], tobacco[*], weaving, fishing, forestry, and salt production.
    The Ilocano people, the third-largest ethnic group in the Philippines, have a highly developed sense of group identity. They think of themselves as different from other Filipinos and are so regarded. Ilocano traits are said to include seriousness, thrift, clannishness, a penchant for violence and vendettas, and above all else, a willingness to work very hard and to go wherever opportunity

beckons. Ilocanos have settled the Cagayan* Valley, parts of the central Luzon plain, the coasts of Zambales and Mindoro, and parts of Mindanao*, displacing other peoples. They have worked in the sugar fields of Hawaii and the Central Valley of California. Their character is a reflection of their harsh homeland, with its eroded hills, worn-out soil, frequent storms, rocky coast, and marginal agriculture. For all that, Ilocos is not isolated from Manila*, being connected by a direct sea route and an easy land route.

Because of its exposed location, Ilocos was visited by Chinese traders and Japanese pirates. Spain's interest was at first mainly strategic. Juan de Salcedo sailed around Luzon in 1572 and reported the Ilocos coast to be thickly settled and prosperous. Four years later he was back with 100 men to establish Vigan as the ecclesiastical and administrative center of Ilocos. A revolt in Pangasinan* in 1660 spread to Ilocos the following year. The rebel leader's name has been given as Juan Manzano by some sources, as Pedro Almazán by others. His revolt was nativist, anti-Spanish, anti-Catholic, and short-lived. The self-styled "King of Ilocos" was hanged by the Spaniards, and no further insurrections disturbed Ilocos for a century, until Diego Silang* and his wife Gabriela led a far more serious rebellion in 1762–1763.

The economy of Ilocos was transformed in the late eighteenth century by the tobacco monopoly. The rules changed from year to year, but its overall effect was to widen the economic and social gulf between the common people and the *principales* ("important people") as the latter collaborated with the Spanish in squeezing the maximum profit from each farm and each farmer. Quotas for tobacco production were assigned, and penalties were imposed for failure to meet them. The leaf was bought cheaply and sold dearly. Corruption flourished. The hardships of life forced Ilocanos to work hard and often to emigrate, but there was little revolutionary agitation in Ilocos in the nineteenth century, when the Tagalog provinces rebelled and finally forced Spain to quit all of the Philippines except Manila.

REFERENCE: Teodoro A. Agoncillo and Oscar M. Alfonso, *A Short History of the Filipino People*, 1960.

Ross Marlay

ILOCOS REVOLT OF 1807. Ilocanos rose in revolt in their homeland on the northwest coast of Luzon* in 1807. Their anger was fanned by the onerous state monopolies on the production of tobacco* and *basi*, a native wine. People were accustomed to a local free market in both commodities and became enraged at the arbitrary restrictions and attendant corruption of the state monopolies. The most interesting feature of this revolt was its clear class character: "Kill all the Dons and Doñas!" was the cry of the insurrectionists. The revolt was quickly suppressed, but it flared up again eight years later. The numerous uprisings in Ilocano history never grew into a true revolutionary movement, however.

REFERENCE: Teodoro A. Agoncillo and Oscar M. Alfonso, *A Short History of the Filipino People*, 1960.

Ross Marlay

ILUSTRADOS. Literally, *ilustrados* means "enlightened ones." The term refers to nineteenth-century Filipino intellectuals whose evolving nationalism created the basis for the Philippine revolution against Spain, Asia's first modern independence movement. Free-trade policies and the opening of the Suez canal brought far-reaching changes to Philippine society. Some educational opportunities had become available to children from wealthy families by the 1860s and 1870s. The *ilustrados* were defined by their fluency in Spanish and their advanced education. Some studied at the University of St. Thomas in Manila*; others took degrees in Barcelona and Madrid. Most came from privileged backgrounds and mestizo* families. They typified a class familiar from other colonies: marginal men not accepted as equals of the Europeans, but far removed from the native village too.

Few *ilustrados* were revolutionary, which is hardly surprising given their wealth and social position. Their goals were reform, legal equality, an end to racial barriers, public schools, and the rationalization of colonial administration. At first, they unanimously opposed independence, instead seeking equality with Spaniards in the framework of empire. Filipino *ilustrados* based in Europe launched the Propaganda Movement* (1880–1895). When Spain proved incapable of reform, some began to think of armed revolution. Most *ilustrados*, including the prominent Dr. José Rizal*, could not endorse violence, but some were driven to it by the logic of events. When Emilio Aguinaldo* proclaimed a Philippine Republic in 1898, he had *ilustrado* backing, which, however, slipped away when the invading Americans promised everything the *ilustrados* had asked for: legal equality, incremental reform, schools, and property rights.

REFERENCE: John N. Schumacher, *The Propaganda Movement, 1880–1895*, 1973.

Ross Marlay

IMMORTAL THIRTY-THREE. The Banda Oriental, today's Uruguay*, had been an apple of discord between Spain and Portugal ever since the Papal bull of Innocent XI established the bishopric of Rio de Janeiro in 1676 with jurisdication extending to the Río de la Plata*. For the colony's protection, the Portuguese then built the fort Colônia do Sacramento in 1680, opposite Buenos Aires*. This was immediately seized by the Spaniards, although it changed hands several times during the eighteenth century while the Banda Oriental as such remained within the Spanish Empire. The struggle for the Banda Oriental, as it was called by the Spaniards in those times, continued in the early nineteenth century. The Portuguese invaded it in 1811 and again in 1816 under General Carlos Federico Lecor. After the defeat of José Gervasio Artigas*, Uruguay's founding father, in the battle of Tacuarembo and his subsequent exile to Paraguay*, the region was incorporated into the Portuguese empire as the Cisplatine

Province[*]. With Brazil's independence in 1822, the area became part of the latter's empire, despite the fact that the *orientales* had everything in common with the Argentines across the river and nothing in common with the Brazilians.

During the early years of the 1820s, a group of *orientales* exiled in Buenos Aires conspired to free their country. Much inspired by Simón Bolívar's[*] victory at Ayacucho[*] (December 9, 1824), the exiles now prepared the invasion in earnest. In the residence of one of them, Juan de la Torre, they prepared the operation, and de la Torre obtained weapons and two tricolor flags with the inscription "Liberty or Death". The Argentine authorities (General Juan Gregorio Las Heras[*]) refused any help in order to avoid a possible conflict with Brazil. At last, in 1825, 33 patriots, the "Immortal Thirty-three", under the leadership of Juan Antonio Lavalleja[*], who had a brave record against the Portuguese and would become the future vicar of Sarandi against the Brazilians, mounted the invasion, also called the Crusade. On April 25, 1825, the Thirty-three crossed the river Paraná, having set out from San Isidro, north of Buenos Aires, and landed at the beach of La Agraciada. Although numerically insignificant, they spontaneously received the support of the population. In Soriano, on April 27, Lavalleja issued a proclamation. On May 7, 1825, the liberators' flag flew from the Cerrito. Lavalleja subsequently summoned a congress, the Assembly of La Florida, on August 25, 1825, which voted for the inclusion of the Banda Oriental into the United Provinces of the Rio de la Plata. This action led to the Argentine-Brazilian war of 1825–1828 and finally ended with the independence of the República Oriental del Uruguay.

REFERENCE: Lorenzo Belinzón, *La revolución emancipadora uruguaya y sus dogmas democráticos*, 1932.

O. Carlos Stoetzer

INCAS. According to one legend, the sun created a son and a daughter, placed them on an island in Lake Titicaca, gave them a golden rod, and instructed them to settle where the staff sank into the earth. At the site where the bar disappeared into the ground, the royal couple, Manco Cápac and his sister-queen Mama Ocllo, obediently built the city of Cuzco[*] and founded an empire. Behind such romantic legends, which enhanced Incan claims to divinity and buttressed their political absolutism, around A.D. 1000 a tribe known as the Incas migrated northward in the Peruvian Andes from the Lake Titicaca area to the Cuzco Valley. Expansion-minded, they promptly embarked upon a policy of conquest. By the early 1500s, their empire extended from Quito[*] in Ecuador[*] to Tucumán[*] in Argentina[*], an area of about 380,000 square miles, or approximately one and one-half times the size of Texas[*]. The Spaniards incorrectly referred to all the Indians[*] of this vast realm as Incas. In fact, that term applied only to the ruling tribe, to the nobility.

With regard to scientific learning, the Incas lagged behind the Mayas[*] and Aztecs[*]. They had only the crudest understanding of the relationship of the earth to other heavenly bodies; they had no system of writing, not even pictographs (our knowledge of them is based largely upon painted pottery, temple ornaments, tapestries, textiles, metal work, and sixteenth- and seventeenth-century chronicles, some unreliable); and their numbering system was cumbersome. They used knotted strings of various colors called *quipus* for record-keeping. A practical people, the Incas seemed more interested in the application of knowledge than in abstract learning. And when it came to pottery, textiles, metal-working in gold, silver, platinum, and copper, road building, and the construction of an integrated empire, they had few if any equals among the pre-Columbian aborigines. Their utilitarian bent was expressed in a royal epigram: "He who attempts to count the stars and does not know how to count the marks and knots of the *quipus* ought to be held in derision."

Politically and socially, the Incan empire was a highly structured despotism, benevolent or cruel depending upon the nature of the Saca Inca, who was an absolute temporal and spiritual leader. Beneath the Saca Inca came the other Incas, nobles who held the most important political, military, and religious positions, followed by a second-class nobility composed of former rulers of conquered territories. At the base of the social pyramid was the mass of commoners, who were set apart by dress and a regimentation that left little or no room for individual choice. The people were divided into groups according to ability and were assigned work on the basis of skill and strength. The daily life of farm workers was tightly governed by the *mita*, a system of forced rotating labor supervised by Incan officials. Though life for commoners was obviously rigorous, the end result, if one accepts the chroniclers at face value, was the virtual elimination of hunger and destitution within the empire. To be sure, from a material standpoint, the people of the empire appear to have been reasonably comfortable. That is, they generally had enough to eat and wear. Superb agriculturalists, the Incas transformed Andean deserts and mountain slopes into arable land. Their system of terraces, aqueducts, irrigation canals, and dams is still a marvel. By storing surpluses in royal granaries and warehouses, they were able to sustain themselves during difficult times.

As empire builders, the Incas surpassed all other pre-Columbian Indians[*]. Whereas the Aztecs ruled by force and made little effort to win the allegiance of subjugated tribes, the Incas governed more subtly and without much brute force, thereby shrewdly transferring the loyalty of the conquered peoples. The Incas always attempted to win new territory through persuasion. An area designated for conquest would be visited by diplomats who sought to convince the people of the advantages of being a part of the empire. Only if this failed was force used, but even then the Incas were restrained. The invading army took no captives for sacrifice, exacted no harsh taxes, and was prohibited from looting.

Once the military conquest was completed, the Incas moved quickly to establish bonds between themselves and their new subjects. First, a host of public officials, road builders, and artisans rushed into the area. Fortresses and government offices were built, and a careful census, which detailed the crafts of the people and the various products produced, was taken. Second, the defeated political leaders were taken to Cuzco for a period of training and then sent back to govern for the Incas. To ensure loyalty, however, their children remained in Cuzco as well-cared-for hostages and were educated in Incan ways. Third, the local gods of a conquered tribe were taken to Cuzco, where they were treated with respect. Meanwhile, the Incas built a temple to the Sun God in a privileged place, and Incan priests set about to convert the local populace. The Incas were not hostile to local deities, so long as the temple to their own god enjoyed a special location. Fourth, the Incas, while banning neither the native tongue nor ancient customs, insisted upon the acceptance of Quechua* as the official language. Finally, the Incas wisely made allowance for local customs, granted privileges to those who performed unusual tasks, and conducted feasts and festivals on holidays. Having established their authority in a new region, the Incas did not tolerate opposition. The slightest sign of rebellion led to deportations of large blocks of people to distant parts of the empire, where, among strangers, the rebels' influence would be diminished.

That Francisco Pizarro* with about 180 men and 27 horses toppled such a mighty empire so quickly in the early 1530s is astonishing. Several factors contributed to the Spaniards' accomplishment. First, fortunately for Pizarro and his band, the empire had recently been torn by civil war and was still suffering the effects of internal strife when the Spanish arrived. Second, Atahuallpa*, the victor in the civil conflict, underestimated the Spanish, whom he held in contempt. Finally, the political absolutism of the Incas ultimately was to their disadvantage. Once Pizarro captured and later executed the Saca Inca Atahuallpa and defeated the other nobles, the masses of corn farmers and craftsmen had little will to resist. For the masses, Pizarro's conquest meant that one set of rulers was replacing another, that Spanish feudalism was replacing Incan feudalism.

REFERENCES: P.A. Means, *Ancient Civilization of the Andes*, 1931; Alfred Metraux, *History of the Incas*, 1970.

John W. Storey

INDIANS. According to most New World archaeologists and anthropologists, the first Americans left Siberia sometime between 40,000 and 25,000 years ago. Around 40,000 B.C., the onset of an ice age lowered temperature levels around the world. Huge glaciers gradually covered Canada and the northern United States, freezing up millions of cubic miles of ocean water. The sea level dropped hundreds of feet as ocean water was absorbed into glacial ice, and the continental shelves around the world surfaced. Land masses became much more extensive. The shallow Bering Sea, North Pacific Ocean, and Arctic Ocean floors appeared, and a land bridge, known now as Beringia, connected Siberia with Alaska. At that point the migration of Siberian hunters, a process that took thousands of years, began. Millenium after millenium, their descendants spread throughout the two New World continents, from Alaska in the north to Tierra del Fuego in the south.

The number of indigenous people present in the Americas at the time of the arrival of the Spanish and Portuguese at the end of the fifteenth century has been a matter of heated scholarly debate. The estimates have ranged from approximately 10,000,000 people to more than 80,000,000; the upper range of that spread is probably more accurate. When the Europeans arrived, the indigenous people were divided into thousands of separate tribal entities, although there were a number of dominant groups. In the Caribbean islands and coastal areas, the fierce Karibs* were expanding their sphere of influence at the expense of the more peaceful Arawak* people. The Maya* Indians were dominant in the Yucatán*, southern Mexico*, and Guatemala*. In the valley of Mexico, the Aztecs* had established one of the New World's greatest civilizations. The Chibcha* people had come to dominate the plateau of what is today Colombia*, and the Incas* had constructed an empire that included contemporary Ecuador*, Peru*, and Bolivia*. In Chile*, the Araucanians* were an intensely independent people who ranged most of the way down the Andes plateau. The Guaraní* Indians dominated much of what is today Paraguay* and southwestern Brazil, while Tupí-speaking Indians ranged up and down the Atlantic coast of Brazil. Christopher Columbus*, convinced that he had reached the real Indies of Asia, called the indigenous people "Indians," a name by which they have been identified ever since.

The arrival of the Spaniards proved to be a catastrophe to the indigenous peoples of the New World. Separated from the Old World for thousands of years, they had no natural immunities to the diseases that accompanied the Europeans. The Indians found themselves facing epidemic death from smallpox, mumps, chickenpox, diphtheria, measles, and a host of other diseases. Within a single generation, almost all of the Arawak and Karib peoples of the Caribbean islands were dead. Precipitous population declines among the indigeous people occurred again and again in Central and South America as a result of contact with European ailments.

In addition to the impact of disease, the Indians also fell victim to Spanish policies in the New World. Historians and anthropologists studying the indigenous people of the New World are usually amazed at the consistency of the historical dynamics at work, whether they are looking at the sixteenth or the twentieth centuries. Beginning with the Spaniards, Europeans and their descendants have consistently approached the indigenous people from one of two perspectives. On the one hand, the Europeans have lusted after Indian economic resources. They created powerful negative stereotypes about the Indians, justifying the conflict necessary to exploit their labor and to drive them off the land. If the Indians really were bloodthirsty savages, they argued, society was better off without them. Spaniards exploited Indian labor through slavery, the *encomienda**, the *repartimiento**, and the *mita**. Although there were debates about better treatment for the Indians through the efforts of people like Bartolomé de las Casas*, the pattern of persecution and exploitation was hardly ameliorated. When the Indian population decline undermined labor exploitation, Spaniards, and later other Europeans, turned their attention to Indian land, concocting a variety of ways, legal and illegal, for driving Indians off the land and expropriating it for European use. Over the centuries, the resources that Europeans wanted changed. Still, whether it was the brazilwood of sixteenth-century Brazil or the oil today in the Ecuadorean Amazon, Europeans have continually tried to push Indians off the land. When the Indians would peaceably relocate to other, less valuable areas, most Europeans were willing to leave them alone, but the key was getting them off the valuable land. If violence was necessary, so be it. All over the New World, those notions led to genocidal assaults on the Indian tribes. The irony, of course, was that time, technology, and population expansion eventually rendered all the land valuable. The penetration by gold prospectors into Yanomamo land in northwestern Brazil today is just the latest chapter in a long history of exploitation and invasion.

The second approach to indigenous people seems more humane, superficially at least, and grew out of a combination of liberal guilt and missionary zeal. Dismayed by the violence inflicted upon indigenous people, some Europeans wanted to protect them, to insulate them from the more aggressive, less morally restrained settlers. They also wanted to change the indigenous people. They accepted their humanity but also their cultural inferiority. Instead of annihilating them to clear the land, however, liberals and missionaries sought to assimilate them into European culture. That is, they sought to remake Indian society, transforming Indians into "law-abiding" farmers who believed in private property, nuclear families, individual aggrandizement, and Jesus Christ. In order to facilitate the conversion of the Indians (and to get the Indians off the land), missionary groups like the Jesuits*, Franciscans*, Dominicans*, and Augustinians* established *reducciones*, *congregaciones*, and missions* to concentrate the Indian populations. In the process, many Indians left their tribal homelands. Those Indians who survived the diseases, slavery*, and genocidal attacks became an underclass of peons and laborers, a status that they still have throughout Latin America. The pattern is the same, whether it was the Jesuits of the sixteenth century or the New Tribes Mission or the Summer Institute of Linguistics in the 1980s. The irony is that although the methods of the assimilationists were far more benign than the genocidal ravages of the Indian haters, the results were the same: the virtual elimination of indigenous civilizations.

REFERENCE: James S. Olson, *The Indians of Central and South America: An Ethnohistorical Dictionary*, 1991.

INDIGO. The cultivation of indigo in the New World dates to pre-Hispanic times. The Indians* of northern Central America harvested wild indigo plants, called *xiquilite*, which they traded widely and used as a dye for textiles. During the late sixteenth century, the Spaniards refined the cultivation of indigo in Central America and developed indigo plantations on the Pacific slopes of El Salvador*, Guatemala*, and Nicaragua*. Spaniards first marketed indigo in 1576, when a shipload was sent from Nicaragua to New Spain*; there it was used in textile *obrajes* (factories). By 1600, indigo had replaced cacao* as the leading export and source of hard currency for the isthmus. Central American indigo was highly valued in the Old World, where it supplanted more expensive blue dyes from the Far East and inferior dyes produced from woad in Northern Europe.

From 1580 to 1620, the indigo industry thrived. *Añileros*, or indigo planters, employed the labor of Indians for cultivating and processing indigo into deep blue dye. Because the work was difficult and dangerous (extended contact with the toxins present in the indigo plant often proved fatal), the industry was limited by the labor supply, and by the mid-seventeenth century, it had stagnated. In the late seventeenth century, the indigenous population resurgence allowed the industry to expand, at which time African slaves* were also added to supplement the native labor force. By 1635, San Vicente, El Salvador, had become the hub of the indigo trade, although other important centers were located in Guatemala and Nicaragua. Indigo remained the most important export of the kingdom of Guatemala throughout the rest of the colonial period. The industry reached its peak during the second half of the eighteenth century, when relaxed Spanish trade restrictions and the nascent textile industry in northern Europe created a significant demand for the rich blue hue.

REFERENCES: Murdo J. MacLeod, *Spanish Central America: A Socioeconomic History, 1520–1720*, 1973; R. L. Woodward, Jr., *Central America: A Nation Divided*, 1983.

Virginia Garrard Burnett

INQUISITION. Founded by King Ferdinand* and Queen Isabella* in 1478, the Inquisition was designed to root out religious heresy in Spain. Because of the Patronato Real* in the New World, the Holy Office of the Inquisition actually came to enforce both religious and political orthodoxy. During most of the sixteenth century, inquisitorial power was exercised by secular and religious bodies, but independent Inquisition tribunals were established in Lima* in 1570, Mexico City* in 1571, and Cartagena* in 1610. Between 1610 and 1819, the Inquisition in Colombia* resulted in 168 convictions for heresy. They concentrated on Christian heresy, Jews, and censorship enforcement to eliminate intellectual heresy. Although some Indians* were tried before the tribunals for idolatry, polygamy, sacrifice, and other "sins," the Inquisition focused most of its attention on Europeans. The Inquisition often exacerbated church-state problems in the New World colonies and frequently became involved in political infighting and corruption as well. With the independence movements in Latin America, the Inquisition was abolished.

REFERENCES: Richard E. Greenleaf, *The Mexican Inquisition of the Sixteenth Century*, 1969; Stanley M. Hordes, "The Inquisition as Economic and Political Agent: The Campaign of the Mexican Holy Office Against the Crypto-Jews in the Mid-Seventeenth Century," *Americas*, 39 (1982), 22–38.

INTENDENCIA. By the middle of the eighteenth century, it was clear to even the most casual observers that the imperial bureaucracy in Spanish America was inefficient and corrupt, and that economic stagnation and declining revenues to the royal treasury were the result. The *intendencia* was a major Bourbon reform introduced by King Charles III* and designed to address those problems. Imposed on Cuba* in 1764, the *intendencia* reached the viceroyalties in Río de la Plata* in 1782, Peru* in 1784, and New Spain* in 1786. By 1790, the system was in place throughout the Spanish Empire. The *intendente* was a royally appointed officer of peninsular birth, and the *intendencia* was a jurisdictional subdivision of a viceroyalty. Each *intendencia* was subdivided into *partidos*, each of which was presided over by a *subdelegado*. The *intendente* and *subdelegado* were charged with overseeing administrative, military, financial, and judicial affairs within their area of jurisdiction. The tendency toward graft and corruption was reduced because the *intendentes* were salaried employees of the Crown. The Crown expected them to expedite the collection of royal taxes and to stimulate commerce and industry. They replaced the *gobernadores, corregidores**, and *alcaldes mayores** and enjoyed the right to communicate directly with the royal government in Spain without having to go through the *audiencia** or viceroy*. Although the officials of the viceroyalties, *audiencias*, and *cabildos** resisted the imposition of the *intendencias*, the latter had come to dominate local government in the Spanish Empire by the time of the wars of independence. The viceroyalty of Peru, for example, was divided into the *intendencias* of Arequipa*, Cuzco*, Huamanga*, Huancavelica*, Tarma*, Trujillo*, and Puno*.

REFERENCES: Lillian Estelle Fisher, *The Intendant System in Spanish America*, 1929; John Lynch, *Spanish Colonial Administration: The Intendancy System in the Viceroyalty of the Río de la Plata*, 1958.

INTERNAL PROVINCES. In 1777, Spain created a new administrative unit known as the Internal Provinces to deal with expanding settlement patterns in northern Mexico as well as continuing problems with hostile Indian* tribes. At first, this unit included all of the northern provinces of New Spain* with the exception of California*. It was headed by a commandant-general and was independent of the viceroy*. The exact authority of the Internal Provinces administration was poorly defined, since each of the constituent provinces had a civil governor who was dependent on the commandant-general in some areas and independent of him in others. Between 1788 and 1793 and 1813 and 1821, the Internal Provinces was divided into western and eastern units. The eastern unit included Coahuila*, Texas*, and New Leon*, while the western unit included Sonora, New Vizcaya*, and New Mexico*; California* was later added. New Vizcaya became part of the *intendencia** of Durango in 1787. In 1793, the Internal Provinces were united into a single unit again, although California, New Leon, and New Santander fell under the viceregal control in Mexico City*. New Santander was returned to the Internal Provinces in 1813 when it was again divided into eastern and western sections. The Internal Provinces unit was dissolved in 1821 when Spanish authority ended in Mexico.

REFERENCES: Luis Navarro García, "La governación y comandancia general de las Provincias Internas del Norte de Nueva España," *Revista del Instituto de historia del Derecho Ricardo Levene*, 14 (1963), 118–51; Luis Navarro García, *Las Provincias Internas en el Siglo XIX*, 1965.

IRADIER Y BULFY, MANUEL. Manuel Iradier y Bulfy was born in the Basque country of Spain in 1854. In 1875, at the head of an organization known as "La Exploradora," Iradier explored the region of what is today Equatorial Guinea and Fernando Po. In 1884, with financing from the Society of Africanists and Colonists*, Iradier went back to the area and, in the course of several months, signed treaties with hundreds of chiefs, giving Spain a territorial claim in West Africa. His book describing the journeys was published as *Africa Tropical* in 1887. Manuel Iradier y Bulfy died in 1911.

REFERENCE: Max Liniger-Goumaz, *Historical Dictionary of Equatorial Guinea*, 1988.

IRALA, DOMINGO MARTÍNEZ DE. See MARTÍNEZ DE IRALA, DOMINGO.

ISABELLA OF CASTILE. Isabella I, patron of the explorer Christopher Columbus*, was born April 22, 1451, in Madrigal. She was queen of Castile* from 1474 until her death on November 26, 1504. In 1469, Isabella married Ferdinand* of Aragón, uniting the two kingdoms of Aragón and Castile, and providing the impetus for a unified modern Spain. With her husband, Isabella was responsible for directing the reconquest of most of the Iberian peninsula from the Muslim Moors. By 1492, with the capture of the Moorish stronghold of Granada, Isabella became convinced of the necessity for Spain to expand its trade with Asia. Along with her chief adviser, royal treasurer Luis de Santangel, Isabella saw merit in the plan of Columbus to find a safe and profitable trade route to the Far East by sailing west across the Atlantic Ocean.

Spain's interest in a western trade route, however, brought it into conflict with the other great nation of explorers. Portugal had been interested in overseas expansion since the days of Prince Henry the Navigator in the early fifteenth century, but it had been focusing its efforts on finding an eastern route to the Indies. In 1494, Isabella attempted to claim all the land mass discovered by Columbus for Spain, but the Treaty of Tordesillas* placed the demarcation line between Spanish and Portuguese interests in the New World west of the mouth of the Amazon. Isabella's failure thus allowed Portugal to colonize the entire eastern two-thirds of South America.

REFERENCES: Irene A. Plunket, *Isabel of Castile*, 1973; J. W. Thompson, *Economic and Social History of Europe in the Later Middle Ages, 1300-1530*, 1958; Denys Hay, *Europe in the Fourteenth and Fifteenth Centuries*, 1966.

William G. Ratliff

ITURBIDE, AGUSTÍN DE. Born in Valladolid[*] (now Morelia), New Spain[*], in 1783 to a wealthy conservative, and royalist, Mexican family, Agustín de Iturbide sympathized very early with the cause of independence but was hostile to any social revolution. He fought on the royalist side at Monte de las Cruces (1811) against Manuel Hidalgo's[*] insurgents, and later against José María Morelos[*]; Iturbide actually contributed to the latter's defeat at Puruaran (1814). Iturbide's military activities centered on the elimination of the insurgents, in which cause he was quite successful. After 1816, he was ordered to provide protection to silver convoys through rebel-infested territory. He appears to have used this new activity for personal enrichment, which is the background for his forced retirement by Viceroy Juan Ruiz de Apodaca[*]. Iturbide attempted to rehabilitate himself, and he thus spent some time in the convent of La Profesa where he met influential people who were talking openly about independence.

The return of liberalism in Spain after the Riego revolt of 1820 precipitated events, since Mexican society was hostile to the radical brand of liberalism emanating from the Peninsula. It was then that Iturbide seized the opportunity that Apodaca offered him when he gave Iturbide the command of the royalist army in 1820. He was defeated by Vicente Guerrero[*] but then reached an understanding with the guerrilla leader. Sensing the mood in the country, he marched to Iguala where, in a typical *pronunciamiento*, he now proclaimed the famous *Plan de Iguala* with its three guarantees: Independence, Only [Catholic] Religion, and Equality between Mexicans and Spaniards. It represented Mexico's conservative reaction against liberal Spain. The army now became the Army of the Three Guarantees. Iturbide offered the Mexican crown to Ferdinand VII[*], in order to free him from the liberal yoke in the Peninsula, and invited him to come over and to rule as a conservative monarch. Ferdinand VII refused and did not recognize Mexican independence.

Although he initially faced difficulties, most of the country eventually rallied to his side, as did important figures, including Antonio López de Santa Anna, Nicolás Bravo, and Guadalupe Victoria[*]. When the new liberal viceroy, Juan O'Donojú, arrived in New Spain[*], he quickly seized the reality and signed the Treaty of Córdoba, which was meaningless since the Spanish Cortes likewise did not accept it. The stage was now set for Iturbide to fill the vacuum. On May 18, 1822, he crowned himself Emperor Agustín I of Mexico, with a congress voting 67 to 15 in his favor. Still, his empire lasted less than ten months. Mounting difficulties and oppositon forced him to abdicate in February 1823 and to leave for Italy. He did not know that the government that followed his abdication had decreed the death penalty in case of his return. And return he did, in 1824. Apprehended, he was shot, like every other leader of the Mexican independence movement. Today, Mexico has still not forgiven Iturbide for his conservative views, his opposition to social reforms, and his military campaigns against Hidalgo and Morelos. Thus, he remains ignored.

REFERENCES: Timothy E. Anthony, "The Rule of Agustín de Iturbide: A Reappraisal," *Journal of Latin American Studies*, 17 (1985), 79–110; William S. Robertson, *Iturbide of Mexico*, 1952.

O. Carlos Stoetzer

ITURRIGARAY Y ARÓSTEGUI, JOSÉ JOAQUÍN VICENTE DE. Born of an aristocratic family from Navarre in Cádiz, Spain, on June 27, 1742, where his father José was serving as a royal official, young José Joaquin Vicente de Iturrigaray followed a military career. At the age of 16, in the year 1759, the year when King Charles III* ascended to the throne, Iturrigaray became a cadet in the Spanish infantry; three years later, he was promoted to second lieutenant and joined the Portuguese campaign. He then rose quickly to captain of the Alcántara regiment, and in 1765, he and his two brothers were jointly admitted to the military Order of Santiago. Among his achievements in those years was his appointment to captain of the Royal Carabineros in 1777 and his participation in the siege of Gibraltar* of 1782 during the Franco-Spanish alliance. In 1786, he married María Francisca Inés de Jaúregui y Aróstegui.

His brilliant career was duly recognized when, in 1789, after 30 years of devoted service, he was promoted to brigadier. The war with revolutionary France in 1793 gave him new opportunities: he joined the Spanish army that invaded the Roussilon. It was in this campaign that Iturrigaray distinguished himself especially in the siege of Perpignan, during the attacks of Villalonga and Coll de Banyuls. His military exploits resulted in his promotion to lieutenant general at the age of 53. He was then appointed governor of Cádiz, and thereafter, in 1800, second commander of Andalucía under General Tomas de Morla, a friend of Manuel Godoy.* His last important position before reaching New Spain was that of commander of the Andalusian army in the campaign against Portugal in 1801. In 1803, he was appointed viceroy* of New Spain*, a position he would hold until 1808.

He arrived in Mexico City* in 1803, and it was through him that the first act of the Mexican emancipation would unfold five years later. He was held in high esteem in view of his distinguished military career, even though he was a favorite of Godoy, the Prince of Peace, and thus was somewhat tarnished. Still, in a relatively short time, Iturrigaray succeeded in gaining the sympathy of the Mexicans, no easy task for a successor of brilliant envoys. His arrival coincided with the famous visit by Alexander von Humboldt*, for whom New Spain was at that time the most cultured nation of Spanish America.

Iturrigaray began his term with the installation of the statue of Charles IV, (which was relocated three times and now stands in a sidestreet between the Zócalo and the Alameda) and the introduction of vaccination. His popularity was quite high, as is evident from a document in the Mexico City *cabildo** that cites his good qualities. The war against Britain required the raising of funds however, and led to the famous *Real Cédula de Consolidación* (December 26, 1804), which affected the religious orders. Aimed against ecclesiastical properties, the action hurt many people and fostered resentment. Another controversial problem was his plan for the defense of the viceroyalty which called for the abandonment of Veracruz*, but the town was able to scuttle the project. Iturrigaray's virtues were generally recognized, especially his interest in public works, but it became known that he was using his high office to increase his personal wealth. His venality, his ties to the unpopular Godoy, and an undignified regime made him an easy target of increased discontent.

When the news of the plot of Aranjuez arrived in Mexico, it caused a sensation—the *criollos** in New Spain interpreting the revolt as a rebellion against an immoral regime and a hated government. Iturrigaray was thus put in a difficult situation, not made easier by the events of Bayonne two weeks later. He thus drifted toward the *criollo* cause, since he could not hope that the Spanish Junta Suprema Central (the regency) would keep him in his position. He aimed at gaining time and may have thought of becoming the first king of an independent New Spain. He called the famous meeting of a Junta General on August 9, 1808, a heterogenous group of some 82 representatives that was to prepare for a Cortes of New Spain. It was in this meeting that the Spanish point of view, expressed by the *oidor** Guillermo de Aguirre*, won. The Spanish party was so enraged about the meeting that it blamed Viceroy Iturrigaray for his embarrassing and highly questionable initiative; he should never have called the meeting in the first place since it opened a Pandora's box of problems. The split now widened between *audiencia** and the viceroy, and, on September 16, 1808, he was deposed and shipped back to Spain. Pedro de Garibay, the choice of the Spanish party, took his place for a short time.

On his return to Spain, Iturrigaray was subjected to the customary *residencia** with the Spanish party of New Spain only too eager to see him punished. His legal troubles lasted seven years, a real ordeal, until he died in Madrid in 1815. The legal proceedings by his widow lasted until 1833 in both Spain and the now-independent Mexico.

REFERENCES: Enrique Lafuent Farrari, *El virrey Iturrigaray y los orígenes de la independencia de Méjico*, 1941; R. Majó Framis, *Vidas de los navegantes, conquistadores y colonizadores españoles de los siglos XVI, XVII y XVIII*. Vol. III: *Colonizadores y fundadores en Indias*, 1954.

O. Carlos Stoetzer

J

JACINTO, EMILIO. Emilio Jacinto was born in 1857 in Trozo, Manila*, the Philippines*. He received an undergraduate degree from the Colegio de San Juan de Letrán and then took a law degree from the Universidad de Santo Tomás. As a young man, Jacinto joined the Katipunan* rebel movement, in which he wrote widely and edited the movement's newspaper. Jacinto's theme was always the independence of the Philippines. Jacinto rose to second in command, just behind José Bonifacio. After Bonifacio's death, Jacinto led the Katipunan army in Majayjay. Jacinto was captured by the Spanish in 1899, and he died while in their custody.

REFERENCE: E. Arsenio Manuel, *Dictionary of Philippine Biography*, 1955.

JAMAICA. Jamaica is a large island of 4,470 square miles, located in the Caribbean Sea about 80 miles south of eastern Cuba*. The island is 144 miles long and 49 miles wide at its widest point. Christopher Columbus* discovered Jamaica on May 1, 1494, during his second voyage to the New World. During his fourth voyage, Columbus was stranded on the northern coast of Jamaica for more than a year in 1503 and 1504. Spanish rule lasted until 1655, and eight Spanish families took control of Jamaica. The Spaniards completely exterminated the native Arawak* Indians who were on the island when Columbus arrived. Population growth was very slow. The Spanish families imported African slaves* to replace the Arawak Indians, and by the middle of the seventeenth century, the Jamaican population was about 3,000 people, most of them of African descent. In the Treaty of Madrid* of 1670, Spain formally ceded Jamaica to Great Britain.

REFERENCES: Aggrey Brown, *Color, Class, and Politics in Jamaica*, 1980; Douglas Hall, *Free Jamaica, 1838-1865: A Study in Economic Growth*, 1961; Katrin Norris, *Jamaica: The Search for an Identity*, 1972.

JAVERIANA UNIVERSITY. Javeriana University was established by the Jesuit* order in Bogotá*, Colombia*, in 1621. When the Jesuits were expelled from the New World in 1767, laymen assumed the direction of the university. Along with the University of San Tomás, Javeriana University was one of the two centers of higher learning in colonial Colombia.

REFERENCE: Robert H. Davis, *Historical Dictionary of Colombia*, 1977.

JENKINS' EAR, WAR OF. The enforcement of Spain's trade monopoly in the West Indies was becoming increasingly difficult in the eighteenth century. The *asiento** that Spain had been forced to grant the English South Sea Company in the Treaty of Utrecht* was an example of Spain's weakening position with regard to that monopoly. Spain relied on *guarda-costas*, privately fitted ships that received remuneration from the sale of the prizes they captured, to prevent unauthorized trade. This system was obviously open to abuse by privateers; without the proper Spanish commissions, they captured foreign ships and kept all the prize for themselves. Even legally sanctioned *guarda-costas* often acted brutally and arbitrarily in seizing ships and declaring their cargoes contraband. As a result, there were many grievances filed against Spain in English courts; there were also claims filed by Spain for English depredations against Spanish shipping. Consequently, unresolved grievances and financial claims were pending resolution in both countries.

It was within this atmosphere that Captain Robert Jenkins appeared in London in 1738 with his famous tale. According to him, his ship, the *Rebecca*, had been seized by a Spanish *guarda-costa* in 1731, and his ear had been cut off in reprisal. William Beckford, M.P., who introduced Jenkins before the House of Commons, later cast doubt on Jenkins's story. True or not, the tale angered members of parliament who promptly resolved that British subjects had the right to sail any waters of the Americas. Public opinion in England, enflamed by jingoistic patriotism and Protestantism, pushed for war with Spain. Hoping to avert war, the two governments pushed forward negotiations for the monetary damages claimed by each country. The Convention of El Pardo was signed on January 14, 1739. The agreement called for Spain to pay England £95,000. This figure was far less than the £160,000 claimed by England and therefore a tacit admission that English claims were inflated. It was also an admission on Spain's part that depredations against foreign shipping had actually occurred. English public opinion was loudly unfavorable to the convention, which was ratified in February 1739. The Duke of Newcastle, prone to heed public opinion, was also concerned about another Franco-Spanish alliance. He therefore maintained the fleet off the Spanish coast to protect Gibraltar* and Minorca. This move angered the Spanish. In retaliation, they said that the £95,000 would not be paid, and they suspended the South Sea Company's *asiento* in May 1739. In August, Keene was recalled from Madrid, and war was declared on October 19, 1739.

As hostilities with Spain opened, the English government assumed that it would also have to fight the French. France had strong dynastic ties with Spain and was England's main rival for trade in Spanish America. Indeed, André Hercule de Fleury, the chief minister of France, was reluctant about entering into a war to aid Spain but did dispatch a fleet to prevent England from seizing Spanish territory in America. The English were initially successful. On November 20, 1739, Admiral Edward Vernon captured Porto Bello and declared the town's trade open. This success was not followed up, however, because Vernon was obliged to search for the French fleet. Later, combined operations against Cartagena* and Santiago de Cuba failed as the forces suffered from yellow fever. The English were able to effect considerable disruption in the flow of treasure back to Spain from the West Indies, forcing Spanish trade to be carried by individual ships that were vulnerable to raiders. This became the pattern of war in the West Indies until 1744, when France openly entered the conflict as the War of the Austrian Succession* unfolded. As a result, war engulfed not only the West Indies but all of colonial North America.

REFERENCE: J. T. Laning, *The Diplomatic History of Georgia: A Study of the Epoch of Jenkins' Ear*, 1936.

Michael Dennis

JEREZ, FRANCISCO DE. Francisco de Jerez was born in Seville*, Spain, around 1497. He went to the New World as a young man and became the personal secretary to Francisco Pizarro*. Jerez was an eyewitness to the conquest of Peru*. His recollections of the conquest, titled *Verdadera relación de la conquista del Perú y Provincia del Cuzco, llamada la Nueva Castilla*, is today considered a key primary source for the study of the conquest. Jerez died around 1563.

REFERENCE: Albert William Bork and Georg Maier, *Historical Dictionary of Ecuador*, 1973.

JESUIT REPUBLICS. Among the most notable and controversial of the Jesuit* activities in the New World were the so-called "Jesuit republics"—a series of *reducciones** established among tropical forest Indian* tribes in what are today Argentina*, Paraguay*, Bolivia*, and Brazil during the late seventeenth and eighteenth centuries. In 1609, Hernando Arias*, the governor of Asunción*, requested that Jesuit missionaries be sent to Paraguay, and they began establishing the missions* within a few years. Their population consisted of from 1,000 to 8,000 Indians, usually Guaraní*; Europeans were excluded. The missions became self-sustaining and economically prosperous enough to begin exporting production surpluses. Their productivity brought them into competition with local Spanish and Brazilian merchants, a fact that greatly increased resentment of the Jesuits and elicited calls for the liquidation of the republics. The republics were tax exempt, governed by canon law, and off-limits to Portuguese and Spanish slavers. The Jesuits also pursued acculturation with a vengeance, trying to prove to skeptics that the Indians were human beings capable of Western learning. In Paraguay, the most important of the Jesuit republics were San Ignacio, San Cosme, Trinidad, and Jesús.

Because of their location, the Jesuit republics were also a source of conflict between Spain and Portugal, both of which claimed the region. Between 1612 and 1656, the Paulistas of Brazil sent slave raiders into the Jesuit missions. On several occasions, those slaving expeditions stole or killed so many people that the Jesuits had to relocate the missions farther to the west. In the Treaty of Madrid* of 1750, which settled the boundary dispute between Spain and Portuguese Brazil, Spain ceded to Brazil an area that contained seven of the Jesuit settlements. When the Indians rebelled against coming under Portuguese authority and having to relocate to Spanish authority, combined Spanish and Portuguese military forces crushed them. The existence of the republics and the resentment of them were a main reason for the expulsion of the Jesuits from Brazil in 1760 and from the Spanish colonies in 1767. At the time of their expulsion, the Jesuits were maintaining 30 missions with 150,000 converts in the border region, 15 *reducciones* in the Gran Chaco, and dozens of missions elsewhere in Latin America. Upon the departure of the Jesuits, the mission areas were either taken over by other religious orders, usually the Franciscans*, or were simply dissolved, leaving the Indians to return to the jungle.

REFERENCE: Philip Caraman, *Lost Paradise: The Jesuit Republics in South America*, 1976.

JESUITS. Jesuits are members of a religious order of the Roman Catholic Church*, the Society of Jesus. The society was founded by Saint Ignatius of Loyola and several followers, including Saint Francis Xavier, in 1534 and confirmed as a religious order by Pope Paul III in 1540. The idea for the creation of the society came to Ignatius, a Spanish nobleman, while he was recovering from a war wound in 1521. The avowed purposes of the society were the spiritual growth of its own members and the salvation of all men and women. The fundamental philosophy of the society is found in *Spiritual Exercises*, written and revised by Ignatius over a period of years. The Jesuit organization was almost military in its highly centralized authority. Ignatius was the first superior general, and he retained that title until his death. Although not created for that purpose, the Society of Jesus rapidly became the most effective instrument of the Counter Reformation*. The weapons of the Jesuits were education, missionary work, the confessional, and stringent obedience and loyalty to the pope. By the early seventeenth century, the Society of Jesus had more than 15,000 members. Jesuit schools were synonymous with excellence in education, and Jesuits were the confessors to the Roman Catholic rulers of Europe. Moreover, the Jesuits established missions in Japan, China, India, the Philippines*, Africa, Latin America, and North America. Because it was founded so late, the Jesuit order did not pioneer missionary work in Spain's New World empire. The Franciscans*, Dominicans*, and Augustinians* led the way, but eventually, the Jesuits assumed the largest role. In 1581, Jesuit missionaries reached the Philippines, and they also taught indigenous people in the Marianas* and Caroline* Islands; when the Jesuits were expelled from Spanish overseas possessions in 1767, 158 priests

also had to leave the Philippines. The first permanent Jesuit mission in Peru*
was established in 1567 and the first in New Spain* was founded in 1572. By
1615, there were 1,180 Jesuit missionaries laboring in the New World, and that
number had nearly doubled to more than 2,300 in 1710. By 1750, the Jesuits
were operating two universities, 102 colleges, and 24 seminaries in the Spanish
colonies of the New World. They also established more than 100 *reducciones*,
known as the Jesuit republics*, for the Indian* tribes, most notably in what are
today Paraguay* and parts of Uruguay*, Brazil, and Argentina*. In all of these
locales, the Jesuits suffered intermittent persecution and often martyrdom, but,
with the exception of Japan from which they were expelled in the early seventeenth century, the Jesuits retained lasting influence. In China, they were the
nucleus of the large Roman Catholic community that developed in that country.
In India, after a slow beginning, Robert de Nobili attracted many converts by
adapting Christianity to the customs of the people. De Nobili's practices drew
criticism from his colleagues and from other sectors of the Roman Catholic
Church, but they proved effective in the East. In Paraguay*, the Jesuits attempted
to save the Indians by establishing the *reducciones*, self-supporting Indian communities from which most whites were barred. In New France, the Jesuits had
successes and failures among the Huron and the Iroquois which are recounted
in detail in the *Jesuit Relations*. Jesuits were instrumental in the exploration of
North America, and a Jesuit priest, Jacques Marquette, accompanied Louis Joliet*
down the Mississippi River to the mouth of the Arkansas River, where it became
clear that there was a waterway from Canada to the Gulf of Mexico.

In the eighteenth century, the Jesuits were opposed by the absolute monarchs,
who resented their involvement in nationalist politics, and by the Enlightenment*
liberals, who resented their conservative philosophy. The Jesuits were banned
from Portugal in 1759, Brazil in 1760, and the Spanish Empire in 1767. Pope
Clement XIV suppressed the Society of Jesus in 1773. The post-Napoleonic period proved more hospitable; Pope Pius VII reestablished it in 1814. In the twentieth century, the Society of Jesuits in the United States has more than 30,000
members, and there are more Jesuits in the United States than in any other country.

REFERENCES: W. V. Bangert, *A History of the Society of Jesus*, 1972; Christopher
Hollis, *The Jesuits—A History*, 1968.

Peter T. Sherrill

JIMÉNEZ, JOSÉ MARIANO. José Mariano Jiménez was born in San Luis
Potosí*, New Spain*, in 1781. He studied and apprenticed as a mining engineer
in San Luis Potosí but he is best remembered for his early conversion to the
cause of Mexican independence. Jiménez rose to the rank of lieutenant general
in the rebel army and saw to the production of large volumes of ordnance. In
1810, Jiménez commanded the rebel army that conquered Saltillo and San Antonio* in the Borderlands*. He was captured by royalist forces in Coahuila* and
executed on July 26, 1811.

REFERENCE: John A. Caruso, *The Liberators of Mexico*, 1967.

JIMÉNEZ DE ENCINO, SALVADOR. Salvador Jiménez de Encino was born in Málaga, Spain, in 1765. He came to America with the entourage of José Antonio de San Alberto, the new Archbishop of Charcas*, and he graduated from the University of Charcas with degrees in law and theology. After graduation, Jiménez returned to Spain where he spent several years as canon of Córdoba and Málaga. In 1815, he was appointed bishop of Popayán* in New Granada* and he assumed the post in 1818. By that time, the wars of independence were well under way. He supported the royalist forces and, when he excommunicated the leading figures of the patriot movement, the congress of Colombia* declared the bishopric at Popayán vacant. In 1822, Jiménez asked to return to Spain, but Simón Bolívar appealed to him not to vacate the church. By then, Jiménez realized that independence was the wave of the future and agreed to stay. He died in Popayán on February 13, 1841.

REFERENCE: G. García Herrera, *Un obispo de historia: El obispo de Popayán, don Salvador Ximénez de Enciso y Cobos Padilla*, 1961.

JIMÉNEZ DE QUESADA, GONZALO. Gonzalo Jiménez de Quesada was born either in Córdoba or Granada, Spain, in 1509, and he spent time in both cities as a youth. He studied law at the University of Salamanca and practiced law for a number of years before coming to Santa Marta* on the northern coast of South America with Pedro Fernández de Lugo in 1536. Jiménez de Quesada left Santa Marta later in 1536 at the head of an expedition exploring the Magdalena River. Eventually the expedition conquered the Chibcha* Indians and founded the city of Santa Fe near contemporary Bogotá*, Colombia*. By 1539, the region was known as New Granada*, and although Jiménez de Quesada vied for the governorship of the province, he was unsuccessful. He spent some time in Spain in the 1540s but returned permanently to New Granada in 1551. Eighteen years later, Gonzalo Jiménez de Quesada led a new expedition in search of the fabled El Dorado* on the east side of the Andes Mountains. The expedition returned empty-handed to Santa Fe in 1572. He is also remembered for his extensive historical writings, particularly his chronicles of the conquest of New Granada. Jiménez died there in 1579.

REFERENCES: Germán Arciniegas, *El caballero de El Dorado*, 1969; R. B. Cumminghame Graham, *The Conquest of New Granada: Being the Life of Gonzalo Jiménez de Quesada*, 1922.

JOINT STOCK COMPANY. Unlike the British and Dutch colonial enterprises, in which investment capital from private companies was the driving force behind imperial expansion, the Spanish Empire was driven by state enterprise, and the Crown retained almost complete control over its colonial domains. The British East India Company and the Dutch East India Company came to exercise sovereign powers over their colonies, and the governments of Great Britain and the Netherlands were able to take over that sovereignty only with the greatest difficulty. That was not the case in the Spanish Empire. There were companies heavily invested in colonial concerns—such as the Caracas Company*, the Havana Company*, the Galicia Company, the Barcelona Company, and the North African Company—but most of them were short-lived and had a difficult time making substantial profits. Regulation and control from the government was just too extensive.

REFERENCE: Carlo Cipolla, *Before the Industrial Revolution: European Society and Economy, 1000–1700,* 1976.

JUARROS, DOMINGO. Domingo Juarros was born in Guatemala* in 1752. He became a Roman Catholic priest and also wrote widely as an historian. Juarros's greatest scholarly achievement was his multivolume *Compendio de la historia de la ciudad de Guatemala,* which was published between 1808 and 1818. It is today considered to be an invaluable primary source for early Guatemalan history. Juarros died in 1820.

REFERENCE: Richard E. Moore, *Historical Dictionary of Guatemala,* 1973.

JUNÍN, BATTLE OF. In 1824, nationalist forces under the command of Simón Bolívar* lost control of Lima* after the mutiny of troops at the garrison in Callao*. Bolívar retreated north to Trujillo*, spent a few months regrouping, and launched an offensive again in June 1824. The Battle of Junín was fought in the highlands, with Bolívar's 9,000 man army fighting against royalist forces under General José Canterac*. Bolívar was assisted in command by General Antonio José de Sucre, and their troops forced the royalists into a retreat toward Lima. Although the battle itself was of little tactical significance, it did hearten Peruvian nationalists and stimulate the independence movement. Royalist forces retreated deeper into the Peruvian highlands, where they were eventually defeated at the Battle of Ayacucho*.

REFERENCE: Clements Markham, *A History of Peru,* 1982.

JURO. The *juro* was a personal property or inheritance tax sometimes imposed by the Spanish Crown in the overseas settlements. In 1639, for example, it was imposed in New Granada*. The *juro* was extremely unpopular among the well-to-do.

REFERENCE: Robert H. Davis, *Historical Dictionary of Colombia,* 1977.

K

KARIB. The word "Karib" (Carib) has been used by ethnologists to describe an Amerindian group as well as a large group of Amerindian languages. Those languages today are scattered widely throughout Venezuela*, Colombia*, Brazil, Guyana, Surinam, French Guiana, Belize*, Peru*, Honduras*, and the Antilles. Included in this group are the Choco languages of Colombia, as well as Carijona, Carare, Pijiao, Muzo, Motilón, and Opone; Acawai, Pemón, Yekuana, Yauarana, and Panare in Venezuela; Rucuyen in French Guiana; Colan and Patagón in Peru; Oyana and Tiriyo in Surinam; Garifuna* in Belize and Honduras; and the Apalai, Aracaju, Upurui, Apiaca, Atroahi, Waimiri, Nahukua, Parucoto, Waiwai, Waiboi, Caxuiana, Saluma, Shikiana, Macushi, Zapara, Yekuana, Pawishana, and Pianokoto in Brazil. The Kariban languages remain one of the most extensive language groups among indigenous people in the New World.

Most ethnologists today argue that the Karib tribes were once a warlike group of Amerindians who lived in the Amazon River Valley. Beginning in the 1200s, some of them began migrating to the northeast where they spread throughout the Guianas. Around A.D. 1300, their migrations pushed them from northeastern South America out to the islands of the Caribbean Sea, where they conquered the more peaceful Arawakan* tribes. The Karib Indians were farmers who raised cassava and lived in small, independent villages. Those Karib groups that conquered the Arawak usually killed the Arawak men and married the Arawak women; the women and their children continued to speak the Arawakan languages while the Karib men spoke the Karib language. By the second generation on the islands, however, the Karib languages died out. By the middle of the fifteenth century, the Karibs had taken over the Lesser Antilles, but their expansion to the Greater Antilles was blocked by the arrival of the Spanish explorers early in the sixteenth century.

The Karib Indians did not survive the presence of the Spaniards. War and disease decimated their numbers, virtually depopulating the islands of Amerindians. On St. Vincent, the surviving Karibs intermarried freely with escaped African slaves, creating a new ethnic group known as Black Karibs or Garifuna. The Garifuna revolted against British rule on St. Vincent in 1795, but the British crushed the rebellion and deported 5,000 Garifuna to the island of Roatan off the coast of Honduras. There, their numbers multiplied and they eventually migrated to the coast, where they now constitute a large ethnic group of 100,000 people in Belize and British Honduras*.

The Karib Indians proper, who use the word Kulina (Kalina, Calina, Caribe, Galibi) to describe themselves, still exist today, though in reduced numbers. On the island of Dominica*, there are approximately 400 of them living on a government reservation, and thousands more live in scattered tribal groups in Guyana, Surinam, and French Guiana.

REFERENCES: Kathleen Adams, *Barama River Carib Narratives*, 1979; Ellen B. Basso, *Carib-Speaking Indians: Culture, Society, and Language*, 1977; Marc de Civrieux, *Los Caribes y la conquista de la Guayana Española*, 1976; William Curtis Farabee, *The Central Caribs*, 1924; Peter Kloos, *The Maroni River Caribs of Surinam*, 1971.

KATIPUNAN. The Katipunan was a secret society founded in 1892 to prepare Filipinos* for a war of independence against Spain. The group's full name was *Kataas-taasan Kagalang-galang na Katipunan ng mga Anak ng Bayan* (often abbreviated KKK) or Highest and Most Respectable Society of the Sons of the Nation. The Spanish had ignored previous pleas for reform. They allowed some freedom for Filipinos to organize in Spain but not in the islands. Dr José Rizal* and other *ilustrados** disavowed revolution, asking only for union with Spain and legal equality for Filipinos. Ironically, Spanish paranoia created the revolution. On the very day that Spanish authorities sent Rizal to internal exile on Mindanao*, July 7, 1892, a middle-class nationalist named Andrés Bonifacio* founded the Katipunan at a secret gathering on Azcarrage Street, Manila*.

The Katipunan's style was awash with secret rituals. Many anticlerical Filipinos had been attracted to Masonry, and Katipuneros mixed Masonic ritual with Catholic and Chinese practices. There were odd induction ceremonies featuring blood oaths, skulls, and swords. There were code names, secret passwords, and ciphered messages. Some of this was necessary for the group to protect itself from discovery, and some was merely designed to create an aura of mystery that would attract superstitious peasants. The Katipunan differed from previous elite meliorist groups in having a membership drawn from the middle and lower classes. Filipino peasants had frequently joined millenarian insurrections led by local messiahs; the Katipunan was able to channel this primitive protest into a forward-looking revolutionary movement, the first in modern Asian history.

Despite its arcane rituals, the Katipunan espoused rational goals: mutual aid among the oppressed; secularism; political and economic reform; and education for the masses. In essence, it sought to create a national Filipino identity. The

Katipunan's by-laws created a virtual shadow government at the national, provincial, and municipal level. For two years, the Katipunan remained dormant, but by 1894, Bonifacio was conducting initiation ceremonies in the mountains above Manila. *Katipuñeros* also began to stockpile weapons. Memberships grew rapidly in 1896, from 300 to perhaps 30,000, due in part to the publication of a newspaper, *Kalayaan* (Freedom) that featured incendiary anti-Spanish articles. The police discovered the press after the first issue was published, but the 2,000 copies of *Kalayaan* that circulated in Manila and the adjoining Tagalog* provinces aroused Filipinos already fed up with clerical abuses and Spain's reactionary colonial policies.

Matters came to a head in 1896 when the Spanish stupidly executed Rizal, who had disavowed the revolution but became its first martyr. The Katipunan had to advance the date of the Filipino declaration of independence to August 23 because the authorities had gotten wind of their plans from a Katipuñero who confessed to a priest. Bonifacio's forces fled from the northern suburbs of Manila to the Marikina hills ten miles away and from there further into the mountains. Meanwhile, Katipuñeros in Cavite province routed the Spanish and quickly gained control of a number of towns under the leadership of Emilio Aguinaldo*. The Katipunan was weakened by personal and regional rivalries. Aguinaldo's faction clashed with that of Bonifacio, and Bonifacio was tried and executed on May 10, 1897. The Katipunan is considered to have come to an end on that date, but it had served its purpose of preparing and instigating the Philippine Revolution.

REFERENCE: Renato Constantino, *A History of the Philippines*, 1975.

Ross Marlay

KINO, EUSEBIO FRANCISCO. Eusebio Francisco Kino was born in Segno, Trent, Italy, and baptized on August 10, 1645. He attended the Jesuit* college in Trent before leaving for Hall, near Innsbruck, Austria, in 1663 to study rhetoric. In 1665, he joined the Jesuits and devoted himself to a theological and scientific education from 1666 to 1678 in preparation for his missionary work. Kino initially petitioned Rome for missionary work in China but was turned down. On March 17, 1678, he received permission to work in New Spain*. He left Europe on January 29, 1681, and arrived in Mexico City* on June 1. In the autumn of 1681, he published a book, *Exposición Astronómica del Cometa*, on the 1680 comet that had stirred controversy among scholars in Mexico City. He stayed in the capital until he was chosen to participate as royal cosmographer, chaplain of the Spaniards, and superior of a scientific and exploring expedition to lower California.*

The reasons for this expedition were to create military bases and colonize unpopulated lands in order to protect the Manila galleons* en route from New Spain to the Philippines*, to Christianize the Indian* population, and to lay the basis for future exploration. The fleet was composed of three ships. *San José y San Francisco*, *La Concepción*, and the escort ship *Balandra* left January 17, 1683, and landed at La Paz, lower California, on April 1. Missionary work and further exploration began after claiming the lands in the name of the Spanish king. On July 14, La Paz was abandoned after the slaughter of 13 Indians in retaliation for the supposed murder of a crew member.

A second California expedition was attempted, and on October 6, 1683, construction began on a fort settlement christened San Bruno. Kino explored and Christianized the interior of California. Attempts were made to close down the mission because no source of wealth or fertile lands existed. The spring and summer of 1684 were spent at San Bruno engaged in pearl-fishing, but not enough was produced to justify the expedition. On December 22, 1685, the Spanish king ordered the suspension of the California mission. Kino found himself on the mainland when he learned of the suspension in April 1686.

Kino returned to Mexico City and remained there until elected missionary for the Indians in New Vizcaya*. He hoped to link the missions* of Sonora with those established in California. On November 20, 1686, he went to Guadalajara*, received instructions for his missionary work, and left for Sonora on December 16. On his arrival at Oposura, he was instructed to go to the Pimería Alta, which included present-day Sonora in the south and Arizona in the north, to work with the Pima Indians. On March 13, 1687, he arrived at his permanent residence, Cosari, renamed "Nuestra Señora de los Dolores". He visited the villages around his residence and built chapels and other structures. In the following years, he explored the surrounding territory and entered present-day Arizona in 1690.

In 1694, Kino began more extensive explorations of the territory. In March, he began construction of a boat to sail down the Magdalena River to the Gulf of California but was ordered to suspend this work by his immediate supervisor. On March 29, 1695, a Pima rebellion broke out, lasting until August 8. Although many missions and settlements were destroyed, Kino's mission was spared.

Kino left for Mexico City in November, arrived on January 8, 1696, and stayed for six months to recruit and get support. Criticism by the new rector of the Pimeriá Alta did not stop Kino from further explorations and missionary activities on his return. In October 1699, an Indian tribe presented Kino with a gift of blue shells. This led him to conclude that a land route to California existed because of the similarity of these shells to some he had seen in California. He began to search for this route to fulfill his wish of linking his mission with that of lower California.

On April 23, 1700, he began another expedition but was recalled before he was able to investigate the hypothesis of the blue shells. On October 7, on still another expedition, he climbed a mountain and saw contiguous land between California and the Pimeriá Alta. In March 1701, a trip to the Colorado River definitely proved that California was not an island but a peninsula. On his return to Dolores he created the map, *Land Passage to California and Its Neighboring New Nations and New Missions of the Company of Jesus in North America*, designed to show that California was a peninsula. This map was subsequently printed in Europe and became a standard. Troubles continued with the authorities because of his relationship with the Pima Indians. In the autumn of 1702 and spring of 1703, he began plans for another expedition but was prevented from taking it.

On September 16, 1710, he made one of his last requests, which was for new bells for Dolores Church. The response from Mexico City was that he would not need them, since New Spain's Jesuit missions had been suppressed. He continued his explorations until his death on March 15, 1711, at the age of 66 in the village of Santa Magdalena. Kino's explorations and missionary work established that California was not an island but a peninsula. He introduced many domestic animals and agricultural products into the region that he explored and built settlements for future colonization of the area. His work as a cartographer, geographer, and explorer would gain him renown in the Old and New World.

REFERENCES: Herbert E. Bolton, *Rim of Christendom: A Biography of Eusebio Francisco Kino, Pacific Coast Pioneer*, 1936; Herbert E. Bolton, *The Padre on Horseback*, 1932.

Carlos Pérez

KRIM AL-KHATTABI, MOHAMMAD ABD EL. Mohammad Abd el-Krim al-Khattabi was born in 1882 and became the leader of the Ait Waryaghar tribe in Spanish Morocco*. He received an Islamic education at home and then went to live in Melilla* where he received a Spanish education. For several years while and just after he was a student, Krim edited a number of anti-French publications that were printed in Spanish. He also rose through the bureaucracy of the Spanish government in Melilla, serving as secretary of the Bureau of Native Affairs, tax assessor, and chief judge. Still, in 1917, Spanish authorities imprisoned him for anti-Spanish rhetoric. He was released soon after but left Melilla and rejoined his tribe. There he organized a guerilla army and began attacking Spanish troops and installations. His greatest victory was at the Battle of Anwal* in 1921, when Krim's Rifian troops thrashed the Spaniards. Krim then proclaimed the Republic of the Rif and organized a cabinet government. In 1926, a combined Franco-Spanish army defeated Krim's forces and forced him to surrender. The French deported Krim to Reunion Island where he spent the next 20 years. In 1947, Krim left Reunion with French permission to live on the Riviera, but he jumped ship at the Suez Canal and was granted asylum in Egypt. Abd el-Krim died in Cairo on February 5, 1963.

REFERENCES: Rupert Furneaux, *Abdel-Krim, Emir of the Rif*, 1967; John P. Halstead, *Rebirth of a Nation: The Origins and Rise of Moroccan Nationalism, 1912-1944*, 1967.

L

LABRADORES. Independent peasant farmers in medieval and early modern Castile* were called *labradores*. The term *labrador* is rather ambiguous; it is sometimes taken to mean taxpaying commoner (*pechero*), as distinguished from the *hidalgo** with tax-exempt status. This distinction, however, often breaks down under scrutiny: In many places, the *hidalgos* did pay taxes, along with their plebeian neighbors; moreover, many *hidalgos* in Golden Age Spain were in exactly the same occupational and property-owning category as their *labrador* neighbors. In fact, in the far north of Castile, nearly the entire population claimed *hidalgo* status, and most of these were peasants or other ordinary working people. Hence, the terms *labrador* and *hidalgo* should not be thought to be incompatible. Some authorities apply the word *labrador* to a peasant landowner in comfortable circumstances, as opposed to poverty-stricken landless day-laborers (*jornaleros* or *trabajadores*). Still, sixteenth- and seventeenth-century documents often speak of *labradores* who were near starvation, and many were tenants who owned little or no land. Thus, we cannot insist that prosperity and landownership were essential *labrador* characteristics.

Some *labradores* were unquestionably wealthy: They employed agricultural workers and owned numerous fields, vineyards, orchards, animals, and houses. These rich *labradores* were a small minority, however. Most *labradores* led a rather modest existence. Typically, they were the owners of at least one yoke of oxen or team of mules, and they probably owned some land as well. Whether rich or poor, the *labradores* by definition were personally involved with the day-to-day activities of growing crops and raising animals. The typical *labrador* occupied a higher socioeconomic position than the typical *jornalero*. In general terms, the *labrador* was considered to be an independent peasant farmer who was better off than the average rural inhabitant. The proportion of *labradores* among the total number of family heads in Golden Age Castilian villages varied widely, from less than 5 to nearly 100 percent.

In Spanish America, the term *labrador* was used in much the same sense as it was in Spain. Colonial *labradores* tended to be of European or mixed race, and they operated medium-sized agricultural operations. In America, as in Spain, it is difficult to classify the *labradores* in socioeconomic terms, because they included large landowners, small landowners, and tenant farmers. As in Spain, some *labradores* were part-time hired workers. They might be thought of as "farmers," to distinguish them from the much more prosperous *hacendados*. The colonial *labradores* often specialized in growing crops for urban markets. Although many eventually lost their lands to nearby large hacienda* owners who had superior resources and political power, many *labradores* survived. All parts of Spanish America had *labradores*, but sometimes they had their own local names. In New Spain*, for example, they were also called *rancheros*. The proportion of *labradores* in frontier zones, such as northern Mexico and southern Chile*, tended to be higher than in other areas.

REFERENCES: David E. Vassberg, *Land and Society in Golden Age Castile*, 1984; Leslie Bethell, ed., *The Cambridge History of Latin America: Colonial Latin America*, 2 vols., 1984.

David E. Vassberg

LADINO. In New Spain*, the term *ladino* referred to acculturated African slaves* who had lived in Spain or the Caribbean before arriving in New Spain. Because *ladinos* already spoke Spanish and understood Spanish ways, they were in much greater demand than *bozales* (slaves brought fresh from Africa). The third category of slaves in New Spain were the *negros criollos* (black slaves born in the New World). In Central America, the word *ladino* did not apply to blacks, but was used interchangeably with the term mestizo*. In Spain, *ladino* was also used to refer to the Jewish Spaniards of the Diaspora.

REFERENCE: Colin MacLaughan and Jaime Rodríguez, *The Forging of the Cosmic Race: A Reinterpretation of Colonial Mexico*, 1980.

Virginia Garrard Burnett

LA GÜERA. Although the Franco-Spanish Convention of 1900* established Spain's claim to the western portion of the Cape Blanc Peninsula on the African coast, the area was not settled until November 1900 when Francisco Bens* established a garrison there and named it La Güera. Spain also enjoyed fishing rights in the neighboring Bay of Levrier, and the Spanish soon constructed a fish processing plant at La Güera. There were 1,200 people living there when the Madrid Agreement* of 1975 ceded La Güera to Mauritania.

REFERENCES: Tony Hodges, *Historical Dictionary of Western Sahara*, 1982; John Mercer, *Spanish Sahara*, 1975.

LAKE MARACAIBO, BATTLE OF. One of the last battles in ending Spanish colonial rule in Venezuela*, the Battle of Lake Maracaibo pitted the recklessly valiant patriot general José Antonio Páez* against combat-seasoned royalist forces. After Páez was forced to break off the siege of Puerto Cabello, the Spanish troops embarked on an unsuccessful expedition against patriot forces. After a series of small battles, all of which the royalists lost, Páez returned to Puerto Cabello to gather a considerable force and sail for Lake Maracaibo. Quickly capturing both the eastern and western peninsulas that formed the entrance to the lake, as well as the strategic castle of San Carlos, an island fortress at the mouth of the lake, the Spaniards navigated the sand bar that blocked entrance to the lake by all but shallow draft vessels.

Mistakenly believing that the Spaniards would be able neither to capture the castle of San Carlos nor to navigate successfully the sand bar at Puertos de Altagracia, Páez moved to attack the royalists while they were penned up in a highly vulnerable position. Arriving at Trujillo, Páez learned that the castle had fallen and the Spanish fleet had crossed into the lake. While the Spaniards now had more room to maneuver, they were still bottled up by the lake and susceptible to attack by a squadron of smaller, more mobile ships under the command of Admiral José Padilla. On July 24, 1823, with 1,300 of Páez's men, the patriot fleet crossed the sand bar. Moving rapidly with a favorable wind, they descended on and boarded the Spanish fleet before its ships could raise anchor. After a fierce three-hour battle in which ten Spanish ships were captured and one sunk, the Spanish surrendered. Although the royalists surrendered all Spanish positions remaining in Venezuela after the defeat at Lake Maracaibo, General José Calzada, the commander of the Spanish garrison at Puerto Cabello, refused to recognize the surrender. Páez moved directly to lay siege to Puerto Cabello, breaching its outer defenses on November 7, 1823. Calzada surrendered the garrison the following day.

REFERENCE: R. B. Cunninghame Graham, *Jose Antonio Páez*, 1929.

Samuel Freeman

LAMAR Y CORTÁZAR, JOSÉ BENIGNO DE. José Benigno de Lamar y Cortázar was born July 12, 1776, in Cuenca, Peru*. He spent his career as a soldier and a politician. As a young man, he joined the Spanish army and fought in the Napoleonic Wars. Assigned to Latin America to fight against the forces of José de San Martín*, Lamar eventually switched over to the rebel side, where he led Peruvian troops in the Battle of Ayacucho*. On August 27, 1827, Lamar was elected president of Peru. A military coup d'état forced him out of office on June 7, 1829, and Lamar was exiled to Costa Rica*. He died in San José*, Costa Rica, on October 11, 1830.

REFERENCE: Manuel de Mendiburu, ed., *Diccionario histórico-biográfico del Perú*, 8 vols., 1874–1890.

LANDA, DIEGO DE. Diego de Landa was born in Cifuentes, Guadalajara, Spain, in 1524 and immigrated to New Spain* as a Franciscan* missionary in 1542. Landa rose through the Franciscan ranks quickly, serving as head of several convents before being selected as the Franciscan provincial for the Yucatán* in 1561. Known for his zealous missionary spirit, Landa was heavy-handed when it came to Indian* policies, especially when the conquered tribes tried to maintain portions of their indigenous beliefs. He was investigated for destroying many Mayan* written documents but was eventually exonerated by the Council of the Indies*. Diego de Landa became bishop of Yucatán in 1572. As bishop, he labored to minimize the exploitation of the Maya Indians by Spanish officials, colonists, and *encomenderos*. Today, Landa is best remembered for his *Relación de las cosas de Yucatán*, a history of Mayan civilization and the Spanish conquest. Diego de Landa died on April 29, 1579.

REFERENCE: A. M. Tozzer, ed., *Landa's Relación de las cosas de Yucatán*, 1941.

LANDÍVAR, RAFAEL. A Guatemalan priest, Rafael Landívar was born in Old Guatemala City, Guatemala*, on October 27, 1731. He attended the University of San Carlos* and then joined the Jesuit* order, through which he pursued an academic career teaching rhetoric and philosophy. Landívar belonged to the small group of poets who composed in Latin, who carried on the tradition of Latin poetry. Landívar was unquestionably the most important of this group. He earned the position of rector of the University of San Marcos* in Guatemala City, but was later expelled from the country, with other Jesuits, in 1767. Taking up residence in Italy, he continued his writings, eventually producing his masterpiece, *Rusticatio Mexicana* (1781), in which he described and exalted Mexico, its geography, and its people. Landívar was a descriptive and sentimental poet who, in spite of his classical style, is viewed by critics as a precursor of the romantic poets and romanticism. Rafael Landívar died in Bologna, Italy, on September 27, 1793.

REFERENCE: J. Matta Gavidia, ed., *Rafael Landívar: El poeta de Guatemala*, 1950.

Sam L. Slick

LA PAZ. The city of La Paz was founded in 1548 by Alonso de Mendoza, under the direction of Pedro de la Gasca*, as a travelers' and shipping station between Lima*, Peru*, the mines of Potosí*, and Lake Titicaca. It was at first called Ciudad de Nuestra Señora de la Paz. Over the centuries, La Paz rose as a commercial center because of its strategic economic location. In 1783, King Charles III* created an *intendencia* in La Paz as part of the viceroyalty of Río de la Plata.* Spanish control of La Paz did not end until 1825. At that point, La Paz became part of the republic of Bolivia.

REFERENCE: David Henige, *Colonial Governors from the Fifteenth Century to the Present*, 1967.

LA PUERTA, BATTLE OF. In the wars of Venezuelan independence, two battles were fought at La Puerta. After the defeat of the First Venezuelan Republic, Simón Bolívar* went to Cartagena*, Colombia*, to help prevent the Spanish destruction of Colombian independence. In early 1813, he convinced authorities in Cartagena to give him a small army. Exceeding his authority, he moved into Venezuela* where his army swelled with volunteers. He defeated the royalist forces, who then retreated to Puerto Cabello to await reinforcements by sea. Bolívar occupied Caracas*, established the Second Republic, and moved to lay siege to Puerto Cabello. Meanwhile, other Spanish loyalist leaders, including Francisco Yañes and Tomás Boves*, prepared a savage counterattack. Boves's army moved against Caracas but was defeated by Campo Elías on October 14. Regrouping, Boves mounted a second threat against Caracas by crippling a patriot army at La Puerta on February 2, 1814, clearing his way to the defenses of Caracas itself. While the Second Republic survived this attack, Boves regrouped once more and slaughtered the patriot army commanded by Bolívar at the second battle of La Puerta on June 15. Boves occupied Caracas a month later, ending the Second Republic.

REFERENCES: William Marsland and Amy Marsland, *Venezuela Through Its History*, 1954; Gerhard Masur, *Simón Bolívar*, 1948.

Samuel Freeman

LARA Y AGUILAR, DOMINGO ANTONIO. Domingo Antonio Lara y Aguilar was born in San Salvador* in 1783 to one of the city's most prominent families. He married the sister of Manuel José Arce* and became a leading figure in the Salvadoran independence movement, particularly in the uprisings of 1811 and 1814. Royalist authorities arrested him in 1814 and kept him in prison until 1819. Between 1821 and 1823, Lara was part of the junta that ruled San Salvador. He died in 1844.

REFERENCE: Philip F. Flemion, *Historical Dictionary of El Salvador*, 1972.

LAS CASAS, BARTOLOMÉ DE. Best known as the Dominican* friar who avidly championed the cause of human rights for the Indians*, Bartolomé de Las Casas was born on November 11, 1484, in Seville*, Spain. Educated at the cathedral academy of Seville, he originally came to the New World as a soldier in the conquest of Cuba*. Horrified by the Spaniards' treatment of the Indians in the Caribbean, Las Casas returned to Spain, gave up his wealth, and at the age of 40, took Dominican vows. In 1522, he wrote the first of his famous treatises in defense of the Indians, *A Very Brief Recital of the Destruction of the Indies*. The work described in graphic and sometimes exaggerated detail the greed, cruelty, and sadism of the Spaniards, and it established Las Casas as Spain's most vocal spokesman for Indian rights. Las Casas's work was also circulated widely among the enemies of Spain, particularly the English, who used it to perpetuate their Black Legend* of Spanish brutality. On a more positive note, his work was influential in persuading the Crown to promulgate the New Laws* in 1542, which were designed to rein in the autonomy and power of Spaniards in the New World by limiting their authority over the Indians.

In 1530, Las Casas wrote another work entitled *The Only Method of Attracting Men to the True Faith*, in which he argued that Indians should be dealt with only through persuasion, affection, and patience. In 1537, the Crown allowed him to put his ideas into action. Las Casas was given a large tract of land in Guatemala* belonging to the warlike Kekchi Indians, whom the Spaniards had been unable to conquer. Las Casas learned the Kekchi language, changed the name of the region from the "Land of War" to the more hopeful "Land of the True Peace" (Verapáz), and traveled all over the area with a team of friars, attempting to convert and befriend the Indians through peaceful persuasion. Under the terms of the royal agreement, Las Casas was allowed to remain in Verapáz for five years; during that time, the experiment was a success. In 1542, however, Spanish settlers moved into the area. The Indians rose up in revolt, killing settlers and friars alike. Las Casas was removed from Guatemala, but in 1544, he was named bishop of Chiapas*, where he continued in his efforts to champion the rights of Indians. He died in Madrid, Spain, on July 18, 1566.

REFERENCES: Lewis Hanke, *The Spanish Struggle for Justice in the Conquest of America*, 1949; Henry Raup Wagner and Helen Rand Parish, *The Life and Writings of Bartolomé de las Casas*, 1967.

Virginia Garrard Burnett

LA SERNA, JOSÉ DE. José de la Serna was born in Jérez de la Frontera, Spain, in 1770. In 1782, he entered the Spanish army in the artillery corps, and during the next three decades, he fought widely throughout Iberia and the Mediterranean against British and French armies. He was assigned to Peru* in 1812 and in 1816, he received command of all royalist forces in Upper Peru (Bolivia*). La Serna invaded Argentina* in 1817, but he failed to dislodge the guerrilla army of Martín Güemes*; La Serna retreated to Upper Peru. Despite his setbacks on the battlefield, he succeeded in politics, and in 1821, he was appointed viceroy* of Peru. Although he tried to reach a political accommodation with José de San Martín*, it was to no avail. La Serna took the royalist forces and retreated into the Peruvian sierra. There he suffered major defeats at Junín* and Ayacucho*. After signing the surrender documents, La Serna returned to Lima* and then to Spain. He died in Cádiz in 1831.

REFERENCES: Enrique Udaondo, *Diccionario biográfico colonial argentino*, 1945; Ione S. Wright and Lisa M. Nekhom, *Historical Dictionary of Argentina*, 1978.

LAS HERAS, JUAN GREGORIO DE. Juan Gregorio de las Heras was born in Buenos Aires* in 1780. He joined the Argentine forces resisting the British invasion of the Río de la Plata* in 1806, and in 1813, he went to Chile* to fight with the patriot forces there. By 1817, Las Heras was a close associate of José de San Martín* and fought at the battles of Chacabuco* and Cancha Rayada*. He became San Martín's chief of staff in 1820. After Chile secured its independence, Las Heras returned to Argentina where he served as governor of Buenos Aires from 1823 to 1826. Las Heras lived out most of the rest of his life in Chile, where he died in 1866.

REFERENCES: Salvatore Bizarro, *Historical Dictionary of Chile*, 1987; José Toribio Medina, *Diccionario biográfico colonial de Chile*, 1906.

LAS MUÑECAS, ILDEFONSO DE. Ildefonso de las Muñecas was born in San Miguel, Tucumán*, in what is today Argentina*, in the late eighteenth century. He took vows as a Roman Catholic priest, received a doctorate in theology from the University of Córdoba* in 1800, and then served as a parish priest in Cuzco*, Peru*. Muñecas was an early, vociferous advocate of independence from Spain. In 1814, he cooperated with Indian leader Mateo Garcia* Pumacahua in the uprising of August 3. Muñecas accompanied the rebels on their invasion of Upper Peru (Bolivia*) and played a key role in their capture of La Paz*. When royalist troops soon regained control of La Paz, Muñecas retreated into the *altiplano* and organized guerrilla forces there. Spanish troops did not capture Muñecas until May 1816; one of them killed him near Lake Titicaca while he was in their custody.

REFERENCE: *New Catholic Encyclopedia*, X:72, 1967.

LAS SIETE PARTIDAS. Juan Donoso Cortés called the code of the Siete Partidas "one of the jewels of the Middle Ages." It was the work of Alfonso the Learned (1252–1284), King of Castile*. Son of Ferdinand III, the Saint (1217–1252), Alfonso's turbulent life was spent between the sword and the pen. A most sophisticated ruler for his times, aloof, magnanimous, but at the same time vacillating, Alfonso was a real scholar. He had ambitions for the Holy Roman Crown, conquered Cádiz and Cartagena, but ended tragically when the Castilian Cortes deposed him in 1282, because of his royal absolutism and his patrimonial divisions.

His major accomplishment was a collection of Castilian laws produced in 1255. Ten years later and with aid from his many lawyers who had studied in Italy and were well acquainted with Roman and canon law, Alfonso offered the Siete Partidas as an improved alternative to his former *fuero real*. The Siete Partidas covered seven legal areas: sources of law, canon law, constitutional law, administrative law, law of procedure, civil law, and penal law. These represented a uniform legal system for the Castilian kingdom and were supposed to replace to the multiplicity of privileges granted to both the towns and the nobility. Alfonso's aim, however, was interpreted by both groups as royal absolutism, with the result that the Siete Partidas were never promulgated, although they became a powerful legal guide that either complemented existing legislature or could be used as reference. The Siete Partidas were important not only in Spain but also in Spanish America.

In Book II, Title 1, Law 2 of the Laws of the Indies, *Recopilación de Leyes de las Indias* (1680), it states that when in doubt, Castilian laws would be applied in accordance with the Laws of Toro of 1505, which had established a system of priorities that in its final instance included the Siete Partidas. At the end of the eighteenth century, when an impressive interest developed in the study of Spanish and Spanish American laws, the Siete Partidas represented a significant element in legal studies, especially in Upper Peru (Bolivia*). The Siete

Partidas were thus referred to in 1810 for the justification of the establishment of "revolutionary" juntas in Spanish America.

REFERENCES: Stanley G. Payne, *A History of Spain and Portugal*, 1973; Agustín Blánquez Fraile, *Historia de España*, 1933; Ricardo Levene, *Manual de Historia del Derecho Argentino*, 1985.

O. Carlos Stoetzer

LATIFUNDIA. The term *latifundia* refers to large, landed estates such as were established in the ancient Roman empire. The term survived to describe as well the large estates of Italy, Spain, and the Spanish colonies of the New World. Economists generally agree that *latifundia* were especially poor arrangements in developing areas because their existence discourages immigration. When large corporations own the estates rather than individuals or families, it is even more economically discouraging because the property tends not to change hands regularly. The Spanish Empire actually encouraged the development of *latifundia*. The New World was conquered at a time when the manorial system of land tenure was still intact throughout much of Spain; it seemed the natural order of things and was transplanted to the colonies. Spanish law provided for the entail, a legal device preventing the break-up of estates upon the death of the owner by requiring inheritance by the eldest son. In addition, the presence of the Indians*, at least in the early stages of colonization, provided a ready source of labor, which permitted the full exploitation of large areas of land. Finally, the Roman Catholic church* acquired enormous amounts of land in the Spanish colonies, stimulating the rise of *latifundia*. The *latifundia* system became the foundation for the tiny upper class and the huge peasant class in the New World colonies.

REFERENCES: William B. Taylor, "Landed Society in New Spain: A View from the South," *Hispanic American Historical Review*, 54 (1974), 387–413; William B. Taylor, *Landlord and Peasant in Colonial Oaxaca*, 1972.

LAUTARO. Born in Chile around 1535, Lautaro was an Araucanian* chief who led a ferocious resistance to the conquest expeditions of the Spaniards. Lautaro served as a slave to Pedro de Valdivia* for several years, but in 1553, he escaped and organized a rebellion against the Spaniards. His forces captured and executed Valdivia in 1553, and in 1554 they seized the city of Concepción. Lautaro failed to capture Santiago* in 1556, and in 1557 he was killed by Spanish forces at the Battle of Mataquito River.

REFERENCE: H. R. S. Pocock, *The Conquest of Chile*, 1967.

LAVALLEJA, JUAN ANTONIO. Juan Antonio Lavalleja was born to a wealthy Spanish ranching family in Minas, Uruguay*, in 1784. In 1811, he joined with the revolutionary forces trying to overthrow Spanish authority. A strong advocate of Uruguayan independence, from Spain as well as from Argentina* and Brazil, Lavalleja led an invasion of Uruguay by the so-called "Thirty-three Volunteers" in 1825 in order to secure Uruguay's independence from Brazil after Spanish power had been crushed. When Brazil and Argentina went to war over Uruguay, Lavalleja led the Uruguayan forces. He became the dictator of the country in 1827. In 1830, he became the provisional president of Uruguay until the constitutional convention elected a permanent president. Dissatisfied with the leadership of President Fructoso Rivera*, Lavalleja led revolts against his administration in 1832 and 1835. Lavalleja emerged as a leader of the Blanco Party in Uruguay in the late 1830s and 1840s, but he perceived an opportunity to depose President Juan Giro, a Blanco colleague, in 1853, when he became one of a ruling triumvirate in Montevideo*. Juan Antonio Lavalleja died in 1853.

REFERENCE: Alfredo Raúl Castellanos, *Juan Antonio Lavalleja, libertador del pueblo oriental: Ensayo biográfico*, 1955.

LAVARDÉN, MANUEL JOSÉ DE. Both a poet and dramatist, Manuel José de Lavardén was born in Buenos Aires* in 1754. He belonged to the neoclassical school of literature. He is generally considered Argentina's* first playwright. He studied law and later became a journalist, but poetry was his first love. He is remembered today primarily because of his famous poem *Oda al Paraná* (1801), in which he paid homage to Argentina's outstanding geography. *Oda* is generally viewed as a precursor of romantic poetry in Latin America. Lavardén is also associated with the formation of colonial theater* in America. Along with some friends, Lavardén helped establish what was probably the first theater in Buenos Aires, the Teatro de la Ranchería. It was there that Lavardén's play, titled *Siropo*, was produced. This work, now lost, dealt with the conflict between the Spanish colonists in Argentina and the indigenous Indian* population. It treated the well-known story of Lucia Miranda, a young Spanish wife who is kidnapped by Indians and becomes the love object of the local cacique*. Lavardén died in 1809.

REFERENCE: Rafael A. Arrieta, ed., *Historia de la literatura argentina*, 1958.

Sam L. Slick

LEGAZPI, MIGUEL LÓPEZ DE. Miguel López de Legazpi was born in Zubarraja, Guipúzcoa, Spain. His birthdate, his early life, and formative years are unknown. It appears that he studied law before his arrival in New Spain* in 1531. He became a member of the Mexico City* *cabildo** on April 4, 1531. Legazpi was *cabildo* secretary when he was appointed to head the expedition to the Philippines*. The Philippines, contested by Portugal and Spain during the early period of discovery and colonization, were effectively colonized by Spain through Legazpi's efforts. Four previous Spanish expeditions to the islands— Ferdinand Magellan's* (1519–1522), García Jofre de Loaysa's (1525–1527), Sebastian Cabot's* (1526), and Álvaro de Saavedra* Cerón's (1527–1529), from New Spain—preceded Legazpi's, which was the culmination of these previous efforts.

In 1559, New Spain's Viceroy Luis de Velasco* advocated another Philippines expedition to the Spanish king, Philip II*. The king followed this suggestion and appointed Andrés de Urdaneta*, an Augustinian* friar and Legazpi's relative and close friend, to the expedition. Urdaneta had been with Loaysa's expedition and had prior knowledge of the islands. On his recommendation, the viceroy* appointed Legazpi commander of the fleet. After the viceroy's death in July 1564, the New Spain *audiencia** took command of preparations for the journey. The expedition's purpose was threefold: to find a return route to New Spain, to bring back spices and riches for trade, and to convert the natives to Christianity. The fleet, composed of two galleons, the *San Pedro* (the flagship) and the *San Pablo*, and two tenders, the *San Juan* and the *San Lucas*, departed from Puerto de la Navidad on November 21, 1564, after many delays. They arrived on February 13, 1565, near the island of Cebu from which further exploration of the archipelago took place. On April 27, 1565, Legazpi returned to Cebu and, after some native resistance, took possession of the town, which he renamed San Miguel.

On June 1, Legazpi sent the *San Pedro*, with Urdaneta aboard, back to New Spain to get provisions and to inform the *audiencia* of the progress of the expedition. Urdaneta proceeded on to Spain to inform the king. The course the *San Pedro* navigated established the route that the Manila galleons* would follow during the length of the colonial period. Through this action, Legazpi fulfilled one of the main purposes of the expedition. When no provisions, men, or instructions arrived in July 1567, Legazpi sent the *San Juan* to New Spain. A year later, in July 1568, he sent the *San Pablo* loaded with spices, but it was wrecked off the Ladrones (Marianas*) islands. Between November 1566 to October 1568, the hardships that the Spanish forces endured increased as a result of Portuguese attacks and a two-month blockade. In January 1569, after the blockade, Legazpi's forces moved from Cebu to the island of Panay, which served as an important steppingstone to the later colonization of the island of Luzon.*

From Panay, Legazpi sent out an expedition under the command of Martín de Goiti, an artillery officer. The expedition encountered Raja Solimán's Moros* who put up fierce resistance. The town of Manila* fell, however, and Goiti took formal possession of the island of Luzon on June 6, 1570. When this force returned to Panay, three ships had finally arrived from New Spain with provisions and instructions that confirmed Legazpi as governor and captain general of the Philippines. The reason for the long delay was the unstable political climate in New Spain during the previous years. These instructions formally set aside Portuguese claims to the archipelago. Permanent settlement began on the island of Cebu when 40 to 50 Spaniards took up residence and established a town council. Legazpi spent the winter of 1570–1571 on the island of Panay and moved to Manila in May 1571. After military campaigns against the natives around Manila, the Spaniards gained effective control of the islands of Cebu, Panay, Mindoro, several smaller islands, and the central area of Luzon. These military campaigns were Legazpi's last because on August 20, 1572, he died suddenly. Guido de Lavesaris, treasurer of the colony, replaced him as governor and captain general.

The accomplishments of Legazpi's expedition are important because he succeeded where four previous expeditions had failed. Legazpi's expedition gave Spain effective possession of the Philippines as a part of the Spanish Empire. It defeated Portuguese claims to the islands by undertaking permanent colonization and settlement. This gave Spain an effective base in the Far East for trade with China. It also established the trade route between New Spain and the Philippines that the Manilla galleons took during the colonial period.

REFERENCES: Edward J. McCarthy, *Spanish Beginnings in the Philippines, 1564–1572*, 1943.; José Sáenz y Díaz, *López De Legazpi (Primero Adelantado y Conquistador de Filipinas)*, 1950.

Carlos Pérez

LEO AFRICANUS. Leo Africanus was born in Granada, Spain, around 1485, to Moorish parents. His Arabic name was al-Hasan ibn-Muhammad al-Wazzan al-Zayyati. After the expulsion of the Moors from Granada in 1492, Leo migrated to Morocco. As a Moroccan diplomatic representative, he traveled widely throughout North and Central Africa and the Middle East in the early 1500s. In 1518, Sicilian pirates working in the eastern Mediterranean captured him and presented him as a slave to Pope Leo X. The pope was impressed with Leo Africanus's learning and freed him after converting him to Christianity in 1520. Leo's geographical text, *Descrittione dell' Africa et delle cose notabili che quivi sono* (1526), became a widely read treatise in Spain and helped shape the Spanish expansion into North Africa* during the sixteenth and seventeenth centuries.

REFERENCE: Jean-León L'Africain, *Description de L'Afrique*, 1956.

LEÓN. León, Nicaragua*, was established by Francisco Hernández* de Córdoba on the shores of Lake Managua in 1524, when the conqueror was sent into Nicaragua by Pedro Arias de Ávila* (Pedrarias) to claim the region from Gil Gonzales* Dávila, who had first explored the area two years earlier. Hernández also founded Granada on Lake Nicaragua in 1524, laying the groundwork for a rivalry between the two towns that would last for centuries. Early on, León, though technically subject to the government in Santiago de Guatemala*, served as a *gobierno*, a virtually autonomous administrative center for the region. The economy of the region in the early sixteenth century was based primarily on sugar* and wheat plantations that were worked by the area's relatively small Indian* population and slaves* brought from Africa. Ecclesiastical authority rested in the diocese of León until 1744, when Guatemala* was made an archdiocese and given authority over all of Central America.

In the mid-sixteenth century, León served as base for expeditions searching for gold in the area now known as New Segovia*. By the late sixteenth century, Spaniards in León were heavily involved in the cacao* trade, for the precious bean used to make chocolate grew in abundance on Nicaragua's fertile Pacific coast. By the seventeenth century, León's involvement in the cacao trade had caused a rivalry with nearby Granada. The rivalry deepened when Guatemala forbade Nicaragua to market cacao from Guayaquil*, in South America, which competed with the Central American product. Granada supported the ruling because the city produced enough of its own cacao to provide itself with hard currency; León, which did not produce enough opposed the ruling adamantly. León's troubles during this time were punctuated by natural disasters that periodically devastated the city. In 1610, volcanic eruptions and earthquakes destroyed León (now León Viejo), and the town was moved to its present location.

León's fortunes improved after Granada was sacked by pirates in 1648 and as Nicaraguan trade shifted from the Caribbean to the Pacific. Although León was also attacked by French pirates from the Southern Sea, it did not suffer as much as Granada. By the beginning of the eighteenth century, it had become, along with the Pacific port of Realejo, one of Nicaragua's most important commercial centers. When Bourbon commercial policies permitted expanded trade between Central America and Peru*, León and Realejo prospered greatly. León became an important commercial entrepot for the pine-pitch trade from New Segovia. Merchants shipped Nicaraguan pitch south to Peru, where it was used to make barrels for the wine industry.

During the Bourbon century, León developed a powerful merchant class. The merchants' power and autonomy eventually pitted them against the royal authorities, whose expanded trade policies had ironically allowed the merchants to prosper in the first place. The Crown attempted to assert royal authority over León by making it an *intendencia** in the early eighteenth century, but local merchants nonetheless remained powerful. The influence of these ''liberal'' merchants was evident at the Cortes of Cádiz* (1810–1814), which authorized a university to be established in León.

REFERENCES: Murdo J. MacLeod, *Spanish Central America: A Socioeconomic History, 1520-1720*, 1973; R. L. Woodward, Jr., *Central America: A Nation Divided*, 1983.

Virginia Garrard Burnett

LEÓN, PEDRO CIEZA DE. See CIEZA DE LEON, PEDRO.

LEÓN PINELO, ANTONIO. Antonio León Pinelo was born in Valladolid, Spain, around 1590. Both of his brothers went to Peru* in the early 1600s, one as a professor at the University of San Marcos* and another as an appointed official with the *audiencia** in Lima*. León Pinelo followed them and arrived in Peru in 1605. He then lived for a time in Buenos Aires* and Córdoba* before settling down in Lima and receiving a degree in theology and canon law from the University of San Marcos in 1616. León Pinelo filled a variety of positions with the government in Peru and Buenos Aires during the next five years, but in 1621, the *cabildo** of Buenos Aires asked him to serve as its spokesman at the royal court. He therefore returned to Spain where he lived out his life. León Pinelo became one of the most prolific writers of the seventeenth century, publishing multiple volumes on life in America as well as on the legal history of the colonies. Antonio León Pinelo died in Madrid on July 21, 1660.

REFERENCE: R. Altamira y Crevea, "La extraña historia de la Recopilación de A. L. P.," *Boletín da Faculdade de direito da Universidade de Coimbra*, 25 (1949), 280–304.

LEPERO. The term *lepero* literally means leper, but it was used to refer to the destitute in colonial New Spain*, so called because of their filthy clothes and propensity for contracting diseases. Although *leperos* were considered by many to be a criminal element, they were more often simply the unemployed who had been pushed from the countryside into the city by economic factors. Racially, a *lepero* might have originated in any group; even Spaniards occasionally found themselves in this unfortunate class. Surviving, if at all, by begging and sleeping on the street, *leperos* were thought by officials to threaten the public order, and they were indeed a public health menace. During the eighteenth century, *leperos* fared especially badly. Weakened by alcoholism, contagious disease, malnutrition, and exposure to the elements, *leperos* were easy victims of epidemics. In the late eighteenth century, thousands died in the streets of Mexico City alone.

REFERENCE: Colin M. MacLachlan and Jaime E. Rodríguez, *The Forging of the Cosmic Race: A Reinterpretation of Colonial Mexico*, 1980.

Virginia Garrard Burnett

LEY QUIÑONES-VARELA. Also known as the "Instruction for the Political and Economic Development of the Overseas Provinces," the *Ley Quiñones-Varela* was drafted by José M. Quiñones of Puerto Rico* and Felix Varela of Cuba* in March 1823. Based on the notions of the Constitution of 1812*, the legislation was passed by the Spanish Cortes. Although the legislation provided for the establishment of a variety of political institutions for the colonies, its fundamental assumption was for internal self-rule. As such, the document represented a shift from the assimilationist approach to colonial rule toward a local autonomy approach. One week after the passage of the law, however, Spain was invaded by the Quadruple Alliance, and the law never went into effect.

REFERENCE: Kenneth R. Farr, *Historical Dictionary of Puerto Rico and the U.S. Virgin Islands*, 1973.

LEYTE. Leyte is the eighth largest island of the Philippines*, with 2,785 square miles, about one-third of which is still tropical hardwood forest. It lies in the eastern Visayas* (central islands), forming a barrier between the huge waves of the open Pacific to the east and the inland Camotes Sea to the west. Leyte is separated from the large island of Samar* only by the narrow San Juanico Strait. The two islands were joined in 1973 when the 7,000-foot-long Marcos bridge was inaugurated. Leyte is only a short boat ride away from other southern Philippine islands such as Bohol*, Mindanao*, and Cebu. The Waray and

Cebuano-speaking people number about 2,000,000. Leyte is not densely populated compared to other Philippine islands, but most of the arable land is already cultivated, so as the population grows, people move to Mindanao. There are copper deposits, but no large mines.

Ferdinand Magellan* landed on Leyte in 1521. The island was governed as an integral part of the Philippines under Spanish, American, and Japanese colonizers, but its remote location excluded Leyte from the mainstream of the nation's economic and cultural life. Economic growth was retarded by two factors: first, Moro* raids on Leyte's west coast; and second, devastating typhoons that annually wiped out villages along the island's east coast. Only two villages, Ormoc and Tacloban, grew into sizable port towns: Tacloban was opened to international trade in 1874, after which coconuts, sugar,* tobacco,* bananas,* and hemp were cultivated for export, but Leyte lacked sufficient level land for true plantations. Most farmers and fishermen were self-sufficient. Leyte endured ferocious battles in World War II, and it was the site of Douglas MacArthur's famous return. Tacloban later gained some notoriety as the birthplace of Imelda Marcos, who showered her hometown with ostentatious development projects of little practical use.

REFERENCE: Frederick Wernstedt and J. E. Spencer, *The Philippine Island World*, 1967.

Ross Marlay

LIBRARIES. Neither the function nor incidence of Spanish colonial libraries is very well known. For many years, particularly in the sixteenth and seventeenth centuries, libraries of significance were primarily the personal property of wealthy aristocrats and important clerics. Seminaries, monasteries, and religious orders also often possessed large collections of books and folia. Eventually, the emerging colonial universities developed modest collections. Perhaps the first library in the New World was that of Juan de Zumárraga*, the first bishop of Mexico, who brought some 200 books to the New World in 1528. Also in Mexico during the sixteenth and seventeenth centuries were the "Biblioteca Turriana," open to the public and eventually given to the National University of Mexico, and the library of the Diocese of Puebla.* In South America, Peru* boasted several major private libraries, including those of Don Pedro de Peralta* Barnuevo, and that of José Eugenio Llano Zapata. Considerable research has been undertaken concerning the early monastic libraries of the New World. Perhaps the most notable of such libraries was that of the Imperial College of Santa Cruz de Tlatelolco, situated in what is today modern Mexico City*. In addition, the monastery of San Francisco in Guadalajara* (Mexico) housed a significant library. In Peru, the Franciscan* monastery of La Recoleta in Arequipa* housed a large library. In the latter part of the colonial period, the monastery of Nuestra Señora de Ocopa in the Peruvian highlands formed a large collection. The Franciscan convent in Trujillo, Venezuela*, likewise contained a noteworthy library.

REFERENCES: Paul H. Bixler, *The Mexican Library*, 1969; Guillermo Furlong Cardiff, *Bibliotecas argentinas durante la dominación hispánica*, 1944; Juan R. Freudenthal, *Development and Current Status of Bibliographic Organization in Chile*, 1972.

Sam L. Slick

LIMA. Lima is the capital city and political center of Peru*. Francisco Pizarro* founded the city in 1535 up the Rimac River from the port of Callao in the coastal plain of Peru. At the time, it was called Ciudad de los Reyes. Throughout the colonial period, Lima was the political and cultural center of Hispanic South America.

LIMA, ARCHDIOCESE OF. The Roman Catholic diocese of Lima was established in 1541 as a suffragen of the archbishopric of Seville*. It was raised to an archdiocese in 1546; at the time, it covered all Spanish territory in South America (except Venezuela* and most of New Granada*), as well as Panama* and Nicaragua*. Eventually the dioceses of Arequipa*, Trujillo*, Huamaga*, Cuzco*, Quito*, Panama, Nicaragua, Popayán*, Charcas*, Santiago* de Chile, Concepción, Paraguay*, and Tucumán* were carved out of it. It was one of the largest archdioceses, in territorial jurisdiction, in history.

REFERENCE: *New Catholic Encyclopedia*, VIII:759–60, 1967.

LIMA, *AUDIENCIA* OF. The *Audiencia* of Lima* was established in Lima, Peru*, in 1542, at the same time that the viceroyalty was formally established. Since the viceroyalty of Peru* was headquartered in Lima, the *audiencia* became a viceregal *audiencia* and existed throughout the colonial period.

REFERENCE: Mark A. Burkholder and D. S. Chandler, *From Impotence to Authority: The Spanish Crown and the American Audiencias, 1687-1808*, 1977.

LINIERS Y BREMOND, SANTIAGO ANTONIO MARÍA DE. Santiago Liniers was born in Niort, France, in 1753. He did a tour in the French army when he was still a teenager, and in 1774 signed on for a tour of duty in the Spanish army. He was assigned to the Río de la Plata* area as the port captain. Liniers came to fame by defending Buenos Aires* and the surrounding area against the British invasion of 1806 and 1807. In 1808, as a reward, Liniers was named viceroy* of Río de la Plata. His fame, however, was short-lived. When Napoleon invaded Spain in 1810, Liniers lost his political base. A French viceroy was simply intolerable to Spanish patriots. Deposed early in 1810, Liniers became involved in opposing the independence movement. Captured by revolutionaries in Córdoba* province, he was executed on August 26, 1810.

REFERENCE: Paul Groussac, *Santiago de Liniers, conde de Buenos Aires*, 1907.

LIRCAY, TREATY OF. Early in 1814, the viceroy* of Peru* dispatched a task force to Chile* under the command of General Gavión Gainza to reinforce royalist troops that were attempting to suppress a patriot revolt. Although defeated at El Quilo, Gainza's advance toward Santiago* continued until he was blocked by forces commanded by Bernardo O'Higgins[*], who recently had been named commander of the patriot forces. With neither commander able to threaten the position of the other and with both armies tired from months of fighting, it was clear that some kind of negotiated settlement was needed.

Acting as mediator, Captain James Hillyar of the Royal British Navy completed negotiations for the Treaty of Lircay on the banks of the Lircay River near Talca on May 3, 1814. Under the terms of the treaty, Chile would cease to fly its distinctive national flag, would recognize the sovereignty of Ferdinand VII[*], and would recognize the Spanish Constitution of 1812[*]. In return, Spain would allow current authorities to remain at their posts, grant Chile substantial autonomy including rights of free trade, and agree to remove its army from Chile within a month. While the treaty may have been a tactical expediency for both sides to buy time, neither O'Higgins nor Gainza placed any faith in the other party's willingness to abide by its terms. While Gainza agreed to the negotiated terms, he was troubled that his actions had gone considerably beyond the viceroy's authorization. The treaty was denounced by some patriots who saw it as closing the door to complete independence from Spain. Chilean support for the treaty was further eroded as General Gainza used every possible excuse to delay his withdrawal until he learned whether Viceroy of Peru José Fernando de Abascal[*] approved of the treaty.

José Miguel Carrera[*], for reasons of personal aggrandizement that were essentially unrelated to dissatisfaction over the treaty, led a coup against the patriot government of Francisco de la Lastra and plunged the patriots into civil war. O'Higgins initially opposed Carrera, but ultimately accepted his government, in part to unify patriot forces against the army of Viceroy de Abascal, who refused to accept the terms of the treaty and ordered a third invasion of Chile. This invasion force was under the command of General Mariano Osorio[*] who would clash decisively with O'Higgins at the Battle of Rancagua[*].

REFERENCES: Sam Collier, *Ideas and Politics of Chilean Independence, 1808-1833*, 1984; Luis Galdames, *A History of Chile*, 1964; Jay Kinsbruner, *Bernardo O'Higgins*, 1968.

Samuel Freeman

LOAYSA, JUAN GARCÍA JOFRE DE. Juan García Jofre de Loaysa was born in Spain in the 1480s and is best remembered for his Pacific explorations in the 1520s. In 1525, Loaysa led seven ships and 450 men on a journey to the Pacific to follow up on the voyage of Ferdinand Magellan[*]. Two ships sank in the Strait of Magellan, and another had to return to New Spain[*] for supplies; a fourth ship deserted. Loaysa then led the three remaining ships into the Pacific Ocean where they reached the Molucca (Spice) Islands in 1527. Loaysa did not live to see the landing because he died of disease during the Pacific crossing.

REFERENCE: Ester G. Maring and Joel M. Maring, *Historical and Cultural Dictionary of the Philippines*, 1973.

LONDON, TREATY OF (1604). Negotiated between Great Britain and Spain and signed on August 19, 1604, the Treaty of London provided for British recognition of Spanish claims to territory that Spain had already effectively occupied but withheld British recognition from unoccupied Spanish territory in the New World. Throughout the last half of the sixteenth century, Protestant England had been locked in a struggle for survival with Catholic Spain. After succeding to the English throne in 1603, however, King James I wanted to settle his disputes with Spain, and King Philip III* agreed. England was also increasingly interested in expanding into the New World, but felt restricted by Spanish claims to North, Central, and South America, as well as to the islands of the Caribbean. In the treaty, England proposed and Spain accepted the doctrine of "effective occupation." England recognized Spain's monopolistic control over territories that it had already settled, but England refused to recognize Spanish claims to unsettled territory. The principal of effective occupation was incorporated in a formal clause in the Truce of Antwerp of 1609, after which it became an increasingly recognized principle of international law.

REFERENCE: R. B. Wernham, ed., *The New Cambridge Modern History*. Volume III: *The Counter Reformation and Price Revolution, 1559-1610*, 1968.

LÓPEZ, ESTANISLAO. Estanislao López was born in Santa Fe, Argentina*, in 1786. By the time he was a teenager, he was fighting Indians* in the northern frontier regions. López enthusiastically joined the rebels after the May Revolution of 1810* and was captured and imprisoned by royalist forces. He escaped from the Montevideo* prison and earned a reputation for military heroism during the next several years. He played an instrumental role in seeing to it that Santa Fe was separated from Buenos Aires*, and in 1819, he was elected governor of Santa Fe. López was re-elected many times until his death in 1838.

REFERENCES: Enrique Udaondo, *Diccionario biográfico colonial argentino*, 1945; Ione S. Wright and Lisa M. Nekhom, *Historical Dictionary of Argentina*, 1978.

LÓPEZ, NARCISO. Narciso López was born in Caracas*, Venezuela*, on September 13, 1798. As a teenager, he joined the Spanish army fighting against Simón Bolívar's* rebel forces, but when the royalists withdrew from Venezuela to Cuba* in 1823, López went with them. After several years, López moved to Spain where he continued his climb through military ranks until he earned the rank of general. He returned to Cuba in 1841 as president of the military tribunal, a judicial body that became widely known for the severity of its judgments. Gradually, however, López grew tired of Spanish rule. Much of his disillusionment was simple politics—he resented many of the leaders who had authority in Cuba—but some of it was personal. López wanted to acquire his fortune, and he had been through a number of unsuccessful business enterprises. He was looking for opportunities. By the late 1840s, López was working with Cuban rebels who wanted the island to be annexed to the United States. Spanish officials found out about the plot, and López fled to the United States. One year later, after raising an army of 600 men, López sailed from New Orleans and landed at Cárdenas in Matanzas Province. His force met heavy resistance from Spanish troops, and López once again fled to the United States. He returned with an army of 400 men in 1851, but he was captured by Spanish troops. Narciso López was tried and executed for treason.

REFERENCE: Jaime Suchlicki, *Historical Dictionary of Cuba*, 1988.

LÓPEZ DE GÓMARA, FRANCISCO. Born in Gómara, Spain, on February 2, 1511, Francisco López de Gómara became a priest during his teenage years. He is best remembered as a Spanish historian who served as the private chaplain of Hernán Cortés[*] for many years and who wrote the *Historia General de las Indias*. Although he admired Cortés, his "chronicle" was a highly inaccurate version of the conquest of New Spain[*], according to Bernal Díaz[*] del Castillo, a soldier who had firsthand knowledge of every single battle. López de Gómara never visited America. He died in Gómara around 1566.

REFERENCES: F. López de Gómara, *Cortés: The Life of the Conqueror of Mexico by His Secretary*, ed. and trans. L. B. Simpson, 1964; Mariano Picón-Salas, *De la conquista a la independencia*, 1944.

Fred Koestler

LÓPEZ DE LEGAZPI, MIGUEL. See LEGAZPI, MIGUEL LÓPEZ DE.

LÓPEZ-JAENA, GRACIANO. Graciano López-Jaena was born on December 20, 1856, in Llongo, the Philippines[*]. In 1880, he became editor of *La Solidaridad*, a leading revolutionary nationalist journal; he was forced to flee the Philippines later that year. He settled in Barcelona, where he joined a series of revolutionary clubs and wrote articles. In 1891, López-Jaena secretly went back to the Philippines, and, under the fictitious name of Diego Laura, he worked for the independence movement in Manila[*]. He was soon discovered by Spanish authorities, and he returned to Spain. López-Jaena died in Barcelona on January 20, 1896.

REFERENCE: E. Manuel Arsenio, *Dictionary of Philippine Biography*, 1955.

LÓPEZ RAYÓN, IGNACIO. Ignacio López Rayón was born in New Spain[*] in 1773 and received a legal education, attaining the rank of attorney. He then spent his career managing the family business, which was heavily invested in mining[*]. During the war for Mexican independence, López Rayón became the personal secretary to Miguel Hidalgo[*]. He also commanded troops after Hidalgo's death and defeated royalist forces in Zacatecas[*]. Royalist forces captured López but did not execute him; he was released from prison. After the revolution, López became mayor of San Luis Potosí[*], Mexico. He died in Guadalajara[*] in 1832.

REFERENCE: John A. Caruso, *The Liberators of Mexico*, 1967.

LOS CONFINES, *AUDIENCIA* **OF.** See GUATEMALA, *AUDIENCIA* OF.

LOUISIANA. The French explorer Robert Cavelier de La Salle claimed all the land drained by the Mississippi River for France in 1682. In 1699, settlers from New France colonized what is today Biloxi, Mississippi, A governor for the new colony of Louisiana was dispatched the same year. In 1718, the capital of the colony was transferred from Biloxi to New Orleans. To prevent the colony from falling under British control, France ceded Louisiana to Spain in 1762, and Spain began to manage it in 1765. Louisiana was under the supervision of the captaincy general of Cuba*. By the terms of the Treaty of San Ildefonso, Spain gave Louisiana back to France in 1800. France did not establish its control until 1803, and within a matter of weeks, France sold the Louisiana territory to the United States.

REFERENCE: Joe Gray Taylor, *Louisiana: A Bicentennial History*, 1976.

LOZANO, PEDRO. Pedro Lozano was born in Madrid, Spain, in 1697. He joined the Jesuit* order in 1711 and was sent to the Río de la Plata* area, where he studied at the University of Córdoba*. During the 1720s, Lozano labored in the missions of Santa Fe and took extensive notes about his travels and observations. In 1730, he was designated the official Jesuit chronicler for the Río de la Plata, and until 1745, when he retired, he traveled widely throughout the region, collecting documents, establishing archives, and writing history. His most important works were *Descripción corográfica del Gran Chaco Gualamba* (1733), *Historia de la Compañía de Jesús en las provincias del Paraguay* (1754–1755), and *Historia de la conquista de la provincia del Paraguay, Río de la Plata y Tucumán* (1873–1875). Lozano died in 1752.

REFERENCES: Enrique Udaondo, *Diccionario biográfico colonial argentino*, 1945; Ione S. Wright and Lisa M. Nekhom, *Historical Dictionary of Argentina*, 1978.

LUNA, JUAN. Juan Luna was born in the Philippines* in 1857 and earned a reputation as one of the islands' greatest painters and artists. In 1881, his painting *Spolairium* won first prize at the Madrid Exposition. Luna became a strong advocate of Philippine independence in the 1890s, and in 1896 he was arrested for writing anti-Spanish propaganda. Luna was exiled to Hong Kong where he died in 1899.

REFERENCE: E. Arsenio Manuel, *Dictionary of Philippine Biography*, 1955.

LUZON. Luzon, with an area of more than 40,000 square miles, is the largest island in the Philippines*. It is so dominant that its history is nearly congruent with that of the nation as a whole. Luzon may be divided into the following regions: (1) Manila* and its environs, the densely populated capital region where nearly all important events in Philippine history have taken place; (2) Central Luzon, the only extensive plain in the islands, where land tenancy disputes have sometimes erupted into open rebellion; (3) Southern Tagalog*, the fertile coconut-growing region south of Manila, home to many writers and political leaders; (4) Ilocos*, the narrow northwestern coastal plain of infertile soil and hard-driving emigrants; (5) the northern cordillera, where non-Christian tribes who do not consider themselves Filipinos* eke out a precarious existence while their mountains are rapidly denuded; (6) the Cagayan* Valley, whose central river flows northward to the sea at the Babuyan Channel; and (7) Bicol, physically and culturally separated on the extreme southeast peninsula of Luzon.

The Philippines were ruled by three imperial powers between 1571 and 1946: Spain, the United States, and Japan. Each controlled the archipelago from Luzon from Manila. That city, with the finest harbor in the Far East, a fertile agricultural hinterland, and a strategic location at the center of all communication and transportation in the islands, dominates the political, cultural, educational, commercial, and industrial life of the nation, in the manner of other Southeast Asian capitals, such as Bangkok, Jakarta, Rangoon, Saigon, and Singapore. All of these great port cities grew up where there had been only muddy fishing villages before the Europeans came. The imperialists came by ship, of course, so they had no use for an inland capital. Manila was where Filipinos met the world and where global commerce entered the islands.

Luzon developed various regional export economies in the nineteenth century in response to the new global market created by the development of steamships and the opening of the Suez Canal (1869). Bicol specialized in abaca. Ilocos grew marvelous tobacco*. The Southern Tagalog area was planted in coconuts. Sugar* estates were established where the swamps of central Luzon were drained to create big fields. Rice and fish remained the staple diet of Filipinos. Under Spanish rule, most large estates were owned by friars. When the United States took over, these lands fell into private hands. The Philippine Islands have never known effective land reform.

Today Luzon exhibits all the pathologies that can thrive on a tropical island transformed by a colonial economy. It has little industry. Its export crops never bring in enough money to pay for imports, so the balance of payments registers a steady outflow. Luzon's population is much too heavily concentrated in the former colonial capital, and that places an impossible burden on services. The land itself is scarred. Protective rain forests that once covered Luzon's mountains, soaking up monsoon rain and then releasing it gradually during the dry season, have been cut down almost everywhere. The soil has laterized (turned to brick), so rain runs off immediately. There are floods from May to September and drought the rest of the year.

REFERENCES: Frederick Wernstedt and J. E. Spencer, *The Philippine Island World*, 1967; Alfred W. McCoy and Edilberto de Jesús, *Philippine Social History*, 1982.

Ross Marlay

M

MABINI, APOLINARIO. Apolinario Mabini is known to generations of Filipino schoolchildren as the "Brains of the Revolution" and the "Sublime Para-
lytic." He was an intense, nationalist intellectual who agitated continually for
Filipino* unity and resistance to foreign domination. He achieved some power,
but his adult life was in fact a series of crushing disappointments. Mabini was
born in 1864 into a Filipino-Chinese mestizo* family without much money. He
worked at odd jobs to get himself through the Colegio de San Juan de Letrán
in Manila*, and in his thirtieth year received a law degree from the University
of St. Thomas. These were the years of swelling Filipino nationalism, and no
one felt more passionate about it than Mabini. Like most other Filipino men of
letters, he at first sought only reforms within the empire. When Dr. José Rizal*
organized the Liga Filipina to petition for such innocent goals, Mabini was one
of its founding members, but then Rizal was arrested and banished. Mabini
seems quickly to have concluded that asking for reforms was hopeless and that
Filipinos should demand, and if necessary seize, full independence. He was
briefly jailed, but he suffered a far more serious setback when stricken with polio
in January 1896.

By 1898, the revolutionaries had gained control of much territory, Emilio
Aguinaldo* had emerged as a leader, and the United States had replaced Spain
as the obstacle to Philippine* independence. Aguinaldo had heard of Mabini's
renown as a scholar and summoned the cripple, who was brought to Aguinaldo
in a hammock. From that moment forward, Aguinaldo and Mabini worked
together, hand in glove. They needed each other: Aguinaldo had great military
talent but few ideas, while Mabini was full of ideas but without the means to
achieve them on account of his physical handicap and his serious lack of political
skill (compounded by his somewhat dour, humorless personality).

More than anything else, Mabini's populist egalitarianism set the wealthy, conservative *ilustrados** against him. He wanted an independent, secularized Philippines, with power in the hands of the common people, and could not bear the thought of compromise, while the *ilustrados* wanted to enhance their own position, even if it meant accepting American sovereignty. Mabini served as premier and foreign minister of the first Philippine Republic for a peso a day, but after only five months, the *ilustrados* ousted him. It made little difference, for the American army was pushing Aguinaldo into the wilds of northern Luzon*. Mabini was physically unable to keep up with the fleeing Aguinaldo but stayed out of American hands as long as he could.

With the situation crumbling around him, Mabini launched another venture in Philippine nationalism: he agitated for a Philippine Catholic church* independent of the Vatican. He had been a Mason and always mistrusted the religious orders; now, in "retirement," he encouraged Gregorio Aglipay to found a schismatic Filipino Catholic Church. Mabini was captured and jailed by the Americans in November 1899. Because he still would not compromise, he was exiled to Guam* and was only brought back to the Philippines in February 1903, three months before his death at age 38. His final disappointment was seeing how enthusiastic Filipinos had become about the new American colonial regime and how little impact his own ideas had made.

REFERENCE: Teodoro Agoncillo, *Filipino Nationalism 1872-1970*, 1974.

Ross Marlay

MACEO Y GRAJALES, ANTONIO. Antonio Maceo y Grajales was born in Santiago, Cuba, in 1848 to a mulatto family that was absolutely committed to Cuban independence. Eventually, his father, ten brothers, and Maceo himself died in the war against Spain. During the Ten Years War*, Maceo rose through the military ranks, earning a reputation as a bold and brilliant strategist. When he refused to accept the Pact of Zanjón ending the Ten Years War, Spanish authorities exiled him from Cuba. By that time, he was a major general in the revolutionary army. He soon became a folk hero among the Cuban black population. In collaboration with Calixto García* Iñiguez, Maceo continued his attacks against the Spanish. He fled to Mexico in 1880 and then spent time in Haiti*, Honduras*, Mexico, and Panama*, agitating for Cuban independence. Maceo went to Costa Rica* where, under the leadership of José Martí*, he assembled a revolutionary army and prepared an invasion of Cuba. In 1895, Maceo returned to Cuba and launched a guerilla war against Spanish troops and government officials. He was killed in battle with Spanish soldiers in 1896.

REFERENCES: Philip Foner, *Antonio Maceo*, 1977; Magdalen M. Pando, *Cuba's Freedom Fighter*, 1980.

MACÍAS NGUEMA BIYOGO NEGUE NDONG, FRANCISCO. Francisco Macías Nguema Biyogo Negue Ndong was born in 1924 to a Fang family in Nfenga, Spanish Equatorial Guinea,* West Africa. He attended a series of Roman

Catholic schools and in 1944 joined the colonial administration, enjoying a number of posts in the forestry service and the public works department. In 1950, Macías received "emancipation" from Spain, and was appointed mayor of Mongomo in 1960. By the early 1960s, he was a member of the Movimiento Nacional de Liberación de Guinea Ecuatorial*, a nationalist political faction intent on securing independence from Spain. At the time, he was also serving as a member of the colonial assembly. Known as a cruel, paranoid megalomaniac, Macías emerged as the head of state of Equatorial Guinea after independence was achieved in 1968. His reputation for dictatorial cruelty only grew. He was overthrown in 1979 in a *coup d'etat* and executed in September 1979.

REFERENCE: Max Liniger-Goumaz, *Historical Dictionary of Equatorial Guinea*, 1988.

MADRID AGREEMENT OF 1975. The controversial Madrid Agreement of November 14, 1975, was between Spain, Morocco, and Mauritania. Under the terms of the agreement, Spain agreed to a temporary tripartite administration in Western Sahara, followed by the permanent withdrawal of Spain by March 1, 1976, and the division of Western Sahara between Mauritania and Morocco. Although Spain claimed that sovereignty rested on the Saharawi people, not in Morocco or Mauritania, the arrival of Moroccan and Mauritanian troops in Western Sahara within weeks of the agreement established such sovereignty, at least in their own minds. The Saharawi people, through the Polisario Front*, bitterly protested the Madrid Agreement in which their hopes for independence were crushed by the replacement of Spanish masters with Moroccan and Mauritanian ones, but their protests were of little avail. The war there continues today.

REFERENCE: Tony Hodges, *Historical Dictionary of Western Sahara*, 1982.

MADRID, TREATY OF (1670). See AMERICAN TREATY.

MADRID, TREATY OF (1750). The Treaty of Madrid of 1750 between Portugal and Spain served to consolidate Portuguese claims in Brazil. During the colonial period, Brazil was expanded beyond the line established by the Treaty of Tordesillas*, west to include the slopes of the Andes, north to the Amazon, and south to the Río de la Plata. Portuguese expansion inevitably led to clashes with Spanish colonial interests in South America. It was Portuguese activity on the northern and southern extremities of Brazil, especially in the upper Paraná region and Paraguay* to the goldfields of Mato Grosso and up the Amazon, that spurred negotiations with Spain. The Spanish-Portuguese territorial negotiations culminated in the Treaty of Madrid, signed January 3, 1750.

The Treaty of Madrid superseded all previous treaties, from Tordesillas in 1494 to Utrecht* in 1713. The treaty attempted to delimit the frontiers of Spanish and Portuguese possessions in America, Africa, and Asia on the basis of logical geographical features and actual occupation. The Treaty of Madrid was a diplomatic triumph for Portugal and King João V, for it officially recognized the contested Portuguese possession of almost half of South America. A secondary result of the treaty was the expulsion of the Jesuits[*] from Portuguese territory. As the Jesuits had been the principal protectors of the numerous Indian[*] tribes in Brazil, their removal allowed for widespread colonial exploitation of Indian lands.

REFERENCES: C. H. Haring, *The Spanish Empire in America*, 1947; Leslie Bethell, ed., *The Cambridge History of Latin America*, Vol. I, 1984.

William G. Ratliff

MA EL-ANIN, CHEIKH. Cheikh Ma el-Anin was born as Mohammed Sidi el-Mustapha in 1830 in Hodh, Mauritania. A brilliant intellectual and gifted leader, Ma el-Anin was educated in Marrakesh, Morocco. By the late nineteenth century, he was urging Saharawi tribesmen to resist the arrival of all Europeans in Africa. He led the guerrilla movement against French Mauritania in the early 1900s and became a heroic figure to subsequent generations of Saharan nationalists. He died on October 28, 1910.

REFERENCES: Tony Hodges, *Historical Dictionary of Western Sahara*, 1982; John Mercer, *Spanish Sahara*, 1975.

MAGELLAN, FERDINAND. Ferdinand Magellan was born in northern Portugal around 1480. During his teenage years, Magellan served as a page to the queen of Portugal, and in his early twenties, he joined several Portuguese expeditions heading for India and Malacca. In 1511, he was with the expedition of Francisco Serrao that conquered Malacca. Magellan returned to Portugal in 1513 to participate in a military campaign against Morocco, but he became discouarged when King Manuel of Portugal refused to finance his proposed voyage to the Moluccas (Spice Islands[*]). In 1517, Magellan turned to King Charles I[*] of Spain who agreed to finance the expedition in hopes of finding a way to the spice-rich Moluccas without having to sail the Portuguese-dominated waters along the coast of Africa.

Magellan set sail with five ships on September 20, 1519, heading for the Canary Islands[*] where they took on provisions. From there, the ships worked their way down the coast of West Africa before heading west toward Brazil, which they reached late in October. They spent more than a year slowly moving down the coast of South America looking for a passage into the Pacific Ocean, which they finally located on October 21, 1520. They sailed west through the strait and reached the Pacific Ocean late in November. The expedition then headed northwest across the Pacific, nearly starving before arriving in the Marianas[*] on March 6, 1521. After stopping over there and resupplying, the expedition sailed to the Philippines[*], where Magellan was killed by hostile natives on April 27, 1521. The expedition, reduced to two ships, made its way to the Moluccas by early November. After taking on supplies and loading up with valuable spices, they sailed for Spain by going around the southern tip of Africa.

They completed the first circumnavigation of the globe on September 8, 1522, when they reached Seville.

REFERENCE: Charles M. Parr, *Ferdinand Magellan, Circumnavigator*, 1964.

MAINE. The U.S.S. *Maine* was the U.S. navy battleship, second class, that was destroyed by an explosion in Havana* harbor on the night of February 15, 1898. Two officers and 250 men were killed by the explosion, and eight more men died later from injuries received in the blast. The *Maine* had been sent to Havana by the administration of William McKinley from Key West, Florida*, on January 24, 1898, in an apparent show of force after riots against Spain's reform policies that promised greater autonomy in the island. Although U.S. Consul General Fitzhugh Lee had warned against the visit, for fear that the opponents of reform might regard it as provocative, the administration ignored his advice. Publicly, the administration insisted that it was merely renewing customary goodwill visits that had been suspended in the days of the administration of Grover Cleveland. Privately, however, the president intended that the *Maine* be on hand to protect American lives and property in the event of renewed violence in Havana.

The ship arrived in Havana harbor on January 25 and was accorded the customary courtesies. The visit appeared to be going well, even during the uproar in the United States over the de Lome letter*. Then, at about 9:40 on the night of February 15, just after the ship's company had retired, the vessel was shaken by a mighty explosion. The commanding officer, Captain Charles D. Sigsbee, had been in his cabin working on correspondence. He felt his way through the dark to the deck and there assembled the survivors. Later, in 1912, he stated that he thought the explosion came from an external source. Convinced that the ship was under attack, he gave the order to prepare to repel boarders. It soon became apparent that the stricken vessel was beyond saving, and Sigsbee ordered the crew to abandon ship as it settled to the bottom of the harbor.

This incident produced the final crisis in Spanish-American relations. News of the *Maine*'s destruction spread across the United States the next morning, with the Hearst press taking the lead in blaming Spain. Subsequently, two different naval boards of inquiry, one American and the other Spanish, investigated the explosion. The Spanish board attributed the explosion to internal causes while the United States naval board blamed it on a "submarine mine," without fixing responsibility upon anyone. This theory was disputed by many foreign naval experts and even questioned by some experts in the U.S. Navy. But among most people in the United States, it was commonly believed that Spanish agents had somehow contrived to fix a mine to the hull of the *Maine* and had blown it up. That assumption and the resultant demands made on Spain by the McKinley administration led the two nations into war.

In 1911, a second naval board of inquiry looked into the destruction of the *Maine*. Its real purpose was to remove the wreckage from its obstructive position in the harbor, but in the process, the operation afforded an opportunity for a thorough examination of the *Maine*. The second board contradicted the findings of the 1898 investigation. It suggested evidence of a magazine explosion in the location where the first board had placed the "submarine mine" explosion. It still purported that a mine had been detonated at another location along the bottom of the ship. The second board, however, offered no other explanations nor appended any evidence to support its contentions.

In 1976, Admiral Hyman G. Rickover, USN, published the results of his definitive study of the *Maine* explosion. His analysis supported the Spanish conclusion that the explosion was from an internal cause, most likely from coal dust that in turn set off nearby magazines. Admiral Rickover also faulted both the inquiries of 1898 and 1911 for assuming that the cause had been external without giving serious consideration to more likely causes.

Given the temper of public opinion in the United States and the intrusive policy of the McKinley administration, it is doubtful that war could have been avoided in 1898 even without the *Maine* incident. But that disaster provided the emotional occasion that made war inevitable and immediate.

REFERENCES: David F. Trask, *The War With Spain in 1898*, 1981; Walter Millis, *The Martial Spirit*, 1931; H. G. Rickover, *How the Battleship Maine Was Destroyed*, 1976.

Joseph M. Rowe, Jr.

MAIPÚ, BATTLE OF. Following the victory by Argentine and Chilean forces over Spanish royalist troops at the battle of Chacabuco* on February 12, 1817, General José de San Martín* took control of Santiago*. There he refused an offer of the governorship of Chile* in favor of General Bernardo O'Higgins* who became supreme director of the newly independent state in April 1817. Over the course of the next year, San Martín's troops advanced to the south, driving the remnants of the Spanish forces into Concepción. Hearing of the defeat at Chacabuco, Joaquín de Pezuela*, the viceroy of Peru*, sent reinforcements by sea to Chile. The able General Mariano Osorio*, who had defeated O'Higgins at Rancagua* October 2, 1814, was put in charge of the king's troops. After the reinforcements, which included the Burgos regiment that had distinguished itself in the Peninsula wars against Napoleon as well as in New World battles, landed at Talcahuano, near Concepción, Osorio combined the fresh troops with the remnants of the Spanish troops in Concepción into a new force of 6,000 well-disciplined troops. In early January, Osorio's troops began a slow march north, even though they did not know where the forces of O'Higgins and San Martín were located. Encamped on the plains of the Cancha River on the north near Rancagua, the independence forces were in the process of changing their positions after receiving word from an inhabitant of the town of Talca that the Spanish army was in the plaza of that city and preparing for attack. The information proved incorrect, and Osorio's forces appeared suddenly during the late afternoon of March 19, 1818. The Spanish troops completely routed the surprised independence forces. In fighting that continued under a full moon until midnight,

O'Higgins showed great personal valor by rallying his troops even after one of his arms was broken by a musket ball. The independence forces then retreated toward Santiago after having lost 120 dead and 22 artillery pieces. The Spanish forces, which lost 200 men, were unable to take advantage of the victory because of a skillful rearguard defense mounted by Argentine troops.

News of the Spanish victory arrived in Santiago on the afternoon of March 21, along with rumors that San Martín was dead and O'Higgins mortally wounded. Many persons reacted with panic. Some families prepared to flee to Mendoza; some took refuge on ships in Valparaíso* harbor, while one royalist supporter prepared a horse with silver trappings to present to the victorious Osorio when he arrived. The panic continued through March 23, even though San Martín sent word that he was safe and in command of 4,000 surviving troops. O'Higgins arrived in Santiago on the morning of March 24 and once again assumed control of the remnants of a government that had begun to disintegrate. San Martín returned on March 25 and held a council of war. Workers were drafted to prepare 10,000 cartridges by melting churchbells down for cannon as well as preparing other supplies in Mendoza before San Martín had crossed the Andes in January 1817. San Martín gathered his forces for another battle and established a new camp on the plains of Maipú, 10 kilometers to the south of Santiago. With the arrival of the rearguard forces of Las Heras on March 28, San Martín's reconstituted forces were able to count upon five Chilean and four Argentine batallions of infantry numbering 4,000, plus one Chilean and two Argentine regiments of cavalry mounted on 1,000 horses.

While Osorio had won the battle of Cancha Rayada, his cavalry was tired and he was operating blindly without knowledge of where San Martín's troops were. Some initial cavalry skirmishing took place on March 28 while the bulk of Osorio's force of 5,500 was marching toward the River Cachapoal, which was crossed on March 31. After crossing the river and reaching a point less than four kilometers from San Martín's forces, Osorio held a council of war on April 4. The Spanish commander apparently proposed that his forces retire to the port of Valparaiso, which was blockaded by a Spanish naval squadron and which he thought offered a better chance of organizing a successful campaign of operations. Apparently his principal commanders objected, and it was decided to engage in battle on the plains of Maipú the next day.

On a clear day, the two forces opened battle against one another's positions, which were about one-half of a mile apart. San Martín's principal position was on the Loma Blanca, a low ridge that dominated access to both the River Maipú and the road to Valparaiso, should a withdrawal there be necessary. The Spanish forces took up what ultimately were defensive positions on another ridge to the south across a flat plain 1,000 meters wide at one point and 250 meters wide at its narrowest. Through it ran a gully 300 meters long and 20 meters deep; at its western end were fenced-in pastures and buildings of the Hacienda Espejo. San Martín's forces opened the actions with strong artillery fire from both the right and left flanks. He then ordered a general advance of Argentine grenadiers against the Spanish line. The Spaniards began an orderly retreat to the buildings and walled enclosures of the Hacienda Espejo farmhouse from which a counterattack was mounted. Over the course of the day, the house reportedly changed hands twenty times.

Toward the end of the day, the Spanish center and one wing apparently gained an advantage, and San Martín's forces appeared doomed to defeat. Around five o'clock in the afternoon, the Spanish Burgos regiment, cut off from cavalry support, attempted to form itself into a new square. At that point, the rebel troops launched a furious charge against what some have called "the flower of the Spanish army." Unable to reform itself into an orderly unit, the confusion within this unit led to panic among the rest of the Spanish troops. San Martín's troops took advantage of the situation, charged at all points, and carried the day. In the midst of the Spanish withdrawal through the gully, Las Heras laid an ambush. The carnage was great as the independence forces bayoneted hundreds of the Spanish troops in the outbuildings of the Espejo farm until Las Heras ordered a halt and accepted the surrender of the Spanish leaders and nearly all of the remaining cavalry and infantry officers. General Osorio apparently abandoned the field around three o'clock in the afternoon when he saw his right and center wings in retreat. He escaped over the Prado ridge with about 280 officers and men and arrived at Talcahuano on April 14. The Spanish lost 12 cannon, four battle flags, 1,000 dead, 3,850 rifles, the military pay chest, and 2,200 troops who were taken as prisoners of war. The forces of San Martín lost about 1,000 dead and wounded, including over half of the Negro slaves from Cuyo Province (Mendoza).

The Spaniards managed to retain a foothold in Valdivia in the south until they were dislodged in a daring naval assault led by Admiral Thomas Cochrane on February 3, 1820. But the battle of Maipú proved decisive, for Argentine and Chilean forces had made it impossible for the Spaniards to maintain and occupy Chilean territory on land while the forces of Bolívar and San Martín were threatening Lima[*] and the heartland of the viceroyalty at that time. It assured the independence of Chile.

REFERENCE: Luis Merino, *La Batalla de Maipú*, 1909.

Neale J. Pearson

MALDONADO Y SOTOMAYOR, PEDRO VICENTE. Pedro Vicente Maldonado y Sotomayor was born in 1709 in Riobamba, Ecuador[*]. A gifted geographer and cartographer who studied at the San Luis Seminary in Quito[*], Maldonado supplied a number of maps for the Ecuadorean region, including his greatest contribution, the *Map of the Kingdom of Quito*. He spent some time as governor and captain general of Atacames and Esmeraldas and then served as chamberlain to King Philip V[*] of Spain. Maldonado died in London on November 17, 1748.

REFERENCES: Albert William Bork and George Maier, *Historical Dictionary of Ecuador*, 1973; Federico González Suárez, *Historia general de la República del Ecuador*, 7 vols., 1890–1903.

MALINCHE. See MARINA, DOÑA.

MALVINAS ISLANDS. The Malvinas Islands, also known as the Falkland Islands, are a British colony, claimed by Argentina*. They comprise an archipelago of almost 12,000 square kilometers and are located some 400 nautical miles from the Argentine coast and 450 miles from the Antarctic. The region is thus larger than either Jamaica* or Puerto Rico*. The archipelago consists of two main islands: West Falkland (Gran Malvina) and the larger East Falkland (Soledad), separated by the Straits of San Carlos, which is 50 miles long and 10 miles wide. There are also 15 islands with an extension of more than 20 square kilometers, 100 if minor islands are counted, and 200 if even smaller ones are included. The closest point to the South American continent is the Isla de los Estados, some 250 miles away. The capital is Port Stanley [Puerto Argentino], the population consisting of roughly 1,800 Kelpers, as the ethnically British population is called. Geologically, the Malvinas are part of Patagonia.

The Falklands were supposedly visited by Amerigo Vespucci* (1501–1502), Binot Palmier de Gonneville (1503–1504), Ferdinand Magellan* (1520), Esteban Gómez (1520), Pedro de Vera and his *Anunciada* (1526), the Alcazaba expedition (1536), the Bishop of Plasencia's *Incógnita* (1540), John Davis and his *Desire* (1592), Richard Hawkins (1594), and Sebald de Weert and his *Geloof* (1600), but only the expeditions of the *Incógnita* and especially of Sebald de Weert have been generally accepted by scholars. In the seventeenth and eighteenth centuries, Dutch, English, and French mariners multiplied their visits. John Strong landed in the islands in 1690 and called them the Falklands in honor of Viscount Falkland (1654–1694), then lord of the admiralty. The French, who arrived there after 1698, came mostly from St. Malo, hence "Malouines", and thereafter the Malvinas in Spanish.

The first colonization attempt was French. Louis Antoine de Bougainville arrived in early 1764. On East Falkland, Bougainville founded St. Louis. The English, unaware of the French presence, established themselves in 1765 on West Falkland and founded Port Egmont. Soon after, they abandoned the base but in 1766 returned with John Macbride. When the Spaniards heard about the French settlement, they protested, whereupon France relinquished its possession and Spain compensated Bougainville for his investment. Realizing the increasing rivalry, Spain now proceeded to occupy the islands and appointed Felipe Ruiz Puente as the first governor (1767). Two years later, the Spaniards discovered the English in the Straits of San Carlos. Governor Francisco Bucareli y Ursúa of Buenos Aires ordered the eviction of the English, which was promptly carried out in 1770. England, however, turned the eviction into a question of honor. Since neither Spain nor France wanted a war, negotiations led to the bizarre secret agreement of 1771 by which England was allowed to return temporarily to the Malvinas. The question of Spanish sovereignty was not affected. In 1774, the English finally and voluntarily abandoned the islands but not without leaving behind a plaque that stated that the islands were under British sovereignty. After

England evacuated the Malvinas, Spain resumed control that same year and maintained it uninterruptedly until 1811 through 20 duly appointed governors. In 1780, the islands became a *presidio*. The Spanish title was reinforced in 1790 through the Nootka Sound Convention, at a moment when the Spanish situation was much more unfavorable than it had been in 1770. The convention specifically acknowledged the status quo in regard to the "eastern and western coasts of South America and the islands adjacent." Argentina inherited the islands in 1811. As a result of its internal anarchy, it did not occupy them until 1820 when the Argentine flag was officially hoisted in the Malvinas by Commander David Jewett from North Parish, New London, Connecticut, who had offered his services to the United Provinces of South America.

REFERENCES: Julius Goebel, *The Struggle for the Falkland Islands: A Study in Legal and Diplomatic History*, 1927; Desmond Rice and Arthur Gavshon, *The Sinking of the Belgrano*, 1984; Alberto R. Coll and Anthony C. Arend, eds., *The Falkland War: Lessons for Strategy, Diplomacy, and International Law*, 1985; Laurio H. Destafani, *Malvinas, Georgias y Sandwich del Sur ante el conflicto con Gran Bretaña*, 1982; Ricardo R. Caillet-Bois, *Una tierra argentina: Las Islas Malvinas*, 1982.

O. Carlos Stoetzer

MANAGUA, DIOCESE OF. The Roman Catholic diocese of Managua was first established by Pope Clement VII in 1531. Its original territory included the area from northwest Nicaragua* to Panama*. It was raised to an archdiocese in 1913.

REFERENCE: *New Catholic Encyclopedia*, IX:141, 1967.

MANCO INCA. Manco Inca was born around 1516 in Peru* and was crowned emperor of the Inca* tribe at Cuzco* at the end of 1533. In effect, Manco Inca was a puppet of Francisco Pizarro*, who hoped to rule the Inca empire by using Manco Inca as his vassal. Manco Inca chafed under Pizarro's heavy-handedness, and in 1535, he escaped from Cuzco. He then led a guerilla campaign against the Spanish invaders that lasted for more than ten years. Manco Inca set up a protected enclave in the Vilcabamba Valley. In 1545, he was assassinated by associates of Diego de Almagro*, whom he had befriended. Manco Inca's son, Túpac Amaru*, then assumed leadership of the Inca empire.

REFERENCE: Burr Cartwright Brundage, *Lords of Cuzco: A History and Description of the Inca People in Their Final Days*, 1967.

MANILA. Manila was the chief port and capital of the Philippines*, the most distant outpost of the Spanish Empire, and leading city of the only Christian nation in Asia. Manila's character is defined by a blend of Filipino*, Chinese, and Spanish cultures. It was natural that Manila Bay, one of the finest harbors in the Far East, should become an entrepot. The city grew up on the eastern shore of the bay, where the Pasig River enters it. When the site was first visited by Martin de Goiti and Juan Salcedo in 1570, it was already a fortified trading town ruled by Raja Solimán, a Muslim related to the ruling family of Brunei. Indonesians and

Chinese came to trade. When the Spaniards landed, the Filipinos already possessed bronze cannons. In the inevitable battle, the native town was burned.

Miguel López de Legazpi* returned on May 19, 1571. He established a fortified position, which was soon attacked by Tagalog* and Pampangan* warships commanded by Raja Solimán and Lakandula, the chief of Tondo, a town across the river from Manila. Solimán was killed. Legazpi proceeded to lay out plans for a major city. He ordered the construction of churches, houses, barracks and, most importantly, a stone fort. The city was granted a royal charter by King Philip II* in 1574 and a coat of arms in 1596.

The history of Manila cannot be understood without reference to the galleon trade that flourished for 250 years (1565–1815). Spanish mariners discovered a route across the Pacific which, though long and perilous, connected their rich New World empire to their foothold in the Orient. Manila was above all else an entrepot through which flowed silks, spices, and porcelain bound for Europe and huge quantities of silver bound for China. The silver did not come from Europe, of course, but rather from the mines of New Spain* and Peru*, where the Spanish forced Indians* to dig it. The silver was then loaded onto ships at Acapulco* and taken to Manila, where it was exchanged for Asian luxury goods. The economies of Spain, New Spain, and China were transformed, while the economic development of the Philippines was actually retarded by the Spaniards' concentration on nonproductive speculation.

The port was shallow, so most loading and unloading employed lighters. The place was vulnerable to earthquakes and typhoons, but offered three advantages: (1) protection from ocean waves; (2) ready access to rich riceland, sugar* fields and fishponds; and (3) a strategic location midway between the Spice Islands* (Moluccas) and China. Legazpi laid out a Spanish city, intramuros ("within the walls"). The Chinese lived in their own quarter, called the Parian. Filipinos lived in surrounding native towns that evolved into suburbs. After devastating fires in 1583 and 1603, the Spanish quarter was rebuilt using easily worked volcanic stone hewn by native and Chinese workers. Paranoia and suspicion plagued relations between the races. The Spaniards and Filipinos hated and feared the Chinese more than they did each other. Many times in the sixteenth century, the Spaniards, imagining Chinese sedition, encouraged Filipinos to massacre them. The Chinese always came back, for the Spanish needed their manufacturing and business talents. In the late eighteenth century, the Chinese settlement was moved north of the river.

Manila might have grown into the greatest city in Asia, but for the fact that Spain could not match Dutch and British power in the Far East. Only when Spanish policy opened Manila to free trade, starting in 1789 and fully by 1834, did Manila grow into a city of warehouses and inter-island trade. The docks were piled with commercial export crops: hemp, tobacco,* sugar and coffee*. Manila was the one place where all the Philippine language groups—Tagalogs, Visayans,* Ilocanos* and many others—mixed with each other and with foreigners. A mestizo* elite emerged claiming to speak for the nations as a whole.

Manila was the center and object of the Philippine Revolution (1896–1898). When the United States intervened in 1898, Spaniards controlled only Intramuros, exactly as they had 321 years earlier. Manila is now the primary city of the Philippines, the center of government, finance, education, trade, industry, communications, and culture.

REFERENCE: William L. Schurz, *The Manila Galleon*, 1959.

Ross Marlay

MANILA, *AUDIENCIA* OF. The *audiencia* of Manila* was established in 1583, shortly after the arrival of the Spaniards in the Philippines*. Throughout the colonial period, it remained the premier European judicial body for the islands. It was suppressed in 1589 but re-established in 1598. In 1599, the *audiencia* decided that in all civil cases involving only Filipinos*, the customary laws of the islands, not Roman or canon law, would apply, and Juan de Plasencia* codified Tagalog* law for the *audiencia's* use. All criminal cases and civil cases not covered by local laws would be decided using Roman or canon law. In this sense, the *audiencia* played an important role in making sure that the legal hispanization of the Philippines occurred smoothly. Until the Mexican Revolution, the *audiencia* of Manila was subject to the viceroyalty of New Spain*. The *audiencia* continued to function until 1898.

REFERENCE: Charles Henry Cunningham, *The Audiencia in the Spanish Colonies as Illustrated by the Audiencia of Manila (1583–1800)*, 1919.

MANILA, DIOCESE OF. The Roman Catholic diocese of Manila* originated in 1571 when Augustinian* missionary priests began to evangelize the region of Luzon* in the Philippines*, which had been conquered by Miguel López de Legazpi. In 1579, Manila became the seat of a Roman Catholic diocese that included all the Spanish settlements in the Far East. The first bishop was Domingo de Salazar. Manila was a suffragen diocese of the archdiocese of Mexico City* until 1595 when it became an archdiocese in its own right. *New Catholic Encyclopedia*, IX:162, 1967.

MANILA GALLEON. Spain conquered most of the New World during her "great century" (1492–1588) but took only one colony in Asia, the Philippines*. For 250 years (1565–1815), all Spanish commerce and communication with its Far Eastern outpost was carried by the annual Manila galleon. Galleon trade was crucially important, not only for Manila Spaniards but also for China and the whole Far East, New Spain*, Peru*, and Spain itself. Spaniards had found truly stupendous quantities of silver in Peru and New Spain. Some of that precious metal was taken across the Pacific in ships plying a long, perilous northern route, sometimes taking half a year to reach Manila*. There, the silver was exchanged for exotic, luxurious Asian goods prized in Europe. The vessel would depart Manila on the easier eastbound journey to Acapulco*, its cargo then carried across Mexico and loaded onto other ships bound for Europe. All other trade routes between Europe and Asia ran the other way, around India. The galleon trade ruined New Spain and Peru, as their wealth was taken away and they received nothing in return. For merchants in Spain, the galleons brought unwanted competition. As for China, the Manila galleon flooded the Celestial Empire with Spanish silver. In fact, Spanish silver dollars became a medium of exchange across Asia, greatly stimulating regional trade.

Manila* was the entrepot. Chinese junks brought porcelains and fine cloth— velvet damask, satins, taffetas, and above all, silken goods already finished as stockings, handkerchiefs, and priests' robes. Indian and Arab ships brought cotton from the Malabar coast and carpets from Persia. Spices from the Moluccas*, ivory and sandalwood from the jungles of Southeast Asia, even slaves and gemstones were all shipped eastward to New Spain and Spain from Manila. On the return voyage, in addition to silver, Spaniards brought horses, cows, and a variety of New World plants that revolutionized farming in Asia, including tobacco*, peanuts, corn*, and tomatoes. The westbound galleon also brought governors and priests, as well as welcome letters that might be two years old before they were delivered.

The fabulous galleon trade benefitted the Philippines little, if at all. Exports stagnated, since few Philippine products were in demand. On the other hand, imported Indian cotton, distributed through a growing network of provincial Chinese middlemen, ruined local cottage industries. The trade encouraged Spanish indolence, since it was much easier to engage in trade and speculation while awaiting the galleon's arrival than to pioneer the interior forests. Manila society became so dependent upon the galleon that if even one disappeared, as the victim of shipwreck or piracy*, fortunes were lost and real economic depression descended on the city. Meanwhile, so many Chinese came to trade and live in Manila that Spaniards and Filipinos*, fearing a "yellow peril," sometimes massacred them in terrible pogroms. The galleon trade petered out in the eighteenth century, as the Spanish Empire sank into decline. Dutch and English traders, with their free trade policies, eroded Manila's significance as an entrepot. The last galleon left for Acapulco in 1815.

REFERENCE: William L. Schurz, *The Manila Galleon*, 1959.

Ross Marlay

MANSO DE VELASCO, JOSÉ ANTONIO. José Antonio Manso de Velasco was born in Logroño, Spain, in 1688. He spent his career in the Spanish army before being appointed lieutenant governor and captain general of Chile* in 1737. He was aggressive in his vision of the future of the colony and is credited with establishing dozens of cities up and down the country. As a reward for his extraordinary performance, the Spanish Crown named him viceroy* of Peru* in 1744. Manso de Velasco remained at that post until he was replaced in 1761 by Manuel de Amat y Junient*. He retired to Spain as the Conde de Superunda, a reward given to him by the Crown. Manso de Velasco died in 1764.

REFERENCE: José Toribio Medina, *Diccionario biográfico colonial de Chile*, 1906.

MAPUCHE. The Mapuche were an Araucanian[*] people who lived between the Picunche and the Huilliche in central Chile[*]. Along with other Araucanian people, the Mapuche put up a fierce resistance to Spanish conquest and have maintained a tribal identity even today.

MARGARITA. Margarita is a small island off the coast of Venezuela[*] in the Caribbean Sea. Between 1525 and 1600, it was under the private control of the Villalobos family, which appointed its governors. The island reverted to the Crown in 1600, and it was under the administrative authority of the *audiencia* of Santo Domingo[*] until 1739, albeit with its own governor. Between 1739 and 1777, the *audiencia* of New Granada[*] supervised Margarita. After 1777, it fell under the control of the captaincy general of Venezuela[*]. Effective royal control of Margarita ceased to exist after 1810, and the island eventually became part of Venezuela.

MARIANA ISLANDS. The Marianas are a series of volcanic islands located in the western Pacific ocean area of Micronesia, approximately 1,500 miles east of the Philippines[*]. The major islands in the group are Guam[*], the southernmost island, Saipan, Tinian, Rota, and Pagan. On a north-south axis, the islands stretch over 450 miles. Ferdinand Magellan[*] first discovered the Marianas in 1521 while on his pioneering circumnavigation of the globe; for the next 375 years, they remained Spanish territory. Colonists from Spain settled Guam in the early 1560s and other locations in the Marianas in 1668. They intermarried with the native people, known to the Spaniards as Chamorros. Spanish control of the Marianas was centered in the Philippines. The political status of the Marianas as a colony of Spain did not change until the Spanish-American War[*]. Spain's defeat at the hands of the United States in 1898 was a strategic disaster— the elimination of Spain as a Pacific power. As part of the Treaty of Paris of 1898[*] that ended the war, Spain ceded the island of Guam as well as the Philipines to the United States. One year later, Spain sold the rest of the Mariana Islands to Germany for $4.5 million.

REFERENCES: J. C. Beaglehole, *The Exploration of the Pacific*, 1968; John W. Coulter, *The Pacific Dependencies of the United States*, 1957; Donald F. McHenry, *Micronesia: Trust Betrayal*, 1975.

MARINA, DOÑA. The area of Coatzacoalcos, in the state of Tabasco, Mexico, is hot and steamy, heavy with vegetation. Most of the roads are still unpaved and ox carts outnumber motor vehicles. Foot trails are the usual paths of transportation, with machetes necessary, since the yearly rains are measured in hundreds of inches, stimulating phenomenal growth of trees and plants. It is an area rich in folklore and unwritten history. This is one of these stories.

Just outside Jaltipán lies a sizable burial mound, covered with jungle growth and believed to be the final resting place of Malinche, better known in Mexican history as Doña Marina, the mistress-linguist of Hernán Cortés[*], the conqueror of the Aztecs*. In 1519, she and 19 other maidens were given to Cortés by the natives of Potonchan, Tabasco. Malinche was baptized and took the name Marina. She quickly distinguished herself as a translator, for she was Aztec (and a Nahuatl* speaker) who had been given to merchants as a child and sold south, where the Maya* language was spoken. She served as interpreter to Cortés, translating from Nahuatl to Yucatec Maya, which was then translated into Spanish by Jerónimo de Aguilar*, who had been shipwrecked among the Maya for eight years. Marina took the honorific title of Doña when she became Cortés's trusted adviser and mistress during the conquest of Mexico. She later bore him an illegitimate son named Martín, who took his father's surname. It is doubtful if Cortés could have been successful in the conquest of the Aztecs without her linguistic and cultural knowledge of the high civilizations of Mexico. It was clear, however, that after the conquest was completed, Cortés considered Malinche a social disadvantage, and he gave her to his captain Xaramilo, commander of one of his sloops. She was not neglected economically, however, having estates in both the Mexico City* area and along the valley of the Coatzacoalcos River. Despite the fact that Cortés returned to Spain and married a noblewoman who bore him a legitimate male heir, Doña Marina retained a high status in Spanish society in Mexico until her death. She is remembered in contemporary Mexico as a traitor to her people.

REFERENCE: Michael C. Meyer and William L. Sherman, *The Course of Mexican History*, 1983.

George A. Agogino

MARINO, SANTIAGO. Born in what is today Venezuela* in 1788, Santiago Marino eventually became one of the premier leaders of Venezuela. During the struggle for independence, Marino was a principal assistant to Simón Bolívar* and director of revolutionary activities in the Guayana* region. After the rebel defeat at the Battle of Carabobo*, Marino fled to Trinidad*, but he returned to Venezuela in 1816. He was a member of the Venezuelan Congress in 1819, and he then served as chief of staff at the second Battle of Carabobo, which won Venezuelan independence. As a military leader, Marino worked for the separation of Venezuela from Gran Colombia*, which was finally accomplished in 1830. Throughout the rest of his career, Marino was a rival of Venezuelan general José Antonio Páez*. In 1848, Marino led the rebel forces that successfully overthrew Páez. Marino was unsuccessful in his own bid for the Venezuelan presidency several times during the 1830s and 1840s. He died in 1854.

REFERENCES: *Diccionario biográfico de Venezuela*, 1953; Manuel Vicente Magallanes, *Los Partidos Políticos en la Evolución Histórica de Venezuela*, 1977.

MARROQUÍN, FRANCISCO. Francisco Marroquín was born to a prominent Spanish family in the Valley of Toranzo in Santander, Spain, in 1477. He entered the Roman Catholic priesthood and accompanied Bishop Juan de Zumárraga* to

Mexico City* in 1528. He served as Zumárraga's vicar-general. In the great dispute of 1529, when Zumárraga condemned several conquistadors*, including Nuño de Guzmán*, for their cruelty to the Indians*, Marroquín excommunicated those who had risen up against the church. Fearing for Marroquín's life, Zumárraga sent him to Guatemala* in 1534 as provost for Guatemala, Honduras*, and El Salvador*. Marroquín brought in Dominican*, Franciscan*, and Mercedarian* priests and taught them the various Indian languages. In 1537, Zumárraga consecrated Marroquín as bishop of Guatemala. A close personal friend of Pedro de Alvarado*, Marroquín did little in his capacity as ecclesiastical "protector of the Indians" and, as executor for Alvarado's estate, glossed over the conquistador's many encroachments on Indian lands and rights. On the other hand, Marroquín was an able leader of the *encomenderos* and colonists in the early years. Marroquín endeavored to see Santiago de Guatemala* (Antigua) firmly established as a viable Spanish capital and demonstrated great leadership during the town's difficult early years. By 1542, Marroquín was able to note of Santiago de Guatemala, "This city has always been an inn and hospital for everyone. It is now and will be since it is on the way to everywhere."

REFERENCES: L. L. Lamadrid, "Bishop Marroquín—Zumárraga's Gift to Central America," *Americas*, 5 (1948–49), 331–41; Miles L. Wortman, *Government and Society in Central America, 1680-1840*, 1982.

Virginia Garrard Burnett

MARSHALL ISLANDS. The Marshall Islands are an archipelago in the central Pacific Ocean between the Gilbert Islands to the southwest and Wake Island to the north. There are 34 islands in two groups. Kwajalein is the largest island in the Ralik chain, while Majuro is the main island of the Ratak chain. Spanish explorers first reached the Marshall Islands in 1526 but they never developed their claim there. Germany established a presence in the Marshall Islands in 1874, and in 1885, Pope Leo XIII arbitrated a dispute between Germany and Spain, confirming Spanish sovereignty over the Marianas* and Caroline Islands* and German control over the Marshalls. When World War I broke out, Japan occupied the Marshall Islands. Japan was confirmed in its possession of the Marshall Islands by the League of Nations under the mandate system.

REFERENCE: Stanley De Smith, *Microstates and Micronesia: Problems of America's Pacific Islands and Other Minute Territories*, 1970.

Joseph M. Rowe, Jr.

MARTÍ, MARIANO. Mariano Martí was born in Bafrim, Tarragona, Spain, in 1721. He received a doctorate in law from the University of Cevera and made a name for himself as the vicar-general of the archbishopric of Tarragona. In 1762, he was consecrated as bishop of Puerto Rico*, and his tenure there was marked by a zealous need to travel widely throughout the diocese and improve church educational facilities. In 1770, he became bishop of Caracas* in what is today Venezuela*. Martí kept excellent records of his travels, and his reports to church leaders constitute a valuable historical record. Martí died in Caracas in 1792.

REFERENCE: J. J. Suria, *El eximio prelado doctor Mariano Martí, obispo de Caracas y Venezuela*, 1962.

MARTÍ Y PÉREZ, JOSÉ. José Martí was born in Havana*, Cuba*, on January 28, 1853, to a military family. As a student, Martí came under the influence of Rafael María de Mendive, an anti-Spanish Cuban nationalist. When Carlos Manuel de Cespedes* launched the Ten Years War* in 1868, Martí became an enthusiastic proponent of Cuban independence. In 1869, along with his close friend Fermín Valdés Domínguez, Martí wrote *El diablo cojuelo*, a satirical political document on freedom of speech and of the press. Martí's first dramatic play, *Abdala*, was a plea for Cuban independence, published in 1869. That same year, he was arrested for sedition and sentenced to six years in prison. He worked at hard labor in prison until early 1871 when he was deported to Spain and released. In the summer of 1871, Martí enrolled in the law school at the University of Madrid, transferred to the University of Zaragoza in 1873, and graduated in 1874. Throughout his law school career, Martí campaigned for Cuban independence and continued his literary career, writing the plays *Adultera* (1872) and *Amor con amor se paga* (1875) and the novel *Amistad funesta* (1875).

In 1875, Martí went to work as a journalist in Mexico City* for *La Revista Universal*. When the Pact of Zanjón* ended the Ten Years War in 1878 and declared a general amnesty for all revolutionaries, Martí returned to Havana. He immediately resumed his political activities, but in 1878, Spanish authorities exiled him once again. Martí moved to New York City where he spent the next 15 years raising money and promoting the cause of Cuban independence. Along with people like Gonzalo Quesado y Arostegui, Antonio Maceo*, Máximo Gómez*, and Juan Gualberto Gómez*, Martí planned and launched the war for Cuban independence in 1895. Martí left New York in the spring of 1895 and joined up with the revolutionary forces in Cuba, where he was killed in a battle with Spanish soldiers on May 19, 1895. He has since become a Cuban national hero.

REFERENCES: Richard B. Gray, *Jose Martí, Cuban Patriot*, 1962; John M. Kirk, *Jose Martí: Mentor of the Cuban Nation*, 1983.

MARTÍNEZ CAMPOS, ARSENIO. Arsenio Martínez Campos was born in Spain in 1831 and spent his career as an officer in the Spanish army. As a young general in 1874, Martínez was given command of Spanish troops trying to quell the Ten Years War* (1868–1878) in Cuba*. He succeeded in crushing the rebellion and was then appointed captain general of Cuba. Martínez tried to be an enlightened leader, campaigning for civil equality between Cubans and Spaniards and a wide range of civil liberties, but he encountered much resistance from Madrid. He spent the late 1880s and early 1890s back in Spain, but when the Cuban rebellion began in 1895, Martínez received the command of Spanish forces in Cuba again. For a year, he tried to achieve a negotiated settlement providing for Cuban autonomy, but when Spanish authorities refused, he resigned his command. Arsenio Martínez Campos died in 1900.

REFERENCE: Jaime Suchlicki, *Historical Dictionary of Cuba*, 1988.

MARTÍNEZ COMPAÑÓN Y BUJANDO, BALTASAR JAIME. Baltasar Jaime Martínez Compañón y Bujando was born in Cabredo, Navarre, Spain, on January 10, 1737. He was ordained a Roman Catholic priest in 1761. He moved to Peru* in 1767 when he was appointed canon of the cathedral, and he steadily gained a reputation in Lima* for his political grace and commitment to the church. He became bishop of Trujillo* in Peru in 1779 and was known for his extensive tours to even the most remote corners of the diocese, his zeal for economic development, and his support for the Indian missions. Martínez was transferred to the diocese of Bogota* in 1788 and he died there, while serving as bishop, on August 17, 1797.

REFERENCE: J. M. Perez Ayala, *Baltasar Jaime Martínez Compañón y Bujando: prelado español de Colómbia y el Perú*, 1955.

MARTÍNEZ DE IRALA, DOMINGO. Domingo Martínez de Irala was born in Vergara, Guipúzcoa, Spain, around 1510 to a wealthy family. He came to the New World with Pedro de Mendoza* and arrived in the Río de la Plata* area in 1535. Martínez de Irala was part of the initial founding of Buenos Aires*. He then served as second in command to Juan de Ayolas in his expedition up the Paraguay River to find a route to Peru*. He became governor of Paraguay* in 1539, a position he held until 1542. Martínez de Irala irritated religious interests by taking seven Indian* wives and encouraging polygamy among his followers, as well as by his active promotion of slavery*. In 1542, Alvar Núñez Cabeza de Vaca* replaced him as governor at the direction of the Crown, but local settlers deposed Cabeza de Vaca in 1544 and restored Irala to the governorship. Domingo Martínez de Irala held the post until his death in 1557. Under his leadership, the Spanish settlement in and around Asunción* became stable and prosperous.

REFERENCE: Machain Lafuente, *Los conquistadores de la Plata*, 1943.

MARTÍNEZ DE ROSAS CORREA, JUAN. Juan Martínez de Rosas Correa was born in Mendoza, Argentina*, in 1759. He attended the University of Córdoba* and then graduated with a doctorate in civil and canon law from the University of San Felipe* in Santiago*, Chile*, in 1786. Martínez taught philosophy, physics, and law for several years before joining the royal service. During the next quarter of a century, Martínez held a variety of posts. Gradually he became an advocate of Chilean independence. He was a supporter of the May Revolution* of 1810 in Argentina and close to the O'Higgins* family in Chile. Martínez was a member of the first revolutionary junta in Chile, but he died in 1813.

REFERENCES: José Toribio Medina, *Diccionario biográfico colonial de Chile*, 1906; Ione S. Wright and Lisa M. Nekhom, *Historical Dictionary of Argentina*, 1978.

MARTINIQUE. Martinique is an island of approximately 60 square miles located in the southern Caribbean, between Dominica* on the north and St. Lucia* on the south. On his second voyage in 1493, Christopher Columbus* first sighted the island, but no European landed there until Columbus's fourth voyage in 1502. After exploring the island, the Spaniards decided that it had little economic value, and they left it to its native Karib* and Arawak* inhabitants. In 1635, Pierre Belain d'Esnambuc took possession of Martinique for France. Because of the sugar* plantations he established, the island became an economic jewel in the French Empire. African slaves* were imported to work the sugar cane fields, and the Karibs and Arawaks died out, victims of European diseases. In 1674, France formally assumed sovereignty over Martinique.

REFERENCES: Herbert Ingram Priestley, *France Overseas: A Study of Modern Imperialism*, 1966; W. Adolphe Roberts, *The French in the West Indies*, 1942.

MATAMOROS, MARIANO. Mariano Matamoros was born in New Spain* in 1770 and became a Roman Catholic priest. As a young man, he became increasingly disillusioned with Spain, with the control it exercised over the economic, social, political, and religious life in Mexico, and with the insufferable arrogance of the *peninsulares*.* In 1811, he joined forces with José María Morelos* y Pavón in fighting the Spanish army, but he was captured in 1814. Spanish authorities transferred him to Valladolid where, after a trial, he was executed for treason on February 3, 1814.

REFERENCE: Lucas Alamán, *Historia de Méjico*, 5 vols., 1968.

MATHEU, DOMINGO. Domingo Matheu was born near Barcelona, Spain, in 1765. He was educated as a mariner and pilot but eventually took a mercantile career when he and his brother Miguel won one of the Cádiz monopolies on New World trade. Matheu established a large mercantile house in Buenos Aires* in 1793 and eventually made a fortune there. He played a key role in the Buenos Aires *cabildo** in the early 1800s. In 1810, Matheu was an enthusiastic supporter of the May Revolution*. He became president of the revolutionary junta in 1811. Throughout the revolutionary period, Matheu used his personal fortune to finance patriot military actions and helped the patriots avoid financial disaster. He retired from public life in 1817 and died in 1831.

REFERENCE: Enrique Udaondo, *Diccionario biográfico argentino*, 1938.

MATIENZO CINTRÓN, ROSENDO. Rosendo Matienzo Cintrón was born in Puerto Rico* in 1855. He pursued a political career and became one of the leading advocates of Puerto Rican independence from Spain. Matienzo backed Luis Muñoz Rivera in forming what became known as the Sagasta Pact* with Spain in 1897, providing for greater Puerto Rican autonomy. When the Spanish-American War* resulted in a change of Puerto Rican sovereignty from Spain to the United States, Matienzo became a member of the new executive council. For the next decade, he advocated statehood in the United States for Puerto Rico, but he eventually became disillusioned. By 1912, Matienzo was campaigning for independence from the United States and for the implementation of a vigorous antitrust program to rid Puerto Rico of the domination of large American corporations. He died in 1913.

REFERENCES: Pedro de Angelis, *Misceláneas puertorriquenas: Colección de artículos históricos-biográficos*, 1894; Clifford A. Hauberg, *Puerto Rico and the Puerto Ricans*, 1974.

MATIENZO Y PERALTA, JUAN DE. Juan de Matienzo y Peralta was born in Spain around 1520 and received a legal education, probably in Valladolid. Between 1544 and 1561, he worked as an attorney and legal writer at the chancery in Valladolid. In 1761, he went to Lima*, Peru*, as the legal adviser to the viceroyalty of Lima* and as an *oidor**. Shortly after his arrival, he was named president of the *audiencia* of Charcas*. He developed a close working relationship with Viceroy Francisco de Toledo.* From that position, Matienzo strongly recommended Spanish development of the Río de la Plata* area, arguing that a port there would make unnecessary the dangerous voyage through the Strait of Magellan. Matienzo died around 1580.

REFERENCES: Enrique Udaondo, *Diccionario biográfico colonial argentino*, 1945; Ione S. Wright and Lisa M. Nekhom, *Historical Dictionary of Argentina*, 1978.

MATLAZAHUATL. *Matlazahuatl*, also known in Nahuatl* as *cocoliztli* (in Maya*, *qucumatz*), was a highly contagious disease, probably pulmonary bubonic plague, which devastated the Indian* population of New Spain* and Central America during the sixteenth century. Its symptoms included nosebleeds, *dolores de costado* (pains in the side), and prostration. Its victims died after three days; the disease was invariably fatal in the Indian population. Although bubonic plague is normally transmitted by flea bite, *matlazahuatl* was usually transmitted by air, making it among the most deadly and contagious diseases brought to the New World by the Spaniards. There were three major pandemics of *matlazahuatl* in Mexico and northern Central America during the sixteenth century. The first pandemic began in 1519, when Cortés's men brought the pestilence to New Spain from Cuba*; it spread south from Mexico into the Guatemalan* highlands, where at least one-third of the population died of the disease. The second pandemic lasted from 1545 to 1548 and reduced the Indian population of Mesoamerica so drastically in Mexico and Central America that it forced the Spaniards to reassess the *encomienda** system. It was in reaction to this decline of population that the Spaniards instituted the *repartimiento** in New Spain as an alternative source of labor. The third pandemic lasted from 1576 to 1581. This appearance of *matlazahuatl* was the most far-reaching, and it drastically reduced the native population as far south as Costa Rica*. From that point on, Costa Rica would be chronically short of labor, making it undesirable for Spanish settlement. By 1600, *matlazahuatl* and other contagious diseases had reduced the native population of Mexico and Central America by as much as 90 percent.

REFERENCE: Murdo J. MacLeod, *Spanish Central America: A Socioeconomic History, 1520-1720*, 1973.

Virginia Garrard Burnett

MAY REVOLUTION. The term May Revolution refers to a series of events in 1810 that launched the Argentine independence movement. In the preceding years, *criollos** in Buenos Aires* had chafed under *peninsular** rule. Resentment among the entire population increased in 1806–1807 when Argentina* received so little help from Spain in repelling the British invasion. In 1808, when France invaded and eventually took over Spain, the independence movement in Argentina received a real boost. At the insistence of local Buenos Aires citizens, Viceroy Baltasar de Cisneros* called an open meeting of the *cabildo** for May 22, 1810. More than 250 people attended the meeting, and at its conclusion, the viceroy was deposed and a revolutionary junta elected in his place. For most Argentines, the May Revolution is the end of the colonial period and the beginning of their national history, although formal independence was not declared until 1816.

REFERENCE: Rodolfo Puiggros, *Los caudillos de la revolución de mayo*, 1942.

MAYA. The term Maya refers to: (1) the largest native language family of Mexico* and Central America; (2) the people who speak one of the languages of this family; and (3) the pre-Conquest civilization developed by the ancestors of these modern Maya speakers. The Mayan language family is composed of 31 languages spoken by over 3,000,000 people living in Guatemala*, Belize*, Honduras*, and the Mexican states of Yucatán*, Campeche, Quintana Roo, Tabasco, Chiapas*, Veracruz*, and adjacent San Luis Potosí*. The languages with the largest number of speakers are Yucatec (spoken in the Mexican states of the Yucatán Peninsula, Belize, and northern Guatemala*), and Mam, Quiché, Cakchiquel, and Kekchi (spoken in the highlands of Guatemala). Two languages, Choltí and Chicomulceltec, are extinct. The distribution of the languages is continuous, with the exception of Huastec which is isolated in northern Veracruz and adjacent San Luis Potosí.

Linguistic evidence indicates the existence of a small proto-Mayan speaking community in the Altos Chuchumatanes of northwestern Guatemala around 2200 B.C. Reconstruction of the proto-Mayan vocabulary indicates that this community was exploiting both highland and lowland habitats. Subsequent migrations resulted in the distribution of Mayan languages observed today. The genetic relationship of the Mayan languages to other Mesoamerican languages is unknown. The study of loan words in the Mayan languages indicates considerable borrowing from the Mixe-Zoquean language family. This borrowing reflects the strong influence on the Maya exercised by the Mixe-Zoquean-speaking peoples of the precocious Olmec* civilization.

Surface survey and excavations in the central and western Guatemalan highlands and in central Chiapas have documented Paleoindian (pre–7000 B.C.) and

Archaic (ca. 7000–2000 B.C.) occupations. At Los Tapiales in the Guatemalan department of Totnoicapán, a Paleoindian campsite occupied in 9000 B.C. has been excavated. Richard MacNeish has established a sequence covering this same time span (ca. 9000–2000 B.C.) in Belize. The exploitation of the abundant riverine and coastal resources in Belize may have led to an earlier shift to a more sedentary life than in the highlands. The transitions from the Archaic hunting, gathering, and fishing economies to those of pottery-producing, sedentary, subsistence farmers is poorly documented and not well understood. It is impossible to identify what language these people spoke.

Beginning around 1000 B.C., a distinctive ceramic tradition developed in Belize and northern lowland Guatemala (the Southern Maya Lowlands). Although there are marked changes through time, the development of this tradition over the next 2,000 years has been well documented. The continuity in this ceramic tradition may reflect an ethnic continuity. If it does, then the presence of Mayan speakers in this area can be documented from at least 1000 B.C. Distributional and hieroglyphic evidence conclusively demonstrates that the great Classic period (A.D. 300–900) sites of this area were built by people who spoke one of the languages of the Cholan group (Chol, Chontal, Chortí, Choltí) or Yucatec.

Between 1000 and 300 B.C., small farming communities spread from their original riverine locations into the interior and throughout the Southern Maya Lowlands. In the following 400 years, some of these developed into large, complex communities with monumental architecture, elaborate stucco sculptures of gods on the building facades, trade in utilitarian and exotic goods over long distances, and abundant evidence of social stratification. A similar growth in the size and complexity characterized communities in the highlands and along the Pacific coast of El Salvador*, Guatemala and Chiapas. Here, these changes began somewhat earlier. The earlier shift to more complex societies may reflect both this area's strategic location along trade routes between Mexico and Central America and Olmec influence and/or colonies in the area. One clear area of Olmec influence is the iconography and calendar system used on free-standing carved monuments (stelae) to convey historical information.

After a florescence between 150 B.C. and A.D. 150, there was a slowing of development in the Southern Maya Lowlands. In the highlands and along the Pacific coast, the break with the past was even more drastic. Large important communities were abandoned. One suggested explanation has been that the eruption of Ilopango volcano in El Salvador in the first half of the third century not only destroyed communities in its immediate area but also disrupted the trade routes critical to the economic well-being of communities throughout the highlands.

At roughly the same time as the eruption of Ilopango, new ceramic forms and decorations appeared in Belize and adjacent parts of northern Guatemala. These forms and decorations had their antecedents in the highlands of El Salvador and Guatemala. Some investigators have suggested that there was a migration of people following the eruption of Ilopango. Others have suggested that there was only a diffusion of objects or ideas. Slightly later, the first free-standing, carved stone monuments appeared at Tikal in northern Guatemala. These depict historical events and record dates in the system developed earlier in the highlands. Thus, there is ample evidence of highland influence prior to the great Classic (A.D. 300–900) florescence in the Southern Maya Lowlands. Archaeologists working in the area have argued that these Maya borrowed ideas and combined them with their own to produce the distinctive culture of the Classic period.

Teotihuacán stepped into the vacuum created by the collapse of communities at the time of the Ilopango eruption. Teotihuacan was the largest, most complex city of pre-Conquest Mexico. From its central location in the northeastern corner of the Valley of Mexico, it established colonies on the Pacific coast of Guatemala and in the Guatemalan highlands at Kaminaljuyu. Tikal was clearly the greatest city of the Early Classic (ca. A.D. 250–550). Hieroglyphic texts reveal that early in this period rulers of the local dynasty were replaced by those of a dynasty tracing its origin to either Teotihuacan or its highland colony of Kaminaljuyu. This alliance and Tikal's strategic location on a portage between the tributaries of the Río Usumacinta that empty into the Gulf of Mexico and the rivers of Belize that empty into the Caribbean may explain its prominence. Hieroglyphic texts document the spread of Tikal's influence, first in its immediate area and then to the Motagua drainage to the southeast and to the Usumacinta drainage to the southwest.

In the middle of the sixth century, Tikal was defeated in war by Caracol in what is now Belize. For a period of approximately 150 years, there were no carved monuments erected at Tikal. Tikal recovered in the seventh and eighth centuries, but it never again exercised the dominant control that it had previously. Rather, there were several small competing states in the Late Classic (A.D. 600–800). The Terminal Classic period (A.D. 800–900) witnessed the collapse of the great Maya state of the Southern Lowlands. The reason for this collapse is poorly understood but probably resulted from a combination of factors, including warfare between the competing Maya states, invasion by "Mexicanized" Maya, and environmental degradation. The latter may have resulted from increasing population, leading to an over-exploitation of the fragile tropical environment.

Although the Southern Maya Lowlands were not completely abandoned, building activities ceased in most of the major centers. Remnant populations have been documented around the lakes of the Petén in Guatemala and in western Belize. For example, the site of Laminai in Belize continued to be occupied. Maya civilization continued to flourish in the Northern Maya Lowlands in the Mexican states of Yucatán, northern Campeche, and northern Quintana Roo. The occupation of portions of this northern area is as early as that in Belize. In the last centuries B.C., Komchen, north of Mérida, was a major trade center controlling the salt deposits of the Yucatán coast. In the Late and Terminal Classic and the Early Postclassic (A.D. 600–1200), there appear to have been two distinct sub-areas in the Northern Maya Lowlands. In the east, the great city of Coba continued a tradition in sculpture and ceramics derived from the Classic centers of the Southern Lowlands. In the Puuc Hills to the west, both architecture and ceramics were distinctive and had fewer similarities with the Southern Maya Lowland tradition.

This latter area came to be dominated by Chichén Itzá in the period from ca. A.D. 1000–1200. Much of the architecture in the area known as "Old Chichén" is like that of other archaeological sites in the Puuc Hills (Uxmal, Kabah, Sayil, Labnah). The area known as "New Chichen" is very different architecturally. The architecture and art of this second area is highly reminiscent of that at the Toltec* capital of Tula in Hidalgo. The traditional interpretation of these similarities has been that a group of Toltec elite led by Quetzalcóatl (Kukulcán in Maya) invaded Chichén Itzá and established control over the local Maya. Alternative explanations have included the arguments that the Putun, a "Mexicanized" group of Cholan-speaking Maya, invaded Chichén Itzá, bringing with them these new ideas, and that the new architectural forms and art style originated in the Maya area and were introduced to Tula.

After more than 200 years of dominance, the power of Chichén Itzá was broken by the Cocom Maya of Mayapán. Mayapán dominated the Northern Maya Lowlands for the next 200 years (1221–1450). Following the collapse of Mayapán's hegemony, the area dissolved into a series of competing petty states. These were conquered by Francisco de Montejo* and his son of the same name between 1527 and 1546. After two unsuccessful attempts (1527–1528 and 1530–1531), the Maya were defeated on a third expedition from 1540 to 1546. Mérida was founded on the ruins of the Maya city of T'ho in January 1542. The definitive defeat of a revolt by the Maya petty states in November 1546 brought the Conquest to a close. The Maya states of the Guatemalan highlands had been defeated earlier by forces under the command of Pedro de Alvarado*. In 1524, Alvarado defeated the Quiché and, in alliance with the Cakchiquel, the Tzutuhil. Several years were required to suppress a rebellion by the former Cakchiquel allies. Still, by 1527, the Conquest of the highlands was completed. The last Maya enclave to be subjugated was the Intza on Lake Petén in the Southern Maya Lowlands. Their capital of Tayasal was finally taken in March 1697.

REFERENCES: Robert S. Chamberlain, *The Conquest and Colonization of Yucatan, 1517-1550*, 1948; Nancy M. Farriss, *Maya Society under Colonial Rule: The Collective Enterprise of Survival*, 1984; John E. Kelly, *Pedro de Alvarado, Conquistador*, 1932; J. E. S. Thompson, *The Rise and Fall of Maya Civilization*, 1966.

Edward B. Sisson

MEDELLÍN. Medellín, the capital city of the department of Antioquia*, Colombia*, was founded in 1616 by Francisco Herrera Campuzano. It very early evolved into a commercial and industrial center.

MEDINA, JUAN DE. Juan de Medina was a native of Spain, born in the 1580s, who entered the Augustinian* order as a young man. He was assigned to the Philippines* in 1610, and he remained there until 1635. Medina is best remembered because of the chronicle he wrote about Filipino and Augustinian history and his own experiences in the islands. Published in Manila* in 1893, it was titled *Historia de los sucesos de la orden de n. gran p. S. Agustín de estas filipinas*. Its overall tone is pessimistic because Juan de Medina realized that the Christianization of the islands would be a very difficult process. Disillusioned and discouraged, Medina decided to return to Spain, but he died in 1635 while traveling on the Manila galleon* to Acapulco*, New Spain.*

REFERENCE: John Leddy Phelan, *The Hispanization of the Philippines: Spanish Aims and Filipino Responses 1565-1700*, 1959.

MELILLA. Melilla is a Spanish city located on the Mediterranean coast of Morocco, approximately 165 miles east of Tangier. The city has been a major port in North Africa* for 2,000 years, but it did not become Spanish territory until 1497. Five years after the expulsion of the Moors from Granada in 1492, Spanish troops crossed the Mediterranean and conquered Melilla. Ever since then, the city has been a Spanish possession administered from the province of Málaga. Its population in the mid-1980s was approximately 82,000 people. When Morocco became independent in 1956, Melilla was one of the areas of the former colony of Spanish Morocco* over which Spain retained sovereignty.

REFERENCE: J. H. Parry, *The Spanish Seaborne Empire*, 1966.

MENDAÑA DE NEIRA, ÁLVARO DE. Álvaro de Mendaña de Neira was born in Galicia, Spain, in 1542. He became a famous Spanish navigator and explorer. Mendaña left Spain for the New World in 1567. In November of the same year, he sailed with two ships from Callao, Peru*, to search for those Pacific islands where one could easily obtain much silver and gold, according to Incan* legends. He also hoped to find the great southern continent usually marked on Renaissance maps as Terra Australis Incognita. Mendaña crossed the Pacific and sighted only one small island in the Ellice group. Not until early February 1568 did this expedition land on Santa Isabel in the central Solomons. Using this island as a base of activities, the Spaniards continued their explorations, remaining in the Solomon archipelago for six months, where they explored and named various islands in this group, including Guadalcanal, Malaita, and San Cristóbal. In August, Mendaña made preparations for the long and arduous journey to western America. After great hardships, the expedition reached the coast of lower California* in mid-December, but the vessels did not finally arrive at the port of Callao, Peru, until September 11, 1569.

Mendaña hoped to establish a colony in the newly discovered Solomon Islands, but he was over 50 before he received another opportunity to sail across the Pacific. In April 1595, Mendaña again left from Callao in an expedition that included his wife, her three brothers, and 378 other persons, including soldiers, sailors, and many women of ill repute. Pedro Fernández de Quiroz, a young, courageous, and capable Portuguese navigator, served as chief pilot. In July, they landed on a group of heavily populated islands that they named Las Marquesas de Mendoza* in honor of the viceroy of Peru. Hundreds of islanders were left dead as a result of various clashes with the Spaniards. The Spaniards left this area and moved westward where they established a settlement on an island that they named Santa Cruz (now Ndemi). Bitter quarrels and dissension among the Spaniards, the breakdown of order and discipline, and bloody conflict with the natives destroyed any hope of the successful colonization at Santa Cruz. Food became scarce and sickness rampant. Many died from tropical fever, including Mendaña himself on October 18, 1595.

In November, Quiroz, now in charge of operations, brought the starving survivors to Manila*, arriving in February 1596. After arriving there, Doña Isabel (Mendaña's widow) married Don Fernando de Castro, a relative of her late husband. The refitted and repaired San Jerónimo sailed from Manila in August 1596, bringing Doña Isabel, her husband, the pilot Quiróz, and others to Acapulco*, New Spain*, on December 11. Mendaña had failed to achieve his goal of establishing a Spanish colony on a firm and lasting foundation, but his exploration efforts did contribute to a better understanding of the geography of the Pacific.

REFERENCES: William A. Amherst and Basil Thomson, eds. and trans., The Discovery of the Solomon Islands by Alvaro de Mendaña in 1568, 2 vols., 1901; John C. Beaglehole, The Exploration of the Pacific, 1966.

MÉNDEZ, RAMÓN IGNACIO. Ramón Ignacio Méndez was born in Barinas, Venezuela*, in 1775. He received doctoral degrees in law and theology from the Royal Pontifical University of Caracas* and was ordained a priest in 1797. Méndez became vicar-general of the diocese of Mérida* in 1802, and from that perspective, he became an early clerical opponent of the Spanish Empire in Venezuela. He served as a deputy to the Constituent Assembly of 1811 and was a signer of the Declaration of Independence of Venezuela. During the wars for independence, Méndez served as the chaplain to Simón Bolívar* and José Páez*. He later served as a deputy in the congresses of Angostura* and Cúcuta*. In 1823, Méndez became the archbishop of Caracas, but he was expelled from Venezuela in 1830 when he tried to protect the church from political interference and secularization. He returned in 1832 but was again expelled for the same reason in 1836. Méndez died in Villeta, Colombia*, in August 1839.

REFERENCE: M. W. Waters, A History of the Church in Venezuela, 1933.

MENDIETA, GERÓNIMO DE. Gerónimo de Mendieta was born in Vitoria, Spain, in 1525. He joined the Franciscan* order and came to New Spain* as a missionary priest. Mendieta became fluent in Nahuatl*, an Indian* language, and became an extremely successful missionary. He was also a scholar and historian, and his Historia eclesiástica indiana is a valuable primary source for historians interested in the history of southwestern colonial New Spain. Mendieta died in the Monastery of St. Francis of Mexico City* in 1604.

REFERENCE: John Leddy Phelan, The Millenial Kingdom of the Franciscans in the New World: A Study of the Writings of Gerónimo de Mendieta (1525–1604), 1956.

MENDOZA, ANTONIO DE. Antonio de Mendoza was born to an aristocratic family in Granada, Spain, in 1490. Before his assignment to the New World, Mendoza served as a diplomat for the royal government of Charles V*. A brilliant administrator and skilled politician, Mendoza was appointed the first viceroy* of New Spain* in 1535, a post he held until 1550. His viceregal administration was unrivaled. Mendoza regularized the laws governing the mining* industry, worked to eliminate the worst abuses in the use of Indian* labor, launched the expansion of New Spain into the northern Borderlands, stimulated the growth of the commercial silver mining industry, imported merino sheep from Spain and began the wool industry, and efficiently collected royal revenues, an ability that only endeared him the more with the royal family in Spain. In 1551, Antonio de Mendoza accepted a new assignment as viceroy of Peru*, but he died in 1552, only one year after assuming the new post.

REFERENCE: Arthur S. Aiton, *Antonio de Mendoza, First Viceroy of New Spain*, 1927.

MENDOZA, PEDRO DE. Pedro de Mendoza was born in Almería, Spain, in 1487, to a wealthy family that was well-connected with King Charles V*. With royal financing, Pedro de Mendoza was charged with conquering the Río de la Plata* area of South America and also the rest of Chile* south of Diego de Almagro's* claim. At the head of a huge expedition, Mendoza crossed the Atlantic Ocean late in 1535. The fleet arrived at the Río de la Plata in 1536, and Mendoza established the settlement of Santa María del Buen Aire, the beginning of Buenos Aires*. The settlers encountered fierce resistance from local Querindi Indians and were forced to abandon the settlement in 1537. On the return voyage to Spain, Pedro de Mendoza died at sea.

REFERENCE: Machain Lafuente, *Los conquistadores de la Plata*, 1943.

MENOCAL, MARIO. A native Cuban born in 1866, Mario Menocal grew up in the United States, graduating from Cornell University in 1885. He spent several years working for American concerns in Nicaragua*, but in 1895, when the revolution broke out in Cuba*, he returned to the island and joined rebel forces. Menocal quickly rose through the ranks to general, with responsibilities as chief of staff to Calixto García* Íñiguez. Menocal earned a reputation in Cuban history as a hero of the independence movement. His subsequent career, however, was nearly as illustrious. Between 1898 and 1900, he served as chief of police in Havana*, but he resigned in 1900 when he established the Cuban-American Sugar Company. He was a millionaire when he won the presidency of Cuba on a Conservative Party ticket in 1912. Menocal's administration was among the most corrupt in Cuban history. When he left office in 1921, his personal assets had swelled to more than $40 million. He managed to stay in power because of American support. World War I, which drove sugar* prices up from 8 to 22 cents a pound also explained his prosperity. Mario Menocal died in 1941.

REFERENCES: Luis Aguilar, *Cuba 1933: Prologue to Revolution*, 1972; Jorge I. Domínguez, *Cuba: Order and Revolution*, 1978; Hugh Thomas, *Cuba: The Pursuit of Freedom*, 1971.

MERCADO Y VILLACORTA, ALONSO DE. Alonso de Mercado y Villacorta was born in Spain around 1620. He spent his career in the Spanish army and in 1655 was appointed governor of Tucumán* in the Río de la Plata* area. He had to suppress the revolt of Pedro Bohórquez* and in 1660 became royal governor of Buenos Aires*, a post he held for three years. Mercado was also president of the first *audiencia* of Buenos Aires*. He was charged with official corruption and removed from office, although a subsequent investigation exonerated him. Mercado was appointed to a second term as governor of Tucumán in 1665. Once again he found himself suppressing another Indian* rebellion led by Pedro Bohórquez. In 1670, Mercado was appointed president of the *audiencia* of Panama*. He died in 1681.

REFERENCE: Ione S. Wright and Lisa M. Nekhom, *Historical Dictionary of Argentina*, 1978.

MERCANTILISM. Mercantilism refers to a set of ideas and practices, associated with the period from 1500 to 1800, by which the national state sought to enhance its power through the use of certain economic policies. The term lacks precise meaning, and the policies advocated in its name were not always consistent. Mercantilist writers and government officials believed that they had the right answers to various problems and acted accordingly. They were less concerned with developing a systematic economic philosophy than with creating policies that would yield national power and prosperity. Consequently, mercantilism is not a very cohesive theory. It manifested itself in different ways in various nations, but was closely associated with the rise of capitalism in Europe and the acquisition of colonial empires. Moving away from medieval values, Europeans began to embrace capitalistic business as the path to wealth and power. Occasionally, there were conflicts between businessmen and mercantilist officials. On balance, however, mercantilism aided the capitalist by supporting him with the power of the government.

Although the ingredients of mercantilism were different in each country, there were certain core policies and concepts that were generally found in all major European nations. One fundamental principle of mercantilism was bullionism, which called for the acquisition and retention of as much gold and silver as possible as the key to national wealth. The example of Spain in the sixteenth century convinced observers of the importance of money. To other European nations, it seemed that Spain had achieved greatness mainly because of the bullion obtained from colonies.

Most of the other policies recommended by mercantilists were linked to bullionism. They called, for example, for the development of gold and silver mines domestically or in colonies. Laws were promulgated either to prohibit entirely or to restrict greatly the export of bullion, the strategy being to keep the gold and silver that flowed into a nation. Some countries, of course, had no gold or silver mines. Under these circumstances, mercantilists advocated increasing exports and decreasing imports so as to gain funds from international trade. This approach became associated with the concept of balance of trade, which maintained that only through an excess of exports over imports could a nation increase its comparative wealth. To achieve a favorable balance of trade, mercantilists called for import and export duties, government promotion of industry, mining, and agriculture, the building of a large merchant marine, and colonial possessions.

On the one hand, mercantilists recommended high tariffs on the importation of manufactured goods and on the exportation of raw materials. On the other, they called for low tariffs on the importation of raw materials and the promotion of the exportation of finished goods. Following this formula, raw materials would be available for domestic industries and foreign industrial products would be kept out. Home industries would occupy a monopolistic position in the domestic market while also being encouraged to export.

Colonies were important for a number of reasons. First, they provided an additional market for the mother country's manufactured goods; second, they served as sources for raw materials; third, colonial trade would provide income for the merchant marine; fourth, the colonial population was a source of inexpensive labor; fifth, colonies provided locations for commercial and military bases; and, sixth, colonies increased a nation's prestige. Under the Spanish mercantilist system, the colonies were dependent directly on the king. Spain tried, but not always successfully, to maintain a trading monopoly with its colonies. Eventually, Spanish control of the colonial trade was so tight that it suffocated economic development and placed Spain at the mercy of countries like England and the Netherlands that had more open economic systems.

REFERENCE: Shepard B. Clough and Charles W. Cole, *Economic History of Europe*, 1952.

Roy E. Thoman

MERCEDARIANS. The Mercedarians were a highly influential Roman Catholic religious order in the New World. Formally known as the Order of Our Lady of Mercy, the Mercedarians established their first convent in Hispaniola[*] in 1514, and it became the base for their work in the New World. They subsequently established two more convents in Hispaniola and one in Cuba[*]. In 1536, they added a convent in Guatemala City[*]; from that base, they spread through Central America, establishing other convents in Ostumcalco, Malacatan, and San Salvador[*], Guatemala[*]; Chuluteca, Tegucigalpa, Gracias a Dios[*], and Tutumbla, Honduras[*]; and León[*], Granada[*], Zebaco, and Samotillo, Nicaragua[*]. Bartolomé Olmedo, a Mercedarian priest, accompanied Hernán Cortés[*] to New Spain[*] in 1519, and eventually they established 23 convents in New Spain. They came to Peru[*] in 1535 and had established 64 convents by 1676. The Mercedarian province of Quito[*], established in 1616, eventually grew to 14 convents, while the province of Santa Bárbara de Tucumán[*], founded in 1593, grew to 20 convents.

REFERENCE: *New Catholic Encyclopedia*, XII:313–14, 1967.

MÉRIDA, DIOCESE OF. The Roman Catholic diocese of Mérida in Venezuela* was established in 1777. Its territory included the region of the Venezuelan Andes as well as what are today the provinces of Maracaibo and Barinas. The first bishop was Juan Ramos de Lora, a Franciscan*. The diocese was raised to an archdiocese in 1923.

REFERENCE: *New Catholic Encyclopedia*, IX:682–83.

MÉRIDA-LA GRITA. In 1575, the Spanish Crown created the province of Espíritu Santo de La Grita in what is today Venezuela* and assigned a governor there. The province fell administratively under the authority of the *audiencia* of New Granada*. Because of population changes, the province was dissolved in 1608 and La Grita was united into a single *corregimiento** with the settlement at Mérida, which was under the jurisdiction of the *audiencia* of Santo Domingo*. Spain then raised Mérida-La Grita to a province in 1625. Maracaibo was added to the province in 1676. To resolve a great deal of administrative confusion, Mérida was transferred to the authority of the *audiencia* of New Granada in 1740, and the name of the entire colony was changed to Maracaibo in 1751. In 1777, Maracaibo became part of the captaincy general of Venezuela. Effective Spanish control over the region was over by 1810, and Maracaibo became part of Gran Colombia* and then Venezuela.

MESSÍA DE LA CERDA, PEDRO. Pedro Messía de la Cerda was born in Spain in 1700. In 1761, he was appointed viceroy* of New Granada*, a post he held until 1772. Messía's tenure as viceroy was marked by a number of challenges and accomplishments. In 1766, he established the tobacco* monopoly, and the next year he had to crush the revolt of the tobacco producers in Neiva. Messía also supervised the expulsion of the Jesuits* from New Granada in 1767 and 1768. He returned to Spain in 1773 and died there in 1783.

REFERENCES: Robert H. Davis, *Historical Dictionary of Colombia*, 1977; José Manuel Groot, *Historia eclesiástica y civil de Nueva Granada*, 5 vols., 1953.

MESTA. In Castile* in the 1200s, *hacer mesta* meant to hold regular meetings of the shepherds and livestock owners of an area, usually in the spring and fall, to separate strays and to deal with other problems. By 1273, the Castilian Crown had chartered the Honrado Concejo de la Mesta de Pastores, which was supposed to be an association of all of the sheepmen of Castile. The royal Mesta was granted various privileges, and under royal protection, it developed into a powerful institution for the expansion and regulation of the nation's pastoral industry. The organization had an administrative hierarchy directly responsible to the Crown. The Mesta, which came to be dominated by wealthy sheepowners, had its own code of pastoral ordinances and sent itinerant *alcalde entregadores* to administer justice throughout the realm. These officials were also responsible for maintaining the privilege of Mesta flocks to use communal pastures, watering places, and resting places along migratory routes. There was constant friction between the Mesta and local residents, both farmers and stockmen. For centuries, the royal government strongly supported the Mesta, as a way to encourage the kingdom's wool and textile industries.

The Mesta reached its peak around 1500, and by the mid-1500s, it had begun to decline. Many pasture lands were cultivated to feed the expanding population and to produce wine, grain, and olive oil for the market in Spain's overseas territories. As the Spanish economy became more agrarian, the Crown gradually began to favor arable interests over the pastoral sector. The royal Mesta tried in vain to defend its traditional privileges, and it entered a lengthy period of decline. In the eighteenth century, the organization was further weakened by reformers, who saw the organization as a hindrance to agrarian development. The Mesta was finally dissolved in 1836 and replaced by the Asociación General de Ganaderos, a much weaker institution that included owners of cattle and goats, as well as sheep.

From the 1500s, the enemies of the royal Mesta succeeded in creating a "black legend," according to which the sheepowners' association acted as an arm of the reactionary feudal oligarchy, holding Castile in thrall and preventing the development of modern agriculture. Recent research has totally discredited the claim that Castilian agriculture was destroyed by the depredations of Mesta sheep. Nevertheless, the black legend far outlived the Mesta itself and continues to be repeated by many twentieth-century historians.

In addition to the royal Mesta, medieval Castile gave birth to numerous municipal *mestas*, particularly in Andalucía. The Andalusian *mestas* were interested primarily in cattle, and they were normally hostile toward the royal *mesta* because their animals often competed for the same pastures. The municipal *mestas* were created by the local *cabildos** and were subservient to the municipal government, merely exercising jurisdiction over local pastoral affairs. One of the chief tasks of each municipal *mesta* was to keep records about the local pastoral sector, including the brands and earmarks of each stockman.

The Andalusian municipal *mestas*—particularly the one in Seville*—became the models for similar municipal *mestas* in the Canary Islands* (established in Tenerife in 1509) and in the Americas. The first American *mesta* was founded in the early 1500s in Hispaniola*, but it was short-lived. Conditions for the development of the livestock industry were far more favorable in New Spain*, where a *mesta* was established at Mexico City* by 1538. As stockraising spread, municipal *mestas* were also installed in other Mexican towns. All of these were patterned after the municipal *mestas* of Andalusia. Elsewhere in Spanish America, despite a royal *cédula* ordering *mestas* created throughout the Indies, no *mestas* were in fact established; from Caracas* to Santiago*, Chile*, and from Bogotá* to Buenos Aires*, pastoral affairs remained directly under the supervision of local cabildos.

REFERENCES: William Dusenberry, *The Mexican Mesta: The Administration of Ranching in Colonial Mexico*, 1963; Jerónimo López-Salazar Pérez, *Mesta, pastos y conflictos en el Campo de Calatrava durante el siglo XVI*, 1987; Charles Julian Bishko, ''The Andalusian Municipal Mestas in the 14th–16th Centuries: Administrative and Social Aspects,'' *Actas del I Congreso de Historia de Andalucía, diciembre de 1976: Andalucía medieval*, I (1978), 347–74.

David E. Vassberg

MESTIZO. The racial classification of mestizo developed through the course of the colonial period in New Spain* and Central America. In Ecuador*, Peru*, Bolivia*, and Chile*, the term *cholo** has the same meaning as *mestizo*. Although technically used to describe a person who was of mixed Indian and Spanish parentage, the term had different connotations at different times. During the sixteenth century, mestizo referred to the illegitimate children of Spaniards and Indians, and the term was used in a pejorative sense. During this period, legitimate children, regardless of genetic make-up, were called ''Spaniards'' if they lived in Spanish society, in effect making them *criollos**. If raised among Indians*, they were considered to be so. Conversely, Indians who became hispanized were often considered to be mestizos.

During this period, the only persons referred to as mestizos were those who, for whatever reason, were considered unacceptable to either group. A marginal group, neither Spanish or Indian, the mestizos shouldered heavy social burdens; they were denied public office, restricted from taking Holy Orders, and forbidden entry into certain craft guilds. Although considered to be *gente de razon* (rational people), they were nonetheless thought to be baser than Spaniards. The only exception to this prejudice was in frontier areas, where mestizos enjoyed a higher status because they were the children of Spaniards.

In the late seventeenth and early eighteenth century, mestizos emerged as a distinct social group, since they were the fastest-growing segment in Mexican society. Because colonial society relied more heavily on socioeconomic factors than on race to determine social status, however, mestizos did not become an outright social class. They became the dominant group in Mexico numerically by the end of the colonial period.

REFERENCE: Colin M. MacLachlan and Jaime E. Rodríguez, *The Forging of the Cosmic Race: A Reinterpretation of Colonial Mexico*, 1980.

Virginia Garrard Burnett

METHUEN, TREATY OF. Portugal's foreign affairs were complicated in the early eighteenth century by the War of the Spanish Succession*. During the war, Portugal sided first with France. Under pressure from England, which dispatched a naval squadron to Portugal in the spring of 1702, it joined the anti-French coalition on May 16, 1703. The same day, Britain and Portugal signed the Lisbon Treaty, which proclaimed a perpetual alliance between the two countries. A second Anglo-Portuguese agreement, the Treaty of Methuen, was signed on December 27, 1703. This treaty, also known as the Methuen Commercial Treaty, was named after Lord John Methuen, the British envoy in Lisbon. Under the terms of the agreement, Great Britain was permitted to export wool cloth to

Portugal (the Portuguese government had banned the import of English woolens in 1677) and Portugal received the right to export its wines to Britain on favorable terms. The political consequences of the treaty, while not explicitly mentioned, were of considerable value to both participants. The Methuen Treaty proved to be the anchor for the continuation of the Anglo-Portuguese alliance that guaranteed the integrity of Portugal and Brazil. The agreement failed to fulfill the commercial aspirations of British merchants, especially their goal of securing eventual direct trade with the Portuguese colonies. In addition, the Methuen Treaty had the indirect result of securing for Britain the crucial western flank for the defense and maintenance of Gibraltar*, the key to Great Britain's emergence as a Mediterranean power.

REFERENCES: A. D. Francis, *The Methuens and Portugal, 1691–1708*, 1966; G. D. Ramsay, *English Overseas Trade During the Centuries of Emergence*, 1957.

William G. Ratliff

MEXICO. See NEW SPAIN.

MEXICO, ARCHDIOCESE OF. The Roman Catholic diocese of Mexico was established in what is today Mexico City* in 1530 by Pope Clement VII. It was raised to an archdiocese in 1546. The first bishop was Juan de Zumárraga*, who first arrived in New Spain* in 1528. The diocese of Mexico included an immense territory, stretching from the Borderlands* region of what are today northern Mexico and the United States, down into Central America, and across the Pacific Ocean to the Philippines*. Subsequent dioceses were established from the original diocese of Mexico in the following order: Carolene-Tlaxcala (1519), Comayagua* (1531), Nicaragua* (1531), Guatemala* (1534), Antequera (1534), Michoacán (1536), Chiapas* (1539), Compostela-Guadalajara* (1548), Yucatán* (1561), Manila* (1579), Guadiana-Durango (1620), Linares (1777), and Sonora (1779).

REFERENCES: J. Bravo Ugarte, *Diocesis y obispos de la Iglesia Mexicana, 1519-1939*, 1941; Joaquín García Icazbalceta, *Don Fray Juan de Zumárraga, primer obispo y arzobispo de México*, 3 vols., 1947.

MEXICO, UNIVERSITY OF. In 1551, Emperor Charles V* ordered the establishment of the Royal and Pontifical University of San Pablo in Mexico, and the university began its teaching operation two years later. Like the University of San Marcos* in Lima* that was founded that same year, the University of Mexico followed the model of Salamanca and Alcalá, projecting Spain's Golden Age and its cultural responsibilities into the New World. From its beginning, the university felt the force of the Counter Reformation and gave pre-eminence to the chair of Scholastic theology. Some of the teachers held the highest degrees from Spanish universities, and their task was "to impugn, to destroy, to vanquish, and to extirpate that which does not conform to the faith." Alonso de la Vera Cruz* became the first rector of the university, in addition to teaching the sacred scriptures and philosophy. He was not only the most outstanding teacher but also the first philosopher in the New World, "the father of all philosophical study in America," who set the trend of philosophy by introducing Aristotle into New Spain. The University of Mexico became one of the leading institutions of higher learning in the New World.

REFERENCES: Ernest J. Burrus, ed., *The Writings of Alonso de la Vera Cruz*, 1967–1975; Samuel Ramos, *Historia de la filosofía en México*, 1943.

MEXICO CITY. By the year 1500 the city of Tenochtitlán[*] had a population of 300,000 people and was the headquarters of the great Aztec[*] empire. Hernán Cortés[*] and his Spanish expedition of conquest first reached Tenochtitlán in 1519, and by 1521 they had conquered the city and vanquished the Aztec empire. Because of its altitude and climate, the Spaniards decided to build their own city there. They immediately began to raze the Aztec buildings and used the stone to fill in the canals and lake and construct their own edifices. According to informal instructions from the Council of the Indies,[*] they constructed a central square and then built the city in a gridiron of square blocks out to the south and the west. The northern and western edges of the city were segregated for the several thousand Indians who had survived the conquest and decided to stay. By 1524 the population of Mexico City was 30,000 people. The *Audiencia* of Mexico City[*] was created in 1528, and in 1535 the crown created the Viceroyalty of New Spain,[*] with its headquarters in Mexico City. The Diocese of Mexico City[*] was established in 1530, and it was raised to an archdiocese in 1546. Five years later the church established the University of Mexico City.[*] Mexico City had become the leading city in the Spanish empire, and its population reached 100,000 people by the late colonial period.

REFERENCE: Charles Gibson, *The Aztecs under Spanish Rule: A History of the Indians of the Valley of Mexico, 1519-1810*, 1964.

MEXICO CITY, *AUDIENCIA* OF. Within a few years of Hernán Cortés's[*] conquest of the Aztec[*] empire in New Spain,[*] it was clear that the colony would become the gem in Spain's overseas empire. Settlement from Spain was rapid, and the *audiencia* of Santo Domingo[*] would be hard pressed to deal with the problems coming from the mainland. In fact, it was evident that New Spain would soon eclipse Santo Domingo[*] in significance. In 1528, the Spanish Crown established the *audiencia* of Mexico City as the primary judicial and legislative body in New Spain, subject only to the Council of the Indies[*]. When the viceroyalty of New Spain was set up in 1535, the *audiencia* of Mexico City became the viceregal *audiencia*,[*] presided over by the viceroy[*]. The territorial jurisdiction of the *audiencia* was gradually circumscribed as new *audiencias* were established: Panama[*] (1538), Guatemala[*] (1542), and New Galicia[*] (1548).

REFERENCE: Mark A. Burkholder and D. S. Chandler, *From Impotence to Authority: The Spanish Crown and the American Audiencias, 1687-1808*, 1977.

MIER NORIEGA Y GUERRA, FRAY SERVANDO TERESA DE. The life of Fray Servando Teresa de Mier Noriega y Guerra was an unbelievable odyssey of ups and downs, triumphs and defeats. He led a life full of adventures, in and out of jail, permanently in opposition to the authorities, and always in rebellion. "Passionate, arrogant, and uncompromising," as Henry Blamford Parkes called him, he was one of the great heroes of the Spanish American revolution. He was a typical Don Quijote, in the best traditions of the Spanish race, but at the same time he was also a realist.

As David Brading has shown us, Fray Servando was able to establish a nationalist ideology "which gave Mexico a basis and a Christian history at the same time that it denied the justice of the Conquest and the rights of the monarchy to rule." He followed the moderate thought of Jovellanos and José María Blanco and thus came close to the conservatism of Edmund Burke and the constitutionalism of Montesquieu. Aristocrat, republican, patriot, and nationalist, he was indeed a Liberal Catholic; in England, he would have been considered a Whig. In his earlier period, he believed that Mexico should follow English institutions; after his later visits to the United States (1816, 1821), he advocated the latter's system. At the end of his turbulent life, however, he warned his countrymen against two evils: Masonry and federalism.

His life is divided into two parts: the first, devoted to the struggle for independence, and the second, dedicated to the solution of Mexico's problems in the 1820s. Born in Monterrey*, New León*, in New Spain*, in 1763, Fray Servando received a thorough education in his hometown and in Mexico. At barely fifteen, he entered the Dominican* order, following the wishes of his father. His restless soul found there ample opportunity to develop. The great event in this early phase centered on two sermons of 1794: in the first, he attacked Rousseau and the French Revolution, as well as the Divine Right of Kings; in the second, which was quite notorious, he claimed that the Indians* had known Christianity 1600 years before the arrival of the Spaniards. Our Lady of Guadalupe* had appeared in the mantle of Saint Thomas, "the apostle of this kingdom." The myth of the apostolic evangelization was thus launched in order to have the Aztecs* accepted as honorable representatives of Mexican antiquity and was simultaneously meant to weaken the rights of the Spanish Crown. While this theory was quite a novelty, and the Church exiled Fray Servando to Spain for this outrageous affirmation, his social compact of [Spanish] America was not. This social compact, "the Magna Carta of [Spanish] America," was the legislation of the native peoples, and was based on the metaphysical link between the various viceroyalties and the Crown. Once the legitimate king (Ferdinand VII*) was no longer the ruler, civil authority automatically reverted to the source whence it had originally come, the people; this was the *pactum translationis* of Francis Suárez*, the true intellectual key to the emancipation of Spanish America. The only interesting difference between Fray Servando's social compact and the one that was invoked in 1810 was the fact that he tied it, not to the conquistador* and settlers, but to the missionaries. Bartolomé de las Casas* was his great hero. This original thesis thus linked the Mexican struggle for independence to both the Indian past and to the church. To this day, his works remain classics of the period: *Cartas de un americano a El Español; Historia de la Revolución de*

Nueva España, and the *Memoria Político-Instructiva* are the most important ones. He died in Mexico City in 1827.

REFERENCES: David A. Brading, *Los orígenes del nacionalismo mexicano*, 1973; Edmundo O'Gorman, "Prólogo" in Servando Teresa de Mier, *Escritos y Memorias*, 1945; Artemio de Valle-Arizpe, *Fray Servando*, 1952; O. Carlos Stoetzer, "Fray Servando Teresa de Mier Noriega y Guerra, el caballero andante de la insurgencia mexicana", *Cuadernos Salmantinos de Filosofía*, 1987.

O. Carlos Stoetzer

MILITIA. Although the use of militias dates back to the Middle Ages, they assumed their major role in the military system of the eighteenth century. In 1734, under a plan devised by the Conde de Montemayor, 33 regiments were raised in the provinces of Castile*. Known as provincial or "disciplined" militia, these regiments differed from previous units in that they operated under a standard table of organization, were provided with uniforms, guns, and equipment, had regular army officers and enlisted men integrated into the chain of command to impart expert training, and drilled regularly. Also awarded the *fuero militar**, these units operated under the 1734 *Ordenanzas de milicias provinciales de España* until 1766. That regulation was superseded by the *Reglamento de 18 de noviembre de 1766* . . . , which increased the number of regiments to 42, and by the 1767 *Real declaración sobre puntos esenciales de la ordenanza de milicias provinciales de España* . . . , which further refined militia governance.

In an age when armies had begun to assume greater mass, the hope was to shape inexpensively a large reserve that in time of crisis might be mobilized, trained intensively, and employed to reinforce the regular army. As the system had evolved by 1767, a regiment consisted of eight companies with 95 men each, including noncommissioned officers. The soldiery numbered 64 fusiliers, eight grenadiers, and eight hussars. The colonels and lieutenant colonels of the command and staff groups were volunteers, but the plans and training officer, the *sargento mayor*, was a regular, as were the adjutants. The company-level officers were volunteers, but the sergeants were regulars, as were the first corporals of grenadiers and hussars. They were assisted in drilling the soldiery by drummers who were also maintained on salary.

Volunteer officers, whose positions were as much political as military, were nominated by the communities and selected by the regional captains general from lists of three, subject to the approval of the ministry of war. Nominees were expected to come from the aristocracy and to enjoy sufficient status to smooth relationships with the local municipal governments, since these were responsible for raising funds to uniform their units, producing censuses of able-bodied men, and accommodating the presence of military privilege in their communities. In 1766, however, the municipalities were relieved of their financial responsibilities by the establishment of a tax on salt throughout Spain to maintain the provincial militia.

Men between the ages of 16 and 40 were eligible for enlistment. The companies were filled annually by lot under the joint supervision of civilian and military authorities, this process required by the potential hardship that mobilization might impose. Single men, for example, were chosen before single men with dependent parents or married men without children, and these before married men with children. A wide range of occupational exemptions were granted to those engaged in vital services, including clerics, physicians, druggists, treasury and judiciary officials, notaries, municipal scribes, teachers, and university students. Although policy varied over time, a man who retired after a specified period of service was eligible to retain his privileges.

Along with the provincial units there existed the urban militia. Urban units were normally sponsored by individual municipalities and could be called to service only in instances of local emergency. Most of the urban militia was located in coastal or border cities. The quality of urban units could vary considerably. They did not receive the same level of training as the provincial militia, and normally only their officers enjoyed the *fuero militar*, although enlisted men also acquired the privilege when mobilized. The urban militia served principally for ceremonial purposes in municipal festivities or for assisting during local disasters, but it might be employed for combat in instances where its immediate locality was threatened by enemy attack.

The colonial militia was not placed on a disciplined footing until the 1760s. Until then, individual units might vary greatly in size, were seldom equipped properly, and drilled infrequently. Others were raised during wartime and disbanded afterwards. Ordinarily, military privileges were restricted to officers except during times of mobilization. Such a militia might adorn parades and even repulse pirates or suppress disorders, but it counted for little in full-scale combat. Some guilds also supported urban militias.

Following Spain's humiliation at Havana* during the Seven Years' War*, Charles III* introduced the disciplined militia system in America, beginning with Cuba*. The man charged with this responsibility was Field Marshal Alejandro O'Reilly, who during late 1763 and early 1764 raised eight battalions of infantry and individual regiments of cavalry and dragoons, adapting the Spanish ordinances of 1734 to the American government. A preliminary regulation was printed in 1765 and, after refinement, reissued in 1769 as the *Reglamento para las milicias . . . de Cuba*. The basic tactical unit for the infantry was the battalion, which numbered 800 soldiers and included eight companies of fusiliers of 90 men each and a separate company of 80 grenadiers. A regiment consisted of two battalions. The Cuban regulation also differed from Spanish practice in that the subinspector general, a regular, occupied the office of lieutenant instead of the municipalities' nominated officers, and Cuban militiamen enjoyed broader military privileges.

In 1764, Lieutenant General Juan de Villalba was sent to New Spain* to establish a disciplined militia; a special plan was likewise sent to Viceroy Manuel de Amat y Junient* of Peru*, and orders were sent to Caracas* and Buenos Aires* to adapt their militia to the Cuban system. In 1765, O'Reilly reorganized the militia of Puerto Rico*. Acting as inspector general of the army of America, he extended his reform to Santo Domingo[*] in 1771 and to New Granada[*] in 1773, also renewing efforts in Buenos Aires and Caracas during this same period. Those units lacking sufficient stature to qualify as disciplined were usually classified as urban, although the distinction was not always clear. The Cuban regulation served as the model for unit organization in most colonies but not Mexico where a separate system evolved that included retention of the narrower Spanish definition of military privilege and the practice of permitting the municipalities to nominate officers. Eventually, most colonies developed separate regulations adapted to local realities.

The quality of the American militia varied considerably, depending largely upon local political and strategic realities. In general, coastal units retained stronger combat capacity than those in the interior districts where the danger of invasion seemed remote and where little was gained and much lost by patterns of defense spending. In 1779–1781, the Cuban militia manned the home front while the regular army won victory in Florida[*]. Volunteer forces of San Juan[*] contributed significantly to crushing the British invasion of 1797. Those of Buenos Aires failed initially in 1806, but eventually rallied to drive out the British and helped to repulse an invasion the following year. On the negative side, arming Americans through the disciplined militia system and entrusting command to powerful criollo[*] aristocrats represented a dangerous erosion of imperial control in the long run, especially when the wars of the French Revolution and Napoleon drained the strength of the regular army and led the Crown to borrow liberally from creole sources to finance its American defenses. During the independence period, the militia very frequently emerged as the core of the patriot armies.

REFERENCES: C. I. Archer, *The Army in Bourbon Mexico, 1760-1810*, 1977; L. G. Campbell, *The Military and Society in Colonial Peru, 1750-1810*, 1978; A.J. Kuethe, *Military Reform and Society in New Granada, 1773-1808*, 1978; A.J. Kuethe, *Cuba, 1753-1815: Crown, Military, and Society*, 1986.

                                                                            Allan J. Kuethe

MINDANAO. Mindanao is the second largest island of the Philippines[*], more than 36,000 square miles in area. Its coastline is highly irregular, with long peninsulas and wide bays. The complex topography includes mountains, plateaus, lakes, swampy river basins, and some remaining virgin jungle in the interior where small tribes dwell in isolation from the outside world. There are also rare species of plants and animals. Mindanao was long considered an island of opportunity, waiting to be developed, but intensive immigration has almost erased its frontier character.

All of Mindanao would be Islamic today had the Spaniards not intervened just after expelling Muslims from Spain itself. They were not happy about traveling halfway around the globe only to run into more Muslims. Spain took Luzon[*] and the Visayas[*] (central islands) and struggled ceaselessly against the Moros[*] (Tausug, Samal, Maguindanao, Maranao, and other groups) but could never really defeat them. To check the spread of Islam, the Spaniards colonized the northern coast of Mindanao with Cebuano-speaking Filipino Christians. Sovereignty over the Philippines went to the United States after the Spanish-American War* of 1898.

REFERENCES: Frederick Wernstedt and J. E. Spencer, *The Philippine Island World*, 1967; Alfred W. McCoy and Edilberto de Jesús, *Philippine Social History*, 1982.

Ross Marlay

MINING. Without question, mining was the most significant industrial sector of the Latin American economy in the colonial era. Although tin, lead, zinc, iron ore, and copper were all extracted, it was the mining of gold and silver that was central to the economy. Gold and silver had been precious commodities to the major Indian* tribes before the Conquest, and when the Spanish conquistadors* came across indigenous groups with large gold supplies, they wanted to take it from them and find the source of the ore. The first gold discoveries came on Hispaniola* in 1500, and after the penetration of New Spain* and Peru* the Spaniards made a number of rich discoveries. Soon after the conquest of the Aztecs* in New Spain, royal officials took control of the Aztec gold mines at Taxco and Pachuco. In the next few decades, new discoveries were made at Taxco in 1536, Zacatecas* in 1546, Guanajuato* in 1550, Pachuco in 1552, and San Luis Potosí* in 1592. A similar pattern was repeated after the conquest of the Incas* in Peru. Rich ore deposits were discovered in the Cauca Valley of Colombia* in 1540, Potosí* in Upper Peru (Bolivia*) in 1545, Castrovirreyna in 1555, Oruro in 1595, and Cerro de Pasco in 1630.

During the 1600s, the total production of silver and gold in the mines of the Spanish Empire exceeded 10 million pesos a year, with the Crown taking 20 percent of all the ore produced in taxes. By the mid-eighteenth century, production had increased to more than 20 million pesos of ore annually. The mining settlements in New Spain, Peru, Bolivia, and Colombia were huge economic stimulants to the surrounding regions, consuming large volumes of meat and grain and providing thousands of jobs to peasant workers, especially after the decline of the Indian population had undermined the original slave labor systems. At the same time, the huge amounts of bullion that Spain imported from the New World triggered a hyperinflation that eventually undermined the entire Iberian economy.

REFERENCES: Carlos Prieto, *Mining in the New World*, 1973; P. J. Blakewell, *Silver Mining and Society in Colonial Mexico: Zacatecas, 1546-1700*, 1971.

MIRANDA, FRANCISCO DE. Francisco de Miranda was born in Caracas*, Venezuela*, in 1750 to a well-to-do merchant family. He entered the army of Spain after graduating from school and fought in North Africa* and the Caribbean during the 1770s and 1780s. In the military, Miranda encountered prejudice and political problems because of his *criollo** background. Native Spaniards looked down upon him as a colonial, and he resented their point of view. He left the army in 1785 and headed for the United States. During the next decade, Miranda spent a great deal of time in the United States, England, and France, and in the process, he became committed to the idea of Spanish-American independence. In the 1790s, he rose to the rank of general in the French army but then shifted his allegiance to England, where he tried to recruit political and financial support for the independence of Spain's colonies in the New World. In 1805, after putting together a small volunteer army, Miranda attacked Venezuela but fled when he failed to inspire a general uprising or secure British naval support. When Venezuela declared its independence in 1810, Miranda returned home and became a leader in the rebellion. When the revolution faltered in 1815, Miranda was arrested by royalist officials. He died in a Spanish prison in 1816.

REFERENCES: William Spence Robertson, *The Life of Miranda*, 1929; Joseph F. Thorning, *Miranda: World Citizen*, 1952.

MISKITO KINGDOM. See MOSQUITIA.

MISKITO INDIANS. The Miskito Indians are actually several indigenous groups, the largest being the Misktu, Rama, and Sumu, who live along the Caribbean coast of Honduras*, Nicaragua*, and Costa Rica*. A fierce and independent people, the Miskito successfully resisted the advances of Spanish *adelantados** and retained their autonomy from the Spaniards throughout the colonial period. The Miskitos' presence on the Atlantic coast thwarted Spanish efforts to develop agriculture and commerce on the Caribbean, and prevented the region from becoming hispanized. Because of their enmity towards the Spaniards, the Miskito supported foreign piracy* against Spanish settlements during the late sixteenth and seventeenth centuries, and often served as middlemen for the contraband trade. They actively cultivated friendly relations with the English. In 1741, the British created a Mosquito Kingdom, also known as Mosquitia, which consisted of Miskito lands running along the Caribbean coast from Cape Gracias a Dios*, Honduras, to southern Costa Rica. The Mosquito Kingdom was nominally ruled by a Mosquito King, crowned by the British, but in practice it served mainly as a base for British contraband operations in Central America. The Miskitos raided Spanish settlements in cooperation with the British during the War of Jenkin's Ear*, the War of Austrian Succession*, and the Seven Years War* during the eighteenth century, and they significantly weakened Spanish defenses on the Caribbean coast. One of the Miskitos' most dramatic attacks occurred in 1747, when the Miskito, under orders of the governor of Jamaica*, attacked the rich cacao* plantations of the Matina Valley of Costa Rica. A decade later, in 1756, the Miskito raided the Matina Valley again, this time killing the governor of Costa Rica.

The Treaty of Paris* signed in 1783 and confirmed in 1786 demanded that the British abandon the Mosquito Coast, and their alliance with the Miskito Indians officially ended. The British continued to send arms to Mosquitia well into the nineteenth century. It was not until 1869, in the Treaty of Managua, that the

British agreed to relinquish all claim to the Nicaraguan Atlantic coast. That same year, the Nicaraguan government created a 7,000-square-mile Miskito reservation in Mosquitia.

REFERENCES: Barbara Nietschmann, *Between Land and Water: The Subsistence Ecology of the Miskito Indians*, 1973; R. L. Woodward, Jr., *Central America: A Nation Divided*, 1983.

Virginia Garrard Burnett

MISSION. In the Spanish colonial empire, the mission became an important vehicle in promoting the conversion of the Indians[*] and extending the power of Spain. In 1573, King Philip II[*] of Spain prohibited the future granting of *encomiendas*[*] as part of the conquest and settlement process, but the Crown still needed an institutional means to consolidate conquest and settlement. The mission became that means. The first missions began at opposite ends of the empire, when Gonzalo Tapia and the Jesuits[*] began establishing missions in northwestern New Spain[*] and Luis de Bolaños[*] and the Franciscans[*] started them in the region of Buenos Aires[*]. Because of the vastness of the empire, the scattered Indian populations, and the shortage in the number of available missionary priests, some method of concentrating the indigenous populations had to be developed. The mission became the institution to accomplish that goal. Missionary priests, primarily from the Jesuit, Franciscan, Augustinian[*], and Dominican[*] orders, scattered throughout Latin America and the Philippines[*]. Capuchin[*] missionaries also arrived in Venezuela[*] in the seventeenth century. Most of the mission work, however, was done by Jesuits and Franciscans. In 1594, for example, the Council of the Indies[*] in Spain instructed the governor and the bishop of the Philippines to divide the Philippines up into contiguous areas among the four religious orders. All of the orders received some parishes in Tagalog[*]-speaking areas, although most of those went to Augustinians and Franciscans. The Jesuits received a much smaller part of the Tagalog area, while the Dominicans were given charge over the Chinese community in the Philippines; most of them lived in the Parian area of Manila[*]. The Augustinians also received the provinces of Pampanga[*] and Ilocos[*] and some of the Visayan[*] islands. The Franciscans received the Bikol-speaking areas of the Camarines[*]. The Dominicans took charge of parishes in Pangasinan[*] and Cagayan[*]. Similar assignments of jurisdictions occurred throughout the empire.

In building the mission, or the *reducción*[*], the priests would construct a church and eventually a town protected by a military garrison. Missionaries would gather the Indians from the area into the mission, where they would be taught religion, farming, and various trades. The missions became the center of political, economic, social, and educational life in the area. With force and persuasion, the priests tried to keep the Indians permanently in the mission, where they could be protected from European slavers and prevented from slipping back to an aboriginal lifestyle. The most successful of the missions were those established in Paraguay[*], northern New Spain[*], California[*], and Leyte[*] in the Philippines.

Because of the missions, Spain was able to extend its control of occupied territory and begin the acculturation process on the Indian tribes.

REFERENCES: *New Catholic Encyclopedia*, IX:944–64, 1967; Robert Ricard, *The Spiritual Conquest of Mexico*, 1966.

MISSIONS. "The Missions" was a rather explicit term in the late seventeenth and eighteenth centuries to describe the territory between Brazil and Paraguay* where Jesuits* had established missions among the various Indian* tribes. Both Brazil and the Banda Oriental (Uruguay*) lusted after The Missions, but when the Jesuits were expelled from South America in 1767, The Missions went into a long economic decline. The Missions territory east of the Uruguay River became Portuguese, and later Brazilian, property in 1801.

REFERENCES: Philip Caraman, *Lost Paradise: The Jesuit Republics in South America*, 1976.

MITA. The *mita* was the Peruvian version of the *repartimiento**. It was a system of forced labor initiated by the Incas* to provide the manpower for their public works projects and their mines. In order to maintain those projects, the Spaniards continued the *mita*, forcing Indian* communities to provide a certain number of workers for specified periods of time, usually a year or more. In Peru*, the *mita* survived throughout the colonial period and was not abolished until 1821.

MOCTEZUMA. See MOTECUHZOMA.

MOGROVEJO, TORIBIO ALFONSO DE. Toribio Alfonso de Mogrovejo was born in November 1538, in Mayorga, León, Spain, to a wealthy landed family. He studied in Valladolid and Salamanca. In 1574, he was named inquisitor of Granada, where he earned a reputation for moderation and efficiency. In 1568, the Council of the Indies* decided to introduce widespread reforms in the colonial government. Francisco de Toledo*, the viceroy* of Lima*, was responsible for carrying them out, and he wanted a sympathetic archbishop in Lima to assist him. In 1579, Mogrovejo was named archbishop of Lima, and he arrived there in 1581. He proved to be an exceptionally able bishop, one who brought important reforms to the Church and the clergy. Those clerical reforms were later adopted throughout the dioceses of Spanish America. Mogrovejo died on March 23, 1606, near Lima. Pope Innocent beatified Mogrovejo on June 26, 1679, and he was proclaimed a saint by Benedict III on April 27, 1726.

REFERENCE: V. Rodríguez Valencia, *Santo Toribio de Mogrovejo, organizador y apóstol de Sud-America*, 1946.

MOHAMMED SIDI IBRAHIM BASSIRI. See BASSIRI, MOHAMMED SIDI IBRAHIM.

MOLINA, PEDRO. Pedro Molina was born in Guatemala* in 1777. He studied medicine at the University of San Carlos*, practiced and taught medicine there, and became active as a radical proponent of Guatemalan independence. Under the pseudonym "Liberato Cauto," he wrote inflammatory articles calling for liberation of the Spanish colonies. In 1829, he served for a year as governor of Guatemala. Molina was also editor of *El Editor Constitucional*. He unsuccessfully opposed Francisco Morazán* for the presidency in 1830. Pedro Molina died in 1854.

REFERENCE: Richard E. Moore, *Historical Dictionary of Guatemala*, 1973.

MOLUCCAS. See SPICE ISLANDS.

MONTE. During the Middle Ages, the forests of Spain suffered progressive shrinkage because of cuttings for fuel and lumber as well as clearings for pasture and agriculture. By the late medieval period, the Castilian forests had been reduced largely to areas that were mountainous or hilly. Consequently, in the Castilian language, *monte* could mean either "mountain" or "forest woodland." Some *montes* were great oak forests, whereas others were scrub brush. The *montes* were a prominent feature of the landscape of medieval and early modern Castile*. They were considered to be common property, and both the Crown and the municipal governments passed regulations to ensure that the benefits of the *montes* were equitably available for all who wished to use them. The *montes* provided pasture and land for cultivated plots, and they were also used for hunting and fishing. Furthermore, they were exploited as a source of lumber, firewood and charcoal, medicinal herbs, cork, fruits and nuts, bees (and the flowers to sustain them), spring water, esparto grass (used to make cordage, mats, and paper), and many other things. The municipal governments of Castile adopted special ordinances to protect their *montes*. Usually there was a blanket authorization to use the *montes* in ways that would not harm them, but it was usually forbidden to cut down trees or to make *rozas* (fire clearings) without special permission, because these threatened to destroy the *montes*. In many areas, the *montes* were exceedingly important to the local economy. They were especially valuable to the poor, who could use their right to free access to the *montes* to eke out an existence by dabbling in this activity and that. Despite royal and municipal safeguards to protect the *montes*, the population pressure of the medieval period and especially of the sixteenth century caused most of Castile's *montes* to shrink in size gradually, typically through illegal *rozas*. The *montes* in Spanish America were also supposed to be for the common benefit and also suffered progressive deforestation as a result of fire clearings, lumbering, and other forms of exploitation.

REFERENCES: David E. Vassberg, *Land and Society in Golden Age Castile*, 1984; Michael R. Weisser, *The Peasants of the Montes: The Roots of Rural Rebellion in Spain*, 1976.

David E. Vassberg

MONTE DE LAS CRUCES, BATTLE OF. On October 30, 1810, Father Miguel Hidalgo*, with a force of some 40,000 men, encountered and defeated several hundred royalist forces under the command of Colonel Torcauto Trujillo just outside Mexico City* at Monte de las Cruces. Royalist survivors retreated to Mexico City where an effort was made to portray the major victory for the revolutionary forces as a royalist victory. The battle also revealed critical weaknesses in Hidalgo's army, however; although the royalists were vastly outnumbered, they fought well against what was little more than a poorly led, disorganized, and ill-armed mob. In particular, the royalist artillery took a devastating toll on Indian attackers who, not understanding artillery, tried to silence cannon by stuffing hats and cloth into them. It was obvious after Las Cruces that, without seasoned officers to train and lead Hidalgo's forces, they would be largely ineffectual against massed royalist forces. The only way that Hidalgo could acquire such leadership was through royalist defections. While there were defectors, their numbers were insufficient. One royalist officer who distinguished himself at Las Cruces was Lieutenant Agustín de Iturbide* who, as a conservative leader, would effect Mexico's independence from Spain in 1821.

REFERENCES: Christon Archer, *The Army in Bourbon Mexico*, 1977; William Robertson, *Rise of the Spanish-American Republics*, 1918; Fayette Robinson, *Mexico and Her Military Chieftans*, 1970.

Samuel Freeman

MONTEGUADO, BERNARDO. Bernardo Monteguado was born in Tucumán*, Río de la Plata*, in 1785. He studied law at the universities of Córdoba* and Chuquisaca and became an early advocate of independence. Monteguado participated in the Chuquisaca Revolt of 1809, and in 1810, he was in Buenos Aires* to be a part of the May Revolution*. Between 1811 and 1815, Monteguado lived in Buenos Aires, edited the *Gaceta de Buenos Aires*, and produced a large volume of writings supporting independence and natural rights. A supporter of Carlos de Alvear*, Monteguado was exiled from Argentina* when Alvear's government fell in 1815. He returned to Argentina in 1817 and became judge advocate of José de San Martín's* army. Monteguado spent the rest of his life with the army fighting in Chile* and Peru*. In 1824, Monteguado established a close relationship with Simón Bolívar* in Lima*, Peru, but he was assassinated in 1825 by an enemy of Bolívar.

REFERENCES: Enrique Udaondo, *Diccionario biográfico colonial argentino*, 1945; Ione S. Wright and Lisa M. Nekhom, *Historical Dictionary of Argentina*, 1978.

MONTEJO, FRANCISCO DE. Born in Spain in 1484, Francisco de Montejo was a friend of Hernán Cortés* and accompanied him to New Spain*. Montejo set out to conquer the Maya* of Yucatán* in 1527. Earlier Spanish incursions into Yucatán had been tentative and unproductive; the peninsula, then thought by the Spaniards to be an island, had first been sighted by Francisco Hernández* de Córdoba in 1517. Hernández had traded with the Maya, but then had been mortally wounded in battle with them. A decade later, Montejo would be the first Spaniard to attempt to engage the Maya again. Like Hernández before him, Montejo was unsuccessful in his first attempt, for the Spaniards found themselves thwarted by the rugged terrain and by their lack of provisions. Even more importantly, Montejo grossly underestimated the fighting skills of the Maya. In one battle alone, 150 Spaniards died at the hands of the Yucatec.

Having failed in his initial attempt to pacify Yucatán and Tabasco, Montejo was made governor of Honduras* in 1536, only to be pushed out by Pedro de Alvarado* the following year. In 1537, Montejo returned to Yucatán, this time joined by his son and nephew, both of whom were also named Francisco de Montejo. The combined leadership of the three proved effective, and by 1542, they had brought most of the region under Spanish control. That year, the Montejos founded Mérida, the capital of Yucatán.

In 1547, a serious insurrection by the Yucatec Maya threatened Spanish domination of the peninsula. A great many Spaniards died in the uprising, many of them settlers and noncombatants, but the Montejos were eventually able to restore calm. An estimated 500 Spaniards were killed in the two decades that it took to conquer Yucatán. Montejo died in 1550. The final victory over the Yucatec Maya took place in 1697, long after Montejo's death, when Tayasal, the Yucatec leader, was captured in the Guatemalan Petén.

REFERENCES: Michael C. Meyer and William L. Sherman, *The Course of Mexican History*, 1983; R. L. Woodward, Jr., *Central America: A Nation Divided*, 1983.

Virginia Garrard Burnett

MONTERREY. The city of Monterrey in the northern reaches of New Spain* was established by Luis de Carvajal in 1596. The settlement served as the control point for the viceroyalty's trade routes through the Sierra Madre mountains.

REFERENCE: Donald C. Briggs and Marvin Alisky, *Historical Dictionary of Mexico*, 1981.

MONTERREY, DIOCESE OF. The Roman Catholic diocese of Monterrey*, at first called the Diocese of Linares, was established in 1777 in New Spain*. Its territorial jurisdiction included the present-day states of Coahuila*, New León*, and Tamaulipas in New Spain and parts of Texas* and Louisiana* in the United States.

REFERENCE: *New Catholic Encyclopedia*, IX:1085–86, 1967.

MONTEVIDEO. Today the capital city of Uruguay*, Montevideo* was founded in 1726 by Bruno Mauricio de Zabala* as part of Spain's geopolitical move to forestall Portuguese expansion into the Banda Oriental*. Its name supposedly comes from the expression "Monte vide eu" ("I see a mountain"), which a sailor on Ferdinand Magellan's* ship uttered in 1520 when he sited low mountains as the expedition proceeded up the La Plata River. In 1726, seven families from Buenos Aires* joined 15 colonist families from the Canary Islands* in establishing the settlement. The city was laid out by military engineers to provide control of the eastern bank of La Plata River and the eastern side of the Plata estuary. Throughout the eighteenth century, the city was a political pawn undergoing attacks by Spanish, British, and Portuguese forces. In 1751, Spain raised Montevideo to the level of a province with its own colonial governor. In 1777, when Portugal ceded the Nova Colonia do Sacramento colony to Spain, it became part of Montevideo. Spanish authority ended in Montevideo in 1814, and for the next sixteen years, Argentina, Portugal, and Great Britain competed for the region. In 1830, the region became independent as Uruguay. When the colonial period ended, the city of Montevideo had a population of approximately 15,000 people.

REFERENCE: Jean L. Willis, *Historical Dictionary of Uruguay*, 1975.

MONTEZUMA. See MOTECUHZOMA.

MONTEZUMA II. See MOTECUHZOMA II.

MONTORO, RAFAEL. Rafael Montoro was born to a wealthy family in Havana*, Cuba*, in 1852. He received a law degree from the University of Madrid and then spent several years in Spain as editor of *Revista Contemporánea* and as an officer in the political and moral sciences section of the Atheneum of Madrid. He returned to Havana in 1877, founded the journal *El Triunfo*, and became involved in the politics of imperialism. Montoro wanted autonomy for Cuba within the Spanish empire rather than complete independence, and he became a member of the Liberal Autonomist Party. Between 1879 and the end of the colonial period in Cuba, Montoro was a Cuban representative in the Spanish Cortes. He refused to participate in the war for independence between 1895 and 1898. When Spain granted Cuba autonomy in 1897, Montoro became secretary of the treasury in the short-lived government. When United States intervention destroyed that government, Montoro retired from public life. He returned for several diplomatic assignments in the early 1900s and died in 1933.

REFERENCE: Jaime Suchlicki, *Historical Dictionary of Cuba*, 1988.

MONTÚFAR, CARLOS DE. Carlos de Montúfar was born in Quito*, Ecuador*, in November 1780. His father, Juan Pío Montúfar y Larrea*, was an early leader of the Ecuadorian independence movement. He was educated in Spain and spent his early military career fighting with Spanish forces against Napoleon. Back in America, Montúfar fought with the independence forces in a number of military campaigns in Gran Colombia*. He was captured by Spanish forces and executed near Buga, Colombia*, on July 31, 1816.

REFERENCES: Albert William Bork and Georg Maier, *Historical Dictionary of Ecuador*, 1973; Federico González Suárez, *Historia General de la República del Ecuador*, 7 vols., 1890–1903.

MONTÚFAR Y CORONADO, MANUEL. Manuel Montúfar y Coronado was born in Guatemala City* in 1791 and became a leading intellectual in the struggle for independence from Spain. Montúfar became widely known in Guatemala* for his articles in the newspaper* *El Editor Constitucional*. He helped to write the state constitution and served as president of the state assembly, but after the Guatemalan civil war, he fled to exile in Mexico, where he died in 1844. He is also remembered for his recollections of the independence movement, published as *Memorias para la historia de la revolución de Centro-América* (1832).
    REFERENCE: Richard E. Moore, *Historical Dictionary of Guatemala*, 1973.

MONTÚFAR Y LARREA, JUAN PÍO DE. Juan Pío de Montúfar y Larrea, the son of Juan Pío Montúfar y Frasso, was born in Quito*, Ecuador*, on June 20, 1759. He was an early leader of the Ecuadorian independence movement. On December 25, 1808, the major independence leaders—José Luis Riofrío, Juan José Salinas, Antonio Ante*, Juan de Dios Morales*, José Manuel Rodríguez de Quiroga, Juan Pablo Arenas, Francisco Javier de Ascazubi, and Pedro Montúfar met at his home to plan the rebellion politically. Montúfar was elected president of the first junta of the rebellion on August 10, 1809. The junta was destroyed in 1810. In 1815, Montúfar renounced his title of nobility. He died in Cádiz, Spain, in 1818.
    REFERENCES: Albert William Bork and Georg Maier, *Historical Dictionary of Ecuador*, 1973; Federico González Suárez, *Historia General de la República del Ecuador*, 7 vols., 1890–1903.

MORA, JOSÉ MARÍA LUIS. José María Luis Mora was born in San Francisco de Chamacuero, New Spain*, in 1794. An important political theorist in Mexico, Mora received a doctorate of theology degree in 1819 from the College of San Ildefonso in Mexico City*. He then spent much of his career teaching law, history, and politics there. Political philosophers remember Mora as the key intellectual figure in the establishment of Mexican political liberalism, and his intellectual contribution to Mexican political philosophy remains a vital one. Mora was also an historian and political essayist. His most important works were *México y sus revoluciones* (1836) and *El clero, la educación y la libertad* (1849). During the latter part of his career, Mora worked with the Mexican diplomatic corps. He died in Paris on July 14, 1850.
    REFERENCES: Charles A. Hale, *Mexican Liberalism in the Age of Mora, 1821-1853*, 1974; Joaquín Ramírez Cabañas, *El doctor Mora*, 1934.

MORALES, JUAN DE DIOS. Juan de Morales was born on April 13, 1767, in what is today the department of Antioquia*, Colombia*. A trained attorney, Morales is remembered as the ''soul of Ecuadorian independence'' because of his role in developing the political philosophy and early policies of the independence juntas in Quito*. Morales died in Quito on August 2, 1810.

REFERENCES: Albert William Bork and Georg Maier, *Historical Dictionary of Ecuador*, 1973; Federico González Suárez, *Historia general de la República del Ecuador*, 7 vols., 1890–1904.

MORALES LEMUS, JOSÉ. José Morales Lemus was born in Cuba[*] in 1808 and raised by a well-to-do family from the Canary Islands[*], who bequeathed to him their fortune. He became a lawyer but as a young man also developed a social conscience that forced him to free all of his slaves. Morales spent the rest of his life campaigning against slavery[*] and for Cuban independence from Spain. Morales was an active participant in the early stages of the Ten Years War[*], but he eventually had to seek exile in New York and the Spaniards confiscated all of his property. In New York, he worked for the Junta Cubana and the Republic in Arms to promote Cuban independence. He died a pauper there in 1870.

REFERENCES: Jaime Suchlicki, *Cuba: From Columbus to Castro*, 1986; Jaime Suchlicki, *Historical Dictionary of Cuba*, 1988.

MORAZÁN, FRANCISCO. Francisco Morazán was born in Tegucigalpa, Honduras[*], on October 3, 1792. He spent his early career in the army and became an early advocate of independence from Spain. Morazán spent much of his political career trying to bring about Central American unity. He was elected president of the Federal Republic of Central America[*] in 1830, but ten years later he was driven from office by Rafael Carrera, at which time Costa Rica[*] left the confederation. Morazán returned with his own army in 1842 and, in a political agreement with his rivals, he was named head of state again. With that, Costa Rica returned to the Federal Republic. Morazán's subsequent attempts to forge a political unity in Central America, however, resulted only in failure and death. Opponents of unification overthrew him in September 1842, and he was executed.

REFERENCE: R. S. Chamberlain, *Francisco Morazán: Champion of Central American Federation*, 1950.

Virginia Garrard Burnett

MORELIA, DIOCESE OF. The Roman Catholic diocese of Morelia was established by Pope Paul III in 1536. At the time, it was called the diocese of Michoacán and included that part of present-day Mexico. The see of the diocese was moved to the city of Valladolid[*] (today's Morelia) in 1580.

REFERENCE: *New Catholic Encyclopedia*, IX:1143–44, 1967.

MORELL DE SANTA CRUZ, PEDRO AGUSTÍN. Pedro Agustín Morell de Santa Cruz was born in Santiago de los Caballeros in Santo Domingo[*] in 1694. He was ordained a Roman Catholic priest in 1718, the same year that he was appointed vicar-general of the cathedral of Santiago de Cuba[*]. Morell became bishop of Nicaragua[*] in 1750, but he is best remembered as an early Cuban historian whose most important works are *La Relación histórica de los primitivos*

obispos y gobernadores de Cuba (1748) and *Historia de la Isla y Catedral de Cuba* (1760). Morell died in Havana* in 1768.
REFERENCE: Carlos de Utrera, "Morell de Santa Cruz," *Clio*, 19 (1951), 57–74.

MORELOS Y PAVÓN, JOSÉ MARÍA. José María Morelos y Pavón was born in Valladolid*, Michoacán, New Spain*, on September 30, 1765. He was a hacienda* laborer until 1790 when he entered the priesthood and began to study at the College of San Nicolás in Valladolid. One of his teachers was Manuel Hidalgo y Castilla*. After completing his studies, Morelos became a priest at Caracuaro in Michoacán, but the liberal ideas that Hidalgo had planted in his mind continued to ferment. In 1810, Morelos decided to follow Hidalgo in the revolt against Spain. Hidalgo assigned him to develop the revolution in southern Mexico, but when Hidalgo died in 1811, Morelos assumed leadership of the rebellion. He proved to have great military skills, and by 1813, much of southern Mexico was under rebel control. In 1813, Morelos convened the Congress of Chilpancingo* which declared Mexican independence. He also began to outline the shape of his own liberalism, which called for universal manhood suffrage, racial equality, abolition of the clerical and military *fueros*, and redistribution of hacienda land to the poor. José María Morelos was captured by Spanish forces and executed on December 22, 1815.
REFERENCE: E. A. Chávez, *Morelos*, 1957.

MORENO, MARIANO. Born in Buenos Aires* in 1778 in a traditional but modest home, Mariano Moreno in his early youth already showed sensitivity, qualities of character, and a clear mind. He began his studies at the Collegium Carolinum in Buenos Aires where his favorite teachers were friar Cayetano Rodríguez* and Mariano Medrano. He was destined for the priesthood and in 1800 entered the University of Chuquisaca, a powerful bastion of traditional scholasticism. From there he graduated in 1801 but then followed his secret wish to study law, which in turn brought him into contact with the writings of the great Hispanic jurists. The most important influence in Chuquisaca seems to have been Victorian de Villava, the great defender of the Indians* and prophet of the May Revolution* in Buenos Aires.

In 1805, Moreno returned to Buenos Aires where he practiced law. In the following years, he did not engage in political activities but on January 1, 1809, he joined the abortive establishment of a junta in Buenos Aires, headed by Martín de Alzaga*. He sided with the latter against Acting Viceroy Santiago Liniers*. By this action, Moreno demonstrated his belief that in the absence of a legal monarchy, Spanish America had the same rights to establish juntas as did the Peninsula. It was also in that year that he published his *Representación de los hacendados y labradores*, an attack on all artificial obstacles to free trade. The document was thus an echo of eighteenth-century economic liberalism.

The May Revolution* propelled Moreno into prominence. He and Juan José Passo became secretaries of the provisional junta. Within the ideological context of the revolution, Moreno represented the extreme Jacobin faction, aiming at independence and a democratic constitution. As legal counsel for the junta, he was the author of several government statements. In the "Manifesto de la Junta con motivo del fusilamiento de Liniers, y otros complicados en la conspiración de Córdoba, 9 de septiembre de 1810," he explained the reasons for the establishment of Buenos Aires junta: With no legal king at the helm, civil authority had reverted automatically whence it had come, the various peoples, including those of the old viceroyalty of Río de la Plata*. Moreno at the time did not believe in a Spanish-American federation but he personally favored Spanish-American union and a very close relationship between the Platine region and Chile*. His ideas for the future constitutional organization were also much inspired by Spanish liberalism. Thus, he wished the revolution to continue in an orderly fashion and not to fall into anarchy, as indeed happened after his premature death. His work in economics followed the ideas exposed in the *Representación*. In education, he published a work attributed to Gaspar Melchor de Jovellanos and wrote a preface to a reprint edition of Jean Jacques Rousseau's *Contrat social*, published in Buenos Aires in 1810.

Maybe he had focused on too many problems at the same time; more and more, he became disillusioned with events. He resigned on December 18, 1810, when the interior provinces demanded inclusion into the junta—the Junta Grande of 21— and he asked to be sent on a mission to London. On board the ship to Europe, he died on March 4, 1811, as a result of poor health, totally exhausted by the energy he had displayed in the historic days of the May Revolution. Ricardo Levene summed up Moreno's historic significance thus: "The sentiments he extolled were: respect of the people, horror of demagoguery, equality before the law, faith in the future greatness of the country and of [Spanish] America, and love for Buenos Aires." In many ways, he remains an enigma, especially his Jacobinism at the time of the May Revolution while his name was on the list of the royalist Alzaga plot of 1809.

REFERENCE: Ricardo Levene, *El pensamiento vivo de Mariano Moreno*, 1942.

O. Carlos Stoetzer

MORET LAW OF 1870. International pressure against the slave trade grew more intense as the nineteenth century progressed. Once the Civil War was over in the United States, slavery* in the New World was doomed. Its last real bastion was in Cuba*, which was still a colony of Spain. Importation of new slaves from Africa to Cuba ended in the late 1860s, but without replenishment of the labor supply, the price of slaves in Cuba rose commensurately. Plantation owners intensely opposed abolition, particularly if the government did not intend to compensate them for their lost property. Intent on securing British diplomatic support in case the United States intervened to liberate Cuba, Spain began putting pressure on the planters to free their slaves. In 1870, Spain passed the Moret Law, which tied slaves to the plantations for a ten-to-fifteen-year period and allowed them to work out their freedom. It also emancipated all slaves over the age of 65 and declared that the children of slaves would in the future be free. In October 1886, Spain ended slavery in Cuba.

REFERENCES: Jaime Suchlicki, *Cuba: From Columbus to Castro*, 1986; Hugh Thomas, *Cuba: The Pursuit of Freedom*, 1971.

MORGA SÁNCHEZ GARAY Y LÓPEZ DE GARFIAS, ANTONIO DE.

Antonio de Morga Sánchez was born in Seville*, Spain, on November 29, 1559. A lawyer trained at the University of Salamanca in Spain, Morga Sánchez practiced and taught in Salamanca. He spent most of his career, however, as a public official in the Spanish imperial bureaucracy. After terms as governor of Manila* in the Philippines* and an *alcalde del crimen* (penal court judge) in Mexico City*, Morga Sánchez was appointed president of the *audiencia* of Quito*, a position he held from 1615 until his death on July 21, 1636.

REFERENCE: Albert William Bork and Georg Maier, *Historical Dictionary of Ecuador*, 1973.

MORILLO Y MORILLO, PABLO.

Born in Spain in 1778, Pablo Morillo y Morillo joined the royal army as a young man and rose through the officer corps until his appointment as a general. In 1816, he was charged with the reconquest of Colombia*, a task he undertook with ruthless zeal. Between 1816 and 1819, he launched a reign of terror that resulted in the executions of hundreds of captured patriot soldiers and leaders. Morillo completed the reconquest and achieved a military stalemate with Simón Bolívar's* forces by 1819. He negotiated a temporary settlement with Bolívar and returned to Spain in 1820. Pablo Morillo y Morillo died in 1837.

REFERENCE: Robert H. Davis, *Historical Dictionary of Colombia*, 1977.

MOROS.

The term ''Moros'' refers to Muslim Filipinos*. Spaniards, having just reconquered Iberia from the Moors, were horrified to be confronted again with Moros, after sailing halfway around the world. The name has pejorative connotations of savagery and treachery, but has been pervasively used anyway. Moros include the four major language groups of Mindanao* and the Sulu Archipelago: Maranao, Maguinandanao, Tausug, and Samal. Speakers of the Bajau, Yakan, Molbog, and Palawan languages may also be considered Moro. Culturally and racially, Moros are not very different from other peoples of the Philippines*, but a heritage of deep distrust and the memory of merciless battles have poisoned relations. Moros have been largely excluded from the national life, yet the government in Manila* (Spanish, American, and now Filipino) has always claimed jurisdiction over all Mindanao and the Sulu Archipelago. The result has been a stalemate between a persistent armed separatist movement and a national government bent on pacifying the Moros.

When Spanish conquistadors* reached the Philippines* in the sixteenth century, Islam was spreading rapidly northeastward from Borneo and had already reached Tagalog* and Pampangan* settlements around Manila Bay. Spain immediately put a stop to that, but if the conquest had been delayed by only 50 years, Islam might have spread to all the Philippine islands. Islam offered models of political units (the rajaship and the sultanate) wider than the disunited villages that Spaniards found so easy to conquer. "Moro wars" were fought almost continuously from 1570 to 1640. Spain could sometimes defeat but never subdue the Muslims. One attempt to occupy the Maranao stronghold around Lake Lanao in central Mindanao was a fiasco. In retaliation, Moros launched devastating raids against Visayan*, Bikolano and Tagalog towns, especially along the coasts of Cebu*, Bohol*, Leyte*, and Luzon*. Most Christian Filipinos in those vulnerable regions lived in constant fear of the Moros.

Spain was intermittently able to defend a stone fort built at Zamboanga, in the heart of Moro territory, but the following areas were never conquered: Sulu, the Lanao highlands, parts of the coasts of Zamboanga and Cotabato, and the southern part of Palawan. The Sulu sultanate grew powerful in the first half of the nineteenth century and briefly asserted itself in international politics until the advent of steamships tipped the balance in favor of the Europeans. Jesuit* missions* in Zamboanga, Iligan and Dapitan ministered to Christians already there, but converted very few Muslims. Spain was still trying to assimilate the Moros when the United States took over, and it soon had to launch its own Moro wars.

REFERENCE: Gregorio F. Zaide, *Philippine Political and Cultural History*, Vol. I, 1957.

Ross Marlay

MOSQUITIA. Mosquitia is the Atlantic coastal region, from Honduras* to the southern border of Costa Rica*, inhabited by the indigenous groups known collectively as the Miskito* Indians. The largest of the groups that make up the Miskito are the Miskitu, the Rama, and the Sumu, who live primarily along the Caribbean coast of modern-day Nicaragua* and Costa Rica. The Miskito, a fierce and independent people, retained their independence from the Spaniards throughout the colonial period, and Mosquitia was never assimilated into Spanish Central America. Because of their enmity towards the Spaniards, the Miskito supported foreign piracy* against Spanish settlements during the late sixteenth and seventeenth centuries, and often served as middlemen for the contraband trade in cacao*, indigo*, and tobacco*.

By the mid-seventeenth century, the British had begun to dominate the contraband trade and actively cultivated friendly relations with the Miskito. It was they who first called the region in which the Miskito lived "Mosquitia". In 1741, the British created the Mosquito Kingdom, which consisted of Miskito lands running from Cape Gracias a Dios*, Honduras, to southern Costa Rica. The British selected and crowned a Mosquito king who nominally ruled the region, but the Mosquito Kingdom was in truth a legal fiction that cloaked the fact that Mosquitia was a base for the British contraband trade in Central America. The British and their Miskito allies also used Mosquitia as a staging ground for raids against Spanish settlements in Nicaragua and Costa Rica. These significantly weakened Spanish defenses on the Caribbean coast.

British activities on the Mosquito coast increased during War of Jenkin's Ear*, the War of Austrian Succession*, and the Seven Years War*. During this time, the British fortified their holdings at Black River, Cape Gracias a Dios, and Bluefields. In 1747, Miskito Indians, acting under orders from the British governor of Jamaica*, drove Spaniards from the cacao-rich Matina Valley of Costa Rica. In 1756, Miskito Indians killed the governor of Costa Rica. Spain periodically attempted to rout the British and Miskito from the area, but failed repeatedly. The course of the struggle for the Caribbean coast of Central America turned briefly in favor of the Spanish in 1779, when they drove the British from Roatan (one of the larger bay islands of Honduras) and Belize*. The ousted British, however, moved south to Mosquitia and used it as a base to step up attacks on Nicaragua. That same year, the British captured Omoa, Nicaragua, and destroyed its fortress. They were later run out by General Matías de Gálvez.

The Treaty of Paris*, which ended the Seven Years War in 1763, ordered the British to leave Mosquitia, but most of the foreigners remained on the coast for several more years. In 1786, a confirmation of the treaty gave the British more rights than they had previously enjoyed to settle in Belize, but it affirmed that they must leave Mosquitia. The confirmed treaty forced a massive British exodus from Mosquitia to Belize, although it did not completely end British interest in the area. In 1816, after the restoration of Ferdinand VII* to the Spanish throne, the British briefly resumed crowning a Mosquito king. Great Britain continued to arm the Miskito into the first years of the nineteenth century and to engage in contraband trade. It was not until 1860, with the signing of the Treaty of Managua, that the British relinquished all claims to the Nicaraguan Atlantic coast.

REFERENCE: R. L. Woodward, Jr., *Central America: A Nation Divided*, 1983.

Virgina Garrard Burnett

MOSQUITO INDIANS. See MISKITO INDIANS.

MOSQUITO COAST. See MOSQUITIA.

MOSQUITO KINGDOM. See MOSQUITIA.

MOTA Y ESCOBAR, ALONSO DE LA. Alonso de la Mota y Escobar was born in Mexico City* in 1556, where he joined the Dominican* order as a young man. He earned a doctorate in theology in Mexico City. After serving for a time as curate in Chiapas*, he went to live in Spain, where he served as a tutor to the prince who would become King Philip II*. He also received a doctorate in canon law from the University of Salamanca. Mota returned to New Spain* and served as a professor and administrator at several institutions of higher learning. In 1697, he was named bishop of Guadalajara*. He quickly earned a reputation as a prelate who tried to protect the Indians* from the worst abuses of Spanish officials and settlers. In 1608, Mota became bishop of Puebla, New Spain. He died there on April 15, 1625.

REFERENCE: Miguel Cuevas, *Historia de la Iglesia en México*, 1946–1947.

MOTECUHZOMA I. Motecuhzoma I was the fifth ruler, or *tlatoani*, of the México, the leaders in the famous Aztec* Triple Alliance. Ruling in Tenochtitlán* from 1440 to 1468, he was one of the strongest and most ambitious of the nine pre-Hispanic México rulers. His full name was Motecuhzoma Ilhuicamina. Motecuhzoma translates as "Angry Lord," and Ilhuicamina means "Archer of the Skies." In the codices*, his name glyph shows either a noble's headband (symbolizing *tecuhtli* or lord) or a stylistic sky pierced by an arrow, and sometimes both. His first name is found in numerous spellings, including the commonly-seen Montezuma. He was also known as Huehue Motecuhzoma (Motecuhzoma the Elder), to distinguish him from the later Motecuhzoma who ruled at the time of the Spanish Conquest.

This first Motecuhzoma was a son of the México ruler Huitzilihuitl (ruled 1391–1415), and a nephew of the immediately preceding ruler, Itzcoatl (ruled 1426–1440). By the time he succeeded to the imperial throne in Tenochtitlán, he was well over 40 years old and brought with him a considerable reputation as a warrior and statesman. Prior to his accession to the highest rank in the land, he had performed as a military leader in distant imperial campaigns and had served as a member of the council of four royal advisers under his uncle. According to the sixteenth century Codex Mendoza (folio 8v), he was considered to be "very serious, severe and virtuous . . . of good temper and judgment." This same codex indicates that he approached wine and women with moderation. This may well have been the case, since he fathered only two children, which is a surprisingly small number, given the practice of polygyny among high-ranking nobles.

During the course of Huehue Motecuhzoma's reign, the position of México nobility became increasingly solidified. Power and privilege became more firmly entrenched in the highest governmental levels, and sumptuary laws favoring the elite were made explicit. His reign provided a focus for displaying the riches won from distant regions, including shimmering tropical feathers, precious stones (such as jadeite and turquoise), and rich metals (gold, silver, and copper). He, like the rulers before and after him, also worked to enlarge the great temple in Tenochtitlán, the city's great ceremonial centerpiece. He also arranged for Nezahualcoyotl, the ruler of neighboring Texcoco, to engineer a huge dike across Lake Texcoco to provide protection against flooding.

Motecuhzoma I was, above all, a military leader. While imperial conquests had begun successfully under his predecessor Itzcoatl, Motecuhzoma's military ambitions led him in conquests from Tenochtitlán, especially to the north, south, and east. His energetic campaigns were interrupted, however, by some of the empire's most significant catastrophes, including a locust plague in 1446, the flooding of Tenochtitlán in 1449, and a disastrous famine that began in 1450 and lasted four years. Despite these setbacks, he displayed a richer and more ambitious political regime than any *tlatoani* before him and set a precedent for military attainments and royal sumptuousness.

REFERENCES: Nigel Davies, *The Aztecs*, 1974; Diego Durán, *Historia de las Indias de Nueva España e Islas de la Tierra Firme*, 1967; Susan Gillespie, *The Aztec Kings*, 1989.

Frances F. Berdan

MOTECUHZOMA II. Motecuhzoma II was the ninth ruler, or *tlatoani*, of the México, the leading power of the Aztec* Triple Alliance. He ruled in the México capital of Tenochtitlán* from 1502 to 1520 and was famous as the great ruler who hosted (and was then enslaved by) Hernán Cortés and his conquistadors*. His complete name was Motecuhzoma Xocoyotzin. Motecuhzoma (also often spelled Montezuma) means "Angry Lord," and Xocoyotzin translates as "The Revered Younger One." This name was doubtlessly given in order to distinguish him from the first Motecuhzoma*, a *tlatoani* who ruled in the previous century. This younger Motecuhzoma was the son of an earlier México ruler, Axayácatl (ruled 1468–1481) and nephew of the immediately preceding ruler, Ahuítzotl (ruled 1486–1502). He was in his mid-thirties at his coronation and had garnered many laurels by that time. As one indication of his martial achievements, he held one of the most exalted military offices in the land just prior to being selected as *tlatoani*.

In addition to being a renowned military officer, Motecuhzoma was known as an astrologer and philosopher. He was also profoundly religious, believing in the power of the gods, the inevitability of fate, and the significance of omens. These attributes came to dominate his attitudes and actions during his frustrating encounter with Cortés and his small band of conquistadors. Motecuhzoma enjoyed an extraordinary lifestyle, reportedly never wearing a cloak more than once and indulging in extravagant multi-course meals. Placing himself above mere mortals, he has frequently been described as haughty, proud, and greatly feared; it was said that his subjects dared not look him in the face.

During his reign, the internal structure of Aztec society became more and more caste-like. Privileges were tightly held by the elite, and a rigidly defined social hierarchy seems to have been the rule. In external matters, Motecuhzoma did little to expand the actual frontiers of the empire; rather, his efforts were directed at consolidating control over areas within those frontiers. With each change in imperial ruler, the conquered areas tended to become restless, particularly under Motecuhzoma's reign. In addition to establishing more definitive control over these areas, he concentrated on the México's age-old enemies, the Tlaxcalans, turning a "flowery war"* into a serious one. By the end of his rule, Tlaxcala was completely hemmed in by imperial subjects.

When Cortés arrived on the Mexican mainland, it was the name of Motecuhzoma that he continually heard uttered with fear and awe. The Spaniard met this god-king in November 1519 at the entrance to Tenochtitlán. Shortly thereafter, Cortés and his men took Motecuhzoma prisoner in his own city. As tensions increased during the winter and spring of 1520, open conflict between the Spaniards (with their Tlaxcalan allies) and the México broke out, and Motecuhzoma was killed. It is not entirely clear if he was killed by the Spaniards or whether dissatisfied México dealt the final blow.

REFERENCES: Nigel Davies, *The Aztecs*, 1974; C. A. Burland, *Montezuma*, 1973; Germán Vázquez, *Moctuzuma*, 1987; Susan Gillespie, *The Aztec Kings*, 1989.

Frances F. Berdan

MOTOLINÍA, BENAVENTE. See BENAVENTE, TORIBIO.

MOTRICO, CONDE DE. See AREILZA, JOSÉ MARÍA DE.

MOVIMIENTO DE UNIÓN NACIONAL DE GUINEA ECUATORIAL. (National Union Movement of Equatorial Guinea). The Movimiento de Unión Nacional de Guinea Ecuatorial (MUNGE) was established in the early 1960s as a moderate nationalist group in Spanish Equatorial Guinea[*] that advocated autonomy for the colony with close ties to Spain. The Spanish government designated MUNGE as the approved nationalist group in Equatorial Guinea. The MUNGE approach to autonomy was not adopted, and when independence came in 1968, MUNGE, as well as all of its leaders, was liquidated by Macías Nguema.

REFERENCE: Max Liniger-Goumaz, *Historical Dictionary of Equatorial Guinea*, 1988.

MOVIMIENTO NACIONAL DE LIBERACIÓN DE GUINEA ECUATORIAL. (National Liberation Movement of Equatorial Guinea.) The Movimiento Nacional de Liberación de Guinea Ecuatorial (MONALIGE) was founded in 1959 by a number of prominent nationalists in Spanish Equatorial Guinea[*]. It was strongly left-wing in its orientation, and it demanded immediate, complete independence from Spain. When independence came in 1968, MONALIGE had become the strongest political organization in the country, but Macias Nguema abolished it in 1970 as part of his drive for absolute power.

REFERENCE: Max Liniger-Goumaz, *Historical Dictionary of Equatorial Guinea*, 1988.

MUNIVE Y ASPEE, LOPE ANTONIO DE. Lope Antonio de Munive y Aspee was born in Marquina, Spain, in 1630. He studied law at the University of Salamanca and practiced law before his appointment as magistrate of the *audiencia* of Lima[*] in 1666. Munive spent two years supervising the mines of Huancavelica[*] between 1674 and 1676; in 1678, he was appointed president of the *audiencia* of Quito.[*] He served in that post for eleven years until his death in 1689.

REFERENCE: Albert William Bork and Georg Maier, *Historical Dictionary of Ecuador*, 1973.

MUÑOS MARÍN, LUIS. Luis Muñoz Marín was born in Puerto Rico* in 1898 but he spent most of his youth in the United States. He graduated from George-town University and, in 1917, when the Jones Act granted U. S. citizenship to all Puerto Ricans, Muñoz joined the Socialist Party of Puerto Rico. He returned to Puerto Rico and began publishing the newspaper *La Democracia*, in which he demanded independence for Puerto Rico and civil and economic rights for small farmers and peasants. Muñoz was elected on the Liberal Party ticket to the Puerto Rican Senate in 1932. He became a strong supporter of Franklin D. Roosevelt and the New Deal, a political position that helped him to secure large amounts of federal aid to ease the pain of the Great Depression. In the process, Muñoz became an increasingly popular figure in Puerto Rico.

In 1938, he broke with the Liberal Party and founded the Popular Democratic Party. By that time, he had decided to postpone indefinitely questions about Puerto Rico's colonial status in favor of agitation on behalf of social and economic rights for poor people. On that platform of workers' rights, minimum wage legislation, agrarian reform, and public works projects, the Popular Democratic Party won the election of 1940 and went on to dominate Puerto Rican political life for a generation. In 1948, Muñoz became the first popularly elected governor in Puerto Rican history. His tenure in office was marked by massive American investment—private as well as public—in Puerto Rico and by a rapidly im-proving standard of living. In 1951, with Muñoz's support, the people of Puerto Rico voted against independence and statehood in favor of commonwealth self-rule within the United States. Muñoz retired from the governorship in 1964. He died in 1980.

REFERENCE: Thomas Aitken, *Poet in the Fortress: The Story of Luis Muñoz Marín*, 1964.

MÜNSTER (WESTPHALIA), TREATY OF. The agreement that ended the Thirty Years War of 1618–1648 in Europe, the Treaty of Westphalia consisted of two peace treaties concluded on October 24, 1648, after lengthy negotiations that had begun in the spring of 1645 in the Westphalian cities of Münster and Osnabruck. The Treaty of Osnabruck was negotiated largely between the Holy Roman Empire and its allies and Sweden and its allies. The Treaty of Münster concerned the Holy Roman Empire and France. The provisions of the Treaty of Westphalia dealt with territorial changes, religious relations, and political ar-rangements throughout Europe. According to the treaty, Sweden received from the Holy Roman Empire, in addition to a large cash indemnity, Rugen Island, all of West Pomerania and part of East Pomerania with the city of Stettin, the city of Wismar, the secularized archbishopric of Bremen, and the bishopric of Verden. Sweden thus gained not only several of the major ports on the Baltic but also, with the town of Bremen, an important North Sea port.

By the Treaty of Münster, France received the former Habsburg possessions in Alsace; French sovereignty over the Lorraine bishoprics of Metz, Toul, and Verdun was confirmed. France and Sweden, as the victorious powers, were declared the chief guarantors of the fulfillment of the provisions of the Treaty of Westphalia. The allies of the victorious powers—the German principalities of Brandenburg, Mecklenburg-Schwerin, and Brunswick-Luneburg—enlarged their territories at the expense of bishoprics and monasteries; the Duke of Bavaria was confirmed in his possession of the Upper Palatinate and in his title of elector. The treaty recognized the German princes' complete independence from the Holy Roman Emperor in conducting domestic and foreign policy, provided that the external alliances were not directed against the interests of the Empire. In matters of religion, the Treaty of Westphalia gave Calvinists in Germany equal rights with the Catholics and Lutherans and legalized the secularization of church lands that had been carried out before 1624.

The Treaty of Westphalia, which consolidated the victory of the anti-Habsburg coalition in the war, was of considerable international significance. The attempt to create a Catholic world empire under the aegis of the Spanish and Austrian Habsburgs had failed, as had their plans for suppressing the Reformation movement in Europe and subjugating the United Netherlands. Both Switzerland and the Netherlands obtained international recognition of their sovereignty. France ensured itself of a dominant position in Western Europe for a century. The treaty, however, did not completely break the power of the Habsburgs. Although in decline since the early seventeenth century, Spain used the Fronde rebellion (1648–1653) in France to prolong the struggle with the French until 1659. The treaty perpetuated German division and political weakness into the nineteenth century, thus maintaining Austria as the dominant power in Central Europe.

REFERENCES: Samuel R. Gardiner, *The Thirty Years War, 1618-1648*, 1972; S. H. Steinberg, *The Thirty Years War and the Conflict for European Hegemony, 1600-1660*, 1966.

William G. Ratliff

MURILLO, PEDRO DOMINGO. Pedro Domingo Murillo was born in 1757 in Bolivia*. An early advocate of Bolivian independence, Murillo engaged in a variety of revolutionary activities, but his rhetoric was always more effective than his political or military planning. On July 16, 1809, Murillo was a leading figure in the La Paz* revolt, and he was named president of the abortive Junta Tuitiva, which tried but failed to rally mass support for the rebellion. Royalist forces arrested Murillo, convicted him of treason, and executed him on January 29, 1810.

REFERENCE: Dwight B. Heath, *Historical Dictionary of Bolivia*, 1972.

N

NAHUATL. Classical Nahuatl was the language spoken by the Aztecs[*] and their neighbors at the time of the Spanish conquest. There are three major dialects of modern Nahuatl. Lexicostatistic data suggest that the three have been separate from one another for a minimum of 11 centuries. The first is spoken primarily in the Mexican states of Mexico, Puebla[*], and Hidalgo; the second is spoken in Michoacán; and the third is spoken in northern Puebla and Veracruz[*]. These are the contemporary dialects of approximately 1.2 million people. Classical Nahuatl and the modern dialects are the southernmost members of the large Uto-Aztecan language family. Most of the languages of this family were spoken in what is today northwestern Mexico and the western United States. The point of dispersal for the family was probably southern California[*]. Cora and Huichol are the languages closest to Nahuatl.

Because it was the language of the Aztec Triple Alliance, Classical Nahuatl (or Mexican) was widely spoken in pre-Columbian Mexico. The language and place names in the language were spread further by the Indians[*] who provided the majority of the troops for the Spanish conquest of Mexico and Guatemala[*]. After the Conquest, Spanish friars quickly learned the language in order to convert the Indians. They created an orthography based on Spanish, began to compose religious writings, and taught native speakers to write their own language. The written language was rapidly adapted to meet the needs of the colonial bureaucracy. There is a great wealth of colonial documents in Classical Nahuatl.

Because of its great importance, the structure and lexicon of Classical Nahuatl are well documented. In 1571, Fray Alonso de Molina published his important dictionary, *Vocabulario de la lengua castellana y mexicana*. In 1645, Horacio Carochi published a grammar, *Arte de la lengua mexicana*. There is an excellent modern dictionary by Remi Simeon, *Dictionnaire de la Langue Nahuatl ou*

Mexicaine published in 1885 and republished in 1963 with an introduction by Jacqueline de Durand-Forest. A second excellent dictionary is Frances Karttunen's 1983 work, *An Analytical Dictionary of Nahuatl*. Important modern grammars in English include J. Richard Andrews, *Introduction to Classical Nahuatl*, and Thelma D. Sullivan, *Compendium of Nahuatl Grammar*.

REFERENCES: Frances F. Berdan, *The Aztec*, 1989; Francisco Clavijero, *The History of Mexico*, 1979; Nigel Davies, *The Aztecs: A History*, 1980; Charles Gibson, *The Aztecs Under Spanish Rule: A History of the Indians of the Valley of Mexico, 1519–1810*, 1964; William Prescott, *The Conquest of Mexico*, 1931; Jacques Soustelle, *The Daily Life of the Aztecs*, 1964.

Edward B. Sisson

NARIÑO, ANTONIO. Not as celebrated as many other heroes of Colombia's[*] fight for independence from Spain, Antonio Nariño is most remembered as the "Precursor" of Colombian independence. He also played an active role throughout the independence period as statesman, military leader, and lawmaker. His life is particularly noted for its great ups and downs—victories followed by defeat and long years in prison for his revolutionary activities. The date of Nariño's birth has been disputed, but April 9, 1765, is now commonly accepted. The well-read son of a prosperous *criollo*[*] family, he was in his early life a friend of the viceroy[*] and held several honored and lucrative posts, including royal treasurer of tithes.

Nariño's status as the Precursor came from the events surrounding his translation and publication of the "Declaration of the Rights of Man and the Citizen" from the French Constituent Assembly, a document proscribed in the Spanish colonies. Much influenced by the ideas of the Enlightenment,[*] the French Revolution, and such North Americans as Benjamin Franklin, Nariño was a leader among the young intellectuals of Santa Fe de Bogotá[*]. His large library included many prohibited books on science and philosophy. About 1789, a *tertulia* (discussion group somewhat similar to the French salons) began to meet in Nariño's house. Within the *tertulia* developed two secret groups that became intellectual cells of revolution. Although he had become increasingly persuaded of the need for revolution, the precise reasons for Nariño's decision to print "The Rights of Man" are unclear. In any event, in late 1793 he printed about 100 copies on his own press. Although some authors have stated that copies of his translation reached most of the colonial capitals, it appears that in order to protect himself, Nariño destroyed all but two copies. The publication led to his conviction by the *audiencia* of New Granada[*] on November 28, 1795, a sentence of imprisonment in Africa, and confiscation of his property.

Nariño escaped in Cádiz, Spain, and began an odyssey to Madrid, Paris, England, Bordeaux, and Venezuela[*]. These travels intensified his republican sentiments and brought him into contact with many of the revolutionary conspirators of the period. Returning in 1797, he made a tour of the provinces, which revealed little support for revolution. Shortly thereafter, he was recaptured in Bogotá and spent six years in prison (which almost broke his health) and six more in rural internment (where he recovered his health and some of his fortune). In 1809, he was again imprisoned for plotting and held until December 1810. Nariño's early actions did not trigger revolt, and some authors have suggested that his contribution as a precursor was more recognized after independence than at the time. From 1811 on, however, he played a direct, major, if truncated role in the independence struggle.

During 1811–1812, Nariño published a newspaper, *La Bagatela*, which he used to criticize the first president of Cundinamarca (the province in which Bogotá is located) and then to defend himself after assuming the presidency in a coup d'etat on September 19, 1811. In 1812, Nariño was made dictator and then on June 24, 1813, president general. This was a period of the conflict among the regional centers of Colombia over independence and regional ascendancy—an era referred to as the Patria Boba (foolish fatherland) for the foolishness and bitterness of the revolutionary governments in the face of the enemy. In September 1813, after a successful defense of Bogotá early in the year, Nariño launched a campaign to liberate the south from the royalists. His army was successful in Popayán*, but in 1814 he was defeated by Pasto and imprisoned till March 23, 1820. Freed from prison in Cádiz by the Riego revolt, he returned home.

The Liberator, Simón Bolívar*, named Nariño vice-president of Colombia to preside over the congress at Rosario de Cúcuta* (May 6-July 5, 1821), which was to write the constitution for the new nation. Nariño had a major influence in shaping the document, particularly its centralist focus. He, however, came into sharp conflict with Francisco Santander*, who supported federalism and saw Nariño as a personal rival for power. Nariño left the Cúcuta convention in ill health and under a cloud of personal scandal (of which his biographers find him innocent). The conflict between the two leaders continued until Nariño's death. Santander defeated him for the vice-presidency of Gran Colombia* on September 7, 1821, and then supported attempts to oust him as senator from Bogotá (1821–1823). Ill and declining since Cúcuta, Nariño died at his home in Villa de Leiva on December 13, 1823.

Although Antonio Nariño is not among the best known of the Colombian heroes of independence, his contribution appears to have been more noted in the twentieth century. Not as famous a precursor as the Venezuelan adventurer Francisco Miranda*, he has nevertheless been described as "the most genuine representative of the progressive and self-denying youth" who prepared the way for independence. He was also a good example of the high intellectual values of the Colombian colonial elites.

REFERENCES: Thomas Blossom, *Nariño, Hero of Colombian Independence*, 1967; John A. Crow, *The Epic of Latin America*, 1948.

Robert E. Biles

NARVÁEZ, PÁNFILO DE. Pánfilo de Narváez was born in Valladolid, Spain, in 1478. He was a Spanish career soldier sent in 1520 by Cuba's* governor, Diego Velásquez*, to New Spain* to arrest Hernán Cortés*, whom Velásquez believed to be insubordinate to his authority. Narváez left Cuba with a large contingent of foot soldiers and 80 horses and landed at Vera Cruz. He traveled to Cempoala, where he attempted to ingratiate himself by means of gifts and promises of ridding the Aztec* empire of Cortés. In Cempoala, Narváez also received gifts and communications from Motecuhzoma II*, who hoped to see Narváez and Cortés destroy one another. Despite Cortés's perhaps disingenuous offer to negotiate with Narváez, the latter refused and planned to travel inland to Tenochtitlán*. Cortés responded that he was dishonored by the whole affair and traveled instead to Vera Cruz with 140 men, leaving Pedro de Alvarado* behind in charge of Tenochtitlán. Cortés attacked Cempoala by dark of night, in the rain, and gained an instant advantage over Narváez. Narváez was stabbed in the eye with a pike and surrendered. Most of Narváez's men joined Cortés's forces and returned with him to Tenochtitlán.

After sending secret messages to the Aztecs telling them to fight Cortés, Narváez returned to the Caribbean. In 1528, he gathered another fighting force and set sail to Florida*, where he hoped to find the fabled lands of Apalachee. He marched overland in search of this chimera, but failed to reunite with his own supply ships. Narváez and his men attempted to sail to Mexico down the Gulf coast in makeshift boats, but almost all, including Narváez himself, perished in the effort. Only four survived, the most notable being Álvar Núñez Cabeza* de Vaca, whose tales of golden cities in the north prompted Spanish exploration of the North American Southwest a decade later.

REFERENCES: Michael C. Meyer and William L. Sherman, *The Course of Mexican History*, 1983; Salvador Madariaga, *Hernán Cortés, Conqueror of Mexico*, 1955.

Virginia Garrard Burnett

NAUFRAGIOS. One of the greatest of the Spanish colonial chronicles, this compelling narrative relates the ill-fated adventures of Pánfilo de Narváez's* expedition to Florida*. Although the enterprise began with some 600 men, a series of misfortunes soon reduced the group to a handful, and eventually to only four. The author of *Naufragios*, Álvar Núñez Cabeza* de Vaca, who served under Narváez as his second-in-command, recounts an almost unbelievable story of survival, suffering, and deprivation. Unlike the majority of chronicles, Cabeza de Vaca's does not treat grandiose battles and exotic deeds, but rather describes pathetic and wretched experiences. The hardships of geography, nature, and calamities at the hands of Indians* are treated by the author with vigor. The narrative proceeds chronologically, beginning with the arrival in Tampa, Florida, and proceeding along the Gulf coast to Galveston Island, Texas*, and across Texas to the Gulf of California*, eventually ending near Culiacán, New Spain*, where the author accidentally met some fellow Spaniards. Clearly man's sheer desire to survive informs the primary narrative thread of *Naufragios*, and it places the work in the general arena of epic literature. Although now known as *Naufragios*, the original title, as published in Zamora, Spain, in 1542, was *Relación que dio Álvar Núñez Cabeza de Vaca de lo acaecido en las Indias*.

Written in the first person, the chronicle is a fast-moving autobiographical account of a white European trapped in the primitive environment of the New World. Finally, aside from the direct and terse narrative style, the work is noteworthy as a splendid source of early ethnography on the Indians of North America.

REFERENCES: Morris Bishop, *The Odyssey of Cabeza de Vaca*, 1933; Cleve Hallenback, *Alvar Núñez Cabeza de Vaca: The Journey and Route of the First European to Cross the Continent of North America, 1534–1536*, 1940.

Sam L. Slick

NEGROES. See BLACKS.

NEW ANDALUCÍA. The region of New Andalucía included what is today eastern Venezuela*. Spaniards settled the area early in the 1520s and founded the town of New Córdoba, or Cumaná, in 1523. It was the first permanent Spanish settlement in South America. In 1569, the Crown officially created the province of New Andalucía with its own governor; it was subject to the *audiencia* of Santo Domingo* until 1739. It then became part of the viceroyalty of New Granada*. In 1777, New Andalucía was placed under the authority of the new captaincy general of Venezuela*, where it remained throughout the wars of independence. In 1821, New Andalucía became part of Gran Colombia* and then of Venezuela.

NEW CALEDONIA. The colony of New Caledonia was established in Darién* in what is today Panama* in 1698. The settlement represented an attempt by some Scottish merchants to establish a colony in the New World. Unfortunately, they selected a most inhospitable location, in terms of weather, for the settlement, and they did not have the financial resources to support it. The settlers abandoned New Caledonia in 1700.

REFERENCE: Robert H. Davis, *Historical Dictionary of Colombia*, 1977.

NEW CARTAGO. See COSTA RICA.

NEW CASTILE, VICEROYALTY OF. See PERU, VICEROYALTY OF.

NEW CÓRDOBA. See NEW ANDALUCÍA.

NEW EXTREMADURA. In 1539, when he embarked on his expedition of conquest in Chile*, Pedro de Valdivia* called the region "New Extremadura." See CHILE.

NEW GALICIA. The region of New Galicia in New Spain* is west of Mexico City* and fell under Spanish control in the 1530s. The *audiencia* of New Galicia* was created in 1549, and it also had jurisdiction over the vast territories extending north of Mexico City all the way up to the Borderlands.* Eventually, the new provinces of Coahuila,* New Vizcaya,* New León,* New Mexico,* Sinaloa and Sonora,* and Texas* were carved out of New Galicia. King Charles III* created the *intendencia** of Guadalajara* in 1787 with the governor of New Galicia serving as indentant. The region became part of Mexico in 1821.

NEW GALICIA, *AUDIENCIA* OF. In 1530 and 1531, Gonzalo Nuño de Guzmán* led an expedition of exploration and conquest into the west central areas of Mexico. As part of that expedition, Guzmán founded the cities of Compostela and Guadalajara*. He eventually declared himself governor of "Greater Spain," a region extending to the west and northwest of Michoacán. The Spanish government ousted Guzmán as governor in 1536, and the colony came to be known as New Galicia*. It included all of New Spain* northwest of Mexico City* and extended all the way into the northern Borderlands*, including California* and the Río Grande area. In 1548, the *audiencia* of New Galicia was established with its headquarters at Compostela, but soon the offices were moved to the larger city of Guadalajara. The *audiencia* of New Galicia was subordinate to the viceroyalty of New Spain* throughout the colonial period.

REFERENCES: Mark A. Burkholder and D. S. Chandler, *From Impotence to Authority: The Spanish Crown and the American Audiencias, 1687–1808*, 1977; John H. Parry, *The Audiencia of New Galicia in the Sixteenth Century: A Study in Spanish Colonial Government*, 1948.

NEW GRANADA. See COLOMBIA.

NEW GRANADA, *AUDIENCIA* OF. The end of the period of conquest and the beginning of the colonial period in Colombia* is more or less marked by the establishment of the royal *audiencia** in Santa Fe de Bogotá* that was decreed July 17, 1549, and installed on April 17, 1550. In 1564, the king set up a president with powers of governor and captain general* with some dependence on the viceroyalty of Peru*. The president's authority covered much of present-day Colombia*, Panama*, and Venezuela*. Although three areas of southern Colombia were under the presidency of Quito*, the beginning of Colombian nationality is often dated from this period. A viceroyalty was established at Santa Fe de Bogotá, 1717–1723, and again, 1739–1810. The viceroyalty of New Granada* included the captaincy general of Venezuela* and the presidency of Quito (Ecuador*). In practice, however, the actual administration of the viceroy covered only New Granada (most of present-day Colombia and Panama).

REFERENCE: Mark A. Burkholder and D. S. Chandler, *From Impotence to Authority: The Spanish Crown and the American Audiencias, 1687–1808*, 1977.

NEW GRANADA, VICEROYALTY OF. The viceroyalty of New Granada was established in 1717 with its headquarters at Santa Fe de Bogotá*. It assumed jurisdiction from the viceroyalty of Peru*, which had previously governed the northern South American continent. Spain set up the viceroyalty to provide greater protection from pirates* for Spanish fleets leaving Portobelo and Cartagena*. Lima* was simply too far away to provide effective military protection. The viceroyalty was discontinued in 1723, with captaincy generals assuming power, but when Spain went to war with Great Britain in 1739, the viceroyalty of New Granada was re-established. Its authority included the *audiencias** of Panama*, Santa Fe de Bogotá, and Quito*.

REFERENCES: Lillian Estelle Fisher, *Viceregal Administration in the Spanish American Colonies*, 1926; José Manuel Groot, *Historia eclesiástica y civil de Nueva Granada*, 5 vols., 1890–1903; Allan J. Kuethe, *Military Reform and Society in New Granada, 1773–1808*, 1978.

NEW LAWS. The New Laws were issued by the Spanish Crown in 1542 in response to the revelations of Bartolomé de Las Casas* concerning the treatment of the Indians* in the New World. The fundamental premise of the New Laws was that no European could exploit Indian labor without the express permission of the Indian. Although they were noble in intent, the New Laws were never enforced because of the storm of protest that greeted them in the New World. The *encomienda** was already a fundamental labor institution in the Americas. In response to the protest, the Crown quickly repealed the provisions in the New Laws that had outlawed the inheritance of *encomiendas* and the establishment of new ones. As a result, the exploitation of Indian labor continued unabated, limited only by the rapid decline of the Indian population because of disease.

REFERENCE: Francisco Morales Padrón, "Las leyes nuevas de 1542–1543: Ordenanzas para la gobernación de las Indias y buen tratamiento y conservación de los indios," *Anuario de estudios americanos*, 16 (1959), 561–619.

NEW LEÓN. In 1582, Spain established the province of New León in northern New Spain* because of increased settlement in the area. It had previously been part of New Vizcaya*. New León fell under the administrative jurisdiction of New Galicia* until 1777 when the Internal Provinces* unit was created. Spain separated New León from the Internal Provinces in 1793. After that date, it was a province of the viceroyalty of New Spain* until it joined the new Republic of Mexico in 1821.

REFERENCE: Peter Gerhard, *The North Frontier of New Spain*, 1982.

NEW MEXICO. Perhaps the first white men to set foot in what is today New Mexico were Alvar Núñez Cabeza de Vaca* and his three associates who were survivors of a shipwreck on the Gulf of Mexico. One of these men was a black named Esteban, who later guided Father Marcos de Niza* to Zuñi Pueblo in west-central New Mexico. Exaggerations of the mineral wealth by Father Marcos sent Francisco Vásquez de Coronado* into the same territory with 300 Spaniards and 800 Indians*, but they failed to find the expected gold. Instead they found only spectacular landscapes and pueblos of adobe. Some of Coronado's officers did explore in this new land. Don Pedro de Tovar discovered the Hopi Indian territory, López de Cárdenas reached the Grand Canyon of the Colorado River, while Coronado himself went as far as the present town of Lyons on the Arkansas

River in Kansas. Exploration was accomplished, but the mineral riches were a disappointment. For the next half century, other expeditions also entered New Mexico territory. These expeditions explored but found little mineral wealth and returned to New Spain* wiser, but no richer.

In 1581, the Franciscan friar Agustín Rodríguez tried to do missionary work in the region, but in 1598, Don Juan de Oñate*, already rich from mining* operations in New Spain, made the first official attempt to colonize New Mexico. Personally funded, he led some 400 people into the region, along with nearly 100 wagons and 7,000 cattle. The same year, he established San Juan de los Caballeros near today's San Juan Pueblo. This was the first permanent colony in New Mexico and the second in what is today the United States. The next year, he established the first capital of New Mexico at San Gabriel near the mouth of the Chama River. For 11 years, it was the regional capital until Santa Fe*, founded in 1610, became the capital of the territory.

In the years that followed, many groups entered the area today called New Mexico, not to seek mineral wealth, but to carve out vast farming and herding areas under Spanish land grants. Between 1598 and 1677, over two dozen Spanish governors, largely qualified leaders, ruled the territory. In the seventeenth century, growing conflict between the Pueblo Indians and the Spanish developed. The problems were economic and religious. Led by a San Juan Indian shaman named Popé, most of the Pueblos were united and plans were made to drive the Spanish from the region. On August 10, 1680, the Indians struck. After a series of conflicts, the Spanish left New Mexico for 12 years. Pope proved as restrictive as the Spanish, however. Once the Spanish had left, the nomadic tribes—Navajo, Apache, Ute, and Comanche—became a major problem to the sedentary Pueblos.

Don Diego de Vargas Zapata Luján Ponce de León reconquered the territory now known as New Mexico. He did so with the promise that if there was no resistance, there would be no punishment. Most Pueblos accepted these conditions. The reconquest was completed by 1692. New Mexico grew slowly through the eighteenth century. It became part of the Internal Provinces* in 1777. The population increased until Mexico became independent from Spain in 1821.

REFERENCE: Warren Beck, *New Mexico: A History of Four Centuries*, 1962.

George A. Agogino

NEW ORLEANS. See LOUISIANA.

NEW ORLEANS, DIOCESE OF. In 1793, the Spanish Crown requested the creation of the Roman Catholic Diocese of Louisiana and the Floridas. The request was granted, and the first bishop appointed was Luis Ignacio de Peñalver*. The diocese covered a immense amount of territory—all the way from the Atlantic Ocean on the Florida* coast to the Rocky Mountains in the west and from Canada to the Gulf of Mexico.

REFERENCE: *New Catholic Encyclopedia*, X:383–85, 1967.

NEW SANTANDER. The term New Santander referred to the sparsely populated reaches of northeastern New Spain*, where settlement and development did not begin until 1746. Between 1749 and 1755, José de Escandón established 24 settlements in the region. It included the area south of the Río Grande in what is today Tamaulipas, Mexico. Settlements developed along the southern bank of the river. Until 1777, New Santander was under the administrative control of the viceregal *audiencia** in Mexico City*, but that year it was transferred to the authority of the Internal Provinces.* Jurisdiction over New Santander was restored to the viceregal *audiencia* in 1793. In 1821, New Santander became the State of Tamualipas in the Republic of Mexico.

REFERENCE: Lawrence Francis Hill, *José de Escandón and the Founding of Nuevo Santander: A Study in Spanish Colonization*, 1926.

NEW SEGOVIA. The term New Segovia was used by the Spanish to refer to their conquest and settlement of northern Luzon* in the Philippines* in 1581. The term was also used to refer to central Nicaragua* in the mid-1550s. See PHILIPPINES and NICARAGUA.

NEW SEGOVIA, DIOCESE OF. The Roman Catholic diocese of New Segovia was established in 1595 as a suffragen to the archdiocese of Manila*. Its first bishop was Miguel de Benavides*. New Segovia was raised to an archdiocese in 1951.

REFERENCE: *New Catholic Encyclopedia*, X:560, 1967.

NEW SPAIN. At the time of the Spanish conquest of what came to be called New Spain, the Aztec* Empire dominated the Valley of Mexico and the surrounding area. The Aztecs had arrived there only recently, in the fourteenth century, when they constructed their capital city, Tenochtitlán*. Motecuhzoma II* came to the Aztec throne in 1502, by which time the Aztec Empire had acquired a powerful military control in central Mexico. As late as the 1490s, Aztec expansion had reached the Gulf of Mexico when Aztec warriors conquered Vera Cruz*. The local tribes hated and resented Aztec power, and the Spaniards were able to exploit those feelings when they arrived a few decades later.

Rumors of fabulous Indian* riches on the mainland of Mexico had been filtering back to Cuba*, Hispaniola*, and Spain for years, and in 1519, Hernán Cortés* received a commission from Diego Velásquez, governor of Cuba, to make contact with the leader of the Aztec Empire. With several hundred soldiers, Cortés landed on the Gulf coast and then marched inland toward the Valley of Mexico, making allies all the way out of Aztec-hating Indian tribes. By the time he reached Tenochtitlán, Cortés's army had swelled to several thousand people. Cortés took Motecuhzoma prisoner and systematically began to plunder the gold of Tenochtitlán. The Aztecs rose up in rebellion in 1520 and expelled the Spaniards, but Cortés returned in 1521 and reconquered the Aztecs. Motecuhzoma had died in the rebellion of 1520 and was succeeded by his son Cuauhtemoc.

From that base in the Valley of Mexico, the Spaniards conquered the rest of Mexico. In 1535, Francisco de Montejo attacked the Mayan* civilization of the Yucatán*, but only after ten years of bloody fighting did the region come under Spanish control. Francisco de Coronado* led an expedition into the northern Borderlands, establishing Spanish claims to northern Mexico, Lower California*, Upper California, and present-day Texas*, New Mexico*, Arizona, and Colorado. By the 1540s, the Spaniards had for all intents and purposes completed their conquest of Mexico. Spain established an *audiencia** in Tenochtitlán in 1528, and in 1535, Spain created the viceroyalty of New Spain with the full array of Crown offices there. Antonio de Mendoza* was the first viceroy*. The Roman Catholic Church established a bishopric in Mexico City* in 1527 and the first bishop, Juan de Zumárraga*, arrived the next year. As the rest of Central America came under Spanish control, the jurisdictional domain of New Spain increased. The viceroyalty of New Spain had jurisdiction over the *audiencias* of Mexico City (1528), Santo Domingo* (1511), Panama* (1538), Guatemala* (1542), and New Galicia*, or Guadalajara* (1548).

The early economy of New Spain, once the Indians had been robbed of their gold, revolved around mining*, ranching, farming, and commerce. During the mid-sixteenth century, rich silver mines were opened at Zacatecas*, Guanajuato*, and Potosí in Mexico, and Spanish treasure ships regularly carried the bullion back to Spain. In rural areas, large haciendas appeared. Spaniards in Mexico raised cattle for meat, tallow, and hides*. They also raised sheep, horses, and a variety of grains. When New Spain expanded north into the Borderlands in the seventeenth century, even larger cattle ranches appeared.

Although the era of conquest was over by the early 1540s, the Indians of New Spain found themselves in a demographic catastrophe. Emperor Charles V* responded to the complaints of Bartolomé de las Casas* by outlawing the *encomienda** in 1520, but Cortés disobeyed royal orders and established the labor institution throughout New Spain, giving Spaniards control over Indian labor. The exploitation from the *encomienda*, combined with the devastating effect of European diseases, reduced the Indian population of New Spain from as many as 25 million people in 1520 to fewer than 1 million in 1605. Most Spanish men living in New Spain married Indian women, and in the process a large mestizo* class emerged.

By the early eighteenth century, Spanish colonial society revolved around four groups. The *peninsulares**—people born in Spain—dominated the civil, religious, and military bureaucracies through Crown appointments. The *criollos** were people of European descent who had been born in New Spain; they tended to dominate commercial and economic life. The mestizos constituted the large working class of artisans, small farmers, soldiers, and small businessmen. At the bottom of the social scale were the surviving Indians. At the end of the colonial period, the population of New Spain exceeded 7 million people.

By the end of the eighteenth century, a growing restlessness had appeared among the people of New Spain. The local *criollo* elite resented the patronizing attitude and monopoly on appointed offices maintained by the *peninsulares*, as well as the commercial restrictions imposed by imperial regulations. Mestizos felt similar hostility, as well as resentment over racism among *criollos* and *peninsulares*. Indians were upset about their poverty and the racism toward them rampant among all other social classes in New Spain. When France invaded and occupied Spain in 1808, this smoldering resentment burst into the independence movement. Miguel Hidalgo* y Castilla launched the war for independence in 1810, and although he was captured and executed in 1811, he had set in motion a political movement that could not be stopped. Eventually, the social classes of New Spain united temporarily to cast off the *peninsular* domination they had come to despise.

José María de Morelos* emerged as the new independence leader, a position he maintained until his capture and execution in 1815. For the next five years, the independence movement degenerated into a series of guerrilla actions, with Vicente Guerrero* the most prominent nationalist. Finally, under the leadership of Agustín de Iturbide, Mexico declared its independence in 1821.

REFERENCES: Ruben V. Austin, *The Development of Economic Policy in Mexico with Special Reference to Economic Doctrines, 1600-1958*, 1987; John F. Bannono, *The Spanish Borderlands Frontier, 1513–1821*, 1974; Louis Hasbrouck, *Mexico from Cortés to Carranza*, 1976.

NEW SPAIN, *AUDIENCIA* OF. See MEXICO CITY, *AUDIENCIA* OF.

NEW SPAIN, VICEROYALTY OF. The viceroyalty of New Spain was established in 1535 with jurisdiction over an enormous area encompassing Mexico, Central America, the Antilles in the Caribbean, the southern half of the United States, and the Philippines*. Because of the size of the viceroyalty, there was considerable administrative independence in the outlying areas. *Audiencias** had been established at Santo Domingo* in 1511 and Mexico City* in 1528, and when the viceroyalty was created in 1535, both came under its direction. Two other *audiencias*—Los Confines or Guatemala* in 1542 and New Galicia* in 1548—also came under its jurisdiction. The *audiencia* at Mexico City was presided over by the viceroys* themselves. The Philippine Islands was created as an *audiencia* at Manila* in 1583 and was separated from the administrative supervision of Mexico City. Along with the viceroyalties of Peru*, New Granada*, and Río de la Plata*, the viceroyalty of New Spain was one of the major administrative units of the Spanish Empire.

REFERENCE: Lillian Estelle Fisher, *Viceregal Administration in the Spanish American Colonies*, 1926.

NEWSPAPERS. Notwithstanding various sorts of news-oriented flyers, newspapers, understood in the contemporary sense, did not appear in the Spanish colonies until the eighteenth century. The first legitimate newspaper, *La Gazeta de México y Noticias de Nueva España*, began circulation in 1722 and lasted six months. In 1728, another newspaper, also called the *Gazeta de México*, was begun and lasted until 1740. Others followed, but with virtually no success and very short duration. Toward the end of the eighteenth century, Manuel Antonio Valdés founded *Gazeta de México, compendio de noticias de Nueva España,* which lasted for some 25 years. In 1805, the first daily newspaper, *Diario de México,* began production. In the decade prior to independence, various newspapers of limited circulation appeared, promoting an anti-Spanish political agenda. Chronologically, Guatemala City* was the site of Spanish America's second newspaper, the *Gazeta de Goathemala* (1729–1731). Other early newspapers included *Gazeta de Lima* (1743–1767?), *Mercurio Peruano* (1791–1795), *Primicias de la Cultura en Quito* (1792), and *Gazeta de Lima* (1793–1795) and (1798–1804). Cuba* was chronologically the fourth region in founding newspapers. These included *Gaceta de la Habana* (1764), *El Pensador* (1764), and *Gazeta de la Habana* (1782). Other early newspapers included *Papel Periódico* (1791–1797) and *El Redactor Americano* (1806–1809) in Bogotá; *Telégrafo Mercantil* (1801–1802) in Buenos Aires*, and the *Gazeta de Caracas* (begun in 1808).

Newspapers appeared much later in the Philippines*. The first newspaper there, a weekly, was *Del Superior Gobierno,* which began publishing in 1811; the first daily was *La Esperanza,* which began its run in 1846. Newspapers were subject to difficult economic problems, scarcity of paper, and suspicious censorship* by the Spanish authorities. The first newspaper published in a Filipino vernacular was *El Locano,* which began in 1889. Nevertheless, newspapers played an important role in a limited number of metropolitan centers in the later colonial period.

REFERENCE: Arthur P. Whitaker, ed., *Latin America in the Enlightenment,* 1958.

Sam L. Slick

NEW TOLEDO. The term New Toledo was used temporarily in the first several decades after the conquest of Peru* and Bolivia* to refer to a region that today includes most of Bolivia and portions of Argentina* and Chile*. It was officially designated the *audiencia* of Charcas* in 1559.

NEW VIZCAYA. The province of New Vizcaya in New Spain* was established in 1562 because of settlement from New Galicia* in what is today north central Mexico, generally the area of the states of Durango and Chihuahua. Spanish interest there was confined primarily to mining*, and settlers were hesitant to go there because of the fierce reputation of the Chichimec* Indians. At first, New Vizcaya had vague boundaries that included most of northern New Spain. As time passed, new provinces were created—New Leon*, New Mexico*, Coahuila*, Sinaloa* and Sonora—which made its boundaries more precise. New Vizcaya became part of the Internal Provinces* in 1777, and in 1786, it became the Intendancy of Durango. In 1821, the region became part of the new Republic of Mexico.

REFERENCES: J. Lloyd Mecham, *Francisco de Ibarra and Nueva Vizcaya*, 1927; Guillermo Porras Muñoz, *Iglesia y estado en Nueva Vizcaya (1562-1821)*, 1980.

NHEENGATU. Nheengatu, also known as Nyengatu, Inekatu, Lingua Geral Amazonica, and Tupi Moderno, is a lingua franca in the region of Colombia* and Brazil drained by the Vaupes River and its tributaries. It is a Tupi*-Guaraní* language that was brought into the area during the rubber boom between 1875 and 1920. Jesuits* originally brought the language up the Amazon in the eighteenth century as a language of mission* instruction. Among multilingual neo-Brazilians and various Indian* tribes, Nheengatu became a way of communicating. In the last several decades, its use has declined, although the language can still be heard along the lower Vaupes River. Today approximately 10,000 people speak Nheengatu.

REFERENCES: Edwin Brooks et al. *Tribes of the Amazon Basin, Brazil 1972*, 1973; Arthur P. Sorenson, Jr., "Multilingualism in the Northwest Amazon," *American Anthropologist*, 69 (1967), 670–84; Robert Lee Spires, "As Linguas Faladas do Brasil," *America Indigena*, 47 (1987), 455–79.

NICARAGUA. Nicaragua, a province of the captaincy general of Guatemala* during the Spanish colonial period, received its name from the principal cacique*, Nicarao or Nicaragua, whom the Spaniards first met. The province, bordered by both the Atlantic and Pacific, contained two large lakes that determined its development and settlement patterns during this period. On September 12, 1502, Christopher Columbus* first discovered the region on his fourth voyage when he was forced to seek refuge in a cape named Gracias a Dios* on the Atlantic side. On the Pacific side, it was Gil González* Dávila who explored Costa Rican* and Nicaraguan territory. He and Andrés Niño left Panama* on January 21, 1522, to explore Central American territory. Niño continued the expedition along the Pacific coast as González went inland. In Nicaragua, he came upon various Indian* groups and was kindly received by them. He came upon the cacique Nicarao and his Indians. Many were baptized, and González received a great deal of gold from them. The cacique Diriangen also talked to González and promised to return; he did, at the head of 3,000 to 4,000 armed Indians to attack the Spaniards. González retreated and arrived in Panama in June 1532 where he left for Santo Domingo* to prepare another expedition.

In 1524, Pedro Arias de Ávila* (Pedrarias), governor of Castilla de Oro*, arranged an expedition under Francisco Hernández* de Córdoba to go to Nicaragua. On his arrival, he faced very little resistance from the Indians. He founded many towns, including Granada* and León*. González landed in Honduras*, moved inland, and met Hernández's troops, who were under the command of Hernando de Soto*. González won the ensuing battle, but he returned to Puerto Caballos when news of another expedition arrived. Meanwhile, Hernández was attempting to free himself from Pedrarias, who sent troops under Martín de Estete to arrest him. Hernández was executed in León in 1526 when Pedrarias arrived. Pedrarias returned to Castilla de Oro, leaving Estete as governor in

León, when Pedro de los Ríos replaced him as governor. Diego López de Salcedo, governor of Honduras, declared Nicaragua under his jurisdiction and went to León in April 1527. Pedrarias convinced de los Ríos to go to Nicaragua, but when he arrived, Salcedo sent him away. Pedrarias received the title of governor of Nicaragua in June 1527 but did not take his post until March 24, 1528. On his arrival, he imprisoned Salcedo for seven months. Pedrarias's administration was noted for its cruelty to the Indians, as was that of his successor, Francisco de Casteneda, who took over upon Pedrarias's death in 1531.

In 1542, the New Laws* put Nicaragua under the jurisdiction of the *audiencia de los Confines** and did away with the governor's position, replacing it with that of *alcalde mayor**. Contreras was given a *residencia** because of his treatment of the Indians and other abuses. Nicaragua's third bishop, Antonio de Valdivieso, demanded enforcement of the royal orders for the protection of the Indians. This inflamed Contreras's sons, Hernando and Pedro, who assassinated the bishop in León on February 26, 1550. They continued their rebellion and went as far as Panama where they were stopped but managed to escape. Juan Gaitán, another rebel coming from Guatemala and Honduras, attacked León but was captured and executed. In 1566, the title of governor was re-established. Explorations of the Atlantic side of the province continued.

At the end of the sixteenth century, León was the capital city, although Granada was the richer of the two. The main economic product was agricultural exports. Besides Spanish and Indian revolts, a major problem was pirate* attacks, which began in 1572 and continued throughout the seventeenth century and into the eighteenth. English pirates joined forces with the Miskito* Indians to sack and burn the province's principal centers. Matagalpa was attacked in 1644, Granada in 1665, 1670, and 1683, León and Realejo in 1685, and various other towns at other times. Pirates commanded the mouth of the San Juan River, impeding commercial traffic. The responses to these attacks was forts and attempts to colonize and settle the Atlantic coast, known as Tologalpa, but these had little success. A major earthquake in 1663 destroyed León. In 1693, the inhabitants of Sebaco, tired of being recruited for the province's defense, rebelled. In 1699, William Pitt established himself in Tegucigalpa.

A difference existed between the Atlantic and Pacific sides of Nicaragua, because the former was colonized by the English with the Miskitos as allies, while the latter had the major Spanish populations. The English used their Atlantic bases to attack and harass the Spaniards and for contraband trade. The governors asked the captain general, as well as the king, for protection, but it was always late in coming and never sufficient. In 1786, a treaty between Spain and England recognized Spain's rights to the Miskito territory. The Miskitos were friendlier toward the Spaniards but still harassed the province. In 1786, Nicaragua was made an intendancy*, and the first intendant, Juan de Ayasa, toured the Atlantic coast trying to pacify the region.

The beginning of the nineteenth century saw both disputes between public functionaries and more Miskito attacks. In 1811, León, Granada, Masaya, Rivas, and other towns revolted. On December 13, 1811, León rebelled against the intendant José Salvador, who resigned to avoid bloodshed. The rebels demanded the establishment of a new government, reductions in the prices of some goods, and the abolition of some taxes. These demands were agreed upon but the rebels continued their revolt until Bishop Nicolás García Jerez established a *junta gubernativa* on December 14, which recognized him as president and intendant of the province. In Granada, a similar revolt occurred in December. It deposed the *peninsular* employees from their offices, replacing them with *criollos**. These former employees went to Masaya where they received help from Captain General José Bustamante* y Guerra, who sent troops under the command of Pedro Gutiérrez. In April 1812, the Granada rebels surrendered and were promised guarantees of which Bustamante did not approve. About 200 rebels were condemned to different punishments, from prison sentences to death.

When Guatemala* declared independence on September 15, 1821, the province's last Spanish intendant, Miguel González Saravia, along with Bishop Jerez, issued the "Acta de los Nublados", in León. This document declared Nicaragua independent from Spain and Guatemala. On October 11, León accepted independence on the terms presented by Agustín Iturbide* and the Mexican Empire. The issue would not be resolved until Guatemala declared in favor of Mexico in 1822.

REFERENCES: Bernardo Portas, *Compendio de la Historia de Nicaragua*, 1927; Sofonias Salvatierra, *Contribuciones a la Historia de Centroamérica*, 2 vols., 1930.

Carlos Pérez

NICUESA, DIEGO DE. Diego de Nicuesa was born in Spain in 1465. With a wealthy family background, Nicuesa was able to secure a large land grant in the New World from the Spanish Crown. Known at first as Veragua and later as Castilla del Oro*, the grant reached from Panama* up to Cape Gracias de Dios* on the north-south axis, and from Nicuesa in the west to Ojeda in the east. In 1510, Nicuesa established his colony on the Caribbean tip of what is today the Panama Canal, but the location was an inauspicious one for both health and economic development. Within a few years, the number of settlers dropped from 700 people to only 70. In 1511, the surviving colonists rebelled at what they considered Nicuesa's heavy-handedness. They put him in a tiny boat and left him at sea. It is presumed that he died there.

REFERENCE: Basil C. Hedrick and Anne K. Hedrick, *Historical Dictionary of Panama*, 1970.

NIZA, MARCOS DE. Marcos de Niza was born around 1500 in Nice, France. He became a missionary priest in the Franciscan* order and traveled widely with Sebastián de Benalcázar*. He arrived in the New World in 1531. Niza was the leader of the first group of Franciscan priests to enter Peru* in 1531, and he traveled widely throughout the region until 1535. In 1535 and 1536, Niza was in Guatemala*, and he arrived in Mexico City* in 1537. In 1539, he led an exploration group out of Mexico City north toward the Borderlands, where he became the first Spaniard to discover Arizona. Niza wrote widely about his journeys. Two books in particular have become important primary sources in the early history of the Spanish New World empire: *Cartas informativas de lo obrado en las provincias del Perú y Quito* and *Las dos líneas de los incas y de los scyris en las provincias del Perú y de Quito*. In 1540, Niza accompanied Francisco Vásquez de Coronado[*] on his expedition to the Borderlands. Niza died in Mexico City[*] on March 25, 1558.

REFERENCE: G. J. Undreiner, "Fray Marcos de Niza and His Journey to Cíbola," *Americas*, 3 (1947), 415–86.

NORTH AFRICA. North Africa was both the beginning and the end of the great history of the Spanish Empire. In 1497, five years after the expulsion of the Moors from Spain, Spanish troops and naval ships crossed the Mediterranean and conquered Melilla[*], which remains a small Spanish enclave in North Africa today. In 1668, Spain acquired Ceuta[*], a North African city directly across from Gibraltar[*], from Portugal. From that point on, however, Spain did not try to penetrate the North African interior until the nineteenth century, when the Spanish colonies of Spanish Morocco[*] and Spanish Sahara[*] were developed. In 1847, Spain established the captaincy general of North Africa, which brought all of the Spanish settlements on the North African coast under the governance of Ceuta. All of those regions were incorporated into Spanish Morocco in 1913. With the independence of Morocco in 1956, Ceuta and Melilla were governed by mayors, with Ceuta attached administratively to Cádiz and Melilla attached to Málaga.

NORTHWEST PASSAGE. It was the quest for the fabled Northwest Passage that inspired most of the great voyages of exploration in the sixteenth and seventeenth centuries and gave birth to the modern age of European imperialism. For centuries, Europe had imported Asian spices across the overland caravan routes in the Middle East, but in the late fifteenth century, the expansion of the Ottoman Empire effectively closed these routes off. The need to find another way to Asia led to the Portuguese voyages of Bartholomew Dias and Vasco da Gama around the Cape of Good Hope to India and the voyages of Christopher Columbus[*] and other Spaniards. By the early 1500s, especially after Pope Alexander VI[*] had delineated the Portuguese and Spanish spheres of influence, the other European powers felt left out of the Asian trade. Spain controlled one route to Asia—across the Atlantic, through the Strait of Magellan, and across the Pacific—while the Portuguese controlled the other—south around the Cape of Good Hope in Africa and east across the Indian Ocean. The Dutch and the English then spent centuries trying to find the Northwest Passage, some other way of getting to Asia besides the southern routes around the tips of South America or Africa. Such a route, of course, did not exist, but it was not until the seventeenth-century declines of the Spanish and Portuguese empires, when the English and Dutch navies were able to make their way to Asia by the more traditional routes anyway, that the search for the Northwest Passage lost some of its urgency.

REFERENCE: Peter Kemp, *The Oxford Companion to Ships and the Sea*, 1976.

NOVALES MUTINY. In 1821, Mexico became independent of Spain, and Spanish officials in the Philippines* became worried about the loyalty of Mexican officers serving in the Spanish army there. They began to replace officers of Mexican birth. In June 1823, Captain Andrés Novales led an uprising of 800 troops. They seized the Manila* barracks and the Governor's Palace. Spanish troops eventually recaptured the area, and Novales was then court-martialed and executed.

REFERENCE: W. Cameron Forbes, *The Philippine Islands*, 2 vols., 1928.

NOVEL OF CHIVALRY. The Spanish novel of chivalry (*novela de cabellería*) is perhaps the earliest thorough manifestation of popular-democratic European narrative directed toward society as a whole (that is, not restricted to aristocratic tastes and/or education). Understood in broadest terms, the novel of chivalry involved knights and their travels to faraway lands of monsters and maidens. These works were melodramatic, exaggerated, and exotic. They were immensely popular among the masses. Spain, France, and England have all laid claim to the origin of the novel of chivalry. Only in Spain, however, did it reach a truly frenzied level of development, fueled by an insatiable reading audience. The first primitive novel of chivalry was probably the Catalán work *Tirant lo Blanch*, but the earliest and most successful was *Amadís de Gaula* (1508).

Perhaps because of the gripping, nearly hypnotic influence that the novel of chivalry exerted upon its readers, the Spanish throne undertook to prohibit the shipment of novels of chivalry to the New World, calling them *historias mentirosas* (deceitful, lying stories). In 1531 and 1543, the Spanish government issued edicts aimed against novels like *Amadis*. The stated motive was to protect the Indian* from confusion between fiction and reality. Interest in the novel of chivalry in Spain crossed all social lines; nobility, clergy (including Ignatius Loyola and Saint Teresa), the military, and women (nuns and secular) all read them. The genre was a literature of passion, provoking among a relatively unsophisticated readership dreams of faraway lands and heroic deeds, exactly the sort of lands and deeds associated with the Spanish conquest of the New World.

It is difficult to overstate the incredible impact of the Spanish novels of chivalry in both Spain and the New World. Quite simply, they informed morality, world views, and artistic tastes. Spaniards incorporated the chivalric codes of honor and valor into their daily lives. Spanish explorers and conquistadors* went to the New World with fixed images of knight errantry on the loose in a mysterious, exotic new land not unlike that described in the imaginative novels. Indeed, some argue that the sheer courage and perseverance of the Spaniards in the New

World was conditioned by the fictional worlds portrayed in the novels of chivalry. The Spaniards' penchant for mythic sites—the Fountain of Youth, the River of the Amazons, and so forth—were likewise conditioned responses stimulated by the novels of chivalry.

REFERENCE: Fernando Alegría, *Historia de la novela hispanoamericana*, 1965.

Sam L. Slick

NÚÑEZ CABEZA DE VACA, ÁLVAR. See CABEZA DE VACA, ÁLVAR NÚÑEZ.

NÚÑEZ DE BALBOA, VASCO. See BALBOA, VASCO NÚÑEZ DE.

NÚÑEZ DE PINEDA Y BASCUÑÁN, FRANCISCO. Francisco Núñez de Pineda y Bascuñán was born in Chilan, Chile*, in 1607, and educated by the Jesuits*. It was there that he received a classical humanistic education. He entered military service as a young man and spent some 40 years of his life fighting in the Indian* wars. In his later years (ca. 1673), he wrote the literary work for which he is remembered: *Cautiverio feliz y razón de las guerras dilatadas de Chile*. *Cautiverio* relates some six months of captivity that Núñez suffered at the hands of the Araucanians* in 1629. It includes a wealth of observations about the Indians and their culture. The author's attitude toward his captors is friendly and positive, and particularly glowing with regard to Maulicán, the chief of the Araucanians. Conversely, Núñez is critical of the Spaniards and their cruelty perpetrated against the noble and courageous Indians.

The literary merit of *Cautiverio* is uneven, and Núñez has often been accused of lacking artistic ability. The autobiographical narration holds the reader's interest, however, and is basically well written. Núñez does, though, have a tendency to lapse into prolonged digressions that detract from the drama portrayed. In addition, Núñez's proclivity for extending the prose with attempts at erudition and Latin distracts the reader. Some critics have spoken more favorably of Núñez's interpolated poems than of his prose, moving some to claim that he was more poet than narrator. Since Núñez wrote *Cautiverio* some 40 years after his actual captivity, it is a work of memories and recollections, unlike a chronicle that tended to be written at the moment of the action. Finally, *Cautiverio* contains an undeniable *criollo** disposition toward the Indian and, more importantly, toward the Spaniard, in that it exalts the native at the expense of the conqueror. Núñez died in 1682.

REFERENCE: Ángel Flores, *The Literature of Spanish America: The Colonial Period*, 1966.

Sam L. Slick

NÚÑEZ DE VELA, BLASCO. Blasco Núñez de Vela was born in Spain in 1490. He rose through court ranks in Spain during the early 1500s, and in 1542 he received his appointment as the first viceroy* of Peru*. Núñez de Vela came to Lima* with orders to enforce the New Laws*, a recently passed set of measures designed to eliminate the worst abuses of the Indians* at the hands of the conquistadors*. He was a dull man with little imagination, however, and he decided immediately upon arriving in Lima to seize the *encomiendas** of the conquistadors, including that of Gonzalo Pizarro*. Pizarro reacted violently, precipitating a civil war. He arrested Núñez de Vela, imprisoned him temporarily, and then released him with orders to return to Spain. Instead, Núñez de Vela headed up to Panama* where he recruited an army to put down Pizarro. When he returned to Peru, Núñez de Vela tried once again to crush Pizarro, but in a pitched battle in 1546, Núñez de Vela was killed.

REFERENCE: Manuel de Mendiburu, *Diccionario histórico-biográfico del Perú*, 8 vols., 1874–90.

O

OAXACA. The city of Oaxaca in southwestern Mexico was founded by Spaniards in 1521 in the center of the Mixtec and Zapotec Indian communities. In 1787, King Charles III* created an *intendencia** for the region of Oaxaca in New Spain*. It became a part of the new Republic of Mexico in 1821.

OAXACA, DIOCESE OF. The Roman Catholic diocese of Oaxaca in New Spain* was established in 1535. It was originally called the diocese of Antequera. For more than 200 years, the diocese of Oaxaca was the center of the Spanish attempts to convert and pacify the various Indian* tribes of southwestern Mexico, especially the Mixtec and Zapotec peoples.
REFERENCE: *New Catholic Encyclopedia*, X:600–601, 1967.

OBANDO, JOSÉ MARÍA. José María Obando was born near Caloto in the lower Cauca Valley of New Granada* in 1795. During the early stages of the wars for independence, Obando fought on the side of the royalist forces, leading guerrilla bands of blacks* and Indians*, but in 1822, after meeting with Simón Bolívar*, he switched sides. Obando fought with the forces of the army of Gran Colombia*. By the late 1820s, upset about Bolívar's assumption of dictatorial powers, Obando fought against him, emerging in the process as the leading caudillo* of southern Colombia*. When Bolívar died in 1830 and Rafael Urdaneta* came to power, Obando led a secessionist movement in southern Colombia, attaching the Cauca Valley to Ecuador*. Urdaneta's government collapsed later in the year, and Obando emerged as a provisional head of state in 1831, a position he held until 1832 when Francisco de Paula Santander* was elected as the first president of the republic of New Granada. On behalf of the new government, Obando then reconquered the Cauca Valley and brought it back to

Colombia. In 1836, Obando failed in an attempt to win the presidency, and by 1839, he was leading a guerrilla army fighting the national government in Pasto province. Defeated by nationalist troops in 1841, Obando fled to Peru*. He returned to Colombia in 1849 when General José Hilario López came to power. Obando's political star rose again. In 1852, he won the presidency, a position he held until 1854 when civil wars in Colombia led to his overthrow. José María Obando was killed in 1860 after he became a leader in an anti-nationalist guerrilla movement.

REFERENCE: Horacio Rodríguez Plata, *José María Obando, íntimo*, 1958.

OFICIAL REAL. The *oficial real*, or royal official, was the royal budget officer. In each Spanish colony, four royal officials were appointed and charged with the collection of taxes and revenues. King Philip II* also gave them judicial authority in tax cases. To pay any bill, all four had to sign every invoice, and it took four separate keys, one held by each royal official, to open official cash boxes where revenues were stored.

REFERENCE: C. H. Haring, *The Spanish Empire in America*, 1947.

O'HIGGINS, BERNARDO. Bernardo O'Higgins was born on August 20, 1778, in Chillan, Chile, in the viceroyalty of Río de la Plata*. O'Higgins was the illegitimate son of Ambrosia O'Higgins, who later became viceroy* of Peru*, and Isabel Riquelme. Although his father took an interest in Bernardo's welfare, he maintained no direct contact and probably met his son on only one occasion. In 1788, the younger O'Higgins was living with his maternal family while being educated by the Franciscans*. His adolescence was spent in Lima*, Peru, following which his father arranged for him to be educated in England. It was in England that O'Higgins cultivated his radical ideas, which were especially surprising in light of the fact that his father was the viceroy of Peru. In England, he met Francisco Miranda*, the champion of Latin American independence. It was his association with Miranda and the Masonic lodge Lautarina, which was dedicated to the independence of Latin America, that instilled in O'Higgins his sense of national pride toward Chile.

Throughout most of his time in Europe, O'Higgins suffered a chronic shortage of funds as a result of mismanagement by his trustees rather than of stinginess on the part of his father. By 1799, O'Higgins was anxious to return to Chile but could not raise the necessary funds for a return voyage. It was not until the death of his father on March 18, 1801, that he could finance his passage home. By 1802, O'Higgins had settled his father's estate and begun the life of a Chilean gentleman farmer working Las Canteras, the large hacienda* that he had inherited on the island of La Laja in southern Chile. He also maintained a house in Chillán, where in 1806 he became a member of the town council.

Before O'Higgins could settle into his new lifestyle, however, Napoleon Bonaparte invaded Spain in 1808, replacing Ferdinand VII* with his brother Joseph Bonaparte. Chileans were now confused about which leader deserved their loyalty. By 1809, economic and political conditions had deteriorated to a point where open rebellion was imminent, a state of affairs brought on more by poor leadership than by neglect from Spain. Politically, Chile was divided into two groups. One group preferred to maintain the present government machinery that was loyal to Ferdinand VII, while the other group called for a national junta, also loyal to the Spanish king. Conditions continued to deteriorate, and on September 18, 1810, the *cabildo abierto* voted to create a national junta in the name of Ferdinand VII. O'Higgins, who was the civil governor of La Laja, swore allegience to the new government. By 1811, Chile had elected a congress in which O'Higgins served as the deputy from Los Angeles. For the next two years, O'Higgins was to play a key role in his country's chaotic political affairs. On December 27, 1811, he was sent to Concepción as a representative of the Santiago* junta to negotiate a truce between the two provinces. Earlier in December, José Miguel Carrera*, the powerful representative from Santiago, had disbanded the congress and transferred power to a five-man junta with residual powers assumed by him. A rival junta in the province of Concepción now threatened to go to war over this presumed grab for power. As a result of the negotiation, a pact of twenty-five articles was signed on January 12, 1812. The pact stated that ultimate authority resided with the people of Chile, and it was agreed that congressional sessions would remain suspended until it was time to adopt a permanent constitution. Until that time, the government would be composed of three individuals, one from each province—Santiago, Concepción, and Coquimbo. Most notably, however, was the eleventh article, which stated that no representative from Spain would be allowed into the country until Ferdinand VII was restored to the throne; even when that occurred, if Chile had not already declared independence, then a new relationship would have to be constructed between the two countries. With regard to contemporary Spain, Chile was unofficially independent. In February 1812, in recognition for his services as congressional deputy, O'Higgins was named a lieutenant colonel of the army.

By early 1813, Chile had a written constitution. With Carrera firmly in control of the government, it appeared that the political turmoil was over. The viceroy of Peru, however, did not believe Chile to be sufficiently subservient to Spain or the viceroy. On March 27, 1813, a disciplinary expedition landed on Chilean soil. O'Higgins called out the militia and, in his first battle, on April 6, he successfully dislodged the royalist troops from Linares. His family, however, fared less well. Both his mother and sister were taken prisoner, and his hacienda was devastated. On November 27, O'Higgins was named general-in-chief of the Army of Restoration, the position held by Carrera. In an earlier attempt to check Carrera's power, O'Higgins had been elevated to the position of governor-intendant of Concepción. In a reorganization of the government, the junta named Francisco de la Lastra supreme director, a position created to dilute Carrera's power further. By the end of March 1814, both the Chilean and Peruvian armies were marching toward Santiago and a showdown. At this point, the British intervened, offering their services to find a peaceful solution. The result was the

Treaty of Lircay*, but it was eventually rejected by the viceroy and a new expedition was sent to Chile. This time the war went badly for the Chileans, and on October 2, 1814, the patriot forces were decisively defeated at Rancagua*. Thousands of Chileans, including O'Higgins and his family, fled across the Andes into Argentina*. While the royalists governed Chile for the next three years, O'Higgins prepared for the reconquest.

In January 1817, O'Higgins returned to Chile with a combined army led by José de San Martín*. This liberation army defeated the royalists in the Battle of Chacabuco* on February 12, 1817. With most of Chile reconquered, O'Higgins was elected supreme director. His election was more the result of his victories than because he enjoyed a following among the people. Men like Carrera, who were associated with Chilean nationalism in the eyes of the people, were either dead or exiled as the result of earlier political struggles. O'Higgins was a figure more associated with the continental independence movement.

Although he held the title of supreme director, O'Higgins was expected to act within the law, and throughout his six year rule, he was often effectively checked by the five-man senate. Although a reformer, politically O'Higgins was more a nineteenth-century liberal than a democrat. The job of setting up a government was difficult because of a nonexistent treasury and the need to secure Chilean territory that remained in the hands of the royalists. Furthermore, he was committed to launch an invasion force to liberate Peru. By May 1818, Chilean independence was secured with the defeat of royalist forces at Maipú*.

With independence secured, O'Higgins set about the task of creating a working government. Many of his policies were laudable and well received by the people. He instituted public works projects that included the construction of canals, roads, and bridges. He was also able to build a national navy, and he successfully mounted a military expedition to liberate Peru. Although a successful administrator, O'Higgins antagonized important elements of Chilean society. The Catholic Church* was angry because O'Higgins retained patronage over the church, and he exercised his power to nominate church officials and to decide which documents could be made public. His policies on religious tolerance were also viewed as an attack on the church. His anti-aristocratic policies included an attempt to abolish primogeniture, the elimination of noble insignia displayed on public doorways, and the abolition of hereditary titles. O'Higgins' greatest blunder, however, was the appointment of José Antonio Rodríguez as finance minister. His commercial regulations were viewed by the business community as an attempt to restrict free trade and, together with his financial irregularities, angered the powerful commercial community.

Events came to a head in May 1822, when O'Higgins ordered a convention to write a new constitution. On October 23, 1822, the new constitution set up a republican government with three branches. The office of supreme director was to be elective with a six-year term. It was stipulated that O'Higgins would serve the first term. This act was viewed as an attempt to perpetuate his power. In response, the province of Concepción rose in revolt and was followed by

Coquimbo. After much negotiation, O'Higgins agreed to relinquish power, transferring his authority to a national junta. Until his death in October 1842, he lived in exile in Peru.

REFERENCE: Jay Kinsbruner, *Bernardo O'Higgins*, 1968.

Michael Dennis

OIDOR. An *oidor* was a judge of an *audiencia*[*] in Spanish America. In the early years of the empire, the vast majority of the *oidores* were *peninsulares*[*], but by the eighteenth century, more and more *criollos*[*] were receiving appointments as *oidores*. By the time of the independence movements, the *criollos* were the majority of the *oidores*. To maintain impartiality, the Crown prohibited *oidores* from owning property, maintaining a business, holding an *encomienda*[*], attending weddings, receiving gifts, marrying in their area of jurisdiction, or even attending social functions. By the eighteenth century, in order to increase royal revenues, the Crown had started appointing men as *oidores* only after they had made large donations to the monarchy, in effect eliminating the efficacy of the administrative regulations that had been designed for impartiality. By the late 1700s, all attempts to guarantee the impartiality of *oidores* had been abandoned.

REFERENCE: C. H. Haring, *The Spanish Empire in America*, 1947.

OJEDA, ALONSO DE. Alonso de Ojeda was born around 1468 in Cuenca, Spain. On Christopher Columbus's[*] second voyage to the New World in 1493, Ojeda commanded one of the ships of the expedition. He played a central role in the exploration of Hispaniola[*] and the conquest of the Indians[*] there. Ojeda returned to Spain in 1495 and then headed up his own expedition to the northern coast of South America in 1499. He was named governor of Coquivacoa, a territory that surrounded the Lake Maracaibo area, in 1500. After voyages of discovery in 1502 and 1505, Ojeda was named governor of New Andalucía[*] (modern Colombia[*]). Ojeda earned a reputation as a ruthless oppressor of Indians, so much that Bartolomé de Las Casas[*] frequently criticized him. Ojeda came on hard times after a new colony he established on the Gulf of Uraba failed. Alonso de Ojeda died in poverty in 1515.

REFERENCE: Samuel Eliot Morrison, *The European Discovery of America: The Southern Voyages, A.D. 1492–1616*, 1974.

OLANETA, PEDRO ANTONIO DE. Pedro Antonio de Olaneta was a prominent *peninsular*[*] who eventually came to command royalist military forces in Upper Peru (Bolivia[*]). He had established a prosperous mercantile establishment in Salta[*], Argentina[*], and he was profoundly loyal to the Crown and the Church. By the early 1820s, Olaneta commanded all the royal armies in the region, but he mistakenly broke ranks with royal forces in Lima[*] when he heard rumors that they had gone over to the revolutionary side. His dissension precipitated the Separatist War of 1824 in which viceregal forces had to fight Olaneta as well as the rebels. Essentially, Olaneta seceded from the viceroyalty of Peru[*] and declared himself the absolute ruler of Chuquisaca. Aware of his misinformation, Olaneta rejoined the viceroyalty of Peru early in 1825 by signing the Treaty of Tarapaca. A relative betrayed him, informing Simón Bolívar* and Antonio de Sucre* of his whereabouts. Pedro Antonio de Olaneta was killed by rebel forces at the Battle of Tumsula on April 1, 1825.

REFERENCE: Dwight B. Heath, *Historical Dictionary of Bolivia*, 1972.

OLID, CRISTÓBAL DE. Born in Spain in 1492, Cristóbal de Olid was one of Hernán Cortés's* closest friends and confidants. He first arrived in Mexico with the conqueror in 1519. Olid was born in the town of Baeza in Andalucía, Spain. He distinguished himself as a valiant soldier during the conquest of the Aztecs* and was the first to charge down the causeway in May 1521 in the final siege of Tenochtitlán*. Cortés ordered Olid to subdue the western outposts of the Aztec Empire in 1522. Olid explored the Pacific coast of Mexico as far as Colima, where fierce opposition forced him to return to Tenochtitlán.

Discontented with his share of the Aztec wealth, Olid set sail for Honduras* in 1523, hoping to find another great civilization. Although Cortés had authorized this expedition, Olid first traveled to Cuba* for provisions. There he allied himself with Diego Velásquez*, the governor of Cuba and Cortés's bitter enemy. From Cuba, Olid sailed to Honduras, where he established the town of Triunfo de la Cruz and proclaimed himself independent of Cortés's authority, much as Cortés had once severed his allegiance to Velásquez. Olid then proceeded to claim Honduras in the name of both himself and Velásquez.

Back in Mexico, Cortés saw this pronouncement as an act of treason and sent a loyal officer, Francisco de las Casas, to arrest Olid. Shortly after las Casas's departure, Cortés, still livid, decided to travel to Honduras personally. The journey southward across the Guatemalan Petén took his forces through rugged, uncharted territory. The Spaniards and Indians* who had accompanied the expedition as guides and porters suffered grievously, and there were many casualties. In the meantime, Olid found his authority confronted from the south by Gil González* Dávila, the explorer of Costa Rica* and Nicaragua*. Shortly thereafter, the party under Las Casas also arrived to challenge Olid. Olid managed to capture both Gonzáles and Las Casas, but both escaped and in turn imprisoned Olid. After a summary trial, Las Casas and González beheaded Olid with a rusty sword in 1524.

REFERENCES: F. A. McNutt, *Fernando Cortes and the Conquest of Mexico, 1485-1547*, 1909; Michael C. Meyer and William L. Sherman, *The Course of Mexican History*, 1983; R. L. Woodward, Jr., *Central America: A Nation Divided*, 1983.

Virginia Garrard Burnett

OLMEC. The term "Olmec" has been used in at least four ways in Mesoamerican archaeological and ethnohistoric literature. (1) Fray Bernardino de Sahagún* reported a group of people named Olmec living in southern Vera Cruz* at the time of the Spanish Conquest. (2) Olmec is the name of a culture that existed on the Gulf coast in southern Vera Cruz, western Tabasco, and northern Chiapas* between 1200 and 600 B.C. (3) Olmec refers to art style(s) characteristic of the Olmec culture but more widely distributed in Mexico and northern Central America. (4) Finally, Olmec has been used as the name of a civilization with a distribution corresponding to that of the art style. Little is known of the Olmec in the first sense.

The Olmec culture, centered on the southern Gulf coast, was characterized by large earthen pyramids and platforms; a distinctive art style depicted on monumental and small stone sculpture, wood, pottery, and ceramic figurines; and trade over long distances for products such as obsidian, jade, and iron ore mirrors. Major Olmec communities include San Lorenzo, Laguna de los Cerros, and Tres Zapotes in Vera Cruz and La Venta in western Tabasco.

The origin of these Olmec is poorly understood. Excavations at San Lorenzo and La Venta have discovered the remains of small farming villages 500 to 700 years older (1700–1200 B.C.) than the earliest Olmec. The ceramics from these villages are quite similar to those recovered from archaeological sites on the Pacific coastal plain of Chiapas and Guatemala*. These settled farming villages on the Pacific coast are older than those in the Olmec area and appear to have been more precocious in the development of social hierarchies. On the basis of the ceramic evidence, it has been argued that the pre-Olmec peoples of the Gulf coast originated on the Pacific coast.

Excavations at San Lorenzo indicate a sudden transition from these pre-Olmec farming villages to the complex Olmec society with its monumental earthworks and sculpture. These diagnostic features appear without local antecedents. Furthermore, there is a marked change in ceramic style. Opinion is divided as to the source of these changes. Some have regarded them as local developments in which the antecedents and transition are poorly understood. Others have argued that the developments were introduced on the Gulf coast, but there are no clear antecedents elsewhere. Finally, it has been argued that the peoples of the Gulf coast combined local and exotic cultural traits to create a unique mestizo culture that we know as Olmec.

Subsequent Olmec history can be divided into three general periods. The first begins with the appearance of Olmec-style monuments at San Lorenzo around 1200 B.C. and ending around 900 B.C. During this period, San Lorenzo was the largest and most powerful community in the heartland. Large earthworks, monumental sculptures, and exotic trade items attest to the existence of a social hierarchy and to the power and organizational ability of the newly emerged Olmec elite. Contemporary objects from the Central Mexican Highlands executed in the Olmec style include abstract motifs on pottery and large, hollow figurines of human infants. Some figurines combine human and fantastic animal traits.

The second period dates from around 900 to 600/500 B.C. During this period, San Lorenzo was abandoned and reoccupied. La Venta, occupied during the pre-Olmec and first Olmec periods, reached its apogee only after 900 B.C. and became the major Olmec community. The Olmec art style, now less naturalistic, was most widespread during this period. Stelae with Olmec iconography occur as far south as Chalchuapa in El Salvador*. The numerous monuments of coastal Guatemala and Chiapas are from this period, as are the jade objects from the Maya* area. Rock art from Chalcatzingo, Morelos, and cave paintings from Guerrero also date from this period.

The final Olmec period, from around 600/500 to 300 B.C., was really an epi-Olmec period, during which La Venta and San Lorenzo were both abandoned. In the heartland, Tres Zapotes was the most important community. The classic form of the art style deteriorated and scenes depicted on stelae became more cluttered. There developed a number of regional styles with their common origin in the earlier Olmec style.

The Olmec style itself is best represented in its monumental sculpture. The earliest Olmec monumental sculpture evidences a surprising stylistic maturity. Monumental sculpture depicts human beings, animals, and composite figures with both human and animal characteristics. There is an emphasis on massive, rounded, dynamic, three-dimensional figures. Human figures include colossal heads, individuals seated with hands on knees, and seated figures depicted as emerging from the mouth of a cave on the side of monumental "altars." Animal figures include ducks, jaguars, monkeys, and plumed serpents. The composite figures characteristically combine human features with features that have traditionally been interpreted as those of the jaguar. Alternative sources for some of these features are the alligator and toad, *Bufo marinus*. Typical Olmec motifs include slanted oval eyes, fangs, claws, flaring upturned upper lips, flat noses, infantile faces, cleft heads, and abstract motifs such as crossed bands, flame eyebrows, and square eyes.

Objects in the Olmec style, especially portable sculptures, are not limited to the heartland on the Gulf coast. Outside the Olmec heartland, the Olmec style appears in a variety of media. Figurines, decorated ceramic vessels, paintings, low-relief rock carvings, small stone carvings, and monumental stone sculpture in Olmec style and Olmec-related styles occur in the central Mexican highlands, in the Chiapas highlands, along the Pacific coast of Chiapas and Guatemala, in the northern Guatemalan lowlands, and in El Salvador.

San José Mogote in the Valley of Oaxaca*, Las Bocas in Puebla*, Gualupita in Morelos, and Tlapacoya and Tlatilco in the Valley of Mexico are famous for their figurines and ceramic vessels. There are no polychrome paintings in the Guerrero rockshelters of Oxtotitlán and Juxtlahuaca. Chalcatzingo in Morelos has Olmec style low-relief rock carvings, and a composite altar. Teopantecuanitlan in Guerrero has monumental sculpture. Carved stone monuments with Olmec iconography occur at Xoc, Pijijiapan, Tzutzuculi, and Padre Piedra in Chiapas, at Abaj Takalik in Guatamela, and at Chalchuapa in El Salvador. Jade in the Olmec style is common in Guerrero and has been recovered from Maya sites in Yucatán* and northern Guatemala.

The traditional interpretations of these data have included the presence of Olmec colonists, missionaries, and/or traders. One persistent interpretation of

Olmec-style objects in the Mexican highlands, especially in the state of Guerrero, has been that the Olmec style originated there. It does appear that some objects with motifs in the Olmec style may be earlier in the highlands. More recent interpretations have stressed the development of trading relationships between Olmec elites on the Gulf coast and emerging local elites in the central Mexican highlands and elsewhere. These arguments focus on the exchange of products such as jade, obsidian, and mirrors for objects with exotic Olmec decorative motifs, objects that would give prestige and legitimacy to their owners and sanctify social hierarchies. Control of this trade has been seen as a source of economic power for the emerging elites.

In the 1940s, Miguel Covarrubias and Mexican archaeologists began to refer to the Olmec as the "Mother Culture." The implication was that the traits that defined Mesoamerica as a distinctive culture area originated with the Olmec. The Olmec civilization was the base from which the later regional cultures of Mesoamerica were derived.

REFERENCES: Ignacio Bernal, *The Olmec World*, 1969; Michael Coe, *America's First Civilization: Discovering the Olmecs*, 1968.

Edward B. Sisson

OLMEDO, JOSÉ JOAQUÍN. José Joaquín Olmedo was born on March 19, 1780, in Guayaquil*, Ecuador*. He studied law at the University of San Marcos* in Lima*, Peru*, and then built a legal career in Guayaquil. Known also as a poet and publicist, Olmedo played an influential role in the Ecuadorian independence movement. He was a deputy to the Cortes of Cádiz* in 1812, where he eloquently condemned the *mita** system of controlling Indian* labor. After the split from Gran Colómbia* in 1830, Olmedo became vice-president of the republic of Ecuador. On March 6, 1845, Olmedo helped lead the group that overthrew the government of Juan José Flores*. He died on February 17, 1847, in Guayaquil.

REFERENCES: Albert William Bork and Georg Maier, *Historical Dictionary of Ecuador*, 1973; Federico González Suárez, *Historia general de la República del Ecuador*, 7 vols., 1890–1904.

OÑA, PEDRO DE. After Alonso Ercilla y Zúñiga*, Pedro de Oña is the next best epic poet of the New World. He was born in southern Chile* in the province of Valdivia in 1570, in a military garrison that served as a supply point for the wars against the Araucanian* Indians. Orphaned at an early age, Oña spent his formative years in Lima*. He attended the University of San Marcos* and took an interest in literature and writing as a student. Although he wrote numerous works, Oña's most famous work is the epic poem *Arauco domado*, which is often invidiously compared with his fellow Chilean Ercilla's *La araucana*. Since Oña was a *criollo**, however, it can be safely stated that *Arauco domado* is the most important epic poem written by a native Latin American. Oña's *Arauco* was published in 1596. It is divided into 19 cantos, consisting of some 1,988 royal octaves. The clear purpose and organizing principle of *Arauco* was that of exalting Viceroy García Hurtado* de Mendoza and the Spaniards' role in the subjugation of the Araucanian Indians. In this sense, Oña's work differs sharply from Ercilla's *La Araucana*, which honors in many ways the courage and suffering of the Araucanian Indians. Most critics feel that although Oña's poetic abilities do not equal Ercilla's in epic tone, Oña exceeds Ercilla with regard to lyrical powers. Indeed, Oña succeeds in depicting colonial Chile in bucolic and sensitive strophes with much style.

The story treated in *Arauco domado* is a straightforward chronology recounting the Spaniards' battles with the Araucanians and their chief Caupolicán* in an effort to put down a rebellion. The Spanish forces were led by the future viceroy*, García Hurtado de Mendoza, who is exalted by the author for his courage and leadership. The war culminates with the capture of the Indian leader Galvarino who is sent back to his followers with his hands amputated. Oña died around 1643.

REFERENCES: Isaac J. Barrera, *Historiografía del Ecuador*, 1956; Michael Rheta Martin and Gabriel Lovett, *Encyclopedia of Latin American History*, 1968.

Sam L. Slick

OÑATE, JUAN DE. Juan de Oñate was born in Guadalajara*, New Spain*, in 1549. He earned his reputation because of his explorations and settlement of the Borderlands regions of New Spain. In 1598, with soldiers and Franciscan* missionaries, Oñate traveled north into what is today New Mexico* and then headed east into Kansas before returning to Mexico City*. Oñate's explorations prepared the way for the subsequent settlement of New Mexico. Oñate died in 1624.

REFERENCES: John F. Bannon, *The Spanish Borderlands Frontier, 1513-1821*, 1970; Peter Gerhard, *The North Frontier of New Spain*, 1982.

OQUENDO, MATEO ROSAS DE. See ROSAS DE OQUENDO, MATEO.

ORÁN. Orán is a city on the coast of North Africa where fleeing Muslims took refuge after the Spanish Crown reconquered Granada in 1492. Spanish forces then occupied the city in 1509 and stationed a governor there. Spain never tried to penetrate to the interior. Forces of the Ottoman Turks seized the city in 1708 and held it until 1732, when Spain recaptured it. Spain finally abandoned Orán in 1792, when the Ottoman Turks took over again.

REFERENCE: David P. Henige, *Colonial Governors from the Fifteenth Century to the Present*, 1970.

ORDAS, DIEGO DE. Diego de Ordas was born in Zamora, Spain, in 1480. He made his way to the New World in 1509 with the expedition of Alonso de Ojeda*, who explored the northern coast of Colombia*. In 1511, Ordas was involved in the conquest of Cuba*, and in 1519 and 1520, he joined with Hernán Cortés's* expedition to the Valley of Mexico. Ordas then returned to Spain for nearly a decade before heading up his own expedition. In 1531, he sailed up the Orinoco River as far as the Meta River. Unsuccessful in locating wealthy

Indian[*] tribes, the expedition returned to the Venezuelan coast, where Ordas was arrested by Spanish officials on the island of Cubagua who contested his right to be exploring the region. Ordas was shipped to Santo Domingo[*] where he was released. On his return voyage to Spain in 1532, Diego de Ordas died en route.

REFERENCE: Florentino P. Embid, *Diego de Ordas, compañero de Cortés y explorador del Orinoco*, 1950.

ORE, LUIS GERÓNIMO DE. Luis Gerónimo de Ore was born in Ayacucho, Peru[*], in 1554. Brilliant and dedicated, he learned to speak Spanish, Quechua[*], and Aymara[*] as a child, and he was ordained a Franciscan[*] priest in 1582. Between 1584 and 1598, Ore labored among the Collagua Indians of Peru and worked on producing catechisms in various Indian[*] languages. His description of that work was published as *Symbolo católico indiano* in 1598. That year, Ore became the vicar of the Franciscan convent in Lima[*], where he taught Quechua and Aymara to prospective missionaries. He went to Rome in 1604 and published *Rituale seu manuale peruanum*—an Indian catechism—in 1607. It was subsequently published in Spanish, Quechua, Aymara, Mochica, Puquina, Guaraní[*], and Portuguese. Ore led a group of Franciscan missionaries to Cuba[*] and Florida[*] in 1614, and he returned to Spain in 1618. One year later, he was appointed bishop of Concepción[*] in Chile[*]. He died there on January 30, 1630.

REFERENCE: Luis Gerónimo de Ore, *The Martyrs of Florida, 1513-1616*, ed. and trans. J. M. Geiger, 1937.

ORELLANA, FRANCISCO DE. Francisco de Orellana was born in Trujillo, Spain, around 1511. As a young man, he headed to the New World where he participated in the conquest of Peru[*]. Orellana founded the city of Guayaquil[*]. In March 1541, he joined Gonzalo Pizarro's[*] expedition into eastern Peru, and after splitting from the main group, Orellana led approximately 50 men into the Amazon basin. Theirs was the first European expedition to sail down the Amazon to the Atlantic Ocean, a journey completed in August 1542. They then sailed northwest along the northern Brazilian coast to the island of Cubagua. Orellana returned to Spain in 1543. In 1544, King Charles I[*] named him governor of New Andalucía[*] and authorized him to colonize those areas not already under Portuguese jurisdiction. He sailed for the New World in May 1545 but died in 1546 while exploring one of the Amazon tributaries.

REFERENCE: Gaspar de Carvajal, *The Discovery of the Amazon*, 1934.

ORIBE, MANUEL. Manuel Oribe was born in Montivideo[*], Río de la Plata[*], in 1792, to one of the city's leading families. He joined the independence movement in 1811 and, for the next ten years, he fought in Uruguay[*] and Argentina[*]. Oribe became associated with Juan Antonio Lavalleja[*] and rose to prominence in the drive for Uruguayan independence. Along with Lavalleja, Oribe was one of the famous "Thirty-Three" people who eventually achieved the country's independence. Under Fructuosa Rivera[*], Uruguay's first president,

Oribe served as minister of war and the navy, and in March 1835, he became Uruguay's second president. When Rivera led a revolt against Oribe in 1836, Oribe formed the Blanco Party to give himself some political strength. Oribe had to resign as president in 1838. He then fled to Buenos Aires*, where he organized a revolt of his own. In 1843, Oribe returned to Uruguay at the head of a military force that soon conquered much of the country. He placed Montevideo under a military siege that lasted nine years but never succeeded. Oribe retired from public life in 1851. He died in 1857.

REFERENCE: Setembrino Pereda, *Los partidos históricos uruguayos*, 1918.

ORTIZ DE DOMÍNGUEZ, JOSEFA. Josefa Ortiz de Domínguez was born in New Spain* in 1768. She married Miguel Domínguez, who became mayor of the city of Querétaro. She was an early advocate of Mexican independence from Spain and allowed rebel leaders to use her home for refuge and planning. In 1810, she was captured and imprisoned in a convent for a short time. Ortiz de Domínguez was released when she promised to cease her revolutionary activities. She died in Mexico City* in 1829.

REFERENCE: John A. Caruso, *The Liberators of Mexico*, 1967.

OSEJO, RAFAEL FRANCISCO. Rafael Francisco Osejo was born in Nicaragua* in 1790. He received an undergraduate degree from the University of León and then began a teaching career, concentrating on law, philosophy, and mathematics. Osejo came from a mixed racial background, which made him an ardent proponent of black, Indian*, and mestizo* rights. In the 1820s, Osejo became a leading advocate of independence in Central America. He was a member of the Junta de Ligados de los Pueblos and then secretary of the first constituent assembly of Costa Rica* in 1822. He became a vociferous opponent of any political affiliation with Agustín Iturbide's* imperial Mexico, and in the later 1820s and early 1830s, he served as a member of the Costa Rican legislature. Rafael Osejo died in 1848.

REFERENCE: Chester Zelaya G., *El bachiller Osejo*, 1971.

OSORIO, MARIANO. Mariano Osorio was born in Spain in 1777 and spent his career in the Spanish army. He received an assignment in Chile* and in 1814 defeated the rebel forces at the Battle of Rancagua*. Impressed with his leadership skills, Viceroy Fernando de Abascal y Souza* appointed him governor of Chile. Osorio held the post from October 9, 1814, to December 26, 1815. Osorio ruled with an iron hand and imprisoned many patriots on the Juan Fernández Islands. Even then, Abascal found him too soft on the rebels and replaced him with Francisco Casimiro Marco* del Pont Ańgel Díaz y Méndez. Osorio continued his military activity, defeating rebel forces at the Battle of Cancha Rayada* in 1818 but suffering a final defeat at the Battle of Maipú* later in the year. Osorio escaped to Peru* after the battle but died in Havana*, Cuba*, in 1819.

REFERENCE: Salvatore Bizarro, *Historical Dictionary of Chile*, 1987.

OTOMÍ. The Otomí were (and are) an important indigenous group in Mexico. Prior to the Spanish conquest, they inhabited considerable portions of central Mexico, primarily to the north and west of the Valley of Mexico. Seven ethnic-linguistic groups are subsumed under the rubric Otomí, and include Otomí proper, Mazahua, Matlatzinca, and Pame. Friar Bernardino de Sahagún* considered the Otomí, as Otonchichimeca, a type of Chichimec* or nomadic hunting-and-gathering group. After stating this, however, he went on to describe the Otomí as well-clothed, "civilized" agriculturalists. There were probably Otomí engaged in both ways of life. Otomí society was complex, with rulers, nobles, priests, and other types of secular and religious officials, but most of the men engaged in farming and the women were expert weavers. The Aztecs* (México) viewed the Otomí as hardworking, but also as gaudy dressers, greedy, and careless managers of their resources. They would scold their children by comparing them with Otomí.

Numerous Otomí city-states fell to the Aztec Triple Alliance in the fifteenth and early sixteenth centuries. The Otomí paid their Aztec overlords tribute in cotton and henequen clothing, warrior costumes, bins of foodstuffs, wood products, lime, and live eagles. The present-day Otomí are distributed in relatively scattered locales throughout central highland Mexico. They number approximately 375,000 people.

REFERENCES: Pedro Carrasco, *Los Otomíes*, 1979; Leonardo Manrique, "The Otomi," in *Handbook of Middle American Indians*, 1969; Bernardino de Sahagún, *Florentine Codex*, 1950–1982.

Frances F. Berdan

OVALLE, FRIAR ALONSO DE. Born to prominent parents in Santiago*, Chile*, in 1601, Ovalle entered the Jesuit* order at the age of 17, against his parents' wishes. He spent some time in Argentina*, but returned to Chile where he gained renown as an educator. He eventually was sent by the Jesuits on missions to Europe where he spent many years. While in Rome, he wrote his famous *Histórica Relación del Reino de Chile y de las misiones y ministerios que ejercita en él la Compañía de Jesús*. According to some, the work was a response to Ovalle's observation that Europeans know nothing whatsoever about colonial Chile. Ovalle died while returning to his homeland in 1650. *Histórica Relación* is divided into eight books. It was written and published in Rome in 1646. Since Ovalle wrote the work without benefit of sufficient documents or the immediate presence of Chile, its people, and its countryside, the historical accuracy of his work is sometimes wanting. It is the grace, elegance, and clarity with which he wrote, however, that confirms *Histórica Relación* as one of colonial Chile's great literary works. Ovalle died in 1651.

REFERENCE: José Toribio Medina, *Historia de la literatura colonial de Chile*, 1878.

Sam L. Slick

OVANDO, NICOLÁS DE. Nicolás de Ovando was born in Spain around 1451. As governor of Hispaniola* (1502–1509), he firmly established royal control over the entire island, transforming it into a stable, productive colony whose accumulated resources made possible the conquests of New Spain* and Peru*. Moreover, the *encomienda** system that Ovando devised for the purpose of legally harnessing native labor became the fundamental institution regulating Spanish-Indian* relations for most of the colonial period, as well as the primary means by which the Spaniards turned conquered lands into colonies. A knight-commander of the Order of Alcantara, Ovando had served the Catholic sovereigns faithfully in the peninsular territories entrusted to his military brotherhood. His appointment to the governorship of Hispaniola in 1501 represented the official abrogation of Christopher Colombus's* viceregal powers, which had been sus-pended in 1500 by Francisco de Bobadilla,* the Crown's special overseas in-vestigator. In their instructions to Bobadilla, King Ferdinand* and Queen Isabella* traced the outlines of the administrative structure that would come to typify Spain's transoceanic bureaucracy.

The new governor entered Santo Domingo* harbor in April 1502, accompanied by a huge fleet carrying 2,500 colonists, including 73 families, the largest ex-pedition yet sent to America. Only 300 Europeans lived on the island at the time of Ovando's arrival. He quickly conducted a royally mandated judicial review of his predecessor Bobadilla's rule, the first recorded instance of a process that Spain's subsequent monarchs would continue to employ as a check on their appointees. A destructive hurricane leveled Santo Domingo later in 1502, per-mitting the governor to rebuild the capital at a more favorable site. The orderly, gridiron pattern that he utilized in the settlement influenced town planners who followed his example in their layouts of other New World municipalities.

Though Ovando obeyed the letter of his orders regarding the collection of Columbus's share of Hispaniola's gold, his personal treatment of the Discoverer was scornful. He denied the Admiral access to the shelter of Santo Domingo just prior to the aforementioned hurricane. Worse, he arrogantly ignored Co-lumbus's storm warnings, a blunder resulting in the loss of 20 vessels, 500 lives, and 200,000 gold *castellanos*. In 1503–1504, the governor tarried several months before sending rescuers to Jamaica*, where Columbus was marooned. By harsh and treacherous means, Ovando broke the power of native chieftains in the eastern and western peripheries of Hispaniola, thereby incorporating them into the island's booming gold-mining economy. In response to his sovereigns' wishes to concentrate Spanish settlers, Ovando oversaw the chartering of 15 white settlements. His organization of the mining* industry substantially boosted pro-duction and royal revenue while reducing taxation rates. Stock-raising was prac-ticed as the island's second most important economic activity. Commerce with Europe crested in 1508. The New World's first hospital was built. Geographic surveys of both Cuba* and Hispaniola were carried out. The colony's prosperity reached its zenith. After Isabella's death in 1504, while a succession crisis shook the homeland, Ovando maintained order in a far-flung possession.

By linking forced Amerindian toil with Christianization and royal tribute, Ovando had salved the queen's conscience, offering a solution to the dilemma stemming from the refusal of recently freed Indian slaves to work for their former overlords. The Iberian *encomienda* was the semi-feudal paradigm applied to the Caribbean island by the resourceful agent of Castile*. Deserving settlers would evangelize and protect native wards who would in turn donate their services to the *encomendero* at the Crown's pleasure. Hispaniola's *encomenderos*, unlike their European counterparts, did not share the cultural ties with their charges that might have ameliorated their behavior toward them. Furthermore, Spain was months away, making abuses difficult to correct promptly. Though the *encomienda* eventually evolved into a gentler, more paternalistic institution, its early grantees regarded it as an arrangement differing little from slavery*. The seeds for a more humane, orderly Indian policy, however, had been sown.

In 1507–1508, Hispaniola's Arawak* population plummeted, in part due to an epidemic originating in Spain. Furthermore, a severe hurricane struck the island in the latter year. These events forced Ovando to look outward. He sent Juan Ponce de León* on a successful expedition to Puerto Rico* and, with the king's permission, inaugurated a genocidal series of slaving forays to the Bahamas*. Ovando was replaced by Diego Columbus*, the Admiral's son, in 1509. The ex-governor, who had requested retirement five years earlier, returned to Spain, wrote his memoirs, published a map of Santo Domingo, and died a wealthy and esteemed man.

REFERENCES: Troy S. Floyd, *The Columbus Dynasty in the Caribbean, 1492-1526*, 1973; Ursula Lamb, *Fray Nicolás de Ovando: Gobernador de las Indias*, 1956.

Frank Marotti

OVIEDO Y VALDÉS, GONZALO FERNÁNDEZ. Gonzalo Fernández Oviedo y Valdés was born in Madrid, Spain, in 1478. He was not only one of the most important chroniclers, but also the first official chronicler of the Indies appointed by the Spanish Crown. Oviedo spent time in Cuba*, Hispaniola*, and the Caribbean coast of Central America. He made an astonishing 12 Atlantic crossings between Spain and the Spanish colonies during his lifetime. His first major work was *Sumario de la Historia Natural de las Indias* (1525), a kind of deeply personal, autobiographical recollection of the author's experiences with the incredible flora, fauna, physical geography, and peoples of the New World. Oviedo's *Sumario* is seen by most as a preview of what was to be his major work: *Historia general y natural de las Indias, islas y Tierra Firme del Mar Océano*, written between 1526 and 1549. In this work, Oviedo not only provided an encompassing view of the New World from 1492 to 1549, but he also articulated a distinctly imperialistic view of Spain's right and destiny to possess and govern the new world. Since Oviedo's defense of Spanish rule was based in part on a disdain for the Indians*, his *Historia* became a counterpoint to Bartolomé de las Casas's* defense of the Indians. He died in Valladolid, Spain, in 1557.

REFERENCE: A. Curtis Wilgus, *The Historiography of Latin America: A Guide to Historical Writing, 1500-1800*, 1975.

Sam L. Slick

P

PÁEZ, JOSÉ ANTONIO. José Antonio Páez, leader of the *llaneros* (plains-men), was one of the major military and political figures of Venezuelan independence and the dominant leader of the new nation from 1829 to 1848. He was born in 1790, the son of a clerk. Like most of his countrymen, he was mestizo*. At the age of 15, he shot a man in self defense and fled to the plains. There the harsh life shaped him and gave him an understanding of the other rough men of the *llanos*. He was physically very powerful and as a leader drew much from his image of strength. He did not become literate until maturity, however, even supposedly not learning to use a knife and fork until after he became a general.

During the war for independence, the *llanero* cavalry was a major force. Although without instruction in tactics, Páez proved a master of guerrilla warfare, in which he participated from 1809 to the expulsion of the Spanish in 1823. He also understood well that the *llaneros* were more motivated by the desire for plunder than by ideology or vague notions of patriotism. Thus, he rose quickly to leadership. He became known as the Lion of Apure, the region in which he operated. Initially, *llaneros* under José Tomás Boves* supported the royalists, but they were beginning to switch to the side of the patriots by 1816 and Páez gained more adherents. In September 1816, he coordinated with the Colombian patriot *llanero* leader, Francisco Santander* and later gave allegiance to the Liberator, Simón Bolívar*. This allegiance was ratified more formally when the two met on January 30, 1818. The two had different styles and goals, and Páez's loyalty was sometimes suspect, yet they worked successfully together. From February 1818 to April 1819, the patriots under Páez and Bolívar generally controlled the Orinoco plains, while the royalists controlled Andean Venezuela. Páez played a key role in victories throughout the independence period—at Queseras del Medio, Carabobo*, and Puerto Cabello.

From 1821 to 1831, military leaders came to dominate a number of provinces of Venezuela*. With Bolívar frequently absent, General Páez emerged as their spokesman and the most powerful Venezuelan leader. On May 16, 1826, he was formally made civil and military chief of Venezuela. On April 30, he revolted against the administration of the Colombian vice-president, Santander, and the dominance by Colombia* under the centralized government of Gran Colombia*. Some writers have also portrayed that conflict as one between the orientation of the caudillo* (represented by Páez) and of constitutional order (represented by Santander). The revolt was not against President Bolívar, whom Páez urged to return and settle the dispute. On January 1, 1827, Bolívar issued an amnesty for those in rebellion. The next day, Páez accepted and reaffirmed loyalty to Bolívar. When Bolívar again departed, he left Páez in command. Some authors have criticized Bolívar for being too generous and thus laying the seeds of future rebellion. In any event, in November and December 1829, Páez led a successful and popular secessionist movement, this time clearly directed against the rule of Colombia and Bolívar. In January 1830, he called for elections for an independent Venezuelan congress. Bolívar was too weak both politically and physically to prevent the separation.

Páez remained the dominant figure of the new nation until 1848 and did not disappear from the national scene until 1863. He served as elected president in 1831–1835 and 1839–1843, with his friends Carlos Soublette* and José Vargas filling the remaining terms. The end of his influence came with the rise of the Liberals. In 1850, after leading unsuccessful revolts, he was exiled to New York, returning as dictator 1861–1863. Unable to re-establish order, he left again for the United States, where he remained, except for a brief period in Argentina*, until his death in New York on May 7, 1873. During his ascendancy, he worked with (some say for) the conservative (but moderate) propertied class of Caracas* in a period that has commonly been seen as prosperous, progressive, and relatively orderly. The role of the Church, for example, was curtailed without the rancor that made the issue of church and state a long-term problem in most other Latin American nations.

Both Páez and his rule have been described in contradictory terms. Some authors have characterized him as greedy, inconstant, lacking discipline, vain, and lusting for power. He has also been seen as careful, tolerant, well liked, fair, egalitarian, not interested in personal gain, governing well and rising from barbarism to civilization. He has been particularly blamed for establishing the tradition of *caudillismo* (personalistic rule by a strong man), which racked Venezuela long after his departure. He has, however, also been considered the best of the caudillos because he was capable both of raising armies and of political maneuver and compromise. He has often been compared to Juan Manuel de Rosas* of Argentina but was less ruthless and more respectful of the rule of law. He has been called the founder of the nation, and to Venezuelans, he generally stands second only to Bolívar.

REFERENCES: Robert L. Gilmore, *Caudillism and Militarism in Venezuela, 1810-1910*, 1964; Salvador de Madariaga, *Bolívar*, 1952; William D. Marsland and Amy L.,

Venezuela Through Its History, 1954; Gerhard Masur, *Simón Bolívar*, 1969; Guillermo Moron, *A History of Venezuela*, 1963.

Robert E. Biles

PAMPANGA. Pampanga is the fertile, densely populated rice-growing province of central Luzon* in the Philippines*. Pampanga is almost entirely flat, except for the foothills of the Zambales Range to the west and the solitary cone of an extinct volcano, Mt. Arayat, that dominate the plain. Pampanga's drainage is to the south. Many rivers join the Río Grande de Pampanga, which empties into Manila Bay through an extensive deltaic swamp. Other parts of the province are also swampy, while the higher ground is planted in rice and sugar*. Most of the soil is fertile. Pampanga province, as its borders stand today, is only the core of a larger area that the Spanish called Lower and Upper Pampanga, the region where speakers of the distinctive Pampangan language lived. Pampangans are strongly loyal to their own ethnic group. Due to its productivity and its proximity (only 35 miles) to Manila*, Pampanga has a history deeply affected by national events. Spaniards first arrived in Manila Bay in 1570. The next year, Martín de Goiti pacified central Luzon and organized Pampanga as a province. Spanish greed soon caused problems: Pampangans were drafted in 1583 to mine gold and were not allowed to return home to plant rice; this policy caused a famine in 1584 and a revolt in 1585. The Pampangans sought allies from Borneo to expel the Europeans, but were betrayed by a Pampangan woman who was married to a Spanish soldier. The uprising was nipped in the bud.

Pampangan history raises many puzzling questions. Although the province was certainly exploited and small revolts flared occasionally, the dominant theme for 300 years was loyalty to Spain, antipathy to other Philippine peoples, and Pampangan readiness to fight for Manila abroad and at home. Indeed, Pampangan troops did for Spain what the Gurkhas did for the British—they served as brave, loyal troops whose sense of honor was not offended by fighting in the employ of foreigners. Various reasons have been offered, including the strong hold that the Catholic Church* exercised in Pampanga and the strong ties that bound peasants to their collaborationist elite. None of the explanations is entirely satisfactory, but the fact remains that, except for an abortive revolt led by Francisco Maniago in 1660, Pampangans gave the Spanish little trouble until the later phases of the revolution in 1898.

In the case of the Maniago revolt, its immediate causes were Spanish cruelty and excessive zeal in enforcing compulsory timber-cutting laws and overtaxation in the form of compulsory rice sales to the government. Spain induced Maniago to surrender in return for amnesty and the relaxation of the onerous tax and labor requisitions. Maniago had little choice, as the silly Spanish governor Manrique de Lara co-opted a Pampangan chief from Arayat, Juan Makapagal. The "revolt" ended with no death or destruction.

Agriculture in Pampanga, as elsewhere in the islands, shifted to meet the demands of the export market after Spanish mercantilist* policy gave way to free trade in the early nineteenth century. The forests in Upper Pampanga were cleared for extensive sugar haciendas*, representing the genesis of the peasant misery plaguing central Luzon today. Even so, Pampangan sugar tenants were able to lead somewhat independent lives; if they felt aggrieved, they still did not rebel. Pampanga was blessedly free of the huge estates known as "friar lands" that caused so much discontent in the Tagalog* provinces. When the Philippine Revolution began in 1896, most of its leaders were Tagalogs. Many Pampangans fought for Spain. When Spain lost to the United States the revolution became the Philippine-American War, and many Pampangans joined General Emilio Aguinaldo* to fight for Philippine independence.

REFERENCES: John A. Larkin, *The Pampangans*, 1972; Marshall S. McLennan, *The Central Luzon Plain*, 1980.

Ross Marlay

PANAMA. Darién was the first Spanish settlement on the North American mainland. In 1509, King Ferdinand* of Spain granted concessions for the settlement of the mainland of the Americas. Alonso de Ojeda* received the territory known as New Andalucía*, which stretched from modern-day Panama's Gulf of Darién eastward. Ojeda attempted to lead an expedition into New Andalucía, but met with great difficulty due to the ruggedness of the terrain and the fierceness of the local Indians*. Ojeda was gravely wounded and returned to Santo Domingo*, leaving Francisco Pizarro*, the future conqueror of Peru*, in command. Ojeda died in 1510 in Santo Domingo, at which time Pizarro was replaced by Martín Francisco de Enciso. Enciso led an expedition to Darién and captured an Indian village on the hot, swampy Caribbean coast. There he established the town of Santa María La Antigua de Darién, or simply Darién.

Enciso was not an able leader, and he relied heavily on the guidance of Vasco Núñez de Balboa*, a Spanish soldier who had stowed away on Enciso's ship to flee indebtedness in Hispaniola*. Balboa eventually accused Enciso of mismanagement, arrested him, and sent him back to Spain. He then consolidated and stabilized Darién. Balboa defeated the Indians of the region and obtained from them sizable amounts of gold and pearls. He established an agricultural economy for Darién, based on Indian labor, and the settlement thrived.

Darién served as the base for Balboa's expedition to find the "Southern Sea" of which local Indians had spoken. On September 29, 1513, Balboa was the first European to sight the Pacific Ocean, claiming all that it bordered for Spain. Back in Spain, Enciso filed formal complaints against Balboa, and the Crown sent Pedro Arias de Ávila* (more commonly known as Pedrarias Dávila) to relieve Balboa's command. While Pedrarias was on his way to Panama, the Crown received word of Balboa's discovery of the Pacific and pragmatically named Balboa "adelantado* of the Southern Sea." Nonetheless, in 1517, Pedrarias had Balboa convicted of treason and beheaded; he then took over command of Darién. The settlement of Darién suffered under Pedrarias's administration. Pedrarias, a rapacious and ruthless man, showed little mercy toward the local natives, and disease, mistreatment, and overwork decimated the local population. In 1519, Pedrarias moved the Spanish population from the pesthole of Darién to the more healthful climate of Panama City on the Pacific coast. In 1524, Darién was abandoned, but Panama City was destroyed by the English pirate Henry Morgan in 1671 and then reconstructed a few miles away.

Located at the isthmus between the Atlantic and Pacific oceans, Panama benefited historically from the transworld commerce, especially from Spanish commercial regulations that required all commerce to and from Peru to move through Panama. It prospered particularly as the point at which gold shipments from Peru were sent to Spain. After 1740, however, Panama City's fortunes declined when Spain permitted the bullion galleons to sail through the Straits of Magellan between Peru and Spain. Panama quickly became a backwater of the empire. With the recreation of the viceroyalty of New Granada* in 1739, Panama came under its jurisdiction and remained there until 1821 when it became part of Gran Colombia*.

REFERENCES: Basil C. Hedrick and Anne K. Hedrick, *Historical Dictionary of Panama*, 1970; R. L. Woodward, Jr., *Central America: A Nation Divided*, 1983.

Virginia Garrard Burnett

PANAMA, *AUDIENCIA* OF. The *audiencia** was a court and regional administrative district founded by royal decree in 1535. It began functioning in 1538. The *Audiencia* of Panama included most of the territory conquered and controlled by Pedro Arias de Ávila* (Pedrarias Dávila) until his death in 1531. This included present-day Panama*, Costa Rica*, and Nicaragua*, although the latter was a disputed territory considered by Pedro de Alvarado* of Guatemala* to be part of the viceroyalty of New Spain*, which was also established in 1535. In 1543, King Philip II* attempted to clarify the issue by eliminating the *audiencia* of Panama and establishing in its place the *Audiencia* of Los Confines*, which had jurisdiction over Tabasco, Yucatán*, and all of the provinces south through Panama. The *audiencia* of Panama was re-established briefly in 1567 after the dissolution of the *audiencia* of Los Confines. It was then placed under the viceroyalty of Peru*. The *audiencia* held jurisdiction over Panama, Costa Rica, and Nicaragua until the northern two territories were incorporated into the new *audiencia* of Guatemala* in 1570. The *audiencia* of Panama was abolished briefly in 1718, re-established in 1722, and then permanently suppressed in 1751.

REFERENCE: Mark A. Burkholder and D. S. Chandler, *From Impotence to Authority: The Spanish Crown and the American Audiencias, 1687–1808*, 1977.

Virginia Garrard Burnett

PANGASINAN. Pangasinan is a Philippine* province of central Luzon*, situated at the northwest end of the great rice-producing plain. Pangasinan has a coastline on the Lingayen Gulf, and its exposed location brought contact with Ming Dynasty Chinese traders, sixteenth-century Spanish explorers, and twentieth-century Japanese invaders. The original inhabitants spoke their own language, related to Ilocano. Juan de Salcedo reconnoitered the coast in 1572 and reported settlements near the shore, but the interior was largely uninhabited. Augustinian[*] fathers founded the city of San Carlos in 1587, and the capital, Dagupan, in 1590. Pangasinan was made a province in 1611. Dominicans[*] spread Catholicism too, but the people retained many elements of their pre-Christian religion.

Spanish efforts to replenish their treasury after war with the Dutch in 1660 ignited rebellions in various provinces on Luzon. Andrés Malong proclaimed himself king of Pangasinan. His followers desecrated Catholic churches and killed Spaniards foolish enough not to have fled to Manila[*]. Malong urged local leaders elsewhere in the north to kill Spaniards too, but his reign lasted only one month. Manila regained control, and Malong was executed. A similar scenario was played out on a larger scale a century later. Spain had gone to war with the British, who occupied Manila. The Spaniards tried to make up their losses by overtaxing the peasants. In 1762, Juan de la Cruz Palaris gathered thousands of followers and expelled all Spaniards in Pangasinan. This time, the rebels controlled Pangasinan for more than a year before the Spaniards attacked with the help of thousands of loyal Ilocano troops. The rebels retreated to the mountains. Palaris was hanged in 1765.

Nineteenth-century economic development brought Pangasinan population growth, intensified agriculture, and increased social tensions. Ilocanos migrated down the coast to establish whole new villages in the marginal zones of Pangasinan, which soon began producing more rice than any other province in the Philippines. Eventually a railroad was built connecting Dagupan to Manila. Some sugar[*] and tobacco[*] were planted, but the provincial economy grew more and more dependent on rice exports. This situation put peasants at the mercy of price fluctuations that they could not understand, much less control.

When the Philippine Revolution began in 1896, Pangasinan was peripheral to the fighting, but a millenial movement known as the Guardia de Honor fought alongside the Katipunan[*]. American troops inherited the problem after taking the Philippines from Spain. At one point, the Americans held in a Pangasinan jail a man who styled himself "God Almighty," along with a "Jesus Christ," a "Virgin Mary," and the "Holy Ghost." Christ and the Holy Ghost were hanged.

REFERENCE: David R. Sturtevant, *Agrarian Unrest in the Philippines*, 1969.

Ross Marlay

PAPAL BULL "ALTITUDO DIVINI CONSIILI." The Papal bull, "Altitudo Divini Consiili," was issued by Pope Paul III on June 1, 1537. In the bull, the pope insisted that the religious should not omit the slightest part of the ceremony of baptism—except in the rite of salt, white robes, and candles—with some neophytes. Instead, the sacrament had to be administered with Holy Water, with each neophyte catechized and exorcised. The Indians[*] had to be impressed with the sacrament. The execution of the bull was ordered by the synod of 1539. According to the bull, there were only four circumstances in which the religious could administer the sacrament without complete ceremonies: siege, shipwreck, grave and dangerous sickness, and insecurity of the country with imminent peril of death. Pope Paul III issued this bull after finding the Franciscans* to be at fault for administering baptism without the complete ceremony. The pope found the religious at fault in principle only, since the essential rite had been respected. As a consequence, a publication was ordered under the title of *Manual de adultos* for the guidance of missionaries. Only two folios of this publication are extant.

REFERENCES: Francisco Morales, *Ethnic and Social Background of the Franciscan Friars in Seventeenth-Century Mexico*, 1930; William Shiels, *King and Church: The Rise and Fall of the Patronato Real*, 1961.

Raysa Amador

PAPAL BULL "DUDUM SIQUIDEM." On September 26, 1493, Pope Alexander VI* issued the bull "Dudum siquidem." The New World discoveries of Christopher Columbus* set in motion an intense rivalry between Spain and Portugal for title to the new lands. Since the pope was Spanish by birth, Ferdinand* and Isabella* pressured him into recognizing Spanish claims to the New World. "Dudum siquidem" gave Spain the freedom to explore in the southern and western Atlantic all the way to "the Indies," in effect nullifying Portuguese claims to the New World. The bull, however, was modified the next year by the Treaty of Tordesillas*.

REFERENCE: H. Vander Linden, "Alexander VI and the Demarcation of the Maritime and Colonial Domains of Spain and Portugal, 1493–1494," *American Historical Review*, 22 (1916–17), 1–20.

PAPAL BULL "EXIMIAE DEVOTIONIS." On November 16, 1501, Pope Alexander VI* issued the bull "Eximiae devotionis," which was central to the development of the Patronato Real* in the New World. In the bull, the pope declared that it was the responsibility of the Spanish Crown to maintain the Roman Catholic Church* in the New World and to propagate the faith among the Indians*. In order to carry out that responsibility, the pope authorized the Crown and royal officials to collect all church tithes in the region and to disburse all church monies there.

REFERENCE: Robert Ricard, *The Spiritual Conquest of Mexico*, 1966.

PAPAL BULL "EXPONI NOBIS FECISTI." Issued by Pope Adrian VI on May 10, 1522, the bull, "Exponi nobis fecisti," granted permission to all the mendicant orders that went to the Indies, especially the Franciscans*, to spread the belief in God among the Indians*. The pope granted the rights and prerogatives of the parish priest to the mendicant orders and authorized them to administer the sacraments. There was a struggle for power between the mendicant orders and the bishops as to who had the right to administer the sacraments in the New World. The essential cause of the bishops' animosity lay in the situation created by this bull and by later papal orders. In effect, the pope allowed the missionaries to come to the Indies to convert and instruct the Indians in the faith. The pope gave the Spanish monarchs and the royal council the right to control missionaries expeditions. These two entities were thus allowed to exercise religious and papal functions.

REFERENCES: Francisco Morales, *Ethnic and Social Background of the Franciscan Friars in Seventeenth-Century Mexico*, 1930; William Shiels, *King and Church: The Rise and Fall of the Patronato Real*, 1961.

Raysa Amador

PAPAL BULL "EXPONIS NOBIS FECISTI." Issued by Pope Pius V on March 24, 1567, this bull gave the religious the most extensive power from the Holy See since Pope Adrian VI's grant of power in 1522 in another bull of the same name. Philip II[*] was obliged to beg the pope not to trouble the Indies with any modification of the customs of receiving the sacraments, as had already been established. The bull of 1567 was an answer to Philip II's request. The religious retained the rights and privileges of parish priests, as well as the power to preach and to administer the sacraments without the express authorization of the bishops. By this time, Pope Pius V had realized the insufficiency of the secular clergy. The text read, "the mendicants could hear confessions without the authorization of the local Ordinaries."

REFERENCES: Francisco Morales, *Ethnic and Social Background of the Franciscan Friars in Seventeenth-Century Mexico*, 1930; William Shiels, *King and Church: The Rise and Fall of the Patronato Real*, 1961.

Raysa Amador

PAPAL BULL "ILLIUS FULCITI PRAESIDIO." This bull was issued by Pope Julius II on December 15, 1504, in Rome. With this bull, the pope constructed a hierarchy of the Church in America. The pope chose the site of the metropolis (headquarter city) to be Santo Domingo[*]. The pope did not refer in this bull to the Patronato Real[*] nor did he recognize the donation of the tithe as already granted by Pope Alexander VI[*] in his bull "Inter caetera" of May 1493. King Ferdinand[*] of Spain protested such a bull because of the conflict of power it created.

REFERENCE: F. Fita, *Boletín de la Real Academia de la Historia*, 1892.

Raysa Amador

PAPAL BULL "INTER CAETERA." This bull was issued by Pope Alexander VI[*] on May 3, 1493. In this bull, the pope conceded to their Catholic majesties Ferdinand[*] and Isabella[*] and to their successors, without any limitation, the full sovereignty of all lands discovered and to be discovered and conquered in the New World by Christopher Colombus[*]. There was also a second bull, with the same title, issued the next day, on May 4, 1493. This bull was a repetition of the bull of the first one; the only changes were that the bull of May 4 made no references to Portugal (such references were saved for another bull that was issued later). In addition, geographical limitations were introduced, establishing a demarcation line. While the bull of May 3 used the terms "lands and islands," the bull of May 4 mentioned "mainland and islands." The most important concept developed in both bulls was that they gave full authority to the Spanish monarchs over the Indies and the New World. The bull praised Christopher Columbus and his fitness for the task of discovering the Indies. The geographical location is mentioned in terms of a line from the north to the south and of the fact that the islands found should lie toward the Azores and Cape Verde. The bull can be found in the Archivo de Indias in Seville* as "Inter Caetera divini maiestari, beneplacita opera."

REFERENCES: Paul Gottschalk, *The Earliest Diplomacy Documents on America*, 1927; William Shiels, *King and Church: The Rise and Fall of the Patronato Real*, 1961.

Raysa Amador

PAPAL BULL "ORTHODOX FIDEI PROPAGATIONEM." This bull was issued by Pope Innocent VIII on December 13, 1486. King Ferdinand* and Queen Isabella* of Spain obtained the universal trust over the churches of the territory of Granada that was about to be conquered. The trust was invoked by the Spanish monarchs when they exercised pontifical concessions regarding the New World. With this bull, the building of churches and their endowments became the responsibilities as well as the rights of the Spanish monarchs. The Church was to give 10 percent of its dowry (a tithe) to the founder and endower, the Spanish monarchs. As a consequence, the Spanish monarchs founded and erected churches in the Indies since this bull gave them the power to do it. They proposed the construction of the metropolis (headquarter city) of Yagua and the suffragans (other dioceses under metropolitan jurisdiction) of Magua and Bynua. In 1504, Pope Julius II in the bull "Illius fulciti praesidio"* recognized the existence of these, but did not refer to the endownment of the tithe or to the trust already granted to the Spanish monarchs by his predecessor.

REFERENCE: Cayetano Bruno, *El derecho público de la Iglesia en las Indias*, 1967.

Raysa Amador

PAPAL BULL "SOLLICITUDO ECCLESIARUM." In 1831, Pope Gregory XVI issued the bull "Sollicitudo Ecclesiarum" in an attempt to resolve a number of tremendous administrative problems caused by the independence movements in Latin America. Throughout the colonial period, the Spanish Crown had controlled all clerical appointments, ecclesiastical courts, collection of revenues, and expenditures of funds because of the Patronato Real*. But when the new governments of Latin America no longer recognized the authority of the king in political matters, they also refused to recognize it in religious matters. The Church was caught in an impasse because the Spanish Crown refused to make clerical appointments in the New World. A number of bishoprics fell vacant and remained so for years. But in 1831, the pope issued the papal bull that announced the Church's intention, regardless of Spanish opinion, to establish normal ecclesiastical relationships with the governments of Latin America. Between 1831 and 1840, all of the vacant bishoprics were filled.

REFERENCE: William Shiels, *King and Church: The Rise and Fall of the Patronato Real*, 1961.

PAPAL BULL "SUBLIMIS DEUS." In 1537, Pope Paul III issued the bull "Sublimis Deus" in response to questions about the humanity of the Indians* of the New World. At the time, widespread exploitation of Indian land and labor, through slavery and the *encomienda**, was decimating the Indian population, even while the Spanish Crown and the Church were intent on converting the natives to Christianity. In the bull, Pope Paul III proclaimed that the Indians were indeed rational human beings capable of conversion to Christianity and that "they were not to be deprived of their liberty or the possession of their property even though they be outside the faith of Jesus Christ . . . nor should they in any case be enslaved." Although the bull gave impetus to the work of people like Bernardino de Minaya and Bartolomé de Las Casas* who were trying to protect the Indians, it was virtually unenforceable in the New World. Exploitation of the Indians continued unabated.

REFERENCES: Lewis Hanke, "Pope Paul III and the American Indians," *Harvard Theological Review*, 30 (1933), 65–162; Robert Ricard, *The Spiritual Conquest of Mexico*, 1966.

PAPAL BULL "UNIVERSALIS ECCLESIAE REGIMINI." In 1508, Pope Julius II issued the bull, "Universalis ecclesiae regimini," which proved to be a central document in the evolution of the Patronato Real* in the Spanish Empire. The bull conferred on the Spanish Crown all rights of church patronage in the New World—control over the establishment and construction of all churches and monasteries, as well as the granting of all ecclesiastical benefices.

REFERENCE: John Lloyd Mecham, *Church and State in Latin America: A History of Politico-Ecclesiastical Relations*, 1934.

PAPAL BULL "VERITAS IPSA." Issued by Pope Paul III on July 4, 1537, this bull recollected that Christ had commanded his apostles to teach all nations without exception, and it declared that nothing justified depriving the Indians*, who were reasonable men, of the blessing of liberty and the light of the Christian faith. The pope's bull was in response to the request of Bishop Julian Garces* and Bishop Bernardino de Minaya on behalf of the Indians. Garces, the Dominican* bishop of Tlaxcala, New Spain*, wrote a long and powerful essay in favor of the Indians to Pope Paul III in 1535. In this document, Bishop Garces urged the pope to take up the defense of the Indians. At a later time, the Dominican Bishop Bernardino de Minaya went to Rome to defend the Indians, also urging the pope to take up the defense of the Indians.

Before issuing "Veritas Ipsa" on July 4, 1537 and *Sublimis Deus* on June 1, 1537, Pope Paul III issued the bull *Altitudo divini consiili*. All of these bulls were issued at a time when Francisco de Vitoria* was debating about theocratic issues regarding the discovery of the New World. It would be of no surprise that Pope Paul III was also influenced by the professor of theology at the University of Salamanca. As one can see, Pope Paul III demonstrated much more interest in the Indians than did any of his predecessors.

REFERENCES: Robert Ricard, *The Spiritual Conquest of Mexico*, 1966.

Raysa Amador

PARAGUAY. Paraguay is one of the more unfortunate nations of the world. Geographically, the country is landlocked and situated between two much larger neighbors, Argentina* and Brazil. Through much of its history, Paraguay has been forced to defend itself from the ambitions of these two rivals. The terrain of Paraguay features extreme contrasts. The eastern one-third of the country—that which is east of the Paraguay River—is a well-watered plateau with rich soil and a pleasant semi-tropical climate. To the west of the Paraguay River is the Chaco, a low, poorly drained plain with extremely poor soil and a climate that features a few weeks of heavy rainfall followed by months of very hot, dry weather. Only a few of the hardiest souls live in the Chaco. Paraguay has the most homogeneous population in Latin America. Nearly all of the 3,500,000 people are mestizos*, the result of miscegenation between the Spanish settlers and the Guaraní* natives. Paraguay is also the only truly bilingual nation in Latin America. The official language is Spanish, but most Paraguayans also speak Guaraní. With little mineral wealth, the country is predominantly agricultural and poor. Industry, transportation, and commerce are controlled by foreigners, mostly Argentines and Brazilians, and much of the more productive land is owned by foreigners. Another misfortune of Paraguay, and probably the major cause of its retarded development, is that it has been governed by a succession of dictators whose rule makes Spanish colonial administration appear benevolent in comparison.

Spanish sovereignty was established in Paraguay in 1537 by an expedition, led by Juan de Ayolas, that had been sent up the Paraguay River to search for the elusive El Dorado*. Because the Guaraní Indians who lived in the region were cooperative and because the area was very fertile, the Spanish founded Asunción* and made it the administrative center for the entire area east of the Andes. Asunción lost favor with Madrid when the Spaniards realized that there was no local wealth to be exploited, that it was not feasible to export Andean gold and silver across the Chaco to Atlantic ports, and that Buenos Aires* was of greater strategic and economic importance. Buenos Aires left Asunción's administrative control in 1617, and Paraguay was transferred in 1776 from the viceroyalty of Peru* to the new viceroyalty of La Plata*. The neglect and isolation perceived by the Paraguayans contributed to the introverted national personality that appeared later.

Colonialism in Paraguay was much less exploitative of Indians* than in the other Spanish colonies, partly because there was less wealth (and thus, less need for labor) and also because the Jesuits* established themselves as the protectors of the Indians. From 1588 until their expulsion from all Spanish colonies in the

New World in 1767, the Jesuits kept the Guaraní in communal enclaves where the Indians were taught Christianity, modern farming methods, and the duty and grace of hard work. Spanish landowners, jealous of the wealth and power of the Jesuits and angry at being deprived of cheap labor, led the first Latin American revolt against Spanish authority. In 1721, the Comuneros* overthrew the local governor, who was protecting the Jesuit missions*, and defied the viceroy* until they were finally defeated in 1735. The revolt was a major factor in Madrid's decision to evict the Jesuits. Without the paternal and authoritarian direction of the priests, the communities disintegrated rapidly after 1767. The Indian population of Paraguay declined precipitously as the Indians fell prey to less paternalistic Spanish landowners and Portuguese slave raiders.

The intransigence exhibited in the Comunero revolt appeared again after 1810 in Paraguay's fight for independence. When the Buenos Aires council in effect declared independence from Spain in 1810, it expected the Asunción council to join them and to remain under the control of Buenos Aires. Long resentful of the power of Buenos Aires, the Paraguayans refused and successfully defeated an Argentine army sent to force compliance. The Asunción council then deposed the Spanish governor and declared the independence of Paraguay in 1811. The government established to replace the colonial administration was the first of Paraguay's dictatorships.

REFERENCES: Harris Gaylord Warren, *Paraguay: An Informal History*, 1949; George Pendle, *Paraguay: A Riverside Nation*, 1967.

Bruce R. Drury

PARDO. The term "pardo" has been used since the colonial period in Spanish America to refer to people of mixed racial heritage, especially individuals with an African-European or African-Indian ancestry. For the most part, *pardos* experienced widespread discrimination and were forbidden to enter universities and the clergy.

REFERENCE: Magnus Morner, *Race Mixture in the History of Latin America*, 1967.

PARIS, TREATY OF (1763). With the end of the War of the Austrian Succession*, Austro-Prussian rivalry over possession of the province of Silesia continued apace. Maria Theresa of Austria, determined to win back her lost territory, entered into secret agreements with Russia, the ultimate purpose of which was the crippling of Brandenburg-Prussia. As British policy in the 1750s continued to be focused on maintaining the balance of power in Europe, London backed Prussia as a counter to French interests in northern Europe. Thus, the Anglo-Prussian Treaty of Westminster (1756) laid the groundwork for British military support of Prussia in any conflict with France or Austria.

The Anglo-French rivalry of the 1750s also included the struggle for overseas empire, especially in North America and India. In North America, Britain most feared the possibility of French expansion into the valuable Ohio and Mississippi valleys. By 1754, an undeclared war already existed between the two powers in North America. The smoldering conflict on the frontier of America, however, was quickly fanned into a conflagration in Europe. In 1756, France agreed to support an old rival, the House of Habsburg, in its claim to Silesia, the restoration of which was to be the condition for the cession of the Southern Netherlands to France. On August 26, 1756, Frederick II of Prussia, aware of the Austro-Russian plan for the dismemberment of Prussia-Brandenburg, attacked Austria, thus opening the Seven Years War pitting Britain and Prussia against France and Austria.

The war in Europe quickly found the French, although defeated in western Prussia, successful in subsidizing the Austro-Russian armies that inflicted a near-decisive defeat on Frederick in the east. Prussia was on the brink of collapse, despite massive British war subsidies, until 1762, when Tsarina Elizabeth of Russia died, bringing to the throne Tsar Peter III, Frederick of Prussia's most devoted admirer. Peter immediately made peace with Prussia, thus forcing Austria into the Treaty of Huburtusburg, signed February 15, 1763, which confirmed the *status quo ante bellum*, most significantly Prussia's retention of Silesia.

In the west, by February 1763, France was forced into peace negotiations with Britain following serious defeats in Europe and North America, most particularly in September 1759, when the French army lost Quebec to British forces under General James Wolfe. Under the terms of the Treaty of Paris, signed February 10, 1763 (which included both Spain and Portugal as signatories), France was forced to cede many of its colonial possessions to Great Britain. In North America, France lost Canada, Cape Breton Island, and all territory east of the Mississippi, excluding New Orleans. In the West Indies, the islands of Dominica[*], St. Vincent, Grenada, and Tobago[*] were ceded to Great Britain. The island of Minorca, which had been captured by the French in 1756, was returned to Great Britain. In return for ceding Florida[*] to Britain, Spain received western Louisiana[*] and a cash compensation from France. French troops were ordered to evacuate the territory of Hanover, and French and Spanish troops were to leave Portugal. Ultimately, France received from Britain several footholds in India, at Pondicherry and Chandernagore. The sugar islands of Guadeloupe[*] and Martinique[*] were restored to the French.

The Seven Years War and the Treaty of Paris were leading causes for both the American and French Revolutions. Until 1789, France, though still possessing sources of colonial income, was no longer a great colonial power. The Spanish Empire remained largely intact, but the British were still determined to penetrate its markets. On the Indian subcontinent, Britain increased its colonial holdings, and the British East India Company continued to press against the weakening indigenous governments and to impose its own authority.

REFERENCES: Z. E. Rashed, *The Peace of Paris, 1763*, 1951; Walter L. Dorn, *Competition for Empire, 1740-1763*, 1940.

William G. Ratliff

PARIS, TREATY OF (1783). After the British defeat at the Battle of Yorktown in 1781, the ministry of Lord Frederick North resigned. The succeeding ministries under Rockingham and Shelburne, pursuant to an act of Parliament, initiated peace negotiations with the United States to end the American Revolution.* The extended negotiations resulted in the signing of preliminary terms of peace on November 30, 1782, leading to a cessation of hostilities on January 20, 1783. The task of reaching peace terms with the other nations involved in the war, however, proved to be even more difficult. France was an ally of the United States in the war, and Spain was an ally of France. Although France was eager to end the war, Spain was somewhat intractable, having failed to achieve its major objective—the recovery of Gibraltar.* Not until September 3, 1783, was the definitive treaty of peace signed at Paris and Versailles.

The Treaty of Paris, which pertained to the American Revolution, secured a generous peace settlement for the new nation. Great Britain acknowledged the independence of the United States; agreed to the boundary between the United States and Canada, a western boundary along the Mississippi River, and the southern boundary with Florida*; granted fishing rights off Newfoundland to Americans; provided for the settlement of prewar debts; made vague references to guaranteeing the property of loyalists and to making compensation for loyalists' property seized; promised to evacuate American territory "with all convenient speed"; provided for the return of prisoners; and guaranteed mutual rights of navigation on the Mississippi River. The American portion of the treaty was signed at Paris because the British representatives refused to go to Versailles to sign the treaty.

The treaty ending the European phase of the war was signed on September 3 at Versailles. Thus, its proper title is the Treaty of Versailles. In it, England retained possession of Gibraltar but returned to Spain, the Floridas in America and Minorca in the Mediterranean. French gains were minimal. England agreed to remove restrictions that had been placed on the French port of Dunkirk and made minor concessions to the French in the West Indies and Africa. The only nation to benefit conclusively from the Wars of the American Revolution was the United States. For good reason, many American diplomatic historians consider the treaty the greatest triumph in the history of American diplomacy.

REFERENCE: Richard B. Morris, *The Peacemakers*, 1965.

Joseph M. Rowe, Jr.

PARIS, TREATY OF (1898). The Treaty of Paris formally ended the Spanish-American War of 1898.* As early as July 1898, Spain had sought French mediation to determine what terms of peace the United States would demand to end the war. As a result of this effort, the two nations signed a protocol on August 12 that provided for a peace treaty to be negotiated at Paris. Hostilities ended under the stipulation that Spain give up Cuba* and cede to the United States the island of Puerto Rico* and also Guam* in the Marianas.* In addition, the United States was to occupy and hold Manila* in the Philippines* until its disposition was determined at the peace conference. Between August 12 and October 1, 1898, when the peace conference convened in Paris, the United States policy toward the Philippines changed. In mid-September, President William

McKinley seemed determined to have only Luzon.* By October 26, however, the President insisted that the United States must have all of the Philippines. Although his explanations for this policy varied from time to time, the decision was clearly based on the commercial advantage that possession of the Philippines would give the United States in the Far East. Spain strongly protested against the injustice of this policy, but was left with no choice but to accede to United States demands. The final treaty, signed on December 10, 1898, contained the following provisions: Spain would give up Cuba, and the United States would occupy the island; Spain would cede to the United States the islands of Puerto Rico in the West Indies and Guam in the Marianas; Spain would cede the Philippine Islands to the United States in return for a payment of $20 million. During the debate over the treaty in the United States Senate, anti-imperialists protested the implications of a new American empire, but ratification was approved on February 6, 1899, by a close vote of 57 to 27. The effect of the war and Treaty of Paris was to diminish Spain's overseas empire and initiate the era of United States imperialism.

REFERENCE: Henry Steel Commager, *Documents of American History*, 1948.

Joseph M. Rowe, Jr.

PATERNO, PEDRO. Pedro A. Paterno was born in the Philippines in 1857. He earned a doctorate at the University of St. Thomas* in Manila*, and he is credited with writing the first novel in the Philippines, *Ninay*, in 1885. Gifted with personal skills of diplomacy, Paterno spent the 1890s trying to negotiate the differences between Emilio Aguinaldo* and the Spaniards, serving as president of the Malolos Congress in 1898, and heading a peace cabinet in 1899, which tried to seek an end to the bloody Philippine-American War. Paterno died in 1911.

REFERENCE: Ester G. Maring and Joel M. Maring, *Historical and Cultural Dictionary of the Philippines*, 1973.

PATIÑO, JOSÉ. Born in Milan in 1666 to Galician nobility, José Patiño devoted his youth to a Jesuit* education. Gaining the attention and esteem of Philip V* during his visit to Italy, Patiño accompanied the monarch to Spain in 1702 to enter royal service. In 1711, he became military intendant of Extremadura and soon thereafter assumed the same office of Catalonia. Patiño's successes and surely his Italian background found favor with de facto Prime Minister Julio Alberoni*. In January 1717, Alberoni named him Marine Intendant-General for Spain, to reside in Cádiz. His authority extending over naval supply and finance, Patiño's primary mission was to organize fleets for Alberoni's ill-fated Italian designs. In May, Alberoni enhanced Patiño's powers by transferring both the Casa de Contratación* and the Consulado* of Seville* to Cádiz, making him president of the Consulado. To placate Seville, Patiño devised an election system for priors and consuls that guaranteed its continuing dominance over the merchant guild, an arrangement that endured until 1743. He also contributed to the formation of the Royal Project of 1720, which updated and codified colonial commercial policy. Apparently owing to his rapport with the royal family, Patiño survived the exile of Alberoni with whom he had developed differences. The fall of the Baron de Ripperda in 1726 led to Patiño's elevation to minister of both finance and marine and the Indies. He consolidated his power by adding war to his duties in 1730 and state in 1734.

Patiño labored mightily to strengthen the foundations of a modern absolutist state and above all to impose order on the royal treasury. In 1734, he established a disciplined militia* system in Castile*, which Charles III* would later extend to the colonies. Patiño's colonial policy aimed to make a reality of Spain's mercantilist* aspirations. He accorded priority to restoring the navy to a complement sufficient for safeguarding commerce, and he waged war on foreign contraband in the colonies. Patiño also assigned high importance to the Havana* shipyard, which constructed impressive numbers of warships, and he strengthened the colonial coast guard. To finance coastal patrols, he extracted from the Consulado of Cádiz a levy of 4 percent on incoming silver and gold. In turn, he favored the guild by permitting it to define its own membership and by a benign supervision over the taxes it administered and the tonnage it registered in its merchant ships. In this sense, Patiño did not anticipate the course of future reform, for he treated the monopoly merchant guild as an ally rather than as an obstacle to modernized mercantilism. Finally, in 1728, he authorized the establishment of the Caracas Company* to secure control over Venezuelan* commerce and in 1734 the Galicia Company to exploit the dyewood of Campeche. The effectiveness of Patiño's policies may be gauged by the British decision to launch a preemptive war against Spain in 1739.

Patiño died on November 3, 1736. He was succeeded in the ministries of marine, the Indies, and finance by the Marqués de Torrenueva and of war and state by Sebastián de la Cuadra.

REFERENCES: José Antonio Escudero, *Los orígenes del Consejo de Ministros en España*, 1979; *Historia general de España*. vol. X.: *La España de las reformas hasta el final del reinado de Carlos IV*, ed. Carlos E. Corona Baratech and José Antonio Armillas Vicente, pt. 2, 1984; Antonio Rodríguez Vila, *Patiño y Campillo: Reseña histórico-biográfica de estos dos ministros de Felipe V*, 1882.

                                                                              Allan J. Kuethe

PATRONATO DE INDÍGENAS. The Patronato de Indígenas (Patronage of the Natives) was established in 1904, ostensibly to protect the Bubi people of Spanish Equatorial Guinea*, but it eventually evolved into a government agency run by the Church with the power to "emancipate" native inhabitants. After 1926, the Patronato de Indígenas enjoyed the power to levy taxes and purchase property as well. It was dissolved in 1960 when the distinction between emancipated and non-emancipated natives was dropped from Spanish colonial policy.

REFERENCE: Max Liniger-Goumaz, *Historical Dictionary of Equatorial Guinea*, 1988.

PATRONATO REAL. The Patronato Real was the absolute control of clerical patronage in the colonies that the papacy gave to the kings of Spain. The leading force behind the institution of the Patronato Real, or "king's patronage," was King Ferdinand*. Papal bulls of 1501 and 1508 gave him authority over the church. On November 16, 1501, Pope Alexander VI* issued the papal bull "Eximiae devotionis,"* in which he declared that it was the responsibility of the Spanish Crown to maintain the Roman Catholic Church* in the New World and to propagate the faith among the Indians*; in order to carry out that responsibility, the pope authorized the Crown and royal officials to collect all church tithes in the region and disburse all church monies there. In 1508, Pope Julius II issued the papal bull "Universalis ecclesiae regimini,"* which conferred on the Spanish Crown all rights of church patronage in the New World—control over the establishment and construction of all churches and monasteries, as well as the granting of all ecclesiastical benefices. As historian Charles Gibson has written, "Patronato Real implied state domination over the church, but it simultaneously allowed for ecclesiastical intrusion into civil and political affairs. In the complexities of law and precedent it was impossible to say where church authority ceased and state authority began." Not surprisingly, the history of the Spanish colonies was characterized by constant struggles for power between viceroys* and bishops. The Spanish Crown maintained this extensive power over the Church throughout the colonial period. During the independence struggles of the early 1800s, Latin American liberals often targeted the political and economic power of the Church as the source of their problems. The Patronato Real came to an end with independence, at which point the Church lost the protection of royal support and had to fight repeated struggles for decades over the collection of tithes, ecclesiastical courts, parochial schools, church property, and clerical appointments.

REFERENCES: Charles Gibson, *Spain in America*, 1966; John Lloyd Mecham, *Church and State in Latin America: A History of Politico-Ecclesiastical Relations*, 1934; Robert Ricard, *The Spiritual Conquest of Mexico*, 1966; W. E. Shiels, *The Rise and Fall of the Patronato Real*, 1961.

PAZOS KANKI, VICENTE. Vicente Pazos Kanki was born on December 30, 1779, in Ilabaya, Bolivia*. He joined the Roman Catholic priesthood and received a degree in theology from the University of Cuzco*. An early advocate of Argentine independence, Pazos wrote articles for *La gaceta* and *El censor*, spent several years in exile in England between 1810 and 1820 to escape Spanish authorities*, and then returned to be a member of the Congress of Tucumán*. He assisted Mariano Moreno* in the revolutionary struggle. After the revolution, Pazos advocated democratic, republican government, a position that again forced him into exile in the United States and Europe. Between 1829 and 1838, and again from 1842 to 1845, Pazos was the Consul General of Bolivia in London. A nineteenth-century romantic, Pazos was a brilliant political essayist and historian, focusing on political events in Latin America and the United States as his subjects. Vicente Pazos Kinki died in London on March 28, 1845.

REFERENCES: Fernando Díez de Medina, *Literatura boliviana*, 1953; Enrique Finot, *Historia de la literatura boliviana*, 1943.

PEDRARIAS. See ÁVILA, PEDRO ARIAS DE.

PEÑA Y MONTENEGRO, ALONSO DE. Alonso de Peña y Montenegro was born in Villa del Padrón, Galicia, Spain, on April 29, 1596. He was educated at the University of Santiago de Compostela, receiving a doctorate in theology in 1621; he went on to become a professor there as well as at the University of Salamanca. He was ordained a priest in 1639. In Salamanca, Peña became close friends with Gaspar Bracamonte y Guzmán, who later became president of the Council of the Indies[*]. In 1653, Peña was appointed bishop of Quito[*], Ecuador[*], a position he assumed in 1654. Peña served as interim president of the *audiencia* of Quito[*] from 1674 to 1678 and is best remembered for his writings on local customs and the people in Ecuador. He died in Quito on May 12, 1687.
    REFERENCE: *New Catholic Encyclopedia*, XI:62, 1967.

PEÑALVER, FERNANDO DE. Fernando de Peñalver was born in Venezuela[*] in 1765 and became an early leader in the revolutionary movement. In 1811, he served as president of the congress of 1811 that drafted the Venezuelan declaration of independence. Peñalver served as a member of Simón Bolívar's[*] Provisional Council of State in 1817, of the Congress of Angostura[*] in 1819, and of the Congress of Cucuta in 1821. Fernando de Peñalver died in 1837.
    REFERENCE: Donna Keyes Rudolph and G. A. Rudolph, *Historical Dictionary of Venezuela*, 1971.

PEÑALVER Y CÁRDENAS, LUIS IGNACIO. Luis Ignacio Peñalver y Cárdenas was born to a prominent family in Havana[*], Cuba[*], on April 13, 1749. He studied at St. Ignatius College, a Jesuit[*] institution in Havana, until 1767, when the Jesuits were expelled from the New World. Peñalver then switched to the University of Havana. He was ordained a priest in 1772. While serving in a number of capacities in the diocese of Santiago[*] de Cuba, he earned his doctorate in theology in 1781. After a terrible hurricane destroyed much of Havana in 1792, Peñalver spent most of his family's fortune helping victims to adjust and rebuilding the city. In 1793, Peñalver was appointed bishop of the diocese of Louisiana[*] and the Floridas[*]. He remained in New Orleans until 1801 when he was appointed archbishop of Guatemala[*]. Peñalver retired in 1806 and died in Havana on July 17, 1810.
    REFERENCE: *New Catholic Encyclopedia*, XI:71–72, 1967.

PENINSULARES. The term *peninsulares* was widely used throughout the Spanish Empire to refer to individuals born in Spain who were residing, usually temporarily, in one of the overseas colonies. For the most part, the *peninsulares* were associated with the colonial bureaucracy, the military, or the Church. They tended to be important officials in one of those capacities, and they were usually on a temporary assignment, hoping to return to Spain and advance in their chosen careers. Backed by political and religious authority, they exercised great power in the colonies, but they were generally resented by the people native to the colonies. *Criollos*[*], *mestizos*[*], and Indians[*] all hated the haughty attitude of the *peninsulares*. When the colonial rebellions spread throughout Latin America, the native classes of the various colonies, even though they often had little in common, were able to unite because of their dislike of the *peninsulares*. Once the revolutions succeeded and the *peninsulares* were expelled, however, racial and class antagonisms badly divided political life in the newly independent countries.

REFERENCES: John K. Chance, *Race and Class in Colonial Oaxaca*, 1978; J. I. Israel, *Race, Class and Politics in Colonial Mexico, 1610–1670*, 1975.

PERALTA DE LA VEGA, JOSÉ MARÍA. José María Peralta de la Vega was born in Jaen, Spain, in 1763. He came to the New World as a young man and settled in Costa Rica[*]. Peralta held official posts with the *ayuntamiento* of Cartago[*], and in 1822, he became president of the Junta Governativa de Costa Rica. Known for his liberalism, Peralta was a member of the Second Constituent Assembly in 1822 and president of the Third Constituent Assembly in 1823. Except for two years, he served as a member of the congress of Costa Rica between 1825 and 1833, and as president of the legislature in 1829, 1832, and 1833. He died in 1836.

REFERENCE: Theodore S. Creedman, *Historical Dictionary of Costa Rica*, 1977.

PERALTA Y BARNUEVO, PEDRO DE. Born in Lima[*], Peru[*], in 1663, Pedro de Peralta y Barnuevo represented the very pinnacle of scholastic-baroque culture in the Spanish colonies. Peralta distinguished himself in a variety of fields; he was a scientist, jurist, theologian, engineer, and historian. In the field of literature, Peralta excelled as a poet, essayist, and dramatist. He was elected rector of the University of San Marcos[*]. In short, he was one of the most remarkable scholars and intellectuals to live in the colonial era. Because his family was both wealthy and important, Peralta operated in the highest circles in colonial Peru. His fame spread readily to Spain, and he was cited by various Spanish intellectuals for his broad erudition. He knew at least seven languages well.

Peralta's literary legacy was extensive and includes over 40 works. He wrote many treatises on technical subjects—astronomy, engineering, and so forth. He also dabbled in history, producing *Historia de España vindicada* (1730), in which he compared the colonizing by the Spaniards in the New World with that of the Romans in Spain. He was both a lyric and epic poet. Regarding the latter, he composed a famous epic poem, *Lima Fundada* (1732), which treats the founding of Lima from Francisco Pizarro's time to 1535. Aside from its literary value, the work is of immense historical value as well. In prose, Peralta's *Pasión y triunfo de Cristo* (1738) stands out. In the field of literature, Peralta is most noted for his dramas. Although only three works have survived, they display significant talent and reflect the theatrical interests of colonial Peru. Two works are decidedly baroque*: *Triunfos de amor y poder* (1711) and *Afectos vencen finezas* (1720). Another play, *La Rodoguna*, is in the neoclassical vein, using Pierre Corneille's *Rodogune* as a model. He died in 1743.

   REFERENCE: Pedro de Peralta y Barnuevo, *Obras dramáticas*, ed. I. A. Leonard, 1937.

Sam L. Slick

PÉREZ, ESTEBAN. Esteban Pérez was the Franciscan* priest who became the patron of Christopher Columbus*. In 1473, Pérez was the guardian of San Esteban de los Olmos in Burgos, Spain, and by 1485, he held the same post in La Rábida. In that year, he provided housing and some financial support to Columbus, whose plans for reaching Asia he accepted completely. He went to the court of Ferdinand* and Isabella* to secure a hearing for Columbus, and on April 17, 1492, Pérez signed the documents authorizing his voyage. He helped secure for Columbus the loyalty of Martín Yáñez* Pinzón, one of the most gifted sailors and navigators of the day. Perez probably accompanied Columbus on his second voyage to the New World in 1493. In 1499, Pérez became vicar provincial of Castile*, and from 1502 to 1505, he served as guardian of Murcia. Esteban Pérez died in 1515.

   REFERENCES: Jean Hippolyte Mariejol, *The Spain of Ferdinand and Isabella*, 1961; Samuel Eliot Morison, *Admiral of the Ocean Sea: A Life of Christopher Columbus*, 2 vols., 1942.

PÉREZ CALAMA, JOSÉ. José Pérez Calama was born in Alberca, Spain, on November 25, 1740. He graduated with a degree in theology and philosophy from the University of Salamanca and then earned a doctorate at the University of Ávila. Pérez taught at the University of Salamanca for several years. He accompanied Bishop Francisco Fabian y Fuero to Puebla*, New Spain* in 1764, and he was ordained a Roman Catholic priest in 1768. Pérez later went to Michoacán as preceptor and then deacon and archdeacon. In 1789, he was appointed bishop of Quito*. Poor health forced him to resign in 1792, and he died at sea later that year while returning to Spain.

   REFERENCE: J. M. Vargas, *Historia de la Iglesia en el Ecuador durante el patronato español*, 1962.

PÉREZ DE RIVAS, ANDRÉS. Andrés Pérez de Rivas was born in Córdoba, Spain, in 1575. He was first ordained a regular priest but in 1602 he joined the Jesuit* order in Córdoba and completed his novitiate in Puebla*, New Spain*. Between 1604 and 1619, Pérez was a missionary priest in northern New Spain, particularly in what became the provinces of Sinaloa* and Sonora. He learned the Indian* languages and kept careful records of his activities. Because of poor health, Pérez left the mission field in 1619 and returned to Mexico City*, where he filled administrative positions for the rest of his life. During those years,

Pérez wrote a number of important historical works, of which the most significant was his *Historia de los triumfos de nuestra santa fé entre gentes los más bárbaros y fieros del Nuevo Orbe* (1645). His other works dealt with the history of the Jesuits in New Spain and with the exploration and conquest of Sinaloa and Sonora. Andrés Pérez de Rivas died in Mexico City on March 26, 1655.

REFERENCE: P. M. Dunne, *Andrés Pérez de Rivas: Pioneer Black Robe of the West Coast, Administrator, Historian*, 1951.

PERU. In 1522, the first news of Peru* reached Panama*. Francisco Pizarro*, Diego de Almagro*, and Hernando de Luque became associates for a Peruvian expedition. In 1524, the expedition departed but returned because it lacked provisions. In the 1526 expedition, Bartolomé Ruiz, a pilot, continued along the coast and "discovered" Peru when he sighted a raft with Indians* who told him about the Incas* and Cuzco*. With this news, Pizarro continued while Almagro returned for provisions. Pizarro stayed on Gallo Island but Panama's governor learned about the privations that his men were undergoing and sent a rescue mission. Pizarro left with 13 men and moved to Gorgona Island. When provisions arrived, he continued to Tumbez and then returned to Panama.

He left for Spain and received a *capitulación**, which made him governor and captain general, in 1529. The Crown provided funds and conferred titles on the men who had been with him on the islands, as well as on his associates. He went to his native town, Trujillo, to pick up his brothers, Hernando, Gonzalo, Juan, and Martín. Almagro felt cheated by Pizarro. In 1531, another expedition left Panama and went to Puña Island where the Spaniards were attacked. They left for Tumbez and found the village destroyed. Pizarro went inland and founded the first Spanish town, San Miguel.

When the Spaniards arrived, an Incan dynastic feud existed between Atahuallpa* of Quito* and Huáscar* of Cuzco. Atahuallpa, the victor, had his army at Cajamarca. Pizarro arrived at Cajamarca on November 15, 1532, and seized Atahuallpa on November 16. In Spanish custody, Atahuallpa ordered Huáscar's execution and bribed the Spaniards with gold for his release. Almagro reached Cajamarca on April 14, 1533. Pizarro condemned Atahuallpa for fratricide and executed him on August 29, 1533. Several conquistadors* disapproved of this action. On October 27, 1533, Pizarro marched to Cuzco and met stiff Indian resistance, but he entered the city on November 15 at the side of Huáscar's brother, Manco Inca*, whom Pizarro supported. The conquest of Quito followed under Sebastián de Benalcázar*. Meanwhile, Pedro de Alvarado* arrived from Guatemala* in 1534 and marched to Quito. Almagro met him and convinced him to leave the enterprise for financial remuneration. Alvarado left but many of his men remained. To prevent further incursions and maintain territorial control, Pizarro founded Lima* on January 18, 1535. Between the capital and San Miguel, he founded Trujillo*.

In July 1535, Almagro left for Chile*, which Pizarro had granted him. In Cuzco, Manco Inca rebelled in April 1536 and put Cuzco under siege, but he retreated to Vilcabamba when he learned of Almagro's return. Almagro forced Cuzco's surrender and entered on April 18, 1537. The civil wars began. Almagro, defeated on April 26, 1538, was executed on July 10 or 12. In Lima, Almagro's men rallied around his son. In June 1541, Francisco Pizarro was assassinated by Almagro's followers. Vaca de Castro, a Crown commissioner, fought Almagro's troops on Sept 16, 1542, defeated them, and executed Almagro's son. He persuaded Gonzalo Pizarro to go to Charcas (later Sucre*).

Gonzalo revolted when the New Laws* of 1542 were introduced. The first Peruvian viceroy, Blasco Núñez de Vela*, attempted to enforce them but met stiff resistance from the conquistadors led by Gonzalo. He entered Cuzco on October 28, 1544. The viceroy was killed in battle in 1546. Pedro de la Gasca* pacified the country and executed Gonzalo Pizarro on April 9, 1548. In January 1550, de la Gasca left Peru in the hands of the *audiencia** until the arrival of Viceroy Antonio de Mendoza*. In 1554, Francisco Hernández Girón arrived in Cuzco. During this period, the consolidation of Spanish power occurred as pacification brought the imposition of colonial organization and institutions into the viceroyalty. In 1551, the University of San Marcos* was founded in Lima. Mendoza died in 1552 and the *audiencia* took over until 1556, when Viceroy Andrés Hurtado de Mendoza arrived. He ordered the execution of anyone with a turbulent history and got the Inca leader, Sayri Túpac, to swear allegiance to the crown. In 1566, the Huancavelica* mercury mines were discovered, which eventually led to the deaths of many Indians.

Under the reign of the fifth viceroy, Francisco de Toledo* (in power 1569–1581), a major reorganization took place, which remained until the eighteenth century. He developed laws to suit the viceroyalty's needs. He executed the last Inca, Túpac Amaru*, in 1572. He put the Indians into *reducciones** and in *mita** for the silver mines. He left the *curacas* (the Indian nobility) to govern the villages. He created a mining* code for the primary export industry. After Toledo left, the Spanish imperial system was firmly entrenched, and no major revolt occurred until 1781.

By 1705, New Spain's* silver production exceeded that of Peru. The Bourbons in Spain brought changes to the imperial system, which had a direct bearing on Peru. In 1724, a rebellion led by José de Antequera* and known as the *Comunero** Revolt* took place in Paraguay*. Antequera was brought to Lima and executed in 1731. Other revolts occurred during the eighteenth century, but that by Juan Santos Atahuallpa (who claimed to be a descendent of Atahuallpa) in 1742 was a millenarian movement that attracted many of the Indians in the jungles of central Peru. The movement continued until the leader's death in 1756. Indian grievances continued as abuses were committed by the *corregidores** through the *repartimiento** de mercancías* and as new taxes were levied. This led to Túpac Amaru II's* rebellion in 1780–1781. It not only involved the Indians but also mestizos* and *criollos**. After Túpac Amaru II's execution, revolts continued in other parts of the viceroyalty. The rebellion accomplished the abolition of the *corregidores* and the *repartimiento de mercancías*. The militia* was also strengthened for internal order, retarding the desire for independence.

Under the Bourbons, other administrative changes were made to deal with the large territorial expanse and the complexity of the viceroyalty by the eighteenth century. The viceroyalty of New Granada* was created in 1739 and the viceroyalty of Río de la Plata* in 1776. These moves oriented trade away from Lima and weakened the viceroyalty of Peru as it was reduced in size. In 1784, the *intendencia** system was introduced, and the *audiencia* of Cuzco* was created in 1787. During this period, botanical expeditions were sent out. In 1791, the first newspaper, *Mercurio Peruano*, was founded.

The beginning of the nineteenth century saw numerous rebellions. In 1811, the Indians of Huanuco rebelled, but they were defeated in 1813. In 1814, Mateo García Pumacahua*, a former royalist supporter against Túpac Amaru II, rebelled and proclaimed himself president of the *audiencia* of Cuzco*. He was defeated in 1815. In Upper Peru (Bolivia*), royalists and patriots battled for control. José de San Martín* sent Argentine troops into Chile* in 1817 to strike at royalist power. He defeated the royalists there in 1818 and landed troops in Peru in 1819. In 1820, the Trujillo *cabildo** declared independence, and other *cabildos* soon followed. These towns were located in the north, as the royalists held power in Lima. When the royalists deserted Lima, San Martín entered and declared independence on July 28, 1821. He organized Free Peru by issuing decrees and calling for parliamentary elections. The northern Peruvian forces joined Simón Bolívar's* forces against the royalists in the *audiencia* of Quito* and defeated them at Pichincha* on April 23, 1822.

Two different ideas existed about Peru's liberation. President José de Riva-Agüero* believed it could be done by Peruvian nationalist forces alone. He went to Trujillo when the royalist forces reoccupied Lima and declared it the capital of Free Peru. The Congress believed that victory could be achieved only through Bolívar's help. They moved to Callao and declared it the capital. The Congress deposed Riva-Agüero and proclaimed the Marqués José Bernardo de Torre Tagle* president. Bolívar landed in Peru, exiled Riva-Agüero, and consolidated his power. In early 1824, the Congress put all military and political power in Bolívar's hands. In August 1824, Bolívar was victorious at Junín*. On December 9, 1824, the patriot forces won at Ayacucho*, thus consummating Peruvian independence with the royalist surrender.

REFERENCES: Henry F. Dobyns and Paul L. Doughty, *Peru: A Cultural History*, 1976; Clements R. Markham, *A History of Peru*, 1982.

Carlos Pérez

PERU, VICEROYALTY OF. The viceroyalty of Peru, originally called the viceroyalty of New Castile, was established in 1542 to provide governmental supervision to the region that Francisco Pizarro* had conquered in the 1530s. It also had authority over the *audiencia** established at Panama* in 1538. The viceroyalty included all Spanish territory from Panama in the north to Tierra del Fuego in the south. Geographical considerations made governmental supervision difficult at best. The Andes Mountains separated Peru from Bolivia*, Paraguay*, and Argentina*. Simple distance made it difficult to closely supervise Chile* in the south and Colombia* in the north. Finally, the fact that Peru was on the Pacific coast and all goods had to cross the Isthmus of Panama and then move across the Atlantic to Spain made for difficult communications. Separate *audiencias* were established at Lima* in 1543, Santa Fe de Bogotá* in 1548, Charcas* (Bolivia*) in 1559, Quito* in 1563, and Santiago* (Chile*) in 1606. The Spanish Crown created the viceroyalty of New Granada* in 1717, dissolved it in 1723, and re-established it in 1739 to assume authority over the *audiencias* of Bogotá, Quito, and Panama. The viceroyalty of Río de La Plata* was established in 1776 with authority over Argentina, Uruguay*, Paraguay, and eastern Bolivia. At that point, the viceroyalty of Peru governed an area that included present-day Peru, Chile, and western Bolivia.

REFERENCES: Lillian Estelle Fisher, *Viceregal Administration in the Spanish American Colonies*, 1927; C. H. Haring, *The Spanish Empire in America*, 1947.

PEZUELA, JOAQUÍN DE LA. A native of Spain, Joaquín de la Pezuela was born in 1761 and pursued a military career. He came to Peru* with royal artillery forces and eventually rose to the command of royalist forces in Upper Peru (Bolivia*). His army defeated General Manuel Belgrano's* army at Vilcapugio and Ayohuma* in 1813, but he lost the Battle of Puerto Márquez in 1815. Pezuela was victorious later in the year at the Battle of Sipe Sipe. That victory earned him the title of Marqués de Viluma and the rank of lieutenant general. He was appointed viceroy of Peru in 1815, but was deposed by his own troops in 1821 and replaced by José de la Serna.* He died in 1830.

REFERENCE: Ione S. Wright and Lisa M. Nekhom, *Historical Dictionary of Argentina*, 1978.

PEZUELA, JUAN MANUEL DE LA. Juan Manuel de la Pezuela was born in 1810 to a father who was the last viceroy of Peru. Pezuela was a unique personality. He was appointed captain general of Cuba* in 1853. There his intense opposition to slavery* immediately came to the forefront. Upon arriving in Havana*, he began publishing articles calling for emancipation of the slaves and strict obedience to international agreements outlawing the slave trade. He enraged the large plantation owners who were convinced that he was bent on their economic and social destruction. In 1854, Pezuela ordered the registration of all slaves and also ordered that all planters who could not prove ownership of individual slaves had to liberate them. Planters put enough pressure on Spain to force his removal that year. Pezuela returned to Spain where he died in 1875.

REFERENCES: Jaime Suchlicki, *Historical Dictionary of Cuba*, 1988; Jaime Suchlicki *Cuba: From Columbus to Castro*, 1986.

PHILIP I. King Philip I of Spain was born in 1478. The son of Maximilian I and Mary of Burgundy, Philip I was the first of a long line of Habsburg rulers to reign over Spain. Philip I assumed the Spanish throne in 1506, and when he married Joanna of Castile* he also became joint ruler of the Netherlands. During his reign, Spain continued explorations of the Greater Antilles, the Caribbean, and Central America, establishing a foothold there that would last for centuries. Philip I died in 1516 and was succeeded by his son, Charles V*, who greatly expanded the empire.

REFERENCE: Edward Gaylord Bourne, *Spain in America, 1450-1580*, 1904.

PHILIP II. King Philip II was born in Valladolid, Spain, on May 21, 1527, the son of Charles I* of Spain and Isabella of Portugal. When his father abdicated the throne in 1556, Philip II formally became King of Spain, Naples, and Sicily. Philip II was the first of the Spanish Habsburg rulers of Spain. He was a most effective ruler, and during his reign Spain became the dominant power in Europe. Not only did Spain establish itself throughout Mexico, Central America, South America, and the Philippines* during his reign, but in 1580 he also seized Portugal, beginning a political union that lasted until 1640. But during Philip II's reign can also be seen the beginning of the end of the Spanish Empire. He was a religious fanatic obsessed with the destruction of Protestantism in England, a goal that was made impossible by the defeat of his Armada in 1588. The bullion riches from the gold and silver mines of the New World were poorly invested, triggering an era of prosperity in Spain without any strengthening of the economic infrastructure. Moreover, the defeat of the Spanish Armada* at the hands of Queen Elizabeth's English fleet was a harbinger of Spain's decline and of the rise of Dutch and British influence in the world. He was also responsible for developing the highly centralized bureaucratic administration of the empire, which created inefficiency, resentment, and corruption. King Philip II died in 1598.

REFERENCES: J. H. Elliott, *Imperial Spain, 1469–1716*, 1963; L. Fernández y Fernández de Retaña, *España en el tiempo de Felipe II*, 1566–1598, 1958.

PHILIP III. King Philip III, the son of King Philip II* of Spain, was born in 1578. He assumed the throne of Spain, Naples, and Sicily upon the death of his father in 1598, but his reign was undistinguished. Economic problems, fueled by serious problems with inflation, began to afflict Spain during Philip III's reign. Philip III turned over the duties of his office to the Duke of Lerma. He died in 1621.

REFERENCE: R. A. Stradling, *Philip IV and the Government of Spain, 1621-1665*, 1988.

PHILIP IV. King Philip IV, the son of King Philip III* of Spain, was born in 1605. He assumed the throne of Spain, Naples, and Sicily upon the death of his father in 1621, but during his reign, Spain began its long decline as a world power. Like his father Philip III, he was an ineffective ruler who let an associate, the Count Olivares, administer the kingdom. The loss of Portugal in 1640 was symbolic of that beginning decline, but English and Dutch penetration of the New World as well as of Asian markets was far more significant. Philip IV died in 1665 and was succeeded by his son Charles II*.

REFERENCE: R. A. Stradling, *Philip IV and the Government of Spain, 1621-1665*, 1988.

PHILIP V. King Philip V, the grandson of King Louis XIV of France, was born on December 19, 1683. King Charles II*, the childless ruler of Spain, designated Philip V as his sucessor, and in 1700, King Philip V thus became the first Bourbon ruler of Spain. His succession to the Spanish throne precipitated the War of the Spanish Succession* throughout Europe and parts of the New World. Philip V's reign was characterized by difficult imperial struggles for power and the continuing decline of Spanish fortunes. As the years passed, Philip V became increasingly morose and uninterested in his responsibilities; more and more power flowed to his second wife, Isabel Farnesio. Philip V abdicated the throne in 1724 in favor of his son Luis, but Luis died after only six months and Philip V returned to power. From then on, he took little interest in affairs of state or colonial questions. He did, however, enrage *criollo** merchants in the New World in 1729 by prohibiting them from direct participation in imperial trade except through a Spanish or *peninsular** agent. He died in 1746 and was succeeded by his son, Ferdinand VI.

REFERENCE: W. T. Hargraves-Mawdsley, *Spain, 1700–1788: A Political, Diplomatic, and Institutional History*, 1978.

PHILIPPINE COMPANY. In 1785, Charles III* founded the Philippine Company to promote trade between Spain and the Philippine* Islands. The company had some economic success in the 1790s and early 1800s, but then its fortunes changed. It failed to gain the full cooperation of Manila* merchants, and it did not exploit what could have been its comparative advantage in trade with Asian countries. Spain abolished the company in 1834.

REFERENCE: Ester G. Maring and Joel M. Maring, *Historical and Cultural Dictionary of the Philippines*, 1973.

PHILIPPINES. An island nation in Southeast Asia, the Philippines are unique in geography, history, and culture. It is the only Christian nation in Asia. Filipinos* are highly educated but very poor. They had a long tutelage in democracy but have had to endure the worst misrule. The roots of the country's problems lie in its colonial history. Other Southeast Asian nations conceive their ''true'' identity to have emerged from pre-colonial kingdoms and empires. Filipinos like to joke that they spent ''300 years in a convent, 50 years in Hollywood, and three years in a concentration camp,'' referring to Spanish, American, and Japanese imperialism. A more accurate metaphor compares the Filipino identity to layers of onionskin. The casual observer sees a superficial veneer of Americanization, but may overlook the Hispanic layer underneath, and not see the Filipino's true Asian identity.

There was no ''Philippines'' before Spain created that political unit from an archipelago of dozens of islands, large and small, inhabited by local groups of Malays who spoke 88 different languages. The islands lay too far east of the

trade route between India and China to have been affected much by the waves
of Hinduism, Buddhism, and Islam that washed over the rest of Southeast Asia.
What Ferdinand Magellan* found when he reached the Visayas* (central islands)
in 1521 was a group of tropical islands where self-sufficient coastal Malays grew
paddy rice and fished. The mountainous, forested interior regions were inhabited
by different tribes, some quite primitive and some who maintained elaborate
rice terraces. The reconquest of Spain for Christendom being fresh in their minds,
the Spaniards were horrified to find that Islam was spreading in the islands.

Spain's motives for taking the islands were threefold: (1) there might be gold
and silver, and there certainly were spice islands nearby; (2) Filipinos, mostly
animists, seemed ripe for conversion; and (3) the archipelago had marvelous
deepwater bays almost on the doorstep of China. Conquest was not too difficult,
as local feuds made it easy to play one group against another. Filipinos were
awed, too, by Catholic religious rituals and clerical garb. Starting with Miguel
López de Legazpi's* settlement at Manila* (1571), Spanish control extended to
all coastal areas of the islands, except Mindanao*.

The islands, an ocean away even from New Spain*, remained always the
remotest part of Spain's empire. Religious orders (Augustinians*, Dominicans*,
Jesuits*, and Franciscans*) cleared vast estates, but most Spaniards preferred to
wait in Manila for the arrival of the Manila galleon* that annually brought mail
and goods from Acapulco*. A stratified class society emerged as Spaniards
conferred titles on tribal chiefs. In the villages, local priests, assisted by retainers
of elite mestizo* families, ran everything. Few Filipinos learned Spanish and
few Spaniards, other than priests, mastered Philippine languages. The authorities
were completely uninterested in teaching anyone to read or write. Insular society
persisted in this sleepy pattern for two centuries until an upswing in global trade
changed everything.

When the last galleon came from Acapulco in 1815, Manila was thrown back
on its own resources. Filipinos now were encouraged to plant export crops:
indigo*, sugar*, rice, hemp, and tobacco*. Spain gave up trying to exclude English
and American merchants, and the transforming effects of world commerce were
felt everywhere. Regional economies depended on a single crop: sugar in central
Luzon* and Negros, tobacco in the Ilocano-speaking coastal regions of northern
Luzon, hemp in Bicol. Chinese immigrants went to live in provincial towns,
where they bought and sold plantation crops, loaned money, and ran retail stores.
The social structure grew more rigid as landowners found new sources of wealth.
Rapid population growth provided plenty of cheap labor.

Free trade in goods eventually brought free circulation of ideas. The mestizo
elite found Spanish arrogance increasingly difficult to endure. Wealthy families
sent their children to be educated in Manila or Spain. Anger focused on the
Spanish monopoly of church posts. Three Filipino priests, Fathers José Burgos,
Mariano Gómez, and Jacinto Zamora, were executed in Cavite* in 1872, becoming the first martyrs to Philippine independence. A sense of national identity
grew where none had existed before. Spaniards called the natives "indios" and

islanders defined themselves by language group: Tagalog*, Cebuano, Ilocano, and so forth. Only in the 1890s did nationalists begin to call themselves "Filipinos."

Revolution was already in the air in 1892 when the brilliant novelist José Rizal* was sent into internal exile in Mindanao. He was executed in 1896, though quite innocent of revolutionary agitation. Fighting broke out that year. The Philippine Revolution (1896–1898) was Asia's first struggle for a modern republic, but it ended inconclusively when General Emilio Aguinaldo* signed the Pact of Biak-na-Bato in 1897, accepting exile in Hong Kong and a generous sum of money. He was brought back by U.S. Admiral George Dewey in 1898, and immediately resumed his revolutionary war against Spain. Aguinaldo believed that after the Americans quickly disposed of Spain's fleet (May 1, 1898) and took Manila in June, they would simply withdraw. He was badly mistaken. Instead, the United States bought the islands from Spain for $20 million. The only problem was that American forces actually controlled only Manila itself. Shooting broke out on February 4, 1899, and the Philippine-American War was on. It was shockingly vicious on both sides, but ended with a complete American victory. The Filipinos traded Spanish imperialism for American imperialism.

REFERENCES: Renato Constantino, *A History of the Philippines*, 1975; Alfred W. McCoy and Edilberto de Jesús, *Philippine Social History*, 1982; John L. Phelan, *The Hispanization of the Philippines*, 1967.

Ross Marlay

PICHINCHA, BATTLE OF. The Battle of Pichincha was the last major engagement in the Ecuadorian war of independence. General Antonio José de Sucre* led the rebel forces and in May 1822, he invaded the Ecuadorian highlands. On May 24, 1822, Sucre established a strong defensive position at the bottom of Mount Pichincha, west of Quito*. Royalist troops attacked but after hours of intense fighting, Sucre's troops prevailed. The next day President Melchor de Aymerich of Quito signed a document of surrender, giving the rebels control of what became the nation of Ecuador*. Simón Bolívar* was quickly accepted as the president of Ecuador.

PIEDRAHITA, LUCAS FERNÁNDEZ DE. See FERNÁNDEZ DE PIEDRAHITA, LUCAS DE.

PIGS. Among the biological transplants that the Spaniards brought to the New World, pigs were among the most important. Unlike cattle, which consume plants indigestible to humans, pigs need concentrated carbohydrates and protein, but they convert one-fifth of what they consume into food for human consumption, compared to only 5 percent for cattle. In the early years of the New World colonies, where carbohydrates and protein were plentiful in the environment and human consumers few, pigs became the ideal food for settlers. Although pigs do not do well in extremely cold climates or intense heat, they found enough shade and moisture in the Americas to thrive. Also, pigs are omnivorous—able to eat a wide variety of products—so they were very adaptable to different habitats. Christopher Columbus[*] brought pigs in 1493, and Spaniards regularly left pigs behind in an area so that future explorers would have plentuful supplies of meat. Pigs multiplied so rapidly that within a few years they would be in abundant supply. This was called the "seeding" of remote areas. Pigs multiplied by the tens of millions, often reverting to a wild state, and for most colonists during most of the colonial period, pork was the main source of protein.

REFERENCE: Alfred W. Crosby, Jr., *Ecological Imperialism: The Biological Expansion of Europe, 900–1900*, 1986.

PINCKNEY'S TREATY OF 1796. Also known as the Treaty of San Lorenzo, Pinckney's Treaty of 1796 was an important diplomatic achievement for the United States. For American settlers living west of the Appalachian mountains, the economic lifeline was the Mississippi River. The only real way for them to ship products to market was down the Ohio and Tennessee rivers to the Mississippi River, and down the Mississippi to New Orleans. Access to New Orleans was critical to economic survival. Thomas Pinckney negotiated the treaty with Spain. The United States secured navigational rights on the Mississippi River, established clear title to the territory of the Old Southwest south to 31 degrees north latitude, and received the right of deposit at New Orleans. Western farmers and shippers now had the economic access they needed to world markets.

REFERENCE: Samuel F. Bemis, *Pinckney's Treaty*, 1960.

PINEDA Y BASCUÑÁN, FRANCISCO NÚÑEZ DE. See NÚÑEZ DE PINEDA Y BASCUÑÁN, FRANCISCO DE.

PINTO DÍAZ, FRANCISCO ANTONIO. Francisco Antonio Pinto Díaz was born in Chile[*] in 1775. He earned a law degree in Santiago[*] in 1808 and in 1810 he joined the independence movement. Eventually he served both Bernardo O'Higgins[*] and José de San Martín[*] as a diplomatic adviser and representative. He became minister of war, interior, and foreign relations in 1824; in 1827, he was elected vice-president of Chile. When President Ramón Freire[*] Serrano resigned in 1827, Pinto Díaz became the new president. When Chile erupted in civil war in 1829, Pinto Díaz resigned the presidency and later emerged as the leader of the Liberal Party. He unsuccessfully ran for the presidency in 1841 and then spent several years in the senate before his death in 1858.

REFERENCES: Lia Cortés and Jordi Fuentes, *Diccionario Político de Chile*, 1967; Luis Galdames, *Historia de Chile*, 1945.

PINZÓN, VICENTE YÁÑEZ. Vicente Yáñez Pinzón was born in Palos, Spain, around 1463. In 1492, he accompanied Christopher Columbus[*] on his epic voyage to the New World, serving as captain of the *Niña*. He sailed for America a second time in November 1499, landing on the coast of Brazil, then sailing west and northwest along the coast, and exploring up the Amazon River for about 30 miles. From the mouth of the Amazon, the expedition headed to Hispaniola*, then the Bahamas*, and finally reached Spain in September 1500. A third voyage between 1502 and 1504 brought Pinzón down the southern coast of Brazil, and on a fourth voyage in 1506 Pinzón explored the Caribbean coast of Central America. Vicente Pinzón died in Spain in 1514.

REFERENCE: James Roxburgh McClymont, *Vicente Yáñez Pinzón*, 1916.

PIPILES. The Pipiles were a Nahuatl* people who migrated from the Central Valley of Mexico to El Salvador* sometime during the first millenium A.D., possibly after the fall of Teotihuacán around A.D. 700. Culturally and linguistically distinct from the Maya* of the southern Mesoamerican region, the Pipiles brought to the area artistic and religious elements from Teotihuacán and from El Tajín, in Vera cruz*. They traded and had extensive communications with the non-Nahuatl peoples of Central America. By the beginning of the sixteenth century, Pipil cultural influences were evident as far south as Costa Rica* and as far north as Guatemala*. The Pipiles established their capital at Cuscatlán*. There the Pipiles defeated Pedro de Alvarado* in 1524, shortly after he had vanquished the Quiche of Guatemala at Xelaju. The next year Alvarado returned to Cuscatlan, which he christened San Salvador*. An uprising of the Cakchiquel forced Alvarado to return to Guatemala and briefly abandon San Salvador, but in 1527 Alvarado's brother Jorge returned to rule the Pipiles. In 1528, when the Pipil population was greatly diminished by disease and deprivation, Jorge de Alvarado moved San Salvador to the Valley of La Bermuda, and Cuscatlán was abandoned.

REFERENCE: R. L. Woodward, Jr., *Central America: A Nation Divided*, 1983.

Virginia Garrard Burnett

PIRACY. Although Spain and Portugal had divided up the New World in the Treaty of Tordesillas* in 1494, the other European powers, especially the English, the French, and the Dutch, did not recognize their sovereignty. Dutch, French, and English pirates, often with the blessings of their respective governments, went after Spanish property in the sixteenth, seventeenth, and eighteenth centuries. French corsairs were operating in Spanish waters within a decade of Christopher Columbus's* discovery, and during the 1500s, they regularly attacked Spanish ports and Spanish shipping along the Gulf coast of New Spain.* English pirates like John Hawkins and Francis Drake* attacked Spanish ships and ports in the latter part of the sixteenth century. Those attacks continued into the eighteenth century. English and Dutch pirates, such as Thomas Cavendish, were active on the west coast of New Spain and targeted the Manila galleons*.

REFERENCES: Peter Gerhard, *Pirates on the West Coast of New Spain, 1575–1742*, 1960; Elisabeth Wallace, *The British Caribbean*, 1977.

PIZARRO, FRANCISCO. Francisco Pizarro was born in Trujillo, Extremadura, Spain, in 1478. He was the illegitimate son of a Spanish soldier and a farmer's daughter. He grew up a social outcast, never attending school or learning to read and write. Like so many other poor people from Extremadura, however, Pizarro found his fortune in the New World. In 1502, he sailed to Hispaniola* with Nicolás de Ovando*; in 1509, Pizarro accompanied Alonso de Ojeda* on his expedition to the Gulf of Uraba; and in 1513, he was among the first to see the Pacific Ocean with Vasco Núñez de Balboa*. By 1524, Pizarro was one of the most prominent political figures in Panama*. As a result of that influence he found financing and received permission to lead an expedition south into the continent of South America where rich Indian* kingdoms were rumored to exist. In 1524 and again between 1526 and 1528, Pizarro led Spanish troops south into Colombia* and northern Peru*, finding evidence along the way that advanced civilizations were indeed nearby. Pizarro traveled back to Spain in 1529 and received royal permission to conquer Peru. He returned to Panama in 1530 to prepare the expedition.

Pizarro's expedition of conquest began in January 1531 when he and his forces left Panama. They landed on the coast of present-day Ecuador* and began a march to the south, which at last brought them to Cuzco*, Peru, in 1533. There they defeated the army of the Incan* king Atahualpa* and executed him. Pizarro founded the city of Lima* in 1535. During the next six years, Pizarro kept control of his new conquest, but not without having to crush several Incan uprisings and fight a civil war with followers of Diego de Almagro*, his chief rival in Peru. On June 26, 1541, Francisco Pizarro was assassinated by an Almagro loyalist.

REFERENCES: John Hemming, *The Conquest of the Incas*, 1970; James Lockhart, *The Men of Cajamarca*, 1972.

PIZARRO, GONZALO. Gonzalo Pizarro was born in Trujillo, Extremadura, Spain, in 1506. He followed his older brother, Francisco Pizarro*, into the New World and participated directly in the conquest of the Inca* empire. The expedition left Panama* in 1531 and landed in Ecuador*. During the next two years, they moved south through Ecuador and Peru*, finally defeating and executing Atahuaupa*, the Inca emperor, in 1533. In return for his support, Francisco Pizarro named Gonzalo governor of Charcas*, which included much of present-day Bolivia*. Francisco and Gonzalo Pizarro fought a civil war against the incursions of Diego de Almagro*, and when Francisco was assassinated by followers of Almagro in 1541, Gonzalo named himself governor of Peru. The next year, King Carlos I* of Spain implemented the New Laws*, which were designed to eliminate the worst abuses that Spanish colonists had imposed on local Indians*, Blasco Núñez de Vela* came to Peru to enforce the New Laws. Gonzalo Pizarro, afraid of losing what he had fought for, violently resisted, throwing the region into civil war. Gonzalo Pizarro died in 1548 when Pedro de la Gasca* arrived with an army to enforce the king's will.

REFERENCES: John Hemming, *The Conquest of the Incas*, 1970; James Lockhart, *The Men of Cajamarca*, 1972.

PIZARRO, PEDRO. Pedro Pizarro was born around 1499 in Toledo, Spain. He came to the New World as the page to his cousin, Francisco Pizarro*, the conqueror of the Inca* empire. Throughout his association with his cousin, Pedro Pizarro kept detailed, written observations of the conquest. Although the manuscript was, not unexpectedly, pro-Spanish and anti-Indian*, it is nevertheless an invaluable primary source for the history of the conquest of Peru*. Pedro Pizarro died in Quito*, Ecuador*, on February 9, 1589, but his manuscript was not discovered until 250 years later in the national library of Spain in Madrid. It was published in 1844 as *Nueva crónica y buen gobierno*.

REFERENCES: Marvin Alisky, *Historical Dictionary of Peru*, 1979; A. Curtis Wilgus, *The Historiography of Latin America: A Guide to Historical Writing, 1500-1800*, 1975.

PLASENCIA, JUAN DE. Juan de Plasencia was born in Extremadura, Spain, and entered the Franciscan* order as a young man. When Franciscans were first sent to Manila* in March 1578, Plasencia was in the first party of priests to arrive. In 1583, he was elected custodian of the Franciscans. During his stay in the Philippines*, Plasencia helped codify Tagalog* law so that the *audiencia* of Manila* could employ local customs in civil suits between Filipinos*. He also wrote the first Tagalog-Spanish catechism and worked at gathering the Filipinos into compact villages where they could be provided with secular and religious education. Juan de Plasencia died in 1590.

REFERENCE: John Leddy Phelan, *The Hispanization of the Philippines: Spanish Aims and Filipino Responses 1565-1700*, 1959.

POLAVIEJA, CAMILO GARCÍA DE. See GARCÍA DE POLAVIEJA, CAMILO.

POLISARIO FRONT. The Polisario Front, formally known as the Popular Front for the Liberation of Saguia el-Hamra and Río de Oro, was formed on May 10, 1973, by militant nationalists who had previously been part of the "Embryonic Movement for the Liberation of the Sahara." Its objective was to destroy the Spanish Empire in the Sahara. Its leader was El-Ouali* Mustapha Sayed. Between 1973 and 1975, the Polisario Front conducted a guerrilla campaign against Spain, which included a variety of military and terrorist attacks. The organization also opposed any attempt by Morocco to annex part or all of Spanish Sahara*. Support for the front grew in 1974 and 1975, especially when it appeared that Spain was preparing to leave Spanish Sahara*. The front also declared its support for an end to slavery*, polygamy, caste differences, sexism, and tribal divisions. During a United Nations visit to Western Sahara in May 1975, it was clear to everyone involved that the front had secured the overwhelming support of the Saharawi people. In October 1975, Spain and the Polisario Front came to terms on independence, whereby all prisoners of war were exchanged and a 15- to 20-year transition would take place concerning Spanish fishing and phosphate claims. The front thought that it had secured its objective. Later in the year, however, the Moroccans and Mauritanians increased their demands for control of Western Sahara. In spite of the earlier agreement with the Polisario Front, Spain signed the Madrid Agreement* in November 1975, which agreed to divide Western Sahara between Mauritania and Morocco. The Polisario Front felt betrayed and launched a new struggle against both Mauritania and Morocco, a struggle that continues today.

REFERENCES: Tony Hodges, *Historical Dictionary of Western Sahara*, 1982; John Mercer, *Spanish Sahara*, 1975.

PONCE DE LEÓN, JUAN. Juan Ponce de León was born in Santervas del Campo, Valladolid province, Spain, around 1460. Although he came from a well-to-do family, Juan Ponce de León looked to the New World for his fortune, sailing with Christopher Columbus* on his second voyage to America in 1493 and settling in Hispaniola*. In 1509, he was named governor of Puerto Rico*, although he lost that position in 1511 to Diego Columbus*, who had a prior claim based on his father's discoveries there. King Ferdinand* then commissioned Ponce de León to take the island of Bimini. Although some historians have claimed that Ponce de León was obsessed with finding the ''fountain of youth,'' there is little evidence for such a claim. In 1513, he led an expedition northwest from Puerto Rico and landed near contemporary St. Augustine*, Florida*, on April 2, 1513. On April 9, during their return voyage, Ponce de León's expedition discovered the Gulf Stream, which opened up a new trade route from the West Indies to Spain. Late in June, the party landed in either Cuba* or the Yucatán* but then returned to Puerto Rico after a short stay. Juan Ponce de León became captain general of Puerto Rico in 1514. He returned to Florida in 1521, planning to establish a permanent settlement there, but he was wounded in a skirmish with local Indians. He died in July 1521 from complications of the wound.

REFERENCE: Edward W. Lawson, *The Discovery of Florida and Its Discoverer, Juan Ponce de León*, 1946.

Virginia Garrard Burnett

PONT, MARCO DEL. Francisco Casimoro Ángel Díaz y Mendez, the Marco del Pont, was born in Spain in Vigo, 1765, and decided on a military career. During the French invasion of Iberia, Marco del Pont was captured and spent the five years between 1809 and 1814 in a French prison. By the time of his release, he was a general in the Spanish army. In 1814, Marco del Pont was appointed governor of Plaza de Tortosa, and at the end of that year, he became captain general of Chile* and president of the royal *audiencia**. He was destined to be the last individual to hold that office. He was taken prisoner by patriot forces after the Battle of Chacabuco* in 1817 and exiled to Argentina*. The Marco del Pont died there in 1821.

REFERENCES: Salvatore Bizarro, *Historical Dictionary of Chile*, 1987; José Toribîo Medina, *Diccionario biográfico colonial de Chile*, 1906.

POPAYÁN. The region known as Popayán was located in southwestern Colombia* and was settled by people moving out of Peru*. Its first governor arrived in 1536. Popayán fell under the authority of the *audiencias** of Peru* (1536–1549), New Granada* (1549–1563), and Quito* (1563–1717). When the *audiencia* of Quito was suppressed in 1717, Popayán came under the viceroyalty of New Granada*. Spanish authority was eliminated in Popayán by 1820, and the region became part of Gran Colombia* after the wars of independence.

POPÉ REBELLION. Following several decades of Spanish assaults on their way of life, the Pueblo Indians* of New Mexico* staged a major rebellion on August 10, 1680. Causes of Pueblo discontent that led to the rebellion included Spanish exploitation of the Pueblo Indians as laborers, the church/state rivalry, smallpox and other epidemics, droughts, Indians raiding towns, and the zealous attempts of Franciscans* to stamp out Pueblo religious practices. One of the key leaders was Popé, a Tewa Indian medicine man from the village of San Juan. Wanting all of the Pueblos to rebel in unison, Popé devised a plan whereby messengers would deliver knotted cords to the Pueblos. Each day one knot was to be untied until none remained, signaling the day of the attack. Spanish authorities, however, learned of the scheme, which, in turn, forced Popé and others to launch their attack a day earlier than planned. The Pueblo Indians went on a rampage throughout New Mexico, killing Spanish men, women, and children and destroying all vestiges of Spanish authority. Spanish survivors fled to Santa Fe*, which was put under seige. The Indians cut off the city's water supply, finally forcing Governor Antonio de Otermín to evacuate Santa Fe on August 21 and head south to El Paso. The Indians had killed over 400 Spaniards, including 21 priests.

The Pueblo Indians held New Mexico for 12 years, defeating Spanish forces sent to reconquer the province. The reconquest was finally achieved by General Diego de Vargas during the period from 1692 to 1694. In 1696, the Pueblo Indians again staged a short-lived revolt that lasted about four months and caused the deaths of 21 colonists and five priests. As a result of the Pueblo Revolt of 1680, Spanish and Pueblo relations eventually improved. For example, the *encomienda** system, a system of exploiting Indians on land grants, ended, and Spanish missionaries toned down their vigorous attacks on Pueblo religion.

REFERENCES: John Francis Bannon, *The Spanish Borderlands Frontier 1513-1821*, 1970; Jack D. Forbes, *Apache, Navaho, and Spaniard*, 1960; Charles W. Hackett and Charmion C. Shelby, eds., *Revolt of the Pueblo Indians of New Mexico and Otermin's Attempted Reconquest, 1680-1682*, 2 vols., 1942.

Raymond Wilson

POPULATION. The size of the indigenous population of the New World at the time of the Spanish conquest remains a scholarly quagmire, with estimates of the total numbers of Indians ranging from 8 million to more than 100 million. The truth, most likely, rests somewhere between those two figures. The greatest concentrations of Indians were in the Valley of Mexico and in the Peruvian and Bolivian Andes. What is certain, however, is that a demographic nightmare took place in the sixteenth century when European diseases created pandemics among the native peoples. The native American population began a steady decline which did not end until the middle of the seventeenth century. By 1650, the population of Latin America, including Brazil, totaled approximately 9,500,000 people. It increased to 10,500,000 by 1750 and 21,000,000 by 1800.

REFERENCE: T. Lynn Smith, *Latin America: Population Studies*, 1961.

POPUL VUH. The "Popul Vuh" is the Quiché Maya* creation story that describes the mythic origins of the Quiché people and their institutions. It also includes the history—part legend and part fact—of the Quiché down to 1550. Although there is considerable doubt as to its literary recording, most scholars believe that a Quiché Indian—Diego Reynos—who had converted to Roman Catholicism recorded the story shortly after the Spanish conquest of the Quiché nation. Father Francisco Ximénez* found the manuscript in his parish church at Chichicastenango in the early 1700s. He then translated it into Latin. The original Quiché text has subsequently been lost.

REFERENCE: Dennis Tedlock, *Popol Vuh*, 1985.

PORRAS, MARTÍN DE. Martín de Porras was a *zambo** of mixed African-Indian ancestry who was born in Peru* in 1579. He joined the Roman Catholic priesthood and devoted the rest of his life to caring for the poor and needy. Porras was eventually canonized by the Roman Catholic Church* and became the patron saint of the Peruvian lower classes.

REFERENCE: Marvin Alisky, *Historical Dictionary of Peru*, 1979.

POTOSÍ. During the early colonial period of Latin American history, the city of Potosí in present-day Bolivia* was the crown jewel of the Spanish Empire. Founded in 1545 after the discovery of incredibly rich veins of silver in the Andes Mountains at Cerro Rico, Potosí was given the name "Real Villa Imperial de Carlos V de España" in 1553. Potosí grew rapidly, reaching a population of 160,000 people by 1600. The mines of Potosí produced the largest volume of silver in the New World. The mercury extraction process increased production in the 1570s and 1580s, and most of the labor in the mines was provided by the *mita** system. By the middle of the 1600s, however, the major silver veins had been exhausted and production dropped dramatically. Potosí was part of the viceroyalty of Peru* until 1777, when it was transferred to the viceroyalty of Río de la Plata*. It was established as an *intendencia** in 1783. Rebel forces deposed and executed Francisco de Paula Sanz, the intendant, in 1810, and for the next decade, Potosí shifted back and forth under the control of rebel and royalist forces. Eventually, most of the *intendencia* became part of Bolivia. At the time of Bolivian independence, the city had fewer than 8,000 people.

PRIMO DE VERDAD Y RAMOS, FRANCISCO. Born in 1760 in Aguascalientes, New Spain*, young Francisco Primo de Verdad y Ramos followed a legal career that catapulted him into fame with the events of 1808. The plot of Aranjuez and the crisis of Bayonne became the catalyst for historic events in the viceregal capital of New Spain. The stronghold of the Mexican party was the *cabildo** of Mexico City*, which now decided to play a significant role at a time when New Spain had already developed a strong national feeling. Among the most conspicuous leaders who aimed at autonomy or independence were the lawyers Francisco Primo de Verdad y Ramos and Juan Francisco de Azcárate. Together with the Mercedarian* friar Melchor de Talamantes Salvador y Baeza, the *marqueses* de Uluapa and de Guardiola, colonel Ignacio Obregón, Count de Santiago and Canon Juan María Beristaín, they represented the core of Mexican nationalism.

When the fateful news from Bayonne was received in New Spain in the middle of July 1808, the *cabildo* of Mexico City took the initiative. It arrogated to itself the right to speak for the entire viceroyalty of New Spain* and called for an extraordinary meeting for July 16, 1808. This meeting, however, accomplished little, so another was convened for July 19. For the *cabildo* of Mexico City, the abdication of Bayonne was an act of force with no right to it. All Spanish sovereigns had given an oath to "this most noble city as the Metropolis of the Kingdom without alienating it, or giving away what it owns in terms of privileges." The *cabildo* concluded that New Spain would sustain the legitimate kings of Spain and that Viceroy José de Iturrigaray* should continue in his post provisionally by the mere fact of the popular will which it, the cabildo, was now interpreting. It also requested the convocation of a *junta general* that was to prepare an assembly of the Cortes of New Spain. These decisions were communicated to the *audiencia** and to the viceroy*. The former opposed the resolutions, but Viceroy Iturrigaray sided with the Mexican party—a unique situation, since at that moment he himself was personifying a kind of king of New Spain.

The meeting of the *junta general* on August 9, 1808, convoked by the viceroy, provided the opportunity for an agreement by both opposing parties: by the *oidor** Guillermo de Aguirre*, the spokesman for the *peninsulares**, and by Primo de Verdad, lawyer of the townhall of Mexico City and the speaker for the *criollos**. It was during this meeting that Primo de Verdad of Aguascalientes made his famous speech. He stated that the reason for the convocation of general Cortes was the simple fact that the legitimate metropolitan authorities had disappeared and that the people, source and origin of sovereignty, ought to resume its authority in order to establish a provisional government that would fill the vacuum caused by the absence and apparent perpetual dethronement of the legitimate Spanish kings. His arguments were based on the legislation of Las Siete Partidas* and represented the *pactum translationis*. In other words, the Spanish people in Spain had implicitly applied the identical thesis when they created juntas, a Junta Suprema Central, and a regency; the Mexicans, having the same rights as the Spaniards, were entitled to establish similar *juntas* and convene *cortes* for the defense of the viceroyalty, since they had never been colonies. The loyalty of New Spain had never been connected to Spain or the Spanish people, except through a metaphysical link to the person of the legitimate king, due to the proprietary character of the Indies. Now that the legitimate ruler was gone, civil authority automatically reverted to the source whence it had come. In Spain, this was the Spanish people; in Mexico, it had to be the Mexican people.

The Mexican party, which was a minority, was soon overruled after Primo de Verdad ended his speech. The Spanish party, headed by the inquisitors, the members of the *consulado**, and the *peninsular* merchants, whose opinion was that of the *oidor* Aguirre, had won the day. Had Primo de Verdad won, Mexico would have achieved independence as early as 1808. On the same night that Viceroy Iturrigaray was seized and shipped back to Spain, September 15, 1808, Primo de Verdad was put in jail. He was to go on trial but was found dead in his cell in October 1808. He may have been murdered.

REFERENCES: Enrique Lafuente Ferrari, *El virrey Iturrigaray y los orígenes de la independencia de Méjico*, 1941; O. Carlos Stoetzer, *The Scholastic Roots of the Spanish American Revolution*, 1979.

O. Carlos Stoetzer

PRINTING. The history of printing in the Spanish colonies is relatively well documented, although certain episodes remain unclear. Various scholars believe that the first printer in the new world was Esteban Martín who, they surmise, in 1534 or 1535, set up a basic printing press in Mexico City* and published what was presumably the first book printed in the Spanish colonies: *Escala Espiritual para Llegar al Cielo*. Prior to Martín's arrival, the first bishop of Mexico, Juan de Zumárraga*, had personally petitioned the Crown for such a press to aid in the instruction of the colonists and Indians*. In 1539, the first commercial press was established in Mexico City by Juan Pablos, who came to Mexico as an employee of Juan Cromberger of Seville, a well-known Spanish printer. Pablos's first work appeared soon thereafter: *Breve y compendiosa Doctrina Christiana en Lengua Mexicana y Castellana*.

The printing press came to Lima*, Peru*, in 1581, thanks to Antonio Ricardo, an Italian printer who had previously worked in Mexico City. He published *Doctrina cristiana y catecismo para instrucción de los indios* in 1584. The seventeenth century witnessed new sites of press activity, most notably Puebla*, Mexico, in 1640, and Guatemala* (chronologically the fourth site), from 1660 to 1679 through the work of José de Pineda Ybarra. Others were established after Pineda's death. Paraguay* saw its first press early in the eighteenth century, thanks to the efforts of the Jesuits* and their desire to convert and catechize the Indians. Havana's* first press has been documented variously as 1707 or 1724. Printing presses were also set up in the following places and years: Oaxaca*, Mexico (1720), Bogotá* (1738–1742), Córdoba*, Argentina* (1766), Santo Domingo* (1782), Vera Cruz*, Mexico (1794), Santiago, Cuba* (1796), Montevideo* (1807), Caracas*, (1808), Puerto Rico* (1808), Guayaquil* (1810).

Although the printing press and printing came very early to the New World, its development was retarded for many reasons. First, colonial society was largely illiterate, resulting in a small reading audience. Secondly, the cost of printing, coupled with a scarcity of paper and supplies, made production economically difficult and many times virtually impossible. Thirdly, all printing was rigidly controlled by the Spanish throne through licensing requirements and marketing restrictions, with violations subject to considerable fines. Finally, censorship of written materials had an inhibiting effect upon the publishers.

Most published works in Spanish America were either religious or didactic in nature. Large numbers of catechisms, books of religious instruction and doctrine, lives of saints, sermons, and so forth were produced. These works were often the products of religious orders, most notably the Franciscans*, Dominicans*, and the Augustinians*. Other works included grammars, vocabularies, and dictionaries of Indian languages, largely for the purpose of conversion and missionary work. Still other books treated philosophy, medicine, and history. Because of strict literary censorship*, however, little creative fiction appeared. The printing press nonetheless exerted a profound influence in the New World. It slowly produced a contingent of printers and journalists, upgraded and increased literacy, and provided the colonists with a source of information not otherwise easily available.

REFERENCE: Arthur P. Whitaker, ed., *Latin America and the Enlightenment*, 1958.

Sam L. Slick

PROPAGANDA MOVEMENT. The Propaganda Movement was an embryonic nationalist movement in the Philippines*. Its primary leaders were José Rizal*, Marcelo del Pilar, and Graciano López-Jaena*. From its inception in 1872 until the establishment of the Katipunan* in 1892, it was the major nationalist movement in the islands. The movement's aims were reform rather than revolution, and it viewed public education as their primary method. It declined in strength during the 1890s when the more radical Katipunan captured Filipino* loyalty.

REFERENCE: W. Cameron Forbes, *The Philippine Islands*, 1928.

PROPIEDAD REALENGA. *Propiedad Realenga* was a term used to describe land once owned by the ruling classes of the Inca* empire in Ecuador*, Peru*, and Bolivia*. Spanish law reserved that land totally and absolutely for the Spanish Crown, which received all the income from such property.

REFERENCE: C. H. Haring, *The Spanish Empire in America*, 1947.

PROPIOS DEL CONCEJO. In medieval and early modern Castile* and throughout the Spanish Empire, municipalities (cities, towns, and villages) owned two types of property: commons, which were set aside for the free use of all *vecinos* (family heads or citizens) of the place; and *propios* (also called *bienes de propios*), which were any other kind of property owned by the municipality as a legal entity. The *propios* were treated legally as the private property of the municipal government and were usually rented out by the town council to provide funds for the municipal treasury. Municipal property of this type had existed in Spain during Roman times, but was expanded during the medieval Reconquista, when Spanish monarchs tried to strengthen the newly founded municipalities by granting them extensive property. Usually the *propios* were in the form of land, but they could be any other type of property, such as a tavern, a mill, a river ferry, or even the right to collect certain taxes.

National and local laws were enacted to guarantee the integrity of the *propios* by protecting them from greedy and unscrupulous local officials and other members of the power elite. Safeguards were provided to prevent abuses, and it was specified that the *propios* could only be rented in public auctions, to the highest bidder. The revenue from some *propios* was earmarked for specific purposes in the public welfare; otherwise, it went into the general municipal treasury. Some towns had little or no property of the *propio* type, whereas cities like Toledo and Trujillo were richly endowed in *propios*. Unlike commons, the *propios* were not legally inalienable, but the Spanish municipalities did not sell their *propios* except in the most pressing emergencies. They preferred to add to them, whenever possible. But the towns displayed no reluctance to mortgage their *propios* when they needed to borrow money. This could be done only through specific royal licenses, but the Crown readily gave its approval, especially since the borrowed funds usually were to be used to pay royal taxes.

In theory, there was a clear legal distinction between commons and *propios*. In practice, the difference was often quite hazy, because some *propios* were used as commons during part of the year and some commons were rented out during parts of the year or in financial emergencies. This ambiguity was the greater becasue many towns had usurped their *propios* from the neighboring commons, and both *propios* and commons had often been usurped from the nearby *tierras baldías**.

REFERENCES: David E. Vassberg, *Land and Society in Golden Age Castile*, 1984; Joaquín Costa y Martínez, *Colectivismo agrario en España: doctrinas y hechos*, 1944.

David E. Vassberg

PROVINCIAS INTERNAS. See INTERNAL PROVINCES.

PUEBLA. The city of Puebla was founded in 1531 by Franciscan* priests. The region of Puebla in eastern New Spain* was created as an *intendencia** in 1787, and in 1821, Puebla became part of the new republic of Mexico.

PUERTO RICO. Historians trace the ancestry of early Indian* tribes of Puerto Rico to the first wave of Asiatic nomads who inhabited the Western hemisphere. One of the early groups were the Ciboney* from whom the Arawaks* were descended. At the time of European contact, the Tainos* of the Arawak branch inhabited Puerto Rico. They were a peaceful, agricultural people who raised corn*, manioc, and cotton. Christopher Columbus* was the first European to contact the island of Puerto Rico. On his second voyage on November 19, 1493, he claimed the island for Spain. At the time, it was called Boriquen (Borinquen); Columbus renamed it San Juan Bautista (St. John the Baptist). The Spanish did not attempt rigid colonization during the first 15 years of occupation. The island was named San Juan, the main city was named Puerto Rico ("Rich Port"), and the Indians were left to their own devices.

This period of indifference ended in 1508 with the arrival of Juan Ponce* de León. As a member of Columbus's maiden crew, he was rewarded with the governorship of Puerto Rico. He initially settled at Caparra, changed the name to Ciudad de Puerto Rico (1511), and began mining for gold. Gold was not to be of major importance on this island except for its decimating effect on the Indian population. Dark, water-filled, poorly ventilated mines were not conducive to good health, and many Indians died. The real "gold" of the area was found upon the introduction of the sugar cane plant from Hispaniola* between 1511 and 1515. African slaves* arrived in 1518 to work the fields. Other crops of economic value during the latter 1500s were cotton, ginger, cacao*, and indigo*. By the seventeenth century, tobacco* was becoming important; within another century, it had become a cash crop. After the introduction of sugar*, the coastal Indian population declined, mostly due to forced labor and such European diseases as measles and smallpox. Those Indians who survived intermarried with the Europeans, thus diluting the Taíno strain.

After 1521, the island became known as Puerto Rico and the main city San Juan. Shortly thereafter, the strategic location of Puerto Rico came to the notice of other European powers. For a 200-year period ending in 1797, the island underwent numerous attacks by the Dutch and the English. San Juan became a heavily fortified, walled city that withstood most attempted takeovers. The English succeeded in 1598 but were eventually doomed by a tropical disease outbreak.

The nineteenth century was marred mainly by outbreaks against Spanish rule. None equaled a major revolution but Spain did acknowledge the actions and gave Puerto Rico the status of a province in 1869. Following quickly was the peaceful abolition of slavery. By the time of the appearance of the United States in 1898, Puerto Rico and Spain had achieved a remarkable compatibility as to the governing of the island. Shortly before United States intervention, Spain had extended limited autonomy to Puerto Rico. At the end of the Spanish-American War* in 1898, Puerto Rico was ceded to the United States.

REFERENCES: Robert Carr, *Puerto Rico*, 1984; Antonio López, *The Puerto Ricans: Their History, Culture, and Society*, 1980.

Catherine G. Harbour

PUERTO RICO, *AUDIENCIA* OF. The *audiencia* of Puerto Rico, also known as the Audiencia Real Territorial de Puerto Rico, was established in 1815. By that time, population growth was heavy enough to justify the existence of such a tribunal in Puerto Rico; moreover, the growing revolutionary movements in Mexico and Central America gave Spain the feeling that more direct control of Puerto Rico was necessary. Until 1831, the *audiencia* of Puerto Rico was closely affiliated with the *audiencia* on Cuba, but it became fully independent of Cuba in 1831.

REFERENCES: Mark A. Burkholder and D. S. Chandler, *From Impotence to Authority: The Spanish Crown and the American Audiencias, 1687-1808*, 1977; Robert Carr, *Puerto Rico*, 1984; Antonio López, *The Puerto Ricans: Their History, Culture, and Society*, 1980.

PUEYRREDÓN, JUAN MARTÍN DE. Juan Martín de Pueyrredón was born in Buenos Aires*, Argentina*, in 1777. He pursued a career as a merchant until the British invasions of 1806–1807, when he became actively involved in the military resistance effort. For a time, Pueyrredón supported the royalist effort in Buenos Aires, but after a visit to Spain, he decided that Spanish decadence was so extensive that Argentina should seek complete independence. Pueyrredón became a supporter of José de San Martín's* independence movement in Argentina. In 1816, the Congress of Tucumán* named him Supreme Director of the United Provinces of La Plata* and at the same time proclaimed independence from Spain. Pueyrredón served out his three-year term but refused to stand for re-election. He died in 1850.

REFERENCE: Enrique Udaondo, *Diccionario biográfico argentino*, 1938.

PUMACAHUA, MATEO GARCÍA. See GARCÍA PUMACAHUA, MATEO.

PUNO. Puno, a region in the far northwestern portion of the viceroyalty of Río de la Plata*, was set up as an *intendencia** in 1783 by King Charles III* as part of the Bourbon reforms. Because of its great distance from the viceregal capital at Buenos Aires*, it was transferred to the viceroyalty of Peru* in 1796. Puno became part of the new republic of Peru* in 1824.

Q

QUECHUA. Quechua (Kechua, Quichua, Kichwa, Keshwa, Quichua) is the language spoken today by the descendants of the Incas* (Inka), as well as of the tribes they conquered, in Peru*, Ecuador*, Colombia*, and Bolivia*. In the 1530s and early 1540s, however, the Spanish conquistadors*, led by Francisco Pizarro*, swiftly brought the Inca Empire under control. Spanish firearms and horses gave them a tremendous advantage in mobility and firepower; European diseases, to which the Indians* had no immunities, devastated tribal populations. Ironically, the absolutism of the Inca Empire proved to be a great Spanish advantage. When Pizarro executed Atahuallpa*, the Inca ruler, he found that the masses of Indians in the Inca Empire had no intention of resisting. They simply viewed Spanish despotism as something similar to Inca despotism.

When the Inca Empire expanded in the fourteenth and fifteenth centuries, it encountered a bewildering variety of languages and dialects. To govern the region, the Incas had to impose their own language. When the Spaniards arrived in the sixteenth century, they employed Quechua as a lingua franca for the *encomienda** as well as for the missions*. As a result, Quechua became a dominant linguistic and ethnic force in the highlands of west-central South America. Today, the northernmost Quechua-speaking tribe in South America is the Inga of Colombia; Almagüero is another Quechua dialect in Colombia. There are also 20,000 Quechuan-speaking Indians in Argentina*, particularly in the barrios of Buenos Aires*. They are classified as the Catamarca-La Rioja and Santiago del Estero groups. With more than 10 million native speakers, Quechua is by far the largest Indian language spoken in either North or South America. The center of Quechua is in the highlands of Peru, Bolivia, and Ecuador, but it has also spread to the highland areas of southern Colombia, northern Chile* and Argentina, the west coast of Peru, and the lowlands of Peru and Bolivia on the east slope of the Andes Mountains. The Quechua-speaking people in Ecuador include such groups as the Quijos, Tenas, Otavalos, Salasacas, and Saraguros. Dynamic and expansionist, Quechua has displaced many other native languages in its region of dominance. In the Peruvian and Bolivian highlands, more than 90 percent of the people understand Quechua, 80 percent speak it, and 50 percent know only it. Quechua is not, however, a monolithic tribal entity. Because it was superimposed by Incas and Spaniards on other tribes and dialects, there are powerful centrifugal ethnic forces among the various Quechua subtribes, who are identified either by their original tribal name, such as the Chachapoya or Chocorbo (Chocorvo), or by the village and region in Peru or Bolivia in which the individuals live, such as the Arequipa or the Huamachuco. Other prominent Quechua-speaking groups in Peru are the Alama, Ancash, Ayacucho, Cajamarca, Chasutino, Huanuco, Junin, Lamano, Lima, Mayna, Pasco, and Ucayali.

There is a tremendous diversity among the Quechua-speaking people, enough to divide them into many different ethnic groups. Linguists have identified two separate Quechuan language groups and seven distinct Quechuan languages: Ayacucho-Cuzco, Ancash-Huanuco, Yaru-Huanuco, Jauja-Huanca, Yauyos, Canaris-Cajamarca, and Chachapoyas-Lamas. Several million Quechua-speaking Indians have crowded into Lima*, Peru, and La Paz*, Bolivia, looking for work in recent years. There they learn to speak Spanish as well as begin to integrate themselves into the urban cash economy. In Bolivia, the Valley of Cochabamba is the center of Quechua culture, and fidelity to the language is very powerful. In Chuquisaca, the dialect is somewhat different but most people are monolingual. South of Potosí, by contrast, most of the Quechuan Indians are bilingual and are increasingly acculturated to neo-Bolivian values and culture. North of La Paz, in the provinces of Muñecas, Bautista Saavedra, and Franz Tamayo, the Indians are monolingual in a pre-Columbian Quechua dialect.

REFERENCES: Paul T. Baker, *Man in the Andes: Multidisciplinary Study of High-Altitude Quechua*, 1976; Lyle Campbell, *Quichoan Linguistic Prehistory*, 1977; Isabel Hernández, "Los Pueblos y Las Lenguas Aborígenes en La Actualidad," *America Indígena*, 47 (1987), 409–23; Billie Jean Isbell, *To Defend Ourselves: Ecology and Ritual in an Andean Village*, 1978; Harold Osborne, *Indians of the Andes: Aymaras and Quechuas*, 1940; Arthur P. Sorenson, Jr., "South American Indian Linguistics at the Turn of the Seventies," in Daniel R. Gross, ed., *Peoples and Cultures of Native South America*, 1973; Alfredo Torero, *El Quechua y la historia social Andina*, 1977.

QUIÑONES, FRANCISCO MARIANO. Francisco Mariano Quiñones was born in Puerto Rico* in 1830. He spent much of his youth in Germany, where he received his education, but upon his return he settled in San Germán, where he established the newspaper *El Espejo*. Quiñones used the newspaper* as a tool to promote his ideas favoring Puerto Rican autonomy within the Spanish Empire, as well as the abolition of slavery*. When Spain granted Puerto Rico the *Carta Autonómica** in 1897, Quiñones was appointed to the cabinet, where he directed internal affairs. After the Spanish-American War*, in which Puerto Rican sovereignty shifted from Spain to the United States, Quiñones served in the first legislature. Francisco Quiñones died in 1908.

REFERENCE: Kenneth R. Farr, *Historical Dictionary of Puerto Rico and the U.S. Virgin Islands*, 1973.

QUINTANO ROO, ANDRÉS. Andrés Quintano Roo was born in Mérida, New Spain*, on November 30, 1787. He received a degree in canon law from the Seminario Conciliar de Mérida, studied law privately, and then enjoyed a career as a revolutionary and journalist. A poet and essayist, Quintano Roo campaigned for independence from Spain. He was a deputy in the Congress of Chilpancingo* and presided over the National Constituent Assembly that declared Mexican independence in 1813. He held a number of important posts in the administrations of Agustín Iturbide*, Guadalupe Victoria*, Vicente Guerrero*, and Antonio López de Santa Anna. Andrés Quintano Roo died in Mexico City* on April 15, 1851.

REFERENCES: José A. Caruso, *The Liberators of Mexico*, 1967; Aurora M. Ocampo de Gómez and Ernesto Prado Velásquez, *Diccionario de escritores mexicanos*, 1967.

QUINTO. The *quinto*, or *quinto real*, was the royal fifth. In the New World empire, the Spanish Crown insisted on receiving 20 percent of the profits from all mining* operations. That yield was established in 1504, and it was somewhat lower than the Old World rate. The Crown hoped to attract investment capital to the New World mines, which were potentially far more lucrative. The royal fifth created much resentment among entrepreneurs in the colonies, and there was widespread avoidance when possible. In the eighteenth century, the Crown gradually reduced the tax to as little as a *diezmo*, or 10 percent.

REFERENCE: Peter J. Bakewell, *Silver Mining and Society in Colonial Mexico: Zacatecas, 1546–1700*, 1971.

QUIROGA, VASCO DE. Born in Madrigal in Old Castile* around 1470, young Vasco studied law in Valladolid and soon gained such a reputation that the bishop of Badajoz, who was also the president of the chancellery at Valladolid, recommended him as *oidor** to the first *audiencia* of New Spain*. This recommendation brought him to the New World. Thus, in 1531 arrived in Mexico where he was specifically entrusted to sit in judgment over Hernán Cortés* and Nuño de Guzmán* for alleged irregularities, especially those of the latter "for the bitter memories left among the Tarascans." Quiroga showed total objectivity and justice in these trials, and with funds earned from his position as *oidor*, he founded the hospital of Santa Fe in Tenochtitlán-Mexico. It was the first hospital of its kind in New Spain.

Thereafter, Vasco de Quiroga was sent to Michoacán to pacify the Tarascan Indians*, who were the victims of the first conquistadors* and had revolted against the abuses committed by Nuño de Guzmán and others. Not only did he succeed in pacifying the Tarascans, he was also able to win their friendship. In 1537, he was appointed bishop of Michoacán. Among his many achievements must be included: the foundation of the College-Seminary of San Nicolás in Pátzcuaro, one of the oldest of its kind in Spanish America; his famous economic measures for the benefit of the natives in his diocese which linked him especially to Thomas More's *Utopia*; and his support of the provincial council of 1555 in the viceregal capital. He is supposed to have been the first to introduce a banana* plantation in New Spain, and he is also credited with the development of several industries in his bishopric. His lifelong devotion to the natives in New Spain through missionary activity and the teaching of new handicrafts earned him eternal gratitude from his Indian pupils and bestowed great honor to the Spanish name, thus making amends for the earlier abuses committed by the first conquistadors. "His reputation for benevolence and idealism became legendary." He planned to attend the Council of Trent but died in 1565 in Uruapan, in his bishopric of Michoacán, before departure.

Vasco de Quiroga represented the echo of the Renaissance and sixteenth-century humanism in New Spain, especially with his attempt to put into practice More's *Utopia*. As a Christian mystic and utopian reformer, he tried to create an ideal society for the Indians under his care; thus, the village-hospitals in Tenochtitlán-Mexico and Michoacán were supposed to bring the natives closer to Spanish-Christian civilization. This he thought to accomplish through a work ethic while protecting the Indians from all kinds of abuses. His idealistic attempt in New Spain represented a vivid example, in both theory and practice, of that magnificent fusion of medieval thought and the currents of Renaissance humanism, similar to what occurred in the Peninsula in the sixteenth century in the eruption of Late Scholasticism. Among his works the following should be mentioned: the *Doctrina para los indios* and the *Reglas y ordenanzas para el gobierno de los hospitales de Santa Fé de México y Michoacán*.

REFERENCES: O. Carlos Stoetzer, *The Scholastic Roots of the Spanish American Revolution*, 1979; Henry Bamford Parkes, *A History of Mexico*, 1962.

O. Carlos Stoetzer

QUITO. Quito is the capital city of Ecuador* as well as of the province of Pichincha. Before the Spanish conquest, Quito became the capital city for the Inca* empire of Atahuallpa*. When the Spaniards captured and executed Atahuallpa, the Inca general Ruminahui destroyed the city. When Sebastián de Benalcázar* and Pedro de Alvarado* completed the conquest, however, they reestablished the city of Quito in 1534. In 1563, Quito became the seat of the *audiencia* of Quito*. The *audiencia* was dissolved between 1718 and 1722, and Quito became part of the viceroyalty of New Granada*; when that viceroyalty was suppressed in 1722, Quito was restored to the viceroyalty of Peru*. When the viceroyalty of New Granada was restored in 1739, the *audiencia* of Quito was transferred back. Between 1809 and 1822, Spanish authority ended in Quito, and until 1830, the region was part of Gran Colombia*. In 1830, Quito and the large surrounding area became the republic of Ecuador.

REFERENCE: Mark A. Buckholder and D. S. Chandler, *From Impotence to Authority: The Spanish Crown and the American Audiencias, 1687–1808*, 1977.

QUITO, *AUDIENCIA* OF. After the period of conquest and civil wars in Ecuador*, political stability was restored. The region became a separate province in 1556, and in 1563, Spain established the *audiencia* of Quito there. It was subject to the viceroyalty of Peru* until 1718, when the viceroyalty of New Granada* was established; at that point, the *audiencia* of Quito was suppressed. It was reconstituted four years later when the viceroyalty was suppressed. Although the viceroyalty of New Granada was re-established in 1740, the *audiencia* of Quito survived. The viceroyalty also contained the *audiencia* of Bogotá* and the *audiencia* of Caracas*. When independence was won, the *audiencias* of Quito, Bogotá, and Caracas all became part of the republic of Gran Colombia*. When Gran Colombia dissolved, the three former *audiencias* eventually became the countries of Ecuador, Colombia*, and Venezuela*.

REFERENCE: Mark A. Buckholder and D. S. Chandler, *From Impotence to Authority: The Spanish Crown and the American Audiencias, 1687–1808*, 1977.

QUITO, DIOCESE OF. The Roman Catholic diocese of Quito was established by Pope Paul III in 1545. It was raised to an archdiocese in 1848.

REFERENCE: *New Catholic Encyclopedia*, XII:33, 1967.

QUITO, UNIVERSITY OF. The city of Quito had a number of universities in the seventeenth and eighteenth centuries. In 1596, the Augustinian* order established the Colegio de San Nicolás Tolentino. The Jesuits* established the University of St. Gregory the Great in 1622 and the Dominicans* founded the College of St. Ferdinand in 1681. The best of the colonial universities was St. Thomas Aquinas, which the Crown established in 1688. In 1776, the royal government consolidated all of these institutions of higher learning into the University of Quito.

REFERENCE: Albert William Bork and Georg Maier, *Historical Dictionary of Ecuador*, 1973.

R

RACE. Some historians have argued that because Spain had been invaded by dark-skinned North African Moors in the eighth century, and because the last of those Moors were not expelled until 1492, the Spanish people were more accustomed to racial diversity than their counterparts in France and England. Whether or not this was so, race played a central role in the social structure of the empire. In virtually every colony, the upper class was composed of what Spaniards called *limpieza de sangre* (purity of blood). Access to positions of trust and power in the church, military, and bureauracy were confined to whites. Because of the shortages of Iberian women, the Spanish male settlers took Indians as wives and mistresses in Mexico, Central America, and South America, and their children became known as *mestizos*,* or mixed-bloods. Although they soon became by far the largest ethnic group in the Spanish colonies, they were nevertheless confined to the working and middle classes. Those Indians who survived the conquest were locked into a caste system in which they filled only the most menial roles in the economy.

In the Caribbean islands, the Indians were completely destroyed by diseases within the first few decades of the conquest. In Cuba,* Puerto Rico,* and Hispaniola,* the Spaniards imported large numbers of African slaves to work the sugar and coffee plantations. Those slaves, of course, became the very bottom level in the social strata. Above them were mulattoes—people of Spanish-African descent—who became the small farmers and working middle class. But just as in Mexico and South America, the upper classes in Cuba, Puerto Rico, and Hispaniola were people of purely European descent. White people were the power brokers in the Spanish empire, and people of color—whether Indian, African, mestizo, or Spanish-African—were exploited economically and powerless politically.

REFERENCE: Colin M. McLachlan and Jaime E. Rodríguez, *The Forging of the Cosmic Race: A Reinterpretation of Colonial Mexico*, 1980.

RAMÍREZ, ALEJANDRO. Alejandro Ramírez was a native of Spain born in 1774. He rose through Spanish political ranks and earned a reputation as a liberal-minded individual who was also an expert in financial matters. In 1812, he was named the first intendant of Puerto Rico*, and he used that post to stimulate education, industry, and agriculture, despite the intense opposition of Governor Salvador Melendez, who felt keenly the loss of personal authority. Ramírez also refined the collection of tax duties and established a lottery to improve the colony's revenue base. Ramírez remained in Puerto Rico until 1817, when he was appointed intendant of Cuba*; there he instituted similar economic reforms. He also abolished the tobacco* monopoly in Cuba and in 1819 saw to it that individuals who could prove they had been living on land for at least 40 years could have title to it. Alejandro Ramírez died in 1821.

REFERENCE: Kenneth R. Farr, *Historical Dictionary of Puerto Rico and the U.S. Virgin Islands*, 1973.

RAMÍREZ DE FUENLEAL, SEBASTIÁN. Sebastián Ramírez de Fuenleal was born in Cuenca, Spain, and was educated at the University of Valladolid. Ramírez became a leading Spanish jurist, serving as a judge in Valladolid, an inquisitor in Seville*, and an *audiencia* judge in Granada. He came to the New World in 1527 as president of the *audiencia* of Santo Domingo* and bishop of the diocese of Santo Domingo*. Ramírez is remembered as an excellent administrator who went on in 1531 to serve as president of the *audiencia* of Mexico City*. He returned to Spain in 1535 and served as bishop of Tuy (1535–38), León (1538–1539), and Cuenca (1539–1542). Ramírez died in Valladolid on January 22, 1547.

REFERENCE: *New Catholic Encyclopedia*, XIII:73, 1967.

RAMÍREZ DE VELASCO, JUAN. Juan Ramírez de Velasco was born in Castilla, Spain, to a distinguished and politically influential family. He entered the Spanish army as a young man and spent the next 30 years in a variety of military campaigns, distinguishing himself by his courage and good judgment. In 1586, King Philip II* appointed him governor of Tucumán* in the Río de la Plata* region, and for the next seven years, Ramírez worked at pacifying the Diaguita and Calchaquí Indians*, establishing new settlements, and placing the livestock industry on a sound footing. He assumed his duties as captain general and governor of Río de la Plata in 1596 but had to retire a year later for health reasons. Ramírez died in Tucumán in the settlement of Santa Fé in 1597.

REFERENCE: Enrique Udaondo, *Diccionario biográfico colonial argentino*, 1945.

RAMOS ARIZPE, JOSÉ MIGUEL. José Miguel Ramos Arizpe was born in San Nicolás de la Capellanía, Coahuila*, New Spain*, on February 15, 1775. He studied at Roman Catholic seminaries in Monterrey* and Guadalajara* before his ordination to the priesthood in 1803. In 1810, Ramos Arizpe was elected to the Cortes in Spain, where he vigorously promoted the political and economic interests of New Spain. In 1814, Ferdinand VII* had Ramos Arizpe imprisoned for treason because of his political philosophy. He was released in 1820 and returned to Mexico in 1822 as a delegate to the constitutional convention. There he was the main author of the constitution of 1824. Ramos Arizpe was also a prominent economist who advocated the abolition of all colonial monopolies, internal free trade, and fewer restrictions on international trade. During the rest of his career, Ramos Arizpe was a spokesman for the federalist political philosophy. He served as minister of justice from 1824 to 1828 and again from 1832 to 1833. José Miguel Ramos Arizpe died in 1843. At the time, he was serving as dean of Puebla* Cathedral.

REFERENCE: John A. Caruso, *The Liberators of Mexico*, 1967.

RANCAGUA, BATTLE OF (1814). In the face of efforts to establish Chilean independence, José Fernando de Abascal*, Spanish viceroy* of Peru*, authorized the invasion of Chile* by royalist forces to re-establish Spanish colonial authority. Patriot forces were split between those of the powerful military caudillo* José Miguel Carrera*, who supported the revolution primarily for the personal power that he gained in a coup d'état on November 15, 1811, and the constitutionalist forces led by Bernardo O'Higgins*. Because of the virtual civil war between the Carrera and the constitutionalist factions, royalists forces under the leadership of General Mariano Osorio* decisively defeated the revolutionary army at the Battle of Rancagua on October 12, 1814.

O'Higgins made a valiant effort to hold his position at Rancagua and to block Osorio's advance on the capital. The necessary unification of patriot forces, which he had recommended, had not been carried out by Carrera, however, who instead dispatched two divisions under the separate command of his relatives; these took positions in the area of Rancagua independent of O'Higgins's forces. Carrera also did not dispatch the munitions and uniforms that O'Higgins had requested from Santiago*. Unable to mount a proper defense, O'Higgins saw the loss of all but about 300 men of the original 1,600 patriot forces. After the battle, O'Higgins and Carrera fled with the remnants of their troops across the Andes to Mendoza. Osorio triumphantly entered Santiago, which Carrera had ordered abandoned, and re-established royalist control. This situation would last for three more years until José de San Martín* and O'Higgins won Chilean independence at the Battle of Chacabuco* in 1818.

While the defeat at Rancagua had been crushing, the seeds of successful revolution had been sown. The rebellion had unleashed an important ideological debate that prevented Chile from acquiesing to Spanish rule. The heroic defense of Rancagua became a patriotic legend and rallying point. Furthermore, the Spanish instituted policies of retribution and repression rather than reconciliation. Within this context, San Martín took command of the northern army and began laying plans for the ultimate liberation of Chile.

REFERENCES: Hubert Herring, *A History of Latin America*, 1961; Jay Kinsbruner, *Bernardo O'Higgins*, 1968; John Lynch, *The Spanish American Revolutions, 1808-1826*, 1973.

Samuel Freeman

REAL. The *real* was the basic unit of Spanish colonial currency. It was established as a monetary unit in 1369. Throughout much of the colonial period, two *reales* equaled a *peseta*; four *reales* were worth a *tostón*; and eight *reales* were worth a *peso*, also known as a *doblón* (a "piece of eight.")

REAL CUERPO DE MINERÍA. The Real Cuerpo de Minería was a trade association of mine owners in colonial America. The Spanish Crown established the Real Cuerpo in New Spain* in 1777. Over the next several years, it was also established in Venezuela*, Guatemala*, New Granada*, Peru*, and Chile*. A five-man body, headed by a director general, was headquartered in Mexico City* and charged with oversight as well as a judicial role as a court of appeals in legal cases concerned with mining* issues. It was actually a tight, well-regulated guild that controlled the industry in the New World. The Real Cuerpo de Minería was dissolved in 1821 after Mexico secured independence.

REFERENCES: Modesto Bargallo, *La minería y la metalurgía en la América española durante la época colonial*, 1955; D. A. Brading, *Miners and Merchants in Bourbon Mexico 1763-1810*, 1971.

RECOPILACIÓN DE LEYES DE LAS INDIAS. With the establishment of each new Spanish colony, the laws of Spain were transplanted to the New World. Over the years, those laws became a confusing mix of contradictory and often trivial rules that colonial authorities often disregarded. During the 1500s and 1600s, laws were passed by the Council of the Indies*, the royal *audiencias**, and the Crown. By the late 1600s, there were so many laws that colonial officials could barely use them. To remedy the confusion, the Crown conducted in the 1670s a careful study and compilation of all the laws passed referring to colonial affairs. Published in 1681 and known as the *Recopilación de Leyes de las Indias*, the compilation listed, described, classified, and cross-referenced 6,377 laws dealing with every part of colonial life. Without question, the *Recopilación* was the most important legal document of the Spanish Empire.

REFERENCE: C. H. Haring, *The Spanish Empire in America*, 1947.

REDUCCIONES (Reductions). See JESUIT REPUBLICS.

REGIDOR. In the Spanish colonial empire, the term *regidor* was used to refer to a member of a local *cabildo**. Each *cabildo* usually had anywhere from four to 12 *regidores*, depending upon the size of the community; the office was a royal appointment.

REFERENCE: C. H. Haring, *The Spanish Empire in America*, 1947.

REMESAL, ANTONIO DE. Antonio de Remesal was born in Spain in 1570. As a young man, he entered the Dominican* order to spend his life as a Roman Catholic priest. He spent three years in Guatemala* between 1613 and 1616; three years later, he published his *Historia de la provincia de S. Vicente de Chyapa y Guatemala*, an early history of Guatemala. Publication of the book caused a furor in Guatemala City* because of Remesal's bitter condemnation of Pedro de Alvarado's* treatment of the Indians*. Today the book remains an important source on the history of colonial Guatemala.

REFERENCE: Richard E. Moore, *Historical Dictionary of Guatemala*, 1973.

RENAISSANCE COLONIAL POETRY. Renaissance colonial poetry, like that of Spain, primarily utilized Italian poetic forms, such as the sonnet and royal octave. It placed heavy emphasis on precision of form, somewhat at the expense of content. Among the best-known renaissance poets were the lyrical poet Francisco de Terrazas*; the two Chilean epic poets Alonso Ercilla y Zúñiga* (1533–1596), author of *La Araucana*, and Pedro de Oña* (1570–1643?), author of *Arauco domado*; and the satirical poet Mateo Rosas* de Oquendo. Baroque poetry, particularly influenced by the great Spanish baroque poet Luis de Góngora, easily took root in the New World. This poetry displayed literary mannerisms and affectation, obscure word play, distortion and adornment, with a purposeful suppression of content and theme in favor of form and stylistics. In baroque poetry, the following names stand out: the transitional figures of Bernardo de Balbuena* (1568–1627), author of *Grandeza Mexicana*, and Diego de Hojeda* (1571–1615), author of *La Cristiada*; the lyric poets Sor Juana Inés de la Cruz* (1648–1695) and Juan del Valle y Caviedes* (1652–1697). Among the more important rococo poets were Juan José Arriola (1698–1768) and Alfonso Méndez Plancarte. Finally, among the neo-classical poets figure the Guatemalan Rafael Landívar* (1731–1793), and the Mexican Frey Manuel de Navarrete. Colonial Cuba* produced many poets of quality, including: Gabriel de Concepción Valdés* (1809–1844), José María Heredia* (1803–1839), the martyr and hero José Martí* (1853–1895), and Julián del Casal* (1863–1893).

REFERENCE: Ángel Flores, *The Literature of Spanish America: The Colonial Period*, 1966.

Sam L. Slick

REPARTIMIENTO. In Spanish the word *repartimiento* means distribution. In the context of the colonial empire, it usually referred to grants of Indian* labor to individuals of Spanish descent as well as the forced sales of Spanish goods to Indians. The *repartimiento*, also called the *cuatequil*, developed when it became clear that the *encomienda** system was not going to be able to supply Indian workers in sufficient numbers. In the beginning, the *repartimiento* was a system of forced labor in which Indians were required to work on private projects of wealthy Spaniards or on public works projects for the colonial government. The vast majority of Indians had to participate in the labor gangs or face severe punishment.

Unlike the *encomienda* system, the Indians were paid wages for their work and were supposedly protected from slavers. By the early seventeenth century, the *repartimiento* had been abolished, except in the mines.

REFERENCE: F. A. Kirkpatrick, "Repartimiento-Encomienda," *Hispanic American Historical Review*, 19 (1939), 372–79.

REQUERIMIENTO. The Spanish conquest of the Indians* proved to be a violent and bloody affair in most areas, but because the Spaniards believed the Indians were rational human beings, they felt some guilt about the destruction of so many lives. To deal with that guilt and absolve themselves of responsibility, the Crown had Juan López de Palacios Rubios draft the *requerimiento* in 1514. It was a document outlining the history of Christianity, the supremacy of the pope, and the obligation of Indians to submit themselves to Spanish authority. All Spanish conquistadors* were required to read the *requerimiento* to the Indians before a battle began. Preferably the document was to be translated into the Indian language. The Indians were supposed to listen to the reading and sign a document indicating that they understood its implications. Then, if they chose to resist, Spain would not be responsible for the subsequent destruction.

The *requerimiento* was hopelessly naive. Often it was read to the Indians in the Spanish language and sometimes at such a distance from them that they could not even hear it. The document encountered opposition from Spaniards and Church officials critical of the prevailing Indian policy, but the *requerimiento* was indeed presented to hundreds of Indian tribes in the sixteenth century.

REFERENCE: Lewis Hanke, "The 'Requerimiento' and Its Interpreters," *Revista de historia de América*, 1 (1938), 25–34.

RESIDENCIA. The *residencia* was a political institution of the Spanish colonial empire. Whenever a governor was leaving office, the *residencia* was a formal investigation of his term of office by the incoming governor. A traveling judge announced public hearings, and accusations and a defense were heard to determine if the previous administration had been fair and efficient. In cases of poor administration and corruption, however, vigorous prosecutions were rarely carried out as the result of a *residencia*. The subsequent report was used to determine if the individual being investigated should be promoted, retired, or imprisoned.

REFERENCE: Richard E. Moore, *Historical Dictionary of Guatemala*, 1973.

RESTREPO, JOSÉ MANUEL. José Manuel Restrepo was born on December 31, 1781, in Emvigada, Antioquia*, New Granada*. He attended the Colegio de San Bartolomé de Bogotá and earned a law degree from the *audiencia* of New Granada* in 1808. During the early years of the independence movement, Restrepo fought against the Spanish and wrote articles on political philosophy. He fled into exile in Jamaica* and then to the United States to escape Spanish prosecution, but when independence was secured, he returned to Colombia*. As an historian, Restrepo wrote the ten-volume *Historia de la revolución de la república de Colombia* (1827) and *Historia de la Nueva Granada* (1836). Restrepo served as governor of Antioquia in 1819 and as minister of the interior in the cabinet of Simón Bolívar*. He died in Bogotá* on April 1, 1863.

REFERENCE: Rafael M. Mesa Ortiz, *Don José Manuel Restrepo*, 1948.

REVENUE. A major purpose behind establishment of the colonial empire was to enrich the coffers of the Spanish Crown. During the course of the sixteenth, seventeenth, and eighteenth centuries, the Crown developed a variety of ways of securing revenues from the colonies. By 1550, those revenues reached 165,000 ducats (1 ducat = 3.5 grams of gold) annually and nearly 3 million ducats by the end of the century. Although those revenues declined in the seventeenth century, they increased to approximately 6 million ducats annually by the end of the eighteenth century. The sources of those revenues were as follows: the *quinto** tax of 20 percent on mine production; *almojarifazgo** taxes on goods arriving at or leaving colonial ports; the *alcabala** sales tax; Indian* tribute payments; sales of public offices; and income from the monopolies on a variety of products coming to the colonies.

REFERENCES: Francisco Gallardo y Fernández, *Orígen, progresos y estado de las rentas de la corona de España, su gobierno y administración*, 8 vols., 1805–1808; C. H. Haring, *The Spanish Empire in America*, 1947.

REVILLAGIGEDO, CONDE DE. Born as Juan Vicente Güemes Pacheco de Padilla in Havana*, Cuba*, in 1740, the count of Revillagigedo was appointed viceroy* of New Spain* in 1789, where he quickly earned a reputation as a tireless, incorruptible administrator. During his five-year term as viceroy, Revillagigedo completed a successful census of the colony, reorganized the military, strengthened the military forts in the Borderlands, commissioned exploration expeditions up the Pacific coast of California*, greatly increased the collection of royal revenues, introduced and reformed the intendancy system, controlled food prices while increasing supplies, made great improvements in the infrastructure of the colony (especially road building, public health, and police services), and imposed restrictions on the way that colonists treated Indians*. Once his term as viceroy was completed, Revillagigedo returned to Cuba where he died in 1799.

REFERENCE: José Calderón Quijano, ed., *Los virreyes de Nueva España en el reinado de Carlos III*, 2 vols., 1967.

RIBERA, PERAFÁN DE. Perafán de Ribera was born in Spain in 1492 and came to the New World to earn his fortune. He was a prominent conquistador* in Central America. Ribera is credited with founding the city of Trujillo* in what is today Honduras*, and in 1568, he became governor of Costa Rica*, a position he held until 1573. Ribera was known for his cruelty, both to the Indians* and to other colonists, and in 1572, he was formally censured by the *audiencia* of Guatemala* for the summary execution of a suspected traitor. He left the governorship of Costa Rica in 1573 and went to live in New Spain*. Perafán de Ribera died in 1577.

REFERENCE: Theodore S. Creedman, *Historical Dictionary of Costa Rica*, 1977.

RICAURTE, ANTONIO DE. Antonio de Ricaurte is a hero of the independence movement in Colombia*, Ecuador*, and Venezuela*. He was born in Leyva, Venezuela, on June 10, 1786, and served as an officer with the army of Simón Bolívar*. On March 25, 1814, Ricaurte refused to retreat from his position, even after the Spanish army had surrounded him. By that time, Ricaurte had ordered all of his men to retreat. When the Spaniards closed in on his position, Ricaurte detonated a powder magazine, killing himself and 300 Spanish troops.

REFERENCE: Albert William Bork and Georg Maier, *Historical Dictionary of Ecuador*, 1973.

RICLA, CONDE DE. Born in Zaragoza, Spain, in 1720, Ambrosio Funes Villalpando was the second son of the Conde de Atares and cousin of the highly influential Conde de Aranda*. At an early age, he entered the regiment of Spanish guards as a cadet, receiving his first commission as captain in the infantry regiment of Soria when only 17. During the War of the Austrian Succession*, he saw extensive action in Italy, rising rapidly in rank to become field marshal in 1747. The following year, he married a woman nearly 20 years his senior, the Condesa de Ricla and Marquesa de Camarasa, a step that brought him both his title and access to the inner circles at court, where he soon became a gentleman of His Majesty's bedchamber entrance. Thereafter, he served successively as governor of Jaca, Zamora, and Cartagena de Levants. Promoted to lieutenant general in 1761, he commanded a division of the army that invaded Portugal during the Seven Years War*.

Ricla's influence in colonial affairs derived from his proposal to introduce the Spanish disciplined militia* system into Cuba* following Spain's humiliation at Havana* during the Seven Years War. Charles III* accepted this plan and named him governor, charging him with taking possession of Havana from the British as provided under the Treaty of Paris* (1763). Ricla also bore instructions to consult with the Havana elite about the means to fund the reformed military. Assigning the actual implementation of his military reform program to Field Marshal Alejandro O'Reilly, but exercising careful supervision, Ricla set about establishing orderly government and worked vigorously to hasten the refortification of Havana. In what proved to be the high point of his career, Ricla showed consummate skill in his negotiations with the Havana elite. Inducing the reluctant Cubans to accept revenue* reform, which included a tripling of the *alcabala** and new excise taxes on the sale of colonial liquors, he in turn vigorously supported their ambitious demands for commercial reform. The 1765 Regulation of Free Trade for the Caribbean Islands, which was later expanded to include the entire empire, was an important measure of Ricla's ability to orchestrate the voice of Havana to be heard at court. On another level, his and O'Reilly's concerns about the chaotic state of the colonial treasury contributed to the establishment of the intendant* system. In conjunction with the military reorganization, these measures became the core of the Bourbon reform program, not only in Cuba but, in later years, throughout America.

His mission in Cuba completed, Governor Ricla was granted permission to return to Spain where he formed part of the powerful Aragonese faction headed by Aranda. In 1772, he became minister of war, a position he held without particular distinction until his death in 1780. He was replaced as captain general of Cuba by Diego Manrique and as minister of war by Minister of Finance Miguel de Múzquiz, who added the second portfolio to his duties.

REFERENCES: Jaime Delgado, "El Conde de Ricla, capitán general de Cuba," *Revista de historia de América*, 1963; Allan J. Kuethe, *Cuba 1753-1815: Crown, Military, and Society*, 1986; Vicente Rodríguez Casado, *La Política y los políticos en el reinado de Carlos III*, 1962.

Allan J. Kuethe

RIF, REPUBLIC OF THE. The Rif Mountains of Morocco have long been inhabited by Berber tribesmen, and during the age of imperialism they were under the political control of the French in Morocco and the Spanish in Spanish Morocco*. The Berbers resented the domination of the French and Spanish, and their opposition to imperialism found expression in the rebellion of Abdel Mohammad Krim* Al-Khattabi. On July 21, 1921, Krim launched an all-out attack on the Spanish military installation at Anwal* in Spanish Morocco. Krim routed the Spaniards, driving them out of Anwal and inflicting 8,688 battlefield deaths on them, along with another 4,500 wounded. The victory permitted Krim to expand his political base among the Berber tribes and extend the rebellion into Ghmara and Jbala. In February 1923, Krim proclaimed the founding of the Republic of the Rif. He organized a government and intended to liberate all of Spanish Morocco from Spanish control. The Republic of the Rif, however, was short-lived. A combined Spanish-French force defeated Krim's army in 1926. Krim was captured and deported, and the Republic of the Rif dissolved.

REFERENCE: Rupert Furneaux, *Abdel-Krim, Emir of the Rif*, 1967.

RIOBAMBA, CONGRESS OF. The Congress of Riobamba convened in Riobamba, Ecuador*, on May 13, 1830, to declare the secession of Ecuador from the Unión de Gran Colombia*. The congress then selected General Juan José Flores* as president of Ecuador. Seven months later, on December 11, 1830, the first constitution of the republic of Ecuador was established.

REFERENCE: Albert William Bork and Georg Maier, *Historical Dictionary of Ecuador*, 1973.

RÍO DE LA PLATA. Sebastian Cabot* first explored the Río de la Plata in 1526, and nine years later, the first Spanish settlers arrived. The city of Buenos Aires* was established in 1536 but it was abandoned in 1537 because the city of Asunción* in what is today Paraguay* seemed more viable and more accessible to the prosperous colonies in Bolivia* and Peru*. The first Spanish governor of the province of Río de la Plata was Pedro de Mendoza*. The province was subject to the *audiencia* of Charcas*. In 1618, in an effort to make the colonial government more efficient and to end the constant political struggles between its two primary regions, the province of Río de la Plata was divided into two new provinces—Asunción and Buenos Aires. See also ARGENTINA.

RÍO DE LA PLATA, VICEROYALTY OF. The viceroyalty of Río de la Plata as established in 1776, splitting off northern Argentina*, Paraguay*, and eastern Bolivia* from the viceroyalty of Peru*. The viceroyalty of Río de la Plata was the fourth and last viceroyalty of the Spanish Empire in the New World. Several factors inspired the Crown to establish the viceroyalty. Spanish officials were worried about possible British attacks on the Río de la Plata area, which the viceroyalty of Peru, because of its distance would be unable to defend. They were also concerned about the expansion of the Portuguese south out of Brazil across the Río de la Plata. Pedro de Cevallos was appointed as the first viceroy*. Under his direction, the region was opened up to international trade, and silver from the mines of Potosí*, instead of being shipped to Spain via Panama*, was rerouted southeast and exported out of Buenos Aires. In 1783, the viceregal *audiencia* was placed in Buenos Aires*. That same year, the Spanish crown divided the viceroyalty into the *intendencias* of Córdoba*, Cochabamba*, La Paz*, Paraguay*, Potosí*, Salta*, Charcas*, and Puno* (transferred from Peru). By the end of the eighteenth century, the viceroyalty was prospering from large exports of beef and hides*. During the revolutionary upheaval in Argentina, the viceregal office relocated to Montevideo* in 1810. Buenos Aires declared its independence in 1816.

REFERENCE: Manfred Kossok, *El vierreinato de Río de la Plata*, 1950.

RÍO DE ORO. The term Río de Oro described an inlet in northwest Africa. Its name came from the traffic in gold dust that had existed there in the fifteenth century. In September 1881, the Society of Canary-African Fishermen built a post there, and in 1884, the Spanish-African Commercial Company* established the settlement of Villa Cisneros on the Dakhla Peninsula. Between 1884 and 1887, Spain issued a series of declarations establishing a protectorate in the area, and, by the 1880s, the name Río de Oro was used for the colony. The Franco-Spanish Convention of 1900* defined the southern and southeastern boundary of Río de Oro with Mauritania. By that time, however, the term was becoming more ambiguous, referring in some diplomatic correspondence to all of Spanish Sahara*. As time passed, the meaning became somewhat more specific. By 1934, Río de Oro meant the territory of Spanish Sahara south of 26° north latitude near Boujdour, while the area to the north between 26° and 27° 40′ was Saguia el-Hamra. The only Spanish settlement in Río de Oro until 1916 was Villa Cisneros. Spain settled La Güera* on Cape Blanc in 1916 and constructed several other military garrisons on the coast during the 1920s and 1930s.

REFERENCE: John Mercer, *Spanish Sahara*, 1975.

RIVA-AGÜERO, JOSÉ DE. José de Riva-Agüero was born in Lima*, Peru*, in 1783 to a Spanish government official. Although he was educated in Spain and spent time in the Spanish army, he became committed as a young man to the idea of Peruvian independence. He returned to Lima in 1809 and became a thorn in the side of royal officials, including many in his own family. For a few years, Riva-Agüero cooperated closely with José de San Martín* and served briefly as the first president of Peru. But in the shifting political fortunes of the early independence movement, Riva-Agüero chose the wrong side. When Simón Bolívar assumed direction of the later stage of the Peruvian independence movement, Riva-Agüero was deposed in 1823. He flirted briefly with royalist officials, trying to forge a constitutional monarchy under a Spanish prince, but independence forces arrested and exiled him to Europe, where he remained until 1833. Upon his return, Riva-Agüero worked closely on the abortive Peru-Bolivia* Confederation and was again exiled, this time for 12 years. He returned to Lima in 1845 and died there in 1858.

REFERENCE: Manuel de Mendiburu, ed., *Diccionario histórico-biográfico del Perú*, 8 vols., 1874–1890.

RIVADAVIA, BERNARDINO. Bernardino Rivadavia was born in Buenos Aires* on May 20, 1780, and educated there at the College of San Carlos. Rivadavia was present at the famous *cabildo* abierto meeting in Buenos Aires on May 25, 1810, when the movement for Argentine independence was launched. Rivadavia became minister of war in the new government in 1811 and subsequently served as minister of finance and government. When the regime was overthrown in 1812, Rivadavia resigned his positions, and for the next two years, he served as diplomatic minister to several European capitals. He returned to Buenos Aires in 1820 to serve once again as minister of government, and after a stint as minister to Great Britain, he was elected president of Argentina* in 1826. Rivadavia resigned in face of the caudillo* revolts of 1827. He spent the years between 1829 and 1834 in Europe. When he returned home in 1834, political enemies charged him with treason and exiled him to Brazil. Bernardino Rivadavia died in Cádiz, Spain, on September 2, 1845.

REFERENCES: Alberto Palcos, *Rivadavia: Ejecutor del Pensamiento de Mayo*, 1960; Ricardo Piccirilli, *Rivadavia y su Tiempo*, 1960.

RIVERA, JOSÉ FRUCTOSA. José Fructosa Rivera was born around 1784 in Pasandu, in what is today Uruguay*, to a working-class family. In 1811, he joined the independence forces and quickly rose through the military ranks. During the period between 1811 and 1820, Rivera was a military leader in resisting the Portuguese invasions of Uruguay. Once Uruguay became part of Brazil, Rivera was given command of an all-Uruguayan unit in the Brazilian army, rising to the rank of general by 1824. But in 1825, Rivera secretly joined forces with Juan Antonio Lavalleja* and became second in command of Uruguayan independence forces. Although he came to resent the dominant role played by Argentines in Uruguayan independence, Rivera broke the back of Brazil by his invasion of southern Brazil in 1828.

When Uruguay won its independence in 1829, Rivera became minister of war, and late in 1830, he was elected the first president of Uruguay. He was immediately embroiled in divisive political factionalism between pro-Brazilian and pro-Argentine officials in the government. Manuel Oribe* succeeded him as president, but in 1836, Rivera led a revolt against Oribe and forced his resignation in 1838. Rivera then became the new president of Uruguay, and somewhat of a liberal, at least in comparison to Oribe's rigid conservatism. He served as president until 1843 but found himself in the middle of a civil war that lasted until 1852. Oribe's forces took control of the countryside and Rivera fled to Brazil, where he remained from 1845 to 1846. He briefly returned to Uruguay in 1847 but was again exiled to Brazil, this time until 1854. Rivera died in 1854 on his return trip to Montevideo*.

REFERENCE: José Gervasio Antuna, *Un caudillo, el general Fructuoso Rivera, prócer del Uruguay*, 1948.

RIZAL, JOSÉ. José Rizal was born in the Philippines* on June 19, 1861, and became the country's national hero. His short life was filled with accomplishment: he has been variously described as a linguist, doctor, patriot, freethinker, novelist, ethnographer, poet, and zoologist. There is no doubt that the man was a genius, the foremost Asian exemplar of Enlightenment* thought. Rizal's novels stimulated the growth of Filipino* nationalism, and his martyr's death symbolized the injustice and cruelty of Spanish rule in the islands. Rizal was of the privileged mestizo* class, which in Philippine colonial society occupied a niche above all darker-skinned natives but below pure-blooded Spaniards. The mestizos, of mixed Chinese-Malay ancestry, were usually wealthy and socially prominent. Rizal's father ran a sugar* plantation in Calamba, Laguna Province, on land that he leased from Dominican* friars. His mother was highly educated. They sent José to the best schools: the Ateneo and the University of St. Thomas* in Manila*, and later to the University of Madrid.

Upper-class *indios* and mestizos (few yet called themselves Filipinos) chafed under Spanish rule and particularly resented the monopoly of high clerical appointments enjoyed by Spaniards. Insular society was outraged by the execution of three Filipino priests in Cavite* in 1872, when Rizal was but eleven years old. It was a formative event: his novels are merciless in their sarcastic depiction of friar abuses. Rizal arrived in Spain in 1882 and became a leader of Filipino students there. He traveled to England, France, and Germany, making the acquaintance of prominent European intellectuals. While studying medicine in Heidelberg (1886), he somehow found time to finish his famous novel, *Noli me Tangere* (literally "Touch Me Not" in Latin, but sometimes translated as *The Social Cancer* or *The Lost Eden*). The book was an immediate sensation in the Philippines, despite condemnation by friars who told people they would fall into mortal sin by reading it.

Rizal returned to his homeland in 1887, but was followed by government agents and soon left again for Europe. In 1890, he annotated a new edition of an old history book, Antonio Morga's* *Sucesos de las Islas Filipinas*, which argued that Filipinos had a national history predating Spanish conquest. In 1891, Rizal finished a second novel, *El Filibusterismo* (the title is sometimes translated as *The Reign of Greed* and sometimes as *The Subversive*). He also contributed to a crusading journal, *La Solidaridad*, published in Spain, where the authorities were considerably more liberal than in Manila. In all this, Rizal never asked for more than justice and political equality. He called for Philippine representation in the Spanish parliament, not independence. He shunned violent revolution, but warned that it might come if Spain ignored the warning signs.

Rizal returned to Manila in 1892, and in July of that year founded an innocuous group, La Liga Filipina, to publicize his reformist agenda. The Spaniards panicked, arrested Rizal, and sent him to internal exile at Dapitan, a backwater town on the coast of Mindanao*. He stayed there for four years, practicing medicine, teaching school, and collecting specimens of local plants and animals. During those years, the Philippine nationalist movement gathered strength without him and veered increasingly toward violent revolution. Rizal wanted no part of it and volunteered to serve as a surgeon with Spanish forces in Cuba*. The Spaniards at first agreed, but then stupidly arrested him.

José Rizal faced a firing squad in Manila on December 30, 1896. His legacy was given three interpretations: (1) American colonial authorities taught generations of Filipinos that Rizal was a ''good'' (because nonrevolutionary) nationalist; (2) numerous Filipino peasants followed millenial cults that taught that Rizal was a Filipino messiah, or even God himself; and (3) modern Filipino nationalists, embarrassed by Rizal's upper-class background and his aversion to violence, have downgraded his importance in favor of such revolutionaries as Andrés Bonifacio* and Emilio Aguinaldo*.

REFERENCE: John Schumacher, *The Propaganda Movement, 1880-1895*, 1973.

Ross Marlay

ROBLEDO, JORGE. Jorge Robledo was born in Spain and sought his fortune in the New World. He came to Peru* with Francisco Pizarro* in 1531, and in 1536, he was authorized to explore the Cauca Valley in what is today Colombia*. Robledo conducted that expedition in 1539 and 1540 and was responsible for establishing settlements in Ansermaviejo, Cartago*, and Santa Fe de Antioquia*. In 1542, Alonso de Heredia arrested Robledo for assuming too much political power, and Robledo had to return to Spain to stand trial. He was acquitted there and came back to New Granada* in 1544. He immediately fell into a jurisdictional dispute with Sebastián Benalcázar* over control of Antioquia and the Cauca Valley. Benalcázar captured Robledo and executed him in 1546.

REFERENCE: Robert H. Davis, *Historical Dictionary of Colombia*, 1977.

ROCAFUERTE, VICENTE. Vicente Rocafuerte, a native of Guayaquil*, Ecuador*, was born on May 3, 1783, and educated in Madrid and Paris. In 1814, he became a member of the Spanish Cortes as the representative from Guayaquil, but when King Ferdinand VII* was restored to the throne and tried to reimpose an authoritarian regime in the empire, Rocafuerte joined the Spanish-American independence movement. Mexico became his base of operations, and between 1824 and 1830, he served as the secretary of the Mexican legation in London. In 1833, Rocafuerte returned to Ecuador and quickly emerged as the leader of the Liberal Party in the national legislature. Between 1835 and 1839, Rocafuerte was president of Ecuador. The Conservative Party came to power in 1839 under the leadership of Juan José Flores*, and Rocafuerte soon led a revolt against the regime. Rocafuerte rose to power again as president of the senate in Quito* before his death in Lima*, Peru*, on May 16, 1847.

REFERENCE: George Blanksten, *Ecuador: Constitutions and Caudillos*, 1951; I. J. Barrera, *Rocafuerte: Estudio histórico-biográfico*, 1911.

RODRÍGUEZ, JOSÉ CAYETANO. José Cayetano Rodríguez was born in Buenos Aires*, in 1761. He became a Franciscan* priest in 1777, and after his ordination, he became a professor at the University of Córdoba*. Rodríguez then went to teach at San Carlos College in Buenos Aires, where he became a strong supporter of the political ideas of Mariano Moreno*. Rodríguez was elected to the Argentine constitutional assembly in 1812, and he edited its minutes until its dissolution in 1815. He became a member of the Congress of Tucumán*, and he was the author of the Act of the Declaration of Independence. After independence, Rodríguez attacked government legislation confiscating church property and imposing clerical reforms. José Cayetano Rodríguez died in Buenos Aires in 1823.

REFERENCE: J. P. Otero, *Fray Cayetano*, 1908.

RODRÍGUEZ, JUAN MANUEL. Juan Manuel Rodríguez was born in 1771 in San Salvador* and became a leading figure in the Salvadoran independence movement. He was part of the November 5, 1811, revolt in San Salvador and served as secretary to the rebel government that ruled the city. In 1813, Rodríguez was elected mayor of San Salvador, and the next year, he led the second Salvadoran uprising against royal authority. Spanish officials imprisoned him for five years for his role in the rebellion. After the declaration of Central American independence, Rodríguez resisted Mexican imperialism and had to seek asylum in the United States. When the Mexican Empire collapsed in 1823, Rodríguez returned to San Salvador and was elected governor of the province. He resigned for health reasons late in 1824. Juan Manuel Rodríguez died in San Salvador in 1843.

REFERENCE: Philip F. Flemion, *Historical Dictionary of El Salvador*, 1972.

RODRÍGUEZ CABRILLO, JUAN. See CABRILLO, JUAN RODRÍGUEZ.

RODRÍGUEZ CAMPOMANES, PEDRO. Pedro Rodríguez Campomanes was born in Asturias, Spain, in 1723. He became a gifted economist and historian who believed that Spain's monopolistic trade practices were stifling the imperial economy. In 1762, Campomanes became president of the Royal Academy of History, and in 1765 he wrote his famous *Tratado de la regalia de la amortización*. Campomanes carefully studied Spain's economic problems and recommended drastic changes in the long-standing Crown practice of granting monopolies. Campomanes was not an advocate of free trade, but he did believe that fewer regulations and increased competition would increase international trade and stimulate the Spanish and colonial economies. Pedro Campomanes died in 1803.

REFERENCES: R. J. Herr, *The Eighteenth Century Revolution in Spain*, 1958; J. R. Sarrailh, *La España ilustrada de la segunda mitad del siglo XVIII*, 1974.

RODRÍGUEZ DE FRANCIA, JOSÉ GASPAR. See FRANCIA, JOSÉ GASPAR RODRÍGUEZ DE.

RODRÍGUEZ FONSECA, JUAN DE. See FONSECA, JUAN DE RODRÍGUEZ.

RODRÍGUEZ FREILE, JUAN. Juan Rodríguez Freile was born in 1566 in New Granada*. Like many New World writers, Rodríguez's literary importance rests upon only one work. He originally embarked on a religious career, but changed to the military and fighting Indians*. His ancestors played a role in the founding of Bogotá and New Granadan society. As a young man, he amassed a considerable amount of money and lived a life of both adventure and leisure. Incredibly, at the age of 70, Rodríguez Freile decided to write a chronicle and history of Bogotá* and New Granada. What emerged was as much fantasy as anything else. His masterpiece was titled *Conquista y descubrimiento del Nuevo Reino de Granada*, but it has mysteriously come to be referred to as *El Carnero*. In it, Rodríguez did not truly attempt to relate the history of New Granada as much as the history of middle and upper society. Although his narrative suggests something of a novel, the work lacks coherent structure, resulting in many disjointed tales and adventures. While not a chronicle, then, it is a societal history that relishes telling spicy anecdotes with picaresque elements, baroque twists, and flashes of local color. He died in 1638.

REFERENCE: Luis María Sánchez López, *Diccionario de escritores colombianos*, 1978.

Sam L. Slick

RODRÍGUEZ ZORRILLA, JOSÉ SANTIAGO. José Rodríguez Zorrilla was born in Santiago*, Chile*, in 1752. He studied at the University of San Felipe* in Santiago and the University of San Marcos* in Lima*, eventually receiving doctorates in theology and law. Rodríguez was ordained a priest in 1775. He was a faculty member for years at the University of San Felipe, and in 1807 he was appointed vicar capitular in Lima. He lost that post in 1810, when he opposed the formation of the ruling junta in Chile and refused to acknowledge the appointment of Martínez de Aldunate as bishop. He also protested the Constitution of 1812's* insistence on dropping the word "Roman" from all references to the Church. In retaliation, the government of Chile refused to recognize his appointment as bishop of Santiago. Rodríguez was exiled from Chile in 1817, returned to Santiago between 1822 and 1825, and then was permanently exiled again by a government that did not trust him. He died in Madrid in 1832.

REFERENCE: C. Silva Cotapos, *Don José Santiago Rodríguez Zorrilla*, 1915.

ROMAN CATHOLIC CHURCH. See CATHOLIC CHURCH.

RONDEAU, JOSÉ. José Rondeau was born in Buenos Aires* in 1773 and became one of Argentina's* and Uruguay's* early heroes. He grew up in Montevideo* and went to school with José Artigas*. Rondeau joined the Spanish army in 1807 and rose to the rank of captain. After spending several years fighting the French in Europe, Rondeau returned to the Río de la Plata* area and joined the revolutionary forces in 1811. By 1814, Rondeau had attained the rank of general, and in 1819, he became Supreme Director of the United Provinces of South America*. Before retiring from public life in 1840, Rondeau served as the minister of war of Argentina. He died in 1844.

REFERENCE: Jean L. Willis, *Historical Dictionary of Uruguay*, 1975.

ROSAS, JUAN MANUEL DE. Juan Manuel de Rosas was born in Buenos Aires* in 1793 to a distinguished family. At the age of eight, he entered the school of Francisco Xavier de Argerich but spent every possible moment at "El Rincón de López," the *estancia* in the Salado district south of Buenos Aires that belonged to his mother's family. There he could roam to his heart's delight, playing with horses, toughening up against all hostile elements, and feeling at ease. It was then that he penetrated deep into the soul of the *gaucho*ature and became identified with him.

At the time of the British invasions (1806–1807), at the age of only 13, he fought in the defense of the city and was personally congratulated by General Santiago de Liniers*. On the other hand, the May Revolution* did not appeal to him, and his name does not appear anywhere in the annals of the struggle for independence. Rosas was opposed to it and saw in it the loss of territorial greatness and the decline of social values—which was not far from the truth. He represented the conservative reaction against the romantic idealism of the small liberal elite of Buenos Aires, whose roots were to be found in the Enlightenment* and the French Revolution. As the voice of the Pampas, Rosas had neither understanding nor sympathy for European concepts for which the Argentina* of his day was totally unprepared.

As early as 1808, his father had handed over to him the administration of "El Rincon de López." It was here that Rosas spent the next years, devoted to agriculture and livestock, far away from the noise of the war of independence. The *estancia* was exploited to the fullest, with methodical precision and an iron discipline. Rosas fought marauding Indians*, but at the same time also had good relations with them. He dominated nomadic *gauchos* and gradually acquired a reputation for order, discipline, and toughness. His *gauchos* feared nothing and would go through fire for him, for such was the admiration and respect he had earned. He thus became the master of the Pampas—his friends loved him and his foes feared him.

In 1813, he married Encarnación Ezcurra y Arguibel, the perfect match: not beautiful, but strong-willed, vigorous, and devoted. It was at this time that Rosas returned the farm to his parents and decided to strike out on his own. He set up a company with Juan Nepomuceno Terrero that soon managed the farm "Los Cerrillos." His company, "Rosas and Terrero," established the first *saladero* (meat-salting factory) in 1815. It was here that Rosas laid the basis for his personal fortune and his growing influence in Argentina. He was a model to his *gauchos* for the austerity of his customs and his love of work. He always took on the hardest tasks and was the most skillful horseman. His ranches became population centers with a rigorous code reminiscent of Robert Owen's New Harmony settlement in Indiana. "A species of lord of the manor, exercising both civil and criminal jurisdiction, Rosas punished drunkenness, idleness, and theft, either expelling from his estates or delivering to the authorities persons who indulged in those vices which he abominated."

It was under Director Juan Martín de Pueyrredón* (in control 1816–1819) that Rosas was offered his first government commission. The background was the fear of a potential Spanish invasion, which prompted the establishment of a Junta de Emigración for the evacuation of the capital's inhabitants. From that moment on, Rosas's voice was heard in Buenos Aires. He submitted a plan for the defense of the country but, since no invasion ever occurred, the plan was simply shelved. In the meantime, the country was heading toward further anarchy. The first constitution in 1819, which was quite centralist, was repudiated by the provinces, and caused the old antagonism between *unitarios* (those favoring a powerful central government) and *federales* (those wanting to retain local powers) to reappear in earnest. The Treaty of Pilar, in 1820, gave Buenos Aires to the *federales*. Rosas had watched events from his farm but then joined the political struggle as head of the southern militia* when requested to come to the aid of the new government. He was appointed commander of the fifth rural regiment, the *colorados*. Of all the troops, his were the only ones with a semblance of discipline. His intervention in favor of Governor Martín Rodríguez was not for a political faction but only in search of peace and in defense of order. Both were largely due to Rosas, who was now promoted to colonel and hailed as "Restorer of Order" and "Pacifier of the Country." At the end of the year, he returned to his farm, deeply disappointed with the government. He felt outraged by those who surrounded Rodriguez, who were mostly *unitarios* who hated Rosas. On top of all this, Indian attacks occurred, which he had anticipated. In 1821, he resigned when the Rodríguez government increasingly took a visible *unitario* position with the return of Bernardino Rivadavia*, whose liberal reforms caused great dissatisfaction among the *estancieros*. In 1824, Rosas declined to serve on a committee on European immigration.

When Juan Gregorio de Las Heras[*] took over the government of Buenos Aires, the country faced two basic problems: the occupation of the Banda Oriental[*], first by the Portuguese (1816) and then by the Brazilians (1822), and the future policies of the new national congress, inaugurated in December of the latter year. Together with his cousins Juan José and Nicolás Anchorena, Rosas financially aided the operation of the "Immortal Thirty-Three"[*] and voiced deep concern about the growing anarchy. He thus foresaw the war with Brazil, which began in 1825, and the civil war with the caudillos[*] of the interior (Juan B. Bustos in Córdoba[*]; Facundo Quiroga in La Rioja; and Estanislao López[*] in Santa Fe). The former conflict derived from the incorporation of the Banda Oriental into the United Provinces of Río de la Plata[*] and the second from Rivadavia's centralist policies. Rosas was asked to take over the defense of the Pampas, since the government believed that Brazil would incite the Indians against Buenos Aires; he accepted the commission but with the reservation that he be granted full powers. Again he felt deceived when the government did not live up to its promises. He thus no longer felt obliged to support the government, which was now facing "the tempest of the war, of political passions and of national dissolution." He resigned with dignified protest.

The increasing anarchy coupled with the war with Brazil now catapulted Rosas into power. Ignored by Rivadavia when the latter became president in 1826, he decided to intervene in response to the uprising of Juan Lavalle and the assassination of Manuel Dorrego (1820). The Junta de Representantes now appointed Rosas governor in the belief that he was the only one who could save the country. His first term as governor of Buenos Aires lasted until 1832. He destroyed the Liga Unitaria and reorganized the country on the basis of the Federal Pact of 1831. He established the nation's unity by allowing the caudillos to do as they pleased, which was probably the only way to keep the country united, and reserved to himself the governorship of Buenos Aires as well as control of foreign relations and finance. After 1832, a series of governors took over under his watchful eye—Juan Ramón González Balcarce[*], Juan José Viamonte, Manuel Vicente de Maza—but disorder again reappeared. Thus, in 1835, he asked for and obtained full powers—"total power . . . for as long as he thinks necessary"—with which he persecuted all liberals and forced unity on the country. It was ironic that his kind of federalism achieved a brand of *unitario* union that the liberals could hardly ever have envisioned.

Rosas turned the clock back in regard to the farsighted policies of Rivadavia: immigration was stopped and Rivadavia's Banco Nacional abolished. Rosas also got into plenty of trouble with foreign powers: with Bolivia[*] in 1837, where Andrés de Santa Cruz[*] had given refuge to *unitarios* and had taken over Tarija, and with Uruguay[*], which Rosas continued to see as an old Argentine territory and where he supported his friend, the *blanco* Manuel Oribe[*], during the 1830s. This intervention led to French support of the Uruguayan liberals although in reality for ulterior motives; by 1838, France had seen the futility and withdrawn. In 1845, however, a joint Anglo-French intervention, again ostensibly to preserve the independence of Uruguay, was more serious, but even this new aggression only helped to make Rosas a national hero. By 1847, the British had withdrawn, by 1848 the French followed suit, and in 1850, both England and France made peace.

By that time, however, the increasing hostility toward Rosas exploded in civil war. Justo José de Urquiza, the governor of Entre Ríos, took the lead and was joined by an alliance of old *unitarios*, Uruguayans, and Brazilians. At Monte Caseros, February 3, 1852, Rosas was defeated and fell from power. Ironically, he settled in England, where he bought a small farm—Burgess Farm—near Southampton, lived peacefully for the next quarter of a century, and died in 1877 at the age of 84. No doubt, Rosas's rule was tyrannical and cruel, but the historical revision begun by Adolfo Saldias has provided a more objective verdict: Rosas terminated anarchy and imposed order and unity. As *restaurador de las leyes*, he made it possible for Argentina, after the period of secession, 1852–1861, to catapult into importance and greatness.

REFERENCES: Carlos Ibarguren, *Juan Manuel de Rosas*, 1961; John Lynch, *Juan Manuel de Rosas, 1829–1852*, 1984.

O. Carlos Stoetzer

ROSAS DE OQUENDO, MATEO. Mateo Rosas de Oquendo was born around 1559 in Seville[*], Spain. He went to reside in the New World at the age of 35. He traveled widely throughout the Spanish Empire, spending considerable time in what are present-day Mexico, Peru[*], and Argentina[*]. He was one of many traveling satirists who commented at length on the comedic in colonial life. It is presumed that he wrote many works that were lost. Those that remain were first published in the nineteenth and twentieth centuries. In his satirical attacks, Rosas de Oquendo's eye spared no one. While in Peru, Rosas wrote *Sátira a las cosas que pasan en el Perú, año de 1598*, a scorching satire on Peruvian society. In Mexico, he wrote *Sátira que hizo un galán a una dama criolla que le alababa mucho a México*, in which he derided the foibles of *criollos*[*] and their lifestyle. Although Rosas wrote with a wry satirical humor, it is his keen observational ability that most captures the modern reader. Indeed, Rosas left some of the most vivid portraits of colonial society extant today. He died around 1621.

REFERENCE: Miguel Ángel Peral, *Diccionario biográfico mexicano*, 1944.

Sam L. Slick

ROZAS. In many parts of Spain and Spanish America, agriculturalists have followed the practice of creating plots for cultivation through setting fires to destroy portions of forest or woodland (*selva* or *monte*). The fire clearings, called *rozas*, are farmed for a few years, until the soil is exhausted; they are then abandoned and allowed to grow back into natural vegetation. The *roza* system, or swidden agriculture, is an itinerant agrarian system involving a prolonged fallow to permit the soil to recuperate its fertility. It is practiced only in areas where climatic and soil conditions are not conducive to permanent agriculture. *Roza* agriculture is a rapid way to prepare large plots for cultivation with a minimum of human labor. It has several advantages over purely mechanical clearing techniques: the fire loosens the soil; it kills weeds; and the ashes temporarily enrich the soil. In tropical areas, this system is also known as slash-and-burn agriculture, from the practice of girdling large trees prior to felling and burning them.

In pre-Hispanic America, this type of agriculture was widely practiced in the Antilles and from Mexico to Chile*. During the Spanish colonial period, it continued to be used, and it continues to be practiced today, particularly in tropical forest areas. The *roza* system, being migratory, is usually associated with dispersed temporary huts rather than European-style permanent villages. In many places, the system has contributed to deforestation.

In Spain, *rozas* were used in medieval and early modern times, sometimes in the itinerant agricultural system described above and sometimes to open up new lands to permanent forms of cultivation. In some places, settlers were given full ownership of *rozas* that they had cleared and plowed in the *monte*. But as Spain's population density increased and as the *montes** diminished in size, the municipal governments began to be concerned over the disappearing pastures, firewood, lumber, acorns, and other fruits of nature. Still, illegal burnings continued to be made, accelerating in the sixteenth century with the expanding population and economy. Many fires in Spanish *montes* were set by shepherds to destroy the thickets and underbrush and to stimulate a tender regrowth that provided succulent pasture in previously unsuitable or inaccessible areas. Often these pastoral clearings were invaded by agriculturalists taking advantage of the opportunity provided by herders. In fact, it often seemed that there was a conspiracy between herders and farmers to destroy the *montes*.

REFERENCES: David E. Vassberg, *Land and Society in Golden Age Castile*, 1984; *The Cambridge History of Latin America: Colonial Latin America*, 2 vols., ed. Leslie Bethell, 1984.

David E. Vassberg

RUIZ DE ALARCÓN Y MENDOZA, JUAN. Routinely considered to be colonial Spanish America's greatest dramatist, Juan Ruiz de Alarcón was born in New Spain* in 1580 to relatively well-to-do parents. He spent his formative years in New Spain and studied the arts at the University of Mexico. But Ruiz de Alarcón's most important years as a writer were not in Mexico, but in Spain. Because of this, many literary critics for years disallowed him as a Mexican writer. Others, however, have contended that Ruiz de Alarcón's works, although clearly written for Spanish theater audiences, reflected a decidedly Mexican point of view. Spanish critics, on the other hand, have attempted to appropriate Ruiz de Alarcón for themselves, presumably because he represents an important chapter in Golden Age letters in Madrid. Whatever the case, Ruiz de Alarcón was a gifted playwright whose origins were very colonial.

Ruiz de Alarcón wrote over 24 plays, the most famous of which are *Las paredes oyen*, *Los pechos privilegiados*, *Ganar amigos*, *La prueba de las promesas*, and *La verdad sospechosa*. The latter work was used by the French playwright Pierre Corneille in his creation of *Le menteur*, a somewhat remarkable fact in that it demonstrates a literary influence from the New World making an impression in Europe, instead of the converse as was the usual pattern. The plays of Ruiz de Alarcón are respected for their human insight, careful construction, and philosophical and moral concern. His works enjoyed great success in Madrid, even though he competed against the greatest of Spanish dramatists, including Lope de Vega, Pedro Calderón de la Barca, and Tirso de Molina. These men, along with Luis de Góngora, Francisco Gómes de Quevedo, and numerous other literary luminaries, shamefully and relentlessly ridiculed the colonial playwright, not only for his New World mannerisms, but also for the severe hunchback and other deformities from which Ruiz de Alarcón suffered.

Ruiz de Alarcón went to Spain to discover his fortune. He first went in 1600, but was forced to return for economic reasons. He returned to Spain in 1613 to spend the rest of his life there. Although he died in relative obscurity in 1639, Ruiz de Alarcón left a permanent mark on both Spanish and New World literary history as one of the greatest dramatists ever to write in the Spanish language.

REFERENCE: A. Castro Real, *Juan Ruiz de Alarcón: Su vida y obra*, 1943.

Sam L. Slick

RUIZ DE APODACA, JUAN. Juan Ruiz de Apodaca was born in Spain in 1767 and arrived in Mexico City[*] as viceroy of New Spain[*] in 1816, right in the middle of the independence movement. He had previously had a naval career and served for four years as governor of Cuba[*]. Ruiz realized that the rebels had the upper hand and that Spain did not have the resources to fight an extended, bloody war of repression, so he adopted a conciliatory posture. He offered amnesty to all rebels who agreed to submit to royalist policies, and he enjoyed several military successes that blunted the rebel movement. In 1820, Ruiz proclaimed that the Constitution of 1812[*], which liberal reformers had passed in Spain, now applied to Mexico; Ferdinand VII[*], recently humbled by revolution in Spain, agreed. It appeared that the rebel movement in New Spain would then subside, but in 1821, Ruiz found himself facing a new insurgency led by Agustín de Iturbide[*]. He recognized immediately that Spain could not stop the independence movement in Mexico. He returned to Spain in 1821 and died there in 1835.

REFERENCE: Artemio de Valle-Arizpe, *Virreyes y virreynas de la Nueva España*, 1933.

RUIZ DE MONTOYA, ANTONIO. Antonio Ruiz de Montoya was born in Lima[*], Peru[*], on November 11, 1583. His father was a wealthy Spanish military officer. Ruiz de Montoya tried the military for a short period of time but then entered the Jesuit* order in Córdoba*, Argentina*, in 1606. He was ordained in 1610. Ruiz then went to Paraguay* for missionary work, and between 1623 and 1637, he was provincial of the Jesuit *reducciones** in Paraguay. It was his task to defend the settlements from the Paulistas attacking out of Brazil. In 1637, Ruiz traveled to Spain where he managed to secure royal protection of the *reducciones*. Ruiz also wrote a number of important studies of the Guaraní language and Roman Catholic catechisms in Guaraní*. He died in Lima*, Peru*, on April 11, 1653.

REFERENCE: G. R. Furlong, *Antonio Ruiz de Montoya y su carta a Comental (1645)*, 1964.

S

SAAVEDRA CERÓN, ÁLVARO DE. Álvaro de Saavedra, a Spanish navigator and explorer, has the distinction of being the first European navigator to sail across the Pacific from the North American coast to the East Indies. Hernán Cortés*, the conqueror of the Aztec* empire, received an order from the emperor Charles V* to send forth an expedition to discover the fate of the *Trinidad*, one of Ferdinand Magellan's* ships. Three vessels, the *Florida*, the *Santiago*, and the *Espíritu Santo*, were prepared and placed under the command of the *hidalgo** Álvaro de Saavedra Cerón, a relative of Cortés. On October 31, 1527, they sailed from Zihuatanejo on the western coast of New Spain*. Early in December, a heavy squall separated the *Florida*, the flagship, from the other two ships, which were swept forward and not seen again by anyone on the flagship. Late in December, the flagship sighted but did not land at the island now known as Guam*. It reached the Philippines* in February and anchored off a small island near the north coast of Mindanao*. While in the Philippines, Saavedra rescued a few men who were survivors from Juan Garcia Jofre de Loaysa's* earlier voyage. He then proceeded to the Moluccas (Spice Islands*) and in March 1528, reached the island of Tidore. Subsequently, Saavedra made two northern cruises in an effort to find a suitable return route to the western coast of North America, but his attempts failed. Saavedra sailed along the coast of New Guinea in the course of these voyages, discovering islands in the Marshall* and Caroline* groups as well as the Admiralty Islands off the northern coast of eastern New Guinea. He died during the second expedition and was buried at sea. The survivors of his company returned to Tidore in December 1529 and surrendered themselves to the Portuguese who kept them in detention for several years before sending them back to Spain.

REFERENCES: Ione Struessy Wright, "The First American Voyage Across the Pacific, 1527–1528: The Voyage of Álvaro de Saavedra Cerón," *Geographical Review*, 24 (1939), 472–82; Ione Struessy Wright, *Voyages of Álvaro de Saavedra Cerón, 1527-1929*, 1951.

SAAVEDRA GUZMÁN, ANTONIO DE. Born in New Spain[*] in 1570, Saavedra was the son of one of the first colonists. He was well connected in both society and politics, holding various public positions. It is known that he assiduously studied fine arts and humanities, with a particular interest in poetry and history. Saavedra reportedly spent some seven years collecting notes and data in order to write his masterpiece, *El Peregrino Indiano* (1599). According to Saavedra, he wrote *El Peregrino* during a 70-day trans-atlantic voyage to Spain. The work consists of over 2,000 octaves and deals with Hernán Cortés's[*] conquest of Mexico, beginning with his expedition's departure from Cuba[*] until the imprisonment of Cuauhtemoc[*]. Critical comment on *El Peregrino* has been uneven. Many consider the work more hisotry (chronicle[*]) than poetry, while others see it as pure epic poetry. In any event, it rates among the important literary works of the sixteenth century in colonial Spanish America. Scholars are not sure about the date of Saavedra Guzman's death.

REFERENCE: Enrique Imbert, *Historia de la literatura hispanoamericana*, 1961.

Sam L. Slick

SACO, JOSÉ ANTONIO. José Antonio Saco was born in Bayamo, Cuba[*], in 1797, and eventually became a noted Cuban intellectual and statesman. He worked as a professor of philosophy at the San Carlos Seminary and edited several journals. When Spanish authorities forbade him to establish a Cuban Academy of Literature, he went to New York in the 1850s, where he published the weekly newspaper *El Mensajero Semanal* and campaigned for the annexation of Cuba by the United States. By the 1860s, Saco was a vociferous opponent of slavery[*] and had abandoned his belief in annexation in favor of Cuban independence. In 1866, he traveled to Madrid to represent Santiago de Cuba before the Junta de Información. José Antonio Saco died in 1879 in Barcelona, Spain. His best-known written works are *Colección de papeles científicos, históricos, políticos y de otros ramos*, *Sobre la Isla de Cuba*, 2 vols. (1858–1859) and *Historia de la esclavitud*.

REFERENCES: Jaime Suchlicki, *Historical Dictionary of Cuba*, 1988; Jaime Suchlicki, *Cuba: From Columbus to Castro*, 1986.

SÁENZ, JOSÉ MARÍA. José María Sáenz was born in Quito[*], Ecuador[*], in the late 1790s. He spent his early career as an officer in the Spanish army, but he switched sides when the independence rebellion occurred, and he served in the famous Infante Battalón. Sáenz fought in Colombia[*] and Ecuador and eventually received the rank of general. Early in the 1830s, he became a political enemy of President Juan José Flores[*] and participated in an insurgent rebellion against him. On April 20, 1834, near Tabacundo, Ecuador, troops loyal to Flores caught up with Sáenz and killed him.

REFERENCE: Albert William Bork and Georg Maier, *Historical Dictionary of Ecuador*, 1973.

SÁENZ, MANUELA. Manuela Sáenz, known in Ecuador as "La Libertadora del Libertador," was born in Quito*, Ecuador*, in December 1793. She married Jaime Thorne, a prominent and wealthy English merchant in Quito, but when the independence movement broke out and he opposed it, she left him. She joined the forces of Simón Bolívar* in 1822. Sáenz is credited with saving Bolívar from an assassination attempt on September 25, 1828—hence the name mentioned above. Manuela Sáenz rose to the rank of colonel in the army of Gran Colombia*. She died in exile on November 23, 1856, in Paita, Peru*.

REFERENCE: Albert William Bork and Georg Maier, *Historical Dictionary of Ecuador*, 1973.

SAGASTA PACT. See CARTA AUTONOMICA.

SAHAGÚN, FRAY BERNARDINO DE. The long life of Friar Bernardino de Sahagún gave the New World (New Spain*) one of its most devoted and best historians and linguists. Sahagún was a liberal spirit, a man of compassion and great learning, and also an early scientific investigator. Born in the province of León, Spain, around 1499, Sahagún arrived in New Spain in 1529. He quickly began a lifelong study of Indian* languages, becoming fluent in Nahuatl* as a young man. Through Sahagún's many close contacts with reliable Indian informants and scribes, he was able to extract and reconstruct a large overview of the Indian's view of the world and man.

Sahagún's major work was the chronicle titled *Historia de las Cosas de la Nueva España* (1569, translated as *The History of Things in New Spain*). *Historia* was originally composed of 12 separate books. Taken as a whole, they are a sweeping and masterly study of Mexican ethnography. It was originally written in Nahuatl by Sahagún's scribes and assistants at the Colegio de Tlatelolco. Sahagún then translated it into both Latin and Spanish. One of the most interesting of the books is the twelfth, which describes the conquest of Mexico from the Indians' point of view. In large part, our contemporary knowledge of both Indian civilization at the time of the conquest and of Nahuatl literature is based upon Sahagún's splendid and extensive *Historia*. He died in Mexico City* around 1590.

REFERENCES: Alfredo Chavero, *Sahagún*, 1877; L. Nicolau D'Olwer, *Historiadores de América: Fray Bernardino de Sahagún, 1499-1590*, 1952.

Sam L. Slick

SAHARAWI POPULAR LIBERATION ARMY. The Saharawi Popular Liberation Army was the military arm of the Polisario Front*, the nationalist group bent on destroying French and Spanish authority in Spanish Sahara*, Spanish Morocco*, and French Morocco. It was poorly equipped and relatively small in numbers between 1973 and 1975 when its target was Spanish imperial power.

Since the Madrid Agreement[*] of 1975, after which Spain began its withdrawal from the region, however, the Saharawi Popular Liberation Army has grown in size and power, with its new target being Moroccan influence.

REFERENCE: Ahmed-Baba Miske, *Front Polisario: l'ame d'un peuple*, 1978.

SAILA OULD ABEIDA OULD AHMED. Saila Ould Abeida Ould Ahmed was born in Togba, Spanish Sahara[*], in 1920. He was a member of the Reguibi ethnic group. Saila collaborated very closely with Spanish imperial interests in the 1970s. He was named president of the Cabildo Provincial in 1965, and in 1966, he presented the Spanish colonial case before the United Nations. Generalíssimo Francisco Franco[*] saw to it that Saila was appointed to the Cortes in 1967 and was named *alcalde*[*] of El-Ayoun. Saila was also elected president of the Djemaa[*], Western Sahara's consultative assembly. Saila was a bitter opponent of Moroccan claims in Western Sahara. After the demise of the Spanish Empire there in 1975, he joined the political groups campaigning for the interests of Mauritania.

REFERENCES: Tony Hodges, *Historical Dictionary of Western Sahara*, 1982; John Mercer, *Spanish Sahara*, 1975.

ST. AUGUSTINE. See EAST FLORIDA.

ST. CHRISTOPHER. St. Christopher, better known as St. Kitts, was first sighted by Christopher Columbus[*] on his second voyage to the Americas in 1493. Columbus named the island St. Christopher because he saw in its shape a resemblance to the saint carrying the Saviour. St. Kitts is a volcanic island and contains a range of rugged mountains and very fertile plains. It was inhabited when the Spanish arrived by fierce Karibs[*] who called the island Liamuiga, meaning "fertile land". Within a couple years of its discovery, Spain's attention was drawn to the larger islands to the west; little or no attention was paid to St. Kitts. After the 1560s, the English "sea dogs"—John Hawkins, Francis Drake[*], and Walter Raleigh—reconnoitered the Caribbean archipelago, exploring possibilities for raiding, trading, and settling the region. While the Spanish refused to surrender their right, which would have allowed other European nations to own the Lesser Antilles, it became obvious to the European latecomers that Spain could not effectively protect the numerous smaller islands of the Caribbean. Furthermore, the unoccupied territories in the Caribbean were "beyond the line" and outside of the territorial limits of European treaties. The English and French seafarers were willing to take their chances, and St. Kitts seemed an excellent staging ground. St. Kitts was colonized by Thomas Warner of Britain in 1623 in cooperation with Pierre Belain d'Esnambuc and a group of French settlers who occupied either end of the island from 1625. Soon afterward, a fierce battle broke out between the English and the French with the Karibs, who were eventually decimated. The Spanish resented the English and the French establishing themselves so strongly and, in 1629, with a fleet of 38 ships, Spain nearly annihilated both the English and French colonies on St. Kitts. Most of the French escaped to neighboring islands, and the English were deported by the Spanish. The sturdy French who remained after the Spanish forces left St. Kitts quickly and re-established the French colony under d'Esnambuc, and the English colonists also returned. In the Anglo-French war of 1666–1667, the French attacked their English neighbors and conquered the whole island, in spite of the assistance rendered to the English governor by Colonel Morgan, the uncle and father-in-law of the famous buccaneer Sir Henry Morgan (later the lieutenant governor of Jamaica). The English part of the island was restored to its former owners by the Treaty of Breda[*] in 1667. Spain had given up its desire to exclude other European powers from settling St. Kitts.

REFERENCE: Richard S. Dunn, *Sugar and Slaves: The Rise of the Planter Class in the English West Indies, 1624-1713*, 1973.

Glenn O. Phillips

ST. DOMINGUE. See SANTO DOMINGO.

ST. KITTS. See ST. CHRISTOPHER.

ST. LUCÍA. St. Lucía is a Caribbean island located in the Lesser Antilles, south of Martinique[*] and northeast of St. Vincent. A large mountain range runs north and south for nearly the entire length of the 233 square miles of this mostly volcanic island. Like most of its neighbors, it was sighted by Christopher Columbus[*] on his voyages to the region; he gave it its modern name after he observed it on St. Lucy's day in 1502 during his fourth voyage. The large Karib[*] population that occupied its lands for centuries called it Hervanorra. The French referred to it as Saint Alouisie or St. Alouziel in their documents.

Like the rest of the Lesser Antilles, St. Lucía was initially considered part of the Spanish Empire. Not possessing any significant mineral resource that would require Spanish colonization in the early years of settlement, it was not settled by Spanish colonists. As on most of the islands in the eastern Caribbean archipelago, a large Karib population had settled before the period of the Spanish exploration, and they resisted European intrusion. Spain's early sixteenth-century interest in St. Lucía was primarily as a Karib slave-raiding site. This was particularly true after the 1511 authorization by the Spanish Crown, which ruled that the Karibs of St. Lucia had refused to become Christians or to allow Christians to enter the island. Since the natives had resisted and killed Spanish Christians, they were cannibalistic; therefore, they could be caught, enslaved, and transported to other parts of the Spanish West Indies to work and, ideally, to be trained in Christian ways. Largely ignored by Spain, St. Lucía became a constant subject of dispute between the French and the English from the mid-seventeenth century.

REFERENCES: Henry Breen, *St. Lucia: Historical, Statistical and Descriptive*, 1970; C. Jesse, "Barbados buys St. Lucia from the Caribs," *Journal of the Barbados Museum and Historical Society*, 32 (1968), 180–86.; C. Jesse, *Outlines of Saint Lucia's History*, 1956.

Glenn O. Phillips

SALAZAR, DOMINGO DE. Domingo de Salazar was born in Labastida, Ebro, Spain, in 1512. He attended the University of Salamanca and in 1546 entered the Dominican* order. A missionary priest, Salazar was assigned to Venezuela* in 1548. After a brief time there, he moved north to New Spain*, where he spent the next decade. Between 1558 and 1561, Salazar accompanied Tristán de Arellano on his expeditions to Florida*; then he returned to labor in Oaxaca* and Puebla*. He relocated to Spain in 1572, and in 1579, King Philip II* appointed him the first bishop of Manila* in the Philippines*. Salazar arrived there in 1581. An opponent of the *encomienda**, Salazar worked to provide humane treatment of the native Filipinos, and in 1587, he invited the Dominicans to come to the islands. Salazar died in Madrid, Spain, on December 4, 1594.

REFERENCES: Lewis Hanke, ed., *Cuerpo de documentos del siglo XVI*, 1943; V. F. O'Daniel, *Dominicans in Early Florida*, 1930.

SALAZAR Y ESPINOSA, JUAN DE. Juan de Salazar y Espinosa was born in Spain in 1508. He was a member of Pedro de Mendoza's* expedition to the Río de la Plata* area. Salazar sailed up the Paraná and Paraguay rivers from the Río de la Plata in 1537. In that year, he founded the city of Asunción*—the first permanent settlement in the southern part of South America. Juan de Salazar died in 1560.

REFERENCE: Machain Lafuente, *Los conquistadores de la Plata*, 1943.

SALINAS Y CÓRDOBA, BUENAVENTURA DE. Buenaventura de Salinas y Córdoba was born in Lima*, Peru*, in 1592. He received a Jesuit* education, but in 1616, he joined the Franciscan* order. Salinas then spent 15 years in a variety of teaching assignments. He became particularly interested in social and political questions, especially the abuses that Spanish *peninsulares**, clerical as well as political, inflicted on the *criollo** population. He published a book in 1630, *Memorial de las historias del Nuevo Mundo*, that offered a blatantly *criollo* interpretation of Spanish imperialism. When Salinas publicly expressed his sentiments during a sermon in Cuzco* in 1635, Bishop Diego de Vera denounced him to the Spanish Crown. Salinas was called to Spain to defend himself. He was quickly cleared there and assigned as regent at Santa María la Nova in Naples. There Salinas became deeply involved in Catalan and Portuguese separatism. He was recalled from Naples and sent back to the Americas as commissary general of the Indies, a post he filled until his death in Cuernavaca, New Spain*, on November 15, 1653.

REFERENCE: W. W. Cook, "Fray Buenaventura de Salinas y Córdoba," in *Memorial de las historias del nuevo mundo*, 1957.

SALTA. The region of Salta consisted of the northern portion of the province of Tucumán*. It was split off from Córdoba* and established as an *intendencia** in 1783. It was under the jurisdiction of the viceroyalty of Río de la Plata*. By 1810, Salta was no longer under Spanish control and eventually became part of Argentina*.

SALVADOR GILIJ, FELIPE. See GILIJ, FELIPE SALVADOR.

SALVATIERRA, JUAN MARÍA. Juan María Salvatierra was born in Milan in what is today Italy on November 15, 1644. A Jesuit* priest, Salvatierra arrived in New Spain* in 1675, while still a novitiate. He continued his studies and was ordained in New Spain. He then spent ten years as a missionary in Sierra de Chinipas before being assigned to missionary work in Lower California*. Along with Juan de Ugarte, Salvatierra raised the funds and in 1697 began the missionary work. He was an indefatigable worker for the next seven years, after which he returned to Mexico City* to serve as the Jesuit provincial. In 1707, Salvatierras returned to Lower California. He worked there until 1717 when he had to retire because of ill health. Juan Salvatierra died in Guadalajara* on July 17, 1717.

REFERENCE: M. R. Venegas, *Juan María de Salvatierra of the Society of Jesus*, 1929.

SAMANO, JUAN. Juan Samano was born in Spain in 1753 and spent his career in the Spanish army; he rose to the rank of field marshal. In order to crush the rebellion of patriot forces in Colombia*, the Spanish Crown appointed him military governor of New Granada* in 1816. Along with General Pablo Morillo y Morillo, Samano supervised the reconquest of New Granada between 1816 and 1819. He was appointed viceroy* of New Granada in 1818. Ill health forced his resignation as viceroy in 1819, and he died one year later.

REFERENCES: Robert H. Davis, *Historical Dictionary of Colombia*, 1977; José Manuel Groot, *Historia eclesiástica y civil de Nueva Granada*, 5 vols., 1953.

SAMAR. Samar is the largest island in the Visayas* (5,000 square miles), but not very densely populated by Philippine* standards. It lies about 300 miles southeast of Manila*. Ferdinand Magellan*, searching for the Spice Islands*, landed on Homonhon, a small island off the south coast of Samar, but continued on his way. Spanish rule rested lightly on the remote, forested, roadless island. The reasons for Samar's underdevelopment are its location and rugged terrain. The long eastern coast faces the open Pacific and takes the brunt of severe annual storms. Structures along this coast are regularly blown down. The population, therefore, is oriented westward, toward the gentler Samar Sea. Most trade passes through the west coast ports of Calbayog and Catbalogan. There are few high mountains, but there is little coastal lowland, either; most of Samar is rolling upland, suitable for hemp production, dry-rice agriculture, and forestry. The

people of Samar speak a language called Waray-Waray, and there are no significant minority groups. There has always been a gap between rich and poor,
as elsewhere in the Philippines, but due to the absence of commercial agriculture
and big haciendas*, class tension did not build to an incendiary level. The only
important Samareno rebellion against Spainsh rule started as a protest against
an order of 1649 drafting men to work in shipyards near Manila. A priest was
killed in the town of Palapag, and, as the insurrection spread to other villages
and to neighboring islands, it assumed an anticlerical character. The rebel leader
Juan Ponce Sumoroy was betrayed by his own troops and his head delivered to
the Spanish. There were no further rebellions on Samar for 200 years.

Jesuits* tried to resettle Samarenos on missions and met with some success,
but less for religious reasons than because the Spanish settlements offered some
protection from Moro* slave raids. In the last half century of Spanish rule, free
trade policies encouraged commercial stands of coconut and hemp. Samar was
still a backwater, though, and played no role in the revolution against Spain. It
was the scene of some of the cruelest fighting of the Philippine-American War,
and the people were not completely pacified until 1911.

REFERENCE: Bruce Cruikshank, "Continuity and Change in the Economic and Administrative History of Nineteenth Century Samar," in Alfred McCoy and Ed. de Jesús,
eds., *Philippine Social History*, 1982.

Ross Marlay

SAN ANTONIO. San Antonio de Valero was the largest of the missions* during
the eighteenth century in the mission district around present-day San Antonio,
Texas*. The Franciscans* established San Antonio de Valero at the headwaters
of the San Antonio River in 1718. San Antonio was established as a link in the
chain of mission-presidios established in the early eighteenth century by the
viceroy of New Spain*, Baltasar de Zúñiga Guzmán, the Marqués de Valero, to
populate the northern Internal Provinces* of New Spain and to prevent foreign
encroachment into Spanish territory. Like all the missions in this system, San
Antonio was protected by a nearby presidio, or garrison, known originally as
San Antonio de Béjar, or Bexar. By 1762, the mission-presidio had a population
of 200 Spanish settlers. San Antonio's distance from Mexico City* and repeated
attacks by the Apache* Indians prevented the mission from thriving, however;
by 1793, it had only 43 permanent settlers. That year, the Franciscans allowed
the mission to be secularized. The compound was turned over to the military
and renamed the Alamo.

REFERENCE: T. R. Fehrenbach, *Lone State: A History of Texas and Texans*, 1985.

Virginia Garrard Burnett

SAN CARLOS, UNIVERSITY OF. The University of San Carlos was first
authorized in 1676, and officially opened in 1681 in Santiago* de Guatemala.
The university was founded by the Dominicans* in an attempt to break the
monopoly held by the Jesuits* in the education of the *criollo* elite of Guatemala*.

The Jesuits' school, the Colegio de Jesús, had been established in Santiago in 1607, and was the first institution of its kind in Central America. The Dominicans founded the University of San Carlos with the help of substantial endowments given by the Pedro Crespo Suárez and Melchor Gonzales families, two *criollo* families that had become wealthy in the sugar* trade. In its early years, the University of San Carlos operated under a budget that was more than three times that of the Colegio de Jesús. Despite its wealth, the University of San Carlos foundered until 1767, when the expulsion of the Jesuits enabled the Dominican-run institution to become the most important center of learning in the region.

REFERENCE: Miles L. Wortman, *Government and Society in Central America, 1680-1840*, 1982.

Virginia Garrard Burnett

SAN CARLOS, UNIVERSITY OF. The University of San Carlos was established in Cebu City, the Philippines*, in 1595 by three Jesuit* missionaries. It remained a Jesuit institution until 1767 when the Jesuits were expelled from the Philippines. The University of San Carlos remained closed from 1767 until 1783, when it reopened as a diocesan institution called the College-Seminary of San Carlos. Dominicans* took it over from 1852 to 1867, and it was then handed over to Vicentians.

REFERENCE: *New Catholic Encyclopedia*, XII:1920, 1967.

SÁNCHEZ CARRIÓN, LUIS. Luis Sánchez Carrión was born in Lima*, Peru*, in 1787. He became an intimate of Simón Bolívar* and an eloquent theorist, advocating republican forms of government. Writing under the pseudonym of "El Solitario," Sánchez called for independence from Spain and democratic republicanism once independence was achieved. During 1824–1825, when some Peruvians were calling for the establishment of a Peruvian monarchy, Sánchez was a vociferous political opponent. He died on June 2, 1825, in Lima.

REFERENCE: Marvin Alisky, *Historical Dictionary of Peru*, 1977.

SÁNCHEZ DE BADAJOZ, HERNÁN. Hernán Sánchez de Badajoz was born in Badajoz, Spain, in 1489. He came to the New World as a young man in 1514 and spent years on various military expeditions in Central America and Peru*. Sánchez made a fortune in Peru in the 1530s. In 1539 he was appointed *adelantado* and captain general of Costa Rica*. In 1540, Sánchez led an expedition through the San Juan River area. He got involved in a bitter struggle for power with Rodrigo de Contreras over territorial control. Sánchez came out on the short end of the struggle; he lost the governorship of Costa Rica in 1541 and was taken to Spain as a prisoner. He died in jail in Valladolid awaiting trial.

REFERENCE: Theodore S. Creedman, *Historical Dictionary of Costa Rica*, 1977.

SAN FELIPE, UNIVERSITY OF. The University of San Felipe was established in 1756 in Santiago*, Chile*. It was named after King Philip V* of Spain. Members of the *cabildo**, concerned about the domination of education by clerics, especially Jesuits*, had lobbied for creation of the university. It began holding classes in 1758. The University of San Felipe became part of the National Institute in 1813.

REFERENCES: Edna Ferguson, *Chile*, 1943; Helen Delpar, *Encyclopedia of Latin America*, 1974.

SAN ILDEFONSO, TREATY OF. The treaty of San Ildefonso of 1777 was the last in a series of eighteenth-century agreements between Spain and Portugal affecting the colonial boundaries of South America. Territorial disputes between Portugal and Spain remained unresolved during the period following the Treaty of Madrid* of 1750, which, among other results, had recognized Portuguese control over most of present-day Brazil. In 1761, the Treaty of El Pardo between Spain and Portugal nullified most of the Portuguese gains inherent in the Treaty of Madrid, thus reopening negotiations over the territorial boundaries between Brazil and Spanish Latin America. The Treaty of San Ildefonso, signed October 1, 1777, was less favorable to Portugal, since its only advantage was to retain sovereignty over a small disputed area in the Rio Grande de São Pedro and the island of Santa Catarina. Spain gained former Portuguese territory in the Seven Missions region between the Uruguay and Ibicui rivers, as well as the Colônia do Sacramento on the Río de la Plata*. The Treaty of San Ildefonso was followed by further attempts at fixing the colonial frontiers in South America, both north and south, culminating in the Treaty of Badajoz of 1801, in which the Portuguese losses under the Treaty of San Ildefonso were confirmed.

REFERENCES: C. H. Haring, *The Spanish Empire in America*, 1947; Leslie Bethell, ed., *The Cambridge History of Latin America*, Vol. I, 1984.

William G. Ratliff

SAN JOSÉ. San José is the capital city of Costa Rica*. The city had its formal beginning in 1738 when Roman Catholic priests constructed a small church and began to encourage farmers in the immediate area to relocate there. Population growth, however, was slow, until sugar*, tobacco*, and coffee* cultivation developed in the late eighteenth and early nineteenth centuries. In 1821, the people of San José unilaterally declared their independence from Spain. In the independence congress that year, delegates moved the capital of the country to San José. At the time of independence, there were approximately 3,000 people living in San José.

REFERENCE: Theodore S. Creedman, *Historical Dictionary of Costa Rica*, 1977.

SAN JOSÉ DE BETANCUR, PEDRO DE. Born in the Canary Islands* in 1627, Hermano Pedro, as Pedro de San José de Betancur was commonly called, came to Guatemala* in 1651. A Franciscan* friar who modeled himself after the founder of his order, Hermano Pedro based his work in Santiago* and ministered to the poor and sick, providing them with both spiritual and medical care. He founded a hospital in Santiago and attracted a following of disciples, from the ranks of both the poor and the wealthy. His most avid disciple was Rodrigo

Arias Maldonado, the former Marquis of Talamanca and governor of Costa Rica, who renounced his former life and status to become Rodrigo de la Cruz. Hermano Pedro died in 1667, leaving behind a will that ordered his followers to establish a *cofradía** to maintain his hospital, but Rodrigo de la Cruz instead used his legacy to establish a new monastic order, the Bethlehemites*, in 1668. Although the Bethlehemites received papal confirmation four years later, they were always viewed with some suspicion by Spanish authorities. The only male religious order to originate in Spanish America, the Bethlehemites established 17 hospitals in Spanish America and one in the Canary Islands, as well as several colleges. In 1670, a small female order of Bethlehemites was also established. Hermano Pedro was credited with miraculous healings after his death. In 1980, he was beatified by Pope John Paul II.

REFERENCE: R. L. Woodward, Jr., *Central America: A Nation Divided*, 1983.

Virginia Garrard Burnett

SAN JUAN. San Juan, the capital city of Puerto Rico*, was founded in 1521 when Spaniards decided to relocate Juan Ponce de León's* settlement at Caparra out to the coast. At the time, San Juan, then called Puerto Rico, had just over 300 inhabitants, and its population growth was slow. Its population reached 1,600 people in 1600 and over 7,000 people in 1800. During the sixteenth and seventeenth centuries, San Juan was the staging area for most of the Spanish exploration expeditions in the Caribbean, and it was recognized as a strategic location for control in the region. When the United States assumed jurisdiction over Puero Rico from Spain in 1898, San Juan's population had reached just over 32,000 people.

REFERENCE: Kenneth R. Farr, *Historical Dictionary of Puerto Rico and the U.S. Virgin Islands*, 1973.

SAN JUAN, DIOCESE OF. The Roman Catholic diocese of San Juan, Puerto Rico*, was established by Pope Julius II in 1511. At the time it was called the diocese of Puerto Rico. It was raised to an archdiocese in 1960.

REFERENCE: *New Catholic Encylclopedia*, XII:1032–33, 1967.

SAN LUIS POTOSÍ. The city of San Luis Potosí in north central Mexico was established in 1550. Gold was discovered there in 1590, and by 1620, it was also a major center of silver mining* in the New World. San Luis Potosí was established as an *intendencia** within New Spain* in 1787. That region eventually became part of the republic of Mexico. See NEW SPAIN.

SAN MARCOS, UNIVERSITY OF. The University of San Marcos was established by decree of the Spanish Crown in 1551 and opened for classes in Lima*, Peru*, in 1571. It eventually developed into one of the most prestigious universities in the New World.

REFERENCE: L. A. Eguiguren, *El fundador de la Universidad de San Marcos*, 1911.

SAN MARTÍN, JOSÉ DE. José de San Martín was born on February 25, 1778, in Yapeyú, in the viceroyalty of Río de la Plata*. His mother was Gregoria Matorras and his father was Juan de San Martín, a professional soldier and government administrator of Yapeyu. The family returned to Spain in 1784, where the younger San Martín was educated at the Seminario de Nobles from 1785 until 1789, at which point he began his military career as a cadet in the Murcia infantry regiment. From 1808 until 1811, he served as an officer against the forces of Napoleon*. Having attained the rank of lieutenant colonel in 1808, he was offered the command of the Sagunto Dragoons following the Battle of Albuera. Instead of accepting, he requested assignment to Lima*, in the vice-royalty of Peru*. He proceeded to Peru via London, where he met other disaffected Spanish-Americans and was recruited by James Duffy, 4th Earl of Fife, to fight against the Seville* Junta (Ferdinand VII* had been imprisoned by Napoleon*). San Martín claimed that he chose to fight for his native land in revolt against the Junta. He was probably motivated by his belief in constitutional liberalism, and he identified with the *criollo** revolutionaries with whom he had earlier become associated in Cádiz. Furthermore, as a *criollo* serving in the Spanish army, he had undoubtedly experienced prejudice from peninsular Spaniards.

Upon his arrival in Buenos Aires* in March 1812, he was given the task of organizing a corps of mounted grenadiers to be used against the Spanish royalists in Peru* who were threatening the government in Argentina*. In September 1812, San Martín reinforced his ties with Argentina when he married María de los Remedios Escalada, the daughter of an upper-class Argentine family. On February 3, 1813, San Martín fought his first engagement, defeating a royalist force at San Lorenzo. Before replacing General Manuel Belgrano* at Tucumán*, San Martín had already come to the conclusion that the Río de la Plata provinces would never be secure until the royalist stronghold in Peru had been crushed. To accomplish this task, he trained the army around Tucumán so that they could sustain a holding operation. Then, on the pretense of ill health, he got himself appointed governor intendant of Cuyo in western Argentina. The capital city, Mendoza, was the key to routes through the Andes mountains. His plan was to travel west from Argentina to Chile* and from there by sea to the Peruvian coast. The design and execution of his plan were carried out with meticulous care; San Martín would not move until he was fully equipped, including his bugles. A setback occurred in October 1814, when the Chilean patriot regime collapsed. San Martín's army benefited from the influx of Chileans, however, including Bernardo O'Higgins*. In January 1817, San Martín set out on his expedition to Chile. Initially, he was able to elude the Spanish by misleading them as to the trail he would take. From January 18 until February 8, 1817, he fought his way across the Andes, concentrating his forces at the enemy's weakest point. He took the main part of his army through passes that reached altitudes of 10,000 to 12,000 feet. On February 12, 1817, San Martín surprised and defeated the royalist army at Casas de Chacabuco* and then occupied Santiago*.

Turning the governorship over to O'Higgins, San Martín took a year to clear the country of the remaining royalist troops, defeating them on April 5, 1818, at the Battle of Maipú*. While the government in Buenos Aires was embroiled in domestic quarrels, San Martín proceeded without their assistance to the next phase of his plan. With a newly created Chilean fleet under the command of Admiral Thomas Cochrane, San Martín sailed from Valparaíso*, landing south of the port of Callao by September 1820. San Martín, not prepared to attack the superiorly defended Lima, waited a year until royalist support had deteriorated and the royalists had withdrawn to the mountains. On July 28, 1821, San Martín entered the city unopposed and declared the independence of Peru, accepting the title "Protector of Peru" from a grateful populace.

In the newly liberated areas, he began to enact a series of liberal reforms, including the gradual emancipation of black slaves* and the abolition of Indian* forced labor. He was criticized, however, for not pursuing the royalists, who remained numerous and well entrenched in the Peruvian Andes. There was also mistrust of San Martín's monarchist views. Earlier, at the Congress of Tucumán* in 1816, he had supported a scheme to establish a limited monarchy under a prince of the Inca* royal family. Prior to his 1821 victory in Peru, San Martín had negotiated with Spain to create an autonomous monarchy in which one of the princes of the Spanish royal family would rule over an independent Peru. Although nothing came of these schemes, San Martín believed that a liberal constitutional monarchy was the best hope for stability in the new nations. San Martín thus faced growing resentment and distrust among Peruvians when he left Peru to meet with Simón Bolívar*. The two great revolutionary leaders met in Guayaquil* in July 1822. Although the content of the meeting was secret, San Martín presumably sought support for his monarchist plans in Peru. He also hoped to secure Guayaquil as a port for Peru. San Martín's request for troops hinged on the type of government that would be established in Peru. Bolívar stood firm in favor of a republic and would not entertain San Martín's plans for creating a constitutional monarchy. Historians have debated the substance of the meeting, but it is clear that although they disagreed over the type of government, both men remained committed to South American independence and felt the need to continue the revolution. Whether he decided to resign before or after his meeting is unclear, but upon his return to Lima on September 20, San Martín resigned as Protector of Peru and departed. In February 1824, he sailed for Europe, where he lived most of the rest of his life in France. He returned to South America in 1828, hoping to aid in the political consolidation of the new nations, but nothing came of his efforts, and he returned to France in 1829. San Martín died in Boulogne-sur-Mer, France, on August 17, 1850.

REFERENCE: Richard Rojas, *San Martín: Knight of the Andes*, 1945.

Michael Dennis

SAN MARTÍN, TOMÁS DE. Tomás de San Martín was born in Palencia, Spain, on March 7, 1482. He professed to become a Dominican* priest in 1498 and then graduated from Santo Tomás in Seville* with a degree in the arts and theology. He went to the New World in 1525 and spent four years there before returning to Spain. San Martín returned to the New World in 1538, where he tried to defend the Indians* against the *encomenderos*. He became the first provincial of the Dominicans in Peru* and presided over the rapid expansion of their activities there. In 1548, at the Dominican convent in Lima*, San Martín began the development of an educational curriculum that evolved into the University of San Marcos*. In 1552, San Martín was appointed bishop of Charcas* but he died in Lima in 1554 before he could assume the position.

REFERENCE: L. A. Eguiguren, *El fundador de la Universidad de San Marcos*, 1911.

SAN SALVADOR. See EL SALVADOR.

SAN SALVADOR. At 2 A.M. on Friday, October 12, 1492, Rodrigo de Triana, on lookout on the *Pinta*, spotted Guanahani, an island in the east-central Bahamas*, the first land that the Christopher Columbus* expedition had encountered since departing from the Canary Islands* 33 days earlier. A thankful Columbus christened it San Salvador (Holy Savior). Triana hoped to receive the lifetime annuity of 10,000 *maravedis* that Spain's monarchs had promised to whoever should initially sight land. Instead, the Admiral himself claimed the prize, which he used to support his mistress. The indignant Triana met a tragic end, either by suicide or in battle as a Muslim convert. Columbus too was haunted by the incident, for in 1891, when he was being considered for Roman Catholic beatification, his detractors termed the conduct unbecoming of a saint.

Over the centuries, nine different islands have been put forth as the original landfall. The Bahamian government in 1926 declared that Watling Island henceforth should be known as San Salvador. Samuel Eliot Morison's classic biography, *Admiral of the Ocean Sea* (1942), seemed to settle the controversy, defending Watling as the site of Columbus's San Salvador. In 1980, the Society for the History of Discoveries decided to reconsider the question. After five years of research, a National Geographic Society team of historians, navigators, archivists, artists, computer experts, cartographers, linguists, and seamen concluded, as had two nineteenth-century sleuths, that uninhabited Samana Cay, 65 miles to the southwest of Watling, best withstood modern scientific scrutiny.

On that morning of October 12, in a colorful ceremony witnessed by royal officials, Columbus solemnly claimed San Salvador for King Ferdinand* and Queen Isabella* of Spain. African trade goods such as caps, bells, and beads were exchanged for parrots, cotton, and wooden lances. Believing that he was in the Indies, in an archipelago near Japan, the Admiral referred to the native Lucayans as "Indians." He praised these peaceful Arawaks* of the Taíno* culture for their beauty and "guileless" nature, marveling at their dugout canoes capable of holding 40 to 45 men. The Genoese-born mariner also lauded the scenic splendor that surrounded him.

The two and one-half days that "the Discoverer" spent on San Salvador proved to be pleasant, if somewhat disappointing. Columbus was eager to find the source of the small golden ornaments that some of the Lucayans sported in their noses. The Admiral expressed a desire to Christianize the natives, but he added that they could easily be enslaved by a small Iberian force. He learned from the Lucayans that warlike overseas Amerindians conducted periodic raids on the island chain. Some San Salvadorans treated the Spaniards as heavenly beings. By the afternoon of Sunday, October 14, the great explorer had begun weaving a path toward Cuba*. On San Salvador, the Spaniards had discovered a "New World."

REFERENCES: Samuel Eliot Morison, *Admiral of the Ocean Sea: A Life of Christopher Columbus*, 2 vols., 1942; Joseph Judge, "Our Search for the True Columbus Landfall," *National Geographic*, 1986.

Frank Marotti

SAN TOMÁS, UNIVERSITY OF. The University of San Tomás was established by Dominican* friars in 1611. Located in Manila*, the Philippines*, it was the preeminent university in the islands during the colonial period.

REFERENCE: Ester G. Maring and Joel M. Maring, *Historical and Cultural Dictionary of the Philippines*, 1973.

SANTA CRUZ DE MAR PEQUEÑA. In 1476, the Castilian knight Diego García de Herrera built a fort on the Sahara coast near Puerto Cansado, which he called Santa Cruz de Mar Pequeña. King Henry IV of Castile* had given him a private concession on the coast opposite his holdings in the Canary Islands*. Spanish interest in the Saharan coast was stimulated by a desire for increased trading opportunities there as well as a need for slaves to work the plantations of the Canary Islands. The indigenous people of the islands were rapidly dying out as a result of Spanish diseases. When Herrera died in 1485, the fort was abandoned, but after the Treaty of Tordesillas* of 1494, which recognized the Spanish claim to the African coast from Cape Boujdour to Massat, Ferdinand* and Isabella* saw to it that Santa Cruz de Mar Pequeña was rebuilt. The fort enjoyed a brisk trade until the 1520s, by which time Spanish interest had shifted to the New World. In 1524, after a bloody attack on the fort by local tribesmen, Spain abandoned it.

REFERENCE: Antonio Rumeu de Armas, *España en el África Átlantica*, 1956.

SANTA CRUZ Y CALAHUMANA, ANDRÉS DE. Andrés de Santa Cruz was born in La Paz*, Bolivia*, on December 5, 1792, to a family that claimed both Spanish and Incan noble ancestry. As a young student, he joined the Spanish army fighting against Argentine and Bolivian rebels, but in 1821, he was converted to the independence movement and within two years, he was serving as chief of staff to José de San Martín* in the liberation army. Santa Cruz fought

in the battles of Junín* and Ayacucho*. In 1826, he became president of Peru*
and in 1829, he became president of Bolivia*. Santa Cruz was an advocate of
Peruvian-Bolivian confederation. Between 1836 and 1839, he served as protector
of the Peruvian-Bolivia Confederation. When Chile* and Argentina* joined forces
against the confederation in 1839, Santa Cruz lost his office and went into exile
in Ecuador*. He spent two years in a Chilean prison between 1843 and 1845.
Upon his release, he moved to Europe where he spent the rest of his life. Between
1845 and 1855, he served as the Bolivian minister to France. Andrés de Santa
Cruz died in France on September 25, 1865.

REFERENCE: A. Crespo Rodas, *Santa Cruz: El condor indio*, 1944.

SANTA CRUZ Y ESPEJO, FRANCISCO EUGENIO. Santa Cruz was a
mestizo* born in Ecuador* in 1747. He struggled with poverty and lack of
advantages but nevertheless earned a degree in medicine. He was known as Dr.
Espejo in Quito*. Santa Cruz was a true product and participant in the Enlightenment*. He studied many languages, theology, philosophy and sciences. He
was an essayist and journalist. He founded Ecuador's first newspaper*: the short-
lived (three months) *Primicia de la Cultura en Quito* (1792). As Santa Cruz's
career developed, he quickly became one of Spain's most ardent critics. In fact,
he relentlessly attacked colonial rule and rulers. This brought him into disfavor
among authorities, all of which further encouraged him in his revolutionary
activities.

Among Santa Cruz's literary works is *El Nuevo Luciano o despertador de
ingenios* (1797), a renaissance-style collection of nine dialogues discussing a
wide range of issues and disciplines. He later published *La Ciencia blancardina*
and *Marco Porcio Catón*, both extensions of his previous work. As a writer,
Santa Cruz was satirical, critical and, from the Spanish point of view, subversive.
Unquestionably his writings served to incite and encourage Ecuador to independence. He died in 1795.

REFERENCE: Federico González Suárez, *Historia general de la República del Ecuador*, 7 vols., 1890–1903.

Sam L. Slick

SANTA FE. Governor Don Pedro de Peralta* of New Mexico* founded the
provincial capital of La Villa de Santa Fe in 1610. Peralta chose the name Santa
Fe, meaning Holy Faith, probably from the city in southern Spain with the same
name. Santa Fe is one of the oldest permanently occupied cities in the United
States. By the 1630s, the population of Santa Fe was about 250 Spaniards, and
in the 1670s, the Spanish population in the upper Río Grande Valley was around
2,800—many of whom lived in and around Santa Fe and engaged in farming
and raising livestock. The remote location of Santa Fe made it dependent on
trade caravans from New Spain* that came by way of El Camino Real (the king's
highway) every three years.

Because of the Pueblo Revolt of 1680, there is a lack of documentation on pre-1680 New Mexico history. The Pueblo Indians successfully forced the Spanish out of New Mexico and destroyed records. The reconquest of New Mexico by General Diego de Vargas in the 1690s reestablished Spanish rule and pacified the Pueblo Indians. Extant documents of the seventeenth century reveal a major power struggle existing between the Franciscan* clergy and civil officials, particularly the governors, in Santa Fe. Each side accused the other of flagrant acts.

Santa Fe continued to attract colonists in the eighteenth and nineteenth centuries. Foreign intruders from France and the United States, however, were serious threats to the Spanish mercantile system. For example, in 1807, Lieutenant Zebulon M. Pike was arrested and taken to Santa Fe and later to Chihuahua. After his release, Pike published his reports in 1811, attracting more interest to the region. Additional problems facing Santa Fe during this period concerned Navajo, Apache*, Comanche, and other Indians* attacking Spanish settlers and Pueblo Indians. Although Indian raids continued to be a major problem, independence from Spain in 1821 opened Santa Fe to legal foreign trade with the United States by way of the Santa Fe Trail, which had an economic impact on both regions.

REFERENCES: John Francis Bannon, *The Spanish Borderlands Frontier, 1513-1821*, 1970; David G. Noble, ed., *Santa Fe: History of an Ancient City*, 1989; Ralph E. Twitchell, *Old Santa Fe*, 1963.

Raymond Wilson

SANTA FE DE BOGOTÁ. See BOGOTÁ.

SANTA FE DE BOGOTÁ, *AUDIENCIA* **OF.** See NEW GRANADA, *AUDIENCIA* OF.

SANTA HERMANDAD. See ACORDADA.

SANTA MARTA-RÍO HACHA. Spanish conquistadors* founded the settlement of Santa Marta in what is today northern Colombia* in 1525, with Rodrigo de Bastidas* as the first governor. Santa Marta then became the base of operations for the conquest expeditions into New Granada*, and was an important export point for Peruvian bullion headed for Spain. The province was under the jurisdiction of the *audiencia* of Santo Domingo* (1525–1719, 1723–1740) and the viceroyalty of New Granada* (1719–1723, 1740–1810). After 1600, the colony was referred to as Santa Marta-Río Hacha. When the wars for independence accelerated, Santa Marta-Río Hacha long remained under Spanish control and was the seat of the viceroyalty of New Granada* after 1810. In 1821, however, when Spanish authority evaporated, Santa Marta-Río Hacha became part of Gran Colombia* and then later of the republic of Colombia*. See COLOMBIA.

SANTANDER, FRANCISCO DE. Francisco de Santander was a Colombian patriot general in the war of independence, vice-president and acting president of Gran Colombia*, and president of New Granada*. He was described by Simón

Bolívar* as "the Man of Laws" and by Colombian historians as the "organizer of victory." He is frequently considered the precursor of Colombian liberalism. Santander was born of the landed gentry in 1792 in Villa del Rosario near Cúcuta on the border of New Granada (now Colombia) with Venezuela*. His younger years spent on the border are said to have influenced his later thinking. He was educated at San Bartolomé in Bogotá* and studied law. In 1810, with the outbreak of the independence movement, he joined the patriot forces and became a successful officer. In 1816, with the Spanish reconquest of New Granada, Santander went to the lightly populated eastern plains. He was a man of courage, but his lack of physical prowess made it difficult for him to gain respect among the rough *llaneros* (plainsmen). He was most successful after joining with Bolívar in 1817. He was promoted to brigadier general in 1818. He proved an effective guerrilla leader in defending the Casanare area of the *llanos* and participated ably in the campaign leading to the Battle of Boyacá*.

According to most writers, Santander was a reasonably competent military officer but was equaled by few as an organizer and administrator of newly liberated territories. The liberator of northern South America, Simón Bolívar, apparently recognized this and made great use of his skills. Following the liberation of Andean New Granada in 1819, Bolívar named Santander vice-president and effectively chief administrator of New Granada. With the creation of Gran Colombia later that year, Santander continued as vice-president of Cundinamarca (the new name for the New Granada portion of the union of Venezuela, Ecuador*, and New Granada). In 1821, Santander was elected vice-president for all Gran Colombia. With President Bolívar generally absent from Bogotá because of military campaigns, Santander served as acting president until 1827, with the exception of a brief period in 1826. (Both Bolívar and Santander were reelected in 1826.)

Santander and Bolívar complemented each other. They represented the two dominant parts of the union—New Granada and Venezuela. Bolívar was a moderate conservative, while Santander was a rather pragmatic liberal, wanting federalism and a wide range of social, economic, and religious changes and willing to experiment to achieve them. Bolívar was talented at organizing on a large scale but cared little for detail. While the simultaneous establishment of a new nation and the implementation of the liberal reforms of the 1821 Congress of Cúcuta* were exceedingly difficult tasks, Santander is generally viewed as having been relatively successful. It was his success in establishing an effective government and in organizing the resources of the nation that allowed Bolívar to continue the military role of liberator. Finally, while Bolívar had little concern for legal formalities, Santander emphasized the rule of law. He would, for example, publish attacks on his opponents in the press, but he did not jail them. It is with respect to his personality that Santander is most criticized. He has often been described as stern, inflexible, ill-tempered, self-righteous, cruel, and hard to love. Nevertheless, he developed a large following.

Over time, regional conflicts intensified, and the differences between the two leaders deepened. The rift reached its nadir when Santander was suspected in the attempted assassination of Bolívar in 1828. The evidence was inconclusive, but Santander was sentenced to death and later allowed to go into exile. He then traveled through Europe and the United States. In 1832, following the dissolution of Gran Colombia, the Bogotá Convention elected Santander president of the new nation of New Granada. Returning from New York, he assumed his duties on October 7. He was subsequently chosen in a popular election and inaugurated on April 1, 1833, serving until 1837. The disorder involved in the destruction of Gran Colombia meant that, to a significant degree, Santander had to begin afresh in organizing the nation's finances, education, and legal system. A strong federalist, he operated under the centralist constitution of 1832. He maintained order rather successfully, improved administration, roughly balanced the budget, and limited the military. He was not able, however, to implement the degree of liberal reforms he wanted. He was more cautious than in his earlier administration but remained intolerant of those associated with Bolívar's dictatorship. Upon leaving the presidency, he led the opposition in the Chamber of Representatives. He died on May 6, 1840, in Bogotá.

REFERENCES: David Bushnell, *The Santander Regime in Gran Colombia*, 1954; David Bushnell and Neill Macaulay, *The Emergence of Latin America in the Nineteenth Century*, 1988; Jesús María Henao and Gerardo Arrubla, *History of Colombia*, 1938; Gerhard Masur, *Simón Bolívar*, 1969.

Robert E. Biles

SANTA ROSA DE LIMA. Santa Rosa de Lima is the patron saint of Peru[*]. Born in Lima[*] in 1586, she was baptized as Isabella de Flores. A profoundly religious child, she made an early decision to join the Dominican[*] order as a nun and then spent the rest of her life cloistered in her own home, working in a garden, praying, and fasting. She was reported to the Inquisition[*] for over-zealous behavior in punishing her own body through fasting, but when the Inquisition exonerated her by proclaiming the saintliness of her behavior, she became widely known throughout Lima. When she died in 1617, her funeral was an extraordinary public observance that assumed near riotous proportions. She was beatified in 1671.

REFERENCE: Marvin Alisky, *Historical Dictionary of Peru*, 1979.

SANTIAGO, MIGUEL DE. Miguel de Santiago was born in Quito[*], Ecuador[*], in 1625. The greatest Ecuadorian painter of the seventeenth century, Santiago is best remembered for the paintings now displayed in the Convent of San Agustín in Quito. He taught art, and his greatest student was Nicolás Javier de Goribar[*]. Santiago died on January 4, 1706, in Quito.

REFERENCE: Albert William Bork and Georg Maier, *Historical Dictionary of Ecuador*, 1973.

SANTIAGO DE CHILE. Santiago is Chile's[*] capital, its largest city, and the center of its economic, cultural, and political life. It is located in central Chile on the Mapocho River at the northern end of the fertile Central Valley. Situated at an altitude of 1,600 to 2,600 feet above sea level, it is flanked on the east by the Cordillera de los Andes, some of whose peaks rise to 20,000 feet and offer an impressive backdrop to the city. To the west at a slightly greater distance are the lower mountain ranges of the Cordillera Marítima. Like many other Latin American capital cities, Santiago has experienced significant urban growth. The city proper had an estimated population (1990) of 3,534,000; the estimated 4,215,000 persons (1990) who live in the metropolitan area constitute over 30 percent of the nation's total population.

The city was founded as Santiago del Nuevo Extremadura (Santiago of the New Frontier) on February 12, 1541, by the Spanish conquistador[*] Pedro de Valdivia[*]. Originally, it was on an island in the middle of the Mapocho River at the foot of a rocky hill that was called Huelen (Sorrow) by the neighboring Picunche Indians and renamed Santa Lucía by Valdivia. The small town was scarcely six months old when Araucanian[*] Indians, nursing bitter memories of cruel treatment by Spaniards in their first Spanish foray into Argentina[*] and Chile in 1535–1537, attacked the city during Valdivia's absence. Although the settlement was nearly destroyed, legend has it that Valdivia and his mistress, Inés de Suárez, gathered their forces on Santa Lucía hill and laid plans to rebuild the city while still surrounded and outnumbered by the Araucanians. After a two-year battle in which some of the adobe houses were rebuilt, help finally arrived from Peru[*] in late 1543.

Almost from the first, Santiago became the effective capital of Chile. In 1561, it became the seat of a bishopric and, from 1609 on, it was the seat of a royal *audiencia*[*]. In 1617, the first of many earthquakes devastated the city. As a consequence of these earthquakes, Santiago has few surviving examples of colonial architecture other than parts of the Palace of the Governors, the Metropolitan Cathedral started in 1558, the Moneda Palace, completed in 1805, which is the present seat of the government, and several churches. The checkerboard outline of the city drawn up by Valdivia was maintained until the early 1800s when the city grew to the north, to the south, and especially to the west. The southern branch of the Mapocho was drained and converted into a public promenade, now known as the Alameda Bernardo O'Higgins[*]. The city was only slightly damaged during the war of independence (1810–1820) since most of the decisive battles took place outside the city limits at Chacabuco[*], Cancha Rayada[*], and Maipú[*]. At the time of the war for independence, Santiago's population was approximately 40,000 people.

REFERENCES: Edna Ferguson, *Chile*, 1943; Helen Delpar, *Encyclopedia of Latin America*, 1974; Hubert Herring, *A History of Latin America from the Beginnings to the Present*, 1962; Nevin O'Winter, *Chile and her People of Today*, 1912.

Neale J. Pearson

SANTIAGO DE CUBA, DIOCESE OF. The Roman Catholic diocese of Santiago de Cuba was established in 1522 after Juan de Witte was appointed bishop of Cuba* in 1518. It was raised to an archbishopric in 1803.
REFERENCE: *New Catholic Encyclopedia*, XII:1073, 1967.

SANTIAGO DE GUATEMALA. Santiago de Guatemala was the name given to the third colonial capital of Guatemala*, now known as Antigua Guatemala. Santiago de Guatemala was moved to this site in the Panchoy Valley in 1542, after a massive earthquake and flood destroyed an earlier capital at Ciudad Vieja on September 10, 1541. The construction of the new capital was overseen by Francisco de la Cueva, who was named governor of Guatemala on the death of his sister Beatriz,* the widow of Pedro de Alvarado*. Santiago de Guatemala became a center of Habsburg prosperity. The architecture of the city, reflected in magnificent houses of aristocrats who made their fortunes largely from the cultivation of indigo* and cochineal* and in the capital's many elaborate ecclesiastical institutions (churches, monasteries, and convents), was a model that smaller Spanish towns in Central America sought to emulate.

Santiago was an ecclesiastical, economic, and intellectual center for the region. The first bishop of Guatemala, Francisco Marroquín* (1535–1563), resided in Santiago and was active in its development; in 1742, the archdiocese of Guatemala was established there, with jurisdiction over the entire kingdom. In 1660, José de Piñeda Ibarra established the first printing* press in Central America, and in 1681, Central America's first university, the University of San Carlos*, opened there. Central America's first newspaper*, the *Gazeta de Guatemala*, was first published in Santiago from 1729 to 1731; the royal mint first minted coins for the kingdom of Guatemala in 1733. In 1773, a massive earthquake ravaged Santiago de Guatemala, forcing the Spaniards to move the capital, known as the Nueva Guatemala, to its present site in the valley of la Hermita.

Virginia Garrard Burnett

SANTIAGO Y LEÓN GARABITO, JUAN DE. Juan de Santiago y León Garabito was born in Palma, Andalucía, Spain, on July 13, 1641, to a prominent Spanish family. Garabito received a doctorate in theology from the University of Salamanca and eventually became the preacher to King Charles II*. He was appointed bishop of Puerto Rico* in 1676, and one year later he was named bishop of Guadalajara*. He had a distinguished tenure as bishop, and he insisted that all priests working among the Indians in the diocese learn the indigenous language. Garabito died on July 11, 1694.
REFERENCE: *New Catholic Encyclopedia*, VI:282, 1967.

SANTILLÁN, FERNANDO DE. A native of Spain and a prominent Roman Catholic priest, Fernando de Santillán arrived in the New World in 1548 to accept a post as magistrate of Lima*, Peru*. In 1564, King Phillip II* named him the first president of the *audiencia* of Quito*. He was appointed bishop of Charcas* in 1572 but died in 1575 before his ordination. Santillán is best remembered for establishing the Royal Hospital in Quito* and for writing the *Historia de los Incas y relaciones de mi gobierno* in 1563.

REFERENCE: Federico González Suárez, *Historia general de la República del Ecuador*, 7 vols., 1890–1903.

SANTO DOMINGO. Santo Domingo is a predominantly mulatto nation that exercises sovereignty over eastern Hispaniola*, an island about 600 miles southeast of Florida.* Prior to Christopher Columbus's* sighting of the republic's northwestern coast on January 4, 1493, Alonzo Pinzón, the captain to the *Pinta*, had disembarked upon its shores. The Arawak* name for the land was Quisqueya. On his second voyage in 1494, Columbus founded the town of Isabela near Pinzón's initial landfall. Two years later, Columbus moved his headquarters to the town of Santo Domingo, a settlement located at a superior site on Quisqueya's southern coast. The socioeconomic, political, and religious patterns that emerged on the island strongly influenced Spain's subsequent colonization efforts.

Columbus proved to be a a poor administrator, stirring the resentment of natives and Europeans alike. After defeating the Arawaks on March 27, 1495, in a full-scale battle, the Discoverer began to extract tribute from them. Later, he was forced to grant Amerindian workers to individual Spaniards in order to regain the loyalty of a prominent rebel, Francisco Roldán. The cultural disruption resulting from this labor requirement, coupled with disease and warfare, precipitated a catastrophic decline in Hispaniola's Arawak community. By 1514, 90 percent of the island's 4,000,000 aborigines had perished. When reports of this chaos reached the Crown, an inspector, Francisco de Bobadilla*, was sent to America. Bobadilla promptly clapped Columbus and his brothers in irons and shipped them to Castile*.

Under Governor Nicolás de Ovando* (1502–1509), Hispaniola thrived. Over 10,000 colonists flocked to the island, building towns, farms, plantations, and ranches, which fueled the conquests of Puerto Rico*, Jamaica*, Cuba*, Panama*, New Spain*, and Peru*. Ovando imported black slaves* in 1503 to replace the rapidly disappearing Arawaks. Columbus's son Diego* nominally ruled from 1509 to 1526. Although he constructed a fine palace in Santo Domingo and initiated the erection of the hemisphere's first cathedral (where his father's remains lie), the distinguished scion saw his power curbed by the institution of a royal tribunal, the *audiencia**, in 1511.

Gold production quickly fell, and more attractive mainland enterprises drew off Quisqueya's settlers so that by 1540 the colony's fortunes had waned. In the next two decades, a large number of inhabitants departed. Shifting trade routes caused Havana* to replace Santo Domingo as Spain's premier West Indian port. Francis Drake* sacked the Quisqueyan capital in 1586. The cultivation of sugar*, a crop first planted by Columbus, suffered from enemy depredations. Smuggling* and foreign incursions occasioned the evacuation of western Hispaniola, thus creating a vacuum filled during the early 1600s by French adventurers from Tortuga*. After a seesaw struggle to expel the interlopers, the Spanish recognized France's ownership of Hispaniola's western third by the Treaty of Ryswick (1697).

While French Saint-Domingue developed into a valuable agricultural enterprise in which slaves outnumbered the free eight to one, Spain's colony languished. A relatively mild servitude prevailed, and ranching dominated the economy, with bondsmen in the minority. A sizable free mulatto segment also existed. Subsequent to a minor economic expansion due to the Bourbon Reforms of 1778, Spanish Hispaniola became embroiled in a black uprising that shook Saint Domingue* in 1791. The Spaniards invaded but were driven back in 1794, when Pierre Dominique Toussaint L'Ouverture, a brilliant black commander, decided to support France's recently arrived revolutionary troops. Spain ceded its Hispaniolan holdings to the French in the Treaty of Basle (1795). Toussaint unified the island in January 1801, after eliminating his rivals by military skill and diplomacy. An expeditionary force dispatched by Napoleon* captured eastern Hispaniola but was forced to abandon the west. On January 1, 1804, Haiti proclaimed its independence.

The French held the former Spanish colony until local residents rebelled in 1809. Spain returned, misruling the territory for 12 years. The restive Quisqueyans expelled the Spaniards in 1821 and sought admission to Simón Bolívar's republic of Gran Colombia*. Jean-Pierre Boyer, Haiti's leader, then moved to reunify Hispaniola. His troops occupied the eastern portion from 1822 to 1844, a period that Dominicans now regard as a time of barbaric repression. In the latter year, patriots led by Juan Pablo Duarte, Francisco del Rosario Sánchez, and Ramón Mella overthrew the Haitians and announced the birth of the Dominican Republic. Fear of another Haitian takeover motivated the new nation's strong men to submit to Spanish rule voluntarily between 1861 and 1865. Following Spain's ouster, the United States, after narrowly rejecting an annexation treaty in 1866, occupied the Dominican Republic in 1916–1924 and again in 1965–1966.

REFERENCES: Ian Bell, *The Dominican Republic*, 1981; Troy S. Floyd, *The Columbus Dynasty in the Caribbean, 1492-1526*, 1973.

Frank Marotti

SANTO DOMINGO, *AUDIENCIA* OF. The *audiencia* of Santo Domingo*, first known as the Audiencia Real de la Española, was founded in 1511 on the island of Hispaniola*. It was the first Spanish *audiencia** in the New World empire and as such was the chief judicial body for Hispaniola, Cuba*, Puerto Rico*, Florida*, Mérida-La Grita-Maracaibo*, Margarita*, New Andalucía*, Santa Marta-Río Hacha*, Guayana*, and Venezuela*. Over the centuries, the regional authority of the *audiencia* of Santo Domingo was gradually circumscribed. New *audiencias* were established in Mexico City* (1528), Panama* (1538), Lima* (1542), Los Confines* (1542), New Galicia* (1548), and Bogotá*

(1549), gradually confining the *audiencia* of Santo Domingo's authority to the Greater Antilles. The *audiencia* was ultimately moved to Cuba and became known as the *audiencia* of Puerto Príncipe.

REFERENCE: Kenneth R. Farr, *Historical Dictionary of Puerto Rico and the U.S. Virgin Islands*, 1973.

SANTO DOMINGO, DIOCESE OF. The Roman Catholic diocese of Santo Domingo* was established in 1511, the first diocese in the New World. It was raised to an archbishopric in 1953.

REFERENCE: *New Catholic Encylcopedia*, XII:1077, 1967.

SANTO DOMINGO, UNIVERSITY OF. The University of Santo Domingo was established in 1538 by Dominican* missionary priests. It was closely connected with the University of Alcalá de Henares and the University of Salamanca. It was named the Royal and Pontifical University of St. Thomas Aquinas, becoming a leading center of learning in the New World during the sixteenth, seventeenth, and eighteenth centuries.

REFERENCE: *New Catholic Encyclopedia*, XII:1077, 1967.

SARMIENTO DE GAMBOA, PEDRO. Pedro Sarmiento de Gamboa was born around 1530 in Alcalá de Henares, Spain. A skilled mapmaker and writer, Sarmiento sought his fortune abroad. In 1567–1568, he was a member of the expedition that discovered the Solomon Islands, and from 1579 to his death in the early 1590s, Sarmiento worked at occupying and fortifying the Strait of Magellan in order to cut off English attacks on Spanish shipping in the Pacific. Sarmiento spent time in English and French Huguenot prisons in the 1580s. He is best remembered for his book *Historia Índica*, written in 1572 while Sarmiento was accompanying Francisco de Toledo*, viceroy of Peru, on a tour of the viceroyalty. The book was an unsympathetic history of the Inca* nation before the Spanish conquest, written to legitimize Spain's claim as the proper ruler of Peru*. He died in Peru in 1591.

REFERENCES: John A. Crow, *The Epic of Latin America*, 1946; Helen Delpar, *Encyclopedia of Latin America*, 1974.

SERNA, JOSÉ DE LA. See LA SERNA, JOSÉ DE.

SERRA, JUNÍPERO. Junípero Serra was born in Petra, Majorca, Spain, on November 11, 1713, to a family of farmers. He joined the Franciscan* order in 1730 and was ordained in 1738. He earned a doctorate in theology from Lullian University. Father Serra labored as a missionary priest in New Spain* from 1750 to 1767. When the Jesuits* were expelled from the New World in 1767 and Franciscans given control over the abandoned missions*, Serra received the settlements in Lower California* as his responsibility. He moved to Upper California in 1769 with Spanish military expeditions. That year he founded his first mission there—at San Diego. By 1782, Serra had founded eight other missions, the last one in 1782 at San Buenaventura. Father Junípero Serra died in Carmel, California, on August 28, 1784.

REFERENCE: M. J. Geiger, *The Life and Times of Junípero Serra*, 1959.

Virginia Garrard Burnett

SERRANO, JOSÉ MARIANO. José Mariano Serrano was born in Chuquisaca (now Sucre*), Bolivia*, in 1788. He graduated from the University of Chuquisaca in 1811 with a law degree and moved to Tucumán*, where he joined the independence movement. At the Congress of Tucumán* in 1816, Serrano represented Charcas* and signed the Argentine declaration of independence. He served as vice-president of the congress until his resignation in 1819. Serrano then returned to Upper Peru* and in 1825 represented Charcas in the patriot assembly. Serrano is credited with drafting the Bolivian declaration of independence. Later he served as president of the supreme court of Bolivia. José Serrano died in 1852.

REFERENCE: Charles W. Arnade, *The Emergence of the Republic of Bolivia*, 1957.

SERVANDO, FRAY. See MIER NORIEGA Y GUERRA, FRAY SERVANDO TERESA DE.

SEVEN YEARS WAR. See PARIS, TREATY OF (1763).

SEVILLE. Seville is the central city of the region of Andalucía in Spain. It sits amidst a large plain on the Guadalquivir River. The city first emerged as an urban settlement in the Roman Empire two centuries before Christ; by 1500, it had a population of approximately 45,000 people. The discovery of the New World in the 1490s quickly transformed Seville into the most prosperous and dynamic city in Spain. The Spanish Crown gave Seville a monopoly on all commercial trade with the New World, designated Seville as home port for the Indies fleet, and stationed the *Casa de la Contratación* there. The archdiocese of Seville was designated as the patriarchal see for the early New World dioceses. By the end of the sixteenth century, the population of Seville exceeded 100,000 people.

REFERENCE: J. Hazañas y la Rúa, *Historia de Sevilla*, 1933.

SIGÜENZA Y GÓNGORA, CARLOS DE. Born in 1645, Carlos Sigüenza y Góngora was the second child and first male in a family of nine children, whose father, Carlos de Sigüenza y Benito, had arrived in New Spain* in 1640 and two years later married Dionisia Suárez de Figueroa y Góngora, who was related to the Peninsular poet Luis de Góngora. The fact that he added the maternal name Góngora to his own meant that he took the Cordoban poet as his model. At the age of 15, he entered the Jesuit* order, taking the first vows six years later. The discipline of the order, however, was not exactly in line with his temperament; as a result of repeated breaches of the rules while pursuing his studies at the College of the Holy Spirit in Puebla*, he was forced to leave the order in 1668. Apparently this dismissal caused him great remorse, guilt, and melancholy. His repeated attempts to gain forgiveness and readmission into the order failed. He was also not a model student at the university. Since he was no longer a member of a religious order, his financial situation became precarious, especially since he had to take care of his numerous brothers and sisters. Still, he managed to survive—quite well in fact—with a number of positions: chief cosmographer of the realm, chaplain of the Hospital del Amor de Dios, general examiner of gunners, university accountant, corrector of the Inquisition*, and a variety of other posts.

Lacking an academic degree, in 1672 he was appointed professor of mathematics and astrology at the University of Mexico, although against powerful opposition. The new chair propelled him into fame. He became the most representative figure of the seventeenth century in New Spain. A baroque scholar, he was the first scientist in New Spain, the symbol of the scientific revolution in the New World who actually prepared New Spain for the new spirit of modernity. He showed an extraordinary intellectual curiosity and independence of mind that "set him apart from the tradition-bound society of theocratic despotism surrounding him." Interested in mathematics, astrology, astronomy, mechanics, and history, he had a reputation for great erudition and was above his intellectual environment and far ahead of his time. He also delved into the great Indian* past of his country and became the foremost authority of pre-Columbian Indian history, as manifested in his lyric *Glorias de Querétaro*, published in 1680. At a time when he resided as a chaplain at the Hospital del Amor de Dios, he became an intimate friend of that other great star of seventeenth-century New Spain: Sister Juana Inés de la Cruz*, who lived only a few blocks away in a Heronymite convent. Long discussions over scientific, literary, and cultural subjects united these two restless and passionate spirits.

In spite of his interest in rationalism and the natural sciences, Sigüenza y Góngora loyally served Church and Crown and remained close to religious orthodoxy, as manifested in his *Primavera indiana* (1668), "a fervent hymn to the Virgin of Guadalupe*," and in his *Oriental planeta evangélico*, a posthumous panegyric to St. Francis Xavier in epic poetry. His other works include the *Manifiesto philosóphico contra los cometas despojados del imperio sobre los tímidos* (1681), *El Belerofonte matemático contra la quimera astrológica*, and the *Libra astronómica y philosóphica* (1681), written against the astronomical viewpoints of the Jesuit Eusebio Francisco Kino*, "the great mission-founder of the American Southwest." Finally, his *Relaciones históricas* include the *Infortunios de Alonso Ramírez*, the *Relación de lo sucedido a la armada de Barlovento*, and the *Trofeo de la justicia española*.

Sigüenza y Góngora was thus very close to the later mind of Benito Jerónimo Feijóo in his attempt to promote modern science and at the same time remain a devout and pious follower of traditional Catholicism. In this, of course, he reflected the typical Spanish genius. He understood, as did Feijóo, the great eighteenth-century Benedictine in the Peninsula, that progress could be achieved without a concomitant loss of the Christian concept of man and of culture. Irving A. Leonard, commenting on the two great geniuses of New Spain at that time, has stated: "If Sister Juana Inés' secret sorrow was the impossibility of escaping into a world of wider horizons, Sigüenza's private grief was the impossibility of returning to the strict rule of a religious community." He died in 1700.

REFERENCE: Irving A. Leonard, *Baroque Times in Old Mexico*, 1971; Guillermo Díaz-Plaja y Francisco Monterde, *Historia de la Literatura Española e Historia de la Literatura Mexicana*, 1955.

O. Carlos Stoetzer

SILANG, DIEGO. Diego Silang was a Philippine[*] Ilocano revolutionary whose military successes startled the Spaniards and drove them from the Ilocos[*] coast of Luzon[*] for six months, from December 1762 to May 1763. Silang's revolt was the most successful of the local insurrections that swept Luzon when the British occupied Manila[*] in October 1762. Diego Silang was well-positioned to lead the rebellion. He was intimately familiar with Spanish culture, having been orphaned and raised by Dominican[*] priests. His background also included having been shipwrecked off the coast of Zambales and held for ransom by Negrito tribesmen. Silang worked as a mail courier who traveled back and forth between Vigan and Manila. He was in the capital in 1762 when the British invaded and immediately returned to Ilocos to urge Spanish authorities there to exempt Ilocanos from the hated tribute payments, for which the Spanish governor imprisoned him.

Silang's followers soon had the upper hand, and the governor had to flee to Manila to save his life. As Silang's authority grew, so did his ambition. First he used force, then he concluded a diplomatic alliance with the British and sent them two boats loaded with treasures his troops had plundered. He pledged his loyalty to King George III. The British, delighted to have a local ally against Spain, reciprocated by naming Silang *alcalde mayor*[*] of Ilocos. Silang's rebellion veered toward religious fanaticism when he appointed Jesus Christ captain general of Ilocos, but he also pillaged friar estates of their cattle and extorted money from individual priests. When Spanish troops attacked, Silang defeated them at the first Battle of Cabuago. Failing to defeat Silang in battle, the Spanish paid Manuel Vicos, a former friend of Silang's, to shoot him in the back. To their chagrin, Silang's heroic wife Gabriela rallied Ilocanos (and even some Tinggian tribesmen) to carry on. Spanish victory at the second Battle of Cabuago did not end the matter, for Gabriela raised a new army to defend Vigan. She was caught and hanged on September 20, 1763. The memory of the brave Diego and Gabriela has assumed mythic proportions in the service of modern Philippine nationalism. She is sometimes referred to as "Ilocandia's Joan of Arc."

REFERENCE: Renato Constantino, *A History of the Philippines*, 1975.

Ross Marlay

SILVER. See MINING.

SIMÓN DOMÍNGUEZ, PEDRO. Pedro Simón Domínguez was born in La Parilla, Cuenca, Spain, in 1581. He joined the Franciscan[*] order as a teenager, and in 1604 he went to New Granada[*] as a missionary. Simón was part of the conquest expedition against the Pijao Indians in 1608. Later he served in a variety of Franciscan posts, including that of provincial. Simón is best remembered for his chronicle of the conquest—*Noticias historiales de las conquistas de Tierrafirme*— published in part in 1627 but not completely until 1892. Simón died in New Granada some time after 1627.

REFERENCE: D. D. Ramos, ''La institución del cronista de Indias combatida por Aguado y Simón,'' *Anuario colombiano de historia social y de la cultura*, 1 (1963), 89–105.

SINALOA AND SONORA. Spanish explorers reached northwestern New Spain[*] as early as 1530, but settlement did not take place for decades. The region of present-day Sonora, Mexico, became an important mining[*] center in New Spain. In 1732, the Spanish Crown separated what are today Sinaloa and Sonora from the province of New Vizcaya[*] and created a new province. The first governor—Manuel Bernal de Huidobro—arrived in 1734. In 1777, Sinaloa and Sonora became part of the Internal Provinces[*], and in 1787, they were established as a new *intendencia*[*]. At the time of independence, they were separated into two individual states of the new republic of Mexico.

SLAVERY. Black people were part of the Spanish Empire from the time of Christopher Columbus's first voyage to the New World, when two black seamen accompanied him. When the Indians[*] proved to be largely unsuitable for slave labor, primarily because of their rapidly declining population, Africans were imported to South America to fill the void. In 1518, King Charles I[*] granted a license for the importation of slaves, making Spain the first country to bring African slaves to the New World. By that time, however, the Portuguese had long been carrying African slaves to European markets. The Spanish grant to import slaves to the New World was known as the *asiento*[*], and during the colonial period, the Portuguese, the Dutch, and finally the English dominated the trade. More than 10 million Africans were forcibly brought to the New World between 1518 and 1886, when all slavery ended in Cuba[*]. Of that total, approximately 15 percent, or 1,500,000 people, ended up in one of the Spanish colonies. Cuba received 700,000 of that total, while the viceroyalty of New Granada[*] had 320,000, the viceroyalty of New Spain[*] 200,000, and the viceroyalty of Peru[*] 100,000. Nearly 80,000 imported African slaves ended up in Puerto Rico[*]. By the early 1800s, people of African descent in Spanish America totaled nearly 800,000 people.

A vast racial mixing also occurred in Spanish America. Because there were usually far more black men than black women on the plantations, black men frequently turned to Indian women for their mates. White men often established sexual liaisons with black slave women on the plantations. Moreover, white men, especially in the early colonial period, frequently established long-term relationships with Indian women. At the end of the colonial period, more than 5 million other Spanish Americans had at least some African ancestry.

The antislavery movement in the Spanish Empire was part of a much larger global phenomenon. Slavery was abolished first in Hispaniola* when blacks rebelled against their masters in the French colony of St. Domingue*. A French diplomat sent there to quell the rebellion proclaimed an end to slavery in 1793. Eight years later, the black Haitian revolutionary Pierre Dominique, Toussaint L'Ouverture, conquered the rest of Hispaniola, or Santo Domingo*, and formally ended slavery there. The revolutionary movements in Latin America set in motion a spirit of liberation. Argentina* abolished slavery in 1813, and Chile* followed suit in 1823. Central America did the same in 1824, as did Mexico in 1829. Slavery was abolished in Colombia* in 1851. Slavery lasted the longest in Cuba because Spaniards were afraid that abolition would destroy the sugar* industry. Slavery was not finally abolished there until 1886.

REFERENCES: Wilbur Zelinsky, "The Historical Geography of the Negro Population of Latin America," *Journal of Negro History*, 34 (1949), 153–221; Philip D. Curtin, *The Atlantic Slave Trade: A Census*, 1969.

SMALLPOX. Of all the diseases that the Europeans brought with them to the New World, smallpox was the most devastating to the native populations. Because it spread from one victim to another by breath, smallpox was one of the world's most communicable diseases. It was especially deadly among children. Smallpox spread into the Americas in 1519 when it appeared in the West Indies, destroying nearly half of the Arawak* population on Hispaniola* and Puerto Rico*. One of Hernán Cortés's* soldiers carried it to Mexico. Smallpox reached Peru even before Francisco Pizarro*, killing thousands of Incas*. Because the disease has an incubation period of 14 days, it is possible for a healthy person to flee a smallpox-ridden area for safety and carry the disease to another region. For the next 300 years, smallpox reduced native populations to sickness and death, paving the way for the triumph of imperial institutions.

REFERENCE: Alfred W. Crosby, Jr., *Ecological Imperialism: The Biological Expansion of Europe, 900- 1900*, 1986.

SMUGGLING. Smuggling was endemic to the Spanish Empire because of the severe restrictions and plentiful monopolies the Crown imposed on colonial trade. *Criollo* merchants and traders, resentful of the restrictions as well as of the arrogance of *peninsular* officials, were only too eager to participate in the illegal traffic. They were supported in this by Dutch, British, French, and Portuguese shippers and merchants anxious to enjoy a share of the lucrative trade opportunities. The Dutch captured Curaçao in 1634, and the island became the base of operations for Dutch trade in the New World. The British conquest of Jamaica* in 1655 likewise provided them a convenient site for exploitation of the illegal trade. France used western Hispaniola*, after its annexation in 1664, as well as Tortuga* for smuggling bases, and the Portuguese regularly brought illegal goods up the Río de la Plata* and then shipped them overland to Upper Peru.

REFERENCES: Woodrow Borah, *Early Trade and Navigation between Mexico and Peru*, 1954; Peter Gerhard, *Pirates on the West Coast of New Spain, 1575-1742*, 1960.

SOCIETY OF AFRICANISTS AND COLONISTS. The Society of Africanists and Colonists was established in 1883 to promote Spanish imperial interests in Africa. It had close ties with such prominent business groups as the Hispanic-African Commercial Company, which had constructed a fort at Dakhla on the coast of Spanish Sahara* in 1884. The society also had powerful connections in the Cortes, the Spanish bureaucracy, and the press. Through its contacts and publications the Society lobbied for Spanish expansion into Africa in the late nineteenth century. The society sponsored the expedition of Emilio Bonelli* to Western Sahara in 1884, and Bonelli began negotiating concessions for the Hispanic-African Commercial Company from local tribal leaders. In 1885, Spain decided to establish a protectorate over the area. The Society of Africanists and Colonists played a key role in the development of Spanish interests in Africa during the late nineteenth century.

REFERENCE: John Mercer, *Spanish Sahara*, 1975.

SOCIETY OF JESUS. See JESUITS.

SOLÍS, JUAN DÍAZ DE. Juan Díaz de Solís was born in Lebrija, Spain, in 1470. He accompanied Vicente Yáñez* Pinzón's expedition to Cuba* in 1508, circumnavigating the island and then moving south along the Caribbean coast of Central America and the northern and eastern coasts of South America. Solís returned to Spain in 1509 and six years later led an expedition that sailed up the Río de la Plata, where Solís was killed in August 1516 by local Indians.

REFERENCE: Samuel Eliot Morison, *The European Discovery of America: The Southern Voyages, A.D. 1492-1616*, 1974.

SOLÍS FOLCH DE CARDONA, JOSÉ. José Solís Folch de Cardona was born to a noble family in Madrid, Spain, on February 16, 1713. He entered the Spanish army as a teenager and eventually achieved the rank of brigadier general in 1747. Solís was appointed viceroy* of New Granada*. Solís's tenure as viceroy was marked by conquest expeditions against the Motilone, Goajiro, Cunacuna, and Andaki Indians, as well as by vigorous attempts to extend Spanish settlement into the upper Orinoco River region. He also encouraged stock raising as an economic activity. Solís was replaced as viceroy in 1761, and he decided to enter the Franciscan* order. He died in New Granada on April 27, 1770.

REFERENCE: D. Samper Ortega, *Don José Solís, virrey del Nuevo Reino de Granada*, 1953.

SOLÓRZANO PEREIRA, JUAN DE. Born in Madrid in 1575 of aristocratic Castilian lineage, young Solórzano went to Salamanca to study law, finishing in 1599. Salamanca at that time was not only a place of truly remarkable scholars, even though the greatest teachers were no longer alive. It was a time of the revival of Roman and canon law (due to the educational reform of 1561 undertaken by Diego de Covarrubias) and of the old Spanish legal tradition. In 1602, Solórzano was appointed substitute teacher for the chair-holder in law. In 1605, he taught the Pandects and in 1608 obtained his doctoral degree. His teaching experience had given him a solid background for his future career in the service of the Spanish Crown.

In 1609, on the recommendation of the then-President of the Council of the Indies*, Pedro de Castro, Count of Lemos, Philip III* appointed him *oidor** of the royal *audiencia* of Lima*. His appointment was made with the particular duty of putting order into the chaotic situation of Spanish legislation overseas, a delicate mission in view of conflicting interests, which he was to accomplish magnificently though not without confrontation. Thus, his activity in the viceroyalty became a great challenge.

His administration centered in Huancavelica* to which the viceroy*, the Prince of Esquilache, had sent him and which turned out to be one of the most successful missions. It was at that time also (1611) that he married Clara Paniagua de Loaysa y Trejo, of a notable Peruvian family. Still, his professional activities did not satisfy him, and, coupled to some disagreeable incidents of which he was the victim, he longed to return to the Peninsula. In 1615, his office had intervened in a smuggling* affair, for which legally he was to receive one-third of the goods seized. However, a royal *cédula* deprived him of this acquisition, and his appeal was denied. He had also taken a stand against the ordinances of Saint Toribio de Mogrovejo concerning tithes and first fruits, and this had annoyed the viceroy. In 1623, Solórzano wrote to the Count-Duke of Olivares for a position in Spain, and a year later, he learned that the office of the attorney-general of the Council of the Indies was thinking of offering him a position there. Then, in 1626 he was ordered to return home, with the Crown requesting him to submit a most secret report to the Council of the Indies with regard to the administration of justice and finances overseas.

In 1627, he left for Spain and rose quickly in the Crown's bureaucracy: *fiscal* (attorney-general) in the Council of Finance and Accounting, then *fiscal* in the Council of the Indies, and finally, after 1629, counselor in that top institution. In 1633, he was also appointed counselor of the High Council of Castile, an appointment that represented more an honor and a balm for his past tribulations in Peru. He was pensioned in 1644, but continued to give advice in legal matters until his death in Madrid in 1655.

His remarkable career in both Spain and Peru in law, politics, and administration gave him an extraordinary insight into the real situation of the Spanish Empire, a duty he performed brilliantly. His literary production was high, and even today many of his writings are still waiting to be unearthed and researched in archives. Besides some minor early contributions, his first great work, the *De Indiarum Iure et Gubernatione*, appeared in 1629. Still Solórzano had to accept a number of changes, since royal censorship* was not too happy about some of the concepts about royal government in the Indies that were aired in the book. Even in 1647, the Council of the Indies was still objecting to some passages that in time were corrected. While waiting for the required royal permission, Solórzano wrote on other related subjects, such as the "Memorial y discurso de las razones que se ofrecen para que el Real y Supremo Consejo de las Indias deba proceder en todos los actos públicos al que llaman de Flandes."

In the same year, 1647, his greatest work appeared: the *Política Indiana* for which he is justly famous. Dedicated to Philip IV*, the work built on his earlier *De Indiarum Iure et Gubernatione* and delved into a variety of subjects related to the Indies: the discovery, acquisition, and retention of the Indies; physical conditions of the New World; the Indians and their government; Indian services to the Spaniards, including the *encomienda**; and ecclesiastical and civil government. The last of his three great works was the *Emlemata Centum Regio Politica* (1653), an eminently classical contribution that projected "a moralist view, an ascetic and transcendental conception of existence, and hence, a profound pedagogic goal."

Solórzano Pereira, one of the greatest of the Spanish jurists of the Indies reflected the Spanish seventeenth century predicament: that is, a need for greater authority in view of the religious disunity in Europe, merged with a commitment still to follow the traditional precepts of the Golden Age. In keeping with the Scholastic traditions of the past, Solórzano believed that absolute kingship was not the best government, but at the time it seemed to be the only solution. As Tulio Halperin Donghi has commented, his traditionalism was based not on a simple repetition of already consolidated positions of the past, but on the fearful distrust of the future.

Integrity, loyalty to king and country, love for justice with a decided defense of law, though "tempered by equity," marked "the most profound Spanish lawyer," as Bartolomé Mitre called him. Ricardo Levene saw in him the great "Defender of the Spanish Americans," and no doubt he always defended the natives and cried out against the abuses of the settlers. At times, he may have been too legalistic and, as a lawyer, too much a defender of the Crown and its prerogatives, but he always stood for freedom and respect of humanity. Finally, he stated in the seventeenth century what Bernardo de Vargas Machuca had already said in the sixteenth: the Indies were not colonies but provinces; as such, they were really parts of Castile* and were united to them in an accessory character.

REFERENCE: F. Javier de Ayala, *Ideas políticas de Juan de Solórzano*, 1946; O. Carlos Stoetzer, *The Scholastic Roots of the Spanish American Revolution*, 1979.

O. Carlos Stoetzer

SOTO, DOMINGO DE. Born in Segovia, Spain, in 1495, and originally baptized Francisco, young Soto first studied in Segovia but then moved to Alcalá where he began his three-year course in the arts in 1512–1513. Thereafter, he traveled to Paris to delve into metaphysics, which he followed with theology in 1517. He fell under the spell of nominalism, but as the latter's pupil, he emerged as one of Vitoria's first converts to Thomism. After two years of theological studies, he returned to Alcalá where in 1520 he was admitted to the Colegio de San Ildefonso. It was here that he held a chair for the arts and passed his first examination in theology. In 1524, however, he resigned, disgusted with the internal problems at the college. He then joined the Benedictines of Montserrat but was thereafter convinced to enter the Dominican* order. This he did in Burgos in 1525, at which time he changed his first name to Domingo. In the same year, he arrived in Salamanca where until 1532 he taught at the Colegio de San Esteban; during 1531–1532 he substituted for Vitoria.

After 1532, Soto began teaching theology at the university while serving as prior of San Esteban several times. While working on his *Commentaries on Aristotle*, which appeared in 1551, he was called to the Council of Trent* where he replaced Vitoria who could not attend. Here he was entrusted with the unpopular task of censoring books for heresy and preparing the conciliar *Index*. He became famous for several positions he took. He stood for the maintenance of Scholastic philosophy and helped to formulate the decree on simultaneity of reform and dogma. After a short visit to Germany, he became the confessor of Emperor Charles V* but soon resigned the position and returned to Salamanca. Here he was chosen in 1552 for the chair of theology. In the next years, he published his major work, *De Iustitia et Iure* which maintained wide popularity in Spain and beyond its borders, as well as in the Indies.

Soto followed in the footsteps of Vitoria in regard to the Indies and the numerous questions that the conquest and colonization had raised. This early interest in the Indies was manifest in his *De Dominio* (1534), in which he, like Vitoria, concluded that the conquest was difficult to justify. Considered to be more neutral in the debates between Bartolomé de Las Casas* and Gines de Sepúlveda, Soto was asked to act as rapporteur to the two famous Juntas of Valladolid (1550–1551), which represent the high point of the great controversy of the sixteenth century regarding the treatment of the Indians* and the legality and morality of the Conquista. It was this Junta that declared further conquests by force as unjust.

In these later years, Soto often acted as mediator in questions that had arisen from the Tridentine Council; he also advised the emperor on many questions. Finally, he defended many worth causes in which justice and freedom were involved. For example, he rose to the defense of Bartolomé Carranza, the Arch-

bishop of Toledo. The latter was condemned despite Soto's efforts, and this may
have hastened his death, which occurred on November 15, 1560, the same year
as Vitoria's.

REFERENCE: Bernice Hamilton, *Political Thought in Sixteenth-Century Spain: A
Study of the Political Ideas of Vitoria, Soto, Suárez, and Molina*, 1963.

O. Carlos Stoetzer

SOTO, HERNANDO DE. Hernando de Soto was born in Jerez de Badajoz, a
town in Extremadura, Spain, around 1500. He left for the New World as a
teenager with Pedro Arias de Ávila's* expedition to Panama* in 1514. Ten years
later he joined Francisco Hernández* de Córdoba's expedition of conquest to
Nicaragua*. In 1531, Hernando de Soto was a leading figure in Francisco Pizarro's* expedition to Peru* and was the first European to meet Atahuallpa*, the
Inca* emperor. Although de Soto had become rich in Peru, he badly wanted a
governorship in the New World. In 1537, the Spanish Crown appointed him
governor of Cuba* and authorized de Soto to conquer the Gulf coast of North
America. The expedition reached present-day Tampa, Florida*, on May 30, 1539.
In search of gold, they explored northern Florida, Georgia, southern Tennessee,
Alabama, and Mississippi. They reached the Mississippi River on May 8, 1541.
They spent the next year exploring northern Arkansas and returned to the Mississippi River. Hernando de Soto died of a fever on May 21, 1542, near Natchez
and was buried in the river.

REFERENCES: Edward Gaylord Bourne, ed., *Narratives of the Career of Hernando
de Soto*, 1904; James Lockhart, *The Men of Cajamarca*, 1972.

SOUBLETTE, CARLOS. Carlos Soublette was born in Venezuela* in 1789
and became an early supporter of the independence movement, becoming an
aide-de-camp to Francisco de Miranda*. Between 1816 and 1822, Soublette was
a loyal supporter of Simón Bolívar*, and in 1821, Bolívar named him vice-
president of Venezuela. When José Antonio Páez* revolted in 1826, Soublette
worked with Bolívar on behalf of Gran Colombia*. By the end of the decade,
however, Soublette had come around to Páez's case and was serving in his
cabinet. Soublette was interim president of Venezuela between 1836 and 1839,
at the request of congress; he won the office outright in 1843, serving as president
until 1847. Because of intense political infighting, Soublette went into exile for
the next decade. He returned in 1858, served briefly in the cabinet of Pedro Gual
in 1861, and died in 1870.

REFERENCE: Donna Keyes Rudolph and G. A. Rudolph, *Historical Dictionary of
Venezuela*, 1971.

SPANISH-AFRICAN COMMERCIAL COMPANY. The Spanish-African
Commercial Company was established in 1883 by the López y López Company,
a huge Spanish commercial enterprise headquartered in Barcelona. Its stated
objective was to increase Spanish-African trade through the establishment of
trading posts and regular steamship service. Well-connected politically and eco-

nomically, the Spanish-African Commercial Company established a trading post at Dakhla on the coast of Spanish Sahara* in 1884. Later in the year, the company helped finance the exploration journey of Emilio Bonelli* as well as his negotiations with local tribal leaders. Although the Spanish government soon established a protectorate over the region, the Spanish-African Commercial Company never realized its hopes for great profits in the region. The company went into liquidation in 1893.

REFERENCE: Tony Hodges, *Historical Dictionary of Western Sahara*, 1982.

SPANISH-AMERICAN WAR. The war between the United States and Spain in 1898 arose out of several developments going back before the beginning of the decade. One was the increasing trade of the United States and subsequent American investment abroad. American businessmen had sunk money into Cuban tobacco* and sugar* production and in various industrial and commercial enterprises. The development that eventually exerted the major influence leading to war was the outbreak of a rebellion in Cuba* against Spanish rule. This uprising began in 1895 and soon took the form of guerilla war that caused widespread destruction of economic and transportation resources, including plantations and other businesses owned by foreigners.

American concern over the situation in Cuba was aroused partly by the destruction of American-owned businesses, but mainly by the public perception of inhumanity exhibited by the Spanish authorities in their conduct of the anti-guerilla operations. Under the Spanish commander, General Valeriano Weyler*, much of the rural population in guerilla-infested areas was relocated to refugee camps where living conditions and poor sanitation facilities caused great suffering and death. The giant American newspaper chains such as Joseph Pulitzer's and William Randolph Hearst's saw the events in Cuba as an opportunity to increase circulation. They did not hesitate to embellish or even to invent stories to attract a wide readership. By early 1898, public pressure upon the administration of President William McKinley to do something to help end the bloodshed led to American efforts to get the Spanish government to agree to a cease-fire and to grant internal self-government to the Cubans. This American interference was widely resented both in Spain and by pro-Spanish people in Cuba. American public opinion became even more anti-Spanish on February 9, 1898, when the New York *Journal* published a private letter in which Enrique Dupuy de Lôme, Spanish minister to the United States, called President William McKinley a "weak . . . common politician."

The impetus to war, already started by American fervor on behalf of the Cubans, became irreversible on the evening of February 15, 1898. That night, American battleship *Maine**, stationed at Havana* to provide a means of evacuating Americans if necessary, was shaken by a huge explosion and sank in the harbor with the loss of 260 of her crew. The United States held Spain responsible, although the cause of the explosion has never been firmly established. The cry "Remember the *Maine*" made it impossible to resist the clamor for war to free the Cubans. After more than two weeks of debate and formal recognition of Cuba's independence, Congress declared war on April 25.

The U.S. Navy was ready for war. On May 1, Commodore George Dewey took the Asiatic squadron past the Corregidor fortifications into Manila* Bay and destroyed the Spanish fleet in the Philippines*, while at about the same time, naval vessels in the Atlantic blockaded Cuban ports. The army meanwhile began a haphazard and inefficient expansion. Americans had no clear strategy except the implied objective of driving the Spaniards out of Cuba. The discovery of the main Spanish fleet in the harbor of Santiago in southeastern Cuba in the latter part of May greatly relieved those who had feared enemy naval bombardment of east coast ports.

The Cuban campaign began on June 22, 1898, when an American army of 17,000 troops under General William R. Shafter landed at Daiquiri, about 15 miles east of Santiago. In the face of strong opposition from a small Spanish force, the ill-organized and poorly equipped American army spent a week driving the Spaniards back to Santiago. Partly because of a lack of coordination and unclear expectations, the Americans got no real help from the Cuban rebels around Santiago, although the guerrillas elsewhere in the island kept the Spanish forces, numbering over 100,000 troops, from concentrating against the Americans.

The culminating stage of the campaign in Cuba came on July 1 when the American army, now assembled before Santiago but increasingly demoralized by supply difficulties and illness, launched assaults against the Spanish fortified positions at El Caney and San Juan Hill. The imagination of Americans was captured by the spectacle of ragged lines of blue-clad American troops under the leadership of Generals Henry W. Lawton, Jacob F. Kent, and Joseph Wheeler, assisted by the irrepressible Colonel Theodore Roosevelt, moving bravely against the heavy fire of the entrenched Spanish defenders. The capture of those positions placed the Spaniards in a difficult position. Unaware of the desperate plight of the American besiegers, running short of ammunition and supplies and with yellow fever beginning to appear among the troops, the Spanish commander in Santiago decided to give up after prolonged negotiations with General Shafter. On July 17, the Spanish garrison of nearly 24,000 men surrendered.

The capture of Santiago was something of an anticlimax. The post had been chosen for attack because of the presence of a Spainsh fleet in the harbor, but by the time Santiago was given up, the fleet was no longer there. On July 3, Admiral Pascual Cervera brought his fleet out in a daring but hopeless attempt to break free of the American naval blockade. In the ensuing running battle westward along the coast, the four Spanish cruisers and their two escorting torpedo boats were all either sunk or driven ashore in flames. The American ships suffered no serious damage and only a few casualties. By the time Santiago was captured, the Spanish government was ready to negotiate a peace treaty. The war had been a disaster for Spain. In addition to the loss of Santiago, the

Spaniards had lost two fleets. Moreover, an American expedition had taken Puerto Rico*, the only other Spanish possession in the New World, while it was obviously only a matter of time before Manila and the Philippines fell. On August 12, 1898, the French ambassador in Washington signed a cease-fire agreement on behalf of the Spanish government, preceding by one day the fall of Manila and the surrender of Spanish forces in the Philippines.

At the peace conference held in Paris from September to December 1898, the Spaniards agreed that Cuba would become independent and that Guam* and Puerto Rico, which had been taken by the Americans, would be annexed by the United States. They opposed American retention of the Philippines, however, because Manila had not been captured until the day after the cease-fire. They accepted $20 million in lieu of the restoration of the Philippines, which the Americans would not permit, and a treaty was signed on December 10. After intense debate about the consequences of establishing an overseas empire, the U.S. Senate approved the treaty on February 6, 1899, shortly after the outbreak of an insurrection by Filipino rebels against the American occupation. The most important result of the war was that it gave the United States an overseas empire, largely in the Pacific. In addition to the Spanish conquests, the annexation of Hawaii was a direct consequence of the war. The acquisition of empire brought the United States directly into the cross currents of international rivalries in the Far East, greatly increased its propensity for interference in the Caribbean, and forced the nation to deal with the many problems of colonial policy.

REFERENCES: Frank Freidel, *The Splendid Little War*, 1958; David F. Frost, *The War with Spain in 1898*, 1981; H. Wayne Morgan, *America's Road to Empire: The War with Spain and Overseas Expansion*, 1965.

Ernest Andrade, Jr.

SPANISH ARMADA. In 1588, Philip II* of Spain sent a fleet of 130 ships, commanded by the Duke of Medina Sidonia and commonly known as the Armada, to facilitate the invasion of England by Spanish troops in the Netherlands. The enterprise was part of an undeclared war between Spain and England that had begun in 1585 and lasted until 1604, overlapping with their involvement in hostilities in the Netherlands and France. Traditionally, the attempted invasion has been regarded as the result of commercial and/or religious rivalry, and the defeat of the Armada has been seen as a decisive victory for well-prepared English naval forces, whose superiority to those of Spain was clearly proven. But the overall picture of the causes, course, and consequences of the Armada campaign is more complex. Neither Philip II nor Elizabeth I of England really wanted a war. While competition for wealth and Catholic-Protestant antagonism were important factors in making the conflict unavoidable, so also were internal pressures in Spain and England and the exceedingly complicated international situation in the 1580s. Moreover, although they had long anticipated a Spanish invasion, the English were caught by surprise by the Armada's arrival at the end of July 1588. Finally, the failure of Philip's scheme was less significant for the subsequent history of the war than other circumstances.

Philip II had a dynastic claim, of a sort, to the English throne because of his marriage to Elizabeth's half-sister, Mary I, from 1554 to 1558. As the leading Catholic ruler in Europe, he was also the focus of the hopes of returning England to the Roman Church. Prior to the 1580s, however, he had shown relatively little interest in plans for a Catholic crusade directed against the British Isles; his orders to the Duke of Alba for an invasion of England at the time of the Ridolfi plot in 1571 were altogether half-hearted, and he gave no support to papal invasions of Ireland in 1579 and 1580. By the beginning of the 1580s, Philip's attitude began to change. In 1580, he inherited the Portuguese throne, but Elizabeth gave sanctuary to the pretender, Dom Antonio, and in 1581–1582, she abetted Antonio's unsuccessful attack on the Azores. She also showed no sign of ceasing her support for the anti-Spanish, Calvinist rebels intent on overthrowing Philip's rule in the Netherlands. After the assassination of their leader, William of Orange, in 1584, she formally took them under her protection. Sir Francis Drake's[*] circumnavigation of the world in 1577–1580 increased Spain's concern about the safety of its empire. These fears were borne out in 1585— after Philip II had seized English ships in Iberian ports—by Drake's raids on Baiona, on Vigo, and on Caribbean shipping and by English attacks on Spain's Newfoundland fishing fleet.

Philip II was also worried by English overtures to Fez-Morocco and the Ottoman Empire in 1584–1585, particularly given the tension caused in Spain by the "New Christians" (converted Moslems, or moriscos). In France, the death of the duke of Anjou in 1584 left the Huguenot Henri (Bourbon) of Navarre as heir to Henri III. Along with Dutch overtures to the latter in 1585, this change raised the specter of an Anglo-French-Dutch alliance against Spain. Finally, Philip's rapprochement with the powerful Catholic Guise family in France made him more amenable to English Catholic schemes to put Mary, Queen of Scots (whose Guise blood had formerly troubled Philip), on England's throne.

As early as 1583, the Marquis of Santa Cruz had suggested an attack on England, which Philip rejected as impractical, but by late 1585, he had changed his mind and was negotiating with Pope Sixtus V for financial aid and the right to name a successor to Mary if she replaced Elizabeth. In March 1586, Santa Cruz proposed sending an invasion force of 55,000 men from Spain, which would require a fleet of over 500 ships, while in June the Duke of Parma suggested transporting 30,000 men across the English Channel from the Netherlands, for which secrecy was essential. Philip began assembling ships and men in various ports and urgently desired the invasion to occur in 1587. Repeated delays prevented this, however, and word of his plans leaked out, giving the English the chance to prepare a defense. Further impetus was given to Philip's enterprise by the execution of Mary, Queen of Scots, in February (for complicity in the Babington Plot of 1586) and by Drake's raid on Cádiz in April, although these were not the causes of the invasion.

The Armada sailed from Lisbon on May 30, but bad weather forced the fleet to put in at La Coruña on June 19 for supplies and repairs; it did not depart again until July 22. By July 18, the English had concluded that the invasion was off, and their fleet sailed from Plymouth to attack Spanish ports, but was driven back by adverse winds. Thus the appearance of the Armada off on July 29 Cornwall on England's southwestern coast surprised the English, but the bulk of their fleet was still at Plymouth under Lord Admiral Charles Howard (Earl of Nottingham) and Drake. It hastily put out to sea, getting the wind advantage on July 31. Superior tactics, greater maneuverability, and the longer range and more rapid fire of their guns gave the English the advantage in skirmishes off Portsmouth, Plymouth, and the Isle of Wight on July 31 and August 2 and 4. But the turning point was Medina Sidonia's halt off Calais on August 6, necessitated by poor communications with Parma; blame for this belongs to Philip. The English sent fire ships among the Spanish on August 7 and thereafter did considerable damage to the Armada before a "Protestant wind" blew the Spanish fleet northward. The English broke off pursuit on August 12, and the Armada had to sail home around Scotland and Ireland, where many men and ships were lost.

The Armada's defeat was not decisive with regard to the war. Drake's expedition against Portugal in 1589 failed, and Philip attempted invasions again in 1596 and 1597, though these were foiled by storms. But the victory of 1588 convinced English Protestants that God was on their side and made loyalists of many English Catholics who could not countenance foreign invasion. It shattered the image of Spanish invincibility and over the long run made peace with the English a compelling alternative in Spanish foreign policy. It also made empire more attractive and attainable for England.

REFERENCES: M. J. Rodriguez-Salgado, et al., *Armada*, 1988; Simon Adams, *The Armada Campaign of 1588*, 1988.

William Robison

SPANISH EQUATORIAL GUINEA. Spanish Equatorial Guinea, now the Republic of Equatorial Guinea, consists of a small enclave on the west coast of equatorial Africa called Río Muni, plus the islands of Bioko (formerly Fernando Po), Annobon, and Corisco, as well as some other very small islands. The island of Bioko was discovered around 1469 by the Portuguese explorer Fernando Po. The Portuguese controlled the commercial activities of the island and the mainland between the Niger and Ogooue rivers (Río Muni) until 1777 when the Portuguese ceded their interests to the Spanish in return for Spanish recognition of the Portuguese claim to the Nova Colônia do Sacramento in Brazil. In 1827, Spain leased the region to the British, who used it as a base to interdict slave traders. Until 1900, the area was explored only along the coast. The French also made formal claims to the bulk of the mainland coast, and the English settled former slaves there throughout the nineteenth century.

With the Treaty of Paris in 1900, the mainland was conceded to Spain and a colonial administration was organized by 1904. The Spanish left the mainland interior unexplored until the 1920s. By 1926–1927, intermittent resistance from the region's dominant ethnic group, the Fang, was defeated. Under colonial rule, the Spanish permitted Fernando Po's indigenous Bubi to assimilate into Spanish commerce and culture. The populations of the mainland, however, were allowed to make little economic progress. After World War II, African nationalist movements began to influence the people of Spanish Guinea. An underground nationalist movement was organized there in 1954. The colonial regime responded quickly. Nationalist leaders Enrique Nvo and Acacio Mane were assassinated, but the movement persisted. In 1958, the colony, formerly governed by an admiral, was named a Spanish province—the Spanish Equatorial Region. Africans were allowed to participate in the political administration. All Africans in the province became citizens of Spain. By 1960, three African representatives were sent to the Spanish Cortes (parliament). Even though the Spanish Equatorial Region was ruled by an appointed governor-general who had military and civilian powers, elections for selected village, municipal, and provincial councils were held. In 1963, limited autonomy was granted, and the province was renamed Equatorial Guinea. A joint legislature and a cabinet of eight African councilors was established, and a president was elected by the legislature. The governor-general was replaced by a high commissioner, who was supposed to leave considerable initiative in formulating laws to the legislature.

Nationalist movements were legally recognized as political parties. The Movimiento de Union Nacional de Guinea Ecuatorial[*] (National Union Movement of Equatorial Guinea or MUNGE) and the Movimiento Nacional de Liberacion de Guinea Ecuatorial National Liberation Movement of Equatorial Guinea (IPGE), all in Río Muni, favored independence of the islands and the mainland as one political entity. The Bubi Union and the Fernandino Democratic Union preferred a separate independence for the island of Fernando Po or a loose federation. MUNGE, headed by Bonifacio Ondo Edu, emerged as the principal party of the provincial government.

Under increasing pressure from the United Nations, the Spanish made plans for Equatorial Guinea's independence by 1968. At the constitutional convention, the five political parties disagreed over the arrangement between the mainland and the islands, as well as over the extent of the future ties with Spain. Francisco Macías[*] Nguema, a Fang, led the protest against the draft constitution, but with its ratification, Macías Nguema ran for president on a constitutional platform favoring a union of the islands and the mainland, as well as close ties to Spain. Once elected, Macías Nguema suspended many of the provisions of the compromise constitution and began a reign of terror, which did not end until he was overthrown in a military coup and executed in 1979. The Republic of Equatorial Guinea was established on October 12, 1968.

REFERENCE: Robin Cohen, ed., *African Islands and Enclaves*, 1983.

Karen Sleezer

SPANISH FOREIGN LEGION. Modeled after the French Foreign Legion, the Spanish Foreign Legion was established in January 1920. The moving force behind formation of the legion was Lieutenant Colonel José Millán Astray.

Second in command was Francisco Franco*, who went on to become the long-time political leader of modern Spain. For years, the volunteer force fought against Moroccan nationalists in Spanish Morocco*. Between 1920 and 1927, they fought 845 engagements and suffered more than 2,000 dead. During the 1930s, the Spanish Foreign Legion fought in the Spanish Civil War, sustaining more than 37,000 casualties. The troops of the Spanish Foreign Legion left Spanish Morocco after Morocco achieved independence in 1956. They fought in Ifni* in 1957–1958. The troops of the Spanish Foreign Legion were withdrawn from Ifni and Spanish Sahara after the Madrid Agreement* of 1975. A small legion contingent still remains in Melilla* and Ceuta*.

REFERENCES: Estado Mayor Central, *La legión española*, 2 vols., 1970–1973; John Mercer, *Spanish Sahara*, 1975.

SPANISH MOROCCO. The Spanish presence in Morocco was the first and among the last ventures of Spain in overseas imperialism. Five years after the expulsion of the Moors from Granada in 1492, Spain crossed the Mediterranean and seized Melilla*, a city on the coast of what is today northeastern Morocco. Spain annexed Ceuta*, a city on the Mediterranean coast about 165 miles east of Tangier, in 1668, winning it from Portugal in the Treaty of Lisbon. Although Spain did not press into the interior from those coastal possessions, it had nevertheless established a foothold in northern Morocco.

The foothold in southern Morocco took much longer to establish. From bases in the Canary Islands*, Spain established a few trading posts along the West African coast in the sixteenth century, but it was soon diverted by the wealthier prospects in the New World. Spain did not return to West Africa until the nineteenth century. Throughout the eighteenth and nineteenth centuries, European sailors were periodically shipwrecked along the coast and sold into slavery, so European countries began negotiating treaties with local potentates. In 1860, Spain won from the rulers of Morocco a 579-square-mile colony at Ifni*, a town on the Atlantic coast approximately 200 miles southwest of Marrakech. Donald Mackenzie of Scotland negotiated the rights to establish a commercial trading post at Cape Juby in 1879, and Spain, concerned about possible British penetration of the area, placed trading posts at Dakhla on the Río de Oro* Bay and at La Güera*. Madrid officially declared these areas Spanish protectorates in December 1884. Still, Spain made no attempt to extend and consolidate its holdings beyond those coastal enclaves.

By the early twentieth century, Germany was expressing interest in Morocco, inspiring Spain, France, and Great Britain to conspire to keep the North African coast in French and Spanish hands. In 1904, they signed a secret agreement recognizing France's and Spain's spheres of influence in Morocco, and the Algeciras Conference of 1906 formalized those claims. Antiforeign political insurgency in Casablanca and Fez in 1912 led to French military intervention from Algeria and the signing of a Franco-Spanish Convention* establishing the French protectorate over most of Morocco, as well as a Spanish protectorate, known as Spanish Morocco, over the country's northern and southern zones. Tangier became an international city.

Spanish Morocco consisted of two zones. The northern zone, known as the Spanish Protectorate in Morocco or the Northern Zone of the Protectorate, stretched from just south of Larache on the Atlantic coast of Morocco east to the Moulouya River and then north to the Mediterranean. The southern zone, separated from the northern zone by more than 500 miles, was known as Cape Juby, Southern Morocco, the Southern Protectorate of Spanish Morocco, Tarafaya, or the Tekna Zone*. Covering more than 8,500 square miles, the Southern Zone included land between the northern boundary of Spanish Sahara* at the latitude of 27° 40¹ north to the Qued Draa and reaching 150 miles into the African interior. In 1934, Ifni and the Northern Zone of Spanish Morocco were united administratively with Spanish Sahara*; in 1946, the Southern Zone of Spanish Morocco was included, creating the new colonial entity of Western Sahara.

But by that time, the seeds of nationalist rebellion had already been sown. During the 1920s, Spain and France found themselves in the middle of a bloody civil war in Morocco and the Northern Zone against the Rif rebels, a group of antiforeign Berber tribesmen led by Abd-el-Krim*. Beginning in 1926, Krim's guerrilla troops repeatedly defeated Spanish troops from bases in the rugged Rif Mountains, which extend along the Moroccan coast from Ceuta to the Algerian border. Only after years of bitter fighting did combined Spanish-French forces crush the rebellion. During the Spanish Civil War in the 1930s, local Moroccan nationalists like Al-Quazzani and Abdelhaleq Torres began pressing their demands for independence from Spain. When Moroccan and Algerian nationalists fought successfully for independence from France in the 1950s, the continuing colonial status of Spanish Morocco was doomed. When Morocco became independent from France in 1956, Spain ceded the Northern Zone of Spanish Morocco to the new country. Two years later, in April 1958, Spain signed the Agreement of Cintra*, handing over the Southern Zone of Spanish Morocco to Morocco. Finally, in 1969, Spain ceded Ifni to Morocco. All that remained of Spanish Morocco were the two tiny enclaves at Ceuta and Melilla.

REFERENCE: Richard M. Brace, *Morocco, Algeria, Tunisia*, 1964.

SPANISH SAHARA. Portugal and Spain first explored the Saharan coastline opposite the Canary Islands* in the fourteenth and fifteenth centuries. The Spanish fort Santa Cruz de Mar Pequeña served as a trading post and a slaveholding base until it was sacked by local tribes in 1524. The Portuguese were evicted in turn from their fort at Agadir in 1541, although they retained control of the island of Arguin until 1638, when it was seized by the Dutch. Meanwhile, imperial ambitions in the Americas diverted the Spaniards, who were not to return to the Sahara coast until the end of the nineteenth century.

Between the late eighteenth century and the 1860s, Western sailors trading at the nearby Canary and Madeira Islands often became shipwrecked along the dangerous Saharan coast and were sold by their captors to nomadic traders. As a consequence, Western interests negotiated a number of peace and trading treaties with local potentates during the second half of the nineteenth century. In 1879, Donald Mackenzie of Scotland signed a trading agreement with Mohammed Ben Beyrouk. As a result, the British North-West Africa Company near Cape Juby became the first successful European commercial operation on the Saharan coast in 350 years, competing with the southern trading activities of the sultan of Morocco. When the business of the BNWA Company began to decline in the early 1890s, MacKenzie's trading station was sold to Morocco (March 13, 1895).

Meanwhile, the Spanish government, fearing that the British might establish a presence on the African coast opposite the Canary Islands, established trading posts at Dakhla on the Río de Oro* Bay (later the settlement of Villa Cisneros) and at La Güera. The Madrid government officially declared these enclaves to be protectorates in December 1884. On April 6, 1887, a Spanish decree consolidated the protectorate to include the whole coastal region from Cape Juby to Cape Blanco. This new territory was under the administration of a subgovernor in Villa Cisneros who was responsible to the captain general of the Canaries. The borders of the protectorate were subsequently extended and more clearly delineated by three Franco-Spanish* conventions in 1900, 1904, and 1912. Despite these extentions, the Spanish presence remained confined, in practice, to the tiny enclaves of Villa Cisneros, Tarafaya, and La Guera on the Bay of Levrier. No attempts were made to occupy the interior until 1934, although in principle, the area, by then known as Río de Oro, extended 150 miles inland.

During the 1930s, under the prodding of France, Spain sought to strengthen its control over Spanish possessions in the Western Sahara region. Unlike the French, who were aggressively trying to pacify their part of the region, the Spanish had established a reasonably amicable relationship with the nomads operating along the nearby trans-Saharan trading routes. Spanish negligence, however, enabled anti-French resistance forces to establish sanctuaries from which they could stage *ghazzis*, or raids, against French positions in the neighboring territories. Following the French call for more control, Spanish occupation stretched inland to include the Saguia el-Hamra region in the north and the small enclave of Ifni*, nominally claimed by Spain since 1860 but not really occupied until the 1930s. In 1934, the Spanish Sahara region and Ifni were unified administratively with the Northern Zone of the Spanish protectorate in Morocco. Ultimate responsibility for the Spanish Sahara rested with the Spanish High Commissioner of Spanish Morocco*. This arrangement was called Spanish Western Sahara or, more simply, Spanish Sahara. As a response to growing Moroccan nationalism, the Southern Zone of Spanish Morocco was attached to Spanish Sahara in 1946. This new overseas entity was dubbed Spanish West Africa*, or AOE (África Occidental Española), with its own governor general in Ifni and with a subgovernor in Western Sahara.

Spanish West Africa was dissolved in January 1958 when the Army of Liberation*, a radical partisan movement that had played a role in gaining Moroccan independence from France in 1956, launched a guerrilla campaign against the Spanish in Ifni and Western Sahara. The Spanish government had no intention of quitting either Ifni or Western Sahara and turned both into Spanish provinces. As a Spanish province, Western Sahara was ruled by its own governor general who had a very wide range of powers but was responsible in military matters to the captain general of the Canary Islands and in administrative matters to the president of Spain.

The threat from the Army of Liberation was largely removed following a joint Spanish-French counter-insurgency operation in February 1958. In April 1958, the Spanish government agreed to hand over the Southern Zone of Spanish Morocco to Morocco in the Agreement of Cintra*. The protectorate over the Northern Zone of Spanish Morocco had come to an end with Moroccan independence in 1956. A detente between Spain and the kingdom of Morocco followed and was further strengthened when Ifni was finally ceded to Morocco in 1969. In 1974, Spain announced its intention of withdrawing from the Spanish Sahara province (by then, generally referred to as Western Sahara). King Hassan II of Morocco and Mokhtar Ould Daddah of Mauritania reiterated their claims to the area, and in September 1974, Spain agreed to partition Western Sahara between them, despite an advisory opinion from the International Court of Justice (October 16, 1975) rejecting the claims. In November 1975, Hassan, in an effort to force the integration of Western Sahara into Morocco, sent 350,000 unarmed Moroccans across the Western Sahara border (the Green March*) and persuaded Spain to yield. On November 14, 1975, in the Madrid Agreement*, the Spanish government withdrew, and on February 26, 1976, the country was formally partitioned. Morocco received the largest and most valuable area, including the richest phosphate deposits in the world; Mauritania got the rest—mostly useless desert. In 1979, Mauritania relinquished its claims in Western Sahara, leaving Morocco to annex the entire territory.

The partition, however, was opposed by the Polisario Front*, an indigenous nationalist group of Western Sahara Saharawi, formed in 1973. From the spring of 1975 on, the Polisario Front received substantial Algerian aid, and on February 27, 1976, declared the formation of the Saharan Arab Democratic Republic (SADR). By the 1980s, the Polisario guerrilla army had swelled to 20,000 men, well equipped and trained by Algeria and Libya. Battles frequently raged between the SADR guerrillas and the Moroccan army. By 1989, neither camp could claim outright victory, but neither seemed ready to compromise. The status of Western Sahara has yet to be resolved.

REFERENCE: John Mercer, *Spanish Sahara*, 1975.

                                                                                        Eric Loew

SPANISH SUCCESSION, WAR OF THE. Before the death of Charles II*, king of Spain, in 1700, both Louis XIV of France and the Habsburg Emperor, Leopold I, had hoped to place a member of his own family on the Spanish throne. Each had married a sister of Charles II, and it was upon these ties that they based their claims. In the last decade of the seventeenth century, an agreement had been worked out, whereby the Spanish possessions would be divided between the two nations, thus preserving the balance of power. When Charles died, however, his will stipulated that Spain and its possessions should pass intact to the grandson of Louis XIV, who would become Philip V* of Spain. Louis's acceptance meant that his influence would extend from Belgium to Gibraltar*, threatening not only the political and military balance, but also threatening British commercial interests on the continent and in America. This threat was further driven home when Spain granted France an *asiento** in August 1701. On September 7, 1701, England joined the United Provinces and the Habsburg empire in forming a grand alliance against France. The Treaty of the Hague forming the alliance pledged the nations to prevent the union of Spain and France, to secure territorial compensation for the Habsburgs, and to gain commercial concessions for the maritime powers. On May 15, 1702, the members of the grand alliance simultaneously declared war on France. Earlier, in May 1701, the emperor had already sent an army to seize the possessions of Spain in northern Italy. For its part, France, could count on Spain and Bavaria as allies. Bavaria gave France an advanced position on Vienna that it would quickly exploit. The grand alliance, however, had the services of the two ablest generals, John Churchill, Duke of Marlborough, and Prince Eugene of Savoy.

With the opening of hostilities, Louis XIV ordered an army to pin down Marlborough in the Low Countries while the main army marched through Bavaria to attack Vienna. Marlborough, without Dutch consent, made an extraordinary march to save Vienna. Joining the armies of Eugene of Savoy and Margrave Louis William I of Baden-Baden, Marlborough took the French by surprise and on August 13, 1704, was victorious over the French at Blenheim. The results were spectacular. Not only was Vienna saved, but 300,000 square miles of terrain was cleared of French troops and Bavaria was occupied by imperial troops.

While Marlborough was marching to save Vienna, an Anglo-Dutch fleet captured the Spanish-held Rock of Gibraltar on August 4. On October 9, 1705, an English fleet captured Barcelona, landing an allied army that protected a revolt in Catalonia against Philip V. Archduke Karl of Austria was established at Madrid as Charles III on June 25, 1706. The sight of the English and Austrians in Spain aroused popular resistance, however, and eventually led to the recovery of Madrid in September 1706. Marlborough, meanwhile, prepared to march into the Spanish Netherlands to engage the main French army led by Villeroi. On May 23, 1706, the two armies met at Ramilles, where the English victory resulted in the capture of Antwerp, Bruges, and Ostend and gave Marlborough a direct supply route to England. It also placed his army 20 miles from France. The new emperor, Joseph I, who had succeeded his father in 1705, was finally enjoying the victories of the armies led by Eugene of Savoy. Savoy had driven the French out of Italy by 1707. As a result of the subsequent Convention of Milan, France abandoned northern Italy, withdrawing all its troops to France. Despite the failure to hold Madrid, the war had gone well for the allies. By August, France was ready to make peace. The allies refused, however, and the war continued.

The year 1707 saw a number of reversals for the alliance. Its armies suffered reversals along the Rhine and failed to capture Toulon. As Marlborough entered the campaign of 1708, he did so with the support of Parliament, which had passed a resolution blocking any peace that allowed the House of Bourbon to retain any part of the Spanish monarchy. In June 1708, Louis sent an army to stop the allied advance into Flanders. Marlborough and Eugene met the French army at Oudenarde on the Scheldt on July 11, 1708. Overwhelming the French army, the allies laid siege to Lille, which fell on December 9. The French were forced to evacuate all of Flanders, and Louis announced that he was ready to negotiate a peace. Negotiations broke down over the insistence by the allies that Louis join them to expel Philip from the Spanish throne.

This demand aroused the French people once again, so the war continued. The new army, met Marlborough on September 11, 1709, at Malplaquet. Although several blunders were committed by the allies, they were victorious, reducing the French to the defensive and preventing them from protecting Mons, which fell to the allies on October 9, 1709. This action firmly established the allies on the Upper Scheldt and protected their conquests in Flanders. In March 1710, Louis again asked the allies for peace. He was now ready to recognize the Archduke Karl as king of Spain. Furthermore, he would offer no assistance to Philip and would even contribute to a fund helping to defray the cost of dethroning him. The allies, however, insisted that Louis unseat Philip alone and do it within two months. The war continued.

French fortunes on the battlefield seemed to be turning when, in December 1710, a French army under the command of Louis's grandson, the Duc de Vendôme, defeated an invading army sent to dethrone Philip. As the new year opened, events off the battlefield also began to work in favor of peace. In England, the Whig government, which had supported Marlborough, was replaced by the Tory Party in 1711. The new government, secretly and without informing its allies, sent Abbé Gaulthier, a French priest, to Paris with a peace offer. Furthermore, on April 7, 1711, Emperor Joseph died, which meant that Archduke Karl would become Emperor Charles VII. England's concern for a European balance was now jeopardized in a different way if the Habsburg Empire also included both Spain and the territory the empire had already won. In light of these new events, England offered to recognize Philip as king of Spain if France would renounce any union with Spain. England further demanded barrier fortresses to protect the United Provinces and Germany, the restitution of French conquests, the recognition of the Protestant succession in England, the expulsion of James III from France, the confirmation that Gibraltar, Newfoundland, and the Hudson Bay region were English, and the transfer of the *asiento* from France to England. The French agreed with minor modifications, and a peace conference was scheduled to meet in Utrecht, where the Peace of Utrecht* was signed by all parties except the emperor. Eugene of Savoy considered the English action a betrayal and continued the war until the Treaty of Rastatt was concluded on March 6, 1714.

The biggest winner of the war was England, which now extended its power into the Mediterranean and increased its holdings in Europe. Although the long war had sapped France's strength, leaving the country depopulated and the mass of its people poverty-stricken, it nonetheless remained strong and vigorous. The war's effects went beyond territorial change, however. It had been the first war to be fought by professional armies, foreshadowing the other wars of the eighteenth century. It was also the first in which religion was not the predominant issue. This war had been fought over commerce and the seapower that spread it to the colonies, thus making it a world war. It also marked the first time that England had become involved in continental politics. Finally, the war had confirmed the system of international relations and the sovereignty of nations already established at Westphalia* in 1648.

REFERENCE: Harold Kamen, *The War of Succession in Spain: 1700-1715*, 1969.

Michael Dennis

SPANISH WEST AFRICA. In 1860, Spain established a vague claim to the area of West Africa and then proclaimed a protectorate there in 1884. On July 20, 1946, Spain established the colony of Spanish West Africa, which incorporated Spanish Sahara* and Ifni* into a single administrative unit. Both of those territories had been part of Spanish Morocco* since 1934, but the Moroccan nationalist rebellion forced Spain to take new steps to maintain its empire in Africa. Spanish West Africa had its governor resident in Ifni with a *subgobernador* in Western Sahara. Spanish West Africa was dissolved in 1958 when Western Sahara and Ifni each became a province of Spain and the Tekna Zone* was ceded to Morocco.

REFERENCE: John Mercer, *Spanish Sahara*, 1975.

SPICE ISLANDS. The romantic, mysterious Spice Islands are the Moluccas of eastern Indonesia. They are not a geographical unit, for they actually consist of several separate island groups and contain a mixture of human races and cultures. The larger Spice Islands are Halmahera, Ceram, Buru, and the Tanimbar group, although some of the smaller islands, such as Ternate, Tidore, and Ambon, were historically more significant. The Spice Islands are situated between Mindanao* on the north, Australia on the south, the Celebes on the west, and New Guinea on the east. They straddle the equator.

Spices were highly prized in Europe, not for their taste but for their ability to preserve meat. Before the age of discovery, spices reached Europe via Javanese seamen, Malay traders, Arab merchants, and Venetian distributors. With all these middlemen, the price was exorbitant in Western Europe. No European actually knew where the fabled Spice Islands were, only that they were very distant. The islands acted as a magnet, drawing first Portugese and Spanish explorers, then Dutch and English merchants. Christopher Columbus* and John Cabot both failed to reach the Spice Islands, but the Portuguese concluded an alliance with the Sultan of Ternate in 1512 and built a fort there ten years later.

Later in the sixteenth century, Portuguese power in Asia waned and that of England and Holland waxed. Sir Francis Drake[*] brought a cargo of spices back to England in 1580. In 1602, the Dutch East India Company was formed to organize the procurement of spices and their shipment to northern Europe.

For the entire first half of the seventeenth century, the Dutch had to fight Spaniards, Englishmen, and Indonesian natives for control of the spice trade. They evicted the Spanish from Ternate in 1608 and massacred a score of Englishmen and Javanese at Amboina (Ambon) in 1623. From 1650 to 1656, they fought to suppress a native rebellion. The Dutch monopoly yielded profits of up to 1,000 percent, but regulating the trade was hard. Foreign privateers had to be chased away, and "bootleg" spice plants had to be uprooted. Overproduction was a constant danger. More than once, the Dutch destroyed planted fields to reduce the supply and drive up the price. They tried assigning clove production exclusively to Amboina, Ternate, and Tidore, while mace and nutmeg went to Amboina and the Banda Islands. Black pepper was more widely cultivated. Dutch interests shifted when changing European tastes created a new, more lucrative market for Javanese coffee. Batavia became the capital of the Netherlands East Indies, and Dutchmen referred to the former Spice Islands as the "great east." Indonesians today think of them as part of the "Outer Islands."

REFERENCE: Anthony Reid, *Southeast Asia in the Age of Commerce, 1450-1680*, 1988.

Ross Marlay

SUÁREZ, FRANCISCO. Young Francisco Suárez was born in Granada, Spain, in 1548. He came from an ancient family that had a distinguished past. He studied at home until 1561 when he moved to Salamanca with his brother Juan. It was the time of a great religious revival which echoed the successful conclusion of the Council of Trent[*]. In 1564, he entered the Jesuit[*] order but not without difficulties, nor were his studies of philosophy devoid of obstacles. Having great modesty, he did not aim at a high position within society. Still, he succeeded and then turned to theology in which he quickly excelled. In 1571, he began teaching philosophy at the Jesuit College of Segovia. It was here that he was ordained. He then moved to Valladolid to teach theology but actually nothing came of it. He went back to Segovia, then to Ávila, and again back to Valladolid where he stayed for the next four years (1576–1580). Despite problems, he succeeded. Due to his growing reputation, he was given the chair of theology at the Jesuit College in Rome. He stayed there for five years.

He returned to Spain, first to Alcalá and then to Salamanca, which was more to his intellectual and spiritual liking. In 1593, Philip II[*] appointed him to the chair of theology at Coimbra. He had little disposition to go to Coimbra but when he did arrive there in 1597, his course was interrupted since he had not yet obtained his doctorate in theology. This he obtained in Evora, but it was too late for him to give the course, so he returned to Salamanca where he lectured on law. These lectures appeared in 1612 under the title *De Legibus ac de Deo*

Legislatore. Shortly thereafter, he published his *Defensio Fidei* (1613), in which he attacked James I of England for his divine-right policies. The controversy became a *cause célèbre* involving Pope Paul V and Cardinal Bellarmine. The net result was that many Jesuit works were publicly burned in England and France. Suárez retired in 1616 and died on September 17, 1617.

With Suárez, Late Scholasticism reached its highest summit. His political thought was of particular import for Spanish-American independence, since justification for the start of the revolution was based on his contract theory. He gave Scholasticism a new dynamism that enabled it to dominate the Spanish-American mind for centuries; his importance lies in the fact, as Richard Mose has written, that "his fresh marshalling of scholastic doctrines, under powerful influences of time and place, encapsuled certain assumptions about political man and certain political dilemmas that pervade Hispanic political life to this day." Suárez followed Bellarmine's theory of the indirect power of the Church in temporal matters. His theory fought the contemporary currents of Niccolo Machiavelli and his followers by emphasizing natural law and exalting the spiritual power of the pope. He also emphasized the rights of the people against the absolutism of the monarchy and particularly the divine-right theories of James I of England. For Suárez, the ruler was invested with the power given by God with the consent of the people through a true compact; the people cannot throw off this power unless this pact is broken or dissolved, as was the case of Ferdinand VII* and the events of May 1808 in Bayonne.

REFERENCES: Bernice Hamilton, *Political Thought in Sixteenth-Century Spain: A Study of the Political Ideas of Vitoria, Soto, Suárez, and Molina*, 1963; O. Carlos Stoetzer, *The Scholastic Roots of the Spanish American Revolution*, 1979.

O. Carlos Stoetzer

SUÁREZ DE PERALTA, JUAN. Considered to be the first of the New World *criollo** chroniclers, Juan Suárez de Peralta was born in New Spain* in the late 1530s. He was related to the Hernán Cortés* family, and his father was one of the original conquistadors*. Because of familial ties and heritage, he enjoyed an early life of privilege, dabbling in horsemanship and society's other leisure activities. His interest in horses resulted in his *Tratado de la caballería de la gineta y brida*, which was one of the first books written in Mexico, but it was in the field of history that Suárez de Peralta was to excel. In 1589, he finished his *Tratado del descubrimiento de las Indias y su conquista*, a fascinating and extremely well-written account of the first decades of the Spanish in New Spain. The work consists of 44 chapters, the first 17 of which treat the origin of the Indians* and the Spanish conquest in Mexico. It is the remaining chapters that offer the reader true novelty, however, for Suárez de Peralta describes in depth Mexico City* in its first decades after Cortés's conquest. Among the author's more interesting observations are those dealing with the already developing distinction between the *peninsulares** of Mexico City and the growing population of *criollos*. Although Suárez de Peralta described himself as a man of little grammar, the fact is that he was an accomplished writer with a notable style, not to mention his natural penchant for writing history. Juan Suárez de Peralta died around 1590.

REFERENCE: Carlos González Peña, *History of Mexican Literature*, 1968.

Sam L. Slick

SUÁREZ Y ROMERO, ANSELMO. Anselmo Suárez y Romero was born in Cuba* in 1818. Eventually he wrote one of the most impressive but little-read novels of the nineteenth century—*Francisco*. Incredible as it now seems, the author wrote the novel at the tender age of 20. Although he wrote it in 1838–1839, some 11 years before the publication of Harriet Beecher Stowe's *Uncle Tom's Cabin*, his book was not published until 1880. Suárez's purpose in writing *Francisco* was to expose the cruelty and mindlessness of slavery* in Cuba. Aside from being an interesting romantic novel of the period, *Francisco* contains a wealth of information and insight into the sugar* plantation mentality and into activity in Cuba in the nineteenth century. *Francisco* documents the cruelty of slavery in the sugar mills and plantations. It has great historical, sociological, and psychological import, and it is well structured and well written. *Francisco* treats the love affair between two slaves; a lovely mulatto, Dorotea, and Francisco, and African-born plantation hand. Their desire to marry is thwarted by the planation owner, whose evil son, Ricardo, eventually manages to extort sexual favors from Dorotea. When Francisco learns of this, he commits suicide; his death ensures the premature death of Dorotea as well. Anselmo Suárez y Romero died in 1878.

REFERENCE: Juan J. Remos, *Proceso Histórico de las Letras Cubanas*, 1958.

Sam L. Slick

SUCRE. Located northeast of Potosí*, Sucre was a major colonial city of Upper Peru (Bolivia*). Sucre was founded in 1538; until it was renamed in honor of Antonio José Sucre* in 1825, it was known as Charcas*, Chuquisaca, and La Plata.

SUCRE, ARCHDIOCESE OF. The Roman Catholic archdiocese of Sucre began in 1551 when Pope Julius III established the diocese of Sucre; it was raised to an archdiocese in 1609. Until 1924, it was called the Archdiocese of La Plata. During much of the colonial period, its territorial jurisdiction included Bolivia*, Argentina*, Chile*, Paraguay*, and Uruguay*.

REFERENCE: *New Catholic Encyclopedia*, XIII:773, 1967.

SUCRE ALCALÁ, ANTONIO JOSÉ DE. Antonio José de Sucre was born in Cumana, Venezuela*, in 1795, to a local aristocratic family. As a teenager in 1810, Sucre joined the patriot army in the rebellion against Spain. He became a loyal follower of Simón Bolívar*, working as an adviser and arms procurer for the leader of the independence movement in Venezuela. Sucre became Bolívar's chief of staff and most trusted aide in 1820. In 1822, Bolívar commissioned Sucre to invade Ecuador* and link up with patriot forces there. Sucre was at the head of the patriot army that won the Battle Pichincha* and seized control of Quito* from royalist forces. Two years later, Sucre played a central role in Bolívar's final destruction of royalist forces at the Battle of Ayacucho*. Sucre spent 1825 mopping up the last royalist resistance in Upper Peru (Bolivia*).

As military commander of Upper Peru, Sucre decided to let the region choose its own political destiny, particularly whether to seek independence or remain with Peru*. The patriots there decided on independence, installing Simón Bolívar as their leader and naming the country Bolivia. Bolívar left the area at the end of 1825, and Sucre became the first constitutional president of the country. Sucre served as president for three years before political problems forced his resignation. He then returned to Quito, Ecuador, where he commanded the military forces of Gran Colombia* in the war with Peru in 1828–1829. Sucre served brilliantly and was rewarded after the war by becoming president of the Gran Colombian congress. On June 4, 1830, Antonio José Sucre was assassinated, most likely by political enemies of Bolívar.

REFERENCES: Charles Arnade, *The Emergence of the Republic of Bolivia*, 1957; Alfonso Rumazo Gonzales, *Sucre, gran mariscal de Ayacucho*, 1963.

SUGAR. Although sugar production was introduced to the Caribbean colonies of Spain in the sixteenth century, it had little significance to the colonial economy until the eighteenth century. During the early stages of the empire, Spain was more interested in extracting gold and silver from the colonies than in developing profitable local industries, but in the eighteenth century, sugar became increasingly important. The center of sugar production was in the Caribbean, especially Cuba*, Puerto Rico*, and Santo Domingo*, although substantial amounts were also produced in Venezuela*, Ecuador*, New Spain*, and Peru*. Beginning in the 1520s, the Casa de la Contratación* began making loans to Cuban sugar planters, but the industry grew slowly. By the 1790s, there were more than 100 plantations on Cuba and more than 10,000 acres in sugar cane production. Sugar production was labor intensive, and it led to substantial importation of African slaves* (approximately 100,000 of them by 1790) to work the fields.

Sugar production exploded in the first half of the nineteenth century. By 1830, there were more than 1,000 plantations in Cuba and 500,000 acres under production. Another 600,000 African slaves were imported to Cuba (and 100,000 to Puerto Rico and Santo Domingo). The New World sugar industry came on hard times, however, in the second half of the nineteenth century. The abolition of slavery created serious labor shortages and disrupted production, while dramatic increases in sugar beet production in Europe undermined world sugar prices. When Cuba and Puerto Rico went from Spanish to United States sovereignty in 1898, the sugar industry was in a severe depression.

REFERENCES: Edward Boorstein, *The Economic Transformation of Cuba*, 1968; Leland Jenks, *Our Cuban Colony: A Study of Sugar*, 1928.

T

TACÓN, MIGUEL. Miguel Tacón was born in Spain in 1775 and became famous in colonial history because of his tenure as captain general of Cuba* between 1834 and 1838. Tacón came to Havana*, Cuba, convinced that a strong hand was necessary to crush Cuban liberalism. He launched an ambitious program of public works construction in Havana and exiled a number of prominent Cuban liberals, including José Antonio Saco*. Tacón was also convinced that *peninsulares** should rule Cuba, not *criollos**. When he prohibited *criollos** from serving in the Cortes, he created an uproar among the local elite. Under pressure, he resigned in 1838 and returned to Spain, where he was named the Viscount of Bayamo and Marqués of the Union of Cuba. He also returned a rich man because of kickbacks he earned in Cuba by not enforcing international agreements against the slave* trade. Miguel Tacón died in Majorca in 1855.

REFERENCES: Jaime Suchlicki, *Historical Dictionary of Cuba*, 1988; Jaime Suchlicki, *Cuba: From Columbus to Castro*, 1986.

TAGALOG PROVINCES. The Philippine* provinces of Bataan, Bulacan, Rizal (formerly Tondo), Cavite, Batangas, and Laguna are inhabited by Tagalog-speaking Filipinos. Tagalogs are not the most numerous ethnic group in the islands (more people speak Cebuano), but they live in the core region of the nation, Manila* and its surrounding area. Settlement patterns and early accounts indicate that the Tagalogs were sea-borne and riverine people; indeed, "Tagailog" means "from the river." When Europeans first saw Manila Bay in 1570, Tagalogs occupied the marshy shores and immediate inland regions of Bataan and Bulacan, as well as the shorelines of two huge lakes, Laguna de Bay, which is low and shallow, a catchment basin for the Pasig, and Lake Taal, which is a giant round caldera, in a region they called Cavite. The coastlines of Balayan

Bay, Batangas Bay, and Tayabas Bay were a sparsely settled Tagalog frontier zone.

Because the Tagalog lands were so strategically situated, Tagalog history is the history of the Philippines, at least in the eyes of the older school of Spanish and American historians. Certainly the Tagalogs, as compared to other Filipinos[*], were exposed more deeply and for a longer time to strong Spanish influences, including Church rule. They were more aware of and affected by international ideas and commerce, more integrated into the world economy, and more penetrated by the new Chinese-Filipino mestizo[*] elite. The Tagalog language had its own pre-Spanish script, and Tagalog literature and poetry are highly developed. Tagalogs have made their language the "national" language (Filipino), but have not gained full acceptance of that from other Filipino groups.

Economic development of the Tagalog provinces rested on three foundations: (1) the traditional village subsistence economy in which peasants planted rice, raised domestic animals, and provided for all their own needs; (2) vast friar estates and ranches; and (3) large- and small-scale commercial agriculture to supply Manila, and later the world market, with rice, sugar[*], hemp, and other products. The friar estates originated in land grants that were generously awarded to early explorers. Many of them had little interest in settling down, and they sold or donated their titles to the Jesuits[*], Augustinians[*], Dominicans[*], and Recollects. The friars rented out some land to tenants, who in turn hired sharecroppers. This was only part of the burden that Tagalogs had to bear—there was also the *polo*, or taxation through compulsory labor in forestry and shipbuilding, for the Spaniards maintained an important naval yard and shipbuilding industry in Cavite.

Considering the exactions of the Spanish and the Tagalogs' numerical inferiority, it is a wonder that there was so little peasant unrest during the three centuries of Spanish rule. The general pattern of hispanization, Christianization, introduction to the market economy, intensification of class inequities, and formation of new elites was mostly evolutionary and peaceful until the late nineteenth century, with the sole exception of agrarian unrest in 1745–1746. In that brief revolt, Jesuit convents were occupied and looted, but loyalist troops suppressed the rebels. In the second half of the nineteenth century, education and modernization created a new Filipino elite—young men who studied in Europe and who at first desired only equality with Spaniards but later led the Philippine Revolution against Spain (1896–1898).

REFERENCE: Dennis M. Roth, "Church Lands in the Agrarian History of the Tagalog Region," in Alfred McCoy and Ed. de Jesús, eds., *Philippine Social History*, 1982.

Ross Marlay

TAÍNO. The Taino were a huge group of perhaps millions of Amerindians occupying Cuba[*], Hispaniola[*], and Puerto Rico[*] at the time of the Spanish conquest of the West Indies in the 1490s and early 1500s. They spoke an Arawakan[*] language. The conventional wisdom among scholars accepts as fact the complete destruction of the Taíno people by 1550, mostly because of disease. Over the years, however, there were reported meetings with small numbers of Indian[*] people in Cuba and Puerto Rico. Miguel Rodríguez Ferrar, a Spanish scientist, encountered Indian communities on the eastern tip of Cuba[*] in 1847, and José Martí[*], the great leader of Cuban independence, claimed to have lived briefly with some Indian groups in Cuba in 1895. Although the Taíno Indians were indeed destroyed as a functional social group, there survived in Puerto Rico and Cuba a few people whose ancestry retained a strong indigenous profile. Today there are a few hundred people who have strong Indian roots in the Baracoa region of eastern Cuba as well as in the mountainous regions of western Puerto Rico. Although they speak Spanish, are Roman Catholic, are integrated into the local economy, and have no sense of a peculiarly Taíno background, they are nevertheless aware of their Indian ancestry.

REFERENCES: José Barreiro, "Indians, in Cuba," *Cultural Survival Quarterly*, 13 (1989), 56–60; Jesse Walter Fewkes, *The Aborigines of Puerto Rico and Neighboring Islands*, 1907.

TARMA. Tarma was created as an *intendencia*[*] within the viceroyalty of Peru[*] in 1784. Spanish authority survived in Tarma until 1823, when royalist forces were driven from the area. The region of Tarma became part of the republic of Peru in 1825.

TECÚM UMÁN. Tecúm Umán was the leader of the Quiché Maya[*] at the time of the Spanish conquest. Remembered today as a valiant and popular leader, Tecúm Umán confronted the Spanish conqueror Pedro de Alvarado[*] and his Cakchiquel Maya allies in July 1524, in battle at the Quiche town of Xelaju[*]. The battle of Xelaju was decisive and bloody. As many as 30,000 Quiché warriors took part, many of whom were slain. According to legend, Tecúm Umán and Pedro de Alvarado fought a personal duel in the midst of the battle. Although Alvarado claimed to have been pinned to his saddle by Tecúm Umán's arrow for nearly four hours, the Spaniard ultimately triumphed. Alvarado killed Tecúm Umán with his own hands, forcing the surrender of the Quiche Maya.

REFERENCE: Jim Handy, *Gift of the Devil: A History of Guatemala*, 1984.

Virginia Garrard Burnett

TEKNA ZONE. The Tekna Zone, also known historically as the Tarfaya Zone or as Spanish Southern Morocco, was a northern strip of Spanish Sahara[*] between the Oued Draa and 27° 40[1] north latitude. It was defined as such in the Franco-Spanish Convention of 1912[*]. In April 1958, under the terms of the Agreement of Cintra,[*] Spain ceded the Tekna Zone to Morocco.

REFERENCE: Tony Hodges, *Historical Dictionary of Western Sahara*, 1982.

TENERIFE. Tenerife, one of the Canary Islands[*], was conquered by Spain in 1495 and received its first governor in 1496. The same person also served as governor of all of the Canary Islands, although each individual island eventually had a governor or chief executive of its own as well. When a permanent captain general was appointed for all the Canary Islands in 1625, he was no longer headquartered at Tenerife but at Grand Canary. After that, the governor of Tenerife was subordinate to the captain general.

TENOCHTITLÁN. Tenochtitlán was the capital city of the powerful México, the military leaders of the Aztec* Triple Alliance (1430–1521). It was founded in the year 1325 as the wandering México sought a foothold in the prosperous basin of Mexico. The México had been led to the lake-dominated valley by their patron god, Huitzilopochtli. They were seeking a sign—an eagle with a snake in its mouth, perched on a prickly pear cactus growing from a rock. This sign appeared as they were being desperately pursued by an angered ruler of the lakeside city of Culhuacán. The pursuit (who had sacrificed and flayed the Culhua ruler's daughter) forced the México into the shallow Lake Texcoco, where they took refuge on a small island. There they settled, first building a humble temple to their god and then going about the business of building a great and powerful city. The city was named Tenochtitlán, meaning "Among the Stone-Cactus Fruit."

The city was built around an enormous ceremonial district, probably measuring some 500 meters square. This area was bounded by a serpent wall and may have contained as many as 78 religious structures. Most of these were temples, each containing its own courtyard and accommodations for priests. The recently excavated Huey Teocalli, or Great Temple, dominated the district. It was dedicated to Tlaloc (rain god) and Huitzilopochtli (god of war and patron of the México). Beyond the central district, which was dedicated to ceremonial activities, lay the palaces of current and past rulers. The palace of Motecuhzoma* II (ruled 1502–1520) contained not only the ruler's substantial polygynous household, but also administrative rooms, such as courthouses, council chambers, tribute storehouses, armories, and even an aviary and zoo.

The remainder of the city was divided into four large quarters, with each quarter split into smaller territorial divisions called *calpulli*. Each *calpulli* contained its own temple, administrative building, and school for training young men in the martial arts. Since the island was small, many of these residential districts extended into the lakebed through the construction of *chinampas*. These "floating gardens," stabilized with tree roots, provided both residential sites and horticultural land for the people of Tenochtitlán. In addition to *chinampa* farmers, the city contained a vast variety of artisans (from producers of expensive feather and stone ornaments to manufacturers of everyday pottery and mats), merchants, imperial bureaucrats, and priests. People from many different ethnic and linguistic groups resided in the city. The systematic construction of *chinampas* yielded a pattern of alternating footpaths and canals throughout the city; comparisons with Venice have frequently been made. The most efficient means of travel to, from, and in the city was by canoe. Vast quantities of goods reached the great marketplace at Tlatelolco, Tenochtitlán's sister-city on an adjacent island, by water transport. In addition, large causeways linked the island cities with the mainland.

By the time of the Spanish conquest (1521), Tenochtitlán was home to some 150,000 to 200,000 people and covered some 12 square miles. It is no surprise that various urban problems arose. One of the most serious was flooding, at least partially solved through the construction of a huge dike across Lake Texcoco in the the late fifteenth century. Population growth was accommodatd by the extension of the *chinampas* and by the distribution of needed goods and services to a large specialized population through an intricate market structure. Hernán Cortés[*] and the Spaniards first entered Tenochtitlán in 1519, but its conquest was not completed until two years later, by which time the struggle had destroyed whole sections of the city. The Spaniards decided to rebuild the city. They drained the lake and established Mexico City[*] on its floor. Mexico City became the seat of the viceroyalty of New Spain[*] and remained by far the most important city in the colony—economically, socially, culturally, and politically. By the end of the colonial period, the Spanish population of Mexico City exceeded 100,000 people.

REFERENCES: Eduardo Matos Moctezuma, *The Great Temple of the Aztecs*, 1988; José Luis de Rojas, *México Tenochtitlán: Economía y Sociedad en el Siglo XVI*, 1986; Rudolf A. M. van Zantwijk, *The Aztec Arrangement*, 1985.

Frances F. Berdan

TEN YEARS WAR. The Ten Years War began on October 10, 1868, when a number of small Cuban planters, led by Carlos Manuel de Céspedes[*], declared eastern Cuba[*] independent of Spain. At the time, Spain was embroiled in its own "Glorious Revolution" and could not spare the resources to crush the rebellion. Céspedes, however, made a fatal error in not coming out in favor of abolition and refusing to invade western Cuba where royalist forces were strong. By not calling for the abolition of slavery[*], Céspedes was unable to marshall much political support from Cuban blacks[*], who constituted the largest block of the population; by not invading western Cuba, he gave royalist forces time to consolidate their resources. In 1876, Spain dispatched a 25,00-man army under General Arsenio Martínez[*] Campos to crush the rebellion. In February 1878, realizing that they did not have the power to expel Martínez Campos, the rebels agreed to an armistice in what became known as the Pact of Zanjoń.

REFERENCE: Jaime Suchlicki, *Cuba: From Columbus to Castro*, 1986.

TERRAZAS, FRANCISCO DE. Francisco de Terrazas was born in Mexico City[*] around 1525 and is generally considered to be the best lyric poet of Mexico during the sixteenth century. Information about his life and activities is largely unknown, but he was apparently related to members of higher society in New Spain[*]. His father was a public functionary in Mexico City where Terrazas grew up. Terrazas was the first native-born poet not only of New Spain but the New World. Terrazas belonged very clearly to the renaissance movement in poetry;

his works reflect Italian poetic forms of the period, including sonnets, tercets, and stanzas of ten octosyllabic lines. His works suggest the influence of Petrarch. Many believe that he learned to write in part from the Spaniard Gutieere de Cetina, who was also a renaissance poet. Although his surviving works are modest in number, Terrazas was relatively well known as a poet in his age. Somewhat surprisingly, he was referred to by Miguel de Cervantes, in the latter's *La Galatea*, as a bright new poetic star. An incomplete epic poem titled *Nuevo Mundo y Conquista*, some sonnets and a work entitled *Epístola amatoria* are all that remain of Terrazas's work. Terrazas died around 1607.

REFERENCE: Carlos González Peña, *History of Mexican Literature*, 1968.

Sam L. Slick

TEXAS. What is today the state of Texas in the United States began as two distinct Spanish colonies in the Borderlands* region. Spaniards established a series of missions* and presidios from San Juan Bautista del Río Grande near contemporary Cerro, Coahuila*, up to the present city of San Antonio*, and then east toward the Sabine River. These included settlements at Goliad and Nacogdoches, as well as the establishment of Mission San Francisco de los Tejas northeast of present-day Crockett, Texas, in 1690. In 1716, Texas was separated from Coahuila an established as a separate province, with Martín de Alarcón as the first governor. Franciscan* missionary priests established the mission of San Antonio de Valero on the San Antonio River in 1718; that settlement evolved into the city of San Antonio. But the geography of the region was inhospitable, and the Apache* and Comanche Indians were hostile. Therefore, the settlements never attracted a sizable immigrant population. By the end of the colonial period in the early 1800s, the total population of these settlements numbered fewer than 5,000 people.

The second Spanish colony was along the Río Grande River. In the middle of the eighteenth century, Spain became increasingly concerned about the potential of French or English penetration of the settlements along the Gulf of Mexico, especially from Tampico north to the mouth of the Guadalupe River. The Spanish Crown commissioned Colonel José de Escandón to colonize the region, and between 1749 and 1755, he went up the Río Grande Valley and established 24 settlements on the river from its mouth up to present-day Laredo. Spain called the colonies Nuevo Santander, or New Santander*. Because it was not located on the main commercial route between Coahuila and San Antonio and because of hostile surrounding Indians*, New Santander developed a self-contained, cohesive, almost insular mentality, with a largely pastoral economy and, by the early 1800s, a population of more than 25,000 people. Escandón became the first governor of New Santander, serving until 1770. After the Mexican Revolution, New Santander became the state of Tamaulipas.

REFERENCE: Robert J. Rosenbaum, *Mexicano Resistance in the Southwest*, 1981.

TEXTILE TRADITION OF MIDDLE AMERICA. Weaving in Middle America extends back in time well over three millennia. The earliest known loom-woven textile dates to approximately 1500 B.C., but sadly, it is only a fragment.

The combination of dry climate and burial practices that preserve ancient cloth did not exist in Mexico-Central America; nonetheless, the area's indigenous pictographic writing system has provided its own form of "textile conservation." The region's pictorial codices* contain hundreds of illustrations of pre-Hispanic garments, many drawn in remarkable detail. These images, together with Spanish colonial descriptive accounts, demonstrate that the same basic mode of dress extended throughout almost all of Mesoamerica.

The fundamental costume for males was a loincloth and cape; the female equivalent was a wrap-around skirt, a sleeveless tunic (the *huipil*), and/or a shoulder shawl (the *quechquemitl*). These garments were woven on the backstrap loom, which, when its warp threads are not attached, is only an assemblage of sticks of various lengths and thicknesses. This deceptively simple device—still in use today—is unique in that the continuous, uncut, warp loops at each end of the loom result in the creation of four-selvage fabrics. The fairly narrow woven cloth can therefore be worn just as it comes off the loom; several webs can be joined at the selvage to create wider garments. The Indians' pre-Hispanic concept of clothing construction was that of uncut, unfitted apparel. This approach was in sharp contrast to that of their conquerors.

Among the innovations that the Spanish introduced into the New World was tailoring: the creation of fitted garments by cutting and sewing together various pieces of cloth. Such attire required broad widths of material, which were created on the European treadle-loom. Accompanying this new technology was the raising of wool-bearing sheep and the establishment of *obrajes* (weaving factories staffed by Indian* men). Changes in the Mesoamerican male costume occurred early on as the result of both the missionary priests' abolishing the "heathen" loincloth and the prolonged exposure to the new culture. In contrast, the modest dress of the Indian women, who had less direct association with the Spaniards, altered far more slowly. This difference in male/female costume acculturation has continued into the modern age.

Many of the more conservative Indian villages of Mexico and Guatemala* are well known today for their distinctive regional dress. There, the women's colorful wrap-around skirts, *huipil*, and *quechquemitl* continue to be woven and worn, albeit they now combine the indigenous cotton and bast fibers with Spanish-introduced wool and present-day synthetics. In contrast, only a few communities feature distinctive male attire. In such Indian towns, the men's costume typically reflects the adoption of clothing traits from the early Spanish colonial period. That same epoch has also left its *mark* in the Central Mexican women's embroidered, short-sleeved blouses, which are often worn together with the *quechquemitl*.

Among the present-day Indians who still wear regional dress, the costumes—what the Indians of Guatemala call *costumbre*—continue to serve as a powerful indicator of social structure, ritual patterns, economic networks, and the commitment to traditional life. Rank, class, status, region, village, religion, or age may be signaled by means of dress. In recent years, however, textiles researchers have discovered that, in certain areas, "one-costume-one-village" is no longer necessarily the case. The fashion impulse appears to play a role in what a woman chooses to weave and wear; *costumbre* no longer demands that a specific blouse or *huipil* be donned in order for a woman to be accepted by her community. To the contrary, knowledge of the outside world is signaled by expertise in weaving a *huipil* identified with another village, and the wearer is admired and respected for her know-how and sophistication.

The ancient Mesoamerican art of skilled weaving continues into the present day. Despite the cataclysmic trauma of the Spanish Conquest, centuries of colonial suppression, and nineteenth- and twentieth-century exploitation of the Indians, weavers continue to produce magnificent, labor-intensive cloth that is increasingly appreciated by the Western world. If the past is indeed prologue, there is promise that the Middle American textile tradition will continue to endure.

REFERENCES: Mary Elizabeth King, "The Prehispanic Textile Industry of Mesoamerica," *The Junius B. Bird Pre-Colombian Textile Conference*, 1979; Patricia Rieff Anawalt, *Indian Clothing Before Cortés*, 1981; Patricia Rieff Anawalt, "The Ramifications of Treadle Loom Introduction in 16th Century Mexico," *Irene Emery Roundtable on Museum Textiles 1977 Proceedings: Looms and Their Products*, 1979.

Patricia Rieff Anawalt

TIERRAS BALDÍAS. During the medieval Reconquista, the monarchs of Castile[*] stimulated the settlement of newly acquired territory through grants to potential colonists. Some royal grants went to specific individuals and new towns, but the Crown also extended a blanket authorization to anyone to settle unoccupied lands. In theory, all lands that had not been formally granted by the monarch remained the property of the Crown (*tierras realengas*), but they were too vast to be controlled effectively. These extensive, ungranted Crown lands were also called *tierras baldías* or *baldíos* (possibly derived from the Arabic *ba'l*, for unirrigated lands). The term "*baldío*" was vague in late medieval and early modern Castile. The *baldíos* were considered to be Crown lands, but many parts of them had been appropriated (or usurped) by individuals or by municipalities, and their legal status was not clear. Because the Crown allowed the public to use the *baldíos* for pasture, hunting, water, and even cultivation, there developed a strong feeling that the *baldíos* were public lands and only vaguely subject to royal control. The towns often added to their community property by encroaching on the adjacent *baldíos*. Consequently, the distinction between *tierras baldías* and *tierras concegiles* often became blurred.

The character of the *baldíos* varied widely, ranging from barren mountain slopes to fertile valley soils that remained uncultivated merely because of physical isolation or low population density. Some places had access to extensive *baldíos* of excellent quality, whereas in other places most of the *baldíos* had been privatized and those remaining were scanty or of poor quality. When portions of the *baldíos* were cultivated, the total amount of public pasture was reduced. To prevent the overcultivation of these lands, many municipal governments asserted the right to license (or deny) permits to plant crops on the *baldíos*. Until the late sixteenth century, the Crown tacitly allowed the municipalities to exercise their authority over the *tierras baldías* under their jurisdiction.

During the late 1550s, the Crown decided to exploit the ill-defined *baldíos* of Castile, to provide funds for the perennially hard-pressed royal treasury. Persons who were occupying portions of the *tierras baldías* without royal permission were given the opportunity to gain clear title to their lands, in exchange for payment. As the Crown realized the money-making potential of this venture, it developed a widespread program to sell the *baldíos* of the kingdom to the highest bidders. Itinerant land commissioners (*jueces de tierras baldías*) were dispatched to the four corners of Castile to sell the *baldíos* to their occupiers or to third parties if the occupiers failed to submit a high enough bid. It was the general policy to give preference to municipalities over individuals; towns were given the first option to purchase the lands used as community property or even to buy all of the *tierras baldías* within their jurisdiction, despite the protests of individuals using those lands. But most *baldío* sales were small ones, to the individual peasants who were occupying the land. Despite the sales to municipalities, which often continued the age-old communal traditions, the program of *baldío* sales resulted in a massive privatization of public lands throughout Castile. Many occupiers of other lands, who had titles of dubious validity, took advantage of the visit of a land commissioner to secure a title confirmation (*composición*) to avoid future problems over the question of ownership. The *baldío* sales program proved to be a major source of revenue for the royal treasury, reaching a peak in the 1580s, then tapering off after the best lands had been sold.

The Spanish brought to America their concept of *tierras baldías*, and applied it to all lands—beyond the recognized Indian[*] communities—that had not been granted by the Crown. As in Spain, the colonial *baldíos* were used as commons, pasture, hunting, and other purposes. And as in Spain, the *tierras baldías* were progressively diminished through illegal or quasi-legal occupation by ranchers and agriculturalists, who were later able to legitimize their claims through *composiciones*.

REFERENCE: David E. Vassberg, "The Spanish Background: Problems Concerning Ownership, Usurpations, and Defense of Common Lands in 16th Century Castile," *Journal of the West*, 27 (1988), 12–23.

David E. Vassberg

TITHES. In the Spanish colonies of the New World, the Roman Catholic Church[*] granted the Crown the authority to collect tithes—a 10 percent tax on agricultural products—if the government would agree to build and maintain ecclesiastical buildings. A papal bull[*] in 1501 permitted this cooperative arrangement between Church and state. The Crown was also authorized to retain one-ninth of all monies collected for its own profits. Because the *encomienda*[*] was a substitute for the tax, most Indians[*] were exempt from paying tithes.

REFERENCE: William E. Sheils, *King and Church: The Rise and Fall of the Patronato Real*, 1961.

TLAXCALA. The Tlaxcalteca, Hernán Cortés's[*] allies in the conquest of the México, or Aztec[*], and of much of New Spain[*], were a group of loosely allied, independent states occupying the area that roughly comprises the present Mexican state of Tlaxcala. The Nahuatl[*]-speaking Tlaxcalteca were one of the Chichimeca[*] tribes that traced its ancestry to the legendary Seven Caves, Chicomostoc. As late arrivals, they displaced Otomí[*]-speaking groups. Thus, although there was an Otomí minority in the sixteenth century, the majority in Tlaxcala spoke Nahuatl.

In the 1420s, the great Acolhua *tlatoani* (leader, or literally "he who speaks"), Nezhaulcoyotl ("hungry coyote"), who was fleeing the wrath of Tezozomoc and Maxtla of Azcapotzalco, sought refuge for six years in Tlaxcala. When the Mexica of Tenochtitlán and the Acolhua of Texcoco rose in rebellion against Maxtla, the Tlaxcalteca and Huexotzinca came to their assistance. Despite this early alliance, the subsequent history of relations between Tlaxcala and its former allies was one of conflict. The military alliance of the independent states that composed Tlaxcala was probably a response to the threat of conquest by the Triple Alliance (Mexica, Acolhua, and Tepanec of Tlacopan).

The Flower Wars[*] (*xochiyaoyotl*) between the Triple Alliance and the states of the Puebla[*]/Tlaxcala Valley (Tlaxcala, Huexotzinco, and Cholollan) began during Motecuhzoma I's[*] reign (1440–1468) in Tenochtitlán and continued intermittently until the Spanish conquest. The function of these flower wars and whether the Triple Alliance could have conquered Tlaxcala or not are questions still debated. Ross Hassig has argued that the flower wars against Tlaxcala were low-intensity conflicts designed to encircle and economically strangle while allowing Triple Alliance expansion elsewhere. Tlaxcala's relations with its erstwhile allies, Huexotzinco and Cholollan,, were characterized as frequently by conflict as by cooperation. Early in the fifteenth century, Huexotzinco was more powerful than Tlaxcala. By the time of the Spanish conquest, Tlaxcala had become the more powerful of the two, and Cholollan had aligned itself with the Triple Alliance.

At the time of the conquest, Maxixcatzin, the *tlatoani* of Ocotelulco, was the supreme military commander of the Tlaxcalan forces. He and the *tlatoani* of Tizatlan exercised political control over neighboring Tlaxcalteca states. In the colonial period, Tlaxcala was divided for administrative purposes into four quadrants governed by the *gobernadores* of Ocotelulco, Tizatlán, Tepeticpac, and Quiahuixtlán. Although this arrangement may have had native antecedents, Charles Gibson has argued that this was a Spanish introduction.

Hernán Cortés arrived in Tlaxcala in early September 1519. After losing two skirmishes (September 2 and 5), the Tlaxcalteca allied themselves with Cortés. Thousands of Tlaxcalteca warriors accompanied Cortés on his march to Tenochtitlán. Following the Spanish defeat by the Mexica in July 1520, Cortés sought refuge in Tlaxcala and used it as a base from which to launch his successful campaign the following year. The Tlaxcalteca provided warriors not only for the conquest of México Tenochtitlán but also for many of the other Spanish campaigns in Mexico and northern Central America. Consequently, Tlaxcalan place names are widely distributed in Mexico, Central America, and even the southwestern United States.

As a reward for their service, the Tlaxcalteca states were not given individually in *encomienda** to Spanish conquistadors. Instead, Tlaxcala was placed in *encomienda* under Crown control. Furthermore, the tribute required of Tlaxcala was reduced. The city of Tlaxcala was founded by the Spaniards early in the colonial period and was located immediately south of the four colonial *cabeceras*.

REFERENCES: Diego Muñoz Camargo, *Historia de Tlaxcala*, 1892; Diego Muñoz Camargo, *Descripción de la ciudad y provincia de Tlaxcala*, 1981; Peter Gerhard, *Geografía Histórica de la Nueva España 1519–1821*, 1986; Charles Gibson, *Tlaxcala in the Sixteenth Century*, 1952; Ross Hassig, *Aztec Warfare*, 1988; Hugo Nutini, *San Bernardino Contla*, 1968; Hugo Nutini, *Ritual Kinship*, 1980; Hugo Nutini, *Todos Santos in Rural Tlaxcala*, 1988.

Edward B. Sisson

TOBACCO. Tobacco, or *nicotiana*, is a crop native to the New World, particularly to the Antilles. By the time of the Spanish conquest of the New World in the sixteenth century, tobacco leaves were smoked by various Native American peoples throughout North America, South America, and the Caribbean. Europeans quickly adopted the practice during the conquest period, and smoking spread to Europe. There was a serious political struggle in Spain over its use in the sixteenth and early seventeenth centuries, because tobacco use was widely considered a bad habit at best and a sin at worst. Still, demand for the product grew rapidly, and in the 1620s, Spain began encouraging its production in Cuba*, Santo Domingo*, and Puerto Rico*, making tobacco a valuable cash crop. In 1717, the Spanish Crown established a monopoly over the tobacco trade. Similar monopolies were imposed in Peru* in 1752, Chile* in 1753, New Spain* in 1764, and New Granada* in 1766. Spain maintained the right to purchase all tobacco grown and imposed tariffs on it. Although tobacco planters protested the tight controls, Spain maintained the monopoly until 1818. The monopoly remained in effect in the Philippines* until 1881. Along with sugar*, tobacco was a major ingredient of commercial agricultural production in the New World.

REFERENCE: Henry Ridley, *The Dispersal of Plants Throughout the World*, 1930.

TOBAGO. Tobago was sighted by Christopher Columbus* at the beginning of his third voyage to the Indies, on July 31, 1498, while on his way to circumnavigating, christening, and settling Trinidad*, the larger neighboring island in the southeastern Caribbean. Columbus's expedition did not land on Tobago but proceeded directly on to the northern Caribbean, landing at Hispaniola*. Still, Columbus's sighting made it part of the early Spanish empire. Tobago changed hands between European powers, including Spain, more often than any other island in the Caribbean. Like most of the small islands of the Lesser Antilles, Tobago was the home of thousands of Amerindians in the late fifteenth century when the Spanish arrived. Large Karib* settlements existed, and this made Spanish colonization of the island most difficult and risky. Many European settlement attempts were made, with little success. In the process, the island began to produce significant amounts of tobacco[*] for traders in the southern region, and the island was widely identified as a corruption of the product, "Tobago". By the mid-1620's, British colonists, long aware of the island's fertile soil and the obvious lack of interest of Spain's informal claim, sought to posses it. Tobago was claimed by the British in 1626 as part of an acquisition by Thomas Warner, who had successfully colonized St. Christopher[*] for the British at the other end of the Antilles a couple of years earlier. The following year, 1627, the island was included in a grant made by Charles I of England to the Earl of Montgomery, but when English settlers from this transaction arrived, they were attacked by the occupying Karibs who were reinforced by other warriors from neighboring islands and the mainland, to the delight of the Spanish colonists who occupied neighboring Trinidad. This repulsion of the English did not dampen their interest in possessing Tobago. Together with Dutch settlers, they worked at creating a hegemony in small parts of the island a few years later.

By the mid-1630s, the English and Dutch influence and trade on Tobago had grown considerably, and the Spanish governor on neighboring Trinidad became apprehensive about the increasing non-Spanish trading activity on the island. He therefore planned a military attack to keep away the non-Spanish presence. In November 1636, the Spanish governor of Trinidad personally headed a Spanish military contingent to force these European intruders out of Tobago. The small Spanish expedition from Trinidad found a fort on Tobago and an international coalition of settlers ready to defend the island. A force of English, Dutch, French and Flemish settlers, as well as persons of African descent on Tobago, were caught unprepared, and the Spanish troops were enough to defeat the international hodge-podge, forcing them to leave Tobago. Spain had made its claim to the island, but never effectively colonized this close neighbor of Spanish Trinidad. Six years later, the British made another serious attempt to settle Tobago and wrest it away from the Spanish Empire, but they were unable to become the sole possessor of this Caribbean prize. For over a century, the British, Dutch, and French contested among themselves for possession of Tobago, which lies about 20 miles northeast of Spanish Trinidad.

In 1642, James, Duke of Courland sent out two shiploads of British settlers. A dozen years later, Dutch settlers financed by two Flushing merchants established themselves on the island's southern coast. A dispute between the Dutch and English groups arose, and in 1658 the Courlanders were completely overpowered by the Dutch, who remained in sole possession of the whole island until 1662. During that year, Cornelius Lampsius, one of the founders of the Dutch settlement on Tobago, was made Baron of Tobago and became proprietor of the island. Tobago became a Dutch dependency under title from the Crown of France. For the next 140 years, the British and the French struggled for complete possession of Tobago. The island changed hands between these powers several more times during the next 100 years, but by then, Spain had resigned itself to not having Tobago in its empire.

REFERENCES: Algernon Aspinall, *The Pocket Guide to the West Indies*, 1935; Samuel E. Morison, *Admiral of the Ocean Sea, A Life of Christopher Columbus*, 2 vols. 1942; Eric Williams, *History of the People of Trinidad and Tobago*, 1982.

Glenn O. Phillips

TOLEDO Y FIGUEROA, FRANCISCO ÁLVAREZ DE. Francisco Álvarez de Toledo y Figueroa was born around 1515 in Spain and spent his career rising through the labyrinth of Spanish court politics and the colonial bureaucracy. In 1569, he received appointment as the fifth viceroy* of Peru*, and he kept that position until 1581. Toledo is remembered as one of the best of the Spanish colonial administrators. Immediately upon arriving in Lima*, he went on an extensive tour of the viceroyalty, trying to provide himself with enough direct information to make informed judgements. Toledo was committed to establishing political order, social welfare, and economic development throughout the viceroyalty. During his tenure there, he established the *mita* labor system to build and maintain public works and detailed codes to govern mining*, irrigation, finance, labor relations, and treatment of the Indians*. Toledo also carried out a widespread resettlement of scattered groups of Indians. Although Toledo was considered an enlightened figure, as least compared to many colonial administrators, he decided in 1572 to execute Túpac Amaru* and the Inca* royal family as a way of subduing the Quechua*-speaking Indians of the viceroyalty. Toledo left his post in Lima in 1581 and died in 1582.

REFERENCE: Roberto Levillier, ed., *Don Francisco de Toledo, supremo organizador del Perú: Su vida, su obra (1515–1582)*, 2 vols., 1935–1940.

TOLSA, MANUEL. Manuel Tolsa was born in Enbuerra, Spain, in 1757. He studied art and sculpture at the academy in Valencia, and in 1790, he went to New Spain* as a professor of sculpture and director of the Academy of San Carlos. Tolsa became one of the colony's leading architects and sculptors. Tolsa's best-known works of art include the facade of the cathedral in Mexico City*— especially the balustrades, the clocktower statues, and the cupola—and the equestrian statue "El Caballito," a depiction of King Charles IV*, which is located today on the Paseo de la Reforma in Mexico City. Tolsa's style was neo-classical. He died in Mexico City on December 25, 1815.

REFERENCE: F. Almela y Vives and A. Igual Ubeda, *El arquitecto y escultor valenciano Manuel Tolsa, 1757–1816*, 1950.

TOLTEC. The Toltec, from Toltecatl literally meaning an "inhabitant of Tollan," ruled a Mesoamerican empire that flourished between A.D. 950 and 1150–1200. Native histories regarded the Toltec as culture heroes, as the creators of human culture. Thus, Toltec came to mean someone who was civilized, educated, and an artisan, or skilled worker. The dynasties of later states sought to legitimize their right to rule by tracing their ancestry to legendary Toltec rulers. Approximately 40 miles north of Mexico City*, the Toltec capital of Tula, or Tollan, is located at the confluence of the Río Tula and Río Rosas near the

modern city of Tula, Hidalgo. The name Tollan means place of reeds, or met-
aphorically, place with many people, a metropolis. Today, the area around Tula
is semiarid and has thin, poor soils. Agriculture is risky without irrigation; the
typical xerophytic vegetation includes mesquite, maguey, and nopal. Archaeological and ethnohistoric data indicate that there has been a severe degradation
of the environment since the Spanish conquest. Earlier, there was more grassland
on the uplands and denser forests along the stream bottoms. The Aztecs* referred
to the area as Teotlalpan, land or garden of the gods; writing in the sixteenth
century, Fray Bernardino de Sahagún* reported abundant crops of maize, squash,
chilis, maguey, cotton, and cacao*.

Tula is strategically located with easy access to the Bajío of Querétaro and
Guanajuato* to the north and west, to the Gulf coast to the east and to the Valley
of Mexico to the south. The immediate area has rich lime deposits, and the
source of the highest quality obsidian in Mexico is nearby. The Toltecs were
not the first to take advantage of these resources. Hamlets and a hilltop center
dating from around 400 to 200 B.C. have been discovered in the area. During
the Early Classic period (ca. A.D. 300–600), Teotihuacán established Chingu, a
provincial center six miles east of Tula, to control the exploitation of lime
deposits. Following the collapse of the Teotihuacan Empire, the area was
abandoned.

Analysis of the ceramics associated with the next inhabitants, the first to inhabit
the archaeological site of Tula (ca. A.D. 700–800), indicates strong ties with the
Bajío. The Coyotlatelco ceramics from the period from ca. A.D. 800–900 are
influenced by those from the Valley of Mexico. The architecture and layout from
Tula Chico are innovations and foreshadow those of Tula Grande, the ceremonial
and administrative center of Tula during its apogee. Dating from ca. A.D. 900–
1000, the distinctive Mazapán ceramic style, with its multiple wavy red lines
on a brown ground, is also like that from the Valley of Mexico and is concentrated
in the southern part of Tula.

These archaeological data are consistent with the ethnohistoric data that indicate that Toltec society was multi-ethnic. Ethnic groups living in Tula included
the Tolteca-Chichimeca* and the Nonoalca. The Tolteca-Chichimeca spoke Nahuatl* and/or Otomí* and traced their origin to the Seven Caves, Chicomoztoc,
located somewhere to the north. The Nonoalca spoke Nahuatl (Popoloca, Mixtec,
Mazatec, and Maya* are other possibilities) and migrated to Tula from the Gulf
coast via Tulancingo in eastern Hidalgo. These immigrants may have been small
groups of elites who organized peoples drawn from the surrounding region.
Beginning ca. A.D. 950, the size and population of Tula grew rapidly. The
ceremonial and administrative center of the city shifted from Tula Chico to Tula
Grande one kilometer to the south. This became the center of a planned, densely
populated city covering 13 square kilometers. Estimates of the population range
from 40,000 to 60,000 or more. Although some may have been farmers, the
great majority of the inhabitants were artisans, specialized craftsmen, and administrators. An additional 60,000 farmers lived in the surrounding countryside.

The largest group of occupational specialists that has been identified archaeo-
logically is the obsidian workers. At first, the obsidian source of Zinapécuaro
in Michoacán provided the bulk of the raw material; through time, the nearby
Pachuca source provided more and more of it. Excavations of workshops indicate
that this was a cottage industry. Control of the Pachuca obsidian may have been
one source of Toltec political and economic power.

Because of the importance of the Toltec in native histories, it was assumed
that they controlled a vast empire. At one time, the ruins of Teotihuacán were
attributed to the Toltec. Wigberto Jiménez Moreno's analysis of contemporary
and ethnohistoric place names, however, conclusively demonstrated that Tula,
not the earlier Teotihuacán, was the Toltec capital. Tula was one of several
regional capitals that flourished in the political vacuum created by the collapse
of Teotihuacán. At its peak, the Toltec empire controlled most of Hidalgo, the
northern Valley of Mexico, parts of the Bajío, and perhaps part of the Toluca
Valley.

In the second half of the twelfth century, the Toltec empire collapsed. The
reasons for its demise are poorly understood. Incursions by Chichimeca groups
from the north and by Huaxtecs from the east have been suggested. There is
evidence that buildings in the ceremonial center were burned, but there is no
such evidence from the residential areas. It is impossible to determine whether
the city was sacked and burned during an invasion, leading to the empire's
collapse, or whether the burning occurred after the empire's decline. Native
histories from the period of the Spanish conquest attribute the Toltec decline to
internal conflict between the rival forces of Topiltzin Quetzalcoátl and either
Tezcatlipoca or Huémac. In one story, Quetzalcoátl is the priestly ruler who is
a patron of the arts and artisans and who abhors human sacrifice. Tezcatlipoca
is a warrior who introduces human sacrifice. Tricked by Tezcatlipoca, Quetz-
alcoatl and his Nonoalca followers flee Tula. In one version, he disappears on
a raft in the eastern sea, the Gulf of Mexico. In a second, he immolates himself.
Huémac, a later ruler, flees Tula for Chapultepec in the Valley of Mexico. In
another story, the conflict is between Quetzalcóatl and Huémac, both of whom
flee Tula.

The first version above is often cited in connection with the architectural and
iconographic similarities between Tula and the Maya[*] city of Chichén Itzá in the
northern Yucatán[*]. The traditional interpretation has been that the Toltec elite, led
by Quetzalcóatl, invaded Chichén Itzá, took control of the city and its Maya population, and rebuilt the city in the image of Tula. Recent work by Mayanists has
indicated that many of the ''Toltec'' innovations at Chichén Itzá have local antecedents. Some investigators now argue that the influence flowed from Chichén Itzá
to Tula. Others argue that ''Mexicanized'' Maya from Tabasco, not Toltec from Tula,
introduced the architectural innovations to Chichen Itza.

It is still not clear how to reconcile the relatively small size of the Toltec
empire, the archaeological data from Chichén Itzá, the various stories about
Quetzalcóatl, the fact that the Quiché Maya elite of highland Guatemala[*] legi-

timized its right to rule by claiming Toltec descent, and linguistic data documenting the appearance in the eleventh or twelfth century of Nahuat-speakers along the Pacific coast of Guatemala and El Salvador*. The ethnohistoric and linguistic data documenting a movement of "Toltec" peoples into the Valley of Mexico, the Puebla-Tlaxcala* Valley, the Tehuacán Valley, and adjacent parts of highland Veracruz is less problematic. This movement, begun during the Toltec apogee, accelerated with the collapse of Tula.

REFERENCES: Richard A. Diehl, *Tula, the Toltec Capital of Ancient Mexico*, 1983; Dan M. Healan, *Tula of the Toltecs*, 1989; Nigel Davies, *The Toltecs until the Fall of Tula*, 1977.

Edward B. Sisson

TORDESILLAS, TREATY OF. In 1493, the Spanish rulers Ferdinand* and Isabella* enlisted papal support to settle disputed land claims with Portugal. Pope Alexander VI* issued four papal bulls that year to resolve conflicting claims over lands explored by Christopher Columbus* and other fifteenth-century voyagers. The first two bulls, *Inter caetera* and *Eximiae devotionis*, confirmed Spain's claims to lands discovered or to be discovered in the West. The third, *Inter caetera*, fixed the north-south line of demarcation along a meridian passing 100 leagues west of the Azores and Cape Verde Islands. Spain was awarded lands west and south of the line, with Portugal receiving lands east and south. The fourth bull, *Dudum siquidem*, extended Spanish grants to include islands and mainland as far as and including India and the Indies. Although King John II of Portugal recognized the pope's authority to allot temporal sovereignty, he was dissatisfied with the pope's disposition because he believed Portugal's claims were insufficently affirmed, which would restrict the movements of its ships trading with its African colonies.

As a result of direct diplomacy, Spain and Portugal concluded the Treaty of Tordesillas on June 7, 1494. The treaty established a new line of demarcation 370 leagues west of the Cape Verde Islands, placing all of Africa, India, and later, Brazil within Portugal's sphere. The treaty was later confirmed by a papal bull, *Ea Quae*, issued by Pope Julius in 1506. As a result of the treaty, relative peace was maintained between Portugal and Spain, since their spheres of influence were realistically defined. Their resources could be directed toward exploration and development of the discoveries rather than war. In fact, the treaty even provided Portugal with the unexpected bonus of New World territory when Brazil was discovered in 1500. The treaty's details, however, remained in dispute until 1777, when both countries simply agreed to drop the matter. In the meantime, the other European powers did not consider themselves to be bound by the treaty and soon began poaching on the Portuguese and Spanish discoveries. Francis I of France spoke for them all when he quipped, "I should very much like to see the passage in Adam's will that divides the New World between my brothers, the Emperor Charles V* [of Spain] and the King of Portugal."

REFERENCE: Charles Edward Nowell, "The Treaty of Tordesillas and the Diplomatic Background of American History," in *Greater America: Essays in Honor of Herbert Eugene Bolton*, 1945.

Michael Dennis

TORQUEMADA, JUAN DE. Juan de Torquemada was born in Spain around 1563 and came to New Spain* as a Franciscan* missionary when he was still a young man. Between 1614 and 1617, Torquemada was the provincial superior of the Franciscans in New Spain, but he is best remembered as a scholar and historian. In 1615, Torquemada published his monumental history of the Franciscans in New Spain—*Monarquia indiana*. Although he borrowed heavily from the earlier work of Gerónimo de Mendieta*, Torquemada's effort is still an important source for historians of colonial Mexico. He died in Mexico City in 1624.

REFERENCE: *New Catholic Encyclopedia*, XIV:204, 1967.

Fred Koestler

TORRE, CARLOS DE LA. Carlos de la Torre was born in Matanzas Province, Cuba*, in 1858. He studied medicine at the University of Havana* and later received a doctorate in natural sciences from the Central University of Madrid. Torre spent his career as a professor of zoology at the University of Havana, but his anticolonial politics angered Spanish officials. Spanish harassment drove him to Mexico during the 1890s, where he taught science in Chihuahua. He returned to the University of Havana when Cuban independence was achieved in 1898. Torre became a founding member of the Nationalist Party and spent the early 1900s serving in the national legislature. He returned to teaching and research in 1905 and spent the rest of his life at the University of Havana. Carlos de la Torre died in 1930.

REFERENCES: Jaime Suchlicki, *Historical Dictionary of Cuba*, 1988; Jaime Suchlicki, *Cuba: From Columbus to Castro*, 1986.

TORREJÓN Y VELASCO, TOMÁS DE. Tomás de Torrejón y Velasco was born in Villarrobledo, Spain, on December 23, 1644. During his childhood, he served as a page in the household of the Count of Lemos. When the count became viceroy* of Peru*, Torrejón accompanied him to Lima*, arriving there in November 1667. After the count's death, Torrejón served as *justicia mayor* in Chachapoyas, Peru, and in 1676, he was appointed chapelmaster of the cathedral in Lima. During his 52-year tenure at the cathedral, Torrejón became known throughout the Hispanic world as a gifted composer and musician. In 1701, his opera *La Estrella de Lima* was performed to celebrate the birthday of Philip V*. Torrejón died in Lima on April 23, 1728.

REFERENCE: *New Catholic Encyclopedia*, XIV:205–06, 1967.

TORRES, CAMILO. Camilo Torres was born in Popayán*, New Granada*, in 1766. A *criollo** who resented Spanish authority, Torres was an outspoken member of the consultative assembly of the viceroyalty of New Granada*. In 1809, he issued his famous *Memorial of Grievances and Rights*, which became the intellectual theme of the Colombian independence movement. When the first junta was established in Colombia* in 1810, Torres served as secretary of state. He believed in a federalist political theory rather than in centralism. Torres was president of the Congress of Leiva and head of the United Provinces of Colombia from 1812 to 1814. Spanish forces captured Torres in 1816 and executed him for treason.

REFERENCES: Robert H. Davis, *Historical Dictionary of Colombia*, 1977; Luis María Sánchez López, *Diccionario de Escritores Colombianos*, 1978.

TORRES BOLLO, DIEGO DE. Diego de Torres Bollo was born in Villalpando, Spain, in 1551. He entered the Jesuit* order in 1571 and was ordained in 1580. Torres went to the New World in the late 1580s and served as superior of Juli, Peru*, and then as rector in Cuzco*, Peru; Quito*, Ecuador*; and Potosí*, Bolivia*. Between 1600 and 1604, Torres represented the order in Rome. He returned to the New World to establish a vice-province in New Granada in 1605 and a province in Paraguay* in 1607. Torres is credited with sending the two first two Jesuit missionaries to found the Jesuit reductions* among the Guaraní* at the end of 1609. In 1615, Torres became rector of the Jesuit school in Córdoba*, Argentina*. He died on August 8, 1638, in Chuquisaca, Bolivia*.

REFERENCE: R. V. Ugarte, "El P. Diego de Torres Bollo y el cardenal Federico Borromeo: Correspondencia inédita," *Boletín del Instituto de investigaciones históricas, Universidad Nacional, Buenos Aires*, 17 (1933–1934), 59–82.

TORRE TAGLE Y PORTOCARRERO, JOSÉ BERNARDO DE. José Bernardo de Torre Tagle y Portocarrero was born in Lima*, Peru*, in 1779, to a noble family. He was actually the fourth Marqués of Torre Tagle. He was serving as governor of Trujillo*, Peru*, when he proclaimed the region independent of Spain on December 29, 1820. In 1822, General José de San Martín* named Torre Tagle as acting chief executive of Peru, and in July 1823, when Spanish forces evacuated Lima, General Antonio de Sucre* named Torre Tagle president of Peru. In September 1823, Torre Tagle voluntarily surrendered that position to Simón Bolívar*. Torre Tagle died in 1841.

REFERENCE: Raul Garbin D., *Diccionario biográfico del Perú*, 1943.

TORTUGA. Tortuga is a small island, approximately 32 miles long by five miles wide, located off the northern coast of Haiti*, eight miles from Port-au-Paix. Today part of Haiti, Tortuga was once Spanish property, but in the early 1600s, as Spanish fortunes began to decline, French pirates* began using the island as a base for attacking Spanish shipping in the Caribbean. During the mid-1600s, those French pirates played a key role in the French conquest of western Hispaniola* and the founding of Haiti.

TOTONACS. The Totonac Indians resided in the coastal and adjacent mountain regions of eastern Mexico at the time of the Spanish arrival. The region of the Totonac was called Totonacapan and extended roughly from Papantla in the north to Cempoala in the south. Totonacapan was largely hot and humid. Aside from the usual agricultural crops of maize, squash, beans, and chilis, the region was noted for its production of liquid amber and cotton. Cultivation of foodstuffs was reliable even during the disastrous central Mexican famine of 1450–1454, when many Aztecs* were forced to sell themselves or their family members as slaves to the Totonac in exchange for subsistence maize. Totonac women were expert weavers and embroiderers; they dressed grandly and braided their hair with feathers. The Franciscan* friar Bernardino de Sahagún* stated that, in all aspects of their appearance, the women were "quite elegant." Likewise, the men dressed well, adorning themselves with multicolored clothing, necklaces, arm bands, and devices made of the prized quetzal feathers.

The region of Totonacapan was subject to Aztec military incursions from the mid-fifteenth century until the Spanish arrival. Despite the establishment of Aztec fortifications throughout the region, rebellion was endemic. Major Totonac centers were Papantla, with an estimated population of 60,000 in 1519, Jalapa (around 120,000), and Cempoala (around 80,000). Cempoala was the first major Indian* center encountered by Hernán Cortés* in his march to the Aztec capital of Tenochtitlán*. The Totonacs of Cempoala joined forces with Cortés and, along with the Tlaxcallan* Indians, contributed significantly to the Spanish conquest. Totonacapan became incorporated into the Spanish regime with comparatively little violence, but the region was ravaged by epidemic diseases during the sixteenth century. Today, approximately 90,000 Totonac speakers reside in the region.

REFERENCES: I. Bernal and E. Dávalos, *Huastecos y Totonacos*, 1953; H. R. Harvey and Isabel Kelly, "The Totonac," in *Handbook of Middle American Indians*, 1969; Isabel Kelly and Ángel Palerm, *The Tajín Totonac*, 1952.

Frances F. Berdan

TRIBUTE (AZTEC). By the time of the Spanish arrival in 1519, the Aztec* empire controlled a large portion of central and southern Mexico. That empire was formed through an alliance of three city-states in the Valley of Mexico (Tenochtitlán*, Texcoco, and Tlacopan) for purposes of military conquest and economic control over conquered peoples. They achieved the latter through the imposition of tribute. When the Aztes succeeded in a military conquest, they demanded that the defeated peoples pay them tribute in goods readily available to them. In most cases, this meant extracting resources produced in that region itself, but at times also referred to goods that filtered into the region through an extensive marketplace system.

Tribute in goods was demanded on a regular schedule from 39 conquered provinces. It was due every 80 days, twice a year, or annually. Clothing was given almost always, feathered warrior costumes and staple foodstuffs (such as maize, beans and chilis) usually, and other items if locally available. These included precious materials, such as jadeite, turquoise, gold, and tropical feathers, as well as more ordinary items, such as reed mats, lumber, gourd bowls, and honey. In addition, these and other conquered city states paid tribute at extraordinary events, such as a ruler's coronation or the dedication of an important temple. Aside from the usual payment in goods, tribute also took other forms: labor on public projects and in rulers' palaces, contributions of troops for Aztec military expeditions, feeding mobile Aztec troops, or provisioning a nearby military garrison.

For the collection of tribute, the Aztec overlords typically placed tribute collectors (*calpixque*) in each conquered district. These officials were, to believe the reports of the Spanish conquistadors[*], quite overbearing and greatly feared in the provinces. Tribute collected by the *calpixque* was used for a variety of purposes. These included support of administrative and military activities, maintenance of the royal palaces, gifts and commissions (especially to valiant warriors), underwriting foreign trade, subsistence support of urban populations, and reserves for emergency situations (such as flooding or famine). In essence, tribute collections contributed substantially to the growth of the imperial urban centers and to the lavish lifestyles of Aztec rulers and high-ranking nobles.

REFERENCES: Frances Berdan, *The Aztecs of Central Mexico*, 1982; Frances Berdan and Jacqueline de Durand-Forest, *The Matrícula de Tributos*, 1980; James Cooper Clark, *The Codex Mendoza*, 1938; Nigel Davies, *The Aztec Empire*, 1987.

Frances F. Berdan

TRINIDAD. Trinidad lies a short distance off northeastern South America in the southern Caribbean. Geologists contend that the 1,862-square-mile island was once part of the mainland. This fertile island, the largest of the Lesser Antilles, has three distinct mountain ranges. Trinidad was first sighted by Christopher Columbus[*] on his third voyage to the Americas on July 31, 1498. Columbus called it after the Trinity on viewing the three very conspicuous peaks in its southern range. The Spanish did not obtain a permanent foothold on the island until 1592, but following soon after Columbus's sighting, other Spanish authorized expeditions came into very close proximity to Trinidad. Two of these were led by Amerigo Vespucci[*] (1499) and Alonso de Ojeda[*] (1502). During the early sixteenth century, some Spanish entrepreneurs illegally used the Indian[*] population on Trinidad to supply the increasing demand for slave labor in other parts of the Indies.

The first serious Spanish colonization attempt was made during 1532 when Don Antonio Sedeño was appointed the Spanish governor and made a settlement at present-day Macurapo. Other unsuccessful efforts were made. Most of them were stimulated by the legend of El Dorado[*]. Spain's greater interest in the more lucrative gold and silver trade allowed for the colony's being almost completely neglected for most of Spain's nearly 300-year rule of Trinidad. In 1592, the town of San José de Oruna was founded seven miles inland as a symbol of

Spanish possession and made the colony's capital. Governor Antonio de Berrío wrote to Spain's King Philip II* in November 1593 that Trinidad was "very fruitful" but observed that "I have only 70 men, yet in this island there are more than 6,000 war Indians." He went on to plead for resources and military protection, but this request went unheeded. Less than two years later, the English explorer Sir Walter Raleigh easily sacked the Trinidad capital, arrested the Spanish governor, and explored the rest of the colony. On Trinidad at "Tierra de Brea," Raleigh was introduced to the "Piche" with which he caulked his ships before sailing away, thereby publicizing the famous Pitch Lake.

The early seventeenth century ushered in a period of massive contraband tobacco* trade in Trinidad that included significant numbers of British and Dutch merchants. Early in 1618, Dr. Salcedo de Merva wrote from Trinidad to the Spanish Crown announcing the beginning of a cacao* industry and requesting slaves to develop it. In order to survive, the Spanish authorities and citizens at Trinidad relied more and more on illegal trade, particularly with the British, French, and Dutch entrepreneurs. The Spanish monopoly system that was the backbone of Spanish economic prosperity was not very effective in Trinidad because Spain was unable to cater to the growing needs of this potentially vibrant colony systematically. The Spanish colonists constantly complained to the authorities in Spain about total neglect of their colony, to no avail. Consequently, poverty and the lack of colonial defenses continued. The main seaport of the colony, Puerto de España, was repeatedly attacked, and it was burnt several times until in 1678 it was resettled near the mouth of the Caroní River.

In spite of Trinidad's lack of silver and gold and its distance from the centers of Spain's commercial activity in the empire, the Spanish government in Madrid attempted to develop and maintain Spanish institutions within the colony. This included the unrealistic monopolistic trading system, the governmental administrative structure, including the offices of the *cabildo**, *alcaldes ordinarios**, *alguacil mayor**, *alferez*, and *regidores**, as well as the role of the Church, all of which suffered from a lack of capable Spanish personnel.

During the early eighteenth century, the fortunes of Spanish Trinidad remained the same; its citizens experienced neglect and hardship but the new cacao industry slowly began to show promising signs as an alternate crop export and brought a brief prosperity until its collapse in 1733. Other setbacks followed, including a widespread smallpox* epidemic in 1741, and so the colony rapidly became depopulated. It was not until the 1780s, when French from neighboring Grenada were allowed to migrate to Trinidad and were given attractive incentives, that the colony began to live up to its economic potential. Between 1777 and 1797, the population increased from 3,432 to 17,718, with the highest percentages arriving after 1783 along with an increased African slave* population that finally surpassed the free population in the early 1790s. During the 1790s, Spanish Trinidad attracted French colonists from Grenada, Martinique*, Guadeloupe*, St. Lucia*, and Cayenne. Before long, a French planter elite, including the St. Laurent family, dominated the colony. On the other hand, the government was effectively administered by Spanish Governor Don José María Chacón. Still militarily unprotected from the growing British naval presence in the region, Spain's declaration of war against Britain in October 1796, on account of events in Europe, precipitated a British invasion within a couple of months. Spain's control of Trinidad was in its final days. On February 12, 1797, a British expedition under Sir Ralph Abercromby and Admiral Harvey left Martinique to capture Trinidad. Almost without a fight, Governor Chacón surrendered Trinidad to Abercromby, and the general's aide-de-camp, Thomas Picton, was appointed the first English governor of Trinidad. The cession was formally confirmed by the Treaty of Amiens in 1802.

REFERENCES: Bridget Brereton, *A History of Modern Trinidad 1783-1962*, 1985; Linda A. Newson, *Aboriginal and Spanish Colonial Trinidad*, 1976; Eric Williams, *A History of the People of Trinidad and Tobago*, 1982.

Glenn O. Phillips

TRUJILLO. Trujillo, Honduras*, was established around 1526 by Francisco de Las Casas, the leader of the expedition sent by Hernán Cortés* to arrest Cristóbal de Olid*, who had defied Cortés and declared his independence in Triunfo de la Cruz, Honduras. Las Casas established Trujillo, located on the Caribbean coast, to serve as a Spanish port and as a center of gold mining*. In its early years, Trujillo prospered due to the presence of alluvial gold, panned for Spanish use by Indian* labor. In 1540, Trujillo produced 10,000 pesos worth of gold, making it the most productive Spanish settlement in Honduras. In 1542, Trujillo produced 15,000 pesos worth of gold. By 1550, Trujillo's gold had nearly played out, and the town began to decline in importance.

Trujillo was also an important source of sarsaparilla, which for a short time was Central America's most important export to Europe. There it was credited with almost magical qualities and thought to cure syphilis, scrofula, fever, and plague. Trujillo's sarsaparilla was considered to be best in Indies in the late sixteenth century, and the city exported large quantities of the root. At the height of the sarsaparilla trade in the 1580s, between 75 and 125 pounds of the root were exported to Spain annually.

Like gold before it, the sarsaparilla boom was short-lived in Trujillo. The wild sarsaparilla growing near the city was quickly exhausted, forcing Indian laborers to travel leagues away to harvest the crop. Moreover, collecting the root was an unhealthy and dangerous task that involved wading in brackish, malarial waters. Harvest times also coincided with local sowing and harvest seasons. In a short time, the exigencies of the sarsaparilla industry caused widespread death and starvation, which precipitated a severe shortage in Indian labor. Nonetheless, sarsaparilla continued to be important crop for Trujillo until the mid-seventeenth century, when demand for the root declined in Europe and its price dropped dramatically.

As a port, Trujillo flourished only briefly. Trujillo was the first Caribbean port in Central America, but when the gold ran out in the mid-sixteenth century and the city declined in importance, Puerto Caballos, 40 leagues to the west, became the primary port for Honduras. Although its importance as a port was minimal by the seventeenth century, Trujillo suffered many incursions by foreign privateers intent on harassing Spanish settlements and diverting the wealth of the Spanish Empire to northern Europe. In 1643, the Dutch captured and sacked Trujillo, nearly destroying the city. From 1660 to 1668, the famous English pirate* Henry Morgan raided Trujillo and used it as a base for contraband trade. Despite a royal order in 1660 that Trujillo should be defended, financial considerations prevailed, and the Spanish virtually abandoned the port until 1789. In 1797, the British attacked the city again. On this one occasion, Spanish defenses proved adequate to the task, and Trujillo successfully vanquished the British invaders.

REFERENCE: Murdo J. MacLeod, *Spanish Central America: A Socioeconomic History, 1520-1720*, 1973.

Virginia Garrard Burnett

TRUJILLO. The region around Trujillo in northern Peru* was set up as a *intendencia* within the viceroyalty of Peru* in 1784. Spanish authority in the region ended when Simón Bolívar's* troops occupied Trujillo in 1824. Trujillo later became part of the republic of Peru.

TRUJILLO, DIOCESE OF. The Roman Catholic diocese of Trujillo was established by Pope Gregory XIII in 1577, but his order was never implemented; in 1609, Pope Paul V re-established it. It was raised to an archbishopric in 1943.

REFERENCE: *New Catholic Encyclopedia*, XIV:323, 1967.

TUCUMÁN. Late in the 1540s, settlers from Peru* began moving into the area of Tucumán in what is today northern Argentina*. Spain set up a province there in 1550 with Juan Núñez del Prado serving as the first governor. For the next century, Tucumán was the jewel of Argentina, the most densely populated and prosperous colony in the region. By 1650, however, Buenos Aires* was rapidly eclipsing Tucumán. Tucumán was under the jurisdiction of the *audiencia* of Charcas* until 1776, when the viceroyalty of Río de la Plata* was created. Tucumán ceased to exist as an administrative unit in 1783 when the Spanish Crown imposed the *intendencia* system. Tucumán was divided into two *intendencias*: Córdoba* and Salta*.

TUCUMÁN, CONGRESS OF. Following the revolution of May 1810, the United Provinces of the Río de la Plata* was created. The confederation included the modern states of Argentina*, Uruguay*, Paraguay*, and southern Bolivia*. By 1816, however, events in South America had changed. The revolution in the north under Simón Bolívar* had been suppressed, and neighboring Chile* was again under Spanish control. The new federation had also found it difficult to maintain political unity, having suffered a succession of revolutionary governments. In March 1816, a constituent congress convened in the northwestern Argentine city of Tucumán* to address many of these problems. Invitations had been sent to Montevideo*, Paraguay, and Upper Peru*. No delegates came from the first two regions and only a few from the last. The 29 delegates to the congress formally declared independence from Spain on July 9, 1819. The most pressing need, however, was to find an acceptable form of government. Pervading the congress was a climate of fear brought about by the incidence of popular violence throughout the country, a trend toward provincial autonomy, and the rise of caudillos*. Further complicating the question of unity, the delegates were not of one mind about the nature of the new government. Many had no exact idea of what they wanted. Some advocated a republican form of government, while those who feared anarchy wanted a monarch.

After declaring independence, the congress created the United Provinces of South America* and appointed Juan Martín de Pueyrredón*, a noted anti-federalist, as supreme dictator. There was some attempt either to establish a European monarch or to restore the Inca* dynasty but nothing ever came of this. Public sentiment was against a monarchy and favored a constitutional republic. By 1820, the United Provinces had fallen into disunity with Paraguay, Uruguay, and Bolivia breaking away and with caudillos in Argentina abetting separatism among the provinces in that country. As a result, the Congress of Tucumán was forced to disband in 1820. The Congress, however, marked a turning point in South American history, establishing the May Revolution* as the goal for the entire continent.

REFERENCE: José Luis Romero, *A History of Argentine Political Thought*, 1963.

Michael Dennis

TÚPAC AMARU. Túpac Amaru was the last of the Inca* emperors. He was born in 1545, about a decade after the conquest of Peru* by the Pizarro* brothers. In the dynastic struggle during the late 1520s and early 1530s between Húascar* and Atahualpa*, the Inca royal family had become badly divided, and Túpac Amaru inherited an imperial position that had lost much of its original power. In the 1570s, however, Spanish authorities were still worried about the possibility of an Indian* uprising, particularly among the surviving, Quechua*-speaking Indians of the former Inca empire. Aware that the Indians still looked to Túpac Amaru for leadership, the Spanish realized that they posed at least a potential revolutionary threat. Early in the 1570s, Viceroy Francisco de Toledo* decided that the elimination of the Inca royal family was the best way to insure that such a rebellion did not materialize. That decision resulted in the execution of Túpac Amaru and his family in 1574.

REFERENCE: Burr Cartwright Brundage, *Lords of Cuzco: A History and Description of the Inca People in Their Final Days*, 1967.

TÚPAC AMARU II. Túpac Amaru II was christened José Gabriel Condorcanquí in 1742. Born into the Peruvian nobility, he was fifth in descent from Túpac Amaru* I, an earlier insurrectionist who was executed by the Spaniards in 1571.

Túpac received an excellent education at the College of Nobles in Cuzco* where he proved to be an outstanding student. At the age of twenty, he succeeded his father as cacique*, or chief, of Tinta (Tuita), an outlying province of the Cuzco region. The Spaniards acknowledged his Inca* descent with the title of Marques de Oropesa. Holding positions of power and prestige, he established a regular association with Spanish priests and officials. He earned his livelihood as a transport agent in the Andes, as the demand for gold, silver, maté, and salt was great.

Under the Spanish regime in Peru*, the native Indians* were at the bottom of the social ladder. They became legal minors or wards of the Spanish Crown. heir religion was suppressed, and their culture was violated. Túpac Amaru II was outraged as he watched the re-establishment of the *repartimiento*￼* and *mita*￼* in 1777. Túpac watched the Spaniards force Indians to work on Spanish-owned farms, serve on construction projects, and labor in the silver mines. He attempted to bring about reform through peaceful means. He first presented a petition to the attorney general in Lima*, asking that the Indians be exempted from paying the unfair labor taxes and performing servile labor. His request was denied. The attorney general claimed that Túpac lacked evidence to substantiate the exploitation of the Indians. In another petition, Túpac included all inhabitants of the Tinta province. That, too, went unheeded. Failing to win support for his measures, Túpac returned to Tinta in late 1778.

In early 1779, peasant unrest had become apparent in the Cuzco region. Taking this unrest as a sign of support, Túpac began to plan his strategy and to organize the rebellious forces. On November 4, 1780, Túpac captured the local *corregidor*￼*, Don Antonio Arriaga, a brutal tyrant who had committed outrages against the Indians. Túpac demanded the abolition of unfair taxes and the replacement of the Spanish-appointed *corregidores* with Indian governors. When these demands also went unheeded, Arriaga was tried and later brutally executed by being forced to drink molten gold in the public square of Tungasuca on November 10, 1780.

By the end of 1780, Túpac Amaru II was the self-proclaimed liberator of the people. This he did for personal and perhaps ideological reasons. Sharing power with the Indian, Tomás Catari*, Túpac initiated a nativist movement that was to last until 1783. Initial support for this movement came from the Indians, mestizos*, and *criollos*￼*. With the promise of rebirth for those who fell in battle against the Spaniards, Túpac gathered an estimated force of 200,000 men. Túpac's movement thus acquired a millenarian tone. He used his forces to wage a bloody war against the Spanish governors in hopes of driving them out of Peru. Thousands of lives were claimed as Túpac's forces, although not armed or trained as well as the Spanish army, fought courageously. Violence swept into Upper Peru and Ecuador*, leaving vast amounts of private property violated. The insurrection, now being led by the Indians, increasingly took on a racial quality. All mestizos and Spaniards were considered enemies, and the rebellious forces held more than 600 Spanish soldiers at Sangarara. All but 28 of these Spanish supporters were either burned or massacred in acts of terrorism that alienated many earlier supporters who then withdrew their support from the movement.

In 1781, by orders of Inspector General José del Valle*, Túpac Amaru II, his family, his captains, and thousands of his followers were captured, tortured, and savagely executed. Túpac's tongue was cut out, and he was drawn and quartered with the use of four horses. Finally, he was decapitated, and the Spanish government ordered that his body parts be placed in leather bags on mules and carried to all the towns where Túpac had incited rebellion.

REFERENCES: Burr Cartwright Brundage, *Lords of Cuzco: A History and Description of the Inca People in Their Final Days*, 1967; Marion Lansing, *Liberators and Heroes of South America*, 1940; Jean Descola, *Daily Life in Colonial Peru*, 1968.

Veula J. Rhodes

TUPI. The term Tupi (Tupy) refers to a huge linguistic group of Amerindian tribes who occupied eastern Brazil and Paraguay at the time of the Portuguese conquest in the sixteenth century. Just when the Portuguese were arriving in Brazil, the Tupi tribes were expanding out of their base in Paraguay* and driving the existing foraging tribes into the Brazilian interior. A vicious battle raged between the Tupi-speaking Indians* and the Ge-speaking Indians for dominance in eastern and southern Brazil, but the Tupi prevailed. The Tupi groups then split into many tribes. Many of those Tupi tribes practiced a ritualistic cannibalism, which gave the Portuguese a moral excuse for exterminating them. Moreover, warfare was a ceremonial ritual among the Tupi, against other Indian groups as well as against one another, so that they were unable to develop the unity necessary to resist Portuguese conquest.

Their own penchant for migration, as well as the inexorable expansion of Portuguese civilization in Brazil, eventually scattered the various Tupi tribes all over Brazil and other regions of South America. The Tupi tribes included the Siriono, Chiriguano*, Guarayu, and Pauserna in Bolivia*; the Guaraní* in Argentina*, Brazil, and Paraguay; the Cocama in Peru*; the Kaiwa in Paraguay and Brazil; the Omagua in Brazil and Peru; the Oyampi-Emerillon in French Guiana and Brazil; and the Tapiete, Chane, and Guayaki in Paraguay. In addition to these Tupi-speaking tribes, there were dozens of Tupi peoples located throughout Brazil, including the Apiaka (Apiaca), Aweti, Canoeiro, Kamayura (Camayura), Kawahib (Cawahib), Pawate (Parinintin, Wirafed), Kayabi (Cayabi), Sheta, Takunape (Tacunyape), Tapirape, Tenetehara (Anambe, Guayayara, Guajajara, Manaje, Tembe, Turiwara, Urubu), Tupi-Guaraní (Tupinamba), Neengatu (Nheengatu*), Arara, Ramarama, Uruku, Urumi, Arikem, Kabishiana, Karitiana, Arue, Digut, Monde, Guarategaya (Amniape, Kanoe, Meken), Kepikiriwat, Makurap, Tupari, Wayoro (Apichum), Kuruaya (Curuaya), Munduruku, Manitsawa, Shipaya, Yuruna, and Purubora.

REFERENCES: Joseph H. Greenberg, *Language in the Americas*, 1987; John Hemming, *Red Gold: The Conquest of the Brazilian Indians, 1500-1760*, 1978.

TZUTUJIL. A highland Maya* Indian* group, the Tzutujil were the indirect descendants of the Classic Lowland Maya of Mesoamerica and, along with the Quiche and Cakchiquel, were one of three powerful Indian tribes of Guatemala* at the beginning of the sixteenth century. The Tzutujil were the smallest and weakest of the three groups. They dominated most of the region around Lake Atitlán. The Tzutujil were the bitter rivals of both the Quiché and Cakchiquels for control of the highlands. In 1501, the Tzutujil were defeated by the Cakchiquel at Zakcab. Although dominated by the Cakchiquel, the Tzutujil have remained culturally and linguistically distinct well into the twentieth century.

REFERENCES: Sandra L. Orellano, ''Ethnohistorical and Archaeological Boundaries of the Tzutujil Maya,'' *Ethnohistory*, 20 (1973), 125–42; Sandra L. Orellano, *The Tzutujil Maya: Continuity and Change, 1250-1630*, 1989.

Virginia Garrard Burnett

U

ULLOA, ANTONIO DE. Antonio de Ulloa was born in Seville*, Spain, in 1716. A prominent naval official for Spain, he was educated at the Guardias Marinas in Cádiz. He first visited the New World as a teenager. In 1735, he received a commission to visit Peru* and Ecuador* and report back to the Crown with his observations. Ulloa spent nine years between 1735 and 1744 traveling in the region, and in 1748, he published his findings as *Relación histórica del viaje a la América meridional*. His other report—*Noticias secretas de América*—was completed in 1749 but not published until 1826. It was highly critical of the ways in which colonial rulers exploited their positions of power for their own benefit and noted how resentful local *criollos** were of such practices. Between 1758 and 1764, Ulloa served as governor of Huancavelica* and of Louisiana* from 1766 to 1768. Ulloa then received the rank of rear admiral and rose to the rank of vice-admiral and chief of Spanish naval operations. His 1772 book *Noticias Americanas* was a valuable survey of eighteenth-century life in Spanish South America. Antonio de Ulloa died in 1795.

REFERENCE: Miguel Pérez, *Antonio de Ulloa*, 1892.

UNITED PROVINCES OF CENTRAL AMERICA. See FEDERAL REPUBLIC OF CENTRAL AMERICA.

UNITED PROVINCES OF LA PLATA. The United Provinces of La Plata was a short-lived federation of the provinces that had made up the viceroyalty of Río de la Plata*. The United Provinces of La Plata was proclaimed by independence forces at Buenos Aires* in 1813. It was immediately debilitated by conflict between centralists, who saw Buenos Aires as the heart and soul of the government, and federalists, who wanted power and authority decentralized. The

Congress of Tucumán* declared the independence of the United Provinces of La Plata in 1816, but there was never any real unity until 1826. At that point, Buenos Aires became the capital city of the combined regions of Paraguay*, Argentina*, and Uruguay*.

REFERENCE: Dwight B. Heath, *Historical Dictionary of Bolivia*, 1972.

UNIVERSITY OF CARACAS. See CARACAS, UNIVERSITY OF.

UNIVERSITY OF MEXICO. See MEXICO, UNIVERSITY OF.

UNIVERSITY OF QUITO. See QUITO, UNIVERSITY OF.

UNIVERSITY OF SAN CARLOS. See SAN CARLOS, UNIVERSITY OF.

UNIVERSITY OF SAN FELIPE. See SAN FELIPE, UNIVERSITY OF.

UNIVERSITY OF SAN MARCOS. See SAN MARCOS, UNIVERSITY OF.

UNIVERSITY OF SANTO DOMINGO. See SANTO DOMINGO, UNIVERSITY OF.

UNIVERSITY OF SAN TOMÁS. See SAN TOMÁS, UNIVERSITY OF.

UPPER PERU. See BOLIVIA.

URDANETA, ANDRÉS DE. Andrés de Urdaneta was born in 1508 in Villafranca de Oria, in the province of Guipúzcoa, Spain. He served as a page in Juan García Jofre de Loaysa's* expedition to the Moluccas (Spice Islands*) from 1524 to 1527. He stayed on in the Moluccas until 1535 when he returned to Spain. Urdaneta joined Pedro de Alvarado's* expedition to New Spain* in 1538, and he fought in the Mixton War there in 1541. Urdaneta stayed in New Spain until 1552, when he joined the Augustinian* religious order there. He was ordained a priest five years later. In 1564, Urdaneta sailed to the Philippines* with Miguel López de Legazpi*. Urdaneta piloted a ship back to New Spain in 1565, opening up the trans-Pacific commercial route that the Manila galleon* would use for centuries. Andrés de Urdaneta died in 1568.

REFERENCE: Mairin Mitchell, *Friar Andrés de Urdaneta, O.S.A.*, 1964.

URDANETA, RAFAEL. Born in Venezuela* in 1789, Rafael Urdaneta eventually became one of Simón Bolívar's* major lieutenants in the Colombian and Venezuelan struggles for independence. After finishing school in Caracas*, Urdaneta moved to Bogotá* in 1804. Six years later, he joined the independence movement, and by 1815 Bolívar had awarded him the rank of general. During the next 20 years, Urdaneta had a varied political career. He served successively as a deputy in the Congress of Guayana, a senator of the Cúcuta Constituent Assembly, president of the senate of Gran Colombia*, and commander of the army of Gran Colombia in Zulia and Cundinamarca between 1824 and 1828. He served as secretary of war and of the navy of Gran Colombia between 1828 and 1830. For a brief period, he was head of state of Gran Colombia in 1830 and 1831, but he resigned and returned to Venezuela. Before his death in Paris in 1845, Urdaneta served as secretary of war and marine for Venezuela.

REFERENCE: *Memorias del General Rafael Urdaneta*, n.d.

URSÚA, PEDRO DE. Pedro de Ursúa was born in Spain around 1510 and came to New Granada* in 1544 with the expedition of Miguel Díaz* de Armendáriz. In 1546, he was appointed military governor of Bogotá*, and in 1549 he founded Pamplona. The next year, Ursúa was appointed governor of Pamplona. Ursúa was assassinated by Lope de Aguirre* in 1550 while he was leading an exploration party in the Amazon River Valley.

REFERENCE: Robert H. Davis, *Historical Dictionary of Colombia*, 1977.

URUGUAY. During the colonial period, present-day Uruguay was known as the Banda Oriental. At first, it did not have much importance for Spain. It was initially governed from Paraguay* until 1617 when the Gobernación del Río de la Plata was created; this agency was headquartered in Buenos Aires*. Not until 1749 would the post of governor of Montevideo* be created, and it was subordinated to Buenos Aires in important matters. In 1776, it was incorporated into the viceroyalty of the Río de la Plata*.

In February 1516, Juan Díaz de Solís* took possession of Uruguay in the Crown's name. The Indians* attacked and killed Solís and some of his men. In 1519, Ferdinand Magellan* visited the region on his expedition to the Philippines*. Between 1526 and 1530, a third expedition under Sebastián Cabot* arrived and established the first settlement, San Salvador, in 1527. The exploration and settlement of Argentine territory also began. The Indians attacked San Salvador, so Cabot left without establishing Spanish hegemony over the region. This region took on new importance with Peru's* discovery in 1527. In 1535, *Adelantado** Pedro de Mendoza* had orders to conquer and colonize the Río de la Plata region, but the Banda Oriental was not given special attention. The region's Indians made colonization difficult. In 1603, governor Hernando Arias* de Saavedra unsuccessfully attempted to conquer the territory. Colonization began in earnest at the beginning of the seventeenth century through the initiative of governors of Buenos Aires. Initially this region provided wood for Buenos Aires. Arias brought the first cattle to the Banda Oriental, and they multiplied quickly. The religious colonization was done by the Franciscans* and Jesuits*. The most important *reducción** was Santo Domingo de Soriano in 1624. Only small groups of Indians were affected by these efforts. The Charruas, the most implacable tribe, resisted evangelization. Lasting colonization efforts were not attempted until the Portuguese threatened the region.

In January 1680, Río de Janeiro's governor founded Colônia do Sacramento. In August 1680, Governor José de Garro attacked Colônia and won. Thus began the battles for control of the Banda Oriental first between Portugal and Spain, and later by Brazil and Buenos Aires. Portugal protested Spain's action, and Colônia was restored in 1683. Portuguese colonization continued as Spain tried unsuccessfully to isolate the colony commercially, but contraband trade between Colônia and Buenos Aires continued. In October 1704, during the War of the Spanish Succession*, governor Alonso de Valdez put Colônia under siege, and by March 1705, the colony was again Spanish. With the Treaty of Utrecht*, Spain granted an *asiento**, which allowed planters to import slaves and led to increased smuggling*. Colônia became a point for Anglo-Portuguese contraband. In December 1723, the Portuguese were spotted in the Bay of Montevideo attempting to establish a settlement. The governor, Bruno Mauricio de Zabala* acted quickly, and the Portuguese abandoned the territory. In February 1724, the fortification and colonization of Montevideo began.

The only interior settlement was Santo Domingo de Soriano. The Portuguese extended themselves along the coast and in the interior to Soriano. The rest of the country was occupied by Indians, gauchos*, and cattle expeditions. Montevideo's jurisdiction encompassed most of the Banda Oriental, except for that under Buenos Aires and a small part occupied by the Jesuit missions*. Montevideo was founded to establish Spanish hegemony and to prevent the contraband trade. Buenos Aires did not want a commercial rival, so trade between Montevideo and the outside was forbidden. Internal rivalries between the authorities, lasting from 1730 until 1749, led to the appointment of a governor in Montevideo, chosen directly from Spain, to administer the region. Up to then, the territory was under the control of either Asunción's* or Buenos Aires's governor. The first governor, José Joaquín de Viana, took possession of his post in 1751. The governors acted with autonomy, governing along with the *cabildo**, and contacted Buenos Aires only in grave cases.

In January 1750, the Treaty of Permuta between Portugal and Spain returned Colônia to Spain. The Portuguese and Spaniards from 1754–1756 engaged in a war against the Guaraní*. The population grew, forts were established, and Maldonado was founded in 1757. During the Seven Years War*, Colônia, under siege for 28 days, surrendered in October 1762. The Portuguese founded a fort in Maldonado's territory, and in January 1763, a combined Anglo-Portuguese fleet tried to reconquer Colônia. The Spanish defeated this fleet and followed up this victory by reconquering other territory then in Portuguese hands. After signing the Treaty of Paris* in 1763, Spain returned Colônia. The Jesuit expulsion in 1767 opened the territory to Portuguese incursions.

In 1776, Uruguay was incorporated into the viceroyalty of the Río de la Plata*. The first viceroy, Pedro de Ceballos*, sent troops to regain territory lost to Portugal. Colônia was retaken on June 3, 1777. Ceballos was ordered to stop all hostilities when the Treaty of San Ildefonso* was signed in October 1777. The treaty established the limits between Portugal and Spain in the Banda Oriental and Spanish domination of the Río de la Plata was established. In 1778, a new law of free trade* contributed to the Banda Oriental's prosperity.

Banda Oriental was under the administrative control of the Spanish Viceroy of La Plata centered in Buenos Aires. When the *criollos* of Buenos Aires deposed the viceroy in 1810, the Uruguayans were expected to be part of an independent Argentina, but the governor of Montevideo refused to recognize the authority of the Buenos Aires junta. José Gervasio Artigas*, a Uruguayan gaucho, then led a rural revolt against the governor. The effort was joined by forces from Buenos Aires, and the Spanish commander in Montevideo finally surrendered in 1814. Artigas, however, refused to accept Argentine domination and forced the Argentines to withdraw in 1815, only to be confronted by Portuguese troops from Brazil* the next year. Artigas's guerrillas were defeated in 1820, and Uruguay became a province of Brazil. Artigas, the architect of Uruguayan nationalism, fled to Paraguay, where he lived in exile until his death in 1850.

Uruguayan nationalists, with Argentine help, went to war against the Brazilians in 1825. After a three year struggle, the British, whose lucrative trade was obstructed by the conflict, persuaded the Brazilians and the Argentines to sign a treaty guaranteeing the security of the independent República Oriental del Uruguay. The British saw an independent Uruguay as a useful buffer between the two giants of South America.

REFERENCES: Mauricio Schurmann Pacheco and María Luisa Cooligham Sanguinetti, *Historia del Uruguay*, 1943; Juan M. de la Sota, *Historia del Territorio Oriental del Uruguay*, 2 vols., 1965.

Carlos Pérez

UTRECHT, TREATY OF. The Treaty of Utrecht is the name for a series of bilateral peace treaties that, along with the Treaty of Rastatt of 1714, ended the War of the Spanish Succession*. The basis of the war was the increasing entropy of the Spanish Empire by the end of the seventeenth century. By 1700, a number of treaties had already attempted to divide the Spanish Empire, largely through the recognition of the claims of the Austrian Habsburgs. The death of the heirless Spanish king, Charles II*, led to a general European conflict after he bequeathed the whole of the Spanish Empire to the Duke of Anjou, the grandson of the king of France, Louis XIV. With Austria, Britain, and the Netherlands allied against France, the first years of the war saw the French armies suffering major defeats by the Duke of Marlborough at the battle of Blenheim, and later at the battles of Ramillies and Oudenarde. The stiffening of French resistance by 1709 at the battle of Malplaquet, combined with British reluctance to carry on the war, led to the opening of peace talks in 1711. Treaties were signed in Utrecht on April 11, 1713, between France and Great Britain, the Dutch Republic of the United Provinces, and on February 6, 1715, between Spain and Portugal.

The treaties recognized the right of Philip V* (formerly the Duke of Anjou) as king of Spain with rights to the Spanish colonial possessions, on the condition that he and his successors renounce all rights to the French crown. Great Britain gained from Spain the island fortress of Gibraltar* and the important coastal town of Mahon. From France, Britain received a number of possessions in North America, most notably the Hudson Bay territory, Newfoundland, and Acadia. Britain also acquired special trading rights with the Spanish colonies in the Americas, especially the right of *asiento**, trading privileges that included the right to introduce African slaves* in Spanish America. The kingdom of Savoy gained Sicily, Montserrat, and part of the duchy of Milan from Spain. Prussia received part of upper Gelderland and several other territories, and France agreed to recognize the royal title of Frederick I as king of Prussia. The treaties marked the definite end of French aggrandizement under the Old Regime and signaled the end of Spain as a significant power in European politics. The Treaty of Utrecht was an important step toward establishing the commercial and colonial supremacy of Great Britain for the succeeding two centuries.

REFERENCES: James Leitch Wright, *Anglo-Spanish Rivalry in North America*, 1971; Henry A. F. Kamen, *The War of Succession in Spain, 1700-1715*, 1969.

William G. Ratliff

V

VALADÉS, DIEGO. Diego Valadés was born in New Spain* in 1533 to a Spanish father and a Tlaxcaltec* Indian* mother. He joined the Franciscan* order and learned a number of Indian languages, including his mother's tongue, as well as Nahuatl*, Otomí*, and Tarasco. Valadés spent time in Seville*, Spain, in the 1570s, and he is best remembered for his scholarly works. In 1579, he published *Retórica christiana*, the first book by a Mexican published in Europe. It was a description of Indian history and culture. Valadés died that year in Perugia.

REFERENCE: E. J. Palomera, *Fray Diego Valadés: El hombre y su época*, 1963.

VALDIVIA, LUIS DE. Luis de Valdivia was born in Granada, Spain, in 1561. He began his training as a Jesuit* novitiate in 1581, and after his ordination, he went to Peru* in 1589. He taught theology and philosophy in Lima* until 1593, when he went to Chile* as rector in Santiago*. Valdivia began extensive travels throughout the land of the Araucanian* Indians in 1597. Based on his observations, he began to call on Spanish officials to implement a policy of defensive pacifism and the abolition of all Indian labor and tribute requirements. Valdivia inspired intense opposition from entrenched economic interests, and in 1609, he went to Spain to lobby on behalf of the Araucanian Indians. He was named visitor general to Chile in 1612, but even then he could do little to stop the Araucanian wars. Valdivia retired to Spain in 1621. He died in Valladolid on November 5, 1642.

REFERENCE: B. T. Blum, "Luis de Valdivia, Defender of the Araucanians," *Mid-America*, 24 (1942), 109–37.

VALDIVIA, PEDRO DE. Pedro de Valdivia was born in La Serena in the province of Extremadura, Spain, around 1502. He joined the army of Spain and, before taking an assignment in the New World in 1535, fought in Italy and Flanders. After spending a year in Venezuela*, Valdivia became a quartermaster in Francisco Pizarro's* army in Peru*. Pizarro commissioned Valdivia to conquer Chile* in 1539, and in 1541, Valdivia founded the city of Santiago*. He spent years battling the Araucanian* Indians before returning to Peru in 1547. There he assisted Pedro de la Gasca* in suppressing Gonzalo Pizarro's* rebellion. He was named governor of Chile in 1548. Pedro de Valdivia resumed his attempt to conquer southern Chile in 1550 but was killed by Araucanian Indians on December 25, 1553.

REFERENCE: H. R. S. Pocock, *The Conquest of Chile*, 1967.

VALENCIA, MARTÍN DE. Martín de Valencia was born in Valencia de Don Juan near León, Spain, in 1473. He joined the Franciscan* order but then became active in a reform movement that culminated in the formation of the Custody of San Gabriel. Valencia was elected its first provincial in 1520. In 1524, Valencia led the first contingent of Franciscan friars—the "Twelve Apostles of Mexico"—into New Spain*, and they arrived at Vera Cruz* in 1524. Valencia labored in New Spain the rest of his life, dying in Tlalmanalco on March 21, 1534.

REFERENCE: S. Escalante Plancarte, *Fray Martín de Valencia*, 1945.

VALLADOLID. In 1787, the Spanish Crown created Valladolid as an intendancy* in the viceroyalty of New Spain*. The intendancy included the Michoacán region of west-central Mexico. It became part of Mexico in 1821.

VALLE, JOSÉ CECILIO DEL. José Cecilio del Valle was born in Choluteca, Honduras*, on November 22, 1770. He was a lawyer from a wealthy Honduran cattle-ranching family and went to Guatemala* in the 1790s, where he became a successful attorney and government official. During the waning years of the eighteenth century, del Valle became a follower of the Enlightenment*. Along with other prominent *criollo* liberals, del Valle formed the Economic Society to promote the economy, the arts, education, and industry in the kingdom of Guatemala. A thoroughly enlightened institution, the Economic Society attempted to deal with liberal issues that more traditional bodies, such as the older University of San Carlos*, failed to address. It sponsored courses in mathematics, political economy, and nonclassical foreign languages, all of which San Carlos—grounded in the earlier ecclesiastical curriculum—declined to provide. The Economic Society was suppressed by the Crown from 1800 to 1811 because of its stridently liberal leanings.

Del Valle nonetheless remained in a position of influence during this period. When José de Bustamante* was named as royal intendant of the kingdom of Guatemala in 1811, del Valle became his close adviser. Advised by del Valle,

Bustamante's efforts to implement Bourbon economic and absolutist policies in Guatemala placed him in direct conflict with the most powerful members of the kingdom's merchant elite, the Aycinena* family, and earned him the enmity of the rich, liberal *criollo* merchant class.

After the restoration in 1820 of the Constitution of 1812, del Valle's liberalism took on a more moderate tone. That year, he began to edit a newspaper* called *El Amigo de la Patria*, which represented the moderate liberalism and opposition to radical change that a faction of the Guatemalan *criollo* elite now embraced. This moderate liberalism, combined with his earlier service to Bustamante, made del Valle the spokesman for the faction of the *criollo* elite that opposed the more radical liberalism represented by the Aycinenas. In reality, the two factions were quite similar, both representing *criollo* aristocratic interests and, to varying degrees, Enlightenment thought.

In 1820, the moderate liberal faction won a narrow victory over the radical liberals when del Valle was elected to the post of first alcalde on the *ayuntamiento*[*] of Guatemala. Challenged by radical liberals, the victory was cut short by Agustín de Iturbide's* *Plan de Iguala*, which brought independence to Mexico and Central America in mid-1821. On September 15, 1821, Guatemala declared its independence from Spain in a document drafted by del Valle. The new government remained fundamentally the same as the colonial administration had been, and del Valle kept his post until Guatemala claimed its independence from Mexico on July 1, 1823. At that time, del Valle became part of the provisional government of the United Provinces of Central America* and one of the guiding lights of the emerging Liberal Party. Del Valle, a moderate until the end, was elected president of the United Provinces of Central America in 1834, but he died before taking office.

REFERENCE: R. L. Woodward, Jr., *Central America: A Nation Divided*, 1983.

Virginia Garrard Burnett

VALLE Y CAVIEDES, JUAN. See CAVIEDES, JUAN VALLE Y.

VALPARAÍSO. Valparaíso, the major port city of Chile*, was founded in 1536 by Juan de Saavedra, but its growth was very slow, depending upon the economic expansion of the colony. As late as the independence period, Valparaíso had a population of only 5,000 people.

VALVERDE, VICENTE DE. Vicente de Valverde was born in Oropeza, Estremadura, Spain. He entered the Dominican* order, studied at Salamanca and Valladolid, and in 1529 accompanied Francisco Pizarro* on his expeditions of conquest in Ecuador* and Peru*. He helped to capture Atahuallpa* at Cajamarca and then baptized the Inca* leader. Tradition has it that Valverde was a heartless priest who insisted on converting Indians* to Roman Catholicism before executing them, but revisionist historians now claim that Valverde accepted the values of his fellow Dominican, Bartolomé de Las Casas*. He actually wanted to protect the Indians from the worst of the Spanish depredations. Vicente de Valverde died on Puna Island in November 1541.

REFERENCE: A. M. Torres, *El padre Valverde*, 1932.

VARELA Y MORALES, FÉLIX FRANCISCO JOSÉ MARÍA DE. Félix Varela was born in 1788 in Havana*, Cuba*, and entered the Roman Catholic priesthood as a young man. He became a professor of philosophy at the San Carlos Seminary in Havana and quickly became a prominent liberal, advocating a variety of church reforms as well as Cuban independence and the abolition of slavery*. Between 1820 and 1823, Varela served as a Cuban representative in the Spanish Cortes, where his liberal Cuban patriotism made him a number of enemies. In 1823, Varela fled into exile in the United States after he learned that his arrest was imminent. He spent the rest of his life in New York City, serving as vicar-general of Roman Catholics there and publishing a Cuban newspaper, *El Habanero*, through which he became Cuba's first true revolutionary. Varela's health failed him and he retired to St. Augustine, Florida*, where he died in 1853.

REFERENCE: J. I. Rodríguez, *Vida del presbitero don Felix Varela*, 1944.

VARONA, ENRIQUE JOSÉ. Born in Cuba* in 1849, Varona was a brilliant literary critic, poet, philosopher, educator, and politician. After the Spanish-American War, he eventually rose to the position of vice-president of the republic. Varona was one of Cuba's greatest intellectual leaders. Essentially self-taught, he was a man of vast culture and knowledge. He was a prolific writer who produced nearly 2,000 items in his lifetime. Varona's initial literary interest was poetry. Among his works are *Poesías* (1878), *Paisajes cubanos y narraciones en verso* (1879), and *Arpas amigas* (1879). In 1880, however, Varona began to publish a series of works promoting positivism, a philosophy that he is credited with having introduced into Cuba.

In conjunction with his positivism, the author simultaneously developed and articulated a position of distrust against literature in general. He became increasingly interested in scientific sociology. This new philosophical orientation allowed Varona to promote actively the independence of Cuba from Spain, a cause in which he became intimately involved. Some of Varona's better known works are *Estudios literarios y filosóficos* (1882), *Artículos y discursos* (1891), *Cuba contra España* (1885), and *El fracaso colonial de España* (1896).

As a journalist, Varona played a key role in the independence of his homeland. At the personal urging of Jose Martí*, Varona went into self-exile in 1895 in order to direct *Patria*, the primary revolutionary journal of the Cuban exile groups. In post-colonial Cuba, Varona achieved even greater accolades as both a writer and politician. He participated in reforming the entire educational system of the island. Varona was one of Cuba's greatest intellectual figures. He died in 1933.

REFERENCES: Juan J. Remos, *Proceso Histórico de las Letras Cubanas*, 1958; Jaime Suchlicki, *Cuba: From Columbus to Castro*, 1986.

                                                                Sam L. Slick

VÁSQUEZ, PABLO. Pablo Vásquez was born in Atlixco, Puebla*, New Spain*, on March 21, 1769. He received a doctorate in theology form the Royal Pontifical University in 1795 and one year later was ordained to the Roman Catholic priesthood. He filled a variety of clerical and faculty positions until 1822, when he was named minister plenipotentiary to the Vatican. In 1825, Vásquez went to Rome to represent the interests of the Mexican government, which wanted papal recognition of Mexican independence and the appointment of bishops to the vacant sees; Spain, of course, objected vigorously. Vásquez lobbied for six years, and in 1831, Pope Gregory XVI appointed six new bishops for Mexico, one of whom was Vásquez, who was named bishop of Puebla. Vásquez died in Cholula, Mexico, on October 7, 1847.

REFERENCE: *New Catholic Encyclopedia*, XIV:582, 1967.

VÁSQUEZ ARCE Y CEBALLOS, GREGORIO. Gregorio Vásquez Arce y Ceballos was born in Bogotá*, New Granada*, in 1638 and became a prolific artist, one of the colonial period's most significant. His themes were almost exclusively religious, and more than 400 of his works survive in the Museum of Colonial Art in Bogotá. Vásquez died in 1711.

REFERENCE: Robert H. Davis, *Historical Dictionary of Colombia*, 1977.

VÁSQUEZ DE CORONADO, FRANCISCO. See CORONADO, FRANCISCO VÁSQUEZ DE.

VÁSQUEZ DE CORONADO, JUAN. See CORONADO, JUAN VÁSQUEZ DE.

VÁSQUEZ DE VELASCO, PEDRO. Pedro Vásquez de Velasco was born in 1603 in Palencia, Ecuador*, and spent his entire career as a public official. He became district attorney of Guatemala* in 1637 and practiced criminal law there. In 1647, Vásquez was appointed district attorney of Lima*, a prestigious post that brought him the presidency of the *audiencia* of Quito* in 1655. In 1661, Vásquez became the president of the *audiencia* of Charcas*, a position he held until his death in 1670. Vásquez's political career is best remembered for his unsuccessful attempt to abolish the *mita** labor system.

REFERENCE: Albert William Bork and Georg Maier, *Historical Dictionary of Ecuador*, 1973.

VEGA, GARCILASO DE LA. See GARCILASO DE LA VEGA.

VELASCO, LUIS DE. A Spanish native born in 1511, Luis de Velasco became the second viceroy* of New Spain*. In 1550, when Antonio de Mendoza* assumed the viceregal office in Lima*, Velasco was appointed to replace him. Velasco's tenure was noted for his insistence on humane treatment of the Indians* as well as the extension of Spanish authority into the region of Durango and the opening of silver mines there. Velasco died in 1564.

REFERENCE: Donald C. Briggs and Marvin Alisky, *Historical Dictionary of Mexico*, 1967.

VELASCO Y PÉREZ PETROCHE, JUAN MANUEL DE. Juan Manuel de Velasco y Pérez Petroche was born on January 6, 1727, in Riobamba, Ecuador*. He entered the Jesuit* order in 1746 and was educated at the Jesuit College of Quito*, where he studied theology, mathematics, and physics. He taught at the Colegio de Popayán. When the Jesuits were expelled from the New World in 1767, Velasco went to Faenza, Italy, and in the 1770s, under a commission from the Spanish monarchy, he wrote *La historia moderna del Reino de Quito*. The book was a discussion of Ecuadorian history and the history of the various Indian* tribes. Velasco died in Faenza, Italy, on June 20, 1792.

REFERENCES: C. M. Larrera, "Acta de defunción del historiador Padre Juan de Velasco y el lugar de su enterramiento," *Boletín de la Academia Nacional de Historia*, 31 (1951), 5–11; Adam Szaszdi, "The Historiography of the Republic of Ecuador," *Hispanic American Historical Review*, 44 (1964), 508–11.

VELÁSQUEZ, DIEGO. Diego Velásquez was born in Cuellar, Spain, in 1465 and is best remembered as the conqueror of Cuba*. He sailed to the New World in 1493 as part of Christopher Columbus's* second voyage. As an aide to Governor Nicolás de Ovando* on Hispaniola*, Velásquez acquired a fortune, and because of his success in quelling Indian* resistance there, he earned a reputation for ferocity and ability. In 1511, Diego Columbus* appointed him governor of Cuba, and Velásquez set out to conquer the island. He landed an expedition at Baracoa on the eastern end of Cuba and then headed inland, defeating the Indian tribes and establishing settlements at Baracoa, Bayamo, Havana*, Puerto Príncipe, Trinidad, and Santiago de Cuba. Velásquez distributed *encomiendas** to his closest associates and served as governor until 1521, when a political dispute with Hernán Cortés* led to his removal. Velásquez was restored to office in 1523 and died in 1524.

REFERENCE: Ramiro Guerra y Sánchez, *Historia de la nación cubana*, 10 vols., 1952.

VENEZUELA. In 1498, on his third voyage to the New World, Christopher Columbus* sailed into the Gulf of Paria and then along the coast of the Orinoco Delta of what is today Venezuela. One year later, Alonso de Ojeda* and Amerigo Vespucci* made a more extensive exploration of the coastal region. During the next two decades, several other Spanish and Portuguese explorers reached the area, but settlement was slow to occur. In 1528, hoping to realize immediate financial gains from its New World discoveries, the Spanish Crown under Charles I* leased Venezuela to the House of Welser*, a prominent German banking group headquartered in Augsburg. Along with the lease went the right to establish cities, develop mineral properties, and an *asiento** to import African slaves*. The Welsers brought in several thousand slaves from West Africa in 1528 and in 1536. The first blacks they brought were primarily people from the Yoruba, Ibo, and Fon tribes. Father Bartolomé de Las Casas* promoted the program because he felt that such a plan would give the Crown control over the trade and guarantee that the slaves were distributed only to individuals willing to give them a Christian education. In 1546, the Spanish Crown refused to renew the lease, and the program was officially terminated in 1556.

Settlement in the area then occurred piecemeal over the next decades. The island of Margarita* off the coast of Venezuela had been given to the Villalobos family as a private domain in 1525. They established a small settlement there, but it reverted to Crown control in 1600. Caracas*, the capital city of Venezuela, was established in 1567 as Santiago de León de Caracas. Its founder was Diego de Losada. The city of Maracaibo was founded in 1569. The Spanish Crown erected the province of Espíritu Santo de La Grita in 1575, and in 1576, Caracas became the colonial capital. Another Spanish settlement developed in Mérida. For the most part, Venezuela was an economic backwater in the sixteenth and seventeenth centuries, its economy revolving around subsistence agriculture, small-scale mining*, and stock raising.

It began to assume commercial importance in the early 1700s with the export to Spain of gold, silver, cacao*, tobacco*, hides*, and indigo* from the region. By the early 1700s, the Dutch had established a near monopoly on the cacao trade coming out of northern South America, and the Spanish Crown resented the loss of revenue. King Philip V* authorized the creation of the Caracas Company* in 1728 to stimulate commerce and trade between Spain and what is today Venezuela. Also known as the Guipuzcoa Company (because Basque investors in Guipúzcoa Province had financed the venture), the Caracas Company first sent a fleet to the New World in 1730. The company was an immediate success, crushing Dutch trade and pirates* in the lower Caribbean and exporting Venezuelan gold, silver, hides, tobacco, indigo, and cacao to Spain. The Crown granted the Caracas Company a monopoly over the Venezuelan trade in 1742, a move that alienated *criollo** traders in Caracas. They revolted violently against the company in 1749, prompting the Crown to relocate the company's board of directors to Spain in 1751. The revolt was led by Juan Francisco de León. After two years of rebellion, which drove even the Spanish governor from the capital, royal troops restored order. The revolt, however, did influence company policy. In 1752, the Caracas Company invited and received substantial *criollo* investment; in 1759, it allowed small cacao merchants to use company warehousing and shipping space to export their product. Under the economic operations of the Caracas Company, Venezuela came into its own economically and became an important political and economic center in the Spanish Empire.

From the beginning of the colonial period until 1717, the region of contemporary Venezuela was under the administrative authority of the *audiencia* of Santo Domingo*. From 1717 to 1723, Venezuela came under the authority of the *audiencia* of Santa Fe (de Bogota*). When the viceroyalty of New Granada* was suppressed, Venezuela returned to the jurisdiction of the *audiencia* of Santo Domingo, where it remained until 1739. For the next three years, Venezuela was back under the authority of the *audiencia* of Santa Fe (de Bogotá), but from 1742 until 1786, Venezuela went back to Santo Domingo's jurisdiction. By 1786, however, with the population growing and the economy expanding, Venezuela deserved its own audiencia. That year, Charles III* established the *audiencia* of Caracas, and it was installed on July 19, 1787. The *audiencia* of Caracas functioned until the end of the colonial period.

The *criollo* revolt against the monopoly of the Caracas Company was a precursor to the subsequent Venezuelan independence movement. Local Venezuelan-born elites resented the social, political, and economic power of the Spanish-born government and church officials, and in 1797, Manual Gual and José María España* led a brief, poorly planned revolt. Spain easily crushed it but the winds of revolutionary sentiment were blowing in Venezuela. In 1806, Francisco Miranda* sailed from New York with a small expedition to liberate Venezuela from Spanish control, but he too was unsuccessful. After the Napoleonic invasion of Spain and the deposing of the Spanish monarchy, the independence movement became irreversible in Venezuela. In April 1810, rebel leaders deposed the captain general of Caracas, and on July 5, 1811, a revolutionary junta was created that formally declared Venezuelan separation from Spain and drew up a constitution. Fighting continued for the next ten years until Simón Bolívar's* forces finally eliminated royalist power. Venezuela was part of Gran Colombia* before finally becoming an independent nation in 1830.

REFERENCES: Roland D. Hussey, *The Caracas Company, 1728–1784: A Study in the History of Spanish Monopolistic Trade*, 1934; John V. Lombardi, *Venezuela: The Search for Order, the Dream of Progress*, 1982; Guillermo Morón, *A History of Venezuela*, 1963.

VENEZUELA, CAPTAINCY GENERAL OF. In 1731, the captaincy general of Venezuela was established as a separate entity, but in 1740, the area came back under the authority of the viceroyalty of New Granada*. The Crown then formed the captaincy general of Caracas on September 8, 1777; its jurisdiction covered most of contemporary Venezuela. The captaincy general of Caracas directed military affairs for the Crown there until the end of the colonial period.

REFERENCE: Donna Keyse Rudolph and G. A. Rudolph, *Historical Dictionary of Venezuela*, 1971.

VERA CRUZ. The region of Vera Cruz, on the Gulf coast of Mexico, was created as an *intendencia** within New Spain* by the Spanish Crown in 1787. In 1821, Vera Cruz became a state in the new Republic of Mexico.

VERA CRUZ, ALONSO DE LA. Born in Caspueñas near Toledo, Spain, in 1504, young Alonso de la Vera Cruz studied first in Alcalá and then under Francisco de Vitoria and Fray Luis de León in Salamanca. He arrived in New Spain* in 1535, the year of the establishment of the viceroyalty and of the famous Seminary of Santa Cruz de Tlaltelolco. He soon joined the Augustinian* order. In 1540, he founded the first Augustinian college in Tiripitio, Michoacán, where for years he taught philosophy to his many students. His successful career included his appointment as provincial vicar in 1543 and as provincial five years later. He was particularly active in founding several convents in Michoacán and in spreading education in New Spain.

In 1551, Emperor Charles V* ordered the establishment of the Royal and Pontifical University of San Pablo in Mexico, which began its teaching operations two years later. Like the University of San Marcos* in Lima*, founded that same year, the University of Mexico also followed the model of Salamanca and Alcalá, projecting Spain's Golden Age and its cultural responsibilities into the New World. From its beginning, the university felt the force of the Counter Reformation* and gave preeminence to the chair of Scholastic theology. Some of the teachers held the highest degrees from Spanish universities and considered that their task was "to impugn, to destroy, to vanquish, and to extirpate that which does not conform to the faith." Alonso de la Vera Cruz became the first rector of the university, in addition to teaching the sacred scriptures and philosophy. He was not only the most outstanding teacher but the first philosopher in the New World, "the father of all philosophical study in America," who also established the trend of philosophy by introducing Aristotle into New Spain. In 1561, he was called back to Spain and stayed there until 1573 when he returned to Mexico. Two years later, he founded the Colegio de San Pablo.

Alonso de la Vera Cruz used his chair of philosophy to spread Scholasticism over the entire region. In his works, including *Recognitio Summularum* (1554), *Dialectica Resolutio* (1556), *Speculum Conjugiorum* (1556), and *Physica Speculatio* (1557), he reflected the Spanish spirit of the times and that special union of Thomistic Scholasticism with the modern spirit of the Renaissance. He was the greatest mind in the Mexico of the sixteenth century. When he died in 1584, Scholasticism was well established, to such an extent that it would dominate the Mexican mind for over 300 years. It was he who had given it its greatest stimulus, although he was also linked to the mysticism of Fray Luis de León and to the other currents of the Spanish [Christian] Renaissance.

REFERENCES: Ernest J. Burrus, ed., *The Writings of Alonso de la Vera Cruz*, 1967–1975; Samuel Ramos, *Historia de la filosofía en México*, 1943; José Tudela, *El legado de España a América*, 1954; Germán Arciniegas, *Latin America: A Cultural History*, 1967; O. Carlos Stoetzer, *The Scholastic Roots of the Spanish American Revolution*, 1979.

O. Carlos Stoetzer

VERA Y PINTADO, BERNARDO. Bernardo Vera y Pintado was born in New Spain* in 1780 but was raised in Santa Fe in what is today Argentina*. In 1799, he came to Santiago*, Chile*, where he earned a degree in law. When the Chilean independence struggle began in 1810, Vera was in the middle of it, and Spanish authorities ordered him to Lima*, Peru*. He avoided making the move and in 1810, when the Chilean junta was formed, Argentina named him as its official representative. He became an assistant editor with the newspaper* *Aurora de Chile* in Santiago in 1812. Vera served as minister of finance and minister of war in the rebel government in 1814, but after the Battle of Rancagua* he had to escape to Mendoza. Vera returned with José de San Martín's* army and fought at the Battle of Chacabuco*. He became editor of the new government's official newspaper, *Gaceta de Santiago de Chile*, in 1817. After the revolution, he served a term in the national legislature and taught law at the national institute. Bernardo Vera y Pintado died in 1827.

REFERENCE: José Toribio Medina, *Diccionario biográfico colonial de Chile*, 1906.

VERTIZ Y SALCEDO, JUAN JOSÉ DE. Juan José de Vertiz y Salcedo was born in Mérida*, Yucatán*, New Spain*, in 1719. His father was the royal governor there. He decided on a military career and fought in a number of Spanish campaigns in Italy and Portugal before being named governor of Río de la Plata* in 1770. Vertiz served as governor until 1776 and in 1778 was named viceroy of Río de la Plata; his tenure lasted until 1783. During those years, Vertiz brought the intendant system to the viceroyalty, saw to the relaxation of a number of trade regulations, expanded the limits of colonial settlement, stimulated the mining* and livestock industries, and greatly improved city services and the infrastructure of Buenos Aires*. Vertiz retired as viceroy in 1784 and returned to Spain where he died in 1799.

REFERENCE: José Torre Revello, *Juan José de Vertiz y Salcedo*, 1970.

VESPUCCI, AMERIGO. Amerigo Vespucci was born on March 9, 1451, in Florence, Italy, where he spent much of his life serving as a financial adviser to the Medici family. While on assignment in Seville*, Spain, for the Medicis, Vespucci met Christopher Columbus* in 1498. His appetite for exploration whetted, Vespucci sailed to the New World in 1499 with the expedition of Alonso de Ojeda*. On the trip, Vespucci explored the northern and eastern coasts of Brazil before returning to Spain in 1500. Vespucci published an account of the voyage in 1504, pushing back the date to 1497 so that he could claim to have discovered the mainland of South America a year before Columbus actually had made landfall. In 1501, Vespucci returned to Brazil with a Portuguese expedition. He became a Spanish citizen in 1505 and was named chief pilot of Spain in 1508. He died on February 22, 1512. Vespucci's fame in history was actually an accident. In 1507, the geographer Martin Waldseemuller published an updated version of Ptolemy's world geography and mistakenly attached Amerigo Vespucci's name to South America instead of Columbus's. The New World has been known as America ever since.

REFERENCES: Roberto Levillier, *Americo Vespucci*, 1966; Frederick J. Pohl, *Americo Vespucci: Pilot Major*, 1944.

VICEROY. The viceroy, the highest official in the Spanish colonial bureaucracy, presided over the largest administrative unit in the empire, the viceroyalty. The viceroy was the direct representative of the Crown in the colonies. Each viceroy was selected by the Spanish Crown and the Council of the Indies*. The viceroy usually came from an important Spanish family and served from three to five years. During the colonial period, there were four viceroyalties: the viceroyalty of New Spain*, the viceroyalty of Peru*, the viceroyalty of New Granada*, and the viceroyalty of the Río de la Plata*. Within his territorial jurisdiction, the viceroy directed the colonial bureaucracy, supervised Indian* policy, administered the royal treasury and the collection of revenues, served as commander in chief of military forces, presided over Church affairs under the Patronato Real*, and headed the *audiencia** in his resident city. In actual practice, however, the viceroy had far less than absolute power. The viceroyalties were far too large, with poor transportation systems, to be governed effectively from the capital city. In addition, the *audiencia* served as a council of advisers to the viceroy and had some check on his authority. Except in extraordinary circumstances, the viceroy could not pass legislation. Instead, he had to seek royal approval of all major decisions and govern according to the existing rules, regulations, and laws. Finally, Church leaders often chafed under viceregal authority and represented a competing constituency.

REFERENCE: C. H. Haring, *The Spanish Empire in America*, 1947.

VICEROYALTY OF NEW CASTILE. See PERU, VICEROYALTY OF.

VICEROYALTY OF NEW GRANADA. See NEW GRANADA, VICEROYALTY OF.

VICEROYALTY OF NEW SPAIN. See NEW SPAIN, VICEROYALTY OF.

VICEROYALTY OF PERU. See PERU, VICEROYALTY OF.

VICEROYALTY OF RÍO DE LA PLATA. See RÍO DE LA PLATA, VICEROYALTY OF.

VICTORIA, GUADELUPE. Guadelupe Victoria was born Miguel Fernández in Durango, New Spain*, in 1785. He studied law in Mexico City* until the independence movement developed at which time he joined the rebel forces. Under attack from Spanish forces, he retreated to the mountains of Vera Cruz and fought guerrilla skirmishes until 1821. When independence came, Victoria soon grew disenchanted with the government of Agustín de Iturbide* and led a successful movement to remove him from office. In 1824, Victoria was elected president. His administration is best remembered for the fact that an elite group of Masons controlled government in Mexico. In 1829, Victoria left office and retired from political life. He died in 1843.

REFERENCES: Wilfred H. Callcot, *Church and State in Mexico, 1822–1857*; Robert Randall, *Real del Monte*, 1972; William S. Robertson, *Iturbide of Mexico*, 1982.

VILLAMIL, JOSÉ DE. José de Villamil was born in New Orleans, Louisiana*, on June 10, 1788. When the independence movement erupted in Ecuador* in 1809 he moved to Guayaquil* and eventually fought in several battles against the Spanish. After independence was secured, Villamil entered the Ecuadorian diplomatic corps. He became the first governor of the Galápagos Islands and then served as minister to the United States in 1852. He died in Guayaquil on May 12, 1866.

REFERENCE: Albert William Bork and Georg Maier, *Historical Dictionary of Ecuador*, 1973.

VILLARROEL, GASPAR DE. Gaspar de Villarroel was born in Riobamba, Ecuador*, in 1587. He was educated at the University of San Marcos* in Lima*, Peru*. A Roman Catholic clergyman who was a member of the Augustinian* order, Villarroel was appointed bishop of Santiago*, Chile*, in 1640, and then archbishop of Arequipa*, Peru, in 1651. He became archbishop of Charcas in 1655, a position he held until his death on October 12, 1665. Few other *criollos* enjoyed as much success in moving up in the clerical, political, or military ranks of the Spanish Empire.

REFERENCE: Albert William Bork and Georg Maier, *Historical Dictionary of Ecuador*, 1973.

VILLAVERDE, CIRILO. Cirilo Villaverde was born in 1812 in Cuba.* He occupies a principal position in the history of nineteenth-century Cuban colonial literature. He began as a romantic writer and slowly moved to *costumbrismo* and realism. His works include the historical novel *El penitente* (1844), the novel of customs *Dos amores* (1858), and *El guajiro* (1842). Villaverde's most important contribution to literature was his antislavery novel, *Cecilia Valdés*. The work is generally considered to be Latin America's first romantic novel. It was first published in 1839, under the title *Cecilia Valdés o la loma del Ángel*. A second, more complete edited version was finished many years later, in 1879 and published in New York in 1882. Both versions were immensely popular in Cuba.

Cecilia Valdés is the story of a young mulatto women who is the child of a black woman from the barrio and a white plantation owner. Cecilia falls in love with the son of the plantation owner, not realizing that he is her half-brother. She is finally rejected and later dies. *Cecilia Valdés* is important not only as literature, but also as a document of its era. It paints with detail the culture of black slaves* in Cuba in the nineteenth century. All of society is treated: plantation members, the poor, Spanish aristocrats, and so forth. The romantic influence of Sir Walter Scott is very present, as well as that of certain Golden Age Spanish classical writers. The novel is well written and developed. It had tremendous impact on the conscience of Cuba relative to the question of morality, slavery, and its subsequent demise.

REFERENCE: Juan J. Remos, *Proceso Histórico de las Letras Cubanas*, 1958.

Sam L. Slick

VIRGIN ISLANDS. The Virgin Islands, composed of a group of seven islands and approximately 90 cays and inlets, were originally inhabited by the Siboney (Ciboney[*]) Indians. Karib[*] Indians lived there when the Europeans first arrived. The Karibs were the scourge of the other Caribbean tribes, for they were extremely hostile, aggressive, and independent. Christopher Columbus[*] became the first European to visit the Virgin Islands when he landed on the island of Ayay (which he renamed Santa Cruz) on November 14, 1493. The Spanish opted not to colonize this nor the other islands because they were more interested in the Greater Antilles. Therefore, other European nations, mainly the English and the Dutch, settled Santa Cruz. The Dutch established present-day Christiansted and the English settled near Fredricksted, both in 1625. The Dutch settlement was joined by French Protestant refugees from St. Christopher[*]. The Dutch abandoned Christiansted in 1645 after Indians killed the governor.

REFERENCES: Darwin D. Creque, *The U.S. Virgin Islands and the Eastern Caribbean*, 1968; James E. Moore, *Everybody's Virgin Islands*, 1979.

Catherine G. Harbour

VIRGIN OF GUADALUPE. See GUADALUPE, VIRGIN OF.

VIRGIN OF THE ANGELS. The Virgin of the Angels has been the patron saint of Costa Rica[*] since 1782. Roman Catholic beliefs hold that in August 1635, a Costa Rican woman named Juana Pereira, who was out collecting wood, claimed to have miraculously received a small black statue of the Virgin Mary. She claimed to have taken the statue to her home in Cartago[*], only to have it disappear and reappear back at the original site of the vision. The story spread rapidly through the region, and eventually the Church decided to build a chapel there in honor of the event. Several churches were built on this site in 1675, 1722, 1790–1805, 1822, 1849, and 1921. (Theodore S. Creedman, *Historical Dictionary of Costa Rica*, 1977.)

VISAYAS. The Visayas (sometimes spelled and pronounced Bisayas) are the central islands of the Philippines[*], between Luzon[*] to the north and Mindanao[*] to the south. The group is defined as much by culture as by geography. The Visayas are usually considered to include the islands of Panay, Negros, Cebu, Bohol[*], Leyte[*], Samar[*], and Masbate, plus innumerable smaller islands in the seas and straits of the region. Visayan languages include the dominant Cebuano, plus Hiligaynon, Aklanon, and Waray-Waray. Generalizations about such a large, diverse region are always dubious, but Visayans characterize themselves as more easy-going than other Filipinos[*]. Nevertheless, the region has a history

of bitter class conflict, particularly in the sugar* regions. Spanish religious authority radiated outward from Cebu City. Other urban centers that developed along with commercial export agriculture include Iliolo on Panay and Bacolod on Negros. There was some revolutionary activity on Panay, but the Philippine Revolution against Spain took place on Luzon*.
REFERENCE: Onofre D. Corpuz, *The Philippines*, 1965.

Ross Marlay

VISITA. The *visita* was an investigation of colonial officials to determine the effectiveness of their administration or the existence of graft and corruption. Usually the Council of the Indies* would authorize a *visita*, which could have any region or political institution as the object of its investigation. The viceroy* could also appoint a *visita* to investigate possible scandals within his area of jurisdiction. The *visitador* had unlimited powers to carry out the investigation, after which he would submit a report to the appropriate authorities. Although the institution of the *visita* seemed an efficient way of reforming the system, it proved unable to do so, primarily because of the extraordinary logistical and philosophical problem. Spain was committed to autocratic, centralized government over a huge colonial empire, an impossible political objective that even the *visita* could not achieve.
REFERENCE: C. H. Haring, *The Spanish Empire in America*, 1947.

VITORIA, FRANCISCO DE. Born in Vitoria in the Basque region of Spain in 1480, young Francisco grew up in Burgos where in 1504 he entered the Dominican* order. Thereafter, he went to Paris where he stayed at the Dominican College of St. Jacques, famous for its association with Saint Thomas Aquinas and Albertus Magnus. In his studies of the arts and theology, Vitoria came under the strong influence of nominalist teachers, especially John Maior, who were largely responsible for the revival of Thomism and thus later influenced profoundly the Late Scholastic school in Spain. Vitoria also became directly involved with the many editions of Saint Thomas's *Summa Theologica* and in the early sixteenth century. He specialized in ethics and was much influenced in this endeavor by both nominalism and the new humanistic currents of the Renaissance. Together with Bartolomé de Las Casas*, he represented in the highest degree the union of Scholasticism with humanism.

In 1523, Vitoria returned to Spain. He had been in Paris for sixteen years. For the next five years, he lectured at the College of San Gregorio in Valladolid, which at that time was the seat of the Council of the Indies*. It was then that he began to delve into the numerous questions regarding the Indies. In 1526, he was elected to the chair of theology at the University of Salamanca. In his lectures, he commented on Saint Thomas Aquinas's *Summa Theologica* and openly criticized all kinds of public servants for their abuses. He also counseled on a variety of subjects, such as the matrimonial difficulties of Henry VIII of

England and Franco-Spanish problems, but in time he became best known for his writings on the Indies.

Vitoria became the great defender of the Indians* and, like Las Casas, was opposed to their exploitation and enslavement. He gave Las Casas significant intellectual help that was highlighted at the time of the great controversy on the Indies, which reached its peak between 1530 and 1550. In 1539, when his lectures on the Indies were held, Vitoria elaborated on the fundamental rights of all men and peoples, criticized the Spanish conquest, and defended the rights of the Indians. He created a theory of liberty and thus established modern international law by attacking not only the temporal power of the pope, but also that of the emperor. Vitoria was among the earliest of the thinkers who applied natural law to international law. It was a middle-of-the-road theory that held the field and actually determined the future against both the concept of a superstate organized on republican lines and the concept that rejected in toto any idea of a natural community uniting all states. For Vitoria, as for the Spanish school in general, there was a natural-law connection among nations. This connection, though it did not result in any authority exercised by the whole over its parts, still involved a system of mutual rights and duties. From this point of view, international law was conceived as binding upon states among themselves, even though they were still in a state of nature by virtue of their sovereignty; it was also binding upon individuals when they were living in a state of nature. Thus, it was not the idolatry or barbarity of the Indians so much as their transgressions against this newly conceived international law which, in Vitoria's view, gave the Spaniards a right to the conquered lands of the Indies.

Vitoria was not only extremely popular with the students, but he succeeded in establishing a real school of his own, since over 20 of his pupils held chairs in Salamanca and two in Alcalá. The New Laws* of 1542 reflected in many ways his class lectures as expounded in *De India I* (1537–1538), *De Indis II*, and *De Iure Belli* (1538–1539). His health could no longer withstand his extraordinary vitality—he died in 1560 at the age of 60.

REFERENCES: Bernice Hamilton, *Political Thought in Sixteenth-Century Spain: A Study of the Political Ideas of Vitoria, Soto, Suárez, and Molina*, 1963; O. Carlos Stoetzer, *The Scholastic Roots of the Spanish American Revolution*, 1979.

O. Carlos Stoetzer

W

WAYNA CÁPAC. See HUAYNA CÁPAC.

WELSER, HOUSE OF. In 1528, the Spanish crown under Charles I*, hoping to realize immediate financial gains from its New World discoveries, leased Venezuela* to the House of Welser, a prominent German banking group head-quartered in Augsburg. Along with the lease went the right to establish cities, develop mineral properties, and import African slaves under an *asiento**. The Welsers brought in several thousand slaves from West Africa in 1528 and again in 1536. The first blacks they brought were primarily people from the Yoruba, Ibo, and Fon tribes. Father Bartolomé de Las Casas* promoted the program because he felt that such a plan would give the Crown control over the trade and guarantee that the slaves were distributed only to individuals willing to give them a Christian education. In 1546, the Spanish Crown refused to renew the lease, and the program was officially terminated in 1556.
REFERENCE: Juan Friede, *Los Welser en la conquista de Venezuela*, 1961.

WESTERN SAHARA. Western Sahara was a shortlived colonial entity in the history of the Spanish Empire. In 1934 Spain united Ifni* and the Northern Zone of Spanish Morocco* with Spanish Sahara*, and when the Southern Zone of Spanish Morocco was added in 1946, the new administrative unit was called Western Sahara. But when Morocco won its independence from France in 1956, Spain agreed to cede the Northern Zone of Spanish Sahara to the new country. Two years later, in the Agreement of Cintra*, Spain also ceded the Southern Zone to Morocco. Ifni was ceded to Morocco in 1969. At that point Western Sahara was practically synonymous again with Spanish Sahara. Western Sahara ceased to exist altogether in 1975 when Spanish Sahara won its independence from Spain.

REFERENCE: John Mercer, *Spanish Sahara*, 1975.

WEST FLORIDA. From the first explorations of Juan Ponce de León[*] in the early sixteenth century, Florida[*] and the Gulf coast came under Spanish control. As a result of the Treaty of Paris of 1763 Great Britain controlled the region between 1763 and 1783. Eventually the Spanish divided the area into East Florida[*] and West Florida. West Florida extended from the Mississippi River east to the Perdido River. When President Thomas Jefferson completed the Louisiana[*] Purchase from France in 1803, he concluded that the territory included what Spain considered West Florida. Spain disagreed, and the two countries disputed the area for the next seven years. Spanish expansionists led a revolt in 1810 and captured Baton Rouge in present-day Louisiana, proclaiming the Republic of West Florida on September 26, 1810. On October 27, 1810, President James Madison declared that the United States owned West Florida from the Mississippi River to the Perdido River. On May 14, 1812, the former Spanish territory of West Florida was incorporated into the Mississippi Territory. Spain protested but there was little to be done. The war for independence had begun in Mexico[*], and Spain was preoccupied there. When the War of 1812 erupted, the United States extended its control of West Florida. General James Wilkinson captured the Spanish fort at what is today Mobile, Alabama, on April 15, 1813. West Florida had become American territory.

REFERENCES: Robert F. Fabel, *The Economy of West Florida, 1763-1783*, 1988; Gloria Jahoda, *Florida: A History*, 1984.

WESTPHALIA, PEACE OF. The Peace of Westphalia, which was concluded in 1648, brought to an end the Thirty Years War. The war had begun in 1618, ostensibly as a religious conflict between Catholics and Protestants; it quickly became a political and economic war that involved all the major powers of Europe. The war began when Bohemia revolted against an attempt by the Holy Roman Emperor, Ferdinand II, to re-Catholicize the country. The Bohemian phase of the war was quickly concluded when the forces of the emperor won an overwhelming victory in 1620. The emperor was now free to reconvert the country, which he proceeded to do. The Spanish Habsburgs joined their fellow Catholics, and the Catholic league was everywhere successful. It was not until 1630 that the fortunes of the Protestants began to take a turn for the better, when King Gustavus Adolphus of Sweden, a devout Protestant, entered the war. In the fall of 1631, he defeated the imperial armies at Breitenfeld, but his victory at Lutzen in 1632 cost him his life. During the final 13 years of fighting, which devastated Germany, the French joined Sweden in an attempt to crush the power of the Austrian and Spanish Habsburgs. The French army handed the Spanish a crushing defeat at the Battle of Rocroi in 1643. It was the first time in 150 years that a Spanish army had been decisively defeated. From this point on,

Spanish power in the world declined as France became the predominant European power. By 1648, the Swedes were threatening Vienna and storming Prague. The dream of Ferdinand II*, who had died in 1637, to re-Catholicize Germany and establish Habsburg control over the empire, had been crushed. On December 25, 1641, the new emperor, Ferdinand III*, agreed to begin peace negotiations with Sweden and France in Westphalia. Negotiations with France would take place in Münster, while those with Sweden would meet in Osnabruck. Continued animosity and disputes would prevent Spain and France from concluding a treaty until 1659. Although the agreed-upon date had been set, continued fighting and diplomatic maneuvering delayed the opening of talks until July 1643 in Osnabruck and April 1644 in Münster.

The Peace of Westphalia included the provisions of the treaties of Münster and Osnabruck, as well as a separate agreement concluded between Spain and the United Netherlands. The territorial settlements concluded in Westphalia confirmed the dissolution of the Holy Roman Empire. The United Provinces (Netherlands) and the Swiss cantons were recognized as sovereign and independent. Dutch conquests on the lower Scheldt were also confirmed, and they gained from Portugal the right to establish outposts in Brazil and Indonesia. France gained Alsace, Metz, Toul, and Verdun. Sweden gained control of Western Peramia and the secularized bishoprics of Bremen and Verden. Bavaria received the Upper Palatinate, and Brandenburg acquired eastern Pomerania and several bishoprics.

The Peace of Westphalia, signed on October 24, 1648, made the German states virtually sovereign. Each of the 300 states gained the right to conduct diplomacy and make treaties with foreign powers. The constitution further stipulated that no laws could be made, no taxes or troops raised, or war declared without the consent of the imperial estates, an event that would be virtually impossible. Although the German states gained their independence, the attainment of that goal retarded German unification until the nineteenth century. The Peace of Westphalia represented a landmark in European political and religious history. Politically, the peace confirmed the modern state system of Europe, in which each nation was a sovereign entity that recognized no higher unifying authority. On the religious side, the Counter Reformation was checked in Germany. Each German sovereign had the power to determine the religion of his state. These choices included Calvinism, which had been added to Lutheranism and Catholicism as acceptable faiths. Furthermore, religion would no longer be the main issue bringing the European nations into conflict.

REFERENCE: George Pages, *The Thirty Years War: 1618-1648*, 1971.

Michael Dennis

WEYLER, VALERIANO. Of German descent, Valeriano Weyler was born in the Canary Islands in 1838. As a young man, he served as the Spanish military attaché to the United States during the Civil War. He went to Cuba* and served there as an officer for the Spanish army during the Ten Years War*; after serving similarly in the Carlista War in Spain, Weyler received his appointment as governor of Cuba in 1896. He was charged with crushing the rebellion there. He undertook the task with enthusiasm and ruled with an iron hand. To deal with Cuban guerrillas, Weyler instituted a policy of herding the rural population into garrisoned towns, where they could be controlled and where the Cuban guerrillas could not recruit or use them for support. The policy was heavy-handed and caused much suffering among Cuban civilians. Spanish liberals in Madrid began to criticize Weyler's policies, as did the American press. Weyler began to lose ground as well when the Filipino rebellion drained Spanish troops out of Cuba. When Spanish Prime Minister Antonio Cánovas was assassinated in June 1897, Weyler lost his political base in Madrid. He resigned as governor of Cuba later in 1897. Valeriano Weyler died in 1930.

REFERENCE: Horatio Rubens, *Liberty*, 1932.

WOMEN. The place of women in the Spanish American colonies was a complex affair which depended on a variety of racial, ethnic, gender, and economic factors. In terms of political power, colonial women could neither vote nor hold public office during the colonial period, and although they exercised great influence within their own households, they had only the most limited political roles in the larger societies. The fundamental demographic and social reality of the sixteenth century, however, was the dearth of Iberian women settling in the New World. The Spanish colonies in the early years consisted overwhelmingly (in as much as 10 to 1 ratios) of Iberian men seeking their fortunes in the New World. Most of those men took Indian women as mistresses and wives, and their children were known as *mestizos*. Eventually, the mestizo population became the largest ethnic group in the New World, vastly outnumbering the Indians or the people of exclusively European descent. Not until the early decades of the seventeenth century did increasing numbers of Iberian women settle in the New World, improving the gender balance in the Iberian population. By that time those Iberian women, either *peninsulares** or *criollos**, constituted the feminine segment of the upper class. Although they enjoyed wealth and prosperity, upper-class women in the Spanish American colonies lived relatively cloistered lives. They exercised no political power in the Spanish bureaucracy, military, or church, and social expectations conspired to keep them out of private business and commerce as well.

Ironically, in spite of more limited economic means, middle- and lower-class women in the Spanish American colonies enjoyed a greater degree of freedom than their upper-class counterparts. Although they had no political power, society allowed them to function in a variety of economic roles outside the household. The vast majority of those women were of mestizo or mixed African-mestizo descent. In fact, because of racial and class prejudice, there was an inverse relationship between poverty and occupational diversity. Working-class women in the Spanish American colonies could be found in a variety of occupations—including farmers, small ranchers, shopkeepers, domestics, bakers, artisans, textile workers, midwives, *curanderas*, and prostitutes. At the bottom of the social structure were African slaves and Indian women, and both groups performed the most menial jobs on ranches and plantations.

The only real exception to the cloistering of upper-class women were the Roman Catholic religious orders for women. Within the church—as teachers, clerical administrators, intellectuals, and health care workers—women religious enjoyed a variety of activities which set them apart from other women in the society.

REFERENCE: Ann M. Pescatello, ed., *Female and Male in Latin America: Essays*, 1973.

WOOL. Although slower to adapt to the environment of the New World and Australia than horses and cattle, sheep were nevertheless one of the most important biological entities of Spanish imperialism. Sheep ranching was a key industry in fifteenth-century Spain, and in 1493, Christopher Columbus* brought sheep with him to the New World. Sheep did not do well in the Caribbean or in the wetter lowlands of South America; unlike pigs and horses, they did not do well on their own in the wild either. But in New Spain* and Peru*, the sheep industry provided meat and wool to the colonial economy. Beginning in 1635, Antonio de Mendoza*, the viceroy* of New Spain, imported high-quality sheep, and by 1680, there were more than 200,000 head there. Sheep ranching also did well in the Peruvian highlands, northern Chile*, and northern Argentina.* Throughout much of colonial Spanish America, wool production was a significant part of the local economy. In the highlands of Peru and Bolivia*, wool production came in four basic varieties. Wool from the llama was a coarse variety, while wool from the alpaca was much finer. Wool from the vicuña was especially fine, but the animal was not domesticated. The lowest quality but most abundant was the wool from sheep. Sheep raising did not reach the region until the arrival of the Spanish. During the colonial period, the centers of wool production were at Texcoco, Guadalajara*, and Saltillo, New Spain; Riobamba, La Tacunga, and Ambato, Ecuador*; and throughout much of Chile and Argentina.

REFERENCE: Alfred W. Crosby, Jr., *The Columbian Exchange: Biological and Cultural Consequences of 1492*, 1972.

X

XELAJÚ. Xelajú was a large Quiche Mayan* town in the western highlands of Guatemala*. In July 1524, Pedro de Alvarado* killed the Quiché leader, Tecúm Uman*, in hand-to-hand combat in Xelajú, thus vanquishing the Quiché Maya and completing Alvarado's conquest of Guatemala. Xelajú was renamed Quezaltenango and remained an influential city in Guatemala throughout the colonial period. It is commonly referred to by its Indian* name, Xclajú, or simply "Xela," to the present day. During the sixteenth and seventeenth centuries, a powerful separatist movement flourished in the populous highland district around Quezaltenango, Sololá, and Totonicapan. This area was known as Los Altos, and Quezaltenango was its recognized capital. The basic grievance of the wealthy landowners and clergy in Los Altos was the discriminatory legal and economic power wielded by Santiago* de Guatemala, the seat of government for both the province and kingdom of Guatemala. The separatists hoped to see Los Altos become a separate province from Guatemala, with Quezaltenango as its official capital. Although the separatist movement based in Quezaltenango never succeeded, the area retained its sense of alienation. Separated from Santiago by bad roads, mountains, and cultural differences—for Los Altos remained a predominantly Indian region—separatist sentiments ran high throughout the colonial period.

REFERENCES: R. L. Woodward, Jr., *Central America: A Nation Divided*, 1983; Miles L. Wortman, *Government and Society in Central America, 1680–1840*, 1982.

Virginia Garrard Burnett

XIMÉNEZ, FRANCISCO. Born in 1666, Francisco Ximénez joined the Dominican* order as a Roman Catholic priest and served in Guatemala*. He is best remembered for his discovery of the *Popul Vuh**, the great creation story and Bible of the Quiche Maya* Indians. Ximénez found the manuscript in a parish church in Chichicastenango. He translated it into Latin from the Quiche texts. A gifted linguist, Ximénez was also the author of *Tesoro de los lenguas Quiché, Cachikel y Tsutuhíl*. Ximénez died in 1729.

REFERENCE: Dennis Tedlock, *Popol Vuh*, 1985.

Y

YÁÑEZ PINZÓN, VICENTE. See PINZÓN, VICENTE YÁÑEZ.

YAQUI AND MAYO INDIANS. The Yaqui Indians live largely along the Yaqui Fuerte river valleys, somewhat more remote than the Mayo Indians who occupy the valley of the Mayo River and are closer to modern civilization. While the two groups are closely related, the Mayo quickly formed alliances with the conquering Spanish and were soon afterward Christianized by Jesuit* clergy. The Yaqui preferred resistance to the Spanish forces, fighting to the death in many instances rather than surrendering. On at least three occasions, the Mayo joined with their close relatives, the Yaqui, and renounced Spanish domination in an attempt to throw off the Spanish yoke. A rebellion in 1740 showed initial success, but was eventually crushed when the Indians were confronted with the power and might of the Spanish army in Mexico. Still, the restless Yaqui and Mayo did not willingly give up their independence, organizing two additional efforts in the nineteenth century, which ended in the capture and execution of native leaders in 1880. The last joint effort occurred in 1917, when both the Mayo and Yaqui Indians served as government soldiers in fighting the forces of Pancho Villa, defeating the Division of the North twice. Villa's forces, used to the noise of gunfire, were psychologically shocked by the silent arrows of the Indians as well as by their use of whistles to signal Indian troop movements throughout the night. Brave men who were used to more conventional fighting wilted before the unconventional Indian tactics.

REFERENCES: G. A. Agogino and B. Ferguson, ''The Mayo Judío Cult,'' *Discover Mexico*, 19 (1979), 12–14; James S. Griffith, *Legacy of Conquest—the Arts of Northwest*

Mexico, 1967; Ernest Henry Gruening, *Mexico and its Heritage*, 1928; Muriel Thayer Painter and E. B. Sayles, *Faith, Flowers, and Fiestas—The Yaqui Indian Year*, 1962.

George A. Agogino

YUCATÁN. The peninsula of Yucatán points northward towards Florida[*] and is made up of a riverless region, where all water flows or is stored beneath the surface. Occasionally, the limestone base of the peninsula splits open over these water resources, forming *cenotes* or water-filled pits, which were essential to the Indian[*] population. The region is the home of the Maya[*] Indians, who in the last 2,000 years, built large, stone, ceremonial centers throughout the peninsula. These centers include Kabah, Chichén Itzá, Izama, Edzna, Labna, Uxmal, Mayapán, and Tulum. The Maya were the direct descendents of the Olmec[*], the first advanced civilization in Meso-America, whose heartland was just to the north of Yucatán. Here, the southern part of Vera Cruz[*] and the northern area of Tabasco, the Olmec culture flourished. Their descendants during the Classic Period were Maya who occupied a good section of southern Mexico and adjacent Meso-America to the south.

The Yucatán Peninsula comprises the Mexican states of Yucatán, Campeche, and Quintana Roo. The name of this final state is not an exotic Maya word but is instead named after a military hero. The vast area of the peninsula is flat with low rolling hills in the Puuc region of the north-central part of the peninsula. Until recently, few roads lead to Yucatán, although currently a modest paved highway system circles the peninsula. The current population, while not exact, runs about 2 million people, mostly Maya Indians. In 1517, Francisco Hernández[*] de Córdoba was the first European to reach Yucatán, and settlement and conquest began a decade later. Even today, ties with the central government of Mexico leave something to be desired, the region often being at odds with the rest of the country. Yucatán's people speak with a decided accent, different from the rest of Mexico; many of them still speak a Maya dialect. Yucatán was part of the *audiencia* of New Spain[*] (Mexico City) from 1527 to 1543; then it was shifted to the *audiencia* of Los Confines[*]. In 1549, it was transferred back to Mexico City[*], but only one year later it became part of the *audiencia* of Guatemala[*]. That lasted until 1560 when it became part of the *audiencia* of New Spain again. The governor's office of Yucatán was elevated to that of a captain general in 1617. In 1789, when Charles III's[*] Bourbon reforms brought the *intendencia*[*] system to New Spain, the Yucatán was organized as the *intendencia* of Mérida. It retained that status until 1821, when the area became part of the Republic of Mexico. See NEW SPAIN.

George A. Agogino

YUCATÁN, CAPTAINCY GENERAL OF. In 1517 and 1518, Francisco Hernández[*] de Córdoba and Juan de Grijalva[*] made preliminary explorations of the Caribbean and Gulf coasts of Mexico, but conquest and settlement of the Yucatán did not begin until ten years later. Between 1527 and 1543, Yucatán was under the administrative jurisdiction of the *audiencia* of New Spain* (Mexico City). It was then transferred to the *audiencia* of Los Confines*. It became part of the *audiencia* of Guatemala* in 1550, and in 1560 was transferred back to Mexico City. It was raised to a captaincy general in 1617. In 1789, the Spanish Crown created an intendancy* out of the Yucatán, and named it the intendancy of Mérida. Yucatán became part of Mexico in 1821. See NEW SPAIN

YUCATÁN, DIOCESE OF. The Roman Catholic diocese of Yucatán*, New Spain*, was established by Pope Leo X in 1519. The first bishop was a Dominican*—Julián Garces*, but the diocese was not implemented until after Francisco de Montejo* completed the conquest of the Yucatán. In 1562, the Franciscan Francisco de Toral was consecrated bishop and occupied the see. It was raised to an archdiocese in 1908.

REFERENCE: *New Catholic Encyclopedia*, XIV:1082–83, 1967.

Z

ZABALA, BRUNO MAURICIO DE. Bruno Mauricio de Zabala was born in Durango, Vizcaya, Spain, in 1682. He joined the Spanish army as a young man and spent nearly 20 years fighting in a variety of campaigns. In 1717, he assumed the post of captain general of Río de la Plata*. His tenure there was marked by his successful resistance against French and Portuguese incursions into the Río de la Plata region and by his suppression of the revolt of the *comuneros** in Paraguay.* In 1726, to strengthen the Spanish foothold in the region, Zabala founded the city of Montevideo.* In 1734, he was named captain general of Chile*, but he died in 1736 before he could assume the post.

REFERENCE: Ione S. Wright and Lisa M. Nekhom, *Historical Dictionary of Argentina*, 1978.

ZACATECAS. The city of Zacatecas, Mexico, was founded in 1548 by Juan de Tolosa, who came across the rich silver deposits mined by the Zacatec Indians. Along with another explorer, Cristóbal de Oñate, Tolosa developed those deposits and became the most wealthy individual in New Spain*. Throughout most of the colonial period, Zacatecas was a prosperous mining* center in New Spain. In 1787, the Spanish Crown, as part of the Bourbon reforms of King Charles III*, created the *intendencia** of Zacatecas in the viceroyalty of New Spain*. In 1821, the region became part of newly independent Mexico.
See NEW SPAIN.

ZAMBO. In colonial Spanish America, the term "zambo" was used to describe an individual of mixed African and Indian* birth. Discriminated against widely throughout the colonies, zambos were forbidden to hold public office and could not seek a formal education or enter the professions.

REFERENCE: James F. King, "The Colored Castes and American Representation in the Cortes of Cádiz," *Hispanic American Historical Review*, 33 (1953), 33–64.

ZANJÓN, PACT OF. See TEN YEARS WAR.

ZAPATA DE CÁRDENAS, LUIS. Luis Zapata de Cárdenas was born in Llerena, Spain, around 1515 to a noble family. He spent several years in the Spanish army before joining the Franciscan* order in 1542. Zapata rose rapidly through the clerical ranks, becoming commissary general in Peru* in 1561 and provincial of San Miguel province in 1566. Zapata was named bishop of Cartagena de Indias* in 1569 but was then consecrated as archbishop of Bogotá* in 1570; he assumed the post in 1573. Zapata campaigned diligently for his priests to learn the Indian* languages. He was also committed to replacing religious *peninsulare** priests with secular *criollo** clergy in the Indian parishes, earning the wrath of the Franciscans*, Dominicans*, and Augustinians*. Zapata died in Bogotá on January 24, 1590.
    REFERENCE: *New Catholic Encyclopedia*, XIV:1112, 1967.

ZAPATA Y SANDOVAL, JUAN. Juan Zapata y Sandoval was born in Mexico City*, New Spain*, to an aristocratic family sometime in the 1570s. He joined the Augustinian* order in 1590. After earning a degree in theology at the University of Mexico*, he went to Spain in 1602, where he taught at the Colegio San Gabriel until 1613. He returned to New Spain* in 1614 as the bishop of Puebla*. He was named bishop of Guatemala* in 1621. Zapata's bishoprics are best remembered because of his commitment to the notion that civil and ecclesiastical appointments in New Spain should go to local *criollos**. That point of view was expressed in his book *De justitia distributiva* (1609). Zapata died in Guatemala City* on January 9, 1630.
    REFERENCE: *New Catholic Encyclopedia*, XIV:1112–13, 1967.

ZARAGOSA, TREATY OF (1529). The Treaty of Tordesillas* of 1494 had settled the immediate rivalry between Portugal and Spain over the Asian spice trade which had resulted from Christopher Columbus's* discovery of America. Ferdinand Magellan's* voyage of 1519–1522 reopened that conflict by proving that a southwestern route to the Spice Islands* (Moluccas) existed. A conference between the two powers was held at Badajoz-Elvas during April and May of 1524 to determine ownership of the Spice Islands. It broke up without reaching a decision. As a result, Emperor Charles V* sent a second expedition of seven ships under the command of García de Loaysa* to the Moluccas by the new southwestern route in order to strengthen his claim. Only one ship survived the Pacific passage to join the survivors of Magellan's ship *Trinidad* on Tidore Island. A third expedition of three ships was dispatched from New Spain* in 1527. Once again, only one ship survived the passage and, like the *Trinidad* of Magellan, it proved unable to find the right sailing route to make a return trip across the Pacific.
    Meanwhile, as early as 1526 Charles V was coming to the conclusion that he needed Portugal as an ally in Europe more than he needed to control the distant

Spice Islands. In that year, he married the Portuguese Infanta and even began negotiating a treaty that would have given up any Spanish claims to the Moluccas. It was not until April 22, 1529, however, that a satisfactory treaty was finally negotiated at Zaragosa. The Treaty of Zaragosa was a vague agreement, probably because Charles V wished to avoid offending his own Cortes of Castile, which opposed any renunciation of Spanish claims to the Moluccas. Instead, in the Treaty of Zaragosa, Charles V pawned his claim to the Moluccas in exchange for 350,000 ducats. When the ownership of the islands was finally decided between Spain and Portugal, he was to return the money if the decision went in favor of Portugal. Meanwhile, Portugal promised to build no new fortifications on the islands, and a line of demarcation was set up 297.5 leagues east of the Moluccas to keep the contending Spanish and Portuguese apart. Final ownership of the Moluccas was never decided. Portugal kept its shaky control over the turbulent islands until the Dutch drove them out at the beginning of the seventeenth century; Charles V kept his money. The Spanish also chose to ignore the treaty's line of demarcation in their settlement of the Philippines[*] later in the sixteenth century.

REFERENCES: Donald Lack, *Asia in the Making of Europe*. Vol. 1: *The Century of Discovery*, 1965; Frances Gardiner Davenport, ed., *European Treaties Bearing on the History of the United States and its Dependencies*, 4 vols., 1917.

Ronald Fritze

ZAYAS Y ALFONSO, ALFREDO. Alfredo Zayas y Alfonso was born on February 21, 1861, in Havana[*], Cuba[*]. After studying at the Colegio El Salvador, he received a law degree in 1882 from the University of Havana. Zayas practiced law in Havana and was an active member of the Revolutionary Party. He served as a prosecuting attorney and as a municipal judge in the 1890s. Spanish authorities imprisoned him in 1896 for treason, and he was exiled in 1897. Zayas returned to Cuba after independence was secured in 1898 and pursued an active political career. During the early 1900s, he served in the Cuban senate and in 1906 led a rebellion against the government of Tomás Estrada Palma. In 1908, he served a term as vice-president of the republic, and between 1921 and 1928, he was president of Cuba. Zayas was also an active historian. He died in Havana in 1934.

REFERENCE: William Belmont Parker, *Cubans of Today*, 1967.

ZENTEÑO DEL POZO Y SILVA, JOSÉ IGNACIO. José Ignacio del Zenteño del Pozo y Silva was born in Santiago[*], Chile[*], in 1786. He became the secretary of José de San Martín[*] and a leader in the Chilean independence movement. Between 1817 and 1821, Zenteño served as minister of finance and war under Bernardo O'Higgins[*], by whom he was charged with raising enough money to support the revolution while destroying the Spanish revenue system. After the revolution, Zenteño served as governor of Valparaíso[*] from 1821 to 1826. He spent much of the rest of his career in the Chilean legislature and as editor of *El Mercurio*, a newspaper[*] in Valparaiso. Zenteño died in 1847.

REFERENCE: José Toribio Medina, *Diccionario biográfico colonial de Chile*, 1906.

ZUMÁRRAGA, JUAN DE. Juan de Zumárraga was born in Durango in the Basque region of Spain in 1468. He studied in Valladolid and became a Franciscan* priest as a young man. Zumárraga rose through the clerical ranks in a variety of assignments before being named bishop of Mexico in 1527 by Charles I*. Zumárraga was deeply concerned about Spanish treatment of the Indians*, and he found himself embroiled in political controversies with the ministers of the *audiencia**. He excommunicated the ministers and reported their activities to Charles I, who then formed a second *audiencia*. The ministers then brought charges against Zumárraga, who returned to Spain in 1532 to defend himself. He survived those charges and returned to Mexico City* in 1533. During his tenure in Mexico City, Zumárraga built schools, hospitals, a printing press, and a university, and he started making Inquisition* investigations as well. He was appointed archbishop of New Spain* in 1547 and died in Mexico City on June 3, 1548.

REFERENCES: Joaquín García Icazbalceta, *Don Fray Juan de Zumárraga primer obispo y arzobispo de México*, 3 vols., 1947; R. E. Greenleaf, *Zumárraga and the Mexican Inquisition, 1536–1543*, 1962.

ZUMAYA, MANUEL DE. Manuel de Zumaya was born in Mexico City*, New Spain*, in 1682 and eventually became one of the greatest musicians of colonial New Spain. He studied organ under José Ydiaquez, who clearly recognized him as a child prodigy. He composed the first opera performed in North America, *La Partenope*, and he served as chapelmaster first in Mexico City and later in Oaxaca*. Manuel de Zumaya died in 1755.

REFERENCE: *New Catholic Encyclopedia*, XIV:1138, 1967.

Appendix A

A HISTORICAL CHRONOLOGY OF THE SPANISH EMPIRE

1402 King Henry III of Castile claims the Canary Islands.

1469 Isabella of Castile marries Ferdinand of Aragon; Spain captures Melilla.

1476 Diego García de Herrera founds Santa Cruz de Mar Pequeña on the coast of West Africa.

1479 Spain and Portugal conclude the Treaty of Alcazovas.

1492 The Moors are expelled from Granada and Spain; Christopher Columbus discovers the New World.

1493 The Papal Bull *Inter caetera* is issued.

1494 The Treaty of Tordesillas is signed by Spain and Portugal.

1496 Forced Indian labor begins on Hispaniola.

1499 Alonso de Ojeda, along with Amerigo Vespucci and Juan de la Cosa, begin exploration of the northern coast of South America.

1501 Rodrigo de Bastidas discovers the Isthmus of Panama.

1503 The Casa de Contratación is established in Seville to control trade with the new Spanish territories, and Queen Isabella authorizes the establishment of *encomiendas*. Christopher Columbus establishes Santa María de Belén in Panama, while Cristóbal de Guerra explores the coast of Colombia.

1504 Juan de la Cosa begins his exploration from the Gulf of Cumaná in Venezuela to the Gulf of Uraba in Colombia.

1506 Juan de Solís and Vicente Yáñes begin their exploration of the Central American coast.

1509 Spain and Portugal conclude the Treaty of Cintra. Spain colonizes the Isthmus of Panama.

1510   Diego Velázquez is commissioned to conquer and settle Cuba, while Alonso de
        Ojeda establishes a settlement on the Gulf of Uraba. The Spanish crown legitimizes
        the *requerimiento*.

1511   The *audiencia* of Santo Domingo is established.

1513   Vasco Núñez de Balboa discovers the Pacific Ocean, and Pedro Arias de Ávila
        is named governor of Castilla del Oro.

1516   Juan de Solís enters the Río de la Plata estuary and names it Mar Dulce. Meanwhile,
        Charles I, the first Habsburg, becomes king of Castile and of Aragon.

1517   Francisco Hernández de Córdoba explores the coast of the Yucatán; the Spanish
        Crown authorizes African slavery as a substitute for Indian slavery.

1518   Juan de Grijalva, sailing from Cuba, explores the Mexican coast from Cozumel
        to Tampico.

1519   The expedition of Ferdinand Magellan begins its circumnavigation of the globe,
        while Hernán Cortés begins the conquest of the Aztec empire of Mexico.

1520   Spain orders the end of the granting of *encomiendas*.

1522   The Spanish occupation of Honduras begins, Gil González Dávila explores the
        Bay of Fonseca, and Pascual de Andagoya explores the Pacific coast of Colombia.

1524   Pedro Arias de Ávila sets out for Honduras from Nicaragua and conquers Gua-
        temala. Francisco Hernández de Córdoba establishes Granada and León, Hon-
        duras, while Francisco Pizarro and Diego de Almagro explore the west coast of
        South America, from Panama south to Ecuador. The Cakchiquel Revolt begins.

1525   Hernán Cortés makes the overland trek from Mexico to Honduras. Juan López
        de Aguirre establishes Trujillo, Honduras, Pedro de Alvarado establishes San
        Salvador, and Rodrigo de Bastidas founds Santa Marta, Colombia.

1526   Diego López de Salcedo becomes the first territorial governor in Honduras; the
        fleet system is inaugurated between Spain and the colonies in order to reduce
        losses to pirates and privateers.

1527   Sebastián Cabot's expedition moves up the Paraná River and establishes the first
        Spanish settlement in the Río de la Plata area—Fort Sancti Spiritus; his expedition
        meets up with that of Diego García. The *audiencia* of Mexico City, the first
        bishopric in New Spain, and the captaincy generals of Guatemala and of Nicaragua
        are established.

1528   Ambrosius Alfinger begins his exploration of the Venezuelan coast, and the Wel-
        sers receive their Venezuelan land grant.

1529   Emperor Charles V signs the *capitulación* giving Francisco Pizarro the rights to
        Peru.

1530   The Cakchiquel Revolt ends.

1531   Martín de Sousa of Portugal visits the Río de la Plata area and triggers the Spanish
        decision to occupy the region.

1532   Francisco Pizarro captures Atahualpa and begins granting *encomiendas* in Peru.

1533   Atahualpa is executed by Francisco Pizarro, and the Spaniards seize Cuzco, Peru.
        The last major Indian resistance on Cuba is crushed, and Pedro de Heredía founds
        Cartagena, Colombia.

1534   Diego de Almagro is proclaimed governor of New Toledo (Chile).

1535   The viceroyalty of New Spain is established, with Antonio de Mendoza as the first viceroy; the *audiencia* of Panama is founded. Francisco Pizarro founds the city of Lima, Peru, Nikolas Federmann begins his explorations in Venezuela and Colombia, and Diego de Almagro enters Chile.

1536   The expedition of Pedro de Mendoza officially founds the city of Buenos Aires, Argentina; Bartolomé de las Casas protests Spanish treatment of Indians.

1537   French corsairs begin to attack Spanish settlements in Central America. Spaniards establish the city of Asunción, Paraguay. Pope Paul III issues the bull *Sublimis Deus*.

1538   Gonzalo Jiménez de Quesada founds Santa Fe de Bogotá, and the *audiencia* of Panama is established.

1539   The Lempira Indian rebellion is crushed in Honduras, but the Gaitana rebellion begins in New Granada. Francisco de Orellano begins his exploration of the Amazon.

1541   Partisans of Diego de Almagro kill Francisco Pizarro. Spaniards establish the cities of Santiago, Chile, and Quito, Ecuador, but the Spanish settlement at Buenos Aires is abandoned.

1542   The *audiencias* of Los Confines and of Lima are established, as is the viceroyalty of Peru. The Spanish Crown proclaims the New Laws, and Francisco de Orellano completes an exploration of the Amazon.

1544   Gonzalo Pizarro leads a coup d'état that contributes to the murder of Viceroy Blasco Núñez de Vela in Peru.

1545   The great silver deposits of Potosí, Bolivia, are discovered.

1546   The great silver deposits of Zacatecas, New Spain, are discovered.

1548   The city of La Paz, Bolivia, is established, as is the *audiencia* of New Galicia. Pedro de la Gasca defeats Gonzalo Pizarro and restores Crown authority in Peru.

1549   The *audiencia* of New Granada (Santa Fe de Bogotá) is established.

1550   Cattle and sheep from Portugal are introduced into the Río de la Plata area.

1551   Juan Núñez del Prado establishes Barco, Argentina.

1553   Pedro de Valdivia is killed in the Lautaro rebellion in Chile.

1556   Philip II comes to the Spanish throne upon the abdication of his father, Emperor Charles V.

1557   Spanish forces finally crush the Lautaro rebellion in Chile, but the Pijao Indian rebellion begins in New Granada.

1558   Elizabeth I succeeds to the English throne, precipitating widespread English privateering against Spanish shipping.

1559   The *audiencia* of Charcas is established, and an expedition under the command of Juan Ladrillero reaches the Strait of Magellan in Chile.

1560   Jesuits enter the Río de la Plata area.

1561   Pedro del Castillo establishes Mendoza, Argentina, and Juan de Cavallón leads the first successful colonization expedition to Costa Rica. Seville's monopoly over all American trade is established.

1563   The *audiencia* of Quito is established.

1565   Diego Villarroel establishes Tucumán, Argentina.

1567   The *audiencia* of Chile is established.

1569   Caracas, Venezuela, is established.

1570   Control over Honduras is given to the captaincy general of Guatemala, while the *audiencia* of Chile is suppressed. The city of Cochabamba, Bolivia, is established.

1571   The Office of the Inquisition is established in Mexico City.

1573   Jerónimo Luis de Cabrera establishes Córdoba, Argentina.

1575   The *alcabala* tax is first collected at the rate of 2 percent; the *audiencia* of Chile is suppressed.

1578   Franciscans establish the first missions in the Río de la Plata area.

1580   Juan de Garay re-establishes the city of Buenos Aires.

1582   Spain establishes political sovereignty over Portugal, Hernando de Lerma establishes Salta, Argentina, and Jesuits arrive in Guatemala.

1583   The *audiencia* of the Philippines is established.

1588   The Spanish Armada is defeated. Torres de Vera y Aragón establishes Corrientes, Argentina.

1593   Jesuits arrive in Chile.

1598   Philip III becomes king of Spain. The Pelantrau Indian Rebellion in Chile begins.

1599   The Araucanian Indians destroy Valdivia, Chile.

1608   Philip III authorizes the enslavement of Indians captured in Chile.

1617   The province of Río de la Plata is separated from Paraguay.

1620   The diocese of Buenos Aires is established.

1621   Philip IV becomes king of Spain.

1630   The Calchaquí rebellion begins in Río de la Plata, but Spaniards achieve a great victory over the Araucanians at La Albarrada, Chile.

1636   The *alcabala* tax is raised to 6 percent.

1637   The Calchaquí rebellion ends in Río de la Plata.

1639   Cristóbal de Acuña explores the Amazon River from Quito to the Atlantic Ocean.

1640   Portugal declares its independence from Spain.

1655   The Araucanian Indians launch a widespread rebellion throughout Chile. The British capture Jamaica.

1658   The second Calchaquí rebellion begins in Río de la Plata.

1661   The *audiencia* of Buenos Aires is established.

1662   A British log-cutting post is established at Belize.

1666   The Calchaquí rebellion ends in Rio de la Plata.

1671   The *audiencia* of Buenos Aires is suppressed.

1672   The Chamorro uprising against Spain takes place in the Mariana Islands.

1674   The Spanish Crown abolishes Indian slavery in Chile.

1680   Portugal establishes the Colônia do Sacramento across the Río de la Plata estuary from Buenos Aires.

1698   William Paterson establishes the unsuccessful Scottish colony at Darién, Panama.

1700   The reign of Philip V, the first of the Bourbon kings, begins.

1701   The War of the Spanish Succession begins.

1704   The British seize Gibraltar.

1713   The War of the Spanish Succession ends.

1714   The Honduras Company is chartered.

1717   The first revolt of the *vegueros* against the tobacco monopoly occurs in Cuba, and the Casa de la Contratación is transferred from Seville to Cádiz.

1718   Spain declares war on France and England. *Encomiendas* are made Crown property, subject to royal taxes, and they rapidly disappear from the New World.

1719   The viceroyalty of New Granada is established.

1720   Spain's war with France and England ends, with France recognizing Spanish sovereignty over Texas.

1721   The Revolt of the Comuneros begins in Paraguay.

1723   The viceroyalty of New Granada is suppressed.

1726   Bruno Mauricio de Zabala establishes the settlement of Montevideo, Uruguay.

1727   Spain declares war on France and England and conducts a four-month siege of Gibraltar.

1728   The Caracas Company is chartered.

1729   Spain's war with France and England ends.

1733   Spain declares war on Austria.

1734   The Galicia Company is chartered.

1735   The Revolt of the Comuneros ends in Paraguay.

1738   Spain's war with Austria ends.

1739   The War of Jenkin's Ear begins; the viceroyalty of New Granada is re-established.

1740   The War of the Austrian Succession begins, and the Havana Company is chartered.

1746   The reign of Ferdinand VI begins, and the War of the Austrian Succession ends.

1748   The Treaty of Aix-la-Chapelle is concluded.

1750   The Guaraní War begins when the Indians refuse to be transferred from Spanish to Portuguese jurisdiction. The Treaty of Madrid is concluded.

1756   The Seven Years War begins.

1759   The reign of Charles III begins.

1761   Treaty of Pardo between Spain and Portugal annuls the Treaty of Madrid of 1750.

1762   England attacks and occupies Havana, Cuba.

1763   The Treaty of Paris ends the Seven Years War.

1765   The *visita* of José de Galvez begins in New Spain.

1767   The Jesuits are expelled from the Spanish Empire.

1771   Spain cedes the Malvinas (Falkland) Islands to Great Britain.

1776   The American Revolution begins. The viceroyalty of Río de la Plata is established, and the *audiencia* of Charcas becomes part of it.

1777   The Treaty of San Ildefonso between Spain and Portugal delineates the Spanish-Portuguese frontiers in South America. The captaincy general of Venezuela is established.

1778   Spain issues the Free Trade Decree and ends the Seville monopoly. The second treaty of Pardo is concluded between Spain and Portugal, whereby Portugal cedes control over Annobón, Fernando Po, and the Guinea coast to Spain, and France takes Fernando Po and Dominica in payment for Louisiana.

1779   Spain declares war on Great Britain and begins the siege of Gibraltar.

1780   The uprising of Túpac Amaru II begins in Peru, and the Revolt of the Comuneros begins in Colombia.

1781   The Philippine Company is established.

1782   The uprising of Túpac Amaro II ends in Peru, and the Revolt of the Comuneros ends in Colombia. The viceroyalty of Ríío de la Plata is divided into eight intendancies.

1783   The Treaty of Versailles/Paris ends the War of American Independence, and the Spanish claim to Florida is upheld. The siege of Gibraltar by Spain ends. The *audiencia* of Buenos Aires is established.

1787   The *audiencia* of Cuzco is established.

1788   The reign of Charles IV begins.

1793   Spain declares war on France.

1794   Antonio Nariño publishes his translation of the Declaration of the Rights of Man.

1795   Spain's war with France ends, and Spain cedes half of Hispaniola to France.

1796   Spain declares war on England.

1797   The Spanish colonies are allowed to trade with neutral non-Spanish ports.

1799   Alexander von Humboldt begins his scientific expeditions in Spanish America.

1800   Spain's war on England ends.

1801   Spain declares war on Portugal.

1802   Bernardo O'Higgins returns to Chile. The Peace of Amiens provides for the return of Minorca to Spain from Great Britain, while Spain cedes Trinidad to Great Britain.

1803   Simón Bolívar travels to Europe seeking assistance for Latin American independence.

1804   St. Dominque (Haiti) declares its independence from France.

1805   Spain declares war on England.

1806   Francisco de Miranda leads his expedition to Venezuela, and the British invade Buenos Aires.

1807   France invades Spain, and the British invade Buenos Aires again. Simón Bolívar returns to Venezuela from Europe.

1808   Charles IV abdicates the Spanish throne, Ferdinand VII is imprisoned by Napoleon, and the rule of Joseph Bonaparte over Spain begins. Viceroy José de Iturrigaray is deported from New Spain.

1809   The uprising of Martín de Alzaga in Buenos Aires fails to exile Viceroy Santiago de Liniers, while the Murillo uprising occurs in La Paz, Bolivia. Mariano Moreno publishes his tract advocating free trade.

1810   Revolutionary junta are established in Caracas, Venezuela, and in Santiago, Chile. The May Revolution takes place in Río de la Plata, but Paraguayans reject the leadership of Buenos Aires. New Granada declares its independence, and in New Spain Miguel Hidalgo launches its independence movement. The Cortes of Cádiz begins to meet.

1811   Paraguay declares its independence from both Spain and the United Provinces of Río de la Plata. Venezuela declares its independence. José M. Delgado leads an independence uprising in San Salvador. The children of slaves born in Chile are declared free.

1812   The Cortes of Cádiz proclaims a liberal Constitution. Patriot forces win the Battle of Tucumán, and José Antonio Aponte leads the slave-free black conspiracy in Cuba.

1813   Simón Bolívar invades Venezuela from Colombia.

1814   Ferdinand VII returns to the Spanish throne and abolishes the constitution of 1812. The Battle of Rancagua takes place in Chile, and the Treaty of Lircay between Chile and Spain is concluded. The Congress of Chilpancingo is held in Mexico, and Uruguay declares its independence.

1815   Royalist forces win the Battle of Sipe-Sipe, which leads to the separation of Upper Peru from the United Provinces of Río de la Plata. The *audiencia* of Puerto Rico is established.

1816   Buenos Aires declares independence, and the Congress of Tucumán declares the independence of the United Provinces of the Río de la Plata. The Congress of Angostura takes place.

1817   Patriot forces win the Battle of Chacabuco in Chile, and José de San Martín declares the independence of Chile. An Anglo-Spanish agreement provides for the suppression of the slave trade in Fernando Po.

1818   Chile wins its independence, following the battles of Cancha Rayada and Maipú.

1819   The Battle of Boyacá takes place in Venezuela; Simón Bolívar captures Bogotá and liberates New Granada from Spanish rule. The constitution of Gran Colombia is proclaimed. Spain cedes Florida to the United States. Spain and the United States conclude the Adams-Oñis Treaty.

1820   The Constitution of 1812 is once again proclaimed, following the Riego revolt in Spain.

1821   The second Battle of Chacabuco takes place in Venezuela, José de San Martín enters Lima, Peru, and Peru declares its independence. Mexico achieves its independence when Viceroy Juan O'Donoju signs the Treaty of Córdoba, and the Act of Central American Independence is proclaimed.

1822 The Battle of Carabobo wins the independence of Colombia and Venezuela. The Battles of Bombona and Pichincha take place in Ecuador; Ecuador joins Gran Colombia. Central America annexes itself to the Mexican Empire, and José de San Martín announces the independence of Peru.

1823 Emperor Agustín Iturbide is overthrown in Mexico, and the Central American Federation secedes from Mexico. Ferdinand VII restores absolute despotism in Spain. Vicente Filisola conquers El Salvador.

1824 The Battle of Junín takes place in Peru, and Patriot forces there win the Battle of Ayacucho. The United Provinces of Central America is established.

1825 Bolivia declares independence, and Uruguay achieves its independence.

1828 Argentina and Brazil agree to the independence of Uruguay.

1830 Gran Colombia disintegrates as Colombia, Venezuela, and Ecuador separate.

1831 Marcelino de Andrés begins his exploration of the Guinea coast.

1837 Spain terminates Cuban representation in the Spanish Cortes.

1838 The Central American Federation begins to disintegrate into Nicaragua, Costa Rica, Honduras, El Salvador, and Guatemala.

1843 Spain formally proclaims its sovereignty over Fernando Po.

1844 "La Escalera" slave conspiracy in Cuba is suppressed.

1859 Spain occupies the Chafarinas Islands, and war begins with Morocco.

1860 The Spanish-Moroccan War ends.

1861 Spain attempts to annex Santo Domingo.

1868 The Ten Years War begins in Cuba, and the "Grito de Lares" movement demands Puerto Rican independence.

1872 The Cavite revolt against Spain erupts in the Philippines.

1878 The Pact of Zanjón ends the Ten Years War in Cuba.

1879 Donald MacKenzie establishes a trading post at Tarfaya.

1883 The Hispanic-African Commercial Company is founded, and the Society of Africanists and Colonists is established in Madrid.

1884 Spain declares a protectorate over Río de Oro, Angra de Cintra, and Cape Blanc.

1886 Spain abolishes slavery in Cuba.

1887 Río de Oro becomes a Spanish colony. José Rizal begins to criticize Spanish rule in the Philippines.

1892 José Martí organizes the Cuban Revolutionary Party. The second Spanish-Moroccan War begins. José Rizal is executed by Spanish officials, and Andrés Bonifacio organizes the Katipunan in the Philippines.

1893 The second Spanish-Moroccan War ends.

1895 An Anglo-Moroccan agreement transfers Tarfaya to Moroccan control. The Cuban war for independence begins, and José Martí is killed there.

1896   General Valeriano Weyler declares a state of emergency in Cuba.

1897   The Pact of Biaknabato leads to the exile of prominent Filipino revolutionary leaders.

1898   The Spanish-American War occurs, and Cuba wins its independence from Spain. The Treaty of Paris ends the war, and Puerto Rico, Guam, and the Philippines become United States territories.

1900   The Franco-Spanish Convention defines the borders of Spanish Guinea and Spanish Sahara.

1904   The Franco-Spanish Convention of 1904 extends the border of Spain's Saharan colony northward.

1906   The Algeciras Conference results in the Act of Algeciras.

1912   The Franco-Spanish Convention results in the establishment of the Spanish protectorate of Spanish Morocco.

1919   The Spanish Foreign Legion is created.

1920   The Rif War in Morocco intensifies as Spain attempts to expand its territory there.

1921   Abd el-Krim proclaims the establishment of the Republic of the Rif and decisively defeats Spanish forces at Anwal.

1925   A joint Franco-Spanish military expedition crushes the Rif rebellion at the Battle of Alhucemas.

1934   Western Sahara is established.

1936   The Spanish Civil War begins.

1938   General Francisco Franco takes on the title of Caudillo and becomes head of the state, the government, the Falange, and the military in Spain.

1939   The Spanish Civil War ends.

1946   Spanish West Africa is established.

1956   Spanish Morocco ceases to exist with the proclamation of Moroccan independence. Spain establishes the Dirección General de Plazas y Provincias Africanas. The Army of Liberation begins its guerrilla war against Spanish forces in Spanish Sahara.

1958   The Agreement of Cintra between Spain and Morocco is concluded; Spanish West Africa is dissolved, and Western Sahara becomes a province of Spain.

1959   Fernando Po and Río Muni are declared Spanish provinces. Spain suppresses the Patronato de Indígenas in Spanish Guinea.

1964   Spain grants self-government to Spanish Guinea.

1966   The colonialism committee of the United Nations calls on Spain to grant full independence to Spanish Guinea.

1967   Spain creates a legislative body, the Djemma, in Spanish Sahara.

1968   Spain announces the independence of Spanish Guinea, and the Republic of Equatorial Guinea, which includes Río Muni, is established. The colonialism committee of the United Nations calls on Spain to grant full independence to Spanish Sahara.

1973   The Polisario Front is established in Spanish Sahara, and the guerrilla war against Spanish authority in Spanish Sahara escalates.

1975   The Madrid Agreement between Spain, Morocco, and Mauritania is reached.

Appendix B

COLONIAL VICEROYS OF THE SPANISH EMPIRE, 1535–1824

VICEROYALTY OF NEW GRANADA

Jorge de Villalongo, Conde de la Cueva (1719–1724)
Sebastián de Eslava y Lazaga (1733–1737)
José Alonso Pizarro, Marqués del Villar (1749–1753)
José Solís Folch de Cardona (1753–1761)
Pedro Mesía de la Cerda, Marqués de la Vega de Armijo (1761–1773)
Manuel de Guiror y Portal de Huarte y Edozain (1773–1776)
Manuel Antonio Flores Maldonado Martínez de Angulo y Bodquín (1776–1782)
Juan de Torreszal Díaz Pimienta (1782)
Juan Francisco Gutiérrez de Piñeres (1782)
Antonio Caballero y Góngora (1782–1788)
Francisco Gil de Taboada Lemos y Villamarín (1789)
José Manuel Ignacio Timoteo de Ezpeleta y Galdeano Dicastillo y del Prado (1789–1797)
Pedro de Mendinueta y Múzquiz (1797–1803)
Antonio Amar y Borbón (1803–1810)
Manuel Bernardo de Álvarez (1810–1811)
Benito Pérez Brito de los Ríos Fernández Valdelomar (1811–1813)
Francisco Montalvo y Ambulodi Arriola y Casabante Valdespino (1813–1818)
Juan José de Sámano y Urribarri de Rebollar y Mazorra (1818–1819)
Juan de la Cruz Mourgeón y Achet (1819–1821)

VICEROYALTY OF NEW SPAIN

Antonio de Mendoza (1535–1550)
Luis de Velasco (1550–1564)
(*Audiencia* control of the viceroyalty, 1564–1566)
Gastón de Peralta, Marqués de Falces (1566–1568)
Martín Enríquez de Almansa (1568–1580)

Lorenzo Suárez de Mendoza, Conde de la Coruña (1580–1582)
Luis de Villanueva y Zapata (1582–1583)
Pedro de Moya y Contreras (1583–1585)
Álvaro Manrique de Zúñiga, Marqués de Villamanrique (1585–1590)
Luis de Velasco, Marqués de Salinas (1590–1595)
Gaspar Zúñiga Acevedo y Fonseca, Marqués de Monterrey (1595–1603)
Juan Manuel Mendoza y Manrique Hurtado y Padilla, Marqués de Montesclaros
    (1603–1607)
Luis de Velasco, Marqués de Salinas (1607–1611)
Francisco García Guerra (1611–1612)
Pedro de Otálora (1612)
Diego Fernández de Cordoba y López de las Roelas Benavides y Melgarejo, Marqués
    de Guadalcázar (1612–1621)
Diego Carrillo de Mendoza y Pimentel, Marqués de Gelves (1621–1624)
Rodrigo Pacheco y Osorio, Marqués de Cerralbo (1624–1635)
Lope Díaz de Armendáriz, Marqués de Cadereyta (1635–1640)
Diego López Pacheco Cabrera y Bobadilla, Duque de Escalona (1640–1642)
Juan de Palafox y Mendoza (1642)
García Sarmiento y Sotomayor Enríquez de Luna, Conde de Salvatierra (1642–1648)
Marcos de Torres y Rueda (1648–1649)
Matías de Peralta (1649–1650)
Luis Enríquez de Guzmán y Coresma, Conde de Alba de Liste (1650–1653)
Francisco Fernández de la Cueva, Duque de Albuquerque (1653–1660)
Juan de Leyva de la Cerda, Conde de Bonos (1660–1664)
Diego Osorio de Escobar y Llamas (1664)
Antonio Sebastián de Toledo Molina y Salazar, Marqués de Mancera (1664–1673)
Pedro Núñez Colón de Portugal y Castro, Duque de Veragua (1673)
Payo Enríquez de Ribera (1673–1680)
Tomás Antonio Manrique de la Cerda y Aragón, Conde de Paredes (1680–1686)
Melchor Portocarrero Lasso de la Vega, Conde de Monclova (1686–1688)
Gaspar de la Cerda Sandoval Silva y Mendoza, Conde de Gálvez (1688–1696)
Juan de Ortega de Montañés (1696–1697)
José Sarmiento de Valladares y Arinas, Conde de Moctezuma (1697–1701)
Juan de Ortega de Montañés (1701–1702)
Francisco Fernández de la Cueva Enríquez, Duque de Alburquerque (1702–1711)
Francisco de Alencastre Noroña y Silva, Duque de Linares (1711–1716)
Baltasar de Zúñiga Guzmán Sotomayor y Mendoza, Marqués de Valero (1716–1722)
Juan de Acuña y Bejarano Astudillo y Marquina, Marqués de Casa Fuerte (1722–1734)
Juan Antonio de Vizarrón y Eguiarreta (1734–1740)
Pedro de Castro y Salazar Figueroa, Duque de la Conquista (1740–1741)
Pedro Malo de Vilavicencio (1741–1742)
Pedro de Cebrián y Agustín, Conde de Fuenclara (1742–1746)
Juan Francisco de Güemes y Horcasitas Gordón y Sáenz de Villamolinedo,
    Conde de Revillagigedo (1746–1755)
Agustín de Ahumada y Villalón, Marqués de las Amarillas (1755–1760)
Francisco de Echévarri (1760)
Francisco Antonio Cagigal de la Vega Salinas y Acevedo (1760–1761)
Joaquín de Montserrat y Ciurana, Marqués de Cruillas (1761–1766)

Carlos Francisco de Croix, Marqués de Croix (1766–1771)
Antonio María de Bucareli y Ursúa Hinostrosa Lasso de la Vega (1771–1779)
Martín de Mayorga (1779–1783)
Matías de Gálvez García Madrid y Cabrera (1783–1784)
Vicente de Herrera y Rivero (1784–1785)
Bernardo Vicente Pólinarde de Gálvez y Galardo (1785–1786)
Eusebio Sánchez Pareja y Beleño (1786–1787)
Alonso Núñez de Haro y Peralta (1787)
Manuel Antonio Flores Maldonado Martínez de Angulo y Bodquín (1787–1789)
Juan Vicente de Güemes Pacheco de Padilla y Horcasitas, Conde de Revillagigedo
    (1789–1794)
Miguel de la Grúa Talamanca y Branciforte, Marqués de Branciforte (1794–1798)
Miguel José de Azanza (1798–1800)
Félix Berenguer de Marquina (1800–1803)
José de Iturrigaray y Aróstegui (1803–1808)
Pedro Garibay (1808–1809)
Francisco Javier de Lizana y Beaumont (1809–1810)
Francisco Javier de Venegas (1810–1813)
Félix María Calleja del Rey, Marqués de Calderón (1813–1816)
Juan Ruiz de Apodaca y Eliza López de Letona y Lasquetty, Conde de Venadito
    (1816–1821)
Francisco Novella Azabal Pérez y Sicardo (1821)

VICEROYALTY OF PERU

Francisco Pizarro (1535–1541)
Diego de Almagro (1541–1542)
Cristóbal Vaca de Castro (1542–1544)
Blasco Núñez de Vela (1544)
Gonzalo Pizarro (1544–1547)
Pedro de la Gasca (1547–1550)
Antonio de Mendoza (1550–1552)
(*Audiencia* control of the viceroyalty, 1552–1556)
Andrés Hurtado de Mendoza, Marqués de Cañete (1556–1561)
Diego López de Zúñiga y Velasco, Conde de Nieva (1561–1564)
Lope García de Castro (1564–1569)
Francisco de Toledo (1569–1581)
Martín Enríquez de Almansa (1581–1583)
(*Audiencia* control of the viceroyalty 1583–1586)
Fernando Torres de Portugal y Mesía Venegas y Ponce de León, Conde de Villadompardo
    (1586–1589)
García Hurtado de Mendoza y Manrique, Marqués de Cañete (1589–1596)
Luis de Velasco, Marqués de Salinas (1596–1604)
Gaspar de Zúñiga Acevedo y Fonseca, Conde de Monterrey (1604–1607)
Juan Manual de Mendoza y Manrique Hurtado y Padilla, Marqués de Montesclaros
    (1607–1615)
Francisco de Borja y Aragón, Príncipe de Esquilache (1615–1621)

Diego Fernández de Córdoba y López de las Roelas Benavides y Melgarejo, Marqués
   de Guadalcázar (1621–1629)
Luis Jerónimo Fernández de Cabrera Bobadilla Cerda y Mendoza, Conde de Chinchón
   (1629–1639)
Pedro de Toledo y Leyva, Marqués de Mancera (1639–1648)
García Sarmiento de Sotomayor Enríquez de Luna, Conde de Salvatierra (1648–1655)
Luis Enríquez de Guzmán y Coresma, Conde de Alba de Liste (1655–1661)
Diego de Benavides y de la Cueva, Conde de Sebastián (1661–1666)
Pedro Antonio Fernández de Castro Andrade y Portugal Conde de Lemos (1666–1674)
Bartolomé de la Cueva Enríquez Arias de Saavedra Pardo Tavera y Ulloa,
   Conde de Castellar (1674–1678)
Melchor Liñán de Cisneros (1678–1681)
Melchor de Navarra y Rocaful, Duque de la Plata (1681–1689)
Melchor Portocarrero Lasso de la Vega, Conde de Monclova (1689–1705)
Manuel Oms de Santa Pau Olim de Semanat y de La Nuza, Marqués de Castell dos Ruís
   (1705–1710)
Diego Ladrón de Guevara (1710–1716)
Carmine Niccolo Caracciolo, Príncipe de Santa Buono (1716–1720)
Diego Morcillo Rubio de Auñón (1720–1724)
José de Armendáriz y Perurena Garrués de Usechi y Urquijo, Marqués de Castellfuerte
   (1724–1736)
José Antonio de Mendoza Camaño y Sotomayor, Marqués de Villagarcí (1736–1745)
José Antonio Manso de Velasco y Sánchez de Samaniego, Conde de Superunda
   (1745–1761)
Manuel de Amat y Junient Planella Aimeric y Santa Pau (1761–1776)
Manuel de Guirior y Portal de Huarte y Edozain, Marqués de Guirior (1776–1780)
Agustín de Jáuregui y Aldecoa (1780–1784)
Teodoro Francisco de Croix, Conde de Croix (1784–1789)
Francisco Gil de Taboada Lemos y Villamarín (1790–1796)
Ambrosio O'Higgins, Marqués de Osorno (1796–1801)
Gabriel de Avilés y del Fierro, Marqués de Avilés (1801–1806)
José Fernando Abascal y Sousa, Marqués de la Concordia (1806–1816)
Joaquín de la Pezuela y Sánchez Muñoz de Velasco (1816–1821)
José de la Serna e Hinojosa (1821–1824)

VICEROYALTY OF RÍO DE LA PLATA

José Juan Vértiz y Salcedo (1778–1784)
Francisco Cristóbal del Campo, Marqués de Loreto (1784–1789)
Nicolás de Arredondo (1789–1795)
Pedro Melo de Portugal y Vilhena (1795–1797)
Antonio Olaguer y Feliú Heredía López y Donec (1797–1799)
Gabriel de Avilés y del Fierro, Marqués de Avilés (1799–1801)
Joaquín del Pino y Rosas Romero Negrete (1801–1804)
Rafael de Sobremonte Núñez Castillo Angulo y Bullón Ramírez de Arellano,
   Marqués de Sobremonte (1804–1807)
Pascual Ruiz Huidobro (1807)

Santiago Antonio María de Liniers y Bremont (1807–1809)
Baltasar Hidalgo y Cisneros y la Torre (1809–1810)

REFERENCE: David P. Henige, *Colonial Governors from the Fifteenth Century to the Present*, 1970.

SELECTED
BIBLIOGRAPHY

Aiton, A. S. *Antonio de Mendoza: First Viceroy of New Spain*. Durham, N. C.: Duke University Press, 1927.

Alba, Victor. *The Communist Party in Spain*. Trans. by Vincent G. Smith. New Brunswick, N. J.: Transaction, 1983.

Alden, Dauril. *Royal Government in Colonial Brazil with Special Reference to the Administration of the Marquis of Lavradio, Viceroy, 1769–1779*. Berkeley and Los Angeles: University of California Press, 1968.

Andrews, Kenneth R. *The Spanish Caribbean: Trade and Plunder, 1530–1630*. New Haven, Conn.: Yale University Press, 1978.

Andrien, Kenneth J. *Crisis and Decline: The Viceroyalty of Peru in the Seventeenth Century*. Albuquerque: University of New Mexico Press, 1985.

Anna, Timothy E. *The Fall of the Royal Government in Mexico City*. Lincoln: University of Nebraska Press, 1978.

————. *The Fall of the Royal Government in Peru*. Lincoln: University of Nebraska Press, 1979.

————. *Spain and the Loss of America*. Lincoln: University of Nebraska Press, 1983.

Archer, Christon I. *The Army in Bourbon Mexico, 1760–1857*. Stanford, Calif.: Stanford University Press, 1985.

Arnada, Charles W. *The Emergence of the Republic of Bolivia*. Gainesville: University of Florida Press, 1957.

Arrom, Silvia Marina. *The Women of Mexico City, 1790–1857*. Stanford, Calif.: Stanford University Press, 1985.

Bakewell, Peter J. *Silver Mining and Society in Colonial Mexico: Zacatecas, 1546–1700*. Cambridge, England: Cambridge University Press, 1971.

Banks, George. *Peru Before Pizarro*. Oxford, England: Phaidon Press, 1977.

Bannon, John Francis. *The Spanish Borderlands Frontier, 1513–1821*. New York: Holt, Rinehart, and Winston, 1970.

Barbier, Jacques A. *Reform and Politics in Bourbon Chile, 1755–1796*. Ottawa, Canada: University of Ottawa Press, 1980.

Ben-Ami, Shlomo. *Fascism from Above: The Dictatorship of Primo de Rivera in Spain, 1923–1930*. Oxford, England: Oxford University Press, 1983.

———. *The Origin of the Second Republic in Spain*. Oxford, England: Oxford University Press, 1978.

Benson, Nettie Lee, ed. *Mexico and the Spanish Cortes, 1810–1822*. Austin: University of Texas Press, 1966.

Bernal, Ignacio. *Mexico Before Cortez: Art, History, and Legend*. Trans. by Willis Barnstone. Garden City, N. Y.: Doubleday, 1975.

Bolton, Herbert E. *Rim of Christendom: A Biography of Eusebio Francisco Kino, Pacific Coast Pioneer*. New York: Macmillan, 1936.

Borah, Woodrow W. *Justice by Insurance: The General Indian Court of Colonial Mexico and the Legal Aides of the Half-Real*. Berkeley and Los Angeles: University of California Press, 1983.

Borah, Woodrow, and Sherburne F. Cook. *The Aboriginal Population of Central Mexico on the Eve of Spanish Conquest*. Berkeley and Los Angeles: University of California Press, 1963.

Bowser, Frederick P. *The African Slave in Colonial Peru, 1524–1650*. Stanford, Calif.: Stanford University Press, 1973.

Boxer, Charles R. *The Dutch in Brazil, 1624–1654*. Oxford, England: Clarendon Press, 1957.

———. *The Golden Age of Brazil, 1695–1750*. Berkeley and Los Angeles: University of California Press, 1962.

———. *The Portuguese Seaborne Empire, 1415–1825*. New York: Knopf, 1969.

———. *Salvador de Sá and the Struggle for Brazil and Angola, 1602–1686*. London, England: University of London, 1952.

Brading, D. A. *Haciendas and Ranchos in the Mexican Bajio Leon 1700–1860*. Cambridge, England: Cambridge University Press, 1978.

———. *Miners and Merchants in Bourbon Mexico*. Cambridge, England: Cambridge University Press, 1970.

Brown, Jonathan C. *A Socioeconomic History of Argentina, 1776–1860*. Cambridge, England: Cambridge University Press, 1979.

Brown, Kendall W. *Bourbons & Brandy: Imperial Reform in Eighteenth-Century Arequipa*. Albuquerque: University of New Mexico Press, 1986.

Bumgartner, Louis E. *José del Valle of Central America*. Durham, N. C.: Duke University Press, 1963.

Burkholder, Mark A. *Politics of a Colonial Career: José Baquíjano and the Audiencia of Lima*. Albuquerque: University of New Mexico Press, 1980.

Burkholder, Mark A., and D. S. Chandler. *From Impotence to Authority: The Spanish Crown and the American Audiencias, 1687–1808*. Columbia: University of Missouri Press, 1977.

Bushnell, Amy. *The King's Coffer: Proprietors of the Spanish Florida Treasury, 1565–1702*. Gainesville: University Presses of Florida, 1981.

Bushnell, David, ed. *The Liberator, Simon Bolivar: Man and Image*. New York: Knopf, 1970.

Callahan, William J. *Church, Politics, and Society in Spain, 1750–1874*. Cambridge, Mass.: Harvard University Press, 1984.

Campbell, Leon G. *The Military and Society in Colonial Peru, 1750–1810*. Philadelphia, Pa.: American Philosophical Society, 1978.

Carr, Raymond. *Modern Spain, 1875–1980*. Oxford, England: Oxford University Press, 1980.

Castro, America. *The Structure of Spanish History*. Trans. by Edmund King. Princeton, N. J.: Princeton University Press, 1954.

Chance, John K. *Race and Class in Colonial Oaxaca*. Stanford, Calif.: Stanford University Press, 1978.

Chevalier, François. *Land and Society in Colonial Mexico: The Great Hacienda*. Trans. by Lesley Byrd Simpson. Berkeley and Los Angeles: University of California Press, 1963.

Christiansen, E. *The Origin of Military Power in Spain, 1800–1854*. London, England: Oxford University Press, 1967.

Clayton, Lawrence A. *Caulkers and Carpenters in a New World: The Shipyards of Colonial Guayaquil*. Athens: Ohio University Center for International Studies, 1980.

Clendinnen, Inga. *Ambivalent Conquests: Maya and Spaniard in Yucatán, 1517–1570*. Cambridge, England: Cambridge University Press, 1987.

Cobo, Bernabe, *History of the Inca Empire*. Trans. and ed. by Roland Hamilton. Austin: University of Texas Press, 1979.

Coe, Michael. *The Maya*. New York: Praeger, 1956.

Cohen, David W., and Jack P. Greene, ed. *Neither Slave nor Free: The Freedmen of African Descent in the Slave Societies of the New World*. Baltimore, Md.: Johns Hopkins University Press, 1972.

Cole, Jeffrey A. *Potosi Mita*. Stanford, Calif.: Stanford University Press, 1985.

Collier, Simon. *Ideas and Politics of Chilean Independence, 1808–1833*. Cambridge, England: Cambridge University Press, 1969.

Conrad, Geoffrey W., and Arthur A. Demarest. *Religion and Empire: The Dynamics of Aztec and Inca Expansionism*. Cambridge, England: Cambridge University Press, 1984.

Conrad, Robert E. *World of Sorrow: The African Slave Trade to Brazil*. Baton Rouge: Louisiana State University Press, 1986.

Cook, Noble David. *Demographic Collapse: Indian Peru, 1520–1620*. Cambridge, England: Cambridge University Press, 1981.

Cortés, Hernán. *Hernán Cortés: Letters from Mexico*. Trans. and ed. A. R. Pagden, with an introduction by J. H. Elliott. New York: Orion Press, 1971.

Costeloe, Michael P. *Response to Revolution: Imperial Spain and the American Revolutions, 1810–1840*. Cambridge, England: Cambridge University Press, 1986.

Crosby, Alfred W. *The Columbian Exchange: Biological and Cultural Consequences of 1492*. Westport, Conn.: Greenwood Press, 1972.

Curtin, Philip D. *The Atlantic Slave Trade: A Census*. Madison: Universiy of Wisconsin Press, 1969.

Cushner, Nicholas P. *Farm and Factory: The Jesuits and the Development of Agrarian Capitalism in Colonial Quito, 1600–1767*. Albany: State University of New York Press, 1982.

———. *Jesuit Ranches and the Agrarian Development of Colonial Argentina, 1650–1767*. Albany: State University of New York Press, 1983.

————. *Lords of the Land: Sugar, Wine, and Jesuit Estates of Coastal Peru, 1600–1767*. Albany: State University of New York Press, 1980.

Davies, Keith A. *Landowners in Colonial Peru*. Austin: University of Texas Press, 1984.

Day, A. Grove. *Coronado's Quest*. Berkeley and Los Angeles: University of California Press, 1940.

Denevan, William M., ed. *The Native Population of the Americas in 1492*. Madison: University of Wisconsin Press, 1976.

Descola, Jean. *Daily Life in Colonial Peru, 1710–1820*. London, England: Allen & Unwin, 1968.

Díaz del Castillo, Bernal. *The True History of the Conquest of New Spain, 1517–1521*. Trans. by A. P. Maudslay. New York: Farrar, Straus, & Giroux, 1966.

Diffie, Bailey W. *A History of Colonial Brazil, 1500–1792*. Ed. by Edwin J. Perkins. Melbourne, Fla.: Krieger, 1987.

Domínguez, Jorge I. *Insurrection or Loyalty: The Breakdown of the Spanish American Empire*. Cambridge: Cambridge University Press, 1980.

Earle, Peter. *The Sack of Panama: Sir Henry Morgan's Adventures on the Spanish Main*. New York: Viking, 1982.

Elliott, J. H. *Imperial Spain, 1469–1716*. New York: New American Library, 1964.

Engerman, Stanley, and Eugene D. Genovese. *Race and Slavery in the Western Hemisphere: Quantitative Studies*. Princeton, N.J.: Princeton University Press, 1975.

Exquemelin, A. O. *The Buccaneers of America*. Trans. by Alexis Brown. Baltimore, Md.: Penguin, 1969.

Farriss, N. M. *Crown and Clergy in Colonial Mexico, 1759–1821: The Crisis of Ecclesiastical Privilege*. London, England: Athlone, 1968.

Farriss, Nancy M. *Maya Society Under Colonial Rule: The Collective Enterprise of Survival*. Princeton, N.J.: Princeton University Press, 1984.

Fisher, John R. *Commercial Relations Between Spain and Spanish America in the Era of Free Trade, 1778–1796*. Liverpool, England: Centre for Latin American Studies, University of Liverpool, 1985.

————. *Government and Society in Colonial Peru: The Intendant System, 1783–1814*. London, England: Athlone, 1970.

————. *Silver Mines and Silver Miners in Colonial Peru, 1776–1824*. Liverpool, England: Centre for Latin American Studies, University of Liverpool, 1977.

Flores Caballero, Romeo. *Counterrevolution: The Role of the Spaniards in the Independence of Mexico, 1804–1838*. Trans. by Jaime E. Rodriguez O. Lincoln: University of Nebraska Press, 1974.

Gallo, Max. *Spain under Franco: A History*. Trans. by Jean Stewart. London, England: Allen & Unwin, 1973.

Gardiner, C. Harvey. *Naval Power in the Conquest of Mexico*. Austin: University of Texas Press, 1956.

Gibson, Charles. *The Aztecs Under Spanish Rule: A History of the Indians of the Valley of Mexico*. Stanford, Calif.: Stanford University Press, 1964.

————. *Spain in America*. New York: Harper & Row, 1966.

Glover, Michael. *The Peninsular War, 1807–1814: A Concise Military History*. London, England: David and Charles, 1974.

Greenleaf, Richard. *The Mexican Inquisition in the Seventeenth Century*. Albuquerque: University of New Mexico Press, 1969.

————. *Zumárraga and the Mexican Inquisition, 1536–1543*. Washington, D.C.: Academy of American Franciscan History, 1961.

————. *The Roman Catholic Church in Colonial Latin America*. New York: Knopf, 1971.

Griffin, Charles C. *The United States and the Disruption of the Spanish Empire, 1800–1822*. New York: Columbia University Press, 1937.

Halperín-Donghi, Tulio. *The Aftermath of Revolution in Latin America*. New York: Harper & Row, 1973.

————. *Politics, Economics, and Society in Argentina in the Revolutionary Period*. Cambridge, England: Cambridge University Press, 1975.

Hamill, Hugh M., Jr. *The Hidalgo Revolt: Prelude to Mexican Independence*. Gainesville: University of Florida Press, 1966.

Hamilton, Earl. *War and Prices in Spain, 1651–1800*. Cambridge, Mass.: Harvard University Press, 1947.

Hamnett, Brian R. *Politics and Trade in Southern Mexico, 1750–1821*. Cambridge, England: Cambridge University Press, 1971.

————. *Roots of Insurgency: Mexican Regions, 1750–1824*. Cambridge, England: Cambridge University Press, 1986.

Hanke, Lewis. *The Imperial City of Potosí: An Unwritten Chapter in the History of Spanish America*. The Hague: Martinus Nijhoff, 1956.

————. *The Spanish Struggle for Justice in the Conquest of America*. Philadelphia: University of Pennsylvania Press, 1949.

Hardoy, Jorge. *Precolumbian Cities*. New York: Walker, 1973.

Haring, C. H. *The Spanish Empire in America*. New York: Oxford University Press, 1947.

Haring, Clarence H. *Trade and Navigation Between Spain and the Indies in the Time of the Hapsburgs*. Cambridge, Mass.: Harvard University Press, 1918.

Harris, Charles A., III. *A Mexican Family Empire: The Latifundio of the Sanchez Navarro Family, 1765–1867*. Austin: University of Texas Press, 1975.

Harrison, Joseph. *An Economic History of Modern Spain*. Manchester, England: Manchester University Press, 1978.

Hassig, Ross. *Aztec Warfare: Imperial Expansion and Political Control*. Norman: University of Oklahoma Press, 1988.

————. *Trade, Tribute, and Transportation: The Sixteenth-Century Political Economy of the Valley of Mexico*. Norman: University of Oklahoma Press, 1985.

Hemming, John. *The Conquest of the Incas*. New York: Harcourt Brace Jovanovich, 1970.

————. *Red Gold: The Conquest of the Brazilian Indians*. Cambridge, Mass.: Harvard University Press, 1978.

————. *The Search for El Dorado*. London, England: Michael Joseph, 1978.

Hennessy, C. A. M. *Modern Spain*. London, England: Historical Association, 1965.

Henschen, Folke. *The History and Geography of Diseases*. Trans. by Joan Tate. New York: Delacorte, 1966.

Herr, Richard. *The Eighteenth-Century Revolution in Spain*. Princeton, N.J.: Princeton University Press, 1958.

Hills, George. *Franco: The Man and His Nation*. London, England: Hale, 1967.

Hoberman, Louisa Schell, and Susan Migden Socolow. *Cities and Society in Colonial Latin America*. Albuquerque: University of New Mexico Press, 1986.

Hoffman, Paul E. *The Spanish Crown and the Defense of the Caribbean, 1535–1585: Precedent, Patrimonialism, and Royal Parsimony*. Baton Rouge: Louisiana State University Press, 1980.

Huddleston, Lee Eldridge. *Origins of the American Indians: European Concepts, 1492–1729*. Austin: University of Texas Press, 1967.

Humboldt, Alexander Von. *Political Essay on the Kingdom of New Spain*. Ed. by Mary Maple Dunn. New York: Knopf, 1973.

Hussey, Roland D. *The Caracas Company, 1728–1784: A Study in the History of Spanish Monopolistic Trade*. Cambridge, Mass.: Harvard University Press, 1934.

Israel, J. I. *Race, Class, and Politics in Colonial Mexico, 1610–1670*. New York: Oxford University Press, 1975.

Jacobsen, Nils, and Hans-Jurgen Puhle, ed. *The Economies of Mexico and Peru During the Late Colonial Period, 1760–1810*. Berlin, G.F.R.: Colloquim Verlag, 1986.

Juan, Jorge, and Antonio de Ulloa. *A Voyage to South America*. Tempe: Arizona State University Press, 1975.

Kamen, Henry. *Spain 1469–1714: A Society of Conflict*. London, England: Longman Group, 1983.

———. *The War of Succession in Spain, 1700–1715*. Bloomington: Indiana University Press, 1969.

Karasch, Mary C. *Slave Life in Rio de Janeiro, 1808–1850*. Princeton, N.J.: Princeton University Press, 1986.

Katz, Friedrich. *The Ancient American Civilizations*. New York: Praeger. 1974.

Kaufmann, W. W. *British Policy and the Independence of Latin America, 1802–1828*. New Haven, Conn: Yale University Press, 1951.

Keith, Robert G. *Conquest and Agrarian Change: Emergence of the Hacienda System on the Peruvian Coast*. Cambridge, Mass.: Harvard University Press, 1976.

Kelly, John E. *Pedro de Alvarado, Conquistador*. Princeton, N.J.: Princeton University Press, 1932.

Kicza, John E. *Colonial Entrepreneurs: Families and Business in Bourbon Mexico*. Albuquerque: University of New Mexico Press, 1983.

Kiemen, Mathias C. *The Indian Policy of Portugal in the Amazon Region, 1614–1693*. Washington, D.C.: Catholic University of America Press, 1954.

Kinsbruner, Jay. *Petty Capitalism in Spanish America: The Pulperos of Puebla, Mexico City, Caracas, and Buenos Aires*. Boulder, Colo.: Westview Press, 1987.

Kirkpatrick, F. A. *The Spanish Conquistadores*. London, England: A. & C. Black, 1946.

Klein, Herbert S. *The Middle Passage: Comparative Studies in the Atlantic Slave Trade*. Princeton, N.J.: Princeton University Press, 1978.

Klein, Julius. *The Mesta: A Study in Spanish Economic History, 1273–1836*. Cambridge, Mass.: Harvard University Press, 1920.

Konrad, Herman. *A Jesuit Hacienda in Colonial Mexico: Santa Lucia, 1576–1767*. Stanford, Calif.: Stanford University Press, 1980.

Korth, Eugene H., S.J. *Spanish Policy in Colonial Chile: The Struggle for Social Justice, 1535–1700*. Stanford, Calif: Stanford University Press, 1968.

Kubler, George. *The Art and Architecture of Ancient America: The Mexican, Maya, and Andean Peoples*. Baltimore, Md. Penguin, 1962.

Kuethe, Allan J. *Cuba, 1753–1815: Crown, Military, and Society*. Knoxville: University of Tennessee Press, 1986.

————. *Military Reform and Society in New Granada, 1773–1808*. Gainesville: University Presses of Florida, 1978.

Kuznesof, Elizabeth A. *Household Economy and Urban Development: Sao Paulo, 1765–1836*. Boulder, Colo.: Westview Press, 1986.

Ladd, Doris M. *The Mexican Nobility at Independence, 1780–1826*. Austin: University of Texas Press, 1976.

Lafaye, Jacques. *Quetzalcóatl and Guadalupe: The Formation of Mexican National Consciousness, 1531–1813*. Trans. by Benjamin Keen. Chicago: University of Chicago Press, 1976.

Lanning, John Tate. *The Eighteenth-Century Enlightenment in the University of San Carlos de Guatemala*. Ithaca, N.Y.: Cornell University Press, 1956.

————. *Pedro de la Torre: Doctor to Conquerors*. Baton Rouge: Louisiana State University Press, 1974.

————. *The Royal Protomedicato: The Regulation of the Medical Profession in the Spanish Empire*. Ed. by John Jay Tepaske. Durham, N.C.: Duke University Press, 1985.

————. *The University in the Kingdom of Guatemala*. Ithaca, N.Y.: Cornell University Press, 1955.

Larson, Brooke. *Colonialism and Agrarian Transformation in Bolivia: Cochabamba, 1550–1900*. Princeton, N.J.: Princeton University Press, 1988.

Lavrin, Asunción, ed. *Latin American Women: Historical Perspectives*. Westport, Conn.: Greenwood Press, 1978.

Lea, Henry Charles. *The Inquisition in the Spanish Dependencies*. New York: Macmillan, 1908.

León-Portilla, Miguel, ed. *The Broken Spears: The Aztec Account of the Conquest of Mexico*. Trans. by Lysander Kemp. Boston: Beacon Press, 1961.

Leonard, Irving A. *Baroque Times in Old Mexico: Seventeenth-Century Persons, Places, and Practices*. Ann Arbor: University of Michigan Press, 1959.

————. *Books of the Brave*. Cambridge, Mass.: Harvard University Press, 1949.

Liss, Peggy K. *Atlantic Empires: The Network of Trade and Revolution, 1713–1826*. Baltimore, Md.: Johns Hopkins University Press, 1982.

————. *Mexico Under Spain, 1521–1556: Society and the Origins of Nationality*. Chicago: University of Chicago Press, 1975.

Lockhart, James. *The Men of Cajamarca: A Social and Biographical Study of the First Conquerors of Peru*. Austin: University of Texas Press, 1972.

————. *Spanish Peru, 1532–1560: A Colonial Society*. Madison: University of Wisconsin Press, 1975.

Lomax, Derek W. *The Reconquest of Spain*. New York: Longman Group, 1978.

Lombardi, John V. *People and Places in Colonial Venezuela*. Bloomington: Indiana University Press, 1976.

López de Gomara, Francisco. *Cortés: The Life of the Conqueror by His Secretary*. Trans. and ed. by Lesley B. Simpson. Berkeley and Los Angeles: University of California Press, 1964.

Lynch, John. *Spain Under the Habsburgs*. 2 vols., revised edition. New York: New York University Press, 1984.

————. *Spanish Colonial Administration, 1782–1810: The Intendant System in the Viceroyalty of the Río de la Plata*. London, England: Athlone, 1958.

Lyon, Eugene. *The Enterprise of Florida: Pedro Menendez de Aviles and the Spanish Conquest of 1565–1568*. Gainesville: University Presses of Florida, 1976.

MacKay, Angus. *Spain in the Middle Ages: From Frontier to Empire, 1000–1500*. London, England: Macmillan, 1977.

MacLachlan, Colin M. *Criminal Justice in Eighteenth-Century Mexico: A Study of the Tribunal of the Acordada*. Berkeley and Los Angeles: University of California Press, 1974.

———. *Spain's Empire in the New World: The Role of Ideas in Institutional and Social Change*. Berkeley and Los Angeles: University of California Press, 1988.

MacLeod, Murdo J. *Spanish Central America: A Socioeconomic History, 1520–1720*. Berkeley and Los Angeles: University of California Press, 1973.

Madariaga, Salvador de. *Spain*. New York: Frederick Praeger, 1958.

Maltby, William S. *The Black Legend in England: The Development of Anti-Spanish Sentiment, 1558–1660*. Durham, N.C.: Duke University Press, 1971.

Markham, Sir Clement. *The Conquest of New Granada*. Port Washington, N.Y.: Kennikat Press, 1971.

Martin, Cheryl English. *Rural Society in Colonial Morelos*. Albuquerque: University of New Mexico Press, 1985.

Martín, Luis. *Daughters of the Conquistadores: Women of the Viceroyalty of Peru*. Albuquerque: University of New Mexico Press, 1983.

———. *The Intellectual Conquest of Peru: The Jesuit College of San Pablo, 1568–1767*. New York: Fordham University Press, 1968.

Marzahl, Peter. *Town in the Empire: Government, Politics, and Society in Seventeenth-Century Popayán*. Austin, Tex.: Institute of Latin American Studies, 1978.

Masur, Gerhard. *Simón Bolívar*. 2d ed. Albuquerque: University of New Mexico Press, 1969.

Maxwell, Kenneth R. *Conflicts and Conspiracies: Brazil and Portugal, 1750–1808*. Cambridge, England: Cambridge University Press, 1973.

McKinley, P. Michael. *Pre-Revolutionary Caracas: Politics, Economy, and Society, 1777–1811*. Cambridge, England: Cambridge University Press, 1973.

McNeill, John Robert. *Atlantic Empires of France and Spain: Louisbourg and Havana, 1700–1763*. Chapel Hill: University of North Carolina Press, 1985.

McNeill, William H. *Plagues and People*. Garden City, N.Y.: Anchor/Doubleday, 1976.

Mellafe, Rolando. *Negro Slavery in Latin America*. Trans. by J. W. S. Judge. Berkeley and Los Angeles: University of California Press, 1975.

Metford, J. C. J. *San Martín the Liberator*. London, England: Longmans Green, 1950.

Metraux, Alfred. *The History of the Incas*. New York: Pantheon, 1969.

Miller, Robert Ryal, ed. *Chronicle of Colonial Lima: The Diary of Josephe and Francisco Mugaburu, 1640–1697*. Norman: University of Oklahoma Press, 1975.

Moore, John Preston. *The Cabildo in Peru Under the Hapsburgs*. Durham, N.C.: Duke University Press, 1954.

Morely, Sylvanus G. *The Ancient Maya*. Revised by G. W. Brainerd. Stanford, Calif.: Stanford University Press, 1965.

Moreno-Franginals, Manuel. *The Sugar Mill: The Socioeconomic Complex of Sugar in Cuba, 1760–1860*. Trans. by Cedric Belfrage. New York: Monthly Review Press, 1976.

Morison, Samuel E. *Admiral of the Ocean Sea: A Life of the Admiral Christopher Columbus*. 2 vols. Boston: Little, Brown, 1942.

———. *The European Discovery of America: The Southern Voyages, 1492–1619*. New York: Oxford University Press, 1974.

Morner, Magnus. *The Political and Economic Activities of the Jesuits in the La Plata Region: The Hapsburg Era*. Stockholm, Sweden: Library and Institute of Ibero-American Studies, 1953.

———. *Race Mixture in the History of Latin America*. Boston: Little Brown, 1967.

Morse, Richard M., ed. *The Bandeirantes: The Role of the Brazilian Pathfinders*. New York: Knopf, 1965.

Newson, Linda. *The Cost of Conquest: Indian Decline in Honduras Under Spanish Rule*. Boulder, Colo.: Westview Press, 1986.

Newton, Arthur P. *The European Nations in the West Indies, 1493–1688*. London, England: A & C Black, 1933.

Nunn, Charles F. *Foreign Immigrants in Early Bourbon Mexico, 1700–1760*. Cambridge, England: Cambridge University Press, 1979.

Oliveira Marques, A. H. de. *History of Portugal*. 2 vols. New York: Columbia University Press, 1972.

Ott, T. O. *The Haitian Revolution, 1789–1804*. Knoxville: University of Tennessee Press, 1973.

Padden, R. C. *The Hummingbird and the Hawk: Conquest and Sovereignty in the Valley of Mexico, 1503–1541*. Columbus: Ohio State University Press, 1967.

Pagden, Anthony. *The Fall of Natural Man: The American Indian and the Origins of Comparative Ethnology*. Cambridge, England: Cambridge University Press, 1982.

Palmer, Colin A. *Slaves of the White God: Blacks in Mexico, 1570–1650*. Cambridge, Mass.: Harvard University Press, 1976.

Parry, J. H. *The Age of Reconnaissance*. New York: Mentor Books, 1964.

———. *The Audiencia of New Galicia in the Sixteenth Century*. Cambridge, England: Cambridge University Press, 1948.

———. *The Sale of Public Office in the Spanish Indies Under the Hapsburgs*. Berkeley and Los Angeles: University of California Press, 1953.

———. *The Spanish Seaborne Empire*. New York: Knopf, 1969.

Payne, Stanley. *A History of Spain and Portugal*. 2 vols. Madison: University of Wisconsin Press, 1973.

———. *Politics and the Military in Modern Spain*. Stanford, Calif.: Stanford University Press, 1967.

———. *Spanish Catholicism: An Historical Overview*. Madison: University of Wisconsin Press, 1984.

Peers, E. Allison. *Spain, the Church, and the Orders*. London, England: Burns, Oates, and Washbourne, 1945.

Phelan, John L. *The Hispanization of the Philippines: Spanish Aims and Filipino Reactions 1565–1700*. Madison: University of Wisconsin Press, 1967.

———. *The Kingdom of Quito in the Seventeenth Century*. Madison: University of Wisconsin Press, 1967.

———. *The Millennial Kingdom of the Franciscans in the New World: A Study of the Writings of Geronimo de Medieta, 1525–1604*. Berkeley and Los Angeles: University of California Press, 1956.

———. *The People and the King—Comunero Revolution in Colombia, 1781*. Madison: University of Wisconsin Press, 1978.

Pike, Ruth. *Enterprise and Adventure: The Genoese in Seville and the Opening of the New World*. Ithaca, N.Y.: Cornell University Press, 1966.

Poole, Stafford. *Pedro Moya de Contreras: Catholic Reform and Royal Power in New Spain, 1571–1591*. Berkeley and Los Angeles: University of California Press, 1987.

Powell, Philip Wayne, *Soldiers, Indians, and Silver*. Berkeley and Los Angeles: University of California Press, 1952.

Prado, Caio, Jr. *The Colonial Background of Modern Brazil*. Trans. by Suzette Macedo. Berkeley and Los Angeles: University of California Press, 1987.

Queiros Mattoso, Katia M. de. *To Be a Slave in Brazil, 1500–1888*. New Brunswick, N.J.: Rutgers University Press, 1986.

Ramirez, Susan E. *Provincial Patriarchs: The Economics of Power in Colonial Peru*. Albuquerque: University of New Mexico Press, 1985.

Ramos Oliveira, Antonio. *Politics, Economics, and Men of Modern Spain, 1808–1946*. Trans. by Teener Hall. London, England: Victor Gollancz, 1949.

Ricard, Robert. *The Spiritual Conquest of Mexico*. Trans. by Lesley B. Simpson. Berkeley and Los Angeles: University of California Press, 1966.

Riley, G. Michael. *Fernando Cortés and the Marquesado in Morelos: A Case Study in the Socioeconomic Development of Sixteenth-Century Mexico*. Albuquerque: University of New Mexico Press, 1973.

Ringrose, David R. *Transportation and Economic Stagnation in Spain, 1750–1850*. Durham N.C.: Duke University Press, 1970.

Robertson, William Spence. *France and Latin-American Independence*. Baltimore, Md.: Johns Hopkins University Press, 1939.

———. *Iturbide of Mexico*. Durham, N.C.: Duke University Press, 1952.

Rodríguez, Mario. *The Cádiz Experiment in Central America, 1808 to 1826*. Berkeley and Los Angeles: University of California Press, 1978.

Rodriguez O. Jaime E. *The Emergence of Spanish America: Vicente Rocafuerte and Spanish Americanism, 1808–1832*. Berkeley and Los Angeles: University of California Press, 1975.

Romoli, Kathleen. *Balboa of Darién: Discoverer of the Pacific*. Garden City, N.Y.: Doubleday, 1953.

Ronan, Charles E., S.J. *Francisco Javier Clavijero, S.J. (1731–1787), Figure of the Mexican Enlightenment: His Life and Works*. Chicago: Loyola University Press, 1978.

Rout, Leslie B., Jr. *The African Experience in Spanish America: 1502 to the Present Day*. Cambridge, England: Cambridge University Press, 1971.

Russell-Wood, A. J. R. *Hidalgos and Philanthropists; The Santa Casa da Misericordia of Bahia, 1550–1755*. Berkeley and Los Angeles: University of California Press, 1969.

———, ed. *From Colony to Nation: Essays on the Independence of Brazil*. Baltimore, Md.: Johns Hopkins University Press, 1975.

Salvucci, Richard J. *Textiles and Capitalism in Mexico: An Economic History of the Obrajes, 1539–1840*. Princeton, N.J.: Princeton University Press, 1987.

Sauer, Carl Ortwin. *Agricultural Origins and Dispersals*. New York: American Geographical Society, 1952.

————. *The Early Spanish Main*. Berkeley and Los Angeles: University of California Press, 1966.

Schurz, William L. *The Manila Galleon*. New York: Dutton, 1939.

Schwaller, John Frederick. *Church and Clergy in Sixteenth-Century Mexico*. Albuquerque: University of New Mexico Press, 1987.

————. *Origins of Church Wealth in Mexico*. Albuquerque: University of New Mexico Press, 1985.

Schwartz, Stuart B. *Sovereignty and Society in Colonial Brazil: The High Court of Bahia and Its Judges, 1609–1751*. Berkeley and Los Angeles: University of California Press, 1981.

Sharp, William F. *Slavery on the Spanish Frontier: The Colombian Chaco, 1680–1810*. Norman: University of Oklahoma Press, 1976.

Sherman, William L. *Forced Native Labor in Sixteenth-Century Central America*. Lincoln: University of Nebraska Press, 1979.

Simpson, Lesley Byrd. *The Encomienda in New Spain: The Beginning of Spanish Mexico*. Berkeley and Los Angeles: University of California Press, 1950.

Smith, Robert S. *The Spanish Guild Merchant: A History of the Consulado, 1250–1700*. Durham, N.C.: Duke University Press, 1940.

Socolo, Susan Migden. *Merchants of Buenos Aires, 1778–1810: Family and Commerce*. Cambridge, England: Cambridge University Press, 1978.

Soustelle, Jacques. *Daily Life of the Aztecs*. Stanford, Calif.: Stanford University Press, 1970.

Spalding, Karen. *Huarochiri: An Andean Society Under Inca and Spanish Rule*. Stanford, Calif.: Stanford University Press, 1984.

Steele, Arthur R. *Flowers for the King: The Expedition of Ruiz and Pavon and the Flora of Peru*. Durham, N.C.: Duke University Press, 1964.

Steinberg, David Joel. *The Philippines: A Singular and a Plural Place*. Boulder, Colo.: Westview Press, 1982.

Stern, Steve J. *Peru's Indian Peoples and the Challenge of Spanish Conquest: Huamanga to 1640*. Madison: University of Wisconsin Press, 1982.

Stoan, Stephen K. *Pablo Morillo and Venezuela, 1815–1820*. Columbus: Ohio State University Press, 1974.

Street, John. *Artigas and the Emancipation of Uruguay*. Cambridge, England: Cambridge University Press, 1959.

Super, John C. *Food, Conquest, and Colonization in Sixteenth-Century Spanish America*. Albuquerque: University of New Mexico Press, 1988.

Sweet, David, and Gary Nash. *Struggle and Survival in Colonial America*. Berkeley and Los Angeles: University of California Press, 1981.

Taylor, William B. *Drinking, Homicide and Rebellion in Colonial Mexican Villages*. Stanford, Calif.: Stanford University Press, 1979.

————. *Landlord and Peasant in Colonial Oaxaca*. Stanford, Calif.: Stanford University Press, 1972.

Tepaske, John J., trans. and ed. *Discourse and Political Reflections on the Kingdom of Peru by Jorge Juan and Antonio de Ulloa*. Norman: University of Oklahoma Press, 1978.

————. *The Governorship of Spanish Florida, 1700–1763*. Durham, N.C.: Duke University Press, 1964.

Tibesar, Antonine. *Franciscan Beginnings in Colonial Peru*. Washington, D.C.: Academy of American Franciscan History, 1953.

Timmons, W. H. *Morelos of Mexico: Priest, Soldier, Statesman*. El Paso: Texas Western Press, 1963.

Trend, J. B. *The Origins of Modern Spain*. New York: Russell and Russell, 1965.

Twinam, Ann. *Miners, Merchants, and Farmers in Colonial Colombia*. Austin: University of Texas Press, 1983.

Vaillant, George. *The Aztecs of Mexico: Origin, Rise and Fall of the Aztec Nation*. Garden City, N.Y.: Doubleday, 1962.

Van Aken, Mark H. *Pan-Hispanism: Its Origins and Development to 1866*. Berkeley: University of California Press, 1959.

Van Oss, C. Adrian. *Colonial Catholicism: A Parish History of Guatemala, 1524–1821*. Cambridge, England: Cambridge University Press, 1986.

Van Young, Eric. *Hacienda and Market in Eighteenth-Century Mexico: The Rural Economy of the Guadalajara Region, 1675–1820*. Berkeley and Los Angeles: University of California Press, 1981.

Vicens Vives, Jaime. *An Economic History of Spain*. Trans. by Frances López-Tropillas. Princeton, N.J.: Princeton University Press, 1969.

Vilar, Pierre. *Spain: A Brief History*. Trans. by Brian Tate. Oxford: Pergamon Press, 1967.

Villamarin, Juan A., and Judith E. Villamarin. *Indian Labor in Mainland Spanish America*. Newark: University of Delaware Latin American Studies Program, 1975.

Wachtel, Nathan. *The Vision of the Vanquished: The Spanish Conquest of Peru Through Indian Eyes, 1530–1570*. New York: Barnes & Noble, 1977.

Walker, Geoffrey J. *Spanish Politics and Imperial Trade, 1700–1789*. Bloomington: Indiana University Press, 1979.

Webb, Kempton E. *Geography of Latin America: A Regional Analysis*. Englewood Cliffs, N.J.: Prentice-Hall, 1972.

Whitaker, Arthur P., ed. *Latin America and the Enlightenment*. 2d ed. Ithaca, N.Y.: Cornell University Press, 1961.

———. *The United States and the Independence of Latin America, 1800–1830*. Baltimore, Md.: Johns Hopkins University Press, 1941.

Wolf, Eric. *Sons of the Shaking Earth: The People of Mexico and Guatemala—Their Land, History, and Culture*. Chicago: University of Chicago Press, 1974.

Woodward, Ralph Lee, Jr. *Class Privilege and Economic Development: The Consulado de Comercio de Guatemala, 1793–1871*. Chapel Hill: University of North Carolina Press, 1966.

Worcester, Donald E. *Sea Power and Chilean Independence*. Gainesville: University of Florida Press, 1962.

Wortman, Miles L. *Government and Society in Central America, 1680–1840*. New York: Columbia University Press, 1982.

Zimmerman, Arthur Franklin. *Francisco de Toledo, Fifth Viceroy of Peru, 1569–1581*. Caldwell, Idaho: Caxton Printers, 1938.

INDEX

Pages for main entries appear in **bold** type.

ABOUT THE
CONTRIBUTORS

George A. Agogino is Distinguished Research Professor in Anthropology at Eastern New Mexico University in Portales, New Mexico.

Mercedes Agogino teaches biology at Eastern New Mexico University in Portales, New Mexico.

Raysa Amador teaches in the department of languages at Adelphi University in Garden City, New York.

Patricia Rieff Anawalt is on the staff of the Museum of Cultural History at the University of California at Los Angeles.

Ernest Andrade, Jr., is a member of the History Department at the University of Colorado, Denver.

Frances F. Berdan teaches in the Department of Anthropology at California State University at San Bernardino.

Robert E. Biles teaches political science at Sam Houston State University in Huntsville, Texas.

Lowell L. Blaisdell is a member of the Department of History at Texas Tech University in Lubbock, Texas.

Virginia Garrard Burnett is a historian on the faculty of the University of Texas at Austin.

Michael Dennis teaches social studies at Cy-Fair High School in Houston, Texas.

Bruce R. Drury is a member of the political science department at Lamar University in Beaumont, Texas.

Samuel Freeman is a political scientist at the University of Texas at Edinburgh, Texas.

Ronald Fritze teaches history at Lamar University in Beaumont, Texas.

Catherine G. Harbour is a graduate student in history at Stephen F. Austin State University in Nacogdoches, Texas.

Craig Hendricks teaches history at Long Beach City College in Long Beach, California.

Fred Koestler is a professor of history at Lee College in Baytown, Texas.

Allan J. Kuethe is a historian at Texas Tech University in Lubbock, Texas.

Eric Loew is a graduate student at Sam Houston State University in Huntsville, Texas.

Ross Marlay is a member of the Department of Political Science at Arkansas State University in State University, Arkansas.

Frank Marotti is a graduate student in history at the University of Hawaii.

Neale J. Pearson teaches political science at Texas Tech University in Lubbock, Texas.

Carlos Pérez is a graduate student in history at the University of California at Berkeley.

Glenn O. Phillips teaches in the Institute for Urban Affairs at Morgan State University in Baltimore, Maryland.

William G. Ratliff teaches history at California State University at Chico, California.

Veula J. Rhodes teaches history at Albany State College in Albany, Georgia.

William Robison teaches in the history department of Southeastern Louisiana University in Hammond, Louisiana.

Joseph M. Rowe, Jr. teaches history at Sam Houston State University in Huntsville, Texas.

Lynda A. Sánchez teaches at Hondo High School in Hondo, New Mexico.

Peter T. Sherrill teaches history at the University of Arkansas at Little Rock, Arkansas.

Mark R. Shulman teaches history at Yale University in New Haven, Connecticut.

Edward B. Sisson teaches in the Department of Anthropology and Sociology at the University of Mississippi in Oxford, Mississippi.

Karen Sleezer is a graduate student in history at Sam Houston State University in Huntsville, Texas.

Sam L. Slick teaches in the Department of Modern Languages at the University of Southern Mississippi in Hattiesburg, Mississippi.

O. Carlos Stoetzer teaches at Fordham University in New York City and is professor of history at the Universidad del Salvador in Buenos Aires, Argentina.

John W. Storey is a historian at Lamar University in Beaumont, Texas.

Roy E. Thoman is a historian at West Texas State University in Canyon, Texas.

David E. Vassberg teaches in the history department at the University of Texas at Edinburgh, Texas.

Raymond Wilson is a historian at Fort Hays State University in Hays, Kansas.